W9-AGU-587

SIXTEEN FAMOUS BRITISH PLAYS

SIXTEEN
Famous British Plays

COMPILED BY BENNETT A. CERF

and

VAN H. CARTMELL

With an Introduction by John Mason Brown

Garden City Publishing Co., Inc.
GARDEN CITY, NEW YORK

1942
GARDEN CITY PUBLISHING CO., INC.

FIRST EDITION

H. W. HAWK
9-18-46 fm

MANUFACTURED IN THE UNITED STATES OF AMERICA

ACKNOWLEDGMENTS

For permission to include the following plays, acknowledgment is here made to the authors of the plays and the publishers under whose imprint they were originally issued:

The Second Mrs. Tanqueray and *The Green Bay Tree* reprinted by permission of Walter H. Baker Company.

Journey's End reprinted by permission of Coward, McCann, Inc.

Milestones, The Circle and *Cavalcade* reprinted by permission of Doubleday, Doran and Company, Inc.

The Green Goddess reprinted by permission of Curtis Brown, Limited.

Dangerous Corner reprinted by permission of Samuel French.

Mr. Pim Passes By reprinted by permission of Alfred A. Knopf, Inc.

The Barretts of Wimpole Street reprinted by permission of Little, Brown and Company.

Outward Bound reprinted by permission of Liveright Publishing Corporation.

The Importance of Being Earnest reprinted by permission of The Modern Library, Inc.

The Corn Is Green reprinted by permission of Random House, Inc.

What Every Woman Knows, Loyalties and *Victoria Regina* reprinted by permission of Charles Scribner's Sons.

FOREWORD

The title *Sixteen Famous British Plays* means, of course, plays that are famous in America. British playgoers have tastes that we Americans are often unable to fathom, and there have been occasions when plays that ran for five years in London withered away within a week in New York.

The sixteen plays in this collection, however, made theatrical history in the United States as well as in Britain, and certainly everybody who is at all interested in the drama will recognize every title as quickly as he did those that we included in our collection of famous American plays, published last year.

We were anxious to head this collection with a play by Bernard Shaw, but the gentleman said "no." He does not want his writings to appear in an anthology, regardless of its scope or possible convenience to the reading public. The only other play that we wanted and failed to obtain was John Balderston's *Berkeley Square,* whose publishers were disinclined to grant the necessary permission. To the authors and publishers of all of the other plays we wanted, and who, in more than one instance, granted our request at some sacrifice to themselves, we offer our grateful thanks.

The plays in this volume are arranged chronologically in the order of their original presentation on the New York stage. We purposely avoided the inclusion of any two plays by the same author. And since the table of contents had been decided upon before John Mason Brown consented to write the introduction, it is obvious that any criticism of the selections must be levelled not at Mr. Brown but at the editors. Both of them are publishers. They can take it!

New York BENNETT A. CERF
January, 1942 VAN H. CARTMELL

CONTENTS

INTRODUCTION

BY JOHN MASON BROWN

Mrs. Wiggs and her Cabbage Patch are not as familiar as they once were. And Mrs. Wiggs, heaven knows, never thought of herself as a rival of the Messrs. Palgrave, Woollcott and Fadiman. Yet without knowing it, in her aproned way, she, too, possessed the courage and the optimism of an anthologist. It was she who, when Lovey Mary was journeying to Niagara, pressed an empty bottle into Lovey Mary's hands, urging her to fill it and to bring it back, so that on her return Mrs. Wiggs could sample in the comfort of her home the grandeur of the Falls.

Although Lovey Mary failed in her mission, Bennett Cerf and Van Cartmell have succeeded to a surprising extent in theirs. As the editors of this volume they, too, have approached a Niagara with the equivalent of a bottle in their hands. Yet from the thousands of plays, many of them of high distinction, written by British dramatists since the modern English theatre came of age, the sixteen included here manage to suggest not only the quality and variety of that drama, but also the characteristics of some of its major contributors.

Mr. Shaw, alas, is missing. One of the few reticences of the Sage of Ayot St. Lawrence happens to be anthologies. This is a pity. Although it may simplify an editor's task by relieving him of the ugly problem of trying to pick the most typical of Mr. Shaw's hydra-headed scripts, it still leaves a void. A collection of representative modern British plays which tries to get along without Mr. Shaw is a Golden Treasury decidedly on the silver standard. It is not *Hamlet* without Hamlet. Far from it. But it is like a history of the Comédie which fails to mention Molière, a study of the eighteenth century which omits Voltaire, or a chronicle of strip-teasers which overlooks Gypsy Rose Lee. Mr. Shaw is as well aware of this as are Mr. Cerf, Mr. Cartmell and I.

What is more, he would be the first to trumpet it, which is not quite the same thing as admitting it.

Why, you may ask, start off by toasting Mr. Shaw at a party he refuses to attend? The reasons are numerous and pressing. If that very Elderly Gentleman, that Methuselah of Cathleen ni Houlihan's other island, haunts this volume Banquo-wise, it is because the theatre which most of these sixteen plays represent could never have existed had it not been for Mr. Shaw.

Everyone knows, from the point of view of quantity, sometimes quality, that the renaissance of the English drama which began before the turn of the century, and survived that catastrophe now referred to as World War I, was one of the most productive periods in the annals of playwriting. To maintain that Mr. Shaw was alone responsible for it, or to picture him as a David who sallied forth single-handed to fight the Goliath of the Victorian drama, would be worse than an exaggeration. It would be a barefaced lie. There were others at work—many others in many other countries, who during the same burgeoning years were fighting the same good fight to emancipate the theatre from the bondage of its old-fashioned puerilities. Widespread, however, as were the changes which swept through the playhouses of the Old World in the nineties, and finally invaded our own stage in the twenties, the temperature of the new theatre they made possible can be taken with almost clinical accuracy by noting how different were not the merits but the assumptions of the English stage in 1940 when *The Corn Is Green* was written from what they had been in 1893 when *The Second Mrs. Tanqueray* (or was it Mrs. Patrick Campbell?) took London by storm.

The whole of London may have succumbed to "that inte-resting play—*The Second Mrs. Tanque-ray.*" Not so the red-bearded critic in the Jaeger jacket who was Mr.

Shaw. He put his hobnail boots down on it. A new old play, he called it, when all England was admiring its novelty and saluting its author as a man of daringly original ideas. Mr. Shaw knew better. Although he did not underestimate its theatrical merits, he realized that if *The Second Mrs. Tanqueray* struck Londoners as outrageous, their outrage was only a measure of their unreadiness for anything more. What was enough for England was not, and never has been, enough for Mr. Shaw. He could not hold his far-ranging mind down to the technical niceties of what he once described as "Pinerotic" plotting. He did not want the English theatre to be a translated version of the French. He hated "Sardoodledom," and had as little respect for the big scenes and table-thumpings of Dumas fils. He was not satisfied with one *raisonneur* however logical; he wanted truth however illogical, and a whole stageful of *raisonneurs* ventriloquizing for Shaw.

In the old theatre of over-colored grease-paint, sweet sentiment and valentine ethics, Mr. Shaw was the Devil's Disciple, both creatively and critically, of the new. And the devil—at least in the literary London of those days—was that surprisingly chilly satan from the north; that brave champion of the Woman who then was New; that enemy of social evils and "the lie" lived; that formidable, dumpy little rebel from Skien; in short (as one of the more scandalized English reviewers of the time had dubbed him) that "nookshotten Norwegian"—Henrik Ibsen.

Mr. Shaw was an Ibsenite as surely as he was a Wagnerite, a Fabian, a Nietzschean, an Erewhonian, or for that matter a cyclist and a vegetarian. But he was no more a perfect Ibsenite than he was a perfect Wagnerite. His treatment of both of his supposed idols was typical of the treatment he has meted out to all the men from whom he has admitted to have borrowed. Invariably his borrowings have been more than loans. They have been arrogant and gleeful invasions of the minds of his so-called "influences," during the course of which Mr. Shaw (at the very moment of swearing allegiance to them) has reduced his "masters" to so many unrecognizable colonials in a giddy intellectual empire of his own. Among his many high talents Mr. Shaw must count the genius which is his for turning his gods into unsuspecting worshippers while genuflecting before them.

If Ibsen and Wagner, when he was through with them, ended up by becoming perfect Shavians, so, with all its imperfections, has the modern English theatre, which is sampled in this volume, long since ceased to be the theatre of those two doubtful Toms—Reade and Robertson—, of H. J. Byron, Dumas fils, Sardou, Shakespeare à la Henry Irving at the Lyceum, actor-managers rampant, or even Henry Arthur Jones and Pinero, those two all-important transitional figures. It has become, at least in its freedom, though not in its mentality or its technique, the theatre of Shaw. Not by any means the actual theatre he dreamed of, wrote for, or would approve of in toto, but still an expression of that new theatre which he had helped to make possible.

Although none of the plays to be found here is experimental in the sense that the word was employed in the Expressionistic twenties, almost all of them—yes, even *Mr. Pim Passes By*, with its talk of bigamy—would have seemed revolutionary to audiences accustomed to *Caste*, *M. P.*, *Society*, *Saints and Sinners*, *The Silver King* or *The Money Spinners*. If even the more daring of them are conservative enough when now read, the explanation lies in other things besides their being British. That they can be accepted without shock or controversy means only that the campaign against prudery which their very existence represents is now forgotten, having long ago been won.

All of these dramas, with the exception of *The Importance of Being Earnest* which speaks a comedic language of Wilde's own, are written in the image of realism. That is to say, they all endeavor to make what happens in them appear as if it could have happened in other places than behind the footlights. The older Victorian playgoers had been willing—if not anxious—to accept the theatre as something happily divorced from life. The playgoers who followed them, and who both in England and in this country have applauded the dramas herein assembled, have been trained to a different expectancy. They take it for granted that blood and grease-paint can mix. Like all playgoers, make-believe is their pleasure, but, unlike their grandfathers, they have grown accustomed to pretending in the interests of life rather than of pretense.

The realistic drama resulting from this changed attitude toward make-believe was, of course, the product of that victory scored by the Naturalists in the Free Theatres, the Independent theatres, the Repertory companies, and the Art Theatres which mushroomed into existence over the whole spread of Europe in the nineties and after the turn of the century. If many of the first realists were identified as Naturalists in the more aggressive days of their youth, it is only because Naturalism was the name under which realism passed when it had to be fought for. The contribution of the insurgent groups which waged their war under Ibsen's banner and turned their backs on the earlier theatre came as more than the triumph of an outward form disguising make-believe as reality. It meant that the theatre of the playwright had replaced the theatre of the actor.

To this new theatre with its new freedoms and its fresh sensing of its own possibilities were drawn a host of authors who would not otherwise have been attracted to the stage. They were far more than jigsaw artists at what had once been prized as theatrical effects. They were men of literary distinction to whom what they had to say mattered more than what they had given others to play. The theatre that enticed them was one in which the mind of Ibsen had demonstrated what could be added to the blueprint of Scribe. In England especially, at the disposal of these new dramatists were the fruits of a whole century of scientific discovery and the benefits of the same century's battling for social reform.

The paradox of the theatre's endeavors to deny itself as a medium (in other words to have its plays seem like life and not like plays) is that the dramatists employing this form could not help speaking for themselves while speaking for others. What was supposed to be a slice of life ended up by being a revelation of the author. Try as he might, the dramatist could not turn himself into a dictaphone. He remained a man observing life and seeing other men, not through their eyes but his own. In short, he continued to be an individualist. And that personal possession of the common facts of life which in an author's transmission of them is known as style is one of the chief delights of the plays which follow.

If some of them have helped to make theatrical history, they have done so unconsciously. A dramatist does not write to make history. That is an historian's job. Theatrical history is something which is thrust upon the playwright by scholars rather than by audiences. It is the product of hindsight and has very little to do with the pleasure of specific instances. And it is as specific instances of audiences satisfied, of single evenings well spent in the theatre, of the challenges of a difficult medium happily met and put to each dramatist's individual uses that all sixteen of these plays have justified themselves.

Had history been the editors' solemn concern, this collection would have been a different affair. Like most anthologists they would have been compelled to include *Michael and His Lost Angel* along with *The Second Mrs. Tanqueray,* because Henry Arthur Jones and Pinero are always "discovered" (to use the guilty verb so dear to the old stage directions) marching forward in the classrooms as the Siamese twins of transition.

The editors would have had to find room, too, for the work of Elizabeth Baker, Stanley Houghton, Granville Barker and St. John Hankin. John Galsworthy would have been represented by such of his earlier (hence innovational) sociological dramas as *Strife* or *Justice* rather than by *Loyalties,* which, though one of his best, was written long after its author's dispassionate approach to a problem had become familiar. *The Admirable Crichton,* because of its toyings with the socially significant, would have probably spoken for Barrie instead of the delights of *What Every Woman Knows.*

Mr. Pim would have been passed by entirely. Such melodramas as *The Green Goddess* and *Dangerous Corner* would have knocked in vain for admittance. Mr. Coward's delegate to history would have been either such a drama of post-war nerves as *The Vortex,* or such a comedy as *Hay Fever, Private Lives,* or *Design for Living* rather than such an untypical pageant of empire as *Cavalcade,* eloquent and supreme of its kind though it happens to be. Some indication would have had to be given of what British dramatists from Stephen Phillips, through T. S. Eliot and right down to Auden and Isherwood have tried to do to bring poetry back to a stage which, in an earlier dramatic renaissance, it had once made glorious. And to cover fully a theatre which, for all its fecundity, has been strangely lacking in dramatists either anxious to, or capable of, dealing with the ecstasies of true tragedy as opposed to the sorrows of the pathetic or the ironic, some place would have been left for such an attempt at the tragic as John Masefield's *Nan.*

But in picking these plays, Mr. Cerf and Mr. Cartmell have fortunately had more than cold history in mind. They have not forgotten the living theatre which is, after all, the theatre playgoers remember with gratitude. All of the plays they have chosen have been popular successes. Moreover, though British, they have not been insular, as English plays have, unfortunately, tended to become in recent years. With the exception of *Cavalcade*, which was applauded here only for one week at the Pasadena Playhouse and then for a considerably longer period on the screen, almost all of them have managed to cross the Atlantic triumphantly. They are plays with which any constant theatregoer in New York is as happily familiar as the same kind of theatregoer would be in London.

Moreover, they are dramas still haunted by the memory of their performances. For most of us George Arliss stalks even now through our libraries with all his sinister suavity as the wicked Rajah in *The Green Goddess*, that melodrama which came to William Archer as the most profitable of dreams, and which was the last kind of play one would ever have expected from the austere Scot who, with Shaw, was one of the sturdiest of Ibsen's champions. The frail poetess who escapes from the vile tyranny of her Victorian father in *The Barretts* is not the Elizabeth Barrett that Robert Browning knew—she is Katherine Cornell in all her shining loveliness. It is Colin Keith-Johnston who, as Stanhope with his frayed nerves, still dominates the dugout in *Journey's End*, that war play as typically British in its reticences as *What Price Glory?* was American in its vitality.

Though gone, it is Mrs. Leslie Carter and John Drew who insist upon being present as Lady Kitty and Lord Porteous, those older social rebels whose disillusionment is played off contrapuntally against the hopes of the younger runaways in Mr. Maugham's wise and witty comedy, *The Circle.* It is James Dale who, as the fetid Mr. Dulcimer, is even now arranging the flowers in *The Green Bay Tree,* and Leo G. Carroll who, as the butler, is handing these same symbolical *fleurs du mal* first to Mr. Dale and then to Laurence Olivier as the boy whose character Mr. Dulcimer has taken away.

Quite properly Laurette Taylor, the Mrs. Midget in the revival of two years back, and Dudley Digges, the heavenly customs' official in the first American production seventeen years ago, join hands in time as the ideal spokesmen for the dead who haunt the decks of that unearthly steamer which is the scene of *Outward Bound. Victoria Regina,* Laurence Housman's amusing series of historical vignettes, is for democrats on this side of the water as much dominated by the house of Hayes as that of Hanover. It is Helen Hayes, too, who for the present generation of playgoers still gives the final bloom of charm to the Shandyisms of Maggie Wylie, the invincible, in *What Every Woman Knows.* And the Ethel Barrymore who may have failed some years back as Paula Tanqueray, is even now contributing the finest performance of her career as the English schoolmistress who invades a Welsh mining town in *The Corn Is Green.*

In a collection of plays as representative as this one is of Britain's popular theatre, I, for one, wish that room could have been found for Ashley Dukes's *The Man with a Load of Mischief,* a script which, though ruined in New York by a lamentable production, is one of the best comedies of manners to have come out of modern England. Or that such a fantasy as John Balderstone's *Berkeley Square* could have been included. Yes, and such a Jules Verne melodrama of what-might-have-happened at No. 10 Downing Street as Robert Nichols's and Maurice Browne's *Wings Over Europe.*

I also wish that since the editors have been too wise to place any academic bans on melodramas, they could have followed *Dangerous Corner* with one more such psychological horror play as Patrick Hamilton's *Rope's End,* Geoffrey Dell's *Payment Deferred,* or Reginald Denham's and Edward Percy's *Ladies in Retirement.* The English excel as much as guignols of this literate sort as we do at straight thrillers, with their clutching hands. And for some of us who are ardent De Quinceyans, these chilling scripts, in which murder is treated as a fine art, have an inordinate fascination.

Only critics, however, expect to get everything for nothing. What really matters in this volume are not the editors' inevitable omissions, which cannot be described as sins, but the virtues of their inclusions. The sixteen plays they have chosen have been "famous" on the modern stage. No one can deny that. They speak not only for themselves and for their authors but for a theatre so free that nowadays we have almost forgotten its freedom ever had to be fought for.

There have been disheartening moments when many of us as Americans, realizing what our stage once owed to England's, have been forced to wonder if the renaissance of the modern British drama represented in these pages had not run its course. One can only hope this is not true. And hoping, be grateful that the final play which speaks here for England (when not only England is threatened but so, too, are all the civilized values for which these dramas stand) is a script possessed of such luminous compassion as *The Corn Is Green.*

New York City
October, 1941

The Second Mrs. Tanqueray

BY ARTHUR W. PINERO

The Second Mrs. Tanqueray was first produced in America at the Star Theatre, New York City, by Daniel Frohman on Oct. 28, 1893. The following is the original cast:

AUBREY TANQUERAY	William Kendal
SIR GEORGE ORREYED, BART.	G. P. Huntley
CAPTAIN HUGH ARDALE	Oscar Adye
CAYLEY DRUMMLE	J. E. Dodson
FRANK MISQUITH, Q. C., M. P.	James East
GORDON JAYNE, M.D.	George H. Gray
MORSE	H. Deane
LADY ORREYED	Nellie Campbell
MRS. CORTELYON	Mary Talbot
ELLEAN	Annie Irish
PAULA	Mrs. Kendal

SCENE

The Present Day.

The Scene of Act One is laid at Mr. Tanqueray's *rooms, No. 2 x, the Albany, in the month of November; the occurrences of the succeeding Acts take place at his house, "Highercoombe," near Willowmere, Surrey, during the early part of the following year.*

THE SECOND MRS. TANQUERAY

ACT ONE

AUBREY TANQUERAY'S *Chambers in the Albany—a richly and tastefully decorated room, elegantly and luxuriously furnished: on the right a large pair of doors opening into another room, on the left at the further end of the room a small door leading to a bed-chamber. A circular table is laid for a dinner for four persons, which has now reached the stage of dessert and coffee. Everything in the apartment suggests wealth and refinement. The fire is burning brightly.*

AUBREY TANQUERAY, MISQUITH, *and* JAYNE *are seated at the dinner-table.* AUBREY *is forty-two, handsome, winning in manner, his speech and bearing retaining some of the qualities of young-manhood.* MISQUITH *is about forty-seven, genial and portly.* JAYNE *is a year or two* MISQUITH'S *senior, soft-speaking and precise—in appearance a type of the prosperous town physician.* MORSE, AUBREY'S *servant, places a little cabinet of cigars and the spirit-lamp on the table beside* AUBREY *and goes out.*

MISQUITH. Aubrey, it is a pleasant yet dreadful fact to contemplate, but it's nearly fifteen years since I first dined with you. You lodged in Piccadilly in those days, over a hat-shop. Jayne, I met you at that dinner, and Cayley Drummle.

JAYNE. Yes, yes. What a pity it is that Cayley isn't here tonight.

AUBREY. Confound the old gossip! His empty chair has been staring us in the face all through dinner. I ought to have told Morse to take it away.

MISQUITH. Odd, his sending no excuse.

AUBREY. I'll walk round to his lodgings later on and ask after him.

MISQUITH. I'll go with you.

JAYNE. So will I.

AUBREY (*opening the cigar-cabinet*). Doctor, it's useless to tempt you, I know. Frank— (MISQUITH *and* AUBREY *smoke*) I particularly wished Cayley Drummle to be one of us tonight. You two fellows and Cayley are my closest, my best friends—

MISQUITH. My dear Aubrey!

JAYNE. I rejoice to hear you say so.

AUBREY. And I wanted to see the three of you round this table. You can't guess the reason.

MISQUITH. You desired to give us a most excellent dinner.

JAYNE. Obviously.

AUBREY (*hesitatingly*). Well—I— (*Glancing at the clock*)—Cayley won't turn up now.

JAYNE. H'm, hardly.

AUBREY. Then you two shall hear it. Doctor, Frank, this is the last time we are to meet in these rooms.

JAYNE. The last time?

MISQUITH. You're going to leave the Albany?

AUBREY. Yes. You've heard me speak of a house I built in the country years ago, haven't you?

MISQUITH. In Surrey.

AUBREY. Well, when my wife died I cleared out of that house and let it. I think of trying the place again.

MISQUITH. But you'll go raving mad if ever you find yourself down there alone.

AUBREY. Ah, but I sha'n't be alone, and that's what I wanted to tell you. I'm going to be married.

JAYNE. Going to be married?

MISQUITH. Married?

AUBREY. Yes—tomorrow.

JAYNE. Tomorrow?

MISQUITH. You take my breath away! My dear fellow, I—I—of course, I congratulate you.

JAYNE. And—and—so do I—heartily.

AUBREY. Thanks—thanks.
(*There is a moment or two of embarrassment.*)

MISQUITH. Er—ah—this is an excellent cigar.

JAYNE. Ah—um—your coffee is remarkable.

AUBREY. Look here; I dare say you two old friends think this treatment very strange, very unkind. So I want you to understand me. You know a marriage often cools friendships. What's the usual course of things? A man's engagement is given out, he is congratulated, complimented upon his choice; the church is filled with troops of friends, and he goes away happily to a chorus of good wishes. He comes back, sets up house in town or country, and thinks to resume the old associations, the old companionships. My dear Frank, my dear good doctor, it's very seldom that it can be done. Generally, a worm has begun to eat its way into those hearty, unreserved, pre-nuptial friendships; a damnable constraint sets in and acts like a wasting disease; and so, believe me, in nine cases out of ten a man's marriage severs for him more close ties than it forms.

MISQUITH. Well, my dear Aubrey, I earnestly hope——

AUBREY. I know what you're going to say, Frank. I hope so, too. In the meantime let's face dangers. I've reminded you of the *usual* course of things, but my marriage isn't even the conventional sort of marriage likely to satisfy society. Now, Cayley's a bachelor, but you two men have wives. By-the-bye, my love to Mrs. Misquith and to Mrs. Jayne when you get home—don't forget that. Well, your wives may not—like—the lady I'm going to marry.

JAYNE. Aubrey, forgive me for suggesting that the lady you are going to marry may not like our wives—mine at least; I beg your pardon, Frank.

AUBREY. Quite so; then I must go the way my wife goes.

MISQUITH. Come, come, pray don't let us anticipate that either side will be called upon to make such a sacrifice.

AUBREY. Yes, yes, let us anticipate it. And let us make up our minds to have no slow bleeding-to-death of our friendship. We'll end a pleasant chapter here tonight, and after tonight start afresh. When my wife and I settle down at Willowmere it's possible that we shall all come together. But if this isn't to be, for Heaven's sake let us recognise that it is simply because it *can't* be, and not wear hypocritical faces and suffer and be wretched. Doctor, Frank—(*holding out his hands, one to* MISQUITH, *the other to* JAYNE)—good luck to all of us!

MISQUITH. But—but—do I understand we are to ask nothing? Not even the lady's name, Aubrey?

AUBREY. The lady, my dear Frank, belongs to the next chapter, and in that her name is Mrs. Aubrey Tanqueray.

JAYNE (*raising his coffee-cup*). Then, in an old-fashioned way, I propose a toast. Aubrey, Frank, I give you "The Next Chapter!"
(*They drink the toast, saying, "The Next Chapter!"*)

AUBREY. Doctor, find a comfortable chair; Frank, you too. As we're going to turn out by-and-bye, let me scribble a couple of notes now while I think of them.

MISQUITH *and* JAYNE. Certainly—yes, yes.

AUBREY. It might slip my memory when I get back.
(AUBREY *sits at a writing-table at the other end of the room, and writes.*)

JAYNE (*to* MISQUITH *in a whisper*). Frank—— (MISQUITH *quietly leaves his chair, and sits nearer to* JAYNE) What is all this? Simply a morbid crank of Aubrey's with regard to ante-nuptial acquaintances?

MISQUITH. H'm! Did you notice *one* expression he used?

JAYNE. Let me think——

MISQUITH. "My marriage is not even the conventional sort of marriage likely to satisfy society."

JAYNE. Bless me, yes! What does that suggest?

MISQUITH. That he has a particular rather than a general reason for anticipating estrangement from his friends, I'm afraid.

JAYNE. A horrible *mésalliance!* A dairymaid who has given him a glass of milk during a day's hunting, or a little anæmic shopgirl! Frank, I'm utterly wretched!

MISQUITH. My dear Jayne, speaking in absolute confidence, I have never been more profoundly depressed in my life.
(MORSE *enters.*)

MORSE (*announcing*). Mr. Drummle.
(CAYLEY DRUMMLE *enters briskly. He is a neat little man of about*

five-and-forty, in manner bright, airy, debonair, but with an undercurrent of seriousness. MORSE *retires.*)

DRUMMLE. I'm in disgrace; nobody realises that more thoroughly than I do. Where's my host?

AUBREY (*who has risen*). Cayley.

DRUMMLE (*shaking hands with him*). Don't speak to me till I have tendered my explanation. A harsh word from anybody would unman me.
(MISQUITH *and* JAYNE *shake hands with* DRUMMLE.)

AUBREY. Have you dined?

DRUMMLE. No—unless you call a bit of fish, a cutlet, and a pancake dining.

AUBREY. Cayley, this is disgraceful.

JAYNE. Fish, a cutlet, and a pancake will require a great deal of explanation.

MISQUITH. Especially the pancake. My dear friend, your case looks miserably weak.

DRUMMLE. Hear me! hear me!

JAYNE. Now then!

MISQUITH. Come!

AUBREY. Well!

DRUMMLE. It so happens that tonight I was exceptionally early in dressing for dinner.

MISQUITH. For which dinner—the fish and cutlet?

DRUMMLE. For *this* dinner, of course—really, Frank! At a quarter to eight, in fact, I found myself trimming my nails, with ten minutes to spare. Just then enter my man with a note—would I hasten, as fast as cab could carry me, to old Lady Orreyed in Bruton Street?—"sad trouble." Now, recollect, please, I had ten minutes on my hands, old Lady Orreyed was a very dear friend of my mother's, and was in some distress.

AUBREY. Cayley, come to the fish and cutlet!

MISQUITH *and* JAYNE. Yes, yes, and the pancake!

DRUMMLE. Upon my word! Well, the scene in Bruton Street beggars description; the women servants looked scared, the men drunk; and there was poor old Lady Orreyed on the floor of her boudoir like Queen Bess among her pillows.

AUBREY. What's the matter?

DRUMMLE (*to everybody*). You know George Orreyed?

MISQUITH. Yes.

JAYNE. I've met him.

DRUMMLE. Well, he's a thing of the past.

AUBREY. Not dead!

DRUMMLE. Certainly, in the worst sense. He's married Mabel Hervey.

MISQUITH. What!

DRUMMLE. It's true—this morning. The poor mother showed me his letter—a dozen curt words, and some of those ill-spelt.

MISQUITH. (*walking up to the fire-place*). I'm very sorry.

JAYNE. Pardon my ignorance—who *was* Mabel Hervey?

DRUMMLE. You don't——? Oh, of course not. Miss Hervey—Lady Orreyed, as she now is—was a lady who would have been, perhaps has been, described in the reports of the Police or the Divorce Court as an actress. Had she belonged to a lower stratum of our advanced civilisation she would, in the event of judicial inquiry, have defined her calling with equal justification as that of a dressmaker. To do her justice, she is a type of a class which is immortal. Physically, by the strange caprice of creation, curiously beautiful; mentally, she lacks even the strength of deliberate viciousness. Paint her portrait, it would symbolise a creature perfectly patrician; lance a vein of her superbly-modelled arm, you would get the poorest *vin ordinaire!* Her affections, emotions, impulses, her very existence—a burlesque! Flaxen, five-and-twenty, and feebly frolicsome; anybody's, in less gentle society I should say everybody's, property! That, doctor, was Miss Hervey who is the new Lady Orreyed. Dost thou like the picture?

MISQUITH. Very good, Cayley! Bravo!

AUBREY (*laying his hand on* DRUMMLE'S *shoulder*). You'd scarcely believe it, Jayne, but none of us really know anything about this lady, our gay young friend here, I suspect, least of all.

DRUMMLE. Aubrey, I applaud your chivalry.

AUBREY. And perhaps you'll let me finish a couple of letters which Frank and Jayne have given me leave to write. (*Returning to the writing-table*) Ring for what you want, like a good fellow!
(AUBREY *resumes his writing.*)

MISQUITH (*to* DRUMMLE). Still, the fish and cutlet remain unexplained.

DRUMMLE. Oh, the poor old woman was so weak that I insisted upon her taking some food, and felt there was nothing for it but to sit down opposite her. The fool! the blackguard!

MISQUITH. Poor Orreyed! Well, he's gone under for a time.

DRUMMLE. For a time! My dear Frank, I tell you he has absolutely ceased to be. (AUBREY, *who has been writing busily, turns his head towards the speakers and listens. His lips are set, and there is a frown upon his face*) For all practical purposes you may regard him as the late George Orreyed. Tomorrow the very characteristics of his speech, as we remember them, will have become obsolete.

JAYNE. But surely, in the course of years, he and his wife will outlive——

DRUMMLE. No, no, Doctor, don't try to upset one of my settled beliefs. You may dive into many waters, but there is *one* social Dead Sea——!

JAYNE. Perhaps you're right.

DRUMMLE. Right! Good God! I wish you could prove me otherwise! Why, for years I've been sitting, and watching and waiting.

MISQUITH. You're in form tonight, Cayley. May we ask where you've been in the habit of squandering your useful leisure?

DRUMMLE. Where? On the shore of that same sea.

MISQUITH. And, pray, what have you been waiting for?

DRUMMLE. For some of my best friends *to come up.* (AUBREY *utters a half-stifled exclamation of impatience; then he hurriedly gathers up his papers from the writing-table. The three men turn to him*) Eh?

AUBREY. Oh, I—I'll finish my letters in the other room if you'll excuse me for five minutes. Tell Cayley the news. (*He goes out.*)

DRUMMLE (*hurrying to the door*). My dear fellow, my jabbering has disturbed you! I'll never talk again as long as I live!

MISQUITH. Close the door, Cayley. (DRUMMLE *shuts the door.*)

JAYNE. Cayley—

DRUMMLE (*advancing to the dinner table*). A smoke, a smoke, or I perish! (*Selects a cigar from the little cabinet.*)

JAYNE. Cayley, marriages are in the air.

DRUMMLE. Are they? Discover the bacillus, Doctor, and destroy it.

JAYNE. I mean, among our friends.

DRUMMLE. Oh, Nugent Warrinder's engagement to Lady Alice Tring. I've heard of that. They're not to be married till the spring.

JAYNE. Another marriage that concerns us a little takes place tomorrow.

DRUMMLE. Whose marriage?

JAYNE. Aubrey's.

DRUMMLE. Aub——! (*Looking towards* MISQUITH) Is it a joke?

MISQUITH. No.

DRUMMLE (*looking from* MISQUITH *to* JAYNE). To whom?

MISQUITH. He doesn't tell us.

JAYNE. We three were asked here tonight to receive the announcement. Aubrey has some theory that marriage is likely to alienate a man from his friends, and it seems to me he has taken the precaution to wish us good-bye.

MISQUITH. No, no.

JAYNE. Practically, surely.

DRUMMLE (*thoughtfully*). Marriage in general, does he mean, or *this* marriage?

JAYNE. That's the point. Frank says——

MISQUITH. No, no, no; I feared it suggested——

JAYNE. Well, well. (*To* DRUMMLE) What do you think of it?

DRUMMLE (*after a slight pause*). Is there a light there? (*Lighting his cigar*) He—wraps the lady—in mystery—you say?

MISQUITH. Most modestly.

DRUMMLE. Aubrey's—not—a very—young man.

JAYNE. Forty-three.

DRUMMLE. Ah! *L'age critique!*

MISQUITH. A dangerous age—yes, yes.

DRUMMLE. When you two fellows go home, do you mind leaving me behind here?

MISQUITH. Not at all.

JAYNE. By all means.

DRUMMLE. All right. (*Anxiously*) Deuce take it, the man's second marriage mustn't be another mistake! (*With his head bent he walks up to the fireplace.*)

JAYNE. You knew him in his short married life, Cayley. Terribly unsatisfactory, wasn't it?

DRUMMLE. Well—(*Looking at the door*) I quite closed that door?

MISQUITH. Yes. (*Settles himself on the sofa;* JAYNE *is seated in an armchair.*)

DRUMMLE (*smoking with his back to the fire*). He married a Miss Herriott; that was in the year eighteen —confound dates—twenty years ago. She was a lovely creature—by Jove, she was; by religion a Roman Catholic. She was one of your cold sort, you know—all marble arms and black velvet. I remember her with painful distinctness as the only woman who ever made me nervous.

MISQUITH. Ha, ha!

DRUMMLE. He loved her—to distraction, as they say. Jupiter, how fervently that poor devil courted her! But I don't believe she allowed him even to squeeze her fingers. She *was* an iceberg! As for kissing, the mere contact would have given him chapped lips. However, he married her and took her away, the latter greatly to my relief.

JAYNE. Abroad, you mean?

DRUMMLE. Eh? Yes. I imagine he gratified her by renting a villa in Lapland, but I don't know. After a while they returned, and then I saw how wofully Aubrey had miscalculated results.

JAYNE. Miscalculated——?

DRUMMLE. He had reckoned, poor wretch, that in the early days of marriage she would thaw. But she didn't. I used to picture him closing his doors and making up the fire in the hope of seeing her features relax. Bless her, the thaw never set in! I believe she kept a thermometer in her stays and always registered ten degrees below zero. However, in time a child came—a daughter.

JAYNE. Didn't that——?

DRUMMLE. Not a bit of it; it made matters worse. Frightened at her failure to stir up in him some sympathetic religious belief, she determined upon strong measures with regard to the child. He opposed her for a miserable year or so, but she wore him down, and the insensible little brat was placed in a convent, first in France, then in Ireland. Not long afterwards the mother died, strangely enough, of fever, the only warmth, I believe, that ever came to that woman's body.

MISQUITH. Don't, Cayley!

JAYNE. The child is living, we know.

DRUMMLE. Yes, if you choose to call it living. Miss Tanqueray—a young woman of nineteen now—is in the Loretto convent at Armagh. She professes to have found her true vocation in a religious life, and within a month or two will take final vows.

MISQUITH. He ought to have removed his daughter from the convent when the mother died.

DRUMMLE. Yes, yes, but absolutely at the end there was reconciliation between husband and wife, and she won his promise that the child should complete her conventual education. He reaped his reward. When he attempted to gain his girl's confidence and affection he was too late; he found he was dealing with the spirit of the mother. You remember his visit to Ireland last month?

JAYNE. Yes.

DRUMMLE. That was to wish his girl good-bye.

MISQUITH. Poor fellow!

DRUMMLE. He sent for me when he came back. I think he must have had a lingering hope that the girl would relent—would come to life, as it were—at the last moment, for, for an hour or so, in this room, he was terribly shaken. I'm sure he'd clung to that hope from the persistent way in which he kept breaking off in his talk to repeat one dismal word, as if he couldn't realise his position without dinning this damned word into his head.

JAYNE. What word was that?

DRUMMLE. Alone—alone.
(AUBREY *enters.*)

AUBREY. A thousand apologies!

DRUMMLE (*gaily*). We are talking about you, my dear Aubrey.
(*During the telling of the story,* MISQUITH *has risen and gone to the fire, and* DRUMMLE *has thrown himself full-length on the sofa.* AUBREY *now joins* MISQUITH *and* JAYNE.)

AUBREY. Well, Cayley, are you surprised?

DRUMMLE. Surp——! I haven't been surprised for twenty years.

AUBREY. And you're not angry with me?

DRUMMLE. Angry! (*Rising*) Because you considerately withhold the name of a lady with whom it is now the object of my life to become acquainted? My dear fellow, you pique my curiosity, you give zest to my existence! And as for a wedding, who on earth wants to attend that familiar and probably draughty function? Ugh! My cigar's out.

AUBREY. Let's talk about something else.

MISQUITH (*looking at his watch*). Not tonight, Aubrey.

AUBREY. My dear Frank!

MISQUITH. I go up to Scotland tomorrow, and there are some little matters—

JAYNE. I am off too.

AUBREY. No, no.

JAYNE. I must: I have to give a look to a case in Clifford Street on my way home.

AUBREY (*going to the door*). Well! (MISQUITH *and* JAYNE *exchange looks with* DRUMMLE. *Opening the door and calling*) Morse, hats and coats! I shall write to you all next week from Genoa or Florence. Now, Doctor, Frank, remember, my love to Mrs. Misquith and to Mrs. Jayne!
(MORSE *enters with hats and coats.*)

MISQUITH *and* JAYNE. Yes, yes—yes, yes.

AUBREY. And your young people!
(*As* MISQUITH *and* JAYNE *put on their coats there is the clatter of careless talk.*)

JAYNE. Cayley, I meet you at dinner on Sunday.

DRUMMLE. At the Stratfields'. That's very pleasant.

MISQUITH (*putting on his coat with* AUBREY'S *aid*). Ah-h!

AUBREY. What's wrong?

MISQUITH. A twinge. Why didn't I go to Aix in August?

JAYNE (*shaking hands with* DRUMMLE). Good night, Cayley.

DRUMMLE. Good night, my dear doctor!

MISQUITH (*shaking hands with* DRUMMLE). Cayley, are you in town for long?

DRUMMLE. Dear friend, I'm nowhere for long. Good night.

MISQUITH. Good night.
(AUBREY, JAYNE, *and* MISQUITH *go out, followed by* MORSE; *the hum of talk is continued outside.*)

AUBREY. A cigar, Frank?

MISQUITH. No, thank you.

AUBREY. Going to walk, Doctor?

JAYNE. If Frank will.

MISQUITH. By all means.

AUBREY. It's a cold night.
(*The door is closed.* DRUMMLE *remains standing with his coat on his arm and his hat in his hand.*)

DRUMMLE (*to himself, thoughtfully*). Now then! What the devil—
(AUBREY *returns.*)

AUBREY (*eyeing* DRUMMLE *a little awkwardly*). Well, Cayley?

DRUMMLE. Well, Aubrey?
(AUBREY *walks up to the fire and stands looking into it.*)

AUBREY. You're not going, old chap?

DRUMMLE (*sitting*). No.

AUBREY (*after a slight pause, with a forced laugh*). Hah! Cayley, I never thought I should feel—shy—with you.

DRUMMLE. Why do you?

AUBREY. Never mind.

DRUMMLE. Now, I can quite understand a man wishing to be married in the dark, as it were.

AUBREY. You can?

DRUMMLE. In your place I should very likely adopt the same course.

AUBREY. You think so?

DRUMMLE. And if I intended marrying a lady not prominently in society, as I presume you do—as I presume you do—

AUBREY. Well?

DRUMMLE. As I presume you do, I'm not sure that *I* should tender her for preliminary dissection at afternoon tea-tables.

AUBREY. No?

DRUMMLE. In fact, there is probably only one person—were I in your position tonight—with whom I should care to chat the matter over.

AUBREY. Who's that?

DRUMMLE. Yourself, of course. (*Going to* AUBREY *and standing beside him*) Of course, yourself, old friend.

AUBREY (*after a pause*). I must seem a brute to you, Cayley. But there are some acts which are hard to explain, hard to defend—

DRUMMLE. To defend—

AUBREY. Some acts which one must trust to time to put right.
(DRUMMLE *watches him for a moment, then takes up his hat and coat.*)

DRUMMLE. Well, I'll be moving.

AUBREY. Cayley! Confound you and your old friendship! Do you think I forget it? Put your coat down! Why did you stay behind here? Cayley, the lady I am going to marry is the lady—who is known as—Mrs. Jarman.
(*There is a pause.*)

DRUMMLE (*in a low voice*). Mrs. Jarman! Are you serious?
(*He walks up to the fireplace, where he leans upon the mantelpiece uttering something like a groan.*)

AUBREY. As you've got this out of me I give you leave to say all you care to say. Come, we'll be plain with each other. You know Mrs. Jarman?

DRUMMLE. I first met her at—what does it matter?

AUBREY. Yes, yes, everything! Come!

DRUMMLE. I met her at Homburg, two—three seasons ago.

AUBREY. Not as Mrs. Jarman?

DRUMMLE. No.

AUBREY. She was then—?

DRUMMLE. Mrs. Dartry.

AUBREY. Yes. She has also seen you in London, she says.

DRUMMLE. Certainly.

AUBREY. In Alford Street. Go on.

DRUMMLE. Please!

AUBREY. I insist.

DRUMMLE (*with a slight shrug of the shoulders*). Some time last year I was asked by a man to sup at his house, one night after the theatre.

AUBREY. Mr. Selwyn Ethurst—a bachelor.

DRUMMLE. Yes.

AUBREY. You were surprised therefore to find Mr. Ethurst aided in his cursed hospitality by a lady.

DRUMMLE. I was unprepared.

AUBREY. The lady you had known as Mrs. Dartry? (DRUMMLE *inclines his head silently*) There is something of a yachting cruise in the Mediterranean too, is there not?

DRUMMLE. I joined Peter Jarman's yacht at Marseilles, in the Spring, a month before he died.

AUBREY. Mrs. Jarman was on board?

DRUMMLE. She was a kind hostess.

AUBREY. And an old acquaintance?

DRUMMLE. Yes.

AUBREY. You have told your story.

DRUMMLE. With your assistance.

AUBREY. I have put you to the pain of telling it to show you that this is not the case of a blind man entrapped by an artful woman. Let me add that Mrs. Jarman has no legal right to that name; that she is simply Miss Ray—Miss Paula Ray.

DRUMMLE (*after a pause*). I should like to express my regret, Aubrey, for the way in which I spoke of George Orreyed's marriage.

AUBREY. You mean you compare Lady Orreyed with Miss Ray? (DRUMMLE *is silent*) Oh, of course! To you, Cayley, all women who have been roughly treated, and who dare to survive by borrowing a little of our philosophy, are alike. You see in the crowd of the ill-used only one pattern; you can't detect the shades of goodness, intelligence, even nobility there. Well, how should you? The crowd is dimly lighted! And, besides, yours is the way of the world.

DRUMMLE. My dear Aubrey, I *live* in the world.

AUBREY. The name we give our little parish of St. James's.

DRUMMLE (*laying a hand on* AUBREY'S *shoulder*). And you are quite prepared, my friend, to forfeit the esteem of your little parish?

AUBREY. I avoid mortification by shifting from one parish to another. I give up Pall Mall for the Surrey hills; leave off varnishing my boots, and double the thickness of the soles.

DRUMMLE. And your skin—do you double the thickness of that also?

AUBREY. I know you think me a fool, Cayley—you needn't infer that

I'm a coward into the bargain. No! I know what I'm doing, and I do it deliberately, defiantly. I'm alone: I injure no living soul by the step I'm going to take; and so you can't urge the one argument which might restrain me. Of course, I don't expect you to think compassionately, fairly even, of the woman whom I —whom I am drawn to—

DRUMMLE. My dear Aubrey, I assure you I consider Mrs.—Miss Jarman—Mrs. Ray—Miss Ray—delightful. But I confess there is a form of chivalry which I gravely distrust, especially in a man of—our age.

AUBREY. Thanks. I've heard you say that from forty till fifty a man is at heart either a stoic or a satyr.

DRUMMLE (*protestingly*). Ah! now—

AUBREY. I am neither. I have a temperate, honourable affection for Mrs. Jarman. She has never met a man who has treated her well—I intend to treat her well. That's all. And in a few years, Cayley, if you've not quite forsaken me, I'll prove to you that it's possible to rear a life of happiness, of good repute, on a—miserable foundation.

DRUMMLE (*offering his hand*). Do prove it!

AUBREY (*taking his hand*). We have spoken too freely of—of Mrs. Jarman. I was excited—angry. Please forget it!

DRUMMLE. My dear Aubrey, when we next meet I shall remember nothing but my respect for the lady who bears your name.
(MORSE *enters, closing the door behind him carefully.*)

AUBREY. What is it?

MORSE (*hesitatingly*). May I speak to you, sir? (*In an undertone*) Mrs. Jarman, sir.

AUBREY (*softly to* MORSE). Mrs. Jarman! Do you mean she is at the lodge in her carriage?

MORSE. No, sir—here. (AUBREY *looks towards* DRUMMLE, *perplexed*) There's a nice fire in your—in that room, sir. (*Glancing in the direction of the door leading to the bedroom.*)

AUBREY (*between his teeth, angrily*). Very well.
(MORSE *retires.*)

DRUMMLE (*looking at his watch*). A quarter to eleven—horrible! (*Taking up his hat and coat*) Must get to bed—up late every night this week. (AUBREY *assists* DRUMMLE *with his coat*) Thank you. Well, good night, Aubrey. I feel I've been deuced serious, quite out of keeping with myself; pray overlook it.

AUBREY (*kindly*). Ah, Cayley!

DRUMMLE (*putting on a neck-handkerchief*). And remember that, after all, I'm merely a spectator in life; nothing more than a man at a play, in fact; only, like the old-fashioned playgoer, I love to see certain characters happy and comfortable at the finish. You understand?

AUBREY. I think I do.

DRUMMLE. Then, for as long as you can, old friend, will you—keep a stall for me?

AUBREY. Yes, Cayley.

DRUMMLE (*gaily*). Ah, ha! Good night! (*Bustling to the door*) Don't bother! I'll let myself out! Good night! God bless yer!

(*He goes out;* AUBREY *follows him.* MORSE *enters by the other door, carrying some unopened letters, which after a little consideration he places on the mantelpiece against the clock.* AUBREY *returns.*)

AUBREY. Yes?

MORSE. You hadn't seen your letters that came by the nine o'clock post, sir; I've put 'em where they'll catch your eye by-and-bye.

AUBREY. Thank you.

MORSE (*hesitatingly*). Gunter's cook and waiter have gone, sir. Would you prefer me to go to bed?

AUBREY (*frowning*). Certainly not.

MORSE. Very well, sir.

(*He goes out.*)

AUBREY (*opening the upper door*). Paula! Paula!

(PAULA *enters and throws her arms round his neck. She is a young woman of about twenty-seven: beautiful, fresh, innocent-looking. She is in superb evening dress.*)

PAULA. Dearest!

AUBREY. Why have you come here?

PAULA. Angry?

AUBREY. Yes—no. But it's eleven o'clock.

PAULA (*laughing*). I know.

AUBREY. What on earth will Morse think?

PAULA. Do you trouble yourself about what servants *think*?

AUBREY. Of course.

PAULA. Goose! They're only machines made to wait upon people—and to give evidence in the Divorce Court. (*Looking round*) Oh, indeed! A snug little dinner!

AUBREY. Three men.

PAULA (*suspiciously*). Men?

AUBREY. Men.

PAULA (*penitently*). Ah! (*Sitting at the table*) I'm so hungry.

AUBREY. Let me get you some game pie, or some—

PAULA. No, no, hungry for this. What beautiful fruit! I love fruit when it's expensive. (*He clears a space on the table, places a plate before her, and helps her to fruit*) I haven't dined, Aubrey dear.

AUBREY. My poor girl! Why?

PAULA. In the first place, I forgot to order any dinner, and my cook, who has always loathed me, thought he'd pay me out before he departed.

AUBREY. The beast!

PAULA. That's precisely what I—

AUBREY. No, Paula!

PAULA. What I told my maid to call him. What next will you think of me?

AUBREY. Forgive me. You must be starved.

PAULA (*eating fruit*). *I* didn't care. As there was nothing to eat, I sat in my best frock, with my toes on the dining-room fender, and dreamt, oh, such a lovely dinner party.

AUBREY. Dear lonely little woman!

PAULA. It was perfect. I saw you at the end of a very long table, opposite me, and we exchanged sly glances now and again over the flowers. We were host and hostess, Aubrey, and had been married about five years.

AUBREY (*kissing her hand*). Five years.

PAULA. And on each side of us was the nicest set imaginable—you know, dearest, the sort of men and women that can't be imitated.

AUBREY. Yes, yes. Eat some more fruit.

PAULA. But I haven't told you the best part of my dream.

AUBREY. Tell me.

PAULA. Well, although we had been married only such a few years, I seemed to know by the look on their faces that none of our guests had ever heard anything—anything—anything peculiar about the fascinating hostess.

AUBREY. That's just how it will be, Paula. The world moves so quickly. That's just how it will be.

PAULA (*with a little grimace*). I wonder! (*Glancing at the fire*) Ugh! Do throw another log on.

AUBREY (*mending the fire*). There. But you musn't be here long.

PAULA. Hospitable wretch! I've something important to tell you. No, stay where you are. (*Turning from him, her face averted*) Look here, that was my dream, Aubrey; but the fire went out while I was dozing, and I woke up with a regular fit of the shivers. And the result of it all was that I ran upstairs and scribbled you a letter.

AUBREY. Dear baby!

PAULA. Remain where you are. (*Taking a letter from her pocket*) This is it. I've given you an account of myself, furnished you with a list of my adventures since I—you know. (*Weighing the letter in her hand*) I wonder if it would go for a penny. Most of it you're acquainted with; *I've* told you a good deal, haven't I?

AUBREY. Oh, Paula!

PAULA. What I haven't told you I dare say you've heard from others. But in case they've omitted anything—the dears—it's all here.

AUBREY. In Heaven's name, why must you talk like this tonight?

PAULA. It may save discussion by-and-bye, don't you think? (*Holding out the letter*) There you are.

AUBREY. No, dear, no.

PAULA. Take it. (*He takes the letter*) Read it through after I've gone, and then—read it again, and turn the matter over in your mind finally. And if, even at the very last moment, you feel you—oughtn't to go to church with me, send a messenger to Pont Street, any time before eleven tomorrow, telling me that you're afraid, and I–I'll take the blow.

AUBREY. Why, what–what do you think I am?

PAULA. That's it. It's because I know you're such a dear good fellow that I want to save you the chance of ever feeling sorry you married me. I really love you so much, Aubrey, that to save you that, I'd rather you treated me as–as the others have done.

AUBREY (*turning from her with a cry*). Oh!

PAULA (*after a slight pause*). I suppose I've shocked you. I can't help it if I have.
(*She sits, with assumed languor and indifference. He turns to her, advances, and kneels by her.*)

AUBREY. My dearest, you don't understand me. I–I can't bear to hear you always talking about–what's done with. I tell you I'll never remember it; Paula, can't you dismiss it? Try. Darling, if we promise each other to forget, to forget, we're bound to be happy. After all, it's a mechanical matter; the moment a wretched thought enters your head, you quickly think of something bright–it depends on one's will. Shall I burn this, dear? (*Referring to the letter he holds in his hand*) Let me, let me!

PAULA (*with a shrug of the shoulders*). I don't suppose there's much that's new to you in it,–just as you like.
(*He goes to the fire and burns the letter.*)

AUBREY. There's an end of it. (*Returning to her*) What's the matter?

PAULA (*rising, coldly*). Oh, nothing! I'll go and put my cloak on.

AUBREY (*detaining her*). What *is* the matter?

PAULA. Well, I think you might have said, "You're very generous, Paula," or at least, "Thank you, dear," when I offered to set you free.

AUBREY (*catching her in his arms*). Ah!

PAULA. Ah! ah! Ha! ha! It's all very well, but you don't know what it cost me to make such an offer. I do so want to be married.

AUBREY. But you never imagined–?

PAULA. Perhaps not. And yet I *did* think of what I'd do at the end of our acquaintance if you had preferred to behave like the rest.
(*Taking a flower from her bodice.*)

AUBREY. Hush!

PAULA. Oh, I forgot!

AUBREY. What would you have done when we parted?

PAULA. Why, killed myself.

AUBREY. Paula, dear!

PAULA. It's true. (*Putting the flower in his buttonhole*) Do you know, I feel certain I should make away with myself if anything serious happened to me.

AUBREY. Anything serious! What, has nothing ever been serious to you, Paula?

PAULA. Not lately; not since a long while ago. I made up my mind then to have done with taking things seriously. If I hadn't, I– However, we won't talk about that.

AUBREY. But now, now, life will be different to you, won't it–quite different? Eh, dear?

PAULA. Oh, yes, now. Only, Aubrey, mind you keep me always happy.

AUBREY. I will try to.

PAULA. I know I couldn't swallow a second big dose of misery. I know that if ever I felt wretched again –truly wretched–I should take a leaf out of Connie Tirlemont's book. You remember? They found her– (*With a look of horror.*)

AUBREY. For God's sake, don't let your thoughts run on such things!

PAULA (*laughing*). Ha, ha, how scared you look! There, think of the time! Dearest, what will my coachman say? My cloak!
(*She runs off, gaily, by the upper door.* AUBREY *looks after her for a moment, then he walks up to the fire and stands warming his feet at the bars. As he does so he raises his head and observes the letters upon the mantelpiece. He takes one down quickly.*)

AUBREY. Ah! Ellean! (*Opening the letter and reading*) "My dear father,–A great change has come over me. I believe my mother in Heaven has spoken to me, and counselled me to turn to you in your loneliness. At any rate, your words have reached my heart, and I no longer feel fitted for this solemn life. I am ready to take my place by you. Dear father, will you receive me?–ELLEAN."
(PAULA *re-enters, dressed in a handsome cloak. He stares at her as if he hardly realised her presence.*)

PAULA. What are you staring at? Don't you admire my cloak?

AUBREY. Yes.

PAULA. Couldn't you wait till I'd gone before reading your letters?

AUBREY (*putting the letter away*). I beg your pardon.

PAULA. Take me downstairs to the carriage. (*Slipping her arm through his*) How I tease you! Tomorrow! I'm so happy! (*They go out.*)

ACT TWO

A morning-room in AUBREY TANQUERAY'S *house, "Highercoombe," near Willowmere, Surrey–a bright and prettily furnished apartment of irregular shape, with double doors opening into a small hall at the back, another door on the left, and a large recessed window through which is obtained a view of extensive grounds. Everything about the room is charming and graceful. The fire is burning in the grate, and a small table is tastefully laid for breakfast. It is a morning in early spring, and the sun is streaming in through the window.*

AUBREY *and* PAULA *are seated at breakfast, and* AUBREY *is silently reading his letters. Two servants, a man and a woman, hand dishes and then retire. After a little while* AUBREY *puts his letters aside and looks across to the window.*

AUBREY. Sunshine! Spring!

PAULA (*glancing at the clock*). Exactly six minutes.

AUBREY. Six minutes?

PAULA. Six minutes, Aubrey dear, since you made your last remark.

AUBREY. I beg your pardon: I was reading my letters. Have you seen Ellean this morning?

PAULA (*coldly*). Your last observation but one was about Ellean.

AUBREY. Dearest, what shall I talk about?

PAULA. Ellean breakfasted two hours ago, Morgan tells me, and then went out walking with her dog.

AUBREY. She wraps up warmly, I hope; this sunshine is deceptive.

PAULA. I ran about the lawn last night, after dinner, in satin shoes. Were you anxious about me?

AUBREY. Certainly.

PAULA (*melting*). Really?

AUBREY. You make me wretchedly anxious; you delight in doing incautious things. You are incurable.

PAULA. Ah, what a beast I am! (*Going to him and kissing him, then glancing at the letters by his side*) A letter from Cayley?

AUBREY. He is staying very near here, with Mrs. —— Very near here.

PAULA. With the lady whose chimneys we have the honour of contemplating from our windows?

AUBREY. With Mrs. Cortelyon—yes.

PAULA. Mrs. Cortelyon! The woman who might have set the example of calling on me when we first threw out roots in this deadly-lively soil! Deuce take Mrs. Cortelyon!

AUBREY. Hush! my dear girl!

PAULA (*returning to her seat*). Oh, I know she's an old acquaintance of yours—and of the first Mrs. Tanqueray. And she joins the rest of 'em in slapping the second Mrs. Tanqueray in the face. However, I have my revenge—she's six-and-forty, and I wish nothing worse to happen to any woman.

AUBREY. Well, she's going to town, Cayley says here, and his visit's at an end. He's coming over this morning to call on you. Shall we ask him to transfer himself to us? Do say yes.

PAULA. Yes.

AUBREY (*gladly*). Ah, ha! old Cayley.

PAULA (*coldly*). He'll amuse *you*.

AUBREY. And you too.

PAULA. Because you find a companion, shall I be boisterously hilarious?

AUBREY. Come, come! He talks London, and you know you like that.

PAULA. London! London or Heaven! which is farther from me!

AUBREY. Paula!

PAULA. Oh! Oh, I am so bored, Aubrey!

AUBREY (*gathering up his letters and going to her, leaning over her shoulder*). Baby, what can I do for you?

PAULA. I suppose, nothing. You have done all you can for me.

AUBREY. What do you mean?

PAULA. You have married me.
(*He walks away from her thoughtfully, to the writing table. As he places his letters on the table he sees an addressed letter, stamped for the post, lying on the blotting-book; he picks it up.*)

AUBREY (*in an altered tone*). You've been writing this morning before breakfast?

PAULA (*looking at him quickly, then away again*). Er—that letter.

AUBREY (*with the letter in his hand*). To Lady Orreyed. Why?

PAULA. Why not? Mabel's an old friend of mine.

AUBREY. Are you—corresponding?

PAULA. I heard from her yesterday. They've just returned from the Riviera. She seems happy.

AUBREY (*sarcastically*). That's good news.

PAULA. Why are you always so cutting about Mabel? She's a kind-hearted girl. Everything's altered; she even thinks of letting her hair go back to brown. She's Lady Orreyed. She's married to George. What's the matter with her?

AUBREY (*turning away*). Oh!

PAULA. You drive me mad sometimes with the tone you take about things! Great goodness, if you come to that, George Orreyed's wife isn't a bit worse than yours! (*He faces her suddenly*) I suppose I needn't have made that observation.

AUBREY. No, there was scarcely a necessity.
(*He throws the letter on to the table, and takes up the newspaper.*)

PAULA. I am very sorry.

AUBREY. All right, dear.

PAULA (*trifling with the letter*). I—I'd better tell you what I've written. I meant to do so, of course. I—I've asked the Orreyeds to come and stay with us. (*He looks at her, and lets the paper fall to the ground in a helpless way*) George was a great friend of Cayley's; I'm sure *he* would be delighted to meet them here.

AUBREY (*laughing mirthlessly*). Ha, ha, ha! They say Orreyed has taken to tippling at dinner. Heavens above!

PAULA. Oh! I've no patience with you! You'll kill me with this life! (*She selects some flowers from a vase on the table, cuts and arranges them, and fastens them in her bodice*) What is my existence, Sunday to Saturday? In the morning, a drive down to the village, with the groom, to give my orders to the tradespeople. At lunch, you and Ellean. In the afternoon, a novel, the newspapers: if fine, another drive—*if* fine! Tea—you and Ellean. Then two hours of dusk; then dinner—you and Ellean. Then a game of Bésique, you and I, while Ellean reads a religious book in a dull corner. Then a yawn from me, another from you, a sigh from Ellean; three figures suddenly rise—"Good night, good night, good night!" (*Imitating a kiss*) "God bless you!" Ah!

AUBREY. Yes, yes, Paula—yes, dearest—that's what it is *now*. But by-and-bye, if people begin to come round us—

PAULA. Hah! That's where we've made the mistake, my friend Aubrey! (*Pointing to the window*) Do you believe these people will *ever* come round us? Your former crony, Mrs. Cortelyon? Or the grim old vicar, or that wife of his whose huge nose is positively indecent? Or the Ullathornes, or the Gollans, or Lady William Petres? I know better! And when the young ones gradually take the place of the old, there will still remain the sacred tradition that the dreadful person who lives at the top of the hill is never, under any circumstances, to be called upon! And so we shall go on here, year in and year out, until the sap is run out of our lives, and we're stale and dry and withered from sheer, solitary respectability. Upon my word, I wonder we didn't see that we should have been far happier if we'd gone in for the devil-may-care, *café*-living sort of life in town! After all, *I* have a set, and you might have joined it. It's true, I did want, dearly, dearly, to be a married woman, but where's the pride in being a married woman among married women who are—married? If— (*Seeing that* AUBREY'S *head has sunk into his hands*) Aubrey! My dear boy! You're not—crying? (*He looks up, with a flushed face.* ELLEAN *enters, dressed very simply for walking. She is a low-voiced, grave girl of about nineteen, with a face somewhat resembling a Madonna. Towards* PAULA *her manner is cold and distant.*)

AUBREY (*in an undertone*). Ellean!

ELLEAN. Good morning, papa. Good morning, Paula.
(PAULA *puts her arms round* ELLEAN *and kisses her.* ELLEAN *makes little response.*)

PAULA. Good morning. (*Brightly*) We've been breakfasting this side of the house, to get the sun. (*She sits at the piano and rattles at a gay melody. Seeing that* PAULA'S *back is turned to them,* ELLEAN *goes to* AUBREY *and kisses him; he returns the kiss almost furtively. As they separate, the servants re-enter, and proceed to carry out the breakfast table.*)

AUBREY (*to* ELLEAN). I guess where you've been: there's some gorse clinging to your frock.

ELLEAN (*removing a sprig of gorse from her skirt*). Rover and I walked nearly as far as Black Moor. The poor fellow has a thorn in his pad; I am going up-stairs for my tweezers.

AUBREY. Ellean! (*She returns to him*) Paula is a little depressed —out of sorts. She complains that she has no companion.

ELLEAN. I am with Paula nearly all the day, papa.

AUBREY. Ah, but you're such a little mouse. Paula likes cheerful people about her.

ELLEAN. I'm afraid I am naturally rather silent; and it's so difficult to seem to be what one is not.

AUBREY. I don't wish that, Ellean.

ELLEAN. I will offer to go down to the village with Paula this morning —shall I?

AUBREY (*touching her hand gently*). Thank you—do.

ELLEAN. When I've looked after Rover, I'll come back to her. (*She goes out;* PAULA *ceases playing, and turns on the music-stool, looking at* AUBREY.)

PAULA. Well, have you and Ellean had your little confidence?

AUBREY. Confidence?

PAULA. Do you think I couldn't feel it, like a pain between my shoulders?

AUBREY. Ellean is coming back in a few minutes to be with you. (*Bending over her*) Paula, Paula dear, is this how you keep your promise?

PAULA. Oh! (*Rising impatiently, and crossing swiftly to the settee, where she sits, moving restlessly*) I *can't* keep my promise; I *am* jealous; it won't be smothered. I see you looking at her, watching her; your voice drops when you speak to her. I know how fond you are of that girl, Aubrey.

AUBREY. What would you have? I've no other home for her. She is my daughter.

PAULA. She is your saint. Saint Ellean!

AUBREY. You have often told me how good and sweet you think her.

PAULA. Good!—yes! Do you imagine *that* makes me less jealous? (*Going to him and clinging to his arm*) Aubrey, there are two sorts of affection—the love for a woman you respect, and the love for the woman you—love. She gets the first from you: I never can.

AUBREY. Hush, hush! You don't realise what you say.

PAULA. If Ellean cared for me only a little, it would be different. I shouldn't be jealous then. Why doesn't she care for me?

AUBREY. She—she—she will, in time.

PAULA. You can't say that without stuttering.

AUBREY. Her disposition seems a little unresponsive; she resembles her mother in many ways; I can see it every day.

PAULA. She's marble. It's a shame. There's not the slightest excuse; for all she knows, I'm as much a saint as she—only married. Dearest, help me to win her over!

AUBREY. Help you?

PAULA. You can. Teach her that it is her duty to love me; she hangs on to every word you speak. I'm sure, Aubrey, that the love of a nice woman who believed me to be like herself would do me a world of good. You'd get the benefit of it as well as I. It would soothe me; it would make me less horribly restless; it would take this —this—mischievous feeling from me. (*Coaxingly*) Aubrey!

AUBREY. Have patience; everything will come right.

PAULA. Yes, if you help me.

AUBREY. In the meantime you will tear up your letter to Lady Orreyed, won't you?

PAULA (*kissing his hand*). Of course I will—anything!

AUBREY. Ah, thank you, dearest! (*Laughing*) Why, good gracious! —ha, ha!—just imagine "Saint Ellean" and that woman side by side!

PAULA (*going back with a cry*). Ah!

AUBREY. What?

PAULA (*passionately*). It's Ellean you're considering, not me? It's all Ellean with you! Ellean! Ellean! (ELLEAN *re-enters.*)

ELLEAN. Did you call me, Paula? (*Clenching his hands,* AUBREY *turns away and goes out*) Is papa angry?

PAULA. I drive him distracted sometimes. There, I confess it!

ELLEAN. Do you? Oh, why do you?

PAULA. Because I—because I'm jealous.

ELLEAN. Jealous?

PAULA. Yes—of you. (ELLEAN *is silent*) Well, what do you think of that?

ELLEAN. I knew it; I've seen it. It hurts me dreadfully. What do you wish me to do? Go away?

PAULA. Leave us! (*Beckoning her with a motion of the head*) Look here! (ELLEAN *goes to* PAULA *slowly and unresponsively*) You could cure me of my jealousy very easily. Why don't you—like me?

ELLEAN. What do you mean by—like you? I don't understand.

PAULA. Love me.

ELLEAN. Love is not a feeling that is under one's control. I shall alter as time goes on, perhaps. I didn't begin to love my father deeply till a few months ago, and then I obeyed my mother.

PAULA. Ah, yes, you dream things, don't you—see them in your sleep? You fancy your mother speaks to you?

ELLEAN. When you have lost your mother it is a comfort to believe that she is dead only to this life, that she still watches over her child. I do believe that of my mother.

PAULA. Well, and so you haven't been bidden to love *me?*

ELLEAN (*after a pause, almost inaudibly*). No.

PAULA. Dreams are only a hash-up of one's day-thoughts, I suppose you know. Think intently of anything, and it's bound to come back to you at night. I don't cultivate dreams myself.

ELLEAN. Ah, I knew you would only sneer!

PAULA. I'm not sneering; I'm speaking the truth. I say that if you cared for me in the daytime I should soon make friends with those nightmares of yours. Ellean, why don't you try to look on me as your second mother? Of course there are not many years between us, but I'm ever so much older than you—in experience. I shall have no children of my own, I know that; it would be a real comfort to me if you would make me feel we belonged to each other. Won't you? Perhaps you think I'm odd—not nice. Well, the fact is I've two sides to my nature, and I've let the one almost smother the other. A few years ago I went through some trouble, and since then I haven't shed a tear. I believe if you put your arms round me just once I should run rupstairs and have a good cry. There, I've talked to you as I've never talked to a woman in my life. Ellean, you seem to fear me. Don't! Kiss me! (*With a cry, almost of despair,* ELLEAN *turns from* PAULA *and sinks on to the settee, covering her face with her hands.*)

PAULA (*indignantly*). Oh! Why is it! How dare you treat me like this? What do you mean by it? What do you mean?
(*A* SERVANT *enters.*)

SERVANT. Mr. Drummle, ma'am.
(CAYLEY DRUMMLE, *in riding-dress, enters briskly. The* SERVANT *retires.*)

PAULA (*recovering herself*). Well, Cayley!

DRUMMLE (*shaking hands with her cordially*). How are you? (*Shaking hands with* ELLEAN, *who rises*) I saw you in the distance an hour ago, in the gorse near Stapleton's.

ELLEAN. I didn't see you, Mr. Drummle.

DRUMMLE. My dear Ellean, it is my experience that no charming young lady of nineteen ever does see a man of forty-five. (*Laughing*) Ha, Ha!

ELLEAN (*going to the door*). Paula, papa wishes me to drive down to the village with you this morning. Do you care to take me?

PAULA (*coldly*). Oh, by all means. Pray tell Watts to balance the cart for three.
(ELLEAN *goes out.*)

DRUMMLE. How's Aubrey?

PAULA. Very well—when Ellean's about the house.

DRUMMLE. And you? I needn't ask.

PAULA (*walking away to the window*). Oh, a dog's life, my dear Cayley, mine.

DRUMMLE. Eh?

PAULA. Doesn't that define a happy marriage? I'm sleek, well-kept, well-fed, never without a bone to gnaw and fresh straw to lie upon. (*Gazing out of the window*) Oh, dear me!

DRUMMLE. H'm! Well, I heartily congratulate you on your kennel. The view from the terrace here is superb.

PAULA. Yes; I can see London.

DRUMMLE. London! Not quite so far, surely?

PAULA. *I* can. Also the Mediterranean, on a fine day. I wonder what Algiers looks like this morning from the sea! (*Impulsively*) Oh, Cayley, do you remember those jolly times on board Peter Jarman's yacht when we lay off—? (*Stopping suddenly, seeing* DRUMMLE *staring at her*) Good gracious! What are we talking about!
(AUBREY *enters.*)

AUBREY (*to* DRUMMLE). Dear old chap! Has Paula asked you?

PAULA. Not yet.

AUBREY. We want you to come to us, now that you're leaving Mrs. Cortelyon—at once, today. Stay a month, as long as you please—eh, Paula?

PAULA. As long as you can possibly endure it—do, Cayley.

DRUMMLE (*looking at* AUBREY). Delighted. (*To* PAULA) Charming of you to have me.

PAULA. My dear man, you're a blessing. I must telegraph to London for more fish! A strange appetite to cater for! Something to do, to do, to do! (*She goes out in a mood of almost childish delight.*)

DRUMMLE (*eyeing* AUBREY). Well?

AUBREY (*with a wearied anxious look*). Well, Cayley?

DRUMMLE. How are you getting on?

AUBREY. My position doesn't grow less difficult. I told you, when I met you last week, of this feverish, jealous attachment of Paula's for Ellean?

DRUMMLE. Yes. I hardly know why, but I came to the conclusion that you don't consider it an altogether fortunate attachment.

AUBREY. Ellean doesn't respond to it.

DRUMMLE. These are early days. Ellean will warm towards your wife by-and-bye.

AUBREY. Ah, but there's the question, Cayley!

DRUMMLE. What question?

AUBREY. The question which positively distracts me. Ellean is so different from—most women; I don't believe a purer creature exists out of heaven. And I—I ask myself, am I doing right in exposing her to the influence of poor Paula's light, careless nature?

DRUMMLE. My dear Aubrey!

AUBREY. That shocks you! So it does me. I assure you I long to urge my girl to break down the reserve which keeps her apart from

Paula, but somehow I can't do it—well, I don't do it. How can I make you understand? But when you come to us you'll understand quickly enough. Cayley, there's hardly a subject you can broach on which poor Paula hasn't some strange, out-of-the-way thought to give utterance to; some curious, warped notion. They are not mere *worldly* thoughts—unless, good God! they belong to the little hellish world which our blackguardism has created: no, her ideas have too little calculation in them to be called worldly. But it makes it the more dreadful that such thoughts should be ready, spontaneous; that expressing them has become a perfectly natural process; that her words, acts even, have almost lost their proper significance for her, and seem beyond her control. Ah, and the pain of listening to it all from the woman one loves, the woman one hoped to make happy and contented, who is really and truly a good woman, as it were, maimed! Well, this is my burden, and I shouldn't speak to you of it but for my anxiety about Ellean. Ellean! What is to be her future? It is in my hands; what am I to do? Cayley, when I remember how Ellean comes to me, from another world I always think—when I realise the charge that's laid on me, I find myself wishing, in a sort of terror, that my child were safe under the ground!

DRUMMLE. My dear Aubrey, aren't you making a mistake?

AUBREY. Very likely. What is it?

DRUMMLE. A mistake, not in regarding your Ellean as an angel, but in believing that, under any circumstances, it would be possible for her to go through life without getting her white robe—shall we say, a little dusty at the hem? Don't take me for a cynic. I am sure there are many women upon earth who are almost divinely innocent; but being on earth, they must send their robes to the laundry occasionally. Ah, and it's right that they should have to do so, for what can they learn from the checking of their little washing-bills but lessons of charity? Now I see but two courses open to you for the disposal of your angel.

AUBREY. Yes?

DRUMMLE. You must either restrict her to a paradise which is, like every earthly paradise, necessarily somewhat imperfect, or treat her as an ordinary flesh-and-blood young woman, and give her the advantages of that society to which she properly belongs.

AUBREY. Advantages?

DRUMMLE. My dear Aubrey, of all forms of innocence mere ignorance is the least admirable. Take my advice, let her walk and talk and suffer and be healed with the great crowd. Do it, and hope that she'll some day meet a good, honest fellow who'll make her life complete, happy, secure. Now you see what I'm driving at.

AUBREY. A sanguine programme, my dear Cayley! Oh, I'm not pooh-poohing it. Putting sentiment aside, of course I know that a fortunate marriage for Ellean would be the best—perhaps the only—solution of my difficulty. But you forget the danger of the course you suggest.

DRUMMLE. Danger?

AUBREY. If Ellean goes among men and women, how can she escape from learning, sooner or later, the history of—poor Paula's—old life?

DRUMMLE. H'm! You remember the episode of the Jeweller's Son in the Arabian Nights? Of course you don't. Well, if your daughter lives, she *can't* escape—what you're afraid of. (AUBREY *gives a half-stifled exclamation of pain*) And when she does hear the story, surely it would be better that she should have some knowledge of the world to help her to understand it.

AUBREY. To understand!

DRUMMLE. To understand, to—philosophise.

AUBREY. To philosophise?

DRUMMLE. Philosophy is toleration, and it is only one step from toleration to forgiveness.

AUBREY. You're right, Cayley; I believe you always are. Yes, yes. But, even if I had the courage to attempt to solve the problem of Ellean's future in this way, I—I'm helpless.

DRUMMLE. How?

AUBREY. What means have I now of placing my daughter in the world I've left?

DRUMMLE. Oh, some friend—some woman friend.

AUBREY. I have none; they're gone.

DRUMMLE. You're wrong there; I know one—

AUBREY (*listening*). That's Paula's cart. Let's discuss this again.

DRUMMLE (*going up to the window and looking out*). It isn't the dog-cart. (*Turning to* AUBREY) I hope you'll forgive me, old chap.

AUBREY. What for?

DRUMMLE. Whose wheels do you think have been cutting ruts in your immaculate drive?
(*A* SERVANT *enters.*)

SERVANT (*to* AUBREY). Mrs. Cortelyon, sir.

AUBREY. Mrs. Cortelyon! (*After a short pause*) Very well. (*The* SERVANT *withdraws*) What on earth is the meaning of this?

DRUMMLE. Ahem! While I've been our old friend's guest, Aubrey, we have very naturally talked a good deal about you and yours.

AUBREY. Indeed, have you?

DRUMMLE. Yes; and Alice Cortelyon has arrived at the conclusion that it would have been far kinder had she called on Mrs. Tanqueray long ago. She's going abroad for Easter before settling down in London for the season, and I believe she has come over this morning to ask for Ellean's companionship.

AUBREY. Oh, I see! (*Frowning*) Quite a friendly little conspiracy, my dear Cayley!

DRUMMLE. Conspiracy! Not at all, I assure you. (*Laughing*) Ha, ha! (ELLEAN *enters from the hall with* MRS. CORTELYON, *a handsome, good-humoured, spirited woman of about forty-five.*)

ELLEAN. Papa—

MRS. CORTELYON (*to* AUBREY, *shaking hands with him heartily*). Well, Aubrey, how are you? I've just been telling this great girl of yours that I knew her when she was a sad-faced, pale baby. How is Mrs. Tanqueray? I have been a bad neighbour, and I'm here to beg forgiveness. Is she indoors?

AUBREY. She's upstairs putting on a hat, I believe.

MRS. CORTELYON (*sitting comfortably*). Ah! (*She looks round:* DRUMMLE *and* ELLEAN *are talking together in the hall*) We used to be very frank with each other, Aubrey. I suppose the old footing is no longer possible, eh?

AUBREY. If so, I'm not entirely to blame, Mrs. Cortelyon.

MRS. CORTELYON. Mrs. Cortelyon? H'm! No, I admit it. But you must make some little allowance for me, *Mr. Tanqueray*. Your first wife and I, as girls, were like two cherries on one stalk, and then I was the confidential friend of your married life. That post, perhaps, wasn't altogether a sinecure. And now—well, when a woman gets to my age I suppose she's a stupid, prejudiced, conventional creature. However, I've got over it and—(*giving him her hand*)—I hope you'll be enormously happy and let me be a friend once more.

AUBREY. Thank you, Alice.

MRS. CORTELYON. That's right. I feel more cheerful than I've done for weeks. But I suppose it would serve me right if the second Mrs. Tanqueray showed me the door. Do you think she will?

AUBREY (*listening*). Here is my wife. (MRS. CORTELYON *rises, and* PAULA *enters, dressed for driving; she stops abruptly on seeing* MRS. CORTELYON) Paula, dear, Mrs. Cortelyon has called to see you.
(PAULA *starts, looks at* MRS. CORTELYON *irresolutely, then after a slight pause barely touches* MRS. CORTELYON'S *extended hand.*)

PAULA (*whose manner now alternates between deliberate insolence and assumed sweetness*). Mrs. —? What name, Aubrey?

AUBREY. Mrs. Cortelyon.

PAULA. Cortelyon? Oh, yes. Cortelyon.

MRS. CORTELYON (*carefully guarding herself throughout against any expression of resentment*). Aubrey ought to have told you that Alice Cortelyon and he are very old friends.

PAULA. Oh, very likely he has mentioned the circumstance. I have quite a wretched memory.

MRS. CORTELYON. You know we are neighbours, Mrs. Tanqueray.

PAULA. Neighbours? Are we really? Won't you sit down? (*They both sit*) Neighbours! That's most interesting!

MRS. CORTELYON. Very near neighbours. You can see my roof from your windows.

PAULA. I fancy I *have* observed a roof. But you have been away from home; you have only just returned.

MRS. CORTELYON. I? What makes you think that?

PAULA. Why, because it is two months since we came to Highercoombe, and I don't remember your having called.

MRS. CORTELYON. Your memory is now terribly accurate. No, I've not been away from home, and it is to explain my neglect that I am here, rather unceremoniously, this morning.

PAULA. Oh, to explain—quite so. (*With mock solicitude*) Ah, you've been very ill; I ought to have seen that before.

MRS. CORTELYON. Ill!

PAULA. You look dreadfully pulled down. We poor women show illness so plainly in our faces, don't we?

AUBREY (*anxiously*). Paula dear, Mrs. Cortelyon is the picture of health.

MRS. CORTELYON (*with some asperity*). I have never *felt* better in my life.

PAULA (*looking round innocently*). Have I said anything awkward? Aubrey, tell Mrs. Cortelyon how stupid and thoughtless I always am!

MRS. CORTELYON (*to* DRUMMLE, *who is now standing close to her*). Really, Cayley—! (*He soothes her with a nod and smile and a motion of his finger to his lip*) Mrs. Tanqueray, I am afraid my explanation will not be quite so satisfactory as either of those you have just helped me to. You may have heard—but, if you have heard, you have doubtless forgotten—that twenty years ago, when your husband first lived here, I was a constant visitor at Highercoombe.

PAULA. Twenty years ago—fancy! I was a naughty little child then.

MRS. CORTELYON. Possibly. Well, at that time, and till the end of her life, my affections were centred upon the lady of this house.

PAULA. Were they? That was very sweet of you.

(ELLEAN *approaches* MRS. CORTELYON, *listening intently to her.*)

MRS. CORTELYON. I will say no more on that score, but I must add this: when, two months ago, you came here, I realised, perhaps for the first time, that I was a middle-aged woman, and that it had become impossible for me to accept without some effort a breaking-in upon many tender associations. There, Mrs. Tanqueray, that is my confession. Will you try to understand it and pardon me?

PAULA (*watching* ELLEAN,—*sneeringly*). Ellean dear, you appear to be very interested in Mrs. Cortelyon's reminiscences; I don't think I can do better than make you my mouthpiece—there is such sympathy between us. What do you say—can we bring ourselves to forgive Mrs. Cortelyon for neglecting us for two weary months?

MRS. CORTELYON (*to* ELLEAN, *pleasantly*). Well, Ellean? (*With a little cry of tenderness* ELLEAN *impulsively sits beside* MRS. CORTELYON *and takes her hand*) My dear child!

PAULA (*in an undertone to* AUBREY). Ellean isn't so very slow in taking to Mrs. Cortelyon!

MRS. CORTELYON (*to* PAULA *and* AUBREY). Come, this encourages me to broach my scheme. Mrs. Tanqueray, it strikes me that you two good people are just now excellent company for each other, while Ellean would perhaps be glad of a little peep into the world you are anxious to avoid. Now, I'm going to Paris tomorrow for a week or two before settling down in Chester Square, so—don't gasp, both of you!—if this girl is willing, and you have made no other arrangements for her, will you let her come with me to Paris, and afterwards remain with me in town during the season? (ELLEAN *utters an exclamation of surprise.* PAULA *is silent*) What do you say?

AUBREY. Paula—Paula dear. (*Hesitatingly*) My dear Mrs. Cortelyon, this is wonderfully kind of you; I am really at a loss to—eh, Cayley?

DRUMMLE (*watching* PAULA *apprehensively*). Kind! Now I must say I don't think so! I begged Alice to take *me* to Paris, and she declined. I am thrown over for Ellean! Ha! ha!

MRS. CORTELYON (*laughing*). What nonsense you talk, Cayley!
(*The laughter dies out.* PAULA *remains quite still.*)

AUBREY. Paula dear.

PAULA (*slowly collecting herself*). One moment. I—I don't quite— (*To* MRS. CORTELYON) You propose that Ellean leaves Highercoombe almost at once, and remains with you some months?

MRS. CORTELYON. It would be a mercy to me. You can afford to be generous to a desolate old widow. Come, Mrs. Tanqueray, won't you spare her?

PAULA. Won't *I* spare her. (*Suspiciously*) Have you mentioned your plan to Aubrey—before I came in?

MRS. CORTELYON. No, I had no opportunity.

PAULA. Nor to Ellean?

MRS. CORTELYON. Oh, no.

PAULA (*looking about her in suppressed excitement*). This hasn't been discussed at all, behind my back?

MRS. CORTELYON. My dear Mrs. Tanqueray!

PAULA. Ellean, let us hear your voice in the matter!

ELLEAN. I should like to go with Mrs. Cortelyon—

PAULA. Ah!

ELLEAN. That is, if—if—

PAULA. If—what?

ELLEAN (*looking towards* AUBREY, *appealingly*). Papa!

PAULA (*in a hard voice*). Oh, of course—I forgot. (*To* AUBREY) My dear Aubrey, it rests with you, naturally, whether I am—to lose—Ellean.

AUBREY. Lose Ellean! (*Advancing to* PAULA) There is no question of losing Ellean. You would see Ellean in town constantly when she returned from Paris; isn't that so, Mrs. Cortelyon?

MRS. CORTELYON. Certainly.

PAULA (*laughing softly*). Oh, I didn't know I should be allowed that privilege.

MRS. CORTELYON. Privilege, my dear Mrs. Tanqueray!

PAULA. Ha, ha! that makes all the difference, doesn't it?

AUBREY (*with assumed gaiety*). All the difference? I should think so! (*To* ELLEAN, *laying his hand upon her head tenderly*) And you are quite certain you wish to see what the world is like on the other side of Black Moor!

ELLEAN. If you are willing, papa, I am quite certain.

AUBREY (*looking at* PAULA *irresolutely, then speaking with an effort*). Then I—I am willing.

PAULA (*rising and striking the table lightly with her clenched hand*). That decides it! (*There is a general movement. Excitedly to* MRS. CORTELYON, *who advances towards her*) When do you want her?

MRS. CORTELYON. We go to town this afternoon at five o'clock, and sleep tonight at Bayliss's. There is barely time for her to make her preparations.

PAULA. I will undertake that she is ready.

MRS. CORTELYON. I've a great deal to scramble through at home too, as you may guess. Good-bye!

PAULA (*turning away*). Mrs. Cortelyon is going. (PAULA *stands looking out of the window, with her back to those in the room.*)

MRS. CORTELYON (*to* DRUMMLE). Cayley—

DRUMMLE (*to her*). Eh?

MRS. CORTELYON. I've gone through it, for the sake of Aubrey and his child, but I—I feel a hundred. Is that a mad-woman?

DRUMMLE. Of course; all jealous women are mad. (*He goes out with* AUBREY.)

MRS. CORTELYON (*hesitatingly, to* PAULA). Good-bye, Mrs. Tanqueray.
(PAULA *inclines her head with the slightest possible movement, then resumes her former position.* ELLEAN *comes from the hall and takes* MRS. CORTELYON *out of the room. After a brief silence,* PAULA *turns with a fierce cry, and hurriedly takes off her coat and hat, and tosses them upon the settee.*)

PAULA. Who's that? Oh! Oh! Oh! (*She drops into the chair as* AUBREY *returns; he stands looking at her.*)

AUBREY. I—you have altered your mind about going out?

PAULA. Yes. Please to ring the bell.

AUBREY (*touching the bell*). You are angry about Mrs. Cortelyon and Ellean. Let me try to explain my reasons—

PAULA. Be careful what you say to me just now! I have never felt like this—except once—in my life. Be careful what you say to me!
(*A* SERVANT *enters.*)

PAULA (*rising*). Is Watts at the door with the cart?

SERVANT. Yes, ma'am.

PAULA. Tell him to drive down to the post-office directly with this. (*Picking up the letter which has been lying upon the table.*)

AUBREY. With that?

PAULA. Yes. My letter to Lady Orreyed. (*Giving the letter to the* SERVANT, *who goes out.*)

AUBREY. Surely you don't wish me to countermand any order of yours to a servant? Call the man back—take the letter from him!

PAULA. I have not the slightest intention of doing so.

AUBREY. I must, then. (*Going to the door. She snatches up her hat and coat and follows him*) What are you going to do?

PAULA. If you stop that letter, I walk out of the house. (*He hesitates, then leaves the door.*)

AUBREY. I am right in believing that to be the letter inviting George Orreyed and his wife to stay here, am I not?

PAULA. Oh, yes—quite right.

AUBREY. Let it go; I'll write to him by-and-bye.

PAULA (*facing him*). You dare!

AUBREY. Hush, Paula!

PAULA. Insult me again and, upon my word, I'll go straight out of the house!

AUBREY. Insult you?

PAULA. Insult me! What else is it? My God! what else is it? What do you mean by taking Ellean from me?

AUBREY. Listen—!

PAULA. Listen to *me!* And how do you take her? You pack her off in the care of a woman who has deliberately held aloof from me, who's thrown mud at me! Yet this Cortelyon creature has only to put foot here once to be entrusted with the charge of the girl you know I dearly want to keep near me!

AUBREY. Paula dear! hear me—!

PAULA. Ah! of course, of course! I can't be so useful to your daughter as such people as this; and so I'm to be given the go-by for any town friend of yours who turns up and chooses to patronise us! Hah! Very well, at any rate, as you take Ellean from me you justify my looking for companions where I can most readily find 'em.

AUBREY. You wish me to fully appreciate your reason for sending that letter to Lady Orreyed?

PAULA. Precisely—I do.

AUBREY. And could you, after all, go back to associates of that order? It's not possible!

PAULA (*mockingly*). What, not after the refining influence of these intensely respectable surroundings? (*Going to the door*) We'll see!

AUBREY. Paula!

PAULA (*violently*). We'll see! (*She goes out. He stands still looking after her.*)

ACT THREE

The drawing-room at "Highercoombe." Facing the spectator are two large French windows, sheltered by a verandah, leading into the garden; on the right is a door opening into a small hall. The fireplace, with a large mirror above it, is on the left-hand side of the room, and higher up in the same wall are double doors recessed. The room is richly furnished, and everything betokens taste and luxury. The windows are open, and there is moonlight in the garden.

LADY ORREYED, *a pretty, affected doll of a woman, with a mincing voice and flaxen hair, is sitting on the ottoman, her head resting against the drum, and her eyes closed.* PAULA, *looking pale, worn, and thoroughly unhappy, is sitting at a table. Both are in sumptuous dinner-gowns.*

LADY ORREYED (*opening her eyes*). Well, I never! I dropped off! (*Feeling her hair*) Just fancy! Where are the men?

PAULA (*icily*). Outside, smoking. (*A* SERVANT *enters with coffee, which he hands to* LADY ORREYED. SIR GEORGE ORREYED *comes in by the window. He is a man of about thirty-five, with a low forehead, a receding chin, a vacuous expression, and an ominous redness about the nose.*)

LADY ORREYED (*taking coffee*). Here's Dodo.

SIR GEORGE. I say, the flies under the verandah make you swear. (*The* SERVANT *hands coffee to* PAULA, *who declines it, then to* SIR GEORGE, *who takes a cup*) Hi! wait a bit! (*He looks at the tray searchingly, then puts back his cup*) Never mind. (*Quietly to* LADY ORREYED) I say, they're dooced sparin' with their liqueur, ain't they?
(*The* SERVANT *goes out at window.*)

PAULA (*to* SIR GEORGE). Won't you take coffee, George?

SIR GEORGE. No, thanks. It's gettin' near time for a whiskey and potass. (*Approaching* PAULA, *regarding* LADY ORREYED *admiringly*) I say, Birdie looks rippin' tonight, don't she?

PAULA. Your wife?

SIR GEORGE. Yaas—Birdie.

PAULA. Rippin'?

SIR GEORGE. Yaas.

PAULA. Quite—quite rippin'.

(*He moves round to the settee.* PAULA *watches him with distaste, then rises and walks away.* SIR GEORGE *falls asleep on the settee.*)

LADY ORREYED. Paula love, I fancied you and Aubrey were a little more friendly at dinner. You haven't made it up, have you?

PAULA. We? Oh, no. We speak before others, that's all.

LADY ORREYED. And how long do you intend to carry on this game, dear?

PAULA (*turning away impatiently*). I really can't tell you.

LADY ORREYED. Sit down, old girl; don't be so fidgety. (PAULA *sits on the upper seat of the ottoman, with her back to* LADY ORREYED) Of course, it's my duty, as an old friend, to give you a good talking-to—(PAULA *glares at her suddenly and fiercely*)—but really I've found one gets so many smacks in the face through interfering in matrimonial squabbles that I've determined to drop it.

PAULA. I think you're wise.

LADY ORREYED. However, I must say that I do wish you'd look at marriage in a more solemn light—just as I do, in fact. It is such a beautiful thing—marriage, and if people in our position don't respect it, and set a good example by living happily with their husbands, what can you expect from the middle classes? When did this sad state of affairs between you and Aubrey actually begin?

PAULA. Actually, a fortnight and three days ago; I haven't calculated the minutes.

LADY ORREYED. A day or two before Dodo and I turned up—arrived.

PAULA. Yes. One always remembers one thing by another; we left off speaking to each other the morning I wrote asking you to visit us.

LADY ORREYED. Lucky for you I was able to pop down, wasn't it, dear?

PAULA (*glaring at her again*). Most fortunate.

LADY ORREYED. A serious split with your husband without a pal on the premises—I should say, without a friend in the house—would be most unpleasant.

PAULA (*turning to her abruptly*). This place must be horribly doleful for you and George just now. At least you ought to consider him before me. Why didn't you leave me to my difficulties?

LADY ORREYED. Oh, we're quite comfortable, dear, thank you—both of us. George and me are so wrapped up in each other, it doesn't matter where we are. I don't want to crow over you, old girl, but I've got a perfect husband. (SIR GEORGE *is now fast asleep, his head thrown back and his mouth open, looking hideous.*)

PAULA (*glancing at* SIR GEORGE). So you've given me to understand.

LADY ORREYED. Not that we don't have our little differences. Why, we fell out only this very morning. You remember the diamond and ruby tiara Charley Prestwick gave poor dear Connie Tirlemont years ago, don't you?

PAULA. No, I do not.

LADY ORREYED. No? Well, it's in the market. Benjamin of Piccadilly has got it in his shop window, and I've set my heart on it.

PAULA. You consider it quite necessary?

LADY ORREYED. Yes, because what I say to Dodo is this—a lady of my station must smother herself with hair ornaments. It's different with you, love—people don't look for so much blaze from you, but I've got rank to keep up; haven't I?

PAULA. Yes.

LADY ORREYED. Well, that was the cause of the little set-to between I and Dodo this morning. He broke two chairs, he was in such a rage. I forgot they're your chairs; do you mind?

PAULA. No.

LADY ORREYED. You know, poor Dodo can't lose his temper without smashing something; if it isn't a chair, it's a mirror; if it isn't that, it's china—a bit of Dresden for choice. Dear old pet! he loves a bit of Dresden when he's furious. He doesn't really throw things *at* me, dear; he simply lifts them up and drops them, like a gentleman. I expect our room upstairs will look rather wrecky before I get that tiara.

PAULA. Excuse the suggestion; perhaps your husband can't afford it.

LADY ORREYED. Oh, how dreadfully changed you are, Paula! Dodo can always mortgage something, or borrow of his ma. What *is* coming to you!

PAULA. Ah! (*She sits at the piano and touches the keys.*)

LADY ORREYED. Oh, yes, do play! That's the one thing I envy you for.

PAULA. What shall I play?

LADY ORREYED. What was that heavenly piece you gave us last night, dear?

PAULA. A bit of Schubert. Would you like to hear it again?

LADY ORREYED. You don't know any comic songs, do you?

PAULA. I'm afraid not.

LADY ORREYED. I leave it to you. (PAULA *plays.* AUBREY *and* CAYLEY DRUMMLE *appear outside the window; they look into the room.*)

AUBREY (*to* DRUMMLE). You can see her face in that mirror. Poor girl, how ill and wretched she looks.

DRUMMLE. When are the Orreyeds going?

AUBREY. Heaven knows! (*Entering the room.*)

DRUMMLE. But *you're* entertaining them; what's it to do with heaven? (*Following* AUBREY.)

AUBREY. Do you know, Cayley, that even the Orreyeds serve a useful purpose? My wife actually speaks to me before our guests—think of that! I've come to rejoice at the presence of the Orreyeds!

DRUMMLE. I dare say; we're taught that beetles are sent for a benign end.

AUBREY. Cayley, talk to Paula again tonight.

DRUMMLE. Certainly, if I get the chance.

AUBREY. Let's contrive it. George is asleep; perhaps I can get that doll out of the way. (*As they advance into the room,* PAULA *abruptly ceases playing and finds interest in a volume of music.* SIR GEORGE *is now nodding and snoring apoplectically*) Lady Orreyed, whenever you feel inclined for a game of billiards I'm at your service.

LADY ORREYED (*jumping up*). Charmed, I'm sure! I really thought you'd forgotten poor little me. Oh, look at Dodo!

AUBREY. No, no, don't wake him; he's tired.

LADY ORREYED. I must, he looks so plain. (*Rousing* SIR GEORGE) Dodo! Dodo!

SIR GEORGE (*stupidly*). 'Ullo!

LADY ORREYED. Dodo dear, you were snoring.

SIR GEORGE. Oh, I say, you could 'a told me that by-and-bye.

AUBREY. You want a cigar, George; come into the billiard-room. (*Giving his arm to* LADY ORREYED) Cayley, bring Paula. (AUBREY *and* LADY ORREYED *go out.*)

SIR GEORGE (*rising*). Hey, what! Billiard-room! (*Looking at his watch*) How goes the—? Phew! 'Ullo, 'Ullo! Whiskey and potass! (*He goes rapidly after* AUBREY *and* LADY ORREYED. PAULA *resumes playing.*)

PAULA (*after a pause*). Don't moon about after me, Cayley; follow the others.

DRUMMLE. Thanks, by-and-bye. (*Sitting*) That's pretty.

PAULA (*after another pause, still playing*). I wish you wouldn't stare so.

DRUMMLE. Was I staring? I'm sorry. (*She plays a little longer, then stops suddenly, rises, and goes to the window, where she stands looking out.* DRUMMLE *moves from the ottoman to the settee*) A lovely night.

PAULA (*startled*). Oh! (*Without turning to him*) Why do you hop about like a monkey?

DRUMMLE. Hot rooms play the deuce with the nerves. Now, it would have done you good to have walked in the garden with us after dinner and made merry. Why didn't you?

PAULA. You know why.

DRUMMLE. Ah, you're thinking of the—difference between you and Aubrey?

PAULA. Yes, I *am* thinking of it.

DRUMMLE. Well, so am I. How long–?

PAULA. Getting on for three weeks.

DRUMMLE. Bless me, it must be! And this would have been such a night to have healed it! Moonlight, the stars, the scent of flowers; and yet enough darkness to enable a kind woman to rest her hand for an instant on the arm of a good fellow who loves her. Ah, ha! It's a wonderful power, dear Mrs. Aubrey, the power of an offended woman! Only realise it! Just that one touch–the mere tips of her fingers–and, for herself and another, she changes the colour of the whole world.

PAULA (*turning to him calmly*). Cayley, my dear man, you talk exactly like a very romantic old lady. (*She leaves the window and sits playing with the knick-knacks on the table.*)

DRUMMLE (*to himself*). H'm, that hasn't done it! Well–ha, ha!–I accept the suggestion. An old woman, eh?

PAULA. Oh, I didn't intend–

DRUMMLE. But why not? I've every qualification–well, almost. And I confess it would have given this withered bosom a throb of grandmotherly satisfaction if I could have seen you and Aubrey at peace before I take my leave tomorrow.

PAULA. Tomorrow, Cayley!

DRUMMLE. I must.

PAULA. Oh, this house is becoming unendurable.

DRUMMLE. You're very kind. But you've got the Orreyeds.

PAULA (*fiercely*). The Orreyeds! I –I hate the Orreyeds! I lie awake at night, hating them!

DRUMMLE. Pardon me, I've understood that their visit is, in some degree, owing to–hem–your suggestion.

PAULA. Heavens! that doesn't make me like them better. Somehow or another, I–I've outgrown these people. This woman–I used to think her "jolly!"–sickens me. I can't breathe when she's near me: the whiff of her handkerchief turns me faint! And she patronises me by the hour, until I–I feel my nails growing longer with every word she speaks!

DRUMMLE. My dear lady, why on earth don't you say all this to Aubrey?

PAULA. Oh, I've been such an utter fool, Cayley!

DRUMMLE (*soothingly*). Well, well, mention it to Aubrey!

PAULA. No, no, you don't understand. What do you think I've done?

DRUMMLE. Done! What, *since* you invited the Orreyeds?

PAULA. Yes; I must tell you–

DRUMMLE. Perhaps you'd better not.

PAULA. Look here! I've intercepted some letters from Mrs. Cortelyon and Ellean to—him. (*Producing three unopened letters from the bodice of her dress*) There are the accursed things! From Paris—two from the Cortelyon woman, the other from Ellean!

DRUMMLE. But why—why?

PAULA. I don't know. Yes, I do! I saw letters coming from Ellean to her father; not a line to me—not a line. And one morning it happened I was downstairs before he was, and I spied this one lying with his heap on the breakfast-table, and I slipped it into my pocket—out of malice, Cayley, pure deviltry! And a day or two afterwards I met Elwes the postman at the Lodge, and took the letters from him, and found these others amongst 'em. I felt simply fiendish when I saw them—fiendish! (*Returning the letters to her bodice*) And now I carry them about with me, and they're scorching me like a mustard plaster!

DRUMMLE. Oh, this accounts for Aubrey not hearing from Paris lately!

PAULA. That's an ingenious conclusion to arrive at! Of course it does! (*With an hysterical laugh*) Ha, ha!

DRUMMLE. Well, well! (*Laughing*) Ha, ha, ha!

PAULA (*turning upon him*). I suppose it *is* amusing!

DRUMMLE. I beg pardon.

PAULA. Heaven knows I've little enough to brag about! I'm a bad lot, but not in mean tricks of this sort. In all my life this is the most caddish thing I've done. How am I to get rid of these letters—that's what I want to know? How am I to get rid of them?

DRUMMLE. If I were you I should take Aubrey aside and put them into his hands as soon as possible.

PAULA. What! and tell him to his face that I—! No, thank you. I suppose *you* wouldn't like to—

DRUMMLE. No, no; I won't touch 'em!

PAULA. And you call yourself my friend?

DRUMMLE (*good-humouredly*). No, I don't!

PAULA. Perhaps I'll tie them together and give them to his man in the morning.

DRUMMLE. That won't avoid an explanation.

PAULA (*recklessly*). Oh, then he must miss them—

DRUMMLE. And trace them.

PAULA (*throwing herself upon the ottoman*). I don't care!

DRUMMLE. I know you don't; but let me send him to you now, may I?

PAULA. Now! What do you think a woman's made of? I couldn't stand it, Cayley. I haven't slept for nights; and last night there was thunder, too! I believe I've got the horrors.

DRUMMLE (*taking the little hand-mirror from the table*). You'll sleep well enough when you deliver those letters. Come, come, Mrs. Aubrey—a good night's rest! (*Holding the mirror before her face*) It's quite time. (*She looks at herself for a moment, then snatches the mirror from him.*)

PAULA. You brute, Cayley, to show me that!

DRUMMLE. Then—may I? Be guided by a fr—a poor old woman! May I?

PAULA. You'll kill me, amongst you!

DRUMMLE. What do you say?

PAULA (*after a pause*). Very well. (*He nods his head and goes out rapidly. She looks after him for a moment, and calls "Cayley! Cayley!" Then she again produces the letters, deliberately, one by one, fingering them with aversion. Suddenly she starts, turning her head towards the door*) Ah!
(AUBREY *enters quickly.*)

AUBREY. Paula!

PAULA (*handing him the letters, her face averted*). There! (*He examines the letters, puzzled, and looks at her enquiringly*) They are many days old. I stole them, I suppose to make you anxious and unhappy. (*He looks at the letters again, then lays them aside on the table.*)

AUBREY (*gently*). Paula, dear, it doesn't matter.

PAULA (*after a short pause*). Why—why do you take it like this?

AUBREY. What did you expect?

PAULA. Oh, but I suppose silent reproaches are really the severest. And then, naturally, you are itching to open your letters. (*She crosses the room as if to go.*)

AUBREY. Paula! (*She pauses*) Surely, surely, it's all over now?

PAULA. All over! (*Mockingly*) Has my step-daughter returned then? When did she arrive? I haven't heard of it!

AUBREY. You can be very cruel.

PAULA. That word's always on a man's lips; he uses it if his soup's cold. (*With another movement as if to go*) Need we—

AUBREY. I know I've wounded you, Paula? But isn't there any way out of this?

PAULA. When does Ellean return? Tomorrow? Next week?

AUBREY (*wearily*). Oh! Why should we grudge Ellean the little pleasure she is likely to find in Paris and in London?

PAULA. I grudge her nothing, if that's a hit at me. But with that woman—?

AUBREY. It must be that woman or another. You know that at present we are unable to give Ellean the opportunity of—of—

PAULA. Of mixing with respectable people.

AUBREY. The opportunity of gaining friends, experience, ordinary knowledge of the world. If you are interested in Ellean, can't you see how useful Mrs. Cortelyon's good offices are?

PAULA. May I put one question? At the end of the London season, when Mrs. Cortelyon has done with Ellean, is it quite understood that the girl comes back to us? (AUBREY *is silent*) Is it? Is it?

AUBREY. Let us wait till the end of the season—

PAULA. Oh! I knew it. You're only fooling me; you put me off with any trash. I believe you've sent Ellean away, not for the reasons you give, but because you don't consider me a decent companion for her, because you're afraid she might get a little of her innocence rubbed off in my company? Come, isn't that the truth? Be honest! Isn't that it?

AUBREY. Yes. (*There is a moment's silence on both sides.*)

PAULA (*with uplifted hands as if to strike him*). Oh!

AUBREY (*taking her by the wrists*). Sit down. Sit down. (*He puts her into a chair; she shakes herself free with a cry*) Now listen to me. Fond as you are, Paula, of harking back to your past, there's one chapter of it you always let alone. I've never asked you to speak of it; you've never offered to speak of it. I mean the chapter that relates to the time when you were—like Ellean. (*She attempts to rise; he restrains her*) No, no.

PAULA. I don't choose to talk about that time. I won't satisfy your curiosity.

AUBREY. My dear Paula, I have no curiosity—I know what you were at Ellean's age. I'll tell you. You hadn't a thought that wasn't a wholesome one, you hadn't an impulse that didn't tend towards good, you never harboured a notion you couldn't have gossiped about to a parcel of children. (*She makes another effort to rise: he lays his hand lightly on her shoulder*) And this was a very few years back—there are days now when you look like a schoolgirl—but think of the difference between the two Paulas. You'll have to think hard, because after a cruel life, one's perceptions grow a thick skin. But, for God's sake, do think till you get these two images clearly in your mind, and then ask yourself what sort of a friend such a woman as you are today would have been for the girl of seven or eight years ago.

PAULA (*rising*). How dare you? I could be almost as good a friend to Ellean as her own mother would have been had she lived. I know what you mean. How dare you?

AUBREY. You say that; very likely you believe it. But you're blind, Paula; you're blind. You! Every belief that a young, pure-minded girl holds sacred—that you once held sacred—you now make a target for a jest, a sneer, a paltry cynicism. I tell you, you're not mistress any longer of your thoughts or your tongue. Why, how often, sitting between you and Ellean, have I seen her cheeks turn scarlet as you've rattled off some tale that belongs by right to the club or the smoking-room! Have you noticed the blush? If you have, has the cause of it ever struck you? And this is the girl you say you love, I admit that you *do* love, whose love you expect in return! Oh, Paula, I make the best, the only, excuse for you when I tell you you're blind!

PAULA. Ellean—Ellean blushes easily.

AUBREY. You blushed as easily a few years ago.

PAULA (*after a short pause*). Well! Have you finished your sermon?

AUBREY (*with a gesture of despair*). Oh, Paula!
(*Going up to the window, and standing with his back to the room.*)

PAULA (*to herself*). A few—years ago! (*She walks slowly towards the door, then suddenly drops upon the ottoman in a paroxysm of weeping*) O God! A few years ago!

AUBREY (*going to her*). Paula!

PAULA (*sobbing*). Oh, don't touch me!

AUBREY. Paula!

PAULA. Oh, go away from me! (*He goes back a few steps, and after a little while she becomes calmer and rises unsteadily; then in an altered tone*) Look here—! (*He advances a step; she checks him with a quick gesture*) Look here! Get rid of these people—Mabel and her husband—as soon as possible! I—I've done with them!

AUBREY (*in a whisper*). Paula!

PAULA. And then—then—when the time comes for Ellean to leave Mrs. Cortelyon, give me—give me another chance! (*He advances again, but she shrinks away*) No, no!
(*She goes out by the door on the right. He sinks on to the settee, covering his eyes with his hands. There is a brief silence, then a* SERVANT *enters.*)

SERVANT. Mrs. Cortelyon, sir, with Miss Ellean.
(AUBREY *rises to meet* MRS. CORTELYON, *who enters, followed by* ELLEAN, *both being in travelling dresses. The* SERVANT *withdraws.*)

MRS. CORTELYON (*shaking hands with* AUBREY). Oh, my dear Aubrey!

AUBREY. Mrs. Cortelyon! (*Kissing* ELLEAN) Ellean dear!

ELLEAN. Papa, is all well at home?

MRS. CORTELYON. We're shockingly anxious.

AUBREY. Yes, yes, all's well. This is quite unexpected. (*To* MRS. CORTELYON) You've found Paris insufferably hot?

MRS. CORTELYON. Insufferably hot! Paris is pleasant enough. We've had no letter from you!

AUBREY. I wrote to Ellean a week ago.

MRS. CORTELYON. Without alluding to the subject I had written to you upon.

AUBREY (*thinking*). Ah, of course—

MRS. CORTELYON. And since then we've both written, and you've been absolutely silent. Oh, it's too bad!

AUBREY (*picking up the letters from the table*). It isn't altogether my fault. Here are the letters—

ELLEAN. Papa!

MRS. CORTELYON. They're unopened.

AUBREY. An accident delayed their reaching me till this evening. I'm afraid this has upset you very much.

MRS. CORTELYON. Upset me!

ELLEAN (*in an undertone to* MRS. CORTELYON). Never mind. Not now, dear—not tonight.

AUBREY. Eh?

MRS. CORTELYON (*to* ELLEAN, *aloud*). Child, run away and take your things off. She doesn't look as if she'd journeyed from Paris today.

AUBREY. I've never seen her with such a colour. (*Taking* ELLEAN'S *hands.*)

ELLEAN (*to* AUBREY, *in a faint voice*). Papa, Mrs. Cortelyon has been so very, very kind to me, but I—I have come home. (*She goes out.*)

AUBREY. Come home! (*To* MRS. CORTELYON) Ellean returns to us then?

MRS. CORTELYON. That's the very point I put to you in my letters, and you oblige me to travel from Paris to Willowmere on a warm day to settle it. I think perhaps it's right that Ellean should be with you just now, although I— My dear friend, circumstances are a little altered.

AUBREY. Alice, you're in some trouble.

MRS. CORTELYON. Well—yes, I *am* in trouble. You remember pretty little Mrs. Brereton who was once Caroline Ardale?

AUBREY. Quite well.

MRS. CORTELYON. She's a widow now, poor thing. She has the *entresol* of the house where we've been lodging in the Avenue de Friedland. Caroline's a dear chum of mine; she formed a great liking for Ellean.

AUBREY. I'm very glad.

MRS. CORTELYON. Yes, it's nice for her to meet her mother's friends. Er—that young Hugh Ardale the papers were full of some time ago—he's Caroline Brereton's brother, you know.

AUBREY. No, I didn't know. What did he do? I forget.

MRS. CORTELYON. Checked one of those horrid mutinies at some faraway station in India. Marched down with a handful of his men and a few faithful natives, and held the place until he was relieved. They gave him his company and a V.C. for it.

AUBREY. And he's Mrs. Brereton's brother?

MRS. CORTELYON. Yes. He's with his sister—*was,* rather—in Paris. He's home—invalided. Good gracious, Aubrey, why don't you help me out? Can't you guess what has occurred?

AUBREY. Alice!

MRS. CORTELYON. Young Ardale—Ellean!

AUBREY. An attachment?

MRS CORTELYON. Yes, Aubrey. (*After a little pause*) Well, I suppose I've got myself into sad disgrace. But really I didn't foresee anything of this kind. A serious, reserved child like Ellean, and a boyish, high-spirited soldier—it never struck me as being likely. (AUBREY *paces to and fro thoughtfully*) I did all I could directly Captain Ardale spoke—wrote to you at once. Why on earth don't you receive your letters promptly, and when you do get them why can't you open them? I endured the anxiety till last night, and then made up my mind—home! Of course, it has worried me terribly. My head's bursting. Are there any salts about? (AUBREY *fetches a bottle from the cabinet and hands it to her*) We've had one of those hateful smooth crossings that won't let you be properly indisposed.

AUBREY. My dear Alice, I assure you I've no thought of blaming you.

MRS. CORTELYON. That statement always precedes a quarrel.

AUBREY. I don't know whether this is the worst or the best luck. How will my wife regard it? Is Captain Ardale a good fellow?

MRS. CORTELYON. My dear Aubrey, you'd better read up the accounts of his wonderful heroism. Face to face with death for a whole week; always with a smile and a cheering word for the poor helpless souls depending on him! Of course it's that that has stirred the depths of your child's nature. I've watched her while we've been dragging the story out of him, and if angels look different from Ellean at that moment, I don't desire to meet any, that's all!

AUBREY. If you were in my position—? But you can't judge.

MRS. CORTELYON. Why, if I had a marriageable daughter of my own, and Captain Ardale proposed for her, naturally I should cry my eyes out all night—but I should thank Heaven in the morning.

AUBREY. You believe so thoroughly in him?

MRS. CORTELYON. Do you think I should have only a headache at this minute if I didn't! Look here, you've got to see me down the lane; that's the least you can do, my friend. Come into my house for a moment and shake hands with Hugh.

AUBREY. What, is he here?

MRS. CORTELYON. He came through with us, to present himself formally tomorrow. Where are my gloves? (AUBREY *fetches them from the ottoman*) Make my apologies to Mrs. Tanqueray, please. She's well, I hope? (*Going towards the door*) I can't feel sorry she hasn't seen me in this condition.

ELLEAN *enters.*

ELLEAN (*to* MRS. CORTELYON). I've been waiting to wish you good night. I was afraid I'd missed you.

MRS. CORTELYON. Good night, Ellean.

ELLEAN (*in a low voice, embracing* MRS. CORTELYON). I can't thank you. Dear Mrs. Cortelyon!

MRS. CORTELYON (*her arms round* ELLEAN, *in a whisper to* AUBREY). Speak a word to her. (MRS. CORTELYON *goes out.*)

AUBREY (*to* ELLEAN). Ellean, I'm going to see Mrs. Cortelyon home. Tell Paula where I am; explain, dear. (*Going to the door.*)

ELLEAN (*her head drooping*). Yes. (*Quickly*) Father! You are angry with me—disappointed?

AUBREY. Angry? No.

ELLEAN. Disappointed?

AUBREY (*smiling and going to her and taking her hand*). If so, it's only because you've shaken my belief in my discernment. I thought you took after your poor mother a little, Ellean; but there's a look on your face tonight, dear, that I never saw on hers—never, never.

ELLEAN (*leaning her head on his shoulder*). Perhaps I ought not to have gone away.

AUBREY. Hush! you're quite happy?

ELLEAN. Yes.

AUBREY. That's right. Then, as you are quite happy, there is something I particularly want you to do for me, Ellean.

ELLEAN. What is that?

AUBREY. Be very gentle with Paula. Will you?

ELLEAN. You think I have been unkind.

AUBREY (*kissing her upon the forehead*). Be very gentle with Paula. (*He goes out, and she stands looking after him; then, as she turns thoughtfully from the door, a rose is thrown through the window and falls at her feet. She picks up the flower wonderingly and goes to the window.*)

ELLEAN (*starting back*). Hugh! (HUGH ARDALE, *a handsome young man of about seven-and-twenty, with a boyish face and manner, appears outside the window.*)

HUGH. Nelly! Nelly dear!

ELLEAN. What's the matter?

HUGH. Hush! Nothing. It's only fun. (*Laughing*) Ha, ha, ha! I've found out that Mrs. Cortelyon's meadow runs up to your father's plantation; I've come through a gap in the hedge.

ELLEAN. Why, Hugh?

HUGH. I'm miserable at The Warren: it's so different from the Avenue de Friedland. Don't look like that! Upon my word I meant just to peep at your home and go back, but I saw figures moving about here, and came nearer, hoping to get a glimpse of you. Was that your father? (*Entering the room.*)

ELLEAN. Yes.

HUGH. Isn't this fun! A rabbit ran across my foot while I was hiding behind that old yew.

ELLEAN. You must go away; it's not right for you to be here like this.

HUGH. But it's only fun, I tell you. You take everything so seriously. Do wish me good night.

ELLEAN. We have said good night.

HUGH. In the hall at The Warren, before Mrs. Cortelyon and a manservant. Oh, it's so different from the Avenue de Friedland!

ELLEAN (*giving him her hand hastily*). Good night, Hugh.

HUGH. Is that all? We might be the merest acquaintances. (*He momentarily embraces her, but she releases herself.*)

ELLEAN. It's when you're like this that you make me feel utterly miserable. (*Throwing the rose from her angrily*) Oh!

HUGH. I've offended you now, I suppose?

ELLEAN. Yes.

HUGH. Forgive me, Nelly. Come into the garden for five minutes; we'll stroll down to the plantation.

ELLEAN. No, no.

HUGH. For two minutes—to tell me you forgive me.

ELLEAN. I forgive you.

HUGH. Evidently. I sha'n't sleep a wink tonight after this. What a fool I am! Come down to the plantation. Make it up with me.

ELLEAN. There is somebody coming into this room. Do you wish to be seen here?

HUGH. I shall wait for you behind that yew tree. You must speak to me. Nelly!

(*He disappears.* PAULA *enters.*)

PAULA. Ellean!

ELLEAN. You—you are very surprised to see me, Paula, of course.

PAULA. Why are you here? Why aren't you with—your friend?

ELLEAN. I've come home—if you'll have me. We left Paris this morning; Mrs. Cortelyon brought me back. She was here a minute or two ago; papa has just gone with her to The Warren. He asked me to tell you.

PAULA. There are some people staying with us that I'd rather you didn't meet. It was hardly worth your while to return for a few hours.

ELLEAN. A few hours?

PAULA. Well, when do you go to London?

ELLEAN. I don't think I go to London, after all.

PAULA (*eagerly*). You—you've quarrelled with her?

ELLEAN. No, no, no, not that; but —Paula! (*In an altered tone*) Paula!

PAULA (*startled*). Eh? (ELLEAN *goes deliberately to* PAULA *and kisses her*) Ellean!

ELLEAN. Kiss me.

PAULA. What—what's come to you?

ELLEAN. I want to behave differently to you in the future. Is it too late?

PAULA. Too—late! (*Impulsively kissing* ELLEAN *and crying*) No—no—no! No—no!

ELLEAN. Paula, don't cry.

PAULA (*wiping her eyes*). I'm a little shaky; I haven't been sleeping. It's all right,—talk to me.

ELLEAN. There is something I want to tell you—

PAULA. Is there—is there?
(*They sit together on the ottoman,* PAULA *taking* ELLEAN'S *hand.*)

ELLEAN. Paula, in our house in the Avenue de Friedland, on the floor below us, there was a Mrs. Brereton. She used to be a friend of my mother's. Mrs. Cortelyon and I spent a great deal of our time with her.

PAULA (*suspiciously*). Oh! (*Letting* ELLEAN'S *hand fall*) Is this lady going to take you up in place of Mrs. Cortelyon?

ELLEAN. No, no. Her brother is staying with her—*was* staying with her. Her brother— (*Breaking off in confusion.*)

PAULA. Well?

ELLEAN (*almost inaudibly*). Paula—
(*She rises and walks away,* PAULA *following her.*)

PAULA. Ellean! (*Taking hold of her*) You're not in love! (ELLEAN *looks at* PAULA *appealingly*) Oh, *you* in love! You! Oh, this is why you've come home! Of course, you can make friends with me now! You'll leave us for good soon, I suppose; so it doesn't much matter being civil to me for a little while!

ELLEAN. Oh, Paula!

PAULA. Why, how you have deceived us—all of us! We've taken you for a cold-blooded little saint. The fools you've made of us! Saint Ellean, Saint Ellean!

ELLEAN. Ah, I might have known you'd only mock me!

PAULA (*her tone changing*). Eh?

ELLEAN. I—I can't talk to you. (*Sitting on the settee*) You do nothing else but mock and sneer, nothing else.

PAULA. Ellean dear! Ellean! I didn't mean it. I'm so horribly jealous, it's a sort of curse on me. (*Kneeling beside* ELLEAN *and embracing her*) My tongue runs away with me. I'm going to alter, I swear I am. I've made some good resolutions, and as God's above me, I'll keep them! If you are in love, if you do ever marry, that's no reason why we shouldn't be fond of each other. Come, you've kissed me of your own accord—you can't take it back. Now we're friends again, aren't we? Ellean dear! I want to know everything, everything. Ellean dear, Ellean!

ELLEAN. Paula, Hugh has done something that makes me very angry. He came with us from Paris today, to see papa. He is staying with Mrs. Cortelyon and—I ought to tell you—

PAULA. Yes, yes. What?

ELLEAN. He has found his way by The Warren meadow through the plantation up to this house. He is waiting to bid me good night. (*Glancing towards the garden*) He is—out there.

PAULA. Oh!

ELLEAN. What shall I do?

PAULA. Bring him in to see me! Will you?

ELLEAN. No, no.

PAULA. But I'm dying to know him. Oh, yes, you must. I shall meet him before Aubrey does. (*Excitedly running her hands over her hair*) I'm so glad. (ELLEAN *goes out by the window*) The mirror—mirror. What a fright I must look! (*Not finding the hand-glass on the table, she jumps on to the settee, and surveys herself in the mirror over the mantelpiece, then sits quietly down and waits*) Ellean! Just fancy! Ellean!
(*After a pause* ELLEAN *enters by the window with* HUGH.)

ELLEAN. Paula, this is Captain Ardale—Mrs. Tanqueray.
(PAULA *rises and turns, and she and* HUGH *stand staring blankly at each other for a moment or two; then* PAULA *advances and gives him her hand.*)

PAULA (*in a strange voice, but calmly*). How do you do?

HUGH. How do you do?

PAULA (*to* ELLEAN). Mr. Ardale and I have met in London, Ellean. Er—Captain Ardale now?

HUGH. Yes.

ELLEAN. In London?

PAULA. They say the world's very small, don't they?

HUGH. Yes.

PAULA. Ellean, dear, I want to have a little talk about you to Mr. Ardale – Captain Ardale – alone. (*Putting her arms round* ELLEAN, *and leading her to the door*) Come back in a little while. (ELLEAN *nods to* PAULA *with a smile and goes out, while* PAULA *stands watching her at the open door*) In a little while—in a little—(*Closing the door and then taking a seat facing* HUGH) Be quick! Mr. Tanqueray has only gone down to The Warren with Mrs. Cortelyon. What is to be done?

HUGH (*blankly*). Done?

PAULA. Done—done. Something must be done.

HUGH. I understand that Mr. Tanqueray had married a Mrs.—Mrs.—

PAULA. Jarman?

HUGH. Yes.

PAULA. I'd been going by that name. You didn't follow my doings after we separated.

HUGH. No.

PAULA (*sneeringly*). No.

HUGH. I went out to India.

PAULA. What's to be done?

HUGH. Damn this chance!

PAULA. Oh, my God!

HUGH. Your husband doesn't know, does he?

PAULA. That you and I—?

HUGH. Yes.

PAULA. No. He knows about others.

HUGH. Not about me. How long were we—?

PAULA. I don't remember, exactly.

HUGH. Do you—do you think it matters?

PAULA. His—his daughter. (*With a muttered exclamation he turns away, and sits with his head in his hands*) What's to be done?

HUGH. I wish I could think.

PAULA. Oh! Oh! What happened to that flat of ours in Ethelbert Street?

HUGH. I let it.

PAULA. All that pretty furniture?

HUGH. Sold it.

PAULA. I came across the key of the escritoire the other day in an old purse! (*Suddenly realising the horror and hopelessness of her position, and starting to her feet with an hysterical cry of rage*) What am I maundering about?

HUGH. For God's sake, be quiet! Do let me think.

PAULA. This will send me mad! (*Suddenly turning and standing over him*) You—you beast, to crop up in my life again like this!

HUGH. I always treated you fairly.

PAULA (*weakly*). Oh! I beg your pardon—I know you did—I— (*She sinks on to the settee crying hysterically.*)

HUGH. Hush!

PAULA. She kissed me tonight! I'd won her over! I've had such a fight to make her love me! and now—just as she's beginning to love me, to bring this on her!

HUGH. Hush, hush! Don't break down!

PAULA (*sobbing*). You don't know! I—I haven't been getting on well in my marriage. It's been my fault. The life I used to lead spoilt me completely. But I'd made up my mind to turn over a new leaf from tonight. From tonight!

HUGH. Paula—

PAULA. Don't you call me that!

HUGH. Mrs. Tanqueray, there is no cause for you to despair in this way. It's all right, I tell you—it *shall* be all right.

PAULA (*shivering*). What are we to do?

HUGH. Hold our tongues.

PAULA. Eh? (*Staring vacantly.*)

HUGH. The chances are a hundred to one against any one ever turning up who knew us when we were together. Besides, no one would be such a brute as to split on us. If anybody did do such a thing we should have to lie! What are we upsetting ourselves like this for, when we've simply got to hold our tongues?

PAULA. You're as mad as I am!

HUGH. Can you think of a better plan?

PAULA. There's only one plan possible—let's come to our senses!—Mr. Tanqueray must be told.

HUGH. Your husband! What, and I lose Ellean! I lose Ellean!

PAULA. You've got to lose her.

HUGH. I won't lose her; I can't lose her!

PAULA. Didn't I read of your doing any number of brave things in India? Why, you seem to be an awful coward!

HUGH. That's another sort of pluck altogether; I haven't this sort of pluck.

PAULA. Oh, I don't ask *you* to tell Mr. Tanqueray. That's my job.

HUGH (*standing over her*). You—you—you'd better! You—

PAULA (*rising*). Don't bully me! I intend to.

HUGH (*taking hold of her; she wrenches herself free*). Look here, Paula, I never treated you badly—you've owned it. Why should you want to pay me out like this? You don't know how I love Ellean!

PAULA. Yes, that's just what I *do* know.

HUGH. I say you don't! She's as good as my own mother. I've been downright honest with her, too. I told her, in Paris, that I'd been a bit wild at one time, and, after a damned wretched day, she promised to forgive me because of what I'd done since in India. She's behaved like an angel to me! Surely I oughtn't to lose her, after all, just because I've been like other fellows! No; I haven't been half as rackety as a hundred men we could think of. Paula, don't pay me out for nothing; be fair to me, there's a good girl—be fair to me!

PAULA. Oh, I'm not considering you at all! I advise you not to stay here any longer: Mr. Tanqueray is sure to be back soon.

HUGH (*taking up his hat*). What's the understanding between us, then? What have we arranged to do?

PAULA. I don't know what you're going to do; I've got to tell Mr. Tanqueray.

HUGH. By God, you shall do nothing of the sort! (*Approaching her fiercely.*)

PAULA. You shocking coward!

HUGH. If you dare! (*Going up to the window*) Mind! If you dare!

PAULA (*following him*). Why, what would you do?

HUGH (*after a short pause, sul-*

lenly). Nothing. I'd shoot myself—that's nothing. Good night.

PAULA. Good night.
(*He disappears. She walks unsteadily to the ottoman, and sits; and as she does so her hand falls upon the little silver mirror, which she takes up, staring at her own reflection.*)

ACT FOUR

The drawing room at "Highercoombe," the same evening.

PAULA *is still seated on the ottoman, looking vacantly before her, with the little mirror in her hand.* LADY ORREYED *enters.*

LADY ORREYED. There you are! You never came into the billiard room. Isn't it maddening—Cayley Drummle gives me sixty out of a hundred, and beats me. I must be out of form, because I know I play remarkably well for a lady. Only last month—(PAULA *rises*) Whatever is the matter with you, old girl?

PAULA. Why?

LADY ORREYED (*staring*). It's the light, I suppose. (PAULA *replaces the mirror on the table*) By Aubrey's bolting from the billiard table in that fashion I thought perhaps—

PAULA. Yes, it's all right.

LADY ORREYED. You've patched it up? (PAULA *nods*) Oh, I am jolly glad—! I mean—

PAULA. Yes, I know what you mean. Thanks, Mabel.

LADY ORREYED (*kissing* PAULA). Now take my advice; for the future—

PAULA. Mabel, if I've been disagreeable to you while you've been staying here, I—I beg your pardon. (*Walking away and sitting down.*)

LADY ORREYED. You disagreeable, my dear? I haven't noticed it. Dodo and me both consider you make a first-class hostess; but then you've had such practice, haven't you? (*Dropping on to the ottoman and gaping*) Oh, talk about being sleepy—!

PAULA. Why don't you—!

LADY ORREYED. Why, dear, I must hang about for Dodo. You may as well know it; he's in one of his moods.

PAULA (*under her breath*). Oh—!

LADY ORREYED. Now, it's not his fault; it was deadly dull for him while we were playing billiards. Cayley Drummle did ask him to mark, but I stopped that; it's so easy to make a gentleman look like a billiard-marker. This is just how it always is; if poor old Dodo has nothing to do, he loses count, as you may say.

PAULA. Hark!
(SIR GEORGE ORREYED *enters, walking slowly and deliberately; he looks pale and watery-eyed.*)

SIR GEORGE (*with mournful indistinctness*). I'm 'fraid we've lef' you a grea' deal to yourself tonight, Mrs. Tanqueray. Attra'tions of billiards. I apol'gise. I say, where's ol' Aubrey?

PAULA. My husband has been obliged to go out to a neighbour's house.

SIR GEORGE. I want his advice on a rather pressing matter connected with my family—my family. (*Sitting*) Tomorrow will do just as well.

LADY ORREYED (*to* PAULA). This is the mood I hate so—drivelling about his precious family.

SIR GEORGE. The fact is, Mrs. Tanqueray, I am not easy in my min' 'bout the way I am treatin' my poor ol' mother.

LADY ORREYED (*to* PAULA). Do you hear that? That's *his* mother, but *my* mother he won't so much as look at!

SIR GEORGE. I shall write to Bruton Street firs' thing in the morning.

LADY ORREYED (*to* PAULA). Mamma has stuck to me through everything —well, you know!

SIR GEORGE. I'll get ol' Aubrey to figure out a letter. I'll drop line to Uncle Fitz too—dooced shame of the ol' feller to chuck me over in this manner. (*Wiping his eyes*) All my family have chucked me over.

LADY ORREYED (*rising*). Dodo!

SIR GEORGE. Jus' because I've married beneath me, to be chucked over! Aunt Lydia, the General, Hooky Whitgrave, Lady Sugnall—my own dear sister!—all turn their backs on me. It's more than I can stan'!

LADY ORREYED (*approaching him with dignity*). Sir George, wish Mrs. Tanqueray good night at once, and come upstairs. Do you hear me?

SIR GEORGE (*rising angrily*). Wha—!

LADY ORREYED. Be quiet!

SIR GEORGE. You presoom to order me about!

LADY ORREYED. You're making an exhibition of yourself!

SIR GEORGE. Look 'ere—!

LADY ORREYED. Come along, I tell you!
(*He hesitates, utters a few inarticulate sounds, then snatches up a fragile ornament from the table, and is about to dash it on the ground.* LADY ORREYED *retreats, and* PAULA *goes to him.*)

PAULA. George!
(*He replaces the ornament.*)

SIR GEORGE (*shaking* PAULA'S *hand*). Good ni', Mrs. Tanqueray.

LADY ORREYED (*to* PAULA). Good night, darling. Wish Aubrey good night for me. Now, Dodo? (*She goes out.*)

SIR GEORGE (*to* PAULA). I say, are you goin' to sit up for ol' Aubrey?

PAULA. Yes.

SIR GEORGE. Shall I keep you comp'ny?

PAULA. No, thank you, George.

SIR GEORGE. Sure?

PAULA. Yes, sure.

SIR GEORGE (*shaking hands*). Good night again.

PAULA. Good night.
(*She turns away. He goes out, steadying himself carefully.* DRUMMLE *appears outside the window, smoking.*)

DRUMMLE (*looking into the room and seeing* PAULA). My last cigar. Where's Aubrey?

PAULA. Gone down to The Warren, to see Mrs. Cortelyon home.

DRUMMLE (*entering the room*). Eh? Did you say Mrs. Cortelyon?

PAULA. Yes. She has brought Ellean back.

DRUMMLE. Bless my soul! Why?

PAULA. I—I'm too tired to tell you, Cayley. If you stroll along the lane you'll meet Aubrey. Get the news from him.

DRUMMLE (*going up to the window*). Yes, yes. (*Returning to* PAULA) I don't want to bother you, only—the anxious old woman, you know. Are you and Aubrey—?

PAULA. Good friends again?

DRUMMLE (*nodding*). Um.

PAULA (*giving him her hand*). Quite, Cayley, quite.

DRUMMLE (*retaining her hand*). That's capital. As I'm off so early tomorrow morning, let me say now—thank you for your hospitality.
(*He bends over her hand gallantly, then goes out by the window.*)

PAULA (*to herself*). "Are you and Aubrey—?" "Good friends again?" "Yes." "Quite, Cayley, quite."
(*There is a brief pause, then* AUBREY *enters hurriedly, wearing a light overcoat and carrying a cap.*)

AUBREY. Paula dear! Have you seen Ellean?

PAULA. I found her here when I came down.

AUBREY. She—she's told you?

PAULA. Yes, Aubrey.

AUBREY. It's extraordinary, isn't it! Not that somebody should fall in love with Ellean, or that Ellean herself should fall in love. All that's natural enough and was bound to happen, I suppose, sooner or later. But this young fellow! You know his history?

PAULA. His history?

AUBREY. You remember the papers were full of his name a few months ago?

PAULA. Oh, yes.

AUBREY. The man's as brave as a lion, there's no doubt about that; and, at the same time, he's like a big good-natured schoolboy, Mrs.

Cortelyon says. Have you ever pictured the kind of man Ellean would marry some day?

PAULA. I can't say that I have.

AUBREY. A grave, sedate fellow I've thought about—hah! She has fallen in love with the way in which Ardale practically laid down his life to save those poor people shut up in the Residency. (*Taking off his coat*) Well, I suppose if a man can do that sort of thing, one ought to be content. And yet—(*Throwing his coat on the settee*) I should have met him tonight, but he'd gone out. Paula dear, tell me how you look upon this business.

PAULA. Yes, I will—I must. To begin with, I—I've seen Mr. Ardale.

AUBREY. Captain Ardale?

PAULA. Captain Ardale.

AUBREY. Seen him?

PAULA. While you were away he came up here, through our grounds, to try to get a word with Ellean. I made her fetch him in and present him to me.

AUBREY (*frowning*). Doesn't Captain Ardale know there's a lodge and a front door to this place? Never mind! What is your impression of him?

PAULA. Aubrey, do you recollect my bringing you a letter—a letter giving you an account of myself—to the Albany late one night—the night before we got married?

AUBREY. A letter?

PAULA. You burnt it; don't you know?

AUBREY. Yes, I know.

PAULA. His name was in that letter.

AUBREY (*going back from her slowly, and staring at her*). I don't understand.

PAULA. Well—Ardale and I once kept house together. (*He remains silent, not moving*) Why don't you strike me? Hit me in the face—I'd rather you did! Hurt me! Hurt me!

AUBREY (*after a pause*). What did you—and this man—say to each other—just now?

PAULA. I—hardly—know.

AUBREY. Think!

PAULA. The end of it all was that I —I told him I must inform you of—what had happened . . . he didn't want me to do that . . . I declared that I would . . . he dared me to. (*Breaking down*) Let me alone!—oh!

AUBREY. Where was my daughter while this went on?

PAULA. I—I had sent her out of the room . . . that is all right.

AUBREY. Yes, yes—yes, yes. (*He turns his head towards the door.*)

PAULA. Who's that?
(*A* SERVANT *enters with a letter.*)

SERVANT. The coachman has just run up with this from The Warren, sir. (AUBREY *takes the letter*) It's

for Mrs. Tanqueray, sir; there's no answer.
(*The* SERVANT *withdraws.* AUBREY *goes to* PAULA *and drops the letter into her lap: she opens it with uncertain hands.*)

PAULA (*reading it to herself*). It's from—him. He's going away—or gone—I think. (*Rising in a weak way*) What does it say? I never could make out his writing. (*She gives the letter to* AUBREY, *and stands near him, looking at the letter over his shoulder as he reads.*)

AUBREY (*reading*). "I shall be in Paris by tomorrow evening. Shall wait there, at Meurice's, for a week, ready to receive any communication you or your husband may address to me. Please invent some explanation to Ellean. Mrs. Tanqueray, for God's sake, do what you can for me."
(PAULA *and* AUBREY *speak in low voices, both still looking at the letter.*)

PAULA. Has he left The Warren, I wonder, already?

AUBREY. That doesn't matter.

PAULA. No, but I can picture him going quietly off. Very likely he's walking on to Bridgeford or Cottering tonight, to get the first train in the morning. A pleasant stroll for him.

AUBREY. We'll reckon he's gone, that's enough.

PAULA. That isn't to be answered in any way?

AUBREY. Silence will answer that.

PAULA. He'll soon recover his spirits, I know.

AUBREY. You know. (*Offering her the letter*) You don't want this, I suppose?

PAULA. No.

AUBREY. It's done with—done with. (*He tears the letter into small pieces. She has dropped the envelope; she searches for it, finds it, and gives it to him.*)

PAULA. Here!

AUBREY (*looking at the remnants of the letter*). This is no good; I must burn it.

PAULA. Burn it in your room.

AUBREY. Yes.

PAULA. Put it in your pocket for now.

AUBREY. Yes. (*He does so.* ELLEAN *enters, and they both turn, guilty, and stare at her.*)

ELLEAN (*after a short silence, wonderingly*). Papa—

AUBREY. What do you want, Ellean?

ELLEAN. I heard from Willis that you had come in; I only want to wish you good night. (PAULA *steals away, without looking back*) What's the matter? Ah! Of course, Paula has told you about Captain Ardale?

AUBREY. Well?

ELLEAN. Have you and he met?

AUBREY. No.

ELLEAN. You are angry with him; so was I. But tomorrow when he calls and expresses his regret—tomorrow—

AUBREY. Ellean—Ellean!

ELLEAN. Yes, papa?

AUBREY. I—I can't let you see this man again. (*He walks away from her in a paroxysm of distress, then, after a moment or two, he returns to her and takes her to his arms*) Ellean! My child!

ELLEAN (*releasing herself*). What has happened, papa? What is it?

AUBREY (*thinking out his words deliberately*). Something has occurred, something has come to my knowledge, in relation to Captain Ardale, which puts any further acquaintanceship between you two out of the question.

ELLEAN. Any further acquaintanceship . . . out of the question?

AUBREY. Yes. (*Advancing to her quickly, but she shrinks from him.*)

ELLEAN. No, no—I am quite well. (*After a short pause*) It's not an hour ago since Mrs. Cortelyon left you and me together here; you had nothing to urge against Captain Ardale then.

AUBREY. No.

ELLEAN. You don't know each other; you haven't even seen him this evening. Father!

AUBREY. I have told you he and I have not met.

ELLEAN. Mrs. Cortelyon couldn't have spoken against him to you just now. No, no, no; she's too good a friend to both of us. Aren't you going to give me some explanation? You can't take this position towards me—towards Captain Ardale—without affording me the fullest explanation.

AUBREY. Ellean, there are circumstances connected with Captain Ardale's career which you had better remain ignorant of. It must be sufficient for you that I consider these circumstances render him unfit to be your husband.

ELLEAN. Father!

AUBREY. You must trust me, Ellean; you must try to understand the depth of my love for you and the—the agony it gives me to hurt you. You must trust me.

ELLEAN. I will, father; but you must trust me a little too. Circumstances connected with Capain Ardale's career?

AUBREY. Yes.

ELLEAN. When he presents himself here tomorrow of course you will see him and let him defend himself?

AUBREY. Captain Ardale will not be here tomorrow.

ELLEAN. Not! You have stopped his coming here?

AUBREY. Indirectly—yes.

ELLEAN. But just now he was talking to me at that window! Nothing had taken place then! And since then nothing can have—! Oh! Why —you have heard something against him from Paula.

AUBREY. From—Paula!

ELLEAN. She knows him.

AUBREY. She has told you so?

ELLEAN. When I introduced Captain Ardale to her she said she had met him in London. Of course! It is Paula who has done this!

AUBREY (*in a hard voice*). I—I hope you—you'll refrain from rushing at conclusions. There's nothing to be gained by trying to avoid the main point, which is that you must drive Captain Ardale out of your thoughts. Understand that! You're able to obtain comfort from your religion, aren't you? I'm glad to think that's so. I talk to you in a harsh way, Ellean, but I feel your pain almost as acutely as you do. (*Going to the door*) I—I can't say anything more to you tonight.

ELLEAN. Father! (*He pauses at the door*) Father, I'm obliged to ask you this; there's no help for it— I've no mother to go to. Does what you have heard about Captain Ardale concern the time when he led a wild, a dissolute life in London?

AUBREY (*returning to her slowly and staring at her*). Explain yourself!

ELLEAN. He has been quite honest with me. One day—in Paris—he confessed to me—what a man's life is —what his life had been.

AUBREY (*under his breath*). Oh!

ELLEAN. He offered to go away, not to approach me again.

AUBREY. And you—you accepted his view of what a man's life is?

ELLEAN. As far as *I* could forgive him, I forgave him.

AUBREY (*with a groan*). Why, when was it you left us? It hasn't taken you long to get your robe "just a little dusty at the hem!"

ELLEAN. What do you mean?

AUBREY. Hah! A few weeks ago my one great desire was to keep you ignorant of evil.

ELLEAN. Father, it is impossible to be ignorant of evil. Instinct. common instinct, teaches us what is good and bad. Surely I am none the worse for knowing what is wicked and detesting it!

AUBREY. Detesting it! Why, you love this fellow!

ELLEAN. Ah, you don't understand! I have simply judged Captain Ardale as we all pray to be judged. I have lived in imagination through that one week in India when he deliberately offered his life back to God to save those wretched, desperate people. In his whole career I see now nothing but that one week; those few hours bring him nearer the saints, I believe, than fifty uneventful years of mere blamelessness would have done! And so, Father, if Paula has reported anything to Captain Ardale's discredit—

AUBREY. Paula—!

ELLEAN. It must be Paula; it can't be anybody else.

AUBREY. You—you'll please keep Paula out of the question. Finally, Ellean, understand me—I have made up my mind. (*Again going to the door.*)

ELLEAN. But wait—listen! I have made up my mind also.

AUBREY. Ah! I recognise your mother in you now!

ELLEAN. You need not speak against my mother because you are angry with me!

AUBREY. I—I hardly know what I'm saying to you. In the morning—in the morning—
(*He goes out. She remains standing, and turns her head to listen. Then, after a moment's hesitation she goes softly to the window, and looks out under the verandah.*)

ELLEAN (*in a whisper*). Paula! Paula!
(PAULA *appears outside the window and steps into the room; her face is white and drawn, her hair is a little disordered.*)

PAULA (*huskily*). Well?

ELLEAN. Have you been under the verandah all the while—listening?

PAULA. N—no.

ELLEAN. You *have* overheard us—I see you have. And it *is* you who have been speaking to my father against Captain Ardale. Isn't it? Paula, why don't you own it or deny it?

PAULA. Oh, I—I don't mind owning it; why should I?

ELLEAN. Ah! You seem to have been very, very eager to tell your tale.

PAULA. No, I wasn't eager. Ellean. I'd have given something not to have had to do it. I wasn't eager.

ELLEAN. Not! Oh, I think you might safely have spared us all for a little while.

PAULA. But Ellean, you forget I—I am your stepmother. It was my—my duty—to tell your father what I—what I knew—

ELLEAN. What you knew! Why, after all, what can you know? You can only speak from gossip, report, hearsay! How is it possible that you—! (*She stops abruptly. The two women stand staring at each other for a moment; then* ELLEAN *backs away from* PAULA *slowly*) Paula!

PAULA. What—what's the matter?

ELLEAN. You—you knew Captain Ardale in London!

PAULA. Why—what do you mean?

ELLEAN. Oh! (*She makes for the door, but* PAULA *catches her by the wrist.*)

PAULA. You shall tell me what you mean!

ELLEAN. Ah! (*Suddenly, looking fixedly into* PAULA*'s face*) You know what I mean.

PAULA. You accuse me!

ELLEAN. It's in your face!

PAULA (*hoarsely*). You—you think I'm—that sort of creature, do you?

ELLEAN. Let me go!

PAULA. Answer me! You've always hated me! (*Shaking her*) Out with it!

ELLEAN. You hurt me!

PAULA. You've always hated me! You shall answer me!

ELLEAN. Well, then, I have always—always—

PAULA. What?

ELLEAN. I have always known what you were!

PAULA. Ah! Who—who told you?

ELLEAN. Nobody but yourself. From the first moment I saw you I knew you were altogether unlike the good women I'd left; directly I saw you I knew what my father had done. You've wondered why I've turned from you! There—that's the reason! Oh, but this is a horrible way for the truth to come home to every one! Oh!

PAULA. It's a lie! It's all a lie! (*Forcing* ELLEAN *down upon her knees*) You shall beg my pardon for it. (ELLEAN *utters a loud shriek of terror*) Ellean, I'm a good woman! I swear I am! I've always been a good woman! You dare to say I've ever been anything else! It's a lie! (*Throwing her off violently.*)
(AUBREY *re-enters.*)

AUBREY. Paula! (PAULA *staggers back as* AUBREY *advances. Raising* ELLEAN) What's this? What's this?

ELLEAN (*faintly*). Nothing. It's—it's my fault. Father, I—I don't wish to see Captain Ardale again. (*She goes out,* AUBREY *slowly following her to the door.*)

PAULA. Aubrey, she—she guesses.

AUBREY. Guesses?

PAULA. About me—and Ardale.

AUBREY. About you—and Ardale?

PAULA. She says she suspected my character from the beginning . . . that's why she's always kept me at a distance . . . and now she sees through— (*She falters; he helps her to the ottoman, where she sits.*)

AUBREY (*bending over her*). Paula, you must have said something—admitted something—

PAULA. I don't think so. It—it's in my face.

AUBREY. What?

PAULA. She tells me so. She's right! I'm tainted through and through; anybody can see it, anybody can find it out. You said much the same to me tonight.

AUBREY. If she has got this idea into her head we must drive it out, that's all. We must take steps to—What shall we do? We had better—better—what—what? (*Sitting and staring before him.*)

PAULA. Ellean! So meek, so demure! You've often said she reminded you of her mother. Yes, I know now what your first marriage was like.

AUBREY. We must drive this idea out of her head. We'll do something. What shall we do?

PAULA. She's a regular woman too. She could forgive *him* easily enough—but *me!* That's just a woman!

AUBREY. What *can* we do?

PAULA. Why nothing! She'd have no difficulty in following up her suspicions. Suspicions! You should have seen how she looked at me! (*He buries his head in his hands. There is silence for a time, then she rises slowly, and goes and sits beside him*) Aubrey.

AUBREY. Yes.

PAULA. I'm very sorry. (*Without meeting her eyes, he lays his hand on her arm for a moment.*)

AUBREY. Well, we must look things straight in the face. (*Glancing around*) At any rate, we've done with this.

PAULA. I suppose so. (*After a brief pause*) Of course, she and I can't live under the same roof any more. You know she kissed me tonight, of her own accord.

AUBREY. I asked her to alter towards you.

PAULA. That was it, then.

AUBREY. I—I'm sorry I sent her away.

PAULA. It was my fault; I made it necessary.

AUBREY. Perhaps now she'll propose to return to the convent—well, she must.

PAULA. Would you like to keep her with you and—and leave me?

AUBREY. Paula—!

PAULA. You needn't be afraid I'd go back to—what I was. I couldn't.

AUBREY. S—sh, for God's sake! We—you and I—we'll get out of this place . . . What a fool I was to come here again!

PAULA. You lived here with your first wife!

AUBREY. We'll get out of this place and go abroad again, and begin afresh.

PAULA. Begin afresh?

AUBREY. There's no reason why the future shouldn't be happy for us—no reason that I can see—

PAULA. Aubrey!

AUBREY. Yes?

PAULA. You'll never forget this, you know.

AUBREY. This?

PAULA. Tonight, and everything that's led up to it. Our coming here, Ellean, our quarrels—cat and dog!—Mrs. Cortelyon, the Orreyeds, this man! What an everlasting nightmare for you!

AUBREY. Oh, we can forget it, if we choose.

PAULA. That was always your cry. How *can* one do it?

AUBREY. We'll make our calculations solely for the future, talk about the future, think about the future.

PAULA. I believe the future is only the past again, entered through another gate.

AUBREY. That's an awful belief.

PAULA. Tonight proves it. You must see now that, do what we will, go where we will, you'll be continually reminded of—what I was. I see it.

AUBREY. You're frightened tonight; meeting this man has frightened you. But that sort of thing isn't likely to recur. The world isn't quite so small as all that.

PAULA. Isn't it! The only great distances it contains are those we carry within ourselves—the distances that separate husbands and wives, for instance. And so it'll be with us. You'll do your best—oh, I know that—you're a good fellow. But circumstances will be too strong for you in the end, mark my words.

AUBREY. Paula—!

PAULA. Of course I'm pretty now—I'm pretty still—and a pretty woman, whatever else she may be, is always—well, endurable. But even now I notice that the lines of my face are getting deeper; so are the hollows about my eyes. Yes, my face is covered with little shadows that usen't to be there. Oh, I know I'm "going off." I hate paint and dye and those messes, but, by-and-bye, I shall drift the way of the others; I sha'n't be able to help myself. And then, some day—perhaps very suddenly, under a queer, fantastic light at night or in the glare of the morning—that horrid, irresistible truth that physical repulsion forces on men and women will come to you, and you'll sicken at me.

AUBREY. I—!

PAULA. You'll see me then, at last, with other people's eyes; you'll see me just as your daughter does now, as all wholesome folks see women like me. And I shall have no weapon to fight with—not one serviceable little bit of prettiness left me to defend myself with! A worn-out creature—broken up, very likely, some time before I ought to be—my hair bright, my eyes dull, my body too thin or too stout, my cheeks raddled and ruddled—a ghost, a wreck, a caricature, a candle that gutters, call such an end what you like! Oh, Aubrey, what shall I be able to say to you then? And this is the future you talk about! I know it—I know it! (*He is still sitting staring forward; she rocks herself to and fro as if in pain*) Oh, Aubrey! Oh! Oh!

AUBREY. Paula—! (*Trying to comfort her.*)

PAULA. Oh, and I wanted so much to sleep tonight! (*Laying her head upon his shoulder. From the distance, in the garden, there comes the sound of* DRUMMLE'S *voice; he is singing as he approaches the house*) That's Cayley, coming back from The Warren. (*Starting up*) He doesn't know, evidently. I—I won't see him! (*She goes out quickly.* DRUMMLE'S *voice comes nearer.* AUBREY *rouses himself and snatches up a book from the table, making a pretence of reading.*

After a moment or two, DRUMMLE *appears at the window and looks in.)*

DRUMMLE. Aha! my dear chap!

AUBREY. Cayley?

DRUMMLE (*coming into the room*). I went down to The Warren after you.

AUBREY. Yes?

DRUMMLE. Missed you. Well—I've been gossiping with Mrs. Cortelyon. Confound you, I've heard the news!

AUBREY. What have you heard?

DRUMMLE. What have I heard! Why—Ellean and young Ardale! (*Looking at* AUBREY *keenly*) My dear Aubrey! Alice is under the impression that you are inclined to look on the affair favourably.

AUBREY (*rising and advancing to* DRUMMLE). You've not—met—Captain Ardale?

DRUMMLE. No. Why do you ask? By-the-bye, I don't know that I need tell you—but it's rather strange. He's not at The Warren tonight.

AUBREY. No?

DRUMMLE. He left the house half an hour ago, to stroll about the lanes; just now a note came from him, a scribble in pencil, simply telling Alice that she would receive a letter from him tomorrow. What's the matter? There's nothing very wrong, is there? My dear chap, pray forgive me if I'm asking too much.

AUBREY. Cayley, you—you urged me to send her away!

DRUMMLE. Ellean! Yes, yes. But—but—by all accounts this is quite an eligible young fellow. Alice has been giving me the history—

AUBREY. Curse him! (*Hurling his book to the floor*) Curse him! Yes, I do curse him—him and his class! Perhaps I curse myself too in doing it. He has only led "a man's life" —just as I, how many of us, have done! The misery he has brought on me and mine it's likely enough we, in our time, have helped to bring on others by this leading "a man's life!" But I do curse him for all that. My God, *I've* nothing more to fear—I've paid *my* fine! And so I can curse him in safety. Curse him! Curse him!

DRUMMLE. In Heaven's name, tell me what's happened?

AUBREY (*gripping* DRUMMLE'S *arm*). Paula! Paula!

DRUMMLE. What?

AUBREY. They met tonight here. They—they—they're not strangers to each other.

DRUMMLE. Aubrey!

AUBREY. Curse him! My poor, wretched wife! My poor, wretched wife!
(*The door opens and* ELLEAN *appears. The two men turn to her. There is a moment's silence.*)

ELLEAN. Father . . . father . . . !

AUBREY. Ellean?

ELLEAN. I–I want you. (*He goes to her*) Father . . . go to Paula! (*He looks into her face, startled*) Quickly–quickly! (*He passes her to go out; she seizes his arm, with a cry*) No, no; don't go! (*He shakes her off and goes.* ELLEAN *staggers back towards* DRUMMLE.)

DRUMMLE (*to* ELLEAN). What do you mean? What do you mean?

ELLEAN. I–I went to her room–to tell her I was sorry for something I had said to her. And I *was* sorry –I *was* sorry. I heard the fall. I–I've seen her. It's horrible.

DRUMMLE. She–she has–!

ELLEAN. Killed–herself? Yes–yes. So everybody will say. But I know –I helped to kill her. If I'd only been merciful! (*She faints upon the ottoman. He pauses for a moment irresolutely–then he goes to the door, opens it, and stands looking out.*)

The Importance of Being Earnest

BY OSCAR WILDE

The Importance of Being Earnest was first produced in America at the Empire Theatre, New York City, by Charles Frohman on April 30, 1895. The following is the original cast:

JOHN WORTHING, *of the Manor House, Woolton, Herefordshire*	Henry Miller
ALGERNON MONCRIEFF, *his friend*	William Faversham
REV. CANON CHASUBLE, D.D., *rector of Woolton*	W. H. Crompton
MERRIMAN, *butler to Mr. Worthing*	J. P. Whitman
LANE, *Mr. Moncrieff's man-servant*	E. Y. Backus
HON. GWENDOLEN FAIRFAX	Viola Allen
LADY BRACKNELL, *her mother*	Ida Vernon
CECILY CARDEW, *John Worthing's ward*	Agnes Miller
MISS PRISM, *her governess*	May Robson

SCENES

ACT ONE

Algernon Moncrieff's Flat in Half-Moon Street, W.

ACT TWO

The Garden at the Manor House, Woolton

ACT THREE

Morning Room of the Manor House, Woolton

Time—The Present

Place—London

THE IMPORTANCE OF BEING EARNEST

ACT ONE

SCENE—*Morning-room in* ALGERNON'S *flat in Half-Moon Street. The room is luxuriously and artistically furnished. The sound of a piano is heard in the adjoining room.*

(LANE *is arranging afternoon tea on the table, and after the music has ceased,* ALGERNON *enters.*)

ALGERNON. Did you hear what I was playing, Lane?

LANE. I didn't think it polite to listen, sir.

ALGERNON. I'm sorry for that, for your sake. I don't play accurately—anyone can play accurately—but I play with wonderful expression. As far as the piano is concerned, sentiment is my forte. I keep science for Life.

LANE. Yes, sir.

ALGERNON. And, speaking of the science of Life, have you got the cucumber sandwiches cut for Lady Bracknell?

LANE. Yes, sir. (*Hands them on a salver.*)

ALGERNON (*inspects them, takes two, and sits down on the sofa*). Oh! . . . by the way, Lane, I see from your book that on Thursday night, when Lord Shoreman and Mr. Worthing were dining with me, eight bottles of champagne are entered as having been consumed.

LANE. Yes, sir; eight bottles and a pint.

ALGERNON. Why is it that at a bachelor's establishment the servants invariably drink the champagne? I ask merely for information.

LANE. I attribute it to the superior quality of the wine, sir. I have often observed that in married households the champagne is rarely of a first-rate brand.

ALGERNON. Good Heavens! Is marriage so demoralizing as that?

LANE. I believe it *is* a very pleasant state, sir. I have had very little experience of it myself up to the present. I have only been married once. That was in consequence of a misunderstanding between myself and a young woman.

ALGERNON (*languidly*). I don't know that I am much interested in your family life, Lane.

LANE. No, sir; it is not a very interesting subject. I never think of it myself.

ALGERNON. Very natural, I am sure. That will do, Lane, thank you.

LANE. Thank you, sir. (LANE *goes out.*)

ALGERNON. Lane's views on marriage seem somewhat lax. Really, if the lower orders don't set us a good example, what on earth is the use of them? They seem, as a class, to have absolutely no sense of moral responsibility.
(*Enter* LANE.)

LANE. Mr. Ernest Worthing.
(*Enter* JACK. LANE *goes out.*)

ALGERNON. How are you, my dear Ernest? What brings you up to town?

JACK. Oh, pleasure, pleasure! What else should bring one anywhere? Eating as usual, I see, Algy!

ALGERNON (*stiffly*). I believe it is customary in good society to take some slight refreshment at five o'clock. Where have you been since last Thursday?

JACK (*sitting down on the sofa*). In the country.

ALGERNON. What on earth do you do there?

JACK (*pulling off his gloves*). When one is in town one amuses oneself. When one is in the country one amuses other people. It is excessively boring.

ALGERNON. And who are the people you amuse?

JACK (*airily*). Oh, neighbours, neighbours.

ALGERNON. Got nice neighbours in your part of Shropshire?

JACK. Perfectly horrid! Never speak to one of them.

ALGERNON. How immensely you must amuse them! (*Goes over and takes sandwich*) By the way, Shropshire is your county, is it not?

JACK. Eh? Shropshire? Yes, of course. Hallo! Why all these cups? Why cucumber sandwiches? Why such reckless extravagance in one so young? Who is coming to tea?

ALGERNON. Oh! merely Aunt Augusta and Gwendolen.

JACK. How perfectly delightful!

ALGERNON. Yes, that is all very well; but I am afraid Aunt Augusta won't quite approve of your being here.

JACK. May I ask why?

ALGERNON. My dear fellow, the way you flirt with Gwendolen is perfectly disgraceful. It is almost as bad as the way Gwendolen flirts with you.

JACK. I am in love with Gwendolen. I have come up to town expressly to propose to her.

ALGERNON. I thought you had come up for pleasure? . . . I call that business.

JACK. How utterly unromantic you are!

ALGERNON. I really don't see anything romantic in proposing. It is very romantic to be in love. But there is nothing romantic about a definite proposal. Why, one may be accepted. One usually is, I believe. Then the excitement is all over. The very essence of romance is uncertainty. If ever I get married, I'll certainly try to forget the fact.

JACK. I have no doubt about that, dear Algy. The Divorce Court was specially invented for people whose memories are so curiously constituted.

ALGERNON. Oh! there is no use speculating on that subject. Divorces are made in Heaven—(JACK *puts out his hand to take a sandwich.* ALGERNON *at once interferes*) Please don't touch the cucumber sandwiches. They are ordered specially for Aunt Augusta. (*Takes one and eats it.*)

JACK. Well, you have been eating them all the time.

ALGERNON. That is quite a different matter. She is my aunt. (*Takes plate from below*) Have some bread and butter. The bread and butter is for Gwendolen. Gwendolen is devoted to bread and butter.

JACK (*advancing to table and helping himself*). And very good bread and butter it is, too.

ALGERNON. Well, my dear fellow, you need not eat as if you were going to eat it all. You behave as if you were married to her already. You are not married to her already, and I don't think you ever will be.

JACK. Why on earth do you say that?

ALGERNON. Well, in the first place girls never marry the men they flirt with. Girls don't think it right.

JACK. Oh, that is nonsense!

ALGERNON. It isn't. It is a great truth. It accounts for the extraordinary number of bachelors that one sees all over the place. In the second place, I don't give my consent.

JACK. Your consent!

ALGERNON. My dear fellow, Gwendolen is my first cousin. And before I allow you to marry her, you will have to clear up the whole question of Cecily. (*Rings bell.*)

JACK. Cecily! What on earth do you mean? What do you mean, Algy, by Cecily? I don't know anyone of the name of Cecily.
(*Enter* LANE.)

ALGERNON. Bring me that cigarette case Mr. Worthing left in the smoking-room the last time he dined here.

LANE. Yes, sir. (LANE *goes out.*)

JACK. Do you mean to say you have had my cigarette case all this time? I wish to goodness you had let me know. I have been writing frantic letters to Scotland Yard about it. I was very nearly offering a large reward.

ALGERNON. Well, I wish you would offer one. I happen to be more than usually hard up.

JACK. There is no good offering a large reward now that the thing is found.

(*Enter* LANE *with the cigarette case on a salver.* ALGERNON *takes it at once.* LANE *goes out.*)

ALGERNON. I think that is rather mean of you, Ernest, I must say. (*Opens case and examines it*) However, it makes no matter, for, now that I look at the inscription, I find that the thing isn't yours after all.

JACK. Of course it's mine. (*Moving to him*) You have seen me with it a hundred times, and you have no right whatsoever to read what is written inside. It is a very ungentlemanly thing to read a private cigarette case.

ALGERNON. Oh! it is absurd to have a hard-and-fast rule about what one should read and what one shouldn't. More than half of modern culture depends on what one shouldn't read.

JACK. I am quite aware of the fact, and I don't propose to discuss modern culture. It isn't the sort of thing one should talk of in private. I simply want my cigarette case back.

ALGERNON. Yes; but this isn't your cigarette case. This cigarette case is a present from someone of the name of Cecily, and you said you didn't know anyone of that name.

JACK. Well, if you want to know, Cecily happens to be my aunt.

ALGERNON. Your aunt!

JACK. Yes. Charming old lady she is, too. Lives at Tunbridge Wells. Just give it back to me, Algy.

ALGERNON (*retreating to back of sofa*). But why does she call herself little Cecily if she is your aunt and lives at Tunbridge Wells? (*Reading*) "From little Cecily with her fondest love."

JACK (*moving to sofa and kneeling upon it*). My dear fellow, what on earth is there in that? Some aunts are tall, some aunts are not tall. That is a matter that surely an aunt may be allowed to decide for herself. You seem to think that every aunt should be exactly like your aunt! That is absurd! For Heaven's sake give me back my cigarette case. (*Follows* ERNEST *round the room.*)

ALGERNON. Yes. But why does your aunt call you her uncle? "From little Cecily, with her fondest love to her dear Uncle Jack." There is no objection, I admit, to an aunt being a small aunt, but why an aunt, no matter what her size may be, should call her own nephew her uncle, I can't quite make out. Besides, your name isn't Jack at all; it is Ernest.

JACK. It isn't Ernest; it's Jack.

ALGERNON. You have always told me it was Ernest. I have introduced you to everyone as Ernest. You answer to the name of Ernest. You look as if your name was Ernest. You are the most earnest-looking person I ever saw in my life. It is perfectly absurd your saying that your name isn't Ernest. It's on your cards. Here is one of them (*Taking it from case*) "Mr. Ernest Worthing, B 4, The Albany." I'll keep this as a proof your name is Ernest if ever you attempt to deny it to me, or to Gwendolen, or to anyone else. (*Puts the card in his pocket.*)

JACK. Well, my name is Ernest in town and Jack in the country, and the cigarette case was given to me in the country.

ALGERNON. Yes, but that does not account for the fact that your small Aunt Cecily, who lives at Tunbridge Wells, calls you her dear uncle. Come, old boy, you had much better have the thing out at once.

JACK. My dear Algy, you talk exactly as if you were a dentist. It is very vulgar to talk like a dentist when one isn't a dentist. It produces a false impression.

ALGERNON. Well, that is exactly what dentists always do. Now, go on! Tell me the whole thing. I may mention that I have always suspected you of being a confirmed and secret Bunburyist; and I am quite sure of it now.

JACK. Bunburyist? What on earth do you mean by a Bunburyist?

ALGERNON. I'll reveal to you the meaning of that incomparable expression as soon as you are kind enough to inform me why you are Ernest in town and Jack in the country.

JACK. Well, produce my cigarette case first.

ALGERNON. Here it is. (*Hands cigarette case*) Now produce your explanation, and pray make it improbable. (*Sits on sofa.*)

JACK. My dear fellow, there is nothing improbable about my explanation at all. In fact it's perfectly ordinary. Old Mr. Thomas Cardew, who adopted me when I was a little boy, made me in his will guardian to his grand-daughter, Miss Cecily Cardew. Cecily, who addresses me as her uncle from motives of respect that you could not possibly appreciate, lives at my place in the country under the charge of her admirable governess, Miss Prism.

ALGERNON. Where is that place in the country, by the way?

JACK. That is nothing to you, dear boy. You are not going to be invited. . . . I may tell you candidly that the place is not in Shropshire.

ALGERNON. I suspected that, my dear fellow! I have Bunburyed all over Shropshire on two separate occasions. Now, go on. Why are you Ernest in town and Jack in the country?

JACK. My dear Algy, I don't know whether you will be able to understand my real motives. You are hardly serious enough. When one is placed in the position of guardian, one has to adopt a very high moral tone on all subjects. It's one's duty to do so. And as a high moral tone can hardly be said to conduce very much to either one's health or one's happiness, in order to get up to town I have always pretended to have a younger brother of the name of Ernest, who lives in the Albany, and gets into the most dreadful scrapes. That, my dear Algy, is the whole truth pure and simple.

ALGERNON. The truth is rarely pure and never simple. Modern life would be very tedious if it were either, and modern literature a complete impossibility!

JACK. That wouldn't be at all a bad thing.

ALGERNON. Literary criticism is not your forte, my dear fellow. Don't try it. You should leave that to people who haven't been at a University. They do it so well in the daily papers. What you really are is a Bunburyist. I was quite right in saying you were a Bunburyist. You are one of the most advanced Bunburyists I know.

JACK. What on earth do you mean?

ALGERNON. You have invented a very useful younger brother called Ernest, in order that you may be able to come up to town as often as you like. I have invented an invaluable permanent invalid called Bunbury, in order that I may be able to go down into the country whenever I choose. Bunbury is perfectly invaluable. If it wasn't for Bunbury's extraordinary bad health, for instance, I wouldn't be able to dine with you at Willis's tonight, for I have been really engaged to Aunt Augusta for more than a week.

JACK. I haven't asked you to dine with me anywhere tonight.

ALGERNON. I know. You are absolutely careless about sending out invitations. It is very foolish of you. Nothing annoys people so much as not receiving invitations.

JACK. You had much better dine with your Aunt Augusta.

ALGERNON. I haven't the smallest intention of doing anything of the kind. To begin with, I dined there on Monday, and once a week is quite enough to dine with one's own relatives. In the second place, whenever I do dine there I am always treated as a member of the family, and sent down with either no woman at all, or two. In the third place, I know perfectly well whom she will place me next to, tonight. She will place me next Mary Farquhar, who always flirts with her own husband across the dinner-table. That is not very pleasant. Indeed, it is not even decent . . . and that sort of thing is enormously on the increase. The amount of women in London who flirt with their own husbands is perfectly scandalous. It looks so bad. It is simply washing one's clean linen in public. Besides, now that I know you to be a confirmed Bunburyist I naturally want to talk to you about Bunburying. I want to tell you the rules.

JACK. I'm not a Bunburyist at all. If Gwendolen accepts me, I am going to kill my brother, indeed I think I'll kill him in any case. Cecily is a little too much interested in him. It is rather a bore. So I am going to get rid of Ernest. And I strongly advise you to do the same with Mr. . . . with your invalid friend who has the absurd name.

ALGERNON. Nothing will induce me to part with Bunbury, and if you ever get married, which seems to me extremely problematic, you will be very glad to know Bunbury. A man who marries without knowing Bunbury has a very tedious time of it.

JACK. That is nonsense. If I marry a charming girl like Gwendolen, and she is the only girl I ever saw in my life that I would marry, I certainly won't want to know Bunbury.

ALGERNON. Then your wife will. You don't seem to realize, that in married life three is company and two is none.

JACK (*sententiously*). That, my dear young friend, is the theory that the corrupt French Drama has been propounding for the last fifty years.

ALGERNON. Yes; and that the happy English home has proved in half the time.

JACK. For heaven's sake, don't try to be cynical. It's perfectly easy to be cynical.

ALGERNON. My dear fellow, it isn't easy to be anything now-a-days. There's such a lot of beastly competition about. (*The sound of an electric bell is heard*) Ah! that must be Aunt Augusta. Only relatives, or creditors, ever ring in that Wagnerian manner. Now, if I get her out of the way for ten minutes, so that you can have an opportunity for proposing to Gwendolen, may I dine with you tonight at Willis's?

JACK. I suppose so, if you want to.

ALGERNON. Yes, but you must be serious about it. I hate people who are not serious about meals. It is so shallow of them.
(*Enter* LANE.)

LANE. Lady Bracknell and Miss Fairfax. (ALGERNON *goes forward to meet them. Enter* LADY BRACKNELL *and* GWENDOLEN.)

LADY BRACKNELL. Good afternoon, dear Algernon, I hope you are behaving very well.

ALGERNON. I'm feeling very well, Aunt Augusta.

LADY BRACKNELL. That's not quite the same thing. In fact the two things rarely go together. (*Sees* JACK *and bows to him with icy coldness.*)

ALGERNON (*to* GWENDOLEN). Dear me, you are smart!

GWENDOLEN. I am always smart! Aren't I, Mr. Worthing?

JACK. You're quite perfect, Miss Fairfax.

GWENDOLEN. Oh! I hope I am not that. It would leave no room for developments, and I intend to develop in *many directions.* (GWENDOLEN *and* JACK *sit down together in the corner.*)

LADY BRACKNELL. I'm sorry if we are a little late, Algernon, but I was obliged to call on dear Lady Harbury. I hadn't been there since her poor husband's death. I never saw a woman so altered; she looks quite twenty years younger. And now I'll have a cup of tea, and one of those nice cucumber sandwiches you promised me.

ALGERNON. Certainly, Aunt Augusta. (*Goes over to tea-table.*)

LADY BRACKNELL. Won't you come and sit here, Gwendolen?

GWENDOLEN. Thanks, mamma, I'm quite comfortable where I am.

ALGERNON (*picking up empty plate in horror*). Good heavens! Lane! Why are there no cucumber sandwiches? I ordered them specially.

LANE (*gravely*). There were no cucumbers in the market this morning, sir. I went down twice.

ALGERNON. No cucumbers!

LANE. No, sir. Not even for ready money.

ALGERNON. That will do, Lane, thank you.

LANE. Thank you, sir. (*Goes out.*)

ALGERNON. I am greatly distressed, Aunt Augusta, about there being no cucumbers, not even for ready money.

LADY BRACKNELL. It really makes no matter, Algernon. I had some crumpets with Lady Harbury, who seems to me to be living entirely for pleasure now.

ALGERNON. I hear her hair has turned quite gold from grief.

LADY BRACKNELL. It certainly has changed its colour. From what cause I, of course, cannot say. (ALGERNON *crosses and hands tea*) Thank you. I've quite a treat for you tonight, Algernon. I am going to send you down with Mary Farquhar. She is such a nice woman, and so attentive to her husband. It's delightful to watch them.

ALGERNON. I am afraid, Aunt Augusta, I shall have to give up the pleasure of dining with you tonight after all.

LADY BRACKNELL (*frowning*). I hope not, Algernon. It would put my table completely out. Your uncle would have to dine upstairs. Fortunately he is accustomed to that.

ALGERNON. It is a great bore, and, I need hardly say, a terrible disappointment to me, but the fact is I have just had a telegram to say that my poor friend Bunbury is very ill again. (*Exchanges glances with* JACK) They seem to think I should be with him.

LADY BRACKNELL. It is very strange. This Mr. Bunbury seems to suffer from curiously bad health.

ALGERNON. Yes; poor Bunbury is a dreadful invalid.

LADY BRACKNELL. Well, I must say, Algernon, that I think it is high time that Mr. Bunbury made up his mind whether he was going to live or to die. This shilly-shallying with the question is absurd. Nor do I in any way approve of the modern sympathy with invalids. I consider it morbid. Illness of any kind is hardly a thing to be encouraged in others. Health is the primary duty of life. I am always telling that to your poor uncle, but he never seems to take much notice . . . as far as any improvement in his ailments goes. I should be much obliged if you would ask Mr. Bunbury, from me, to be kind enough not to have a relapse on Saturday, for I rely on you to arrange my music for me. It is my last reception and one wants something that will encourage conversation, particularly at the end of the season when everyone has practically said whatever they had to say, which, in most cases, was probably not much.

ALGERNON. I'll speak to Bunbury, Aunt Augusta, if he is still conscious, and I think I can promise you he'll be all right by Saturday. You see, if one plays good music, people don't listen, and if one plays bad music people don't talk. But I'll run over the programme I've drawn out, if you will kindly come into the next room for a moment.

LADY BRACKNELL. Thank you, Algernon. It is very thoughtful of you. (*Rising, and following* ALGERNON) I'm sure the programme will be delightful, after a few expurgations. French songs I cannot possibly allow. People always seem to think that they are improper, and either look shocked, which is vulgar, or laugh, which is worse. But German sounds a thoroughly respectable language, and indeed, I believe is so. Gwendolen, you will accompany me.

GWENDOLEN. Certainly, mamma. (LADY BRACKNELL *and* ALGERNON *go into the music-room,* GWENDOLEN *remains behind.*)

JACK. Charming day it has been, Miss Fairfax.

GWENDOLEN. Pray don't talk to me about the weather, Mr. Worthing. Whenever people talk to me about the weather, I always feel quite certain that they mean something else. And that makes me so nervous.

JACK. I do mean something else.

GWENDOLEN. I thought so. In fact, I am never wrong.

JACK. And I would like to be allowed to take advantage of Lady Bracknell's temporary absence . . .

GWENDOLEN. I would certainly advise you to do so. Mamma has a way of coming back suddenly into a room that I have often had to speak to her about.

JACK (*nervously*). Miss Fairfax, ever since I met you I have admired you more than any girl . . . I have ever met since . . . I met you.

GWENDOLEN. Yes, I am quite aware of the fact. And I often wish that in public, at any rate, you had been more demonstrative. For me you have always had an irresistible fascination. Even before I met you I was far from indifferent to you. (JACK *looks at her in amazement*) We live, as I hope you know, Mr. Worthing, in an age of ideals. The fact is constantly mentioned in the more expensive monthly magazines, and has reached the provincial pulpits I am told: and my ideal has always been to love some one of the name of Ernest. There is something in that name that inspires absolute confidence. The moment Algernon first mentioned to me that he had a friend called Ernest, I knew I was destined to love you.

JACK. You really love me, Gwendolen?

GWENDOLEN. Passionately!

JACK. Darling! You don't know how happy you've made me.

GWENDOLEN. My own Ernest!

JACK. But you don't really mean to say that you couldn't love me if my name wasn't Ernest?

GWENDOLEN. But your name is Ernest.

JACK. Yes, I know it is. But supposing it was something else? Do you mean to say you couldn't love me then?

GWENDOLEN (*glibly*). Ah! that is clearly a metaphysical speculation, and like most metaphysical speculations has very little reference at all to the actual facts of real life, as we know them.

JACK. Personally, darling, to speak quite candidly, I don't much care about the name of Ernest . . . I don't think that name suits me at all.

GWENDOLEN. It suits you perfectly. It is a divine name. It has a music of its own. It produces vibrations.

JACK. Well, really, Gwendolen, I must say that I think there are lots of other much nicer names. I think, Jack, for instance, a charming name.

GWENDOLEN. Jack? . . . No, there is very little music in the name Jack, if any at all, indeed. It does not thrill. It produces absolutely no vibrations. . . . I have known several Jacks, and they all, without exception, were more than usually plain. Besides, Jack is a notorious domesticity for John! And I pity any woman who is married to a man called John. She would probably never be allowed to know the entrancing pleasure of a single moment's solitude. The only really safe name is Ernest.

JACK. Gwendolen, I must get christened at once—I mean we must get married at once. There is no time to be lost.

GWENDOLEN. Married, Mr. Worthing?

JACK (*astounded*). Well . . . surely. You know that I love you, and you led me to believe, Miss Fairfax, that you were not absolutely indifferent to me.

GWENDOLEN. I adore you. But you haven't proposed to me yet. Nothing has been said at all about marriage. The subject has not even been touched on.

JACK. Well . . . may I propose to you now?

GWENDOLEN. I think it would be an admirable opportunity. And to spare you any possible disappointment, Mr. Worthing, I think it only fair to tell you quite frankly beforehand that I am fully determined to accept you.

JACK. Gwendolen!

GWENDOLEN. Yes, Mr. Worthing, what have you got to say to me?

JACK. You know what I have got to say to you.

GWENDOLEN. Yes, but you don't say it.

JACK. Gwendolen, will you marry me? (*Goes on his knees.*)

GWENDOLEN. Of course I will, darling. How long you have been about it! I am afraid you have had very little experience in how to propose.

JACK. My own one, I have never loved anyone in the world but you.

GWENDOLEN. Yes, but men often propose for practice. I know my brother Gerald does. All my girl-friends tell me so. What wonderfully blue eyes you have, Ernest! They are quite, quite blue. I hope you will always look at me just like that, especially when there are other people present.
(*Enter* LADY BRACKNELL.)

LADY BRACKNELL. Mr. Worthing! Rise, sir, from this semi-recumbent posture. It is most indecorous.

GWENDOLEN. Mamma! (*He tries to rise; she restrains him*) I must beg you to retire. This is no place for you. Besides, Mr. Worthing has not quite finished yet.

LADY BRACKNELL. Finished what, may I ask?

GWENDOLEN. I am engaged to Mr. Worthing, mamma. (*They rise together.*)

LADY BRACKNELL. Pardon me, you are not engaged to anyone. When you do become engaged to some one, I or your father, should his health permit him, will inform you of the fact. An engagement should come on a young girl as a surprise, pleasant or unpleasant, as the case may be. It is hardly a matter that she could be allowed to arrange for herself. . . . And now I have a few questions to put to you, Mr. Worthing. While I am making these inquiries, you, Gwendolen, will wait for me below in the carriage.

GWENDOLEN (*reproachfully*). Mamma!

LADY BRACKNELL. In the carriage, Gwendolen! (GWENDOLEN *goes to the door. She and* JACK *blow kisses to each other behind* LADY BRACKNELL'S *back.* LADY BRACKNELL *looks vaguely about as if she could not understand what the noise was. Finally turns round*) Gwendolen, the carriage!

GWENDOLEN. Yes, mamma. (*Goes out, looking back at* JACK.)

LADY BRACKNELL (*sitting down*). You can take a seat, Mr. Worthing. (*Looks in her pocket for notebook and pencil.*)

JACK. Thank you, Lady Bracknell, I prefer standing.

LADY BRACKNELL (*pencil and notebook in hand*). I feel bound to tell you that you are not down on my list of eligible young men, although I have the same list as the dear Duchess of Bolton has. We work together, in fact. However, I am quite ready to enter your name, should your answers be what a really affectionate mother requires. Do you smoke?

JACK. Well, yes, I must admit I smoke.

LADY BRACKNELL. I am glad to hear it. A man should always have an occupation of some kind. There are far too many idle men in London as it is. How old are you?

JACK. Twenty-nine.

LADY BRACKNELL. A very good age to be married at. I have always been of opinion that a man who desires to get married should know either everything or nothing. Which do you know?

JACK (*after some hesitation*). I know nothing, Lady Bracknell.

LADY BRACKNELL. I am pleased to hear it. I do not approve of anything that tampers with natural ignorance. Ignorance is like a delicate exotic fruit; touch it and the bloom is gone. The whole theory of modern education is radically unsound. Fortunately in England, at any rate, education produces no effect whatsoever. If it did, it would prove a serious danger to the upper classes, and probably lead to acts of violence in Grosvenor Square. What is your income?

JACK. Between seven and eight thousand a year.

LADY BRACKNELL (*makes a note in her book*). In land, or in investments?

JACK. In investments, chiefly.

LADY BRACKNELL. That is satisfactory. What between the duties expected of one during one's lifetime, and the duties exacted from one after one's death, land has ceased to be either a profit or a pleasure. It gives one position, and prevents one from keeping it up. That's all that can be said about land.

JACK. I have a country house with some land, of course, attached to it, about fifteen hundred acres, I believe; but I don't depend on that for my real income. In fact, as far as I can make out, the poachers are the only people who make anything out of it.

LADY BRACKNELL. A country house! How many bedrooms? Well, that point can be cleared up afterwards. You have a town house, I hope? A girl with a simple, unspoiled nature, like Gwendolen, could hardly be expected to reside in the country.

JACK. Well, I own a house in Belgrave Square, but it is let by the year to Lady Bloxham. Of course, I can get it back whenever I like, at six months' notice.

LADY BRACKNELL. Lady Bloxham? I don't know her.

JACK. Oh, she goes about very little. She is a lady considerably advanced in years.

LADY BRACKNELL. Ah, now-a-days that is no guarantee of respectability of character. What number in Belgrave Square?

JACK. 149.

LADY BRACKNELL (*shaking her head*). The unfashionable side. I thought there was something. However, that could easily be altered.

JACK. Do you mean the fashion, or the side?

LADY BRACKNELL (*sternly*). Both, if necessary, I presume. What are your politics?

JACK. Well, I am afraid I really have none. I am a Liberal Unionist.

LADY BRACKNELL. Oh, they count as Tories. They dine with us. Or come in the evening, at any rate. Now to minor matters. Are your parents living?

JACK. I have lost both my parents.

LADY BRACKNELL. Both? . . . That seems like carelessness. Who was your father? He was evidently a man of some wealth. Was he born in what the Radical papers call the purple of commerce, or did he rise from the ranks of the aristocracy?

JACK. I am afraid I really don't know. The fact is, Lady Bracknell, I said I had lost my parents. It would be nearer the truth to say that my parents seem to have lost me . . . I don't actually know who I am by birth. I was . . . well, I was found.

LADY BRACKNELL. Found!

JACK. The late Mr. Thomas Cardew, an old gentleman of a very charitable and kindly disposition, found me, and gave me the name of Worthing, because he happened to have a first-class ticket for Worthing in his pocket at the time. Worthing is a place in Sussex. It is a seaside resort.

LADY BRACKNELL. Where did the charitable gentleman who had a first-class ticket for this seaside resort find you?

JACK (*gravely*). In a hand-bag.

LADY BRACKNELL. A hand-bag?

JACK (*very seriously*). Yes, Lady Bracknell. I was in a hand-bag—a somewhat large, black leather hand-bag, with handles to it—an ordinary hand-bag in fact.

LADY BRACKNELL. In what locality did this Mr. James, or Thomas, Cardew come across this ordinary hand-bag?

JACK. In the cloak-room at Victoria Station. It was given to him in mistake for his own.

LADY BRACKNELL. The cloak-room at Victoria Station?

JACK. Yes. The Brighton line.

LADY BRACKNELL. The line is immaterial. Mr. Worthing, I confess I feel somewhat bewildered by what you have just told me. To be born, or at any rate bred, in a hand-bag, whether it had handles or not, seems to me to display a contempt for the ordinary decencies of family life that remind one of the worst excesses of the French Revolution. And I presume you know what that unfortunate movement led to? As for the particular locality in which the hand-bag was found, a cloak-room at a railway station might serve to conceal a social indiscretion—has probably, indeed, been used for that purpose before now—but it could hardly be regarded as an assured basis for a recognised position in good society.

JACK. May I ask you then what you would advise me to do? I need hardly say I would do anything in the world to ensure Gwendolen's happiness.

LADY BRACKNELL. I would strongly advise you, Mr. Worthing, to try and acquire some relations as soon as possible, and to make a definite effort to produce at any rate one parent, of either sex, before the season is quite over.

JACK. Well, I don't see how I could possibly manage to do that. I can produce the hand-bag at any moment. It is in my dressing-room at home. I really think that should satisfy you, Lady Bracknell.

LADY BRACKNELL. Me, sir! What has it to do with me? You can hardly imagine that I and Lord Bracknell would dream of allowing our only daughter—a girl brought up with the utmost care—to marry into a cloak-room, and form an alliance with a parcel? Good morning, Mr. Worthing! (LADY BRACKNELL *sweeps out in majestic indignation.*)

JACK. Good morning! (ALGERNON, *from the other room, strikes up the Wedding March.* JACK *looks perfectly furious, and goes to the door*) For goodness' sake don't play that ghastly tune, Algy! How idiotic you are! (*The music stops, and* ALGERNON *enters cheerily.*)

ALGERNON. Didn't it go off all right, old boy? You don't mean to say Gwendolen refused you? I know it is a way she has. She is always refusing people. I think it is most ill-natured of her.

JACK. Oh, Gwendolen is as right as a trivet. As far as she is concerned, we are engaged. Her mother is perfectly unbearable. Never met such a Gorgon . . . I don't really know what a Gorgon is like, but I am quite sure that Lady Bracknell is one. In any case, she is a monster, without being a myth, which is rather unfair. . . . I beg your pardon, Algy, I suppose I shouldn't talk about your own aunt in that way before you.

ALGERNON. My dear boy, I love hearing my relations abused. It is the only thing that makes me put up with them at all. Relations are simply a tedious pack of people, who haven't got the remotest knowledge of how to live, nor the smallest instinct about when to die.

JACK. Oh, that is nonsense!

ALGERNON. It isn't!

JACK. Well, I won't argue about the matter. You always want to argue about things.

ALGERNON. That is exactly what things were originally made for.

JACK. Upon my word, if I thought that, I'd shoot myself . . . (*A pause*) You don't think there is any chance of Gwendolen becoming like her mother in about a hundred and fifty years, do you, Algy?

ALGERNON. All women become like their mothers. That is their tragedy. No man does. That's his.

JACK. Is that clever?

ALGERNON. It is perfectly phrased! and quite as true as any observation in civilized life should be.

JACK. I am sick to death of cleverness. Everybody is clever now-a-days. You can't go anywhere without meeting clever people. The thing has become an absolute public nuisance. I wish to goodness we had a few fools left.

ALGERNON. We have.

JACK. I should extremely like to meet them. What do they talk about?

ALGERNON. The fools? Oh! about the clever people, of course.

JACK. What fools!

ALGERNON. By the way, did you tell Gwendolen the truth about your being Ernest in town, and Jack in the country?

JACK (*in a very patronising manner*). My dear fellow, the truth isn't quite the sort of thing one tells to a nice, sweet, refined girl. What extraordinary ideas you have about the way to behave to a woman!

ALGERNON. The only way to behave to a woman is to make love to her, if she is pretty, and to someone else if she is plain.

JACK. Oh, that is nonsense.

ALGERNON. What about your brother? What about the profligate Ernest?

JACK. Oh, before the end of the week I shall have got rid of him. I'll say he died in Paris of apoplexy. Lots of people die of apoplexy, quite suddenly, don't they?

ALGERNON. Yes, but it's hereditary, my dear fellow. It's a sort of thing that runs in families. You had much better say a severe chill.

JACK. You are sure a severe chill isn't hereditary, or anything of that kind?

ALGERNON. Of course it isn't!

JACK. Very well, then. My poor brother Ernest is carried off suddenly in Paris, by a severe chill. That gets rid of him.

ALGERNON. But I thought you said that . . . Miss Cardew was a little too much interested in your poor brother Ernest? Won't she feel his loss a good deal?

JACK. Oh, that is all right. Cecily is not a silly, romantic girl, I am glad to say. She has got a capital appetite, goes for long walks, and pays no attention at all to her lessons.

ALGERNON. I would rather like to see Cecily.

JACK. I will take very good care you never do. She is excessively pretty, and she is only just eighteen.

ALGERNON. Have you told Gwendolen yet that you have an excessively pretty ward who is only just eighteen?

JACK. Oh! one doesn't blurt these things out to people. Cecily and Gwendolen are perfectly certain to be extremely great friends. I'll bet you anything you like that half an hour after they have met, they will be calling each other sister.

ALGERNON. Women only do that when they have called each other a lot of other things first. Now, my dear boy, if we want to get a good table at Willis's, we really must go and dress. Do you know it is nearly seven?

JACK (*irritably*). Oh! it always is nearly seven.

ALGERNON. Well, I'm hungry.

JACK. I never knew you when you weren't. . . .

ALGERNON. What shall we do after dinner? Go to a theatre?

JACK. Oh, no! I loathe listening.

ALGERNON. Well, let us go to the Club?

JACK. Oh, no! I hate talking.

ALGERNON. Well, we might trot round to the Empire at ten?

JACK. Oh, no! I can't bear looking at things. It is so silly.

ALGERNON. Well, what shall we do?

JACK. Nothing!

ALGERNON. It is awfully hard work doing nothing. However, I don't mind hard work where there is no definite object of any kind.
(*Enter* LANE.)

LANE. Miss Fairfax.
(*Enter* GWENDOLEN. LANE *goes out.*)

ALGERNON. Gwendolen, upon my word!

GWENDOLEN. Algy, kindly turn your back. I have something very particular to say to Mr. Worthing.

ALGERNON. Really, Gwendolen, I don't think I can allow this at all.

GWENDOLEN. Algy, you always adopt a strictly immoral attitude towards life. You are not quite old enough to do that. (ALGERNON *retires to the fireplace.*)

JACK. My own darling!

GWENDOLEN. Ernest, we may never be married. From the expression on mamma's face I fear we never shall. Few parents now-a-days pay any regard to what their children say to them. The old-fashioned respect for the young is fast dying out. Whatever influence I ever had over mamma, I lost at the age of three. But although she may prevent us from becoming man and wife, and I may marry someone else, and marry often, nothing that she can possibly do can alter my eternal devotion to you.

JACK. Dear Gwendolen.

GWENDOLEN. The story of your romantic origin, as related to me by mamma, with unpleasing comments, has naturally stirred the deeper fibres of my nature. Your Christian name has an irresistible fascination. The simplicity of your character makes you exquisitely incomprehensible to me. Your town address at the Albany I have. What is your address in the country?

JACK. The Manor House, Woolton, Hertfordshire. (ALGERNON, *who has been carefully listening, smiles to himself, and writes the address on his shirt-cuff. Then picks up the Railway Guide.*)

GWENDOLEN. There is a good postal service, I suppose? It may be necessary to do something desperate. That, of course, will require serious consideration. I will communicate with you daily.

JACK. My own one!

GWENDOLEN. How long do you remain in town?

JACK. Till Monday.

GWENDOLEN. Good! Algy, you may turn round now.

ALGERNON. Thanks, I've turned round already.

GWENDOLEN. You may also ring the bell.

JACK. You will let me see you to your carriage, my own darling?

GWENDOLEN. Certainly.

JACK (*to* LANE, *who now enters*). I will see Miss Fairfax out.

LANE. Yes, sir. (JACK *and* GWENDOLEN *go off.* LANE *presents several letters on a salver to* ALGERNON. *It is to be surmised that they are bills, as* ALGERNON, *after looking at the envelopes, tears them up.*)

ALGERNON. A glass of sherry, Lane.

LANE. Yes, sir.

ALGERNON. Tomorrow, Lane, I'm going Bunburying.

LANE. Yes, sir.

ALGERNON. I shall probably not be back till Monday. You can put up my dress clothes, my smoking jacket, and all the Bunbury suits . . .

LANE. Yes, sir. (*Handing sherry.*)

ALGERNON. I hope tomorrow will be a fine day, Lane.

LANE. It never is, sir.

ALGERNON. Lane, you're a perfect pessimist.

LANE. I do my best to give satisfaction, sir.
(*Enter* JACK. LANE *goes off.*)

JACK. There's a sensible, intellectual girl! the only girl I ever cared for in my life. (ALGERNON *is laughing immoderately*) What on earth are you so amused at?

ALGERNON. Oh, I'm a little anxious about poor Bunbury, that's all.

JACK. If you don't take care, your friend Bunbury will get you into a serious scrape some day.

ALGERNON. I love scrapes. They are the only things that are never serious.

JACK. Oh, that's nonsense, Algy. You never talk anything but nonsense.

ALGERNON. Nobody ever does. (JACK *looks indignantly at him, and leaves the room.* ALGERNON *lights a cigarette, reads his shirt-cuff and smiles.*)

ACT TWO

SCENE—*Garden at the Manor House. A flight of gray stone steps leads up to the house. The garden, an old-fashioned one, full of roses. Time of year, July. Basket chairs, and a table covered with books, are set under a large yew tree.*

(MISS PRISM *discovered seated at the table.* CECILY *is at the back watering flowers.*)

MISS PRISM (*calling*). Cecily, Cecily! Surely such a utilitarian occupation as the watering of flowers is rather Moulton's duty than yours? Especially at a moment when intellectual pleasures await you. Your German grammar is on the table. Pray open it at page fifteen. We will repeat yesterday's lesson.

CECILY (*coming over very slowly*). But I don't like German. It isn't at all a becoming language. I know perfectly well that I look quite plain after my German lesson.

MISS PRISM. Child, you know how anxious your guardian is that you should improve yourself in every way. He laid particular stress on your German, as he was leaving for town yesterday. Indeed, he always lays stress on your German when he is leaving for town.

CECILY. Dear Uncle Jack is so very serious! Sometimes he is so serious that I think he cannot be quite well.

MISS PRISM (*drawing herself up*). Your guardian enjoys the best of health, and his gravity of demeanour is especially to be commended in one so comparatively young as he is. I know no one who has a higher sense of duty and responsibility.

CECILY. I suppose that is why he often looks a little bored when we three are together.

MISS PRISM. Cecily! I am surprised at you. Mr. Worthing has many troubles in his life. Idle merriment and triviality would be out of place in his conversation. You must remember his constant anxiety about that unfortunate young man, his brother.

CECILY. I wish Uncle Jack would allow that unfortunate young man, his brother, to come down here sometimes. We might have a good influence over him, Miss Prism. I am sure you certainly would. You know German, and geology, and things of that kind influence a man very much. (CECILY *begins to write in her diary.*)

MISS PRISM (*shaking her head*). I do not think that even I could produce any effect on a character that, according to his own brother's admission, is irretrievably weak and vacillating. Indeed, I am not sure that I would desire to reclaim him. I am not in favour of this modern mania for turning bad people into good people at a moment's notice. As a man sows so let him reap. You must put away your diary, Cecily. I really don't see why you should keep a diary at all.

CECILY. I keep a diary in order to enter the wonderful secrets of my life. If I didn't write them down I should probably forget all about them.

MISS PRISM. Memory, my dear Cecily, is the diary that we all carry about with us.

CECILY. Yes, but it usually chronicles the things that have never happened, and couldn't possibly have happened. I believe that Memory is responsible for nearly all the three-volume novels that Mudie sends us.

MISS PRISM. Do not speak slightingly of the three-volume novel, Cecily. I wrote one myself in earlier days.

CECILY. Did you really, Miss Prism? How wonderfully clever you are! I hope it did not end happily? I don't like novels that end happily. They depress me so much.

MISS PRISM. The good ended happily, and the bad unhappily. That is what Fiction means.

CECILY. I suppose so. But it seems very unfair. And was your novel ever published?

MISS PRISM. Alas! no. The manuscript unfortunately was abandoned. I use the word in the sense of lost or mislaid. To your work, child, these speculations are profitless.

CECILY (*smiling*). But I see dear Dr. Chasuble coming up through the garden.

MISS PRISM (*rising and advancing*). Dr. Chasuble! This is indeed a pleasure.
(*Enter* CANON CHASUBLE.)

CHASUBLE. And how are we this morning? Miss Prism, you are, I trust, well?

CECILY. Miss Prism has just been complaining of a slight headache. I think it would do her so much good to have a short stroll with you in the park, Dr. Chasuble.

MISS PRISM. Cecily, I have not mentioned anything about a headache.

CECILY. No, dear Miss Prism, I know that, but I felt instinctively that you had a headache. Indeed I was thinking about that, and not about my German lesson, when the Rector came in.

CHASUBLE. I hope, Cecily, you are not inattentive.

CECILY. Oh, I am afraid I am.

CHASUBLE. That is strange. Were I fortunate enough to be Miss Prism's pupil, I would hang upon her lips. (MISS PRISM *glares*) I spoke metaphorically.—My metaphor was drawn from bees. Ahem! Mr. Worthing, I suppose, has not returned from town yet?

MISS PRISM. We do not expect him till Monday afternoon.

CHASUBLE. Ah yes, he usually likes to spend his Sunday in London. He is not one of those whose sole aim is enjoyment, as, by all accounts, that unfortunate young man, his brother, seems to be. But I must not disturb Egeria and her pupil any longer.

MISS PRISM. Egeria? My name is Lætitia, Doctor.

CHASUBLE (*bowing*). A classical allusion merely, drawn from the Pagan authors. I shall see you both no doubt at Evensong.

MISS PRISM. I think, dear Doctor, I will have a stroll with you. I find I have a headache after all, and a walk might do it good.

CHASUBLE. With pleasure, Miss Prism, with pleasure. We might go as far as the schools and back.

MISS PRISM. That would be delightful. Cecily, you will read your Political Economy in my absence. The chapter on the Fall of the Rupee you may omit. It is somewhat too sensational. Even these metallic problems have their melodramatic side.
(*Goes down the garden with* DR. CHASUBLE.)

CECILY (*picks up books and throws them back on table*). Horrid Political Economy! Horrid Geography! Horrid, horrid German!
(*Enter* MERRIMAN *with a card on a salver.*)

MERRIMAN. Mr. Ernest Worthing has just driven over from the station. He has brought his luggage with him.

CECILY (*takes the card and reads it*). "Mr. Ernest Worthing, B 4 The Albany, W." Uncle Jack's brother! Did you tell him Mr. Worthing was in town?

MERRIMAN. Yes, Miss. He seemed very much disappointed. I mentioned that you and Miss Prism were in the garden. He said he was anxious to speak to you privately for a moment.

CECILY. Ask Mr. Ernest Worthing to come here. I suppose you had better talk to the housekeeper about a room for him.

MERRIMAN. ~~Yes, Miss.~~ (MERRIMAN *goes off.*)

CECILY. I have never met any really wicked person before. I feel rather frightened. I am so afraid he will look just like everyone else. (*Enter* ALGERNON, *very gay and debonair*) He does!

ALGERNON (*raising his hat*). You are my little cousin Cecily, I'm sure.

CECILY. You are under some strange mistake. I am not little. In fact, I am more than usually tall for my age. (ALGERNON *is rather taken aback*) But I am your cousin Cecily. You, I see from your card, are Uncle Jack's brother, my cousin Ernest, my wicked cousin Ernest.

ALGERNON. Oh! I am not really wicked at all, cousin Cecily. You mustn't think that I am wicked.

CECILY. If you are not, then you

have certainly been deceiving us all in a very inexcusable manner. I hope you have not been leading a double life, pretending to be wicked and being really good all the time. That would be hypocrisy.

ALGERNON (*looks at her in amazement*). Oh! of course I have been rather reckless.

CECILY. I am glad to hear it.

ALGERNON. In fact, now you mention the subject, I have been very bad in my own small way.

CECILY. I don't think you should be so proud of that, though I am sure it must have been very pleasant.

ALGERNON. It is much pleasanter being here with you.

CECILY. I can't understand how you are here at all. Uncle Jack won't be back till Monday afternoon.

ALGERNON. That is a great disappointment. I am obliged to go up by the first train on Monday morning. I have a business appointment that I am anxious . . . to miss.

CECILY. Couldn't you miss it anywhere but in London?

ALGERNON. No; the appointment is in London.

CECILY. Well, I know, of course, how important it is not to keep a business engagement, if one wants to retain any sense of the beauty of life, but still I think you had better wait till Uncle Jack arrives. I know he wants to speak to you about your emigrating.

ALGERNON. About my what?

CECILY. Your emigrating. He has gone up to buy your outfit.

ALGERNON. I certainly wouldn't let Jack buy my outfit. He has no taste in neckties at all.

CECILY. I don't think you will require neckties. Uncle Jack is sending you to Australia.

ALGERNON. Australia! I'd sooner die.

CECILY. Well, he said at dinner on Wednesday night, that you would have to choose between this world, the next world, and Australia.

ALGERNON. Oh, well! The accounts I have received of Australia and the next world, are not particularly encouraging. This world is good enough for me, cousin Cecily.

CECILY. Yes, but are you good enough for it?

ALGERNON. I'm afraid I'm not that. That is why I want you to reform me. You might make that your mission, if you don't mind, cousin Cecily.

CECILY. I'm afraid I've not time, this afternoon.

ALGERNON. Well, would you mind my reforming myself this afternoon?

CECILY. That is rather Quixotic of you. But I think you should try.

ALGERNON. I will. I feel better already.

CECILY. You are looking a little worse.

ALGERNON. That is because I am hungry.

CECILY. How thoughtless of me. I should have remembered that when one is going to lead an entirely new life, one requires regular and wholesome meals. Won't you come in?

ALGERNON. Thank you. Might I have a button-hole first? I never have any appetite unless I have a button-hole first.

CECILY. A Maréchal Niel? (*Picks up scissors.*)

ALGERNON. No, I'd sooner have a pink rose.

CECILY. Why? (*Cuts a flower.*)

ALGERNON. Because you are like a pink rose, cousin Cecily.

CECILY. I don't think it can be right for you to talk to me like that. Miss Prism never says such things to me.

ALGERNON. Then Miss Prism is a short-sighted old lady. (CECILY *puts the rose in his button-hole*) You are the prettiest girl I ever saw.

CECILY. Miss Prism says that all good looks are a snare.

ALGERNON. They are a snare that every sensible man would like to be caught in.

CECILY. Oh! I don't think I would care to catch a sensible man. I shouldn't know what to talk to him about.

(*They pass into the house.* MISS PRISM *and* DR. CHASUBLE *return.*)

MISS PRISM. You are too much alone, dear Dr. Chasuble. You should get married. A misanthrope I can understand—a womanthrope, never!

CHASUBLE (*with a scholar's shudder*). Believe me, I do not deserve so neologistic a phrase. The precept as well as the practice of the Primitive Church was distinctly against matrimony.

MISS PRISM (*sententiously*). That is obviously the reason why the Primitive Church has not lasted up to the present day. And you do not seem to realize, dear Doctor, that by persistently remaining single, a man converts himself into a permanent public temptation. Men should be careful; this very celibacy leads weaker vessels astray.

CHASUBLE. But is a man not equally attractive when married?

MISS PRISM. No married man is ever attractive except to his wife.

CHASUBLE. And often, I've been told, not even to her.

MISS PRISM. That depends on the intellectual sympathies of the woman. Maturity can always be depended on. Ripeness can be trusted. Young women are green. (DR. CHASUBLE *starts*) I spoke horticulturally. My metaphor was drawn from fruits. But where is Cecily?

CHASUBLE. Perhaps she followed us to the schools.

(*Enter* JACK *slowly from the back of the garden. He is dressed in the deepest mourning, with crape hatband and black gloves.*)

MISS PRISM. Mr. Worthing!

CHASUBLE. Mr. Worthing?

MISS PRISM. This is indeed a surprise. We did not look for you till Monday afternoon.

JACK (*shakes* MISS PRISM's *hand in a tragic manner*). I have returned sooner than I expected. Dr. Chasuble, I hope you are well?

CHASUBLE. Dear Mr. Worthing, I trust this garb of woe does not betoken some terrible calamity?

JACK. My brother.

MISS PRISM. More shameful debts and extravagance?

CHASUBLE. Still leading his life of pleasure?

JACK (*shaking his head*). Dead!

CHASUBLE. Your brother Ernest dead?

JACK. Quite dead.

MISS PRISM. What a lesson for him! I trust he will profit by it.

CHASUBLE. Mr. Worthing, I offer you my sincere condolence. You have at least the consolation of knowing that you were always the most generous and forgiving of brothers.

JACK. Poor Ernest! He had many faults, but it is a sad, sad blow.

CHASUBLE. Very sad indeed. Were you with him at the end?

JACK. No. He died abroad; in Paris, in fact. I had a telegram last night from the manager of the Grand Hotel.

CHASUBLE. Was the cause of death mentioned?

JACK. A severe chill, it seems.

MISS PRISM. As a man sows, so shall he reap.

CHASUBLE (*raising his hand*). Charity, dear Miss Prism, charity! None of us are perfect. I myself am peculiarly susceptible to draughts. Will the interment take place here?

JACK. No. He seems to have expressed a desire to be buried in Paris.

CHASUBLE. In Paris! (*Shakes his head*) I fear that hardly points to any very serious state of mind at the last. You would no doubt wish me to make some slight allusion to this tragic domestic affliction next Sunday. (JACK *presses his hand convulsively*) My sermon on the meaning of the manna in the wilderness can be adapted to almost any occasion, joyful, or, as in the present case, distressing. (*All sigh*) I have preached it at harvest celebrations, christenings, confirmations, on days of humiliation and festal days. The last time I delivered it was in the Cathedral, as a charity sermon on behalf of the Society for the Prevention of Discontentment among the Upper Orders. The Bishop, who was present, was much struck by some of the analogies I drew.

JACK. Ah, that reminds me, you mentioned christenings I think, Dr. Chasuble? I suppose you know how to christen all right? (DR. CHASUBLE *looks astounded*) I mean, of course, you are continually christening, aren't you?

MISS PRISM. It is, I regret to say, one of the Rector's most constant duties in this parish. I have often spoken to the poorer classes on the subject. But they don't seem to know what thrift is.

CHASUBLE. But is there any particular infant in whom you are interested, Mr. Worthing? Your brother was, I believe, unmarried, was he not?

JACK. Oh, yes.

MISS PRISM (*bitterly*). People who live entirely for pleasure usually are.

JACK. But it is not for any child, dear Doctor. I am very fond of children. No! the fact is, I would like to be christened myself, this afternoon, if you have nothing better to do.

CHASUBLE. But surely, Mr. Worthing, you have been christened already?

JACK. I don't remember anything about it.

CHASUBLE. But have you any grave doubts on the subject?

JACK. I certainly intend to have. Of course, I don't know if the thing would bother you in any way, or if you think I am a little too old now.

CHASUBLE. Not at all. The sprinkling, and, indeed, the immersion of adults is a perfectly canonical practice.

JACK. Immersion!

CHASUBLE. You need have no apprehensions. Sprinkling is all that is necessary, or indeed I think advisable. Our weather is so changeable. At what hour would you wish the ceremony performed?

JACK. Oh, I might trot around about five if that would suit you.

CHASUBLE. Perfectly, perfectly! In fact I have two similar ceremonies to perform at that time. A case of twins that occurred recently in one of the outlying cottages on your own estate. Poor Jenkins the carter, a most hard-working man.

JACK. Oh! I don't see much fun in being christened along with other babies. It would be childish. Would half-past five do?

CHASUBLE. Admirably! Admirably! (*Takes out watch*) And now, dear Mr. Worthing, I will not intrude any longer into a house of sorrow. I would merely beg you not to be too much bowed down by grief. What seem to us bitter trials at the moment are often blessings in disguise.

MISS PRISM. This seems to me a blessing of an extremely obvious kind.
(*Enter* CECILY *from the house.*)

CECILY. Uncle Jack! Oh, I am pleased to see you back. But what horrid clothes you have on! Do go and change them.

MISS PRISM. Cecily!

CHASUBLE. My child! my child! (CECILY *goes towards* JACK; *he kisses her brow in a melancholy manner.*)

CECILY. What is the matter, Uncle Jack? Do look happy! You look as if you had a toothache and I have such a surprise for you. Who do you think is in the dining-room? Your brother!

JACK. Who?

CECILY. Your brother Ernest. He arrived about half an hour ago.

JACK. What nonsense! I haven't got a brother.

CECILY. Oh, don't say that. However badly he may have behaved to you in the past he is still your brother. You couldn't be so heartless as to disown him. I'll tell him to come out. And you will shake hands with him, won't you, Uncle Jack? (*Runs back into the house.*)

CHASUBLE. These are very joyful tidings.

MISS PRISM. After we had all been resigned to his loss, his sudden return seems to me peculiarly distressing.

JACK. My brother is in the dining-room? I don't know what it all means. I think it is perfectly absurd. (*Enter* ALGERNON *and* CECILY *hand in hand. They come slowly up to* JACK.)

JACK. Good heavens! (*Motions* ALGERNON *away.*)

ALGERNON. Brother John, I have come down from town to tell you that I am very sorry for all the trouble I have given you, and that I intend to lead a better life in the future. (JACK *glares at him and does not take his hand.*)

CECILY. Uncle Jack, you are not going to refuse your own brother's hand?

JACK. Nothing will induce me to take his hand. I think his coming down here disgraceful. He knows perfectly well why.

CECILY. Uncle Jack, do be nice. There is some good in everyone. Ernest has just been telling me about his poor invalid friend, Mr. Bunbury, whom he goes to visit so often. And surely there must be much good in one who is kind to an invalid, and leaves the pleasures of London to sit by a bed of pain.

JACK. Oh, he has been talking about Bunbury, has he?

CECILY. Yes, he has told me all about poor Mr. Bunbury, and his terrible state of health.

JACK. Bunbury! Well, I won't have him talk to you about Bunbury or about anything else. It is enough to drive one perfectly frantic.

ALGERNON. Of course I admit that the faults were all on my side. But I must say that I think that Brother John's coldness to me is peculiarly painful. I expected a more enthusiastic welcome, especially considering it is the first time I have come here.

CECILY. Uncle Jack, if you don't shake hands with Ernest I will never forgive you.

JACK. Never forgive me?

CECILY. Never, never, never!

JACK. Well, this is the last time I shall ever do it. (*Shakes hands with* ALGERNON *and glares.*)

CHASUBLE. It's pleasant, is it not, to see so perfect a reconciliation? I think we might leave the two brothers together.

MISS PRISM. Cecily, you will come with us.

CECILY. Certainly, Miss Prism. My little task of reconciliation is over.

CHASUBLE. You have done a beautiful action today, dear child.

MISS PRISM. We must not be premature in our judgments.

CECILY. I feel very happy. (*They all go off.*)

JACK. You young scoundrel, Algy, you must get out of this place as soon as possible. I don't allow any Bunburying here.
(*Enter* MERRIMAN.)

MERRIMAN. I have put Mr. Ernest's things in the room next to yours, sir. I suppose that is all right?

JACK. What?

MERRIMAN. Mr. Ernest's luggage, sir. I have unpacked it and put it in the room next to your own.

JACK. His luggage?

MERRIMAN. Yes, sir. Three portmanteaus, a dressing-case, two hatboxes, and a large luncheon-basket.

ALGERNON. I am afraid I can't stay more than a week this time.

JACK. Merriman, order the dog-cart at once. Mr. Ernest has been suddenly called back to town.

MERRIMAN. Yes, sir. (*Goes back into the house.*)

ALGERNON. What a fearful liar you are, Jack. I have not been called back to town at all.

JACK. Yes, you have.

ALGERNON. I haven't heard anyone call me.

JACK. Your duty as a gentleman calls you back.

ALGERNON. My duty as a gentleman has never interfered with my pleasures in the smallest degree.

JACK. I can quite understand that.

ALGERNON. Well, Cecily is a darling.

JACK. You are not to talk of Miss Cardew like that. I don't like it.

ALGERNON. Well, I don't like your clothes. You look perfectly ridiculous in them. Why on earth don't you go up and change? It is perfectly childish to be in deep mourning for a man who is actually staying for a whole week with you in your house as a guest. I call it grotesque.

JACK. You are certainly not staying with me for a whole week as a guest or anything else. You have got to leave . . . by the four-five train.

ALGERNON. I certainly won't leave you so long as you are in mourning. It would be most unfriendly. If I were in mourning you would stay with me, I suppose. I should think it very unkind if you didn't.

JACK. Well, will you go if I change my clothes?

ALGERNON. Yes, if you are not too long. I never saw anybody take so long to dress, and with such little result.

JACK. Well, at any rate, that is better than being always over-dressed as you are.

ALGERNON. If I am occasionally a little over-dressed, I make up for it by being always immensely over-educated.

JACK. Your vanity is ridiculous, your conduct an outrage, and your presence in my garden utterly absurd. However, you have got to catch the four-five, and I hope you will have a pleasant journey back to town. This Bunburying, as you call it, has not been a great success for you. (*Goes into the house.*)

ALGERNON. I think it has been a great success. I'm in love with Cecily, and that is everything. (*Enter* CECILY *at the back of the garden. She picks up the can and begins to water the flowers*) But I must see her before I go, and make arrangements for another Bunbury. Ah, there she is.

CECILY. Oh, I merely came back to water the roses. I thought you were with Uncle Jack.

ALGERNON. He's gone to order the dog-cart for me.

CECILY. Oh, is he going to take you for a nice drive?

ALGERNON. He's going to send me away.

CECILY. Then have we got to part?

ALGERNON. I am afraid so. It's a very painful parting.

CECILY. It is always painful to part from people whom one has known for a very brief space of time. The absence of old friends one can endure with equanimity. But even a momentary separation from anyone to whom one has just been introduced is almost unbearable.

ALGERNON. Thank you.
(*Enter* MERRIMAN.)

MERRIMAN. The dog-cart is at the door, sir. (ALGERNON *looks appealingly at* CECILY.)

CECILY. It can wait, Merriman . . . for . . . five minutes.

MERRIMAN. Yes, miss.
(*Exit* MERRIMAN.)

ALGERNON. I hope, Cecily, I shall not offend you if I state quite frankly and openly that you seem to me to be in every way the visible personification of absolute perfection.

CECILY. I think your frankness does you great credit, Ernest. If you will allow me I will copy your remarks into my diary. (*Goes over to table and begins writing in diary.*)

ALGERNON. Do you really keep a diary? I'd give anything to look at it. May I?

CECILY. Oh, no. (*Puts her hand over it*) You see, it is simply a very young girl's record of her own thoughts and impressions, and consequently meant for publication. When it appears in volume form I hope you will order a copy. But pray, Ernest, don't stop. I delight in taking down from dictation. I have reached "absolute perfection." You can go on. I am quite ready for more.

ALGERNON (*somewhat taken aback*). Ahem! Ahem!

CECILY. Oh, don't cough, Ernest. When one is dictating one should speak fluently and not cough. Besides, I don't know how to spell a cough. (*Writes as* ALGERNON *speaks.*)

ALGERNON (*speaking very rapidly*). Cecily, ever since I first looked upon your wonderful and incomparable beauty, I have dared to love you wildly, passionately, devotedly, hopelessly.

CECILY. I don't think that you should tell me that you love me wildly, passionately, devotedly, hopelessly. Hopelessly doesn't seem to make such sense, does it?

ALGERNON. Cecily!
(*Enter* MERRIMAN.)

MERRIMAN. The dog-cart is waiting, sir.

ALGERNON. Tell it to come round next week, at the same hour.

MERRIMAN (*looks at* CECILY, *who makes no sign*). Yes, sir.
(MERRIMAN *retires.*)

CECILY. Uncle Jack would be very much annoyed if he knew you were staying on till next week, at the same hour.

ALGERNON. Oh, I don't care about Jack. I don't care for anybody in the whole world but you. I love you, Cecily. You will marry me, won't you?

CECILY. You silly you! Of course. Why, we have been engaged for the last three months.

ALGERNON. For the last three months?

CECILY. Yes, it will be exactly three months on Thursday.

ALGERNON. But how did we become engaged?

CECILY. Well, ever since dear Uncle Jack first confessed to us that he had a younger brother who was very wicked and bad, you of course have formed the chief topic of conversation between myself and Miss Prism. And of course a man who is much talked about is always very attractive. One feels there must be something in him after all. I daresay it was foolish of me, but I fell in love with you, Ernest.

ALGERNON. Darling! And when was the engagement actually settled?

CECILY. On the 4th of February last. Worn out by your entire ignorance of my existence, I determined to end the matter one way or the other, and after a long struggle with myself I accepted you under this dear old tree here. The next day I bought this little ring in your name, and this is the little bangle with the true lovers' knot I promised you always to wear.

ALGERNON. Did I give you this? It's very pretty, isn't it?

CECILY. Yes, you've wonderfully good taste, Ernest. It's the excuse I've always given for your leading such a bad life. And this is the box in which I keep all your dear letters. (*Kneels at table, opens box, and produces letters tied up with blue ribbon.*)

ALGERNON. My letters! But my own sweet Cecily, I have never written you any letters.

CECILY. You need hardly remind me of that, Ernest. I remember only too well that I was forced to write your letters for you. I wrote always three times a week, and sometimes oftener.

ALGERNON. Oh, do let me read them, Cecily?

CECILY. Oh, I couldn't possibly. They would make you far too conceited. (*Replaces box*) The three you wrote me after I had broken off the engagement are so beautiful, and so badly spelled, that even now I can hardly read them without crying a little.

ALGERNON. But was our engagement ever broken off?

CECILY. Of course it was. On the 22nd of last March. You can see the entry if you like. (*Shows diary*) "Today I broke off my engagement with Ernest. I feel it is better to do so. The weather still continues charming."

ALGERNON. But why on earth did you break it off? What had I done? I had done nothing at all. Cecily, I am very much hurt indeed to hear you broke it off. Particularly when the weather was so charming.

CECILY. It would hardly have been a really serious engagement if it hadn't been broken off at least once. But I forgave you before the week was out.

ALGERNON (*crossing to her, and kneeling*). What a perfect angel you are, Cecily.

CECILY. You dear romantic boy. (*He kisses her, she puts her fingers through his hair*) I hope your hair curls naturally, does it?

ALGERNON. Yes, darling, with a little help from others.

CECILY. I am so glad.

ALGERNON. You'll never break off our engagement again, Cecily?

CECILY. I don't think I could break it off now that I have actually met you. Besides, of course, there is the question of your name.

ALGERNON. Yes, of course. (*Nervously.*)

CECILY. You must not laugh at me, darling, but it had always been a girlish dream of mine to love some one whose name was Ernest. (ALGERNON *rises,* CECILY *also*) There is something in that name that seems to inspire absolute confidence. I pity any poor married woman whose husband is not called Ernest.

ALGERNON. But, my dear child, do you mean to say you could not love me if I had some other name?

CECILY. But what name?

ALGERNON. Oh, any name you like—Algernon, for instance. . . .

CECILY. But I don't like the name of Algernon.

ALGERNON. Well, my own dear, sweet, loving little darling, I really can't see why you should object to the name of Algernon. It is not at all a bad name. In fact, it is rather an aristocratic name. Half of the chaps who get into the Bankruptcy Court are called Algernon. But seriously, Cecily . . . (*Moving to her*) . . . if my name was Algy, couldn't you love me?

CECILY (*rising*). I might respect you, Ernest, I might admire your character, but I fear that I should not be able to give you my undivided attention.

ALGERNON. Ahem! Cecily! (*Picking up hat*) Your Rector here is, I suppose, thoroughly experienced in the practice of all the rites and ceremonials of the church?

CECILY. Oh, yes. Dr. Chasuble is a most learned man. He has never written a single book, so you can imagine how much he knows.

ALGERNON. I must see him at once on a most important christening—I mean on most important business.

CECILY. Oh!

ALGERNON. I sha'n't be away more than half an hour.

CECILY. Considering that we have been engaged since February the 14th, and that I only met you today for the first time, I think it is rather hard that you should leave me for so long a period as half an hour. Couldn't you make it twenty minutes?

ALGERNON. I'll be back in no time. (*Kisses her and rushes down the garden.*)

CECILY. What an impetuous boy he is. I like his hair so much. I must enter his proposal in my diary. (*Enter* MERRIMAN.)

MERRIMAN. A Miss Fairfax has just called to see Mr. Worthing. On very important business, Miss Fairfax states.

CECILY. Isn't Mr. Worthing in his library?

MERRIMAN. Mr. Worthing went over in the direction of the Rectory some time ago.

CECILY. Pray ask the lady to come out here; Mr. Worthing is sure to be back soon. And you can bring tea.

MERRIMAN. Yes, miss. (*Goes out.*)

CECILY. Miss Fairfax! I suppose one of the many good elderly women who are associated with Uncle Jack in some of his philanthropic work in London. I don't quite like women who are interested in philanthropic work. I think it is so forward of them.
(*Enter* MERRIMAN.)

MERRIMAN. Miss Fairfax.
(*Enter* GWENDOLEN. *Exit* MERRIMAN.)

CECILY (*advancing to meet her*). Pray let me introduce myself to you. My name is Cecily Cardew.

GWENDOLEN. Cecily Cardew? (*Moving to her and shaking hands*) What a very sweet name! Something tells me that we are going to be great friends. I like you already more than I can say. My first impressions of people are never wrong.

CECILY. How nice of you to like me so much after we have known each other such a comparatively short time. Pray sit down.

GWENDOLEN (*still standing up*). I may call you Cecily, may I not?

CECILY. With pleasure!

GWENDOLEN. And you will always call me Gwendolen, won't you?

CECILY. If you wish.

GWENDOLEN. Then that is all quite settled, is it not?

CECILY. I hope so. (*A pause. They both sit down together.*)

GWENDOLEN. Perhaps this might be a favorable opportunity for my mentioning who I am. My father is Lord Bracknell. You have never heard of papa, I suppose?

CECILY. I don't think so.

GWENDOLEN. Outside the family circle, papa, I am glad to say, is entirely unknown. I think that is quite as it should be. The home seems to me to be the proper sphere for the man. And certainly once a man begins to neglect his domestic duties he becomes painfully effeminate, does he not? And I don't like that. It makes men so very attractive. Cecily, mamma, whose views on education are remarkably strict, has brought me up to be extremely short-sighted; it is part of her system; so do you mind my looking at you through my glasses?

CECILY. Oh, not at all, Gwendolen. I am very fond of being looked at.

GWENDOLEN (*after examining* CECILY *carefully through a lorgnette*). You are here on a short visit, I suppose.

CECILY. Oh, no, I live here.

GWENDOLEN (*severely*). Really? Your mother, no doubt, or some female relative of advanced years, resides here also?

CECILY. Oh, no. I have no mother, nor, in fact, any relations.

GWENDOLEN. Indeed?

CECILY. My dear guardian, with the assistance of Miss Prism, has the arduous task of looking after me.

GWENDOLEN. Your guardian?

CECILY. Yes, I am Mr. Worthing's ward.

GWENDOLEN. Oh! It is strange he never mentioned to me that he had a ward. How secretive of him! He grows more interesting hourly. I am not sure, however, that the news inspires me with feelings of unmixed delight. (*Rising and going to her*) I am very fond of you, Cecily; I have liked you ever since I met you. But I am bound to state that now that I know that you are Mr. Worthing's ward, I cannot help expressing a wish you were—well, just a little older than you seem to be—and not quite so very alluring in appearance. In fact, if I may speak candidly——

CECILY. Pray do! I think that whenever one has anything unpleasant to say, one should always be quite candid.

GWENDOLEN. Well, to speak with perfect candour, Cecily, I wish that you were fully forty-two, and more than usually plain for your age. Ernest has a strong upright nature. He is the very soul of truth and honour. Disloyalty would be as impossible to him as deception. But even men of the noblest possible moral character are extremely susceptible to the influence of the physical charms of others. Modern, no less than Ancient History, supplies us with many most painful examples of what I refer to. If it were not so, indeed, History would be quite unreadable.

CECILY. I beg your pardon, Gwendolen, did you say Ernest?

GWENDOLEN. Yes.

CECILY. Oh, but it is not Mr. Ernest Worthing who is my guardian. It is his brother—his elder brother.

GWENDOLEN (*sitting down again*). Ernest never mentioned to me that he had a brother.

CECILY. I am sorry to say they have not been on good terms for a long time.

GWENDOLEN. Ah! that accounts for it. And now that I think of it I have never heard any man mention his brother. The subject seems distasteful to most men. Cecily, you have lifted a load from my mind. I was growing almost anxious. It would have been terrible if any cloud had come across a friendship like ours, would it not? Of course you are quite, quite sure that it is not Mr. Ernest Worthing who is your guardian?

CECILY. Quite sure. (*A pause*) In fact, I am going to be his.

GWENDOLEN (*enquiringly*). I beg your pardon?

CECILY (*rather shy and confidingly*). Dearest Gwendolen, there is no reason why I should make a secret of it to you. Our little county newspaper is sure to chronicle the fact next week. Mr. Ernest Worthing and I are engaged to be married.

GWENDOLEN (*quite politely, rising*). My darling Cecily, I think there must be some slight error. Mr. Ernest Worthing is engaged to me. The announcement will appear in the *Morning Post* on Saturday at the latest.

CECILY (*very politely, rising*). I am afraid you must be under some misconception. Ernest proposed to me exactly ten minutes ago. (*Shows diary.*)

GWENDOLEN (*examines diary through her lorgnette carefully*). It is certainly very curious, for he asked me to be his wife yesterday afternoon at 5.30. If you would care to verify the incident, pray do so. (*Produces diary of her own*) I never travel without my diary. One should always have something sensational to read in the train. I am so sorry, dear Cecily, if it is any disappointment to you, but I am afraid *I* have the prior claim.

CECILY. It would distress me more than I can tell you, dear Gwendolen, if it caused you any mental or physical anguish, but I feel bound to point out that since Ernest proposed to you he clearly has changed his mind.

GWENDOLEN (*meditatively*). If the poor fellow has been entrapped into any foolish promise I shall consider it my duty to rescue him at once, and with a firm hand.

CECILY (*thoughtfully and sadly*). Whatever unfortunate entanglement my dear boy may have got into, I will never reproach him with it after we are married.

GWENDOLEN. Do you allude to me, Miss Cardew, as an entanglement? You are presumptuous. On an occasion of this kind it becomes more than a moral duty to speak one's mind. It becomes a pleasure.

CECILY. Do you suggest, Miss Fairfax, that I entrapped Ernest into an engagement? How dare you? This is no time for wearing the shallow mask of manners. When I see a spade I call it a spade.

GWENDOLEN (*satirically*). I am glad to say that I have never seen a spade. It is obvious that our social spheres have been widely different.

(*Enter* MERRIMAN, *followed by the footman. He carries a salver, tablecloth, and plate-stand.* CECILY *is about to retort. The presence of the servants exercises a restraining influence, under which both girls chafe.*)

MERRIMAN. Shall I lay tea here as usual, miss?

CECILY (*sternly, in a calm voice*). Yes, as usual. (MERRIMAN *begins to clear and lay cloth. A long pause.* CECILY *and* GWENDOLEN *glare at each other.*)

GWENDOLEN. Are there many interesting walks in the vicinity, Miss Cardew?

CECILY. Oh, yes, a great many. From the top of one of the hills quite close one can see five counties.

GWENDOLEN. Five counties! I don't think I should like that. I hate crowds.

CECILY (*sweetly*). I suppose that is why you live in town? (GWEN-

DOLEN *bites her lip, and beats her foot nervously with her parasol.*)

GWENDOLEN (*looking round*). Quite a well-kept garden this is, Miss Cardew.

CECILY. So glad you like it, Miss Fairfax.

GWENDOLEN. I had no idea there were any flowers in the country.

CECILY. Oh, flowers are as common here, Miss Fairfax, as people are in London.

GWENDOLEN. Personally I cannot understand how anybody manages to exist in the country, if anybody who is anybody does. The country always bores me to death.

CECILY. Ah! This is what the newspapers call agricultural depression, is it not? I believe the aristocracy are suffering very much from it just at present. It is almost an epidemic amongst them, I have been told. May I offer you some tea, Miss Fairfax?

GWENDOLEN (*with elaborate politeness*). Thank you. (*Aside*) Detestable girl! But I require tea!

CECILY (*sweetly*). Sugar?

GWENDOLEN (*superciliously*). No, thank you. Sugar is not fashionable any more. (CECILY *looks angrily at her, takes up the tongs and puts four lumps of sugar into the cup.*)

CECILY (*severely*). Cake or bread and butter?

GWENDOLEN (*in a bored manner*). Bread and butter, please. Cake is rarely seen at the best houses nowadays.

CECILY (*cuts a very large slice of cake, and puts it on the tray*). Hand that to Miss Fairfax. (MERRIMAN *does so, and goes out with footman.* GWENDOLEN *drinks the tea and makes a grimace. Puts down cup at once, reaches out her hand to the bread and butter, looks at it, and finds it is cake. Rises in indignation.*)

GWENDOLEN. You have filled my tea with lumps of sugar, and though I asked most distinctly for bread and butter, you have given me cake. I am known for the gentleness of my disposition, and the extraordinary sweetness of my nature, but I warn you, Miss Cardew, you may go too far.

CECILY (*rising*). To save my poor, innocent, trusting boy from the machinations of any other girl there are no lengths to which I would not go.

GWENDOLEN. From the moment I saw you I distrusted you. I felt that you were false and deceitful. I am never deceived in such matters. My first impressions of people are invariably right.

CECILY. It seems to me, Miss Fairfax, that I am trespassing on your valuable time. No doubt you have many other calls of a similar character to make in the neighborhood. (*Enter* JACK.)

GWENDOLEN (*catching sight of him*). Ernest! My own Ernest!

JACK. Gwendolen! Darling! (*Offers to kiss her.*)

GWENDOLEN (*drawing back*). A moment! May I ask if you are engaged to be married to this young lady? (*Points to* CECILY.)

JACK (*laughing*). To dear little Cecily! Of course not! What could have put such an idea into your pretty little head?

GWENDOLEN. Thank you. You may. (*Offers her cheek.*)

CECILY (*very sweetly*). I knew there must be some misunderstanding, Miss Fairfax. The gentleman whose arm is at present around your waist is my dear guardian, Mr. John Worthing.

GWENDOLEN. I beg your pardon?

CECILY. This is Uncle Jack.

GWENDOLEN (*receding*). Jack! Oh! (*Enter* ALGERNON.)

CECILY. Here is Ernest.

ALGERNON (*goes straight over to* CECILY *without noticing anyone else*). My own love! (*Offers to kiss her.*)

CECILY (*drawing back*). A moment, Ernest! May I ask you—are you engaged to be married to this young lady?

ALGERNON (*looking round*). To what young lady? Good heavens! Gwendolen!

CECILY. Yes, to good heavens, Gwendolen, I mean to Gwendolen.

ALGERNON (*laughing*). Of course not! What could have put such an idea into your pretty little head?

CECILY. Thank you. (*Presenting her cheek to be kissed*) You may. (ALGERNON *kisses her.*)

GWENDOLEN. I felt there was some slight error, Miss Cardew. The gentleman who is now embracing you is my cousin, Mr. Algernon Moncrieff.

CECILY (*breaking away from* ALGERNON). Algernon Moncrieff! Oh! (*The two girls move towards each other and put their arms round each other's waists as if for protection.*)

CECILY. Are you called Algernon?

ALGERNON. I cannot deny it.

CECILY. Oh!

GWENDOLEN. Is your name really John?

JACK (*standing rather proudly*). I could deny it if I liked. I could deny anything if I liked. But my name certainly is John. It has been John for years.

CECILY (*to* GWENDOLEN). A gross deception has been practiced on both of us.

GWENDOLEN. My poor wounded Cecily!

CECILY. My sweet, wronged Gwendolen!

GWENDOLEN (*slowly and seriously*). You will call me sister, will you not? (*They embrace.* JACK *and* ALGERNON *groan and walk up and down.*)

CECILY (*rather brightly*). There is

just one question I would like to be allowed to ask my guardian.

GWENDOLEN. An admirable idea! Mr. Worthing, there is just one question I would like to be permitted to put to you. Where is your brother Ernest? We are both engaged to be married to your brother Ernest, so it is a matter of some importance to us to know where your brother Ernest is at present.

JACK (*slowly and hesitatingly*). Gwendolen—Cecily—it is very painful for me to be forced to speak the truth. It is the first time in my life that I have ever been reduced to such a painful position, and I am really quite inexperienced in doing anything of the kind. However I will tell you quite frankly that I have no brother Ernest. I have no brother at all. I never had a brother in my life, and I certainly have not the smallest intention of ever having one in the future.

CECILY (*surprised*). No brother at all?

JACK (*cheerily*). None!

GWENDOLEN (*severely*). Had you never a brother of any kind?

JACK (*pleasantly*). Never. Not even of any kind.

GWENDOLEN. I am afraid it is quite clear, Cecily, that neither of us is engaged to be married to anyone.

CECILY. It is not a very pleasant position for a young girl suddenly to find herself in. Is it?

GWENDOLEN. Let us go into the house. They will hardly venture to come after us there.

CECILY. No, men are so cowardly, aren't they? (*They retire into the house with scornful looks.*)

JACK. This ghastly state of things is what you call Bunburying, I suppose?

ALGERNON. Yes, and a perfectly wonderful Bunburying it is. The most wonderful Bunbury I have ever had in my life.

JACK. Well, you've no right whatsoever to Bunbury here.

ALGERNON. That is absurd. One has a right to Bunbury anywhere one chooses. Every serious Bunburyist knows that.

JACK. Serious Bunburyist! Good heavens!

ALGERNON. Well, one must be serious about something, if one wants to have any amusement in life. I happen to be serious about Bunburying. What on earth you are serious about I haven't got the remotest idea. About everything, I should fancy. You have such an absolutely trivial nature.

JACK. Well, the only small satisfaction I have in the whole of this wretched business is that your friend Bunbury is quite exploded. You won't be able to run down to the country quite so often as you used to do, dear Algy. And a very good thing, too.

ALGERNON. Your brother is a little off colour, isn't he, dear Jack? You won't be able to disappear to London quite so frequently as your wicked custom was. And not a bad thing, either.

JACK. As for your conduct towards Miss Cardew, I must say that your taking in a sweet, simple, innocent girl like that is quite inexcusable. To say nothing of the fact that she is my ward.

ALGERNON. I can see no possible defence at all for your deceiving a brilliant, clever, thoroughly experienced young lady like Miss Fairfax. To say nothing of the fact that she is my cousin.

JACK. I wanted to be engaged to Gwendolen, that is all. I love her.

ALGERNON. Well, I simply wanted to be engaged to Cecily. I adore her.

JACK. There is certainly no chance of your marrying Miss Cardew.

ALGERNON. I don't think there is much likelihood, Jack, of you and Miss Fairfax being united.

JACK. Well, that is no business of yours.

ALGERNON. If it was my business, I wouldn't talk about it. (*Begins to eat muffins*) It is very vulgar to talk about one's business. Only people like stock-brokers do that, and then merely at dinner parties.

JACK. How you can sit there, calmly eating muffins, when we are in this horrible trouble, I can't make out. You seem to me to be perfectly heartless.

ALGERNON. Well, I can't eat muffins in an agitated manner. The butter would probably get on my cuffs. One should always eat muffins quite calmly. It is the only way to eat them.

JACK. I say it's perfectly heartless your eating muffins at all, under the circumstances.

ALGERNON. When I am in trouble, eating is the only thing that consoles me. Indeed, when I am in really great trouble, as anyone who knows me intimately will tell you, I refuse everything except food and drink. At the present moment I am eating muffins because I am unhappy. Besides, I am particularly fond of muffins. (*Rising.*)

JACK (*rising*). Well, that is no reason why you should eat them all in that greedy way. (*Takes muffins from* ALGERNON.)

ALGERNON (*offering tea-cake*). I wish you would have tea-cake instead. I don't like tea-cake.

JACK. Good heavens! I suppose a man may eat his own muffins in his own garden.

ALGERNON. But you have just said it was perfectly heartless to eat muffins.

JACK. I said it was perfectly heartless of you, under the circumstances. That is a very different thing.

ALGERNON. That may be. But the muffins are the same. (*He seizes the muffin-dish from* JACK.)

JACK. Algy, I wish to goodness you would go.

ALGERNON. You can't possibly ask me to go without having some dinner. It's absurd. I never go without my dinner. No one ever does, except vegetarians and people like that. Besides I have just made arrangements with Dr. Chasuble to be christened at a quarter to six under the name of Ernest.

JACK. My dear fellow, the sooner you give up that nonsense the better. I made arrangements this morning with Dr. Chasuble to be christened myself at 5.30, and I naturally will take the name of Ernest. Gwendolen would wish it. We can't both be christened Ernest. It's absurd. Besides, I have a perfect right to be christened if I like. There is no evidence at all that I ever have been christened by anybody. I should think it extremely probable I never was, and so does Dr. Chasuble. It is entirely different in your case. You have been christened already.

ALGERNON. Yes, but I have not been christened for years.

JACK. Yes, but you have been christened. That is the important thing.

ALGERNON. Quite so. So I know my constitution can stand it. If you are not quite sure about your ever having been christened, I must say I think it rather dangerous your venturing on it now. It might make you very unwell. You can hardly have forgotten that someone very closely connected with you was very nearly carried off this week in Paris by a severe chill.

JACK. Yes, but you said yourself that a severe chill was not hereditary.

ALGERNON. It usedn't to be, I know —but I daresay it is now. Science is always making wonderful improvements in things.

JACK (*picking up the muffin-dish*). Oh, that is nonsense; you are always talking nonsense.

ALGERNON. Jack, you are at the muffins again! I wish you wouldn't. There are only two left. (*Takes them*) I told you I was particularly fond of muffins.

JACK. But I hate tea-cake.

ALGERNON. Why on earth then do you allow tea-cake to be served up for your guests? What ideas you have of hospitality!

JACK. Algernon! I have already told you to go. I don't want you here. Why don't you go?

ALGERNON. I haven't quite finished my tea yet, and there is still one muffin left. (JACK *groans, and sinks into a chair.* ALGERNON *still continues eating.*)

CURTAIN

ACT THREE

SCENE—*Morning-room at the Manor House.* GWENDOLEN *and* CECILY *are at the window, looking out into the garden.*

GWENDOLEN. The fact that they did not follow us at once into the house, as anyone else would have done, seems to me to show that they have some sense of shame left.

CECILY. They have been eating muffins. That looks like repentance.

GWENDOLEN (*after a pause*). They don't seem to notice us at all. Couldn't you cough? They're looking at us. What effrontery!

CECILY. They're approaching. That's very forward of them.

GWENDOLEN. Let us preserve a dignified silence.

CECILY. Certainly. It's the only thing to do now.
(*Enter* JACK, *followed by* ALGERNON. *They whistle some dreadful popular air from a British opera.*)

GWENDOLEN. This dignified silence seems to produce an unpleasant effect.

CECILY. A most distasteful one.

GWENDOLEN. But we will not be the first to speak.

CECILY. Certainly not.

GWENDOLEN. Mr. Worthing, I have something very particular to ask you. Much depends on your reply.

CECILY. Gwendolen, your common sense is invaluable. Mr. Moncrieff, kindly answer me the following question. Why did you pretend to be my guardian's brother?

ALGERNON. In order that I might have an opportunity of meeting you.

CECILY (*to* GWENDOLEN). That certainly seems a satisfactory explanation, does it not?

GWENDOLEN. Yes, dear, if you believe him.

CECILY. I don't. But that does not affect the wonderful beauty of his answer.

GWENDOLEN. True. In matters of grave importance, style, not sincerity, is the vital thing. Mr. Worthing, what explanation can you offer to me for pretending to have a brother? Was it in order that you might have an opportunity of coming up to town to see me as often as possible?

JACK. Can you doubt it, Miss Fairfax?

GWENDOLEN. I have the gravest doubts upon the subject. But I intend to crush them. This is not the moment for German scepticism. (*Moving to* CECILY) Their explanations appear to be quite satisfactory, especially Mr. Worthing's. That seems to me to have the stamp of truth upon it.

CECILY. I am more than content with what Mr. Moncrieff said. His voice alone inspires one with absolute credulity.

GWENDOLEN. Then you think we should forgive them?

CECILY. Yes. I mean no.

GWENDOLEN. True! I had forgotten. There are principles at stake that one cannot surrender. Which of us should tell them? The task is not a pleasant one.

CECILY. Could we not both speak at the same time?

GWENDOLEN. An excellent idea! I nearly always speak at the same time as other people. Will you take the time from me?

CECILY. Certainly. (GWENDOLEN *beats time with uplifted finger.*)

GWENDOLEN AND CECILY (*speaking together*). Your Christian names are still an insuperable barrier. That is all!

JACK AND ALGERNON (*speaking together*). Our Christian names! Is that all? But we are going to be christened this afternoon.

GWENDOLEN (*to* JACK). For my sake you are prepared to do this terrible thing?

JACK. I am.

CECILY (*to* ALGERNON). To please me you are ready to face this fearful ordeal?

ALGERNON. I am!

GWENDOLEN. How absurd to talk of the equality of the sexes! Where questions of self-sacrifice are concerned, men are infinitely beyond us.

JACK. We are. (*Clasps hands with* ALGERNON.)

CECILY. They have moments of physical courage of which we women know absolutely nothing.

GWENDOLEN (*to* JACK). Darling!

ALGERNON (*to* CECILY). Darling! (*They fall into each other's arms. Enter* MERRIMAN. *When he enters he coughs loudly, seeing the situation.*)

MERRIMAN. Ahem! Ahem! Lady Bracknell!

JACK. Good heavens!
(*Enter* LADY BRACKNELL. *The couples separate in alarm. Exit* MERRIMAN.)

LADY BRACKNELL. Gwendolen! What does this mean?

GWENDOLEN. Merely that I am engaged to be married to Mr. Worthing, Mamma.

LADY BRACKNELL. Come here. Sit down. Sit down immediately. Hesitation of any kind is a sign of mental decay in the young, of physical weakness in the old. (*Turns to*

JACK) Apprised, sir, of my daughter's sudden flight by her trusty maid, whose confidence I purchased by means of a small coin, I followed her at once by a luggage train. Her unhappy father is, I am glad to say, under the impression that she is attending a more than usually lengthy lecture by the University Extension Scheme on the Influence of a Permanent Income on Thought. I do not propose to undeceive him. Indeed I have never undeceived him on any question. I would consider it wrong. But of course, you will clearly understand that all communication between yourself and my daughter must cease immediately from this moment. On this point, as indeed on all points, I am firm.

JACK. I am engaged to be married to Gwendolen, Lady Bracknell!

LADY BRACKNELL. You are nothing of the kind, sir. And now, as regards Algernon! . . . Algernon!

ALGERNON. Yes, Aunt Augusta.

LADY BRACKNELL. May I ask if it is in this house that your invalid friend Mr. Bunbury resides?

ALGERNON (*stammering*). Oh, no! Bunbury doesn't live here. Bunbury is somewhere else at present. In fact, Bunbury is dead.

LADY BRACKNELL. Dead! When did Mr. Bunbury die? His death must have been extremely sudden.

ALGERNON (*airily*). Oh, I killed Bunbury this afternoon. I mean poor Bunbury died this afternoon.

LADY BRACKNELL. What did he die of?

ALGERNON. Bunbury? Oh, he was quite exploded.

LADY BRACKNELL. Exploded! Was he the victim of a revolutionary outrage? I was not aware that Mr. Bunbury was interested in social legislation. If so, he is well punished for his morbidity.

ALGERNON. My dear Aunt Augusta, I mean he was found out! The doctors found out that Bunbury could not live, that is what I mean—so Bunbury died.

LADY BRACKNELL. He seems to have had great confidence in the opinion of his physicians. I am glad, however, that he made up his mind at the last to some definite course of action, and acted under proper medical advice. And now that we have finally got rid of this Mr. Bunbury, may I ask, Mr. Worthing, who is that young person whose hand my nephew Algernon is now holding in what seems to me a peculiarly unnecessary manner?

JACK. That lady is Miss Cecily Cardew, my ward. (LADY BRACKNELL *bows coldly to* CECILY.)

ALGERNON. I am engaged to be married to Cecily, Aunt Augusta.

LADY BRACKNELL. I beg your pardon?

CECILY. Mr. Moncrieff and I are engaged to be married, Lady Bracknell.

LADY BRACKNELL (*with a shiver, crossing to the sofa and sitting down*). I do not know whether there is anything peculiarly exciting in the air of this particular part of Hertfordshire, but the number of engagements that go on seems to me considerably above the proper average that statistics have laid down for our guidance. I think some preliminary enquiry on my part would not be out of place. Mr. Worthing, is Miss Cardew at all connected with any of the larger railway stations in London? I merely desire information. Until yesterday I had no idea that there were any families or persons whose origin was a Terminus. (JACK *looks perfectly furious, but restrains himself.*)

JACK (*in a clear, cold voice*). Miss Cardew is the grand-daughter of the late Mr. Thomas Cardew of 149, Belgrave Square, S.W.; Gervase Park, Dorking, Surrey; and the Sporran, Fifeshire, N.B.

LADY BRACKNELL. That sounds not unsatisfactory. Three addresses always inspire confidence, even in tradesmen. But what proof have I of their authenticity?

JACK. I have carefully preserved the Court Guide of the period. They are open to your inspection, Lady Bracknell.

LADY BRACKNELL (*grimly*). I have known strange errors in that publication.

JACK. Miss Cardew's family solicitors are Messrs. Markby, Markby, and Markby.

LADY BRACKNELL. Markby, Markby, and Markby? A firm of the very highest position in their profession. Indeed I am told that one of the Mr. Markbys is occasionally to be seen at dinner parties. So far I am satisfied.

JACK (*very irritably*). How extremely kind of you, Lady Bracknell! I have also in my possession, you will be pleased to hear, certificates of Miss Cardew's birth, baptism, whooping cough, registration, vaccination, confirmation, and the measles; both the German and the English variety.

LADY BRACKNELL. Ah! A life crowded with incident, I see; though perhaps somewhat too exciting for a young girl. I am not myself in favour of premature experiences. (*Rises, looks at her watch*) Gwendolen! the time approaches for our departure. We have not a moment to lose. As a matter of form, Mr. Worthing, I had better ask you if Miss Cardew has any little fortune?

JACK. Oh, about a hundred and thirty thousand pounds in the Funds. That is all. Good-bye, Lady Bracknell. So pleased to have seen you.

LADY BRACKNELL (*sitting down again*). A moment, Mr. Worthing. A hundred and thirty thousand pounds! And in the Funds! Miss Cardew seems to me a most attractive young lady, now that I look at her. Few girls of the present day have any really solid qualities, any of the qualities that last, and improve with time. We live, I regret to say, in an age of surfaces. (*To* CECILY) Come over here, dear. (CECILY *goes across*) Pretty child! your dress is sadly simple, and your hair seems almost as Nature might have left it. But we can soon alter all that. A thoroughly experienced French maid produces a really marvellous result in a very brief space of time. I remember recommending one to young Lady Lancing, and after three months her own husband did not know her.

JACK (*aside*). And after six months nobody knew her.

LADY BRACKNELL (*glares at* JACK *for a few moments. Then bends, with a practised smile, to* CECILY). Kindly turn round, sweet child. (CECILY *turns completely round*) No, the side view is what I want. (CECILY *presents her profile*) Yes, quite as I expected. There are distinct social possibilities in your profile. The two weak points in our age are its want of principle and its want of profile. The chin a little higher, dear. Style largely depends on the way the chin is worn. They are worn very high, just at present. Algernon!

ALGERNON. Yes, Aunt Augusta!

LADY BRACKNELL. There are distinct social possibilities in Miss Cardew's profile.

ALGERNON. Cecily is the sweetest, dearest, prettiest girl in the whole world. And I don't care twopence about social possibilities.

LADY BRACKNELL. Never speak disrespectfully of society, Algernon. Only people who can't get into it do that. (*To* CECILY) Dear child, of course you know that Algernon has nothing but his debts to depend upon. But I do not approve of mercenary marriages. When I married Lord Bracknell I had no fortune of any kind. But I never dreamed for a moment of allowing that to stand in my way. Well, I suppose I must give my consent.

ALGERNON. Thank you, Aunt Augusta.

LADY BRACKNELL. Cecily, you may kiss me!

CECILY (*kisses her*). Thank you, Lady Bracknell.

LADY BRACKNELL. You may also address me as Aunt Augusta for the future.

CECILY. Thank you, Aunt Augusta.

LADY BRACKNELL. The marriage, I think, had better take place quite soon.

ALGERNON. Thank you, Aunt Augusta.

CECILY. Thank you, Aunt Augusta.

LADY BRACKNELL. To speak frankly, I am not in favour of long engagements. They give people the opportunity of finding out each other's character before marriage, which I think is never advisable.

JACK. I beg your pardon for interrupting you, Lady Bracknell, but this engagement is quite out of the question. I am Miss Cardew's guardian, and she cannot marry without my consent until she comes of age. That consent I absolutely decline to give.

LADY BRACKNELL. Upon what grounds, may I ask? Algernon is an extremely, I may almost say an ostentatiously, eligible young man. He has nothing, but he looks everything. What more can one desire?

JACK. It pains me very much to have to speak frankly to you, Lady Bracknell, about your nephew, but the fact is that I do not approve at all of his moral character. I suspect him of being untruthful. (ALGERNON *and* CECILY *look at him in indignant amazement.*)

LADY BRACKNELL. Untruthful! My nephew Algernon? Impossible! He is an Oxonian.

JACK. I fear there can be no possible doubt about the matter. This afternoon, during my temporary absence in London on an important question of romance, he obtained admission to my house by means of the false pretence of being my brother. Under an assumed name he drank, I've just been informed by my butler, an entire pint bottle of my Perrier-Jouet, Brut, '89; a wine I was specially reserving for myself. Continuing his disgraceful deception, he succeeded in the course of the afternoon in alienating the affections of my only ward. He subsequently stayed to tea, and devoured every single muffin. And what makes his conduct all the more heartless is, that he was perfectly well aware from the first that I have no brother, that I never had a brother, and that I don't intend to have a brother, not even of any kind. I distinctly told him so myself yesterday afternoon.

LADY BRACKNELL. Ahem! Mr. Worthing, after careful consideration I have decided entirely to overlook my nephew's conduct to you.

JACK. That is very generous of you, Lady Bracknell. My own decision, however, is unalterable. I decline to give my consent.

LADY BRACKNELL (*to* CECILY). Come here, sweet child. (CECILY *goes over*) How old are you, dear?

CECILY. Well, I am really only eighteen, but I always admit to twenty when I go to evening parties.

LADY BRACKNELL. You are perfectly right in making some slight alteration. Indeed, no woman should ever be quite accurate about her age. It looks so calculating. . . . (*In meditative manner*) Eighteen, but admitting to twenty at evening parties. Well, it will not be very long before you are of age and free from the restraints of tutelage. So I don't think your guardian's consent is, after all, a matter of any importance.

JACK. Pray excuse me, Lady Bracknell, for interrupting you again, but it is only fair to tell you that according to the terms of her grandfather's will Miss Cardew does not come legally of age till she is thirty-five.

LADY BRACKNELL. That does not seem to me to be a grave objection. Thirty-five is a very attractive age. London society is full of women of the very highest birth who have, of their own free choice, remained thirty-five for years. Lady Dubleton is an instance in point. To my own knowledge she has been thirty-five ever since she arrived at the age of forty, which was many years ago now. I see no reason why our dear Cecily should not be even still more attractive at the age you mention than she is at present. There will be a large accumulation of property.

CECILY. Algy, could you wait for me till I was thirty-five?

ALGERNON. Of course I could, Cecily. You know I could.

CECILY. Yes, I felt it instinctively, but I couldn't wait all that time. I hate waiting even five minutes for anybody. It always makes me rather cross. I am not punctual myself, I know, but I do like punctuality in others, and waiting, even to be married, is quite out of the question.

ALGERNON. Then what is to be done, Cecily?

CECILY. I don't know, Mr. Moncrieff.

LADY BRACKNELL. My dear Mr. Worthing, as Miss Cardew states positively that she cannot wait till she is thirty-five—a remark which I am bound to say seems to me to show a somewhat impatient nature—I would beg of you to reconsider your decision.

JACK. But my dear Lady Bracknell, the matter is entirely in your hands. The moment you consent to my marriage with Gwendolen, I will most gladly allow your nephew to form an alliance with my ward.

LADY BRACKNELL (*rising and drawing herself up*). You must be quite aware that what you propose is out of the question.

JACK. Then a passionate celibacy is all that any of us can look forward to.

LADY BRACKNELL. That is not the destiny I propose for Gwendolen. Algernon, of course, can choose for himself. (*Pulls out her watch*) Come, dear, (GWENDOLEN *rises*) we have already missed five, if not six, trains. To miss any more might expose us to comment on the platform.

(*Enter* DR. CHASUBLE.)

CHASUBLE. Everything is quite ready for the christenings.

LADY BRACKNELL. The christenings, sir! Is not that somewhat premature?

CHASUBLE (*looking rather puzzled, and pointing to* JACK *and* ALGERNON). Both these gentlemen have expressed a desire for immediate baptism.

LADY BRACKNELL. At their age? The idea is grotesque and irreligious! Algernon, I forbid you to be baptised. I will not hear of such excesses. Lord Bracknell would be highly displeased if he learned that that was the way in which you wasted your time and money.

CHASUBLE. Am I to understand then that there are to be no christenings at all this afternoon?

JACK. I don't think that, as things are now, it would be of much practical value to either of us, Dr. Chasuble.

CHASUBLE. I am grieved to hear such sentiments from you, Mr. Worthing. They savour of the heretical views of the Anabaptists, views that I have completely refuted in four of my unpublished sermons. However, as your present mood seems to be one peculiarly secular, I will return to the church at once. Indeed, I have just been informed by the pew-opener that for the last hour and a half Miss Prism has been waiting for me in the vestry.

LADY BRACKNELL (*starting*). Miss Prism! Did I hear you mention a Miss Prism?

CHASUBLE. Yes, Lady Bracknell. I am on my way to join her.

LADY BRACKNELL. Pray allow me to detain you for a moment. This matter may prove to be one of vital importance to Lord Bracknell and myself. Is this Miss Prism a female of repellent aspect, remotely connected with education?

CHASUBLE (*somewhat indignantly*). She is the most cultivated of ladies, and the very picture of respectability.

LADY BRACKNELL. It is obviously the same person. May I ask what position she holds in your household?

CHASUBLE (*severely*). I am a celibate, madam.

JACK (*interposing*). Miss Prism, Lady Bracknell, has been for the last three years Miss Cardew's esteemed governess and valued companion.

LADY BRACKNELL. In spite of what I hear of her, I must see her at once. Let her be sent for.

CHASUBLE (*looking off*). She approaches; she is nigh.
(*Enter* MISS PRISM *hurriedly.*)

MISS PRISM. I was told you expected me in the vestry, dear Canon. I have been waiting for you there for an hour and three-quarters. (*Catches sight of* LADY BRACKNELL, *who has fixed her with a stony glare.* MISS PRISM *grows pale and quails. She looks anxiously round as if desirous to escape.*)

LADY BRACKNELL (*in a severe, judicial voice*). Prism! (MISS PRISM *bows her head in shame*) Come here, Prism! (MISS PRISM *approaches in a humble manner*) Prism! Where is that baby? (*General consternation. The Canon starts back in horror.* ALGERNON *and* JACK *pretend to be anxious to shield* CECILY *and* GWENDOLEN *from hearing the details of a terrible public scandal*) Twenty-eight years ago, Prism, you left Lord Bracknell's house, Number 104, Upper Grosvenor Street, in charge of a perambulator that contained a baby, of the male sex. You never returned. A few weeks later, through the elaborate investigations of the Metropolitan police, the perambulator was discovered at midnight, standing by itself in a remote corner of Bayswater. It contained the manuscript of a three-volume novel of more than usually revolting sentimentality. (MISS PRISM *starts in involuntary indignation*) But the baby was not there! (*Everyone looks at* MISS PRISM) Prism, where is that baby? (*A pause.*)

MISS PRISM. Lady Bracknell, I admit with shame that I do not know. I only wish I did. The plain facts of the case are these. On the morning of the day you mention, a day that is forever branded on my memory, I prepared as usual to take the baby out in its perambulator. I had also with me a somewhat old but capacious hand-bag in which I had intended to place the manuscript of a work of fiction that I had written during my few unoccupied hours. In a moment of mental abstraction, for which I never can forgive myself, I deposited the manuscript in the bassinette, and placed the baby in the hand-bag.

JACK (*who has been listening attentively*). But where did you deposit the hand-bag?

MISS PRISM. Do not ask me, Mr. Worthing.

JACK. Miss Prism, this is a matter of no small importance to me. I insist on knowing where you deposited the hand-bag that contained that infant.

MISS PRISM. I left it in the cloakroom of one of the larger railway stations in London.

JACK. What railway station?

MISS PRISM (*quite crushed*). Victoria. The Brighton line. (*Sinks into a chair.*)

JACK. I must retire to my room for a moment. Gwendolen, wait here for me.

GWENDOLEN. If you are not too long, I will wait here for you all my life.
(*Exit* JACK *in great excitement.*)

CHASUBLE. What do you think this means, Lady Bracknell?

LADY BRACKNELL. I dare not even suspect, Dr. Chasuble. I need hardly tell you that in families of high position strange coincidences are not supposed to occur. They are hardly considered the thing. (*Noises heard overhead as if someone was throwing trunks about. Everybody looks up.*)

CECILY. Uncle Jack seems strangely agitated.

CHASUBLE. Your guardian has a very emotional nature.

LADY BRACKNELL. This noise is extremely unpleasant. It sounds as if he was having an argument. I dislike arguments of any kind. They are always vulgar, and often convincing.

CHASUBLE (*looking up*). It has stopped now. (*The noise is redoubled.*)

LADY BRACKNELL. I wish he would arrive at some conclusion.

GWENDOLEN. This suspense is terrible. I hope it will last.
(*Enter* JACK *with a hand-bag of black leather in his hand.*)

JACK (*rushing over to* MISS PRISM). Is this the hand-bag, Miss Prism? Examine it carefully before you speak. The happiness of more than one life depends on your answer.

MISS PRISM (*calmly*). It seems to be mine. Yes, here is the injury it received through the upsetting of a Gower Street omnibus in younger and happier days. Here is the stain on the lining caused by the explosion of a temperance beverage, an incident that occurred at Leamington. And here, on the lock, are my initials. I had forgotten that in an extravagant mood I had had them placed there. The bag is undoubtedly mine. I am delighted to have it so unexpectedly restored to me. It has been a great inconvenience being without it all these years.

JACK (*in a pathetic voice*). Miss Prism, more is restored to you than this hand-bag. I was the baby you placed in it.

MISS PRISM (*amazed*). You?

JACK (*embracing her*). Yes . . . mother!

MISS PRISM (*recoiling in indignant astonishment*). Mr. Worthing! I am unmarried!

JACK. Unmarried! I do not deny that is a serious blow. But after all, who has the right to cast a stone against one who has suffered? Cannot repentance wipe out an act of folly? Why should there be one law for men and another for women? Mother, I forgive you. (*Tries to embrace her again.*)

MISS PRISM (*still more indignant*). Mr. Worthing, there is some error. (*Pointing to* LADY BRACKNELL) There is the lady who can tell you who you really are.

JACK (*after a pause*). Lady Bracknell, I hate to seem inquisitive, but would you kindly inform me who I am?

LADY BRACKNELL. I am afraid that the news I have to give you will not altogether please you. You are the son of my poor sister, Mrs. Moncrieff, and consequently Algernon's elder brother.

JACK. Algy's elder brother! Then I have a brother after all. I knew I had a brother! I always said I had a brother! Cecily,—how could you have ever doubted that I had a brother? (*Seizes hold of* ALGERNON) Dr. Chasuble, my unfortunate brother. Miss Prism, my unfortunate brother. Gwendolen, my unfortunate brother. Algy, you young scoundrel, you will have to treat me with more respect in the future. You have never behaved to me like a brother in all your life.

ALGERNON. Well, not till today, old boy, I admit. I did my best, however, though I was out of practice. (*Shakes hands.*)

GWENDOLEN (*to* JACK). My own! But what own are you? What is your Christian name, now that you have become someone else?

JACK. Good heavens! . . . I had quite forgotten that point. Your decision on the subject of my name is irrevocable, I suppose?

GWENDOLEN. I never change, except in my affections.

CECILY. What a noble nature you have, Gwendolen!

JACK. Then the question had better be cleared up at once. Aunt Augusta, a moment. At the time when Miss Prism left me in the hand-bag, had I been christened already?

LADY BRACKNELL. Every luxury that money could buy, including christening, had been lavished on you by your fond and doting parents.

JACK. Then I was christened! That is settled. Now, what name was I given? Let me know the worst.

LADY BRACKNELL. Being the eldest son you were naturally christened after your father.

JACK (*irritably*). Yes, but what was my father's Christian name?

LADY BRACKNELL (*meditatively*). I cannot at the present moment recall what the General's Christian name was. But I have no doubt he had one. He was eccentric, I admit. But only in later years. And that was the result of the Indian climate, and marriage, and indigestion, and other things of that kind.

JACK. Algy! Can't you recollect what our father's Christian name was?

ALGERNON. My dear boy, we were never even on speaking terms. He died before I was a year old.

JACK. His name would appear in the Army Lists of the period, I suppose, Aunt Augusta?

LADY BRACKNELL. The General was essentially a man of peace, except in his domestic life. But I have no doubt his name would appear in any military directory.

JACK. The Army Lists of the last forty years are here. These delightful records should have been my constant study. (*Rushes to bookcase and tears the books out*) M. Generals . . . Mallam, Maxbohm, Magley, what ghastly names they have—Markby, Migsby, Mobbs, Moncrieff! Lieutenant 1840, Captain, Lieutenant-Colonel, Colonel, General 1869, Christian names, Ernest John. (*Puts book very quietly down and speaks quite calmly*) I always told you, Gwendolen, my name was Ernest, didn't I? Well, it is Ernest after all. I mean it naturally is Ernest.

LADY BRACKNELL. Yes, I remember that the General was called Ernest. I knew I had some particular reason for disliking the name.

GWENDOLEN. Ernest! My own Ernest! I felt from the first that you could have no other name!

JACK. Gwendolen, it is a terrible thing for a man to find out suddenly that all his life he has been speaking nothing but the truth. Can you forgive me?

GWENDOLEN. I can. For I feel that you are sure to change.

JACK. My own one!

CHASUBLE (*to* MISS PRISM). Lætitia! (*Embraces her.*)

MISS PRISM (*enthusiastically*). Frederick! At last!

ALGERNON. Cecily! (*Embraces her*) At last!

JACK. Gwendolen! (*Embraces her*) At last!

LADY BRACKNELL. My nephew, you seem to be displaying signs of triviality.

JACK. On the contrary, Aunt Augusta, I've now realized for the first time in my life the vital Importance of Being Earnest.

CURTAIN

What Every Woman Knows

BY J. M. BARRIE

What Every Woman Knows was first produced in America at the Empire Theatre, New York City, by Charles Frohman on Dec. 28, 1908. The following is the original cast:

JOHN SHAND	Richard Bennett
ALICK WYLIE	R. Peyton Carter
DAVID WYLIE	David Torrence
JAMES WYLIE	Fred Tyler
MAGGIE WYLIE	Maude Adams
MR. VENABLES	Lumsden Hare
COMTESSE DE LA BRIÈRE	Ffolliott Paget
LADY SYBIL LAZENBY	Beatrice Agnew
MAID	Lillian Spencer
FIRST ELECTOR	James L. Cachart
SECOND ELECTOR	Wallace Jackson
THIRD ELECTOR	W. H. Gilmore

WHAT EVERY WOMAN KNOWS

ACT ONE

JAMES WYLIE *is about to make a move on the dambrod, and in the little Scotch room there is an awful silence befitting the occasion.* JAMES *with his hand poised—for if he touches a piece he has to play it,* ALICK *will see to that—raises his red head suddenly to read* ALICK'S *face. His father, who is* ALICK, *is pretending to be in a panic lest* JAMES *should make this move.* JAMES *grins heartlessly, and his fingers are about to close on the "man" when some instinct of self-preservation makes him peep once more. This time* ALICK *is caught: the unholy ecstasy on his face tells as plain as porridge that he has been luring* JAMES *to destruction.* JAMES *glares; and, too late, his opponent is a simple old father again.* JAMES *mops his head, sprawls in the manner most conducive to thought in the* WYLIE *family, and, protruding his underlip, settles down to a reconsideration of the board.* ALICK *blows out his cheeks, and a drop of water settles on the point of his nose.*

You will find them thus any Saturday night (after family worship, which sends the servant to bed); and sometimes the pauses are so long that in the end they forget whose move it is.

It is not the room you would be shown into if you were calling socially on MISS WYLIE. *The drawing-room for you, and* MISS WYLIE *in a coloured merino to receive you; very likely she would exclaim, "This is a pleasant surprise!" though she has seen you coming up the avenue and has just had time to whip the dust-cloths off the chairs, and to warn* ALICK, DAVID *and* JAMES, *that they had better not dare come in to see you before they have put on a dickey. Nor is this the room in which you would dine in solemn grandeur if invited to drop in and take pot-luck, which is how the* WYLIES *invite, it being a family weakness to pretend that they sit down in the dining-room daily. It is the real living room of the house, where* ALICK, *who will never get used to fashionable ways, can take off his collar and sit happily in his stocking soles, and* JAMES *at times would do so also; but catch* MAGGIE *letting him.*

There is one very fine chair, but, heavens, not for sitting on; just to give the room a social standing in an emergency. It sneers at the other chairs with an air of insolent superiority, like a haughty bride who has married into the house for money. Otherwise the furniture is homely; most of it has come from that smaller house where the WYLIES *began. There is the large and shiny chair which can be turned into a bed if you look the other way for a moment.* JAMES *cannot sit on this chair without gradually sliding down it till he is lying luxuriously on the small of his back, his legs indicating, like the hands of a clock, that it is ten past twelve; a position in which* MAGGIE *shudders to see him receiving company.*

The other chairs are horse-hair, than which nothing is more comfortable if there be a good slit down the seat. The seats are heavily dented, because all the WYLIE *family sit down with a dump. The draught-board is on the edge of a large centre table, which also displays four books placed at equal distances from each other, one of them a Bible, and another the family album. If these were the only books they would not justify* MAGGIE *in calling this chamber the library, her dogged name for it; while* DAVID *and* JAMES *call it the west-room and* ALICK *calls it "the room," which is to him the natural name for any apartment without a bed in it. There is a bookcase of pitch pine, which contains six hundred books, with glass doors to prevent your getting at them.*

No one does try to get at the books, for the WYLIES *are not a reading family. They like you to gasp when you see so much literature gathered together in one prison-house, but they gasp themselves at the thought that there are persons, chiefly clergymen, who, having finished one book, coolly begin another. Nevertheless it was not all vainglory that made* DAVID *buy this library: it was rather a mighty respect for education, as something that he has missed. This same feeling makes him take in the* Contemporary Review *and stand up to it like a man.* ALICK, *who also has a respect for education, tries to read the* Contemporary, *but becomes dispirited, and may be heard muttering over its pages, "No, no use, no use, no," and sometimes even "Oh hell."* JAMES *has no respect for education; and* MAGGIE *is at present of an open mind.*

They are WYLIE AND SONS *of the local granite quarry, in which* ALICK *was throughout his working days a mason. It is* DAVID *who has raised them to this position; he climbed up himself step by step (and hewed the steps), and drew the others up after him.* "WYLIE BROTHERS," ALICK *would have had the firm called, but* DAVID *said No, and* JAMES *said No, and* MAGGIE *said No; first honour must be to their father; and* ALICK *now likes it on the whole, though he often sighs at having to shave every day; and on some snell mornings he still creeps from his couch at four and even at two (thinking that his mallet and chisel are calling him), and begins to pull on his trousers, until the grandeur of them reminds him that he can go to bed again. Sometimes he cries a little, because there is no more work for him to do for ever and ever; and then* MAGGIE *gives him a spade (without telling* DAVID) *or* DAVID *gives him the logs to saw (without telling* MAGGIE).

We have given JAMES *a longer time to make his move than our kind friends in front will give him, but in the meantime something has been happening.* DAVID *has come in, wearing a black coat and his Sabbath boots, for he has been to a public meeting.* DAVID *is nigh forty years of age, whiskered like his father and brother (*ALICK'*s whiskers being worn as a sort of cravat round the neck), and he has the too-brisk manner of one who must arrive anywhere a little before anyone else. The painter who did the three of them for fifteen pounds (you may observe the canvases on the walls) has caught this characteristic, perhaps accidentally, for* DAVID *is almost stepping out of his frame, as if to hurry off somewhere; while* ALICK *and* JAMES *look as if they were pinned to the wall for life. All the six of them, men and pictures, however, have a family resemblance, like granite blocks from their own quarry. They are as Scotch as* *peat for instance, and they might exchange eyes without any neighbour noticing the difference, inquisitive little blue eyes that seem to be always totting up the price of things.*

The dambrod players pay no attention to DAVID, *nor does he regard them. Dumping down on the sofa he removes his 'lastic sides, as his Sabbath boots are called, by pushing one foot against the other, gets into a pair of hand-sewn slippers, deposits the boots as according to rule in the ottoman, and crosses to the fire. There must be something on* DAVID'S *mind tonight, for he pays no attention to the game, neither gives advice (than which nothing is more maddening) nor exchanges a wink with* ALICK *over the parlous condition of* JAMES'S *crown. You can hear the wag-at-the-wall clock in the lobby ticking. Then* DAVIID *lets himself go; it runs out of him like a hymn:*

DAVID. Oh, let the solid ground
Not fail beneath my feet,
Before my life has found
What some have found so sweet.

(This is not a soliloquy, but is offered as a definite statement. The players emerge from their game with difficulty.)

ALICK *(with* JAMES'S *crown in his hand).* What's that you're saying, David?

DAVID *(like a public speaker explaining the situation in a few well-chosen words).* The thing I'm speaking about is Love.

JAMES *(keeping control of himself).* Do you stand there and say you're in love, David Wylie?

DAVID. Me; what would I do with the thing?

JAMES *(who is by no means without pluck).* I see no necessity for calling it a thing.

(They are two bachelors who all their lives have been afraid of nothing but Woman. DAVID *in his sportive days—which continue—has done roguish things with his arm when conducting a lady home under an umbrella from a soiree, and has both chuckled and been scared on thinking of it afterwards.* JAMES, *a commoner fellow altogether, has discussed the sex over a glass, but is too canny to be in the company of less than two young women at a time.)*

DAVID *(derisively).* Oho, has she got you, James?

JAMES *(feeling the sting of it).* Nobody has got me.

DAVID. They'll catch you yet, lad.

JAMES. They'll never catch me. You've been nearer catched yourself.

ALICK. Yes, Kitty Menzies, David.

DAVID *(feeling himself under the umbrella).* It was a kind of a shave that.

ALICK *(who knows all that is to be known about women and can speak of them without a tremor).* It's a curious thing, but a man cannot help winking when he hears that one of his friends has been catched.

DAVID. That's so.

JAMES (*clinging to his manhood*). And fear of that wink is what has kept the two of us single men. And yet what's the glory of being single?

DAVID. There's no particular glory in it, but it's safe.

JAMES (*putting away his aspirations*). Yes, it's lonely, but it's safe. But who did you mean the poetry for, then?

DAVID. For Maggie, of course.
(*You don't know* DAVID *and* JAMES *till you know how they love their sister* MAGGIE.)

ALICK. I thought that.

DAVID (*coming to the second point of his statement about Love*). I saw her reading poetry and saying those words over to herself.

JAMES. She has such a poetical mind.

DAVID. Love. There's no doubt as that's what Maggie has set her heart on. And not merely love, but one of those grand noble loves; for though Maggie is undersized she has a passion for romance.

JAMES (*wandering miserably about the room*). It's terrible not to be able to give Maggie what her heart is set on.
(*The others never pay much attention to* JAMES, *though he is quite a smart figure in less important houses.*)

ALICK (*violently*). Those idiots of men.

DAVID. Father, did you tell her who had got the minister of Galashiels?

ALICK (*wagging his head sadly*). I had to tell her. And then I—I—bought her a sealskin muff, and I just slipped it into her hands and came away.

JAMES (*illustrating the sense of justice in the Wylie family*). Of course, to be fair to the man, he never pretended he wanted her.

DAVID. None of them wants her; that's what depresses her. I was thinking, father, I would buy her that gold watch and chain in Snibby's window. She hankers after it.

JAMES (*slapping his pocket*). You're too late, David; I've got them for her.

DAVID. It's ill done of the minister. Many a pound of steak has that man had in this house.

ALICK. You mind the slippers she worked for him?

JAMES. I mind them fine; she began them for William Cathro. She's getting on in years, too, though she looks so young.

ALICK. I never can make up my mind, David, whether her curls make her look younger or older.

DAVID (*determinedly*). Younger. Whisht! I hear her winding the clock. Mind, not a word about the minister to her, James. Don't even mention religion this day.

JAMES. Would it be like me to do such a thing?

DAVID. It would be very like you. And there's that other matter: say not a syllable about our having a reason for sitting up late tonight. When she says it's bed-time, just all pretend we're not sleepy.

ALICK. Exactly, and when—
(*Here* MAGGIE *enters, and all three are suddenly engrossed in the dambrod. We could describe* MAGGIE *at great length. But what is the use? What you really want to know is whether she was good-looking. No, she was not. Enter* MAGGIE, *who is not good-looking. When this is said, all is said. Enter* MAGGIE, *as it were, with her throat cut from ear to ear. She has a soft Scotch voice and a more resolute manner than is perhaps fitting to her plainness; and she stops short at sight of* JAMES *sprawling unconsciously in the company chair.*)

MAGGIE. James, I wouldn't sit on the fine chair.

JAMES. I forgot again. (*But he wishes she had spoken more sharply. Even profanation of the fine chair has not roused her. She takes up her knitting, and they all suspect that she knows what they have been talking about.*)

MAGGIE. You're late, David, it's nearly bed-time.

DAVID (*finding the subject a safe one*). I was kept late at the public meeting.

ALICK (*glad to get so far away from Galashiels*). Was it a good meeting?

DAVID. Fairish. (*With some heat*) That young John Shand *would* make a speech.

MAGGIE. John Shand? Is that the student Shand?

DAVID. The same. It's true he's a student at Glasgow University in the winter months, but in summer he's just the railway porter here; and I think it's very presumptuous of a young lad like that to make a speech when he hasn't a penny to bless himself with.

ALICK. The Shands were always an impudent family, and jealous. I suppose that's the reason they haven't been on speaking terms with us this six years. Was it a good speech?

DAVID (*illustrating the family's generosity*). It was very fine; but he needn't have made fun of *me*.

MAGGIE (*losing a stitch*). He dared?

DAVID (*depressed*). You see I can *not* get started on a speech without saying things like "In rising *for* to make a few remarks."

JAMES. What's wrong with it?

DAVID. He mimicked me, and said "Will our worthy chairman come for to go for to answer my questions?" and so on; and they roared.

JAMES (*slapping his money pocket*). The sacket.

DAVID. I did feel bitterly, father, the want of education. (*Without knowing it, he has a beautiful way of pronouncing this noble word.*)

MAGGIE (*holding out a kind hand to him*). David.

ALICK. I've missed it sore, David. Even now I feel the want of it in the very marrow of me. I'm shamed to think I never gave you your chance. But when you were young I was so desperate poor, how could I do it, Maggie?

MAGGIE. It wasn't possible, father.

ALICK (*gazing at the book-shelves*). To be able to understand these books! To up with them one at a time and scrape them as clean as though they were a bowl of brose. Lads, it's not to riches, it's to scholarship that I make my humble bow.

JAMES (*who is good at bathos*). There's ten yards of them. And they were selected by the minister of Galashiels. He said—

DAVID (*quickly*). James.

JAMES. I mean—I mean—

MAGGIE (*calmly*). I suppose you mean what you say, James. I hear, David, that the minister of Galashiels is to be married on that Miss Turnbull.

DAVID (*on guard*). So they were saying.

ALICK. All I can say is she has made a poor bargain.

MAGGIE (*the damned*). I wonder at you, father. He's a very nice gentleman. I'm sure I hope he has chosen wisely.

JAMES. Not him.

MAGGIE (*getting near her tragedy*). How can you say that when you don't know her? I expect she is full of charm.

ALICK. Charm? It's the very word he used.

DAVID. Havering idiot.

ALICK. What *is* charm, exactly, Maggie?

MAGGIE. Oh, it's—it's a sort of bloom on a woman. If you have it, you don't need to have anything else; and if you don't have it, it doesn't much matter what else you have. Some women, the few, have charm for all; and most have charm for one. But some have charm for none. (*Somehow she has stopped knitting. Her men-folk are very depressed.* JAMES *brings his fist down on the table with a bang.*)

JAMES (*shouting*). I have a sister that has charm.

MAGGIE. No, James, you haven't.

JAMES (*rushing at her with the watch and chain*). Ha'e, Maggie. (*She lets them lie in her lap.*)

DAVID. Maggie, would you like a silk?

MAGGIE. What could I do with a silk? (*With a gust of passion*) You might as well dress up a little brown hen.
(*They wriggle miserably.*)

JAMES (*stamping*). Bring him here to me.

MAGGIE. Bring whom, James?

JAMES. David, I would be obliged if you wouldn't kick me beneath the table.

MAGGIE (*rising*). Let's be practical; let's go to our beds.
(*This reminds them that they have a job on hand in which she is not to share.*)

DAVID (*slily*). I don't feel very sleepy yet.

ALICK. Nor me either.

JAMES. You've just taken the very words out of my mouth.

DAVID (*with unusual politeness*). Good night to you, Maggie.

MAGGIE (*fixing the three of them*). *All* of you unsleepy, when, as is well known, ten o'clock is your regular bed-time?

JAMES. Yes, it's common knowledge that we go to our beds at ten. (*Chuckling*) That's what we're counting on.

MAGGIE. Counting on?

DAVID. You stupid whelp.

JAMES. What have *I* done?

MAGGIE (*folding her arms*). There's something up. You've got to tell me, David.

DAVID (*who knows when he is beaten*). Go out and watch, James.

MAGGIE. Watch?
(JAMES *takes himself off, armed, as* MAGGIE *notices, with a stick.*)

DAVID (*in his alert business way*). Maggie, there are burglars about.

MAGGIE. Burglars? (*She sits rigid, but she is not the kind to scream.*)

DAVID. We hadn't meant for to tell you till we nabbed them; but they've been in this room twice of late. We sat up last night waiting for them, and we're to sit up again tonight.

MAGGIE. The silver plate.

DAVID. It's all safe as yet. That makes us think that they were either frightened away these other times, or that they are coming back for to make a clean sweep.

MAGGIE. How did you get to know about this?

DAVID. It was on Tuesday that the polissman called at the quarry with a very queer story. He had seen a man climbing out at this window at ten past two.

MAGGIE. Did he chase him?

DAVID. It was so dark he lost sight of him at once.

ALICK. Tell her about the window.

DAVID. We've found out that the catch of the window has been pushed back by slipping the blade of a knife between the woodwork.

MAGGIE. David.

ALICK. The polissman said he was carrying a little carpet bag.

MAGGIE. The silver plate *is* gone.

DAVID. No, no. We were thinking that very likely he has bunches of keys in the bag.

MAGGIE. Or weapons.

DAVID. As for that, we have some pretty stout weapons ourselves in the umbrella stand. So, if you'll go to your bed, Maggie–

MAGGIE. Me? and my brothers in danger.

ALICK. There's just one of them.

MAGGIE. The polissman just saw one.

DAVID (*licking his palms*). I would be very pleased if there were three of them.

MAGGIE. I watch with you. I would be very pleased if there were four of them.

DAVID. And they say she has no charm!
(JAMES *returns on tiptoe as if the burglars were beneath the table. He signs to every one to breathe no more, and then whispers his news.*)

JAMES. He's there. I had no sooner gone out than I saw him sliding down the garden wall, close to the rhubarbs.

ALICK. What's he like?

JAMES. He's an ugly customer. That's all I could see. There was a little carpet bag in his hand.

DAVID. That's him.

JAMES. He slunk into the rhodydendrons, and he's there now, watching the window.

DAVID. We have him. Out with the light.
(*The room is beautified by a chandelier fitted for three gas jets, but with the advance of progress one of these has been removed and the incandescent light put in its place. This alone is lit.* ALICK *climbs a chair, pulls a little chain, and the room is now but vaguely lit by the fire. It plays fitfully on four sparkling faces.*)

MAGGIE. Do you think he saw you, James?

JAMES. I couldn't say, but in any case I was too clever for him. I looked up at the stars, and yawned loud at them as if I was tremendous sleepy.
(*There is a long pause during which they are lurking in the shadows. At last they hear some movement, and they steal like ghosts from the room. We see* DAVID *turning out the lobby light; then the door closes and an empty room awaits the intruder with a shudder of expectancy. The window opens and shuts as softly as if this were a mother peering in to see whether her baby is asleep. Then the head of a man shows between the curtains. The remainder of him follows. He is carrying a little carpet bag. He stands irresolute; what puzzles him evidently is that the Wylies should have retired to rest without lifting that piece of coal off the fire. He opens the door and peeps into the lobby, listening to the wag-at-the-wall clock. All seems serene, and he turns on the light. We see him clearly now. He is* JOHN SHAND, *age twenty-one, boots muddy, as an indignant carpet can testify. He wears a shabby topcoat and a cockerty bonnet; otherwise he is in the well-worn corduroys of a railway porter. His movements, at first stealthy, become almost homely as he feels*

that he is secure. He opens the bag and takes out a bunch of keys, a small paper parcel, and a black implement that may be a burglar's jemmy. This cool customer examines the fire and piles on more coals. With the keys he opens the door of the bookcase, selects two large volumes, and brings them to the table. He takes off his topcoat and opens his parcel, which we now see contains sheets of foolscap paper. His next action shows that the "jemmy" is really a ruler. He knows where the pen and ink are kept. He pulls the fine chair nearer to the table, sits on it, and proceeds to write, occasionally dotting the carpet with ink as he stabs the air with his pen. He is so occupied that he does not see the door opening, and the Wylie family staring at him. They are armed with sticks.)

ALICK (*at last*). When you're ready, John Shand.
(JOHN *hints back, and then has the grace to rise, dogged and expressionless.*)

JAMES (*like a railway porter*). Ticket, please.

DAVID. You can't think of anything clever for to go for to say now, John.

MAGGIE. I hope you find that chair comfortable, young man.

JOHN. I have no complaint to make against the chair.

ALICK (*who is really distressed*). A native of the town. The disgrace to your family. I feel pity for the Shands this night.

JOHN (*glowering*). I'll thank you, Mr. Wylie, not to pity my family.

JAMES. Canny, canny.

MAGGIE (*that sense of justice again*). I think you should let the young man explain. It mayn't be so bad as we thought.

DAVID. Explain away, my billie.

JOHN. Only the uneducated would need an explanation. I'm a student, (*with a little passion*) and I'm desperate for want of books. You have all I want here; no use to you but for display; well, I came here to study. I come twice weekly. (*Amazement of his hosts.*)

DAVID (*who is the first to recover*). By the window.

JOHN. Do you think a Shand would so far lower himself as to enter your door? Well, is it a case for the police?

JAMES. It is.

MAGGIE (*not so much out of the goodness of her heart as to patronise the Shands*). It seems to me it's a case for us all to go to our beds and leave the young man to study; but not on that chair. (*And she wheels the chair away from him.*)

JOHN. Thank you, Miss Maggie, but I couldn't be beholden to you.

JAMES. My opinion is that he's nobody, so out with him.

JOHN. Yes, out with me. And you'll be cheered to hear I'm likely to be a nobody for a long time to come.

DAVID (*who had been beginning to respect him*). Are you a poor scholar?

JOHN. On the contrary, I'm a brilliant scholar.

DAVID. It's siller, then?

JOHN (*glorified by experiences he has shared with many a gallant soul*). My first year at college I lived on a barrel of potatoes, and we had just a sofa-bed between two of us; when the one lay down the other had to get up. Do you think it was hardship? It was sublime. But this year I can't afford it. I'll have to stay on here, collecting the tickets of the illiterate, such as you, when I might be with Romulus and Remus among the stars.

JAMES (*summing up*). Havers.

DAVID (*in whose head some design is vaguely taking shape*). Whisht, James. I must say, young lad, I like your spirit. Now tell me, what's your professors' opinion of your future.

JOHN. They think me a young man of extraordinary promise.

DAVID. You have a name here for high moral character.

JOHN. And justly.

DAVID. Are you serious-minded?

JOHN. I never laughed in my life.

DAVID. Who do you sit under in Glasgow?

JOHN. Mr. Flemister of the Sauchiehall High.

DAVID. Are you a Sabbath-school teacher?

JOHN. I am.

DAVID. One more question. Are you promised?

JOHN. To a lady?

DAVID. Yes.

JOHN. I've never given one of them a single word of encouragement. I'm too much occupied thinking about my career.

DAVID. So. (*He reflects, and finally indicates by a jerk of the head that he wishes to talk with his father behind the door.*)

JAMES (*longingly*). Do you want me too? (*But they go out without even answering him.*)

MAGGIE. I don't know what maggot they have in their heads, but sit down, young man, till they come back.

JOHN. My name's Mr. Shand, and till I'm called that I decline to sit down again in this house.

MAGGIE. Then I'm thinking, young sir, you'll have a weary wait. (*While he waits you can see how pinched his face is. He is little more than a boy, and he seldom has enough to eat.* DAVID *and* ALICK *return presently, looking as sly as if they had been discussing some move on the dambrod, as indeed they have.*)

DAVID (*suddenly become genial*). Sit down, Mr. Shand, and pull in your chair. You'll have a thimbleful of something to keep the cold out? (*Briskly*) Glasses, Maggie. (*She wonders, but gets glasses and decanter from the sideboard, which* JAMES *calls the chiffy.* DAVID *and* ALICK, *in the most friendly manner, also draw up to the table*) You're not a totaller, I hope?

JOHN (*guardedly*). I'm practically a totaller.

DAVID. So are we. How do you take it? Is there any hot water, Maggie?

JOHN. If I take it at all, and I haven't made up my mind yet, I'll take it cold.

DAVID. You'll take it hot, James?

JAMES (*also sitting at the table but completely befogged*). No, I—

DAVID (*decisively*). I think you'll take it hot, James.

JAMES (*sulking*). I'll take it hot.

DAVID. The kettle, Maggie.
(JAMES *has evidently to take it hot so that they can get at the business now on hand, while* MAGGIE *goes kitchenward for the kettle.*)

ALICK. Now, David, quick, before she comes back.

DAVID. Mr. Shand, we have an offer to make you.

JOHN (*warningly*). No patronage.

ALICK. It's strictly a business affair.

DAVID. Leave it to me, father. It's this— (*But to his annoyance the suspicious* MAGGIE *has already returned with the kettle*) Maggie, don't you see that you're not wanted?

MAGGIE (*sitting down by the fire and resuming her knitting*). I do, David.

DAVID. I have a proposition to put before Mr. Shand, and women are out of place in business transactions.
(*The needles continue to click.*)

ALICK (*sighing*). We'll have to let her bide, David.

DAVID (*sternly*). Woman. (*But even this does not budge her.*) Very well then, sit there, but don't interfere, mind. Mr. Shand, we're willing, the three of us, to lay out £300 on your education if—

JOHN. Take care—

DAVID (*slowly, which is not his wont*). On condition that five years from now, Maggie Wylie, if still unmarried, can claim to marry you, should such be her wish; the thing to be perfectly open on her side, but you to be strictly tied down.

JAMES (*enlightened*). So, so.

DAVID (*resuming his smart manner*). Now, what have you to say? Decide.

JOHN (*after a pause*). I regret to say—

MAGGIE. It doesn't matter what he regrets to say, because I decide against it. And I think it was very ill-done of you to make any such proposal.

DAVID (*without looking at her*). Quiet, Maggie.

JOHN (*looking at her*). I must say, Miss Maggie, I don't see what reasons *you* can have for being so set against it.

MAGGIE. If you would grow a beard, Mr. Shand, the reasons wouldn't be quite so obvious.

JOHN. I'll never grow a beard.

MAGGIE. Then you're done for at the start.

ALICK. Come, come.

MAGGIE. Seeing I have refused the young man—

JOHN. Refused!

DAVID. That's no reason why we shouldn't have his friendly opinion. Your objections, Mr. Shand?

JOHN. Simply, it's a one-sided bargain. I admit I'm no catch at present; but what could a man of my abilities not soar to with three hundred pounds? Something far above what she could aspire to.

MAGGIE. Oh, indeed.

DAVID. The position is that without the three hundred you can't soar.

JOHN. You have me there.

MAGGIE. Yes, but—

ALICK. You see *you're* safe-guarded, Maggie; you don't need to take him unless you like, but he has to take you.

JOHN. That's an unfair arrangement also.

MAGGIE. I wouldn't dream of it without that condition.

JOHN. Then you *are* thinking of it?

MAGGIE. Poof.

DAVID. It's a good arrangement for you, Mr. Shand. The chances are you'll never have to go on with it, for in all probability she'll marry soon.

JAMES. She's tremendous run after.

JOHN. Even if that's true, it's just keeping me in reserve in case she misses doing better.

DAVID (*relieved*). That's the situation in a nutshell.

JOHN. Another thing. Supposing I was to get fond of her?

ALICK (*wistfully*). It's very likely.

JOHN. Yes, and then suppose she was to give me the go by?

DAVID. You have to risk that.

JOHN. Or take it the other way. Supposing as I got to know her I *could not* endure her?

DAVID (*suavely*). You have both to take risks.

JAMES (*less suavely*). What you need, John Shand, is a clout on the head.

JOHN. Three hundred pounds is no great sum.

DAVID. You can take it or leave it.

ALICK. No great sum for a student studying for the ministry!

JOHN. Do you think that with that amount of money I would stop short at being a minister?

DAVID. That's how I like to hear you speak. A young Scotsman of your ability let loose upon the world with £300, what could he not do? It's almost appalling to think of; especially if he went among the English.

JOHN. What do you think, Miss Maggie?

MAGGIE (*who is knitting*). I have no thoughts on the subject either way.

JOHN (*after looking her over*). What's her age? She looks young, but they say it's the curls that does it.

DAVID (*rather happily*). She's one of those women who are eternally young.

JOHN. I can't take that for an answer.

DAVID. She's twenty-five.

JOHN. I'm just twenty-one.

JAMES. I read in a book that about four years' difference in the ages is the ideal thing. (*As usual he is disregarded.*)

DAVID. Well, Mr. Shand?

JOHN (*where is his mother!*). I'm willing if she's willing.

DAVID. Maggie?

MAGGIE. There can be no "if" about it. It must be an offer.

JOHN. A Shand give a Wylie such a chance to humiliate him? Never.

MAGGIE. Then all is off.

DAVID. Come, come, Mr. Shand, it's just a form.

JOHN (*reluctantly*). Miss Maggie, will you?

MAGGIE (*doggedly*). Is it an offer?

JOHN (*dourly*). Yes.

MAGGIE (*rising*). Before I answer I want first to give you a chance of drawing back.

DAVID. Maggie.

MAGGIE (*bravely*). When they said that I have been run after they were misleading you. I'm without charm; nobody has ever been after me.

JOHN. Oho!

ALICK. They will be yet.

JOHN (*the innocent*). It shows at least that you haven't been after them.
(*His hosts exchange a self-conscious glance.*)

MAGGIE. One thing more; David said I'm twenty-five, I'm twenty-six.

JOHN. Aha!

MAGGIE. Now be practical. Do you withdraw from the bargain, or do you not?

JOHN (*on reflection*). It's a bargain.

MAGGIE. Then so be it.

DAVID (*hurriedly*). And that's settled. Did you say you would take it hot, Mr. Shand?

JOHN. I think I'll take it neat. (*The others decide to take it hot, and there is some careful business here with the toddy ladles.*)

ALICK. Here's to you, and your career.

JOHN. Thank you. To you, Miss Maggie. Had we not better draw up a legal document? Lawyer Crosbie could do it on the quiet.

DAVID. Should we do that, or should we just trust to one another's honour?

ALICK (*gallantly*). Let Maggie decide.

MAGGIE. I think we would better have a legal document.

DAVID. We'll have it drawn up tomorrow. I was thinking the best way would be for to pay the money in five yearly instalments.

JOHN. I was thinking, better bank the whole sum in my name at once.

ALICK. I think David's plan's the best.

JOHN. I think not. Of course if it's not convenient to you—

DAVID (*touched to the quick*). It's perfectly convenient. What do you say, Maggie?

MAGGIE. I agree with John.

DAVID (*with an odd feeling that* MAGGIE *is now on the other side*). Very well.

JOHN. Then as that's settled I think I'll be stepping. (*He is putting his papers back in the bag.*)

ALICK (*politely*). If you would like to sit on at your books—

JOHN. As I can come at any orra time now I think I'll be stepping. (MAGGIE *helps him into his topcoat.*)

MAGGIE. Have you a muffler, John?

JOHN. I have. (*He gets it from his pocket.*)

MAGGIE. You had better put it twice round. (*She does this for him.*)

DAVID. Well good night to you, Mr. Shand.

ALICK. And good luck.

JOHN. Thank you. The same to you. And I'll cry in at your office in the morning before the 6.20 is due.

DAVID. I'll have the document ready for you. (*There is the awkward pause that sometimes follows great events*) I think, Maggie, you might see Mr. Shand to the door.

MAGGIE. Certainly. (JOHN *is going by the window*) This way, John.

(*She takes him off by the more usual exit.*)

DAVID. He's a fine frank fellow; and you saw how cleverly he got the better of me about banking the money. (*As the heads of the conspirators come gleefully together*) I tell you, father, he has a grand business head.

ALICK. Lads, he's canny. He's cannier than any of us.

JAMES. Except maybe Maggie. He has no idea what a remarkable woman Maggie is.

ALICK. Best he shouldn't know. Men are nervous of remarkable women.

JAMES. She's a long time in coming back.

DAVID (*not quite comfortable*). It's a good sign. H'sh. What sort of a night is it, Maggie?

MAGGIE. It's a little blowy. (*She gets a large dust-cloth which is lying folded on a shelf, and proceeds to spread it over the fine chair. The men exchange self-conscious glances.*)

DAVID (*stretching himself*). Yes—well, well, oh yes. It's getting late. What is it with you, father?

ALICK. I'm ten forty-two.

JAMES. I'm ten forty.

DAVID. Ten forty-two.
(*They wind up their watches.*)

MAGGIE. It's high time we were bedded. (*She puts her hands on their shoulders lovingly, which is the very thing they have been trying to avoid*) You're very kind to me.

DAVID. Havers.

ALICK. Havers.

JAMES (*but this does not matter*) Havers.

MAGGIE (*a little dolefully*). I'm a sort of sorry for the young man, David.

DAVID. Not at all. You'll be the making of him. (*She lifts the two volumes*) Are you taking the books to your bed, Maggie?

MAGGIE. Yes. I don't want him to know things I don't know myself. (*She departs with the books; and* ALICK *and* DAVID, *the villains, now want to get away from each other.*)

ALICK. Yes—yes. Oh yes—ay, man—it is so—umpha. You'll lift the big coals off, David.
(*He wanders away to his spring mattress.* DAVID *removes the coals.*)

JAMES (*who would like to sit down and have an argy-bargy*). It's a most romantical affair. (*But he gets no answer*) I wonder how it'll turn out? (*No answer*) She's queer, Maggie. I wonder how some clever writer has never noticed how queer women are. It's my belief you could write a whole book about them. (DAVID *remains obdurate*) It was very noble of her to tell him she's twenty-six. (*Muttering as he too wanders away*) But I thought she was twenty-seven.
(DAVID *turns out the light.*)

ACT TWO

Six years have elapsed and JOHN SHAND'*s great hour has come. Perhaps his great hour really lies ahead of him, perhaps he had it six years ago; it often passes us by in the night with such a faint call that we don't even turn in our beds. But according to the trumpets this is* JOHN'*s great hour; it is the hour for which he has long been working with his coat off; and now the coat is on again (broadcloth but ill-fitting), for there is no more to do but await results. He is standing for Parliament, and this is election night.*

As the scene discloses itself you get, so to speak, one of JOHN SHAND'S *posters in the face. Vote for* SHAND. SHAND, SHAND, SHAND. *Civil and Religious Liberty, Faith, Hope, Freedom. They are all fly-blown names for* SHAND. *Have a placard about* SHAND, *have a hundred placards about him, it is snowing* SHAND *tonight in Glasgow; take the paste out of your eye, and you will see that we are in one of* SHAND'S *committee rooms. It has been a hairdresser's emporium, but* SHAND, SHAND, SHAND *has swept through it like a wind, leaving nothing but the fixtures; why shave, why have your head doused in those basins when you can be brushed and scraped and washed up for ever by simply voting for* SHAND?

There are a few hard chairs for yelling SHAND *from, and then rushing away. There is an iron spiral staircase that once led to the ladies' hairdressing apartments, but now leads to more* SHAND, SHAND, SHAND. *A glass door at the back opens on to the shop proper, screaming Civil and Religious Liberty,* SHAND, *as it opens, and beyond is the street crammed with still more* SHAND *pro and con. Men in every sort of garb rush in and out, up and down the stair, shouting the magic word. Then there is a lull, and down the stair comes* MAGGIE WYLIE, *decidedly over-dressed in blue velvet and (let us get this over) less good-looking than ever. She raises her hands to heaven, she spins round like a little teetotum. To her from the street, suffering from a determination of the word* SHAND *to the mouth, rush* ALICK *and* DAVID. ALICK *is thinner (being older),* DAVID *is stouter (being older), and they are both in tweeds and silk hats.*

MAGGIE. David—have they—is he? quick, quick!

DAVID. There's no news yet, no news. It's terrible.
(*The teetotum revolves more quickly.*)

ALICK. For God's sake, Maggie, sit down.

MAGGIE. I can't, I can't.

DAVID. Hold her down.
(*They press her into a chair;* JAMES *darts in, stouter also. His necktie has gone; he will never again be able to attend a funeral in that hat.*)

JAMES (*wildly*). John Shand's the

man for you. John Shand's the man for you. John Shand's the man for you.

DAVID (*clutching him*). Have you heard anything?

JAMES. Not a word.

ALICK. Look at her.

DAVID. Maggie (*he goes on his knees beside her, pressing her to him in affectionate anxiety*) It was mad of him to dare.

MAGGIE. It was grand of him.

ALICK (*moving about distraught*). Insane ambition.

MAGGIE. Glorious ambition.

DAVID. Maggie, Maggie, my lamb, best be prepared for the worst.

MAGGIE (*husky*). I am prepared.

ALICK. Six weary years has she waited for this night.

MAGGIE. Six brave years has John toiled for this night.

JAMES. And you could have had him, Maggie, at the end of five. The document says five.

MAGGIE. Do you think I grudge not being married to him yet? Was I to hamper him till the fight was won.

DAVID (*with wrinkled brows*). But if it's lost? (*She can't answer.*)

ALICK (*starting*). What's that?
(*The three listen at the door; the shouting dies down.*)

DAVID. They're terrible still; what can make them so still?
(JAMES *spirits himself away.* ALICK *and* DAVID *blanch to hear* MAGGIE *speaking softly as if to* JOHN.)

MAGGIE. Did you say you had lost, John? Of course you would lose the first time, dear John. Six years. Very well, we'll begin another six tonight. You'll win yet. (*Fiercely*) Never give in, John, never give in!
(*The roar of the multitude breaks out again and comes rolling nearer.*)

DAVID. I think he's coming.
(JAMES *is fired into the room like a squeezed onion.*)

JAMES. He's coming!
(*They may go on speaking, but through the clang outside none could hear. The populace seem to be trying to take the committee room by assault. Out of the scrimmage a man emerges dishevelled and bursts into the room, closing the door behind him. It is* JOHN SHAND *in a five-guinea suit, including the hat. There are other changes in him also, for he has been delving his way through loamy ground all those years. His right shoulder, which he used to raise to pound a path through the crowd, now remains permanently in that position. His mouth tends to close like a box. His eyes are tired, they need some one to pull the lids over them and send him to sleep for a week. But they are honest eyes still, and faithful, and could even light up his face at times with a smile, if the mouth would give a little help.*)

JOHN (*clinging to a chair that he may not fly straight to heaven*).

I'm in; I'm elected. Majority two hundred and forty-four; I'm John Shand, *M.P.*

(*The crowd have the news by this time and their roar breaks the door open.* JAMES *is off at once to tell them that he is to be Shand's brother-in-law. A teardrop clings to* ALICK'S *nose;* DAVID *hits out playfully at* JOHN, *and* JOHN *in an ecstasy returns the blow.*)

DAVID. Fling yourself at the door, father, and bar them out. Maggie, what keeps you so quiet now?

MAGGIE (*weak in her limbs*). You're sure you're in, John.

JOHN. Majority 244. I've beaten the baronet. I've done it, Maggie, and not a soul to help me; I've done it alone. (*His voice breaks; you could almost pick up the pieces*) I'm as hoarse as a crow, and I have to address the Cowcaddens Club yet; David, pump some oxygen into me.

DAVID. Certainly, Mr. Shand. (*While he does it,* MAGGIE *is seeing visions.*)

ALICK. What are you doing, Maggie?

MAGGIE. This is the House of Commons, and I'm John, catching the Speaker's eye for the first time. Do you see a queer little old wifie sitting away up there in the Ladies' Gallery? That's me. Mr. Speaker, sir, I rise to make my historic maiden speech. I am no orator, sir; voice from Ladies' Gallery, "Are you not, John? you'll soon let them see that"; cries of "Silence, woman," and general indignation. Mr. Speaker, sir, I stand here diffidently with my eyes on the Treasury Bench; voice from the Ladies' Gallery, "And you'll soon have your coat-tails on it, John"; loud cries of "Remove that little old wifie," on which she is forcibly ejected, and the honourable gentleman resumes his seat in a torrent of admiring applause.

(ALICK *and* DAVID *waggle their proud heads.*)

JOHN (*tolerantly*). Maggie, Maggie.

MAGGIE. You're not angry with me, John?

JOHN. No, no.

MAGGIE. But you glowered.

JOHN. I was thinking of Sir Peregrine. Just because I beat him at the poll he took a shabby revenge; he congratulated me in French, a language I haven't taken the trouble to master.

MAGGIE (*becoming a little taller*). Would it help you, John, if you were to marry a woman that could speak French?

DAVID (*quickly*). Not at all.

MAGGIE (*gloriously*). Mon cher Jean, laissez-moi parler le français, voulez-vous un interprète?

JOHN. Hullo!

MAGGIE. Je suis la sœur française de mes deux frères écossais.

DAVID (*worshipping her*). She's been learning French.

JOHN (*lightly*). Well done.

MAGGIE (*grandly*). They're arriving.

ALICK. Who?

MAGGIE. Our guests. This is London, and Mrs. John Shand is giving her first reception. (*Airily*) Have I told you, darling, who are coming tonight? There's that dear Sir Peregrine. (*To* ALICK) Sir Peregrine, this *is* a pleasure. Avez-vous. . . . So sorry we beat you at the poll.

JOHN. I'm doubting the baronet would sit on you, Maggie.

MAGGIE. I've invited a lord to sit on the baronet. *Voilà!*

DAVID (*delighted*). You thing! You'll find the lords expensive.

MAGGIE. Just a little cheap lord. (JAMES *enters importantly*) My dear Lord Cheap, this is kind of you.
(JAMES *hopes that* MAGGIE'S *reason is not unbalanced.*)

DAVID (*who really ought to have had education*). How de doo, Cheap?

JAMES (*bewildered*). Maggie—

MAGGIE. Yes, do call me Maggie.

ALICK (*grinning*). She's practising her first party, James. The swells are at the door.

JAMES (*heavily*). That's what I came to say. They *are* at the door.

JOHN. Who?

JAMES. The swells; a carriage and pair. (*He gives* JOHN *three cards.*)

JOHN. "Mr. Tenterden."

DAVID. Him that was speaking for you?

JOHN. The same. He's a whip and an Honourable. "Lady Sybil Tenterden." (*Frowns*) Her! She's his sister.

MAGGIE. A married woman?

JOHN. No. "The Comtesse de la Brière."

MAGGIE (*the scholar*). She must be French.

JOHN. Yes; I think she's some relation. She's a widow.

JAMES. But what am I to say to them? ("*Mr. Shand's compliments, and he will be proud to receive them" is the very least that the Wylies expect.*)

JOHN (*who was evidently made for great ends*). Say I'm very busy, but if they care to wait I hope presently to give them a few minutes.

JAMES (*thunderstruck*). Good God, Mr. Shand!
(*But it makes him* JOHN'S *more humble servant than ever, and he departs with the message.*)

JOHN (*not unaware of the sensation he has created*). I'll go up and let the crowd see me from the window.

MAGGIE. But—but—what are we to do with these ladies?

JOHN (*as he tramps upwards*). It's your reception, Maggie; this will prove you.

MAGGIE (*growing smaller*). Tell me what you know about this Lady Sybil?

JOHN. The only thing I know about her is that she thinks me vulgar.

MAGGIE. You?

JOHN. She has attended some of my meetings, and I'm told she said that.

MAGGIE. What could the woman mean?

JOHN. I wonder. When I come down I'll ask her.
(*With his departure* MAGGIE'S *nervousness increases.*)

ALICK (*encouragingly*). In at them, Maggie, with your French.

MAGGIE. It's all slipping from me, father.

DAVID (*gloomily*). I'm sure to say "for to come for to go."
(*The newcomers glorify the room, and* MAGGIE *feels that they have lifted her up with the tongs and deposited her in one of the basins. They are far from intending to be rude; it is not their fault that thus do swans scatter the ducks. They do not know that they are guests of the family, they think merely that they are waiting with other strangers in a public room; they undulate enquiringly, and if* MAGGIE *could undulate in return she would have no cause for offence. But she suddenly realises that this is an art as yet denied her, and that though* DAVID *might buy her evening gowns as fine as theirs (and is at this moment probably deciding to do so), she would look better carrying them in her arms than on her person. She also feels that to emerge from wraps as they are doing is more difficult than to plank your money on the counter for them. The* COMTESSE *she could forgive, for she is old; but* LADY SYBIL *is young and beautiful and comes lazily to rest like a stately ship of Tarsus.*)

COMTESSE (*smiling divinely, and speaking with such a pretty accent*). I hope one is not in the way. We were told we might wait.

MAGGIE (*bravely climbing out of the basin*). Certainly—I am sure—if you will be so—it is—
(*She knows that* DAVID *and her father are very sorry for her. A high voice is heard orating outside.*)

SYBIL (*screwing her nose deliciously*). He is at it again, Auntie.

COMTESSE. Mon Dieu! (*Like one begging pardon of the universe*) It is Mr. Tenterden, you understand, making one more of his delightful speeches to the crowd. Would you be so charming as to shut the door?
(*This to* DAVID *in such appeal that she is evidently making the petition of her life.* DAVID *saves her.*)

MAGGIE (*determined not to go under*). J'espère que vous—trouvez —cette—réunion—intéressante?

COMTESSE. Vous parlez français? Mais c'est charmant! Voyons, causons un peu. Racontez-moi tout de ce grand homme, toutes les choses merveilleuses qu'il a faites.

MAGGIE. I—I—Je connais—(*Alas!*)

COMTESSE (*naughtily*). Forgive me, Mademoiselle, I thought you spoke French.

SYBIL (*who knows that* DAVID *admires her shoulders*). How wicked of you, Auntie. (*To* MAGGIE) I assure you none of us can understand her when she gallops at that pace.

MAGGIE (*crushed*). It doesn't matter. I will tell Mr. Shand that you are here.

SYBIL (*drawling*). Please don't trouble him. We are really only waiting till my brother recovers and can take us back to our hotel.

MAGGIE. I'll tell him.
(*She is glad to disappear up the stair.*)

COMTESSE. The lady seems distressed. Is she a relation of Mr. Shand?

DAVID. Not for to say a relation. She's my sister. Our name is Wylie.
(*But granite quarries are nothing to them.*)

COMTESSE. How do you do. You are the committee man of Mr. Shand?

DAVID. No, just friends.

COMTESSE (*gaily to the basins*). Aha! I know you. Next, please! Sybil, do you weigh yourself, or are you asleep?
(LADY SYBIL *has sunk indolently into a weighing-chair.*)

SYBIL. Not quite, Auntie.

COMTESSE (*the mirror of la politesse*). Tell me all about Mr. Shand. Was it here that he—picked up the pin?

DAVID. The pin?

COMTESSE. As *I* have read, a self-made man always begins by picking up a pin. After that, as the memoirs say, his rise was rapid. (DAVID, *however, is once more master of himself, and indeed has begun to tot up the cost of their garments.*)

DAVID. It wasn't a pin he picked up, my lady; it was £300.

ALICK (*who feels that* JOHN'S *greatness has been outside the conversation quite long enough*). And his rise wasn't so rapid, just at first, David!

DAVID. He had his fight. His original intention was to become a minister; he's university-educated, you know; he's not a workingman member.

ALICK (*with reverence*). He's an M.A. But while he was a student he got a place in an iron cementer's business.

COMTESSE (*now far out of her depths*). Iron cementer?

DAVID. They scrape boilers.

COMTESSE. I see. The fun men have, Sybil!

DAVID (*with some solemnity*). There have been millions made in scraping boilers. They say, father, he went into business so as to be able to pay off the £300.

ALICK (*slily*). So I've heard.

COMTESSE. Aha—it was a loan? (DAVID *and* ALICK *are astride their great subject now.*)

DAVID. No, a gift—of a sort—from some well-wishers. But they wouldn't hear of his paying it off, father!

ALICK. Not them!

COMTESSE (*restraining an impulse to think of other things*). That was kind, charming.

ALICK (*with a look at* DAVID). Yes. Well, my lady, he developed a perfect genius for the iron cementing.

DAVID. But his ambition wasn't satisfied. Soon he had public life in his eye. As a heckler he was something fearsome; they had to seat him on the platform for to keep him quiet. Next they had to let him into the Chair. After that he did all the speaking; he cleared all roads before him like a fire-engine; and when this vacancy occurred, you could hardly say it did occur, so quickly did he step into it. My lady, there are few more impressive sights in the world than a Scotsman on the make.

COMTESSE. I can well believe it. And now he has said farewell to boilers?

DAVID (*impressively*). Not at all; the firm promised if he was elected for to make him their London manager at £800 a year.

COMTESSE. There is a strong man for you, Sybil; but I believe you *are* asleep.

SYBIL (*stirring herself*). Honestly I'm not. (*Sweetly to the others*) But *would* you mind finding out whether my brother is drawing to a close?

(DAVID *goes out, leaving poor* ALICK *marooned. The* COMTESSE *is kind to him.*)

COMTESSE. Thank you very much. (*Which helps* ALICK *out*) Don't you love a strong man, sleepy-head?

SYBIL (*preening herself*). I never met one.

COMTESSE. Neither have I. But if you *did* meet one, would he wake you up?

SYBIL. I dare say he would find there were two of us.

COMTESSE (*considering her.*) Yes, I think he would. Ever been in love, you cold thing?

SYBIL (*yawning*). I have never shot up in flame, Auntie.

COMTESSE. Think you could manage it?

SYBIL. If Mr. Right came along.

COMTESSE. As a girl of today it would be your duty to tame him.

SYBIL. As a girl of today I would try to do my duty.

COMTESSE. And if it turned out that *he* tamed you instead?

SYBIL. He would have to do that if he were *my* Mr. Right.

COMTESSE. And then?

SYBIL. Then, of course, I should adore him. Auntie, I think if I ever really love it will be like Mary Queen of Scots, who said of her Bothwell that she could follow him round the world in her nighty.

COMTESSE. My petite!

SYBIL. I believe I mean it.

COMTESSE. Oh, it is quite my conception of your character. Do you know, I am rather sorry for this Mr. John Shand.

SYBIL (*opening her fine eyes*). Why? He is quite a boor, is he not?

COMTESSE. For that very reason. Because his great hour is already nearly sped. That wild-bull manner that moves the multitude—they will laugh at it in your House of Commons.

SYBIL (*indifferent*). I suppose so.

COMTESSE. Yet if he had education—

SYBIL. Have we not been hearing how superbly he is educated?

COMTESSE. It is such as you or me that he needs to educate him now. *You* could do it almost too well.

SYBIL (*with that pretty stretch of neck*). I am not sufficiently interested. I retire in your favour. How would you begin?

COMTESSE. By asking him to drop in, about five, of course. By the way, I wonder is there a Mrs. Shand?

SYBIL. I have no idea. But they marry young.

COMTESSE. If there is not, there is probably a lady waiting for him, somewhere in a boiler.

SYBIL. I dare say.
(MAGGIE *descends.*)

MAGGIE. Mr. Shand will be down directly.

COMTESSE. Thank you. Your brother has been giving us such an interesting account of his career. I forget, Sybil, whether he said that he was married.

MAGGIE. No, he's not married; but he will be soon.

COMTESSE. Ah! (*She is merely making conversation*) A friend of yours?

MAGGIE (*now a scorner of herself*). I don't think much of her.

COMTESSE. In that case, tell me all about her.

MAGGIE. There's not much to tell. She's common, and stupid. One of those who go in for self-culture; and then when the test comes they break down. (*With sinister enjoyment*) She'll be the ruin of him.

COMTESSE. But is not that sad! Figure to yourself how many men with greatness before them have been shipwrecked by marrying in the rank from which they sprang.

MAGGIE. I've told her that.

COMTESSE. But she will not give him up?

MAGGIE. No.

SYBIL. Why should she if he cares for her? What is her name?

MAGGIE. It's—Maggie.

COMTESSE (*still uninterested*). Well, I am afraid that Maggie is to do for John. (JOHN *comes down*) Ah, our hero!

JOHN. Sorry I have kept you waiting. The Comtesse?

COMTESSE. And my niece Lady Sybil Tenterden. (SYBIL's *head inclines on its stem*) She is not really all my niece; I mean I am only half of her aunt. What a triumph, Mr. Shand!

JOHN. Oh, pretty fair, pretty fair. Your brother has just finished addressing the crowd, Lady Sybil.

SYBIL. Then we must not detain Mr. Shand, Auntie.

COMTESSE (*who unless her heart is touched thinks insincerity charming*). Only one word. I heard you speak last night. Sublime! Just the sort of impassioned eloquence that your House of Commons loves.

JOHN. It's very good of you to say so.

COMTESSE. But we must run. *Bon soir.*
(SYBIL *bows as to some one far away.*)

JOHN. Good-night, Lady Sybil. I hear you think I'm vulgar.
(*Eyebrows are raised.*)

COMTESSE. My dear Mr. Shand, what absurd—

JOHN. I was told she said that after hearing me speak.

COMTESSE. Quite a mistake, I—

JOHN (*doggedly*). Is it not true?

SYBIL (*"waking up"*). You seem to know, Mr. Shand; and as you press me so unnecessarily—well, yes, that is how you struck me.

COMTESSE. My child!

SYBIL (*who is a little agitated*). He would have it.

JOHN (*perplexed*). What's the matter? I just wanted to know, because if it's true I must alter it.

COMTESSE. There, Sybil, see how he values your good opinion.

SYBIL (*her svelte figure giving like a fly-rod*). It is very nice of you to put it in that way, Mr. Shand. Forgive me.

JOHN. But I don't quite understand yet. Of course, it can't matter to me, Lady Sybil, what you think of me; what I mean is, that I mustn't be vulgar if it would be injurious to my career.
(*The fly-rod regains its rigidity.*)

SYBIL. I see. No, of course, I could not affect your career, Mr. Shand.

JOHN (*who quite understands that he is being challenged*). That's so, Lady Sybil, meaning no offence.

SYBIL (*who has a naughty little impediment in her voice when she is most alluring*). Of course not. And we are friends again?

JOHN. Certainly.

SYBIL. Then I hope you will come to see me in London as I present no terrors.

JOHN (*he is a man, is* JOHN). I'll be very pleased.

SYBIL. Any afternoon about five.

JOHN. Much obliged. And you can teach me the things I don't know yet, if you'll be so kind.

SYBIL (*the impediment becoming more assertive*). If you wish it, I shall do my best.

JOHN. Thank you, Lady Sybil. And who knows there may be one or two things I can teach you.

SYBIL (*it has now become an angel's hiccough*). Yes, we can help one another. Good-bye till then.

JOHN. Good-bye. Maggie, the ladies are going.
(*During this skirmish* MAGGIE *has stood apart. At the mention of her name they glance at one another.* JOHN *escorts* SYBIL, *but the* COMTESSE *turns back. She says:*)

"Are you, then, *the* Maggie? (MAGGIE *nods rather defiantly and the* COMTESSE *is distressed*) But if I had known I would not have said those things. Please forgive an old woman."

"It doesn't matter."

"I—I dare say it will be all right. Mademoiselle, if I were you I would not encourage those *tête-à-têtes* with Lady Sybil. I am the rude one, but she is the dangerous one; and I am afraid his impudence has attracted her. *Bon voyage,* Miss Maggie."

"Good-bye—but I *can* speak French. Je parle français. Isn't that right?"

"But, yes, it is excellent. (*Making things easy for her*) C'est très bien."

"Je me suis embrouillée—la dernière fois."

"Good! Shall I speak more slowly?"

"No, no. Non, non, faster, faster."

"J'admire votre courage!"

"Je comprends chaque mot."

"Parfait! Bravo!"

"Voilà!"

"Superbe!"
(*The* COMTESSE *goes, applauding; and* MAGGIE *has a moment of elation, which however has passed before* JOHN *returns for his hat.*)

"Have you more speaking to do, John?"
(*He is somehow in high good-humour.*)

"I must run across and address the Cowcaddens Club. (*He sprays his throat with a hand-spray*) I wonder if I *am* vulgar, Maggie?"

"You are not, but *I* am."

"Not that *I* can see."

"Look how over-dressed I am, John! I knew it was too showy

when I ordered it, and yet I could not resist the thing. But I will tone down, I will. What did you think of Lady Sybil?"

"That young woman had better be careful. She's a bit of a beson, Maggie."

"She's beautiful, John."

"She has a neat way of stretching herself. For playing with she would do as well as another."
(MAGGIE *looks at him wistfully.*)

"You couldn't stay and have a talk for a few minutes?"

"If you want me, Maggie. The longer you keep them waiting, the more they think of you."

"When are you to announce that we're to be married, John?"

"I won't be long. You've waited a year more than you need have done, so I think it's your due I should hurry things now."

"I think it's noble of you."

"Not at all, Maggie; the nobleness has been yours in waiting so patiently. And your brothers would insist on it at any rate. They're watching me like cats with a mouse."

"It's so little I've done to help."

"Three hundred pounds."

"I'm getting a thousand per cent. for it."

"And very pleased I am you should think so, Maggie."

"Is it terrible hard to you, John?"

"It's not hard at all. I can say truthfully, Maggie, that all, or nearly all, I've seen of you in these six years has gone to increase my respect for you."

"Respect!"

"And a bargain's a bargain."

"If it wasn't that you're so glorious to me, John, I would let you off."
(*There is a gleam in his eye, but he puts it out.*)

"In my opinion, Maggie, we'll be a very happy pair."
(*She accepts this eagerly.*)

"We know each other so well, John, don't we?"

"I'm an extraordinary queer character, and I suppose nobody knows me well except myself; but I know you, Maggie, to the very roots of you."
(*She magnanimously lets this remark alone.*)

"And it's not as if there was any other woman you—fancied more, John."

"There's none whatever."

"If there ever should be—oh, if there ever should be! Some woman with charm."

"Maggie, you forget yourself. There couldn't be another woman once I was a married man."

"One has heard of such things."

"Not in Scotsmen, Maggie; not in Scotsmen."

"I've sometimes thought, John, that the difference between us and the English is that the Scotch are hard in all other respects but soft with women, and the English are hard with women but soft in all other respects."

"You've forgotten the grandest moral attribute of a Scotsman, Maggie, that he'll do nothing which might damage his career."

"Ah, but John, whatever you do, you do it so tremendously; and if you were to love, what a passion it would be."

"There's something in that, I suppose."

"And then, what could I do? For the desire of my life now, John, is to help you to get everything you want, except just that I want you to have me, too."

"We'll get on fine, Maggie."

"You're just making the best of it. They say that love is sympathy, and if that's so mine must be a great love for you, for I see all you are feeling this night and bravely hiding; I feel for you as if I was John Shand myself." (JOHN *sighs.*)

"I had best go to the meeting, Maggie."

"Not yet. Can you look me in the face, John, and deny that there is surging within you a mighty desire to be free, to begin the new life untrammelled?"

"Leave such maggots alone, Maggie."

"It's a shame of me not to give you up."

"I would consider you a very foolish woman if you did."

"If I were John Shand I would no more want to take Maggie Wylie with me through the beautiful door that has opened wide for you than I would want to take an old pair of shoon. Why don't you bang the door in my face, John? (*A tremor runs through* JOHN.)

"A bargain's a bargain, Maggie." (MAGGIE *moves about, an eerie figure, breaking into little cries. She flutters round him, threateningly.*)

"Say one word about wanting to get out of it, and I'll put the lawyers on you."

"Have I hinted at such a thing?"

"The document holds you hard and fast."

"It does."
(*She gloats miserably.*)

"The woman never rises with the man. I'll drag you down, John. I'll drag you down."

"Have no fear of that, I won't let you. I'm too strong."

"You'll miss the prettiest thing in the world, and all owing to me."

"What's that?"

"Romance."

"Poof."

"All's cold and grey without it, John. They that have had it have slipped in and out of heaven."

"You're exaggerating, Maggie."

"You've worked so hard, you've had none of the fun that comes to most men long before they're your age."

"I never was one for fun. I cannot call to mind, Maggie, ever having laughed in my life."

"You have no sense of humour."

"Not a spark."

"I've sometimes thought that if you had, it might make you fonder of me. I think one needs a sense of humour to be fond of me."

"I remember reading of some one that said it needed a surgical operation to get a joke into a Scotsman's head."

"Yes, that's been said."

"What beats me, Maggie, is how you could insert a joke with an operation." (*He considers this and gives up.*)

"That's not the kind of fun I was thinking of. I mean fun with the lasses, John—gay, jolly, harmless fun. They could be impudent fashionable beauties now, stretching themselves to attract you, like that hiccoughing little devil, and running away from you, and crooking their fingers to you to run after them."
(JOHN *draws a big breath.*)

"No, I never had that."

"It's every man's birthright, and you would have it now but for me."

"I can do without, Maggie."

"It's like missing out all the Saturdays."

"You feel sure, I suppose, that an older man wouldn't suit you better, Maggie?"

"I couldn't feel surer of anything. You're just my ideal."

"Yes, yes. Well, that's as it should be."
(*She threatens him again.*)

"David has the document. It's carefully locked away."

"He would naturally take good care of it."
(*The pride of the Wylies deserts her.*)

"John, I make you a solemn promise that, in consideration of the circumstances of our marriage, if you should ever fall in love I'll act differently from other wives."

"There will be no occasion, Maggie."
(*Her voice becomes tremulous.*)

"John, David doesn't have the document. He thinks he has, but I have it here." (*Somewhat heavily* JOHN *surveys the fatal paper.*)

"Well do I mind the look of it, Maggie. Yes, yes, that's it. Umpha."

"You don't ask why I've brought it."

"Why did you?"

"Because I thought I might perhaps have the courage and the womanliness to give it back to you. (JOHN *has a brief dream*) Will you never hold it up against me in the future that I couldn't do that?"

"I promise you, Maggie, I never will."

"To go back to the Pans and take up my old life there, when all these six years my eyes have been centred on this night! I've been waiting for this night as long as you have been; and now to go back there, and wizen and dry up, when I might be married to John Shand!"

"And you will be, Maggie. You have my word."

"Never—never—never. (*She tears up the document. He remains seated immovable, but the gleam returns to his eye. She rages first at herself and then at him*) I'm a fool, a fool, to let you go. I tell you, you'll rue this day, for you need me, you'll come to grief without me. There's nobody can help you as I could have helped you. I'm essential to your career, and you're blind not to see it."

"What's that, Maggie? In no circumstances would I allow any meddling with my career."

"You would never have known I was meddling with it. But that's over. Don't be in too great a hurry to marry, John. Have your fling with the beautiful dolls first. Get the whiphand of the haughty ones, John. Give them their licks. Every time they hiccough let them have an extra slap in memory of me. And be sure to remember this, my man, that the one who marries you will find you out."

"Find me out?"

"However careful a man is, his wife always finds out his failings."

"I don't know, Maggie, to what failings you refer. (*The Cowcaddens Club has burst its walls, and is pouring this way to raise the new Member on its crest. The first wave hurls itself against the barber's shop with cries of "Shand, Shand, Shand." For a moment* JOHN *stems the torrent by planting his back against the door*) You are acting under an impulse, Maggie, and I can't take advantage of it. Think the matter over, and we'll speak about it in the morning."

"No, I can't go through it again. It ends tonight and now. Good luck, John." (*She is immediately submerged in the sea that surges through the door, bringing much wreckage with it. In a moment the place is so full that another cupful could not find standing room. Some slippery ones are squeezed upwards and remain aloft as warnings.* JOHN *has jumped on to the stair, and harangues the flood vainly like another Canute. It is something about freedom and noble minds, and, though unheard, goes to all heads, including the speaker's. By the time he is audible sentiment has him for her own.*)

"But, gentlemen, one may have too much even of freedom. (*No, no*) Yes, Mr. Adamson. One may want to be tied. (*Never, never*) I say yes, Willie Cameron; and I have found a young lady who I am proud to say is willing to be tied to me. I'm to be married. (*Uproar*) Her name's Miss Wylie. (*Transport*) Quiet; she's here now. (*Frenzy*) She was here! Where are you, Maggie?" (*A small voice* –"I'm here." *A hundred great voices* – "Where–where–where?" *The small voice*–"I'm so little none of you can see me.")

(*Three men, name of Wylie, buffet their way forward. Anon is heard the voice of* DAVID.)

"James, father, have you grip of her?"

"We've got her."

"Then hoist her up."

(*The queer little elated figure is raised aloft. With her fingers she can just touch the stars. Not unconscious of the nobility of his behaviour, the hero of the evening points an impressive finger at her.*)

"Gentlemen, the future Mrs. John Shand!" ("*Speech, speech.*") "No, no, being a lady she can't make a speech, but–"

(*The heroine of the evening surprises him.*)

"I can make a speech, and I will make a speech, and it's in two words, and they're these–(*holding out her arms to enfold all the members of the Cowcaddens Club*)–My Constituents!" (*Dementia.*)

ACT THREE

A few minutes ago the COMTESSE DE LA BRIÈRE, *who has not recently been in England, was shown into the London home of the* SHANDS. *Though not sufficiently interested to express her surprise in words, she raised her eyebrows on finding herself in a charming room; she had presumed that the* SHAND *scheme of decoration would be as impossible as themselves.*

It is the little room behind the dining-room for which English architects have long been famous; "Make something of this, and you will indeed be a clever one," they seem to say to you as they unveil it. The COMTESSE *finds that* JOHN *has undoubtedly made something of it. It is his "study" (mon Dieu, the words these English use!) and there is nothing in it that offends; there is so much not in it too that might so easily have been there. It is not in the least ornate; there are no colours quarrelling with each other (unseen, unheard by the blissful occupant of the revolving chair); the* COMTESSE *has not even the gentle satisfaction of noting a "suite" in stained oak. Nature might have taken a share in the decorations, so restful are they to the eyes; it is the working room of a man of culture, probably lately down from Oxford; at a first meeting there is nothing in it that pretends to be what it is not. Our visitor is a little disappointed, but being fair-minded blows her absent host a kiss for disappointing her.*

He has even, she observes with a twinkle, made something of the most difficult of his possessions, the little wife. For MAGGIE, *who is here receiving her, has been quite creditably toned down. He has put her into a little grey frock that not only deals gently with her personal defects, but is in harmony with the room. Evidently, however, she has not "risen" with him, for she is as stupid as ever; the* COMTESSE, *who remembers having liked her the better of the two, could shake her for being so stupid. For instance, why is she not asserting herself in that other apartment?*

The other apartment is really a correctly solemn dining-room, of which we have a glimpse through partly open folding-doors. At this moment it is harbouring MR. SHAND'S *ladies' committee, who sit with pens and foolscap round the large table, awaiting the advent of their leader. There are nobly wise ones and some foolish ones among them, for we are back in the strange days when it was considered "unwomanly" for women to have minds. The* COMTESSE *peeps at them with curiosity, as they arrange their papers or are ushered into the dining-room through a door which we cannot see. To her frivolous ladyship they are a species of wild fowl, and she is specially amused to find her niece among them. She demands an explanation as soon as the communicating doors close.*

"Tell me since when has my dear Sybil become one of these ladies? It is not like her."

(MAGGIE *is obviously not clever enough to understand the woman question. Her eye rests longingly on a half-finished stocking as she innocently but densely replies:*)

"I think it was about the time that my husband took up their cause."

(*The* COMTESSE *has been hearing tales of* LADY SYBIL *and the barbarian; and after having the grace to hesitate, she speaks with the directness for which she is famed in Mayfair.*)

"Mrs. Shand, excuse me for saying that if half of what I hear be true, your husband is seeing that lady a great deal too often. (MAGGIE *is expressionless; she reaches for her stocking, whereat her guest loses patience*) Oh, mon Dieu, put that down; you can buy them at two francs the pair. Mrs. Shand, why do not you compel yourself to take an intelligent interest in your husband's work?"

"I typewrite his speeches."

"But do you know what they are about?"

"They are about various subjects."

"Oh!"

(*Did* MAGGIE *give her an unseen quizzical glance before demurely resuming the knitting? One is not certain, as* JOHN *has come in, and this obliterates her. A "Scotsman on the make," of whom* DAVID *has spoken reverently, is still to be read—in a somewhat better-bound volume—in* JOHN SHAND'S *person; but it is as doggedly honest a face as ever; and he champions women, not for personal ends, but because his blessed days of poverty gave him a light upon their needs. His self-satisfaction, however, has increased, and he has pleasantly forgotten some things. For instance, he can now call out "Porter" at railway stations without dropping his hands for the barrow.* MAGGIE *introduces the* COMTESSE, *and he is still undaunted.*)

"I remember you well—at Glasgow."

"It must be quite two years ago, Mr. Shand."
(JOHN *has no objection to showing that he has had a classical education.*)

"*Tempus fugit,* Comtesse."

"I have not been much in this country since then, and I return to find you a coming man."
(*Fortunately his learning is tempered with modesty.*)

"Oh, I don't know, I don't know."

"The Ladies' Champion."
(*His modesty is tempered with a respect for truth.*)

"Well, well."

"And you are about, as I understand, to introduce a bill to give women an equal right with men to grow beards (*which is all she knows about it.* JOHN *takes the remark literally.*)

"There's nothing about beards in it, Comtesse. (*She gives him time to cogitate, and is pleased to note that there is no result*) Have you typed my speech, Maggie?"

"Yes; twenty-six pages." (*She produces it from a drawer. Perhaps* JOHN *wishes to impress the visitor.*)

"I'm to give the ladies' committee a general idea of it. Just see, Maggie, if I know the peroration: 'In conclusion, Mr. Speaker, these are the reasonable demands of every intelligent Englishwoman'—I had better say British woman—'and I am proud to nail them to my flag' "—
(*The visitor is properly impressed.*)

"Oho! defies his leaders!"

" 'So long as I can do so without embarrassing the Government.' "

"Ah, ah, Mr. Shand!"

" 'I call upon the Front Bench, sir, loyally but firmly' "—

"Firm again!"

". . . 'either to accept my Bill, or to promise *without delay* to bring in one of their own; and if they decline to do so I solemnly warn them that though I will not press the matter to a division just now' "—

"Ahem!"

" 'I will bring it forward again in the near future.' And now, Comtesse, *you* know that I'm not going to divide—and not another soul knows it."

"I am indeed flattered by your confidence."

"I've only told you because I don't care who knows now."

"Oh!"
(*Somehow* MAGGIE *seems to be dissatisfied.*)

"But why is that, John?"

"I daren't keep the Government in doubt any longer about what I mean to do. I'll show the whips the speech privately to-night."
(*But still* MAGGIE *wants to know.*)

"But not to go to a division is hedging, isn't it? Is that strong?"

"To make the speech at all, Maggie, is stronger than most would dare. They would *do* for me if I went to a division."

"Bark but not bite?"

"Now, now, Maggie, you're out of your depth."

"I suppose that's it."
(*The* COMTESSE *remains in the shallows.*)

"But what will the ladies say, Mr. Shand?"

"They won't like it, Comtesse, but they've got to lump it."
(*Here the* MAID *appears with a card for* MAGGIE, *who considers it quietly.*)

"Any one of importance?"

"No."

"Then I'm ready, Maggie."
(*This is evidently an intimation that she is to open the folding-doors, and he makes an effective entrance into the dining-room, his thumb in his waistcoat. There is a delicious clapping of hands from the committee, and the door closes. Not till then does* MAGGIE, *who has grown thoughtful, tell her maid to admit the visitor.*)

"Another lady, Mrs. Shand?"

"The card says 'Mr. Charles Venables.'"
(*The* COMTESSE *is really interested at last.*)

"Charles Venables! Do *you* know him?"

"I think I call to mind meeting one of that name at the Foreign Office party."

"One of that name! He who is a Minister of your Cabinet. But as you know him so little why should he call on you?"

"I wonder." (MAGGIE'S *glance wanders to the drawer in which she has replaced* JOHN'S *speech.*)

"Well, well, I shall take care of you, petite."

"Do *you* know him?"

"Do I know him! The last time I saw him he asked me to—to—hem! —ma chérie, it was thirty years ago."

"Thirty years!"

"I was a pretty woman then. I dare say I shall detest him now; but if I find I do not—let us have a little plot—I shall drop this book; and then perhaps you will be so charming as—as not to be here for a little while?"
(MR. VENABLES, *who enters, is such a courtly seigneur that he seems to bring the eighteenth century with him; you feel that his sedan chair is at the door. He stoops over* MAGGIE'S *plebeian hand.*)

"I hope you will pardon my calling, Mrs. Shand; we had such a pleasant talk the other evening." (MAGGIE, *of course, is at once deceived by his gracious manner.*)

"I think it's kind of you. Do you know each other? The Comtesse de la Brière."
(*He repeats the name with some emotion, and the* COMTESSE *half mischievously, half sadly, holds a hand before her face.*)

"Comtesse."

"Thirty years, Mr. Venables."
(*He gallantly removes the hand that screens her face.*)

"It does not seem so much."
(*She gives him a similar scrutiny.*)

"Mon Dieu, it seems all that."
(*They smile rather ruefully.* MAGGIE *like a kind hostess relieves the tension.*)

"The Comtesse has taken a cottage in Surrey for the summer."

"I am overjoyed."

"No, Charles, you are not. You no longer care. Fickle one! And it is only thirty years."
(*He sinks into a chair beside her.*)

"Those heavenly evenings, Comtesse, on the Bosphorus."

"I refuse to talk of them. I hate you." (*But she drops the book, and* MAGGIE *fades from the room. It is not a very clever departure, and the old diplomatist smiles. Then he sighs a beautiful sigh, for he does all things beautifully.*)

"It is moonlight, Comtesse, on the Golden Horn."

"Who are those two young things in a caïque?"

"Is he the brave Leander, Comtesse, and is she Hero of the Lamp?"

"No, she is the foolish wife of the French Ambassador, and he is a good-for-nothing British attaché trying to get her husband's secrets out of her."

"Is it possible! They part at a certain garden gate."

"Oh, Charles, Charles!"

"But you promised to come back; I waited there till dawn. Blanche, if you *had* come back—"

"How is Mrs. Venables?"

"She is rather poorly. *I* think it's gout."

"And you?"

"I creak a little in the mornings."

"So do I. There is such a good man at Wiesbaden."

"The Homburg fellow is better. The way he patched me up last summer—Oh, Lord, Lord!"

"Yes, Charles, the game is up; we are two old fogies. (*They groan in unison; then she raps him sharply on the knuckles*) Tell me, sir, what are you doing here?"

"Merely a friendly call."

"I do not believe it."

"The same woman; the old delightful candour."

"The same man; the old fibs. (*She sees that the door is asking a question*) Yes, come, Mrs. Shand, I have had quite enough of him; I warn you he is here for some crafty purpose."

MAGGIE (*drawing back timidly*). Surely not?

VENABLES. Really, Comtesse, you make conversation difficult. To show that my intentions are innocent, Mrs. Shand, I propose that you choose the subject.

MAGGIE (*relieved*). There, Comtesse.

VENABLES. I hope your husband is well?

MAGGIE. Yes, thank you (*With a happy thought*) I decide that we talk about him.

VENABLES. If you wish it.

COMTESSE. Be careful; *he* has chosen the subject.

MAGGIE. *I* chose it, didn't I?

VENABLES. You know you did.

MAGGIE (*appealingly*). You admire John?

VENABLES. Very much. But he puzzles me a little. You Scots, Mrs. Shand, are such a mixture of the practical and the emotional that you escape out of an Englishman's hand like a trout.

MAGGIE (*open-eyed*). Do we?

VENABLES. Well, not you, but your husband. I have known few men make a worse beginning in the House. He had the most atrocious bow-wow public park manner—

COMTESSE. I remember that manner!

MAGGIE. No, he hadn't.

VENABLES (*soothingly*). At first. But by his second session he had shed all that, and he is now a pleasure to listen to. By the way, Comtesse, have you found any dark intention in that?

COMTESSE. You wanted to know whether he talks over these matters with his wife; and she has told you that he does not.

MAGGIE (*indignantly*). I haven't said a word about it, have I?

VENABLES. Not a word. Then, again, I admire him for his impromptu speeches.

MAGGIE. What is impromptu?

VENABLES. Unprepared. They have contained some grave blunders, not so much of judgment as of taste—

MAGGIE (*hotly*). *I* don't think so.

VENABLES. Pardon me. But he has righted himself subsequently in the neatest way. I have always found that the man whose second thoughts are good is worth watching. Well, Comtesse, I see you have something to say.

COMTESSE. You are wondering whether she can tell you who gives him his second thoughts.

MAGGIE. Gives them to John? I would like to see anybody try to give thoughts to John.

VENABLES. Quite so.

COMTESSE. Is there anything more that has roused your admiration, Charles?

VENABLES (*purring*). Let me see. Yes, we are all much edified by his humour.

COMTESSE (*surprised indeed*). His humour? That man!

MAGGIE (*with hauteur*). Why not?

VENABLES. I assure you, Comtesse, some of the neat things in his speeches convulse the house. A word has even been coined for them—Shandisms.

COMTESSE (*slowly recovering from a blow*). Humour!

VENABLES. In conversation, I admit, he strikes one as being—ah—somewhat lacking in humour.

COMTESSE (*pouncing*). You are wondering who supplies his speeches with the humour.

MAGGIE. Supplies John?

VENABLES. Now that you mention it, some of his Shandisms do have a curiously feminine quality.

COMTESSE. You have thought it might be a woman.

VENABLES. Really, Comtesse—

COMTESSE. I see it all. Charles, you thought it might be the wife!

VENABLES (*flinging up his hands*). I own up.

MAGGIE (*bewildered*). Me?

VENABLES. Forgive me, I see I was wrong.

MAGGIE (*alarmed*). Have I been doing John any harm?

VENABLES. On the contrary, I am relieved to know that there are no hairpins in his speeches. If he is at home, Mrs. Shand, may I see him? I am going to be rather charming to him.

MAGGIE (*drawn in two directions*). Yes, he is—oh, yes—but—

VENABLES. That is to say, Comtesse, if he proves himself the man I believe him to be.
(*This arrests* MAGGIE *almost as she has reached the dining-room door.*)

MAGGIE (*hesitating*). He is very busy just now.

VENABLES (*smiling*). I think he will see me.

MAGGIE. Is it something about his speech?

VENABLES (*the smile hardening*). Well, yes, it is.

MAGGIE. Then I dare say I could tell you what you want to know without troubling him, as I've been typing it.

VENABLES (*with a sigh*). I don't acquire information in that way.

COMTESSE. I trust not.

MAGGIE. There's no secret about it. He is to show it to the Whips to-night.

VENABLES (*sharply*). You are sure of that?

COMTESSE. It is quite true, Charles. I heard him say so; and indeed he repeated what he called the "peroration" before me.

MAGGIE. I know it by heart. (*She plays a bold game*) "These are the demands of all intelligent British women, and I am proud to nail them to my flag"—

COMTESSE. The very words, Mrs. Shand.

MAGGIE (*looking at her imploringly*). "And I don't care how they may embarrass the Government." (*The* COMTESSE *is bereft of speech, so suddenly has she been introduced to the real* MAGGIE SHAND) "If the right honourable gentleman will give us his pledge to introduce a similar bill this session I will willingly withdraw mine; but otherwise I solemnly warn him that I will press the matter now to a division."
(*She turns her face from the great man; she has gone white.*)

VENABLES (*after a pause*). Capital.
(*The blood returns to* MAGGIE's *heart.*)

COMTESSE (*who is beginning to enjoy herself very much*). Then you are pleased to know that he means to, as you say, go to a division?

VENABLES. Delighted. The courage of it will be the making of him.

COMTESSE. I see.

VENABLES. Had he been to hedge we should have known that he was a pasteboard knight and have disregarded him.

COMTESSE. I see.
(*She desires to catch the eye of* MAGGIE, *but it is carefully turned from her.*)

VENABLES. Mrs. Shand, let us have him in at once.

COMTESSE. Yes, yes, indeed.
(MAGGIE's *anxiety returns, but she has to call* JOHN *in.*)

JOHN (*impressed*). Mr. Venables! This is an honour.

VENABLES. How are you, Shand?

JOHN. Sit down, sit down. (*Becoming himself again*) I can guess what you have come about.

VENABLES. Ah, you Scotsmen.

JOHN. Of course I know I'm harassing the Government a good deal—

VENABLES (*blandly*). Not at all, Shand. The Government are very pleased.

JOHN. You don't expect me to believe that.

VENABLES. I called here to give you the proof of it. You may know that we are to have a big meeting at Leeds on the 24th, when two Ministers are to speak. There is room for a third speaker, and I am authorised to offer that place to you.

JOHN. To me!

VENABLES. Yes.

JOHN (*swelling*). It would be—the Government taking me up.

VENABLES. Don't make too much of it; it would be an acknowledgment that they look upon you as one of their likely young men.

MAGGIE. John!

JOHN (*not found wanting in a trying hour*). It's a bribe. You are offering me this on condition that I don't make my speech. How can you think so meanly of me as to believe that I would play the women's cause false for the sake of my own advancement. I refuse your bribe.

VENABLES (*liking him for the first time*). Good. But you are wrong. There are no conditions, and we want you to make your speech. Now do you accept?

JOHN (*still suspicious*). If you make me the same offer after you have read it. I insist on your reading it first.

VENABLES (*sighing*). By all means. (MAGGIE *is in an agony as she sees* JOHN *hand the speech to his leader. On the other hand, the* COMTESSE *thrills*) But I assure you we look on the speech as a small matter. The important thing is your intention of going to a division; and we agree to that also.

JOHN (*losing his head*). What's that?

VENABLES. Yes, we agree.

JOHN. But—but—why, you have been threatening to excommunicate me if I dared.

VENABLES. All done to test you, Shand.

JOHN. To test me?

VENABLES. We know that a division on your Bill can have no serious significance; we shall see to that. And so the test was to be whether you had the pluck to divide the House. Had you been intending to talk big in this speech, and then hedge, through fear of the Government, they would have had no further use for you.

JOHN (*heavily*). I understand. (*But there is one thing he cannot understand, which is, why* VENABLES *should be so sure that he is not to hedge.*)

VENABLES (*turning over the pages carelessly*). Any of your good things in this, Shand?

JOHN (*whose one desire is to get the pages back*). No, I—no—it isn't necessary you should read it now.

VENABLES (*from politeness only*). Merely for my own pleasure. I shall look through it this evening. (*He rolls up the speech to put it in his pocket.* JOHN *turns despairingly to* MAGGIE, *though well aware that no help can come from her.*)

MAGGIE. That's the only copy there is, John. (*To* VENABLES) Let me make a fresh one, and send it to you in an hour or two.

VENABLES (*good-naturedly*). I could not put you to that trouble,

Mrs. Shand. I will take good care of it.

MAGGIE. If anything were to happen to you on the way home, wouldn't whatever is in your pocket be considered to be the property of your heirs?

VENABLES (*laughing*). Now there is forethought! Shand, I think that after that—! (*He returns the speech to* JOHN, *whose hand swallows it greedily*) She is Scotch too, Comtesse.

COMTESSE (*delighted*). Yes, she is Scotch too.

VENABLES. Though the only persons likely to do for me in the street, Shand, are your ladies' committee. Ever since they took the horse out of my brougham, I can scent them a mile away.

COMTESSE. A mile? Charles, peep in there.
(*He softly turns the handle of the dining-room door, and realises that his scent is not so good as he had thought it. He bids his hostess and the* COMTESSE *good-bye in a burlesque whisper and tiptoes off to safer places.* JOHN *having gone out with him,* MAGGIE *can no longer avoid the* COMTESSE'*s reproachful eye. That much-injured lady advances upon her with accusing finger.*)

"So, madam!"
(MAGGIE *is prepared for her.*)

"I don't know what you mean."

"Yes, you do. I mean that there *is* some one who 'helps' our Mr. Shand."

"There's not."

"And it *is* a woman, and it's you."

"I help in the little things."

"The little things! You are the Pin he picked up and that is to make his fortune. And now what I want to know is whether your John is aware that you help at all."
(JOHN *returns, and at once provides the answer.*)

"Maggie, Comtesse, I've done it again!"

"I'm so glad, John."
(*The* COMTESSE *is in an ecstasy.*)

"And all because you were not to hedge, Mr. Shand."
(*His appeal to her with the wistfulness of a schoolboy makes him rather attractive.*)

"You won't tell on me, Comtesse! (*He thinks it out*) They had just guessed I would be firm because they know I'm a strong man. You little saw, Maggie, what a good turn you were doing me when you said you wanted to make another copy of the speech."
(*She is dense.*)

"How, John?"

"Because now I can alter the end."
(*She is enlightened.*)

"So you can!"

"Here's another lucky thing, Maggie: I hadn't told the ladies' committee that I was to hedge, and so they need never know. Comtesse, I tell you there's a little cherub who sits up aloft and looks after the career of John Shand."

(*The* COMTESSE *looks not aloft but toward the chair at present occupied by* MAGGIE.)

"Where does she sit, Mr. Shand?" (*He knows that women are not well read.*)

"It's just a figure of speech." (*He returns airily to his committee room; and now again you may hear the click of* MAGGIE's *needles. They no longer annoy the* COMTESSE; *she is setting them to music.*)

"It is not down here she sits, Mrs. Shand, knitting a stocking?"

"No, it isn't."

"And when I came in I gave him credit for everything; even for the prettiness of the room!"

"He has beautiful taste."

"Good-bye, Scotchy."

"Good-bye, Comtesse, and thank you for coming."

"Good-bye—Miss Pin." (MAGGIE *rings genteelly.*)

"Good-bye." (*The* COMTESSE *is now lost in admiration of her.*)

"You divine little wife. He can't be worthy of it, no man could be worthy of it. Why do you do it?" (MAGGIE *shivers a little.*)

"He loves to think he does it all himself; that's the way of men. I'm six years older than he is. I'm plain, and I have no charm. I shouldn't have let him marry me. I'm trying to make up for it."

(*The* COMTESSE *kisses her and goes away.* MAGGIE, *somewhat foolishly, resumes her knitting.*)

(*Some days later this same room is listening—with the same inattention—to the outpouring of* JOHN SHAND's *love for the lady of the hiccoughs. We arrive—by arrangement—rather late; and thus we miss some of the most delightful of the pangs. One can see that these two are playing no game, or, if they are, that they little know it. The wonders of the world (so strange are the instruments chosen by Love) have been revealed to* JOHN *in hiccoughs; he shakes in* SYBIL's *presence; never were more swimming eyes; he who has been of a wooden face till now, with ways to match, has gone on flame like a piece of paper; emotion is in flood in him. We may be almost fond of* JOHN *for being so worshipful of love. Much has come to him that we had almost despaired of his acquiring, including nearly all the divine attributes except that sense of humour. The beautiful* SYBIL *has always possessed but little of it also, and what she had has been struck from her by Cupid's flail. Naked of the saving grace, they face each other in awful rapture.*)

"In a room, Sybil, I go to you as a cold man to a fire. You fill me like a peal of bells in an empty house." (*She is being brutally treated by the dear impediment, for which hiccough is such an inadequate name that even to spell it is an abomination though a sign of ability. How to describe a sound that is noiseless? Let us put it thus, that when* SYBIL *wants to say something very much there are little obstacles in her way; she falters, falls per-*

haps once, and then is over, the while her appealing orbs beg you not to be angry with her. We may express those sweet pauses in precious dots, which some clever person can afterwards string together and make a pearl necklace of them.)

"I should not . . . let you say it, . . . but . . . you . . . say it so beautifully."

"You must have guessed."

"I dreamed . . . I feared . . . but you were . . . Scotch, and I didn't know what to think."

"Do you know what first attracted me to you, Sybil? It was your insolence. I thought, 'I'll break her insolence for her.' "

"And I thought . . . 'I'll break his str . . . ength!' "

"And now your cooing voice plays round me; the softness of you, Sybil, in your pretty clothes makes me think of young birds. (*The impediment is now insurmountable; she has to swim for it, she swims toward him*) It is you who inspire my work." (*He thrills to find that she can be touched without breaking.*)

"I am so glad . . . so proud . . ."

"And others know it, Sybil, as well as I. Only yesterday the Comtesse said to me, 'No man could get on so fast unaided. *Cherchez la femme,* Mr. Shand.' "

"Auntie said that!"

"I said 'Find her yourself, Comtesse.' "

"And she?"

"She said 'I have found her,' and I said in my blunt way, 'You mean Lady Sybil,' and she went away laughing."

"Laughing?"

"I seem to amuse the woman." (SYBIL *grows sad.*)

"If Mrs. Shand— It is so cruel to her. Whom did you say she had gone to the station to meet?"

"Her father and brothers."

"It is so cruel to them. We must think no more of this. It is mad . . . ness."

"It's fate. Sybil, let us declare our love openly."

"You can't ask that, now in the first moment that you tell me of it."

"The one thing I won't do even for you is to live a life of underhand."

"The . . . blow to her."

"Yes. But at least she has always known that I never loved her."

"It is asking me to give . . . up everything, every one, for you."

"It's too much." (JOHN *is humble at last.*)

"To a woman who truly loves, even that is not too much. Oh! it is not I who matter—it is you."

"My dear, my dear."

"So gladly would I do it to save you; but, oh, if it were to bring you down!"

"Nothing can keep me down if I have you to help me."

"I am dazed, John, I . . ."

"My love, my love."

"I . . . oh . . . here . . ."

"Be brave, Sybil, be brave."

". . . . ."

(*In this bewilderment of pearls she melts into his arms.* MAGGIE *happens to open the door just then; but neither fond heart hears her.*)

"I can't walk along the streets, Sybil, without looking in all the shop windows for what I think would become you best. (*As awkwardly as though his heart still beat against corduroy, he takes from his pocket a pendant and its chain. He is shy, and she drops pearls over the beauty of the ruby which is its only stone*) It is a drop of my blood, Sybil."
(*Her lovely neck is outstretched, and he puts the chain round it.* MAGGIE *withdraws as silently as she had come; but perhaps the door whispered "d–n," or (humorously) "d . . n" as it closed, for* SYBIL *wakes out of Paradise.*)

"I thought– Did the door shut?"

"It was shut already."
(*Perhaps it is only that* SYBIL *is bewildered to find herself once again in a world that has doors.*)

"It seemed to me–"

"There was nothing. But I think I hear voices; they may have arrived."

(*Some pretty instinct makes* SYBIL *go farther from him.* MAGGIE *kindly gives her time for this by speaking before opening the door.*)

"That will do perfectly, David. The maid knows where to put them. (*She comes in*) They've come, John; they *would* help with the luggage. (JOHN *goes out.* MAGGIE *is agreeably surprised to find a visitor*) How do you do, Lady Sybil? This is nice of you."

"I was so sorry not to find you in, Mrs. Shand." (*The impediment has run away. It is only for those who love it.*)

"Thank you. You'll sit down?"

"I think not; your relatives–"

"They will be so proud to see that you are my friend." (*If* MAGGIE *were less simple her guest would feel more comfortable. She tries to make conversation.*)

"It is their first visit to London?"
(*Instead of relieving her anxiety on this point,* MAGGIE *has a long look at the gorgeous armful.*)

"I'm glad you are so beautiful, Lady Sybil."
(*The beautiful one is somehow not flattered. She pursues her investigations with growing uneasiness.*)

"One of them is married now, isn't he? (*Still there is no answer;* MAGGIE *continues looking at her, and shivers slightly*) Have they travelled from Scotland to-day? Mrs. Shand, why do you look at me so? The door did open! (MAGGIE *nods*) What are you to do?"

"That would be telling. Sit down, my pretty."

(*As* SYBIL *subsides into what the Wylies with one glance would call the best chair,* MAGGIE'S *men-folk are brought in by* JOHN, *all carrying silk hats and looking very active after their long rest in the train. They are gazing about them. They would like this lady, they would like* JOHN, *they would even like* MAGGIE *to go away for a little and leave them to examine the room. Is that linen on the walls, for instance, or just paper? Is the carpet as thick as it feels, or is there brown paper beneath it? Had* MAGGIE *got anything off that bookcase on account of the worm-holes?* DAVID *even discovers that we were simpletons when we said there was nothing in the room that pretended to be what it was not. He taps the marble mantelpiece, and is favourably impressed by the tinny sound.*)

DAVID. Very fine imitation. It's a capital house, Maggie.

MAGGIE. I'm so glad you like it. Do you know one another? This is my father and my brothers, Lady Sybil.

(*The lovely form inclines toward them.* ALICK *and* JOHN *remain firm on their legs, but* JAMES *totters.*)

JAMES. A ladyship! Well done, Maggie.

ALICK (*sharply*). James! I remember you, my lady.

MAGGIE. Sit down, father. This is the study.

(JAMES *wanders round it inquisitively until called to order.*)

SYBIL. You must be tired after your long journey.

DAVID (*drawing the portraits of himself and partners in one lightning sketch*). Tired, your ladyship? We sat on cushioned seats the whole way.

JAMES (*looking about him for the chair you sit on*). Every seat in this room is cushioned.

MAGGIE. You may say all my life is cushioned now, James, by this dear man of mine. (*She gives* JOHN'S *shoulder a loving pressure, which* SYBIL *feels is a telegraphic communication to herself in a cypher that she cannot read.* ALICK *and the* BROTHERS *bask in the evidence of* MAGGIE'S *happiness.*)

JOHN (*uncomfortably*). And is Elizabeth hearty, James?

JAMES (*looking down his nose in the manner proper to young husbands when addressed about their wives*). She's very well, I thank you kindly.

MAGGIE. James is a married man now, Lady Sybil.

(SYBIL *murmurs her congratulations.*)

JAMES. I thank you kindly. (*Courageously*) Yes, I'm married. (*He looks at* DAVID *and* ALICK *to see if they are smiling; and they are*) It wasn't a case of being catched; it was entirely of my own free will. (*He looks again; and the mean fellows are smiling still*) Is your ladyship married?

SYBIL. Alas! no.

DAVID. James! (*Politely*) You will be yet, my lady.

(SYBIL *indicates that he is kind indeed.*)

JOHN. Perhaps they would like you to show them their rooms, Maggie?

DAVID. Fine would we like to see all the house as well as the sleeping accommodation. But first— (*He gives his father the look with which chairmen call on the next speaker.*)

ALICK. I take you, David. (*He produces a paper parcel from a roomy pocket*) It wasn't likely, Mr. Shand, that we would forget the day.

JOHN. The day?

DAVID. The second anniversary of your marriage. We came purposely for the day.

JAMES (*his fingers itching to take the parcel from his father*). It's a lace shawl, Maggie, from the three of us, a pure Tobermory; you would never dare wear it if you knew the cost.
(*The shawl in its beauty is revealed, and* MAGGIE *hails it with little cries of joy. She rushes at the donors and kisses each of them just as if she were a pretty woman. They are much pleased and give expression to their pleasure in a not very dissimilar manner.*)

ALICK. Havers.

DAVID. Havers.

JAMES. Havers.

JOHN. It's a very fine shawl. (*He should not have spoken, for he has set* JAMES's *volatile mind working.*)

JAMES. You may say so. What did you give her, Mr. Shand?

JOHN (*suddenly deserted by God and man*). Me?

ALICK. Yes, yes, let's see it.

JOHN. Oh–I–(*He is not deserted by* MAGGIE, *but she can think of no way out.*)

SYBIL (*prompted by the impediment, which is in hiding, quite close*). Did he . . . forget?
(*There is more than a touch of malice in the question. It is a challenge, and the Wylies as a family are almost too quick to accept a challenge.*)

MAGGIE (*lifting the gage of battle*). John forget? Never! It's a pendant, father.
(*The impediment bolts.* JOHN *rises.*)

ALICK. A pendant? One of those things on a chain? (*He grins, remembering how once, about sixty years ago, he and a lady and a pendant—but we have no time for this.*)

MAGGIE. Yes.

DAVID (*who has felt the note of antagonism and is troubled*). You were slow in speaking of it, Mr. Shand.

MAGGIE (*this is her fight*). He was shy, because he thought you might blame him for extravagance.

DAVID (*relieved*). Oh, that's it.

JAMES (*licking his lips*). Let's see it.

MAGGIE (*a daughter of the devil*). Where did you put it, John?

(JOHN'S *mouth opens but has nothing to contribute.*)

SYBIL (*the impediment has stolen back again*). Perhaps it has been . . . mislaid.
(*The* BROTHERS *echo the word incredulously.*)

MAGGIE. Not it. I can't think where we laid it down, John. It's not on that table, is it, James? (*The Wylies turn to look, and* MAGGIE'S *hand goes out to* LADY SYBIL: JOHN SHAND, *witness. It is a very determined hand, and presently a pendant is placed in it*) Here it is! (ALICK *and the* BROTHERS *cluster round it, weigh it and appraise it.*)

ALICK. Preserve me. Is that stone real, Mr. Shand?

JOHN (*who has begun to look his grimmest*). Yes.

MAGGIE (*who is now ready, if he wishes it, to take him on too*). John says it's a drop of his blood.

JOHN (*wishing it*). And so it is.

DAVID. Well said, Mr. Shand.

MAGGIE (*scared*). And now, if you'll all come with me, I think John has something he wants to talk over with Lady Sybil. (*Recovering and taking him on*) Or would you prefer, John, to say it before us all?

SYBIL (*gasping*). No!

JOHN (*flinging back his head*). Yes, I prefer to say it before you all.

MAGGIE. (*flinging back hers*). Then sit down again. (*The Wylies wonderingly obey.*)

SYBIL. Mr. Shand, Mr. Shand!—

JOHN. Maggie knows, and it was only for her I was troubled. Do you think I'm afraid of *them?* (*With mighty relief*) Now we can be open.

DAVID (*lowering*). What is it? What's wrong, John Shand?

JOHN (*facing him squarely*). It was to Lady Sybil I gave the pendant, and all my love with it. (*Perhaps* JAMES *utters a cry, but the silence of* ALICK *and* DAVID *is more terrible.*)

SYBIL (*whose voice is smaller than we had thought*). What are you to do? (*It is to* MAGGIE *she is speaking.*)

DAVID. She'll leave it for us to do.

JOHN. That's what I want.
(*The lords of creation look at the ladies.*)

MAGGIE (*interpreting*). You and I are expected to retire, Lady Sybil, while the men decide our fate. (SYBIL *is ready to obey the law, but* MAGGIE *remains seated*) Man's the oak, woman's the ivy. Which of us is it that's to cling to you, John?
(*With three stalwarts glaring at him,* JOHN *rather grandly takes* SYBIL'S *hand. They are two against the world.*)

SYBIL (*a heroine*). I hesitated, but I am afraid no longer; whatever he asks of me I will do. (*Evidently the first thing he asks of her is to await him in the dining-room*) It will mean surrendering everything for him. I am glad it means all that. (*She passes into the dining-room looking as pretty as a kiss.*)

MAGGIE. So that settles it.

ALICK. I'm thinking that doesn't settle it.

DAVID. No, by God! (*But his love for* MAGGIE *steadies him. There is even a note of entreaty in his voice*) Have you nothing to say to her, man?

JOHN. I have things to say to her, but not before you.

DAVID (*sternly*). Go away, Maggie. Leave him to us.

JAMES (*who thinks it is about time that he said something*). Yes, leave him to us.

MAGGIE. No, David, I want to hear what is to become of me; I promise not to take any side. (*And sitting by the fire she resumes her knitting. The four regard her as on an evening at The Pans a good many years ago.*)

DAVID (*barking*). How long has this been going on?

JOHN. If you mean how long has that lady been the apple of my eye, I'm not sure; but I never told her of it until today.

MAGGIE (*thoughtfully and without dropping a stitch*). I think it wasn't till about six months ago, John, that she began to be very dear to you. At first you liked to bring in her name when talking to me, so that I could tell you of any little things I might have heard she was doing. But afterwards, as she become more and more to you, you avoided mentioning her name.

JOHN (*surprised*). Did you notice that?

MAGGIE (*in her old-fashioned way*). Yes.

JOHN. I tried to be done with it for your sake. I've often had a sore heart for you, Maggie.

JAMES. You're proving it!

MAGGIE. Yes, James, he had. I've often seen him looking at me very sorrowfully of late because of what was in his mind; and many a kindly little thing he has done for me that he didn't used to do.

JOHN. You noticed that too!

MAGGIE. Yes.

DAVID (*controlling himself*). Well, we won't go into that; the thing to be thankful for is that it's ended.

ALICK (*who is looking very old*). Yes, yes, that's the great thing.

JOHN. All useless, sir, it's not ended; it's to go on.

DAVID. There's a devil in you, John Shand.

JOHN (*who is an unhappy man just now*). I dare say there is. But do you think he had a walk over, Mr. David?

JAMES. Man, I could knock you down!

MAGGIE. There's not one of you could knock John down.

DAVID (*exasperated*). Quiet, Maggie. One would think you were taking his part.

MAGGIE. Do you expect me to desert him at the very moment that he needs me most?

DAVID. It's him that's deserting you.

JOHN. Yes, Maggie, that's what it is.

ALICK. Where's your marriage vow? And your church attendances?

JAMES (*with terrible irony*). And your prize for moral philosophy?

JOHN (*recklessly*). All gone whistling down the wind.

DAVID. I suppose you understand that you'll have to resign your seat.

JOHN (*his underlip much in evidence*). There are hundreds of seats, but there's only one John Shand.

MAGGIE (*but we don't hear her*). That's how I like to hear him speak.

DAVID (*the ablest person in the room*). Think, man, I'm old by you, and for long I've had a pride in you. It will be beginning the world again with more against you than there was eight years ago.

JOHN. I have a better head to begin it with than I had eight years ago.

ALICK (*hoping this will bite*). She'll have her own money, David!

JOHN. She's as poor as a mouse.

JAMES (*thinking possibly of his Elizabeth's mother*). We'll go to her friends, and tell them all. They'll stop it.

JOHN. She's of age.

JAMES. They'll take her far away.

JOHN. I'll follow, and tear her from them.

ALICK. Your career—

JOHN (*to his credit*). To hell with my career. Do you think I don't know I'm on the rocks. What can you, or you, or you, understand of the passions of a man! I've fought, and I've given in. When a ship founders, as I suppose I'm foundering, it's not a thing to yelp at. Peace all of you. (*He strides into the dining-room, where we see him at times pacing the floor.*)

DAVID (*to* JAMES, *who gives signs of a desire to take off his coat*). Let him be. We can't budge him. (*With bitter wisdom*) It's true what he says, true at any rate about me. What do I know of the passions of a man! I'm up against something I don't understand.

ALICK. It's something wicked.

DAVID. I dare say it is, but it's something big.

JAMES. It's that damned charm.

MAGGIE (*still by the fire*). That's it. What was it that made you fancy Elizabeth, James?

JAMES (*sheepishly*). I can scarcely say.

MAGGIE. It was her charm.

DAVID. *Her* charm!

JAMES (*pugnaciously*). Yes, *her* charm.

MAGGIE. She had charm for James. (*This somehow breaks them up.* MAGGIE *goes from one to another with an odd little smile flickering on her face.*)

DAVID. Put on your things, Maggie, and we'll leave his house.

MAGGIE (*patting his kind head*). Not me, David. (*This is a* MAGGIE *they have known but forgotten; all three brighten.*)

DAVID. You haven't given in!
(*The smile flickers and expires.*)

MAGGIE. I want you all to go upstairs, and let me have my try now.

JAMES. Your try?

ALICK. Maggie, you put new life into me.

JAMES. And into me.
(DAVID *says nothing; the way he grips her shoulder says it for him.*)

MAGGIE. I'll save him, David, if I can.

DAVID. Does he deserve to be saved after the way he has treated you?

MAGGIE. You stupid David. What has that to do with it.
(*When they have gone,* JOHN *comes to the door of the dining-room. There is welling up in him a great pity for* MAGGIE, *but it has to subside a little when he sees that the knitting is still in her hand. No man likes to be so soon supplanted.* SYBIL *follows, and the two of them gaze at the active needles.*)

MAGGIE (*perceiving that she has visitors*). Come in, John. Sit down, Lady Sybil, and make yourself comfortable. I'm afraid we've put you about. (*She is, after all, only a few years older than they and scarcely looks her age; yet it must have been in some such way as this that the little old woman who lived in a shoe addressed her numerous progeny.*)

JOHN. I'm mortal sorry, Maggie.

SYBIL (*who would be more courageous if she could hold his hand*). And I also.

MAGGIE (*soothingly*). I'm sure you are. But as it can't be helped I see no reason why we three shouldn't talk the matter over in a practical way.
(SYBIL *looks doubtful, but* JOHN *hangs on desperately to the word practical.*)

JOHN. If you could understand, Maggie, what an inspiration she is to me and my work.

SYBIL. Indeed, Mrs. Shand, I think of nothing else.

MAGGIE. That's fine. That's as it should be.

SYBIL (*talking too much*). Mrs. Shand, I think you are very kind to take it so reasonably.

MAGGIE. That's the Scotch way. When were you thinking of leaving me, John?
(*Perhaps this is the Scotch way also; but* SYBIL *is English, and from the manner in which she starts you would say that something has fallen on her toes.*)

JOHN (*who has heard nothing fall*). I think, now that it has come to a breach, the sooner the better. (*His tone becomes that of* JAMES *when asked after the health of his wife*) So long as it is convenient to you, Maggie.

MAGGIE (*making a rapid calculation*). It couldn't well be before Wednesday. That's the day the laundry comes home.
(SYBIL *has to draw in her toes again.*)

JOHN. And it's the day the House rises. (*Stifling a groan*) It may be my last appearance in the House.

SYBIL (*her arms yearning for him*). No, no, please don't say that.

MAGGIE (*surveying them sympathetically*). You love the House, don't you, John, next to her? It's a pity you can't wait till after your speech at Leeds. Mr. Venables won't let you speak at Leeds, I fear, if you leave me.

JOHN. What a chance it would have been. But let it go.

MAGGIE. The meeting is in less than a month. Could you not make it such a speech that they would be very loth to lose you?

JOHN (*swelling*). That's what was in my mind.

SYBIL (*with noble confidence*). And he could have done it.

MAGGIE. Then we've come to something practical.

JOHN (*exercising his imagination with powerful effect*). No, it wouldn't be fair to you if I was to stay on now.

MAGGIE. Do you think I'll let myself be considered when your career is at stake. A month will soon pass for me; I'll have a lot of packing to do.

JOHN. It's noble of you, but I don't deserve it, and I can't take it from you.

MAGGIE. Now's the time, Lady Sybil, for you to have one of your inspiring ideas.

SYBIL (*ever ready*). Yes, yes—but what?
(*It is odd that they should both turn to* MAGGIE *at this moment.*)

MAGGIE (*who has already been saying it to herself*). What do you think of this: I can stay on here with my father and brothers; and you, John, can go away somewhere and devote yourself to your speech?

SYBIL. Yes.

JOHN. That might be. (*Considerately*) Away from both of you. Where could I go?

SYBIL (*ever ready*). Where?

MAGGIE. I know.
(*She has called up a number on the telephone before they have time to check her.*)

JOHN (*on his dignity*). Don't be in such a hurry, Maggie.

MAGGIE. Is this Lamb's Hotel? Put me on to the Comtesse de la Brière, please.

SYBIL (*with a sinking*). What do you want with Auntie?

MAGGIE. Her cottage in the country would be the very place. She invited John and me.

JOHN. Yes, but—

MAGGIE (*arguing*). And Mr. Venables is to be there. Think of the impression you could make on *him*, seeing him daily for three weeks.

JOHN. There's something in that.

MAGGIE. Is it you, Comtesse? I'm Maggie Shand.

SYBIL. You are not to tell her that—?

MAGGIE. No. (*To the* COMTESSE) Oh, I'm very well, never was better. Yes, yes; you see I can't, because my folk have never been in London before, and I must take them about and show them the sights. But John could come to you alone; why not?

JOHN (*with proper pride*). If she's not keen to have me, I won't go.

MAGGIE. She's very keen. Comtesse, I could come for a day by and by to see how you are getting on. Yes—yes—certainly. (*To* JOHN) She says she'll be delighted.

JOHN (*thoughtfully*). You're not doing this, Maggie, thinking that my being absent from Sybil for a few weeks can make any difference? Of course it's natural you should want us to keep apart, but—

MAGGIE (*grimly*). I'm founding no hope on keeping you apart, John.

JOHN. It's what other wives would do.

MAGGIE. I promised to be different.

JOHN (*his position as a strong man assured*). Then tell her I accept. (*He wanders back into the dining-room.*)

SYBIL. I think—(*she is not sure what she thinks*)—I think you are very wonderful.

MAGGIE. Was that John calling to you?

SYBIL. Was it? (*She is glad to join him in the dining-room.*)

MAGGIE. Comtesse, hold the line a minute—(*She is alone, and she has nearly reached the end of her self-control. She shakes emotionally and utters painful little cries; there is something she wants to do, and she is loth to do it. But she does it*) Are you there, Comtesse? There's one other thing, dear Comtesse; I want you to invite Lady Sybil also; yes, for the whole time that John is there. No, I'm not mad; as a great favour to me; yes, I have a very particular reason, but I won't tell you what it is; oh, call me Scotchy as much as you like, but consent; do, do, do. Thank you, thank you, good-bye.
(*She has control of herself now, and is determined not to let it slip from her again. When they reappear the stubborn one is writing a letter.*)

JOHN. I thought I heard the telephone again.

MAGGIE (*looking up from her labours*). It was the Comtesse; she says she's to invite Lady Sybil to the cottage at the same time.

SYBIL. Me!

JOHN. To invite Sybil? Then of course I won't go, Maggie.

MAGGIE (*wondering seemingly at these niceties*). What does it matter? Is anything to be considered except the speech? (*It has been admitted that she was a little devil*) And, with Sybil on the spot, John, *to help you and inspire you*, what a speech it will be!

JOHN (*carried away*). Maggie, you really are a very generous woman.

SYBIL (*convinced at last*). She is indeed.

JOHN. And you're queer too. How many women in the circumstances would sit down to write a letter.

MAGGIE. It's a letter to you, John.

JOHN. To me?

MAGGIE. I'll give it to you when it's finished, but I ask you not to open it till your visit to the Comtesse ends.

JOHN. What is it about?

MAGGIE. It's practical.

SYBIL (*rather faintly*). Practical? (*She has heard the word so frequently today that it is beginning to have a Scotch sound. She feels she ought to like* MAGGIE, *but that she would like her better if they were farther apart. She indicates that the doctors are troubled about her heart, and murmuring her adieux she goes.* JOHN, *who is accompanying her, pauses at the door.*)

JOHN (*with a queer sort of admiration for his wife*). Maggie, I wish I was fond of you.

MAGGIE (*heartily*). I wish you were, John.

(*He goes, and she resumes her letter. The stocking is lying at hand, and she pushes it to the floor. She is done for a time with knitting.*)

ACT FOUR

Man's greatest invention is the lawn-mower. All the birds know this, and that is why, when it is at rest, there is always at least one of them sitting on the handle with his head cocked, wondering how the delicious whirring sound is made. When they find out, they will change their note. As it is, you must sometimes have thought that you heard the mower very early in the morning, and perhaps you peeped in négligé *from your lattice window to see who was up so early. It was really the birds trying to get the note.*

On this broiling morning, however, we are at noon, and whoever looks will see that the whirring is done by MR. VENABLES. *He is in a linen suit with the coat discarded (the bird is sitting on it), and he comes and goes across the* COMTESSE'S *lawns, pleasantly mopping his face. We see him through a crooked bowed window generously open, roses intruding into it as if to prevent its ever being closed at night; there are other roses in such armfuls on the tables that one could not easily say where the room ends and the garden begins.*

In the COMTESSE'S *pretty comic drawing-room (for she likes the comic touch when she is in England) sits* JOHN SHAND *with his hostess, on chairs at a great distance from each other. No linen garments for* JOHN, *nor flannels, nor even knickerbockers; he envies the English way of dressing for trees and lawns, but is too Scotch to be able to imitate it; he wears tweeds, just as he would do in his native country where they would be in kilts. Like many another Scot, the first time he ever saw a kilt was on a Sassenach; indeed kilts were only invented, like golf, to draw the English north.* JOHN *is doing nothing, which again is not a Scotch accomplishment, and he looks rather miserable and dour. The* COMTESSE *is already at her Patience cards, and occasionally she smiles on him as if not displeased with his long silence. At last she speaks:*

"I feel it rather a shame to detain you here on such a lovely day, Mr. Shand, entertaining an old woman."

"I don't pretend to think I'm entertaining you, Comtesse."

"But you *are*, you know."

"I would be pleased to be told how?"

(*She shrugs her impertinent shoulders, and presently there is another heavy sigh from* JOHN.)

"Again! Why do not you go out on the river?"

"Yes, I can do that." (*He rises.*)

"And take Sybil with you." (*He sits again*) "No?"

"I have been on the river with her twenty times."

"Then take her for a long walk through the Fairloe woods."

"We were there twice last week."

"There is a romantically damp little arbour at the end of what the villagers call the Lovers' Lane."

"One can't go there every day. I see nothing to laugh at."

"Did I laugh? I must have been translating the situation into French."

(*Perhaps the music of the lawn-mower is not to* JOHN'S *mood, for he betakes himself to another room.* MR. VENABLES *pauses in his labours to greet a lady who has appeared on the lawn, and who is* MAGGIE. *She is as neat as if she were one of the army of typists (who are quite the nicest kind of women), and carries a little bag. She comes in through the window, and puts her hands over the* COMTESSE'S *eyes. The* COMTESSE *says:*)

"They are a strong pair of hands, at any rate."

"And not very white, and biggish for my size. Now guess."

(*The* COMTESSE *guesses, and takes*

both the hands in hers as if she valued them. She pulls off MAGGIE's *hat as if to prevent her flying away.*)

"Dear abominable one, not to let me know you were coming.'"

"It is just a surprise visit, Comtesse. I walked up from the station. (*For a moment* MAGGIE *seems to have borrowed* SYBIL's *impediment*) How is—everybody?"

"He is quite well. But, my child, he seems to me to be a most unhappy man."
(*This sad news does not seem to make a most unhappy woman of the child. The* COMTESSE *is puzzled, as she knows nothing of the situation save what she has discovered for herself.*)

"Why should that please you, O heartless one?"

"I won't tell you."

"I could take you and shake you, Maggie. Here have I put my house at your disposal for so many days for some sly Scotch purpose, and you will not tell me what it is."

"No."

"Very well then, but I have what you call a nasty one for you. (*The* COMTESSE *lures* MR. VENABLES *into the room by holding up what might be a foaming glass of lemon squash*) Alas, Charles, it is but a flower vase. I want you to tell Mrs. Shand what you think of her husband's speech."
(MR. VENABLES *gives his hostess a reproachful look.*)

"Eh—ah—Shand will prefer to do that himself. I promised the gardener—I must not disappoint him—excuse me—"

"You must tell her, Charles."

"Please, Mr. Venables, I should like to know."
(*He sits down with a sigh and obeys.*)

"Your husband has been writing the speech here, and by his own wish he read it to me three days ago. The occasion is to be an important one; and, well, there are a dozen young men in the party at present, all capable of filling a certain small ministerial post. (*He looks longingly at the mower, but it sends no message to his aid*) And as he is one of them I was anxious that he should show in this speech of what he is capable."

"And hasn't he?"
(*Not for the first time* MR. VENABLES *wishes that he was not in politics.*)

"I am afraid he has."

"What is wrong with the speech, Charles?"

"Nothing—and he can still deliver it. It is a powerful, well-thought-out piece of work, such as only a very able man could produce. But it has no *special quality* of its own —none of the little touches that used to make an old stager like myself want to pat Shand on the shoulder. (*The* COMTESSE's *mouth twitches, but* MAGGIE *declines to notice it*) He pounds on manfully enough, but, if I may say so, with a wooden leg. It is as good, I dare say, as the rest of them could have done; but they start with such inherited advantages, Mrs. Shand, that he had to do better."

"Yes, I can understand that."

"I am sorry, Mrs. Shand, for he interested me. His career has set me wondering whether if *I* had begun as a railway porter I might not still be calling out, 'By your leave.'"
(MAGGIE *thinks it probable but not important.*)

"Mr. Venables, now that I think of it, surely John wrote to me that you were dissatisfied with his first speech, and that he was writing another."
(*The* COMTESSE'S *eyes open very wide indeed.*)

"I have heard nothing of that, Mrs. Shand. (VENABLES *shakes his wise head*) And in any case, I am afraid—" (*He still hears the wooden leg.*)

"But you said yourself that his second thoughts were sometimes such an improvement on the first."
(*The* COMTESSE *comes to the help of the baggage.*)

"I remember your saying that, Charles."

"Yes, that has struck me. (*Politely*) Well, if he has anything to show me— In the meantime—"
(*He regains the lawn, like one glad to escape attendance at* JOHN'S *obsequies. The* COMTESSE *is brought back to speech by the sound of the mower—nothing wooden in it.*)

"What are you up to now, Miss Pin? You know as well as I do that there is no such speech."
(MAGGIE'S *mouth tightens.*)

"I do not."

"It is a duel, is it, my friend?"
(*The* COMTESSE *rings the bell and* MAGGIE'S *guilty mind is agitated.*)

"What are you ringing for?"

"As the challenged one, Miss Pin, I have the choice of weapons. I am going to send for your husband to ask him if he has written such a speech. After which, I suppose, *you* will ask me to leave you while you and he write it together."
(MAGGIE *wrings her hands.*)

"You are wrong, Comtesse; but please don't do that."

"You but make me more curious, and my doctor says that I must be told everything. (*The* COMTESSE *assumes the pose of her sex in melodrama*) Put your cards on the table, Maggie Shand, *or*—(*she indicates that she always pinks her man.* MAGGIE *dolefully produces a roll of paper from her bag*) What precisely is that?"
(*The reply is little more than a squeak.*)

"John's speech."

"You have written it yourself!"
(MAGGIE *is naturally indignant.*)

"It's typed."

"You guessed that the speech he wrote unaided would not satisfy, and you prepared this to take its place!"

"Not at all, Comtesse. It is the draft of his speech that he left at home. That's all."

"With a few trivial alterations by yourself, I swear. Can you deny it?"
(*No wonder that* MAGGIE *is outraged. She replaces* JOHN'S *speech in the bag with becoming hauteur.*)

"Comtesse, these insinuations are unworthy of you. May I ask where is my husband?"
(*The* COMTESSE *drops her a curtsy.*)

"I believe your Haughtiness may find him in the Dutch garden. Oh, I see through you. You are not to show him your speech. But you are to get him to write another one, and somehow all your additions will be in it. Think not, creature, that you can deceive one so old in iniquity as the Comtesse de la Brière."
(*There can be but one reply from a good wife to such a charge, and at once the* COMTESSE *is left alone with her shame. Anon a footman appears. You know how they come and go.*)

"You rang, my lady?"

"Did I? Ah, yes, but why? (*He is but lately from the ploughshare and cannot help her. In this quandary her eyes alight upon the bag. She is unfortunately too abandoned to feel her shame: she still thinks that she has the choice of weapons. She takes the speech from the bag and bestows it on her servitor*) Take this to Mr. Venables, please, and say it is from Mr. Shand. (THOMAS—*but in the end we shall probably call him* JOHN—*departs with the little explosive; and when* MAGGIE *returns she finds that the* COMTESSE *is once more engaged on her interrupted game of Patience*) You did not find him?"
(*All the bravery has dropped from* MAGGIE'S *face.*)

"I didn't see him, but I heard him. *She* is with him. I think they are coming here."
(*The* COMTESSE *is suddenly kind again.*)

"Sybil? Shall I get rid of her?"

"No, I want her to be here, too. Now I shall know."
(*The* COMTESSE *twists the little thing round.*)

"Know what?"

"As soon as I look into his face I shall know."
(*A delicious scent ushers in the fair* SYBIL, *who is as sweet as a milking stool. She greets* MRS. SHAND *with some alarm.*)

MAGGIE. How do you do, Lady Sybil? How pretty you look in that frock. (SYBIL *rustles uncomfortably*) You are a feast to the eye.

SYBIL. Please, I wish you would not.
(*Shall we describe* SYBIL'S *frock, in which she looks like a great strawberry that knows it ought to be plucked; or would it be easier to watch the coming of* JOHN? *Let us watch* JOHN.)

JOHN. You, Maggie! You never wrote that you were coming.
(*No, let us watch* MAGGIE. *As soon as she looked into his face she was to know something of importance.*)

MAGGIE (*not dissatisfied with what she sees*). No, John, it's a surprise visit. I just ran down to say good-bye.
(*At this his face falls, which does not seem to pain her.*)

SYBIL (*foreseeing another horrible Scotch scene*). To say good-bye?

COMTESSE (*thrilling with expectation*). To whom, Maggie?

SYBIL (*deserted by the impediment, which is probably playing with rough boys in the Lovers' Lane*). Auntie, do leave us, won't you?

COMTESSE. Not I. It is becoming far too interesting.

MAGGIE. I suppose there's no reason the Comtesse shouldn't be told, as she will know so soon at any rate?

JOHN. That's so. (SYBIL *sees with a sinking that he is to be practical also.*)

MAGGIE. It's so simple. You see, Comtesse, John and Lady Sybil have fallen in love with one another, and they are to go off as soon as the meeting at Leeds has taken place.
(*The* COMTESSE'S *breast is too suddenly introduced to Caledonia and its varied charms.*)

COMTESSE. Mon Dieu!

MAGGIE. I think that's putting it correctly, John.

JOHN. In a sense. But I'm not to attend the meeting at Leeds. My speech doesn't find favour. (*With a strange humility*) There's something wrong with it.

COMTESSE. I never expected to hear you say that, Mr. Shand.

JOHN (*wondering also*). I never expected it myself. I meant to make it the speech of my career. But somehow my hand seems to have lost its cunning.

COMTESSE. And you don't know how?

JOHN. It's inexplicable. My brain was never clearer.

COMTESSE. You might have helped him, Sybil.

SYBIL (*quite sulkily*). I did.

COMTESSE. But I thought she was such an inspiration to you, Mr. Shand.

JOHN (*going bravely to* SYBIL'S *side*). She slaved at it with me.

COMTESSE. Strange. (*Wickedly becoming practical also*) So now there is nothing to detain you. Shall I send for a fly, Sybil?

SYBIL (*with a cry of the heart*). Auntie, do leave us.

COMTESSE. I can understand your impatience to be gone, Mr. Shand.

JOHN (*heavily*). I promised Maggie to wait till the 24th, and I'm a man of my word.

MAGGIE. But I give you back your word, John. You can go now.
(JOHN *looks at* SYBIL, *and* SYBIL *looks at* JOHN, *and the impediment*

arrives in time to take a peep at both of them.)

SYBIL (*groping for the practical, to which we must all come in the end*). He must make satisfactory arrangements about you first. I insist on that.

MAGGIE (*with no more imagination than a hen*). Thank you, Lady Sybil, but I have made all my arrangements.

JOHN (*stung*). Maggie, that was my part.

MAGGIE (*the hens are saying it all the time*). You see, my brothers feel they can't be away from their business any longer; and so, if it would be convenient to you, John, I could travel north with them by the night train on Wednesday.

SYBIL. I–I–. The way you put things–!

JOHN. This is just the 21st.

MAGGIE. My things are all packed. I think you'll find the house in good order, Lady Sybil. I have had the vacuum cleaners in. I'll give you the keys of the linen and the silver plate; I have them in that bag. The carpet on the upper landing is a good deal frayed, but–

SYBIL. Please, I don't want to hear any more.

MAGGIE. The ceiling of the dining-room would be the better of a new lick of paint–

SYBIL (*stamping her foot, small fours*). Can't you stop her?

JOHN (*soothingly*). She's meaning well. Maggie, I know it's natural to you to value those things, because your outlook on life is bounded by them; but all this jars on me.

MAGGIE. Does it?

JOHN. Why should you be so ready to go?

MAGGIE. I promised not to stand in your way.

JOHN (*stoutly*). You needn't be in such a hurry. There are three days to run yet. (*The French are so different from us that we shall probably never be able to understand why the* COMTESSE *laughed aloud here*) It's just a joke to the Comtesse.

COMTESSE. It seems to be no joke to you, Mr. Shand. Sybil, my pet, are you to let him off?

SYBIL (*flashing*). Let him off? If he wishes it. Do you?

JOHN (*manfully*). I want it to go on. (*Something seems to have caught in his throat: perhaps it is the impediment trying a temporary home*) It's the one wish of my heart. If you come with me, Sybil, I'll do all in a man's power to make you never regret it.
(*Triumph of the Vere de Veres.*)

MAGGIE (*bringing them back to earth with a dump*). And I can make my arrangements for Wednesday?

SYBIL (*seeking the* COMTESSE'*s protection*). No, you can't. Auntie, I am not going on with this. I'm very

sorry for you, John, but I see now —I couldn't face it—
(*She can't face anything at this moment except the sofa pillows.*)

COMTESSE (*noticing* JOHN'S *big sigh of relief*). So *that* is all right, Mr. Shand!

MAGGIE. Don't you love her any more, John? Be practical.

SYBIL (*to the pillows*). At any rate I have tired of him. Oh, best to tell the horrid truth. I am ashamed of myself. I have been crying my eyes out over it—I thought I was such a different kind of woman. But I am weary of him. I think him—oh, so dull.

JOHN (*his face lighting up*). Are you sure that is how you have come to think of me?

SYBIL. I'm sorry; (*With all her soul*) but yes—yes—yes.

JOHN. By God, it's more than I deserve.

COMTESSE. Congratulations to you both.
(SYBIL *runs away; and in the fulness of time she married successfully in Cloth of Silver, which was afterwards turned into a bedspread.*)

MAGGIE. You haven't read my letter yet, John, have you?

JOHN. No.

COMTESSE (*imploringly*). May I know to what darling letter you refer?

MAGGIE. It's a letter I wrote to him before he left London. I gave it to him closed, not to be opened until his time here was ended.

JOHN (*as his hand strays to his pocket*). Am I to read it now?

MAGGIE. Not before her. Please go away, Comtesse.

COMTESSE. Every word you say makes me more determined to remain.

MAGGIE. It will hurt you. (*Distressed*) Don't read it, John; tear it up.

JOHN. You make me very curious, Maggie. And yet I don't see what can be in it.

COMTESSE. But you feel a little nervous? Give *me* the dagger.

MAGGIE (*quickly*). No. (*But the* COMTESSE *has already got it.*)

COMTESSE. May I? (*She must have thought they said Yes, for she opens the letter. She shares its contents with them*) "Dearest John, It is at my request that the Comtesse is having Lady Sybil at the cottage at the same time as yourself."

JOHN. What?

COMTESSE. Yes, she begged me to invite you together.

JOHN. But why?

MAGGIE. I promised you not to behave as other wives would do.

JOHN. It's not understandable.

COMTESSE. "You may ask why I do this, John, and my reason is, I think that after a few weeks of Lady Sybil, every day, and all day, you will become sick to death of her. I am also giving her the chance to help you and inspire you with your work, so that you may both learn what her help and her inspiration amount to. Of course, if your love is the great strong passion you think it, then those weeks will make you love her more than ever and I can only say good-bye. But if, as I suspect, you don't even now know what true love is, then by the next time we meet, dear John, you will have had enough of her.—Your affectionate wife, MAGGIE." Oh, why was not Sybil present at the reading of the will! And now, if you two will kindly excuse me, I think I must go and get that poor sufferer the eau de Cologne.

JOHN. It's almost enough to make a man lose faith in himself.

COMTESSE. Oh, don't say that, Mr. Shand.

MAGGIE (*defending him*). You mustn't hurt him. If you haven't loved deep and true, that's just because you have never met a woman yet, John, capable of inspiring it.

COMTESSE (*putting her hand on* MAGGIE'S *shoulder*). Have you not, Mr. Shand?

JOHN. I see what you mean. But Maggie wouldn't think better of me for any false pretences. She knows my feelings for her now are neither more nor less than what they have always been.

MAGGIE (*who sees that he is looking at her as solemnly as a volume of sermons printed by request*). I think no one could be fond of me that can't laugh a little at me.

JOHN. How could that help?

COMTESSE (*exasperated*). Mr. Shand, I give you up.

MAGGIE. I admire his honesty.

COMTESSE. Oh, I give you up also. Arcades ambo. Scotchies both.

JOHN (*when she has gone*). But this letter, it's not like you. By Gosh, Maggie, you're no fool.
(*She beams at this, as any wife would.*)
But how could I have made such a mistake? It's not like a strong man. (*Evidently he has an inspiration.*)

MAGGIE. What is it?

JOHN (*the inspiration*). *Am* I a strong man?

MAGGIE. You? Of course you are. And self made. Has anybody ever helped you in the smallest way?

JOHN (*thinking it out again*). No, nobody.

MAGGIE. Not even Lady Sybil?

JOHN. I'm beginning to doubt it. It's very curious, though, Maggie, that this speech should be disappointing.

MAGGIE. It's just that Mr. Venables hasn't the brains to see how good it is.

JOHN. That must be it. (*But he is too good a man to rest satisfied with this*) No, Maggie, it's not. Somehow I seem to have lost my neat way of saying things.

MAGGIE (*almost cooing*). It will come back to you.

JOHN (*forlorn*). If you knew how I've tried.

MAGGIE (*cautiously*). Maybe if you were to try again; and I'll just come and sit beside you, and knit. I think the click of the needles sometimes put you in the mood.

JOHN. Hardly that; and yet many a Shandism have I knocked off while you were sitting beside me knitting. I suppose it was the quietness.

MAGGIE. Very likely.

JOHN (*with another inspiration*). Maggie!

MAGGIE (*again*). What is it, John?

JOHN. What if it was you that put those queer ideas into my head!

MAGGIE. Me?

JOHN. Without your knowing it, I mean.

MAGGIE. But how?

JOHN. We used to talk bits over; and it may be that you dropped the seed, so to speak.

MAGGIE. John, could it be this, that I sometimes had the idea in a rough womanish sort of way and then you polished it up till it came out a Shandism?

JOHN (*slowly slapping his knee*). I believe you've hit it, Maggie: to think that you may have been helping me all the time—and neither of us knew it.

(*He has so nearly reached a smile that no one can say what might have happened within the next moment if the* COMTESSE *had not reappeared.*)

COMTESSE. Mr. Venables wishes to see you, Mr. Shand.

JOHN (*lost, stolen, or strayed a smile in the making*). Hum.

COMTESSE. He is coming now.

JOHN (*grumpy*). Indeed.

COMTESSE (*sweetly*). It is about your speech.

JOHN. He has said all he need say on that subject, and more.

COMTESSE (*quaking a little*). I think it is about the second speech.

JOHN. What second speech?

(MAGGIE *runs to her bag and opens it.*)

MAGGIE (*horrified*). Comtesse, you have given it to him.

COMTESSE (*impudently*). Wasn't I meant to?

JOHN. What is it? What second speech?

MAGGIE. Cruel, cruel. (*Willing to go on her knees*) You had left the first draft of your speech at home, John, and I brought it here with—with a few little things I've added myself.

JOHN (*a seven-footer*). What's that?

MAGGIE (*four foot ten at most*). Just trifles—things I was to suggest to you—while I was knitting—and then, if you liked any of them you could have polished them—and turned them into something good. John, John—and now she has shown it to Mr. Venables.

JOHN (*thundering*). As my work, Comtesse?
(*But the* COMTESSE *is not of the women who are afraid of thunder.*)

MAGGIE. It is your work—nine-tenths of it.

JOHN (*in the black cap*). You presumed, Maggie Shand! Very well, then, here he comes, and now we'll see to what extent you've helped me.

VENABLES. My dear fellow. My dear Shand, I congratulate you. Give me your hand.

JOHN. The speech?

VENABLES. You have improved it out of knowledge. It is the same speech, but those new touches make all the difference. (JOHN *sits down heavily*) Mrs. Shand, be proud of him.

MAGGIE. I am. I am, John.

COMTESSE. You always said that his second thoughts were best, Charles.

VENABLES (*pleased to be reminded of it*). Didn't I? didn't I? Those delicious little touches! How good that is, Shand, about the flowing tide.

COMTESSE. The flowing tide?

VENABLES. In the first speech it was something like this—"Gentlemen, the Opposition are calling to you to vote for them and the flowing tide, but I solemnly warn you to beware lest the flowing tide does not engulf you." The second way is much better.

COMTESSE. What is the second way, Mr. Shand?
(JOHN *does not tell her.*)

VENABLES. This is how he puts it now. (JOHN *cannot help raising his head to listen*) "Gentlemen, the Opposition are calling to you to vote for them and the flowing tide, but I ask you cheerfully to vote for us and *dam* the flowing tide."
(VENABLES *and his old friend the* COMTESSE *laugh heartily, but for different reasons.*)

COMTESSE. It *is* better, Mr. Shand.

MAGGIE. *I* don't think so.

VENABLES. Yes, yes, it's so virile. Excuse me, Comtesse, I'm off to read the whole thing again. (*For the first time he notices that* JOHN *is strangely quiet*) I think this has rather bowled you over, Shand.
(JOHN'S *head sinks lower.*)
Well, well, good news doesn't kill.

MAGGIE (*counsel for the defence*). Surely the important thing about the speech is its strength and knowledge and eloquence, the things that were in the first speech as well as in the second.

VENABLES. That of course is largely true. The wit would not be enough without them, just as they were not enough without the wit. It is the combination that is irresistible. (JOHN'S *head rises a little*) Shand, you are our man, remember that, it is emphatically the best thing you have ever done. How this will go down at Leeds.

(*He returns gaily to his hammock; but lower sinks* JOHN'S *head, and even the* COMTESSE *has the grace to take herself off.* MAGGIE'S *arms flutter near her husband, not daring to alight.*)

"You heard what he said, John. It's the combination. Is it so terrible to you to find that my love for you had made me able to help you in the little things?"

"The little things! It seems strange to me to hear you call me by my name, Maggie. It's as if I looked on you for the first time."

"Look at me, John, for the first time. What do you see?"

"I see a woman who has brought her husband low."

"Only that?"

"I see the tragedy of a man who has found himself out. Eh, I can't live with you again, Maggie."

(*He shivers.*)

"Why did you shiver, John?"

"It was at myself for saying that I couldn't live with you again, when I should have been wondering how for so long you have lived with me. And I suppose you have forgiven me all the time. (*She nods*) And forgive me still? (*She nods again*) Dear God!"

"John, am I to go? or are you to keep me on? (*She is now a little bundle near his feet*) I'm willing to stay because I'm useful to you, if it can't be for a better reason. (*His hand feels for her, and the bundle wriggles nearer*) It's nothing unusual I've done, John. Every man who is high up loves to think that he has done it all himself; and the wife smiles, and lets it go at that. It's our only joke. Every woman knows that. (*He stares at her in hopeless perplexity*) Oh, John, if only you could laugh at me."

"I can't laugh, Maggie."

(*But as he continues to stare at her a strange disorder appears in his face.* MAGGIE *feels that it is to be now or never.*)

"Laugh, John, laugh. Watch me; see how easy it is."

(*A terrible struggle is taking place within him. He creaks. Something that may be mirth forces a passage, at first painfully, no more joy in it than in the discoloured water from a spring that has long been dry. Soon, however, he laughs loud and long. The spring water is becoming clear.* MAGGIE *claps her hands. He is saved.*)

Milestones

BY ARNOLD BENNETT AND
EDWARD KNOBLOCK

TO

FRANK VERNON

WHO HAVING BROUGHT THE AUTHORS TOGETHER INSTRUCTED THEM TO COLLABORATE IN A PLAY AND WHO WHEN THEY HAD OBEYED HIM PUT THE PLAY ON THE STAGE WITH AN ART WHICH EVOKED THEIR LIVELIEST GRATITUDE

Milestones was first produced in America at the Liberty Theatre, New York City, by Klaw and Erlanger on September 17, 1912, and closed on March 22, 1913. The following is the original cast:

JOHN RHEAD	Leslie Faber
GERTRUDE RHEAD	Auriol Lee
MRS. RHEAD	Eugenie Vernie
ROSE SIBLEY ROSE RHEAD	Gillian Scaife
SAMUEL SIBLEY	Warburton Gamble
EMILY RHEAD LADY MONKHURST	Gladys Mason
NED PYM LORD MONKHURST	A. G. Onslow
LORD MONKHURST	Douglas Imbert
NANCY SIBLEY	Edith Barwell
RICHARD SIBLEY	Frank Arundel
ARTHUR PREECE	Frederick Lloyd
THOMPSON	William O. Fazan
WEBSTER	Frederick Penley

Directed by Frank Vernon

SCENE

The Scene is laid throughout in the drawing-room of a house in Kensington Gore.

The First Act is in 1860

The Second Act is in 1885

The Third Act is in 1912

MILESTONES

ACT ONE

1860

The Scene represents the drawing-room of a house in Kensington Gore. The house is quite new at the time: all the decorations, pictures and furniture are of the mid-Victorian period. On the left three long windows look out on Kensington Gardens. On the right a large double door leads into the back drawing-room. A single door on the same side of the room leads to the hall and stairs. In the centre at back a large fireplace with a fire burning in it. The blinds and curtains are drawn; the lamps are lighted.

It is about half-past nine at night of the 29th of December, 1860.

MRS. RHEAD, *a woman of nearly sixty, is sitting on the sofa, crocheting some lace, which is evidently destined to trim petticoats. Her hair is dressed in the style of* 1840, *though her dress is of the* 1860 *period. Near her, in an armchair, sits* ROSE SIBLEY, *a gentle, romantic-looking girl of twenty-one, who is dressed in the height of fashion of the period. She is at work on a canvas wool-work pattern. Cups of after-dinner coffee stand near both ladies.*

MRS. R. Do permit me to look at your work one moment, my dear Rose.

ROSE. With pleasure, Mrs. Rhead.

MRS. R. Very pretty indeed. Nothing could be in better taste than these Berlin wool patterns.

ROSE. I got the design from the *Englishwoman's Domestic Magazine.* It's to be one of three cushions for father's study.

MRS. R. I had an idea of doing the same sort of thing for my husband, after we moved into the new house here, three years ago. But then, when he died, I hadn't the heart to go on. So I'm crocheting lace now, instead, for Gertrude's trousseau. Will you have some more coffee?

ROSE. No, thank you.

MRS. R. Just a drop. Gertrude, pour out– (*She looks about*) Now where has Gertrude disappeared to?

ROSE. She left the room some moments ago.

MRS. R. Even between dinner and coffee she must be off.

ROSE. But why?

MRS. R. Do I know, my dear? Just managing the house and managing it, and managing it. Upon my word,

Gertrude performs the duties of the place as if it were the foundry and she were John. My son and daughter are so alike.

ROSE (*interjecting enthusiastically*). One's as splendid as the other.

MRS. R. She keeps account-books now.

ROSE (*rather startled*). Of the house?

MRS. R. (*nods*). And she says she shall show John a balance-sheet at quarter-day. Did you ever hear of such behaviour?

ROSE. She always was very active, wasn't she? It's in the blood.

MRS. R. It is not in mine, and I am her mother. No! It is all due to these modern ways; that is what it is.

ROSE. I suppose John's rather pleased.

MRS. R. Yes, John! But what about *your* brother? Will he be pleased? Is Gertrude going to make him the wife his position demands?

ROSE. I'm sure he'll be delighted to have his house managed as this one's managed.

MRS. R. But will it stop at that? Once one begins these modern ways, one never knows where they will end.

ROSE. I must say I was surprised she ever accepted Sam.

MRS. R. (*deprecatingly*). Surprised? But why?

ROSE. We Sibleys are such an extremely old-fashioned family. Look at father! And I do believe Sam's worse. Yes, I do believe Sam's worse than father. Thank goodness they have your son for a partner—two such slow-coaches, as they are.

MRS. R. Slow-coaches! My dear, remember the respect due to your father.

ROSE (*eagerly*). Oh, I adore father, and Sam, too! I wouldn't have either of them altered for the world. But I do think Sam's very fortunate in getting Gertrude.

MRS. R. She also is very fortunate, very fortunate indeed. I have the highest respect for Sam's character, and my hope and prayer is that he and Gertrude will influence each other for nothing but good. But, between you and me, my dear, the first six months will be—well—lively, to say the least. (GERTRUDE RHEAD *enters by the door from the hall, carrying in her hand a cloak of the latest pattern of the period. She is twenty-one, high-spirited, independent, afraid of no one.*)

ROSE. What on earth's that, Gertrude?

GERT. I've just been upstairs to get it. Help me, will you? I wanted to show it you. (ROSE *helps* GERTRUDE *with the cloak*) I only bought it today, with the money John gave me for Christmas. Thank you—Well?

ROSE. Very daring, isn't it? I suppose it's quite the latest?

GERT. Next year's. Mother says it's "fast."

MRS. R. I hope you'll put it away before the men come up.

GERT. (*with assumed innocence*). Why?

MRS. R. Because Samuel will surely not approve of it.

GERT. I bet you he will.

MRS. R. Gertrude!

GERT. The truth is, Rose, mother's only taken a prejudice against it because I brought it home myself this afternoon in a hansom cab.

ROSE (*staggered*). Alone? In a hansom cab?

MRS. R. You may well be shocked, dear. My lady refuses the carriage, because of keeping the horses standing in this terrible frost. And then she actually hails a hansom-cabriolet! What Samuel would say if he knew I dare not imagine.

GERT. Well, what harm is there in it, mamma darling? (*Caresses her*) I do wish you'd remember we're in the year 1860—and very near '61. You really must try to keep up with the times. Why, girls will be riding on the tops of omnibuses some day.

ROSE (*protesting*). Gertrude!

MRS. R. I hope I sha'n't live to see it. (*Enter* THOMPSON, *a young butler, from the hall. He collects the coffee cups, putting them all on a tray.*)

GERT. Is the hot-water apparatus working properly, Thompson?

THOMPSON. Moderate, miss.

GERT. (*rather annoyed*). It ought to work perfectly.

ROSE. What's the hot-water apparatus?

GERT. It's for the bath-room, you know.

ROSE. Yes. I know you'd got a bath-room.

GERT. It's just the latest device. John had it put in the week mother was down at Brighton. It was his Christmas surprise for her.

ROSE. Yes, but I don't understand.

GERT. It's quite simple. We have a boiler behind the kitchen range, and pipes carry the hot water up to the bath. There's one tap for hot and another for cold.

ROSE. How wonderful!

GERT. So when you want a hot bath all you have to do——

MRS. R. (*drily*). All we have to do is to tell cook to put down a shoulder of mutton to roast. Very modern!

GERT. (*caressing her mother again*). Horrid old dear! Thompson, why is it working only moderately?

THOMPSON (*by the door*). No doubt because cook had orders that the beef was to be slightly underdone, miss. (*Exit quickly with tray.*)

GERT. (*to* ROSE). That was to please your carnivorous daddy, Rose, and he never came.

MRS. R. I do hope there's been no trouble down at the foundry between him and my son.

ROSE. So do I.

GERT. Why are you both pretending? You know perfectly well there has been trouble between them. You must have noticed the chilliness when our respective brothers met tonight.

ROSE. I assure you, Gertrude, I know *nothing*. Sam said not a single word in the carriage.

GERT. Well, wasn't that enough? Or does he never speak in the carriage?

ROSE (*to* MRS. RHEAD). Has John said anything?

MRS. R. I understood you to say that the reason your father didn't come to dinner was that he had an urgent appointment, quite unexpectedly, at the last moment.

ROSE. Yes, he asked me to tell you and make his excuses.

GERT. Urgent appointment at his club—most likely!

MRS. R. I wonder what the trouble can have been.

GERT. You don't, mother. You know! It's the old story—Sam and his father with their set ideas, pulling one way; and John with his go-ahead schemes, pulling the other—with the result——

MRS. R. The result is that we've had one of the most mournful dinners tonight that I have ever had the pleasure of giving.

GERT. I know! What a good thing we asked Ned Pym. If he hadn't come to the rescue with his usual facetious, senseless chatter, I do believe Sam and John——

MRS. R. (*quickly, stopping her*). Here are the gentlemen! Gertrude, take that cloak off. (*Enter from the hall* SAMUEL SIBLEY, NED PYM, *and* JOHN RHEAD. SAMUEL SIBLEY *is twenty-eight, heavy, with a serious face, a trifle pompous, but with distinct dignity.* NED PYM, *who is a little over twenty, is the young dandy of the day; handsome, tall, with excellent manners, which allow him to carry off his facetious attitude rather successfully.* JOHN RHEAD *comes last. He is twenty-five, full of determination and purpose. He knows what he wants and is going to get it.*)

MRS. R. (*in a smooth tone to* ROSE). Have you seen the new number of *Great Expectations,* dear?

NED. What's this, Gertrude? Charades?

GERT. (*flouncing her cloak half defiantly at* SAM). Paris!

NED (*coming between* SAM *and* GERTRUDE). Evidently it has lost nothing on the journey over.

GERT. Ned, would you mind . . . I'm showing to to Sam. (*To* SAM) Don't you like it?

SAM (*forcing himself*). On my betrothed, yes.

NED (*facetiously*). By the exercise of extreme self-control the lover conceals his enthusiasm for the cloak of his mistress.

GERT. (*appealing to* SAM). But you do like it—don't you?

SAM (*evasively*). Isn't it rather original?

GERT. Of course it is. That's just the point.

SAM (*surprised*). Just the point?

GERT. (*taking the cloak off and flinging it half pettishly on a chair*). Oh!

JOHN. It's original, and therefore it has committed a crime. (*Looking at* SAM) Isn't that it, Sam?

SAM (*gives* JOHN *a look and turns to* MRS. RHEAD *with an obvious intention of changing the conversation*). What were you saying about *Great Expectations*, Mrs. Rhead?

MRS. R. (*at a loss*). What *were* we saying about *Great Expectations*?

NED. Well, I can tell you one thing about it; it's made my expectations from my uncle smaller than ever. (*He sits by* MRS. RHEAD.)

MRS. R. Oh, how is dear Lord Monkhurst?

NED. He's very well and quarrelsome, thank you. And his two sons, my delightful cousins, are also in excellent health. Well, as I was going to tell you; you know how my uncle has turned against Dickens since *Little Dorrit*. I happened to say something about *Great Expectations* being pretty fairish, and he up and rode over me like a troop of cavalry.

MRS. R. (*puzzled*). A troop of cavalry?

NED. It was at his Christmas party, too, worse luck. He as good as told me I disagreed with him on purpose to annoy him. Now I cannot agree with him solely and simply because he allows me seven hundred a year, can I?

ROSE. Is he so difficult to get on with?

NED. Difficult? He's nothing but a faddist! An absolute old faddist! What can you do with a man that's convinced that spirits 'll turn his dining-table, and that Bacon wrote Shakespeare; and that the Benecia Boy's a better man than Tom Sayers?

MRS. R. It seems a great pity you cannot do something to please your uncle.

NED. Would you believe it? He even wanted me to join the Rifle Volunteers. Now, I ask you, can you see me in the Rifle Volunteers, me among a lot of stockbrokers and chimney-sweeps?

GERT. We cannot, Ned.

NED. And in order to raise my patriotism last night—(*Slapping his knee violently*) By Jove! (*He jumps up*) By Heavens! Jiggered! Jiggered!

GERT. *and* ROSE. Ned!

NED. I am a ruined man! You see before you, kind friends, a man ruined and without hope! Last night my uncle sent me a ticket for the launching of the *Warrior*.

SAM (*with a sneer*). The *Warrior!* You didn't miss much!

NED. But my beloved aunt was commanded to be in attendance on Her Royal Highness at the said function. . . . Well, I forgot all about it. I repeat I forgot all about it. My uncle will certainly call this the last straw. There will be no quarterly cheque for me on New Year's Day.

ROSE. What *is* the *Warrior*?

JOHN (*bursting out*). The *Warrior* is a steam-frigate—first vessel of the British Navy to be built entirely of iron. She's over six thousand tons burden, and she represents the beginning of a new era in iron.

ROSE (*adoringly*). How splendid!

JOHN (*responding quickly to her mood*). Ah, you agree with me!

ROSE (*enthusiastically*). Of course! (*She breaks off self-consciously*) Of course I agree with you.

JOHN (*after a slight pause—quickly*). This 29th of December marks a great day in the history of the British Navy.

SAM (*with a slight superior smile, trying to be gay*). Nonsense. All this day marks is the folly of the Admiralty. You may take it as an absolute rule that whatever the Admiralty does is wrong. Always has been, always will be. The *Great Eastern* was the champion White Elephant of the age. And now the *Warrior* has gone her one better.

JOHN. Sam, you don't know what you're saying. How can you talk about the *Warrior* when you've never even so much as laid eyes on the ship?

SAM. Well, have *you*?

JOHN. Yes—I went to the launch to-day.

SAM. You?

MRS. R. Why did you go, John? You never said a word to me.

JOHN. I went on business.

SAM. You told me you had an appointment with the bank.

JOHN. I only said that because I couldn't stop to argue just then.

SAM. So you said what wasn't so.

JOHN. I said what was necessary at the moment. I wasn't going to leave you in the dark; never fear.

SAM (*curtly controlling himself*). I see. (*A slight pause, then* SAM *turns abruptly to* GERTRUDE *and says gently*) Come and sing, dear. I haven't heard you sing for over a fortnight.

GERT. (*moved by the quarrel—after a pause in a low voice*). What shall I sing?

SAM. Sing *Nita, Juanita.*

GERT. No! I heard Madame Sainton Dolby sing it last week.

SAM. Do!—to please me. (GERTRUDE *turns towards the double doors and goes off in silence with* SAM. NED *is about to follow instantly, but* MRS. RHEAD *stops him.*)

MRS. R. (*whispering*). Give them just one instant alone.

NED. I beg pardon. My innocence at fault. (*The song is heard. A pause*) Is that long enough? (MRS. RHEAD *taps him, then she goes off after the others, followed by* NED. *A slight pause.*)

ROSE (*moving towards the doors*). What a lovely voice she has!

JOHN (*abruptly, closing the doors*). I want to talk to you.

ROSE (*nervous and self-conscious*). To me?

JOHN. I wish I'd asked you to come to that launch.

ROSE. Where was it?

JOHN. At Greenhithe; only two stations beyond the foundry. Would you have come?

ROSE. I should have loved to . . . if Gertrude had come too.

JOHN (*musing*). You should have seen her go into the water—the wave she made! All that iron—and rivets! Iron, mind you. . . . And then float like a cork. I never was at a launch before, and it gave me a thrill, I can tell you. And I'm not easily thrilled.

ROSE (*adoringly, but restraining herself*). I'm sure you're not. I do wish I'd seen it. It must have been almost sublime.

JOHN. You'd have understood. You'd have felt like I did. Do you know how I know that?

ROSE (*shaking her head*). No——

JOHN. By the way you said "how splendid" when I was telling the others just now.

ROSE. Really!

JOHN. Fact! That gave me more encouragement in my schemes than any words I ever heard.

ROSE. Please don't say that. Gertrude is always on your side. She's so like you in every way.

JOHN. Yes, Gertrude's all right. But she's got no poetry in her, Gertrude hasn't. That's the difference between you and her. She's very go-ahead; but she doesn't feel. You feel.

ROSE (*breathless*). Do I, John? (*She looks down.*)

JOHN. I'll tell you something—tears came into my eyes when that frigate took the water. Couldn't help it! (ROSE *raises her eyes to his*) In thirty years every big ship in the world will be built of iron. Very few people today believe in iron for ship-building, and I know there's a lot of silly, easy sarcasm about it—especially in the papers. But it's coming! It's coming!

ROSE (*religiously*). I'm sure you're right.

JOHN. If only your father and your brother thought as you do!

ROSE (*faintly*). Yes.

JOHN. I'm in the minority, you see; two partners against one. If my father had lived, I know which side *he'd* have been on! I shouldn't have been in the minority then.

ROSE. You'd have been equal.

JOHN (*enthusiastically*). No! We should certainly have rolled your excellent father and brother straight into the Thames!

ROSE (*amiably protesting*). Please——

JOHN (*smiling*). Forgive me—you know what I mean, don't you?

ROSE. I love to see you when you are enthusiastic!

JOHN. It's so plain. We've got probably the largest iron foundry on Thames-side. But our business isn't increasing as quickly as it used to do. It can't. We've come to about the limit of expansion on present lines. Ship-building is simply waiting for us. There it is—asking to be picked up! We're *in* iron. We know all about iron. The ships of the future will be built of nothing but iron. And we're right in the middle of the largest port in the world. What more can anyone want? But no! They won't see it! They—will—not—see—it!

ROSE. I wonder why they won't!

JOHN. Simply because they can't.

ROSE. Then one oughtn't to blame them.

JOHN. Blame them! Good Heavens, no! I don't blame them. I'm fond of them, and I rather feel for them. But that's just why I want to smash them to smithereens! They've got to yield. The people who live in the past *must* yield to the people who live in the future. Otherwise, the earth would begin to turn the other way round, and we should be back again in the eighteenth century before we knew where we were, making for the Middle Ages.

ROSE. Then you think a conflict is unavoidable?

JOHN. Absolutely unavoidable! That's the point. It's getting nearer every hour. . . . Why is your father not here tonight?

ROSE. I don't know, but I was afraid——

JOHN. *I* know and *Sam* knows. It must be because he has heard somehow of an enterprise I am planning, and the news has upset him. He's vexed.

ROSE. Poor dear old thing! Then you've started a scheme already?

JOHN (*nods*). I have. But I can't carry it out alone.

ROSE. If there is one man in the world who could stand alone, I should have said you were that man.

JOHN. I know. That's the impression I give. And yet nobody ever needed help more than I do. I'm not all on the surface, you know.

ROSE. What sort of help?

JOHN. Sympathy—understanding.

ROSE (*low*). I see.

JOHN. Of course you see! And that's why I suddenly decided I must have a bit of a chat with you—this very night. It's forced on me. And I feel I'm rather forcing it on you.

But I can't help it—honestly I can't. Rose, you're on my side, aren't you?

ROSE. I believe you're in the right.

JOHN. Would you like to see me win—(*silence*)—or lose?

ROSE. I don't think I could bear to see you beaten.

JOHN. Well, then, help me! When you look at me with that trustful look of yours, I can do anything—anything. No other woman's eyes ever had the same effect on me. It's only because you believe in me. No, that isn't the only reason; it isn't the chief reason. The chief reason is that I'm in love with you—there you have it!

ROSE (*sinking her head*). Oh!——

JOHN (*coming to her*). Curious! I've known you all my life. But I wasn't aware of all that you meant to me, until these difficulties began. You're essential to me. You can't imagine how much depends on just you!

ROSE. Really?

JOHN. You're too modest, too womanly to realise it. Why, sometimes a tone of yours, a mere inflection, almost knocks me over—You aren't crying, surely? What are you crying for?

ROSE. It's too much for me, coming like this, with no warning.

JOHN. Rose, be mine! I'll work for you, I'll succeed for you. No woman in this country shall have a finer position than yours.

ROSE. I don't want a fine position—except for you.

JOHN. I'm not hard, really.

ROSE. But I like you to be hard. It's when you're inflexible and brutal that I like you the most.

JOHN. Then you do like me a little—sometimes? (*Kisses her hands.*)

ROSE. I can't help telling you. I didn't hope for this. Yes, I did. But the hope seemed absurd. Is this real—now?

JOHN. My love!

ROSE. John, you say I don't realise how much I mean to you. Perhaps I do though. But it's impossible for *you* to realise how I want to give my life to you, to serve you. No *man* could realise that. A woman could. I shall be your slave. (JOHN *looks at her with a little start*) Yes, I know it sounds queer for me to be talking like this. But I must. It thrills me to tell you. . . . I shall be your slave.

JOHN. Don't make me afraid, my darling!

ROSE. Afraid?

JOHN. Afraid of being unworthy.

ROSE. Please. . . . (*A slight pause*) Has the singing stopped?

JOHN. A long time ago.

ROSE. They'll be coming in, perhaps.

JOHN (*vaguely without conviction*). No.

ROSE. What will your mother and Gertrude say?

JOHN. You know as well as I do, they'll be absolutely delighted.

ROSE. And father?

JOHN (*alertly*). Rose, you're mine, whatever happens?

ROSE. Oh, nothing must happen now! Nothing shall happen!

JOHN. But suppose I couldn't carry out my scheme without quarrelling with your father? And he refused his consent to our being married?

ROSE. My heart would be yours for ever and ever. But I couldn't marry without father's consent.

JOHN. But——

ROSE. I couldn't——

JOHN. Why not?

ROSE. It would not be right.

JOHN. But you love me?

ROSE. Yes, but I love father, too. And he's getting very old. And he's very dependent on me. In any case to give me up would be a great sacrifice for him. To lose me against his will—well, I don't know what would happen!

JOHN. As things are just now—he's bound to refuse.

ROSE. But are you so sure he won't have anything to do with your scheme?

JOHN. You heard Sam!

ROSE. Yes; but you haven't discussed your plans very thoroughly with Sam. He seemed quite surprised.

JOHN. Suppose I speak to Sam tonight; tell him everything. At any rate, I shall know then where I stand.

ROSE. Tonight?

JOHN. Now! I *might* win him over. Anyhow, he'll do what he can to make things smooth for us with your father—surely! After all, he's engaged to Gertrude!

ROSE. Just as you think best. . . . And Sam's very fond of me, though he never shows it.

JOHN. Let me get it over now, instantly. Will you go in to the others? (ROSE *looks at him in silence, then rises and goes to the double doors.* JOHN *stops her and solemnly and passionately kisses her, then opens the doors and she passes through.*)

JOHN (*calling into the other room*). I say, Sam! Mother, I want a word with Sam alone. (SAMUEL *enters by the double doors.* JOHN *closes them behind him.*)

SAM (*suspicious, and not over friendly*). What is it? Not business, I hope?

JOHN (*with a successful effort to be cordial*). No, no!

SAM (*following* JOHN's *lead, and to make conversation*). I was wondering what you and Rosie were palavering about.

JOHN. Samuel, you've gone right into the bull's-eye at the first shot—Sam. I've just been through a very awkward moment.

SAM. Oh, I see! That's it, is it?

JOHN. I've made a proposal of marriage to my partner's sister. Startling, ain't it?

SAM. No! If you care to know, I was talking to your mother about it last week.

JOHN. About what?

SAM. About the betting odds—whether it was more likely to come off this year or next. Your mother was right, and I was wrong—by a couple of days.

JOHN (*startled*). But you'd none of you the slightest ground. I've never shown— Certainly Rose has never shown——

SAM (*teasingly*). No, of course not. But you know how people *will* gossip, and jump to conclusions, don't you? I know, I went through it myself, not very long ago either. I remember the clever way in which you all knew about it before I'd got half-way to the end of my first sentence.

JOHN. Sam, you're devilish funny.

SAM. Even the dullest old Tory is funny once in his life. Am I right in assuming that Rose did not unconditionally refuse your offer?

JOHN. She did me the honour to accept it.

SAM. I must confess I'm not entirely surprised that she didn't spurn you.

JOHN. All right, old cock. Keep it up. I don't mind. But when you're quite done, you might congratulate me.

SAM (*not effusively*). I do, of course.

JOHN. I suppose you'll admit, even as a brother, that I'd have to go rather far before I met a woman with half Rose's qualities.

SAM. Yes, Rosie's all right. Of course she's cold; she hasn't got what I call poetry in her. That's the difference between her and Gertrude.

JOHN (*facing him*). Do you honestly think Rose has no poetry in her? Rose?

SAM. Easy does it, my tulip! Have it your own way!

JOHN (*good-humouredly*). I suppose where sisters are concerned, all brothers are alike.

SAM. Well, I'm looking at one. We're a pair.

JOHN. Shake! (*They shake hands,* SAM *rather perfunctorily*) Now, Sam, I'm going to rely on you.

SAM. What for?

JOHN. I don't think you had any fault to find with my attitude towards your engagement, had you? I welcomed it with both arms. Well, I want you to do the same with me.

SAM. But, my dear fellow, I'm nobody in the affair. You're the head of a family; I'm not.

JOHN. But you have enormous influence with the head of a family, my boy.

SAM (*rather falsely*). Why! Are you anticipating trouble with the governor?

JOHN. I'm not anticipating it—but you know as well as I do—probably much better—that he ain't very friendly disposed this last day or two. The plain truth is—he's sulking. Now why? Nothing whatever has passed between us except just every-day business.

SAM. Well, the fact is, he suspects you're keeping something nasty up your sleeve for him.

JOHN. Has he told you?

SAM (*somewhat pugnaciously*). Yes, he has.

JOHN. And what is it I'm supposed to have up my sleeve?

SAM. Look here, Jack. I'm not here to be cross-examined. If there's anything up your sleeve, you're the person to know what it is. It's not my sleeve we're talking about. Why don't you play with the cards on the table?

JOHN. I'm only too anxious to play with the cards on the table.

SAM. Then it is business you really wanted to talk about after all!

JOHN (*movement of irritation concealed*). I expect your father's heard about me and Macleans, though how it's got abroad I can't imagine.

SAM. Macleans? Macleans of Greenhithe?

JOHN. Yes. That's what's worrying the old man, isn't it?

SAM. I don't know.

JOHN. He hasn't mentioned Macleans to you?

SAM. He has not. He isn't a great talker, you know. He merely said to me he suspected you were up to something.

JOHN. And what did you say?

SAM. Briefly, I said I thought you *were*. (*Disgustedly*) But, by gad! I never dreamed you were hobnobbing with the Maclean gang.

JOHN. Macleans are one of the oldest ship-building firms in the South of England. I went to the launch today with Andrew Maclean.

SAM. What's ship-building got to do with us?

JOHN. It's got nearly everything to do with us. Or it will have. Now listen, Sammy. I've arranged a provisional agreement for partnership between Macleans and ourselves.

SAM. You've——

JOHN. Half a minute. Macleans are rather flattered at the idea of a connection with the august firm of Sibley, Rhead and Sibley.

SAM. By God! I should think they were. (*Walks away.*)

JOHN. They've had an output of over 25,000 tons this year. All wood. Naturally they want to go in for iron. They'll pay handsomely for our help and experience. In fact, I've got a draft agreement, my boy, that is simply all in our favour.

SAM. Did you seriously suppose——

JOHN. Let me finish. It's a brilliant agreement. In three years it'll mean the doubling of our business. And we shall have the satisfaction of being well-established in the great industry of the future. Your father's old. I don't expect him to be very enthusiastic about a new scheme. But you're young, and you can influence him. He'll be retiring soon, and you and I will be together—just the two of us. We're marrying each other's sisters. And we shall divide an enormous fortune, my boy.

SAM. And have you had the impudence to try to make an agreement behind our backs?

JOHN (*controlling himself*). I've made no agreement. I've only got the offer. It's open to you to refuse or accept. I only held my tongue about it so as to keep the job as easy as possible.

SAM. You had no right to approach anyone without consulting us.

JOHN. I was going to tell you tomorrow. But I guessed from your father's attitude these last two days that something had leaked out. That's why I'm telling you first, Sam—tonight. Come now, look at the thing calmly—reasonably. Don't condemn it offhand. A very great deal depends on your decision—more than you think.

SAM. I don't see that anything particular depends on my decision. If we refuse, we refuse. And we shall most decidedly refuse.

JOHN. But it's impossible you should be so blind to the future! Impossible!

SAM. See here, John! Don't you make the mistake of assuming that any man who doesn't happen to agree with you is a blind fool. To begin with, it isn't polite. I know you *do* think we're blind, old-fashioned, brainless dolts, father and I. We've both felt that for some time.

JOHN. I think you're blind to the future of iron ships, that's all.

SAM. Well, shall I tell you what we think of *you*? We think you've got a bee in your bonnet. That's all. We think you're a faddist in the style of Ned Pym's noble uncle!

JOHN (*his lips curling*). Me like Lord Monkhurst! Ha!

SAM. Precisely. Don't you go and imagine that all the arguments are on one side. They aren't. Five-sixths of the experts in England have no belief whatever in the future of iron ships. You know that! Iron ships indeed! And what about British oak? Would you build ships of the self-same material as bridges? Why not stone ships, then? Oh, yes, I know there's a number of faddists up and down the land—anything in the nature of a novelty is always bound to attract a certain type of brain. Unfortunately we happen to have that type of brain just now in the Cabinet. I quite agree with my father that the country is going to the dogs. Another Reform Bill this year! And actually an attempt to repeal the paper duty. But, of course, people who believe in iron ships would naturally want to unsettle the industrial classes by a poisonous flood of cheap newspapers! However, we've had enough commonsense left to knock both those schemes on the head. And I've no doubt the sagacity of the country will soon also put an end to this fantastic notion of iron ships.

JOHN (*quietly*). I see.

SAM. Oh, don't think I'm not fond of iron! Iron means as much to me as it does to you. But I flatter myself I can keep my balance. (*More quietly*) We didn't expect this of you, John, with your intellect.

JOHN (*as before*). Very well.

SAM. I've made it clear, haven't I?

JOHN. Quite.

SAM. That's all right.

JOHN (*still quietly*). Only I shall dissolve partnership.

SAM. Dissolve partnership? What for?

JOHN. I shall go on with Macleans alone.

SAM. You don't mean it.

JOHN. I mean every single word of it! (*He rises. They look at each other.*)

SAM. Then I can tell you one thing! You won't marry Rosie.

JOHN. Why sha'n't I marry Rosie?

SAM. After such treachery.

JOHN (*raising his voice*). Treachery! I merely keep my own opinion—I leave you to yours.

SAM. Do you think father will let you drag Rose into this fatuous scheme of yours? Do you think he'll give his daughter to a traitor?

JOHN (*sarcastic and cold*). Don't get on stilts. (*Then suddenly bursting out*) And what has my marriage got to do with you? When I want your father's opinion, I'll go to your father for it.

SAM. Don't try to browbeat me, John. I know my father's mind, and what's more, you know I know it. And I repeat, my father will never let his daughter marry a——

JOHN (*shouting*). Silence! (*Enter* MRS. RHEAD *by the double doors, followed by* NED PYM, GERTRUDE *and* ROSE. *The women remain silent.*)

NED (*facetiously coming forward*). Why silence? Go on. We've only come in because we thought it might interest us. What's it all about? A hint will suffice.

JOHN. Ned, you're a blundering donkey, and you will be a blundering donkey to the end of your life.

NED. My one desire is to please.

GERT. (*coming to* SAM, *in a quiet, firm tone*). Sam, what's the matter?

SAM. Nothing! We must go! Rosie, get ready. (*Very respectfully to*

MRS. RHEAD) I'm sorry to break up the evening.

GERT. But you can't go like this.

SAM (*with deference*). My dear Gertrude, please leave matters to your brother and me. You're a woman, and there are things——

GERT. (*stopping him*). It is possible I am a woman, but I'm a reasonable creature, and I intend to be treated as such.

MRS. R. (*very upset*). My dear child, remember you are speaking to your future husband.

GERT. That's just why I'm speaking as I am. I ask Sam what's the matter—(*Scornfully*)—and he says "Nothing." Am I a child? Are we all children?

SAM (*curtly*). Come, now, Rose.

GERT. And why must Rose go off like this? She's engaged to John.

SAM. Who told you?

GERT. Her eyes told me when she came out of this room.

MRS. R. We all knew it, and no word said. We've been expecting it for weeks. (MRS. RHEAD *and* ROSE *embrace.*)

SAM. You are mistaken, Gertrude. Rose is not engaged to John, and she is not likely to be.

GERT. You object?

SAM. I do, and I know my father well.

GERT. You object to John for a brother-in-law? John! Why?—You might at least condescend to tell Rosie, if not me. It's an affair that rather interests her, you see.

SAM. If you must know, John is going to leave our firm.

MRS. R. John?

SAM. He thinks my father and I are old-fashioned, and so he's leaving us.

MRS. R. John! Leave the firm. Surely you're not thinking of breaking up Rhead and Sibley?

SAM. Sibley, Rhead—and Sibley.

MRS. R. It was Rhead and Sibley in my young days, when your father and John's were founding it. John, you cannot mean it!

SAM (*sarcastically*). He's going to build iron ships.

GERT. And is that any reason why you should make poor Rosie unhappy and spoil her life?

SAM. I do not propose to argue.

GERT. The man who does not propose to argue with me is not going to be my husband.

MRS. R. Gertrude!

GERT. (*looking at* SAM). I mean it. (SAM *bows.*)

MRS. R. Please don't listen to her, Sam.

SAM. All my apologies, Mrs. Rhead.

GERT. And you, Rosie, what do you say to all this?

ROSE (*humbly and tearfully*). I—I hardly understand. Sam, what is the matter?

JOHN (*coming to* ROSE). It's quite simple. I believe in the future of iron ships and I have the courage of my convictions. Therefore you are not to be allowed to marry me. You see the connection is perfectly clear. But you shall marry me, all the same!

SAM (*confidently*). You don't know my sister.

NED (*to* SAM, *facetiously*). And you don't know John.

SAM (*turning to* NED, *firmly*). Ned, go and order my carriage, there's a good fellow.

NED (*going off by the door into the hall*). Oh, very well. (*He closes the door behind him.*)

MRS. R. John, John, why are you so set in your own ideas? Everything was going perfectly smoothly. We were all so happy. And now you must needs fall out with your partners over iron ships. Do you prefer your iron ships to Rose's happiness and your own? *Is everything* to be sacrificed to iron ships?

JOHN. There need be no question of sacrifice, if——

SAM. If you can have it your own way. Of course. Mrs. Rhead, your son wants to risk the ruin of all of us. Now, so far as we Sibleys are concerned, we won't allow him to do so. If he still persists in his purpose, very well, that's *his* look-out. Only—he can hardly be surprised if Rose's family object—and very strongly—to letting him make her his wife. One does not entrust one's daughter or one's sister to a traitor.

GERT. Sam, don't be childish!

SAM (*drawing himself up*). I beg your pardon.

MRS. R. John, I'm your mother. Listen to me. Give up this idea of yours. For my sake—for the sake of all of us.

JOHN. I cannot.

MRS. R. But if it means so much unhappiness.

JOHN. I should be ashamed of myself if I gave it up. I believe in it. It's my religion.

MRS. R. John, I beg you not to be profane.

JOHN (*a little quieter*). I cannot give up my idea, mother. I should be a coward to give it up. I should be miserable for the rest of my days. I could never look anyone in the face, not even my wife. (*Enter* NED *from the hall.*)

NED (*to* SAM *in a flunkey's voice*). Carriage is waiting, my lord.

SAM. Now, Rose! Good evening, Mrs. Rhead.

GERT. *Just a moment.* (*Drawing a ring off her finger*) Ned! Hand this ring to Mr. Sibley with my compliments.

NED. Must I?

GERT. Yes.

NED (*taking the ring*). The donkey becomes a beast of burden. (*Handing ring to* SAM) Sam, you get this, but you lose something that's worth a lot more.

SAM (*taking the ring*). Of course I have no alternative.

ROSE. Good-bye, John.

MRS. R. John, she's going. Will you let her?

JOHN (*rigidly*). I cannot give up my idea.

SAM (*going into the hall as* ROSE *stands hesitating*). Come along, child. I'm waiting.

ROSE (*moving a step towards* JOHN). Stick to your idea! Let me go! I love you all the more for it!

JOHN. Don't worry, Rose. The future is on our side.

ROSE (*looking straight at him*). I— (*Her emotion gets the better of her; she turns quickly and hurries from the room*).

GERT. (*blankly, in spite of herself*). The future! (*She sinks down on a sofa and bursts into sobs.* JOHN *stands, looking after* ROSE.)

CURTAIN

ACT TWO

1885

The Scene represents the same drawing-room as in Act One. But twenty-five years have passed. We are now in the year 1885. *Consequently great changes have occurred. The furniture has been re-arranged and added to. The flowered carpet of the first Act has given place to an Indian carpet. There are new ornaments amongst some of the old ones. The room is over-crowded with furniture in the taste of the period.*

It is about four o'clock of an afternoon in June. The curtains are drawn back and the sun is shining brightly outside.

ROSE SIBLEY, *now* MRS. JOHN RHEAD, *forty-six years of age and dressed in the fashion of* 1885, *her hair slightly grey at the temples, is seated writing some notes at a desk near the windows.* NED PYM *enters from the hall, followed by* JOHN RHEAD. *The former has developed into a well-preserved, florid, slightly self-sufficient man of forty-six. The latter, now fifty, has not changed so much physically except that his hair is grey and his features have become much firmer. But his manner has grown even more self-assured than it was in the first Act. He is in fact a person of authority; the successful man whose word is law.*

JOHN. Oh, you *are* there, Rosie. I've brought a person of importance to see you.

ROSE (*rising*). Ned—— (*They shake hands.*)

NED. Now please don't say what you were going to say.

ROSE. And what was I going to say?

NED. That I'm quite a stranger since I came into the title.

ROSE (*curtseying and teasing*). Lord Monkhurst, we are only too flattered—I was merely going to say that you look younger than ever.

NED (*seriously*). Don't I? That's what everyone says. Time leaves me quite unchanged, don't you know.

JOHN. In every way. How old *are* you, Ned?

NED (*with a sigh*). Well, I shall never see thirty again.

JOHN. What about forty?

NED. Or forty either. But my proud boast is I'm nearer forty than fifty.

JOHN. Well, it can only be by a couple of months.

NED. Sh!—It's a lot more than you say, Jack.

JOHN. I was fifty in April. There's just five years' difference between us.

ROSE (*to Ned*). You look more like John's son.

NED. Say nephew; don't be too hard on him.

ROSE. But I do wish you would go out of mourning. It doesn't suit you.

NED. Not these beautiful continuations?

ROSE. No!

NED. Well, I'm awfully sorry. But I can't oblige you yet. Please remember I've got three sudden deaths to work off. I think that when a man loses a harsh but beloved uncle in a carriage accident, and two amiable cousins through a misunderstanding about toadstools, all in twelve months, why—(*gesture*)—the least he can do is to put himself unreservedly into the hands of his tailor.

ROSE. I——

JOHN (*stopping her, kindly but rather tyrannically*). Now enough of this graceful badinage. Ned and I are here on business. What are you up to, there, Rose?

ROSE (*with eager submissiveness*). I was doing the invitations for the dinner, or rather for the reception.

JOHN. Good. I've got some more names in my study. You'd better come in there with me.

ROSE. Yes, love.

NED. Am I invited to this dinner? I generally get very hungry about eight o'clock at nights.

ROSE (*teasing*). Yes, I *think* I put you down. It's our wedding-day.

NED. Don't tell me how long you've been married. It would age me!

ROSE. Considering that we have a daughter who is turned twenty-two.

JOHN. Yes, Ned, you must face the facts bravely. Old Mr. Sibley died in January, 1860——

ROSE. Sixty-one, love.

JOHN (*after a frown at being corrected*). Sixty-one. And we were married in June of the following year. Surely you recall the face Sam pulled when he gave my little Rosie away.

ROSE. But, love, it was a great concession for him to give me away at all, wasn't it?

JOHN. Oh, yes!

ROSE. By the bye, he's coming up to town this afternoon.

JOHN. What, here?

NED. Oh! But I ought to see old Sam.

ROSE. Stay for tea, and you'll see *him* and his wife, too.

NED. His wife? His what did you say?

ROSE. Now, Ned, it's no use pretending you don't know all about it.

NED. I remember hearing a couple of years ago, before I went to India, that Sam had staggered his counting-house by buying one of these new type-writing machines, and getting a young woman to work it for him.

ROSE. That's the person. Her name is Nancy.

NED. Is it? Only fancy; Nancy, Nancy, in the counting-*house!* I say —are these girl-clerks or clerk-girls going to be a regular thing? What's coming over the world?

JOHN (*shakes his head*). Passing craze! Goes with all this Votes-for-Women agitation and so on. You'll see, it won't last a year—not a year! Of course, Sam—susceptible bachelor of fifty and over—just the man to fall a victim. Inevitable!

ROSE. She's a very well-meaning, honest creature.

NED. You intimate with her, Rose?

ROSE. I went to see her several times after she had her baby. They're living at Brockley.

NED. Baby! Brockley! No more typewriting then. The typewriter has served its turn—eh? Of course it was a great catch for her.

JOHN. Yes, but it wouldn't have been if Samuel hadn't sold out.

NED. How much did he retire with about?

JOHN. Well, you see he was losing three thousand a year. He got £20,000 net cash.

NED. I'm not a financier, but £20,000 cash in exchange for a loss of £3,000 a year doesn't seem so bad! Think of the money he'd have made though, if he'd taken up with your ideas!

JOHN (*ironically*). You recollect the folly of iron ships? And the bee in my bonnet? (*Laughs*) There were only four wooden steamships built in this country last year. The rest were iron; and I was responsible for half a dozen of 'em.

NED. What's all this talk about steel for ships?

JOHN (*disdainfully*). Just talk.

NED. Well, of course, if you're building at the rate of six steamers a year, I can understand your generosity in the matter of subscriptions.

ROSE. He *is* generous, isn't he?

NED. Told your wife about your latest contribution?

JOHN. No, I was just going to.

ROSE (*proudly*). John tells me everything.

JOHN. And Rosie always approves, don't you, Rosie? Ah! The new generation can't show such wives.

ROSE (*eagerly*). Well?

JOHN. I've decided to give ten thousand pounds to the party funds—politics, you know.

NED. You see, it's to save the country. That's what it amounts to practically, in these days. *I* know, since I've gone into politics.

ROSE. How noble! I'm so glad, John.

NED. And the great secret—shall I tell her, or will you, Jack?

JOHN. Go on.

NED. How should you like your husband to be a baronet, Rose?

ROSE. A baronet?

NED. Sir John Rhead, Bart., and Lady Rhead!

ROSE (*ecstatic*). Is he going to be?

NED. As soon as our side comes into power—and we shall be in power in a month. John'll be on the next Honours' List.

ROSE. In a month!

NED. The Budget's bound to be thrown out. They're trying to increase the taxes on beer and spirits—I've studied the question deeply. I know what will happen.

ROSE. How magnificent!

JOHN. Then you approve? (*Rose kisses John fondly*) That's all we've called in for, just to make sure.

ROSE (*weeping*). I——

JOHN. What's the matter?

ROSE. I'm only sorry we haven't had a son.

NED. There, there! I'm sure you did your best, Rose.

ROSE (*to John*). Are they making you a baronet because you're giving ten thousand to the party funds?

NED. My dear woman! Of course not! That's pure coincidence.

ROSE (*convinced*). Oh!

NED. Your beloved John will be made a baronet solely on account of his splendid services to commerce. Doesn't he deserve it?

ROSE. No one better. Do you know, I can scarcely believe it. Who–? Tell me all about it.

JOHN. Well, it's thanks to Ned in the first place.

ROSE. To Ned?

NED (*pretending to be hurt*). You needn't be so surprised, Rose. You seem to be unaware that I've gone into politics. Don't you read the newspapers?

ROSE. No, I leave the newspapers to my daughter.

NED. If you did, you'd know that I made a sensation in the Indian Debate, in the House of Lords. All that Afghanistan business, don't you know.

ROSE. Really!

NED. Oh, I became quite a nob, at once. Bit of luck me having gone to India, wasn't it? I'd spent the best part of a month in India; so, of course, I knew all about it.

ROSE (*solemnly*). Of course.

NED. The leader of the Opposition said I had a great future!

JOHN. No doubt.

NED (*simply*). I shall specialise in India and the Navy. You see my father being a rear-admiral, I ought to be familiar with the subject. If fellows like me don't begin to take an interest in our neglected Navy, England'll be playing second fiddle to Russia in five years' time. Mark my word, in 1890. In 1890.

ROSE. Perhaps you'll be in the Government some day?

NED. There's no "perhaps" about it. I shall! There's only one difficulty.

ROSE. What's that?

NED (*mysteriously and important*). I'm told I ought to marry.

JOHN (*rather self-consciously*). Nothing simpler.

NED. I know! I've had seventeen indirect offers this last six months, and that's a fact.

ROSE. None suitable?

NED. I'm afraid of 'em. It's no joke going and marrying a perfect stranger. I want somebody I know —somebody I've known all my life, or at least all hers.

ROSE. And can't you find her?

NED. I can. I *have* done.

ROSE. Who is it, may one ask?

NED. Jack knows.

JOHN (*turning to Rose and clearing his throat*). Ned would like to marry into *our* family, Rose.

NED (*eagerly*). You know I've been dead sweet on Emily for a couple of years at least.

ROSE (*after a pause*). I know you're very fond of her, and she of you.

NED (*as above*). You think she is, really?

ROSE. But it seems so queer.

JOHN (*peremptorily*). How queer? We're respectable enough for the young rascal, aren't we?

ROSE. Of course. It would be ideal—ideal! My poor little Emily!

NED. Well, I've got that off my chest. I'll be moving. I must be at the Carlton at three-thirty to settle up John's business with the panjandrum.

ROSE. You'll come back for tea. *She'll* be here. (*Enter from the hall Emily and Gertrude. Both are dressed to go out. Emily is a handsome girl of twenty-two. She has fine qualities, combining her father's pluck with her mother's loving nature. But she has been rather spoilt by her parents. Gertrude follows. She has grown into a faded, acidy spinster with protective impulses for her niece, Emily, on whom she spends all her suppressed maternal feelings.*)

EMILY (*slightly disconcerted*). Why, father! How is it you aren't at the works this afternoon earning our bread-and-butter?

JOHN (*delighted*). Such impertinence!

ROSE. Emily, I really wonder at you! What your grandmother Rhead would have said to such manners if she'd been alive, I daren't think. And Lord Monkhurst here, too!

EMILY. Well, mamma, you see, grandmother isn't alive! (*To* NED, *who, after shaking hands with* GERTRUDE, *advances towards her*) And as for dear old Uncle Ned—(NED, JOHN *and* ROSE *are all somewhat put about by this greeting.* NED *hesitates, his hand half out*) Aren't you going to shake hands, then?

NED (*shaking hands*). Why "uncle"? You've never called me uncle before?

EMILY. Haven't I? It seems to suit you.

NED. I'm severely wounded. And I shall retire into my wigwam until you make it up to me.

ROSE. You really are very pert, Emily.

EMILY (*affectionately*). I should have thought you would adore being my uncle. I'm sure I like you lots more than I like Uncle Sam, for instance.

NED. That's better. I'm peeping out of my wigwam now. Only I won't be your uncle. I won't be anybody's uncle. I don't mind being your cousin, if that's any use to you.

GERT. (*sharply*). He's afraid of being taken for the same age as your auntie, darling.

NED (*to* GERTRUDE). Half a moment, Gertrude, and I'll try to think of a compliment that will turn your flank.

GERT. My flank, Ned?

NED. I mean——

EMILY (*to her parents and* NED). Where were you all off to?

ROSE. Your father and I are going to the study.

NED. And I'm going on an errand, but I shan't be long.

JOHN. And may we ask where you and Auntie Gertrude are "off to," Miss Inquisitive?

GERT. Oh, Mr. Preece is calling for us to take us to the Royal Academy.

EMILY. And then we shall have tea at the new Hotel Métropole, in Northumberland Avenue. It's the very latest thing.

JOHN (*in a different tone*). Preece? But he was here last Sunday.

EMILY. Yes, it was then we arranged it.

JOHN. I don't like the idea of your seeing so much of Preece. And your mother doesn't like it, either.

ROSE. No, indeed!

GERT. But why not? He's the cleverest man in your works. You've often said so.

JOHN. He may be the cleverest man in my works; but he isn't going to be the cleverest man in my house. Who gave him leave to take half a day off, I should like to know?

GERT. He said he had business in the West End.

EMILY (*to* NED). Now if you want to make yourself useful as a cousin, please explain to these called-so parents that they oughtn't to spoil me one day, and rule me with a rod of iron the next. It's not fair. It's very bad for my disposition.

NED (*to* JOHN). Is this man-about-town the same Preece you were telling me of?

EMILY. There you are, you see! He tells everyone about Mr. Preece. He's as proud as Punch of Mr. Preece.

JOHN (*more kindly*). Arthur Preece is a youth that I discovered in my drawing office. Last year I took out a patent for him for bending metal plates at a low temperature; and it's attracted some attention. But our relations are purely business.

GERT. Still, it was you who first asked him to the house.

JOHN (*drily*). It was. And Rose kept him for tea. It's all our fault as usual. However—(*rising*)—you'll kindly tell Master Preece that you can't give yourselves the pleasure of his society this afternoon.

EMILY. But why?

JOHN (*continuing*). And if he's obstreperous, inform him that *I* am in my study, and rather anxious to know exactly what his business in the West End is.

EMILY (*insisting*). But why, father?

JOHN (*firmly*). Simply because your mother and I wish you to be in this afternoon. Uncle Sam and Aunt Nancy are coming, for one thing.

EMILY (*disdainfully*). Uncle Sam! Aunt Nancy!

ROSE. Emily! I won't have you bandying words with your father; you seem to have lost all sense of respect.

EMILY (*to* NED *angrily*). Aren't they tyrants! (*She goes to a little table and takes off her bonnet, in a quick annoyed way.*)

ROSE (*very politely and nicely to* GERTRUDE). Gertrude, if *you* aren't going out, could you come into the study about those addresses?

GERT. (*somewhat snappishly, taking* EMILY'S *bonnet*). Of course! (*She goes out quickly.*)

JOHN (*to* NED). Well, you've got to be off then, for the moment. (*All are near the door now, except* EMILY, *who is drawing off her gloves savagely.*)

ROSE (*in a low voice to* NED). Till tea, then. (*She goes out, nodding her head significantly.*)

NED (*hesitating*). Yes. (*To* JOHN) But I must just kiss the hand of this new cousin of mine first.

JOHN (*in a peculiar tone*). Oh! All right! (*He follows* ROSE.)

NED (*going up to* EMILY, *whose face is turned away ingratiatingly*). Now, I'm not included in this frown, am I?

EMILY (*facing him and bursting out*). But don't you think it's a shame, seriously?

NED. Of course if you've *promised* Mr. Preece, and don't want to disappoint him——

EMILY (*with false lightness*). Oh, Mr. Preece is nothing to me! Only I *do* want to know where I am. The fact is they let me do as I like in little things, and they're frightfully severe in big things. Not really big things, but—you know——

NED. Middling big things.

EMILY. After all I'm twenty-two.

NED. A mature age.

EMILY (*huffy*). Oh! Naturally you take their side!

NED. Honour bright, I don't! I tell you I feel far more like your age than theirs. I'm much younger than your father—much! That's why I don't like being called uncle.

EMILY. Really?

NED. Really.

EMILY (*confidentially*). And there's another thing. They oughtn't to treat Auntie Gertrude like that, ought they? She's got more brains than anybody else here.

NED. Than your father?

EMILY. No, not than father. I meant mother, and Uncle Sam, and me—and you——

NED. I see.

EMILY. Who is it runs the house? You don't suppose it's mother, do you? Mother is absorbed in father, quite absorbed in him. No! It's auntie does everything. And yet she's nobody, simply nobody. She arranges to take me out, and they stop it without so much as apologising to her.

NED. Well, you see, she's an old maid.

EMILY. I don't care whether she's an old maid or not. She's the only friend I have. Father and mother are most awfully fond of me and all that, and mother *is* sweet, isn't she? But still that makes no difference. There are two camps in this house; they're in one, and auntie and I are in the other. And I tell you we have to be regular conspirators, in self-defence. Of course I'm trusting you.

NED (*who has been playing with a book he has picked up from a table*). You may.

EMILY. For instance, they won't let me read Ouida. They don't even like auntie to read Ouida.

NED. This isn't Ouida.

EMILY. I know it isn't. That's William Black. They're always throwing William Black at me, and I hate him. I want to read Ouida.

NED. You must wait till you're married.

EMILY. I won't. And I do so want to go to the Hotel Métropole.

NED. I thought it was the Royal Academy.

EMILY. The Academy too.

NED. Look here, Emily. Suppose I arrange a little theatre party?

EMILY. Not with father and mother. They'll want to go to something silly.

NED. No. Just your auntie and me—and you, of course.

EMILY. Will you?

NED. Rather!

EMILY. You're quite coming out. But will they allow it?

NED. You bet they will.

EMILY. Where?

NED. Anywhere you like.

EMILY. Do you know *The Mikado's* been running three months, and I haven't seen it yet?

NED. "Here's a 'How d'you do!'" The Savoy then.

EMILY. Oh! Hurrah! Hurrah! Thanks; you are a dear.

NED (*pleased*). Am I? That's all right then. Au revoir. (*Turns to the door.*)

EMILY (*calling him back*). Cousin! (*She beckons him to come to her*) What's this secret between you and father and mother?

NED. What secret?

EMILY (*crossly*). Now you needn't pretend. I could see it as plain as anything when I came in. And when they went out too, for that matter.

NED. I can't stand being bullied.

EMILY. Tell me, and I won't bully you.

NED (*solemnly*). You're going to be related to a baronet.

EMILY (*disturbed*). They don't want me to marry a baronet, do they?

NED. Foolish creature! No. It's the opposite camp that's about to receive a title.

EMILY (*delighted*). Father—a baronet!

NED. I'm just off to make the final arrangements now.

EMILY. Truly?

NED. Don't be misled by my modest exterior. I'm a terrific nob—really. (*He turns to go.*)

EMILY (*as he is going*). Didn't you say something about kissing my hand? One of your jokes, I suppose. (NED *comes and kisses it, then hurries to the door. As he opened it he looks back and says "The Mikado," and hurries out.* EMILY *stands a moment in thought, a smile on her lips. Then she hums, quite unconsciously, "For he's going to marry Yum-Yum, Yum-Yum!" Goes back to the table on which the William Black is lying, picks it up—opens it, reading a bit, then flings the book aside, muttering in disgust, "Black!"* THOMPSON *enters. He has grown old in the service of the* RHEADS.)

THOMPSON (*announcing*). Mr. Preece. (*He withdraws.* ARTHUR PREECE *enters. His age is twenty-five; he is a man of the clerk class, whose talent and energy have made him what he is. He is full of enthusiasm, earnest, but with a rough sense of humour. Rather short and stocky in figure, but important. His clothes are neat and useful—but very simple.*)

PREECE (*excited*). Good afternoon, Miss Rhead. I'm afraid I'm a little early.

EMILY (*putting on the manner of a woman of the world*). Not at all, Mr. Preece. I'm sure Auntie Gertrude will be delighted.

PREECE (*vaguely*). She's not here now, your aunt?

EMILY (*looking round*). No.

PREECE (*eagerly*). I wonder if I should have time to tell you something before she comes in. It isn't that it's a secret. But nobody knows yet, and I should like you to be the first.

EMILY. How very kind of you, Mr. Preece!

PREECE. I've only just known it myself.

EMILY. It seems to be very thrilling.

PREECE. It is, rather. It's just this. I've succeeded in making mild steel nearly five per cent. lighter than it's ever been made before. Nearly five per cent. lighter, and no extra cost.

EMILY. Really! How much is five per cent.?

PREECE. It's one-twentieth part. You know, it's enormous.

EMILY. I suppose it is.

PREECE. I dare say you don't quite realise what it means—this enormous change in the specific gravity. But it *is* enormous.

EMILY. What is specific gravity? In a word?

PREECE. It's—well—Now supposing —Do you mind if I explain that to you some other time? I'd like to, awfully!

EMILY. Oh! Any time!

PREECE. It's quite O.K., you know. And the thing comes to this. Assume the steel for a biggish ship cost £20,000. Under my new process you'd get the same result with steel that weighed about a twentieth less and cost, roughly, £19,000. Net saving of nearly one thousand pounds!

EMILY (*impressed*). And did you——

PREECE (*continuing*). And not only that. As the hull weighs so much less, you can carry a proportionately heavier cargo in the same bottom.

EMILY. Well, I never heard of such a thing! And am I really the first to know?

PREECE. You are.

EMILY. And you found out this all alone?

PREECE. Oh, yes! Except the manager, nobody has any idea of what I've been experimenting on.

EMILY. Not even father?

PREECE. No.

EMILY. I suppose he knows you *are* experimenting.

PREECE. Of course. That's my job. That's what he took me out of the drawing office for. I'm always experimenting on something.

EMILY. I expect you're what they call an inventor.

PREECE (*humorously*). I expect I am. (*Eagerly*) I'd practically finished this experiment a week ago. But I had to make sure whether there was any manganese left in the steel. I've been getting a friend at the City and Guilds of London Institute to analyse it for me—you know, the big, red building in Exhibition Road. I've just come from there.

EMILY. So *that* was your business in the West End? (PREECE *nods*) I'm sure auntie and I hadn't an idea it was anything half so romantic.

PREECE. It *is* romantic, isn't it?

EMILY. No wonder you're so excited.

PREECE. Am I? Well, I don't care! It's all right. That's all I care about. Here's a bit of the steel now. (*He offers her a small sample.*)

EMILY. Is it for me? May I keep it?

PREECE. I want you to.

EMILY. Rather a strange thing for a girl to keep, isn't it?

PREECE. You don't mind——

EMILY. I'd part with all my jewellery before I parted with this. D'you know, it makes me feel very proud. And when I think of poor old father not knowing *anything* about it——

PREECE. I shall tell him tomorrow if he can spare time to see me.

EMILY. Spare time to see *you*—why?

PREECE. Oh! you don't know, but Mr. Rhead's a sort of crowned head on the works. You can't walk into his office as if it was a public-house, I can tell you.

EMILY. But it's so important for him.

PREECE. Rather! Much more important for him than for me.

EMILY. Why?

PREECE. Under our agreement! Our agreement has five years to run yet, and during that time everything I do belongs to the firm. I only get a percentage on whatever my inventions bring in.

EMILY. What percentage?

PREECE. Ten. For every hundred pounds profit I get ten pounds and the firm gets ninety.

EMILY. But what a frightful shame! It ought to be the other way about—you ninety pounds and the firm ten.

PREECE. Oh, no! It's fair enough—really! They pay me a very good salary. And you must remember if Mr. Rhead hadn't taken me out of the drawing office, I should be there now getting two pounds a week!

EMILY. I don't care! I think it's a frightful shame. I shall tell father.

PREECE (*half playfully*). Please don't unless you want to ruin me with him. I owe just about everything to your father.

EMILY. But it's so horridly unfair.

PREECE. Oh, no! I assure you. I shall have all the money I want, and more. And it will always be *my* invention. That's the point.

EMILY. Then you don't care for money?

PREECE. Yes, I do. I want enough. In fact, I want a good deal. But what's interesting is to *do* things, and to do 'em better and quicker, and less clumsily than ever they were done before. If I can make nineteen tons of steel do the work of twenty—Well, I reckon I've accomplished something for the world.

EMILY. I like that. It's very original.

PREECE. Not my notion, you know. I'm a disciple of William Morris.

EMILY. Oh! He's a poet, isn't he?

PREECE. You should read *The Earthly Paradise.*

EMILY. I should love to.

PREECE. If people would read a bit more William Morris, and less of these silly gim-crack novels about lord and actresses—Ouida and so on—What's the matter?

EMILY. Nothing. (*With a certain self-satisfaction*) William Black's silly too, isn't he?

PREECE. Of course.

EMILY (*firmly*). I'm going to read *The Earthly Paradise*.

PREECE. Let me lend it you. I've got a signed copy, from the author.

EMILY. You know an author!

PREECE. I know William Morris. I was up at his stable last night.

EMILY. His stable?

PREECE. He gives lectures in a stable behind his house at Hammersmith. I wish you'd heard him pitching into the House of Lords. "A squad of dukes."

EMILY. But why?

PREECE. Oh, because they aren't interested in the right thing.

EMILY. What is the right thing?

PREECE. The right thing is to make the world fit to live in.

EMILY. But isn't it?

PREECE. Have you ever been to the East End?

EMILY. I did some slumming once, just to see. But I was so ashamed to go into their awful houses, that I never tried again.

PREECE (*getting up, excited*). That's grand! That's grand! That's just how I feel. Everyone feels like that that's got any imagination and any sense of justice. We *ought* to be ashamed of the East End. At least the governing classes ought. Not for the poor, but for themselves. They ought to go and get buried if they can't govern better than that.

EMILY (*after a pause, rising as in thought; moved*). But how are you going to change it?

PREECE. Not by slumming, that's a certainty. You can only change it by getting some decent laws passed, and by playing fair, and doing your job, and thinking a great deal less about eating and drinking, and fine clothes, and being in the swim and all that sort of nonsense. Do you know what I am going to do as soon as I can afford? I'm going to be a Member of Parliament.

EMILY (*low*). Why did you offer to take us to the Hotel Métropole?

PREECE (*confused*). I thought you'd like it. I—I——

EMILY. You despise it yourself.

PREECE. I'm human.

EMILY. But—— (*She draws close to him.*)

PREECE. I'm very ambitious. I want a whole lot of things. But if I thought I could find someone—find a woman, who—who feels as I feel; who'd like before everything to help to make the world decent—I'd——

EMILY. I—— (*Profoundly stirred, she falls into his arms.*)

PREECE. Emily! (*He kisses her long, holding her close.*)

EMILY (*gently releases herself and walks away. With effort*). I haven't told you. I forgot. Father doesn't wish me to go out with you this afternoon. He's here now, in the study. (GERTRUDE *enters from the hall, without her bonnet this time.*)

GERT. Good afternoon, Mr. Preece. (*They shake hands. To* EMILY) I suppose you—er—told Mr. Preece that the excursion is countermanded? (*She goes to the fireplace.*)

EMILY. Yes, Mr. Preece was just going. (*Gently*) Good afternoon. (*She holds out her hand to* PREECE, *who hesitates.* EMILY *repeats in firmer tone*) Good afternoon. (*In a tender voice*) Please! (*With a smile*) Another time! (PREECE *shakes hands and, bowing to* GERTRUDE, *retires. As he departs* GERTRUDE *rings the bell by the fireplace.*)

GERT. Well, I've been catching it, I can tell you!

EMILY (*shaken*). What about?

GERT. About you. They simply asked me to go into the study so that I could be talked to—for your good, my girl.

EMILY. They weren't rude, were they?

GERT. You know your mother's always almost most considerate. She's an angel. But your father rubbed it in finely. How many times had you seen the young man?—If ever alone?—What on earth was I thinking of?—What on earth was your mother doing to have noticed nothing? (As if your mother ever noticed anything!) And so on! Of course, I told them pretty straight that they were making a most ridiculous fuss about nothing.

EMILY. Well, anyhow, I've let him kiss me.

GERT. You've let him kiss you? When?

EMILY. Just now. Here.

GERT. But what——

EMILY. Don't ask me. I don't know, I really don't. But I've felt it coming for some time.

GERT. Do you mean to say he walked in here and proposed to you straight off, and you accepted him?

EMILY. I didn't accept him, because he didn't propose. He was talking about his ideas.

GERT. What ideas?

EMILY (*with a vague gesture*). Oh, about the world in general, and all that he means to do. He's made another marvellous invention, only no one knows except me. It was the excited way he talked—somehow—I couldn't help it—before I knew what we were doing, he'd got his arms round me.

GERT. (*rather sternly, in spite of her tender feeling*). Well, Emily, I must say I'm very surprised.

EMILY. So am I.

GERT. Of course you're engaged to him?

EMILY. Am I?

GERT. And it'll be all my fault. However, it's got to be seen through to the end now.

EMILY. He has very strange ideas. They sound splendid when he's explaining them. But d'you know, he thinks Ouida's silly.

GERT. Does he?

EMILY. And he really doesn't care about money and fashion and all that sort of thing. He despises going to the Hotel Métropole. He only offered to go there because he thought it would please our horrid little minds—I was so ashamed.

GERT. But surely you knew all this before—at least you guessed it?

EMILY. I didn't, auntie. I never thought about his ideas, never! I just——

GERT. You just simply fell into his arms as soon as you heard them, that's all. Well, surely in that case, you must admire these ideas of his tremendously. (*She sits in an armchair.*)

EMILY. I don't know. Yes. I *admire* them, but——

GERT. Listen, young woman! Are you in love with him, or aren't you?

EMILY. I—I—— How can you tell whether you're in love with a man or not?

GERT. Supposing you were alone with him here, now—would you let him kiss you again? (*Pause.*)

EMILY. I——

GERT. Now, out with it!

EMILY. I shouldn't be able to stop him, should I?

GERT. That's enough.

EMILY. Yes. But then what about father? He would be frightfully angry, I can see that. Oh, I do hate unpleasantness, auntie. And Mr. Preece's ideas are really very peculiar.

GERT (*after a look at* EMILY). Listen, Emily! I was once engaged to be married.

EMILY. Oh, auntie! I always knew you must have been. Do tell me. Who was it?

GERT. Your Uncle Sam.

EMILY. (*staggered*). Not Uncle Sam?

GERT. You're surprised, naturally. But you musn't be too hard. Remember it was twenty-five years ago, Uncle Sam was a splendid fellow then. He's old now. We're all old, except you—and Mr. Preece. You've got the only thing worth having, you two.

EMILY (*sitting at* GERTRUDE'S *feet*). What's that?

GERT. Youth. Your Uncle Sam lived the miserable life of a bachelor till he was fifty. He'd have been a very different man if I'd married him. And I should have been a very different woman.

EMILY. Why did you break it off?

GERT. I broke it off because there were difficulties; and because I thought his ideas were peculiar; and because I hated unpleasantness! And now look at me! Couldn't I have ruled a house and a family?

Couldn't I have played the hostess? (*In another tone*) Today the one poor little joy I have in life is to pretend I'm your mother. Look at my position here. I'm only——

EMILY (*passionately*). Oh, auntie, don't! I can't bear to hear you say it. I know!

GERT. We were opposite in every way, your uncle and I, but I–I loved him.

EMILY (*softly*). Do you still love him, auntie?

GERT. (*in a flat tone of despair*). No! Love dies out.

EMILY (*after a moment*). Why didn't you marry somebody else?

GERT. There *was* nobody else. There never is anybody else when you've made the mistake I made. Marry! I could have chosen among a dozen men! But they were all the wrong men. Emily! Fancy pouring out tea every day of your life for the wrong man. Every breakfast time–every afternoon! And there he sits, and nothing will move him. Think of that, Emily–think of that. (*A pause.*)

EMILY (*embracing her again*). Oh, auntie! *I* love you awfully!

GERT. You must show some courage, my girl. Don't be afraid of anything–and especially not of arguments and threats. What does unpleasantness matter, after all? It's over in a month; but a mistake lasts for ever.

EMILY. You'll help me?

GERT. That's all I live for. (*She kisses* EMILY *tenderly*) Is that Sam's voice? (THOMPSON *enters.*)

THOMPSON (*announcing*). Mr. and Mrs. Sibley. (*He retires*) (SAMUEL SIBLEY *and his wife* NANCY *enter.* SAMUEL, *who is now fifty-three, has grown into a rather flabby nonentity, grey-haired with longish side whiskers and glasses. His manner is important and fussy.* NANCY *is a buxom, Yorkshire woman of thirty-two, round-faced, good-natured, full of energy. She wears the fashionable jersey of* 1885 *and a very definite "bustle."*)

SAM. Well, Gertrude? Well, my little Emmie! (*He kisses* EMILY, *who gives her cheek unwillingly; then shakes hands with* GERTRUDE.)

GERT. How are you, Sam; and you, Mrs. Sam?

NANCY. Nicely, thank you! (*Shaking hand vigorously with* GERTRUDE *and* EMILY) Everybody well, here?

EMILY. Yes, thank you.

NANCY. That's fine! Then your mother got Sam's letter saying we were coming?

EMILY (*drily*). Oh, yes!

NANCY. I said to Sam it would happen be best to write and tell you. So he wrote–(*with a look at* SAM) –finally.

SAM (*with a serious tone*). We nearly didn't come.

GERT. Anything wrong?

SAM. Infant's temperature up at a hundred last night. However, it was normal this morning.

NANCY. You know he takes the baby's temperature every night.

EMILY. Oh, do you, uncle? How funny!

SAM. I don't see anything funny about it, niece. Good thing if some parents took their responsibilities a bit more seriously.

NANCY. I must say Sam makes a very good father.

GERT. Let me see—how old is Dickie now?

SAM. We never call him Dickie—Richard, better; less nonsensical. (*He settles down solemnly in a chair.*)

NANCY. You've no idea what I call him when you're not there, Sam! (*To* GERTRUDE) He was two on the second of this month. He talks like anything! You ought to see him and his father together. It's killing! The little thing's so *exactly* like Sam.

EMILY (*examining* SAM). Is he? We must go down to Brockley, mustn't we, auntie?

NANCY (*drily*). I've been expecting you for the better part of some time. (*Then cordially*) I should love you to come as soon as I've got a new cook. (*With emphasis*) Oh, my!

GERT. Are you having trouble?

NANCY. Trouble's not the word. And as for the nurse-maid! If it wasn't for Sam being free——

GERT. D'you take your share, Sam?

NANCY. By the hour he wheels that child up and down.

EMILY. Not in the street?

SAM. Why not, niece? Anything to be ashamed of in being a father?

NANCY. That's what we came up for today, to buy a new perambulator. He did try to repair the other in the little workshop he's made himself at the end of the garden—and most useful he is for odd jobs. Upon my word, he's busy from morning to night! But we thought it better to buy a new pram altogether.

SAM (*discontented*). Nancy would insist on having one of those new things with indiarubber tyres, as they call them.

NANCY (*very definitely*). Now, Sam. I thought we'd done with that question.

SAM. Yes; but rubber tyres on gravel paths! It's obvious they'll not last a——

NANCY. I told you Mrs. Caton across the road told me——

SAM. Oh, very well! Very well! Only it's very light and flimsy.

EMILY (*restless*). I think I'll go and tell father and mother you're here. (*Going towards the door.*)

NANCY (*rising, very convinced*). Come and see for yourself what you think of the pram and the rubber tyres.

EMILY (*rising*). It it here?

NANCY. Yes, in the hall.

SAM. I deemed it imprudent to let them send it down by train. So we brought it away on the roof of a four-wheeler.

EMILY (*patronisingly*). Well, let's go and inspect it, Aunt Nancy. (EMILY *and* NANCY *go off.*)

GERT. (*waiting till the door is closed; in low, quiet tones*). Sam, I'm so glad you've come. There's going to be another tragedy in this house, if some of us don't do something.

SAM. *Another* tragedy? What do you mean?

GERT. I just mean a tragedy. That child's head over heels in love with young Arthur Preece, at the works, and John simply won't hear of it.

SAM. Why?

GERT. (*shrugs her shoulders*). Why, indeed? Sam, if there's any discussion while you're here I want you to help me all you can.

SAM. But really, Gertrude, How can I meddle in an affair like that? I have my own responsibilities.

GERT. Sam, it's many years since I asked the slightest favour of you.

SAM (*moved, friendly*). Come, come. Don't go so far back as all that. We're all very comfortable as we are, I think. (*The door opens.*)

GERT. (*quick and low*). But will you? You've got more influence than I have.

SAM (*low*). All right. (*Pats her arm*) All right. (*Enter* ROSE *and* JOHN.)

JOHN (*coming up to* SAM *a little patronisingly*). Sam, glad to see you! How's the precious family getting on? Any new trouble lately?

SAM (*a little sharply*). Oh, no! And what about yours? (*In a significant, bantering tone*) Any new trouble lately?

JOHN. Mine? Trouble? No!

ROSE (*kissing* SAM *fondly*). Your wife's here?

SAM. She's downstairs somewhere——

JOHN (*interrupting sharply*). Where's Emily?

GERT. She's just gone with Mrs. Sam to look at a new——

JOHN (*interrupting again*). Preece hasn't been, has he?

GERT. He's been and gone.

JOHN. Were you here?

GERT. I was here part of the time.

JOHN. You ought to have been here all the time. What did you tell him?

GERT. Emily told him you wished us to stay at home this afternoon.

JOHN (*nodding curtly*). So much for that.

SAM. So even *you* are not quite without 'em, Jack?

JOHN. Not quite without what?

SAM. Family troubles.

JOHN. What in heaven's name are you driving at?

SAM. Nothing. I only gathered from your tone that Preece was considered—er—dangerous.

JOHN (*hedging*). Oh, no! I'm merely taking precautions. Preece is an excellent fellow in his way—brilliant even.

SAM. But you wouldn't care for him as a son-in-law.

JOHN (*positively*). I should not.

ROSE (*shaking her head*). No!

SAM. I've always understood he had a great career before him.

JOHN. So he has, undoubtedly. You should see what he's got me to do at the works. Made me instal the telephone. And his latest is that he wants me to put down an electric light plant. What do you think of that?

SAM. He must be very enthusiastic.

GERT. I should think he just is!

JOHN. Why, the boy's invention-mad. He thinks of nothing else.

SAM. Well, if you ask me I'd sooner have that kind of madness than most kinds I meet with. Seems to me people have gone mad on bicycles or banjo-playing or this lawn-tennis, as it's called. It was different in our day, Jack, when young men took an interest in volunteering and the defence of their country. I've quite decided when our boy grows up——

GERT. (*putting a hand on* SAM'S *arm*). Sam!—Emily may be back any moment. We were talking about Arthur Preece.

SAM. So we were. (*Turns again to* JOHN) Well, Jack——

JOHN (*annoyed*). Look here, Sam—I don't mind being frank with you. Her mother and I have somebody else in view for Emily.

SAM. Oh!

GERT. (*bitterly*). I thought as much. (*A slight pause.*)

JOHN (*carelessly to* SAM). Have you heard I'm going to have a title?

SAM. No! What title?

JOHN. Baronet.

GERT. (*quickly*). You never told me.

ROSE (*soothingly*). It only came out this afternoon, Gertrude dear.

SAM. Oh—ho.

JOHN (*still with an affectation of carelessness*). And what's more, Emily can marry—under the very happiest auspices—into the peerage. That's why we don't want her to see too much of young Preece.

SAM. And may one ask who is the Peer?

JOHN. Monkhurst, of course.

SAM. Ned!

GERT. Ned?

ROSE. Wouldn't it be ideal, Sam!

SAM. He's keen—Ned?

JOHN. Very! Put that in your pipe and smoke it, my boy. (EMILY *and* NANCY *re-enter rather suddenly. All the others have a self-conscious air.*)

JOHN (*rather negligently*). Well, Nancy. How are you? It seems the infant's grown out of his pram. (*Shakes hands.*)

NANCY (*rather proud of being able to call the great man "John" and yet trying not to be proud*). Glad to see you, John. (ROSE *and* NANCY *embrace. An awkward pause.*)

EMILY (*with suspicion*). What's the matter here? More secrets?

GERT. (*in an outburst*). It's being arranged that you are to marry Lord Monkhurst.

JOHN (*nonplussed, coldly angry*). Gertrude, are you stark staring mad—blurting things out like that?

ROSE (*shocked*). Gertrude, dear—really!

GERT. (*firmly*). She'd better know, hadn't she?

JOHN. You——

NANCY (*blandly*). Well, anyhow, the fat's in the fire now, isn't it, John?

JOHN (*turning to* NANCY). Sorry you've been let in for a bit of a scene, Nancy.

NANCY (*cheerfully*). Oh! Don't mind me. I know what family life is—my word! I'm from Yorkshire! Best to have it out fair and square—that's my experience.

SAM. That's what she always says when the infant's obstreperous. Why, the night before last, just as we were getting off to sleep——

JOHN. There's nothing to have out!

GERT. Oh, yes, there is. Emily's in love with Arthur Preece.

JOHN. What's this?

EMILY (*very nervous; to* GERTRUDE). What do you mean—it's being arranged for me to marry Lord Monkhurst? Me—marry old Ned!

JOHN. He's not old.

EMILY. Isn't he old enough to be my father?

JOHN. Certainly not.

SAM (*mischievously*). I doubt it.

JOHN (*turning on him*). You're the last man to talk about difference of age between husband and wife.

ROSE (*smoothing over the awkwardness*). But you're very happy, aren't you, dear?

SAM. Naturally.

NANCY. I don't see that age matters—so long as people really fancy each other. I'm sure Sam gets younger every day.

JOHN. Of course! (*Turning to* EMILY *angrily*) What's this tale about you being in love with Preece?

EMILY. I——

JOHN. Has he been proposing to you?

EMILY. No.

JOHN (*disdainfully*). Then how can you be in love with him?

EMILY (*resenting his tone*). Well, I *am* in love with him, if you want to know, father.

JOHN. You have the audacity——

NANCY. Come, John, it's not a crime.

JOHN. Preece is not of our class at all. It's a gross mistake to marry out of your class.

NANCY (*bantering*). Now, John, that's not very tactful, seeing that Sam married out of *his* class.

SAM. Don't be foolish, Nan! I married a lady. Even a marquis couldn't do more.

JOHN. My dear Nancy, you belong to the family—that's enough! Preece is quite a different affair. Just a common clerk until I——

EMILY. I can't see what more you want. He has the most beautiful manners, and, as for money, he'll make lots.

JOHN. How will he make lots?

EMILY. With his inventions. You haven't heard about his latest. But I have. He's told me. Here it is. (*Hands piece of steel to her father.*)

JOHN (*taking it*). And what's this?

EMILY. I don't know exactly. But it's very wonderful. It's steel, I think—a new kind.

JOHN (*drily*). Yes. I see it's steel.

EMILY. And I think it's a great shame for you to take nine-tenths of all the money from his inventions, and for *him* to only have one-tenth.

JOHN (*flashing up*). What? Has he been whining to you in that style?

EMILY (*passionately*). No, he hasn't been whining to me in that style. He hasn't been whining at all. He thought it was quite fair. It only came out by pure accident, and I promised I'd never breathe a word. You must forget what I've said.

JOHN. I'll teach him——

EMILY (*more passionately*). If you ever say a single thing, father, I'll run away and never come back.

ROSE. Child! please! (*She tries to soothe her.*)

SAM (*to calm the stress*). Hand over, Jack. (*Takes the piece of steel and looks at it*) I fully admit I was wrong about iron. But even *you* won't prophesy that steel's going to take the place of iron for ships!

JOHN (*shortly*). I don't think it is in *my* works. But, as for prophesying—I don't prophesy. Heavens knows no one can accuse me of being conservative in my ideas. But I must say the new generation seems to be going clean off its head. If one of these up-to-date inventors came along and told me he'd made a flying-machine, I should keep my nerve. I shouldn't blench.

SAM. Good! Good!

GERT. Now you're at flying-machines! What have flying-machines got to do with Emily's happiness? If she wants to marry young Preece——

EMILY. Yes, if I want to marry him, why shouldn't I?

ROSE. Because your father objects.

EMILY. Oh, mother. Didn't you marry father, in spite of everyone?

JOHN. Who's told you that?

EMILY. I know. (*General glances at* GERTRUDE.)

ROSE (*indignant*). Do you mean to compare young Preece with your father?

EMILY. Why not? You loved father, and I——

JOHN. I'll tell you why not. I was independent. I was my own master. Young Mr. Preece isn't. That's why.

GERT. (*sarcastically*). Surely it's a free country—for men!

JOHN. It's not a country where honest men break their contracts. Young Preece can't patent an invention without me. Can't do anything without me. If I like, I can force him to mark time for five years, five solid years.

EMILY. Does that mean that if I married him in spite of you——

ROSE (*horrified*). Child! Well may you say we've spoilt you!

JOHN (*calmly*). It means that if he had the impudence to marry you, I'd scotch him—*that* I would.

EMILY. But why? Who's going to suffer? How can my marriage affect anybody but me?

JOHN. Don't talk like a little fool. Your marriage is the most important thing in the whole world to your mother and me. And if you persist in doing something against our will, I shall retaliate—that's all.

EMILY (*with a despairing gesture*). I can't make out your objections to Mr. Preece. Why, he's a genius; everyone *knows* he's a genius.

JOHN. And what if he is? Are geniuses to be the kings of the earth? Not quite! Geniuses have to be kept in order like criminals. If there's one thing above all to be said in favour of the English character, it is that we've known the proper way to treat geniuses.

SAM. I'm inclined to agree with you there.

JOHN (*to* EMILY). Oh, it isn't Preece's class I object to. He's presentable enough. The whole truth is he's a highly dangerous sort of young man we're breeding in these days. He—makes you feel—uncomfortable. In the works, under discipline, admirable. Outside the works—no, no! And no! I've been following Master Preece's activities far more closely than he thinks. He little guesses I know he's a Socialist!

SAM. A Socialist! Good God! Gertrude, you never told me that. A Socialist!

GERT. Why are men always so frightened by names?

JOHN. A Socialist. (*To* EMILY, *an ultimatum*) And I don't intend you to marry him. If you do, you ruin him. That's the long and short of it. Now, Emily, have we heard the last of Preece—or not?

ROSE (*to* EMILY). Darling!

GERT. I really think you ought——

JOHN (*curtly*). Pardon me, Gertrude. This isn't your affair. It's my daughter's.

GERT. (*to* EMILY). Your father is right. It's your affair. It depends solely on you.

EMILY (*weeping imploringly*). What am I to do, auntie? (GERTRUDE *turns away with a movement of pain and disgust.*)

EMILY. I don't want to make everybody miserable.

GERT. (*reproachfully*). Oh, Emily!

EMILY. I couldn't stand—in Mr. Preece's light! I couldn't.

JOHN. There! There! Of course you couldn't.

ROSE (*comforting her*). My poor lamb!

JOHN. And don't go and suppose I want to compel you to marry Monkhurst—or anybody. You're absolutely free.

GERT. (*sniffs audibly*). H'm!

JOHN (*glaring at* GERTRUDE *to* EMILY). Only, as your aunt *has* dragged in his name, I don't see any harm in telling you this much. He adores you. We all like him. His wife will have a position second to none in London Society. But don't let that influence you. Take him or refuse him as you please; your mother and I won't complain.

ROSE. Indeed we sha'n't, my love.

JOHN. Still a marriage like this is not to be sneezed at. Is it, Emily? (*Pause*) I say, *is* it?

EMILY (*trying to smile; weakly*). No.

JOHN (*continuing*). Not that I think it wouldn't be a big slice of luck for Monkhurst, too! There's only one Emily! (*He pats her*) And then my title——

NANCY. Your title, John?

JOHN (*carelessly*). Haven't you heard?

NANCY. No!

JOHN (*as above*). Baronetcy!

NANCY (*staggered*). Wonders'll never cease. (*To* ROSE) What a pity you've got no son, dear!

ROSE (*with a trace of bitterness*). Don't crow over us, dear! (*She clasps* EMILY *to her.*)

SAM (*with a sigh of regret for himself*). Well, well! And I've retired into private life!

JOHN (*surveying him patronisingly*). And you've retired into private life. You're safe at Brockley. But then you see you hadn't got a bee in your bonnet.

SAM (*accepting the sarcasm with a foolish smile*). Well, well!

NANCY (*sharply*). I don't see that there's any need for so much well-welling.

JOHN. Come and give your father a kiss, Em. (EMILY *obeys.*)

GERT. (*rising as she does so, full of emotion*). I—— (THOMPSON *enters followed by a* FOOTMAN. *They bring in tea.* GERTRUDE *pulls herself together. There is a slight pause while the* SERVANTS *arrange the tea-things. They leave the room.*)

ROSE. Emily, dear, will you pour out?

EMILY (*demurely*). Yes, mother.

ROSE. I hope Ned won't be late.

NANCY. Is Lord Monkhurst coming for tea?

ROSE. He promised to.

NANCY. Oh, dear! If I'd known I was going to meet him—— (*She rises and arranges her bustle and the draperies of her skirt*) I do hope he won't notice that pram. A pram in a hall looks so common. (*She reseats herself.* THOMPSON *enters.*)

THOMPSON (*announcing*). Lord Monkhurst! (*He retires.*)

GERT. (*passionately*). Here's your lord! (NED *enters rapidly.*)

NED. Well, kind friends. Hullo, Sam!

SAM. Hullo, Ned! (*They shake hands*) By the way, my wife—Nancy, Lord Monkhurst. (NANCY *flustered, bows.*)

NED (*going towards* EMILY). Delighted! Any of that tea for me?

GERT. (*with great feeling*). And there's your tea—your daily tea, for the rest of your life.

JOHN (*angrily*). Gertrude!

GERT. No, I will speak! Ned, what would *you* do, if I told you that——

EMILY (*pleading*). Aunt Gertrude, please——

GERT. Emily?

EMILY (*weakly*). It's all right, auntie.

GERT. All right? Oh, very well! (*Desperately*) What's the use! (*She turns and walks quickly out of the room.*)

NED (*surprised at* GERTRUDE'S *tone*). What's the matter with dear Gertrude?

JOHN. Nothing. One of her moods. (*Drawing up a chair, with authority*) Now then, Emily,—tea!

CURTAIN

ACT THREE

1912

The same drawing-room, but now in 1912, *it has undergone an entire change. All of the old mid-Victorian furniture has been crowded out by furniture of later style. Changes of ornaments, etc. The lights are electric; so is the bell by the fireplace.*

It is a June evening, about half-past ten at night. Signs of festivity—flowers, presents (in gold) are standing about. It is the evening of the Golden Wedding of JOHN *and* ROSE. WEBSTER, *a smart, military-looking butler of forty, is arranging a tray of whiskey and soda. The door to the hall opens, and a* FOOTMAN *enters.*

FOOTMAN (*announcing*). Lord Monkhurst. (*He withdraws*) (*Lord Monkhurst enters. He is a young man-about-town of twenty-two, tall, hollow-chested, careless in his manners, very self-assured and properly bored.*)

MONK. I say, Webster.

WEBSTER. Good evening, my lord.

MONK (*cheerfully*). I suppose dinner's over?

WEBSTER (*looking at his watch*). It's half-past ten, my lord.

MONK. Of course, they'll all say I'm late for dinner.

WEBSTER. Oh, no, my lord. Shall I order some dinner for your lordship?

MONK. No. Who's here now?

WEBSTER. Lady Monkhurst and Miss Muriel; Miss Rhead, Mrs. Samuel Sibley, and Mr. Richard Sibley.

MONK. Yes. I know *he's* here. Many people at the reception this afternoon?

WEBSTER. Droves, my lord.

MONK. I suppose these ghastly things are the presents?

WEBSTER. As your lordship says.

MONK. Dashed if I can understand why my grandfather should make such a fuss about his golden wedding. (*Very cheerfully*) Was he very angry at me not turning up?

WEBSTER. Considering his age, no, my lord. I took the liberty of suggesting to him that this might be one of your busy weeks, my lord, and that your lordship could never tell beforehand——

MONK. You're a clever chap, Webster. Why the devil did you leave the army?

WEBSTER. Probably because, as your lordship says, I'm clever. There's more brains outside the army than in it, my lord. And like turns to like.

MONK (*laughing in a superior way*). Ha! ha! Really!

WEBSTER. Fact is, I enlisted under a misapprehension, when I was in a temper. I have to thank your lordship's late father for helping me to re-enter my old profession, and under the most auspicious circumstances.

MONK. Well, we could do with more fellahs like you. I've not yet found any serjeant to draw my sketch maps for me half as well as you used to. (*He is looking over the tray with drinks.*)

WEBSTER. Ah, my lord! Those half-guineas came in very handy, very handy. Glorious times, no doubt. But I wouldn't go back.

MONK. Bring me a benedictine, will you?

(EMILY, *now* LADY MONKHURST, *forty-eight, enters by the double doors. She has developed into a handsome, well-preserved woman of the world. She wears an evening dress of rich brocade, and magnificent pearls.*)

MONK. Well, mater, I don't see much sign of the fatted calf.

EMILY (*annoyed*). Gerald, your poor father was witty; you are merely facetious. I wish you could cure yourself.

MONK. Now, what's the matter now?

EMILY. What's the matter? You must needs choose your grandparents' golden wedding to go to Sandown. You promised me you'd be back early, at any rate in time for the tail end of the reception; and you don't even appear for dinner. Your grandfather is very displeased.

MONK. If a fellow keeps a stable, he keeps a stable. Somebody's got to look after the gees in these days. And then—— (*Hesitates.*)

EMILY. Please don't tell me your car broke down. I've heard that too often.

MONK. It didn't—this time.

EMILY. Have you dined?

MONK. I have.

EMILY. Whom with? (*Silence*) One of your numerous "lady friends," I presume. Gerald, I'm ashamed of you.

MONK. You've no right to be ashamed of me. If you want to know, I dined at the House of Lords.

EMILY. At the House of Lords?

MONK. At the House of Lords. They telephoned to me at Sandown to come up for an important division, and I was kept hanging about there till after ten o'clock. Jolly amusing place, the House of Lords.

EMILY (*rather taken aback*). Why didn't you tell me at first?

MONK. Because I just wanted to teach you a lesson, mater. You're always ragging me about something or other.

EMILY. You might at least have telephoned.

MONK. When a chap's doing his duty to his country, he can't always think about telephoning.

EMILY. My dear Gerald, if you mean to follow in your father's footsteps, nobody will be more delighted than your mother. There'd be nothing to prevent you from being Master of the Horse, if you chose. Only, my chick——

MONK. Only your what?

EMILY. You must alter your manner of living.

MONK. My manner of living, my dear mater, is my own affair. (*With meaning*) If you'd leave me alone, and look after your other "chick" a little bit more——

EMILY. What do you mean? Muriel?

MONK. Precisely. The Honourable Muriel.

EMILY. Why?

MONK. Oh! I know Muriel can do no wrong. Still, I spotted her at the top of the stairs just now practically in the arms of the good Richard.

EMILY. Richard!

MONK (*intoning*). And Samuel took to wife Nancy, and begat Richard. And Samuel passed away in the fulness of years and his son Richard reigned in his stead. And Richard looked upon Muriel, and lo! she was beautiful in the eyes of Richard——

EMILY. Hush, Gerald! Aren't you mistaken? I've never seen the slightest thing——

MONK. That shows how blind you are, then! Of course I'm not mistaken.

EMILY. Are you sure?

MONK. Do you take me for a fool, mater?

EMILY (*positively*). Richard, indeed! I shall put a stop to it.

MONK (*almost savagely*). I should jolly well think you would. (*Enter* WEBSTER *from the hall with a liqueur on a salver.* MONKHURST *takes it and drinks it slowly.*)

EMILY. Webster, will you kindly ask Miss Muriel to come here?

WEBSTER. Very good, my lady. (*He goes out.* MONKHURST *nods knowingly to his mother as if to say, "Now you'll see!"* NANCY *enters by the double doors. She has grown into a rather red-faced, plump, old woman of fifty-eight. She is good-natured, but is quick to retort. Her laugh is rather loud, her manner more definite than ever.*)

NANCY. Good evening, young man.

MONK. Good evening.

NANCY. So you've come at——

EMILY (*interrupting her*). Aunt Nancy, I've just had to send for Muriel to come here.

NANCY. What's amiss?

EMILY. I—well—I hardly like——

MONK. Your excellent son Richard has been seen trying to kiss my sister.

NANCY. What was *she* doing?

EMILY. Well, that's not the point.

NANCY. And supposing he *was* trying to kiss Muriel?

EMILY. I must say, Aunt Nancy, you don't seem very surprised.

NANCY. Who *would* be? You invite young people to a golden wedding, and then you're startled when you catch 'em kissing. What else do you expect?

EMILY. I expected a good deal else.

NANCY. Then you're likely to be disappointed. As a matter of fact, I knew Richard was going to kiss Muriel tonight.

EMILY. Who told you?

NANCY. *He* did, of course. At least, he let out to me he was going to propose to her. He usually gets what he wants, you know.

EMILY (*angrily surprised*). H'm!

MONK (*very definitely*). He won't get what he wants this time.

NANCY. Oh?

MONK. You must see that my sister can't marry an engineer.

NANCY. Well—why not an engineer? What are *you*? I can tell you what you might have been, if you hadn't been born in the right bedroom: you might have been a billiard-marker. What have you done? Tell me a single thing you've done?

MONK. I've—oh! What tripe!

EMILY. Really, Aunt Nancy——

NANCY. Yes, my son *is* an engineer. And if you want to know what sort of an engineer he is, go to Mr. Arthur Preece.

MONK (*disdainfully*). Who's Preece?

NANCY (*imitating his tone*). Ask your mother who *Preece* is.

EMILY (*self-consciously*). Aunt Nancy!

NANCY (*continuing*). You aren't old enough to remember Mr. Preece as an engineer, but, at any rate, you know he's in the House of Commons, whereas you're only in the House of Lords. And I'd like you to tell me where your grandfather'd have been last week with all his workmen on strike—but for Mr. Preece!

MONK. Oh, *that* Preece!

NANCY. Exactly. And it's that Preece that thinks the world of my son. My son's been out to Canada, and look how he got on in Winnipeg! And now he's going out again, whose capital is he taking but your grandfather's? I should like to see your grandfather trust *you* with thirty thousand pounds and a ticket to Canada.

MONK. I'm in no need of capital, thank ye.

NANCY. Lucky for you you aren't! My husband left me very badly off, poor man, but I could count on Richard. A pretty look-out for your mother if she'd had to count on you!

EMILY (*impatient*). Really, Aunt Nancy——

NANCY (*nettled*). Well, you leave my son alone.
(*Enter from the hall* MURIEL *and* RICHARD. MURIEL *is a handsome girl of twenty-four, rather thin and eager with a high forehead, and with much distinction. She has herself under absolute control. Richard is a tall, broad, darkish fellow of twenty-seven, with a clean-shaven heavy face and rough hair. He is very taciturn.*)

EMILY. Muriel, it was you that I asked for.

MURIEL (*quite calmly*). We were both just coming to tell you.

EMILY. Tell me what?

MURIEL. We're engaged.

EMILY. Does Richard leave you to say this to me?

MURIEL. Well, you know he was never a great talker.

RICHARD. There it is—we're engaged.

NANCY (*to* MURIEL). How matter-of-fact you are, you girls, nowdays. (*She caresses* RICHARD.)

MURIEL. Well, nobody seems strikingly enthusiastic here.

EMILY. I should think not. I don't like these underhand ways.

MURIEL. What underhand ways? Surely you didn't expect Richard to announce in advance the exact place and hour he was going to propose to me.

EMILY. Please don't try to imitate your dear father. You're worse than Gerald sometimes.

MURIEL. Oh, very well, mamma! What else?

EMILY. Do you mean to tell me you're seriously thinking of going out to Canada—to Winnipeg—for the rest of your days?

MURIEL. Of course, mama! I'm sure I shall be happier there than here.

EMILY. You'll leave England?

MURIEL. Certainly. Politics are much more satifactory over there, except for woman's suffrage. All the questions that all the silly statesmen are still wrangling about here have been settled over there ages ago.

EMILY. My poor girl!

MURIEL. Mamma, I wish you wouldn't say "my poor girl."

EMILY. What have politics to do with happiness?

MURIEL. They have a great deal to do with mine. But, of course, what most attracts me is all those thousands of square miles of wheat fields, and Richard making reaping-machines for them. The day I first see one of Richard's new machines at work on a Canadian wheat-farm will be the happiest day of my life—except today.

NANCY (*amazed at these sentiments*). Well, you're a caution.

MONK (*with disgust*). Why not marry an agricultural implement while you're about it?

RICHARD (*threateningly*). You shut up!

MURIEL. But aren't you glad, mamma?

EMILY. I can't discuss the matter now.

MURIEL. But what is there to discuss?

EMILY (*after a pause*). Muriel, I tell you at once, both of you, I sha'n't allow this marriage.

MURIEL. Not allow it? My poor mamma!

MONK. Certainly not.

RICHARD. I've told you to shut up once.

EMILY. And your grandfather won't allow it, either.

MURIEL. Of course, mamma, you and I have always been devoted to each other. You've made allowances for me, and I've made allowances for you. But you must please remember that we're in the year 1912. I've promised to marry Richard, and I shall marry him. There's no question of being "allowed." And if it comes to that, why shouldn't I marry him, indeed?

EMILY. You—your father's daughter, to think of going out to Winnipeg as the wife of a—your place is in London.

RICHARD (*stiffening at the sight of trouble*). But I say, Cousin Emily——

MURIEL (*gentle, but firmly*). Richard—please. (*Turning to her mother*) Mamma, you really do shock me. Just because I'm the Honourable Muriel Pym! (*Laughs*) I won't say you're a snob, because everybody's a snob, in some way or other. But you don't understand the new spirit, not in the least—and I'm so sorry. Why! Hasn't it occurred to you even yet that the aristocracy racket's played out? (ROSE *and* JOHN *enter by the double doors. They have both grown very old,* ROSE *being seventy-three and* JOHN *seventy-seven.* ROSE *has become short-sighted, white-haired and stoutish.* JOHN *has grown a little deaf; his hair is thin, his eyes sunken, his complexion of wax, his features sharply defined.* GERTRUDE *follows them, now seventy-three. She has grown into a thin shrivelled old woman, erect, hard with a high, shrill voice and keen, clear eyes.*)

ROSE. Oh! It's here they seem to be collected. (*To* MONKHURST) Is that you, Gerald? Wherever has the poor lamb been? (*She kisses him.*)

MONK. Grandma, congratulations. (*To* JOHN) Congratulations, sir.

JOHN (*sternly*). Is this what you call good manners, boy?

MONK. Sorry, sir. I was kept.

JOHN (*sarcastically*). Kept?

MONK. At the House of Lords. A division.

MURIEL. Good Heavens! Break it to us gently. Has his grandma's lamb gone into politics?

MONK (*haughtily, ignoring his sister*). They telephoned me from headquarters. I thought you would prefer me——

JOHN. Certainly, my boy. (*Shakes his hand*) You couldn't have celebrated our golden wedding in a fashion more agreeable to us than by recording your first vote in the House of Lords. Could he, granny?

ROSE (*feebly*). Bless us! Bless us!

JOHN. What was the division?

MONK (*mumbling*). Er—the Trades Union Bill, sir. Third reading.

JOHN (*not hearing*). What did you say?

MONK (*louder*). Trades Union Bill, sir.

MURIEL. Oh, my poor lamb! The Trades Union Bill division isn't to be taken till tomorrow!

MONK (*hastily*). What am I thinking of? It must have been the Extended Franchise Bill, then. . . . Anyhow, I voted.

JOHN (*coughing*). H'm! H'm!

GERT (*drawing a shawl round her shoulders, fretfully*). Couldn't we have that window closed?

ROSE. Auntie Gertrude, how brave you are! I daren't have asked. I declare I'm a martyr to this ventilation in my old age.

GERT. I daresay I'm very old-fashioned, but when I was young we didn't try to turning a drawing-room into a park.

ROSE (*to* RICHARD, *as he closes the window*). Thank you, Richard.

JOHN (*pettishly*). Put a match to the fire, boy, and have done with it. (*Richard goes to the fireplace, kneels down, and lights the fire.*)

GERT. What's the matter, Emily?

EMILY (*who has begun to weep*). Oh, Auntie Gertrude!

NANCY (*soothingly*). Come, come, Emily.

JOHN. What's that? What's that?

ROSE (*peering at* EMILY). What is it, John?

JOHN. Monkhurst, have you been upsetting your mother again?

MURIEL. I think it's *us*, grandpapa.

JOHN. What does she say?

MURIEL. I'm afraid it's us—Richard and me. We're engaged to be married. (MURIEL *points to* RICHARD, *who is still on his knees busy with the fire.*)

ROSE. Oh, my dear—how sudden! What a shock! What a shock! I can understand your mother crying. I must cry myself. Come and kiss me! It's astonishing how quietly you young people manage these things nowadays. (*Embraces* MURIEL.)

JOHN. Who's engaged to be married? Who's engaged to be married?

RICHARD (*loudly, rising and dusting his hands*). Muriel and I, sir.

JOHN. Mu–Mu——! What the devil do you mean, sir? Emily, what in God's name are you thinking of?

EMILY (*whimpering*). It's just as much of a surprise to me as to anybody. I don't approve of it.

MONK. I've told them already you would never approve, sir.

NANCY. You haven't, young man. It was your mother who told us that.

JOHN (*to* NANCY). I asked you to my golden wedding, Nancy——

NANCY. You did, Sir John. I shouldn't have come without.

JOHN. Do you countenance this—affair?

NANCY. What's wrong with it?

ROSE (*timidly*). Yes, John. What's wrong with it? Why shouldn't my Muriel marry her Richard?

JOHN. What's wrong with it, d'you say? What——!

EMILY (*passionately*). I won't agree to it.

JOHN (*to* NANCY). Nothing wrong with it, from your point of view. Nothing! (*Laughing*) Only I sha'n't have it. I won't have it.

ROSE. Grandpa, why do you always try to cross me?

JOHN. I? You?

ROSE. I've been yielding to you in everything for fifty years. I think I'm old enough to have my own way now—just once.

JOHN (*startled*). What's come over you?

ROSE. Nothing's come over me. But I really——

JOHN (*subduing her*). Be silent, granny!

NANCY. We thought you thought very highly of Richard.

JOHN. So I do. But what's that got to do with it? It's nothing but this genius business over again.

NANCY. Genius business?

JOHN. Yes. I shall be told Richard's a genius, therefore he must be allowed to marry Muriel. Nonsense! I had just the same difficulty with her mother twenty-six years ago. You ought to remember; you were there! Hadn't I, Emily?

EMILY (*faintly*). Yes.

JOHN (*not hearing*). What's that?

EMILY. Yes, father. Yes.

JOHN. Of course I had. I wouldn't have it then, and I won't have it now. What? Here's a young fellow, a very smart engineer. Insists on going to Canada. Wants capital! Well, I give it him! I tell him he may go. Everything's settled. And then, if you please, he calmly announces his intention of carrying off my granddaughter—him!

ROSE. If she's your granddaughter, he's my nephew.

JOHN (*glaring at her*). Sh!

ROSE. No! I wo——

JOHN (*continuing, staring at* ROSE). My granddaughter has got to marry something very different from an engineer.

NANCY. If she did she might marry something that'll turn her hair grey a good deal sooner.

JOHN. I have my plans for Muriel.

EMILY. Imagine Muriel in Winnipeg!

MURIEL. What plans, granddad? You've never told me about any plans.

JOHN. Not told you! At your age, your mother had a conspicuous place in London society. And it's your duty to carry on the family tradition. Your mother didn't marry into the peerage so that you could gallivant up and down Winnipeg as the wife of a manufacturing engineer. You have some notion of politics, though it's a mighty queer one——

MURIEL. I hardly think my politics would further your plan, granddad. I should have supposed the whole of my career would have made it plain that I have the greatest contempt for official politics.

JOHN. Your "career"! Your "contempt"! (*Laughs good-humouredly, then more softly*) My child——

MURIEL (*nettled*). I'm not a child.

JOHN (*angrily*). Enough! Don't make yourself ridiculous. (*More quietly*) Your mother and your brother think as I do. Let that suffice.

RICHARD. Pardon me, sir, but suppose it won't suffice?

JOHN (*furious*). I—I——

MURIEL (*violently*). Granddad, do please keep calm.

JOHN (*as above*). I'm perfectly calm, I believe.

NANCY (*to* GERTRUDE). Then he'd believe anything!

MURIEL. You don't seem to have understood that we're engaged to be married.

GERT. I must say——

JOHN. And what must *you* say? You'll side with my wife against me, and the girl's own mother, I suppose?

GERT. I fail to see any objection whatever.

JOHN. Do you, indeed! Well, objection or no objection, I mean it to be stopped—now, at once.

MURIEL. But how shall you stop it, granddad?

JOHN. If I hear one more word of this, one more word—there'll be no thirty thousand pounds for Richard. Not from me, at any rate. And I don't imagine that your mother will help him, or Monkhurst either. Where is he?

MONK. Not much.

MURIEL. But that won't stop it, granddad!

ROSE (*rising, and going to the hall door*). John, you're a hard, hard old man. The one thing I ask of you, and on our golden wedding day, too, and you won't even listen. You shut me up as though I were a—a— I do think it's a shame. The poor things. (*She goes out in tears.*)

NANCY (*hurrying out after her*). Rose! Rose! Don't!

JOHN. Here I arrange a nice little family dinner to celebrate the occasion. I invite no outsiders, so that we shall be nice and homely and comfortable. And this is how you treat me. You induce your grandmother to defy me—the first time in her life. You bring your mother to tears, and you——

EMILY. There's nothing to be said in favour of it—nothing. The very thought of it——

RICHARD. I'm awfully sorry.

JOHN. No, you aren't, sir. So don't be impudent.
(WEBSTER *enters.*)

WEBSTER. Mr. Arthur Preece, Sir John. I've shown him into the study.

JOHN. Very good.
(WEBSTER *goes out.*)

GERT. Why can't Mr. Preece come up here?

JOHN. Because he's come to see me on private business, madam. Private, do I say? It's public enough. Everybody knows that I can't keep my own workmen in order without the help of a Labour M.P. The country's going to the dogs! My own father used to say so, and I never believed him. But it's true. (*He goes to the door.*)

MONK. May I come with you, sir? (*With a superior glance at* MURIEL) These family ructions——

JOHN. Come! (JOHN *goes off, followed by* MONKHURST.)

GERT (*meaningly*). Richard, go and see where your mother is, will you? (*Richard follows the others. A slight pause.*)

EMILY (*still weakly and tearfully*). How your poor grandmother is upset!

MURIEL. Yes, I'm very sorry.

EMILY. That's something.

MURIEL. It's such a humiliating sight. No real arguments. No attempt to understand *my* point of view! Nothing but blustering and bullying and stamping up and down. He wants to make out that I'm still a child with no will of my own. But it's he who's the child.

GERT. Come, come, Muriel.

MURIEL. Yes, it is. A spoilt child! When anything happens that doesn't just please him, there's a fine exhibition of temper. Don't we all know it. And this is the great Sir John Rhead! Bah!

EMILY (*amazed*). Muriel!

MURIEL. Oh, of course it isn't his fault! Everyone's always given him his own way—especially grandma. It's positively pathetic; grandma trying to turn against him now. Poor old thing! As if she could! Now!

EMILY. Muriel, your cold-bloodedness absolutely frightens me.

MURIEL. But, mother, I'm not cold-blooded. It's only common-sense.

GERT. (*clumsily caressing* EMILY). Darling!

EMILY. Common-sense will be the finish of me; I've no one left in the world now.

GERT. (*hurt*). Then I suppose I'm too old to count. And yet for nearly fifty years I've lived for nobody but you. Many and many a time I should have been ready to die—yes, glad to—only you were there.

EMILY (*affectionately*). And yet you're against me now.

GERT. I only want you not to have any regrets.

EMILY. Any regrets! My life has been all regrets. Look at me.

GERT. Not all your life, dear—your marriage. (MURIEL *looks up.*)

EMILY (*firmly, and yet frightened with a look at* MURIEL). Hush, auntie!

GERT. Why? Why should I hush? You say your life's been all regrets, if you care about being honest with Muriel, you ought to tell her now that you did not marry the man you were in love with.

EMILY (*in an outburst*). Don't believe it, Muriel. No one could have been a kinder husband than your father was, and I always loved him.

MURIEL (*intimidated by these revelations of feelings*). Mother!

GERT. Then what do you regret? You had an affection for Ned, but if you had loved him as you loved —the other one—what is there to regret? And now you seem to be doing your best to make regrets for Muriel—and—and—oh, Emily, why do you do it?

MURIEL (*moved, but controlling herself*). Yes, mamma! Why? I'm sure I'm open to hear reason on any subject—even marriage.

EMILY (*blackly*). Reason! Reason! There you are again! My child, you're my oldest, and I've loved you beyond everybody. You've never been attached to me. It isn't your fault, and I don't blame you. Things happen to be like that, that's all. You don't know how hard you are. If you did, you'd be ready to bite your tongue off. Here I am, with you and Gerald. Gerald is not bad at heart, but he's selfish and he's a fool. I could never talk freely to him, as I do to you. One day he'll be asking me to leave Berkeley Square, and I shall go and finish my days in the country. And here you calmly announce you're off to Canada, and you want my *reasons* for objecting! There's only one reason—all the others are nothing—mere excuses—and you couldn't guess that one reason. You have to be told. If you cared for me, you wouldn't force me to the shame of telling you.

MURIEL (*whispering*). Shame?

EMILY. Isn't it humiliating for a mother to have to tell her daughter, who never's even thought of it, that she cannot bear to lose her,—cannot bear?—Canada!

MURIEL (*throwing herself at her mother's knees*). Mother, I'll never leave you! (*She sobs, burying her face in her mother's lap.*)

GERT. (*softly*). All this self-sacrifice is a sad mistake. (*To* MURIEL) None of us can live for ever. When your mother is gone—what will you do then?

MURIEL (*climbing up and kissing her mother*). I'll never leave you!

EMILY. My child!

GERT. (*gently*). It's wrong of you, Emily! All wrong!

(ARTHUR PREECE *enters from the hall. His hair and moustache have grown grey. His expression and manner slightly disillusioned and cynical. In figure he is the same.*)

PREECE. Good evening.

MURIEL (*on seeing him, rises quickly rather like a school-girl*). Good evening. (*She goes out rapidly.* PREECE *looks after her a little surprised.*)

EMILY (*at once the woman of the world*). Good evening. You've soon finished your business with father.

PREECE (*puzzled by the appearance of things*). Good evening. (*He shakes hands with* EMILY) What is the matter? The old gentleman really wasn't equal to seeing me. I just told him what I had to tell him about the strikers, and then he said I'd perhaps better come up here. I think he wanted to be alone.

EMILY. Poor dear!

PREECE. Nothing serious, I hope?

GERT. (*briskly, shaking* PREECE *by the hand*). The usual thing, Mr. Preece, the usual thing! A new generation has got to the marrying age. You know what it is. I know what it is. Now, Emily, don't begin to cry again. People who behave as selfishly as you're doing have no right to weep—except for their sins.

EMILY (*protesting*). Auntie, this can't possibly interest Mr. Preece.

GERT. (*still more briskly*). Don't talk that kind of conventional nonsense, Emily! You know quite well it *will* interest Mr. Preece extremely. (*Rising*) Now just tell him all about it and see what he says. (*With a peculiar tone*) I suppose you'll admit he ought to be a good judge of such matters? (*She moves to the door.*)

EMILY. Where are you going?"

GERT. (*imitating* EMILY *slightly*). That can't possibly interest you. (*Wearily*) I'm out of patience. (*She goes out of the room.*)

EMILY (*trying to force a light tone*). I hope you had some good news about the workmen for my poor old father. What a finish for his golden wedding day!

PREECE (*following her lead*). Yes, I think his little affair's pretty well fixed up—anyhow for the present. He's shown himself pretty reasonable. If he'd continued to be as obstinate as he was at the start, the thing would have run him into a lot of money.

EMILY. I wonder he doesn't retire.

PREECE. He's going to. There's to be a Limited Company.

EMILY. Father—a Limited Company! He told you?

PREECE. Yes.

EMILY. Then he must have been feeling it's getting too much for him.

PREECE. Well, considering his years—seventy-seven, isn't it? Some of us will be beaten long before that age. (*He sighs.*)

EMILY. Why that sigh? You aren't getting ready to give up, are you?

PREECE. No, I expect I shall go on till I drop.

EMILY. I should have thought you had every reason to be satisfied with what you have done.

PREECE. Why?

EMILY. Unless you regret giving up steel for politics.

PREECE. No. I don't regret that. I'd done all I really wanted to do there. I'd forced your father to take up steel on a big scale. I'd made more than all the money I needed. And other processes were coming along, better than mine.

EMILY. I wonder how many men there are who've succeeded as you have done, both in politics and out of politics.

PREECE. Do you think I've succeeded in politics?

EMILY. You haven't held office, but I've always understood it was because you preferred to be independent.

PREECE. It was. I could have sold my soul over and over again for a seat at an Under-Secretary's desk. I wouldn't even lead the Labour Party.

EMILY. But everyone knows you're the strongest man in the Labour Party.

PREECE. Well, if I am—the strongest man in the Labour Party is rather depressed.

EMILY. Why?

PREECE. Difficult to say. Twenty years ago, I thought the millennium would be just about established in 1912. Instead of that, it's as far off as ever. It's even further off.

EMILY. Further off?

PREECE. Yes. And yet a lot of us have worked. By God, we have! But there's a different spirit now.

The men are bitter. They can't lead themselves and they won't be led. They won't be led. And nobody knows what's going to happen next. Except that trouble's going to happen. I often wonder why I was cursed with the reforming spirit. How much happier I should have been if I'd cared for nothing in this world but my own work—like young Richard Sibley, for instance.

EMILY. Isn't he interested in reform?

PREECE. Not he! He's an engineer, only an engineer. He minds his own business. I suppose he's here tonight.

EMILY. Yes.

PREECE (*in an ordinary tone*). Why won't you let him marry Miss Muriel?

EMILY (*startled*). Then father's told you?

PREECE. Not a word. But Richard and I are great pals. He's told me his plans. Why shouldn't they marry?

EMILY (*weakly*). Muriel won't go to Canada.

PREECE. Won't go to Canada? But I understand she had a tremendous notion of Canada.

EMILY. She's promised me she won't go.

PREECE. But why should she do that?

EMILY (*half breaking down*). Oh, I know I'm selfish. But—but—I should be quite alone, if she went. And then, it's not what we'd anticipated for her. We naturally hoped——

PREECE. Oh! Of course, if you're in the marriage market——

EMILY. No. Really it's not that—at least as far as I'm concerned. I should be so utterly alone. And she's promised me. If she deserted me——

PREECE. Deserted—rather a strong word——

EMILY. Please don't be hard! You don't know how unhappy I am. You admit you're discouraged.

PREECE. I said "depressed."

EMILY. Well, depressed, then. Can't you feel for others?

PREECE (*rather roughly*). And who made me admit it? Who kept questioning me and worming it out of me? You wouldn't leave it alone. You're like all the other women—and I've had to do with a few.

EMILY (*affronted*). Please—

PREECE. It isn't sufficient for you to make a man unhappy. You aren't satisfied till he admits you've made him unhappy.

EMILY (*protesting*). Oh!

PREECE. How many times have I seen you since this cursed strike brought me among the family again? Half a dozen, perhaps. And every single time I've noticed you feeling your way towards it. And tonight you've just got there.

EMILY. Arthur, you must forgive me. It's quite true. We can't help it.

PREECE. What should I care about lost millenniums and labour troubles ahead, if I'd any genuine personal interest in my own? Not a jot. Not a tinker's curse! Do you remember you let me kiss you—once?

EMILY. Forgive me! I know I oughtn't to be forgiven. But life's so difficult. Ever since I've been seeing you again I've realised how miserable I am—it's such a long time since. It seems as it was some other girl and not me—twenty-six years ago—here! And yet it's like yesterday. (*She sobs.*)
(PREECE *embraces her first roughly and then very tenderly.*)

PREECE. My child!

EMILY. I'm an old woman.

PREECE. You said it was like yesterday—when you were twenty-three—so it is. (*They kiss again.*)

EMILY (*with a little laugh*). This will kill father.

PREECE. Not it. Your father has a remarkable constitution. It's much more likely to kill the Labour Party.
(JOHN *enters, agitated and weary.*)

JOHN (*brusquely*). Where's your mother? She's not in the other room. I thought she was in here. I want to see her.

EMILY. She's probably gone to her own room—poor dear!

JOHN. Can't you go and find her? (*He sits down, discouraged.*)

EMILY (*coming over to him*). Father, I've been thinking it over, and I'm afraid we shall have to agree to Muriel's marriage.

JOHN. We shall have to agree to it? I sha'n't agree to it.

EMILY. As Mr. Preece says——

JOHN. Mr. Preece?

EMILY. You know how friendly he is to Richard—as Mr. Preece says, why shouldn't they marry?

PREECE. I merely ventured to put the question, Sir John.

JOHN. Why shouldn't they? Because they shouldn't. Isn't that enough? (*To* EMILY) A quarter of an hour ago you yourself agreed in the most positive way that there was nothing whatever to be said in favour of such a match.

EMILY. I was rather overlooking the fact that they're in love with each other—(*glancing at* PREECE) —a quarter of an hour ago.

JOHN. Are all you women gone mad tonight? Preece, do you reckon *you* understand women?

PREECE. Now and then one gets a glimpse, sir.

JOHN (*realising state of affairs between* PREECE *and* EMILY). H'm!

EMILY (*noticing her father watch her, rather self-consciously*). After all, what difference can it make to us? We sh'a'nt be here as long as they will.

JOHN. What? What?

EMILY (*louder*). We sha'n't be here as long as they will, I say.

JOHN. That's it! Tell me I'm an old man! Of course, it can't make any difference to us. I was looking at the matter solely from their point of view. How can it affect me—*whom* Muriel marries?

EMILY. Well, then! Let them judge for themselves. You agree? (JOHN *stares before him obstinately*) Father——(JOHN *shakes his head impatiently*) Dad!

JOHN (*looking up like a sulky child*). Oh, have it your own way. I'm not the girl's mother. If you've made up your mind, there's nothing more to be said.

EMILY. And Richard's capital?

JOHN. Oh, it's all lying ready. (*Shrugs his shoulders*) May as well have it, I suppose.

EMILY. You're a dear!

JOHN. I'm not a dear, and I hate to be called a dear.

EMILY. What a shocking untruth! I shall go and tell them, I think. (*She goes to the door.*)

JOHN (*calling her back*). Emily!

EMILY. Yes.

JOHN. Don't let them come in here. I couldn't bear it.

EMILY. Oh, but——

JOHN. I couldn't stand the strain of another scene. It's late now—I'm an old man, and people have no right to upset me in this way.

EMILY. Couldn't they just say good-night?

JOHN. Very well. They must say good-night and go at once. Another day——

EMILY (*very soothingly*). I'll tell them you're very tired. (*She nods smilingly at her father and leaves the room. A slight pause.*)

PREECE. A difficult job, being the head of a family.

JOHN. I've done with it, Preece. I've decided that tonight—that's what a golden wedding comes to in these days. Things aren't what they were. In my time a man was at any rate master in his own house and in his own works. Seemed natural enough! But you've changed all that.

PREECE. I've changed it?

JOHN (*continuing confidentially*). Why, even my own wife's gone against me tonight. My own wife! (*Troubled*) Did you ever hear of such a thing?

PREECE. I *have* heard of it, Sir John.

JOHN (*grimly*). You laugh. Wait till you're married.

PREECE. I may have to wait a long time.

JOHN. Eh, what? A long time? Don't try to hoodwink me, Preece. I know what you all say when I'm not there. "Old Rhead." "Be breaking up soon, the old man!" But I'm not yet quite doddering. (*Pointedly*) You'll be married inside six months—and every newspaper in London will be full of it. Yes, answer that. My workmen go out on strike, and you poke your nose in and arrange it for me. Then my family go out on strike, and upon my soul, you poke your damned nose in there, too, and arrange that for me—on your own terms. Tut—tut! Shake hands, man! You and your like are running the world to the devil, and I'm too old to step in and knock you down. But—but—I wish you luck, my lad. You're a good sort. (*They shake hands.* EMILY, NANCY, MURIEL, RICHARD *and* GERTRUDE *all enter from the hall.*)

PREECE. Well, good-night, Sir John.

EMILY (*cheerfully*). We're just coming to say good-night, grandpapa. I'm sure you must be very tired. We've said good-night to granny.

JOHN (*feebly*). Where is she? Where is granny?

NANCY (*heartily shaking hands*). Good-night, John, and thank you for a very pleasant time. (*She goes to* GERTRUDE, *who now stands near the door, and kisses her good-night.*)

RICHARD (*heartily shaking hands*). Thank you, sir. (NANCY *passes out by the door.* GERTRUDE *now shakes hands with* RICHARD, *who follows his mother.*)

EMILY (*kisses* JOHN). Good-night, dear. (JOHN, *turning from* EMILY, *moves with a generous gesture to* MURIEL, *who, however, keeps a very stiff demeanor and shakes hands in cold silence.* EMILY *has reached* GERTRUDE. *They both watch* MURIEL.)

EMILY (*with a shade of disappointment turns to* GERTRUDE). Good-night, auntie. (GERTRUDE *and* EMILY *embrace, then* EMILY *passes quickly out of the door.*)

JOHN (*stiffly, looking about*). Where's Monkhurst?

GERT. Oh, he is gone! He said he had an appointment at the Club.

JOHN. What Club? The Carlton?

MURIEL (*shaking hands with* GERTRUDE). The Automobile, you may depend. (*She goes off by the door quickly.*)

GERT. Well, this day is over. (WEBSTER *enters from the hall.*)

WEBSTER. Any orders, Sir John?

JOHN. None.

GERT. Can't we have some of the blaze of electricity turned off?

JOHN. As you like. (WEBSTER *extinguishes several clusters with the switches at the door, then goes out. The room is left in a discreet light.*)

JOHN (*almost plaintively*). Where's Rose? (ROSE *enters timidly from the hall.*)

GERT. Here she is.

ROSE (*going up to* JOHN). John, forgive me for having dared to differ from my dear husband.

JOHN (*taking her hand softly*). Old girl—(*then half humorously shaking his head*)—you'll be the death of me, if you do it again.

GERT. I think I'm going to bed.

JOHN. No, not yet.

ROSE. Gertrude, will you do me a favour, on my golden wedding-day?

GERT. What is it?

ROSE. Sing for us.

GERT. Oh! My singing days are over long ago.

JOHN (*persuasively*). Go on—go on. There's nobody but us to hear.

GERT. Really it is—— (*Stops*) Very well. (GERTRUDE *goes through the double doors.* ROSE *draws her lace shawl round her.*)

JOHN. Let's sit by the fire if you're cold. (*He moves a chair in place for her gallantly.* ROSE *sits to the left of the fire.* JOHN *takes a seat to the right of the fire. The song "Juanita" is heard in a cracked and ancient voice, very gently and faintly.*)

ROSE (*softly, by the fire*). When I think of all this room has seen——

JOHN (*looking into the fire*). Ah!

ROSE. I'm sure it's very pleasant to remember.

JOHN. Ah! That's because you're pleasant. I've said it before, and I say it again. The women of today aren't what women used to be. They're hard. They've none of the old charm. Unsexed—that's what they are—unsexed. (*Muriel enters quickly from the hall in a rich white cloak. She pauses smiling, then hurries delicately across to her grandfather and embraces him; releases him, shyly takes a flower from her bosom, drops it into his hand, turns and gives her grandmother a smile, whispering "Good-night. They're waiting for me," and hurries out again.*)

JOHN (*looking at the flower*). We live and learn.

ROSE (*nodding her head*). Yes, John. (*The song continues.*)

CURTAIN

The Green Goddess

BY WILLIAM ARCHER

The Green Goddess was first produced in America at the Booth Theatre, New York City, by Winthrop Ames on January 18, 1921, and closed on February 4, 1922. The following is the original cast:

The Raja of Rukh	George Arliss
Watkins	Ivan F. Simpson
Major Antony Crespin	Herbert Waring
Lucilla	Olive Wyndham
Dr. Basil Traherne	Cyril Keightley
Lieut. Denis Cardew	Herbert Ransome
The High Priest	David A. Leonard
The Temple Priest	Ronald Colman
An Ayah	Helen Nowell

Staged by Winthrop Ames

SCENE

A remote region at the back of the Himalayas

THE GREEN GODDESS

ACT ONE

A region of gaunt and almost treeless mountains, uniformly grey in tone, except in so far as the atmosphere lends them colour. Clinging to the mountain wall in the background, at an apparent distance of about a mile, is a vast barbaric palace, with long stretches of unbroken masonry, crowned by arcades and turrets.

The foreground consists of a small level space between two masses of rock. In the rock on the right a cave-temple has been roughly hewn. Two thick and rudely carved pillars divide it into three sections. Between the pillars, in the middle section, can be seen the seated figure of a six-armed Goddess, of forbidding aspect, coloured dark green. In front of the figure is a low altar with five or six newly severed heads of goats lying at its base. The temple is decorated with untidy and mouldering wreaths and other floral offerings.

The open space between the two rock masses forms a rudely paved forecourt to the temple. It is bordered by small idols and three or four round-headed stone posts, painted green.

Mountain paths wind off behind the rocks, and through the low shrubs, both to right and left.

Projecting over the rock-mass on the left can be seen the wing of an aeroplane, the nacelle and under-carriage hidden. It has evidently just made a rather disastrous forced landing. The pilot and two passengers are in the act of extricating themselves from the wreck, and clambering down the cliff. The pilot is DR. BASIL TRAHERNE; *the passengers are* MAJOR ANTONY CRESPIN *and his wife* LUCILLA. TRAHERNE (35) *is a well-set-up man, vigourous and in good training.* CRESPIN (40), *somewhat heavy and dissipated-looking, is in khaki.* LUCILLA (28), *is a tall, slight, athletic woman, wearing a tailor-made tweed suit. All three on their first appearance wear aviation helmets and leather coats. The coats they take off as occasion offers.*

Their proceedings are watched with wonder and fear by a group of dark and rudely clad natives, rather Mongolian in feature. They chatter eagerly among themselves. A man of higher stature and more Aryan type, the PRIEST *of the temple, seems to have some authority over them.*

As soon as all three newcomers have descended, the PRIEST *gives some directions to a young man among the bystanders, who makes off at great speed. He is a messenger to the castle.*

LUCILLA (*to* CRESPIN, *who is at a difficult point, and about to jump*). Take care, Antony! Let Dr. Traherne give you a hand.

TRAHERNE (*already on the ground*). Yes.

CRESPIN. Hang it all, I'm not such a crock as all that. (*Jumps heavily, but safely.*)

TRAHERNE. Are you all right, Mrs. Crespin? Not very much shaken?

LUCILLA. Not a bit.

TRAHERNE. It was a nasty bump.

LUCILLA. You managed splendidly.

CRESPIN. Come on, Lu—sit on that ledge, and I can swing you down.

TRAHERNE. Let me——
(CRESPIN *and* TRAHERNE *support her as she jumps lightly to the ground.*)

LUCILLA. Thank you.

CRESPIN. That last ten minutes was pretty trying. I don't mind owning that my nerves are all of a twitter. (*Producing a pocket flask, and pouring some of its contents into the cup*) Have a mouthful, Traherne?

TRAHERNE. No, thank you.

CRESPIN (*to* LUCILLA). You won't, I know. I will. (*Drinks off the brandy, then pours and drinks again*) That's better!—And now—where are we, Doctor?

TRAHERNE. I have no notion.

CRESPIN. Let's ask the populace.
(*The natives have been standing at some distance, awe-struck, but chattering eagerly among themselves. The* PRIEST, *intently watching, is silent.* CRESPIN *advances towards him, the natives meanwhile shrinking back in fear. The* PRIEST *salaams slightly and almost contemptuously.* CRESPIN *addresses him in Hindustani, which he evidently does not understand. He in turn pours forth a speech of some length, pointing to the temple and the palace.* CRESPIN *can make nothing of it. While this is proceeding:*)

TRAHERNE (*in a low voice, to* LUCILLA). You were splendid, all through!

LUCILLA. I had perfect faith in you.

TRAHERNE. If I'd had another pint of petrol, I might have headed for that sort of esplanade behind the castle——

LUCILLA. Yes, I saw it.

TRAHERNE. —and made an easy landing. But I simply had to try for this place, and trust to luck.

LUCILLA. It wasn't luck, but your skill, that saved us.

TRAHERNE. You are very good to me.

CRESPIN (*turning*). It's no use—he doesn't understand a word of Hindustani. You know Russian, don't you, Doctor?

TRAHERNE. A little.

CRESPIN. We must be well on towards Central Asia. Suppose you try him in Russian. Ask him where the deuce we are, and who owns the shooting-box up yonder.
(TRAHERNE *says something to the* PRIEST *in Russian.*)

THE PRIEST (*his face lighting up, points to the earth, and then makes an enveloping gesture to signify the whole country, saying*). Rukh, Rukh, Rukh, Rukh.

CRESPIN. What the deuce is he Rooking about?

TRAHERNE. Goodness knows.

LUCILLA. I believe I know. Wait a minute. (*Feeling in her pockets*) I thought I had the paper with me. I read in the *Leader*, just before we started, that the three men who murdered the Political Officer at Abdulabad came from a wild region at the back of the Himalayas, called Rukh.

TRAHERNE. Now that you mention it, I have heard of the place. (*He turns to the* PRIEST *and says a few more words in Russian, pointing to the Palace. The* PRIEST *replies "Raja Sahib" several times over.*)

CRESPIN. Oh, it's Windsor Castle, is it? Well, we'd better make tracks for it. Come, Lucilla.
(*The* PRIEST, *much excited, stops his way, pouring forth a stream of unintelligible language.* TRAHERNE *says something to him in Russian, whereupon he pauses and then says two or three words, slowly and with difficulty—one of them "Raja."*)

TRAHERNE. His Russian is even more limited than mine; but I gather that the Raja has been sent for and will come here.

CRESPIN (*lighting a cigarette*). All right—then we'd better await developments. (*Seats himself on a green-painted stone. As the* PRIEST *sees this, he makes a rush, hustles* CRESPIN *off, with wild exclamations, and then, disregarding him, makes propitiatory gestures, and mutters formulas of deprecation, to the stone.*)

CRESPIN (*very angry, lays his hand on his revolver-case*). Confound you, take care what you're doing! You'd better treat us civilly, or——

TRAHERNE (*laying a hand on his arm*). Gently, gently, Major. This is evidently some sort of sacred enclosure, and you were sitting on one of the gods.

CRESPIN. Well, curse him, he might have told me——

TRAHERNE. If he had you wouldn't have understood. The follow seems to be the priest—you see, he's begging the god's pardon.

CRESPIN. If I knew his confounded lingo I'd jolly well make him beg mine.

TRAHERNE. We'd better be careful not to tread on their corns. We have Mrs. Crespin to think of.

CRESPIN. Confound it, sir, do you think I don't know how to take care of my own wife?

TRAHERNE. I think you're a little hasty, Major—that's all. These are evidently queer people, and we're dependent on them to get us out of our hobble.

LUCILLA (*down, left*). Do you think I could sit on this stone without giving offence to the deities?

TRAHERNE. Oh yes, that seems safe enough. (*After* LUCILLA *is seated*)

I don't know how to apologise for having got you into this mess.

LUCILLA. Don't talk nonsense, Dr. Traherne. Who can foresee a Himalayan fog?

TRAHERNE. The only thing to do was to get above it, and then, of course, my bearings were gone.

LUCILLA. Now that we're safe, I should think it all great fun if it weren't for the children.

CRESPIN. Oh, they don't expect us for a week, and surely it won't take us more than that to get back to civilisation.

TRAHERNE. Or, at all events, to a telegraph line.

LUCILLA. I suppose there's no chance of flying back?

TRAHERNE. Not the slightest, I'm afraid. I fancy the old 'bus is done for.

LUCILLA. Oh, Dr. Traherne, what a shame! And you'd only had it a few weeks!

TRAHERNE. What does it matter so long as you are safe?

LUCILLA. What does it matter so long as we're all safe?

CRESPIN. That's not what Traherne said. Why pretend to be blind to his—chivalry?

TRAHERNE (*trying to laugh it off*). Of course I'm glad you're all right, Major, and I'm not sorry to be in a whole skin myself. But ladies first, you know.

CRESPIN. The perfect knight errant, in fact!

TRAHERNE. Decidedly "errant." I couldn't well have gone more completely astray.

LUCILLA. Won't you look at the machine and see if it's quite hopeless?

TRAHERNE. Yes, at once. (*He goes towards the wreck of the aeroplane and passes out of sight. The populace clustered in and around the temple on the right are intent upon the marvel of the aeroplane, but the* PRIEST *fixes his gaze upon* CRESPIN *and* LUCILLA.)

CRESPIN (*sits beside* LUCILLA *on the stone*). Well, Lucilla!

LUCILLA. Well?

CRESPIN. That was a narrow squeak.

LUCILLA. Yes, I suppose so.

CRESPIN. All's well that ends well, eh?

LUCILLA. Of course.

CRESPIN. You don't seem very grateful to Providence.

LUCILLA. For sending the fog?

CRESPIN. For getting us down safely—all three.

LUCILLA. It was Dr. Traherne's nerve that did that. If he hadn't kept his head——

CRESPIN. We should have crashed. One or other of us would probably have broken his neck; and if Providence had played up, it might have been the right one.

LUCILLA. What do you mean?

CRESPIN. It might have been me. Then you'd have thanked God, right enough!

LUCILLA. Why will you talk like this, Antony? If I hadn't sent Dr. Traherne away just now, you'd have been saying these things in his hearing.

CRESPIN. Well, why not? He's quite one of the family! Don't tell me he doesn't know all about the "state of our relations," as they say in the divorce court.

LUCILLA. If he does, it's not from me. No doubt he knows what the whole station knows.

CRESPIN. And what does the whole station know? Why, that your deadly coldness drives me to drink. I've lived for three years in an infernal clammy fog like that we passed through. Who's to blame if I take a whiskey-peg now and then, to keep the chill out?

LUCILLA. Oh, Antony, why go over it all again? You know very well it was drink—and other things—that came between us; not my coldness, as you call it, that drove you to drink.

CRESPIN. Oh, you good women! You patter after the parson, "Forgive us as we forgive those that trespass against us." But you don't know what forgiveness means.

LUCILLA. What's the use of it, Antony? Forgive? I have "forgiven" you. I don't try to take the children from you, though it might be better for them if I did. But to forgive is one thing, to forget another. When a woman has seen a man behave as you have behaved, do you think it is possible for her to forget it, and to love him afresh? There are women in novels, and perhaps in the slums, who have such short memories; but I am not one of them.

CRESPIN. No, by Jove, you're not! So a man's whole life is to be ruined——

LUCILLA. Do you think yours is the only life to be ruined?

CRESPIN. Ah, there we have it! I've not only offended your sensibilities; I am in your way. You love this other man, this model of all the virtues!

LUCILLA. You have no right to say that.

CRESPIN (*disregarding her protest*). He's a paragon. He's a wonder. He's a mighty microbe-killer before the Lord; he's going to work Heaven knows what miracles, only he hasn't brought them off yet. And you're cursing the mistake you made in marrying a poor devil of a soldierman instead of a first-class scientific genius. Come! Make a clean breast of it! You may as well!

LUCILLA. I have nothing to answer. While I continue to live with you, I owe you an account of my actions —but not of my thoughts.

CRESPIN. Your actions? Oh, I know very well you're too cold—too confounded respectable—to kick over the traces. And then you have the children to think of.

LUCILLA. Yes; I have the children.

CRESPIN. Besides, there's no hurry. If you only have patience for a year or two, I'll do the right thing for once, and drink myself to death.

LUCILLA. You have only to keep yourself a little in hand to live to what they call "a good old age."

CRESPIN. 'Pon my soul, I've a mind to try to, though goodness knows my life is not worth living. I was a fool to come on this crazy expedition——

LUCILLA. Why, it was you yourself that jumped at Dr. Traherne's proposal.

CRESPIN. I thought we'd get to the kiddies a week earlier. They'd be glad to see me, poor little things. They don't despise their daddy.

LUCILLA. It shan't be my fault, Antony, if they ever do. But you don't make it easy to keep up appearances.

CRESPIN. Oh, Lu, Lu, if you would treat me like a human being—if you would help me and make life tolerable for me, instead of a thing that won't bear looking at except through the haze of drink—we might retrieve the early days. Heaven knows I never cared two pins for any woman but you——

LUCILLA. No, the others, I suppose, only helped you, like whiskey, to see the world through a haze. *I* saw the world through a haze when I married you; but you have dispelled it once for all. Don't force me to tell you how impossible it is for me to be your wife again. I am the mother of your children —that gives you a terrible hold over me. Be content with that.

TRAHERNE (*still unseen, calls*): Oh, Mrs. Crespin! (*He appears, clambering down from the aeroplane*) I've found in the wreck the newspaper you spoke of—you were right about Rukh.

CRESPIN (*as* TRAHERNE *comes forward*). What does it say?

TRAHERNE (*reads*). "Abdulabad, Tuesday. Sentence of death has been passed on the three men found guilty of the murder of Mr. Haredale. It appears that these miscreants are natives of Rukh, a small and little-known independent state among the northern spurs of the Himalayas."

LUCILLA. Yes, that's what I read.

TRAHERNE. This news isn't the best possible passport for us in our present situation.

LUCILLA. But if we're hundreds of miles from anywhere, it can't be known here yet.

CRESPIN (*lighting a cigarette*). In any case, they wouldn't dare to molest us.

TRAHERNE. All the same it might be safest to burn this paragraph in case there's anybody here that can read it. (*He tears a strip out of the paper, lights it at* CRESPIN's *match, watches it burn till he has to drop the flaming remnant of it, upon which he stamps.* LUCILLA *takes the rest of the small local paper and lays it beside her leather coat on the stone, left. The* PRIEST *intently watches all these proceedings. Meanwhile strange ululations, mingled with the throb of tom-toms and the clash of cymbals, have made themselves faintly heard from the direction of the mountain path, right.*)

CRESPIN. Hallo! What's this?

TRAHERNE. Sounds like the march of the Great Panjandrum.

(*The sounds rapidly approach. The natives all run to the point where the path debouches on the open space. They prostrate themselves, some on each side of the way. A wild procession comes down the mountain path. It is headed by a gigantic Negro flourishing two naked sabers, and gyrating in a barbaric war-dance. Then come half a dozen musicians with tom-toms and cymbals. Then a litter carried by four bearers. Through its gauze curtains the figure of the* RAJA *can be indistinctly seen. Immediately behind the litter comes* WATKINS, *an English valet, demure and correct, looking as if he had just strolled in from St. James Street. The procession closes with a number of the* RAJA'S *bodyguard, in the most fantastic, parti-coloured attire, and armed with antique match-locks, some of them with barrels six or seven feet long. The* RAJA'S *litter is set down in front of the temple.* WATKINS *opens the curtains and gives his arm to the* RAJA *as he alights. The* RAJA *makes a step towards the European party in silence. He is a tall, well-built man of forty, dressed in the extreme of Eastern gorgeousness.* CRESPIN *advances and salutes.*)

CRESPIN. Does Your Highness speak English?

RAJA. Oh, yes, a little. (*As a matter of fact he speaks it irreproachably.*)

CRESPIN (*pulling himself together and speaking like a soldier and a man of breeding*). Then I have to apologise for our landing uninvited in your territory.

RAJA. Uninvited, but, I assure you, not unwelcome.

CRESPIN. We are given to understand that this is the State of Rukh.

RAJA. The kingdom of Rukh, Major—if I rightly read the symbols on your cuff.

CRESPIN (*again salutes*). Major Crespin. Permit me to introduce my wife——

RAJA (*with a profound salaam*). I am delighted, Madam, to welcome you to my secluded dominions. You are the first lady of your nation I have had the honour of receiving.

LUCILLA. Your Highness is very kind.

CRESPIN. And this is Dr. Basil Traherne, whose aeroplane—or what is left of it—you see.

RAJA. Doctor Traherne? The Doctor Traherne, whose name I have so often seen in the newspaper? "The Pasteur of Malaria."

TRAHERNE. The newspapers make too much of my work. It is very incomplete.

RAJA. But you are an aviator as well?

TRAHERNE. Only as an amateur.

RAJA. I presume it is some misadventure—a most fortunate misadventure for me—that has carried you so far into the wilds of the Himalayas?

TRAHERNE. Yes—we got lost in the clouds. Major and Mrs. Crespin were coming up from the plains to see their children at a hill station——

RAJA. Pahari, no doubt?

TRAHERNE. Yes, Pahari—and I was rash enough to suggest that I might save them three days' travelling by taking them up in my aeroplane.

RAJA. Madam is a sportswoman, then?

LUCILLA. Oh, I have been up many times.

CRESPIN (*with a tinge of sarcasm*). Yes, many times.

LUCILLA. It was no fault of Dr. Traherne's that we went astray. The weather was impossible.

RAJA. Well, you have made a sensation here, I can assure you. My people have never seen an aeroplane. They are not sure—simple souls—whether you are gods or demons. But the fact of your having descended in the precincts of a temple of our local goddess—(*with a wave of his hand towards the idol*) allow me to introduce you to her—is considered highly significant.

CRESPIN. I hope, sir, that we shall find no difficulty in obtaining transport back to civ—to India.

RAJA. To civilisation, you were going to say? Why hesitate, my dear sir? We know very well that we are barbarians. We are quite reconciled to the fact. We have had some five thousand years to accustom ourselves to it. This sword (*touching his scimitar*) is a barbarous weapon compared with your revolver; but it was worn by my ancestors when yours were daubing themselves blue and picking up a precarious livelihood in the woods. (*Breaking off hastily to prevent any reply*) But Madam is standing all this time! Watkins, what are you thinking of? Some cushions. (WATKINS *piles some cushions from the litter so as to form a seat for* LUCILLA. *Meanwhile the* RAJA *continues*) Another litter for Madam, and mountain-chairs for the gentlemen, will be here in a few minutes. Then I hope you will accept the hospitality of my poor house.

LUCILLA. We are giving a great deal of trouble, Your Highness.

RAJA. A great deal of pleasure, Madam.

CRESPIN. But I hope, sir, there will be no difficulty about transport back to—India.

RAJA. Time enough to talk of that, Major, when you have rested and recuperated after your adventure. You will do me the honor of dining with me this evening? I trust you will not find us altogether uncivilised.

LUCILLA (*lightly*). Your Highness will have to excuse the barbarism of our attire. We have nothing to wear but what we stand up in.

RAJA. Oh, I think we can put that all right. Watkins!

WATKINS (*advancing*). Your 'Ighness!

RAJA. You are in the confidence of our Mistress of the Robes. How does our wardrobe stand?

WATKINS. A fresh consignment of Paris models come in only last week, Your 'Ighness.

RAJA. Good! Then I hope, Madam, that you may find among them some rag that you will deign to wear.

LUCILLA. Paris models, Your Highness! And you talk of being uncivilised!

RAJA. We do what we can, Madam. I sometimes have the pleasure of entertaining European ladies—though not, hitherto, Englishwomen—in my solitudes; and I like to mitigate the terrors of exile for them. Then, as for civilisation, you know, I have always at my elbow one of its most finished products. Watkins!

WATKINS (*stepping forward*). Your 'Ighness!

RAJA. You will recognise in Watkins, gentleman, another representative of the Ruling Race. (WATKINS, *with downcast eyes, touches his hat to* CRESPIN *and* TRAHERNE) I assure you he rules me with an iron hand—not always in a velvet glove. Eh, Watkins?

WATKINS. Your 'Ighness will 'ave your joke.

RAJA. He is my Prime Minister and all my Cabinet—but more particularly my Lord Chamberlain. No one can touch him at mixing a cocktail or making a salad. My entire household trembles at his nod; even my *chef* quails before him. Nothing comes amiss to him; for he is, like myself, a man without prejudices. You may be surprised at my praising him to his face in this fashion; you may foresee some danger of—what shall I say—swelled head. But I know my Watkins; there is not the slightest risk of his outgrowing that modest bowler. He knows his value to me, and he knows that he would never be equally appreciated elsewhere. I have guarantees for his fidelity—eh, Watkins?

WATKINS. I know when I'm well off, if that's what Your 'Ighness means.

RAJA. I mean a little more than that—but no matter. I have sometimes thought of instituting a peerage, in order that I might raise Watkins to it. But I mustn't let my admiration for British institutions carry me too far.—Those scoundrels of bearers are taking a long time, Watkins.

WATKINS. The lady's litter 'ad to 'ave fresh curtains, Your 'Ighness. They won't be a minute, now.

RAJA. You were speaking of transport, Major—is your machine past repair, Dr. Traherne?

TRAHERNE. Utterly, I'm afraid.

RAJA. Let us look at it. (*Turns and finds that his bodyguards are all clustered on the path, looking at it. He gives a sharp word of command. They scamper into a sort of loose order, up, right*) Ah, yes—propeller smashed—planes crumpled up——

TRAHERNE. Under-carriage wrecked——

RAJA. I'm afraid we can't offer to repair the damage for you.

TRAHERNE. I'm afraid not, sir.

RAJA. A wonderful machine! Yes, Europe has something to boast of. I wonder what the Priest here thinks of it. (*He says a few words to the* PRIEST, *who salaams, and replies volubly at some length*) He says it is the great roc—the giant bird, you know, of our Eastern stories. And he declares that he plainly saw his Goddess hovering over you as you descended, and guiding you towards her temple.

TRAHERNE. I wish she could have guided us towards the level ground I saw behind your castle. I could have made a safe landing there.

RAJA. No doubt—on my parade ground—almost the only level spot in my dominions.

LUCILLA. These, I suppose, are your bodyguards?

RAJA. My household troops, Madam.

LUCILLA. How picturesque they are!

RAJA. Oh, a relic of barbarism, I know. I can quite understand the contempt with which my friend the Major is at this moment regarding them.

CRESPIN. Irregular troops, Raja. Often first-class fighting men.

RAJA. And you think that, if irregularity is the virtue of irregular troops, these—what is the expression, Watkins?

WATKINS. Tyke the cyke, Your 'Ighness?

RAJA. That's it—take the cake—that is what you are thinking?

CRESPIN. Well, they would be hard to beat, sir.

RAJA. I repeat—a relic of barbarism. You see, I have strong conservative instincts—I cling to the fashions of my fathers—and my people would be restive if I didn't. I maintain these fellows, as his Majesty the King-Emperor keeps up the Beefeaters in the Tower. But I also like to move with the times, as perhaps you will allow me to show you. (*He blows two short blasts on a silver whistle hanging round his neck. Instantly from behind every rock and shrub—from every bit of cover—there emerges a soldier, in spick-and-span European uniform* (*Russian in style*), *armed with the latest brand of magazine rifles. They stand like statues at attention*)

CRESPIN. Good Lord!

TRAHERNE. Hallo!

RAJA (*to* LUCILLA, *who makes no move*). I trust I did not startle you, Madam?

LUCILLA. Oh, not at all. I'm not nervous.

RAJA. You, of course, realise that this effect is not original. I have plagiarised it from the excellent Walter Scott:

"These are Clan-Alpine's warriors true,
And, Saxon, I am Roderick Dhu!"

But I think you'll admit, Major, that my men know how to take cover.

CRESPIN. By the Lord, sir, they must move like cats—for you can't have planted them there before we arrived.

RAJA. No, you had given me no notice of your coming.

LUCILLA. Perhaps the Goddess did.

RAJA. Not she, Madam. She keeps her own counsel. These men followed me down from the palace and have taken up position while we have been speaking. (*The* RAJA *gives a word of command, and the men rapidly assemble and form in two ranks, an officer on their flank.*)

CRESPIN. A very smart body of men, Raja. Allow me to congratulate you on their training.

RAJA. I am greatly flattered, Major. I superintend it myself.—Ah, here comes the litter. (*Down the path comes a litter borne, like the* RAJA'*s, by four men. It is followed by two mountain-chairs carried by two men apiece*) Permit me, Madam, to hand you to your palanquin. (*He offers* LUCILLA *his hand. As she rises she picks up her leather coat, and the newspaper falls to the ground. The* RAJA *notices it*) Forgive me, Madam. (*Picks up the paper and looks at it*) A newspaper, only two days old! This is such a rarity you must allow me to glance at it. (*He opens the paper and sees that a strip has been torn out from the back page*) Ah! the telegraphic news gone! What a pity! In my seclusion, I hunger for tidings from the civilized world. (*The* PRIEST *comes forward and speaks to him eagerly, suggesting in pantomime* TRAHERNE'*s action in burning the paper, and pointing to the ashes on the ground, at which the* RAJA *looks*) You burned this column?

TRAHERNE. Unfortunately, I did.

RAJA. Ah! (*Pause*) I know your motive, Dr. Traherne, and I appreciate it. You destroyed it out of consideration for my feelings, wishing to spare me a painful piece of intelligence. That was very thoughtful—but quite unnecessary. I already know what you tried to conceal.

CRESPIN. You know—!

TRAHERNE. Your Highness knows —! (*Simultaneously.*)

RAJA. I know that three of my subjects, accused of a political crime, have been sentenced to death.

TRAHERNE. How is it possible—?

RAJA. Bad news flies fast, Dr. Traherne. But one thing you can perhaps tell me—is there any chance of their sentences being remitted?

TRAHERNE. I am afraid not, Your Highness.

CRESPIN. Remitted? I should rather say not. It was a cold-blooded, unprovoked murder.

RAJA. Unprovoked, you think? Well, I won't argue the point. And the execution is to be——?

TRAHERNE. I think tomorrow—or the day after.

RAJA. Tomorrow or the day after—yes. (*Turning to* LUCILLA) Forgive me, Madam—I have kept you waiting.

TRAHERNE. Does Your Highness know anything of these men?

RAJA (*over his shoulder, as he hands* LUCILLA *into the litter*). Know them? Oh, yes—they are my brothers. (*He seats himself on his own litter and claps his hands twice. Both litters are raised and move off,* LUCILLA'S *first. The regular soldiers line the way, in single rank. They salute as the litters pass.* WATKINS *follows the* RAJA'S. CRESPIN *and* TRAHERNE *seat themselves in their chairs. As they do so:*)

CRESPIN. His brothers? What did he mean?

TRAHERNE (*shrugging his shoulders*). Heaven knows!

CRESPIN. I don't half like our host, Traherne. There's too much of the cat about him.

TRAHERNE. Or of the tiger. And how the mischief had he got the news?

(*As the two chairs move off,* CRESPIN *first, the two ranks of soldiers close round them. The irregulars and musicians, headed by the dancing Negro, bring up the rear. The* PRIEST *prostrates himself, as if in thanksgiving, before the Goddess.*)

ACT TWO

A spacious and well-proportioned room, opening at the back upon a wide loggia. Beyond the loggia can be seen distant snow-peaks and a strip of sky. Late afternoon light.

The room is furnished in a once splendid but now very old-fashioned and faded style. Furniture of black picked out with gold, and upholstered in yellow damask. A great crystal chandelier in the middle of the ceiling, and under it a circular ottoman. Right, a large two-leaved door; left, a handsome marble fireplace, with a mirror over it. Candlesticks with crystal pendants at each end of the mantelpiece, and in the middle a bronze statuette, some eighteen inches high, representing the many-armed Goddess. A wood fire laid, but unlighted. Near the fireplace, two quite modern saddle-bag armchairs, out of keeping with the stiffness of the remaining furniture. A small table near the door, right, with modern English and French books on it. A handsome gramophone in the corner, right. On the walls, left and right, some very bad paintings of fine-looking Orientals in gorgeous attire. Electric lights.

TRAHERNE *discovered at back, centre, looking out over the landscape. He does not go out upon the loggia (which can be entered both right and left without passing through the room) because two turbaned servants are there, under the direction of an old and dignified Major-domo, arranging a luxurious dinner table, with four covers.* TRAHERNE *stands motionless for a moment. Then enters* CRESPIN *by the door, right, ushered in by a servant, who salaams and retires.*

CRESPIN. Ah, there you are, Doctor.

TRAHERNE (*turning*). Hullo! How did you get on?

CRESPIN. All right. Had a capital tub. And you?

TRAHERNE. Feeling more like a human being. And what about Mrs. Crespin? I hope she's all right.

CRESPIN. She was taken off by an ayah as soon as we got in—presumably to the women's quarters.

TRAHERNE. And you let her go off alone?

CRESPIN. What the blazes could I do? I couldn't thrust myself into the women's quarters.

TRAHERNE. You could have kept her with you.

CRESPIN. Do you think she'd have stayed? And, come to that, what business is it of yours?

TRAHERNE. It's any man's business to be concerned for a woman's safety.

CRESPIN. Well, well—all right. But there was nothing I could have done or that she would let me do. And I don't think there's any danger.

TRAHERNE. Let us hope not.

CRESPIN. It's a vast shanty this.

TRAHERNE. It's a palace and a fortress in one.

CRESPIN. A devilish strong place before the days of big guns. But a couple of howitzers would soon make it look pretty foolish.

TRAHERNE. No doubt; but how would you get them here?

CRESPIN (*looking at the dinner table*). I say—it looks as if our friend were going to do us well. (*One of the servants comes in with a wine-cooler. When the man has gone,* CRESPIN *picks up the bottle and looks at the label*) Perrier Jouet, nineteen-o-six, by the lord! (*He strolls over to the ottoman, and seats himself, facing the fireplace*) It's a rum start this, Traherne. I suppose you intellectual chaps would call it romantic.

TRAHERNE (*examining the figure of the Goddess on the mantelpiece*). More romantic than agreeable, I should say. I don't like the looks of this lady.

CRESPIN. What is she?

TRAHERNE. The same figure we saw in the little temple, where we landed.

CRESPIN. How many arms has she got?

TRAHERNE. Six.

CRESPIN. She could give you a jolly good hug, anyway.

TRAHERNE. You wouldn't want another.

CRESPIN. Where do you suppose we really are, Traherne?

TRAHERNE. On the map, you mean?

CRESPIN. Of course.

TRAHERNE. Oh, in the never-never land. Somewhere on the way to Bokhara. I've been searching my memory for all I ever heard about Rukh. I fancy very little is known, except that it seems to send forth a peculiarly poisonous breed of fanatics.

CRESPIN. Like those who did poor Haredale in?

TRAHERNE. Precisely.

CRESPIN. D'you think our host was serious when he said they were his brothers? Or was he only pulling our leg, curse his impudence?

TRAHERNE. He probably meant caste-brothers, or simply men of the same race. But, even so, it's awkward.

CRESPIN. I don't see what these beggars, living at the back of the north wind, have got to do with Indian politics. We've never interfered with them.

TRAHERNE. Oh, it's a case of Asia for the Asians. Ever since the Japanese beat the Russians, the whole continent has been itching to kick us out.

CRESPIN. So that they may cut each other's throats at leisure, eh?

TRAHERNE. We Westerners never cut each other's throats, do we? (WATKINS *has entered at the back, right, carrying a silver centre-piece for the table. He sets it down and is going out to the left, when* CRESPIN *catches sight of him and hails him.*)

CRESPIN. Hallo! You there! What's your name! (WATKINS *stops*) Just come here a minute, will you?

WATKINS. Meaning me, sir? (*He advances into the room. There is a touch of covert insolence in his manner.*)

CRESPIN. Yes, you, Mr.——? Mr.——

WATKINS. Watkins is my name, sir.

CRESPIN. Right ho! Watkins. Can you tell us where we are, Watkins?

WATKINS. They calls the place Rukh, sir.

CRESPIN. Yes, yes, we know that. But where is Rukh?

WATKINS. I hunderstand these mountains is called the 'Imalayas, sir.

CRESPIN. Confound it, sir, we don't want a lesson in geography!

WATKINS. No, sir? My mistake, sir.

TRAHERNE. Major Crespin means that we want to know how far we are from the nearest point in India.

WATKINS. I really couldn't say, sir. Not so very far, I dessay, as the crow flies.

TRAHERNE. Unfortunately we're not in a position to fly with the crow. How long does the journey take?

WATKINS. They tell me it takes about three weeks to Cashmere.

CRESPIN. They tell you! Surely you must remember how long it took you?

WATKINS. No, sir, excuse me, sir—I've never been in India.

CRESPIN. Not been in India? And I was just thinking, as I looked at you, that I seemed to have seen you before.

WATKINS. Not in India, sir. We might 'ave met in England, but I don't call to mind having that pleasure.

CRESPIN. But if you haven't been in India, how the mischief did you get here?

WATKINS. I came with 'Is 'Ighness, sir, by way of Tashkent. All our dealin's with Europe is by way of Russia.

TRAHERNE. But it's possible to get to India direct, and not by way of Central Asia?

WATKINS. Oh, yes, it's done, sir. But I'm told there are some very tight places to negotiate—like the camel and the needle's eye, as you might say.

TRAHERNE. Difficult travelling for a lady, eh?

WATKINS. Next door to himpossible, I should guess, sir.

CRESPIN. A nice look-out, Traherne! (*To* WATKINS) Tell me, my man—is His Highness—h'm—married?

WATKINS. Oh, yessir—very much so, sir.

CRESPIN. Children?

WATKINS. He has fifteen sons, sir.

CRESPIN. The daughters don't count, eh?

WATKINS. I've never 'ad a hopportunity of counting 'em, sir.

TRAHERNE. He said the men accused of assassinating a political officer were his brothers——

WATKINS (*quickly*). Did 'e say that, sir?

TRAHERNE. Didn't you hear him? What did he mean?

WATKINS. I'm sure I couldn't say, sir. 'Is 'Ighness is what you'd call a very playful gentleman, sir.

TRAHERNE. But I don't see the joke in saying that.

WATKINS. No, sir? P'raps 'Is 'Ighness'll explain, sir. (*A pause.*)

CRESPIN. Your master spoke of visits from European ladies—do they come from Russia?

WATKINS. From various parts, I understand, sir.

CRESPIN. Any here now?

WATKINS. I really couldn't say, sir.

TRAHERNE. They don't dine with His Highness?

WATKINS. Oh no, sir. 'Is 'Ighness sometimes sups with them.

CRESPIN. And my wife—Mrs. Crespin——?

WATKINS. Make your mind easy, sir—the lady won't meet any hundesirable characters, sir. I give strict orders to the—the female what took charge of the lady.

TRAHERNE. She is to be trusted?

WATKINS. Habsolutely, sir. She is—in a manner of speakin',—my wife, sir.

CRESPIN. Mrs. Watkins, eh?

WATKINS. Yessir—I suppose you would say so.

TRAHERNE. But now look here, Watkins—you say we're three weeks away from Cashmere—yet the Raja knew of the sentence passed on these subjects of his, who were tried only three days ago. How do you account for that?

WATKINS. I can't, sir. All I can say is, there's queer things goes on here.

TRAHERNE. Queer things? What do you mean?

WATKINS. Well, sir, them priests you know—they goes in a lot for what 'Is 'Ighness calls magic——

TRAHERNE. Oh come, Watkins—you don't believe in that!

WATKINS. Well, sir, p'raps not. I don't, not to say, believe in it. But there's queer things goes on. I can't say no more, nor I can't say no less. If you'll excuse me, sir, I must just run my eye over the dinner-table. 'Is 'Ighness will be here directly. (*He retires, inspects the table, makes one or two changes, and presently goes out by the back, left.*)

CRESPIN. That fellow's either a cunning rascal or a cursed fool. Which do you think?

TRAHERNE. I don't believe he's the fool he'd like us to take him for.—(*Enter* LUCILLA, *right, ushered in by a handsome* AYAH. *She is dressed in a gauzy gown of quite recent style, dark blue or crimson. Not in the least décolletée. At most the sleeves might be open, so as to show her arms to the elbow. No ornaments except a gold locket on a little gold chain round her neck. The costume is absolutely plain, but in striking contrast to her travelling dress. Her hair is beautifully arranged.*)

LUCILLA (*to the* AYAH). Thank you. (*The* AYAH *disappears.* LUCILLA *advances, holding out her skirt a little*) Behold the Paris model!

CRESPIN. My eye, Lu, what a ripping frock!

TRAHERNE. Talk of magic, Major! There's something in what our friend says.

LUCILLA. What is that? What about magic?

CRESPIN. We'll tell you afterwards. Let's have your adventures first.

LUCILLA. No adventures precisely—only a little excursion into the Arabian Nights.

TRAHERNE. Do tell us!

LUCILLA (*evidently a little nervous, yet not without enjoyment of the experience*). Well, my guide—the woman you saw—led me along corridor after corridor, and upstairs and downstairs, till we came to a heavy bronze door where two villainous-looking blacks, with crooked swords, were on guard. I didn't like the looks of them a bit; but I was in for it and had to go on. They drew their swords and flourished a sort of salute, grinning with all their teeth. Then the ayah clapped her hands twice, some one inspected us through a grating in the door, and the ayah said a word or two——

TRAHERNE. No doubt "Open sesame!"

LUCILLA. The door was opened by a hideous, hump-backed old woman, just like the wicked fairy in a pantomime. She didn't actually bite me, but she looked as if she'd like to—and we passed on. More corridors, with curtained doorways, where I had a feeling that furtive eyes were watching me—though I can't positively say I saw them. But I'm sure I heard whisperings and titterings——

CRESPIN. Good Lord! If I'd thought they were going to treat you like that, I'd have——

LUCILLA. Oh, there was nothing you could have done; and, you see, no harm came of it. At last the woman led me into a large sort of wardrobe room, lighted from above, and almost entirely lined with glazed presses full of frocks. Then she slid back a panel, and there was a marble-lined bathroom!—a deep pool, with a trickle of water flowing into it from a dolphin's head of gold—just enough to make the surface ripple and dance. And all around were the latest Bond Street luxuries—shampooing bowls and brushes, bottles of essences, towels on hot rails and all the rest of it. The only thing that was disagreeable was a sickly odour from some burning pastilles—oh, and a coal-black bath-woman.

TRAHERNE. It suggests a Royal Academy picture—"The Odalisque's Pool."

CRESPIN. Or a soap advertisement.

TRAHERNE. Same thing.

LUCILLA. Well, I wasn't sorry to play the odalisque for once; and when I had finished, lo and behold! the ayah had laid out for me half-a-dozen gorgeous and distinctly risky dinner-gowns. I had to explain to her in gestures that I couldn't live up to any of them, and would rather put on my old travelling dress. She seemed quite frightened at the idea——

CRESPIN. Ha ha! She'd probably have got the sack—perhaps literally—if she'd let you do that.

LUCILLA. Anyway, she at last produced this comparatively inoffensive frock. She did my hair, and wanted to finish me off with all sorts of necklaces and bangles, but I stuck to my old locket with the babies' heads.

CRESPIN. Well, all's well that ends well, I suppose. But if I'd foreseen all this "Secrets of the Zenana" business, I'm dashed if I wouldn't——

LUCILLA (*cutting him short*). What were you saying about magic when I came in?

TRAHERNE. Only that this man, Watkins—he's the husband of your ayah, by the way—says queer things go on here, and pretends to believe in magic.

LUCILLA. Do you know, Antony, when the Raja was speaking about him down there, it seemed to me that his face was somehow familiar to me.

CRESPIN. There, Doctor! What did I say? I knew I'd seen him before, but I'm blowed if I can place him.

LUCILLA. I wish I could get a good look at him.

(WATKINS *enters, back, left, with something for the table.*)

TRAHERNE. There he is. Shall I call him in?

LUCILLA. Say I want him to thank his wife from me.

TRAHERNE (*calls*). Watkins!

WATKINS. Sir?

TRAHERNE. Mrs. Crespin would like to speak to you. (WATKINS *comes forward.*)

LUCILLA. I hear, Watkins, that the ayah who so kindly attended to me is your wife.

WATKINS. That's right, ma'am.

LUCILLA. She gave me most efficient assistance, and, as she seems to know no English, I couldn't thank her. Will you be good enough to tell her how much I appreciated all she did for me?

WATKINS. Thank you kindly, ma'am. She'll be proud to hear it. (*Pause*) Is that all, ma'am?

LUCILLA. That's all, thank you, Watkins.

(*He returns to the loggia, but goes to the other side of the dinner-table and keeps an eye on the three.*)

CRESPIN. You've a good memory for faces, Lu. Do you spot him?

LUCILLA. Don't let him see we're talking about him. I believe I do know him, but I'm not quite sure. Do you remember, the first year we were in India, there was a man of the Dorsets that used often to be on guard outside the mess-room?

CRESPIN. By heaven, you've hit it!

TRAHERNE. Take care! He's watching.

LUCILLA. You remember he deserted, and was suspected of having murdered a woman in the bazaar.

CRESPIN. I believe it's the very man.

LUCILLA. It's certainly very like him.

CRESPIN. And he swears he's never been in India!

TRAHERNE. Under the circumstances, he naturally would.

LUCILLA. At all events, he's not a man to be trusted.

(*At this moment the* RAJA *enters by the door, right. He is in faultless European evening dress—white waistcoat, white tie, etc. No jewels, except the ribbon and star of a Russian order. Nothing oriental about him except his turban and his complexion.*)

RAJA (*as he enters*). Pray forgive me, Madam, for being the last to appear. The fact is, I had to hold a sort of Cabinet Council—or shall I say a conclave of prelates?—with regard to questions arising out of your most welcome arrival.

CRESPIN. May we hope, Raja, that you were laying a dawk for our return?

RAJA. Pray, pray, Major, let us postpone that question for the moment. First, let us fortify ourselves; after dinner we will talk seriously. If you are in too great a hurry to desert me, must I not conclude, Madam, that you are dissatisfied with your reception?

LUCILLA. How could we possibly be so ungrateful, Your Highness? Your hospitality overwhelms us.

RAJA. I trust my Mistress of the Robes furnished you with all you required?

LUCILLA. With all and more than all. She offered me quite a bewildering array of gorgeous apparel.

RAJA. Oh, I am glad. I had hoped that perhaps your choice might have fallen on something more—(*He indicates by gestures, "décoletée"*) But no—I was wrong—Madam's taste is irreproachable.

(*A servant enters from behind with cocktails on a silver salver.* LUCILLA *refuses. The men accept.* LUCILLA *picks up a yellow French book on one of the tables.*)

RAJA. You see, Madam, we fall behind the age here. We are still in the Anatole France period. If he bores you, here (*picking up another book*) is a Maurice Barrès that you may find more amusing.

LUCILLA. Oh, I too am in the Anatole France period, I assure you. (*Reads*) "Sur la Pierre Blanche"—isn't that the one you were recommending to me, Dr. Traherne?

TRAHERNE. Yes, I like it better than some of his later books.

RAJA (*picking up a silver-grey book*). As for Bernard Shaw, I suppose he's quite a back number; but I confess his impudence entertains me. What do you say, Major?

CRESPIN. Never read a line of the fellow—except in *John Bull*.

LUCILLA and TRAHERNE (*simultaneously*). In *John Bull!*

CRESPIN. Somebody told me he wrote in *John Bull*—doesn't he?

RAJA. Are you fond of music, Mrs. Crespin? (*Goes to the gramaphone, and turns over some records, till he finds one which he lays on the top of the pile*) Suppose we have some during dinner. (WATKINS *enters from the back, left*) Watkins, just start this top record, will you. (WATKINS *does so.*)

(*At this moment the* MAJOR-DOMO *enters from the back, and says a few words.*)

RAJA. Ah! *Madame est servie!* Allow me— (*He offers* LUCILLA *his arm and leads her to the table. The others follow*) Will you take this seat, Madam? You here, Major —Dr. Traherne! (*He himself sits to the left of the table;* LUCILLA *on his right;* TRAHERNE *opposite him; and* CRESPIN *opposite* LUCILLA, *with his back to the sunset, which is now flooding the scene.*) (*As the servants offer dishes*) I can recommend this caviar, Major—and you'll take a glass of maraschino with it—Russian fashion.
(*Just as they sit down the gramophone reels out the first bars of a piece of music.*)

LUCILLA (*after listening a moment*). Oh, what is that?

RAJA. Don't you know it?

LUCILLA. Oh yes, but I can't think what it is.

RAJA. Gounod's "Funeral March of a Marionette"—a most humorous composition. May I pour you a glass of maraschino? (*He goes on talking as the curtain falls. When it rises again, the glow has faded, and some big stars are pulsing in the strip of purple sky. The party is just finishing dinner. Dessert is on the table, which is lighted by electric lamps.* WATKINS *stands behind the* RAJA'S *chair. The* MAJOR-DOMO *and other servants hover round. The* RAJA *has just finished a story, at which all laugh. A short pause.*)

LUCILLA. What a heavenly night!

RAJA. Yes, our summer climate is far from bad.

LUCILLA. The air is like champagne.

RAJA. A little over-frappé for some tastes. What do you say, Madam? Shall we have coffee indoors? There is an edge to the air at these altitudes, as soon as the sun has gone down.

LUCILLA (*shivers slightly*). Yes, I do feel a little chilly.

RAJA. Watkins, send for a shawl for Madam. (*Rising*) And ah—let us have the fire lighted. (WATKINS *goes off to the left. The* RAJA *says a word to the* MAJOR-DOMO, *who touches a switch in one of the pillars of the loggia opening. The chandelier and wall-lamps of the salon burst into brilliant light.*)

RAJA (*offering his arms to* LUCILLA). Let me find you a comfortable seat, Madam. (*He leads her to the farther back of the two arm-chairs*) When the fire is lighted, I think you will find this quite pleasant. Take the other chair, Major. (CRESPIN *does so*) I must really refurnish this salon. My ancestors had no notion of comfort. To tell the truth, I use the room only on state occasions, like the present. (*Bowing to* LUCILLA) I have a much more modern snuggery upstairs, which I hope you will see tomorrow.
(*Servants hand round coffee, liqueurs, cigars, cigarettes, during what follows. One of them lights the fire, of aromatic wood.*)

RAJA (*to* TRAHERNE *who has remained at the loggia opening, looking out into the night*). Star-gazing, Dr. Traherne?

TRAHERNE. I beg your pardon. (*Comes forward.*)

LUCILLA. Dr. Traherne is quite an astronomer.

RAJA. As much at home with the telescope as with the microscope, eh?

TRAHERNE. Oh no. I'm no astronomer. I can pick out a few of the constellations,—that's all.

RAJA. For my part, I look at the stars as little as possible. As a spectacle they're monotonous, and they don't bear thinking of.
(*The* AYAH, *entering by door, right, brings* LUCILLA *a shawl, which the* RAJA *places on her shoulders.*)

LUCILLA. What an exquisite shawl!

RAJA. And most becoming—don't you think so, Doctor? (TRAHERNE *is gazing at* LUCILLA) My Mistress of the Robes has chosen well! (*He makes a motion of noiseless applause to the* AYAH, *who grins and exit, right.*)

LUCILLA. Why won't the stars bear thinking of, Raja?

RAJA. Well, dear lady, don't you think they're rather ostentatious? I was guilty of a little showing-off today, when I played that foolish trick with my regular troops. But think of the Maharaja up yonder (*pointing upwards*) who night after night whistles up his glittering legions, and puts them through their deadly punctual drill, as much as to say, "See what a devil of a fellow *I* am!" Do you think it quite in good taste, Madam?

TRAHERNE (*laughing*). I'm afraid you're jealous, Raja. You don't like having to play second fiddle to a still more absolute ruler.

RAJA. Perhaps you're right, Doctor —perhaps it's partly that. But there's something more to it. I can't help resenting— (*To* CRESPIN, *to whom a servant is offering liqueurs*) Let me recommend the kümmel, Major. I think you'll find it excellent.

TRAHERNE. What is it you resent?

RAJA. Oh, the respect paid to mere size—to the immensity, as they call it, of the universe. Are we to worship a god because he's big?

TRAHERNE. If you resent his bigness, what do you say to his littleness? The microscope, you know, reveals him no less than the telescope.

RAJA. And reveals him in the form of death-dealing specks of matter, which you, I understand, Doctor, are impiously proposing to exterminate.

TRAHERNE. I am trying to marshal the life-saving against the death-dealing powers.

RAJA. To marshal God's right hand against his left, eh? or *vice versa?* But I admit you have the pull of the astronomers, in so far as you deal in life, not in dead mechanism. (*Killing a gnat on the back of his hand*) This mosquito that I have just killed—I am glad to see you smoke, Madam: it helps to keep them off—this mosquito, or any smallest thing that has life in it, is to me far more admirable than a whole lifeless universe. What do you say, Major?

CRESPIN (*smoking a cigar*). I say, Raja, that if you'll tell that fellow to give me another glass of kümmel, I'll let you have your own way about the universe. (*The* RAJA *says a word to one of the servants, who refills* CRESPIN'*s glass.*)

LUCILLA. But what if the mechanism, as you call it, isn't dead? What if the stars are swarming with life?

TRAHERNE. Yes—suppose there are planets, which of course we can't see, circling round each of the great suns we do see? And suppose they are all inhabited?

RAJA. I'd rather not suppose it. Isn't one inhabited world bad enough? Do we want it multiplied by millions?

LUCILLA. Haven't you just been telling us that a living gnat is more wonderful than a dead universe?

RAJA. Wonderful? Yes, by all means —wonderful as a device for torturing and being tortured. Oh, I'm neither a saint nor an ascetic—I take life as I find it—I am tortured and I torture. But there's one thing I'm really proud of—I'm proud to belong to the race of the Buddha, who first found out that life was a colossal blunder.

LUCILLA (*in a low voice*). Should you like the sky to be starless? That seems to me—forgive me, Prince—the last word of impiety.

RAJA. Possibly, Madam. How my esteemed fellow-creatures were ever bluffed into piety is a mystery to me. Not that I'm complaining. If men could not be bluffed by the Raja above, much less would they be bluffed by us Rajas below. And though life is a contemptible business, I don't deny that power is the best part of it.

TRAHERNE. In short, your Highness is a Superman.

RAJA. Ah, you read Nietzsche? Yes, if I weren't of the kindred of the Buddha, I should like to be of the race of that great man.
(*The servants have now all withdrawn.*)

LUCILLA (*looking out*). There is the moon rising over the snowfields. I hope you wouldn't banish her from the heavens?

RAJA. Oh no—I like her silly, good-natured face. And she's useful to lovers and brigands and other lawless vagabonds, with whom I have great sympathy. Besides, I don't know that she's so silly either. She seems to be for ever raising her eyebrows in mild astonishment at human folly.

CRESPIN. All this is out of my depths, your Highness. We've had a rather fatiguing day. Mightn't we——?

RAJA. To be sure. I only waited till the servants had gone. Now, are you all quite comfortable?

LUCILLA. Quite.

TRAHERNE. Perfectly, thank you.

CRESPIN. Perfectly.

RAJA (*smoking a cigar, and standing with his back to the fire*). Then we'll go into committee upon your position here.

CRESPIN. If you please, sir.

RAJA. I'm afraid you may find it rather disagreeable.

CRESPIN. Communications bad, eh? We have a difficult journey before us?

RAJA. A long journey, I fear—yet not precisely difficult.

CRESPIN. It surely can't be so very far, since you had heard of the sentence passed on those assassins.

RAJA. I am glad, Major, that you have so tactfully spared me the pain of re-opening that subject. We should have had to come to it, sooner or later. (*An embarrassed pause.*)

TRAHERNE. When your Highness said they were your brothers, you were, of course, speaking figuratively. You meant your tribesmen?

RAJA. Not at all. They are sons of my father—not of my mother.

LUCILLA. And we intrude upon you at such a time! How dreadful!

RAJA. Oh, pray don't apologise. Believe me, your arrival has given great satisfaction.

TRAHERNE. How do you mean?

RAJA. I'll explain presently. But first——

CRESPIN (*interrupting*). First, let us understand each other. You surely can't approve of this abominable crime?

RAJA. My brothers are fanatics, and there is no fanaticism in me.

LUCILLA. How do they come to be so different from you?

RAJA. That is just what I was going to tell you. I was my father's eldest son, by his favourite wife. Through my mother's influence (my poor mother—how I loved her!) I was sent to Europe. My education was wholly European. I shed all my prejudices. I became the open-minded citizen of the world whom I hope you recognise in me. My brothers, on the other hand, turned to India for their culture. The religion of our people has always been a primitive idolatry. My brothers naturally fell in with adherents of the same superstition, and they worked each other up to a high pitch of frenzy against the European exploitation of Asia.

TRAHERNE. Had you no restraining influence upon them?

RAJA. Of course I might have imprisoned them—or had them strangled—the traditional form of argument in our family. But why should I? As I said, I have no prejudices—least of all in favor of the British raj. We are of Indian race, though long severed from the Motherland—and I do not love her tyrants.

CRESPIN (*who has had quite enough to drink*). In short, sir, you defend this wicked murder?

RAJA. Oh, no—I think it foolish and futile. But there is a romantic as well as a practical side to my nature, and, from the romantic point of view, I rather admire it.

CRESPIN (*rising*). Then, sir, the less we intrude on your hospitality the better. If you will be good enough to furnish us with transport tomorrow morning——

RAJA. That is just where the difficulty arises——

CRESPIN. No transport, hey?

RAJA. Materially it might be managed; but morally I fear it is—excuse the colloquialism, Madam—no go.

CRESPIN. What the blazes do you mean, sir——?

LUCILLA (*trying to cover his bluster*). Will your Highness be good enough to explain?

RAJA. I mentioned that the religion of my people is a primitive superstition? Well, since the news has spread that three Feringhis have dropped from the skies precisely at the time when three princes of the royal house are threatened with death at the hands of the Feringhi government,—and dropped, moreover, in the precincts of a temple—my subjects have got it into their heads that you have been personally conducted hither by the Goddess whom they especially worship.

LUCILLA. The Goddess——?

RAJA (*turning to the statuette*). Here is her portrait on the mantelpiece—much admired by connoisseurs. (LUCILLA *cannot repress a shudder*) I need not say that I am far from sharing the popular illusion. Your arrival is, of course, the merest coincidence—for me, a charming coincidence. But my people hold unphilosophic views. I understand that even in England the vulgar are apt to see the Finger of Providence in particularly fortunate —or unfortunate—occurrences.

CRESPIN. Then the upshot of all this palaver is that you propose to hold us as hostages, to exchange for your brothers?

RAJA. That is not precisely the idea, my dear sir. My theologians do not hold that an exchange is what the Goddess decrees. Nor, to be quite frank, would it altogether suit my book.

LUCILLA. Not to get your brothers back again?

RAJA. You may have noted in history, Madam, that family affection is seldom the strong point of Princes. Is it not Pope who remarks on their lack of enthusiasm for "a brother near the throne"? My sons are mere children, and were I to die—we are all mortal—there might be trouble about the succession. In our family, uncles seldom love nephews.

LUCILLA. So you would raise no finger to save your brothers?

RAJA. That is not my only reason. Supposing it possible that I could bully the Government of India into giving up my relatives, do you think it would sit calmly down under the humiliation? No, no, dear lady. It might wait a few years to find some decent pretext, but assuredly we should have a punitive expedition. It would cost thousands of lives and millions of money, but what would that matter? Prestige would be restored, and I should end my days in a maisonette in Petrograd. It wouldn't suit me at all. Hitherto I have escaped the notice of your Government by a policy of masterly inactivity, and I propose to adhere to that policy.

CRESPIN. Then I don't see how——

TRAHERNE (*simultaneously*). Surely you don't mean——?

RAJA. We are approaching the crux of the matter—a point which I fear you may have some difficulty in appreciating. I would beg you to remember that, though I am what is commonly called an autocrat, there is no such thing under the sun as real despotism. All government is government by consent of the people. It is very stupid of them to consent—but they do. I have studied the question—I took a pretty good degree at Cambridge, in Moral and Political Science—and I assure you that, though I have absolute power of life and death over my subjects, it is only their acquiescence that gives me that power. If I defied their prejudices or their passions, they could upset my throne tomorrow.

CRESPIN. (*angrily*). Will you be so kind as to come to the point, sir?

RAJA. Gently, Major! We shall reach it soon enough. (*To* LUCILLA) Please remember, too, Madam, that an autocracy is generally a theocracy to boot, and mine is a case in point. I am a slave to theology. The clerical party can do what it pleases with me, for there is no other party to oppose it. True, I am my own Archbishop of Canterbury—but "I have a partner: Mr. Jorkins"—I have a terribly exacting Archbishop of York. I fear I may have to introduce you to him tomorrow.

LUCILLA. You are torturing us, your Highness. Like my husband, I beg you to come to the point.

RAJA. The point is, dear lady, that the theology on which, as I say, my whole power is founded, has not yet emerged from the Mosaic stage of development: it demands an eye for an eye, a tooth for a tooth—
(*A long pause*)
a life for a life.
(*Another pause.*)

TRAHERNE. You mean to say——

RAJA. Unfortunately, I do.

LUCILLA. You would kill us——?

RAJA. Not I, Madam—the clerical party. And only if my brothers are executed. If not, I will merely demand your word of honour that what has passed between us shall never be mentioned to any human soul—and you shall go free.

CRESPIN. But if your brother assassins are hanged—as assuredly they will be—you will put to death in cold blood——

RAJA (*interrupting*). Oh, not in cold blood, Major. There is nothing cold-blooded about the clerical party when "white goats," as their phrase goes, are to be sacrificed to the Goddess.

TRAHERNE. Does your Goddess demand the life of a woman?

RAJA. Well, on that point she might not be too exacting. "On trouve avec le Ciel des accommodements." If Madam would be so gracious as to favour me with her—society——
(LUCILLA *after gazing at him for a moment speechless, realises his meaning and springs up with a cry of rage and shame.*)

TRAHERNE. Scoundrel!

CRESPIN (*draws his revolver*). Another word, and I shoot you like a dog!

RAJA. Oh, no, Major—that wouldn't help a bit. You would only be torn to pieces instead of beheaded. Besides, I have had your teeth drawn. That precaution was taken while you were at your bath.

CRESPIN (*examines his revolver and finds it empty*). Curse it!

LUCILLA (*raising her head and addressing both men*). Promise you won't leave me alone! If we must die, let me die first.

RAJA. The order of the ceremony, Madam, will not be at these gentlemen's choice. (LUCILLA *makes a gesture of despair*) But do not be alarmed. No constraint shall be put upon your inclinations. Dr. Traherne reproached me with lack of consideration for your sex, and I hinted that, if you so pleased, your sex should meet with every consideration. I gather that you do not so please? Well, I scarcely hoped you would—I do not press the point. None the less, the suggestion remains open. And now, I'm afraid I've been talking a great deal. You must be fatigued.
(*The* MAJOR-DOMO *appears at the door, right, with a slip of paper on a salver. The* RAJA *motions him to advance, goes to meet him, takes the paper and looks at it.*)

RAJA. Ah, this is interesting! If you will wait a few minutes, I may have some news for you. Excuse me. (*Exit, right, followed by the* MAJOR-DOMO.)
(*The three stare at each other for a moment in speechless horror.*)

LUCILLA. And we were saved this morning—only for this!

TRAHERNE. Courage! There must be some way out.

CRESPIN. The whole thing's a confounded piece of bluff! Ha, ha, ha! The scoundrel almost took me in.

LUCILLA (*throwing herself down on the ottoman, in a passion of tears*). My babies! Oh, my babies! Never to see them again! To leave them all alone in the world! My Ronny! My little Iris! What can we do? What can we do? Antony! Dr. Traherne! Think of something—something——

CRESPIN. Yes, yes, Lu—we'll think of something——

TRAHERNE. There's that fellow Watkins—we might bribe him——

LUCILLA. Oh, offer him every penny we have in the world——

TRAHERNE. I'm afraid he's a malicious scoundrel. He must have known what was hanging over our heads, and, looking back, I seem to see him gloating over it.

LUCILLA. Still—still—perhaps he can be bought. Antony! Think of the children! Oh, do let us try.

CRESPIN. But even if he would, he couldn't guide us through the mountains.

LUCILLA. Oh, he could hire some one else.

TRAHERNE. I don't believe we can possibly be so far from the frontier as he makes out.

LUCILLA. How far did he say?

TRAHERNE. Three weeks' journey. Yet they know all about things that happened less than a week ago.
(*Suddenly all the lights in the room go down very perceptibly. All look round in surprise.*)

LUCILLA. What is that? (*A sort of hissing and chittering sound is heard faintly but unmistakably*) What an odd sound!

TRAHERNE. Major! Do you hear that!

CRESPIN. Do I hear it? I should say so!

TRAHERNE. Wireless!

CRESPIN (*much excited*). Wireless, by Jupiter! They're sending out a message.

TRAHERNE. That accounts for it! They're in wireless communication with India!

LUCILLA (*to* TRAHERNE). Antony knows all about wireless.

CRESPIN. I should rather think so! Wasn't it my job all through the war! If I could hear more distinctly now—and if they're transmitting in clear—I could read their message.

TRAHERNE. That may be our salvation!

CRESPIN. If we could get control of the wireless for five minutes, and call up the aerodrome at Amil-Serai——

LUCILLA. What then?

CRESPIN. Why, we'd soon bring the Raja to his senses.

LUCILLA (*to* CRESPIN). Where do you suppose the installation is?

CRESPIN. Somewhere overhead I should say.

TRAHERNE. We must go very cautiously, Major. We must on no account let the Raja suspect that we know anything about wireless telegraphy, else he'd take care we should never get near the installation.

CRESPIN. Right you are, Traherne—I'll lie very low.

LUCILLA (*tearing off the shawl*). And how are we to behave to that horrible man?

CRESPIN. We must keep a stiff upper lip, and play the game.

LUCILLA. You mean pretend to take part in his ghastly comedy of hospitality and politeness?

TRAHERNE. If you can, it would be wisest. His delight in showing off his European polish is all in our favor. But for that he might separate us and lock us up. We must avoid that at all costs.

LUCILLA. Oh, yes, yes——

CRESPIN. You've always had plenty of pluck, Lu–. Now's the time to show it.

LUCILLA (*putting on the shawl again*). You can trust me. The thought of the children knocked me over at first; but I'm not afraid to die. (*The chittering sound ceases, and the lights suddenly go up again*) The noise has stopped.

CRESPIN. Yes, they've left off transmitting, and ceased to draw on the electric current.

TRAHERNE. He'll be back presently. Don't let us seem to be consulting. (TRAHERNE *seats himself in an easy chair.* LUCILLA *sits on the ottoman.* CRESPIN *lights a cigar and takes the* RAJA's *place before the fire.*)

CRESPIN. Curse it! I can't remember the wave-length and the call for Amil-Serai. I was constantly using it at one time.

TRAHERNE. It'll come back to you.

CRESPIN. I pray to the Lord it may! (*The* RAJA *enters, right.*)

RAJA. I promised you news, and it has come.

CRESPIN. What news?

RAJA. My brothers' execution is fixed for the day after tomorrow.

LUCILLA. Then the day after tomorrow——?

RAJA. Yes—at sunset. (*A pause*) But meanwhile I hope you will regard my poor house as your own. This is Liberty Hall. My tennis courts, my billiard-room, my library are all at your disposal. I should not advise you to pass the palace gates—it would not be safe, for popular feeling, I must warn you, runs very high. Besides, where could you go? There are three hundred miles of almost impassable country between you and the nearest British post.

TRAHERNE. In that case, Prince, how do you communicate with India? How has this news reached you?

RAJA. Does that puzzle you?

TRAHERNE. Naturally.

RAJA. You don't guess?

TRAHERNE. We have been trying to. The only thing we could think of was that you must be in wireless communication.

RAJA. You observed nothing to confirm the idea?

TRAHERNE. Why, no.

RAJA. Did you notice that the lights suddenly went down?

TRAHERNE. Yes, and at the same time we heard a peculiar hissing sound.

RAJA. None of you knew what it meant?

TRAHERNE. No.

RAJA. Then you have no knowledge of wireless telegraphy?

TRAHERNE. None.

RAJA. I may tell you, then, that that hissing is the sound of wireless transmission. I am in communication with India.

TRAHERNE (*to the others*). You see, I was right.

CRESPIN. You have a wireless expert here then?

RAJA. Watkins,—that invaluable fellow—he is my operator.

TRAHERNE. And with whom do you communicate?

RAJA. Do you think that quite a fair question, Doctor? Does it show your usual tact? I have my agents—I can say no more. (*Pause*) Shall I ring for the ayah, Madam, to see you to your room?

LUCILLA. If you please. (*As he has his finger on the bell, she says*) No; stay a moment. (*Rises and advances towards him*) Prince, I have two children. If it weren't for them, don't imagine that any of us would beg a favour at your hands. But for their sakes won't you instruct your agent to communicate with Simla and try to bring about an exchange —your brothers' lives for ours?

RAJA. I am sorry, Madam, but I have already told you why that is impossible. Even if your Government agreed, it would assuredly take revenge on me for having extorted such a concession. No whisper of your presence here must ever reach India, or—again forgive the vulgarism—my goose is cooked.

LUCILLA. The thought of my children does not move you?

RAJA. My brothers have children—does the thought of them move the Government of India? No, Madam, I am desolated to have to refuse you, but you must not ask for the impossible. (*He presses the bell.*)

LUCILLA. Does it not strike you that, if you drive us to desperation, we may find means of cheating your Goddess? What is to prevent me, for instance, from throwing myself from that loggia?

RAJA. Nothing, dear lady, except that clinging to the known, and shrinking from the unknown, that all of us feel, even while we despise it. Besides, it would be foolishly precipitate, in every sense of the word. While there is life there is hope. You can't read my mind. For aught you can tell, I may have no intention of proceeding to extremities, and may only be playing a little joke upon you. I hope you have observed that I have a sense of humour. (*The* AYAH *enters*) Ah, here is the ayah. Good night, Madam; sleep well. (*Bows her to the door. Exit* LUCILLA *with* AYAH) Gentlemen, a whiskey and soda. No? Then good night, good night. (*Exeunt* CRESPIN *and* TRAHERNE.) (*The* RAJA *takes from the table a powerful electric torch, and switches it on. Then he switches off the lights of the room, which is totally dark except for the now moonlit background. He goes up to the idol on the mantelpiece, throws the light of the torch upon it, and makes it an ironic salaam. Then he lights himself towards the door, left.*)

CURTAIN

ACT THREE

The RAJA's *Snuggery. An entirely European and modern room; its comfort contrasting with the old-fashioned, comfortless splendour of the scene of Act Two.*

A door in front, left, opens on the billiard-room; another, a little farther back, leads to the rest of the palace. A large and solid folding door in the back wall, centre. To the right, a large open window with a shallow balcony, which has the effect of being at a great height, and commands a view across the valley to the snow peaks beyond.

On the right, near the window, a handsome pedestal writing table, with a large and heavy swivel chair behind it. Silver fittings on the table, all in perfect order. Close to the nearer end of the writing table, a revolving bookcase, containing the Encyclopaedia Britannica and other books of reference. On the top of it a tantalus with a syphon and glasses. Close up to the writing table, and about of equal length, a deeply upholstered green leather sofa. Further over towards the left, a small table with smoking appliances. On each side of the table a comfortable green leather arm-chair. No small chairs. Low bookcases, filled with serious-looking modern books, against the walls, wherever there is space for them. On the top of one of the bookcases, a large bronze bust of Napoleon. A black and white portrait of Nietzsche on the wall, along with some sporting prints.

CRESPIN *discovered alone, wandering around the room, nervous and irritable. He tries the door at back; it is locked. Opens the door down left, and closes it, muttering "Billiards, begad!" Crosses to the writing table, examines the articles upon it, and picks up a paper which proves to be "La Vie Parisienne." He throws it down with the comment, "French muck!" Notices a paper on the couch, picks it up and says with disgust, "Russian." Then he comes down to the revolving bookcase, glances at the books and spins it angrily. After a moment's hesitation, he pours some whiskey into a tumbler and fills it from the siphon. Is on the point of drinking, but hesitates, then says, "No!" Goes to the balcony and throws out the contents of the glass. As he is setting the glass down,* TRAHERNE *enters, second door left, ushered in by a* SOLDIER, *who salutes and exits.*

CRESPIN. There! You think you've caught me!

TRAHERNE. Caught you?

CRESPIN. Lushing. But I haven't been. I threw the stuff out of the window. For Lucilla's sake, I must keep all my wits about me.

TRAHERNE. Yes, if we can all do that, we may pull through yet.

CRESPIN. Did you sleep?

TRAHERNE. Not a wink. And you?

CRESPIN. Dozed and woke again fifteen times in a minute. A beast of a night!

TRAHERNE. Have you news of Mrs. Crespin?

CRESPIN. She sent me this *chit.* (*Hands him a scrap of paper.*)

TRAHERNE (*reads*). "Have slept and am feeling better. Keep the flag flying." What pluck she has!

CRESPIN. Yes, she's game—always was.

TRAHERNE. She reminds me of the women in the French Revolution. We might all be in the Conciergerie, waiting to hear the tumbrils.

CRESPIN. It would be more endurable if we were in prison. It's this appearance of freedom—the scoundrel's cursed airs of politeness and hospitality—that makes the thing such a nightmare. (*Mechanically mixing himself a whiskey and soda*) Do you believe we're really awake, Traherne? If I were alone, I'd think the whole thing was a blasted nightmare; but Lucilla and you seem to be dreaming it too. (*Raising the glass to his lips, he remembers and puts it down again, saying:*) Curse it!

TRAHERNE. Some day we may look back upon it as on a bad dream.

CRESPIN. He does you well, curse him! They served me a most dainty *chota hazri* this morning, and with it a glass of rare old *fine champagne.*

TRAHERNE (*pointing to the door, down left*). Where does that door lead?

CRESPIN. To the billiard-room. Billiards! Ha, ha!

TRAHERNE (*at door, centre*). And this one?

CRESPIN. I don't know. It's locked—and a very solid door, too.

TRAHERNE. Do you know what I think?

CRESPIN. Yes, and I agree with you.

TRAHERNE. Opening off the fellow's own sanctum——

CRESPIN. It's probably the wireless room.
(*They exchange significant glances.*)

TRAHERNE (*indicating the window*). And what's out here?

CRESPIN. Take a look.

TRAHERNE (*looking over*). A sheer drop of a hundred feet.

CRESPIN. And a dry torrent below. How if we were to pick up our host, Traherne, and gently drop him on those razor-edged rocks?

TRAHERNE (*shrugs his shoulders*). As he said last night, they'd only tear us to pieces the quicker.

CRESPIN. If it weren't for Lucilla, I'm cursed if I wouldn't do it all the same.
(*The* RAJA *enters, second door left, dressed in spick-and-span up-to-date riding attire. He crosses to the writing table.*)

RAJA. Good morning, Major; good morning, Doctor. How do you like my snuggery? I hope you have slept well? (*They make no answer*) No? Ah, perhaps you find this altitude trying? Never mind. We have methods of dealing with insomnia.

CRESPIN. Come now, Raja, a joke's a joke, but this cat-and-mouse business gets on one's nerves. Make arrangements to send us back to the nearest British outpost, and we'll give you our Bible oath to say nothing about the—pleasantry you've played on us.

RAJA. Send you back, my dear Major? I assure you, if I were ever so willing, it would be as much as my place is worth. You don't know how my faithful subjects are looking forward to tomorrow's ceremony. If I tried to cancel it, there would be a revolution. You must be reasonable, my dear sir.

CRESPIN. Do you think we would truckle to you, curse you, if it weren't for my wife's sake? But for her we'll make any concession—promise you anything.

RAJA. What can you promise that is worth a brass farthing to me? (*With sudden ferocity*) No. Asia has a long score against you swaggering, blustering, whey-faced lords of creation, and, by all the gods! I mean to see some of it paid tomorrow! (*Resuming his suave manner*) But in the meantime there is no reason why we shouldn't behave like civilised beings. How would you like to pass the morning? I'm sorry I can't offer you any shooting. I musn't lead you into temptation. What do you say to billiards? It soothes the nerves. (*Opening the door*) Here is the billiard-room. I have a little business to attend to, but I'll join you presently.

CRESPIN. Of all the infernal purring devils——!

RAJA. Dignity, Major, dignity! (TRAHERNE *interposes and shepherds the* MAJOR *off. The click of billiard-balls is presently heard. The* RAJA *seats himself at the writing table and presses a bell. Then he takes up a pad of paper and pencil, and taps his teeth, cogitating what to write. In a few moments* WATKINS *enters.*)

WATKINS. Your Highness rang?

RAJA. Come in, Watkins. Just close the billiard-room door, will you? (WATKINS *looks into the billiard-room and then closes the door.*)

WATKINS. They're good pluck'd uns, sir; I will say that.

RAJA. Yes, there's some satisfaction in handling them. I'm glad they're not abject—it would quite spoil the sport.

WATKINS. Quite so, sir.

RAJA. But it has occurred to me, Watkins, that perhaps it's not quite safe to have them so near the wireless room. Their one chance would be to get into communication with India. They appeared last night to know nothing about the wireless, but I have my doubts. Tell me, Watkins—have they made any attempt to bribe you?

WATKINS. Not yet, sir.

RAJA. Ha, that looks bad. It looks as if they had something else up their sleeves, and were leaving bribery to the last resort. I want to test their ignorance of wireless. I want you, in their presence, to send out some message that is bound to startle or enrage them, and see if they show any sign of understanding it.

WATKINS (*grinning*). That's a notion, sir.

RAJA. But I can't think of a message.
(*The* AYAH *opens the second door, left, ushers in* LUCILLA, *and exit.* LUCILLA *has resumed her travelling dress. The* RAJA *has been examining the lock of the wireless room, and is thus partly concealed by the entrance door as it opens, so that* LUCILLA *is well into the room before she observes him. He comes forward.*)

RAJA. Ah, Mrs. Crespin, I was just thinking of you. Think of angels and you hear their wings. Won't you sit down?

LUCILLA (*ignoring his invitation*). I thought my husband was here.

RAJA. He's not far off. (*To* WATKINS, *pointing to the centre door*) Just wait in there for a few minutes; I may have instructions for you.
(WATKINS *produces a key-ring, selects a key, unlocks the door of the wireless-room, and goes in, closing the door behind him.*)

RAJA (*to* LUCILLA, *who has stood motionless*). Do, pray, sit down. I want so much to have a chat with you. (LUCILLA *seats herself, in silence*) I hope you had everything you required?

LUCILLA. Everything.

RAJA. The ayah?

LUCILLA. Was most attentive.

RAJA. And you slept——?

LUCILLA. More or less.

RAJA. More rather than less, if one may judge by your looks.

LUCILLA. Does it matter?

RAJA. What can matter more than the looks of a beautiful woman?

LUCILLA (*listening*). What's that?

RAJA. The click of billiard-balls. Your husband and Dr. Traherne are passing the time.

LUCILLA (*rising*). If you'll excuse me, I'll join them.

RAJA. Oh, pray spare me a few moments. I want to speak to you seriously.

LUCILLA (*sitting down again*). Well —I am listening.

RAJA. You are very curt, Mrs. Crespin. I'm afraid you bear me malice,—you hold me responsible for the doubtless trying situation in which you find yourself.

LUCILLA. Who else is responsible?

RAJA. Who? Why chance, fate, the gods, Providence—whoever, or whatever, pulls the strings of this unaccountable puppet-show. Did *I* bring you here? Did *I* conjure up the fog? Could I have prevented your dropping from the skies? And when once you had set foot in the Goddess's precinct, it was utterly out of my power to save you—at any rate the men of your party. If I raised a finger to thwart the Goddess, it would be the end of my rule—perhaps of my life.

LUCILLA. You know that is not true. You could easily smuggle us away, and then face the people out. What about your troops?

RAJA. A handful, dear lady—a toy army. It amuses me to play at soldiers. They could no nothing against priests and people, even if they were to be depended upon. And they, too, worship the Goddess.

LUCILLA. What you really mean, Raja, is that you dare not risk it—you haven't the courage.

RAJA. You take a mean advantage, Madam. You abuse the privilege of your sex in order to taunt me with cowardice.

LUCILLA. Let us say, then, that you haven't the will to save us.

RAJA. Reflect one moment, Madam—why should I have the will, at the risk of all I possess, to save Major Crespin and Dr. Traherne? Major Crespin is your husband—does that recommend him to me? Forgive me if I venture to guess that it doesn't greatly recommend him to you. He is an only too typical specimen of a breed I detest: pigheaded, bullnecked, blustering, overbearing. Dr. Traherne is an agreeable man enough—I daresay a man of genius——

LUCILLA. If you kill him—if you cut short his work—you kill millions of your own race, whom he would have saved.

RAJA. I don't know that I care very much about the millions you speak of. Life is a weed that grows again as fast as death mows it down. At all events, he is an Englishman, a Feringhi—and, may I add, without indiscretion, that the interest you take in him—oh, the merest friendly interest, I am sure—does not endear him to me. One is, after all, a man, and the favour shown to another man by a beautiful woman—(LUCILLA *rises and moves towards the billiard-room. The* RAJA *interposes*) Please, please, Mrs. Crespin, bear with me if I transgress your Western conventions. Can I help being an Oriental? Believe me, I mean no harm; I wanted to talk to you about——

LUCILLA. Well?

RAJA. You spoke last night of—your children. (LUCILLA *turns away, her self-control wavering*) I think you said—a boy and a little girl.

LUCILLA (*throws herself down on the couch in a fit of weeping*). My babies, my babies!

RAJA. I feel for you, Mrs. Crespin, I do indeed. I would do anything——

LUCILLA (*looking up, vehemently*). Prince, if I write them a letter of farewell, will you give me your word of honour that it shall reach them?

RAJA. Ah, there, Madam, you must pardon me! I have already said that the last thing I desire is to attract the attention of the Government of India.

LUCILLA. I will say nothing to show where I am, or what has befallen me. You shall read it yourself.

RAJA. An ingenious idea! You would have it come fluttering down out of the blue upon your children's heads, like a message from a Mahatma. But, the strength of my position, you see, is that no one will ever know what has become of you. You will simply disappear in the uncharted sea of the Himalayas, as a ship sinks with all hands in the ocean. If I permitted any word from you to reach India, the detective instinct, so deeply implanted in your race, would be awakened, and the Himalayas would be combed out with a tooth-comb. No, Madam, I cannot risk it.

LUCILLA (*her calm recovered*). Cannot? You dare not! But you can and dare kill defenseless men and women. Raja, you are a pitiful coward.

RAJA. Forgive me if I smile at your tactics. You want to goad me into chivalry. If every man were a coward who took life without risking his own, where would your British sportsmen be?

LUCILLA. I beg your pardon—a savage is not necessarily a coward. And now let me go to my husband.

RAJA. Not yet, Mrs. Crespin—one more word. You are a brave woman, and I sincerely admire you——

LUCILLA. Please—please——

RAJA. Listen to me. It will be worth your while. I could not undertake to send a letter to your children—but it would be very easy for me to have them carried off and brought to you here.

LUCILLA (*starts, and faces him*). What do you mean?

RAJA. I mean that, in less than a month, you may have your children in your arms, uninjured, unsuspecting, happy—if——

LUCILLA. If?

RAJA. If—oh, in your own time, of your own free will—you will accept the homage it would be my privilege to offer you.

LUCILLA. That!

RAJA. You have the courage to die, dear lady—why not have the courage to live?
(*Pause.*)
You believe, I daresay, that tomorrow, when the ordeal is over, you will awaken in a new life, and that there your children will rejoin you. Suppose it were so: suppose that in forty—fifty—sixty years, they passed over to you: would they be your children? Can God Himself give you back their childhood? What I offer you is a new life, not problematical, but assured; a new life, without passing through the shadow of death; a future utterly cut off from the past, except that your children will be with you, not as vague shades, but living and loving. They must be quite young; they would soon forget all that had gone before. They would grow to manhood and womanhood under your eyes; and ultimately, perhaps, when the whole story was forgotten, you might, if you wished it,

return with them to what you call civilisation.

And meanwhile, you are only on the threshold of the best years of your life. You would pass them, not as a memsahib in a paltry Indian cantonment, but as the absolute queen of an absolute king. I do not talk to you of romantic love. I respect you too much to think you accessible to silly sentiment. But that is just it: I respect as much as I admire you; and I have never pretended to respect any other woman. Therefore I say you should be my first and only Queen. Your son, if you gave me one, should be the prince of princes; my other sons should all bow down to him and serve him. For, though I hate the arrogance of Europe, I believe that from a blending of the flower of the East with the flower of the West, the man of the future —the Superman—may be born. (LUCILLA *has sat motionless through all this speech, her elbows on the end of the couch, twisting her handkerchief in her hands and gazing straight in front of her. There is now a perceptible pause before she speaks in a toneless voice.*)

LUCILLA. Is that all? Have you quite done?

RAJA. I beg you to answer.

LUCILLA. I can't answer the greater part of what you have been saying, for I have not heard it; at least I have not understood it. All I have heard is "In less than a month you may have your children in your arms," and then again, "Can God Himself give you back their childhood?" These words have kept hammering at my brain till—(*showing her handkerchief*) you see—I have bit my lip to keep from shrieking aloud. I think the devil must have put them in your mouth——

RAJA. Pooh! You don't believe in these old bugbears.

LUCILLA. Perhaps not. But there is such a thing as diabolical temptation, and you have stumbled upon the secret of it.

RAJA. Stumbled!

LUCILLA. Mastered the art of it, if you like—but not in your long harangue. All I can think of is, "Can God Himself give you back their childhood?" and "In a month you may have them in your arms."

RAJA (*eagerly*). Yes, yes—think of that. In three or four weeks you may have your little ones——

LUCILLA (*rising and interrupting him vehemently*). Yes—but on what conditions? That I should desert my husband and my friend—should let them go alone to their death—should cower in some back room of this murderous house of yours, listening to the ticking of the clock, and thinking, "Now—now—the stroke has fallen"—stopping my ears so as not to hear the yells of your bloodthirsty savages—and yet, perhaps, hearing nothing else to my dying day. No, prince!—you said something about not passing through the shadow of death; but if I did this I should not pass through it, but live in it, and bring my children into it as well. What would be the good of having them in my arms if I could not look them in the face? (*She passes to the billiard-room door.*)

RAJA. That is your answer?

LUCILLA. The only possible answer. (*She enters the billiard-room and closes the door.*)

RAJA (*looking after her, to himself*). But not the last word, my lady! (*He sits at the writing table, and begins to write, at the same time calling, not very loudly,* "WATKINS!" *The valet immediately appears, center.*)

WATKINS. Yessir?

RAJA (*tearing a sheet off the pad and handing it to him*). Read that.

WATKINS. A message to be sent out, sir?

RAJA. Yes.

WATKINS (*reading*). "The lady has come to terms. She will enter His Highness's household." Quite so, sir. What suite will she occupy?

RAJA. My innocent Watkins! Do you think it's true? What have I to do with a stuck-up Englishwoman? It's only a bait for the Feringhis. You shall send it out in their hearing, and if either of them can read the Morse code, the mischief's in it if he doesn't give himself away.

WATKINS. Beg pardon, sir; I didn't quite catch on.

RAJA. If they move an eyelash I'll take care they never see the inside of this room again.

WATKINS. Am I to send this to India, sir?

RAJA. To anywhere or nowhere. Reduce the current, so that no one can pick it up. So long as it's heard in this room, that's all I want.

WATKINS. But when am I to send it, sir?

RAJA. Listen. I'll get them in here on the pretext of a little wireless demonstration, and then I'll tell you to send out an order to Tashkent for champagne. That'll be your cue. Go ahead—and send slowly.

WATKINS. Shall I ask you whether I'm to code it, sir?

RAJA. You may as well. It'll give artistic finish to the thing.

WATKINS. Very good, Your 'Ighness. But afterwards,—if, as you was saying, they was to try to corrupt me, sir——

RAJA. Corrupt you? That would be painting the lily with a vengeance.

WATKINS (*with a touch of annoyance*). Suppose they tries to get at me, sir—what are your instructions?

RAJA. How do you mean?

WATKINS. Shall I let on to take the bait?

RAJA. You may do exactly as you please. I have the most implicit confidence in you, Watkins.

WATKINS. You are very good, sir.

RAJA. I know that anything they can offer you would have to be paid either in England or in India, and that you daren't show your nose in either country. You have a very comfortable job here——

WATKINS. My grateful thanks to you, sir.

RAJA. And you don't want to give the hangman a job, either in Lahore or in London.

WATKINS. The case in a nutshell, sir. But I thought if I was to pretend to send a message for them, it might keep them quiet-like.

RAJA. Very true, Watkins. It would not only keep them quiet, but the illusion of security would raise their spirits, which would be a humane action. I am always on the side of humanity.

WATKINS. Just so, sir. Then I'll humour them.

RAJA. Yes, if they want you to send a message. If they try to "get at," not only you, but the instrument, call the guard and let me know at once.

WATKINS. Certainly, sir.

RAJA. Now open the door and stand by. You have the message?

WATKINS (*producing the slip from his pocket, reads*): "The lady has come to terms. She–"

RAJA (*interrupting*). Yes, that's right. (*As* WATKINS *is opening the door*) Oh, look here–when you've finished, you'd better lock the door, and say, "Any orders, sir?" If I say "No orders, Watkins," it'll mean I'm satisfied they don't understand. If I think they do understand, I'll give you what orders I think necessary.

WATKINS. Very good, sir. (*He opens the folding doors wide, revealing a small room, in which is a wireless installation.*)

RAJA (*at billiard-room door*). Oh, Major, you were saying you had no experience of wireless. If you've finished your game, it might amuse you to see it at work. Watkins is just going to send out a message. Would Mrs. Crespin care to come?

CRESPIN (*at door*). Yes–why not? Will you come, Lucilla?
(CRESPIN *enters, followed by* LUCILLA *and* TRAHERNE. *The* RAJA *eyes them closely so that they have no opportunity to make any sign to each other.*)

RAJA. This, you see, is the apparatus. All ready, Watkins? (*To the others*) Won't you sit down? (*To* WATKINS) You have the order for Tashkent?

WATKINS (*producing paper*). Yes, Your 'Ighness; but I haven't coded it.

RAJA. Oh, never mind; send it in clear. Even if some outsider does pick it up, I daresay we can order three cases of champagne without causing international complications. (CRESPIN *and* TRAHERNE *sit in the arm-chairs, left.* LUCILLA *is about to sit on the couch, but seeing the* RAJA *make a move to sit beside her, she passes behind the writing table and sits in the swivel chair. The* RAJA *sits on the sofa.* WATKINS *begins to transmit–pauses.*)

RAJA. He's waiting for the reply signal.
(*A pause.*)

CRESPIN. May I take one of your excellent cigars, Raja?

RAJA. By all means.
(CRESPIN *lights a cigar.*)

WATKINS. I've got them. (*Proceeds to send the message: "The lady has come to terms," etc.*)

CRESPIN (*a moment after the transmission has begun, says in a low voice to the* RAJA). May we speak?

RAJA. Oh, yes—you won't be heard in Tashkent.

CRESPIN (*holding out his cigarette case*). Have a cigarette, Traherne.

TRAHERNE. Thanks. (*He takes a cigarette.* CRESPIN *strikes a match and lights the cigarette, saying meanwhile:*)

CRESPIN. Let us smoke and drink, for tomorrow we—— (*Blows out the match.*)
(*Silence until the transmission ends.*)

RAJA. That's how it's done!

TRAHERNE. How many words did he send?

RAJA. What was it, Watkins? "Forward by tomorrow's caravan twelve cases champagne. Usual brand. Charge our account"; was that it?

WATKINS. That's right, sir.

RAJA. Twelve words.

CRESPIN. And can they really make sense out of these fireworks?

RAJA. I hope so—else we shall run short of champagne.

WATKINS (*locking the folding door*). Any orders, Your 'Ighness?

RAJA. No orders, Watkins.
(*As he is going out,* WATKINS *meets at the door a* SOLDIER, *who says a few words to him.*)

WATKIS (*turning*). The 'Igh Priest is waiting to see Your 'Ighness.

RAJA. Oh, show him in.
(WATKINS *ushers in the* HIGH PRIEST OF THE GODDESS, *and then exit. The* HIGH PRIEST'S *personality is unmistakably sinister. The* RAJA, *after a word of greeting, turns to the others.*)

RAJA. I mentioned my Archbishop of York. This is he. Allow me to introduce you. Your Grace, Mrs. Crespin—Major Crespin—Dr. Traherne. (*The* PRIEST, *understanding the situation, makes a sort of contemptuous salaam*) The Archbishop's manners are not good. You will excuse him. He regards you, I regret to say, as unclean creatures, whose very presence means pollution. He would be a mine of information for an anthropologist. (*He exchanges a few words with the* PRIEST, *and turns again to his guests*) His Grace reminds me of some arrangements for tomorrow's ceremony, which, as Archbishop of Canterbury, I must attend to in person. You will excuse me for half an hour? Pray make yourselves at home. Tiffin at half past twelve. (*He speaks a few words to the* PRIEST, *who replies in a sort of growl*) His grace says *au revoir*—and so do I. (*Exit, followed by the* PRIEST. *Both* TRAHERNE *and* LUCILLA *are about to speak.* CRESPIN *motions them to be cautious. He goes to the billiard-room, opens the door, looks around and closes it again.* LUCILLA *examines the balcony.* TRAHERNE *slips up to the centre door and noiselessly tests it.*)

TRAHERNE (*to* CRESPIN). What was the message?

CRESPIN. It said that the lady had accepted her life—on his terms.

TRAHERNE. Oh!—a trap for us.

CRESPIN. Yes. A put-up job.

LUCILLA. You gave no sign, Antony. I think he must have been reassured.

TRAHERNE. Evidently; or he wouldn't have left us here.

CRESPIN. What to do now?

TRAHERNE. Can we break open the door?

CRESPIN. No good. It would make a noise. We'd be interrupted, and then it would be all up.

TRAHERNE. Well, then, the next step is to try to bribe Watkins.

CRESPIN. I don't believe it's a bit of good.

TRAHERNE. Nor I. The fellow's a thorough-paced scoundrel. But we might succeed, and if we don't even try they'll suspect that we're plotting something else. If we can convince them that we're at our wits' end, we've the better chance of taking them off their guard.

LUCILLA. Yes—you see that, Antony?

CRESPIN. Perhaps you're right. But, even if the cursed scoundrel can be bought, what good is it if I can't remember the wave-length and the call for Amil-Serai?

LUCILLA. You'll think of it all of a sudden.

CRESPIN. Not if I keep racking my brains for it. If I could get my mind off it, the cursed thing might come back to me.

TRAHERNE. All the more reason for action. But first, we must settle what message to send if we get the chance.

LUCILLA (*sits at writing-table*). Dictate—I'll write.

TRAHERNE. What about this? "Major Crespin, wife, Traherne imprisoned, Rukh, Raja's palace, lives in danger."
(LUCILLA *writes on an envelope which she takes from the paper-case.*)

CRESPIN. We want something more definite.

LUCILLA. How would this do? "Death threatened tomorrow evening. Rescue urgent."

TRAHERNE. Excellent.
(LUCILLA *finishes the message, and hands it to* CRESPIN.)

CRESPIN (*reads*). "Major Crespin, wife, Traherne, imprisoned, Rukh, Raja's palace. Death threatened tomorrow evening. Rescue urgent." (*Takes the paper*) Right. I'll keep it ready.

TRAHERNE. Now, how to get hold of Watkins?

LUCILLA (*at the table*). There's a bell there. Shall I try it?

TRAHERNE. Hold on a moment. We have to decide what to do if he won't take money, and we have to use force in order to get his keys.

CRESPIN (*looking around*). There's nothing here to knock him on the head with—not even a chair you can lift——

TRAHERNE. Not a curtain cord to truss him up with——

LUCILLA. The first thing would be to gag him, wouldn't it? (*Takes off her scarf*) Would this do for that?

TRAHERNE. Capital! (*Takes the scarf, ties a knot in it, and places it on the upper end of the sofa.*)

CRESPIN. What about a billiard cue?

TRAHERNE. If he saw it around he'd smell a rat.

CRESPIN. Then there's only one thing——

TRAHERNE. What?

(CRESPIN *points to the balcony, and makes a significant gesture.*)

LUCILLA. Oh! (*Shrinks away from the window.*)

TRAHERNE. I'm afraid it can't be helped. There's a drop of a good hundred feet.

CRESPIN. None too much for him.

TRAHERNE. When he locked that door he put the key in his trousers pocket. We must remember to get it before——

LUCILLA. But if you kill him and still don't remember the call, we shall be no better off than we are now.

TRAHERNE. We shall be no worse off.

CRESPIN. Better, by Jove! For if I can get three minutes at that instrument, the Raja can't tell whether we have communicated or not. (*He takes up the glass of whiskey-and-soda which he has poured out before.*)

LUCILLA. Oh, Antony!

CRESPIN. Don't be a fool, Lu. (*Gulps down the drink, and says as he pours out more whiskey*) It's because I'm so unnaturally sober that my brain won't work. (*Drinks the whiskey raw*) Now ring that bell. (LUCILLA *does so*) You do the talking, Traherne. The fellow's cursed insolence gets on my nerves.

TRAHERNE. All right. (*Sits at the writing table.*)

CRESPIN. Look out——

(*Enter* WATKINS, *second door, left.*)

WATKINS. You rang, sir? (*Standing by the door.*)

TRAHERNE. Yes, Watkins, we want a few words with you. Do you mind coming over here? We don't want to speak loud.

WATKINS. There's no one understands English, sir.

TRAHERNE. Please oblige me, all the same.

WATKINS (*coming forward*). Now, sir!

TRAHERNE. I daresay you can guess what we want with you.

WATKINS. I'm no 'and at guessin', sir. I'd rather you'd put it plain.

TRAHERNE. Well, you know that we've fallen into the hands of bloodthirsty savages? You know what is proposed for tomorrow?

WATKINS. I've 'eard as your numbers is up.

TRAHERNE. You surely don't intend to stand by and see us murdered —three of your own people, and one of them a lady?

WATKINS. My own people, is it? And a lady—!

LUCILLA. A woman, then, Watkins.

WATKINS. What has my own people ever done for me—or women either —that I should lose a cushy job and risk my neck for the sake of the three of you? I wouldn't do it for all your bloomin' England, I tell you straight.

CRESPIN. It's no good, Traherne. Come down to tin tacks.

TRAHERNE. Only a sighting shot, Major. It was just possible we might have misread our man.

WATKINS. You did if you took 'im for a V.C. 'ero wot 'ud lay down his life for England, 'ome and beauty. The first thing England ever done for me was to 'ave me sent to a reformatory for pinching a silver rattle off of a young haristocrat in a p'rambulator. That, and the likes of that, is wot I've got to thank England for. And why did I do it? Because my mother would have bashed my face in if I'd have come back empty-handed. That's wot 'ome and beauty has meant for me. W'y should I care more for a woman being scragged than what I do for a man?

TRAHERNE. Ah, yes, I quite see your point of view. But the question now is: What'll you take to get us out of this?

WATKINS. Get out of this! If you was to offer me millions, 'ow could I do that?

TRAHERNE. By going into that room and sending this message through to the Amil-Serai aerodrome. (CRESPIN *hands* WATKINS *the message. He reads it through and places it on the table.*)

WATKINS. So that's the game, is it?

TRAHERNE. That, as you say, is the game.

WATKINS. You know what you're riskin'?

TRAHERNE. What do you mean?

WATKINS. W'y, if the Guv'nor suspected as you'd got a word through to India, ten to one he'd wipe you off the slate like that (*snapping his fingers*) without waiting for tomorrow.

CRESPIN. That makes no difference. We've got to face it.

TRAHERNE. Come now! On your own showing, Mr. Watkins, loyalty to your master oughtn't to stand in your way. I don't suppose gratitude is one of your weaknesses.

WATKINS. Gratitude! To 'im? What for? I'm not badly off here, to be sure, but it's nothing to wot I does for 'im; and I 'ate 'im for 'is funny little ways. D'you think I don't see that he's always pulling my leg?

TRAHERNE. Well, then, you won't mind selling him. We've only to settle the price.

WATKINS. That's all very fine, sir; but what price 'ave you gents to offer?

TRAHERNE. Nothing down—no spot cash—that's clear. You'll have to take our word for whatever bargain we come to.

WATKINS. Your word! How do I know——?

TRAHERNE. Oh, our written word. We'll give it to you in writing.

WATKINS (*after thinking for a moment*). If I was to 'elp you out, there must be no more fairy-tales about any of you 'avin' seen me in India.

TRAHERNE. All right. We accept your assurance that you never were there.

WATKINS. And see here, Dr. Traherne—you know very well I couldn't stay here after I'd helped you to escape—leastways, if I stayed, it'd be in my grave. You'll 'ave to take me with you—and for that I can only have your word. Supposing you could get the message through, and the English was to come, no writing could bind you if you chose to leave me in the lurch.

TRAHERNE. Quite true. I'm afraid you'll have to trust us for that. But I give you my word of honour that we would be as careful of your safety as if you were one of ourselves. I suppose you know that, strange as you may think it, there are people in the world that would rather die than break a solemn promise.

CRESPIN. Even to a hound like you, Watkins.

WATKINS. I advise you to keep a civil tongue in yer 'ead, Major. Don't forget that I 'ave you in the 'ollow of my 'and.

TRAHERNE. True, Watkins; and the hollow of your hand is a very disagreeable place to be in. That's why we're willing to pay well to get out of it. Come, now, what shall we say?

WATKINS. Well, what about a little first instalment? You ain't quite on your uppers, are you, now? You could come down with something, be it ever so humble?

TRAHERNE (*examining his pocketbook*). I have 300 rupees and five ten-pound notes. (*Places the money on the table.*)

WATKINS. And you, Major?

CRESPIN. Two hundred and fifty rupees. (*Crosses and lays the notes on the table*) Oh, and some loose change.

WATKINS (*nobly*). Oh, never mind the chicken-feed! And the lady?

LUCILLA. I gave my last rupee to your wife, Watkins.

WATKINS. Well, that's about £120 to go on with.

TRAHERNE (*placing his hand on the heap of notes*). There. That's your first instalment. Now what about the balance? Shall we say £1000 apiece?

WATKINS. A thousand apiece! Three thousand pounds! You're joking, Dr. Traherne! Wot would £3000 be to me in England? W'y, I'd 'ave to take to valetting again. No, no, sir! If I'm to do this job, I must 'ave enough to make a gentleman of me.
(CRESPIN, TRAHERNE *and* LUCILLA *burst out laughing.*)

WATKINS. Well, you are the queerest lot as ever I come across. Your lives is 'anging by a 'air, and yet you can larf!

LUCILLA (*hysterically*). It's your own fault, Watkins. Why will you be so funny? (*Her laughter turns to tears and she buries her face in the end of the couch, shaken with sobs.*)

TRAHERNE. I'm afraid what you ask is beyond our means, Watkins. But I double my bid—two thousand apiece.

WATKINS. You'll 'ave to double it again sir, and a little more. You write me out an I. O. U. for fifteen thousand pounds, and I'll see wot can be done.

CRESPIN. Well, you are the most consummate——

WATKINS. If your lives ain't worth five thousand apiece to you, there's nothing doing. For my place here is worth fifteen thousand to me. And there's all the risk, too—I'm not charging you nothing for that.

TRAHERNE. We appreciate your generosity, Watkins. Fifteen thousand be it!

WATKINS. Now you're talking.
(TRAHERNE *rapidly writes and signs the I. O .U. and hands it to* WATKINS.)

WATKINS. That's right, sir; but the Major must sign it, too.

CRESPIN (*crosses to the table, on which* WATKINS *places the paper, writes, throws down the pen*). There you are, curse you!

TRAHERNE. Now get to work quick, and call up Amil-Serai.

WATKINS. Right you are, sir. (*Picks up the envelope and begins, in a leisurely way, unlocking the centre door.*)

CRESPIN. Isn't there some special call you must send out to get Amil-Serai?

WATKINS. Oh, yes, sir, I know it. (WATKINS *takes his seat at the instrument, with his back to the snuggery, and begins to work it.*)

CRESPIN (*whispers*). That's not a service call.
(*A pause.*)

WATKINS. Right! Got them, sir. Now the message.

CRESPIN (*as* WATKINS *works the key,* CRESPIN *spells out*). "The—

white–goats–are–ready–for–" (*To* TRAHERNE) No, but the black sheep is! Come on! (CRESPIN *tiptoes up toward* WATKINS *followed by* TRAHERNE. *As he passes the upper end of the sofa* CRESPIN *picks up* LUCILLA'S *scarf and hands it to* TRAHERNE, *meantime producing his own handkerchief.* LUCILLA *rises, her hand pressed to her mouth. The men steal up close behind* WATKINS. *Suddenly* TRAHERNE *jams the gag in* WATKINS'S *mouth, and ties the ends of the scarf.* WATKINS *attempts a cry, but it trails off into a gurgle.* CRESPIN *meantime grips* WATKINS'S *arms behind, and ties the wrists with his handkerchief.* TRAHERNE *makes fast the gag, and the two lift him, struggling, and carry him towards the window.* WATKINS'S *head falls back and his terror-stricken eyes can be seen over the swathing gag. They rest him for a moment on the balustrade.*)

TRAHERNE. Must we——?

CRESPIN. Nothing else for it–one, two, three! (*They heave him over.* LUCILLA, *who has been watching, petrified, gives a gasping cry.*)

CRESPIN. At least we haven't taken it lying down! (*He pours out some whiskey and is about to drink when he pauses, puts down the glass, and then cries in great excitement*) Hold on! Don't speak! (*A pause*) I have it! (*Another pause*) Yes, by Jupiter, I have it! I've remembered the call! Can you lock that door?

LUCILLA (*at second door left*). No key this side!

TRAHERNE (*whispering, and running to the door*). Don't open it. There are soldiers in the passage. I'll hold it. (*He stations himself before the door.* CRESPIN *rushes to the instrument and rapidly examines it.*)

CRESPIN. The scoundrel had reduced the current. (*Makes an adjustment with feverish haste*) Now the wave length! (*More adjustment. He begins to transmit. A pause.*)

TRAHERNE. Do you get any answer?

CRESPIN. No, no; I don't expect any –I'm sure they haven't the power. But it's an even chance that I get them all the same. (*He goes on transmitting hurriedly while* TRAHERNE *and* LUCILLA *stand breathless,* TRAHERNE *with his shoulder to the door.*)

TRAHERNE. Some one's coming up the passage! Go on! Go on! I'll hold the door.
(*Another slight pause, while* CRESPIN *transmits feverishly. Suddenly* TRAHERNE *braces himself against the door, gripping the handle. After a moment, there is a word of command outside, the sound of shoulders heaved against the door, and it is gradually pushed open by three guards.* TRAHERNE *is shoved back by its motion.*)
(*The* RAJA *enters, rushes forward and grasps the situation.*)

RAJA. Ah! When the cat's away——
(*He whips out a revolver and fires.*)

CRESPIN. Got me, by Heaven! (*He falls forward over the instrument, but immediately recovers himself, and rapidly unmakes the adjustments.* LUCILLA *and* TRAHERNE *catch him as he staggers back from the instrument, and lay him on the couch.*)

TRAHERNE (*kneeling and supporting him*). Brandy!

(LUCILLA *gets the glass. They put it to his lips. The* RAJA *meanwhile goes to the wireless table, sees the draft message and reads it.*)

RAJA (*holding out the paper*). How much of this did you get through?

CRESPIN (*raising himself a little*). Curse you—none! (*Falls back dead.*)

LUCILLA (*crying out*). Antony!

RAJA. All over, eh?

(TRAHERNE, *still kneeling, makes an affirmative sign. At this moment a noise is heard outside, and three soldiers burst open the door and rush in. One of them speaks to the* RAJA, *pointing to the window, the other two rush up to* TRAHERNE, *seize him and drag him over to the left.* LUCILLA *remains kneeling by* CRESPIN'S *body. The* RAJA *goes calmly over to the window and looks out.*)

RAJA (*returning to the centre*). Tut tut—most inconvenient. And foolish on your part—for now, if my brothers should be reprieved, we cannot hear of it. (*Looks at the message reflectively*) Otherwise, the situation remains unchanged. We adhere to our program for tomorrow. The Major has only a few hours' start of you.

CURTAIN

ACT FOUR

A gloomy hall, its roof supported by four wooden columns, two in a row, rudely carved with distorted animal and human figures. The walls are also of rudely carved wood, and are pierced all round, at the height of about twelve feet, by a sort of clerestory—a series of oblong slits or unglazed windows through which the sky can be seen. The general tone of the wood is dark brown, but the interstices between the carvings have here and there been filled in with dull red. There is a high curtained doorway, left, leading to a sort of robing-room. Opposite to it, right, a two-leaved wooden door, closed with a heavy wooden bolt. An oblong hole in the door, with a sliding shutter, enables the guard within to inspect whoever approaches from without. At the back, centre, is a wide opening, curtained at the beginning of the Act. When the curtains are withdrawn, they reveal a sort of balcony or tribune, raised by two steps above the level of the hall, over the balustrade of which can be seen the head and shoulders of a colossal image of the Goddess, apparently at a distance of some fifty yards. Between the two foremost columns, on a dais of two steps, a wide throne, which has for its backing a figure of the Goddess carved in high relief, amid a good deal of barbaric tracery.

The figure is green, but there are touches of gold in her crown, her ornaments, and in the tracery. A low brazier rests on the ground in front of the throne.

The hall is a sort of anteroom to the public place of sacrifice without. Late afternoon light comes in through the clerestory on the left.

When the curtain rises, a group of Priests is gathered round the doorway, left, while the CHIEF PRIEST *stands at the center, holding the curtains a little way apart and looking out. A Priest is on guard at the door, right.*

For a moment after the rise of the curtain, there is a regular and subdued murmur from the crowd without. Then it swells into a chorus of execrations. The CHIEF PRIEST *gives an order to the other Priests, left, one of whom goes off through the doorway. The guard at the door, right, slips back the shutter and looks out, then unbolts the door, and admits* TRAHERNE, *strapped to a mountain chair, and guarded by two soldiers, who withdraw. At the same time, the* RAJA, *in splendid Eastern attire, enters, left.*

RAJA. Well, Doctor, it doesn't appear that any "god from the machine" is going to interfere with our program.

TRAHERNE. You are bringing a terrible vengeance upon yourself.

RAJA. Think, my dear Doctor. If, as the Major said, he did not get your S. O. S. through, I have nothing to fear. If he lied, and did get it through, nothing can ultimately save me, and I may as well be hung for a sheep as for a lamb.

TRAHERNE (*writhing in his bonds*). You might have spared me this.

RAJA. A ritual detail, Doctor; not quite without reason. Persons lacking in self-control might throw themselves to the ground or otherwise disarrange the ceremony. (*He speaks a word, and the bearers promptly release* TRAHERNE, *and carry the chair out, right.*)

TRAHERNE. What have you done with Mrs. Crespin?

RAJA. Don't be alarmed. She'll be here in due time.

TRAHERNE. Listen to me, Raja. Do what you will with me, but let Mrs. Crespin go. Send her to India or to Russia, and I am sure, for her children's sake, she will swear to keep absolute silence as to her husband's fate and mine.

RAJA. You don't believe, then, that I couldn't save you if I would?

TRAHERNE. Believe it? No!

RAJA. You are quite right, my dear Doctor. I am not a High Priest for nothing. I might work the oracle. I might get a command from the Goddess to hurt no hair upon your heads.

TRAHERNE. Then what devilish pleasure do you find in putting us to death?

RAJA. Pleasure? The pleasure of a double vengeance. Vengeance for today—my brothers—and vengeance

for centuries of subjection and insult. Do you know what brought you here? It was not blind chance, any more than it was the Goddess. It was my will, my craving for revenge, that drew you here by a subtle, irresistible magnetism. My will is my religion—my god. And by that god I have sworn that you shall not escape me. (*Yells from the crowd outside*) Ah, they are bringing Mrs. Crespin.
(*The* PRIEST *unbolts the door, right, and* LUCILLA *is carried in.*)

RAJA. I apologise, Madam, for the manners of my people. Their fanaticism is beyond my control. (*He says a word to the bearers, who release* LUCILLA. TRAHERNE *gives her his hand, and she steps from the chair, which the bearers remove, right.*)

TRAHERNE. How long have we left?

RAJA. Till the sun's rim touches the crest of the mountain. A blast of our great mountain horn will announce the appointed hour, and you will be led out to the sacred enclosure. You saw the colossal image of the Goddess out yonder? (*He points to the back. They look at each other in silence.*)

TRAHERNE. Will you grant us one last request?

RAJA. By all means, if it is in my power. In spite of your inconsiderate action of yesterday——

TRAHERNE. Inconsiderate——?

RAJA. Watkins, you know—poor Watkins—a great loss to me! But *à la guerre comme à la guerre!* I bear no malice for a fair act of war. I am anxious to show you every consideration.

TRAHERNE. Then you will leave us alone for the time that remains to us.

RAJA. Why, by all means. And oh, by the way, you need have no fear of the ceremony—being protracted. It will be brief and—I—trust—painless. The High Church Party are not incapable of cruelty; but I have resolutely set my face against it. (LUCILLA *has meanwhile stood stonily gazing in front of her. The* RAJA *reflects for a moment, and then goes up to her*) Before I go, Madam, may I remind you of my offer of yesterday? It is not yet too late. (LUCILLA *takes no notice*) Is it just to your children to refuse? (*She looks at him stonily, saying nothing. After a pause*) Immovable? So be it! (*He turns to go. At this moment a great yell of triumphant hatred goes up from the populace.*)

RAJA. Your husband's body, Madam. They are laying it at the feet of the Goddess.

LUCILLA. You promised me——

RAJA. That it should be burnt. I will keep my promise. But you see I had three brothers—a head for a head. (*He goes into the inner chamber, encircled by his Priests. Only the* GUARD *at the door, right, remains, half hidden by the door jamb.* LUCILLA *and* TRAHERNE *are left alone.* LUCILLA *sinks down upon the broad base of the foremost pillar, left.*)

LUCILLA. So this is the end!

TRAHERNE. What offer did that devil make you?

LUCILLA. Oh, I didn't mean to tell you, but I may as well. He is an ingenious tormentor. He offered yesterday to let me live, and to kidnap the children and bring them here to me—you know on what terms.

TRAHERNE. To bring the children here?

LUCILLA. He said in a month I might have them in my arms. Think of it! Ronny and Iris in my arms!
(*A pause.* TRAHERNE *stands with his back to her.*)

TRAHERNE (*in a low and unsteady voice*). Are you sure you did right to refuse?

LUCILLA. Do you mean——?

TRAHERNE (*louder and almost harshly*). Are you sure it is not wrong to refuse?

LUCILLA. Oh, how can you—? Right? Wrong? What are right and wrong to me now? If I could see my children again, would any scruple of "right" or "wrong" make me shrink from anything that was possible? But this is so utterly, utterly impossible.

TRAHERNE. Forgive me. You know it would add an unspeakable horror to death if I had to leave you here. But I felt I must ask you whether you had fully considered——

LUCILLA. I have thought of nothing else through all these torturing hours.

TRAHERNE. How brave you are!

LUCILLA. Not brave, not brave. If I could live, I would—there, I confess it! But I should die of shame and misery, and leave my children—to that man. Or, if I did live, what sort of a mother should I be to them? They would be much better without me! Oh my precious, precious darlings! (*She clasps her arms across her breast, and rocks herself in agony. A short silence.*)

TRAHERNE (*lays his hand on her shoulder*). Lucilla!

LUCILLA (*looking up*). Oh, Basil, say you think it won't be altogether bad for them! They will never know anything of their father now, but what was good. And their mother will simply have vanished into the skies. They will think she has flown away to heaven—and who knows but it may be true? There may be something beyond this hell.

TRAHERNE. We shall know soon, Lucilla.

LUCILLA. But to go away and leave them without a word—! Poor little things, poor little things.

TRAHERNE. They will remember you as something very dear and beautiful. The very mystery will be like a halo about you.

LUCILLA. Shall I see them again, Basil? Tell me that.
(*A pause.*)

TRAHERNE. Who knows? Even to comfort you, I won't say I am certain. But I do sincerely think you may.

LUCILLA (*smiling woefully*). You think there is a sporting chance?

TRAHERNE. More than that. This life is such a miracle—could any other be more incredible?

LUCILLA. But even if I should meet them in another world, they would not be my Ronny and Iris, but a strange man and a strange woman, built up of experiences in which I had had no share. Oh, it was cunning, cunning, what that devil said to me! He said "God Himself cannot give you back their childhood."

TRAHERNE. How do you know that God is going to take their childhood from you? You may be with them this very night—with them, unseen, but perhaps not unfelt, all the days of their life.

LUCILLA. You are saying that to make what poor Antony called a "haze" for me—to soften the horror of darkness that is waiting for us? Don't give me "dope," Basil—I can face things without it.

TRAHERNE. I mean every word of it. (*A pause*) Why do you smile?

LUCILLA. At a thought that came to me—the thought of poor Antony as a filmy, purified spirit. It seems so unthinkable.

TRAHERNE. Why unthinkable? Why may he not still exist, though he has left behind him the nerves, the cravings, that tormented him—and you. You have often told me that there was something fine in the depths of his nature; and you know how he showed it yesterday.

LUCILLA. Oh, if I could only tell the children how he died!

TRAHERNE. But his true self was chained to a machine that was hopelessly out of gear. The chain is broken: the machine lies out there—scrapped. Do you think that he was just that machine, and nothing else?

LUCILLA. I don't know. I only feel that Antony spiritualised would not be Antony. And you, Basil—if Antony leaves his—failings, you must leave behind your work. Do you want another life in which there is no work to be done—no disease to be rooted out? (*With a mournful smile*) Don't tell me you don't long to take your microscope with you wherever you may be going.

TRAHERNE. Perhaps there are microscopes awaiting me there.

LUCILLA. Spirit microscopes for spirit microbes? You don't believe that, Basil.

TRAHERNE. I neither believe nor disbelieve. In all we can say of another life we are like children blind from birth, trying to picture the form and colours of the rainbow.

LUCILLA. But if the forms and colours we know are of no use to us, what comforts are we to find in formless, colourless possibilities? If we are freed from all human selfishness, shall I love my children more than any other woman's? Can I love a child I cannot kiss, that cannot look into my eyes and kiss me back again?

TRAHERNE (*starting up*). Oh, Lucilla, don't!

LUCILLA. What do you mean?

TRAHERNE. Don't remind me of all we are losing! I meant to leave it all unspoken—the thought of him lying out there seemed to tie my tongue. But we have only one moment on this side of eternity. Lucilla, shall I go on? (*After a perceptible pause,* LUCILLA *bows her head*) Do you think it is with a light heart that I turn my back upon the life of earth and all it might have meant for you and me —for you and me, Lucilla!

LUCILLA. Yes, Basil, for you and me.

TRAHERNE. Rather than live without you, I am glad to die with you; but oh, what a wretched gladness compared with that of living with you and loving you! I wonder if you guess what it has meant to me, ever since we met at Dehra Dun, to see you as another man's wife, bound to him by ties I couldn't ask you to break. It has been hell, hell! (*Looking up with a mournful smile*) My love has not been quite selfish, Lucilla, since I can say I really do love your children, though I know they have stood between me and heaven.

LUCILLA. Yes, Basil, I know. I have known from the beginning.

TRAHERNE. Oh, Lucilla, have we not been fools, fools? We have sacrificed to an idol as senseless as that—(*with a gesture towards the image*) all the glory and beauty of life! What do I care for a bloodless, shadowy life—life in the abstract, with all the senses extinct? Is there not something in the depths of our heart that cries out "We don't want it! Better eternal sleep!"?

LUCILLA. Oh, Basil—you are going back on your own wisdom.

TRAHERNE. Wisdom! What has wisdom to say to love, thwarted and unfulfilled? You were right when you said that it is a mockery to speak of love without hands to clasp, without lips to kiss. We may be going to some pale parody of life; but in our cowardice we have killed love for ever and ever.

LUCILLA. No, Basil, don't call it cowardice. I, too, regret—perhaps as much as you—that things were —as they were. But not even your love could have made up to me for my children. (*A trumpet-blast is heard—a prolonged deep, wailing sound*) There is the signal! Good-bye, dear love. (*She holds out her hands to him. They kiss and stand embraced, until, at a sound of tom-toms and a low muttered chant from behind the curtains, left, they part, and stand hand in hand, facing the doorway. Suddenly, at a great shattering note from a gong, the curtains of the doorway part, and a procession of chanting* PRIESTS *enters, all wearing fantastic robes and headdresses, and all, except the* CHIEF PRIEST, *masked. The* RAJA *follows them, also wearing a priestly headdress, and gorgeously robed. Behind him come three dark-robed and masked figures, carrying heavy swords. Musicians bring up the rear. The* PRIESTS *group themselves round the throne.*)

RAJA (*to* TRAHERNE *and* LUCILLA, *who are standing in front of the throne*). May I trouble you to move a little aside? I am, for the moment, not a king, but a priest, and must observe a certain dignity. Ridiculous, isn't it?

(*They move over to the right of the throne. He advances in stately fashion and seats himself on it.*)

RAJA (*to* LUCILLA). Must I do violence to my feelings, Madam, by including you in the approaching ceremony? There is still time. (LUCILLA *is silent*) We autocrats are badly brought up. We are not accustomed to having our desires, or even our whims, thwarted.

TRAHERNE (*interrupting*). Will you never cease tormenting this lady?

RAJA (*totally disregarding him*). Remember my power. If I may not take you back to my palace as my Queen, I can send you back as my slave. (*A pause*) Have you nothing to say?

LUCILLA. Nothing.

RAJA. I repeat my offer as to your children.

LUCILLA. I would die a hundred times rather than see them in your hands.

RAJA. Remember, too, that, if I so will it, you cannot save them by dying. I can have them kidnaped —or—I can have them killed.

(LUCILLA *shrieks.* TRAHERNE, *with a cry of "Devil!" makes a leap at the* RAJA'S *throat, pinning him against the back of the throne. The* PRIESTS *instantly pull* TRAHERNE *off, pinion him, and drag him over to the left. They talk furiously to each other, and the* CHIEF PRIEST *prostrates himself before the* RAJA, *apparently in urgent supplication. The* RAJA, *who is now to the left of the throne,* LUCILLA *remaining on the right, quits them with some difficulty, and then turns to* TRAHERNE.)

RAJA. Chivalrous but ill-advised, Dr. Traherne. I regret it, and so will you. My colleagues here insist that, as you have laid impious hands on the chief of their sacred caste, your death alone will not appease the fury of the Goddess. They insist on subjecting you to a process of expiation—a ritual of great antiquity—but——

TRAHERNE. You mean torture?

RAJA. Well—yes. (LUCILLA *rushes forward with a cry*) Not you, Madam—not you——

LUCILLA. I must speak to you—speak to you alone! Send Dr. Traherne away.

TRAHERNE. Lucilla! What are you thinking of! Lucilla——!

(*The* RAJA *motions to the* PRIESTS, *who do something to* TRAHERNE *which causes him to crumple up, and his voice dies away.*)

LUCILLA. I beg you—I beg you! One minute—no more!

(*The* RAJA *looks at her for a moment, then shrugs his shoulders and gives an order.* TRAHERNE *is dragged through the doorway, left.* LUCILLA, *in her desperation, has rushed up the steps of the throne. She now sinks, exhausted, upon the end of the throne itself.*)

LUCILLA. Let him go, send him back to India unharmed, and—it shall be as you wish.

RAJA. Soho! You will do for your lover—to save him a little additional pain—what you would not do to have your children restored to you! Suppose I agree—would he accept this sacrifice?

LUCILLA. No, no, he wouldn't—but he must have no choice. That is part of the bargain. Send him—bound hand and foot, if need be—down to Kashmir, and put him over the frontier——

RAJA. You don't care what he thinks of you?

LUCILLA. He will know what to think?

RAJA. And I, too, Madam, know what to think. (*Kneeling with one knee on the throne, he seizes her by the shoulders and turns her face towards him*) Come, look me in the eyes and tell me that you honestly intend to fulfil your bargain! (*Her head droops*) I knew it! You are playing with me! But the confiding barbarian is not so simple as you imagine. No woman has ever tried to fool me that has not repented it. You think, when you have to pay up, you will fob me off with your dead body. Let me tell you, I have no use for you dead —I want you with all the blood in your veins, with all the pride in that cursed sly brain of yours. I want to make my plaything of your beauty, my mockery of your pride. I want to strip off the delicate English lady, and come down to the elemental woman, the handmaid and the instrument of man. (*Changing his tone*) Come now, I'll make you a plain offer. I will put Dr. Traherne over the frontier, and, as they set him free, my people shall hand him a letter written by you at my dictation. You will tell him that you have determined to accept my protection and make this your home. Consequently, you wish to have your children conveyed to you here——

LUCILLA. Never—never—never! I will make no bargain that involves my children.

RAJA. You see! You will give me no hostages for the fulfilment of your bond. But a pledge of your good faith I must have. For without a pledge, Madam, I don't believe in it one little bit.

LUCILLA. What pledge?

RAJA. Only one is left—Dr. Traherne himself. I may—though it will strain my power to the uttermost—save his life, while keeping him in prison. Then, when you have fulfilled your bond I will let him go free. But the moment you attempt to evade your pledge, by death or by escape, I will hand him over to the priests to work their will with; and I will put no restraint upon their savage instincts. (*Pause*) Choose, my dear lady, choose!

(*The subdued murmur of the crowd below, which has been faintly audible during the foregoing scene, ceases, and in the silence is heard a faint, but rapidly increasing, whirr and throb.* LUCILLA, *who has been crouching on the steps of the throne, looks up slowly, hope dawning in her face. For a few seconds she says nothing, waiting to assure herself that she can believe her ears. Then she says in a low voice, with a sort of sob of relief:*)

LUCILLA. Aeroplanes! (*She springs up with a shriek*) The aeroplanes!

Basil! Basil! The aeroplanes! (*She rushes out through the doorway, left, thrusting aside the incoming* PRIESTS, *who are too amazed to oppose her. The* RAJA *does not at first alter his attitude but looks up and listens intently. The curtains shutting off the balcony at the back are violently torn apart by the guard outside, who shout to the* RAJA *and point upward. Sounds of consternation and terror proceed from the unseen crowd. The* RAJA *goes to the back and looks out. At the same moment* LUCILLA *and* TRAHERNE *rush in from the doorway, left.*)

LUCILLA. See! See! They are circling lower and lower! Is it true, Basil? Are we saved?

TRAHERNE. Yes, Lucilla, we are saved.

LUCILLA. Oh, thank God! I shall see my babies again! (*She sways, almost fainting.* TRAHERNE *supports her.*)

RAJA. So the Major lied like a gentleman! Good old Major! I didn't think he had it in him. (*The* GUARDS *call his attention; he looks out from the balcony, and gives an order, then turns down again*) One of the machines has landed. An officer is coming this way—he looks a mere boy.

TRAHERNE. The conquerors of the air have all been mere boys.

RAJA. I have given orders that he shall be brought here unharmed. Perhaps I had better receive him with some ceremony. (*He goes back to the throne and seats himself, cross-legged. At his command the* PRIESTS *range themselves about him.*)

RAJA. You said just now, Dr. Traherne, that you were saved. Are you so certain of that?

TRAHERNE. Certain?

RAJA. How many men does each of these humming-birds carry?

TRAHERNE. Two or three, but——

RAJA. I counted six planes—say at the outside, twenty men. Even my toy army can cope with that number.
(*There is a growing clamour outside. The* RAJA *gives an order to the* PRIEST *at the door, right. He throws it wide open.* FLIGHT-LIEUTENANT CARDEW *saunters in, escorted by three soldiers.*)

RAJA. Who are you, sir?

CARDEW. One moment! (*Crosses to* LUCILLA, *who holds out both her hands. He takes them cordially but coolly*) Mrs. Crespin! I'm very glad we're in time. (*Turns to* TRAHERNE) Dr. Traherne, I presume? (*Shakes hands with him*) And Major Crespin?

TRAHERNE. Shot while transmitting our message.

CARDEW. I'm so sorry, Mrs. Crespin. (*To* TRAHERNE) By whom? (TRAHERNE *indicates the* RAJA, *who has meanwhile watched the scene impassively.*)

RAJA. I am sorry to interrupt these effusions, but——

CARDEW. Who are you, sir?

RAJA. I am the Raja of Rukh. And you?

CARDEW. Flight-Lieutenant Cardew. I have the honor to represent his Majesty, the King-Emperor.

RAJA. The King-Emperor? Who is that, pray? We live so out of the world here, I don't seem to have heard of him.

CARDEW. You will in a minute, Raja, if you don't instantly hand over his subjects.

RAJA. His subjects? Ah, I see you mean the King of England. What terms does his Majesty propose?

CARDEW. We make no terms with cut-throats. (*Looks at his wrist watch*) If I do not signal your submission within three minutes of our landing——
(*A bomb is heard to fall at some distance. Great consternation among the* PRIESTS, *etc.*)

RAJA (*unperturbed*). Ah! bombs!

CARDEW. Precisely.

RAJA. I fancied your Government affected some scruples as to the slaughter of innocent civilians.

CARDEW. There has been no slaughter—as yet. That bomb fell in the ravine, where it could do no harm. So will the next one— (*Bomb—nearer. Increasing hubbub without*) But the third—well, if you're wise you'll throw up the sponge, and there won't be a third.

RAJA. Throw up the sponge, Lieutenant—? I didn't quite catch your name?

CARDEW. Cardew.

RAJA. Ah, yes, Lieutenant Cardew. Why on earth should I throw up the sponge? Your comrades up yonder can no doubt massacre quite a number of my subjects—a brave exploit!—but when they've spent their thunderbolts, they'll just have to fly away again—if they can. A bomb may drop on this temple, you say? In that case, you and your friends will escort me—in fragments—to my last abode. Does that prospect allure you? I call your bluff, Lieutenant Cardew. (*A third bomb—very loud. The* PRIESTS *rush up to the* RAJA, *and fall before him in panic-stricken supplication, with voluble remonstrances, pointing to the Idol in the background. The* RAJA *hesitates for a moment, then proceeds.*)

RAJA. My priests, however, have a superstitious dread of these eggs of the Great Roc. They fear injury to the Sacred Image. For myself, I am always averse from bloodshed. You may, if you please, signal to your squadron commander my acceptance of your terms.

CARDEW. I thought you would come to reason. (*Shaking out his flag in preparation for signaling, he hurries across to where the white beam of a searchlight is visible outside the doorway, right. He disappears for a moment.*)

RAJA. This comes of falling behind the times. If I had had anti-aircraft guns——

TRAHERNE. Thank your stars you hadn't!

CARDEW (*returning*). All clear for the moment, Raja. You have no further immediate consequences to fear.

RAJA. What am I to conclude from your emphasis on immediate?

CARDEW (*after whispering to* TRAHERNE). I need scarcely remind you, sir, that you can only hand over the body of one of your prisoners.

RAJA. Major Crespin murdered a faithful servant of mine. His death at my hands was a fair act of war.

CARDEW. His Majesty's Government will scarcely view it in that light.

RAJA. His Majesty's Government has today, I believe, taken the lives of three kinsmen of mine. Your side has the best of the transaction by four lives to one.

CARDEW (*shrugging his shoulders*). Will you assign us an escort through the crowd?

RAJA. Certainly. (*Gives an order to the officer of regulars, who hurries out, right*) The escort will be here in a moment. (*To* LUCILLA *and* TRAHERNE) It only remains for me to speed the parting guest. I hope we may one day renew our acquaintance—oh, not here! I plainly foresee that I shall have to join the other Kings in Exile. Perhaps we may meet at Homburg or Monte Carlo, and talk over old times. Ah, here is the escort.

(*The escort has formed at the door, right.* TRAHERNE, LUCILLA *and* CARDEW *cross to it, the* RAJA *following them up.*)

Good-bye, dear lady. I lament the Major's end. Perhaps I was hasty; but, you know, "'Tis better to have loved and lost," etc. And oh—Mrs. Crespin! (*As she is going out,* LUCILLA *looks back at him with horror*) My love to the children! (*The Priests and others are all clustered on the balcony, looking at the aeroplanes. The* RAJA *turns back from the door, lights a cigarette at the brazier, takes a puff, and says:*) Well, well—she'd probably have been a deuce of a nuisance.

CURTAIN

Mr. Pim Passes By

BY A. A. MILNE

Mr. Pim Passes By was first produced in America at the Garrick Theatre, New York City, by The Theatre Guild, Inc. on February 28, 1921, and closed on October 1, 1921. The following is the original cast:

George Marden	Dudley Digges
Olivia	Laura Hope Crews
Dinah	Phyllis Porah
Lady Marden	Helen Westley
Brian Strange	Leonard Moody
Carraway Pim	Erskine Sanford
Anne	Peggy Harvey

Directed by Philip Moeller
Designed by Lee Simonson

MR. PIM PASSES BY

ACT ONE

The morning-room at Marden House (Buckinghamshire) decided more than a hundred years ago that it was all right, and has not bothered about itself since. Visitors to the house have called the result such different adjectives as "mellow," "old-fashioned," "charming"—even "baronial" and "antique"; but nobody ever said it was "exciting." Sometimes OLIVIA *wants it to be more exciting, and last week she let herself go over some new curtains. At present they are folded up and waiting for her; she still has the rings to put on. It is obvious that the curtains alone will overdo the excitement; they will have to be harmonised with a new carpet and cushions.* OLIVIA *has her eye on just the things, but one has to go carefully with* GEORGE. *What was good enough for his great-great-grandfather is good enough for him. However, we can trust* OLIVIA *to see him through it, although it may take time.*

There are two ways of coming into the room; by the open windows leading from the terrace or by the door. On this pleasant July morning MR. PIM *chooses the latter way—or rather* ANNE *chooses it for him; and old* MR. PIM, *wistful, kindly, gentle, little* MR. PIM, *living in some world of his own whither we cannot follow, ambles after her.*

ANNE. I'll tell Mr. Marden you're here, sir. Mr. Pim, isn't it?

PIM (*coming back to this world*). Yes—er—Mr. Carraway Pim. He doesn't know me, you understand, but if he could just see me for a moment—er—— (*He fumbles in his pockets*) I gave you that letter?

ANNE. Yes, sir, I'll give it to him.

PIM (*bringing out a letter which is not the one he was looking for, but which reminds him of something else he has forgotten*). Dear me!

ANNE. Yes, sir?

PIM. I ought to have sent a telegram, but I can do it on my way back. You have a telegraph office in the village?

ANNE. Oh, yes, sir. If you turn to the left when you get outside the gates, it isn't more than a hundred yards down the hill.

PIM. Thank you, thank you. Very stupid of me to have forgotten.

(ANNE *goes out.* MR. PIM *wanders about the room humming to himself, and looking vaguely at the pictures. He has his back to the door as* DINAH *comes in. She is nineteen, very pretty, very happy, and full of boyish high spirits and conversation.*)

DINAH. Hullo!

PIM (turning round). Ah, good morning, Mrs. Marden. You must forgive my—er——

DINAH. Oh, I say, I'm not Mrs. Marden. I'm Dinah.

PIM (*with a bow*). Then I will say, Good morning, Miss Diana.

DINAH (*reproachfully*). Now, look here, if you and I are going to be friends you mustn't do that. Dinah, *not* Diana. Do remember it, there's a good man, because I get so tired of correcting people. Have you come to stay with us?

PIM. Well no, Miss—er—Dinah.

DINAH (*nodding*). That's right. I can see I shan't have to speak to *you* again. Now tell me *your* name, and I bet you I get it right first time. And do sit down.

PIM (*sitting down*). Thank you. My name is—er—Pim, Carraway Pim——

DINAH. Pim, that's easy.

PIM. And I have a letter of introduction to your father——

DINAH. Oh no; now you're going wrong again, Mr. Pim. George isn't my father; he's my uncle. *Uncle* George—he doesn't like me calling him George. Olivia doesn't mind—I mean she doesn't mind being called Olivia, but George is rather touchy. You see, he's been my guardian since I was about two, and then about five years ago he married a widow called Mrs. Telworthy—that's Olivia—so she became my Aunt Olivia, only she lets me drop the Aunt. Got that?

PIM (*a little alarmed*). I—I think so, Miss Marden.

DINAH (*admiringly*). I say, you *are* quick, Mr. Pim. Well, if you take my advice, when you've finished your business with George, you will hang about a bit and see if you can't see Olivia. She's simply devastating. I don't wonder George fell in love with her.

PIM. It's only the merest matter of business—just a few minutes with your uncle—I'm afraid I shall hardly——

DINAH. Well, you must please yourself, Mr. Pim. I'm just giving you a friendly word of advice. Naturally, I was awfully glad to get such a magnificent aunt, because, of course, marriage *is* rather a toss-up, isn't it, and George might have gone off with anybody. It's different on the stage, where guardians always marry their wards, but George couldn't marry *me* because I'm his niece. Mind you, I don't say that I should have had him, because between ourselves he's a little bit old-fashioned.

PIM. So he married—er—Mrs. Marden instead.

DINAH. Mrs. Telworthy—don't say you've forgotten already, just when you were getting so good at names. Mrs. Telworthy. You see, Olivia married the Telworthy man and went to Australia with him, and he drank himself to death in the bush, or wherever you drink yourself to death out there, and Olivia came home to England, and met my uncle, and he fell in love with her and proposed to her, and he came into my room that night—I was about fourteen—and turned on the light and said, "Dinah, how would you like to have a beautiful aunt of your very own?" And I said: "Congratulations, George." That was the first time I called him George. Of course, I'd seen it coming for *weeks*. Telworthy, isn't it a funny name?

PIM. Very singular. From Australia, you say?

DINAH. Yes, I always say that he's probably still alive, and will turn up here one morning and annoy George, because that's what first husbands always do in books, but I'm afraid there's not much chance.

PIM (*shocked*). Miss Marden!

DINAH. Well, of course, I don't really *want* it to happen, but it *would* be rather exciting, wouldn't it? However, things like that never seem to occur down here, somehow. There was a hay-rick burnt last year about a mile away, but that isn't quite the same thing, is it?

PIM. No, I should say that that was certainly different.

DINAH. Of course, something very, very wonderful did happen last night, but I'm not sure if I know you well enough—— (*She looks at him hesitatingly.*)

PIM (*uncomfortably*). Really, Miss Marden, I am only a—a passer-by, here today and gone tomorrow. You really mustn't——

DINAH. And yet there's something about you, Mr. Pim, which inspires confidence. The fact is—(*in a stage whisper*)—I got engaged last night!

PIM. Dear me, let me congratulate you.

DINAH. I expect that's why George is keeping you such a long time. Brian, my young man, the well-known painter—only nobody has ever heard of him—he's smoking a pipe with George in the library and asking for his niece's hand. Isn't it exciting? You're really rather lucky, Mr. Pim—I mean being told so soon. Even Olivia doesn't know yet.

PIM (*getting up*). Yes, yes. I congratulate you, Miss Marden. Perhaps it would be better——
(ANNE *comes in.*)

ANNE. Mr. Marden is out at the moment sir—— Oh, I didn't see you, Miss Dinah.

DINAH. It's all right, Anne. *I'm* looking after Mr. Pim.

ANNE. Yes, Miss. (*She goes out.*)

DINAH (*excitedly*). That's me. They can't discuss me in the library without breaking down, so they're walking up and down outside, and slashing at the thistles in order to conceal their emotion. *You* know. I expect Brian——

PIM (*looking at his watch*). Yes, I think, Miss Marden, I had better go now and return a little later. I have a telegram which I want to send, and perhaps by the time I came back——

DINAH. Oh, but how disappointing of you, when we were getting on together so nicely. And it was just going to be your turn to tell me all about *yourself*.

PIM. I have really nothing to tell, Miss Marden. I have a letter of introduction to Mr. Marden, who in turn will give me, I hope, a letter to a certain distinguished man whom it is necessary for me to meet. That is all. (*Holding out his hand*) And now, Miss Marden——

DINAH. Oh, I'll start you on your way to the post office. I want to know if you're married, and all that sort of thing. You've got heaps to tell me, Mr. Pim. Have you got your hat? That's right. Then we'll —hullo, here's Brian.

(BRIAN STRANGE *comes in at the windows. He is what* GEORGE *calls a damned futuristic painter-chap, aged twenty-four. To look at, he is a very pleasant boy, rather untidily dressed.*)

BRIAN (*nodding*). How do you do?

DINAH (*seizing him*). Brian, this is Mr. Pim. Mr. Carraway Pim. He's been telling me all about himself. It's so interesting. He's just going to send a telegram, and then he's coming back again. Mr. Pim, this is Brian—*you* know.

BRIAN (*smiling and shaking hands*). How do you do?

DINAH (*pleadingly*). You *won't* mind going to the post office by yourself, will you, because, you see, Brian and I—(*she looks lovingly at* BRIAN).

PIM (*because they are so young*). Miss Dinah and Mr.—er—Brian, I have only come into your lives for a moment, and it is probable that I shall now pass out of them for ever, but you will allow an old man——

DINAH. Oh, not old!

PIM (*chuckling happily*). Well, a middle-aged man—to wish you both every happiness in the years that you have before you. Good-bye, good-bye.

(*He disappears gently through the windows.*)

DINAH. Brian, he'll get lost if he goes that way.

BRIAN (*going to the windows and calling after him*). Round to the left, sir. . . . That's right. (*He comes back into the room*) Rum old bird. Who is he?

DINAH. Darling, you haven't kissed me yet.

BRIAN (*taking her in his arms*). I oughtn't to, but then one never ought to do the nice things.

DINAH. Why oughtn't you?

(*They sit on the sofa together.*)

BRIAN. Well, we said we'd be good until we'd told your uncle and aunt all about it. You see, being a guest in their house——

DINAH. But, darling child, what *have* you been doing all this morning *except* telling George?

BRIAN. *Trying* to tell George.

DINAH (*nodding*). Yes, of course, there's a difference.

BRIAN. I think he guessed there was something up, and he took me down to see the pigs—he said he had to see the pigs at once—I don't know why; an appointment perhaps. And we talked about pigs all the way, and I couldn't say, "Talking about pigs, I want to marry your niece——"

DINAH (*with mock indignation*). Of course you couldn't.

BRIAN. No. Well, you see how it was. And then when we'd finished talking about pigs, we started talking *to* the pigs——

DINAH (*eagerly*). Oh, *how* is Arnold?

BRIAN. The little black-and-white one? He's very jolly, I believe, but naturally I wasn't thinking about him much. I was wondering how to begin. And then Lumsden came up, and wanted to talk pig-food, and the atmosphere grew less and less romantic, and—and I gradually drifted away.

DINAH. Poor darling. Well, we shall have to approach him through Olivia.

BRIAN. But I always wanted to tell her first; she's so much easier. Only you wouldn't let me.

DINAH. That's *your* fault, Brian. You would tell Olivia that she ought to have orange-and-black curtains.

BRIAN. But she *wants* orange-and-black curtains.

DINAH. Yes, but George says he's not going to have any futuristic nonsense in an honest English country house, which has been good enough for his father and his grandfather and his great-grandfather, and—and all the rest of them. So there's a sort of strained feeling between Olivia and George just now, and if Olivia were to—sort of recommend you, well, it wouldn't do you much good.

BRIAN (*looking at her*). I see. Of course I know what *you* want, Dinah.

DINAH. What do I want?

BRIAN. You want a secret engagement, and notes left under doormats, and meetings by the withered thorn, when all the household is asleep. *I* know you.

DINAH. Oh, but it is such fun! I love meeting people by withered thorns.

BRIAN. Well, I'm not going to have it.

DINAH (*childishly*). Oh, George! Look at us being husbandy!

BRIAN. You babe! I adore you. (*He kisses her and holds her away from him and looks at her*) You know, you're rather throwing yourself away on me. Do you mind?

DINAH. Not a bit.

BRIAN. We shall never be rich, but we shall have lots of fun, and meet interesting people, and feel that we're doing something worth doing, and not getting paid nearly enough for it, and we can curse the Academy together and the British Public, and—oh, it's an exciting life.

DINAH (*seeing it*). I shall love it.

BRIAN. I'll make you love it. You shan't be sorry, Dinah.

DINAH. You shan't be sorry either, Brian.

BRIAN (*looking at her lovingly*). Oh, I know I shan't. . . . What will Olivia think about it? Will she be surprised?

DINAH. She's never surprised. She always seems to have thought of things about a week before they happen. George just begins to get hold of them about a week *after* they've happened. (*Considering him*) After all, there's no reason why George *shouldn't* like you, darling.

BRIAN. I'm not his sort, you know.

DINAH. You're more Olivia's sort. Well, we'll tell Olivia this morning.

OLIVIA (*coming in*). And what are you going to tell Olivia this morning? (*She looks at them with a smile*) Oh, well, I think I can guess.

Shall we describe OLIVIA? *But you will know all about her before the day is over.*

DINAH (*jumping up*). Olivia, darling!

BRIAN (*following*). Say you understand, Mrs. Marden.

OLIVIA. Mrs. Marden, I am afraid, is a very dense person, Brian, but I think if you asked Olivia if she understood——

BRIAN. Bless you, Olivia. I knew you'd be on our side.

DINAH. Of course she would.

OLIVIA. I don't know if it's usual to kiss an aunt-in-law, Brian, but Dinah is such a very special sort of niece that—(*she inclines her cheek and* BRIAN *kisses it*).

DINAH. I say, you *are* in luck today, Brian.

OLIVIA (*going over to her chair by the work-table and getting to business with the curtains*). And how many people have been told the good news?

BRIAN. Nobody yet.

DINAH. Except Mr. Pim.

BRIAN. Oh, does *he*——

OLIVIA. Who's Mr. Pim?

DINAH. Oh, he just happened—I say, are those *the* curtains? Then you're going to have them after all?

OLIVIA (*with an air of surprise*). After all what? But I decided on them long ago. (*To* BRIAN) You haven't told George yet?

BRIAN. I began to, you know, but I never got any farther than "Er—there's just—er——"

DINAH. George *would* talk about pigs all the time.

OLIVIA. Well, I suppose you want me to help you.

DINAH. Do, darling.

BRIAN. It would be awfully decent of you. Of course, I'm not quite his sort really——

DINAH. You're *my* sort.

BRIAN. But I don't think he objects to me, and——

(GEORGE *comes in, a typical, narrow-minded, honest country gentleman of forty-odd.*)

GEORGE (*at the windows*). What's all this about a Mr. Pim? (*He kicks some of the mud off his boots*) Who is he? Where is he? I had most important business with Lumsden, and the girl comes down and cackles about a Mr. Pim, or Ping, or something. Where did I put his card? (*Bringing it out*) Carraway Pim. Never heard of him in my life.

DINAH. He said he had a letter of introduction, Uncle George.

GEORGE. Oh, *you* saw him, did you? Yes, that reminds me, there *was* a letter—(*he brings it out and reads it*).

DINAH. He had to send a telegram. He's coming back.

OLIVIA. Pass me those scissors, Brian.

BRIAN. These? (*He picks them up and comes close to her.*)

OLIVIA. Thank you. (*She indicates* GEORGE'S *back. "Now?" says* BRIAN *with his eyebrows. She nods.*)

GEORGE (*reading*). Ah well, a friend of Brymer's. Glad to oblige him. Yes, I know the man he wants. Coming back, you say, Dinah? Then I'll be going back. Send him down to the farm, Olivia, when he comes. (*To* BRIAN) Hallo, what happened to *you*?

OLIVIA. Don't go, George, there's something we want to talk about.

GEORGE. Hallo, what's this?

BRIAN (*to* OLIVIA). Shall I——?

OLIVIA. Yes.

BRIAN (*stepping out*). I've been wanting to tell you all this morning, sir, only I didn't seem to have an opportunity of getting it out.

GEORGE. Well, what is it?

BRIAN. I want to marry Dinah, sir.

GEORGE. You want to marry Dinah? God bless my soul!

DINAH (*rushing to him and putting her cheek against his coat*). Oh, do say you like the idea, Uncle George.

GEORGE. Like the idea! Have you heard of this nonsense, Olivia?

OLIVIA. They've just this moment told me, George. I think they would be happy together.

GEORGE (*to* BRIAN). And what do you propose to be happy together *on*?

BRIAN. Well, of course, it doesn't amount to much at present, but we shan't starve.

DINAH. Brian got fifty pounds for a picture last March!

GEORGE (*a little upset by this*). Oh! (*Recovering gamely*) And how many pictures have you sold since?

BRIAN. Well, none, but——

GEORGE. None! And I don't wonder. Who the devil is going to buy pictures with triangular clouds and square sheep? And they call that

Art nowadays! Good God, man, (*waving him to the windows*) go outside and *look* at the clouds!

OLIVIA. If he draws round clouds in future, George, will you let him marry Dinah?

GEORGE. What—what? Yes, of course, you *would* be on his side—all this Futuristic nonsense. I'm just taking these clouds as an example. I suppose I can see as well as any man in the county, and I say that clouds *aren't* triangular.

BRIAN. After all, sir, at my age one is naturally experimenting, and trying to find one's (*with a laugh*) —well, it sounds priggish, but one's medium of expression. I shall find out what I want to do directly, but I think I shall always be able to earn enough to live on. Well, I have for the last three years.

GEORGE. I see, and now you want to experiment with a wife, and you propose to start experimenting with *my* niece?

BRIAN (*with a shrug*). Well, of course, if you——

OLIVIA. You could help the experiment, darling, by giving Dinah a good allowance until she's twenty-one.

GEORGE. Help the experiment! I don't *want* to help the experiment.

OLIVIA (*apologetically*). Oh, I thought you did.

GEORGE. You will talk as if I was made of money. What with taxes always going up and rents always going down, it's as much as we can do to rub along as we are, without making allowances to everybody who thinks she wants to get married. (*To* BRIAN) And that's thanks to you, my friend.

BRIAN (*surprised*). To me?

OLIVIA. You never told me, darling. What's Brian been doing?

DINAH (*indignantly*). He hasn't been doing anything.

GEORGE. He's one of your Socialists who go turning the country upside down.

OLIVIA. But even Socialists must get married sometimes.

GEORGE. I don't see any necessity.

OLIVIA. But you'd have nobody to damn after dinner, darling, if they all died out.

BRIAN. Really, sir, I don't see what my politics and my art have got to do with it. I'm perfectly ready not to talk about either when I'm in your house, and as Dinah doesn't seem to object to them——

DINAH. I should think she doesn't.

GEORGE. Oh, you can get round the women, I daresay.

BRIAN. Well, it's Dinah I want to marry and live with. So what it really comes to is that you don't think I can support a wife.

GEORGE. Well, if you're going to do it by selling pictures, I don't think you can.

BRIAN. All right, tell me how much you want me to earn in a year, and I'll earn it.

GEORGE (*hedging*). It isn't merely a question of money. I just mention that as one thing—one of the important things. In addition to that, I think you are both too young to marry. I don't think you know your own minds, and I am not at all persuaded that, with what I venture to call your outrageous tastes, you and my niece will live happily together. Just because she thinks she loves you, Dinah may persuade herself now that she agrees with all you say and do, but she has been properly brought up in an honest English country household, and—er—she—well, in short, I cannot at all approve of any engagement between you. (*Getting up*) Olivia, if this Mr.—er—Pim comes, I shall be down at the farm. You might send him along to me. (*He walks towards the windows.*)

BRIAN (*indignantly*). Is there any reason why I shouldn't marry a girl who has been properly brought up?

GEORGE. I think you know my views, Strange.

OLIVIA. George, wait a moment, dear. We can't quite leave it like this.

GEORGE. I have said all I want to say on the subject.

OLIVIA. Yes, darling, but I haven't begun to say all that *I* want to say on the subject.

GEORGE. Of course, if you have anything to say, Olivia, I will listen to it; but I don't know that this is quite the time, or that you have chosen—(*looking darkly at the curtains*)—quite the occupation likely to—er—endear your views to me.

DINAH (*mutinously*). I may as well tell you, Uncle George, that *I* have got a good deal to say, too.

OLIVIA. I can guess what you are going to say, Dinah, and I think you had better keep it for the moment.

DINAH (*meekly*). Yes, Aunt Olivia.

OLIVIA. Brian, you might take her outside for a walk. I expect you have plenty to talk about.

GEORGE. Now mind, Strange, no love-making. I put you on your honour about that.

BRIAN. I'll do my best to avoid it, sir.

DINAH (*cheekily*). May I take his arm if we go up a hill?

OLIVIA. I'm sure you'll know how to behave—both of you.

BRIAN. Come on, then, Dinah.

DINAH. Righto.

GEORGE (*as they go*). And if you do see any clouds, Strange, take a good look at them. (*He chuckles to himself*) Triangular clouds—I never heard of such nonsense. (*He goes back to his chair at the writing-table*) Futuristic rubbish . . . Well, Olivia?

OLIVIA. Well, George?

GEORGE. What are you doing?

OLIVIA. Making curtains, George. Won't they be rather sweet? Oh, but I forgot—you don't like them.

GEORGE. I don't like them, and what is more, I don't mean to have them in my house. As I told you yesterday, this is the house of a simple country gentleman, and I don't want any of these new-fangled ideas in it.

OLIVIA. Is marrying for love a new-fangled idea?

GEORGE. We'll come to that directly. None of you women can keep to the point. What I am saying now is that the house of my fathers and forefathers is good enough for me.

OLIVIA. Do you know, George, I can hear one of your ancestors saying that to his wife in their smelly old cave, when the new-fangled idea of building houses was first suggested. "The Cave of my Fathers is——"

GEORGE. That's ridiculous. Naturally we must have progress. But that's just the point. (*Indicating the curtains*) I don't call this sort of thing progress. It's—ah—retrogression.

OLIVIA. Well, anyhow, it's pretty.

GEORGE. There I disagree with you. And I must say once more that I will not have them hanging in my house.

OLIVIA. Very well, George. (*But she goes on working.*)

GEORGE. That being so, I don't see the necessity of going on with them.

OLIVIA. Well, I must do something with them now I've got the material. I thought perhaps I could sell them when they're finished—as we're so poor.

GEORGE. What do you mean—so poor?

OLIVIA. Well, you said just now that you couldn't give Dinah an allowance because rents had gone down.

GEORGE (*annoyed*). Confound it, Olivia! Keep to the point! We'll talk about Dinah's affairs directly. We're discussing our own affairs at the moment.

OLIVIA. But what is there to discuss?

GEORGE. Those ridiculous things.

OLIVIA. But we've finished that. You've said you wouldn't have them hanging in your house, and I've said, "Very well, George." Now we can go on to Dinah and Brian.

GEORGE (*shouting*). But put those beastly things away.

OLIVIA (*rising and gathering up the curtains*). Very well, George. (*She puts them away, slowly, gracefully. There is an uncomfortable silence. Evidently somebody ought to apologise.*)

GEORGE (*realising that he is the one*). Er—look here, Olivia, old girl, you've been a jolly good wife to me, and we don't often have rows, and if I've been rude to you about this—lost my temper a bit perhaps, what?—I'll say I'm sorry. May I have a kiss?

OLIVIA (*holding up her face*). George, darling! (*He kisses her*) Do you love me?

GEORGE. You know I do, old girl.

OLIVIA. As much as Brian loves Dinah?

GEORGE (*stiffly*). I've said all I want to say about that. (*He goes away from her.*)

OLIVIA. Oh, but there must be lots you want to say—and perhaps don't like to. Do tell me, darling.

GEORGE. What it comes to is this. I consider that Dinah is too young to choose a husband for herself, and that Strange isn't the husband I should choose for her.

OLIVIA. You were calling him Brian yesterday.

GEORGE. Yesterday I regarded him as a boy, now he wants me to look upon him as a man.

OLIVIA. He's twenty-four.

GEORGE. And Dinah's nineteen. Ridiculous!

OLIVIA. If he'd been a Conservative, and thought that clouds were round, I suppose he'd have seemed older, somehow.

GEORGE. That's a different point altogether. That has nothing to do with his age.

OLIVIA (*innocently*). Oh, I thought it had.

GEORGE. What I am objecting to is these ridiculously early marriages before either party knows its own mind, much less the mind of the other party. Such marriages invariably lead to unhappiness.

OLIVIA. Of course, *my* first marriage wasn't a happy one.

GEORGE. As you know, Olivia, I dislike speaking about your first marriage at all, and I had no intention of bringing it up now, but since you mention it—well, that is a case in point.

OLIVIA (*looking back at it*). When I was eighteen, I was in love. Or perhaps I only thought I was, and I don't know if I should have been happy or not if I had married him. But my father made me marry a man called Jacob Telworthy; and when things were too hot for him in England—"too hot for him"—I think that was the expression we used in those days—then we went to Australia, and I left him there, and the only happy moment I had in all my married life was on the morning when I saw in the papers that he was dead.

GEORGE (*very uncomfortable*). Yes, yes, my dear, I know. You must have had a terrible time. I can hardly bear to think about it. My only hope is that I have made up to you for it in some degree. But I don't see what bearing it has upon Dinah's case.

OLIVIA. Oh, none, except that *my* father *liked* Jacob's political opinions and his views on art. I expect that that was why he chose him for me.

GEORGE. You seem to think that I wish to choose a husband for

Dinah. I don't at all. Let her choose whom she likes as long as he can support her and there's a chance of their being happy together. Now, with regard to this fellow——

OLIVIA. You mean Brian?

GEORGE. He's got no money, and he's been brought up in quite a different way from Dinah. Dinah may be prepared to believe that—er—all cows are blue, and that—er—waves are square, but she won't go on believing it for ever.

OLIVIA. Neither will Brian.

GEORGE. Well, that's what I keep telling him, only he won't see it. Just as I keep telling you about those ridiculous curtains. It seems to me that I am the only person in the house with any eyesight left.

OLIVIA. Perhaps you are, darling; but you must let us find out our own mistakes for ourselves. At any rate, Brian is a gentleman; he loves Dinah, Dinah loves him; he's earning enough to support himself, and you are earning enough to support Dinah. I think it's worth risking, George.

GEORGE (*stiffly*). I can only say the whole question demands much more anxious thought than you seem to have given it. You say that he is a gentleman. He knows how to behave, I admit; but if his morals are as topsy-turvy as his tastes and—er—politics, as I've no doubt they are, then—er—— In short, I do *not* approve of Brian Strange as a husband for my niece and ward.

OLIVIA (*looking at him thoughtfully*). You *are* a curious mixture, George. You were so very unconventional when you married me, and you're so very conventional when Brian wants to marry Dinah. . . . George Marden to marry the widow of a convict!

GEORGE. Convict! What do you mean?

OLIVIA. Jacob Telworthy, convict—I forget his number—surely I told you all this, dear, when we got engaged?

GEORGE. Never!

OLIVIA. I told you how he carelessly put the wrong signature to a cheque for a thousand pounds in England; how he made a little mistake about two or three companies he'd promoted in Australia; and how——

GEORGE. Yes, yes, but you never told me he was *convicted*!

OLIVIA. What difference does it make?

GEORGE. My dear Olivia, if you can't see that—a convict!

OLIVIA. So, you see, we needn't be too particular about our niece, need we?

GEORGE. I think we had better leave your first husband out of the conversation altogether. I never wished to refer to him; I never wish to hear about him again. I certainly had not realised that he was actually—er—*convicted* for his—er——

OLIVIA. Mistakes.

GEORGE. Well, we needn't go into that. As for this other matter, I don't for a moment take it seriously. Dinah is an exceptionally pretty girl, and young Strange is a good-looking boy. If they are attracted to each other, it is a mere outward attraction which I am convinced will not lead to any lasting happiness. That must be regarded as my last word in the matter, Olivia. If this Mr.–er–what was his name, comes, I shall be down at the farm. (*He goes out by the door.*)

(*Left alone,* OLIVIA *brings out her curtains again, and gets calmly to work upon them.*)

(DINAH *and* BRIAN *come in by the windows.*)

DINAH. Finished?

OLIVIA. Oh no, I've got all these rings to put on.

DINAH. I meant talking to George.

BRIAN. We walked about outside——

DINAH. Until we heard him *not* talking to you any more——

BRIAN. And we didn't kiss each other once.

DINAH. Brian was very George-like. He wouldn't even let me tickle the back of his neck. (*She goes up suddenly to* OLIVIA *and kneels by her and kisses her*) Darling, being George-like is a very nice thing to be–I mean a nice thing for other people to be–I mean–oh, you know what I mean. But say that he's going to be decent about it.

OLIVIA. Of course he is, Dinah.

BRIAN. You mean he'll let me come here as–as——

DINAH. As my young man?

OLIVIA. Oh, I think so.

DINAH. Olivia, you're a wonder. Have you really talked him round?

OLIVIA. I haven't said anything yet. But I daresay I shall think of something.

DINAH (*disappointedly*). Oh!

BRIAN (*making the best of it*). After all, Dinah, I'm going back to London tomorrow——

OLIVIA. You can be good for one more day, Dinah, and then when Brian isn't here, we'll see what we can do.

DINAH. Yes, but I didn't want him to go back tomorrow.

BRIAN (*sternly*). Must. Hard work before me. Earn thousands a year. Paint the Mayor and Corporation of Pudsey, life-size, including chains of office; paint slice of haddock on plate. Copy Landseer for old gentleman in Bayswater. Design antimacassar for middle-aged sofa in Streatham. Earn a living for you, Dinah.

DINAH (*giggling*). Oh, Brian, you're heavenly. What fun we shall have when we're married.

BRIAN (*stiffly*). Sir Brian Strange, R.A., if you please, Miss Marden. Sir Brian Strange, R.A., writes: "Your Sanogene has proved a most excellent tonic. After completing the third acre of my Academy picture 'The Mayor and Corporation of Pudsey' I was completely exhausted, but one bottle of Sanogene revived me, and I finished the remaining seven acres at a single sitting."

OLIVIA (*looking about her*). Brian, find my scissors for me.

BRIAN. Scissors. (*Looking for them*) Sir Brian Strange, R.A., looks for scissors. (*Finding them*) Aha! Once more we must record an unqualified success for the eminent Academician. Your scissors.

OLIVIA. Thank you so much.

DINAH. Come on, Brian, let's go out. I feel open-airy.

OLIVIA. Don't be late for lunch, there's good people. Lady Marden is coming.

DINAH. Aunt Juli-ah! Help! (*She faints in* BRIAN's *arms*) That means a clean pinafore. Brian, you'll jolly well have to brush your hair.

BRIAN (*feeling it*). I suppose there's no time now to go up to London and get it cut?
(*Enter* ANNE, *followed by* PIM.)

ANNE. Mr. Pim!

DINAH (*delighted*). Hullo, Mr. Pim! Here we are again! You can't get rid of us so easily, you see.

PIM. I—er—dear Miss Marden——

OLIVIA. How do you do, Mr. Pim? I can't get up, but do come and sit down. My husband will be here in a minute. Anne, send somebody down to the farm——

ANNE. I think I heard the Master in the library, madam.

OLIVIA. Oh, will you tell him then?

ANNE. Yes, madam. (ANNE *goes out.*)

OLIVIA. You'll stay to lunch, of course, Mr. Pim?

DINAH. Oh, do!

PIM. It's very kind of you, Mrs. Marden, but——

DINAH. Oh, you simply must, Mr. Pim. You haven't told us half enough about yourself yet. I want to hear all about your early life.

OLIVIA. Dinah!

PIM. Oh, we are almost, I might say, old friends, Mrs. Marden.

DINAH. Of course we are. He knows Brian, too. There's more in Mr. Pim than you think. You *will* stay to lunch, won't you?

PIM. It's very kind of you to ask me, Mrs. Marden, but I am lunching with the Trevors.

OLIVIA. Oh, well, you must come to lunch another day.

DINAH. The reason why we like Mr. Pim so much is that he was the first person to congratulate us. We feel that he is going to have a great influence on our lives.

PIM (*to* OLIVIA). I, so to speak, stumbled on the engagement this morning and—er——

OLIVIA. I see. Children, you must go and tidy yourselves up. Run along.

BRIAN. Sir Brian and Lady Strange never run; they walk. (*Offering his arm*) Madam!

DINAH (*taking it*). Au revoir, Mr. Pim. (*Dramatically*) We—shall—meet—*again!*

PIM (*chuckling*). Good morning, Miss Dinah.

BRIAN. Good morning. (*He and* DINAH *go out.*)

OLIVIA. You must forgive them, Mr. Pim. They're such children. And naturally they're rather excited just now.

PIM. Oh, not at all, Mrs. Marden.

OLIVIA. Of course you won't say anything about their engagement. We only heard about it five minutes ago, and nothing has been settled yet.

PIM. Of course, of course!
(*Enter* GEORGE.)

GEORGE. Ah, Mr. Pim, we meet at last. Sorry to have kept you waiting before.

PIM. The apology should come from me, Mr. Marden for having—er—

GEORGE. Not at all. Very glad to meet you now. Any friend of Brymer's. You want a letter to this man Fanshawe?

OLIVIA. Shall I be in your way at all?

PIM. Oh, no, no, please don't.

GEORGE. It's only just a question of a letter. (*Going to his desk*) Fanshawe will put you in the way of seeing all that you want to see. He's a very old friend of mine. (*Taking a sheet of notepaper*) You'll stay to lunch, of course?

PIM. I'm afraid I am lunching with the Trevors—

GEORGE. Oh, well, they'll look after you all right. Good chap, Trevor.

PIM (*to* OLIVIA). You see, Mrs. Marden, I have only recently arrived from Australia after travelling about the world for some years, and I'm rather out of touch with my—er—fellow-workers in London.

OLIVIA. Oh yes. You've been in Australia, Mr. Pim?

GEORGE (*disliking Australia*). I shan't be a moment, Mr. Pim. (*He frowns at* OLIVIA.)

PIM. Oh, that's all right, thank you. (*To* OLIVIA) Oh yes, I have been in Australia more than once in the last few years.

OLIVIA. Really? I used to live at Sydney many years ago. Do you know Sydney at all?

GEORGE (*detesting Sydney*). H'r'm! Perhaps I'd better mention that you are a friend of the Trevors?

PIM. Thank you, thank you. (*To* OLIVIA) Indeed yes, I spent several months in Sydney.

OLIVIA. How curious. I wonder if we have any friends in common there.

GEORGE (*hastily*). Extremely unlikely, I should think. Sydney is a very big place.

PIM. True, but the world is a very small place, Mr. Marden. I had a remarkable instance of that, coming over on the boat this last time.

GEORGE. Ah! (*Feeling that the conversation is now safe, he resumes his letter.*)

PIM. Yes. There was a man I used to employ in Sydney some years ago, a bad fellow, I'm afraid, Mrs. Marden, who had been in prison for some kind of fraudulent company-promoting and had taken to drink and—and so on.

OLIVIA. Yes, yes, I understand.

PIM. Drinking himself to death I should have said. I gave him at the most another year to live. Yet to my amazement the first person I saw as I stepped on board the boat that brought me to England last week was this fellow. There was no mistaking him. I spoke to him, in fact; we recognised each other.

OLIVIA. Really?

PIM. He was travelling steerage; we didn't meet again on board, and as it happened at Marseilles, this poor fellow—er—now what *was* his name? A very unusual one. Began with a—a T, I think.

OLIVIA (*with suppressed feeling*). Yes, Mr. Pim, yes? (*She puts out a hand to* GEORGE.)

GEORGE (*in an undertone*). Nonsense, dear!

PIM (*triumphantly*). I've got it! Telworthy!

OLIVIA. Telworthy!

GEORGE. Good God!

PIM (*a little surprised at the success of his story*). An unusual name, is it not? Not a name you could forget when once you had heard it.

OLIVIA (*with feeling*). No, it is not a name you could forget when once you had heard it.

GEORGE (*hastily coming over to* PIM). Quite so, Mr. Pim, a most remarkable name, a most odd story altogether. Well, well, here's your letter, and if you're sure you won't stay to lunch——

PIM. I'm afraid not, thank you. You see, I——

GEORGE. The Trevors, yes. I'll just see you on your way—— (*To* OLIVIA) Er—my dear——

OLIVIA (*holding out her hand, but not looking at him*). Good-bye, Mr. Pim.

PIM. Good-bye, good-bye!

GEORGE (*leading the way through the windows*). This way, this way. Quicker for you.

PIM. Thank you, thank you.
(GEORGE *hurries* MR. PIM *out.* OLIVIA *sits there and looks into the past. Now and then she shudders.* GEORGE *comes back.*)

GEORGE. Good God! Telworthy! Is it possible?
(*Before* OLIVIA *can answer,* LADY MARDEN *is announced. They pull themselves together and greet her.*)

ACT TWO

Lunch is over and coffee has been served on the terrace. Conversation drags on, to the satisfaction of LADY MARDEN, *but of nobody else.* GEORGE *and* OLIVIA *want to be alone; so do* BRIAN *and* DINAH. *At last* BRIAN *murmurs something about a cigarette-case; and, catching* DINAH'S *eye, comes into the house. He leans against the sofa and waits for* DINAH.

DINAH (*loudly as she comes in*). Have you found it?

BRIAN. Found what?

DINAH (*in her ordinary voice*). That was just for *their* benefit. I said I'd help you find it. It *is* your cigarette-case we're looking for, isn't it?

BRIAN (*taking it out*). Yes. Have one?

DINAH. No, thank you, darling. Aunt Juli-ah still thinks it's unladylike. . . . Have you ever seen her beagling?

BRIAN. No. Is that very ladylike?

DINAH. Very. . . . I say, what has happened, do you think?

BRIAN. Everything. I love you, and you love me.

DINAH. Silly! I meant between George and Olivia. Didn't you notice them at lunch?

BRIAN. I noticed that you seemed to be doing most of the talking. But then I've noticed that before sometimes. Do you think Olivia and your uncle have quarrelled because of *us*?

DINAH. Of course not. George may *think* he has quarrelled, but I'm quite sure Olivia hasn't. No, I believe Mr. Pim's at the bottom of it. He's brought some terribly sad news about George's investments. The old home will have to be sold up.

BRIAN. Good. Then your uncle won't mind your marrying me.

DINAH. Yes, darling, but you must be more dramatic about it than that. "George," you must say, with tears in your eyes, "I cannot pay off the whole of the mortgage for you. I have only two and ninepence; but at least let me take your niece off your hands." Then George will thump you on the back and say gruffly, "You're a good fellow, Brian, a damn good fellow," and he'll blow his nose very loudly, and say, "Confound this cigar, it won't draw properly." (*She gives us a rough impression of* GEORGE *doing it.*)

BRIAN. Dinah, you're a heavenly idiot. And you've simply got to marry me, uncles or no uncles.

DINAH. It will have to be "uncles," I'm afraid, because, you see, I'm his ward, and I can get sent to

Chancery or Coventry or somewhere beastly, if I marry without his consent. Haven't *you* got anybody who objects to your marrying *me*?

BRIAN. Nobody, thank Heaven.

DINAH. Well, that's rather disappointing of you. I saw myself fascinating your aged father at the same time that you were fascinating George. I should have done it much better than you. As a George-fascinator you aren't very successful, sweetheart.

BRIAN. What am I like as a Dinah-fascinator?

DINAH. Plus six, darling.

BRIAN. Then I'll stick to that and leave George to Olivia.

DINAH. I expect she'll manage him all right. I have great faith in Olivia. But you'll marry me, anyhow, won't you, Brian?

BRIAN. I will.

DINAH. Even if we have to wait till I'm twenty-one?

BRIAN. Even if we have to wait till you're fifty-one.

DINAH (*holding out her hands to him*). Darling!

BRIAN (*uneasily*). I say, don't do that.

DINAH. Why not?

BRIAN. Well, I promised I wouldn't kiss you.

DINAH. Oh! . . . Well, you might just *send* me a kiss. You can look the other way as if you didn't know I was here.

BRIAN. Like this?
(*He looks the other way, kisses the tips of his fingers, and flicks it carelessly in her direction.*)

DINAH. That was a lovely one. Now here's one coming for you.
(*He catches it gracefully and conveys it to his mouth.*)

BRIAN (*with a low bow*). Madam, I thank you.

DINAH (*curtseying*). Your servant, Mr. Strange.

OLIVIA (*from outside*). Dinah!

DINAH (*jumping up*). Hullo!
(OLIVIA *comes in through the windows, followed by* GEORGE *and* LADY MARDEN, *the latter a vigorous young woman of sixty-odd, who always looks as if she were beagling.*)

OLIVIA. Aunt Julia wants to see the pigs, dear. I wish you'd take her down. I'm rather tired, and your uncle has some business to attend to.

LADY MARDEN. I've always said that you don't take enough exercise, Olivia. Look at me—sixty-five and proud of it.

OLIVIA. Yes, Aunt Julia, you're wonderful.

DINAH. How old would Olivia be if she took exercise?

GEORGE. Don't stand about asking silly questions, Dinah. Your aunt hasn't much time.

BRIAN. May I come, too, Lady Marden?

LADY MARDEN. Well, a little exercise wouldn't do *you* any harm, Mr. Strange. You're an artist, ain't you?

BRIAN. Well, I try to paint.

DINAH. He sold a picture last March for——

GEORGE. Yes, yes, never mind that now.

LADY MARDEN. Unhealthy life. Well, come along.
(*She strides out, followed by* DINAH *and* BRIAN. GEORGE *sits down at his desk with his head in his hand, and stabs the blotting-paper with a pen.* OLIVIA *takes the curtains with her to the sofa and begins to work on them.*)

GEORGE (*looking up and seeing them*). Really, Olivia, we've got something more important, more vital to us than curtains, to discuss, now that we *are* alone at last.

OLIVIA. I wasn't going to discuss them, dear.

GEORGE. I'm always glad to see Aunt Julia in my house, but I wish she hadn't chosen this day of all days to come to lunch.

OLIVIA. It wasn't Aunt Julia's fault. It was really Mr. Pim who chose the wrong day.

GEORGE (*fiercely*). Good Heavens, is it true?

OLIVIA. About Jacob Telworthy?

GEORGE. You told me he was dead. You always said that he was dead. You—you——

OLIVIA. Well, I always thought that he was dead. He was as dead as anybody could be. All the papers said he was dead.

GEORGE (*scornfully*). The papers!

OLIVIA (*as if this would settle it for* GEORGE). The *Times* said he was dead. There was a paragraph about him. Apparently even his death was fraudulent.

GEORGE. Yes, yes, I'm not blaming you, Olivia, but what are we going to do, that's the question, what are we going to do? My God, it's horrible! You've never been married to me at all! You don't seem to understand.

OLIVIA. It is a little difficult to realise. You see, it doesn't seem to have made any difference to our happiness.

GEORGE. No, that's what's so terrible. I mean—well, of course, we were quite innocent in the matter. But, at the same time, nothing can get over the fact that we—we had no right to—to be happy.

OLIVIA. Would you rather we had been miserable?

GEORGE. You're Telworthy's wife, that's what you don't seem to understand. You're Telworthy's wife. You—er—forgive me, Olivia, but it's the horrible truth—you committed bigamy when you married me. (*In horror*) Bigamy!

OLIVIA. It is an ugly word, isn't it?

GEORGE. Yes, but don't you understand—— (*He jumps up and comes over to her*) Look here, Olivia, old girl, the whole thing is nonsense, eh? It isn't your husband, it's some other Telworthy that this fellow met. That's right, isn't it? Some other shady swindler who turned up on the boat, eh? This sort of thing doesn't happen to people like *us*—committing bigamy and all that. Some other fellow.

OLIVIA (*shaking her head*). I knew all the shady swindlers in Sydney, George. . . . They came to dinner. . . . There were no others called Telworthy.

(GEORGE *goes back despondently to his seat.*)

GEORGE. Well, what are we going to do?

OLIVIA. You sent Mr. Pim away so quickly. He might have told us things. Telworthy's plans. Where he is now. You hurried him away so quickly.

GEORGE. I've sent a note round to ask him to come back. My one idea at the moment was to get him out of the house—to hush things up.

OLIVIA. You can't hush up two husbands.

GEORGE (*in despair*). You can't. Everybody will know. Everybody!

OLIVIA. The children, Aunt Julia, they may as well know now as later. Mr. Pim must, of course.

GEORGE. I do not propose to discuss my private affairs with Mr. Pim——

OLIVIA. But he's mixed himself up in them rather, hasn't he, and if you're going to ask him questions——

GEORGE. I only propose to ask him one question. I shall ask him if he is absolutely certain of the man's name. I can do that quite easily without letting him know the reason for my inquiry.

OLIVIA. You couldn't make a mistake about a name like Telworthy. But he might tell us something about Telworthy's plans. Perhaps he's going back to Australia at once. Perhaps he thinks I'm dead, too. Perhaps—oh, there are so many things I want to know.

GEORGE. Yes, yes, dear. It would be interesting to—that is, one naturally wants to know these things, but of course it doesn't make any real difference.

OLIVIA (*surprised*). No difference?

GEORGE. Well, that is to say, you're as much his wife if he's in Australia as you are if he's in England.

OLIVIA. I am not his wife at all.

GEORGE. But, Olivia, surely you understand the position——

OLIVIA (*shaking her head*). Jacob Telworthy may be alive, but I am not his wife. I ceased to be his wife when I became yours.

GEORGE. You never *were* my wife. That is the terrible part of it. Our union—you make me say it, Olivia—has been unhallowed by the Church. Unhallowed even by the Law. Legally, we have been living in—living in—well, the point is, how does the Law stand? I imagine that

Telworthy could get a—a divorce. . . . Oh, it seems impossible that things like this can be happening to *us*.

OLIVIA (*joyfully*). A divorce?

GEORGE. I—I imagine so.

OLIVIA. But then we could *really* get married, and we shouldn't be living in—living in—whatever we were living in before.

GEORGE. I can't understand you, Olivia. You talk about it so calmly, as if there was nothing blameworthy in being divorced, as if there was nothing unusual in my marrying a divorced woman, as if there was nothing wrong in our having lived together for years without having been married.

OLIVIA. What seems wrong to me is that I lived for five years with a bad man whom I hated. What seems right to me is that I lived for five years with a good man whom I love.

GEORGE. Yes, yes, my dear, I know. But right and wrong don't settle themselves as easily as that. We've been living together when you were Telworthy's wife. That's *wrong*.

OLIVIA. Do you mean wicked?

GEORGE. Well, no doubt the Court would consider that we acted in perfect innocence——

OLIVIA. What Court?

GEORGE. These things have to be done legally, of course. I believe the proper method is a nullity suit, declaring our marriage null and—er—void. It would, so to speak, wipe out these years of—er——

OLIVIA. Wickedness?

GEORGE. Of irregular union, and—er—then——

OLIVIA. Then I could go back to Jacob. . . . Do you really mean that, George?

GEORGE (*uneasily*). Well, dear, you see—that's how things are—one can't get away from—er——

OLIVIA. What you feel is that Telworthy has the greater claim? You are prepared to—make way for him?

GEORGE. Both the Church and the Law would say that I had no claim at all, I'm afraid. I—I suppose I haven't.

OLIVIA. I see. (*She looks at him curiously*) Thank you for making it so clear, George.

GEORGE. Of course, whether or not you go back to—er—Telworthy is another matter altogether. That would naturally be for you to decide.

OLIVIA (*cheerfully*). For me and Jacko to decide.

GEORGE. Er—Jacko?

OLIVIA. I used to call my first husband—I mean my only husband—Jacko. I didn't like the name of Jacob, and Jacko seemed to suit him somehow. . . . He had very long arms. Dear Jacko.

GEORGE (*annoyed*). You don't seem to realise that this is not a joke, Olivia.

OLIVIA. (*a trifle hysterically*). It may not be a joke, but it *is* funny, isn't it?

GEORGE. I must say I don't see anything funny in a tragedy that has wrecked two lives.

OLIVIA. Two? Oh, but Jacko's life isn't wrecked. It has just been miraculously restored to him. And a wife, too. There's nothing tragic for Jacko in it.

GEORGE (*stiffly*). I was referring to *our* two lives—yours and mine.

OLIVIA. Yours, George? Your life isn't wrecked. The Court will absolve you of all blame; your friends will sympathise with you, and tell you that I was a designing woman who deliberately took you in; your Aunt Julia——

GEORGE (*overwrought*). Stop it! What do you mean? Have you no heart? Do you think I *want* to lose you, Olivia? Do you think I *want* my home broken up like this? Haven't you been happy with me these last five years?

OLIVIA. Very happy.

GEORGE. Well then, how can you talk like that?

OLIVIA (*pathetically*). But you want to send me away.

GEORGE. There you go again. I don't *want* to. I have hardly had time to realise just what it will mean to me when you go. The fact is I simply daren't realise it. I daren't think about it.

OLIVIA (*earnestly*). Try thinking about it, George.

GEORGE. And you talk as if I *wanted* to send you away!

OLIVIA. Try thinking about it, George.

GEORGE. You don't seem to understand that I'm not *sending* you away. You simply aren't mine to keep.

OLIVIA. Whose am I?

GEORGE. Your husband's. Telworthy's.

OLIVIA (*gently*). If I belong to anybody but myself, I think I belong to you.

GEORGE. Not in the eyes of the Law. Not in the eyes of the Church. Not even in the eyes of—er——

OLIVIA. The County?

GEORGE (*annoyed*). I was about to say "Heaven."

OLIVIA (*unimpressed*). Oh!

GEORGE. That this should happen to *us!*

(*He gets up and walks about the room, wondering when he will wake up from this impossible dream.* OLIVIA *works in silence. Then she stands up and shakes out her curtains.*)

OLIVIA (*looking at them*). I do hope Jacko will like these.

GEORGE. What! You—— (*Going up to her*) Olivia, Olivia, have you no heart?

OLIVIA. Ought you to talk like that to another man's wife?

GEORGE. Confound it, is this just a joke to you?

OLIVIA. You must forgive me, George; I am a little over-excited—at the thought of returning to Jacob, I suppose.

GEORGE. Do you *want* to return to him?

OLIVIA. One wants to do what is right. In the eyes of—er—Heaven.

GEORGE. Seeing what sort of man he is, I have no doubt that you could get a separation, supposing that he didn't—er—divorce you. I don't know *what* is best. I must consult my solicitor. The whole position has been sprung on us, and —(*miserably*) I don't know, I don't know. I can't take it all in.

OLIVIA. Wouldn't you like to consult your Aunt Julia too? She could tell you what the County—I mean what Heaven really thought about it.

GEORGE. Yes, yes, Aunt Julia has plenty of common sense. You're quite right, Olivia. This isn't a thing we can keep from the family.

OLIVIA. Do I still call her *Aunt* Julia?

GEORGE (*looking up from his pacings*). What? What? (ANNE *comes in*) Well, what is it?

ANNE. Mr. Pim says he will come down at once, sir.

GEORGE. Oh, thank you, thank you. (ANNE *goes out.*)

OLIVIA. George, Mr. Pim has got to know.

GEORGE. I don't see the necessity.

OLIVIA. Not even for me? When a woman suddenly hears that her long-lost husband is restored to her, don't you think she wants to ask questions? Where is he living, and how is he looking, and——

GEORGE (*coldly*). Of course, if you are interested in these things——

OLIVIA. How can I help being? Don't be so silly, George. We *must* know what Jacko——

GEORGE (*annoyed*). I wish you wouldn't call him by that ridiculous name.

OLIVIA. My husband——

GEORGE (*wincing*). Yes, well—your husband?

OLIVIA. Well, we must know his plans—where we can communicate with him, and so on.

GEORGE. I have no wish to communicate with him.

OLIVIA. I'm afraid you'll have to, dear.

GEORGE. I don't see the necessity.

OLIVIA. Well, you'll want to—to apologise to him for living with his wife for so long. And as I belong to him, he ought to be told where he can—call for me.

GEORGE (*after a struggle*). You put it in a very peculiar way, but I see your point. (*With a shudder*) Oh, the horrible publicity of it all!

OLIVIA (*going up to him and comforting him*). Poor George. Dear, don't think I don't sympathise with you. I understand so exactly what you are feeling. The publicity! It's terrible.

GEORGE (*miserably*). I want to do what's right, Olivia. You believe that?

OLIVIA. Of course I do. It's only that we don't quite agree as to what is right and what is wrong.

GEORGE. It isn't a question of agreeing. Right is right, and wrong is wrong, all the world over.

OLIVIA (*with a sad little smile*). But more particularly in Buckinghamshire, I think.

GEORGE. If I only considered myself, I should say: "Let us pack this man Telworthy back to Australia. He would make no claim. He would accept money to go away and say nothing about it." If I consulted simply my own happiness, Olivia, that is what I should say. But when I consult—er——

OLIVIA (*surprised*). Mine?

GEORGE. My conscience——

OLIVIA. Oh!

GEORGE. Then I can't do it. It's wrong. (*He is at the window as he says this.*)

OLIVIA (*making her first and last appeal*). George, aren't I worth a little——

GEORGE (*turning round*). H'sh! Dinah! (*Loudly for* DINAH'S *benefit*) Well, then I'll write to him and—— Ah, Dinah, where's Aunt Julia?

DINAH (*coming in*). We've seen the pigs, and now she's discussing the Art of Landseer with Brian. I just came to ask——

OLIVIA. Dinah, dear, bring Aunt Julia here. And Brian too. We have things we want to talk about with you all.

GEORGE (*outraged*). Olivia!

DINAH. Righto. What fun! (*Exit* DINAH.)

GEORGE. Olivia, you don't seriously suggest that we should discuss these things with a child like Dinah and a young man like Strange, a mere acquaintance.

OLIVIA. Dinah will have to know. I'm very fond of her, George. You can't send me away without telling Dinah. And Brian is my friend. You have your solicitor and your aunt and your conscience to consult—mayn't I even have Brian?

GEORGE (*forgetting*). I should have thought that your *husband*——

OLIVIA. Yes, but we don't know where Jacko is.

GEORGE. I was not referring to—er —Telworthy.

OLIVIA. Well then?

GEORGE. Well, naturally I—you mustn't—— Oh, this is horrible! (*He comes back to his desk as the others come in.*)

OLIVIA (*getting up*). George and I have had some rather bad news, Aunt Julia. We wanted your advice. Where will you sit?

LADY MARDEN. Thank you, Olivia. I can sit down by myself. (*She does so, near* GEORGE. DINAH *sits on the sofa with* OLIVIA, *and* BRIAN *half leans against the back of it. There is a hush of expectation. . . .*) What is it? Money, I suppose. Nobody's safe nowadays.

GEORGE (*signalling for help*). Olivia——

OLIVIA. We've just heard that my first husband is still alive.

DINAH. Telworthy!

BRIAN. Good Lord!

LADY MARDEN. George!

DINAH (*excitedly*). And only this morning I was saying that nothing ever happened in this house! (*Remorsefully to* OLIVIA) Darling, I don't mean that. Darling one!

LADY MARDEN. What does this mean, George? I leave you for ten minutes—barely ten minutes—to go and look at the pigs, and when I come back you tell me that Olivia is a bigamist.

BRIAN (*indignantly*). I say——

OLIVIA (*restraining him*). H'sh!

BRIAN (*to* OLIVIA). If this is a row, I'm on your side.

LADY MARDEN. Well, George?

GEORGE. I'm afraid it's true, Aunt Julia. We heard the news just before lunch—just before you came. We've only this moment had an opportunity of talking about it, of wondering what to do.

LADY MARDEN. What was his name —Tel—something——

OLIVIA. Jacob Telworthy.

LADY MARDEN. So he's alive still?

GEORGE. Apparently. There seems to be no doubt about it.

LADY MARDEN (*to* OLIVIA). Didn't you *see* him die? I should always want to *see* my husband die before I married again. Not that I approve of second marriages, anyhow. I told you so at the time, George.

OLIVIA. *And* me, Aunt Julia.

LADY MARDEN. Did I? Well, I generally say what I think.

GEORGE. I ought to tell you, Aunt Julia, that no blame attaches to Olivia over this. Of that I am perfectly satisfied. It's nobody's fault, except——

LADY MARDEN. Except Telworthy's. *He* seems to have been rather careless. Well, what are you going to do about it?

GEORGE. That's just it. It's a terrible situation. There's bound to be so much publicity. Not only all this, but—but Telworthy's past and—and everything.

LADY MARDEN. I should have said that it was Telworthy's present which was the trouble. Had he a past as well?

OLIVIA. He was a fraudulent company promoter. He went to prison a good deal.

LADY MARDEN. George, you never told me this!

GEORGE. I—er——

OLIVIA. I don't see *why* he should want to talk about it.

DINAH (*indignantly*). What's it got to do with Olivia, anyhow? It not *her* fault.

LADY MARDEN (*sarcastically*). Oh no, I daresay it's mine.

OLIVIA (*to* GEORGE). You wanted to ask Aunt Julia what was the right thing to do.

BRIAN (*bursting out*). Good Heavens, what *is* there to do except the one and only thing? (*They all look at him and he becomes embarrassed*) I'm sorry. You don't want *me* to——

OLIVIA. *I* do, Brian.

LADY MARDEN. Well, go on, Mr. Strange. What would *you* do in George's position?

BRIAN. Do? Say to the woman I loved, "You're *mine*, and let this other damned fellow come and take you from me if he can!" And he couldn't—how could he?—not if the woman chose *me*.
(LADY MARDEN *gazes at* BRIAN *in amazement,* GEORGE *in anger.* OLIVIA *presses his hand gratefully. He has said what she has been waiting—oh, so eagerly—for* GEORGE *to say.*)

DINAH (*adoringly*). Oh, Brian! (*In a whisper*) It *is* me, isn't it, and not Olivia?

BRIAN. You baby, of course!

LADY MARDEN. I'm afraid, Mr. Strange, your morals are as peculiar as your views on Art. If you had led a more healthy life——

BRIAN. This is not a question of morals or of art, it's a question of love.

DINAH. Hear, hear!

LADY MARDEN (*to* GEORGE). Isn't it that girl's bedtime yet?

OLIVIA (*to* DINAH). We'll let her sit up a little longer if she's good.

DINAH. I will be good, Olivia, only I thought anybody, however important a debate was, was allowed to say "Hear, hear!"

GEORGE (*coldly*). I really think we could discuss this better if Mr. Strange took Dinah out for a walk. Strange, if you—er——

OLIVIA. Tell them what you have settled first, George.

LADY MARDEN. Settled? What is there to be settled? It settles itself.

GEORGE (*sadly*). That's just it.

LADY MARDEN. The marriage must be annulled—is that the word, George?

GEORGE. I presume so.

LADY MARDEN. One's solicitor will know all about that of course.

BRIAN. And when the marriage has been annulled, what then?

LADY MARDEN. Presumably Olivia will return to her husband.

BRIAN (*bitterly*). And *that's* morality! As expounded by Bishop Landseer!

GEORGE (*angered*). I don't know what you mean by Bishop Landseer. Morality is acting in accordance with the Laws of the Land and the Laws of the Church. I am quite prepared to believe that *your* creed embraces neither marriage nor monogamy, but my creed is different.

BRIAN (*fiercely*). My creed includes both marriage *and* monogamy, and monogamy means sticking to the woman you love, as long as she wants you.

LADY MARDEN (*calmly*). You suggest that George and Olivia should go on living together, although they have never been legally married, and wait for this Telworthy man to divorce her, and then—bless the man, what do you think the County would say?

BRIAN (*scornfully*). Does it matter?

DINAH. Well, if you really want to know, the men would say, "Gad, she's a fine woman; I don't wonder he sticks to her," and the women would say, "I can't *think* what he sees in her to stick to her like that," and they'd both say, "After all, he may be a damn fool, but you can't deny he's a sportsman." That's what the County would say.

GEORGE (*indignantly*). Was it for this sort of thing, Olivia, that you insisted on having Dinah and Mr. Strange in here? To insult me in my own house?

LADY MARDEN. I can't think what young people are coming to nowadays.

OLIVIA. I think, dear, you and Brian had better go.

DINAH (*getting up*). We will go. But I'm just going to say one thing, Uncle George. Brian and I *are* going to marry each other, and when we are married we'll stick to each other, how*ever* many of our dead husbands and wives turn up! (*She goes out indignantly, followed by* BRIAN.)

GEORGE. Upon my word, this is a pleasant discussion.

OLIVIA. I think the discussion is over, George. It is only a question of where I shall go, while you are bringing your—what sort of suit did you call it?

LADY MARDEN (*to* GEORGE). Nullity suit. I suppose that is the best thing?

GEORGE. It's horrible. The awful publicity. That it should be happening to *us*, that's what I can't get over.

LADY MARDEN. I don't remember anything of the sort in the Marden Family before, ever.

GEORGE (*absently*). Lady Fanny.

LADY MARDEN (*recollecting*). Yes, of course; but that was two hundred years ago. The standards were different then. Besides, it wasn't quite the same, anyhow.

GEORGE (*absently*). No, it wasn't quite the same.

LADY MARDEN. No. We shall all feel it. Terribly.

GEORGE (*his apology*). If there were any other way! Olivia, what *can* I do? It *is* the only way, isn't it? All that that fellow said—of course, it sounds very well—but as things are. . . . *Is* there anything in marriage, or isn't there? You believe that there is, don't you? You aren't one of these Socialists. Well, then, *can* we go on living together when you're another man's wife? It isn't only what people will say, but it *is* wrong, isn't it? . . . And supposing he doesn't divorce you, are we to go on living together, unmarried, for *ever*? Olivia, you seem to think that I'm just thinking of the publicity—what people will say. I'm not. I'm not. That comes in any way. But I want to do what's right, what's best. I don't mean what's best for *us*, what makes us happiest, I mean what's really best, what's rightest. What anybody else would do in my place. *I* don't know. It's so unfair. You're not my wife at all, but I want to do what's right. . . . Oh, Olivia, Olivia, you do understand, don't you?

(*They have both forgotten* LADY MARDEN. OLIVIA *has never taken her eyes off him as he makes his last attempt to convince himself.*)

OLIVIA (*almost tenderly*). So very very well, George. Oh, I understand just what you are feeling. And oh, I do so wish that you could—(*with a little sigh*)—but then it wouldn't be George, not the George I married—(*with a rueful little laugh*)—or didn't quite marry.

LADY MARDEN. I must say, I think you are both talking a little wildly.

OLIVIA (*repeating it, oh, so tenderly*). Or didn't—quite—marry. (*She looks at him with all her heart in her eyes. She is giving him his last chance to say "Damn Telworthy; you're mine!" He struggles desperately with himself. . . . Will he?—will he? . . . But we shall never know, for at that moment* ANNE *comes in.*)

ANNE. Mr. Pim is here, sir.

GEORGE (*emerging from the struggle with an effort*). Pim? Pim? Oh, ah, yes, of course. Mr. Pim. (*Looking up*) Where have you put him?

OLIVIA. I want to see Mr. Pim, too, George.

LADY MARDEN. Who on earth is Mr. Pim?

OLIVIA. Show him in here, Anne.

ANNE. Yes, madam. (*She goes out.*)

OLIVIA. It was Mr. Pim who told us about my husband. He came across with him in the boat, and recognised him as the Telworthy he knew in Australia.

LADY MARDEN. Oh! Shall I be in the way?

GEORGE. No, no. It doesn't matter, does it, Olivia?

OLIVIA. Please stay.

(ANNE *enters followed by* MR. PIM.)

ANNE. Mr. Pim.

GEORGE (*pulling himself together*). Ah, Mr. Pim! Very good of you to have come. The fact is—er—— (*It is too much for him; he looks despairingly at* OLIVIA.)

OLIVIA. We're so sorry to trouble you, Mr. Pim. By the way, do you know Lady Marden? (MR. PIM *and* LADY MARDEN *bow to each other*) Do come and sit down, won't you? (*She makes room for him on the sofa next to her*) The fact is, Mr. Pim, you gave us rather a surprise this morning, and before we had time to realise what it all meant, you had gone.

MR. PIM. A surprise, Mrs. Marden? Dear me, not an unpleasant one, I hope?

OLIVIA. Well, rather a—surprising one.

GEORGE. Olivia, allow me a moment. Mr. Pim, you mentioned a man called Telworthy this morning. My wife used to—that is to say, I used to—that is, there are reasons——

OLIVIA. I think we had better be perfectly frank, George.

LADY MARDEN. I am sixty-five years of age, Mr. Pim, and I can say that I've never had a moment's uneasiness by telling the truth.

MR. PIM (*after a desperate effort to keep up with the conversation*). Oh! . . . I—er—I'm afraid I am rather at sea. Have I—er—left anything unsaid in presenting my credentials to you this morning? This Telworthy whom you mention—I seem to remember the name——

OLIVIA. Mr. Pim, you told us this morning of a man whom you had met on the boat, a man who had come down in the world, whom you had known in Sydney. A man called Telworthy.

MR. PIM (*relieved*). Ah yes, yes, of course. I did say Telworthy, didn't I? Most curious coincidence, Lady Marden. Poor man, poor man! Let me see, it must have been ten years ago——

GEORGE. Just a moment, Mr. Pim. You're quite sure that his name was Telworthy?

MR. PIM. Telworthy—Telworthy—didn't I say Telworthy? Yes, that was it—Telworthy. Poor fellow!

OLIVIA. I'm going to be perfectly frank with you, Mr. Pim. I feel quite sure that I can trust you. This man Telworthy whom you met is my husband.

MR. PIM. Your husband? (*He looks in mild surprise at* GEORGE) But—er——

OLIVIA. My first husband. His death was announced six years ago. I had left him some years before that, but there seems no doubt from your story that he's still alive. His record—the country he comes from—above all, the very unusual name—Telworthy.

MR. PIM. Telworthy—yes—certainly a most peculiar name. I remember saying so. Your first husband? Dear me! Dear me!

GEORGE. You understand, Mr. Pim, that all this is in absolute confidence.

MR. PIM. Of course, of course.

OLIVIA. Well, since he is my husband, we naturally want to know something about him. Where is he now, for instance?

MR. PIM (*surprised*). Where is he now? But surely I told you? I told you what happened at Marseilles?

GEORGE. At Marseilles?

MR. PIM. Yes, yes, poor fellow, it was most unfortunate. (*Quite happy again*) You must understand, Lady Marden, that although I had met the poor fellow before in Australia, I was never in any way intimate——

GEORGE (*thumping the desk*). Where is he *now*, that's what we want to know?

(MR. PIM *turns to him with a start.*)

OLIVIA. Please, Mr. Pim!

MR. PIM. Where is he now? But—didn't I tell you of the curious fatality at Marseilles—poor fellow—the fish-bone?

ALL. Fish-bone?

MR. PIM. Yes, yes, a herring, I understand.

OLIVIA (*understanding first*). Do you mean he's dead?

MR. PIM. Dead—of course—didn't—I——?

OLIVIA (*laughing hysterically*). Oh, Mr. Pim, you—oh, what a husband to have—oh, I—— (*But that is all she can say for the moment.*)

LADY MARDEN. Pull yourself together, Olivia. This is so unhealthy for you. (*To* PIM) So he really *is* dead this time?

MR. PIM. Oh, undoubtedly, undoubtedly. A fish-bone lodged in his throat.

GEORGE (*trying to realise it*). Dead!

OLIVIA (*struggling with her laughter*). I think you must excuse me, Mr. Pim—I can never thank you enough—a herring—there's something about a herring—morality depends on such little things—George, you—— (*Shaking her head at him in a weak state of laughter, she hurries out of the room.*)

MR. PIM. Dear me! Dear me!

GEORGE. Now, let us have this quite clear, Mr. Pim. You say that the man, Telworthy, Jacob Telworthy, is dead?

MR. PIM. Telworthy, yes—didn't I say Telworthy? This man I was telling you about——

GEORGE. He's dead?

MR. PIM. Yes, yes, he died at Marseilles.

LADY MARDEN. A dispensation of Providence, George. One can look at it in no other light.

GEORGE. Dead! (*Suddenly annoyed*) Really, Mr. Pim, I think you might have told us before.

MR. PIM. But I—I *was* telling you—I——

GEORGE. If you had only told us the whole story at once, instead of in two—two instalments like this, you would have saved us all a good deal of anxiety.

MR. PIM. Really, I——

LADY MARDEN. I am sure Mr. Pim meant well, George, but it seems a pity he couldn't have said so before. If the man was dead, *why* try to hush it up?

MR. PIM (*lost again*). Really, Lady Marden, I——

GEORGE (*getting up*). Well, well, at any rate, I am much obliged to you, Mr. Pim, for having come down to us this afternoon. Dead! *De mortuis,* and so forth, but the situation would have been impossible had he lived. Good-bye! (*Holding out his hand*) Good-bye!

LADY MARDEN. Good-bye, Mr. Pim.

MR. PIM. Good-bye, good-bye! (GEORGE *takes him to the door*) Of course, if I had—(*to himself*) Telworthy—I *think* that was the name. (*He goes out, still wondering.*)

GEORGE (*with a sigh of thankfulness*). Well! This is wonderful news, Aunt Julia.

LADY MARDEN. Most providential! . . . You understand, of course, that you are not married to Olivia?

GEORGE (*who didn't*). Not married?

LADY MARDEN. If her first husband only died at Marseilles a few days ago——

GEORGE. Good Heavens!

LADY MARDEN. Not that it matters. You can get married quietly again. Nobody need know.

GEORGE (*considering it*). Yes . . . yes. Then all these years we have been—er—— Yes.

LADY MARDEN. Who's going to know?

GEORGE. Yes, yes, that's true. . . . And in perfect innocence, too.

LADY MARDEN. I should suggest a Registry Office in London.

GEORGE. A Registry Office, yes.

LADY MARDEN. Better go up to town this afternoon. Can't do it too quickly.

GEORGE. Yes, yes. We can stay at an hotel——

LADY MARDEN (*surprised*). George!

GEORGE. What?

LADY MARDEN. *You* will stay at your club.

GEORGE. Oh—ah—yes, of course, Aunt Julia.

LADY MARDEN. Better take your solicitor with you to be on the safe side. . . . To the Registry Office, I mean.

GEORGE. Yes.

LADY MARDEN (*getting up*). Well, I must be getting along, George. Say good-bye to Olivia for me. And those children. Of course, you won't allow this absurd love-business between them to come to anything?

GEORGE. Most certainly not. Good-bye, Aunt Julia!

LADY MARDEN (*indicating the windows*). I'll go *this* way. (*As she goes*) And get Olivia out more, George. I don't like these hysterics. You want to be firm with her.

GEORGE (*firmly*). Yes, yes! Good-bye!
(*He waves to her and then goes back to his seat.*)

(OLIVIA *comes in, and stands in the middle of the room looking at him. He comes to her eagerly.*)

GEORGE (*holding out his hands*). Olivia! Olivia!
(*But it is not so easy as that.*)

OLIVIA (*drawing herself up proudly*). Mrs. Telworthy!

ACT THREE

OLIVIA *is standing where we left her at the end of the last act.*

GEORGE (*taken aback*). Olivia, I—I don't understand.

OLIVIA (*leaving melodrama with a little laugh and coming down to him*). Poor George! Did I frighten you rather?

GEORGE. You're so strange to-day. I don't understand you. You're not like the Olivia I know.
(*They sit down on the sofa together.*)

OLIVIA. Perhaps you don't know me very well after all.

GEORGE (*affectionately*). Oh, that's nonsense, old girl. You're just my Olivia.

OLIVIA. And yet it seemed as though I wasn't going to be your Olivia half an hour ago.

GEORGE (*with a shudder*). Don't talk about it. It doesn't bear thinking about. Well, thank Heaven that's over. Now we can get married again quietly and nobody will be any the wiser.

OLIVIA. Married again?

GEORGE. Yes, dear. As you—er—(*he laughs uneasily*) said just now, you are Mrs. Telworthy. Just for the moment. But we can soon put that right. My idea was to go up this evening and—er—make arrangements, and if you come up to-morrow morning, if we can manage it by then, we could get quietly married at a Registry Office, and—er—nobody any the wiser.

OLIVIA. Yes, I see. You want me to marry you at a Registry Office to-morrow?

GEORGE. If we can arrange it by then. I don't know how long these things take, but I should imagine there would be no difficulty.

OLIVIA. Oh no, that part ought to be quite easy. But—— (*She hesitates.*)

GEORGE. But what?

OLIVIA. Well, if you want to marry me tomorrow, George, oughtn't you to propose to me first?

GEORGE (*amazed*). Propose?

OLIVIA. Yes. It is usual, isn't it, to propose to a person before you marry her, and—and we want to do the usual thing, don't we?

GEORGE (*upset*). But you—but we . . .

OLIVIA. You see, dear, you're George Marden, and I'm Olivia Telworthy, and you—you're attracted by me, and think I would make you a good wife, and you want to marry me. Well, naturally you propose to me first, and—tell me how much you are attracted by me, and what a good wife you think I shall make, and how badly you want to marry me.

GEORGE (*falling into the humour of it, as he thinks*). The baby! Did she want to be proposed to all over again?

OLIVIA. Well, she did rather.

GEORGE (*rather fancying himself as an actor*). She shall then. (*He adopts what he considers to be an appropriate attitude*) Mrs. Telworthy, I have long admired you in silence, and the time has now come to put my admiration into words. Er—— (*But apparently he finds a difficulty.*)

OLIVIA (*hopefully*). Into words.

GEORGE. Er——

OLIVIA (*with the idea of helping*). Oh, Mr. Marden!

GEORGE. Er—may I call you Olivia?

OLIVIA. Yes, George.

GEORGE (*taking her hand*). Olivia—I—— (*He hesitates.*)

OLIVIA. I don't want to interrupt, but oughtn't you to be on your knees? It is—usual, I believe. If one of the servants came in, you could say you were looking for my scissors.

GEORGE. Really, Olivia, you must allow me to manage my own proposal in my own way.

OLIVIA (*meekly*). I'm sorry. Do go on.

GEORGE. Well, er—confound it, I love you. Will you marry me?

OLIVIA. Thank you, George, I will think it over.

GEORGE (*laughing*). Silly girl! Well then, tomorrow morning. No wedding-cake, I'm afraid, Olivia. (*He laughs again*) But we'll go and have a good lunch somewhere.

OLIVIA. I will think it over, George.

GEORGE (*good-humouredly*). Well, give us a kiss while you're thinking.

OLIVIA. I'm afraid you mustn't kiss me until we are actually engaged.

GEORGE (*laughing uneasily*). Oh, we needn't take it as seriously as all that.

OLIVIA. But a woman must take a proposal seriously.

GEORGE (*alarmed at last*). What do you mean?

OLIVIA. I mean that the whole question, as I heard somebody say once, demands much more anxious thought than either of us has given it. These hasty marriages——

GEORGE. Hasty!

OLIVIA. Well, you've only just proposed to me, and you want to marry me tomorrow.

GEORGE. Now you're talking perfect nonsense, Olivia. You know quite well that our case is utterly different from—from any other.

OLIVIA. All the same, one has to ask oneself questions. With a young girl like—well, with a young girl, love may well seem to be all that matters. But with a woman of my age, it is different. I have to ask myself if you can afford to support a wife.

GEORGE (*coldly*). Fortunately that is a question that you can very easily answer for yourself.

OLIVIA. Well, but I have been hearing rather bad reports lately. What with taxes always going up, and rents always going down, some of our landowners are getting into rather straitened circumstances. At least, so I'm told.

GEORGE. I don't know what you're talking about.

OLIVIA (*surprised*). Oh, isn't it true? I heard of a case only this morning—a landowner who always seemed to be very comfortably off, but who couldn't afford an allowance for his only niece when she wanted to get married. It made me think that one oughtn't to judge by appearances.

GEORGE. You know perfectly well that I can afford to support a wife as my wife *should* be supported.

OLIVIA. I'm so glad, dear. Then your income—you aren't getting anxious at all?

GEORGE (*stiffly*). You know perfectly well what my income is. I see no reason for anxiety in the future.

OLIVIA. Ah, well, then we needn't think about that any more. Well, then, there is another thing to be considered.

GEORGE. I can't make out what you're up to. Don't you want to get married; to—er—legalise this extraordinary situation in which we are placed?

OLIVIA. I want to be sure that I am going to be happy, George. I can't just jump at the very first offer I have had since my husband died, without considering the whole question very carefully.

GEORGE. So I'm under consideration, eh?

OLIVIA. Every suitor is.

GEORGE (*sarcastically, as he thinks*). Well, go on.

OLIVIA. Well, then, there's your niece. You have a niece who lives with you. Of course Dinah is a delightful girl, but one doesn't like marrying into a household in which there is another grown-up woman. But perhaps she will be getting married herself soon?

GEORGE. I see no prospect of it.

OLIVIA. I think it would make it much easier if she did.

GEORGE. Is this a threat, Olivia? Are you telling me that if I do not allow young Strange to marry Dinah, you will not marry me?

OLIVIA. A threat? Oh, no, George.

GEORGE. Then what does it mean?

OLIVIA. I'm just wondering if you love me as much as Brian loves Dinah. You *do* love me?

GEORGE (*from his heart*). You know I do, old girl. (*He comes to her.*)

OLIVIA. You're not just attracted by my pretty face? . . . *Is* it a pretty face?

GEORGE. It's an adorable one. (*He tries to kiss it, but she turns away.*)

OLIVIA. How can I be sure that it is not *only* my face which makes you think that you care for me? Love which rests upon a mere outward attraction cannot lead to any lasting happiness—as one of our thinkers has observed.

GEORGE. What's come over you, Olivia? I don't understand what you're driving at. Why should you doubt my love?

OLIVIA. Ah!—Why?

GEORGE. You can't pretend that we haven't been happy together. I've—I've been a good pal to you, eh? We—we suit each other, old girl.

OLIVIA. Do we?

GEORGE. Of course we do.

OLIVIA. I wonder. When two people of our age think of getting married, one wants to be very sure that there is real community of ideas between them. Whether it is a comparatively trivial matter, like the right colour for a curtain, or some very much more serious question of conduct which arises, one wants to feel that there is some chance of agreement between husband and wife.

GEORGE. We—we love each other, old girl.

OLIVIA. We do now, yes. But what shall we be like in five years' time? Supposing that after we have been married five years, we found ourselves estranged from each other upon such questions as Dinah's future, or the decorations of the drawing-room, or even the advice to give to a friend who had innocently contracted a bigamous marriage? How bitterly we should regret then our hasty plunge into a matrimony which was no true partnership, whether of tastes, or of ideas, or even of consciences! (*With a sigh*) Ah me!

GEORGE (*nastily*). Unfortunately for your argument, Olivia, I can answer you out of your own mouth. You seem to have forgotten what you said this morning in the case of—er—young Strange.

OLIVIA (*reproachfully*). Is it quite fair, George, to drag up what was said this morning?

GEORGE. You've brought it on yourself.

OLIVIA. I? . . . Well, and what did I say this morning?

GEORGE. You said that it was quite enough that Strange was a gentleman and in love with Dinah for me to let them marry each other.

OLIVIA. Oh! . . . *Is* that enough, George?

GEORGE (*triumphantly*). You said so.

OLIVIA (*meekly*). Well, if you think so, too, I—I don't mind risking it.

GEORGE (*kindly*). Aha, my dear! You see!

OLIVIA. Then you do think it's enough?

GEORGE. I—er—— Yes, yes, I—I think so.

OLIVIA (*going to him*). My darling one! Then we can have a double wedding. How jolly!

GEORGE (*astounded*). A double one!

OLIVIA. Yes. You and me, Brian and Dinah.

GEORGE (*firmly*). Now look here, Olivia, understand once and for all, I am not to be blackmailed into giving my consent to Dinah's engagement. Neither blackmailed nor tricked. Our marriage has nothing whatever to do with Dinah's.

OLIVIA. No, dear. I quite understand. They may take place about the same time, but they have nothing to do with each other.

GEORGE. I see no prospect of Dinah's marriage taking place for many years.

OLIVIA. No, dear, that was what I said.

GEORGE (*not understanding for the moment*). You said . . . ? I see. Now, Olivia, let us have this perfectly clear. You apparently insist on treating my—er—proposal as serious.

OLIVIA (*surprised*). Wasn't it serious? Were you trifling with me?

GEORGE. You know quite well what I mean. You treat it as an ordinary proposal from a man to a woman who have never been more than acquaintances before. Very well then. Will you tell me what you propose to do, if you decide to—ah—refuse me? You do not suggest that we should go on living together—unmarried?

OLIVIA (*shocked*). Of course not, George! What would the County—I mean Heaven—I mean the Law—I mean, of *course* not! Besides, it's so unnecessary. If I decide to accept you, of *course* I shall marry you.

GEORGE. Quite so. And if you—ah—decide to refuse me? What will you do?

OLIVIA. Nothing.

GEORGE. Meaning by that?

OLIVIA. Just that, George. I shall stay here—just as before. I like this house. It wants a little re-decorating perhaps, but I do like it, George. . . . Yes, I shall be quite happy here.

GEORGE. I see. You will continue to live down here—in spite of what you said just now about the immorality of it.

OLIVIA (*surprised*). But there's nothing immoral in a widow living alone in a big country house, with perhaps the niece of a friend of hers staying with her, just to keep her company.

GEORGE (*sarcastic*). And what shall *I* be doing, when you've so very kindly taken possession of my house for me?

OLIVIA. I don't know, George. Travelling, I expect. You could come down sometimes with a chaperone. I suppose there would be nothing wrong in that.

GEORGE (*indignant*). Thank you! And what if I refuse to be turned out of my house?

OLIVIA. Then, seeing that we can't *both* be in it, it looks as though you'd have to turn *me* out. (*Casually*) I suppose there are legal ways of doing these things. You'd have to consult your solicitor again.

GEORGE (*amazed*). Legal ways?

OLIVIA. Well, you couldn't *throw* me out, could you? You'd have to get an injunction against me—or prosecute me for trespass—or something. It would make an awfully unusual case, wouldn't it? The papers would be full of it.

GEORGE. You must be mad!

OLIVIA (*dreamily*). Widow of well-known ex-convict takes possession of J.P.'s house. Popular country gentleman denied entrance to his own home. Doomed to travel.

GEORGE (*angrily*). I've had enough of this. Do you mean all this nonsense?

OLIVIA. I do mean, George, that I am in no hurry to go up to London and get married. I love the country just now, and (*with a sigh*) after this morning, I'm—rather tired of husbands.

GEORGE (*in a rage*). I've never heard so much—damned nonsense in my life. I will leave you to come to your senses. (*He goes out indignantly.*)

(OLIVIA, *who has forgiven him already, throws a loving kiss after him, and then turns triumphantly to her dear curtains. She takes them, smiling, to the sofa, and has just got to work again, when* MR. PIM *appears at the open windows.*)

PIM (*in a whisper*). Er, may I come in, Mrs. Marden?

OLIVIA (*turning round in surprise*). Mr. Pim!

PIM (*anxiously*). Mr. Marden is—er—not here?

OLIVIA (*getting up*). Do you want to see him? I will tell him.

PIM. No, no, no! Not for the world! (*He comes in and looks anxiously at the door*) There is no immediate danger of his returning, Mrs. Marden?

OLIVIA (*surprised*). No, I don't think so. What is it? You——

PIM. I took the liberty of returning by the window in the hope of—er—coming upon you alone, Mrs. Marden.

OLIVIA. Yes?

PIM (*still rather nervous*). I—er—Mr. Marden will be very angry with me. Quite rightly. I blame myself entirely. I do not know how I can have been so stupid.

OLIVIA. What is it, Mr. Pim? Has my husband come to life again?

PIM. Mrs. Marden, I throw myself on your mercy entirely. The fact is—his name was Polwittle.

OLIVIA (*at a loss*). Whose? My husband's?

PIM. Yes, yes. The name came back to me suddenly, just as I reached the gate. Polwittle, poor fellow.

OLIVIA. But, Mr. Pim, my husband's name was Telworthy.

PIM. No, no, Polwittle.

OLIVIA. But, really I ought to . . .

PIM (*firmly*). Polwittle. It came back to me suddenly just as I reached the gate. For the moment, I had thoughts of conveying the news by letter. I was naturally disinclined to return in person, and—— Polwittle. (*Proudly*) If you remember, I always said it was a curious name.

OLIVIA. But who *is* Polwittle?

PIM (*in surprise at her stupidity*). The man I have been telling you about, who met with the sad fatality at Marseilles. Henry Polwittle—or was it Ernest? No, Henry, I think. Poor fellow.

OLIVIA (*indignantly*). But you said his name was Telworthy! How *could* you?

PIM. Yes, yes, I blame myself entirely.

OLIVIA. But how could you *think* of a name like Telworthy, if it wasn't Telworthy?

PIM (*eagerly*). Ah, that is the really interesting thing about the whole matter.

OLIVIA. Mr. Pim, all your visits here to-day have been interesting.

PIM. Yes, but you see, on my first appearance here this morning, I was received by—er—Miss Diana.

OLIVIA. Dinah.

PIM. Miss Dinah, yes. She was in—er—rather a communicative mood, and she happened to mention, by way of passing the time, that before your marriage to Mr. Marden you had been a Mrs.—er——

OLIVIA. Telworthy.

PIM. Yes, yes, Telworthy, of course. She mentioned also Australia. By some process of the brain—which strikes me as decidedly curious—when I was trying to recollect the name of the poor fellow on the boat, whom you remember I had also met in Australia, the fact that this other name was also stored in my memory, a name equally peculiar—this fact I say . . .

OLIVIA (*seeing that the sentence is rapidly going to pieces*). Yes, I understand.

PIM. I blame myself, I blame myself entirely.

OLIVIA. Oh, you mustn't do that, Mr. Pim. It was really Dinah's fault for inflicting all our family history on you.

PIM. Oh, but a charming young woman. I assure you I was very much interested in all that she told me. (*Getting up*) Well, Mrs.—er—Marden, I can only hope that you will forgive me for the needless distress I have caused you to-day.

OLIVIA. Oh, you mustn't worry about that—please.

PIM. And you will tell your husband—you will break the news to him?

OLIVIA (*smiling to herself*). I will—break the news to him.

PIM. You understand how it is that I thought it better to come to you in the first place?

OLIVIA. I am very glad you did.

PIM (*holding out his hand*). Then I will say good-bye, and—er——

OLIVIA. Just a moment, Mr. Pim. Let us have it quite clear this time. You never knew my husband, Jacob Telworthy, you never met him in Australia, you never saw him on the boat, and nothing whatever happened to him at Marseilles. Is that right?

PIM. Yes, yes, that is so.

OLIVIA. So that, since he was supposed to have died in Australia six years ago, he is presumably still dead?

PIM. Yes, yes, undoubtedly.

OLIVIA (*holding out her hand with a charming smile*). Then good-bye, Mr. Pim, and thank you so much for—for all your trouble.

PIM. Not at all, Mrs. Marden. I can only assure you I——

DINAH (*from the window*). Hullo, here's Mr. Pim! (*She comes in, followed by* BRIAN.)

PIM (*anxiously looking at the door in case* MR. MARDEN *should come in*). Yes, yes, I—er——

DINAH. Oh, Mr. Pim, you mustn't run away without even saying how do you do! Such old friends as we are. Why, it is ages since I saw you! Are you staying to tea?

PIM. I'm afraid I——

OLIVIA. Mr. Pim has to hurry away, Dinah. You mustn't keep him.

DINAH. Well, but you'll come back again?

PIM. I fear that I am only a passer-by, Miss—er—Dinah.

OLIVIA. You can walk with him to the gate, dear.

PIM (*gratefully to* OLIVIA). Thank you. (*He edges towards the window*) If you would be so kind, Miss Dinah——

BRIAN. I'll catch you up.

DINAH. Come along then, Mr. Pim. (*As they go out*) I want to hear all about your *first* wife. You haven't really told me anything yet. (OLIVIA *resumes her work, and* BRIAN *sits on the back of the sofa looking at her.*)

BRIAN (*awkwardly*). I just wanted to say, if you don't think it cheek, that I'm—I'm on your side, if I may be, and if I can help you at all I should be very proud of being allowed to.

OLIVIA (*looking up at him*). Brian, you dear. That's sweet of you. . . . But it's quite all right now, you know.

BRIAN. Oh, I'm so glad.

OLIVIA. Yes, that's what Mr. Pim came back to say. He'd made a mistake about the name. (*Smiling*) George is the only husband I have.

BRIAN (*surprised*). What? You mean that the whole thing—that Pim—— (*With conviction*) Silly ass!

OLIVIA (*kindly*). Oh, well, he didn't mean to be. (*After a pause*) Brian, do you know anything about the Law?

BRIAN. I'm afraid not. I hate the Law. Why?

OLIVIA (*casually*). Oh, I just—I was wondering—thinking about all the shocks we've been through to-day. Second marriages, and all that.

BRIAN. Oh! It's a rotten business.

OLIVIA. I suppose there's nothing wrong in getting married to the *same* person twice?

BRIAN. A hundred times if you like, I should think.

OLIVIA. Oh?

BRIAN. After all, in France, they always go through it twice, don't they? Once before the Mayor or somebody, and once in church.

OLIVIA. Of course they do! How silly of me. . . . I think it's rather a nice idea. They ought to do it in England more.

BRIAN. Well, once will be enough for Dinah and me, if you can work it. (*Anxiously*) D'you think there's any chance, Olivia?

OLIVIA (*smiling*). Every chance, dear.

BRIAN (*jumping up*). I say, do you really? Have you squared him? I mean, has he——

OLIVIA. Go and catch them up now. We'll talk about it later on.

BRIAN. Bless you. Righto.
(*As he goes out by the windows,* GEORGE *comes in at the door.* GEORGE *stands looking after him, and then turns to* OLIVIA, *who is absorbed in her curtains. He walks up and down the room, fidgeting with things, waiting for her to speak. As she says nothing, he begins to talk himself, but in an obviously unconcerned way. There is a pause after each answer of hers, before he gets out his next remark.*)

GEORGE (*casually*). Good-looking fellow, Strange.

OLIVIA (*equally casually*). Brian—yes, isn't he? And such a nice boy. . . .

GEORGE. Got fifty pounds for a picture the other day, didn't he? Hey?

OLIVIA. Yes. Of course he has only just begun. . . .

GEORGE. Critics think well of him, what?

OLIVIA. They all say he has genius. Oh, I don't think there's any doubt about it. . . .

GEORGE. Of course, I don't profess to know anything about painting.

OLIVIA. You've never had time to take it up, dear.

GEORGE. I know what I like, of course. Can't say I see much in this new-fangled stuff. If a man can paint, why can't he paint like —Rubens or—or Reynolds?

OLIVIA. I suppose we all have our own styles. Brian will find his directly. Of course, he's only just beginning. . . .

GEORGE. But they think a lot of him, what?

OLIVIA. Oh yes!

GEORGE. H'm! . . . Good-looking fellow.
(*There is rather a longer silence this time.* GEORGE *continues to hope that he is appearing casual and unconcerned. He stands looking at* OLIVIA'S *work for a moment.*)

GEORGE. Nearly finished 'em?

OLIVIA. Very nearly. Are my scissors there?

GEORGE (*looking round*). Scissors?

OLIVIA. Ah, here they are. . . .

GEORGE. Where are you going to put 'em?

OLIVIA (*as if really wondering*). I don't quite know. . . . I *had* thought of this room, but—I'm not quite sure.

GEORGE. Brighten the room up a bit.

OLIVIA. Yes. . . .

GEORGE (*walking over to the present curtains*). H'm. They *are* a bit faded.

OLIVIA (*shaking out hers, and looking at them critically*). Sometimes I think I love them, and sometimes I'm not quite sure.

GEORGE. Best way is to hang 'em up and see how you like 'em then. Always take 'em down again.

OLIVIA. That's rather a good idea, George!

GEORGE. Best way.

OLIVIA. Yes. . . . I think we might do that. . . . The only thing is—— (*she hesitates*).

GEORGE. What?

OLIVIA. Well, the carpet and the chairs, and the cushions and things——

GEORGE. What about 'em?

OLIVIA. Well, if we had new curtains——

GEORGE. You'd want a new carpet, eh?

OLIVIA (*doubtfully*). Y—yes. Well, new chair-covers anyhow.

GEORGE. H'm. . . . Well, why not?

OLIVIA. Oh, but——

GEORGE (*with an awkward laugh*). We're not so hard up as all that, you know.

OLIVIA. No, I suppose not. (*Thoughtfully*) I suppose it would mean that I should have to go up to London for them. That's rather a nuisance.

GEORGE (*extremely casual*). Oh, I don't know. We might go up together one day.

OLIVIA. Well, of course if we *were* up—for anything else—we could just look about us, and see if we could find what we want.

GEORGE. That's what I meant. (*There is another silence.* GEORGE *is wondering whether to come to closer quarters with the great question.*)

OLIVIA. Oh, by the way, George——

GEORGE. Yes?

OLIVIA (*innocently*). I told Brian, and I expect he'll tell Dinah, that Mr. Pim had made a mistake about the name.

GEORGE (*astonished*). You told Brian that Mr Pim——

OLIVIA. Yes—I told him that the whole thing was a mistake. It seemed the simplest way.

GEORGE. Olivia! Then you mean that Brian and Dinah think that —that we have been married all the time?

OLIVIA. Yes. . . . They both think so now.

GEORGE (*coming close to her*). Olivia, does that mean that you *are* thinking of marrying me?

OLIVIA. At your old Registry Office?

GEORGE (*eagerly*). Yes!

OLIVIA. Tomorrow?

GEORGE. Yes!

OLIVIA. Do you want me to *very* much?

GEORGE. My darling, you know I do!

OLIVIA (*a little apprehensive*). We should have to do it very quietly.

GEORGE. Of course, darling. Nobody need know at all. We don't *want* anybody to know. And now that you've put Brian and Dinah off the scent, by telling them that Mr. Pim made a mistake—— (*He breaks off, and says admiringly*) That was very clever of you, Olivia. I should never have thought of that.

OLIVIA (*innocently*). No, darling. . . . You don't think it was wrong, George?

GEORGE (*his verdict*). An innocent deception . . . perfectly harmless.

OLIVIA. Yes, dear, that was what I thought about—about what I was doing.

GEORGE. Then you will come to-morrow? (*She nods*) And if we happen to see the carpet, or anything that you want——

OLIVIA. Oh, what fun!

GEORGE (*beaming*). And a wedding lunch at the Carlton, what? (*She nods eagerly*) And—and a bit of a honeymoon in Paris?

OLIVIA. Oh, George!

GEORGE (*hungrily*). Give us a kiss, old girl.

OLIVIA (*lovingly*). George! (*She holds up her cheek to him. He kisses it, and then suddenly takes her in his arms.*)

GEORGE. Don't ever leave me, old girl.

OLIVIA (*affectionately*). Don't ever send me away, old boy.

GEORGE (*fervently*). I won't . . . (*Awkwardly*) I—I don't think I would have, you know. I—I——
(DINAH *and* BRIAN *appear at the windows, having seen* MR. PIM *safely off.*)

DINAH (*surprised*). Oo, I say! (GEORGE *hastily moves away.*)

GEORGE. Hallo!

DINAH (*going up impetuously to him*). Give *me* one, too, George; Brian won't mind.

BRIAN. Really, Dinah, you are the limit.

GEORGE (*formally, but enjoying it*). Do you mind, Mr. Strange?

BRIAN (*a little uncomfortably*). Oh, I say, sir——

GEORGE. We'll risk it, Dinah. (*He kisses her.*)

DINAH (*triumphantly to* BRIAN). Did you notice that one? That wasn't just an ordinary affectionate kiss. It was a special bless-you-my-children one. (*To* GEORGE) Wasn't it?

OLIVIA. You do talk nonsense, darling.

DINAH. Well, I'm so happy, now that Mr. Pim has relented about your first husband——
(GEORGE *catches* OLIVIA'S *eye and smiles; she smiles back; but they are different smiles.*)

GEORGE (*the actor*). Yes, yes, stupid fellow, Pim, what?

BRIAN. Absolute idiot.

DINAH. —And now that George has relented about *my* first husband.

GEORGE. You get on much too quickly, young woman. (*To* BRIAN) So you want to marry my Dinah, eh?

BRIAN (*with a smile*). Well, I do rather, sir.

DINAH (*hastily*). Not at once, of course, George. We want to be engaged for a long time first, and write letters to each other, and tell each other how much we love each other, and sit next to each other when we go out to dinner.

GEORGE (*to* OLIVIA). Well, *that* sounds fairly harmless, I think.

OLIVIA (*smiling*). I think so. . . .

GEORGE (*to* BRIAN). Then you'd better have a talk with me—er—Brian.

BRIAN. Thank you very much, sir.

GEORGE. Well, come along then. (*Looking at his watch*) I am going up to town after tea, so we'd better——

DINAH. I say! Are you going to London?

GEORGE (*with the smile of the conspirator*). A little business. Never you mind, young lady.

DINAH (*calmly*). All right. Only, bring me back something nice.

GEORGE (*to* BRIAN). Shall we walk down and look at the pigs?

BRIAN. Righto!

OLIVIA. Don't go far, dear. I may want you in a moment.

GEORGE. All right, darling, we'll be on the terrace. (*They go out together.*)

DINAH. Brian and George always try to discuss me in front of the pigs. So tactless of them. Are you going to London, too, darling?

OLIVIA. Tomorrow morning.

DINAH. What are you going to do in London?

OLIVIA. Oh, shopping, and—one or two little things.

DINAH. With George?

OLIVIA. Yes. . . .

DINAH. I say, wasn't it lovely about Pim?

OLIVIA. Lovely?

DINAH. Yes; he told me all about it. Making such a hash of things, I mean.

OLIVIA (*innocently*). Did he make a hash of things?

DINAH. Well, I mean keeping on coming like that. And if you look at it all round—well, for all he had to say, he needn't really have come at all.

OLIVIA (*smiling to herself*). I shouldn't quite say that, Dinah. (*She stands up and shakes out the curtains.*)

DINAH. I say, aren't they jolly?

OLIVIA (*demurely*). I'm so glad everybody likes them. Tell George I'm ready, will you?

DINAH. I say, is *he* going to hang them up for you?

OLIVIA. Well, I thought he could reach best.

DINAH. Righto! What fun! (*At the windows*) George! George! (*To* OLIVIA) Brian is just telling George about the five shillings he's got in the Post Office. . . . George!

GEORGE (*from the terrace*). Coming! (*He hurries in, the model husband.* BRIAN *follows.*)

OLIVIA. Oh, George, just hang these up for me, will you?

GEORGE. Of course, darling. I'll get the steps from the library. (*He hurries out.* BRIAN *takes out his sketching block. It is obvious that his five shillings has turned the scale. He bows to* DINAH. *He kisses* OLIVIA'S *hand with an air. He motions to* DINAH *to be seated.*)

DINAH (*impressed*). What is it?

BRIAN (*beginning to draw*). Portrait of Lady Strange.

(GEORGE *hurries in with the steps, and gets to work. There is a great deal of curtain, and for the moment he becomes slightly involved in it. However, by draping it over his head and shoulders, he manages to get successfully up the steps. There we may leave him. But we have not quite finished with* MR. PIM. *It is a matter of honour with him now that he should get his little story quite accurate before passing out of the* MARDENS' *life for ever. So he comes back for the last time; for the last time we see his head at the window. He whispers to* OLIVIA.)

MR. PIM. Mrs. Marden! I've just remembered. His name was *Ernest* Polwittle—*not* Henry. (*He goes off happily. A curious family the* MARDENS. *Perhaps somebody else would have committed bigamy if he had not remembered in time that it was Ernest. . . . Ernest. . . . Yes. . . . Now he can go back with an easy conscience to the Trevors.*)

The Circle

BY W. SOMERSET MAUGHAM

The Circle was first produced in America at the Selwyn Theatre, New York City, by The Selwyns on September 12, 1921, and closed on February 4, 1922. The following is the original cast:

ARNOLD CHAMPION-CHENEY, M. P.	Robert Rendel
FOOTMAN	Charles L. Sealy
MRS. SHENSTONE	Maxine MacDonald
ELIZABETH	Estelle Winwood
EDWARD LUTON	John Halliday
CLIVE CHAMPION-CHENEY	Ernest Lawford
BUTLER	Walter Soderling
LORD PORTEOUS	John Drew
LADY CATHERINE CHAMPION-CHENEY	Mrs. Leslie Carter

THE CIRCLE

ACT ONE

The Scene is a stately drawing-room at Aston-Adey, with fine pictures on the walls and Georgian furniture. Aston-Adey has been described, with many illustrations, in Country Life. *It is not a house, but a place. Its owner takes a great pride in it, and there is nothing in the room which is not of the period. Through the French windows at the back can be seen the beautiful gardens which are one of the features.*

It is a fine summer morning.

ARNOLD *comes in. He is a man of about thirty-five, tall and good-looking, fair, with a clean-cut, sensitive face. He has a look that is intellectual, but somewhat bloodless. He is very well dressed.*

ARNOLD (*calling*). Elizabeth! (*He goes to the window and calls again*) Elizabeth! (*He rings the bell. While he is waiting he gives a look round the room. He slightly alters the position of one of the chairs. He takes an ornament from the chimney-piece and blows the dust from it. A* FOOTMAN *comes in*) Oh, George! see if you can find Mrs. Cheney, and ask her if she'd be good enough to come here.

FOOTMAN. Very good, sir. (*The* FOOTMAN *turns to go.*)

ARNOLD. Who is supposed to look after this room?

FOOTMAN. I don't know, sir.

ARNOLD. I wish when they dust they'd take care to replace the things exactly as they were before.

FOOTMAN. Yes, sir.

ARNOLD (*dismissing him*). All right. (*The* FOOTMAN *goes out. He goes again to the window and calls.*)

ARNOLD. Elizabeth! (*He sees* MRS. SHENSTONE) Oh, Anna, do you know where Elizabeth is?

(MRS. SHENSTONE *comes in from the garden. She is a woman of forty, pleasant and of elegant appearance.*)

ANNA. Isn't she playing tennis?

ARNOLD. No, I've been down to the tennis court. Something very tiresome has happened.

ANNA. Oh?

ARNOLD. I wonder where the deuce she is.

ANNA. When do you expect Lord Porteous and Lady Kitty?

ARNOLD. They're motoring down in time for luncheon.

ANNA. Are you sure you want me to be here? It's not too late yet, you know. I can have my things packed and catch a train for somewhere or other.

ARNOLD. No, of course we want you. It'll make it so much easier if there are people here. It was exceedingly kind of you to come.

ANNA. Oh, nonsense!

ARNOLD. And I think it was a good thing to have Teddie Luton down.

ANNA. He is so breezy, isn't he?

ARNOLD. Yes, that's his great asset. I don't know that he's very intelligent, but, you know, there are occasions when you want a bull in a china shop. I sent one of the servants to find Elizabeth.

ANNA. I daresay she's putting on her shoes. She and Teddie were going to have a single.

ARNOLD. It can't take all this time to change one's shoes.

ANNA (*with a smile*). One can't change one's shoes without powdering one's nose, you know.
(ELIZABETH *comes in. She is a very pretty creature in the early twenties. She wears a light summer frock.*)

ARNOLD. My dear, I've been hunting for you everywhere. What *have* you been doing?

ELIZABETH. Nothing! I've been standing on my head.

ARNOLD. My father's here.

ELIZABETH (*startled*). Where?

ARNOLD. At the cottage. He arrived last night.

ELIZABETH. Damn!

ARNOLD (*good-humouredly*). I wish you wouldn't say that, Elizabeth.

ELIZABETH. If you're not going to say "Damn" when a thing's damnable, when are you going to say "Damn"?

ARNOLD. I should have thought you could say, "Oh, bother!" or something like that.

ELIZABETH. But that wouldn't express my sentiments. Besides, at that speech day when you were giving away the prizes you said there were no synonyms in the English language.

ANNA (*smiling*). Oh, Elizabeth! it's very unfair to expect a politician to live in private up to the statements he makes in public.

ARNOLD. I'm always willing to stand by anything I've said. There *are* no synonyms in the English language.

ELIZABETH. In that case I shall be regretfully forced to continue to say "Damn" whenever I feel like it.
(EDWARD LUTON *shows himself at the window. He is an attractive youth in flannels.*)

TEDDIE. I say, what about this tennis?

ELIZABETH. Come in. We're having a scene.

TEDDIE (*entering*). How splendid! What about?

ELIZABETH. The English language.

TEDDIE. Don't tell me you've been splitting your infinitives.

ARNOLD (*with the shadow of a frown*). I wish you'd be serious, Elizabeth. The situation is none too pleasant.

ANNA. I think Teddie and I had better make ourselves scarce.

ELIZABETH. Nonsense! You're both in it. If there's going to be any unpleasantness we want your moral support. That's why we asked you to come.

TEDDY. And I thought I'd been asked for my blue eyes.

ELIZABETH. Vain beast! And they happen to be brown.

TEDDIE. Is anything up?

ELIZABETH. Arnold's father arrived last night.

TEDDIE. Did he, by Jove! I thought he was in Paris.

ARNOLD. So did we all. He told me he'd be there for the next month.

ANNA. Have you seen him?

ARNOLD. No! he rang me up. It's a mercy he had a telephone put in the cottage. It would have been a pretty kettle of fish if he'd just walked in.

ELIZABETH. Did you tell him Lady Catherine was coming?

ARNOLD. Of course not. I was flabbergasted to know he was here. And then I thought we'd better talk it over first.

ELIZABETH. Is he coming along here?

ARNOLD. Yes. He suggested it, and I couldn't think of any excuse to prevent him.

TEDDIE. Couldn't you put the other people off?

ARNOLD. They're coming by car. They may be here any minute. It's too late to do that.

ELIZABETH. Besides, it would be beastly.

ARNOLD. I knew it was silly to have them here. Elizabeth insisted.

ELIZABETH. After all, she *is* your mother, Arnold.

ARNOLD. That meant precious little to her when she—went away. You can't imagine it means very much to me now.

ELIZABETH. It's thirty years ago. It seems so absurd to bear malice after all that time.

ARNOLD. I don't bear malice, but the fact remains that she did me the most irreparable harm. I can find no excuse for her.

ELIZABETH. Have you ever tried to?

ARNOLD. My dear Elizabeth, it's no good going over all that again. The facts are lamentably simple. She had a husband who adored her, a wonderful position, all the money she could want, and a child of five. And she ran away with a married man.

ELIZABETH. Lady Porteous is not a very attractive woman, Arnold. (*To* ANNA) Do you know her?

ANNA (*smiling*). "Forbidding" is the word, I think.

ARNOLD. If you're going to make little jokes about it, I have nothing more to say.

ANNA. I'm sorry, Arnold.

ELIZABETH. Perhaps your mother couldn't help herself—if she was in love?

ARNOLD. And had no sense of honour, duty, or decency? Oh, yes, under those circumstances you can explain a great deal.

ELIZABETH. That's not a very pretty way to speak of your mother.

ARNOLD. I can't look on her as my mother.

ELIZABETH. What you can't get over is that she didn't think of you. Some of us are more mother and some of us more woman. It gives me a little thrill when I think that she loved that man so much. She sacrificed her name, her position, and her child to him.

ARNOLD. You really can't expect the said child to have any great affection for the mother who treated him like that.

ELIZABETH. No, I don't think I do. But I think it's a pity after all these years that you shouldn't be friends.

ARNOLD. I wonder if you realise what it was to grow up under the shadow of that horrible scandal. Everywhere, at school, and at Oxford, and afterwards in London, I was always the son of Lady Kitty Cheney. Oh, it was cruel, cruel!

ELIZABETH. Yes, I know, Arnold. It was beastly for you.

ARNOLD. It would have been bad enough if it had been an ordinary case, but the position of the people made it ten times worse. My father was in the House then, and Porteous—he hadn't succeeded to the title—was in the House too; he was Under-Secretary for Foreign Affairs, and he was very much in the public eye.

ANNA. My father always used to say he was the ablest man in the party. Every one was expecting him to be Prime Minister.

ARNOLD. You can imagine what a boon it was to the British public. They hadn't had such a treat for a generation. The most popular song of the day was about my mother. Did you ever hear it? "Naughty Lady Kitty. Thought it such a pity . . ."

ELIZABETH (*interrupting*). Oh, Arnold, don't!

ARNOLD. And then they never let people forget them. If they'd lived quietly in Florence and not made a fuss the scandal would have died down. But those constant actions between Lord and Lady Porteous kept on reminding everyone.

TEDDIE. What were they having actions about?

ARNOLD. Of course my father divorced his wife, but Lady Porteous refused to divorce Porteous. He tried to force her by refusing to support her and turning her out of her house, and heaven knows what. They were constantly wrangling in the law courts.

ANNA. I think it was monstrous of Lady Porteous.

ARNOLD. She knew he wanted to marry my mother, and she hated my mother. You can't blame her.

ANNA. It must have been very difficult for them.

ARNOLD. That's why they've lived in Florence. Porteous has money. They found people there who were willing to accept the situation.

ELIZABETH. This is the first time they've ever come to England.

ARNOLD. My father will have to be told, Elizabeth.

ELIZABETH. Yes.

ANNA (*to* ELIZABETH). Has he ever spoken to you about Lady Kitty?

ELIZABETH. Never.

ARNOLD. I don't think her name has passed his lips since she ran away from this house thirty years ago.

TEDDIE. Oh, they lived here?

ARNOLD. Naturally. There was a house-party, and one evening neither Porteous nor my mother came down to dinner. The rest of them waited. They couldn't make it out. My father sent up to my mother's room, and a note was found on the pin-cushion.

ELIZABETH (*with a faint smile*). That's what they did in the Dark Ages.

ARNOLD. I think he took a dislike to this house from that horrible night. He never lived here again, and when I married he handed the place over to me. He just has a cottage now on the estate that he comes to when he feels inclined.

ELIZABETH. It's been very nice for us.

ARNOLD. I owe everything to my father. I don't think he'll ever forgive me for asking these people to come here.

ELIZABETH. I'm going to take all the blame on myself, Arnold.

ARNOLD (*irritably*). The situation was embarrassing enough anyhow. I don't know how I ought to treat them.

ELIZABETH. Don't you think that'll settle itself when you see them?

ARNOLD. After all, they're my guests. I shall try and behave like a gentleman.

ELIZABETH. I wouldn't. We haven't got central heating.

ARNOLD (*taking no notice*). Will she expect me to kiss her?

ELIZABETH (*with a smile*). Surely.

ARNOLD. It always makes me uncomfortable when people are effusive.

ANNA. But I can't understand why you never saw her before.

ARNOLD. I believe she tried to see me when I was little, but my father thought it better she shouldn't.

ANNA. Yes, but when you were grown up?

ARNOLD. She was always in Italy. I never went to Italy.

ELIZABETH. It seems to me so pathetic that if you saw one another in the street you wouldn't recognise each other.

ARNOLD. Is it my fault?

ELIZABETH. You've promised to be very gentle with her and very kind.

ARNOLD. The mistake was asking Porteous to come too. It looks as though we condoned the whole thing. And how am I to treat him? Am I to shake him by the hand and slap him on the back? He absolutely ruined my father's life.

ELIZABETH (*smiling*). How much would you give for a nice motor accident that prevented them from coming?

ARNOLD. I let you persuade me against my better judgment, and I've regretted it ever since.

ELIZABETH (*good-humouredly*). I think it's very lucky that Anna and Teddie are here. I don't foresee a very successful party.

ARNOLD. I'm going to do my best. I gave you my promise and I shall keep it. But I can't answer for my father.

ANNA. Here is your father.
(MR. CHAMPION-CHENEY *shows himself at one of the French windows.*)

C.-C. May I come in through the window, or shall I have myself announced by a supercilious flunkey?

ELIZABETH. Come in. We've been expecting you.

C.-C. Impatiently, I hope, my dear child. (MR. CHAMPION-CHENEY *is a tall man in the early sixties, spare, with a fine head of gray hair and an intelligent, somewhat ascetic face. He is very carefully dressed. He is a man who makes the most of himself. He bears his years jauntily. He kisses* ELIZABETH *and then holds out his hand to* ARNOLD.)

ELIZABETH. We thought you'd be in Paris for another month.

C.-C. How are you, Arnold? I always reserve to myself the privilege of changing my mind. It's the only one elderly gentlemen share with pretty women.

ELIZABETH. You know Anna.

C.-C. (*shaking hands with her*). Of course I do. How very nice to see you here! Are you staying long?

ANNA. As long as I'm welcome.

ELIZABETH. And this is Mr. Luton.

C.-C. How do you do? Do you play bridge?

LUTON. I do.

C.-C. Capital. Do you declare without top honours?

LUTON. Never.

C.-C. Of such is the kingdom of heaven. I see that you are a good young man.

LUTON. But, like the good in general, I am poor.

C.-C. Never mind; if your principles are right, you can play ten shillings a hundred without danger. I never play less, and I never play more.

ARNOLD. And you—are you going to stay long, father?

C.-C. To luncheon, if you'll have me.
(ARNOLD *gives* ELIZABETH *a harassed look.*)

ELIZABETH. That'll be jolly.

ARNOLD. I didn't mean that. Of course you're going to stay for luncheon. I meant, how long are you going to stay down here?

C.-C. A week.
(*There is a moment's pause. Everyone but* CHAMPION-CHENEY *is slightly embarrassed.*)

TEDDIE. I think we'd better chuck our tennis.

ELIZABETH. Yes. I want my father-in-law to tell me what they're wearing in Paris this week.

TEDDIE. I'll go and put the rackets away. (TEDDIE *goes out.*)

ARNOLD. It's nearly one o'clock, Elizabeth.

ELIZABETH. I didn't know it was so late.

ANNA (*to* ARNOLD). I wonder if I can persuade you to take a turn in the garden before luncheon.

ARNOLD (*jumping at the idea*). I'd love it. (ANNA *goes out of the window, and as he follows her he stops irresolutely*) I want you to look at this chair I've just got. I think it's rather good.

C.-C. Charming.

ARNOLD. About 1750, I should say. Good design, isn't it? It hasn't been restored or anything.

C.-C. Very pretty.

ARNOLD. I think it was a good buy, don't you?

C.-C. Oh, my dear boy! you know I'm entirely ignorant about these things.

ARNOLD. It's exactly my period . . . I shall see you at luncheon, then. (*He follows* ANNA *through the window.*)

C.-C. Who is that young man?

ELIZABETH. Mr. Luton. He's only just been demobilised. He's the manager of a rubber estate in the F.M.S.

C.-C. And what are the F.M.S. when they're at home?

ELIZABETH. The Federated Malay States. He joined up at the beginning of the war. He's just going back there.

C.-C. And why have we been left alone in this very marked manner?

ELIZABETH. Have we? I didn't notice it.

C.-C. I suppose it's difficult for the young to realise that one may be old without being a fool.

ELIZABETH. I never thought you that. Everyone knows you're very intelligent.

C.-C. They certainly ought to by now. I've told them often enough. Are you a little nervous?

ELIZABETH. Let me feel my pulse. (*She puts her finger on her wrist*) It's perfectly regular.

C.-C. When I suggested staying to luncheon Arnold looked exactly like a dose of castor oil.

ELIZABETH. I wish you'd sit down.

C.-C. Will it make it easier for you? (*He takes a chair*) You have evidently something very disagreeable to say to me.

ELIZABETH. You won't be cross with me?

C.-C. How old are you?

ELIZABETH. Twenty-five.

C.-C. I'm never cross with a woman under thirty.

ELIZABETH. Oh, then I've got ten years.

C.-C. Mathematics?

ELIZABETH. No. Paint.

C.-C. Well?

ELIZABETH (*reflectively*). I think it would be easier if I sat on your knees.

C.-C. That is a pleasing taste of yours, but you must take care not to put on weight.
(*She sits down on his knees.*)

ELIZABETH. Am I bony?

C.-C. On the contrary. . . . I'm listening.

ELIZABETH. Lady Catherine's coming here.

C.-C. Who's Lady Catherine?

ELIZABETH. Your—Arnold's mother.

C.-C. Is she? (*He withdraws himself a little and* ELIZABETH *gets up.*)

ELIZABETH. You mustn't blame Arnold. It's my fault. I insisted. He was against it. I nagged him till he gave way. And then I wrote and asked her to come.

C.-C. I didn't know you knew her.

ELIZABETH. I don't. But I heard she was in London. She's staying at Claridge's. It seemed so heartless not to take the smallest notice of her.

C.-C. When is she coming?

ELIZABETH. We're expecting her in time for luncheon.

C.-C. As soon as that? I understand the embarrassment.

ELIZABETH. You see, we never expected you to be here. You said you'd be in Paris for another month.

C.-C. My dear child, this is your house. There's no reason why you shouldn't ask whom you please to stay with you.

ELIZABETH. After all, whatever her faults, she's Arnold's mother. It seemed so unnatural that they should never see one another. My heart ached for that poor lonely woman.

C.-C. I never heard that she was lonely, and she certainly isn't poor.

ELIZABETH. And there's something else. I couldn't ask her by herself. It would have been so—so insulting. I asked Lord Porteous, too.

C.-C. I see.

ELIZABETH. I daresay you'd rather not meet them.

C.-C. I daresay they'd rather not meet me. I shall get a capital luncheon at the cottage. I've noticed you always get the best food if you come in unexpectedly and have the same as they're having in the servants' hall.

ELIZABETH. No one's ever talked to me about Lady Kitty. It's always been a subject that everyone has avoided. I've never even seen a photograph of her.

C.-C. The house was full of them when she left. I think I told the butler to throw them in the dustbin. She was very much photographed.

ELIZABETH. Won't you tell me what she was like?

C.-C. She was very like you, Elizabeth, only she had dark hair instead of red.

ELIZABETH. Poor dear! it must be quite white now.

C.-C. I daresay. She was a pretty little thing.

ELIZABETH. But she was one of the great beauties of her day. They say she was lovely.

C.-C. She had the most adorable little nose, like yours. . . .

ELIZABETH. D'you like my nose?

C.-C. And she was very dainty, with a beautiful little figure; very light on her feet. She was like a *marquise* in an old French comedy. Yes, she was lovely.

ELIZABETH. And I'm sure she's lovely still.

C.-C. She's no chicken, you know.

ELIZABETH. You can't expect me to look at it as you and Arnold do. When you've loved as she's loved you may grow old, but you grow old beautifully.

C.-C. You're very romantic.

ELIZABETH. If everyone hadn't made such a mystery of it I daresay I shouldn't feel as I do. I know she did a great wrong to you and a great wrong to Arnold. I'm willing to acknowledge that.

C.-C. I'm sure it's very kind of you.

ELIZABETH. But she loved and she dared. Romance is such an illusive thing. You read of it in books, but it's seldom you see it face to face. I can't help it if it thrills me.

C.-C. I am painfully aware that the husband in these cases is not a romantic object.

ELIZABETH. She had the world at her feet. You were rich. She was a figure in society. And she gave up everything for love.

C.-C. (*dryly*). I'm beginning to suspect it wasn't only for her sake and for Arnold's that you asked her to come here.

ELIZABETH. I seem to know her already. I think her face is a little sad, for a love like that doesn't leave you gay, it leaves you grave, but I think her pale face is unlined. It's like a child's.

C.-C. My dear, how you let your imagination run away with you!

ELIZABETH. I imagine her slight and frail.

C.-C. Frail, certainly.

ELIZABETH. With beautiful thin hands and white hair. I've pictured her so often in that Renaissance Palace that they live in, with old Masters on the walls and lovely carved things all round, sitting in a black silk dress with old lace round her neck and old-fashioned diamonds. You see, I never knew my mother; she died when I was a baby. You can't confide in aunts with huge families of their own. I want Arnold's mother to be a mother to me. I've got so much to say to her.

C.-C. Are you happy with Arnold?

ELIZABETH. Why shouldn't I be?

C.-C. Why haven't you got any babies?

ELIZABETH. Give us a little time. We've only been married three years.

C.-C. I wonder what Hughie is like now!

ELIZABETH. Lord Porteous?

C.-C. He wore his clothes better than any man in London. You know he'd have been Prime Minister if he'd remained in politics.

ELIZABETH. What was he like then?

C.-C. He was a nice-looking fellow. Fine horseman. I suppose there was something very fascinating about him. Yellow hair and blue eyes, you know. He had a very good figure. I liked him. I was his parliamentary secretary. He was Arnold's godfather.

ELIZABETH. I know.

C.-C. I wonder if he ever regrets!

ELIZABETH. I wouldn't.

C.-C. Well, I must be strolling back to my cottage.

ELIZABETH. You're not angry with me?

C.-C. Not a bit.

(*She puts up her face for him to kiss. He kisses her on both cheeks and then goes out. In a moment* TEDDIE *is seen at the window.*)

TEDDIE. I saw the old blighter go.

ELIZABETH. Come in.

TEDDIE. Everything all right?

ELIZABETH. Oh, quite, as far as he's concerned. He's going to keep out of the way.

TEDDIE. Was it beastly?

ELIZABETH. No, he made it very easy for me. He's a nice old thing.

TEDDIE. You were rather scared.

ELIZABETH. A little. I am still. I don't know why.

TEDDIE. I guessed you were. I thought I'd come and give you a little moral support. It's ripping here, isn't it?

ELIZABETH. It is rather nice.

TEDDIE. It'll be jolly to think of it when I'm back in the F.M.S.

ELIZABETH. Aren't you homesick sometimes?

TEDDIE. Oh, everyone is now and then, you know.

ELIZABETH. You could have got a job in England if you'd wanted to, couldn't you?

TEDDIE. Oh, but I love it out there. England's ripping to come back to, but I couldn't live here now. It's like a woman you're desperately in love with as long as you don't see her, but when you're with her she maddens you so that you can't bear her.

ELIZABETH (*smiling*). What's wrong with England?

TEDDIE. I don't think anything's wrong with England. I expect something's wrong with me. I've been away too long. England seems to me full of people doing things they don't want to because other people expect it of them.

ELIZABETH. Isn't that what you call a high degree of civilisation?

TEDDIE. People seem to me so insincere. When you go to parties in London they're all babbling about art, and you feel that in their hearts they don't care twopence about it. They read the books that everybody is talking about because they don't want to be out of it. In the F.M.S. we don't get very many books, and we read those we have over and over again. They mean so much to us. I don't think the people over there are half so clever as the people at home, but one gets to know them better. You see, there are so few of us that we have to make the best of one another.

ELIZABETH. I imagine that frills are not much worn in the F.M.S. It must be a comfort.

TEDDIE. It's not much good being pretentious where everyone knows exactly who you are and what your income is.

ELIZABETH. I don't think you want too much sincerity in society. It would be like an iron girder in a house of cards.

TEDDIE. And then, you know, the place is ripping. You get used to a blue sky and you miss it in England.

ELIZABETH. What do you do with yourself all the time?

TEDDIE. Oh, one works like blazes. You have to be a pretty hefty fellow to be a planter. And then there's ripping bathing. You know, it's lovely, with palm trees all along the beach. And there's shooting. And now and then we have a little dance to a gramophone.

ELIZABETH (*pretending to tease him*). I think you've got a young woman out there, Teddie.

TEDDIE (*vehemently*). Oh, no!
(*She is a little taken aback by the earnestness of his disclaimer. There is a moment's silence, then she recovers herself.*)

ELIZABETH. But you'll have to marry and settle down one of these days, you know.

TEDDIE. I want to, but it's not a thing you can do lightly.

ELIZABETH. I don't know why there more than elsewhere.

TEDDIE. In England if people don't get on they go their own ways and jog along after a fashion. In a place like that you're thrown a great deal on your own resources.

ELIZABETH. Of course.

TEDDIE. Lots of girls come out because they think they're going to have a good time. But if they're empty-headed, then they're just faced with their own emptiness and they're done. If their husbands can afford it they go home and settle down as grass-widows.

ELIZABETH. I've met them. They seem to find it a very pleasant occupation.

TEDDIE. It's rotten for their husbands, though.

ELIZABETH. And if the husbands can't afford it?

TEDDIE. Oh, then they tipple.

ELIZABETH. It's not a very alluring prospect.

TEDDIE. But if the woman's the right sort she wouldn't exchange it for any life in the world. When all's said and done it's we who've made the Empire.

ELIZABETH. What sort is the right sort?

TEDDIE. A woman of courage and endurance and sincerity. Of course, it's hopeless unless she's in love with her husband.
(*He is looking at her earnestly and she, raising her eyes, gives him a long look. There is silence between them.*)

TEDDIE. My house stands on the side of a hill, and the cocoanut trees wind down to the shore. Azaleas grow in my garden, and camellias, and all sorts of ripping flowers. And in front of me is the winding coast line, and then the blue sea. (*A pause*) Do you know that I'm awfully in love with you?

ELIZABETH (*gravely*). I wasn't quite sure. I wondered.

TEDDIE. And you? (*She nods slowly*) I've never kissed you.

ELIZABETH. I don't want you to.
(*They look at one another steadily. They are both grave.* ARNOLD *comes in hurriedly.*)

ARNOLD. They're coming, Elizabeth.

ELIZABETH (*as though returning from a distant world*). Who?

ARNOLD (*impatiently*). My dear! My mother, of course. The car is just coming up the drive.

TEDDIE. Would you like me to clear out?

ARNOLD. No, no! For goodness' sake stay.

ELIZABETH. We'd better go and meet them, Arnold.

ARNOLD. No, no; I think they'd much better be shown in. I feel simply sick with nervousness.
(ANNA *comes in from the garden.*)

ANNA. Your guests have arrived.

ELIZABETH. Yes, I know.

ARNOLD. I've given orders that luncheon should be served at once.

ELIZABETH. Why? It's not half-past one already, is it?

ARNOLD. I thought it would help. When you don't know exactly what to say you can always eat.
(*The* BUTLER *comes in and announces.*)

BUTLER. Lady Catherine Champion-Cheney! Lord Porteous!
(LADY KITTY *comes in followed by* PORTEOUS, *and the* BUTLER *goes out.* LADY KITTY *is a gay little lady, with dyed red hair and painted cheeks. She is somewhat outrageously dressed. She never forgets that she has been a pretty woman and she still behaves as if she were twenty-five.* LORD PORTEOUS *is a very bald, elderly gentleman in loose, rather eccentric clothes. He is snappy and gruff. This is not at all the couple that Elizabeth expected, and for a moment she stares at them with round, startled eyes.* LADY KITTY *goes up to her with outstretched hands.*)

LADY KITTY. Elizabeth! Elizabeth! (*She kisses her effusively*) What an adorable creature! (*Turning to* PORTEOUS) Hughie, isn't she adorable?

PORTEOUS (*with a grunt*). Ugh!
(ELIZABETH, *smiling now, turns to him and gives him her hand.*)

ELIZABETH. How d'you do?

PORTEOUS. Damnable road you've got down here. How d'you do, my dear? Why d'you have such damnable roads in England?
(LADY KITTY'S *eyes fall on* TEDDIE *and she goes up to him with her arms thrown back, prepared to throw them round him.*)

LADY KITTY. My boy, my boy! I should have known you anywhere!

ELIZABETH (*hastily*). That's Arnold.

LADY KITTY (*without a moment's hesitation*). The image of his father! I should have known him anywhere! (*She throws her arms round his neck*) My boy, my boy!

PORTEOUS (*with a grunt*). Ugh!

LADY KITTY. Tell me, would you have known me again? Have I changed?

ARNOLD. I was only five, you know, when—when you . . .

LADY KITTY (*emotionally*). I remember as if it was yesterday. I went up into your room. (*With a sudden change of manner*) By the way, I always thought that nurse drank. Did you ever find out if she really did?

PORTEOUS. How the devil can you expect him to know that, Kitty?

LADY KITTY. You've never had a child, Hughie; how can you tell what they know and what they don't?

ELIZABETH (*coming to the rescue*). This is Arnold, Lord Porteous.

PORTEOUS (*shaking hands with him*). How d'you do? I knew your father.

ARNOLD. Yes.

PORTEOUS. Alive still?

ARNOLD. Yes.

PORTEOUS. He must be getting on. Is he well?

ARNOLD. Very.

PORTEOUS. Ugh! Takes care of himself, I suppose. I'm not at all well. This damned climate doesn't agree with me.

ELIZABETH (*to* LADY KITTY). This is Mrs. Shenstone. And this is Mr. Luton. I hope you don't mind a very small party.

LADY KITTY (*shaking hands with* ANNA *and* TEDDIE). Oh, no, I shall enjoy it. I used to give enormous parties here. Political, you know. How nice you've made this room!

ELIZABETH. Oh, that's Arnold.

ARNOLD (*nervously*). D'you like this chair? I've just bought it. It's exactly my period.

PORTEOUS (*bluntly*). It's a fake.

ARNOLD (*indignantly*). I don't think it is for a minute.

PORTEOUS. The legs are not right.

ARNOLD. I don't know how you can say that. If there is anything right about it, it's the legs.

LADY KITTY. I'm sure they're right.

PORTEOUS. You know nothing whatever about it, Kitty.

LADY KITTY. That's what you think. *I* think it's a beautiful chair. Hepplewhite?

ARNOLD. No, Sheraton.

LADY KITTY. Oh, I know. "The School for Scandal."

PORTEOUS. Sheraton, my dear. Sheraton.

LADY KITTY. Yes, that's what I say. I acted the screen scene at some amateur theatricals in Florence, and Ermeto Novelli, the great Italian tragedian, told me he'd never seen a Lady Teazle like me.

PORTEOUS. Ugh!

LADY KITTY (*to* ELIZABETH). Do you act?

ELIZABETH. Oh, I couldn't. I should be too nervous.

LADY KITTY. I'm never nervous. I'm a born actress. Of course, if I had my time over again I'd go on the stage. You know, it's extraordinary how they keep young. Actresses, I mean. I think it's because they're always playing different parts. Hughie, do you think Arnold takes after me or after his father? Of course I think he's the very image of me. Arnold, I think I ought to tell you that I was received into the Catholic Church last winter. I'd been thinking about it for years, and last time we were at Monte Carlo I met such a nice monsignore. I told him what my difficulties were and he was too wonderful. I knew Hughie wouldn't approve, so I kept it a secret. (*To* ELIZABETH) Are you interested in religion? I think it's too wonderful. We must have a long talk about it one of these days. (*Pointing to her frock*) Callot?

ELIZABETH. No, Worth.

LADY KITTY. I knew it was either Worth or Callot. Of course, it's line that's the important thing. I go to Worth myself, and I always say to him, "Line, my dear Worth, line." What *is* the matter, Hughie?

PORTEOUS. These new teeth of mine are so damned uncomfortable.

LADY KITTY. Men are extraordinary. They can't stand the smallest discomfort. Why, a woman's life is uncomfortable from the moment she gets up in the morning till the moment she goes to bed at night. And d'you think it's comfortable to sleep with a mask on your face?

PORTEOUS. They don't seem to hold up properly.

LADY KITTY. Well, that's not the fault of your teeth. That's the fault of your gums.

PORTEOUS. Damned rotten dentist. That's what's the matter.

LADY KITTY. I thought he was a very nice dentist. He told me *my* teeth would last till I was fifty. He has a Chinese room. It's so interesting; while he scrapes your teeth he tells you all about the dear Empress Dowager. Are you interested in China? I think it's too wonderful. You know they've cut off their pigtails. I think it's such a pity. They were so picturesque. (*The* BUTLER *comes in.*)

BUTLER. Luncheon is served, sir.

ELIZABETH. Would you like to see your rooms?

PORTEOUS. We can see our rooms after luncheon.

LADY KITTY. I must powder my nose, Hughie.

PORTEOUS. Powder it down here.

LADY KITTY. I never saw anyone so inconsiderate.

PORTEOUS. You'll keep us all waiting half an hour. I know you.

LADY KITTY (*fumbling in her bag*). Oh, well, peace at any price, as Lord Beaconsfield said.

PORTEOUS. He said a lot of damned silly things, Kitty, but he never said that.

(LADY KITTY'S *face changes. Perplexity is followed by dismay, and dismay by consternation.*)

LADY KITTY. Oh!

ELIZABETH. What is the matter?

LADY KITTY (*with anguish*). My lip-stick!

ELIZABETH. Can't you find it?

LADY KITTY. I had it in the car. Hughie, you remember that I had it in the car.

PORTEOUS. I don't remember anything about it.

LADY KITTY. Don't be so stupid, Hughie. Why, when we came through the gates I said: "My home, my home!" and I took it out and put some on my lips.

ELIZABETH. Perhaps you dropped it in the car.

LADY KITTY. For heaven's sake send some one to look for it.

ARNOLD. I'll ring.

LADY KITTY. I'm absolutely lost without my lip-stick. Lend me yours, darling, will you?

ELIZABETH. I'm awfully sorry. I'm afraid I haven't got one.

LADY KITTY. Do you mean to say you don't use a lip-stick?

ELIZABETH. Never.

PORTEOUS. Look at her lips. What the devil d'you think she wants muck like that for?

LADY KITTY. Oh, my dear, what a mistake you make! You *must* use a lip-stick. It's so good for the lips. Men like it, you know. I couldn't *live* without a lip-stick.
(CHAMPION-CHENEY *appears at the window holding in his upstretched hand a little gold case.*)

C.-C. (*as he comes in*). Has anyone here lost a diminutive utensil containing, unless I am mistaken, a favourite preparation for the toilet?
(ARNOLD *and* ELIZABETH *are thunderstruck at his appearance and even* TEDDIE *and* ANNA *are taken aback. But* LADY KITTY *is overjoyed.*)

LADY KITTY. My lip-stick!

C.-C. I found it in the drive and I ventured to bring it in.

LADY KITTY. It's Saint Antony. I said a little prayer to him when I was hunting in my bag.

PORTEOUS. Saint Antony be blowed! It's Clive, by God!

LADY KITTY (*startled, her attention suddenly turning from the lip-stick*). Clive!

C.-C. You didn't recognise me. It's many years since we met.

LADY KITTY. My poor Clive, your hair has gone quite white!

C.-C. (*holding out his hand*). I hope you had a pleasant journey down from London.

LADY KITTY (*offering him her cheek*). You may kiss me, Clive.

C.-C. (*kissing her*). You don't mind, Hughie?

PORTEOUS (*with a grunt*). Ugh!

C.-C. (*going up to him cordially*). And how are you, my dear Hughie?

PORTEOUS. Damned rheumatic if you want to know. Filthy climate you have in this country.

C.-C. Aren't you going to shake hands with me, Hughie?

PORTEOUS. I have no objection to shaking hands with you.

C.-C. You've aged, my poor Hughie.

PORTEOUS. Some one was asking me how old you were the other day.

C.-C. Were they surprised when you told them?

PORTEOUS. Surprised! They wondered you weren't dead.
(*The* BUTLER *comes in.*)

BUTLER. Did you ring, sir?

ARNOLD. No. Oh, yes, I did. It doesn't matter now.

C.-C. (*as the* BUTLER *is going*). One moment. My dear Elizabeth, I've come to throw myself on your mercy. My servants are busy with their own affairs. There's not a thing for me to eat in my cottage.

ELIZABETH. Oh, but we shall be delighted if you'll lunch with us.

C.-C. It either means that or my immediate death from starvation. You don't mind, Arnold?

ARNOLD. My dear father!

ELIZABETH (*to the* BUTLER). Mr. Cheney will lunch here.

BUTLER. Very good, ma'am.

C.-C. (*to* LADY KITTY). And what do you think of Arnold?

LADY KITTY. I adore him.

C.-C. He's grown, hasn't he? But then you'd expect him to do that in thirty years.

ARNOLD. For God's sake let's go in to lunch, Elizabeth!

ACT TWO

The Scene is the same as in the preceding Act.

It is afternoon. When the curtain rises PORTEOUS *and* LADY KITTY, ANNA *and* TEDDIE *are playing bridge.* ELIZABETH *and* CHAMPION-CHANEY *are watching.* PORTEOUS *and* LADY KITTY *are partners.*

C.-C. When will Arnold be back, Elizabeth?

ELIZABETH. Soon, I think.

C.-C. Is he addressing a meeting?

ELIZABETH. No, it's only a conference with his agent and one or two constituents.

PORTEOUS (*irritably*). How anyone can be expected to play bridge when people are shouting at the top of their voices all round them, I for one cannot understand.

ELIZABETH (*smiling*). I'm so sorry.

ANNA. I can see your hand, Lord Porteous.

PORTEOUS. It may help you.

LADY KITTY. I've told you over and over again to hold your cards up. It ruins one's game when one can't help seeing one's opponent's hand.

PORTEOUS. One isn't obliged to look.

LADY KITTY. What was Arnold's majority at the last election?

ELIZABETH. Seven hundred and something.

C.-C. He'll have to fight for it if he wants to keep his seat next time.

PORTEOUS. Are we playing bridge, or talking politics?

LADY KITTY. I never find that conversation interferes with my game.

PORTEOUS. You certainly play no worse when you talk than when you hold your tongue.

LADY KITTY. I think that's a very offensive thing to say, Hughie. Just because I don't play the same game as you do you think I can't play.

PORTEOUS. I'm glad you acknowledge it's not the same game as I play. But why in God's name do you call it bridge?

C.-C. I agree with Kitty. I hate people who play bridge as though they were at a funeral and knew their feet were getting wet.

PORTEOUS. Of course you take Kitty's part.

LADY KITTY. That's the least he can do.

C.-C. I have a naturally cheerful disposition.

PORTEOUS. You've never had anything to sour it.

LADY KITTY. I don't know what you mean by that, Hughie.

PORTEOUS (*trying to contain himself*). Must you trump my ace?

LADY KITTY (*innocently*). Oh, was that your ace, darling?

PORTEOUS (*furiously*). Yes, it was my ace.

LADY KITTY. Oh, well, it was the only trump I had. I shouldn't have made it anyway.

PORTEOUS. You needn't have told them that. Now she knows exactly what I've got.

LADY KITTY. She knew before.

PORTEOUS. How could she know?

LADY KITTY. She said she'd seen your hand.

ANNA. Oh, I didn't. I said I could see it.

LADY KITTY. Well, I naturally supposed that if she could see it she did.

PORTEOUS. Really, Kitty, you have the most extraordinary ideas.

C.-C. Not at all. If anyone is such a fool as to show me his hand, of course I look at it.

PORTEOUS (*fuming*). If you study the etiquette of bridge, you'll discover that onlookers are expected not to interfere with the game.

C.-C. My dear Hughie, this is a matter of ethics, not of bridge.

ANNA. Anyhow, I get the game. And rubber.

TEDDIE. I claim a revoke.

PORTEOUS. Who revoked?

TEDDIE. You did.

PORTEOUS. Nonsense. I've never revoked in my life.

TEDDIE. I'll show you. (*He turns over the tricks to show the faces of the cards*) You threw away a club on the third heart trick and you had another heart.

PORTEOUS. I never had more than two hearts.

TEDDIE. Oh, yes, you had. Look here. That's the card you played on the last trick but one.

LADY KITTY (*delighted to catch him out*). There's no doubt about it, Hughie. You revoked.

PORTEOUS. I tell you I did not revoke. I never revoke.

C.-C. You did, Hughie. I wondered what on earth you were doing.

PORTEOUS. I don't know how anyone can be expected not to revoke when there's this confounded chatter going on all the time.

TEDDIE. Well, that's another hundred to us.

PORTEOUS (*to* CHAMPION-CHENEY). I wish you wouldn't breathe down my neck. I never can play bridge when there's somebody breathing down my neck.

(*The party have risen from the bridge-table, and they scatter about the room.*)

ANNA. Well, I'm going to take a book and lie down in the hammock till it's time to dress.

TEDDIE (*who has been adding up*). I'll put it down in the book, shall I?

PORTEOUS (*who has not moved, setting out the cards for a patience*). Yes, yes, put it down. I never revoke. (ANNA *goes out.*)

LADY KITTY. Would you like to come for a little stroll, Hughie?

PORTEOUS. What for?

LADY KITTY. Exercise.

PORTEOUS. I hate exercise.

C.-C. (*looking at the patience*). The seven goes on the eight. (PORTEOUS *takes no notice.*)

LADY KITTY. The seven goes on the eight, Hughie.

PORTEOUS. I don't choose to put the seven on the eight.

C.-C. That knave goes on the queen.

PORTEOUS. I'm not blind, thank you.

LADY KITTY. The three goes on the four.

C.-C. All these go over.

PORTEOUS (*furiously*). Am I playing this patience, or are you playing it?

LADY KITTY. But you're missing everything.

PORTEOUS. That's my business.

C.-C. It's no good losing your temper over it, Hughie.

PORTEOUS. Go away, both of you. You irritate me.

LADY KITTY. We were only trying to help you, Hughie.

PORTEOUS. I don't want to be helped. I want to do it by myself.

LADY KITTY. I think your manners are perfectly deplorable, Hughie.

PORTEOUS. It's simply maddening when you're playing patience and people won't leave you alone.

C.-C. We won't say another word.

PORTEOUS. That three goes. I believe it's coming out. If I'd been such a fool as to put that seven up I shouldn't have been able to bring these down. (*He puts down several cards while they watch him silently.*)

LADY KITTY and C.-C. (*together*). The four goes on the five.

PORTEOUS (*throwing down the cards violently*). Damn you! why don't you leave me alone? It's intolerable.

C.-C. It was coming out, my dear fellow.

PORTEOUS. I know it was coming out. Confound you!

LADY KITTY. How petty you are, Hughie!

PORTEOUS. Petty, be damned! I've told you over and over again that I will not be interfered with when I'm playing patience.

LADY KITTY. Don't talk to me like that, Hughie.

PORTEOUS. I shall talk to you as I please.

LADY KITTY (*beginning to cry*). Oh, you brute! You brute! (*She flings out of the room.*)

PORTEOUS. Oh, damn! now she's going to cry.
(*He shambles out into the garden.* CHAMPION-CHENEY, ELIZABETH *and* TEDDIE *are left alone. There is a moment's pause.* CHAMPION-CHENEY *looks from* TEDDIE *to* ELIZABETH, *with an ironical smile.*)

C.-C. Upon my soul, they might be married. They frip so much.

ELIZABETH (*frigidly*). It's been nice of you to come here so often since they arrived. It's helped to make things easy.

C.-C. Irony? It's a rhetorical form not much favoured in this blessed plot, this earth, this realm, this England.

ELIZABETH. What exactly are you getting at?

C.-C. How slangy the young women of the present day are! I suppose the fact that Arnold is a purist leads you to the contrary extravagance.

ELIZABETH. Anyhow you know what I mean.

C.-C. (*with a smile*). I have a dim, groping suspicion.

ELIZABETH. You promised to keep away. Why did you come back the moment they arrived?

C.-C. Curiosity, my dear child. A surely pardonable curiosity.

ELIZABETH. And since then you've been here all the time. You don't generally favour us with so much of your company when you're down at your cottage.

C.-C. I've been excessively amused.

ELIZABETH. It has struck me that whenever they started fripping you took a malicious pleasure in goading them on.

C.-C. I don't think there's much love lost between them now, do you?

(TEDDIE *is making as though to leave the room.*)

ELIZABETH. Don't go, Teddie.

C.-C. No, please don't. I'm only staying a minute. We were talking about Lady Kitty just before she arrived. (*To* ELIZABETH) Do you remember? The pale, frail lady in black satin and old lace.

ELIZABETH (*with a chuckle*). You are a devil, you know.

C.-C. Ah, well, he's always had the reputation of being a humorist and a gentleman.

ELIZABETH. Did *you* expect her to be like that, poor dear?

C.-C. My dear child, I hadn't the vaguest idea. You were asking me the other day what she was like when she ran away. I didn't tell you half. She was so gay and so natural. Who would have thought that animation would turn into such frivolity, and that charming impulsiveness lead to such a ridiculous affectation?

ELIZABETH. It rather sets my nerves on edge to hear the way you talk of her.

C.-C. It's the truth that sets your nerves on edge, not I.

ELIZABETH. You loved her once. Have you no feeling for her at all?

C.-C. None. Why should I?

ELIZABETH. She's the mother of your son.

C.-C. My dear child, you have a charming nature, as simple, frank, and artless as hers was. Don't let pure humbug obscure your common sense.

ELIZABETH. We have no right to judge. She's only been here two days. We know nothing about her.

C.-C. My dear, her soul is as thickly rouged as her face. She hasn't an emotion that's sincere. She's tinsel. You think I'm a cruel, cynical old man. Why, when I think of what she was, if I didn't laugh at what she has become I should cry.

ELIZABETH. How do you know she wouldn't be just the same now if she'd remained your wife? Do you think your influence would have had such a salutary effect on her?

C.-C. (*good-humouredly*). I like you when you're bitter and rather insolent.

ELIZABETH. D'you like me enough to answer my question?

C.-C. She was only twenty-seven when she went away. She might have become anything. She might have become the woman you expected her to be. There are very few of us who are strong enough to make circumstances serve us. We are the creatures of our environment. She's a silly, worthless woman because she's led a silly, worthless life.

ELIZABETH (*disturbed*). You're horrible today.

C.-C. I don't say it's I who could have prevented her from becoming this ridiculous caricature of a pretty woman grown old. But life could. Here she would have had the friends fit to her station, and a decent activity, and worthy interests. Ask her what her life has been all these years among divorced women and kept women and the men who consort with them. There is no more lamentable pursuit than a life of pleasure.

ELIZABETH. At all events she loved and she loved greatly. I have only pity and affection for her.

C.-C. And if she loved what d'you think she felt when she saw that she had ruined Hughie? Look at him. He was tight last night after dinner and tight the night before.

ELIZABETH. I know.

C.-C. And she took it as a matter of course. How long do you suppose he's been getting tight every night? Do you think he was like that thirty years ago? Can you imagine that that was a brilliant young man, whom everyone expected to be Prime Minister? Look at him now. A grumpy sodden old fellow with false teeth.

ELIZABETH. You have false teeth, too.

C.-C. Yes, but damn it all, they fit. She's ruined him and she knows she's ruined him.

ELIZABETH (*looking at him suspiciously*). Why are you saying all this to me?

C.-C. Am I hurting your feelings?

ELIZABETH. I think I've had enough for the present.

C.-C. I'll go and have a look at the gold-fish. I want to see Arnold when he comes in. (*Politely*) I'm afraid we've been boring Mr. Luton.

TEDDIE. Not at all.

C.-C. When are you going back to the F.M.S.?

TEDDIE. In about a month.

C.-C. I see. (*He goes out.*)

ELIZABETH. I wonder what he has at the back of his head.

TEDDIE. D'you think he was talking at you?

ELIZABETH. He's as clever as a bagful of monkeys.
(*There is a moment's pause.* TEDDIE *hesitates a little and when he speaks it is in a different tone. He is grave and somewhat nervous.*)

TEDDIE. It seems very difficult to get a few minutes alone with you. I wonder if you've been making it difficult?

ELIZABETH. I wanted to think.

TEDDIE. I've made up my mind to go away tomorrow.

ELIZABETH. Why?

TEDDIE. I want you altogether or not at all.

ELIZABETH. You're so arbitrary.

TEDDIE. You said you—you said you cared for me.

ELIZABETH. I do.

TEDDIE. Do you mind if we talk it over now?

ELIZABETH. No.

TEDDIE (*frowning*). It makes me feel rather shy and awkward. I've repeated to myself over and over again exactly what I want to say to you, and now all I'd prepared seems rather footling.

ELIZABETH. I'm so afraid I'm going to cry.

TEDDIE. I feel it's all so tremendously serious and I think we ought to keep emotion out of it. You're rather emotional, aren't you?

ELIZABETH (*half smiling and half in tears*). So are you for the matter of that.

TEDDIE. That's why I wanted to have everything I meant to say to you cut and dried. I think it would be awfully unfair if I made love to you and all that sort of thing, and you were carried away. I wrote it all down and thought I'd send it to you as a letter.

ELIZABETH. Why didn't you?

TEDDIE. I got the wind up. A letter seems so—so cold. You see, I love you so awfully.

ELIZABETH. For goodness' sake don't say that.

TEDDIE. You mustn't cry. Please don't, or I shall go all to pieces.

ELIZABETH (*trying to smile*). I'm sorry. It doesn't mean anything really. It's only tears running out of my eyes.

TEDDIE. Our only chance is to be awfully matter-of-fact.
(*He stops for a moment. He finds it quite difficult to control himself. He clears his throat. He frowns with annoyance at himself.*)

ELIZABETH. What's the matter?

TEDDIE. I've got a sort of lump in my throat. It is idiotic. I think I'll have a cigarette. (*She watches him in silence while he lights a cigarette*) You see, I've never been in love with anyone before, not really. It's knocked me endways. I don't know how I can live without you now. . . . Does that old fool know I'm in love with you?

ELIZABETH. I think so.

TEDDIE. When he was talking about Lady Kitty smashing up Lord Porteous' career I thought there was something at the back of it.

ELIZABETH. I think he was trying to persuade me not to smash up yours.

TEDDIE. I'm sure that's very considerate of him, but I don't happen to have one to smash. I wish I had. It's the only time in my life I've wished I were a hell of a swell so that I could chuck it all and show you how much more you are to me than anything else in the world.

ELIZABETH (*affectionately*). You're a dear old thing, Teddie.

TEDDIE. You know, I don't really know how to make love, but if I did I couldn't do it now because I just want to be absolutely practical.

ELIZABETH (*chaffing him*). I'm glad you don't know how to make love. It would be almost more than I could bear.

TEDDIE. You see, I'm not at all romantic and that sort of thing. I'm just a common or garden business man. All this is so dreadfully serious and I think we ought to be sensible.

ELIZABETH (*with a break in her voice*). You owl!

TEDDIE. No, Elizabeth, don't say things like that to me. I want you to consider all the *pros* and *cons*, and my heart's thumping against my chest, and you know I love you, I love you, I love you.

ELIZABETH (*in a sigh of passion*). Oh, my precious!

TEDDIE (*impatiently, but with himself, rather than with* ELIZABETH). Don't be idiotic, Elizabeth. I'm not going to tell you that I can't live without you and a lot of muck like that. You know that you mean everything in the world to me. (*Almost giving it up as a bad job*) Oh, my God!

ELIZABETH (*her voice faltering*). D'you think there's anything you can say to me that I don't know already?

TEDDIE (*desperately*). But I haven't said a single thing I wanted to. I'm a business man and I want to put it all in a business way, if you understand what I mean.

ELIZABETH (*smiling*). I don't believe you're a very good business man.

TEDDIE (*sharply*). You don't know what you're talking about. I'm a first-rate business man, but somehow this is different. (*Hopelessly*) I don't know why it won't go right.

ELIZABETH. What are we going to do about it?

TEDDIE. You see, it's not just because you're awfully pretty that I love you. I'd love you just as much if you were old and ugly. It's you I love, not what you look like. And it's not only love; love be blowed! It's that I *like* you so tremendously. I think you're such a ripping good sort. I just want to be with you. I feel so jolly and happy just to think you're there. I'm so awfully *fond* of you.

ELIZABETH (*laughing through her tears*). I don't know if this is your idea of introducing a business proposition.

TEDDIE. Damn you, you won't let me.

ELIZABETH. You said "Damn you."

TEDDIE. I meant it.

ELIZABETH. Your voice sounded as if you meant it, you perfect duck!

TEDDIE. Really, Elizabeth, you're intolerable.

ELIZABETH. I'm doing nothing.

TEDDIE. Yes, you are, you're putting me off my blow. What I want to say is perfectly simple. I'm a very ordinary business man.

ELIZABETH. You've said that before.

TEDDIE (*angrily*). Shut up. I haven't got a bob besides what I earn. I've got no position. I'm nothing. You're rich and you're a big pot and you've got everything that anyone can want. It's awful cheek my saying anything to you at all. But after all there's only one thing that really matters in the world, and that's love. I love you. Chuck all this, Elizabeth, and come to me.

ELIZABETH. Are you cross with me?

TEDDIE. Furious.

ELIZABETH. Darling!

TEDDIE. If you don't want me tell me so at once and let me get out quickly.

ELIZABETH. Teddie, nothing in the world matters anything to me but you. I'll go wherever you take me. I love you.

TEDDIE (*all to pieces*). Oh, my God!

ELIZABETH. Does it mean as much to you as that? Oh, Teddie!

TEDDIE (*trying to control himself*). Don't be a fool, Elizabeth.

ELIZABETH. It's you're the fool. You're making me cry.

TEDDIE. You're so damned emotional.

ELIZABETH. Damned emotional yourself. I'm sure you're a rotten business man.

TEDDIE. I don't care what you think. You've made me so awfully happy. I say, what a lark life's going to be!

ELIZABETH. Teddie, you are an angel.

TEDDIE. Let's get out quick. It's no good wasting time. Elizabeth.

ELIZABETH. What?

TEDDIE. Nothing. I just like to say Elizabeth.

ELIZABETH. You fool!

TEDDIE. I say, can you shoot?

ELIZABETH. No.

TEDDIE. I'll teach you. You don't know how ripping it is to start out from your camp at dawn and travel through the jungle. And you're so tired at night and the sky's all starry. It's a fair treat. Of course I didn't want to say anything about all that till you'd decided. I'd made up my mind to be absolutely practical.

ELIZABETH (*chaffing him*). The only practical thing you said was that love is the only thing that really matters.

TEDDIE (*happily*). Pull the other leg next time, will you? I should have to have one longer than the other.

ELIZABETH. Isn't it fun being in love with some one who's in love with you?

TEDDIE. I say, I think I'd better clear out at once, don't you? It seems rather rotten to stay on in—in this house.

ELIZABETH. You can't go tonight. There's no train.

TEDDIE. I'll go tomorrow. I'll wait in London till you're ready to join me.

ELIZABETH. I'm not going to leave a note on the pin-cushion like Lady Kitty, you know. I'm going to tell Arnold.

TEDDIE. Are you? Don't you think there'll be an awful bother?

ELIZABETH. I must face it. I should hate to be sly and deceitful.

TEDDIE. Well, then, let's face it together.

ELIZABETH. No, I'll talk to Arnold by myself.

TEDDIE. You won't let anyone influence you?

ELIZABETH. No.
(*He holds out his hand and she takes it. They look into one another's eyes with grave, almost solemn affection. There is the sound outside of a car driving up.*)

ELIZABETH. There's the car. Arnold's come back. I must go and bathe my eyes. I don't want them to see I've been crying.

TEDDIE. All right. (*As she is going*) Elizabeth.

ELIZABETH (*stopping*). What?

TEDDIE. Bless you.

ELIZABETH (*affectionately*). Idiot! (*She goes out of the door and* TEDDIE *through the French window into the garden. For an instant the room is empty.* ARNOLD *comes in. He sits down and takes some papers out of his despatch-case.* LADY KITTY *enters. He gets up.*)

LADY KITTY. I saw you come in. Oh, my dear, don't get up. There's no reason why you should be so dreadfully polite to me.

ARNOLD. I've just rung for a cup of tea.

LADY KITTY. Perhaps we shall have the chance of a little talk. We don't seem to have had five minutes by ourselves. I want to make your acquaintance, you know.

ARNOLD. I should like you to know that it's not by my wish that my father is here.

LADY KITTY. But I'm so interested to see him.

ARNOLD. I was afraid that you and Lord Porteous must find it embarrassing.

LADY KITTY. Oh, no. Hughie was his greatest friend. They were at Eton and Oxford together. I think your father has improved so much since I saw him last. He wasn't good-looking as a young man, but now he's quite handsome.
(*The* FOOTMAN *brings in a tray on which are tea-things.*)

LADY KITTY. Shall I pour it out for you?

ARNOLD. Thank you very much.

LADY KITTY. Do you take sugar?

ARNOLD. No. I gave it up during the war.

LADY KITTY. So wise of you. It's so bad for the figure. Besides being patriotic, of course. Isn't it absurd that I should ask my son if he takes sugar or not? Life is really very quaint. Sad, of course, but oh, so quaint! Often I lie in bed at night and have a good laugh to myself as I think how quaint life is.

ARNOLD. I'm afraid I'm a very serious person.

LADY KITTY. How old are you now, Arnold?

ARNOLD. Thirty-five.

LADY KITTY. Are you really? Of course, I was a child when I married your father.

ARNOLD. Really. He always told me you were twenty-two.

LADY KITTY. Oh, what nonsense! Why, I was married out of the nursery. I put my hair up for the first time on my wedding-day.

ARNOLD. Where is Lord Porteous?

LADY KITTY. My dear, it sounds too absurd to hear you call him Lord Porteous. Why don't you call him—Uncle Hughie?

ARNOLD. He doesn't happen to be my uncle.

LADY KITTY. No, but he's your godfather. You know, I'm sure you'll like him when you know him better. I'm so hoping that you and Elizabeth will come and stay with us in Florence. I simply adore Elizabeth. She's too beautiful.

ARNOLD. Her hair is very pretty.

LADY KITTY. It's not touched up, is it?

ARNOLD. Oh, no.

LADY KITTY. I just wondered. It's rather a coincidence that her hair should be the same colour as mine. I suppose it shows that your father and you are attracted by just the same thing. So interesting, heredity, isn't it?

ARNOLD. Very.

LADY KITTY. Of course, since I joined the Catholic Church I don't believe in it any more. Darwin and all that sort of thing. Too dreadful. Wicked, you know. Besides, it's not very good form, is it?

(CHAMPION-CHENEY *comes in from the garden.*)

C.-C. Do I intrude?

LADY KITTY. Come in, Clive. Arnold and I have been having such a wonderful heart-to-heart talk.

C.-C. Very nice.

ARNOLD. Father, I stepped in for a moment at the Harveys' on my way back. It's simply criminal what they're doing with that house.

C.-C. What are they doing?

ARNOLD. It's an almost perfect Georgian house and they've got a lot of dreadful Victorian furniture. I gave them my ideas on the subject, but it's quite hopeless. They said they were attached to their furniture.

C.-C. Arnold should have been an interior decorator.

LADY KITTY. He has wonderful taste. He gets that from me.

ARNOLD. I suppose I have a certain *flair*. I have a passion for decorating houses.

LADY KITTY. You've made this one charming.

C.-C. D'you remember, we just had chintzes and comfortable chairs when we lived here, Kitty.

LADY KITTY. Perfectly hideous, wasn't it?

C.-C. In those days gentlemen and ladies were not expected to have taste.

ARNOLD. You know, I've been looking at this chair again. Since Lord Porteous said the legs weren't right I've been very uneasy.

LADY KITTY. He only said that because he was in a bad temper.

C.-C. His temper seems to me very short these days, Kitty.

LADY KITTY. Oh, it is.

ARNOLD. You feel he knows what he's talking about. I gave seventy-five pounds for that chair. I'm very seldom taken in. I always think if a thing's right you feel it.

C.-C. Well, don't let it disturb your night's rest.

ARNOLD. But, my dear father, that's just what it does. I had a most horrible dream about it last night.

LADY KITTY. Here is Hughie.

ARNOLD. I'm going to fetch a book I have on Old English furniture. There's an illustration of a chair which is almost identical with this one.
(PORTEOUS *comes in.*)

PORTEOUS. Quite a family gathering, by George!

C.-C. I was thinking just now we'd make a very pleasing picture of a typical English home.

ARNOLD. I'll be back in five minutes. There's something I want to show you, Lord Porteous. (*He goes out.*)

C.-C. Would you like to play piquet with me, Hughie?

PORTEOUS. Not particularly.

C.-C. You were never much of a piquet player, were you?

PORTEOUS. My dear Clive, you people don't know what piquet is in England.

C.-C. Let's have a game then. You may make money.

PORTEOUS. I don't want to play with you.

LADY KITTY. I don't know why not, Hughie.

PORTEOUS. Let me tell you that I don't like your manner.

C.-C. I'm sorry for that. I'm afraid I can't offer to change it at my age.

PORTEOUS. I don't know what you want to be hanging around here for.

C.-C. A natural attachment to my home.

PORTEOUS. If you'd had any tact you'd have kept out of the way while we were here.

C.-C. My dear Hughie, I don't understand your attitude at all. If I'm willing to let bygones be bygones why should you object?

PORTEOUS. Damn it all, they're not bygones.

C.-C. After all, I am the injured party.

PORTEOUS. How the devil are you the injured party?

C.-C. Well, you did run away with my wife, didn't you?

LADY KITTY. Now, don't let's go into ancient history. I can't see why we shouldn't all be friends.

PORTEOUS. I beg you not to interfere, Kitty.

LADY KITTY. I'm very fond of Clive.

PORTEOUS. You never cared two straws for Clive. You only say that to irritate me.

LADY KITTY. Not at all. I don't see why he shouldn't come and stay with us.

C.-C. I'd love to. I think Florence in spring-time is delightful. Have you central heating?

PORTEOUS. I never liked you, I don't like you now, and I never shall like you.

C.-C. How very unfortunate! because I liked you, I like you now, and I shall continue to like you.

LADY KITTY. There's something very nice about you, Clive.

PORTEOUS. If you think that, why the devil did you leave him?

LADY KITTY. Are you going to reproach me because I loved you? How utterly, utterly, utterly detestable you are!

C.-C. Now, now, don't quarrel with one another.

LADY KITTY. It's all his fault. I'm the easiest person in the world to live with. But really he'd try the patience of a saint.

C.-C. Come, come, don't get upset, Kitty. When two people live together there must be a certain amount of give and take.

PORTEOUS. I don't know what the devil you're talking about.

C.-C. It hasn't escaped my observation that you are a little inclined to frip. Many couples are. I think it's a pity.

PORTEOUS. Would you have the very great kindness to mind your own business?

LADY KITTY. It is his business. He naturally wants me to be happy.

C.-C. I have the very greatest affection for Kitty.

PORTEOUS. Then why the devil didn't you look after her properly?

C.-C. My dear Hughie, you were my greatest friend. I trusted you. It may have been rash.

PORTEOUS. It was inexcusable.

LADY KITTY. I don't know what you mean by that, Hughie.

PORTEOUS. Don't, don't, don't try and bully me, Kitty.

LADY KITTY. Oh, I know what you mean.

PORTEOUS. Then why the devil did you say you didn't?

LADY KITTY. When I think that I sacrificed everything for that man! And for thirty years I've had to live in a filthy marble palace with no sanitary conveniences.

C.-C. D'you mean to say you haven't got a bathroom?

LADY KITTY. I've had to wash in a tub.

C.-C. My poor Kitty, how you've suffered!

PORTEOUS. Really, Kitty, I'm sick of hearing of the sacrifices you made. I suppose you think I sacrificed nothing. I should have been Prime Minister by now if it hadn't been for you.

LADY KITTY. Nonsense!

PORTEOUS. What do you mean by that? Everyone said I should be Prime Minister. Shouldn't I have been Prime Minister, Clive?

C.-C. It was certainly the general expectation.

PORTEOUS. I was the most promising young man of my day. I was bound to get a seat in the Cabinet at the next election.

LADY KITTY. They'd have found you out just as I've found you out. I'm sick of hearing that I ruined your career. You never had a career to ruin. Prime Minister! You haven't the brain. You haven't the character.

C.-C. Cheek, push, and a gift of the gab will serve very well instead, you know.

LADY KITTY. Besides, in politics it's not the men that matter. It's the women at the back of them. I could have made Clive a Cabinet Minister if I'd wanted to.

PORTEOUS. Clive?

LADY KITTY. With my beauty, my charm, my force of character, my wit, I could have done anything.

PORTEOUS. Clive was nothing but my political secretary. When I was Prime Minister I might have made him Governor of some Colony or other. Western Australia, say. Out of pure kindliness.

LADY KITTY (*with flashing eyes*). D'you think I would have buried myself in Western Australia? With my beauty? My charm?

PORTEOUS. Or Barbadoes, perhaps.

LADY KITTY (*furiously*). Barbadoes! Barbadoes can go to—Barbadoes.

PORTEOUS. That's all you'd have got.

LADY KITTY. Nonsense! I'd have India.

PORTEOUS. I would never have given you India.

LADY KITTY. You would have given me India.

PORTEOUS. I tell you I wouldn't.

LADY KITTY. The King would have given me India. The nation would have insisted on my having India. I would have been a vice-reine or nothing.

PORTEOUS. I tell you that as long as the interests of the British Empire—Damn it all, my teeth are coming out! (*He hurries from the room.*)

LADY KITTY. It's too much. I can't bear it any more. I've put up with him for thirty years and now I'm at the end of my tether.

C.-C. Calm yourself, my dear Kitty.

LADY KITTY. I won't listen to a word. I've quite made up my mind. It's finished, finished, finished. (*With a change of tone*) I was so touched when I heard that you never lived in this house again after I left it.

C.-C. The cuckoos have always been very plentiful. Their note has a personal application which, I must say, I have found extremely offensive.

LADY KITTY. When I saw that you didn't marry again I couldn't help thinking that you still loved me.

C.-C. I am one of the few men I know who is able to profit by experience.

LADY KITTY. In the eyes of the Church I am still your wife. The Church is so wise. It knows that in the end a woman always comes back to her first love. Clive, I am willing to return to you.

C.-C. My dear Kitty, I couldn't take advantage of your momentary vexation with Hughie to let you take a step which I know you would bitterly regret.

LADY KITTY. You've waited for me a long time. For Arnold's sake.

C.-C. Do you think we really need bother about Arnold? In the last thirty years he's had time to grow used to the situation.

LADY KITTY (*with a little smile*). I think I've sown my wild oats, Clive.

C.-C. I haven't. I was a good young man, Kitty.

LADY KITTY. I know.

C.-C. And I'm very glad, because it has enabled me to be a wicked old one.

LADY KITTY. I beg your pardon. (ARNOLD *comes in with a large book in his hand.*)

ARNOLD. I say, I've found the book I was hunting for. Oh! isn't Lord Porteous here?

LADY KITTY. One moment, Arnold. Your father and I are busy.

ARNOLD. I'm so sorry. (*He goes out into the garden.*)

LADY KITTY. Explain yourself, Clive.

C.-C. When you ran away from me, Kitty, I was sore and angry and miserable. But above all I felt a fool.

LADY KITTY. Men are so vain.

C.-C. But I was a student of history, and presently I reflected that I shared my misfortune with very nearly all the greatest men.

LADY KITTY. I'm a great reader myself. It has always struck me as peculiar.

C.-C. The explanation is very simple. Women dislike intelligence, and when they find it in their husbands they revenge themselves on them in the only way they can, by making them—well, what you made me.

LADY KITTY. It's ingenious. It may be true.

C.-C. I felt I had done my duty by society and I determined to devote the rest of my life to my own entertainment. The House of Commons had always bored me excessively and the scandal of our divorce gave me an opportunity to resign my seat. I have been relieved to find that the country got on perfectly well without me.

LADY KITTY. But has love never entered your life?

C.-C. Tell me frankly, Kitty, don't you think people make a lot of unnecessary fuss about love?

LADY KITTY. It's the most wonderful thing in the world.

C.-C. You're incorrigible. Do you really think it was worth sacrificing so much for?

LADY KITTY. My dear Clive, I don't mind telling you that if I had my time over again I should be unfaithful to you, but I should not leave you.

C.-C. For some years I was notoriously the prey of a secret sorrow. But I found so many charming creatures who were anxious to console that in the end it grew rather fatiguing. Out of regard to my health I ceased to frequent the drawing-rooms of Mayfair.

LADY KITTY. And since then?

C.-C. Since then I have allowed myself the luxury of assisting financially a succession of dear little things, in a somewhat humble sphere, between the ages of twenty and twenty-five.

LADY KITTY. I cannot understand the infatuation of men for young girls. I think they're so dull.

C.-C. It's a matter of taste. I love old wine, old friends and old books, but I like young women. On their twenty-fifth birthday I give them a diamond ring and tell them they must no longer waste their youth and beauty on an old fogey like me. We have a most affecting scene, my technique on these occasions is perfect, and then I start all over again.

LADY KITTY. You're a wicked old man, Clive.

C.-C. That's what I told you. But, by George! I'm a happy one.

LADY KITTY. There's only one course open to me now.

C.-C. What is that?

LADY KITTY (*with a flashing smile*). To go and dress for dinner.

C.-C. Capital. I will follow your example.
(*As* LADY KITTY *goes out* ELIZABETH *comes in.*)

ELIZABETH. Where is Arnold?

C.-C. He's on the terrace. I'll call him.

ELIZABETH. Don't bother.

C.-C. I was just strolling along to my cottage to put on a dinner jacket. (*As he goes out*) Arnold. (*Exit* C.-C.)

ARNOLD. Hulloa! (*He comes in*) Oh, Elizabeth, I've found an illustration here of a chair which is almost identical with mine. It's dated 1750. Look!

ELIZABETH. That's very interesting.

ARNOLD. I want to show it to Porteous. (*Moving a chair which has been misplaced*) You know, it does exasperate me the way people will not leave things alone. I no sooner put a thing in its place than somebody moves it.

ELIZABETH. It must be maddening for you.

ARNOLD. It is. You are the worst offender. I can't think why you don't take the pride that I do in the house. After all, it's one of the show places in the country.

ELIZABETH. I'm afraid you find me very unsatisfactory.

ARNOLD (*good-humouredly*). I don't know about that. But my two subjects are politics and decoration. I should be a perfect fool if I didn't see that you don't care two straws about either.

ELIZABETH. We haven't very much in common, Arnold, have we?

ARNOLD. I don't think you can blame me for that.

ELIZABETH. I don't. I blame you for nothing. I have no fault to find with you.

ARNOLD (*surprised at her significant tone*). Good gracious me! What's the meaning of all this?

ELIZABETH. Well, I don't think there's any object in beating about the bush. I want you to let me go.

ARNOLD. Go where?

ELIZABETH. Away. For always.

ARNOLD. My dear child, what *are* you talking about?

ELIZABETH. I want to be free.

ARNOLD (*amused rather than disconcerted*). Don't be ridiculous, darling. I daresay you're run down and want a change. I'll take you over to Paris for a fortnight if you like.

ELIZABETH. I shouldn't have spoken to you if I hadn't quite made up my mind. We've been married for three years and I don't think it's been a great success. I'm frankly bored by the life you want me to lead.

ARNOLD. Well, if you'll allow me to say so, the fault is yours. We lead a very distinguished, useful life. We know a lot of extremely nice people.

ELIZABETH. I'm quite willing to allow that the fault is mine. But how does that make it any better? I'm only twenty-five. If I've made a mistake I have time to correct it.

ARNOLD. I can't bring myself to take you very seriously.

ELIZABETH. You see, I don't love you.

ARNOLD. Well, I'm awfully sorry. But you weren't obliged to marry me. You've made your bed and I'm afraid you must lie on it.

ELIZABETH. That's one of the falsest proverbs in the English language. Why should you lie on the bed you've made if you don't want to? There's always the floor.

ARNOLD. For goodness' sake don't be funny, Elizabeth.

ELIZABETH. I've quite made up my mind to leave you, Arnold.

ARNOLD. Come, come, Elizabeth, you must be sensible. You haven't any reason to leave me.

ELIZABETH. Why should you wish to keep a woman tied to you who wants to be free?

ARNOLD. I happen to be in love with you.

ELIZABETH. You might have said that before.

ARNOLD. I thought you'd take it for granted. You can't expect a man to go on making love to his wife after three years. I'm very busy. I'm awfully keen on politics and I've worked like a dog to make this house a thing of beauty. After all, a man marries to have a home, but also because he doesn't want to be bothered with sex and all that sort of thing. I fell in love with you the first time I saw you and I've been in love ever since.

ELIZABETH. I'm sorry, but if you're not in love with a man his love doesn't mean very much to you.

ARNOLD. It's so ungrateful. I've done everything in the world for you.

ELIZABETH. You've been very kind to me. But you've asked me to lead a life I don't like and that I'm not suited for. I'm awfully sorry to cause you pain, but now you must let me go.

ARNOLD. Nonsense! I'm a good deal older than you are and I think I have a little more sense. In your interests as well as in mine I'm not going to do anything of the sort.

ELIZABETH (*with a smile*). How can you prevent me? You can't keep me under lock and key.

ARNOLD. Please don't talk to me as if I were a foolish child. You're my wife and you're going to remain my wife.

ELIZABETH. What sort of a life do you think we should lead? Do you think there'd be any more happiness for you than for me?

ARNOLD. But what is it precisely that you suggest?

ELIZABETH. Well, I want you to let me divorce you.

ARNOLD (*astounded*). Me? Thank you very much. Are you under the impression I'm going to sacrifice my career for a whim of yours?

ELIZABETH. How will it do that?

ARNOLD. My seat's wobbly enough as it is. Do you think I'd be able to hold it if I were in a divorce case? Even if it were a put-up job, as most divorces are nowadays, it would damn me.

ELIZABETH. It's rather hard on a woman to be divorced.

ARNOLD (*with sudden suspicion*). What do you mean by that? Are you in love with some one?

ELIZABETH. Yes.

ARNOLD. Who?

ELIZABETH. Teddie Luton.
(*He is astonished for a moment, then bursts into a laugh.*)

ARNOLD. My poor child, how can you be so ridiculous? Why, he hasn't a bob. He's a perfectly commonplace young man. It's so absurd I can't even be angry with you.

ELIZABETH. I've fallen desperately in love with him, Arnold.

ARNOLD. Well, you'd better fall desperately out.

ELIZABETH. He wants to marry me.

ARNOLD. I daresay he does. He can go to hell.

ELIZABETH. It's no good talking like that.

ARNOLD. Is he your lover?

ELIZABETH. No, certainly not.

ARNOLD. It shows that he's a mean skunk to take advantage of my hospitality to make love to you.

ELIZABETH. He's never even kissed me.

ARNOLD. I'd try telling that to the horse marines if I were you.

ELIZABETH. It's because I wanted to do nothing shabby that I told you straight out how things were.

ARNOLD. How long have you been thinking of this?

ELIZABETH. I've been in love with Teddie ever since I knew him.

ARNOLD. And you never thought of me at all, I suppose.

ELIZABETH. Oh, yes, I did. I was miserable. But I can't help myself. I wish I loved you, but I don't.

ARNOLD. I recommend you to think very carefully before you do anything foolish.

ELIZABETH. I have thought very carefully.

ARNOLD. By God! I don't know why I don't give you a sound hiding. I'm not sure if that wouldn't be the best thing to bring you to your senses.

ELIZABETH. Oh, Arnold, don't take it like that.

ARNOLD. How do you expect me to take it? You come to me quite calmly and say: "I've had enough of you. We've been married three years and I think I'd like to marry somebody else now. Shall I break up your home? What a bore for you! Do you mind my divorcing you? It'll smash up your career, will it? What a pity!" Oh, no, my girl, I may be a fool, but I'm not a damned fool.

ELIZABETH. Teddie is leaving here by the first train tomorrow. I warn you that I mean to join him as soon as he can make the necessary arrangements.

ARNOLD. Where is he?

ELIZABETH. I don't know. I suppose he's in his room.

(ARNOLD *goes to the door and calls.*)

ARNOLD. George! (*For a moment he walks up and down the room impatiently.* ELIZABETH *watches him. The* FOOTMAN *comes in.*)

FOOTMAN. Yes, sir.

ARNOLD. Tell Mr. Luton to come here at once.

ELIZABETH. Ask Mr. Luton if he wouldn't mind coming here for a moment.

FOOTMAN. Very good, madam. (*Exit* FOOTMAN.)

ELIZABETH. What are you going to say to him?

ARNOLD. That's my business.

ELIZABETH. I wouldn't make a scene if I were you.

ARNOLD. I'm not going to make a scene. (*They wait in silence*) Why did you insist on my mother coming here?

ELIZABETH. It seemed to me rather absurd to take up the attitude that I should be contaminated by her when . . .

ARNOLD (*interrupting*). When you were proposing to do exactly the same thing. Well, now you've seen her what do you think of her? Do you think it's been a success? Is that the sort of woman a man would like his mother to be?

ELIZABETH. I've been ashamed. I've been so sorry. It all seemed dreadful and horrible. This morning I happened to notice a rose in the garden. It was all overblown and bedraggled. It looked like a painted old woman. And I remembered that I'd looked at it a day or two ago. It was lovely then, fresh and blooming and fragrant. It may be hideous now, but that doesn't take away from the beauty it had once. That was real.

ARNOLD. Poetry, by God! As if this were the moment for poetry!
(TEDDIE *comes in. He has changed into a dinner jacket.*)

TEDDIE (*to* ELIZABETH). Did you want me?

ARNOLD. *I* sent for you. (TEDDIE *looks from* ARNOLD *to* ELIZABETH. *He sees that something has happened*) When would it be convenient for you to leave this house?

TEDDIE. I was proposing to go tomorrow morning. But I can very well go at once if you like.

ARNOLD. I do like.

TEDDIE. Very well. Is there anything else you wish to say to me?

ARNOLD. Do you think it was a very honourable thing to come down here and make love to my wife?

TEDDIE. No, I don't. I haven't been very happy about it. That's why I wanted to go away.

ARNOLD. Upon my word you're cool.

TEDDIE. I'm afraid it's no good saying I'm sorry and that sort of thing. You know what the situation is.

ARNOLD. Is it true that you want to marry Elizabeth?

TEDDIE. Yes. I should like to marry her as soon as ever I can.

ARNOLD. Have you thought of me at all? Has it struck you that you're destroying my home and breaking up my happiness?

TEDDIE. I don't see how there could be much happiness for you if Elizabeth doesn't care for you.

ARNOLD. Let me tell you that I refuse to have my home broken up by a twopenny-halfpenny adventurer who takes advantage of a foolish woman. I refuse to allow myself to be divorced. I can't prevent my wife from going off with you if she's determined to make a damned fool of herself, but this I tell you: nothing will induce me to divorce her.

ELIZABETH. Arnold, that would be monstrous.

TEDDIE. We could force you.

ARNOLD. How?

TEDDIE. If we went away together openly you'd have to bring an action.

ARNOLD. Twenty-four hours after you leave this house I shall go down to Brighton with a chorus-girl. And neither you nor I will be able to get a divorce. We've had enough divorces in our family. And now get out, get out, get out!
(TEDDIE *looks uncertainly at* ELIZABETH.)

ELIZABETH (*with a little smile*). Don't bother about me. I shall be all right.

ARNOLD. Get out! Get out!

ACT THREE

The Scene is the same as in the preceding Acts.

It is the night of the same day as that on which takes place the action of the second Act.

CHAMPION-CHENEY *and* ARNOLD, *both in dinner jackets, are discovered,* CHAMPION-CHENEY *is seated.* ARNOLD *walks restlessly up and down the room.*

C.-C. I think, if you'll follow my advice to the letter, you'll probably work the trick.

ARNOLD. I don't like it, you know. It's against all my principles.

C.-C. My dear Arnold, we all hope that you have before you a distinguished political career. You can't learn too soon that the most useful thing about a principle is that it can always be sacrificed to expediency.

ARNOLD. But supposing it doesn't come off? Women are incalculable.

C.-C. Nonsense! Men are romantic. A woman will always sacrifice herself if you give her the opportunity. It is her favourite form of self-indulgence.

ARNOLD. I never know whether you're a humorist or a cynic, father.

C.-C. I'm neither, my dear boy; I'm merely a very truthful man. But people are so unused to the truth that they're apt to mistake it for a joke or a sneer.

ARNOLD (*irritably*). It seems so unfair that this should happen to me.

C.-C. Keep your head, my boy, and do what I tell you.

(LADY KITTY *and* ELIZABETH *come in.* LADY KITTY *is in a gorgeous evening gown.*)

ELIZABETH. Where is Lord Porteous?

C.-C. He's on the terrace. He's smoking a cigar. (*Going to window*) Hughie!

(PORTEOUS *comes in.*)

PORTEOUS (*with a grunt*). Yes? Where's Mrs. Shenstone?

ELIZABETH. Oh, she had a headache. She's gone to bed.

(*When* PORTEOUS *comes in* LADY KITTY *with a very haughty air purses her lips and takes up an illustrated paper.* PORTEOUS *gives her an irritated look, takes another illustrated paper and sits himself down at the other end of the room. They are not on speaking terms.*)

C.-C. Arnold and I have just been down to my cottage.

ELIZABETH. I wondered where you'd gone.

C.-C. I came across an old photograph album this afternoon. I meant to bring it along before dinner, but I forgot, so we went and fetched it.

ELIZABETH. Oh, do let me see it! I love old photographs.
(*He gives her the album, and she, sitting down, puts it on her knees and begins to turn over the pages. He stands over her.* LADY KITTY *and* PORTEOUS *take surreptitious glances at one another.*)

C.-C. I thought it might amuse you to see what pretty women looked like five-and-thirty years ago. That was the day of beautiful women.

ELIZABETH. Do you think they were more beautiful then than they are now?

C.-C. Oh, much. Now you see lots of pretty little things, but very few beautiful women.

ELIZABETH. Aren't their clothes funny?

C.-C. (*pointing to a photograph*). That's Mrs. Langtry.

ELIZABETH. She has a lovely nose.

C.-C. She was the most wonderful thing you ever saw. Dowagers used to jump on chairs in order to get a good look at her when she came into a drawing-room. I was riding with her once, and we had to have the gates of the livery stable closed when she was getting on her horse because the crowd was so great.

ELIZABETH. And who's that?

C.-C. Lady Lonsdale. That's Lady Dudley.

ELIZABETH. This is an actress, isn't it?

C.-C. It is, indeed. Ellen Terry. By George! how I loved that woman!

ELIZABETH (*with a smile*). Dear Ellen Terry!

C.-C. That's Bwabs. I never saw a smarter man in my life. And Oliver Montagu. Henry Manners with his eye-glass.

ELIZABETH. Nice-looking, isn't he? And this?

C.-C. That's Mary Anderson. I wish you could have seen her in "A Winter's Tale." Her beauty just took your breath away. And look! There's Lady Randolph. Bernal Osborne—the wittiest man I ever knew.

ELIZABETH. I think it's too sweet. I love their absurd bustles and those tight sleeves.

C.-C. What figures they had! In those days a woman wasn't supposed to be as thin as a rail and as flat as a pancake.

ELIZABETH. Oh, but aren't they laced in? How could they bear it?

C.-C. They didn't play golf then, and nonsense like that, you know. They hunted, in a tall hat and a long black habit, and they were very gracious and charitable to the poor in the village.

ELIZABETH. Did the poor like it?

C.-C. They had a very thin time if they didn't. When they were in London they drove in the Park every afternoon, and they went to ten-course dinners, where they never met anybody they didn't know. And they had their box at the opera when Patti was singing or Madame Albani.

ELIZABETH. Oh, what a lovely little thing! Who on earth is that?

C.-C. That?

ELIZABETH. She looks so fragile, like a piece of exquisite china, with all those furs on and her face up against her muff, and the snow falling.

C.-C. Yes, there was quite a rage at that time for being taken in an artificial snowstorm.

ELIZABETH. What a sweet smile, so roguish and frank, and debonair! Oh, I wish I looked like that! Do tell me who it is!

C.-C. Don't you know?

ELIZABETH. No.

C.-C. Why—it's Kitty.

ELIZABETH. Lady Kitty! (*To* LADY KITTY) Oh, my dear, do look! It's too ravishing. (*She takes the album over to her impulsively*) Why didn't you tell me you looked like that? Everybody must have been in love with you. (LADY KITTY *takes the album and looks at it. Then she lets it slip from her hands and covers her face with her hands. She is crying*) (*In consternation*) My dear, what's the matter? Oh, what have I done? I'm so sorry.

LADY KITTY. Don't, don't talk to me. Leave me alone. It's stupid of me.

(ELIZABETH *looks at her for a moment perplexed, then, turning round, slips her arm in* CHAMPION-CHENEY'S *and leads him out on to the terrace.*)

ELIZABETH (*as they are going, in a whisper*). Did you do that on purpose?

(PORTEOUS *gets up and goes over to* LADY KITTY. *He puts his hand on her shoulder. They remain thus for a little while.*)

PORTEOUS. I'm afraid I was very rude to you before dinner, Kitty.

LADY KITTY (*taking his hand which is on her shoulder*). It doesn't matter. I'm sure I was very exasperating.

PORTEOUS. I didn't mean what I said, you know.

LADY KITTY. Neither did I.

PORTEOUS. Of course I know that I'd never have been Prime Minister.

LADY KITTY. How can you talk such nonsense, Hughie? No one would have had a chance if you'd remained in politics.

PORTEOUS. I haven't the character.

LADY KITTY. You have more character than anyone I've ever met.

PORTEOUS. Besides, I don't know that I much wanted to be Prime Minister.

LADY KITTY. Oh, but I should have been so proud of you. Of course you'd have been Prime Minister.

PORTEOUS. I'd have given you India, you know. I think it would have been a very popular appointment.

LADY KITTY. I don't care twopence about India. I'd have been quite content with Western Australia.

PORTEOUS. My dear, you don't think I'd have let you bury yourself in Western Australia?

LADY KITTY. Or Barbadoes.

PORTEOUS. Never. It sounds like a cure for flat feet. I'd have kept you in London. (*He picks up the album and is about to look at the photograph of* LADY KITTY. *She puts her hand over it.*)

LADY KITTY. No, don't look. (*He takes her hand away.*)

PORTEOUS. Don't be so silly.

LADY KITTY. Isn't it hateful to grow old?

PORTEOUS. You know, you haven't changed much.

LADY KITTY (*enchanted*). Oh, Hughie, how can you talk such nonsense?

PORTEOUS. Of course you're a little more mature, but that's all. A woman's all the better for being rather mature.

LADY KITTY. Do you really think that?

PORTEOUS. Upon my soul I do.

LADY KITTY. You're not saying it just to please me?

PORTEOUS. No, no.

LADY KITTY. Let me look at the photograph again. (*She takes the album and looks at the photograph complacently*) The fact is, if your bones are good, age doesn't really matter. You'll always be beautiful.

PORTEOUS (*with a little smile, almost as if he were talking to a child*). It was silly of you to cry.

LADY KITTY. It hasn't made my eyelashes run, has it?

PORTEOUS. Not a bit.

LADY KITTY. It's very good stuff I use now. They don't stick together either.

PORTEOUS. Look here, Kitty, how much longer do you want to stay here?

LADY KITTY. Oh, I'm quite ready to go whenever you like.

PORTEOUS. Clive gets on my nerves. I don't like the way he keeps hanging about you.

LADY KITTY (*surprised, rather amused, and delighted*). Hughie, you don't mean to say you're jealous of poor Clive?

PORTEOUS. Of course I'm not jealous of him, but he does look at you in a way that I can't help thinking rather objectionable.

LADY KITTY. Hughie, you may throw me downstairs like Amy Robsart; you may drag me about the floor by the hair of my head; I don't care, you're jealous. I shall never grow old.

PORTEOUS. Damn it all, the man was your husband.

LADY KITTY. My dear Hughie, he never had your style. Why, the moment you come into a room everyone looks and says: "Who the devil is that?"

PORTEOUS. What? You think that, do you? Well, I daresay there's something in what you say. These damned Radicals can say what they like, but, by God, Kitty! when a man's a gentleman—well, damn it all, you know what I mean.

LADY KITTY. I think Clive has degenerated dreadfully since we left him.

PORTEOUS. What do you say to making a bee-line for Italy and going to San Michele?

LADY KITTY. Oh, Hughie! It's years since we were there.

PORTEOUS. Wouldn't you like to see it again—just once more?

LADY KITTY. Do you remember the first time we went? It was the most heavenly place I'd ever seen. We'd only left England a month, and I said I'd like to spend all my life there.

PORTEOUS. Of course I remember. And in a fortnight it was yours, lock, stock and barrel.

LADY KITTY. We were very happy there, Hughie.

PORTEOUS. Let's go back once more.

LADY KITTY. I daren't. It must be all peopled with the ghosts of our past. One should never go again to a place where one has been happy. It would break my heart.

PORTEOUS. Do you remember how we used to sit on the terrace of the old castle and look at the Adriatic? We might have been the only people in the world, you and I, Kitty.

LADY KITTY (*tragically*). And we thought our love would last for ever.

(*Enter* CHAMPION-CHENEY.)

PORTEOUS. Is there any chance of bridge this evening?

C.-C. I don't think we can make up a four.

PORTEOUS. What a nuisance that boy went away like that! He wasn't a bad player.

C.-C. Teddie Luton?

LADY KITTY. I think it was very funny his going without saying good-bye to anyone.

C.-C. The young men of the present day are very casual.

PORTEOUS. I thought there was no train in the evening.

C.-C. There isn't. The last train leaves at 5.45.

PORTEOUS. How did he go then?

C.-C. He went.

PORTEOUS. Damned selfish I call it.

LADY KITTY (*intrigued*). Why did he go, Clive?

(CHAMPION-CHENEY *looks at her for a moment reflectively.*)

C.-C. I have something very grave to say to you. Elizabeth wants to leave Arnold.

LADY KITTY. Clive! What on earth for?

C.-C. She's in love with Teddie Luton. That's why he went. The men of my family are really very unfortunate.

PORTEOUS. Does she want to run away with him?

LADY KITTY (*with consternation*). My dear, what's to be done?

C.-C. I think you can do a great deal.

LADY KITTY. I? What?

C.-C. Tell her, tell her what it means. (*He looks at her fixedly. She stares at him.*)

LADY KITTY. Oh, no, no!

C.-C. She's a child. Not for Arnold's sake. For her sake. You must.

LADY KITTY. You don't know what you're asking.

C.-C. Yes, I do.

LADY KITTY. Hughie, what shall I do?

PORTEOUS. Do what you like. I shall never blame you for anything.
(*The* FOOTMAN *comes in with a letter on a salver. He hesitates on seeing that* ELIZABETH *is not in the room.*)

C.-C. What is it?

FOOTMAN. I was looking for Mrs. Champion-Cheney, sir.

C.-C. She's not here. Is that a letter?

FOOTMAN. Yes, sir. It's just been sent up from the "Champion Arms."

C.-C. Leave it. I'll give it to Mrs. Cheney.

FOOTMAN. Very good, sir. (*He brings the tray to* CLIVE, *who takes the letter. The* FOOTMAN *goes out.*)

PORTEOUS. Is the "Champion Arms" the local pub?

C.-C. (*looking at the letter*). It's by way of being a hotel, but I never heard of anyone staying there.

LADY KITTY. If there was no train I suppose he had to go there.

C.-C. Great minds. I wonder what he has to write about! (*He goes to the door leading on to the garden*) Elizabeth!

ELIZABETH (*outside*). Yes.

C.-C. Here's a note for you.
(*There is silence. They wait for* ELIZABETH *to come. She enters.*)

ELIZABETH. It's lovely in the garden tonight.

C.-C. They've just sent this up from the "Champion Arms."

ELIZABETH. Thank you. (*Without embarrassment she opens the letter. They watch her while she reads it. It covers three pages. She puts it away in her bag.*)

LADY KITTY. Hughie, I wish you'd fetch me a cloak. I'd like to take a little stroll in the garden, but after thirty years in Italy I find these English summers rather chilly. (*Without a word* PORTEOUS *goes out.* ELIZABETH *is lost in thought*) I want to talk to Elizabeth, Clive.

C.-C. I'll leave you. (*He goes out.*)

LADY KITTY. What does he say?

ELIZABETH. Who?

LADY KITTY. Mr. Luton.

ELIZABETH (*gives a little start. Then she looks at* LADY KITTY). They've told you?

LADY KITTY. Yes. And now they have I think I knew it all along.

ELIZABETH. I don't expect you to have much sympathy for me. Arnold is your son.

LADY KITTY. So pitifully little.

ELIZABETH. I'm not suited for this sort of existence. Arnold wants me to take what he calls my place in Society. Oh, I get so bored with those parties in London. All those middle-aged painted women, in beautiful clothes, lolloping round ball-rooms with rather old young men. And the endless luncheons where they gossip about so-and-so's love affairs.

LADY KITTY. Are you very much in love with Mr. Luton?

ELIZABETH. I love him with all my heart.

LADY KITTY. And he?

ELIZABETH. He's never cared for anyone but me. He never will.

LADY KITTY. Will Arnold let you divorce him?

ELIZABETH. No, he won't hear of it. He refuses even to divorce me.

LADY KITTY. Why?

ELIZABETH. He thinks a scandal will revive all the old gossip.

LADY KITTY. Oh, my poor child!

ELIZABETH. It can't be helped. I'm quite willing to accept the consequences.

LADY KITTY. You don't know what it is to have a man tied to you only by his honour. When married people don't get on they can separate, but if they're not married it's impossible. It's a tie that only death can sever.

ELIZABETH. If Teddie stopped caring for me I shouldn't want him to stay with me for five minutes.

LADY KITTY. One says that when one's sure of a man's love, but when one isn't any more—oh, it's so different. In those circumstances one's got to keep a man's love. It's the only thing one has.

ELIZABETH. I'm a human being. I can stand on my own feet.

LADY KITTY. Have you any money of your own?

ELIZABETH. None.

LADY KITTY. Then how can you stand on your own feet? You think

I'm a silly, frivolous woman, but I've learned something in a bitter school. They can make what laws they like, they can give us the suffrage, but when you come down to bedrock it's the man who pays the piper who calls the tune. Woman will only be the equal of man when she earns her living in the same way that he does.

ELIZABETH (*smiling*). It sounds rather funny to hear you talk like that.

LADY KITTY. A cook who marries a butler can snap her fingers in his face because she can earn just as much as he can. But a woman in your position and a woman in mine will always be dependent on the men who keep them.

ELIZABETH. I don't want luxury. You don't know how sick I am of all this beautiful furniture. These over-decorated houses are like a prison in which I can't breathe. When I drive about in a Callot frock and a Rolls-Royce I envy the shop-girl in a coat and skirt whom I see jumping on the tailboard of a bus.

LADY KITTY. You mean that if need be you could earn your own living?

ELIZABETH. Yes.

LADY KITTY. What could you be? A nurse or a typist. It's nonsense. Luxury saps a woman's nerve. And when she's known it once it becomes a necessity.

ELIZABETH. That depends on the woman.

LADY KITTY. When we're young we think we're different from every-one else, but when we grow a little older we discover we're all very much of a muchness.

ELIZABETH. You're very kind to take so much trouble about me.

LADY KITTY. It breaks my heart to think that you're going to make the same pitiful mistake that I made.

ELIZABETH. Oh, don't say it was that, don't, don't.

LADY KITTY. Look at me, Elizabeth, and look at Hughie. Do you think it's been a success? If I had my time over again do you think I'd do it again? Do you think he would?

ELIZABETH. You see, you don't know how much I love Teddie.

LADY KITTY. And do you think I didn't love Hughie? Do you think he didn't love me?

ELIZABETH. I'm sure he did.

LADY KITTY. Oh, of course in the beginning it was heavenly. We felt so brave and adventurous and we were so much in love. The first two years were wonderful. People cut me, you know, but I didn't mind. I thought love was everything. It *is* a little uncomfortable when you come upon an old friend and go towards her eagerly, so glad to see her, and are met with an icy stare.

ELIZABETH. Do you think friends like that are worth having?

LADY KITTY. Perhaps they're not very sure of themselves. Perhaps they're honestly shocked. It's a test one had better not put one's friends to if one can help it. It's rather bitter to find how few one has.

ELIZABETH. But one has some.

LADY KITTY. Yes, they ask you to come and see them when they're quite certain no one will be there who might object to meeting you. Or else they say to you: "My dear, you know I'm devoted to you, and I wouldn't mind at all, but my girl's growing up—I'm sure you understand; you won't think it unkind of me if I don't ask you to the house?"

ELIZABETH (*smiling*). That doesn't seem to me very serious.

LADY KITTY. At first I thought it rather a relief, because it threw Hughie and me together more. But you know, men are very funny. Even when they are in love they're not in love all day long. They want change and recreation.

ELIZABETH. I'm not inclined to blame them for that, poor dears.

LADY KITTY. Then we settled in Florence. And because we couldn't get the society we'd been used to we became used to the society we could get. Loose women and vicious men. Snobs who like to patronise people with a handle to their names. Vague Italian Princes who were glad to borrow a few francs from Hughie and seedy countesses who liked to drive with me in the Cascine. And then Hughie began to hanker after his old life. He wanted to go big game shooting, but I dared not let him go. I was afraid he'd never come back.

ELIZABETH. But you knew he loved you.

LADY KITTY. Oh, my dear, what a blessed institution marriage is—for women, and what fools they are to meddle with it! The Church is so wise to take its stand on the indi—indi—

ELIZABETH. Solu—

LADY KITTY. Bility of marriage. Believe me, it's no joke when you have to rely only on yourself to keep a man. I could never afford to grow old. My dear, I'll tell you a secret that I've never told a living soul.

ELIZABETH. What is that?

LADY KITTY. My hair is not naturally this colour.

ELIZABETH. Really.

LADY KITTY. I touch it up. You would never have guessed, would you?

ELIZABETH. Never.

LADY KITTY. Nobody does. My dear, it's white, prematurely of course, but white. I always think it's a symbol of my life. Are you interested in symbolism? I think it's too wonderful.

ELIZABETH. I don't think I know very much about it.

LADY KITTY. However tired I've been I've had to be brilliant and gay. I've never let Hughie see the aching heart behind my smiling eyes.

ELIZABETH (*amused and touched*). You poor dear.

LADY KITTY. And when I saw he was attracted by some one else the fear and the jealousy that seized me! You see, I didn't dare make a scene as I should have done if I'd been married—I had to pretend not to notice.

ELIZABETH (*taken aback*). But do you mean to say he fell in love with anyone else?

LADY KITTY. Of course he did eventually.

ELIZABETH (*hardly knowing what to say*). You must have been very unhappy.

LADY KITTY. Oh, I was, dreadfully. Night after night I sobbed my heart out when Hughie told me he was going to play cards at the club and I knew he was with that odious woman. Of course, it wasn't as if there weren't plenty of men who were only too anxious to console me. Men have always been attracted by me, you know.

ELIZABETH. Oh, of course, I can quite understand it.

LADY KITTY. But I had my self-respect to think of. I felt that whatever Hughie did I would do nothing that I should regret.

ELIZABETH. You must be very glad now.

LADY KITTY. Oh, yes. Notwithstanding all my temptations I've been absolutely faithful to Hughie in spirit.

ELIZABETH. I don't think I quite understand what you mean.

LADY KITTY. Well, there was a poor Italian boy, young Count Castel Giovanni, who was so desperately in love with me that his mother begged me not to be too cruel. She was afraid he'd go into a consumption. What could I do? And then, oh, years later, there was Antonio Melita. He said he'd shoot himself unless I—well, you understand I couldn't let the poor boy shoot himself.

ELIZABETH. D'you think he really would have shot himself?

LADY KITTY. Oh, one never knows, you know. Those Italians are so passionate. He was really rather a lamb. He had such beautiful eyes. (ELIZABETH *looks at her for a long time and a certain horror seizes her of this dissolute, painted old woman.*)

ELIZABETH (*hoarsely*). Oh, but I think that's—dreadful.

LADY KITTY. Are you shocked? One sacrifices one's life for love and then one finds that love doesn't last. The tragedy of love isn't death or separation. One gets over them. The tragedy of love is indifference. (ARNOLD *comes in.*)

ARNOLD. Can I have a little talk with you, Elizabeth?

ELIZABETH. Of course.

ARNOLD. Shall we go for a stroll in the garden?

ELIZABETH. If you like.

LADY KITTY. No, stay here. I'm going out anyway. (*Exit* LADY KITTY.)

ARNOLD. I want you to listen to me for a few minutes, Elizabeth. I was so taken aback by what you told me just now that I lost my head. I was rather absurd and I beg your pardon. I said things I regret.

ELIZABETH. Oh, don't blame yourself. I'm sorry that I should have given you occasion to say them.

ARNOLD. I want to ask you if you've quite made up your mind to go.

ELIZABETH. Quite.

ARNOLD. Just now I seem to have said all that I didn't want to say and nothing that I did. I'm stupid and tongue-tied. I never told you how deeply I loved you.

ELIZABETH. Oh, Arnold!

ARNOLD. Please let me speak now. It's so very difficult. If I seemed absorbed in politics and the house, and so on, to the exclusion of my interest in you, I'm dreadfully sorry. I suppose it was absurd of me to think you would take my great love for granted.

ELIZABETH. But, Arnold, I'm not reproaching you.

ARNOLD. I'm reproaching myself. I've been tactless and neglectful. But I do ask you to believe that it hasn't been because I didn't love you. Can you forgive me?

ELIZABETH. I don't think that there's anything to forgive.

ARNOLD. It wasn't till today when you talked of leaving me that I realised how desperately in love with you I was.

ELIZABETH. After three years?

ARNOLD. I'm so proud of you. I admire you so much. When I see you at a party, so fresh and lovely, and everybody wondering at you, I have a sort of little thrill because you're mine, and afterwards I shall take you home.

ELIZABETH. Oh, Arnold, you're exaggerating.

ARNOLD. I can't imagine this house without you. Life seems on a sudden all empty and meaningless. Oh, Elizabeth, don't you love me at all?

ELIZABETH. It's much better to be honest. No.

ARNOLD. Doesn't my love mean anything to you?

ELIZABETH. I'm very grateful to you. I'm sorry to cause you pain. What would be the good of my staying with you when I should be wretched all the time?

ARNOLD. Do you love that man as much as all that? Does my unhappiness mean nothing to you?

ELIZABETH. Of course it does. It breaks my heart. You see, I never knew I meant so much to you. I'm so touched. And I'm so sorry, Arnold, really sorry. But I can't help myself.

ARNOLD. Poor child, it's cruel of me to torture you.

ELIZABETH. Oh, Arnold, believe me, I have tried to make the best of it. I've tried to love you, but I can't. After all, one either loves or one doesn't. Trying is no help. And now I'm at the end of my tether. I can't help the consequences—I must do what my whole self yearns for.

ARNOLD. My poor child, I'm so afraid you'll be unhappy. I'm so afraid you'll regret.

ELIZABETH. You must leave me to my fate. I hope you'll forget me and all the unhappiness I've caused you.

ARNOLD. (*There is a pause.* ARNOLD *walks up and down the room reflectively. He stops and faces her.*) If you love this man and want to go to him I'll do nothing to prevent you. My only wish is to do what is best for you.

ELIZABETH. Arnold, that's awfully kind of you. If I'm treating you badly at least I want you to know that I'm grateful for all your kindness to me.

ARNOLD. But there's one favour I should like you to do me. Will you?

ELIZABETH. Oh, Arnold, of course I'll do anything I can.

ARNOLD. Teddie hasn't very much money. You've been used to a certain amount of luxury, and I can't bear to think that you should do without anything you've had. It would kill me to think that you were suffering any hardship or privation.

ELIZABETH. Oh, but Teddie can earn enough for our needs. After all, we don't want much money.

ARNOLD. I'm afraid my mother's life hasn't been very easy, but it's obvious that the only thing that's made it possible is that Porteous was rich. I want you to let me make you an allowance of two thousand a year.

ELIZABETH. Oh, no, I couldn't think of it. It's absurd.

ARNOLD. I beg you to accept it. You don't know what a difference it will make.

ELIZABETH. It's awfully kind of you, Arnold. It humiliates me to speak about it. Nothing would induce me to take a penny from you.

ARNOLD. Well, you can't prevent me from opening an account at my bank in your name. The money shall be paid in every quarter whether you touch it or not, and if you happen to want it, it will be there waiting for you.

ELIZABETH. You overwhelm me, Arnold. There's only one thing I want you to do for me. I should be very grateful if you would divorce me as soon as you possibly can.

ARNOLD. No, I won't do that. But I'll give you cause to divorce me.

ELIZABETH. You!

ARNOLD. Yes. But of course you'll have to be very careful for a bit. I'll put it through as quickly as possible, but I'm afraid you can't hope to be free for over six months.

ELIZABETH. But, Arnold, your seat and your political career!

ARNOLD. Oh, well, my father gave up his seat under similar circumstances. He's got along very comfortably without politics.

ELIZABETH. But they're your whole life.

ARNOLD. After all one can't have it both ways. You can't serve God and Mammon. If you want to do the decent thing you have to be prepared to suffer for it.

ELIZABETH. But I don't want you to suffer for it.

ARNOLD. At first I rather hesitated at the scandal. But I daresay that was only weakness on my part. Under the circumstances I should have liked to keep out of the Divorce Court if I could.

ELIZABETH. Arnold, you're making me absolutely miserable.

ARNOLD. What you said before dinner was quite right. It's nothing for a man, but it makes so much difference to a woman. Naturally I must think of you first.

ELIZABETH. That's absurd. It's out of the question. Whatever there's to pay I must pay it.

ARNOLD. It's not very much I'm asking you, Elizabeth.

ELIZABETH. I'm taking everything from you.

ARNOLD. It's the only condition I make. My mind is absolutely made up. I will never divorce you, but I will enable you to divorce me.

ELIZABETH. Oh, Arnold, it's cruel to be so generous.

ARNOLD. It's not generous at all. It's the only way I have of showing you how deep and passionate and sincere my love is for you. (*There is a silence. He holds out his hand*) Good-night. I have a great deal of work to do before I go to bed.

ELIZABETH. Good-night.

ARNOLD. Do you mind if I kiss you?

ELIZABETH (*with agony*). Oh, Arnold!

(*He gravely kisses her on the forehead and then goes out.* ELIZABETH *stands lost in thought. She is shattered.* LADY KITTY *and* PORTEOUS *come in.* LADY KITTY *wears a cloak.*)

LADY KITTY. You're alone, Elizabeth?

ELIZABETH. That note you asked me about, Lady Kitty, from Teddie . . .

LADY KITTY. Yes?

ELIZABETH. He wanted to have a talk with me before he went away. He's waiting for me in the summer house by the tennis court. Would Lord Porteous mind going down and asking him to come here?

PORTEOUS. Certainly. Certainly.

ELIZABETH. Forgive me for troubling you. But it's very important.

PORTEOUS. No trouble at all. (*He goes out.*)

LADY KITTY. Hughie and I will leave you alone.

ELIZABETH. But I don't want to be left alone. I want you to stay.

LADY KITTY. What are you going to say to him?

ELIZABETH (*desperately*). Please don't ask me questions. I'm so frightfully unhappy.

LADY KITTY. My poor child!

ELIZABETH. Oh, isn't life rotten? Why can't one be happy without making other people unhappy?

LADY KITTY. I wish I knew how to help you. I'm simply devoted to you. (*She hunts about in her mind for something to do or say*) Would you like my lip-stick?

ELIZABETH (*smiling through her tears*). Thanks. I never use one.

LADY KITTY. Oh, but just try. It's such a comfort when you're in trouble.

(*Enter* PORTEOUS *and* TEDDIE.)

PORTEOUS. I brought him. He said he'd be damned if he'd come.

LADY KITTY. When a lady sent for him? Are these the manners of the young men of today?

TEDDIE. When you've been solemnly kicked out of a house once I think it seems rather pushing to come back again as though nothing had happened.

ELIZABETH. Teddie, I want you to be serious.

TEDDIE. Darling, I had such a rotten dinner at that pub. If you ask me to be serious on the top of that I shall cry.

ELIZABETH. Don't be idiotic, Teddie. (*Her voice faltering*) I'm so utterly wretched.

(*He looks at her for a moment gravely.*)

TEDDIE. What is it?

ELIZABETH. I can't come away with you, Teddie.

TEDDIE. Why not?

ELIZABETH (*looking away in embarrassment*). I don't love you enough.

TEDDIE. Fiddle!

ELIZABETH (*with a flash of anger*). Don't say "Fiddle" to me.

TEDDIE. I shall say exactly what I like to you.

ELIZABETH. I won't be bullied.

TEDDIE. Now look here, Elizabeth, you know perfectly well that I'm in love with you, and I know perfectly well that you're in love with me. So what are you talking nonsense for?

ELIZABETH (*her voice breaking*). I can't say it if you're cross with me.

TEDDIE (*smiling very tenderly*). I'm not cross with you, silly.

ELIZABETH. It's harder still when you're being rather an owl.

TEDDIE (*with a chuckle*). Am I mistaken in thinking you're not very easy to please?

ELIZABETH. Oh, it's monstrous. I was all wrought up and ready to do anything, and now you've thoroughly put me out. I feel like a great big fat balloon that some one has put a long pin into. (*With a sudden look at him*) Have you done it on purpose?

TEDDIE. Upon my soul I don't know what you're talking about.

ELIZABETH. I wonder if you're really much cleverer than I think you are.

TEDDIE (*taking her hands and making her sit down*). Now tell me exactly what you want to say. By the way, do you want Lady Kitty and Lord Porteous to be here?

ELIZABETH. Yes.

LADY KITTY. Elizabeth asked us to stay.

TEDDIE. Oh, I don't mind, bless you. I only thought you might feel rather in the way.

LADY KITTY (*frigidly*). A gentlewoman never feels in the way, Mr. Luton.

TEDDIE. Won't you call me Teddie? Everybody does, you know.
(LADY KITTY *tries to give him a withering look, but she finds it very difficult to prevent herself from smiling.* TEDDIE *strokes* ELIZABETH'S *hands. She draws them away.*)

ELIZABETH. No, don't do that. Teddie, it wasn't true when I said I didn't love you. Of course I love you. But Arnold loves me, too. I didn't know how much.

TEDDIE. What has he been saying to you?

ELIZABETH. He's been very good to me, and so kind. I didn't know he could be so kind. He offered to let me divorce him.

TEDDIE. That's very decent of him.

ELIZABETH. But don't you see, it ties my hands. How can I accept such a sacrifice? I should never forgive myself if I profited by his generosity.

TEDDIE. If another man and I were devilish hungry and there was only one mutton chop between us, and he said, "You eat it," I wouldn't waste a lot of time arguing. I'd wolf it before he changed his mind.

ELIZABETH. Don't talk like that. It maddens me. I'm trying to do the right thing.

TEDDIE. You're not in love with Arnold; you're in love with me. It's idiotic to sacrifice your life for a slushy sentiment.

ELIZABETH. After all, I did marry him.

TEDDIE. Well, you made a mistake. A marriage without love is no marriage at all.

ELIZABETH. *I* made the mistake. Why should he suffer for it? If anyone has to suffer it's only right that I should.

TEDDIE. What sort of a life do you think it would be with him? When two people are married it's very difficult for one of them to be unhappy without making the other unhappy too.

ELIZABETH. I can't take advantage of his generosity.

TEDDIE. I daresay he'll get a lot of satisfaction out of it.

ELIZABETH. You're being beastly, Teddie. He was simply wonderful. I never knew he had it in him. He was really noble.

TEDDIE. You are talking rot, Elizabeth.

ELIZABETH. I wonder if you'd be capable of acting like that.

TEDDIE. Acting like what?

ELIZABETH. What would you do if I were married to you and came and told you I loved somebody else and wanted to leave you?

TEDDIE. You have very pretty blue eyes, Elizabeth. I'd black first one and then the other. And after that we'd see.

ELIZABETH. You damned brute!

TEDDIE. I've often thought I wasn't quite a gentleman. Had it ever struck you?
(*They look at one another for a while.*)

ELIZABETH. You know, you are taking an unfair advantage of me. I feel as if I came to you quite unsuspectingly and when I wasn't looking you kicked me on the shins.

TEDDIE. Don't you think we'd get on rather well together?

PORTEOUS. Elizabeth's a fool if she don't stick to her husband. It's bad enough for the man, but for the woman—it's damnable. I hold no brief for Arnold. He plays bridge like a foot. Saving your presence, Kitty, I think he's a prig.

LADY KITTY. Poor dear, his father was at his age. I daresay he'll grow out of it.

PORTEOUS. But you stick to him, Elizabeth, stick to him. Man is a gregarious animal. We're members of a herd. If we break the herd's laws we suffer for it. And we suffer damnably.

LADY KITTY. Oh, Elizabeth, my dear child, don't go. It's not worth it. It's not worth it. I tell you that, and I've sacrificed everything to love. (*A pause.*)

ELIZABETH. I'm afraid.

TEDDIE (*in a whisper*). Elizabeth.

ELIZABETH. I can't face it. It's asking too much of me. Let's say good-bye to one another, Teddie. It's the only thing to do. And have pity on me. I'm giving up all my hope of happiness.
(*He goes up to her and looks into her eyes.*)

TEDDIE. But I wasn't offering you happiness. I don't think my sort of love tends to happiness. I'm jealous. I'm not a very easy man to get on with. I'm often out of temper and irritable. I should be fed to the teeth with you sometimes, and so would you be with me. I daresay we'd fight like cat and dog, and sometimes we'd hate each other. Often you'd be wretched and bored stiff and lonely, and often you'd be frightfully homesick, and then you'd regret all you'd lost. Stupid women would be rude to you because we'd run away together. And some of them would cut you. I don't offer you peace and quietness. I offer you unrest and anxiety. I don't offer you happiness. I offer you love.

ELIZABETH (*stretching out her arms*). You hateful creature, I absolutely adore you!
(*He throws his arms round her and kisses her passionately on the lips.*)

LADY KITTY. Of course the moment he said he'd give her a black eye I knew it was finished.

PORTEOUS (*good-humouredly*). You are a fool, Kitty.

LADY KITTY. I know I am, but I can't help it.

TEDDIE. Let's make a bolt for it now.

ELIZABETH. Shall we?

TEDDIE. This minute.

PORTEOUS. You're damned fools, both of you, damned fools! If you like you can have my car.

TEDDIE. That's awfully kind of you. As a matter of fact I got it out of the garage. It's just along the drive.

PORTEOUS (*indignantly*). How do you mean, you got it out of the garage?

TEDDIE. Well, I thought there'd be a lot of bother, and it seemed to me the best thing would be for Elizabeth and me not to stand upon the order of our going, you know. Do it now. An excellent motto for a business man.

PORTEOUS. Do you mean to say you were going to steal my car?

TEDDIE. Not exactly. I was only going to bolshevise it, so to speak.

PORTEOUS. I'm speechless. I'm absolutely speechless.

TEDDIE. Hang it all, I couldn't carry Elizabeth all the way to London. She's so damned plump.

ELIZABETH. You dirty dog!

PORTEOUS (*spluttering*). Well, well, well! . . . (*Helplessly*) I like him, Kitty, it's no good pretending I don't. I like him.

TEDDIE. The moon's shining, Elizabeth. We'll drive all through the night.

PORTEOUS. They'd better go to San Michele. I'll wire to have it got ready for them.

LADY KITTY. That's where we went when Hughie and I . . . (*faltering*) Oh, you dear things, how I envy you!

PORTEOUS (*mopping his eyes*). Now don't cry, Kitty. Confound you, don't cry.

TEDDIE. Come, darling.

ELIZABETH. But I can't go like this.

TEDDIE. Nonsense! Lady Kitty will lend you her cloak. Won't you?

LADY KITTY (*taking it off*). You're capable of tearing it off my back if I don't.

TEDDIE (*putting the cloak on* ELIZABETH). And we'll buy you a toothbrush in London in the morning.

LADY KITTY. She must write a note for Arnold. I'll put it on her pincushion.

TEDDIE. Pincushion be blowed! Come, darling. We'll drive through the dawn and through the sunrise.

ELIZABETH (*kissing* LADY KITTY *and* PORTEOUS). Good-bye. Good-bye. (TEDDIE *stretches out his hand and she takes it. Hand in hand they go out into the night.*)

LADY KITTY. Oh, Hughie, how it all comes back to me! Will they suffer all we suffered? And have we suffered all in vain?

PORTEOUS. My dear, I don't know that in life it matters so much what you do as what you are. No one can learn by the experience of another because no circumstances are quite the same. If we made rather a hash of things perhaps it was because we were rather trivial people. You can do anything in this world if you're prepared to take the consequences, and consequences depend on character. (*Enter* CHAMPION-CHENEY, *rubbing his hands. He is as pleased as Punch.*)

C.-C. Well, I think I've settled the hash of that young man.

LADY KITTY. Oh!

C.-C. You have to get up very early in the morning to get the better of your humble servant.

(*There is the sound of a car starting.*)

LADY KITTY. What is that?

C.-C. It sounds like a car. I expect it's your chauffeur taking one of the maids for a joy-ride.

PORTEOUS. Whose hash are you talking about?

C.-C. Mr. Edward Luton's, my dear Hughie. I told Arnold exactly what to do and he's done it. What makes a prison? Why, bars and bolts. Remove them and a prisoner won't want to escape. Clever, I flatter myself.

PORTEOUS. You were always that, Clive, but at the moment you're obscure.

C.-C. I told Arnold to go to Elizabeth and tell her she could have her freedom. I told him to sacrifice himself all along the line. I know what women are. The moment every obstacle was removed to her marriage with Teddie Luton, half the allurement was gone.

LADY KITTY. Arnold did that?

C.-C. He followed my instructions to the letter. I've just seen him. She's shaken. I'm willing to bet five hundred pounds to a penny that she won't bolt. A downy old bird, eh? Downy's the word. Downy.
(*He begins to laugh. They laugh, too. Presently they are all three in fits of laughter.*)

CURTAIN

Loyalties

BY JOHN GALSWORTHY

Loyalties was first produced in America at the Gaiety Theatre, New York City, by Charles Dillingham on September 27, 1922, and closed on April 29, 1923. The following is the original cast:

(*In the Order of Appearance*)

Charles Winsor, Owner of Meldon Court, near Newmarket	H. G. Stoker
Lady Adela, His Wife	Cathryn Young
Ferdinand De Levis, Young, rich, and new	James Dale
Treisure, Winsor's Butler	Henry Carvill
General Canynge, A Racing Oracle	Felix Aylmer
Margaret Orme, A Society Girl	Jeannette Sherwin
Captain Ronald Dancy, D.S.O., Retired	Charles Quartermaine
Mabel, His Wife	Diana Bourbon
Inspector Dede, Of the County Constabulary	Victor Tandy
Robert, Winsor's Footman	Deering Wells
A Constable, Attendant on Dede	Henry Morrell
Augustus Borring, A Clubman	Deering Wells
Lord St. Erth, A Peer of the Realm	Laurence Hanray
A Footman, Of the Club	Henry Morrell
Major Colford, A Brother Officer of Dancy's	Wilfred Seagram
Edward Graviter, A Solicitor	Henry Morrell
A Young Clerk, Of Twisden & Graviter's	Deering Wells
Gilman, A Large Grocer	Victor Tandy
Jacob Twisden, Senior Partner of Twisden & Graviter's	Laurence Hanray
Ricardos, An Italian, in Wine	Henry Carvill

SCENES

ACT ONE

SCENE I

Charles Winsor's Dressing-room at Meldon Court, near Newmarket, of a night in early October

SCENE II

De Levis's Bedroom at Meldon Court, a few minutes later

ACT TWO

SCENE I

The Card Room of a London Club between four and five in the afternoon, three weeks later

SCENE II

The Sitting-room of the Dancys' Flat, the following morning

ACT THREE

SCENE I

Old Mr. Jacob Twisden's Room at Twisden & Graviter's in Lincoln's Inn Fields, at four in the afternoon, three months later

SCENE II

The same, next morning at half-past ten

SCENE III

The Sitting-room of the Dancys' Flat, an hour later

LOYALTIES

ACT ONE

SCENE I

The dressing-room of CHARLES WINSOR, *owner of Meldon Court, near Newmarket; about eleven-thirty at night. The room has pale grey walls, unadorned; the curtains are drawn over a window Back Left Centre. A bed lies along the wall, Left. An open door, Right Back, leads into* LADY ADELA'S *bedroom; a door, Right Forward, into a long corridor, on to which abut rooms in a row, the whole length of the house's left wing.* WINSOR'S *dressing-table, with a light over it, is Stage Right of the curtained window. Pyjamas are laid out on the bed, which is turned back. Slippers are handy, and all the usual gear of a well-appointed bed-dressing-room.* CHARLES WINSOR, *a tall, fair, good-looking man about thirty-eight, is taking off a smoking jacket.*

WINSOR. Hallo! Adela!

V. OF LADY A. (*from her bedroom*). Hallo!

WINSOR. In bed?

V. OF LADY A. No.

(*She appears in the doorway in under-garment and a wrapper. She, too, is fair, about thirty-five, rather delicious, and suggestive of porcelain.*)

WINSOR. Win at Bridge?

LADY A. No fear.

WINSOR. Who did?

LADY A. Lord St Erth and Ferdy De Levis.

WINSOR. That young man has too much luck—the young bounder won two races today; and he's as rich as Crœsus.

LADY A. Oh! Charlie, he did look so exactly as if he'd sold me a carpet when I was paying him.

WINSOR (*changing into slippers*). His father did sell carpets, wholesale, in the City.

LADY A. Really? And you say I haven't intuition! (*With a finger on her lips*) Morison's in there.

WINSOR (*motioning towards the door, which she shuts*). Ronny Dancy took a tenner off him, anyway, before dinner.

LADY A. No! How?

WINSOR. Standing jump on to a bookcase four feet high. De Levis had to pay up, and sneered at him for making money by parlour tricks. That young Jew gets himself disliked.

LADY A. Aren't you rather prejudiced?

WINSOR. Not a bit. I like Jews. That's not against him—rather the contrary these days. But he pushes himself. The General tells me he's deathly keen to get into the Jockey Club. (*Taking off his tie*) It's amusing to see him trying to get round old St Erth.

LADY A. If Lord St Erth and General Canynge backed him he'd get in if he *did* sell carpets!

WINSOR. He's got some pretty good horses. (*Taking off his waistcoat*) Ronny Dancy's on his bones again, I'm afraid. He had a bad day. When a chap takes to doing parlour stunts for a bet—it's a sure sign. What made him chuck the Army?

LADY A. He says it's too dull, now there's no fighting.

WINSOR. Well, he can't exist on backing losers.

LADY A. Isn't it just like him to get married now? He really is the most reckless person.

WINSOR. Yes. He's a queer chap. I've always liked him, but I've never quite made him out. What do you think of his wife?

LADY A. Nice child; awfully gone on him.

WINSOR. Is *he*?

LADY A. Quite indecently—both of them. (*Nodding towards the wall, Left*) They're next door.

WINSOR. Who's beyond them?

LADY A. De Levis; and Margaret Orme at the end. Charlie, do you realise that the bathroom out there has to wash those four?

WINSOR. I know.

LADY A. Your grandfather was crazy when he built this wing; six rooms in a row with balconies like an hotel, and only one bath—if we hadn't put ours in.

WINSOR (*looking at his watch*). Half-past eleven. (*Yawns*) Newmarket always makes me sleepy. You're keeping Morison up.

(LADY ADELA *goes to the door, blowing a kiss.* CHARLES *goes up to his dressing-table and begins to brush his hair, sprinkling on essence. There is a knock on the corridor door.*)

Come in.

(DE LEVIS *enters, clad in pyjamas and flowered dressing-gown. He is a dark, good-looking, rather Eastern young man. His face is long and disturbed.*)

Hallo! De Levis! Anything I can do for you?

DE LEVIS (*in a voice whose faint exoticism is broken by a vexed excitement*). I say, I'm awfully sorry, Winsor, but I thought I'd better tell you at once. I've just had—er—rather a lot of money stolen.

WINSOR. What! (*There is something of outrage in his tone and glance, as who should say: "In my house?"*) How do you mean *stolen*?

DE LEVIS. I put it under my pillow and went to have a bath; when I came back it was gone.

WINSOR. Good Lord! How much?

DE LEVIS. Nearly a thousand—nine hundred and seventy, I think.

WINSOR. Phew! (*Again the faint tone of outrage, that a man should have so much money about him.*)

DE LEVIS. I sold my Rosemary filly today on the course to Kentman the bookie, and he paid me in notes.

WINSOR. What? That weed Dancy gave you in the Spring?

DE LEVIS. Yes. But I tried her pretty high the other day; and she's in the Cambridgeshire. I was only out of my room a quarter of an hour, and I locked my door.

WINSOR (*again outraged*). You locked——

DE LEVIS (*not seeing the fine shade*). Yes, and had the key here. (*He taps his pocket*) Look here! (*He holds out a pocket-book*) It's been stuffed with my shaving papers.

WINSOR (*between feeling that such things don't happen, and a sense that he will have to clear it up*). This is damned awkward, De Levis.

DE LEVIS (*with steel in his voice*). Yes. I should like it back.

WINSOR. Have you got the numbers of the notes?

DE LEVIS. No.

WINSOR. What were they?

DE LEVIS. One hundred, three fifties, and the rest tens and fives.

WINSOR. What d'you want me to do?

DE LEVIS. Unless there's anybody you think——

WINSOR (*eyeing him*). Is it likely?

DE LEVIS. Then I think the police ought to see my room. It's a lot of money.

WINSOR. Good Lord! We're not in Town; there'll be nobody nearer than Newmarket at this time of night—four miles.
(*The door from the bedroom is suddenly opened and* LADY ADELA *appears. She has on a lace cap over her finished hair, and the wrapper.*)

LADY A. (*closing the door*). What is it? Are you ill, Mr. De Levis?

WINSOR. Worse; he's had a lot of money stolen. Nearly a thousand pounds.

LADY A. Gracious! Where?

DE LEVIS. From under my pillow, Lady Adela—my door was locked—I was in the bathroom.

LADY A. But how fearfully thrilling!

WINSOR. Thrilling! What's to be done? He wants it back.

LADY A. Of course! (*With sudden realisation*) Oh! But—— Oh! it's quite too unpleasant!

WINSOR. Yes! What am I to do? Fetch the servants out of their rooms? Search the grounds? It'll make the devil of a scandal.

DE LEVIS. Who's next to me?

LADY A. (*coldly*). Oh! Mr. De Levis!

WINSOR. Next to you? The Dancys on this side, and Miss Orme on the other. What's that to do with it?

DE LEVIS. They may have heard something.

WINSOR. Let's get them. But Dancy was downstairs when I came up. Get Morison, Adela! No. Look here! When *was* this exactly? Let's have as many alibis as we can.

DE LEVIS. Within the last twenty minutes, certainly.

WINSOR. How long has Morison been up with you?

LADY A. I came up at eleven, and rang for her at once.

WINSOR (*looking at his watch*). Half an hour. Then she's all right. Send her for Margaret and the Dancys—there's nobody else in this wing. No; send her to bed. We don't want gossip. D'you mind going yourself, Adela?

LADY A. Consult General Canynge, Charlie.

WINSOR. Right. Could you get him too? D'you really want the police, De Levis?

DE LEVIS (*stung by the faint contempt in his tone of voice*). Yes, I do.

WINSOR. Then, look here, dear! Slip into my study and telephone to the police at Newmarket. There'll be somebody there; they're sure to have drunks. I'll have Treisure up, and speak to him. (*He rings the bell.*)

(LADY ADELA *goes out into her room and closes the door.*)

WINSOR. Look here, De Levis! This isn't an hotel. It's the sort of thing that doesn't happen in a decent house. Are you sure you're not mistaken, and didn't have them stolen on the course?

DE LEVIS. Absolutely. I counted them just before putting them under my pillow; then I locked the door and had the key here. There's only one door, you know.

WINSOR. How was your window?

DE LEVIS. Open.

WINSOR (*drawing back the curtains of his own window*). You've got a balcony like this. Any sign of a ladder or anything?

DE LEVIS. No.

WINSOR. It must have been done from the window, unless someone had a skeleton key. Who knew you'd got that money? Where did Kentman pay you?

DE LEVIS. Just round the corner in the further paddock.

WINSOR. Anybody about?

DE LEVIS. Oh, yes!

WINSOR. Suspicious?

DE LEVIS. I didn't notice anything.

WINSOR. You must have been marked down and followed here.

DE LEVIS. How would they know my room?

WINSOR. Might have got it somehow. (*A knock from the corridor*) Come in.
(TREISURE, *the Butler, appears, a silent, grave man of almost supernatural conformity.* DE LEVIS *gives him a quick, hard look, noted and resented by* WINSOR.)

TREISURE (*to* WINSOR). Yes, sir?

WINSOR. Who valets Mr. De Levis?

TREISURE. Robert, sir.

WINSOR. When was he up last?

TREISURE. In the ordinary course of things, about ten o'clock, sir.

WINSOR. When did he go to bed?

TREISURE. I dismissed at eleven.

WINSOR. But did he go?

TREISURE. To the best of my knowledge. Is there anything *I* can do, sir?

WINSOR (*disregarding a sign from* DE LEVIS). Look here, Mr. De Levis has had a large sum of money taken from his bedroom within the last half hour.

TREISURE. Indeed, sir!

WINSOR. Robert's quite all right, isn't he?

TREISURE. He is, sir.

DE LEVIS. How do you know?
(TREISURE'S *eyes rest on* DE LEVIS.)

TREISURE. I am a pretty good judge of character, sir, if you'll excuse me.

WINSOR. Look here, De Levis, eighty or ninety notes must have been pretty bulky. You didn't have them on you at dinner?

DE LEVIS. No.

WINSOR. Where did you put them?

DE LEVIS. In a boot, and the boot in my suitcase, and locked it.
(TREISURE *smiles faintly.*)

WINSOR (*again slightly outraged by such precautions in his house*). And you found it locked—and took them from there to put under your pillow?

DE LEVIS. Yes.

WINSOR. Run your mind over things, Treisure—has any stranger been about?

TREISURE. No, sir.

WINSOR. This seems to have happened between 11.15 and 11.30. Is that right? (DE LEVIS *nods*) Any noise—anything outside – anything suspicious anywhere?

TREISURE (*running his mind—very still*). No, sir.

WINSOR. What time did you shut up?

TREISURE. I should say about eleven-fifteen, sir. As soon as Major Colford and Captain Dancy had finished billiards. What was Mr. De Levis doing out of his room, if I may ask, sir?

WINSOR. Having a bath; with his room locked and the key in his pocket.

TREISURE. Thank you, sir.

DE LEVIS (*conscious of indefinable suspicion*). Damn it! What do you mean? I *was*.

TREISURE. I beg your pardon, sir.

WINSOR (*concealing a smile*). Look here, Treisure, it's infernally awkward for everybody.

TREISURE. It is, sir.

WINSOR. What do you suggest?

TREISURE. The proper thing, sir, I suppose, would be a cordon and a complete search—in our interests.

WINSOR. I entirely refuse to suspect anybody.

TREISURE. But if Mr. De Levis feels otherwise, sir?

DE LEVIS (*stammering*). I? All I know is—the money was there, and it's gone.

WINSOR (*compunctious*). Quite! It's pretty sickening for you. But so it is for anybody else. However, we must do our best to get it back for you.
(*A knock on the door.*)

WINSOR. Hallo!
(TREISURE *opens the door, and* GENERAL CANYNGE *enters.*)
Oh! It's you, General. Come in. Adela's told you?
(GENERAL CANYNGE *nods. He is a slim man of about sixty, very well preserved, intensely neat and self-contained, and still in evening dress. His eyelids droop slightly, but his eyes are keen and his expression astute.*)

WINSOR. Well, General, what's the first move?

CANYNGE (*lifting his eyebrows*). Mr. De Levis presses the matter?

DE LEVIS (*flicked again*). Unless you think it's too plebeian of me, General Canynge — a thousand pounds.

CANYNGE (*drily*). Just so! Then we must wait for the police, Winsor. Lady Adela has got through to them. What height are these rooms from the ground, Treisure?

TREISURE. Twenty-three feet from the terrace, sir.

CANYNGE. Any ladders near?

TREISURE. One in the stables, sir, very heavy. No others within three hundred yards.

CANYNGE. Just slip down, and see whether that's been moved.

TREISURE. Very good, General. (*He goes out.*)

DE LEVIS (*uneasily*). Of course, he —I suppose you——

WINSOR. We do.

CANYNGE. You had better leave this in our hands, De Levis.

DE LEVIS. Certainly; only, the way he——

WINSOR (*curtly*). Treisure has been here since he was a boy. I should as soon suspect myself.

DE LEVIS (*looking from one to the other—with sudden anger*). You seem to think——! What was I to do? Take it lying down and let whoever it is get clear off? I suppose it's natural to want my money back?
(CANYNGE *looks at his nails;* WINSOR *out of the window.*)

WINSOR (*turning*). Of course, De Levis!

DE LEVIS (*sullenly*). Well, I'll go to my room. When the police come, perhaps you'll let me know. (*He goes out.*)

WINSOR. Phew! Did you ever see such a dressing-gown?
(*The door is opened.* LADY ADELA *and* MARGARET ORME *come in. The latter is a vivid young lady of about twenty-five in a vivid wrapper; she is smoking a cigarette.*)

LADY A. I've told the Dancys—she was in bed. And I got through to Newmarket, Charles, and Inspector Dede is coming like the wind on a motor cycle.

MARGARET. Did he say "like the wind," Adela? He must have imagination. Isn't this gorgeous? Poor little Ferdy!

WINSOR (*vexed*). You might take it seriously, Margaret; it's pretty beastly for us all. What time did *you* come up?

MARGARET. I came up with Adela. Am I suspected, Charles? How thrilling!

WINSOR. Did you hear anything?

MARGARET. Only little Ferdy splashing.

WINSOR. And saw nothing?

MARGARET. Not even that, alas!

LADY A. (*with a finger held up*). *Leste! Un peu leste!* Oh! Here are the Dancys. Come in, you two!
(MABEL *and* RONALD DANCY *enter. She is a pretty young woman with bobbed hair, fortunately, for she has just got out of bed, and is in her nightgown and a wrapper.* DANCY *is in his smoking jacket. He has a pale, determined face with high cheek-bones, small, deep-set dark eyes, reddish crisp hair, and looks like a horseman.*)

WINSOR. Awfully sorry to disturb you, Mrs. Dancy; but I suppose you and Ronny haven't heard anything. De Levis's room is just beyond Ronny's dressing-room, you know.

MABEL. I've been asleep nearly half an hour, and Ronny's only just come up.

CANYNGE. Did you happen to look out of your window, Mrs. Dancy?

MABEL. Yes. I stood there quite five minutes.

CANYNGE. When?

MABEL. Just about eleven, I should think. It was raining hard then.

CANYNGE. Yes, it's just stopped. You saw nothing?

MABEL. No.

DANCY. What time does he say the money was taken?

WINSOR. Between the quarter and half past. He'd locked his door and had the key with him.

MARGARET. How quaint! Just like an hotel. Does he put his boots out?

LADY A. Don't be so naughty, Meg.

CANYNGE. When exactly did *you* come up, Dancy?

DANCY. About ten minutes ago. I'd only just got into my dressing-room before Lady Adela came. I've been writing letters in the hall since Colford and I finished billiards.

CANYNGE. You weren't up for anything in between?

DANCY. No.

MARGARET. The mystery of the grey room.

DANCY. Oughtn't the grounds to be searched for footmarks?

CANYNGE. That's for the police.

DANCY. The deuce! Are they coming?

CANYNGE. Directly. (*A knock*) Yes? (TREISURE *enters*) Well?

TREISURE. The ladder has not been moved, General. There isn't a sign.

WINSOR. All right. Get Robert up, but don't say anything to him. By the way, we're expecting the police.

TREISURE. I trust they will not find a mare's nest, sir, if I may say so. (*He goes.*)

WINSOR. De Levis has got wrong with Treisure. (*Suddenly*) But, I say, what would any of us have done if *we'd* been in his shoes?

MARGARET. A thousand pounds? I can't even conceive having it.

DANCY. We probably shouldn't have found it out.

LADY A. No—but if we had.

DANCY. Come to you—as he did.

WINSOR. Yes; but there's a way of doing things.

CANYNGE. We shouldn't have wanted the police.

MARGARET. No. That's it. The hotel touch.

LADY A. Poor young man; I think we're rather hard on him.

WINSOR. He sold that weed you gave him, Dancy, to Kentman, the bookie, and these were the proceeds.

DANCY. Oh!

WINSOR. He'd tried her high, he said.

DANCY (*grimly*). He would.

MABEL. Oh! Ronny, what bad luck!

WINSOR. He must have been followed here. (*At the window*) After rain like that, there ought to be footmarks.
(*The splutter of a motor cycle is heard.*)

MARGARET. Here's the wind!

WINSOR. What's the move now, General?

CANYNGE. You and I had better see the Inspector in De Levis's room,

Winsor. (*To the others*) If you'll all be handy, in case he wants to put questions for himself.

MARGARET. I hope he'll want me; it's just too thrilling.

DANCY. I hope he won't want me; I'm dog-tired. Come on, Mabel. (*He puts his arm in his wife's.*)

CANYNGE. Just a minute, Charles. (*He draws close to* WINSOR *as the others are departing to their rooms.*)

WINSOR. Yes, General?

CANYNGE. We must be careful with this Inspector fellow. If he pitches hastily on somebody in the house it'll be very disagreeable.

WINSOR. By Jove! It *will.*

CANYNGE. We don't want to rouse any ridiculous suspicion.

WINSOR. Quite. (*A knock*) Come in! (TREISURE *enters.*)

TREISURE. Inspector Dede, sir.

WINSOR. Show him in.

TREISURE. Robert is in readiness, sir; but I could swear he knows nothing about it.

WINSOR. All right.

(TREISURE *reopens the door, and says: "Come in, please." The* INSPECTOR *enters, blue, formal, moustachioed, with a peaked cap in his hand.*)

WINSOR. Good-evening, Inspector. Sorry to have brought you out at this time of night.

INSPECTOR. Good evenin', sir. Mr. Winsor? You're the owner here, I think?

WINSOR. Yes. General Canynge.

INSPECTOR. Good evenin', General. I understand, a large sum of money?

WINSOR. Yes. Shall we go straight to the room it was taken from? One of my guests, Mr. De Levis. It's the third room on the left.

CANYNGE. We've not been in there yet, Inspector; in fact, we've done nothing, except to find out that the stable ladder has not been moved. We haven't even searched the grounds.

INSPECTOR. Right, sir; I've brought a man with me. (*They go out.*)

Curtain. Interval of a Minute.

SCENE II*

The bedroom of DE LEVIS *is the same in shape as* WINSOR'S *dressing-room, except that there is only one door—to the corridor. The furniture, however, is differently arranged; a small four-poster bedstead stands against*

* The same set is used for this Scene, with the different arrangement of furniture, as specified.

the wall, Right Back, jutting into the room. A chair, on which DE LEVIS'S *clothes are thrown, stands at its foot. There is a dressing-table against the wall to the left of the open windows, where the curtains are drawn back and a stone balcony is seen. Against the wall to the right of the window is a chest of drawers, and a washstand is against the wall, Left. On a small table to the right of the bed an electric reading lamp is turned up, and there is a light over the dressing-table. The* INSPECTOR *is standing plumb centre looking at the bed, and* DE LEVIS *by the back of the chair at the foot of the bed.* WINSOR *and* CANYNGE *are close to the door, Right Forward.*

INSPECTOR (*finishing a note*). Now, sir, if this is the room as you left it for your bath, just show us exactly what you did after takin' the pocket-book from the suit case. Where was that, by the way?

DE LEVIS (*pointing*). Where it is now—under the dressing-table.
(*He comes forward to the front of the chair, opens the pocket-book, goes through the pretence of counting his shaving papers, closes the pocket-book, takes it to the head of the bed and slips it under the pillow. Makes the motion of taking up his pyjamas, crosses below the* INSPECTOR *to the wash-stand, takes up a bath sponge, crosses to the door, takes out the key, opens the door.*)

INSPECTOR (*writing*). We now have the room as it was when the theft was committed. Reconstruct accordin' to 'uman nature, gentlemen—assumin' the thief to be in the room, what would he try first?—the clothes, the dressin'-table, the suit case, the chest of drawers, and last the bed.
(*He moves accordingly, examining the glass on the dressing-table, the surface of the suit cases, and the handles of the drawers, with a spy-glass, for finger-marks.*)

CANYNGE (*sotto voce to* WINSOR). The order would have been just the other way.
(*The* INSPECTOR *goes on hands and knees and examines the carpet between the window and the bed.*)

DE LEVIS. Can I come in again?

INSPECTOR (*standing up*). Did you open the window, sir, or was it open when you first came in?

DE LEVIS. I opened it.

INSPECTOR. Drawin' the curtains back first?

DE LEVIS. Yes.

INSPECTOR (*sharply*). Are you sure there was nobody in the room already?

DE LEVIS (*taken aback*). I don't know. I never thought. I didn't look under the bed, if you mean that.

INSPECTOR (*jotting*). Did not look under bed. Did you look under it after the theft?

DE LEVIS. No. I didn't.

INSPECTOR. Ah! Now, what *did* you do after you came back from your bath? Just give us that precisely.

DE LEVIS. Locked the door and left the key in. Put back my sponge, and took off my dressing-gown and put it there. (*He points to the foot-rails of the bed*) Then I drew the curtains, again.

INSPECTOR. Shutting the window?

DE LEVIS. No. I got into bed, felt for my watch to see the time. My hand struck the pocket-book, and somehow it felt thinner. I took it out, looked into it, and found the notes gone, and these shaving papers instead.

INSPECTOR. Let me have a look at those, sir. (*He applies the spy-glasses*) And then?

DE LEVIS. I think I just sat on the bed.

INSPECTOR. Thinkin' and cursin' a bit, I suppose. Ye-es?

DE LEVIS. Then I put on my dressing-gown and went straight to Mr. Winsor.

INSPECTOR. Not lockin' the door?

DE LEVIS. No.

INSPECTOR. Exactly. (*With a certain finality*) Now, sir, what time did you come up?

DE LEVIS. About eleven.

INSPECTOR. Precise, if you can give it to me.

DE LEVIS. Well, I *know* it was eleven-fifteen when I put my watch under my pillow, before I went to the bath, and I suppose I'd been about a quarter of an hour undressing. I should say after eleven, if anything.

INSPECTOR. Just undressin'? Didn't look over your bettin' book?

DE LEVIS. No.

INSPECTOR. No prayers or anything?

DE LEVIS. No.

INSPECTOR. Pretty slippy with your undressin' as a rule?

DE LEVIS. Yes. Say five past eleven.

INSPECTOR. Mr. Winsor, what time did the gentleman come to you?

WINSOR. Half-past eleven.

INSPECTOR. How do you fix that, sir?

WINSOR. I'd just looked at the time, and told my wife to send her maid off.

INSPECTOR. Then we've got it fixed between 11.15 and 11.30. (*Jots*) Now, sir, before we go further I'd like to see your butler and the footman that valets this gentleman.

WINSOR (*with distaste*). Very well, Inspector; only—my butler has been with us from a boy.

INSPECTOR. Quite so. This is just clearing the ground, sir.

WINSOR. General, d'you mind touching that bell?

(CANYNGE *rings a bell by the bed.*)

INSPECTOR. Well, gentlemen, there are four possibilities. Either the thief was here all the time, waiting under the bed, and slipped out after this gentleman had gone to Mr. Winsor. Or he came in with a key that fits the lock; and I'll want to see all the keys in the house. Or he came in with a skeleton key and out by the window, probably droppin' from the balcony. Or he came in by the window with a rope or ladder and out the same way. (*Pointing*) There's a footmark here from a big boot which has been out of doors since it rained.

CANYNGE. Inspector—you er—walked up to the window when you first came into the room.

INSPECTOR (*stiffly*). I had not overlooked that, General.

CANYNGE. Of course.
(*A knock on the door relieves a certain tension.*)

WINSOR. Come in.
(*The footman* ROBERT, *a fresh-faced young man, enters, followed by* TREISURE.)

INSPECTOR. You valet Mr.—Mr. De Levis, I think?

ROBERT. Yes, sir.

INSPECTOR. At what time did you take his clothes and boots?

ROBERT. Ten o'clock, sir.

INSPECTOR (*with a pounce*). Did you happen to look under his bed?

ROBERT. No, sir.

INSPECTOR. Did you come up again, to bring the clothes back?

ROBERT. No, sir; they're still downstairs.

INSPECTOR. Did you come up again for anything?

ROBERT. No, sir.

INSPECTOR. What time did you go to bed?

ROBERT. Just after eleven, sir.

INSPECTOR (*scrutinising him*). Now, be careful. Did you go to bed at all?

ROBERT. No, sir.

INSPECTOR. Then why did you say you did? There's been a theft here, and anything you say may be used against you.

ROBERT. Yes, sir. I meant, I went to my room.

INSPECTOR. Where is your room?

ROBERT. On the ground floor, at the other end of the right wing, sir.

WINSOR. It's the extreme end of the house from this, Inspector. He's with the other two footmen.

INSPECTOR. Were you there alone?

ROBERT. No, sir. Thomas and Frederick was there too.

TREISURE. That's right; I've seen them.

INSPECTOR (*holding up his hand for silence*). Were you out of the room again after you went in?

ROBERT. No, sir.

INSPECTOR. What were you doing, if you didn't go to bed?

ROBERT (*to* WINSOR). Beggin' youı pardon, sir, we were playin' Bridge.

INSPECTOR. Very good. You can go. I'll see *them* later on.

ROBERT. Yes, sir. They'll say the same as me.
(*He goes out, leaving a smile on the face of all except the* INSPECTOR *and* DE LEVIS.)

INSPECTOR (*sharply*). Call him back.
(TREISURE *calls "Robert," and the* FOOTMAN *re-enters.*)

ROBERT. Yes, sir?

INSPECTOR. Did you notice anything particular about Mr. De Levis's clothes?

ROBERT. Only that they were very good, sir.

INSPECTOR. I mean—anything peculiar?

ROBERT (*after reflection*). Yes, sir.

INSPECTOR. Well?

ROBERT. A pair of his boots this evenin' was reduced to one, sir.

INSPECTOR. What did you make of that?

ROBERT. I thought he might have thrown the other at a cat or something.

INSPECTOR. Did you look for it?

ROBERT. No, sir; I meant to draw his attention to it in the morning.

INSPECTOR. Very good.

ROBERT. Yes, sir. (*He goes again.*)

INSPECTOR (*looking at* DE LEVIS). Well, sir, there's *your* story corroborated.

DE LEVIS (*stiffly*). I don't know why it should need corroboration, Inspector.

INSPECTOR. In my experience, you can never have too much of that. (*To* WINSOR) I understand there's a lady in the room on this side (*pointing Left*) and a gentleman on this (*pointing Right*). Were they in their rooms?

WINSOR. Miss Orme was; Captain Dancy not.

INSPECTOR. Do they know of the affair?

WINSOR. Yes.

INSPECTOR. Well, I'd just like the keys of their doors for a minute. My man will get them.
(*He goes to the door, opens it, and speaks to a constable in the corridor.*)
(*To* TREISURE) You can go with him.
(TREISURE *goes out.*)
In the meantime I'll just examine the balcony.
(*He goes out on the balcony, followed by* DE LEVIS.)

WINSOR (*to* CANYNGE). Damn De Levis and his money! It's deuced invidious, all this, General.

CANYNGE. The Inspector's no earthly.
(*There is a simultaneous re-entry of the* INSPECTOR *from the balcony and of* TREISURE *and the* CONSTABLE *from the corridor.*)

CONSTABLE (*handing key*). Room on the left, sir. (*Handing key*) Room on the right, sir.
(*The* INSPECTOR *tries the keys in the door, watched with tension by the others. The keys fail.*)

INSPECTOR. Put them back.
(*Hands keys to* CONSTABLE, *who goes out, followed by* TREISURE.)
I'll have to try every key in the house, sir.

WINSOR. Inspector, do you really think it necessary to disturb the whole house and knock up all my guests? It's most disagreeable, all this, you know. The loss of the money is not such a great matter. Mr. De Levis has a very large income.

CANYNGE. You could get the numbers of the notes from Kentman the bookmaker, Inspector; he'll probably have the big ones, anyway.

INSPECTOR (*shaking his head*). A bookie. I don't suppose he will, sir. It's come and go with them, all the time.

WINSOR. We don't want a Meldon Court scandal, Inspector.

INSPECTOR. Well, Mr. Winsor, I've formed my theory.
(*As he speaks,* DE LEVIS *comes in from the balcony.*)
And I don't say to try the keys is necessary to it; but strictly, I ought to exhaust the possibilities.

WINSOR. What do you say, De Levis? D'you want everybody in the house knocked up so that their keys can be tried?

DE LEVIS (*whose face, since his return, expresses a curious excitement*). No, I don't.

INSPECTOR. Very well, gentlemen. In my opinion the thief walked in before the door was locked, probably during dinner; and was under the bed. He escaped by dropping from the balcony—the creeper at that corner (*he points stage Left*) has been violently wrenched. I'll go down now, and examine the grounds, and I'll see you again, sir. (*He makes another entry in his note-book*) Good-night, then, gentlemen!

CANYNGE. Good-night!

WINSOR (*with relief*). I'll come with you, Inspector.
(*He escorts him to the door, and they go out.*)

DE LEVIS (*suddenly*). General, I know who took them.

CANYNGE. The deuce you do! Are you following the Inspector's theory?

DE LEVIS (*contemptuously*). That ass! (*Pulling the shaving papers out of the case*) No! The man who put those there was clever and cool enough to wrench that creeper off the balcony, as a blind. Come and look here, General. (*He goes to the window; the* GENERAL *follows.* DE LEVIS *points stage Right*) See the rail of my balcony, and the rail of the next? (*He holds up the cord of his dressing-gown, stretching his arms out*) I've measured it with this. Just over seven feet, that's all! If a man can take a standing jump on to a narrow bookcase four feet high and balance there, he'd make nothing of that. And, look here! (*He goes out on the balcony and returns with a bit of broken creeper in his hand, and holds it out into the light*) Someone's stood on that —the stalk's crushed—the inner corner too, where he'd naturally stand when he took his jump back.

CANYNGE (*after examining it—stiffly*). That other balcony is young Dancy's, Mr. De Levis; a soldier and a gentleman. This is an extraordinary insinuation.

DE LEVIS. Accusation.

CANYNGE. What!

DE LEVIS. I have intuitions, General; it's in my blood. I see the whole thing. Dancy came up, watched me into the bathroom, tried my door, slipped back into his dressing-room, saw my window was open, took that jump, sneaked the notes, filled the case up with these, wrenched the creeper there (*he points stage Left*) for a blind, jumped back, and slipped downstairs again. It didn't take him four minutes altogether.

CANYNGE (*very gravely*). This is outrageous, De Levis. Dancy says he was downstairs all the time. You must either withdraw unreservedly, or I must confront you with him.

DE LEVIS. If he'll return the notes and apologise, I'll do nothing—except cut him in future. He gave me that filly, you know, as a hopeless weed, and he's been pretty sick ever since, that he was such a flat as not to see how good she was. Besides, he's hard up, I know.

CANYNGE (*after a vexed turn up and down the room*). It's mad, sir, to jump to conclusions like this.

DE LEVIS. Not so mad as the conclusion Dancy jumped to when he lighted on my balcony.

CANYNGE. Nobody could have taken this money who did not know you had it.

DE LEVIS. How do you know that he didn't?

CANYNGE. Do you know that he did?

DE LEVIS. I haven't the least doubt of it.

CANYNGE. Without any proof. This is very ugly, De Levis. I must tell Winsor.

DE LEVIS (*angrily*). Tell the whole blooming lot. You think I've no feelers, but I've felt the atmosphere here, I can tell you, General. If I were in Dancy's shoes and he in mine, your tone to me would be very different.

CANYNGE (*suavely frigid*). I'm not aware of using any tone, as you call it. But this is a private house, Mr. De Levis, and something is due to our host and to the *esprit de corps* that exists among gentlemen.

DE LEVIS. Since when is a thief a gentleman? Thick as thieves—a good motto, isn't it?

CANYNGE. That's enough! (*He goes to the door, but stops before opening it*) Now, look here! I have some knowledge of the world.

Once an accusation like this passes beyond these walls no one can foresee the consequences. Captain Dancy is a gallant fellow, with a fine record as a soldier; and only just married. If he's as innocent as—Christ—mud will stick to him, unless the real thief is found. In the old days of swords, either you or he would not have gone out of this room alive. If you persist in this absurd accusation, you will *both* of you go out of this room dead in the eyes of Society: you for bringing it, he for being the object of it.

DE LEVIS. Society! Do you think I don't know that I'm only tolerated for my money? Society can't add injury to insult and have my money as well, that's all. If the notes are restored I'll keep my mouth shut; if they're not, I shan't. I'm certain I'm right. I ask nothing better than to be confronted with Dancy; but, if you prefer it, deal with him in your own way—for the sake of your *esprit de corps.*

CANYNGE. 'Pon my soul, Mr. De Levis, you go too far.

DE LEVIS. Not so far as I shall go, General Canynge, if those notes aren't given back.
(WINSOR *comes in.*)

WINSOR. Well, De Levis, I'm afraid that's all we can do for the present. So very sorry this should have happened in my house.

CANYNGE (*after a silence*). There's a development, Winsor. Mr. De Levis accuses one of your guests.

WINSOR. What?

CANYNGE. Of jumping from his balcony to this, taking the notes, and jumping back. I've done my best to dissuade him from indulging the fancy—without success. Dancy must be told.

DE LEVIS. You can deal with Dancy in your own way. All I want is the money back.

CANYNGE (*drily*). Mr. De Levis feels that he is only valued for his money, so that it is essential for him to have it back.

WINSOR. Damn it! This is monstrous, De Levis. I've known Ronald Dancy since he was a boy.

CANYNGE. You talk about adding injury to insult, De Levis. What do you call such treatment of a man who gave you the mare out of which you made this thousand pounds?

DE LEVIS. I didn't want the mare; I took her as a favour.

CANYNGE. With an eye to possibilities, I venture to think—the principle guides a good many transactions.

DE LEVIS (*as if flicked on a raw spot*). In my race, do you mean?

CANYNGE (*coldly*). I said nothing of the sort.

DE LEVIS. No; you don't *say* these things, any of you.

CANYNGE. Nor did I think it.

DE LEVIS. Dancy does.

WINSOR. Really, De Levis, if this is the way you repay hospitality——

DE LEVIS. Hospitality that skins my feelings and costs me a thousand pounds!

CANYNGE. Go and get Dancy, Winsor; but don't say anything to him. (WINSOR *goes out.*)

CANYNGE. Perhaps you will kindly control yourself, and leave this to me.
(DE LEVIS *turns to the window and lights a cigarette.* WINSOR *comes back, followed by* DANCY.)

CANYNGE. For Winsor's sake, Dancy, we don't want any scandal or fuss about this affair. We've tried to make the police understand that. To my mind the whole thing turns on our finding who knew that De Levis had this money. It's about that we want to consult you.

WINSOR. Kentman paid De Levis round the corner in the further paddock, he says.
(DE LEVIS *turns round from the window, so that he and* DANCY *are staring at each other.*)

CANYNGE. Did you hear anything that throws light, Dancy? As it was your filly originally, we thought perhaps you might.

DANCY. I? No.

CANYNGE. Didn't hear of the sale on the course at all?

DANCY. No.

CANYNGE. Then you can't suggest anyone who could have known? Nothing else was taken, you see.

DANCY. De Levis is known to be rolling, as I am known to be stony.

CANYNGE. There are a good many people still rolling, besides Mr. De Levis, but not many people with so large a sum in their pocket-books.

DANCY. He won two races.

DE LEVIS. Do you suggest that I bet in ready money?

DANCY. I don't know how you bet, and I don't care.

CANYNGE. You can't help us, then?

DANCY. No, I can't. Anything else? (*He looks fixedly at* DE LEVIS.)

CANYNGE (*putting his hand on* DANCY'S *arm*). Nothing else, thank you, Dancy.
(DANCY *goes.* CANYNGE *puts his hand up to his face. A moment's silence.*)

WINSOR. You see, De Levis? He didn't even know you'd got the money.

DE LEVIS. Very conclusive.

WINSOR. Well! You *are*——!
(*There is a knock on the door, and the* INSPECTOR *enters.*)

INSPECTOR. I'm just going, gentlemen. The grounds, I'm sorry to say, have yielded nothing. It's a bit of a puzzle.

CANYNGE. You've searched thoroughly?

INSPECTOR. We have, General. I can pick up nothing near the terrace.

WINSOR (*after a look at* DE LEVIS, *whose face expresses too much*).

H'm! You'll take it up from the other end, then, Inspector?

INSPECTOR. Well, we'll see what we can do with the bookmakers about the numbers, sir. Before I go, gentlemen—you've had time to think it over—there's no one you suspect in the house, I suppose?
(DE LEVIS's *face is alive and uncertain.* CANYNGE *is staring at him very fixedly.*)

WINSOR (*emphatically*). No.
(DE LEVIS *turns and goes out on to the balcony.*)

INSPECTOR. If you're coming in to the racing tomorrow, sir, you might give us a call. I'll have seen Kentman by then.

WINSOR. Right you are, Inspector. Good-night, and many thanks.

INSPECTOR. You're welcome, sir. (*He goes out.*)

WINSOR. Gosh! I thought that chap (*with a nod towards the balcony*) was going to——! Look here, General, we *must* stop his tongue. Imagine it going the rounds. They may never find the real thief, you know. It's the very devil for Dancy.

CANYNGE. Winsor! Dancy's sleeve was damp.

WINSOR. How d'you mean?

CANYNGE. Quite damp. It's been raining.
(*The two look at each other.*)

WINSOR. I—I don't follow—— (*His voice is hesitative and lower, showing that he does.*)

CANYNGE. It was coming down hard; a minute out in it would have been enough—— (*He motions with his chin towards the balcony.*)

WINSOR (*hastily*). He must have been out on his balcony since.

CANYNGE. It stopped before I came up, half an hour ago.

WINSOR. He's been leaning on the wet stone, then.

CANYNGE. With the outside of the *upper* part of the arm?

WINSOR. Against the wall, perhaps. There may be a dozen explanations. (*Very low and with great concentration*) I entirely and absolutely refuse to believe anything of the sort against Ronald Dancy—in my house. Dash it, General, we must do as we'd be done by. It hits us all—it hits us all. The thing's intolerable.

CANYNGE. I agree. Intolerable. (*Raising his voice*) Mr. De Levis!
(DE LEVIS *returns into view, in the centre of the open window.*)

CANYNGE (*with cold decision*). Young Dancy was an officer and is a gentleman; this insinuation is pure supposition, and you must not make it. Do you understand me?

DE LEVIS. My tongue is still mine, General, if my money isn't!

CANYNGE (*unmoved*). Must not. You're a member of three Clubs, you want to be member of a fourth. No one who makes such an insinuation against a fellow-guest in a country house, except on absolute proof, can do so without complete ostracism. Have we your word to say nothing?

DE LEVIS. Social blackmail? H'm!

CANYNGE. Not at all—simple warning. If you consider it necessary in your interests to start this scandal—no matter how, we shall consider it necessary in ours to dissociate ourselves completely from one who so recklessly disregards the unwritten code.

DE LEVIS. Do you think your code applies to me? Do you, General?

CANYNGE. To anyone who aspires to be a gentleman, sir.

DE LEVIS. Ah! But you haven't known *me* since I was a boy.

CANYNGE. Make up your mind.
(*A pause.*)

DE LEVIS. I'm not a fool, General. I know perfectly well that you can get me outed.

CANYNGE (*icily*). Well?

DE LEVIS (*sullenly*). I'll say nothing about it, unless I get more proof.

CANYNGE. Good! We have implicit faith in Dancy.
(*There is a moment's encounter of eyes; the* GENERAL'S *steady, shrewd, impassive;* WINSOR'S *angry and defiant;* DE LEVIS'S *mocking, a little triumphant, malicious. Then* CANYNGE *and* WINSOR *go to the door, and pass out.*)

DE LEVIS (*to himself*). Rats!

CURTAIN

ACT TWO

SCENE I

Afternoon, three weeks later, in the card room of a London Club. A fire is burning, Left. A door, Right, leads to the billiard-room. Rather Left of Centre, at a card table, LORD ST. ERTH, *an old John Bull, sits facing the audience; to his right is* GENERAL CANYNGE, *to his left* AUGUSTUS BORRING, *an essential Clubman, about thirty-five years old, with a very slight and rather becoming stammer or click in his speech. The fourth Bridge player,* CHARLES WINSOR, *stands with his back to the fire.*

BORRING. And the r-rub.

WINSOR. By George! You do hold cards, Borring.

ST. ERTH (*who has lost*). Not a patch on the old whist—this game. Don't know why I play it—never did.

CANYNGE. St. Erth, shall we raise the flag for whist again?

WINSOR. No go, General. You can't go back on pace. No getting a man to walk when he knows he can fly. The young men won't look at it.

BORRING. Better develop it so that t-two can sit out, General.

ST. ERTH. We ought to have stuck to the old game. Wish I'd gone to Newmarket, Canynge, in spite of the weather.

CANYNGE (*looking at his watch*). Let's hear what's won the Cambridgeshire. Ring, won't you, Winsor?
(WINSOR *rings.*)

ST. ERTH. By the way, Canynge, young De Levis was blackballed.

CANYNGE. What!

ST. ERTH. I looked in on my way down.
(CANYNGE *sits very still, and* WINSOR *utters a disturbed sound.*)

BORRING. But of c-course he was, General. What did you expect?
(*A* FOOTMAN *enters.*)

FOOTMAN. Yes, my lord?

ST. ERTH. What won the Cambridgeshire?

FOOTMAN. Rosemary, my lord. Sherbet second; Barbizon third. Nine to one the winner.

WINSOR. Thank you. That's all.
(FOOTMAN *goes.*)

BORRING. Rosemary! And De Levis sold her! But he got a good p-price, I suppose.
(*The other three look at him.*)

ST. ERTH. Many a slip between price and pocket, young man.

CANYNGE. Cut! (*They cut.*)

BORRING. I say, is that the yarn that's going round about his having had a lot of m-money stolen in a country house? By Jove! He'll be pretty s-sick.

WINSOR. You and I, Borring.
(*He sits down in* CANYNGE's *chair, and the* GENERAL *takes his place by the fire.*)

BORRING. Phew! Won't Dancy be mad! He gave that filly away to save her keep. He was rather pleased to find somebody who'd take her. Kentman must have won a p-pot. She was at thirty-threes a fortnight ago.

ST. ERTH. All the money goes to fellows who don't know a horse from a haystack.

CANYNGE (*profoundly*). And care less. Yes! We want men racing to whom a horse means something.

BORRING. I thought the horse m-meant the same to everyone, General—chance to get the b-better of one's neighbour.

CANYNGE (*with feeling*). The horse is a noble anmal, sir, as you'd know if you'd owed your life to them as often as I have.

BORRING. They always try to *take* mine, General. I shall never belong to the noble f-fellowship of the horse.

ST. ERTH (*drily*). Evidently. Deal!
(*As* BORRING *begins to deal the*

door is opened and MAJOR COLFORD *appears—a lean and moustached cavalryman.*)

BORRING. Hallo, C-Colford.

COLFORD. General!
(*Something in the tone of his voice brings them all to a standstill.*)

COLFORD. I want your advice. Young De Levis in there (*he points to the billiard-room from which he has just come*) has started a blasphemous story——

CANYNGE. One moment. Mr. Borring, d'you mind——

COLFORD. It makes no odds, General. Four of us in there heard him. He's saying it was Ronald Dancy robbed him down at Winsor's. The fellow's mad over losing the price of that filly now she's won the Cambridgeshire.

BORRING (*all ears*). Dancy! Great S-Scott!

COLFORD. Dancy's in the Club. If he hadn't been I'd have taken it on myself to wring the bounder's neck.
(WINSOR *and* BORRING *have risen.* ST. ERTH *alone remains seated.*)

CANYNGE (*after consulting* ST. ERTH *with a look*). Ask De Levis to be good enough to come in here. Borring, you might see that Dancy doesn't leave the Club. We shall want him. Don't say anything to him, and use your tact to keep people off.
(BORRING *goes out, followed by* COLFORD.)

WINSOR. Result of hearing he was blackballed—pretty slippy.

CANYNGE. St. Erth, I told you there was good reason when I asked you to back young De Levis. Winsor and I knew of this insinuation; I wanted to keep his tongue quiet. It's just wild assertion; to have it bandied about was unfair to Dancy. The duel used to keep people's tongues in order.

ST. ERTH. H'm! It never settled anything, except who could shoot straightest.

COLFORD (*reappearing*). De Levis says he's nothing to add to what he said to you before, on the subject.

CANYNGE. Kindly tell him that if he wishes to remain a member of this Club he must account to the Committee for such a charge against a fellow-member. Four of us are here, and form a quorum.
(COLFORD *goes out again.*)

ST. ERTH. Did Kentman ever give the police the numbers of those notes, Winsor?

WINSOR. He only had the numbers of two—the hundred, and one of the fifties.

ST. ERTH. And they haven't traced 'em?

WINSOR. Not yet.
(*As he speaks,* DE LEVIS *comes in. He is in a highly-coloured, not to say excited state.* COLFORD *follows him.*)

DE LEVIS. Well, General Canynge! It's a little too strong all this—a little too strong. (*Under emotion his voice is slightly more exotic.*)

CANYNGE (*calmly*). It is obvious, Mr. De Levis, that you and Captain Dancy can't both remain members of this Club. We ask you for an explanation before requesting one resignation or the other.

DE LEVIS. You've let me down.

CANYNGE. What!

DE LEVIS. Well, I shall tell people that you and Lord St. Erth backed me up for one Club, and asked me to resign from another.

CANYNGE. It's a matter of indifference to me, sir, what you tell people.

ST. ERTH (*drily*). You seem a venomous young man.

DE LEVIS. I'll tell you what seems to me venomous, my lord—chasing a man like a pack of hounds because he isn't your breed.

CANYNGE. You appear to have your breed on the brain, sir. Nobody else does, so far as I know.

DE LEVIS. Suppose I had robbed Dancy, would you chase him out for complaining of it?

COLFORD. My God! If you repeat that——

CANYNGE. Steady, Colford!

WINSOR. You make this accusation that Dancy stole your money in my house on no proof—no proof; and you expect Dancy's friends to treat you as if you were a gentleman! That's too strong, if you like!

DE LEVIS. No proof? Kentman told me at Newmarket yesterday that Dancy *did* know of the sale. He told Goole, and Goole says that he himself spoke of it to Dancy.

WINSOR. Well—if he did?

DE LEVIS. Dancy told you he *didn't* know of it in General Canynge's presence, and mine. (*To* CANYNGE) You can't deny that, if you want to.

CANYNGE. Choose your expressions more nicely, please!

DE LEVIS. Proof! Did they find any footmarks in the grounds below that torn creeper? Not a sign! You saw how he can jump; he won ten pounds from me that same evening betting on what he knew was a certainty. That's your Dancy—a common sharper!

CANYNGE (*nodding towards the billiard-room*). Are those fellows still in there, Colford?

COLFORD. Yes.

CANYNGE. Then bring Dancy up, will you? But don't say anything to him.

COLFORD (*to* DE LEVIS). You may think yourself damned lucky if he doesn't break your neck.
(*He goes out. The three who are left with* DE LEVIS *avert their eyes from him.*)

DE LEVIS (*smouldering*). I have a memory, and a sting too. Yes, my lord—since you are good enough to call me venomous. (*To* CANYNGE) I quite understand—I'm marked for Coventry now, whatever happens. Well, I'll take Dancy with me.

ST. ERTH (*to himself*). This Club has always had a decent, quiet name.

WINSOR. Are you going to retract, and apologise in front of Dancy and the members who heard you?

DE LEVIS. No fear!

ST. ERTH. You must be a very rich man, sir. A jury is likely to take the view that money can hardly compensate for an accusation of that sort.
(DE LEVIS *stands silent.*)

CANYNGE. Courts of law require proof.

ST. ERTH. He can make it a criminal action.

WINSOR. Unless you stop this at once, you may find yourself in prison. *If* you can stop it, that is.

ST. ERTH. If I were young Dancy, nothing should induce me.

DE LEVIS. But you didn't steal my money, Lord St. Erth.

ST. ERTH. You're deuced positive, sir. So far as I could understand it, there were a dozen ways you could have been robbed. It seems to me you value other men's reputations very lightly.

DE LEVIS. Confront me with Dancy and give me fair play.

WINSOR (*aside to* CANYNGE). Is it fair to Dancy not to let him know?

CANYNGE. Our duty is to the Club now, Winsor. We must have this cleared up.

(COLFORD *comes in, followed by* BORRING *and* DANCY.)

ST. ERTH. Captain Dancy, a serious accusation has been made against you by this gentleman in the presence of several members of the Club.

DANCY. What is it?

ST. ERTH. That you robbed him of that money at Winsor's.

DANCY (*hard and tense*). Indeed! On what grounds is he good enough to say that?

DE LEVIS (*tense too*). You gave me that filly to save yourself her keep, and you've been mad about it ever since; you knew from Goole that I had sold her to Kentman and been paid in cash, yet I heard you myself deny that you knew it. You had the next room to me, and you can jump like a cat, as we saw that evening; I found some creepers crushed by a weight on my balcony on that side. When I went to the bath your door was open, and when I came back it was shut.

CANYNGE. That's the first we have heard about the door.

DE LEVIS. I remembered it afterwards.

ST. ERTH. Well, Dancy?

DANCY (*with intense deliberation*). I'll settle this matter with any weapons, when and where he likes.

ST. ERTH (*drily*). It can't be settled that way—you know very well. You must take it to the Courts, unless he retracts.

DANCY. Will you retract?

DE LEVIS. Why did you tell General Canynge you didn't know Kentman had paid me in cash?

DANCY. Because I didn't.

DE LEVIS. Then Kentman and Goole lied—for no reason?

DANCY. That's nothing to do with me.

DE LEVIS. If you were downstairs all the time, as you say, why was your door first open and then shut?

DANCY. Being downstairs, how should I know? The wind probably.

DE LEVIS. I should like to hear what your wife says about it.

DANCY. Leave my wife alone, you damned Jew!

ST. ERTH. Captain Dancy!

DE LEVIS (*white with rage*). Thief!

DANCY. Will you fight?

DE LEVIS. You're very smart—dead men tell no tales. No! Bring your action, and we shall see.
(DANCY *takes a step towards him, but* CANYNGE *and* WINSOR *interpose.*)

ST. ERTH. That'll do, Mr. De Levis; we won't keep you. (*He looks round*) Kindly consider your membership suspended till this matter has been threshed out.

DE LEVIS (*tremulous with anger*). Don't trouble yourselves about my membership. I resign it. (*To* DANCY) You called me a damned Jew. My race was old when you were all savages. I am proud to be a Jew. *Au revoir,* in the Courts.
(*He goes out, and silence follows his departure.*)

ST. ERTH. Well, Captain Dancy?

DANCY. If the brute won't fight, what am I to do, sir?

ST. ERTH. We've told you—take action, to clear your name.

DANCY. Colford, you saw me in the hall writing letters after our game.

COLFORD. Certainly I did; you were there when I went to the smoking-room.

CANYNGE. How long after you left the billiard-room?

COLFORD. About five minutes.

DANCY. It's impossible for me to prove that I was there all the time.

CANYNGE. It's for De Levis to prove what he asserts. You heard what he said about Goole?

DANCY. If he told me, I didn't take it in.

ST. ERTH. This concerns the honour of the Club. Are you going to take action?

DANCY (*slowly*). That is a very expensive business, Lord St. Erth, and I'm hard up. I must think it over. (*He looks round from face to face*) Am I to take it that there is a doubt in your minds, gentlemen?

COLFORD (*emphatically*). No.

CANYNGE. That's not the question, Dancy. This accusation was overheard by various members, and we represent the Club. If you don't take action, judgment will naturally go by default.

DANCY. I might prefer to look on the whole thing as beneath contempt.
(*He turns and goes out. When he is gone there is an even longer silence than after* DE LEVIS'S *departure.*)

ST. ERTH (*abruptly*). I don't like it.

WINSOR. I've known him all his life.

COLFORD. You may have my head if he did it, Lord St. Erth. He and I have been in too many holes together. By Gad! My toe itches for that fellow's butt end.

BORRING. I'm sorry; but has he t-taken it in quite the right way? I should have thought—hearing it s-suddenly——

COLFORD. Bosh!

WINSOR. It's perfectly damnable for him.

ST. ERTH. More damnable if he did it, Winsor.

BORRING. The Courts are b-beastly distrustful, don't you know.

COLFORD. His word's good enough for me.

CANYNGE. We're as anxious to believe Dancy as you, Colford, for the honour of the Army and the Club.

WINSOR. Of course, he'll bring a case, when he's thought it over.

ST. ERTH. What are we to do in the meantime?

COLFORD. If Dancy's asked to resign, you may take my resignation too.

BORRING. I thought his wanting to f-fight him a bit screeny.

COLFORD. Wouldn't you have wanted a shot at the brute? A law court? Pah!

WINSOR. Yes. What'll be his position even if he wins?

BORRING. Damages, and a stain on his c-character.

WINSOR. Quite so, unless they find the real thief. People always believe the worst.

COLFORD (*glaring at* BORRING). They do.

CANYNGE. There *is* no decent way out of a thing of this sort.

ST. ERTH. No. (*Rising*) It leaves a bad taste. I'm sorry for young Mrs. Dancy—poor woman!

BORRING. Are you going to play any more?

ST. ERTH (*abruptly*). No, sir. Good night to you. Canynge, can I give you a lift?
(*He goes out, followed by* CANYNGE.)

BORRING (*after a slight pause*). Well, I shall go and take the t-temperature of the Club.
(*He goes out.*)

COLFORD. Damn that effeminate stammering chap! What can we do for Dancy, Winsor?

WINSOR. Colford! (*A slight pause*) The General felt his coat sleeve that night, and it was wet.

COLFORD. Well! What proof's that? No, by George! An old schoolfellow, a brother officer, and a pal.

WINSOR. If he did do it——

COLFORD. He didn't. But if he did, I'd stick to him, and see him through it, if I could.

(WINSOR *walks over to the fire, stares into it, turns round and stares at* COLFORD, *who is standing motionless.*)

COLFORD. Yes, by God!

CURTAIN

*SCENE II**

Morning of the following day. The DANCYS' *flat. In the sitting-room of this small abode* MABEL DANCY *and* MARGARET ORME *are sitting full face to the audience, on a couch in the centre of the room, in front of the imaginary window. There is a fireplace, Left, with fire burning; a door below it, Left; and a door on the Right, facing the audience, leads to a corridor and the outer door of the flat, which is visible. Their voices are heard in rapid exchange; then as the curtain rises, so does* MABEL.

MABEL. But it's monstrous!

MARGARET. Of course! (*She lights a cigarette and hands the case to* MABEL, *who, however, sees nothing but her own thoughts*) De Levis might just as well have pitched on me, except that I can't jump more than six inches in these skirts.

MABEL. It's wicked! Yesterday afternoon at the Club, did you say? Ronny hasn't said a word to me. Why?

MARGARET (*with a long puff of smoke*). Doesn't want you bothered.

MABEL. But—— Good heavens!—— Me!

MARGARET. Haven't you found out, Mabel, that he isn't exactly communicative? No desperate character is.

MABEL. Ronny?

MARGARET. Gracious! Wives *are* at a disadvantage, especially early on. You've never hunted with him, my dear. I have. He takes more sudden decisions than any man I ever knew. He's taking one now, I'll bet.

MABEL. That beast, De Levis! I was in our room next door all the time.

* NOTE.—This should be a small set capable of being set quickly within that of the previous scene.

MARGARET. Was the door into Ronny's dressing-room open?

MABEL. I don't know; I–I think it was.

MARGARET. Well, you can say so in Court anyway. Not that it matters. Wives are liars by law.

MABEL (*staring down at her*). What do you mean–Court?

MARGARET. My dear, he'll have to bring an action for defamation of character, or whatever they call it.

MABEL. Were they talking of this last night at the Winsors'?

MARGARET. Well, you know a dinner-table, Mabel–Scandal is heaven-sent at this time of year.

MABEL. It's terrible, such a thing–terrible!

MARGARET (*gloomily*). If only Ronny weren't known to be so broke.

MABEL (*with her hands to her forehead*). I can't realise–I simply can't. If there's a case would it be all right afterwards?

MARGARET. Do you remember St. Offert–cards? No, you wouldn't–you were in high frocks. Well, St. Offert got damages, but he also got the hoof, underneath. He lives in Ireland. There isn't the slightest connection, so far as I can see, Mabel, between innocence and reputation. Look at me!

MABEL. We'll fight it tooth and nail!

MARGARET. Mabel, you're pure wool, right through; everybody's sorry for you.

MABEL. It's for *him* they ought——

MARGARET (*again handing the cigarette-case*). Do smoke, old thing.
(MABEL *takes a cigarette this time, but does not light it.*)
It isn't altogether simple. General Canynge was there last night. You don't mind my being beastly frank, do you?

MABEL. No. I want it.

MARGARET. Well, he's all for *esprit de corps* and that. But he was awfully silent.

MABEL. I hate half-hearted friends. Loyalty comes before everything.

MARGARET. Ye-es; but loyalties cut up against each other sometimes, you know.

MABEL. I *must* see Ronny. D'you mind if I go and try to get him on the telephone?

MARGARET. Rather not. (MABEL *goes out by the door left*) Poor kid! (*She curls herself into a corner of the sofa, as if trying to get away from life. The bell rings.* MARGARET *stirs, gets up, and goes out into the corridor, where she opens the door to* LADY ADELA WINSOR, *whom she precedes into the sitting-room*) Enter the second murderer! D'you know that child knew nothing?

LADY A. Where is she?

MARGARET. Telephoning. Adela, if there's going to be an action, we shall be witnesses. I shall wear black georgette with an écru hat. Have you ever given evidence?

LADY A. Never.

MARGARET. It must be too frightfully thrilling.

LADY A. Oh! Why did I ever ask that wretch De Levis? I used to think him pathetic. Meg—did you know—— Ronald Dancy's coat was wet? The General happened to feel it.

MARGARET. So that's why he was so silent.

LADY A. Yes; and after the scene in the Club yesterday he went to see those bookmakers, and Goole—what a name!—is sure he told Dancy about the sale.

MARGARET (*suddenly*). I don't care. He's my third cousin. Don't you feel you *couldn't*, Adela?

LADY A. Couldn't—what?

MARGARET. Stand for De Levis against one of ourselves?

LADY A. That's very narrow, Meg.

MARGARET. Oh! I know lots of splendid Jews, and I rather liked little Ferdy; but when it comes to the point——! *They* all stick together; why shouldn't we? It's in the blood. Open your jugular, and see if you haven't got it.

LADY A. My dear, my great-grandmother was a Jewess. I'm very proud of her.

MARGARET. Inoculated. (*Stretching herself*) Prejudices, Adela—or are they loyalties—I don't know—criss-cross—we all cut each other's throats from the best of motives.

LADY A. Oh! I shall remember that. Delightful! (*Holding up a finger*) You got it from Bergson, Meg. Isn't he wonderful?

MARGARET. Yes; have you ever read him?

LADY A. Well—no. (*Looking at the bedroom door*) That poor child! I quite agree. I shall tell everybody it's ridiculous. You don't really think Ronald Dancy——?

MARGARET. I don't know, Adela. There are people who simply can't live without danger. I'm rather like that myself. They're all right when they're getting the D.S.O. or shooting man-eaters; but if there's no excitement going, they'll make it—out of sheer craving. I've seen Ronny Dancy do the maddest things for no mortal reason except the risk. He's had a past, you know.

LADY A. Oh! Do tell!

MARGARET. He did splendidly in the war, of course, because it suited him; but—just before—don't you remember—a very queer bit of riding?

LADY A. No.

MARGARET. Most dare-devil thing—but not quite. You must remember—it was awfully talked about. and then, of course, right up to his marriage—— (*She lights a cigarette.*)

LADY A. Meg, you're very tantalising!

MARGARET. A foreign-looking girl—most plummy. Oh! Ronny's got charm—this Mabel child doesn't know in the least what she's got hold of!

LADY A. But they're so fond of each other!

MARGARET. That's the mistake. The General isn't mentioning the coat, is he?

LADY A. Oh, no! It was only to Charles.
(MABEL *returns.*)

MARGARET. Did you get him?

MABEL. No; he's not at Tattersall's, nor at the Club.
(LADY ADELA *rises and greets her with an air which suggests bereavement.*)

LADY A. Nobody's going to believe this, my dear.

MABEL (*looking straight at her*). Nobody who does need come here, or trouble to speak to *us* again.

LADY A. That's what I was afraid of; you're going to be defiant. Now don't! Just be perfectly natural.

MABEL. So easy, isn't it? I could kill anybody who believes such a thing.

MARGARET. You'll want a solicitor, Mabel. Go to old Mr. Jacob Twisden.

LADY A. Yes; he's so comforting.

MARGARET. He got my pearls back once—without loss of life. A frightfully good fireside manner. Do get him here, Mabel, and have a heart-to-heart talk, all three of you!

MABEL (*suddenly*). Listen! There's Ronny!
(DANCY *comes in.*)

DANCY (*with a smile*). Very good of you to have come.

MARGARET. Yes. We're just going. Oh! Ronny, this is quite too——
(*But his face dries her up; and sidling past, she goes.*)

LADY A. Charles sent his—love——
(*Her voice dwindles on the word, and she, too, goes.*)

DANCY (*crossing to his wife*). What have they been saying?

MABEL. Ronny! Why didn't you tell me?

DANCY. I wanted to see De Levis again first.

MABEL. That wretch! How dare he? Darling! (*She suddenly clasps and kisses him. He does not return the kiss, but remains rigid in her arms, so that she draws away and looks at him*) It's hurt you awfully, I know.

DANCY. Look here, Mabel! Apart from that muck—this is a ghastly tame-cat sort of life. Let's cut it and get out to Nairobi. I can scare up the money for that.

MABEL (*aghast*). But how can we? Everybody would say——

DANCY. Let them! We shan't be here.

MABEL. I couldn't bear people to think——

DANCY. I don't care a damn what people think—monkeys and cats. I never could stand their rotten menagerie. Besides, what does it matter how I act; if I bring an action and get damages—if I pound him to a jelly—it's all no good! I can't *prove* it. There'll be plenty of people unconvinced.

MABEL. But they'll find the real thief.

DANCY (*with a queer little smile*). Will staying here help them to do that?

MABEL (*in a sort of agony*). Oh! I couldn't—it looks like running away. We *must* stay and fight it!

DANCY. Suppose I didn't get a verdict—you never can tell.

MABEL. But you must—I was there all the time, with the door open.

DANCY. Was it?

MABEL. I'm almost sure.

DANCY. Yes. But you're my wife.

MABEL (*bewildered*). Ronny, I don't understand—suppose I'd been accused of stealing pearls!

DANCY (*wincing*). I can't.

MABEL. But I might—just as easily. What would you think of me if I ran away from it?

DANCY. I see. (*A pause*) All right! You shall have a run for your money. I'll go and see old Twisden.

MABEL. Let me come! (DANCY *shakes his head*) Why not? I can't be happy a moment unless I'm fighting this.
(DANCY *puts out his hand suddenly and grips hers.*)

DANCY. You *are* a little brick!

MABEL (*pressing his hand to her breast and looking into his face*). Do you know what Margaret called you?

RONNY. No.

MABEL. A desperate character.

DANCY. Ha! I'm not a tame cat, any more than she.
(*The bell rings.* MABEL *goes out to the door and her voice is heard saying coldly.*)

MABEL. Will you wait a minute, please? (*Returning*) It's De Levis—to see you. (*In a low voice*) Let me see him alone first. Just for a minute! Do!

DANCY (*after a moment's silence*). Go ahead! (*He goes out into the bedroom.*)

MABEL (*going to the door, Right*). Come in. (DE LEVIS *comes in, and stands embarrassed*) Yes?

DE LEVIS (*with a slight bow*). Your husband, Mrs. Dancy?

MABEL. He is in. Why do you want to see him?

DE LEVIS. He came round to my rooms just now, when I was out. He threatened me yesterday. I don't choose him to suppose I'm afraid of him.

MABEL (*with a great and manifest effort at self-control*). Mr. De

Levis, you are robbing my husband of his good name.

DE LEVIS (*sincerely*). I admire your trustfulness, Mrs. Dancy.

MABEL (*staring at him*). How can you do it? What do you want? What's your motive? You can't possibly believe that my husband is a *thief!*

DE LEVIS. Unfortunately.

MABEL. How dare you? How dare you? Don't you know that I was in our bedroom all the time with the door open? Do you accuse me too?

DE LEVIS. No, Mrs. Dancy.

MABEL. But you do. I must have seen, I must have heard.

DE LEVIS. A wife's memory is not very good when her husband is in danger.

MABEL. In other words, I'm lying.

DE LEVIS. No. Your wish is mother to your thought, that's all.

MABEL (*after staring again with a sort of horror, turns to get control of herself. Then turning back to him*). Mr. De Levis, I appeal to you as a gentleman to behave to us as you would we should behave to you. Withdraw this wicked charge, and write an apology that Ronald can show.

DE LEVIS. Mrs. Dancy, I am not a gentleman, I am only a—damned Jew. Yesterday I might possibly have withdrawn to spare you. But when my race is insulted I have nothing to say to your husband, but as he wishes to see me, I've come. Please let him know.

MABEL (*regarding him again with that look of horror—slowly*). I think what you are doing is too horrible for words.

(DE LEVIS *gives her a slight bow, and as he does so* DANCY *comes quickly in, Left. The two men stand with the length of the sofa between them.* MABEL, *behind the sofa, turns her eyes on her husband, who has a paper in his right hand.*)

DE LEVIS. You came to see me.

DANCY. Yes. I want you to sign this.

DE LEVIS. I will sign nothing.

DANCY. Let me read it: "I apologise to Captain Dancy for the reckless and monstrous charge I made against him, and I retract every word of it."

DE LEVIS. Not much!

DANCY. You will sign.

DE LEVIS. I tell you this is useless. I will sign nothing. The charge is true; you wouldn't be playing this game if it weren't. I'm going. You'll hardly try violence in the presence of your wife; and if you try it anywhere else——look out for yourself.

DANCY. Mabel, I want to speak to him alone.

MABEL. No, no!

DE LEVIS. Quite right, Mrs. Dancy. Black and tan swashbuckling will only make things worse for him.

DANCY. So you shelter behind a woman, do you, you skulking cur! (DE LEVIS *takes a step, with fists clenched and eyes blazing.* DANCY, *too, stands ready to spring—the moment is cut short by* MABEL *going quickly to her husband.*)

MABEL. Don't, Ronny. It's undignified! He isn't worth it.
(DANCY *suddenly tears the paper in two, and flings it into the fire.*)

DANCY. Get out of here, you swine! (DE LEVIS *stands a moment irresolute, then, turning to the door, he opens it, stands again for a moment with a smile on his face, then goes.* MABEL *crosses swiftly to the door, and shuts it as the outer door closes. Then she stands quite still, looking at her husband—her face expressing a sort of startled suspense.*)

DANCY (*turning and looking at her*). Well! Do you agree with him?

MABEL. What do you mean?

DANCY. That I wouldn't be playing this game unless——

MABEL. Don't! You hurt me!

DANCY. Yes. You don't know much of me, Mabel.

MABEL. Ronny!

DANCY. What did you say to that swine?

MABEL (*her face averted*). That he was robbing *us.* (*Turning to him suddenly*) Ronny—you—didn't? I'd rather know.

DANCY. Ha! I thought that was coming.

MABEL (*covering her face*). Oh! How horrible of me—how horrible!

DANCY. Not at all. The thing looks bad.

MABEL (*dropping her hands*). If *I* can't believe in you, who can? (*Going to him, throwing her arms round him, and looking up into his face*) Ronny! If all the world—*I'd* believe in you. You know I would.

DANCY. That's all right, Mabs! That's all right! (*His face, above her head, is contorted for a moment, then hardens into a mask*) Well, what shall we do?

MABEL. Oh! Let's go to that lawyer—let's go at once!

DANCY. All right. Get your hat on. (MABEL *passes him, and goes into the bedroom, Left.* DANCY, *left alone, stands quite still, staring before him. With a sudden shrug of his shoulders he moves quickly to his hat and takes it up just as* MABEL *returns, ready to go out. He opens the door; and crossing him, she stops in the doorway, looking up with a clear and trustful gaze as*)

THE CURTAIN FALLS

ACT THREE

SCENE I

Three months later. Old MR. JACOB TWISDEN'S *Room, at the offices of Twisden & Graviter, in Lincoln's Inn Fields, is spacious, with two large windows at back, a fine old fireplace, Right, a door below it, and two doors, Left. Between the windows is a large table sideways to the window wall, with a chair in the middle on the right-hand side, a chair against the wall, and a client's chair on the left-hand side.*

GRAVITER, TWISDEN'S *much younger partner, is standing in front of the right-hand window looking out on to the Fields, where the lamps are being lighted, and a taxi's engine is running down below. He turns his sanguine, shrewd face from the window towards a grandfather clock, between the doors, Left, which is striking "four." The door, Left Forward, is opened.*

YOUNG CLERK (*entering*). A Mr. Gilman, sir, to see Mr. Twisden.

GRAVITER. By appointment?

YOUNG CLERK. No, sir. But important, he says.

GRAVITER. I'll see him.
(*The* CLERK *goes.* GRAVITER *sits right of table. The* CLERK *returns, ushering in an oldish* MAN, *who looks what he is, the proprietor of a large modern grocery store. He wears a dark overcoat and carries a pot hat. His gingery-grey moustache and mutton-chop whiskers give him the expression of a cat.*)

GRAVITER (*sizing up his social standing*). Mr. Gilman? Yes.

GILMAN (*doubtfully*). Mr. Jacob Twisden?

GRAVITER (*smiling*). His partner. Graviter my name is.

GILMAN. Mr. Twisden's not in, then?

GRAVITER. No. He's at the Courts. They're just up; he should be in directly. But he'll be busy.

GILMAN. Old Mr. Jacob Twisden—I've heard of him.

GRAVITER. Most people have.
(*A pause.*)

GILMAN. It's this Dancy-De Levis case that's keepin' him at the Courts, I suppose? (GRAVITER *nods*) Won't be finished for a day or two? (GRAVITER *shakes his head*) No. Astonishin' the interest taken in it.

GRAVITER. As you say.

GILMAN. The Smart Set, eh? This Captain Dancy got the D.S.O., didn't he? (GRAVITER *nods*) Sad to have a thing like that said about you. I thought he gave his evidence well; and his wife too. Looks as if this De Levis had got some private spite. *Searchy la femme*, I said to Mrs. Gilman only this morning, before I——

GRAVITER. By the way, sir, what is your business?

GILMAN. Well, my business here—— No, if you'll excuse me, I'd rather wait and see old Mr. Jacob Twisden. It's delicate, and I'd like his experience.

GRAVITER (*with a shrug*). Very well; then, perhaps, you'll go in there. (*He moves towards the door, Left Back.*)

GILMAN. Thank you. (*Following*) You see, I've never been mixed up with the law——

GRAVITER (*opening the door*). No?

GILMAN. And I don't want to begin. When you do, you don't know where you'll stop, do you? You see, I've only come from a sense of duty; and—other reasons.

GRAVITER. Not uncommon.

GILMAN (*producing card*). This is my card. Gilman's — several branches, but this is the 'ead.

GRAVITER (*scrutinising card*). Exactly.

GILMAN. Grocery—I daresay you know me; or your wife does. They say old Mr. Jacob Twisden refused a knighthood. If it's not a rude question, why was that?

GRAVITER. Ask him, sir; ask him.

GILMAN. I said to my wife at the time, "He's holdin' out for a baronetcy."

(GRAVITER *closes the door with an exasperated smile.*)

YOUNG CLERK (*opening the door, Left Forward*). Mr. Winsor, sir, and Miss Orme.

(*They enter, and the* CLERK *withdraws.*)

GRAVITER. How d'you do, Miss Orme? How do you do, Winsor?

WINSOR. Twisden not back, Graviter?

GRAVITER. Not yet.

WINSOR. Well, they've got through De Levis's witnesses. Sir Frederic was at the very top of his form. It's looking quite well. But I hear they've just subpœnaed Canynge after all. His evidence is to be taken tomorrow.

GRAVITER. Oho!

WINSOR. I said Dancy ought to have called him.

GRAVITER. We considered it. Sir Frederic decided that he could use him better in cross-examination.

WINSOR. Well! I don't know that. Can I go and see him before he gives evidence tomorrow?

GRAVITER. I should like to hear Mr. Jacob on that, Winsor. He'll be in directly.

WINSOR. They had Kentman, and Goole, the Inspector, the other bobby, my footman, Dancy's banker, and his tailor.

GRAVITER. Did we shake Kentman or Goole?

WINSOR. Very little. Oh! by the way, the numbers of those two notes were given, and I see they're published in the evening papers. I suppose the police wanted that. I tell you what I find, Graviter—a general feeling that there's something behind it all that doesn't come out.

GRAVITER. The public wants its money's worth—always does in these Society cases; they brew so long beforehand, you see.

WINSOR. They're looking for something lurid.

MARGARET. When I was in the box, I thought they were looking for me. (*Taking out her cigarette case*) I suppose I mustn't smoke, Mr. Graviter?

GRAVITER. Do!

MARGARET. Won't Mr. Jacob have a fit?

GRAVITER. Yes, but not till you've gone.

MARGARET. Just a whiff. (*She lights a cigarette.*)

WINSOR (*suddenly*). It's becoming a sort of Dreyfus case—people taking sides quite outside the evidence.

MARGARET. There are more of the chosen in Court every day. Mr. Graviter, have you noticed the two on the jury?

GRAVITER (*with a smile*). No; I can't say——

MARGARET. Oh! but quite distinctly. Don't you think they ought to have been challenged?

GRAVITER. De Levis might have challenged the other ten, Miss Orme.

MARGARET. Dear me, now! I never thought of that. (*As she speaks, the door Left Forward is opened and old* MR. JACOB TWISDEN *comes in. He is tallish and narrow, sixty-eight years old, grey, with narrow little whiskers curling round his narrow ears, and a narrow bow ribbon curling round his collar. He wears a long, narrow-tailed coat, and strapped trousers on his narrow legs. His nose and face are narrow, shrewd, and kindly. He has a way of narrowing his shrewd and kindly eyes. His nose is seen to twitch and sniff.*)

TWISDEN. Ah! How are you, Charles? How do you do, my dear?

MARGARET. Dear Mr. Jacob, I'm smoking. Isn't it disgusting? But they don't allow it in Court, you know. Such a pity! The Judge might have a hookah. Oh! wouldn't he look sweet—the darling!

TWISDEN (*with a little, old-fashioned bow*). It does not become everybody as it becomes you, Margaret.

MARGARET. Mr. Jacob, how charming! (*With a slight grimace she puts out her cigarette.*)

GRAVITER. Man called Gilman waiting in there to see you specially.

TWISDEN. Directly. Turn up the light, would you, Graviter?

GRAVITER (*turning up the light*). Excuse me. (*He goes.*)

WINSOR. Look here, Mr. Twisden——

TWISDEN. Sit down; sit down, my dear. (*And he himself sits behind the table, as a cup of tea is brought in to him by the* YOUNG CLERK, *with two Marie biscuits in the saucer*) Will you have some, Margaret?

MARGARET. No, dear Mr. Jacob.

TWISDEN. Charles?

WINSOR. No, thanks.
(*The door is closed.*)

TWISDEN (*dipping a biscuit in the tea*). Now, then?

WINSOR. The General knows something which on the face of it looks rather queer. Now that he's going to be called, oughtn't Dancy to be told of it, so that he may be ready with his explanation, in case it comes out?

TWISDEN (*pouring some tea into the saucer*). Without knowing, I can't tell you.
(WINSOR *and* MARGARET *exchange looks, and* TWISDEN *drinks from the saucer.*)

MARGARET. Tell him, Charles.

WINSOR. Well! It rained that evening at Meldon. The General happened to put his hand on Dancy's shoulder, and it was damp.
(TWISDEN *puts the saucer down and replaces the cup in it. They both look intently at him.*)

TWISDEN. I take it that General Canynge won't say anything he's not compelled to say.

MARGARET. No, of course; but, Mr. Jacob, they might ask; they know it rained. And he is such a George Washington.

TWISDEN (*toying with a pair of tortoise-shell glasses*). They didn't ask either of *you*. Still—no harm in your telling Dancy.

WINSOR. I'd rather *you* did it, Margaret.

MARGARET. I daresay. (*She mechanically takes out her cigarette-case, catches the lift of* TWISDEN'S *eyebrows, and puts it back.*)

WINSOR. Well, we'll go together. I don't want Mrs. Dancy to hear.

MARGARET. Do tell me, Mr. Jacob; is he going to win?

TWISDEN. I think so, Margaret; I think so.

MARGARET. It'll be too frightful if he doesn't get a verdict, after all this. But I don't know what we shall do when it's over. I've been sitting in that Court all these three days, watching, and it's made me feel there's nothing we like better than seeing people skinned. Well, bye-bye, bless you!
(TWISDEN *rises and pats her hand.*)

WINSOR. Half a second, Margaret. Wait for me. (*She nods and goes out*) Mr. Twisden, what do you really think?

TWISDEN. I am Dancy's lawyer, my dear Charles, as well as yours.

WINSOR. Well, can I go and see Canynge?

TWISDEN. Better not.

WINSOR. If they get that out of him, and recall me, am I to say he told me of it at the time?

TWISDEN. You didn't feel the coat yourself? And Dancy wasn't present? Then what Canynge told you is not evidence. *We'll* stop your being asked.

WINSOR. Thank Goodness. Goodbye! (WINSOR *goes out.*)

(TWISDEN, *behind his table, motionless, taps his teeth with the eyeglasses in his narrow, well-kept hand. After a long shake of his head and a shrug of his rather high shoulders he sniffs, goes to the window and opens it. Then crossing to the door, Left Back, he throws it open and says:*)

TWISDEN. At your service, sir. (GILMAN *comes forth, nursing his pot hat*) Be seated. (TWISDEN *closes the window behind him, and takes his seat.*)

GILMAN (*taking the client's chair, to the left of the table*). Mr. Twisden, I believe? My name's Gilman, head of Gilman's Department Stores. You have my card.

TWISDEN (*looking at the card*). Yes. What can we do for you?

GILMAN. Well, I've come to you from a sense of duty, sir, and also a feelin' of embarrassment. (*He takes from his breast pocket an evening paper*) You see, I've been followin' this Dancy case—it's a good deal talked of in Putney—and I read this at half-past two this afternoon. To be precise, at 2.25. (*He rises and hands the paper to* TWISDEN, *and with a thick gloved forefinger indicates a passage*) When I read these numbers, I 'appened to remember givin' change for a fifty-pound note—don't often 'ave one in, you know—so I went to the cash-box out of curiosity, to see that I 'adn't got it. Well, I 'ad; and here it is. (*He draws out from his breast pocket and lays before* TWISDEN *a fifty-pound banknote*) It was brought in to change by a customer of mine three days ago, and he got value for it. Now, that's a stolen note, it seems, and you'd like to know what I did. Mind you, that customer of mine I've known 'im—well—eight or nine years; an Italian he is—wine salesman, and so far's I know, a respectable man —foreign-lookin', but nothin' more. Now, this was at 'alf-past two, and I was at my head branch at Putney, where I live. I want you to mark the time, so as you'll see I 'aven't wasted a minute. I took a cab and I drove straight to my customer's private residence in Putney, where he lives with his daughter—Ricardos his name is, Paolio Ricardos. They tell me there he's at his business shop in the City. So off I go in the cab again, and there I find him. Well, sir, I showed this paper to him and I produced the note. "Here," I said, "you brought this to me and you got value for it." Well, that man was taken aback. If I'm a judge, Mr. Twisden, he was taken aback, not to speak in a guilty way, but he was, as you might say, flummoxed. "Now," I said to him, "where did you get it—that's the point?" He took his time to answer, and then he said: "Well, Mr. Gilman," he said, "you know me; I am an honourable man. I can't tell you offhand, but I am above the board." He's foreign, you know, in his expressions. "Yes," I said, "that's all very well," I said, "but here I've got a stolen note and you've got the value for it. Now I tell you," I said, "what I'm going to do; I'm going straight with this note to Mr. Jacob Twisden, who's got this Dancy-De Levis case in 'and. He's a well-known Society lawyer," I said, "of great experience." "Oh!" he said, "that is what you do?"—funny the way he speaks! "Then I come with you!"—And I've got him in the cab below. I want to tell you everything before he comes up. On the way I tried to get something out of him, but I couldn't—I could *not*. "This is very awkward," I said at last. "It is, Mr. Gilman," was his reply; and he began to talk about his Sicilian claret—a very good wine, mind you; but under the circumstances it seemed to me uncalled for. Have I made it clear to you?

TWISDEN (*who has listened with extreme attention*). Perfectly, Mr. Gilman. I'll send down for him. (*He touches a hand-bell. The* YOUNG CLERK *appears at the door, Left Forward*) A gentleman in a taxi—waiting. Ask him to be so good as to step up. Oh! and send Mr. Graviter here again.
(*The* YOUNG CLERK *goes out.*)

GILMAN. As I told you, sir, I've been followin' this case. It's what you might call piquant. And I should be very glad if it came about that this helped Captain Dancy. I take an interest, because, to tell you the truth, (*confidentially*) I don't like—well, not to put too fine a point upon it—'Ebrews. They work harder; they're more sober; they're honest; and they're everywhere. I've nothing against them, but the fact is—they get *on* so.

TWISDEN (*cocking an eye*). A thorn in the flesh, Mr. Gilman.

GILMAN. Well, I prefer my own countrymen, and that's the truth of it. (*As he speaks,* GRAVITER *comes in by the door Left Forward.*)

TWISDEN (*pointing to the newspaper and the note*). Mr. Gilman has brought this, of which he is holder for value. His customer, who changed it three days ago, is coming up.

GRAVITER. The fifty-pounder! I see. (*His face is long and reflective*).

YOUNG CLERK (*entering*). Mr. Ricardos, sir. (*He goes out.*)
(RICARDOS *is a personable, Italian-looking man in a frock coat, with a dark moustachioed face and dark hair a little grizzled. He looks anxious, and bows.*)

TWISDEN. Mr. Ricardos? My name is Jacob Twisden. My partner. (*Holding up a finger, as* RICARDOS *would speak*) Mr. Gilman has told us about this note. You took it to him, he says, three days ago; that is, on Monday, and received cash for it?

RICARDOS. Yes, sare.

TWISDEN. You were *not* aware that it was stolen?

RICARDOS (*with his hand to his breast*). Oh! no, sare.

TWISDEN. You received it from——?

RICARDOS. A minute, sare; I would weesh to explain——(*with an expressive shrug*) in private.

TWISDEN (*nodding*). Mr. Gilman, your conduct has been most prompt. You may safely leave the matter in our hands, now. Kindly let us retain this note; and ask for my cashier as you go out and give him (*He writes*) this. He will reimburse you. We will take any necessary steps ourselves.

GILMAN (*in slight surprise, with modest pride*). Well, sir, I'm in your 'ands. I must be guided by you, with your experience. I'm glad you think I acted rightly.

TWISDEN. Very rightly, Mr. Gilman —very rightly. (*Rising*) Good-afternoon!

GILMAN. Good-afternoon, sir. Good-afternoon, gentlemen! (*To* TWISDEN) I'm sure I'm very 'appy to have made your acquaintance, sir. It's a well-known name.

TWISDEN. Thank you.
(GILMAN *retreats, glances at* RICARDOS, *and turns again.*)

GILMAN. I suppose there's nothing else I ought to do, in the interests of the law? I'm a careful man.

TWISDEN. If there is, Mr. Gilman, we will let you know. We have your address. You may make your mind easy; but don't speak of this. It might interfere with Justice.

GILMAN. Oh! I shouldn't dream of it. I've no wish to be mixed up in anything conspicuous. That's not my principle at all. Good-day, gentlemen. (*He goes.*)

TWISDEN (*seating himself*). Now, sir, will you sit down. (*But* RICARDOS *does not sit; he stands looking uneasily across the table at* GRAVITER) You may speak out.

RICARDOS. Well, Mr. Tweesden and sare, this matter is very serious for me, and very delicate—it concairns my honour. I am in a great difficulty.

TWISDEN. When in difficulty—complete frankness, sir.

RICARDOS. It is a family matter, sare, I——

TWISDEN. Let me be frank with you. (*Telling his points off with fingers*) We have your admission that you changed this stopped note for value. It will be our duty to inform the Bank of England that it has been traced to you. You will have to account to them for your possession of it. I suggest to you that it will be far better to account frankly to us.

RICARDOS (*taking out a handkerchief and quite openly wiping his hands and forehead*). I received this note, sare, with others, from a gentleman, sare, in settlement of a debt of honour, and I know nothing of where he got them.

TWISDEN. Hm! that is very vague. If that is all you can tell us, I'm afraid——

RICARDOS. Gentlemen, this is very painful for me. It is my daughter's good name—— (*He again wipes his brow*).

TWISDEN. Come, sir, speak out!

RICARDOS (*desperately*). The notes were a settlement to her from this gentleman, of whom she was a great friend.

TWISDEN (*suddenly*). I am afraid we must press you for the name of the gentleman.

RICARDOS. Sare, if I give it to you, and it does 'im 'arm, what will my daughter say? This is a bad matter for me. He behaved well to her; and she is attached to him still; sometimes she is crying yet because she lost him. And now we betray him, perhaps, who knows? This is very unpleasant for me. (*Taking up the paper*) Here it gives the number of another note—a 'undred-pound note. I 'ave that too. (*He takes a note from his breast pocket.*)

GRAVITER. How much did he give you in all?

RICARDOS. For my daughter's settlement one thousand pounds. I understand he did not wish to give a cheque because of his marriage. So I did not think anything about it being in notes, you see.

TWISDEN. When did he give you this money?

RICARDOS. The middle of Octobare last.

TWISDEN (*suddenly looking up*). Mr. Ricardos, was it Captain Dancy?

RICARDOS (*again wiping his forehead*). Gentlemen, I am so fond of my daughter. I have only the one, and no wife.

TWISDEN (*with an effort*). Yes, yes; but I must know.

RICARDOS. Sare, if I tell you, will you give me your good word that my daughter shall not hear of it?

TWISDEN. So far as we are able to prevent it—certainly.

RICARDOS. Sare, I trust you.—It was Captain Dancy.
(*A long pause.*)

GRAVITER (*suddenly*). Were you blackmailing him?

TWISDEN (*holding up his hand*). My partner means, did you press him for this settlement?

RICARDOS. I did think it my duty to my daughter to ask that he make compensation to her.

TWISDEN. With threats that you would tell his wife?

RICARDOS (*with a shrug*). Captain Dancy was a man of honour. He said: "Of course I will do this." I trusted him. And a month later I did remind him, and he gave me this money for her. I do not know where he got it—I do not know. Gentlemen, I have invested it all on her—every penny—except this note, for which I had the purpose to buy her a necklace. That is the swearéd truth.

TWISDEN. I must keep this note. (*He touches the hundred-pound note*) You will not speak of this to anyone. *I* may recognise that you were a holder for value received—others might take a different view. Good-day, sir. Graviter, see Mr. Ricardos out, and take his address.

RICARDOS (*pressing his hands over the breast of his frock coat—with a sigh*). Gentlemen, I beg you—remember what I said. (*With a roll of his eyes*) My daughter—I am not happee. Good-day. (*He turns and goes out slowly, Left Forward, followed by* GRAVITER.)

TWISDEN (*to himself*). Young Dancy! (*He pins the two notes together and places them in an envelope, then stands motionless except for his eyes and hands, which restlessly express the disturbance within him.* GRAVITER *returns, carefully shuts the door, and going up to him, hands him* RICARDOS' *card. Looking at the card*) Villa Benvenuto. This will have to be verified, but I'm afraid it's true. That man was not acting.

GRAVITER. What's to be done about Dancy?

TWISDEN. Can you understand a gentleman——?

GRAVITER. I don't know, sir. The war loosened "form" all over the place. I saw plenty of that myself. And some men have no moral sense. From the first I've had doubts.

TWISDEN. We can't go on with the case.

GRAVITER. Phew! . . . (*A moment's silence*) Gosh! It's an awful thing for his wife.

TWISDEN. Yes.

GRAVITER (*touching the envelope*). Chance brought this here, sir. That man won't talk—he's too scared.

TWISDEN. Gilman.

GRAVITER. Too respectable. If De Levis got those notes back, and the rest of the money, anonymously?

TWISDEN. But the case, Graviter; the case.

GRAVITER. I don't believe this alters what I've been thinking.

TWISDEN. Thought is one thing—knowledge another. There's duty to our profession. Ours is a fine calling. On the good faith of solicitors a very great deal hangs. (*He crosses to the hearth as if warmth would help him.*)

GRAVITER. It'll let him in for a prosecution. He came to us in confidence.

TWISDEN. Not as against the law.

GRAVITER. No. I suppose not. (*A pause*) By Jove, I don't like losing this case. I don't like the admission we backed such a wrong 'un.

TWISDEN. Impossible to go on. Apart from ourselves, there's Sir Frederic. We must disclose to him—can't let him go on in the dark. Complete confidence between solicitor and counsel is the essence of professional honour.

GRAVITER. What are you going to do then, sir?

TWISDEN. See Dancy at once. Get him on the 'phone.

GRAVITER (*taking up the telephone*). Get me Captain Dancy's flat. . . . What? . . . (*To* TWISDEN) Mrs. Dancy is here. That's *à propos* with a vengeance. Are you going to see her, sir?

TWISDEN (*after a moment's painful hesitation*). I must.

GRAVITER (*telephoning*). Bring Mrs. Dancy up. (*He turns to the window.* MABEL DANCY *is shown in, looking very pale.* TWISDEN *advances from the fire, and takes her hand.*)

MABEL. Major Colford's taken Ronny off in his car for the night. I thought it would do him good. I said I'd come round in case there was anything you wanted to say before tomorrow.

TWISDEN (*taken aback*). Where have they gone?

MABEL. I don't know, but he'll be home before ten o'clock tomorrow. Is there anything?

TWISDEN. Well, I'd like to see him before the Court sits. Send him on here as soon as he comes.

MABEL (*with her hand to her forehead*). Oh! Mr. Twisden, when will it be over? My head's getting awful sitting in that Court.

TWISDEN. My dear Mrs. Dancy, there's no need at all for you to come down tomorrow; take a rest and nurse your head.

MABEL. Really and truly?

TWISDEN. Yes; it's the very best thing you can do.
(GRAVITER *turns his head, and looks at them unobserved.*)

MABEL. How do you think it's going?

TWISDEN. It went very well today; very well indeed.

MABEL. You must be awfully fed up with us.

TWISDEN. My dear young lady, that's our business. (*He takes her hand.* MABEL'*s face suddenly quivers. She draws her hand away, and covers her lips with it*) There, there! You want a day off badly.

MABEL. I'm so tired of——! Thank you so much for all you're doing. Good night! Good night, Mr. Graviter!

GRAVITER. Good night, Mrs. Dancy. (MABEL *goes.*)

GRAVITER. D'you know, I believe she knows.

TWISDEN. No, no! She believes in him implicitly. A staunch little woman. Poor thing!

GRAVITER. Hasn't that shaken you, sir? It has me.

TWISDEN. No, no! I–I can't go on with the case. It's breaking faith. Get Sir Frederic's chambers.

GRAVITER (*telephoning, and getting a reply, looks round at* TWISDEN). Yes?

TWISDEN. Ask if I can come round and see him.

GRAVITER (*telephoning*). Can Sir Frederic spare Mr. Twisden a few minutes now if he comes around? (*Receiving reply*) He's gone down to Brighton for the night.

TWISDEN. H'm! What hotel?

GRAVITER (*telephoning*). What's his address? What . . . ? (*To* TWISDEN) The Bedford.

TWISDEN. I'll go down.

GRAVITER (*telephoning*). Thank you. All right. (*He rings off.*)

TWISDEN. Just look out the trains down and up early to-morrow.
(GRAVITER *takes an A B C, and* TWISDEN *takes up the Ricardos card.*)

TWISDEN. Send to this address in Putney, verify the fact that Ricardos has a daughter, and give me a trunk call to Brighton. Better go yourself, Graviter. If you see her, don't say anything, of course —invent some excuse. (GRAVITER *nods*) I'll be up in time to see Dancy.

GRAVITER. By George! I feel bad about this.

TWISDEN. Yes. But professional honour comes first. What time is that train? (*He bends over the A B C.*)

CURTAIN

SCENE II

The same room on the following morning at ten-twenty-five, by the Grandfather clock.

The YOUNG CLERK *is ushering in* DANCY, *whose face is perceptibly harder than it was three months ago, like that of a man who has lived under great restraint.*

DANCY. He wanted to see me before the Court sat.

YOUNG CLERK. Yes, sir. Mr. Twisden will see you in one minute. He had to go out of town last night. (*He prepares to open the waiting-room door.*)

DANCY. Were *you* in the war?

YOUNG CLERK. Yes.

DANCY. How can you stick this?

YOUNG CLERK (*with a smile*). My trouble was to stick that, sir.

DANCY. But you get no excitement from year's end to year's end. It'd drive me mad.

YOUNG CLERK (*shyly*). A case like this is pretty exciting. I'd give a lot to see us win it.

DANCY (*staring at him*). Why? What is it to you?

YOUNG CLERK. I don't know, sir. It's—it's like football—you want your side to win. (*He opens the waiting-room door. Expanding*) You see some rum starts, too, in a lawyer's office in a quiet way.
(DANCY *enters the waiting-room, and the* YOUNG CLERK, *shutting the door, meets* TWISDEN *as he comes in, Left Forward, and takes from him overcoat, top hat, and a small bag.*)

YOUNG CLERK. Captain Dancy's waiting, sir. (*He indicates the waiting-room.*)

TWISDEN (*narrowing his lips*). Very well. Mr. Graviter gone to the Courts?

YOUNG CLERK. Yes, sir.

TWISDEN. Did he leave anything for me?

YOUNG CLERK. On the table, sir.

TWISDEN (*taking up an envelope*). Thank you.
(*The* CLERK *goes.*)

TWISDEN (*opening the envelope and reading*). "All corroborates." H'm! (*He puts it in his pocket and takes out of an envelope the two notes, lays them on the table, and covers them with a sheet of blotting-paper; stands a moment preparing himself, then goes to the door of the waiting-room, opens it, and says:*) Now, Captain Dancy. Sorry to have kept you waiting.

DANCY (*entering*). Winsor came to me yesterday about General Canynge's evidence. Is that what you wanted to speak to me about?

TWISDEN. No. It isn't that.

DANCY (*looking at his wrist watch*). By me it's just on the half-hour, sir.

TWISDEN. Yes. I don't want you to go to the Court.

DANCY. Not?

TWISDEN. I have very serious news for you.

DANCY (*wincing and collecting himself*). Oh!

TWISDEN. These two notes. (*He uncovers the notes*) After the Court rose yesterday we had a man called Ricardos here. (*A pause*) Is there any need for me to say more?

DANCY (*unflinching*). No. What now?

TWISDEN. Our duty was plain; we could not go on with the case. I have consulted Sir Frederic. He felt—he felt that he must throw up his brief, and he will do that the moment Court sits. Now I want to talk to you about what you're going to do.

DANCY. That's very good of you, considering.

TWISDEN. I don't pretend to understand, but I imagine you may have done this in a moment of reckless bravado, feeling, perhaps, that as you gave the mare to De Levis, the money was by rights as much yours as his. (*Stopping* DANCY, *who is about to speak, with a gesture*) To satisfy a debt of honour to this —lady; and, no doubt, to save your wife from hearing of it from the man Ricardos. Is that so?

DANCY. To the life.

TWISDEN. It was mad, Captain Dancy, mad!—— But the question now is: What do you owe to your wife? She doesn't dream—I suppose?

DANCY (*with a twitching face*). No.

TWISDEN. We can't tell what the result of this collapse will be. The police have the theft in hand. They may issue a warrant. The money could be refunded, and the costs paid—somehow that can all be managed. But it may not help. In any case, what end is served by your staying in the country? You can't save your honour—that's gone. You can't save your wife's peace of mind. If she sticks to you—do you think she will?

DANCY. Not if she's wise.

TWISDEN. Better go! There's a war in Morocco.

DANCY (*with a bitter smile*). Good old Morocco!

TWISDEN. Will you go, then, at once, and leave me to break it to your wife?

DANCY. I don't know yet.

TWISDEN. You must decide quickly, to catch a boat train. Many a man has made good. You're a fine soldier.

DANCY. There are alternatives.

TWISDEN. Now, go straight from this office. You've a passport, I suppose; you won't need a *visa* for France, and from there you can find means to slip over. Have you got money on you? (DANCY *nods*) We will see what we can do to stop or delay proceedings.

DANCY. It's all damned kind of you. (*With difficulty*) But I must think of my wife. Give me a few minutes.

TWISDEN. Yes, yes; go in there and think it out.

(*He goes to the door, Right, and opens it.* DANCY *passes him and goes out.* TWISDEN *rings a bell and stands waiting.*)

CLERK (*entering*). Yes, sir?

TWISDEN. Tell them to call a taxi.

CLERK (*who has a startled look*). Yes, sir. Mr. Graviter has come in, sir, with General Canynge. Are you disengaged?

TWISDEN. Yes.
(*The* CLERK *goes out, and almost immediately* GRAVITER *and* CANYNGE *enter.*)
Good-morning, General. (*To* GRAVITER) Well?

GRAVITER. Sir Frederic got up at once and said that since the publication of the numbers of those notes, information had reached him which forced him to withdraw from the case. Great sensation, of course. I left Bromley in charge. There'll be a formal verdict for the defendant, with costs. Have you told Dancy?

TWISDEN. Yes. He's in there deciding what he'll do.

CANYNGE (*grave and vexed*). This is a dreadful thing, Twisden. I've been afraid of it all along. A soldier! A gallant fellow, too. What on earth got into him?

TWISDEN. There's no end to human nature, General.

GRAVITER. You can see queerer things in the papers, any day.

CANYNGE. That poor young wife of his! Winsor gave me a message for you, Twisden. If money's wanted quickly to save proceedings, draw on him. Is there anything *I* can do?

TWISDEN. I've advised him to go straight off to Morocco.

CANYNGE. I don't know that an asylum isn't the place for him. He must be off his head at moments. That jump—crazy! He'd have got a verdict on that alone—if they'd seen those balconies. I was looking at them when I was down there last Sunday. Daring thing, Twisden. Very few men, on a dark night—— He risked his life twice. That's a shrewd fellow—young De Levis. He spotted Dancy's nature.
(*The* YOUNG CLERK *enters.*)

CLERK. The taxi's here, sir. Will you see Major Colford and Miss Orme?

TWISDEN. Graviter—— No; show them in.
(*The* YOUNG CLERK *goes.*)

CANYNGE. Colford's badly cut up.
(MARGARET ORME *and* COLFORD *enter.*)

COLFORD (*striding forward*). There must be some mistake about this, Mr. Twisden.

TWISDEN. Hssh! Dancy's in there. He's admitted it.
(*Voices are subdued at once.*)

COLFORD. What? (*With emotion*) If it were my own brother, I couldn't feel it more. But—damn it! What right had that fellow to chuck up the case—without letting him know, too. I came down with Dancy this morning, and he knew nothing about it.

TWISDEN (*coldly*). That was unfortunately unavoidable.

COLFORD. Guilty or not, you ought to have stuck to him—it's not playing the game, Mr. Twisden.

TWISDEN. You must allow me to judge where my duty lay, in a very hard case.

COLFORD. I thought a man was safe with his solicitor.

CANYNGE. Colford, you don't understand professional etiquette.

COLFORD. No, thank God!

TWISDEN. When you have been as long in your profession as I have been in mine, Major Colford, you will know that duty to your calling outweighs duty to friend or client.

COLFORD. But I serve the Country.

TWISDEN. And I serve the Law, sir.

CANYNGE. Graviter, give me a sheet of paper. I'll write a letter for him.

MARGARET (*going up to* TWISDEN). Dear Mr. Jacob—pay De Levis. You know my pearls—put them up the spout again. Don't let Ronny be——

TWISDEN. Money isn't the point, Margaret.

MARGARET. It's ghastly! It really is.

COLFORD. I'm going in to shake hands with him. (*He starts to cross the room.*)

TWISDEN. Wait! We want him to go straight off to Morocco. Don't upset him. (*To* COLFORD *and* MARGARET) I think you had better go. If, a little later, Margaret, you could go round to Mrs. Dancy——

COLFORD Poor little Mabel Dancy! It's perfect hell for her.
(*They have not seen that* DANCY *has opened the door behind them.*)

DANCY. It is!
(*They all turn round in consternation.*)

COLFORD (*with a convulsive movement*). Old boy!

DANCY. No good, Colford. (*Gazing round at them*) Oh! clear out. I can't stand commiseration—and let me have some air.
(TWISDEN *motions to* COLFORD *and* MARGARET *to go; and as he turns to* DANCY, *they go out.* GRAVITER *also moves towards the door. The* GENERAL *sits motionless.* GRAVITER *goes out.*)

TWISDEN. Well?

DANCY. I'm going home, to clear up things with my wife. General Canynge, I don't quite know why I did the damned thing. But I did, and there's an end of it.

CANYNGE. Dancy, for the honour of the Army, avoid further scandal if you can. I've written a letter to a friend of mine in the Spanish War Office. It will get you a job in their war. (CANYNGE *closes the envelope.*)

DANCY. Very good of you. I don't know if I can make use of it.
(CANYNGE *stretches out the letter, which* TWISDEN *hands to* DANCY, *who takes it.* GRAVITER *reopens the door.*)

TWISDEN. What is it?

GRAVITER. De Levis is here.

TWISDEN. De Levis? Can't see him.

DANCY. Let him in!
(*After a moment's hesitation* TWISDEN *nods, and* GRAVITER *goes out. The three wait in silence with their eyes fixed on the door, the* GENERAL *sitting at the table,* TWISDEN *by his chair,* DANCY *between him and the door Right.* DE LEVIS *comes in and shuts the door. He is advancing towards* TWISDEN *when his eyes fall on* DANCY, *and he stops.*)

TWISDEN. You wanted to see me?

DE LEVIS (*moistening his lips*). Yes. I came to say that—that I overheard—I am afraid a warrant is to be issued. I wanted you to realise—it's not *my* doing. I'll give it no support. I'm content. I don't want my money. I don't even want costs. Dancy, do you understand?
(DANCY *does not answer, but looks at him with nothing alive in his face but his eyes.*)

TWISDEN. We are obliged to you, sir. It was good of you to come.

DE LEVIS (*with a sort of darting pride*). Don't mistake me. I didn't come because I feel Christian; I am a Jew. I will take no money—not even that which was stolen. Give it to a charity. I'm proved right. And now I'm done with the damned thing. Good-morning!
(*He makes a little bow to* CANYNGE *and* TWISDEN, *and turns to face* DANCY, *who has never moved. The two stand motionless, looking at each other, then* DE LEVIS *shrugs his shoulders and walks out. When he is gone there is a silence.*)

CANYNGE (*suddenly*). You heard what he said, Dancy. You have no time to lose.
(*But* DANCY *does not stir.*)

TWISDEN. Captain Dancy?
(*Slowly, without turning his head, like a man in a dream,* DANCY *walks across the room, and goes out.*)

CURTAIN

SCENE III

The DANCYS' *sitting-room, a few minutes later.*

MABEL DANCY *is sitting alone on the sofa with a newspaper on her lap; she is only just up, and has a bottle of smelling-salts in her hand. Two or three other newspapers are dumped on the arm of the sofa. She topples the one off her lap and takes up another as if she couldn't keep away from them; drops it in turn, and sits staring before her, sniffing at the salts. The door, Right, is opened and* DANCY *comes in.*

MABEL (*utterly surprised*). Ronny! Do they want me in Court?

DANCY. No.

MABEL. What is it, then? Why are you back?

DANCY. Spun.

MABEL (*blank*). Spun? What do you mean? What's spun?

DANCY. The case. They've found out through those notes.

MABEL. Oh! (*Staring at his face*) Who?

DANCY. Me!

MABEL (*after a moment of horrified stillness*). Don't, Ronny! Oh! No! Don't! (*She buries her face in the pillows of the sofa.*)
(DANCY *stands looking down at her.*)

DANCY. Pity you wouldn't come to Africa three months ago.

MABEL. Why didn't you tell me then? I would have gone.

DANCY. You wanted this case. Well, it's fallen down.

MABEL. Oh! Why didn't I face it? But I couldn't—I *had* to believe.

DANCY. And now you can't. It's the end, Mabel.

MABEL (*looking up at him*). No.
(DANCY *goes suddenly on his knees and seizes her hand.*)

DANCY. Forgive me!

MABEL (*putting her hand on his head*). Yes; oh, yes! I think I've known a long time, really. Only—why? What made you?

DANCY (*getting up and speaking in jerks*). It was a crazy thing to do;

but, damn it, I was only looting a looter. The money was as much mine as his. A decent chap would have offered me half. You didn't see the brute look at me that night at dinner as much as to say: "You blasted fool!" It made me mad. That wasn't a bad jump—twice over. Nothing in the war took quite such nerve. (*Grimly*) I rather enjoyed that evening.

MABEL. But—money! To keep it!

DANCY (*sullenly*). Yes, but I had a debt to pay.

MABEL. To a woman?

DANCY. A debt of honour—it wouldn't wait.

MABEL. It was—it was to a woman. Ronny, don't lie any more.

DANCY (*grimly*). Well! I wanted to save your knowing. I'd promised a thousand. I had a letter from her father that morning, threatening to tell you. All the same, if that tyke hadn't jeered at me for parlour tricks!—But what's the good of all this now? (*Sullenly*) Well—it may cure you of loving me. Get over that, Mab; I never was worth it—and I'm done for!

MABEL. The woman—have you—since——?

DANCY (*energetically*). No! You supplanted her. But if you'd known I was leaving a woman for you, you'd never have married me. (*He walks over to the hearth.*)
(MABEL *too gets up. She presses her hands to her forehead, then walks blindly round to behind the sofa and stands looking straight in front of her.*)

MABEL (*coldly*). What has happened, exactly?

DANCY. Sir Frederic chucked up the case. I've seen Twisden; they want me to run for it to Morocco.

MABEL. To the war there?

DANCY. Yes. There's to be a warrant out.

MABEL. A prosecution? Prison? Oh, go! Don't wait a minute! Go!

DANCY. Blast them!

MABEL. Oh, Ronny! Please! Please! Think what you'll want. I'll pack. Quick! No! Don't wait to take things. Have you got money?

DANCY (*nodding*). This'll be goodbye, then!

MABEL (*after a moment's struggle*). Oh! No! No, no! I'll follow—I'll come out to you there.

DANCY. D'you mean you'll stick to me?

MABEL. Of course I'll stick to you. (DANCY *seizes her hand and puts it to his lips. The bell rings.*)

MABEL (*in terror*). Who's that?
(*The bell rings again.* DANCY *moves towards the door.*)
No! Let *me!*
(*She passes him and steals out to the outer door of the flat, where she stands listening. The bell rings again. She looks through the slit of the letter-box. While she is gone* DANCY *stands quite still, till she comes back.*)

MABEL. Through the letter-box—I can see—— It's—it's police. Oh! God! . . . Ronny! I can't bear it.

DANCY. Heads up, Mab! Don't show the brutes!

MABEL. Whatever happens, I'll go on loving you. If it's prison—*I'll wait.* Do you understand? I don't care what you did—I don't *care!* I'm just the same. I will be just the same when you come back to me.

DANCY (*slowly*). That's not in human nature.

MABEL. It is. It's in *me.*

DANCY. I've crocked up your life.

MABEL. No, no! Kiss me!
(*A long kiss, till the bell again startles them apart, and there is a loud knock.*)

DANCY. They'll break the door in. It's no good—we must open. Hold them in check a little. I want a minute or two.

MABEL (*clasping him*). Ronny! Oh, Ronny! It won't be for long—I'll be waiting! I'll be waiting—I swear it.

DANCY. Steady, Mab! (*Putting her back from him*) Now!
(*He opens the bedroom door, Left, and stands waiting for her to go. Summoning up her courage, she goes to open the outer door. A sudden change comes over* DANCY'S *face; from being stony it grows almost maniacal.*)

DANCY (*under his breath*). No! No! By God! No!
(*He goes out into the bedroom, closing the door behind him.*)
(MABEL *has now opened the outer door, and disclosed* INSPECTOR DEDE *and the* YOUNG CONSTABLE *who were summoned to Meldon Court on the night of the theft, and have been witnesses in the case. Their voices are heard.*)

MABEL. Yes?

INSPECTOR. Captain Dancy in, madam?

MABEL. I am not quite sure—I don't think so.

INSPECTOR. I wish to speak to him a minute. Stay here, Grover. Now, madam!

MABEL. Will you come in while I see?
(*She comes in, followed by the* INSPECTOR.)

INSPECTOR. I should think you must be sure, madam. This is not a big place.

MABEL. He was changing his clothes to go out. I think he has gone.

INSPECTOR. What's that door?

MABEL. To our bedroom.

INSPECTOR (*moving towards it*). He'll be in there, then.

MABEL. What do you want, Inspector?

INSPECTOR (*melting*). Well, madam, it's no use disguising it. I'm exceedingly sorry, but I've a warrant for his arrest.

MABEL. Inspector!

INSPECTOR. I'm sure I've every sympathy for you, madam; but I must carry out my instructions.

MABEL. And break my heart?

INSPECTOR. Well, madam, we're—we're not allowed to take that into consideration. The Law's the Law.

MABEL. Are you married?

INSPECTOR. I am.

MABEL. If you—your wife——
(*The* INSPECTOR *raises his hand, deprecating.*)
(*Speaking low*) Just half an hour! Couldn't you? It's two lives—two whole lives! We've only been married four months. Come back in half an hour. It's such a little thing—nobody will know. Nobody. Won't you?

INSPECTOR. Now, madam—you must know my duty.

MABEL. Inspector, I beseech you—just half an hour.

INSPECTOR. No, no—don't you try to undermine me—I'm sorry for you; but don't you try it! (*He tries the handle, then knocks at the door.*)

DANCY'S VOICE. One minute!

INSPECTOR. It's locked. (*Sharply*) Is there another door to that room? Come, now! (*The bell rings.*)
(*Moving towards the door, Left; to the* CONSTABLE.)
Who's that out there?

CONSTABLE. A lady and gentleman, sir.

INSPECTOR. What lady and——Stand by, Grover!

DANCY'S VOICE. All right! You can come in *now.*

(*There is the noise of a lock being turned. And almost immediately the sound of a pistol shot in the bedroom.* MABEL *rushes to the door, tears it open, and disappears within, followed by the* INSPECTOR, *just as* MARGARET ORME *and* COLFORD *come in from the passage, pursued by the* CONSTABLE. *They, too, all hurry to the bedroom door and disappear for a moment; then* COLFORD *and* MARGARET *reappear, supporting* MABEL, *who faints as they lay her on the sofa.* COLFORD *takes from her hand an envelope, and tears it open.*)

COLFORD. It's addressed to *me.* (*He reads it aloud to* MARGARET *in a low voice.*)

"DEAR COLFORD,—This is the only decent thing I can do. It's too damned unfair to her. It's only another jump. A pistol keeps faith. Look after her. Colford—my love to her, and you."
(MARGARET *gives a sort of choking sob, then, seeing the smelling bottle, she snatches it up, and turns to revive* MABEL.)

COLFORD. Leave her! The longer she's unconscious, the better.

INSPECTOR (*re-entering*). This is a very serious business, sir.

COLFORD (*sternly*). Yes, Inspector; you've done for my best friend.

INSPECTOR. I, sir? He shot himself.

COLFORD. Hari-kari.

INSPECTOR. Beg pardon?

COLFORD (*he points with the letter to* MABEL). For her sake, and his own.

INSPECTOR (*putting out his hand*). I'll want that, sir.

COLFORD (*grimly*). You shall have it read at the inquest. Till then—it's addressed to me, and I stick to it.

INSPECTOR. Very well, sir. Do you want to have a look at him?

(COLFORD *passes quickly into the bedroom, followed by the* INSPECTOR. MARGARET *remains kneeling beside* MABEL. COLFORD *comes quickly back.* MARGARET *looks up at him. He stands very still.*)

COLFORD. Neatly—through the heart.

MARGARET (*wildly*). Keeps faith! We've all done that. It's not enough.

COLFORD (*looking down at* MABEL). All right, old boy!

THE CURTAIN FALLS

Outward Bound

BY SUTTON VANE

TO DIANA, MY WIFE

Outward Bound was first produced in America at the Ritz Theatre, New York City, by William Harris, Jr., on January 7, 1924, and closed on May 10, 1924. The following is the original cast:

SCRUBBY	J. M. Kerrigan
ANN	Margalo Gillmore
HENRY	Leslie Howard
MR. PRIOR	Alfred Lunt
MRS. CLIVEDEN-BANKS	Charlotte Granville
REV. WILLIAM DUKE	Lyonel Watts
MRS. MIDGET	Beryl Mercer
MR. LINGLEY	Eugene Powers
REV. FRANK THOMSON	Dudley Digges

Staged by Robert Milton

Settings by Livingston Platt

SCENES

On board ship

ACT ONE

In harbour. Morning

ACT TWO

At sea. The same evening

ACT THREE

About six days later

SCENE I

Afternoon

SCENE II

The night of the same day

Time: The present

OUTWARD BOUND

ACT ONE

The curtain rises on a room which suggests rather than represents the lounge smoke-room of a small ocean liner. There is a bar on the right with the usual array of glasses and bottles on the counter and on the shelves behind it. On the extreme left is a small writing table, and the rest of the furniture consists of the usual small round tables and swivel arm-chairs that are found in the smoke-room on most liners. Around the room at the back is a red cushioned wall-seat. The carpet is of warm neutral tone. There are three doors: one behind the bar, another leading off left and a third, centre, opening on to the deck. This centre door is wide open, and behind it can be seen the liner railings. The colour of the sky at the back arrests the attention at once. It is a curious colour—vague and almost nondescript. There are four portholes in the back wall, fitted up with small curtains which are now drawn. Three large lights hang from the ceiling, and some small lamp brackets on the walls.

The sun is shining, and it is a clear still morning. Behind the bar stands SCRUBBY, *busy polishing the glasses—preparatory to the boat sailing. He is dressed in the usual uniform of a ship's steward. His manner is always calm and reposeful, and his voice gentle and kindly. He is an elderly man, typically English.*

ANN *is seen to pass along the deck, and she comes through the centre door into the room. She is wearing a hat and coat, underneath which is a simple but very smart clinging frock of green. She is young, but one sees at once that she is terribly nervous. She pauses and looks round in a frightened manner. Then* SCRUBBY *clinks a glass and she turns and sees him.*

ANN. Oh, I beg your pardon—good morning.

SCRUBBY. Good morning, madam.

ANN. I'm sorry to bother you, but I'm afraid we've lost our way.

SCRUBBY. Where do you want to get to, madam?

ANN. The cabins, of course.

SCRUBBY. Cabins?

ANN. Yes! Where we sleep. I'm afraid I'm awfully stupid. I've never been on the sea before.

SCRUBBY. The old ship will be highly flattered. You'll find all the berths right forward (*points to the left*) down there.

ANN. Thank you very much. (*She goes up to the centre and speaks to someone outside.*) Henry, come along, dear, I was quite right, this is the way. (HENRY *enters from the deck. He is wearing a well-cut lounge suit and a dark soft hat. He is an ardent young man, about thirty years old. He is good looking, quietly emotional, serious and sincere. He is rather mystic in manner, and behaves like a dazed man who has recently received a severe shock.*)

HENRY. Sorry, I was looking at the sea. What did you say?

ANN. This *is* the way, dear.

HENRY. Oh, good! We'll probably find all our stuff in the cabin already. How did you find out?

ANN. *He* told me. (*Indicating* SCRUBBY.)

HENRY. Oh!—good morning!

SCRUBBY. Good morning, sir.
(ANN *moves down to left.*)

HENRY. Bit confusing these boats, aren't they?

SCRUBBY. Yes, sir, to begin with.

ANN. Come along, dear.

HENRY. I say, I'm feeling awfully tired.

ANN. Do you wonder?—after what you've been through?

HENRY. No, I suppose I don't. I can't quite focus it all even now, you know. By Jove, we'll have a gorgeous trip though, won't we?

ANN. Yes, dear.

HENRY. The rest—the peace and—and—

ANN. Don't worry so, dear.

HENRY. And the forgetfulness—

ANN. Of course, dear, don't worry.

HENRY. No, I won't, I won't! (*To* SCRUBBY) Thanks for telling my—my wife the way.

ANN. Give me your hand.

HENRY. What's that?

ANN. Give me your hand, dear.

HENRY. Oh! You treat me like a child! I'm quite all right really.

ANN. Give me your hand. (*He goes to her, takes her hand*) There!

HENRY. Thanks for the hand.

ANN. Come along.
(*They go off together, left, and a moment later* TOM PRIOR *enters by the centre door.* PRIOR *is a slight young man, highly strung. He is not specifically drunk at the moment, but rather more displays the mellow and bland cock-sureness of a youth who for some time has kept himself going with constant stimulants. He is wearing a lounge suit, and is very cheerful and smiling.*)

TOM. Oh!—er—good morning, steward.

SCRUBBY. Good morning, sir.

TOM. This is the smoke-room, I suppose?

SCRUBBY. Yes, sir.

TOM. Look here, then—er—how long before we sail?

SCRUBBY. About a quarter of an hour—sir—or more—or less.

TOM. Then I say, could I—er—I get a drink?

SCRUBBY. Certainly, sir.

TOM. Bravo! (*He crosses to the bar*) I want it.

SCRUBBY. What shall I get you, sir?

TOM. A Scotch.

SCRUBBY. Any soda-water, sir?

TOM. No, thank you.

SCRUBBY. All Scotch!

TOM. As a matter of fact, steward, you'll probably see a lot of me during this trip. Yes, you'll get to know me quite well, so I thought I'd warn you to begin with.

SCRUBBY (*serves drink*). The warning is an honour, sir.

TOM. Yes, thanks. How much is it?

SCRUBBY. Oh, you needn't pay, sir.

TOM. What!

SCRUBBY. If you'll just sign this. (*Presents chit book.*)

TOM. Oh, yes, of course, I'd forgotten that catch. Have one yourself?

SCRUBBY. No thank you, sir.

TOM (*drinks*). Ah, that's better. As a matter of fact, steward, I'd a rather thick night last night—

SCRUBBY. Indeed, sir.

TOM. Yes—yes—and I want pulling together. By Jove—it must have been a jolly thick night because I can't remember anything about it now. But never mind. (*Drinks again*) It's a gorgeous morning, anyway.

SCRUBBY. It is, sir. A pity some people should be alive to spoil it.

TOM. What's that?

SCRUBBY. I was talking to myself, sir.

TOM. I say, steward, how many passengers have we got?

SCRUBBY. Not many, sir, it's our slack time of year.

TOM. The last time I came out—why—it must be over ten years ago —I was going tea planting, and—and—I was only about nineteen—and— (*Pause*) Phew, how time flies! Get me some cigarettes.

SCRUBBY. Yes, sir! Egyptians, Turkish or Virginian?

TOM. Gold Flake. What's the old Captain like?

SCRUBBY. Very decent sort I've heard say, sir. Very respected, I *know*.

TOM. Oh, I don't like that sort—not on these small ships. Now when I went out before—

SCRUBBY. Your cigarettes, sir.

TOM. Thank you. And get me another drink. The same.

(MRS. CLIVEDEN-BANKS *enters from the centre and goes down to* TOM.

She is a withered old harridan of fifty odd—probably once beautiful. Smartly frocked in travelling costume. She carries an armful of magazines.)

MRS. C-BANKS. Aha! I thought I knew that voice!

TOM. What! (*Rises, turns*) Oh, really! Good gracious! Mrs. Cliveden-Banks! How are you? What a surprise! (*Shakes hands.*)

MRS. C-BANKS. I saw your name on the passenger list, so I asked for the bar at once, and here you are! (*Sits left of table.*)

TOM. Delighted. Come and sit down. What are you doing here? (*Sits above table.*)

MRS. C-BANKS. Joining my dear husband. And I'm afraid we're in for a very dull trip. There is nobody on board—at least nobody who *is* anybody. Though, of course, the poor creatures can't help that. You follow me. What I say I mean in the most kindly manner—but still, there it is.

TOM. We must try and cheer each other up, then, Mrs. Banks.

MRS. C-BANKS. Yes, all friends at sea, of course. By the way, my name is *Cliveden*-Banks. You know, of course, but it's such a long while since we met. There was a plain Mrs. Banks in the divorce court lately—so silly of her—and so plain, judging from the Daily Mirror—a total stranger, of course. Still it's made me very particular about my hyphen. Not that I am ever likely to appear in a divorce court.

TOM. No, most unlikely. (*With a significant appraisal of her.*)

MRS. C-BANKS. Still you see what I mean.
(SCRUBBY *puts drink on table.*)

TOM. Of course. Thank you. Mrs. *Cliveden*-Banks, will you have a drink?

MRS. C-BANKS. Thank you—what are you drinking—ginger ale?

TOM. No—er—whiskey.

MRS. C-BANKS. At this time in the morning?

TOM. Whiskey at any time in the morning, afternoon or evening.

MRS. C-BANKS. I'm afraid you're still a naughty boy. I'll have a ginger ale. (SCRUBBY *proceeds to fetch her the drink*) When I said there was nobody on board, dear Mr. Prior, between you and me, there is one person on board to whom I shall take a strong objection. He's a clergyman.

TOM. Poor blighter! I should pity rather than blame him.

MRS. C-BANKS. Oh, don't you know? Clergymen at sea are dreadfully unlucky. We shall probably all go to the bottom. If we do I shall blame the clergyman entirely. In my opinion steamship companies have no right to let clergymen travel at all. The clergy ought to stay at home in their own parishes and do good, not go gadding about all over the world putting other people's lives in danger.

SCRUBBY. Your ginger ale, madam! (*Puts drink on table.*)

MRS. C-BANKS. Thank you, steward. (*Takes drink.*) Isn't that so?

SCRUBBY. Isn't what so, madam?

MRS. C-BANKS. Oh, you must have been listening to what I was saying.

SCRUBBY. I assure you, madam, I was not.

MRS. C-BANKS. How odd! (TOM *signs for drink*) I was remarking that the sea-faring men regard the presence of a clergyman on board your ship as highly unlucky.

SCRUBBY. I believe there is a superstition to that effect, madam, yes. (*Returns behind bar.*)

MRS. C-BANKS. There! I told you so. Well, the best thing we can do is to cut the fellow dead. Nicely, of course, but firmly.

TOM. Just as you like. But will we save the boat by doing it?

MRS. C-BANKS. How droll you are!

TOM. Look out! Talk of the—

(THE REV. WILLIAM DUKE *enters left, crosses to desk and looks for writing paper and envelope. As he does so he speaks to* TOM. DUKE *is a very sincere, earnest young clergyman.*)

DUKE. Good morning, sir.

TOM (*in a loud voice to* MRS. C-BANKS). How is the Colonel?

MRS. C-BANKS. Dear. Benjamin, I regret to say, is feeling the heat dreadfully. I should have joined him last year, but somehow I never got time. The penalty of popularity. My great friend, Mabel, the Duchess of Middleford—*you don't* know her, of course, she was only saying to me at the Palace the other day—

DUKE (*as he sits at writing desk with paper, etc., turns to* TOM). Good morning.

TOM. Eh—oh, good morning.

MRS. C-BANKS. Who is that man?

TOM. Really, Mrs. Cliveden-Banks, I dunno—I—

MRS. C-BANKS. How strange! Peculiar people one must meet, mustn't one, in public places? Never mind. Let me see, where was I?

TOM. With your great friend whom I don't know.

MRS. C-BANKS. Oh, yes, of course. (REV. WILLIAM DUKE *sits left and writes*) And then that strange man whom we neither of us know interrupted by wishing you good morning. Never mind. Mabel pointed out to me very clearly that I was in danger of neglecting my duty. She said to me quite plainly, almost brutally, and she can be very brutal sometimes—"My dear Genevieve," she said, "you must remember you are a daughter of the Empire, a soldier's *daughter*—a soldier's *wife*. Your place is by your husband's side in far, far India." In fact she was so insistent on my leaving England that if I didn't know her really well, I should have felt she wanted to get rid of me. Still I have taken her advice, I have abandoned London's gaieties and go to help poor dear Benjamin rule a lot of black men. Frankly I hate the idea.

DUKE (*still sitting at table, turns*). I'm awfully sorry to bother you, madam, but could you tell me what the date is?

MRS. C-BANKS. What was that?

DUKE. I ought to know, of course, seeing that it's the date we sail, but my memory's so—

MRS. C-BANKS. Did you say the date?

DUKE. Yes, if you please.

MRS. C-BANKS. The *date*?

DUKE. If you would—

MRS. C-BANKS. You're trying to start a conversation with me, aren't you?

DUKE (*laughs*). Well, frankly, as we're all to be shipmates, the sooner we get to know each other the better, don't you think?

MRS. C-BANKS. That, young man, is a matter of opinion.

DUKE. Oh, I'm awfully sorry if—I didn't think introductions were necessary on board ship.

MRS. C-BANKS. Possibly they may not have been in the days of Walter Raleigh. Not having been there myself at the time, I cannot say for certain. But customs change at sea, young man, even though the Church remains exactly where it always was. Under the circumstances, therefore, there can be no question of me giving you a date.

DUKE. I beg your pardon—I'll find it out for myself.

MRS. C-BANKS. Was that cutting enough, dear Mr. Prior?

TOM. Oh yes, most; but what did it mean?

MRS. C-BANKS. I don't know.
(MRS. MIDGET *wanders on from the deck. A poor charwoman in black little bonnet, black shawl and dress —her best. Very humble, simple and obviously out of place in these strange surroundings. But sweet and motherly.*)

MRS. MIDGET. You'll excuse me, mum, but—

MRS. C-BANKS (*looking up and seeing her*). Good gracious!

MRS. MIDGET. You'll excuse me speaking up as it were, but I must say something to someone. And as you're the only other lady I've seen about, bar myself, I must ask you to give me a—

MRS. C-BANKS. Mr. Prior, am I to be attacked from all sides?

MRS. MIDGET (*starts suddenly on hearing name*). Mr. Prior?

TOM. Any objection?

MRS. MIDGET. No, very pleased to meet you. You see, mum, I 'ad to follow yer because yer see, mum, I've been struck all of a 'eap.

MRS. C-BANKS. You've been what?

MRS. MIDGET. Struck all of a 'eap.

MRS. C-BANKS. Mr. Prior, rescue me. And you had better do something for this good woman, too. It appears she has been struck all of a heap—whatever that may mean.

TOM. Well—what's the trouble?

MRS. MIDGET. Well, sir, thanking you, it's like this, as it were—

MRS. C-BANKS. "As it were." How quaint! "As it was" is correct, of course—we all know that from our Prayer Book. Go on.

MRS. MIDGET. Well, sir, it were like this, *as it was;* only last Saturday, Mrs. Roberts and I were talking about the sheets being damp, and I says—

MRS. C-BANKS. Ah! Sheets—damp. The good woman is, of course, a stewardess.

TOM. Are you?

MRS. MIDGET. Am I what?

TOM. A stewardess on this boat?

MRS. MIDGET. No, I'm a passenger.

MRS. C-BANKS. She's a passenger! Oh, I see it, she's a passenger! I see it all! The whole thing has come to me in a flash! She's a passenger. Don't worry yourself any more, Mr. Prior, I have solved the good woman's trouble. She's a passenger and she's lost her way; haven't you, good woman?

MRS. MIDGET. Exactly, mum.

MRS. C-BANKS. Mr. Prior, tell that steward fellow to tell somebody to take the good woman back to her proper place immediately. She's been wandering. She's on the wrong deck, she's in the wrong class. Goodbye, good woman, goodbye. So glad to have been so helpful.

MRS. MIDGET. Thank you, mum.

TOM (*going to her*). Oh, steward, just get someone to show this woman steerage – er – third class deck—or something, will you?

SCRUBBY (*turns to* TOM). The third class, sir?

TOM. Yes, please.

SCRUBBY. I think you've made some mistake, sir. There is only one class on the boat.
(REV. WILLIAM DUKE *finishes his letter and goes out left.*)

MRS. C-BANKS (*faintly*). What was that?

TOM. Only one class?

SCRUBBY. Yes, sir. It's the same on all this line.

MRS. C-BANKS. What was that?

TOM. Oh, sorry—I didn't know. (*Returning*) Er—Mrs. Cliveden-Banks—

MRS. C-BANKS. Mr. Prior, did I, or did I not hear that fellow say there is only one class on this boat?

TOM. He said so, certainly.

MRS. C-BANKS. Mr. Prior, the thing's impossible.

TOM. Well, he ought to know.

MRS. C-BANKS. How dare she—how dare my secretary book me a passage on a vessel with only one class? How am I to know who are the ladies and gentlemen, and who are not?

TOM. Now, now, don't get excited.

MRS. C-BANKS. Excited! Mr. Prior, a terrible thought has struck me. That woman there—

TOM. Well, what about her?

MRS. C-BANKS. She probably eats.

TOM. Extremely likely, I should say.

MRS. C-BANKS. Well then—if she eats—and if there's only one class—she will eat in the same place as we shall. It can't be done, I shall disembark immediately.

TOM. Now look here, Mrs. Banks—Mrs. Cliveden-Banks—she's probably only a lady's maid or something.

MRS. C-BANKS. Who would have a maid like that—outside a theatrical boarding house?

TOM. The idea of your landing is absurd. Don't get nervy about nothing. We can easily avoid her. If you're really upset—

MRS. C-BANKS. And I am, I am!

TOM. Then I'll question her.

MRS. C-BANKS. Yes. Do, do, quickly. It would be quite impossible for me to lunch at the same table with a woman who has been struck all of a heap.

TOM. Come here, will you? I—er—we want to help you if we possibly can. (*Drinks.*)

MRS. MIDGET. Thank you, sir.

TOM. Excuse me. (*Finishes drink*) Thanks. Now, what is—your name?

MRS. MIDGET. Midget.

TOM. What?

MRS. MIDGET. Midget.

MRS. C-BANKS. That, to begin with, is an alibi. No one could possibly be called Midget.

MRS. MIDGET (*warming in quick resentment*). Oh, couldn't they? Well, I'll show you whether they could or not all right. Midget's as good a name as any other name, Midget is. And don't you forget it, old Mrs. 'Igh and Mighty. My name's Midget all right, Midget married me all right, and I can prove it, and I've got my lines, which was a job to get as I admit.

MRS. C-BANKS. How dreadfully sordid!

MRS. MIDGET. But when it comes to utter strangers tellin' me as I don't know what my own name is, then I speaks up and unabashed, as I would do in front of the 'ole street. I've nothing to 'ide, I've not, I'm not one of these—

MRS. C-BANKS. That will do, that will do. The world is full of troubles, we know. Doubtless you have had yours, my good—er—my woman.

MRS. MIDGET. I 'ave 'ad trouble, I confess.

TOM. But what's your present one—that's what—what we want to know?

MRS. MIDGET. Where am I?

TOM. On board—on board this ship.

MRS. MIDGET. Yes, but what for?

TOM. How should *I* know? Are your tickets and luggage all right?

MRS. MIDGET. I suppose so. I'm not one to worry over little things.

TOM. Have you been to your cabin yet?

MRS. MIDGET. No.

TOM. What's the number?

MRS. MIDGET. 'Ow do I know if I ain't been there?

TOM. I say—you're not tight, are you?

MRS. MIDGET. Tight?

TOM. Blotto—squiffy—gone away.

MRS. MIDGET. Not me. "To T.," I am.

TOM. How wise of you. (*Drinks*) Well, are you ill?

MRS. MIDGET. Now, that's what I'm a-wondering. Am I ill? I don't think so. I don't feel ill. And yet I said to Mrs. Roberts last Thursday —or was it Wednesday?—never mind, I said to 'er anyway I says—"What I want" says I—or did she say it to me? Never mind, it don't make no difference, one of us says to the other, "What I or you want," according to whichever of us *did* say it, "is a thorough 'oliday." And then—wait a minute—I remember now—it's all coming back—I've come on 'ere to meet somebody.

TOM. Oh, that's it, is it?

MRS. MIDGET. Yes, at the other end. It was our parson's idea. "A thorough 'oliday" of course! 'Ow silly of me to forget. But of course I ain't 'ad much to eat today and what with the excitement and one thing and another, and Mrs. Roberts—

TOM. Damn Mrs. Roberts!

MRS. MIDGET. Oh, I do, sir—often.

TOM. Look here, what you want's a sandwich and a drink, and a good sleep. Then you'll remember everything. Someone should have brought you here, of course. But if you're being met at the other end, there's nothing to worry about.

MRS. MIDGET. Thank you, sir.

MRS. C-BANKS. The woman is obviously light-headed. Have her removed.

TOM. Steward, can you find out this passenger's stewardess for me —for her? Have her put in her charge, see she gets everything she should have. Nervous you know, never been to sea.

SCRUBBY. Certainly, sir. (*Crosses left from behind bar.*)

MRS. C-BANKS. I should certainly suggest a sleep for her. A long, long sleep—in fact, if I were in her place I should take a complete rest, have all my meals in my own cabin, and never come on deck at all. I'm sure she would feel better if she did that.

MRS. MIDGET. Much obliged. But I 'ope to be 'opping about like a cricket in an 'our or two.

SCRUBBY. This way, madam.

MRS. MIDGET (*flattered by the attention*). Thank you, *Captain.*
(SCRUBBY *and* MRS. MIDGET *go off together left.*)

SCRUBBY. Straight ahead.

MRS. C-BANKS. I should like to burn Miss Longton. Miss Longton is my secretary.

TOM (*looking after them*). Do you think that woman was speaking the truth?

MRS. C-BANKS. No. She's probably one of a gang of international crooks. Look at the way she scraped acquaintance with me. Personally I shall be on my guard against her. (*Low muffled siren heard*) What do you think that is?

TOM. Sailing shortly, I suppose.

MRS. C-BANKS. Then I shall go on deck and wave farewell to the dear old white cliffs. (*Rises*) By the way, I'm told on many parts of the coast they're crumbling fast. Still, England, England, there is no country like her.

TOM. Thank goodness.

MRS. C-BANKS. Why do you say that?

TOM. I don't. That's what other countries say.

MRS. C-BANKS. How naughty you are. Well, come along and protect me from the mob.

TOM. No, thanks, if you'll excuse me. I'd far rather remain here and slip away from my native land oblivious of her disregard for me.

MRS. C-BANKS. Which means—?

TOM. That I'm going to have another drink.

MRS. C-BANKS. You're a bad lad. Still, I'll see you later.
(*She passes through the centre door and goes left along the deck.*)

TOM. I suppose so. Confound the woman. (*Drinks and lights cigarette.*)
(REV. WILLIAM DUKE *reappears from the left.*)
Oh, I say, Padre!

DUKE. How is the Colonel?

TOM. Padre.

DUKE. Were you speaking to me, sir?

TOM. Yes. I want to—to apologise.

DUKE (*centre*). What for?

TOM. Cutting you stone dead like the silly old woman I was with.

DUKE. Oh, that's all right.

TOM. Sure?

DUKE. Sure!

TOM. Positive?

DUKE. Positive!

TOM. Good. Have a drink? (*Leading him to bar.*)

DUKE. Thanks.

TOM. The fellow will be back in a second.

DUKE. Good.

TOM. Cigarette?

DUKE. Thanks.

TOM. Hot, isn't it?

DUKE. Yes. Hot.

TOM. Yes—er—do you think we shall have—er—smooth passage?

DUKE. Quite. I mean—I hope so.

TOM. So do I.

DUKE. I suppose we all do.

TOM. Er—yes. I suppose we all do. I say, I must tell you, of course, that I should never have behaved as I did just now, pretending not to see you and all that, but of course I'm a very weak character.

DUKE. Strong of you to admit it.

TOM. Yes, I'm easily swayed. No stamina. (*Drinks*) I can't think why. And the old cat was drivelling along, and she persuaded me not to see you. Told me you were unlucky.

DUKE. Ha!

TOM. So I agreed not to. I always agree with anyone I'm with. She was to blame entirely.

DUKE. I have always found it an unwise habit to run down other people. They have a nasty way of getting to hear about it and retaliating—with interest.

TOM. You're not going to preach a sermon, are you?

DUKE. Good Lor', no! I say, do you know the slums?

TOM. Good heavens, no!

DUKE. Take my advice then and don't; I do. I've known them for the last eight years. And I'm sick of the slums and people I was trying to keep straight with sermons—official and otherwise—and the drizzle, and the smell of tea in urns with the Vicar—oh yes, the Vicar more than anything. No, no, no more sermons from me for a bit. But I beg your pardon, I must be boring you.

TOM. Not at all so far. You must have had a pretty rotten time! (SCRUBBY *re-enters from the left and goes to bar.*)

DUKE. Oh, I don't know, I'm awfully keen on my job. I want a rest, that's all.

TOM. "A thorough 'oliday," in fact. Hello, here's our man. This will do you good. What's it to be?

DUKE. Beer, please.

TOM. Er—steward—er—what *is* your name?

SCRUBBY. Scrubby.

TOM. Midget and Scrubby. Good Lor'! Oh, well, it can't be helped, I suppose. A Bass please, and a—the same.

SCRUBBY. Yes, sir.

DUKE. I think everybody ought to be awfully keen, don't you?

TOM. What do you mean? Sort of getting up in the morning before breakfast and having a cold bath? Because if you do, I don't.

DUKE. No, no, not necessarily that, of course. But keen every moment of the day, keen on something—never wasting a moment—at it, always at it, as it were. Now there's the trip for instance, that we're going on. We must arrange to enjoy every moment of it.

TOM. Why?

DUKE. Because we're meant to.

TOM. Oh!

DUKE. We must organise amongst ourselves. I've thought out lots of jolly little ideas.

TOM. Such as—?

DUKE. Well—for instance—we'll get up a concert.

TOM. Oh! that will be jolly. *Must* we get up a concert?

DUKE. Of course.

TOM. How awful! Why must we?

DUKE. Just to amuse the other passengers.

TOM. *Would* it amuse the other passengers?

DUKE. And ourselves, too.

TOM. Oh, I see.

DUKE. It always *is* done, you know.

TOM. Some habits want breaking—

DUKE. Do you sing?

TOM. No.

DUKE. That's a pity.

TOM. Do you recite?

DUKE. Er—no—

TOM. That's excellent! (SCRUBBY *serves drinks.*)

SCRUBBY. Your drinks, sir, and it's quite all *right.*

TOM. What's quite all *right?*

SCRUBBY. The lady, sir.

TOM. Which lady?

SCRUBBY. The lady you wanted put in charge of her stewardess.

TOM. Oh yes, of course. That lady. Thanks very much.

SCRUBBY. Thank you, sir.

DUKE. I say, I really oughtn't to know, but I'd always understood you couldn't get a drink on board a ship until she sailed?

TOM. Neither you can as a rule. That never struck me—don't say anything.

DUKE. It's very queer.

TOM. It's very lucky. Cheero!

DUKE. Cheero!

TOM. Got any other gadget on you for the passengers' amusement? Perhaps you'd like me to walk the plank or something?

DUKE. We ought to have some sports, of course.

TOM. Why did I put the idea into your head?

DUKE. You can help with the organisation. You need not participate.

TOM. Right. I'll organise anything you like—from here. Cheery spot this.
(*Through the centre door enters* MR. LINGLEY. *He is a hard and unpleasant business man, aged fifty-five or sixty. He is loud and officious, and is obviously self-made. He has on a travelling cap and a heavy overcoat, and he is carrying an attaché case, containing business papers. He is evidently in a great hurry.*)

LINGLEY. Ah, good morning, gentlemen. My name's Lingley.

TOM. Hurray!

LINGLEY. I've had a narrow shave—nearly missed her.

DUKE. Duke's my name. Very warm today, sir.

LINGLEY. Damn warm—I beg your pardon, I didn't notice your collar—very warm. Steward, get me a drink. (*Sits at table left.*)

SCRUBBY. Whiskey and soda, sir?

LINGLEY. No, confound you, ginger ale with some ice. Yes, I left it a bit too late, another five minutes and I'd have missed her.

DUKE. We'll soon be off then?

LINGLEY. We're sailing now.

TOM. Land of hope and glory—au revoir! (*Drinks.*)

DUKE. You motored here?

LINGLEY. No, flew—in my office two hours ago. Now I must get on with things. (*Opens attaché case and lays out papers.*)
(SCRUBBY *brings him his drink.*)

DUKE (*to* TOM). There you are, you see, the man's keen.

TOM. I *know* the blighter.

LINGLEY (*to* SCRUBBY). How much?

SCRUBBY. You needn't pay, sir.

LINGLEY. I always pay. How much?

SCRUBBY. One shilling, sir.

LINGLEY. Damn—er—*very* expensive still—here is *one* shilling.

SCRUBBY. Thank you, sir.

LINGLEY. What for? (SCRUBBY *returns behind bar*) I haven't tipped you.

DUKE. I hope you won't be so busy, sir, that we shan't see you on the trip.

LINGLEY. Once in my state-room I don't suppose I'll leave it—till we touch—er—er—Marseilles.

DUKE. I hope it's interesting work, sir.

LINGLEY. No, it isn't, but it keeps me busy—I am an M.P. you know.
(SCRUBBY *disappears through the door right.*)

DUKE. Oh! Pleased to meet you.

LINGLEY. Not at all. I'm on the London County Council as well, incidentally I own twenty-one music-halls, a chain of cinemas, two gold mines and a Methodist chapel. Naturally they want looking after.

DUKE. Naturally. What are you doing with the chapel?

LINGLEY. Having it pulled down.

TOM. Sportsman!

LINGLEY. You—you there!

TOM. Me?

LINGLEY. Yes! I know your face, don't I? I never forget a face.

TOM. How that must sadden your sweet life at times.

LINGLEY. Where have I seen it before?

TOM. Oh, in your office. You gave me a job once. It lasted two days.

LINGLEY. What was the matter?

TOM. Your office! I couldn't stand the atmosphere, so I drowned it in drink.

LINGLEY. I remember. I remember. You were sacked mechanically.

TOM. Yes. You wouldn't give me a second chance.

LINGLEY. No one has ever given *me* a second chance. I shall never expect one. I shall certainly never ask for one.

TOM. As you said when you sacked me mechanically. In my opinion, Mr. Lingley, L.C.C., M.P., you're a pompous old idiot.

LINGLEY (*rising*). How dare you! How—you must be crazy.

TOM. I'm not in your ghastly office now. I can say what I like. (*Shouts*) You're a blue-nosed baboon! There! I've dreamt I said that to you for weeks, and now I've said it.

LINGLEY. If you're not careful, Mr. —Mr.—er—er—I'll—I'll—

TOM. If *you're* not careful, Mr. Lingley, I'll make you walk the plank at the sports.

LINGLEY. Mr. Prior, you are obviously drunk now.

TOM. I am drunk, I admit—but I had trusted not obviously.

DUKE. Dear, dear, dear, dear!

TOM. Yes, that remark helps matters such a lot, doesn't it?

LINGLEY. I shall go on deck. Where are my papers? I've been irritated. The doctors said I must not be irritated. I've too much to do to be irritated.

DUKE. Oh, I'm sure Mr. Prior didn't mean—

TOM. I did. Every word of it. Shut up! He's a pink-eyed rabbit. He's a rotter, he's a grasper—

LINGLEY. Silence, sir! For goodness' sake, silence! I shan't be able to concentrate after this interruption. I came here for peace, damn you. I've been thinking too hard as it is

—and now this little gnat—he's destroyed what I'd nearly completed in my mind. Damn you, sir, I'm sick of opposition. Damn you—you— (*The long low siren is heard again*) Oh, my God! (*Falls into chair.*)

DUKE. Mr. Lingley, what is it? (*Goes to Lingley.*)
(TOM *goes to* LINGLEY *glass in hand.*)

LINGLEY. Wait—wait!

DUKE. You're looking ill.

LINGLEY. Yes, I am ill, I'm feeling ill, I am. Suddenly. I must have help, I was warned about this. An arm, please—and some of that stuff you're drinking. (TOM *gives him drink and supports him*) Thank you. I shall be all right in a minute.

DUKE. I'll get the doctor.

LINGLEY. No. He'll only irritate me. I know what to do. I've been told what to do. Absolute quiet and fresh air. I'll go on deck. (*Feels in pocket*) Oh yes, I'd forgotten. I'm to take one of these. (TOM *takes phial from his pocket and gives him a tabloid*) Thank you. I must keep quiet, calm and not think. I shall be all right in a minute, and I'll see another man the moment I get to—get to— (*Looks from one to the other*) Where *am* I going to?

DUKE. Marseilles you said, sir.

LINGLEY. Oh, yes, of course, Marseilles. (*Pause*) What am I going to Marseilles for?

DUKE. Don't worry now.

LINGLEY. No, don't worry, that's right. I felt quite faint for the moment, Mr. Duke; your drink has done me good. I'll go on deck and sit down.

DUKE. I'll see you there.

LINGLEY. Thank you. I prefer to be alone. I'm quite all right. I shall soon remember everything. I know what I'm doing. Oh, I've forgotten my papers.
(DUKE *supports him towards the centre door.*)

DUKE. Leave them—they can wait—I'll look after them.

LINGLEY. No, no, give them to me. (TOM *gives them.*)

DUKE. I wish you'd let me come and—

LINGLEY. Please don't worry me! It's all right this time, I know it is, if I'm not worried. Thank you. I know what I'm doing, of course—I know—already I'm better. I'm going to meet someone, that's all. But was it Aaronson or was it Bantock?

DUKE. Remember what your doctor said, don't worry!

LINGLEY (*going towards the door*). Of course not—no. That was the worst attack I've had so far. But I'm better now—yes—and the quiet and sea air will soon clear my mind completely. Thank you. I wish I could remember if it was Aaronson or Bantock! Thank you, Mr. Duke, for your very kind assistance.
(*He goes out slowly on to the deck and passes out of sight to the right.* DUKE *follows up after him.*)

TOM. Padre!

DUKE (*stopping*). Well?

TOM. What was it?

DUKE. I don't know—some sudden sort of attack—I'm going to stop by him. (*Starting to follow* LINGLEY.)

TOM. Padre!

DUKE. Well? (*Returning.*)

TOM. It was my fault, I suppose.

DUKE. Oh no, I—

TOM. Are you angry with me?

DUKE. Why should I be?

TOM. You know.

DUKE. Drink is a terrible—

TOM. It seemed to do *him* good.

DUKE. That's different.

TOM. You promised no sermons, anyway.

DUKE. What made you start it?

TOM. You said everyone should be keen on something. Drink's my hobby. Let's leave it at that.

DUKE. Please don't joke about it.

TOM. All right. If you won't be angry with me—I hate people to be angry with me. But I wasn't joking.

DUKE. I'll see you later. In fact I hope to see a lot of you on the voyage. (*Starting out centre.*)

TOM. Thanks. That's what I said to the steward. (*Stopping him again*) Padre!

DUKE (*returning*). Well—well!

TOM. One moment.

DUKE. What is it?

TOM. In strict confidence—now we're friends again—has it struck you by any chance that there's anything queer about this boat? Strictly between ourselves.

DUKE. No, it hasn't.

TOM. It has me.

DUKE. How do you mean?

TOM. I think there's something jolly queer about her. By Jove, if I were right it *would* be a joke!

DUKE. I don't follow you.

TOM. It's difficult to explain. But Mr. Lingley—and—and—oh, I'm not quite sure myself. It may be only my—

DUKE. Imagination?

TOM. Exactly. Only somehow I don't think it is.

DUKE. Go on. I must hurry.

TOM. Yes. Well (*turns to* DUKE), there was a sort of charwoman here just now—you didn't see her—a very decent sort of soul, of course, but—well—hardly the kind of person you'd expect to find here. And she couldn't remember where she was going. Excepting she was going to meet someone.

(*Turns to him*) Now this Lingley fellow's just told us the same thing in different words. He couldn't remember where he was going either, at least not clearly. And I've noticed lots of other little things. For instance, it's absurd sailing with our passenger list—there are so few of us. I tell you it's queer—and—

DUKE. Really I can't follow you.

TOM. Then there's old Mrs. Banks drivelling on about joining her husband— Good Lor'! It's just struck me.

DUKE. What has?

TOM. Colonel Cliveden-Banks kicked the bucket over a month ago. Surely she can't have forgotten *that*. Or—or would *that* be her father?

DUKE. Mr. Prior, if you take my advice, you'll follow Mr. Lingley's example and get some fresh air on deck.

TOM. Yes, I think I will. All the same it *is* queer. (*Rises to above table*) Certain you're not angry with me?

DUKE. Oh yes, certain. Shipmates, eh? (*Shakes hands.*)

TOM. Oh, yes, shipmates. But I bet you cut me the moment we land.

DUKE. Rot!
(*He follows* LINGLEY *on to the deck.* HENRY *has entered and is lighting his pipe from a match which he has taken from the table up left.*)

TOM. Excuse me, sir, after you. (*Coming up to him, takes his match and lights his cigarette from it*) Thanks. I say, do you mind if I ask you a question?

HENRY. Of course not.

TOM. It's rather a queer question.

HENRY. Go on.

TOM. Do—you—know—where—you—are—going—to?

HENRY. Are you a Salvation Army man or what?

TOM. No, I'm quite serious.

HENRY. Of course I know where I'm going to.

TOM. On this boat?

HENRY. Certainly.

TOM. Thank goodness! I'm going to get some fresh air!
(*He goes out on to the deck.* HENRY *goes up towards the deck, looks out.* ANN *enters left.*)

ANN. Why did you run away?

HENRY. Wanted a match.

ANN. I had some.

HENRY. A bit nervy, too. (*Coming down centre.*)

ANN. You've no need to be now—we've sailed.

HENRY. Really!

ANN. Yes. I saw the water moving by the porthole.

HENRY (*runs up centre and looks out*). You're right. Why, we're well out. Almost open water.

ANN. Yes, dear.

HENRY. Give me your hand.

ANN. Hold tight to it.

HENRY. Queer. It's just like an ordinary sailing.

ANN. Is it? (*Pause.*)

HENRY. A man just now asked me if I knew where I was going. I said I did.

ANN. That was right.

HENRY. Funny question though, wasn't it?

ANN. Oh, I don't know.

HENRY. He said it was queer. You don't think he—

ANN. Of course not, dear. Can you smell the sea? (*Crosses below settee.*)

HENRY. Yes, fine, isn't it?

ANN. I hope it will be terribly rough with lots of spray and wind.

HENRY. Why?

ANN. You can hold me closer.

HENRY. Ann! Ann! I've been worrying, I've been thinking just now—these modern inventions that doctors have—and things like that, you know.

ANN. You prosaic old thing—aren't you?

HENRY. They couldn't possibly call us back even now, could they?

ANN. Of course not, dear. How could they? We're safe enough as long as we hold tight.

HENRY. It was a risk, though, wasn't it?

ANN. Yes, dear.

HENRY. If—supposing—if it hadn't happened.

ANN. My dear, we always knew it would.

HENRY. Yes, but if it hadn't.

ANN. But we knew.

HENRY. I think you were always more certain than I was.

ANN (*sits*). Well then, I knew for both of us.

HENRY (*sits*). Yes, that's right. You knew. Ann, I trust you so in things I can't quite understand. Of course I trust you in things I can understand, too. But you seem to know so much more about the big things than I do.

ANN. Perhaps I only pretend to.

HENRY. Oh, no, you know all right. Give me another light, will you? (*Bus.*) Thanks. It's nice being able to smoke. Ann?

ANN. Well, dear.

HENRY. You're quite, quite sure?

ANN. Quite sure, dear.

HENRY. Isn't ours a terribly big secret?

ANN. Isn't it?

HENRY. Yes, Ann, I love you.

ANN. I love you, Henry.

HENRY. Always?

ANN. Always.

HENRY. Ann, I wonder how the dog is?

ANN. You baby—poor old Jock! Oh, they'll look after him all right.

HENRY. I hope so. I say, Ann, when dogs die, what do you think happens to them?

ANN. I dunno. There must be a heaven for dogs—at least there ought to be.

HENRY. What a jolly place it must be! No cats in it, of course.

ANN. Of course not. Just lots of bones and meat and water. And hot fires to lie in front of in the winter.

HENRY. What about the kind masters?

ANN. I'd forgotten them. Oh, I expect there's some arrangement so that the good dogs can't remember the kind masters.

HENRY. *We* remember, though.

ANN. Yes. *You* were a very kind master.

HENRY (*rises*). It's queer. (*Over to centre*) Poor old Jock. (*Turns*) I say, Ann, you don't think—

ANN. What?

HENRY. Any of these other people can possibly know.

ANN. Our secret? Of course they can't.

HENRY. It *is* a wonderful secret.

ANN (*rises*). I told you, Henry, how it would be as long as we believed.

HENRY. And yet? (*Over to her*) I wonder if it's safe—even now.

ANN. What makes you say that?

HENRY. I can't quite remember, Ann, not clearly, not yet—it's coming back gradually of course, but—but—

ANN. Yes, dear?

HENRY. Ann, haven't you and I sinned in some way?

ANN. We've been true to each other. How can we have sinned?

HENRY. If we had, Ann, could they separate us?

ANN. Hold my hand tightly.

HENRY. I'm trying so hard to remember.

ANN. What, dear?

HENRY. What it is we've done that isn't right.

ANN. We've done nothing that isn't right.

HENRY. No. Not in our light, of course. But have we from other—from the world's—

ANN. We've never cared for the world. We're not going to care for it now.

HENRY. If we were wrong and if it were something very, very wrong, they couldn't separate us, could they?

ANN. That sort of thing's all over now, Henry. You've forgotten our secret.

HENRY. No, I haven't, it's all perfect, of course—excepting this one thing. (TOM *enters from the deck and unobserved by them stands quietly at the back leaning against doorway*) Don't laugh—don't laugh at me, Ann, I'm only trying to remember, and asking for your help. But it seems (*sits*) to me this thing—this crime, if it is one—that we've committed, is something big, and yet that it's—now don't laugh—that it's only something to do with gas.

ANN (*sits beside him*). Gas?

HENRY. Yes.

ANN. You silly.

HENRY. It seems to me that before we left the flat—

ANN. Our sad little flat!

HENRY. I forgot—to turn off—the gas.

ANN. You terrible silly! Of course you did. We—agreed—that. That's what we agreed.

HENRY. There's nothing very wrong in not turning off gas!

ANN. Don't worry, dear. Take my hand.

HENRY. Nothing so bad that they could separate us for it. You can't blame people for not turning off gas! And yet, I'd have sworn—Ann, you're quite certain that there isn't something else we've done? Something big?

ANN. There's nothing else, dear, I'm certain. You've nothing to be ashamed of.

HENRY. I love you so.

ANN. Thank you, Henry. Don't worry, dear.

HENRY. I wish I could remember *how* we got here. We wanted to so long. Anyway, now we have.

ANN. Let's go out on to the deck.

HENRY. Yes, let's—bless you. (*Both turn and see* TOM) Hello, sir.

TOM (*quietly*). Hello!

HENRY. We didn't notice you—

TOM. It's all right. I just came back to—

HENRY. May I introduce my wife? Ann, this is the gentleman who asked me if I knew where I was going.

ANN. How do you do?

TOM. How do you do? (TOM *is a changed man. His tone is quiet and sad, and he stands perfectly rigid. The awful truth which has dawned upon him has completely sobered him. There is a pause. Then* ANN *goes out on to the deck, and* HENRY *follows her.)*

HENRY (*as he exits*). We'll see you later. We've sailed, you know.
(SCRUBBY *appears behind the bar.*)

TOM. Yes, I am right. (*Comes to bar*) Scrubby!

SCRUBBY. Yes, sir?

TOM. I am right, aren't I, Scrubby?

SCRUBBY. Right, sir, in the head, do you mean?

TOM. You know what I mean.

SCRUBBY. Right about what, sir?

TOM. You—I—all of us on this boat.

SCRUBBY. What about all of us on this boat, sir?

TOM (*trembling with apprehension*). We are—now answer me truthfully—we are all *dead, aren't we?*

SCRUBBY (*after a pause. Very quietly with firm conviction*). Yes, sir, we are all dead. Quite dead. They don't find out so soon as you have as a rule.

TOM (*pause*). Queer! (*Sits left of table.*)

SCRUBBY. Not when you get used to it, sir.

TOM. How long have you been—you been—oh, you know?

SCRUBBY. Me, sir? Oh, I was lost young.

TOM. You were what?

SCRUBBY. Lost young, sir.

TOM. I don't understand.

SCRUBBY. No, sir, you wouldn't, not yet. But you'll get to know lots of things as the voyage goes on.

TOM. Tell me—tell me one thing—*now.*

SCRUBBY. Anything I can, sir.

TOM (*terrified*). Where—where are we sailing for?

SCRUBBY. Heaven, sir. (*Pause*) And hell, too. (*Pause*) It's the same place, you see.
(*The curtain falls, with* TOM, *in a state of apprehension, gazing blankly at* SCRUBBY.)

ACT TWO

The scene is unchanged, but it is evening. The curtains are drawn over the portholes, and the electric lights are on. The centre door is open from time to time, and it is pitch black outside.

On the left is seated MRS. CLIVEDEN-BANKS *in evening frock.* MR. LINGLEY *is with her, seated at the table on the right.*

LINGLEY. Well, I'm feeling very much better.

MRS. C-BANKS. I am so glad.

LINGLEY. I didn't quite catch your name at dinner. Being introduced during the soup has its disadvantages. The lady sitting next to us made it a little difficult to hear concisely.

MRS. C-BANKS. Mrs. Cliveden-Banks. Yes, I foresaw trouble with her this morning. Er—Mrs. Midget.

LINGLEY. Thank you. I say, Mrs. Midget.

MRS. C-BANKS. No, no! No. *I* am Cliveden-Banks.

LINGLEY. I apologise. What strikes me is that this line can't be paying any dividends— Why, there's nobody on board.

MRS. C-BANKS. Bother dividends as long as I'm comfortable!

LINGLEY. This I think is the best place.

MRS. C-BANKS. Quite a jolly little snuggery. (THE REVEREND WILLIAM DUKE *enters and comes down centre*) At least it *was*.

LINGLEY. Join me in a cigar, Duke?

REVEREND W. DUKE. Thank you.

MRS. C-BANKS (*after a glance at* DUKE). And I was so comfortable. Where on earth can I go to now, I wonder? (*Rises.*)

LINGLEY. Oh! don't go.

DUKE. I hope you are not leaving on my account?

MRS. C-BANKS. Your hope is shattered, young man, I am.

DUKE. Mrs. Cliveden-Banks. I don't know what I've done to offend you. I can't help being a parson. But I do know that you'll make it very uncomfortable for the others if you go on like this. So come, look over my shortcomings just for the trip. Remember that "to err is human, to forgive divine."

MRS. C-BANKS. Are you suggesting I have ever erred?

DUKE. In your case, I am certain such a thing would be impossible.

MRS. C-BANKS. Oh! very well. I sacrifice myself for the others' sake, I am a generous woman. How do you do? (*Shaking hands*) But remember, Mr. Duke, if you *do* drown us all, I'll never speak to you again. (*Sits on settee.*)

DUKE. Splendid! (*Sits right of table right*) Now, where are those other two? We might get up some bridge. We *must* all do something our first night out.

MRS. C-BANKS. What other two do you mean?

DUKE. They—er—at dinner. They sat by themselves. Seemed awfully nice—quiet. I don't know their names—I think the girl's called Ann.

MRS. C-BANKS. Oh! that couple! Oh! dear! Did you like the look of *them?*

DUKE. Yes, didn't you?

MRS. C-BANKS. No, I thought there was something funny about them.

LINGLEY. "Funny"?

DUKE. What do you mean by that?

MRS. C-BANKS. I don't know. It just struck me they were funny. Not nice. I may be wrong. I hope I am. But that *is* my opinion. Not nice. Funny.
(MRS. MIDGET *wanders in from the deck. Now hatless.*)

MRS. MIDGET. May I come in?

MRS. C-BANKS. Now I *shall* go.

DUKE (*rises*). Yes, come in, Mrs. Midget, come in.

MRS. MIDGET (*entering*). It's a bit lonely in the street.

DUKE. "Street"?

MRS. MIDGET. Out there.

MRS. C-BANKS. She means the deck —how quaint.

DUKE. It's more cheerful in here, isn't it?

MRS. MIDGET. Oh, much.

DUKE. Sit down. You're not nervous, now, are you?

MRS. MIDGET (*sits at table, right centre*). Not of you, sir. You wear just the same sort of collar as our parson does. I wish I was back in the Lambeth Road.

MRS. C-BANKS (*to* LINGLEY). I can't stand the creature. I really can't—she's too impossible. I shall squash her. Good evening, Mrs. Midget. We heard you at dinner. Very warm, this evening, isn't it?

MRS. MIDGET. Yes, dearie. 'Ellish 'ot. Beggin' your Reverence's pardon. I've come out all of a sweat. (*Wiping her neck with handkerchief.*)

MRS. C-BANKS. Dear me! Have you really? How embarrassing. What a day you have had, haven't you? First of all you're struck into a heap and now you've come out all of a —yes, exactly. Yet, I suppose you travel a great deal?

MRS. MIDGET. Every day. Lambeth to the Bank and from the Bank back to Lambeth. Workin' in the City as I did—do.

MRS. C-BANKS. The City! How enthralling! Big financial interests, I presume?

MRS. MIDGET. No—charrin'. And in the old times we always managed Margate in the summer. Nice spot, Margate, ain't it?

MRS. C-BANKS. I know nothing against it. I have never been there, of course.

MRS. MIDGET. Never been to Margate! (*To* DUKE) Would you believe it?

DUKE. Yes.

MRS. MIDGET. Oh! you'd love Margate a treat, mum. What with the paddling and everything. Do you like cocoanuts?

MRS. C-BANKS. Cocoanuts? Oh, good Lord no!

MRS. MIDGET. Ah! Then you mightn't like Margate. They grow very good ones there though. At least they used to. Cors I ain't been there since I lost all my money. Do you know, all of yer, believe me or believe me not, I once had a house of my very own.

MRS. C-BANKS. How magnificent!

MRS. MIDGET. Yes, wasn't it? Though of course it wasn't *all* my own. No. Semi-detached, and lodgers yer know. Payin' guests and very well it *did* pay for donkey's years. Well enough for me to make my son a gentleman anyway, and send him to college to prove it.

MRS. C-BANKS. Quite romantic. Perhaps I have met your dear boy? Where is he now? Cambridge or Cologne?

MRS. MIDGET. Well, 'avin' become a gentleman 'e naturally lost all 'is money. And 'is money was my money. And I ain't seen him since. 'E hasn't seen me, not to know me, since 'e was a little boy. I got my brother-in-law, 'e's rich, to take him over and manage things for me. You see I didn't want to disgrace 'im. 'E's been a good boy.

LINGLEY. Sounds it.

MRS. MIDGET (*resentfully*). 'E *was*, I tell yer. But you know what it is yerself, sir.

LINGLEY. I do not—I have never lost a penny in my life.

MRS. MIDGET. Ah! then you can't be a gentleman.

LINGLEY. What?

MRS. MIDGET. Now the gentlemen my—my boy mixed with *were* gents. Always broke, bless 'em, and then 'avin' "another one" just to make 'em forget about it. And my boy the life and soul of the 'ole crowd. At least so the letter told me from the brother-in-law. And you can't 'ave your cake and eat it, as the sayin' goes, nor your gin and drink it *as* you well know, sir.

LINGLEY. Confound it, madam, I do *not* know.

DUKE. Sorrow's sent to try us, Mrs. Midget.

MRS. MIDGET. Cors it's sent to try us. What else could it be sent for? And it does try us very much.

DUKE. Yes—but sometimes as in your case—

MRS. C-BANKS. Mr. Duke means you would never have the steady poise, you would not be the woman of the world you so obviously are unless—

MRS. MIDGET. You're trying to pull my leg, aren't you?

DUKE. I'm afraid Mrs. Cliveden-Banks *was* trying to. I certainly didn't mean that.

MRS. MIDGET. Thank you, sir. (*Rises and crosses centre to* MRS. CLIVEDEN-BANKS) Mum, I may not know the manners of Society, and if them is such as yours I do *not* want to. With which terse remark I shuts up, being sorry for anything I've said. (*Moves up centre.*)

DUKE. Yes, yes, quite, quite. Well, we must all *do* something, you know, time is getting on. What about those cards?

MRS. MIDGET (*coming down right*). Oh! I'd love a game o' cards. (*sits*)

Mr. Prior was only telling me this afternoon before 'e—well, 'e was telling me that 'e played cards.

LINGLEY. Prior—pooh!

MRS. MIDGET. I like 'im anyway.

DUKE. Very unfortunate—Prior—Yes, yes, dear, dear, dear.

MRS. C-BANKS. Poor Mr. Prior! But I hear he's always like that nowadays. A thoroughly bad lot in fact. Not that I would say so in public of course—but just between ourselves I mean. Oh! (*Laughs*) What a sight he was and what an exhibition he made of himself. I shall never forget it. Never! (*Laughs again*) Mr. Lingley, he called you a—dear, dear me—I can't help smiling but he called you a—(*laughs*) didn't he?

LINGLEY. Never mind what he called me, madam.

MRS. C-BANKS. Well, you *are* rather like one, you know, if you don't mind my saying so. Where is he now, I wonder?

LINGLEY. Sleeping it off if he's a wise man.

DUKE. Which he isn't.

MRS. C-BANKS. He wasn't at dinner naturally. I expect you all noticed it.

DUKE. Of course, of course. It's a great shame, a great pity. (TOM *enters; he is very pale, tense and very quiet*) Ah! Prior!

MRS. C-BANKS. Mr. Prior! Why, we were just talking about you—

TOM. Indeed.

MRS. C-BANKS. Yes, I was only saying what a steady hand—

TOM. Don't waste any more of your breath than is absolutely necessary, Mrs. Cliveden-Banks. Nor any of you, either.

MRS. C-BANKS. I beg your pardon.

DUKE. What's the matter now?

TOM. We're trapped, that's all.

DUKE (*rises*). Trapped!

TOM. Yes, trapped. Every one of us—all of us on this boat, we're done for.

MRS. C-BANKS. What, *already!* (*Threateningly pointing to* DUKE) Mr. *Duke!!*—

TOM. I mean it. You needn't believe me if you don't want to. It's true all the same. We're dead people!

LINGLEY. Oh, run away, run away, young man, and sleep it off.

TOM. I'm sober enough now. And the boat's not sinking. I don't mean that either.

LINGLEY. What in blazes do you mean, sir?

TOM. Duke, come here. Feel my pulse. Draw a chalk line on the floor and make me walk it if you want to. (DUKE *moves up to him*) Look at my eyes. Now—I am sober, aren't I?

DUKE. Yes, I think so.

TOM. The last time I heard a clergyman say "Yes, I think so" was on the music halls. Funny I shall never go to a music hall again.

MRS. MIDGET (*rises*). Why doesn't someone put the poor young man to bed? It would be much kinder.

TOM. Quiet, please. I don't want to frighten you—any of you—but I feel—I ought to try and convince you. You admit I'm sober. You'll have to take my word I'm not mad.

LINGLEY. I should want more than your word for that.

TOM. You shall have it. You shall have the word of the—the man who calls himself a steward, and the words of two of our fellow passengers. The two who I see are not here.

LINGLEY. But what about, sir? What are you driving at?

TOM (*comes down left centre*). I began to suspect this morning before lunch. Nobody seemed to know where they were going to. I'd forgotten myself, though I didn't admit it. I didn't want to. I didn't dare to. I daren't now. When I was quite convinced, I got drunk. That was only natural. All my life I've started to face facts by getting drunk. Well—when—when I woke up again—about an hour ago, you were all in the saloon. I was frightened, terribly frightened. At last I got out of my cabin and went over the ship. I made myself. Yes, over her, all over her. Into the officers' quarters and everything. No one said a word to me for a very simple reason. There's no one on board *to* say anything. No captain, no crew, no nothing.

MRS. C-BANKS. If there's *no* crew on board this ship, Mr. Prior, may I ask who waited on *me* at dinner?

TOM. There's no one at all on board this ship, excepting we five—and those two—and the steward. *He* waited on you at dinner. He's in charge of the ship. I made myself find out. Do you know where that steward is now? He's in the rigging—sitting cross-legged—high up in the rigging. I've just seen him.

MRS. MIDGET. It's takin' 'im in a funny way, ain't it?

DUKE (*advancing on* TOM). Really, Prior, I think that—

TOM (*turning to* DUKE). I don't know what I'm talking about? Very well, then, answer me this. Who have you, any of you, seen on board this ship since she sailed? Excepting ourselves? Mrs. Midget, perhaps you can help. (*Going to* MRS. MIDGET) When I sent you to your stewardess this morning, did you see her?

MRS. MIDGET. See who? I saw no one except the fellow I went with. And first rate he looked after me. Got me a cup of tea and—

TOM. I tell you I—(*Turns to* DUKE) Padre—Padre, think carefully, who exactly have *you* spoken to?

DUKE. I—really, I—I have seen men about of course.

TOM. Have you? Have you indeed? What sort of men, sailors?

DUKE. Yes, I think so.

TOM. In the same way that you thought I was sober.

MRS. C-BANKS. You don't expect us to talk to sailors, do you, Mr. Prior, able bodied though they may be?

TOM. Have any of you met anybody else then? A purser, an officer of any sort, even a stoker?

LINGLEY. That reminds me. In your gigantic tour of this vessel did you by any chance strike the engine room?

TOM. No, I couldn't find it.

LINGLEY. A pity! I'd hoped you were going to say the ship was worked by elastic—ha, ha, ha. (MRS. CLIVEDEN-BANKS *laughs also.*)

TOM. Joke if you want to. If that *is* a joke. Well, Padre, speak up.

DUKE. Well, I—I must have met someone of course.

TOM. You *should* have met someone, you mean. But you've not. Padre, where are *you* landing?

DUKE. Landing? I'm going to—of course I'm going to—mind your own business.

TOM. Where are you landing?

DUKE. I'm taking a little holiday, that's all. I'm going first to—to—

TOM. You see you can't remember. I'm right! I knew I was. Why, look at the quiet way we sailed. Was anybody here to see any of us off? No, you know they weren't. Because you can't see people off—not right off—to where we're going.

LINGLEY. I wish you'd get out, sir; we want to play cards.

TOM. Cards—pah! Lingley, Lingley (*down to* LINGLEY), you're impossible! Why I should try to warn *you*, I don't know. Still, can you really, honestly, tell me you've seen nothing queer about this boat?

LINGLEY. Nothing whatever—excepting you. She's exactly the same as any other boat—go away.

TOM. Is she? Is she indeed? (HENRY *and* ANN *appear at the center door and cross down left. They are, as ever, close together and almost always hand in hand, and aloof from the others.*)

TOM. Well, I'll tell you one little thing I noticed about her that struck me as slightly different. This boat doesn't carry a port light—no—and she doesn't carry a starboard one either! *Now* is she the same as any other? *Now* can you settle down to your cards?

LINGLEY. You *are* mad?

TOM. Go and look then! Get on deck. You can find out if you go forward for yourself, and if you can see 'em—you're mad.

LINGLEY. I shouldn't make such a fool of myself.

TOM (*seeing* ANN *and* HENRY). Ah!—you're just in time.

HENRY. What for?

TOM. To give these people their chance—to stop them from making fools of themselves—to back me up.

HENRY. I don't quite follow.

TOM. You know—you knew this morning.

HENRY. Knew what?

TOM. You've been on deck?

HENRY. Just now.

TOM. Notice anything wrong?
(*A pause.*)

HENRY. With what?

TOM. Oh! don't pretend—don't lie to me.

HENRY. Really, I *don't* understand.

TOM. Then you don't understand how you got here, either, I suppose? How either of you got here. (*Up to them*) Gas, my dear sir, sheer gas.

ANN. Henry, don't speak to him! (*Moves down a step*) He frightens me.

TOM. Yes, I suppose I do. I know as well, you see.

MRS. C-BANKS. He's trying to frighten us, that's all.

LINGLEY. Madam, I must apologise for our fellow passenger. He—he is not—ahem—well.

TOM (*moves down a step*). Of course I'm not well. Under the circumstances I should have thought that would have been obvious.

LINGLEY (*rises*). Mr. Duke, I see an unpleasant duty will have to be performed. As a clergyman you must be more used to unpleasantness than any of us. Will you please perform it.

DUKE. What do you want me to do?

LINGLEY. Get him to the doctor—or lock him up.
(DUKE *moves slightly to centre door.*)

TOM (*up to centre door*). The doctor! I tell you there *is* no doctor. No one! and if you try any of that sort of thing on, I'll make trouble.

MRS. C-BANKS. Oh, dear, how selfish.

TOM. But I tell you what you *can* do if you like—

LINGLEY. Well?

TOM. I'll make a bargain with you.

LINGLEY. What is it?

TOM. Go out there—one of you men and convince yourselves about those lights. Then if I'm wrong—well, I'll go quietly.

MRS. MIDGET. That seems fair, poor fellow.

TOM. Well? What do you say? Mr. Lingley, will you oblige?

LINGLEY. I should never dream of interfering with the ship's discipline.

TOM (*to* HENRY). It's no good asking *you*, of course?

HENRY. No.

TOM. Padre—you're the only one left—what do you say?

DUKE. If I do it—just to satisfy you—you'll keep your word?

TOM. Yes.

DUKE. Very well then.

LINGLEY. Preposterous! (*Sits on settee.*)

TOM. Thank you. (DUKE *goes slowly to doorway*) Oh! Duke, the truth.

DUKE. Of course. (DUKE *goes quietly out on to the deck.*)

LINGLEY. Weak, weak.

MRS. C-BANKS. Ah! the Church was always like that!

TOM. Don't you run the Church down so. Take my advice, you may want her help very badly before long. Wait until I'm proved right.

MRS. C-BANKS. I simply ignore you, Mr. Prior. You won't be right. That is why I ignore you.
(DRAKE'S *drum is faintly heard, a heavily muffled and mysterious and irregular beating.*)

LINGLEY. Childish weak foolishness giving in to you. *I've* never given in to anyone. No one's ever given in to me. I should never expect them to. You're drunk, sir, and you're in the wrong, sir, and—
(*The drum stops.*)

TOM. Quiet. (*Rises*) I can hear something—out there.

HENRY. What is it?

TOM. Wait a minute—it's stopped now.

LINGLEY. I didn't hear anything.

TOM. I did. It sounded like a drum.

LINGLEY. A drum?

TOM. Yes. A muffled drum.

MRS. C-BANKS. Very possibly it *was* a muffled drum.

LINGLEY. Very possibly it was imagination.

MRS C-BANKS. What's the good of talking about things out there in the cold, anyway? Let's concentrate on making it nice and comfortable in here for our cards, (*to* TOM) which we hope to start the moment you've gone.

TOM (*moving towards her*). Mrs. Cliveden-Banks, you're an ostrich! I'm sorry, but you are. You're in danger, great danger of something out there—something, I don't know what it is—but it may affect your very soul—yet all you can think about is light and warmth and cards in here. So the only word for you *is* ostrich.

LINGLEY (*to* MRS. C-BANKS). Dear me, dear me, I can't help smiling, but he called you a—didn't he?

ANN (*looking out on to the deck*). Oh! why doesn't he come back? (*In terrified impatience.*)

HENRY. Steady, steady. (*To others*) My wife is easily upset. (*Draws her away from door.*)

MISS MIDGET. Poor dear.

LINGLEY. It's too bad of you, Prior.

TOM. Is it?

ANN. What has happened to him?

TOM. To whom?

ANN. The clergyman—of course.

TOM. Oh! Duke! Who knows? Perhaps he can't get back. He's only been a second away.

ANN. You don't think—
(*Drum starts again, beating irregularly and a trifle more loudly.*)

TOM. I don't think, because I don't know any more than you do. Hark! (*a pause*) Listen, there it is again. The drum!

LINGLEY. Um! *I* must be getting deaf!
(DUKE *appears as if breathless—a pause. He is pale and agitated, terrified—but tries to conceal it.*)

TOM (*tensely anxious*). Well—well?

LINGLEY. Well—speak, Mr. Duke. (*A pause.*)

ANN (*with a great effort at dissembling*). It's—all right, of course.

LINGLEY. Duke? (*Another pause*) It *is* all right?

DUKE. Of course.

LINGLEY. Everything?

DUKE. Everything.
(*Drum stops.*)

MRS. C-BANKS. I knew it would be all the time.

TOM (*rushing up and throwing himself on* DUKE). You liar! You liar! Come with me—I'll show you. (*Grabs him by throat.*)
(LINGLEY *rises.*)

DUKE (*struggling with him*). Prior! (MRS. MIDGET *rises.* LINGLEY *seizes* TOM'S *neck.* ANN *and* HENRY *up left huddled together in alarm*) You promised to go quietly.

TOM. You swore to tell the truth! *You clergyman*, you dirty liar!

DUKE. Got him, Lingley?

TOM (*struggling violently*). I'll show you! No more lies! Now we're dead, you bloody liar! I won't be cheated! I *will* make you understand! I'm trying to help, I tell you —I'm only trying to help—

LINGLEY. Be quiet, sir.
(*They bring* TOM *to chair left of table right. He sinks to chair and with head buried in arms on table sobs hysterically but quietly—exhausted.*)

MRS. C-BANKS. Well, if I'm wanted, I'll be in the ladies' waiting room. (*Going left*) A long letter, you know, while the details are still fresh. (*Turns*) Coming, dear? (*Sees she is speaking to* MRS. MIDGET—*turns at door*) Oh, no! (*She goes out with her nose in the air.* MRS. MIDGET *crosses and exits left following* MRS. CLIVEDEN-BANKS. *All stand quietly for a moment's pause.*)

HENRY (*to* ANN). Dear?

ANN (*as she goes*). I'll wait on deck. (*Exit centre.*)

LINGLEY (*to* HENRY). Shut those doors.
(HENRY *closes centre door.*)

LINGLEY. *And now, sir.*

DUKE (*coming down to* PRIOR). Prior, I apologise.

LINGLEY. What do you mean?

DUKE. That Mr. Prior was perfectly right.

LINGLEY. What?

DUKE. There *is* no—there's no starboard—no—

LINGLEY. There's *not!*

DUKE. No. There's no light on the boat at all. She's black as pitch.

LINGLEY. Impossible.

DUKE. Look for yourself.

LINGLEY (*alarmed now, crosses to centre door, opens it and glances out into the dark, then shuts it. Then hesitates and turns*). But—the bridge?

DUKE. As far as I could see there's nothing—nothing anywhere.

LINGLEY. Nothing—nobody?

DUKE. I'm not even certain that we're moving.

LINGLEY (*coming back*). Good heavens, man, why didn't you tell us this at once?

DUKE. I didn't want to alarm the ladies.

LINGLEY. Women drown as easily as men.

DUKE. Is this a question of drowning? Something must be done—we must all *do* something immediately.

TOM. Exactly, but what?

LINGLEY (*thoroughly rattled*). To begin with—well—somebody—somebody ought to ring a bell.

TOM. And get someone else to explain.

LINGLEY. Duke—do you—do you believe in all this?

DUKE. I don't understand it.

LINGLEY (*to* HENRY). And you, sir?

HENRY. I don't understand it either.

TOM. That's not true! And you know it's not true!

DUKE. Prior! Now look here, when did you first feel certain, in your mind, about all this?

TOM (*pointing at* HENRY—*sits at table*). After I'd heard something he said. I spoke to the steward, I asked him if—he told me the truth, I'm sure—it seems we're sailing for (*pause*)—both Hell and Heaven.

DUKE. Very interesting from a professional point of view, of course.

TOM. If there's anything else you want to know, better ask *nim, the steward.* (*Goes toward bar.*)

DUKE. Where is he now, I wonder?

LINGLEY. Still sitting high up in the rigging, I expect.

TOM. Don't be sarcastic! He was there.

LINGLEY. Was he? (*Rises, takes one step towards* TOM) Then how did you see him if it's all dark outside?

TOM (*vaguely*). That never struck me. But he was there.

(SCRUBBY *enters from left and softly strolls across towards centre.*)

DUKE (*rises*). We must hurry. Whilst we're talking like this we may be drifting on to the rocks—crashing into something or—

SCRUBBY (*always very kindly, very quiet and compassionate—like a tolerant elder to children*). No, sir, you won't do that.

LINGLEY. Now look here, my man. What is all this nonsense? I can't stand excitement. My doctor ordered rest and quiet. Where's the captain? Take me to him.

SCRUBBY. Oh, he left long ago, sir.

LINGLEY. Enough of that! Understand? By Gad, when I get back to London I'll report—

SCRUBBY. I'm afraid you won't get back to London, sir—

LINGLEY. No more of your impertinence! Take me to the captain! —do you hear? You're only a damned servant—take me to him—

DUKE. Mr. Lingley, I think we should *all* keep our tempers.

SCRUBBY. That's all right, sir, I've known a lot of them to get angry at first. (*Crossing to right.*)

LINGLEY. A lot of whom?

SCRUBBY. People like you, sir, who are just beginning.

LINGLEY. Beginning?

SCRUBBY. To be passengers.

TOM. What you told me this morning *was* true, wasn't it?

SCRUBBY. That we're dead, sir? Yes, quite dead if that's what you mean.

LINGLEY. You speak for yourself.

DUKE. It *is* queer. (*Sits right of table right.*)

SCRUBBY. Why, sir? We didn't think it was queer when we were born.

LINGLEY. Now listen. I don't want any mysteries.

SCRUBBY. There are none, sir.

LINGLEY. And I mean to get in touch with someone at once—ah! I have it, the wireless!

SCRUBBY. She doesn't carry any, sir.

LINGLEY. That's illegal anyway! Duke! (*A pause*) Duke?

DUKE. I'm afraid I can't suggest anything.

LINGLEY. But—but—! (*Suddenly overcome with fear*) I must get out of this—I must get out of it.

SCRUBBY. That, sir, is impossible until after the examination. (*Going behind bar.*)

LINGLEY. What examination?

SCRUBBY. You'll find out later, sir.

LINGLEY. The ladies ought to be warned immediately.

SCRUBBY. I should leave them to find out for themselves, sir, if I were you. I have known some of them not to like the idea to begin with and get hysterical. It is kinder to let them find out for themselves.

DUKE. They will find out?

SCRUBBY. Undoubtedly, sir.

LINGLEY (*suddenly seeing* HENRY). Damn it—don't stand there saying nothing—get upset!

HENRY. I am—of course.

LINGLEY. You're a bright lot, all of you, aren't you? So helpful—but—but—what are we to do? What are we to do? (*To* DUKE) *You're* always talking about doing things? What are we to do?

DUKE. I really—don't know. Of course, if we were all quite certain—a prayer—

LINGLEY. Is praying going to bring the captain or the crew to life?

TOM. Or *any* of us for that matter.

SCRUBBY. There's no danger, gentlemen, if *that's* what you're frightened of.

LINGLEY. Isn't there?

SCRUBBY. No, sir.

LINGLEY. *I'm* not frightened.

DUKE. I am. How many times have *you* made this passage, steward?

SCRUBBY. About five thousand times, sir.

LINGLEY. Five—

SCRUBBY. Yes. I was lost young.

DUKE. And it's always been like this?

SCRUBBY. Not always, sir. No. As I was telling this gentleman (*referring to* PRIOR), the passengers don't find out so quickly as a rule. I suppose it's because of the half-ways we've got on board this trip.

DUKE. Half-ways?

SCRUBBY. Yes, sir, it sometimes *does* work like that.

LINGLEY. There is no point in standing here talking to a lunatic. The question is, "What is—?"

SCRUBBY. —to be done? That's what they *all* ask, sir. There's *nothing* to be done. Just go on as if nothing had happened.

TOM. How simple.

SCRUBBY. Quite, sir, quite. You'll find everything simple now. Until it comes to the examination.

LINGLEY. Don't talk to me as if I were a schoolboy.

SCRUBBY. It *is* rather like going to school, sir.

LINGLEY. Stop! It's all right. Everything's all right. I've solved the whole thing suddenly.

HENRY. Have you? (*Still up left aloof.*)

LINGLEY. Of course I have. I'm asleep. I'm safe really. I'm simply asleep.

TOM. What am I?—part of the nightmare?

LINGLEY. I've had dreams like this before. Go away, go away, all you people. It's no good your waiting! I'm Lingley of Lingley, Ltd. Not one of you can touch me. I turned myself into a company years ago. Only go away now. (*A pause and then he turns to the steward*) *I am asleep,* aren't I?

SCRUBBY. Yes, sir—sound asleep—or just waking.

LINGLEY. Good, good. Now get away, get away, all you people. I shall go. (*Moves about settee*) I will go. (*Crosses to door left*) Isn't that lucky! I *can* go. You know, in *some* dreams, you can't. (LINGLEY *walks off left.*)

SCRUBBY (*following him*). Don't worry, gentlemen, I'll look after him. (SCRUBBY *follows him.*)

DUKE. A good sleep would be the very best thing for Lingley.

TOM. Would it?

DUKE. Eh?

TOM. Well, I mean—you know—would it help now?

DUKE. Oh! yes, of course—I'd forgotten—I really don't know. I—I don't understand. I'm quite a young man and there's such a lot of work to be done after my holiday.

TOM. Try some of this whiskey—it still seems to work. (*Going to bar.*)

DUKE (*rises*). No, I don't think I will if you'll excuse me, in case we —we meet anyone.

TOM (*toying idly with glass*). I'm awfully sorry. I'm afraid I'm a fearful rotter, I'm so used to it. Any crises you know— (*He sits on front of table*) I say—I say— (*Pause*) Charles Reade—or some other rotten novelist once said, "Never too late to mend," didn't he? Do you think there's any truth in novels? And then there was that other chap —the Great One, you know, in the Bible, he said—he— There you are, you see; that's the sort of fellow I am! I've forgotten what *he* said.

DUKE. Does it really much matter what either of them said? Isn't it more to the point what *you* have got to say?

TOM. No sermons! But, if you please, I would like to talk to you seriously if you'd listen to me, out there in the dark.

DUKE (*rises*). Shall we go out there —in the dark—and talk to each other, shipmate?

TOM (*humorously*). This is a great chance for *you,* isn't it?

DUKE. We must both, my dear Prior, keep our sense of humour. (*Moves up to door centre. To* HENRY *at door*) Coming out, sir? (*With* TOM *to door arm in arm.*)

HENRY. No, not yet. (*Still up left.*)

DUKE. See you later then. (*He goes out.*)

HENRY. Yes.

TOM. I say, your wife's out there, isn't she?

HENRY. Yes.

TOM. Shall I send her to you?

HENRY. Oh—thank you.

TOM (*returning a step from door*). You must have known or you wouldn't have let her be out there alone.

HENRY. I knew *nothing*. I know nothing now. Good night.

TOM. I suppose so. (*He walks out on to the deck and disappears. There is a pause and then* HENRY *calls "Ann!" Another pause. He calls again.* ANN *enters from the deck.*)

HENRY. Ann— (*a pause*) Come here. (*Crosses right to above table.*)

ANN. What is it? (*She goes to left of* HENRY.)

HENRY. Come here.

ANN. I'm with you.

HENRY. Ann—listen—they know we're dead—they're—they're finding out our secret.

ANN (*frightened*). I know! I know they are! (*They look at each other.*)

HENRY. What will they *do* to us, dear?

ANN (*getting closer to him*). They won't separate us—will they?

CURTAIN

ACT THREE

SCENE I

It is an afternoon some days later. There is a small table near the bar with a water carafe and a glass, a hand bell and papers on it. Chairs are arranged round it in a circle as if for a meeting. Otherwise the scene is unchanged.

MR. LINGLEY *is pacing up and down the room in an agitated manner, watch in hand.*

LINGLEY. Four thirty—four thirty-*one!* Tut, tut, tut! (*Goes to table*) Late, late. Now let's see— (*Counting the chairs*) Mrs. Cliveden-Banks—Mr. Duke—two—four—six— (*Touching armchair at head and fingering water bottle*) Myself here —yes, that's right. (*The siren is heard. Takes out watch again*) Four thirty-one and a half—four thirty-*two*. Oh, tut, tut, tut! (TOM *walks in from the deck.* LINGLEY *stops in his walk on seeing him*) Good gracious, fancy *you* being the first!

TOM. First for what?

LINGLEY. The meeting, sir!

TOM. Oh, I'd forgotten about your rotten old meeting.

LINGLEY. Where are the others?

TOM. On deck. It may interest you to know we've just sighted land. (*Sits at table.*)

LINGLEY. Land, Mr. Prior? Land! (*Delighted.*)

TOM. Yes. We've just sighted *hell.*

LINGLEY. Oh.

TOM. It looks quite a jolly little spot from here. The padre's arranging a sweepstake on the exact time it will take us to get in. He's suddenly developed a sense of humour.

LINGLEY. Sense of humour and sweepstakes when we're all—all—! What's the use of a sense of humour to a dead man? (*Pacing to and fro, up and down.*)

TOM. I dunno! I've never asked one.

LINGLEY. Oh, why don't they *come?*

TOM. You're getting the wind up a bit, aren't you? Oh, I don't blame you, Lingley of Lingley Limited, for I shouldn't be surprised if over there a nice private little gridiron isn't being warmed up for your personal reception.

LINGLEY. Will you be quiet, you foolish boy!
(SCRUBBY *enters left.*)

SCRUBBY (*indicating the table*). Everything correct, sir?

LINGLEY. Eh?

SCRUBBY. Enough chairs, sir?

LINGLEY. Oh! yes, very nice indeed, very nice, Mr. Scrubby. Er—here is half-a-crown for your trouble. Thank you.

SCRUBBY. Thank *you*, sir.

LINGLEY. What for? Half-a-crown is no use to me now. Wait! Please tell the others—the others—my shipmates—that they're late for the meeting.

SCRUBBY (*as he goes out centre*). Certainly, sir.

LINGLEY. Thank you, Mr. Scrubby, thank you.

TOM. What's the object of this meeting, anyway?

LINGLEY. Can't you see?

TOM. Yes. That's why I asked. (*To bar.*)

LINGLEY. We're approaching our destination, and I want to make this one last effort. I feel we should talk the matter over in a rational spirit—and as a business man I've called this meeting.

TOM. You *would.* And, as has probably been your custom, you think that a committee report and minutes, and balance sheets and all that bunkum may impress the examiner as they do shareholders and *other* examiners. Of course you'll be chairman?

LINGLEY. Naturally. I seem to be the only one qualified.

TOM. You admit it.

LINGLEY. By right of experience and proved ability—Prior, when I was a boy—

TOM. Were you ever a boy? Poor parents!

LINGLEY. When I was seventeen I could only manage one egg for breakfast.

TOM. I can never manage *any* breakfast myself.

LINGLEY. *Afford* one egg, I mean. At six thirty A.M. I used to walk to my work.

TOM. On the egg? (*Sits right.*)

LINGLEY. And after business I'd walk home again. That was the beginning of Lingley, Limited. When I was seventeen I made my motto "Try to rely on yourself." At thirty-seven I made it "Rely on yourself."

TOM. So you fired *me.*

LINGLEY. At forty-seven I made it "Rely on yourself *absolutely*"; because if you fail all your friends will only say, "It serves you right."

TOM. *Had* you any friends at forty-seven?

LINGLEY. You're incorrigible! And I thought *you* were concerned in this—this dilemma.

TOM. I *am.*
(MRS. CLIVEDEN-BANKS *enters through the centre door. She is in the very deepest mourning.*)

MRS. C-BANKS. I must apologise for being late! I've been playing sweepstake.

LINGLEY. Mrs. Cliveden-Banks! Why this dress?

MRS. C-BANKS. Our present circumstances!
(TOM *sits left. His attitude toward the subsequent proceedings is one of contempt.*)

LINGLEY. Will you sit here?

MRS. C-BANKS. It's nice to be able to, isn't it? (*Sits in the first chair left of table*) And the object of this meeting, Mr. Lingley, is—er—?

LINGLEY. Well—er—is this company alive or dead?

TOM. And the next question on the agenda?

LINGLEY (*a pause; sits*). What is going to happen to us? Mr. Prior—as a prospective shareholder—I ask you what you think?

TOM. Lingley—do you know anything about Elizabethan furniture?

LINGLEY. Nothing whatever.

TOM. Neither do I. That's why I never talk about it.

LINGLEY. But it is the right thing to do, isn't it?

TOM. To solemnly sit down and discuss if we've immortal souls or if we haven't? And if we have, to pool 'em. (*Sarcastically*) Undoubtedly. (*Rises*) "We must combine" —the most hopeful refuge for an embarrassed business man like you.

LINGLEY. Exactly. We must all face this examiner together.
(REV. W. DUKE *enters. He is quite different and most cheerful.*)

DUKE. Hello, Tom! Hello, Lingley! (*To* MRS. CLIVEDEN-BANKS) Hello, Banky!

MRS. C-BANKS. Banky!

DUKE. Yes. (*He shakes her shoulders*) Banky, Banky! We're dead now, so my job's over and I can be quite natural; do what I like and say what I like, Banky. (*Over* LINGLEY'S *right shoulder*) Prior, have you heard this one—I've been dying to spring it for ages—"There was a young girl of Hong-Kong."

MRS. C-BANKS (*convulsed with laughter*). Oh, *I* know that one.

LINGLEY. Sir! You ought to be ashamed of yourself. We are about to hold a Board Meeting.

DUKE. Sorry. I overheard one of my ex-choir boys reciting that in the Vestry. I remember his voice was breaking at the time. Damn badly. (*Sits below* TOM.)

LINGLEY. Supposing your Bishop heard you say "damn."

DUKE. Impossible, unless he's listening in.

LINGLEY. You've evidently become unbalanced.

MRS. MIDGET (*entering centre*). Is this the meeting 'ouse?

LINGLEY. Yes, Mrs. Midget. Sit here, will you? Very good of you to come. I hope you—your family are well and—

MRS. MIDGET (*sits at left of table below* MRS. CLIVEDEN-BANKS). What the 'ell are you talking about?

MRS. C-BANKS. Please do not mention hell, Mrs. Midget; it's rather a ticklish subject at the moment.

LINGLEY. Now, are we all here?

TOM. We're all here.

MRS. MIDGET. The young couple aren't 'ere.

LINGLEY. *They* never say anything, anyway. Shall we begin?

MRS. C-BANKS. Begin.

LINGLEY. Very well, then. (*Rises*) Ahem! (*Rings bell on table.*)

TOM. They're off!

LINGLEY. Ladies and gentlemen—

MRS. MIDGET. 'Ear, 'ear!

MRS. C-BANKS. Be quiet!

MRS. MIDGET. I was only thanking 'im for the compliment.

LINGLEY. Ladies *and* gentlemen—"de mortuis nil nisi bonum."

TOM. Oh, get on with it!

LINGLEY. I intend to. *Ladies* and gentlemen—I am a business man.

DUKE. Quite.

LINGLEY. I have never done anything in my life without a reason.

DUKE. Quite.

LINGLEY. I would like firstly, therefore, to explain that my reason for calling this meeting is, if I may put it in this manner, to draw up a clean balance sheet.

DUKE. Quite.

LINGLEY. Now, secondly—if I may say so—

TOM. You may say anything you like, old boy, only for goodness' sake say it.

LINGLEY. Sir! I—

MRS. C-BANKS. Order, please. Order.

TOM. I'll have the same, with a splash.

LINGLEY. Oh, please don't all keep interrupting.

MRS. C-BANKS. Well, they always say "order" at meetings—

DUKE. Quite!

LINGLEY. Where was I?

DUKE. Drawing up a balance sheet.

TOM. "Laughter."

LINGLEY. And trying to explain my reason for doing so.

DUKE. Quite.

TOM. Quite *what?*

LINGLEY. My reasons—

TOM. *Have* you any?

LINGLEY (*sits down in disgust*). I shall say no more.

TOM. *Good.*

MRS. MIDGET. Oh, sir, don't rob the gentleman of his amusement! 'E may not 'ave much more opportunity.

LINGLEY. I only thought, in view of the shortness of time at our command, *and* the nature of the harbour we are rapidly approaching,—I shall therefore call on Mr. Duke for a few words. He should, professionally, know more of the matter than we do. Ahem! The Rev. W. Duke, M. C.

DUKE (*without rising*). All I can say is—if we *are* all dead then let us hope we have done our jobs to the best of our ability.

LINGLEY. I've never been late for an appointment in my life.

DUKE. And now that we're nearing this—this dread examiner, we think something should be done. And we've put off really thinking what to do till the last moment. Naturally we *would,* we're all English.

MRS. C-BANKS. Rule Britannia!

DUKE. You ask for my professional advice! I have none to give. The steward himself has none to give.

MRS. MIDGET. You might pray for us, sir.

DUKE. I would if I thought my prayer would be worth anything. But now I don't understand. To pray for something one doesn't understand is to be an idolater.

MRS. MIDGET. Oh, we mustn't be one of those.

DUKE. It's the first time in my—it's the first *time* I've never known what to do. It's a strange business, this being dead. (*The drum is heard again.* ANN *and* HENRY *appear in the centre. A pause and then the* REV. MR. DUKE *notices the couple*) Oh, come in. (ANN *and* HENRY *come in and stand away from the others*) By the way. I suppose we're all agreed on that point?

LINGLEY. What point?

TOM. Ask these two.

LIGLEY. What point?

DUKE. *Are we all dead or are we not?*

LINGLEY. That's what I called this meeting to decide. (*To* ANN *and* HENRY) You two, won't you sit down? (*No reply, they simply huddle closer together, and stand aloof left*) No? No. Very well, then. The motion in front of us is, I think, perfectly plain to all. "Are we—" Who will speak first?

MRS. C-BANKS. I will. For I think it's a most impertinent question to be asked. If I am dead, why can't I be dead in private? Personally, I believe I *am* dead. My corsets have never fitted so comfortably anyway.

LINGLEY. Mr. Prior?

TOM. I *know*. And I don't care a damn one way or the other.

MRS. C-BANKS. The man's a plebiscite.

LINGLEY. Mr. Duke?

DUKE. Agreed. Mr. Lingley?

LINGLEY (*pause*). I agree. Mrs. Midget?

MRS. MIDGET. Ladies and gents, all I want to know is this, and I really don't know what's goin' on. But if it *'as* 'appened—it would greatly please me to know that I've been *done proper*.

LINGLEY. I beg your pardon.

MRS. MIDGET. You know, the street, the neighbours, the sherry wine and cake—and flowers.

LINGLEY. This is beside the point—do you think you're dead or do you not?

MRS. MIDGET. Oh, I leave it entirely to you, sir.

LINGLEY. I take it in favour of the motion. And now you two young people?

TOM. They know. They've always known.

LINGLEY. Please, please, let them answer for themselves. Well? Well, what do you say?

HENRY. We have nothing to say.

LINGLEY. I suppose we must disregard your evidence. As far as the rest of us are concerned, I think there is nothing more to be done than to enter the verdict that this board (*commences to write*) "certifies itself to be dead." And the next thing for me to decide—is the most effective way—in all our interests—to meet and talk with this examiner.

TOM. Do you mean we want to get out of it if we can?

LINGLEY. If we can. And—if we can't—we want to get out of it as lightly as we can.

MRS. C-BANKS. Go on.

LINGLEY. And we're under a great disadvantage. You see we do not know what sort of a person this examiner is, who is suddenly to pounce upon us. He is bound to be a hard, stern business man. In which case, I suggest I am the one best fitted to deal with him.

TOM. Hear, hear!

DUKE. Supposing he isn't anything like that? Supposing he is something even *you* can't understand? Supposing he is really *the* examiner? Don't you think we all ought to speak for ourselves?—if we can.

LINGLEY. It's if we *can't* I'm thinking of.

DUKE. I wish we knew. I certainly wish we knew.
(SCRUBBY *enters from behind bar.*)

MRS. C-BANKS. Why not ask that steward person about him? They must have met before.

TOM. Not a bad idea at all, Mrs. Cliveden-Banks.

LINGLEY. The steward! Exactly, will someone go and fetch him?

SCRUBBY. You want *me*, sir?

LINGLEY. What the—!

SCRUBBY. I have been here all the time.

LINGLEY. But, we—

SCRUBBY. You wanted to ask me about the examiner, sir?

LINGLEY. Yes, if you would be so good.

SCRUBBY. What did you want to know exactly, sir?

LINGLEY. Well, he can't be tipped, that of course is obvious—but between ourselves—what sort of a person is he?

SCRUBBY. I can't say. I don't know. It all depends.

LINGLEY. Depends on what?

SCRUBBY. Yourselves, sir. I have seen some men and women before him cry for—but no, I can't say. (*He crosses right towards door centre.*)

LINGLEY. Tell us just this, Mr. Scrubby, what do you think we really ought to do—how exactly should we approach him?

SCRUBBY. I have been asked that question nearly five thousand times, sir; I have always answered that it is better to leave the approaching to him. (*Starts to go out centre.*)

DUKE. Scrubby, have I any chance?

SCRUBBY (*standing in door silhouetted against the golden light outside*). You *all* have chances, sir.

DUKE. What's he like?

SCRUBBY. He's the wind and the skies and the earth, sir. He knows the furthest eddy of the high tide up the remotest cove. He knows the simpleness of beauty and the evilest thoughts of the human mind. He'll know all your evil thoughts.

DUKE (*quickly*). God!

SCRUBBY. Yes, sir, he will. (*Looks out on to the deck*) Would you excuse me now, please? I can tell no more; and a seagull has just fallen on to the deck. I'm afraid it may have broken its wing. If so, I must try and mend it.

ANN. Poor thing!

SCRUBBY. Yes, madam, it's very sad the way the birds die in these strange waters. (*He walks off along the deck.*)

DUKE. Just like the first day at school again.

TOM. *Now* do you want to deal with him—collectively? Or will you just make yourself responsible for your own sins?

LINGLEY. Oh, come, come, come! We mustn't all get jumpy. I still think we ought to be prepared though my own conscience is perfectly clear.

MRS. C-BANKS. Then you'd better worry about *ours*, dear Mr. Lingley. Come, tabulate us, as it were.

LINGLEY. Excellent. Then I can put all the cases before this—this examiner briefly and to the point.

MRS. C-BANKS. It should save us a great amount of trouble.

LINGLEY. So, if you will all just give me a few details about yourselves—and any special little reference you might like me to bring forward. Mrs. Cliveden-Banks, let me start with you. What shall I say about *you* to this—er—examiner?

MRS. C-BANKS. I should just say I am—or *was*—Mrs. Cliveden-Banks—and leave it at that.

LINGLEY. Um! Oh, very well; you, Mrs. Midget?

MRS. MIDGET. Oh, I dunno.

LINGLEY. Oh, dear, dear, dear! Is that really all?

MRS. MIDGET. Yes, please, sir.

LINGLEY. All right—not at all satisfactory, but I suppose all right—in my hands. I can answer for myself of course. You, Mr. Prior?

TOM. Oh, say, I'm an old drunk. Or rather a young one.

LINGLEY. That won't help you very much.

TOM. How do *you* know?

LINGLEY. But you must have had some redeeming qualities that will help you? For instance, were you good to your mother or—did you go to Oxford?

TOM. Put down the truth—he will know it anyway.

LINGLEY. Really, you're none of you being very helpful. (*Writes*) A drunk—er—a Mrs. Cliveden-Banks—er—and an I dunno.

MRS. C-BANKS. I should prefer to precede the drunk.

LINGLEY. Very well. (*To* HENRY) Now, sir, how *can* you assist me?

HENRY. I can't.

LINGLEY. But—you then, madam?

ANN. He speaks for both of us.

HENRY. We have nothing to say.

LINGLEY. It is really most discourteous of you! Mr. Duke, I can rely on *you* at any rate.

DUKE. You can rely on me for *one* piece of information.

LINGLEY. Thank you very much.

DUKE. I now entirely agree with Mr. Prior for calling you a pompous old idiot!

TOM. Cheers.

LINGLEY. What?—just because I'm trying to do my duty!

DUKE. Your duty! Your rubbish! You're doing what you are because you're in a blue funk! And I don't blame you. I'm in a blue funk, too! But not so much as to make an utter ass of myself by trying to get out of this with balance sheets and board meetings! You want to try and impress this examiner with your cleverness, your business importance, your supposed interest in your fellow creatures. You're hoping to save your own skin that way. And I think it's pretty rotten!

LINGLEY. Indeed. Destructive criticism is very simple. Then perhaps *you* can advise me.

DUKE. I can advise nothing.

LINGLEY. Um! That's *very* useful.

MRS. MIDGET. Oh, sir, not just *one* word of 'elp?

DUKE. That is different. If I can *help* I will. But you mustn't take anything I say in the nature of advice. The blind leading the blind, you know. I can only tell you what I am going to do myself, and I may be wrong.

TOM. *What* are you going to do, Duke? (*Staccato.*)

DUKE. I have been trying to look into myself silently, trying to examine my past thoughtfully and humbly—to seek out all the faults and not try to excuse them. But to know all that I am responsible for; and when I see my life, lying before me like a blurred map, I am going to pray to be able to make one more prayer. But for myself; I am not fit to pray for others. If any of you care to do likewise please do so if it will comfort you. Look back.

MRS. C-BANKS. I *could* look back, of course, but I don't intend to. Remember Mrs. Lot.

MRS. MIDGET. Thank you, sir.

DUKE. No, no, now that's just what I didn't *want* you to do. You see, Mrs. Midget—try to understand—we're just shipmates, you and I—trying to help one another. I'm not a captain any longer. I cannot pray for others. Perhaps the realisation of that is the beginning of my punishment. I've *lost* my job.

LINGLEY. I don't suppose it was worth much anyway.

DUKE. It was the most glorious job in the world. I suppose a man never really knows he's incompetent until he's sacked, and I can't, I can't understand and I *ought* to. It's my *job* to; and it's beastly hard

not to be able to. It's heartbreaking—it's— (*To* PRIOR) Give me a cigarette.
(*The siren is heard again.* HENRY *moves away from* ANN.)

LINGLEY. Well, let's get down to hard facts—I suggest.

DUKE. Too late. Didn't you hear?

LINGLEY. What?

ANN. *I* heard.

TOM. What?

DUKE. The siren.

TOM (*after a pause suddenly hysterical*). I didn't hear anything—I didn't hear anything.
(DUKE *and* TOM *rise.* TOM *in sudden panic.*)

DUKE. Now, now, Prior.

TOM. I didn't, I didn't! (*Another pause*) But I can feel something though, can't you?

DUKE. No.

TOM. The boat's stopped.

DUKE. Exactly. We're in.
(*Another pause. The siren is repeated.*)

TOM. No, no! I won't face it! I daren't! It's all been bluff on my part! Let me get away! Let me get—!

DUKE (*rising with hand on* PRIOR). Prior, my boy!

TOM. I can't face it. I want to get away! Make the boat go on!

ANN. Henry! (*She gets closer to him.*)

TOM. Let me get away. (*Struggling to get away.*)

DUKE. We can none of us get away. We've stopped for good now. This is the judgment.

TOM (*pulling himself together*). No, it can't be. Here in the smoke-room of a liner?

DUKE. Why *shouldn't* it be here in the smoke-room of a liner? Have any of us really ever troubled very much to think where-and-how-and-when it might be?

ANN (*quietly*). Henry. They won't *separate* us—they *can't.*
(HENRY *merely holds her closer—as if in defiance.*)

DUKE. We're for it now all right.
(DUKE *sits right of table with his face buried in his hands.*)

TOM. We must stick together. Duke, man, you *must* pray even if the words are meaningless. Don't desert duty at the last moment. We're in the night and I want a prayer. I want a prayer from a man, I don't care if he's a clergyman or not.

MRS. MIDGET (*going to* DUKE). You *ought* to pray, your Reverence.

TOM. Even if you can't understand what for—you understand *us.*

DUKE. You really think I ought to, Mrs. Midget?

MRS. MIDGET (*bending over him*). Yes, sir, pardon the liberty.

There's no 'arm in 'abits—if they're *good* 'abits; and prayer *is* a good 'abit.

DUKE (*without rising—but slowly facing front and with utter simplicity and sincerity*). Forgive me then, for I don't know—"Gentle Jesus, meek and mild, look upon a little child—children—pardon our simplicity, suffer us to come to Thee. God bless father and mother, Harriet (she was my nurse), all kind friends, make me a good boy. Amen." That was the first prayer I ever learnt, so it's probably the finest. Say it to yourselves if you want to; and remember—Harriet—she was a worthy soul.

ANN (*after a long pause*). Henry, let's hide. (*She takes his hand and they drift off together, left.*)

MRS. MIDGET. I feel better.
(SCRUBBY *enters from the left, giving a glance back as he does so.*)

SCRUBBY (*brightly—and businesslike*). We're in, ladies and gentlemen, we're in.

DUKE. Yes, yes, we know.

SCRUBBY. The examiner is just coming on board. His cutter's alongside. He'll *be* with you in a second. (*He goes out on to the deck.*)

DUKE. We can do nothing now.

MRS. C-BANKS (*in a whisper*). Mr. Lingley—Mr. Lingley !

LINGLEY. Well?

MRS. C-BANKS. Well—hadn't we better all stand up? (*All rise.*)

LINGLEY. Eh? Oh, yes, of course, it would be more polite.

DUKE. Politeness!

SCRUBBY (*appearing and announcing*). The Examiner.

TOM (*quickly and quietly appealingly*). Duke!

DUKE. Quiet.
(THE REV. FRANK THOMSON *is heard shouting off, right.*)

THOMSON. Hello, hello, hello there, I say! Where is everyone? Where are you, Duke? (*He appears in the centre. An elderly and massive clergyman, rotund, rubicund and jovial. He is dressed in white drill and a topee. But he wears a clergyman's collar and black bib*) Ah, there you are! Duke, my old boy, how are you?

DUKE. Good—! My—! Well—! Well, I'm dashed if it isn't old "grease spot." (*Crossing and shaking hands.*)

THOMSON. It is, sir, and greasier than ever. Phew! This climate! Well, I am glad to see you after all this time. How are you, Duke? Have a good passage? You're looking fit. (*Taking off topee and wiping forehead.*)

DUKE. I'm not *feeling* it.

THOMSON. I only heard this morning your boat was due in this afternoon. I'd seen your name on the passenger list of course—so I hurried down especially to meet you, I'd been up country. (*Sits at table left.*)

DUKE. Thank you.

THOMSON. Well, how goes everything? I'm bursting for news! How's Fergusson—still in the same old place?

DUKE. No, they've made him a bishop now.

THOMSON. Good Lor', they *would*. Well, I hope he likes it. And what's become of Maltby; and that little fellow with the red hair and spectacles? I never could remember his name. (*Lights a cigarette*) And do you still go for your blow-out at Simpson's every pay day, you young rascal? Tell me, what's the meat like there now?

DUKE (*greatly agitated and in no mood for* THOMSON'S *frivolity*). Thomson, I'm delighted to see you again, of course, and I'm dying to tell you everything afterwards—*if I can*—but can't you realise—at this moment—how terribly worried I am?

THOMSON. Worried—worried about what?

DUKE. This—this person.

THOMSON. What person?

DUKE. This person—or whoever it is—who's just coming to examine us.

THOMSON. The examiner! Oh, I shouldn't worry about him!

DUKE. What—do—you—mean?

THOMSON. *I'm* the examiner! (*General movement.*)

DUKE. You—you are!

THOMSON. Well, I'm one of 'em anyway. We've got dozens on the job. And they *will* shove all the duds on to it. My dear boy, our profession is not what it used to be. Terribly overcrowded, too, believe me.

DUKE. You're—my—examiner?

THOMSON. Yes—you're under *my* orders now. And I tell you, my boy, you'll have to mind your p's and q's; and *how* you'll have to slog at it! But I've fixed your "digs" up for you all right; they're not up to much, but clean, in the same house as myself; the old woman's quite a decent sort. And it's near your work, right in the centre of the parish, so you couldn't do better, really.

DUKE. *Work?*

THOMSON. I find it quite handy myself.

DUKE. "Parish—slog at it." Thomson, Thomson, you don't mean I haven't lost my job after all? Don't torture me, tell me quickly.

THOMSON. Of course you haven't lost it. You haven't started it yet. You're just beginning it.

DUKE. Not lost my job? Still got my job. Oh, thank you! Oh, thank God! I will work harder now every moment, I swear I will, Mr. Thomson. Harder than ever! Oh, do you all hear? My job I was so keen on —it's not been taken from me after all. My—oh! (*sits at table, left, and quietly cries*)—job.

THOMSON (*patting him on shoulder*). There, there, boy, there, there! Whatever made you think it would be taken from you? (DUKE *sobs*) There, there, it's quite all right.

MRS. C-BANKS (*at back on the seat with* LINGLEY). I'm very glad to see they know each other so well—but what about us?

LINGLEY. This might be a suitable moment to approach him.

MRS. C-BANKS. Try.

LINGLEY. I will. (*Importantly crossing to examiner who takes no notice*) Sir—ahem—my name is Lingley—of Ling—

THOMSON. Go away.

LINGLEY. I have advocated myself —or rather my fellow passengers have advocated me—their spokesman as it were—

THOMSON (*still attending to* DUKE). Go away.

LINGLEY. And I thought this might be a good moment to approach a somewhat—

THOMSON (*turning on him positively*). Will you go away, sir?

LINGLEY. Certainly. (*Retires*) I've no wish to stay where I'm not wanted. (*Goes back to his seat.*)

MRS. C-BANKS. How very rude!

LINGLEY. I don't believe he's the examiner at all.

MRS. C-BANKS. Of course, Mr. Duke will get off lightly. (*Rises*) A friend at court, you see. Influence! Ah! It's always the same. Shall *I* say something to him?

LINGLEY. Good Lor', madam, *no.*

THOMSON (*to* DUKE). Feeling better now?

DUKE. I'm very sorry, sir. But it means such a lot to me. You understand.

THOMSON. Perfectly. I had exactly the same feeling when it happened to *me.* But you've nothing to worry about except your work.

DUKE. I'm full of energy.

THOMSON. Then you can start your apprenticeship now and help me with this bunch. By the way, there aren't many of you.

DUKE. No, sir.

THOMSON. Then it won't take long and we can get on shore for dinner.

LINGLEY. Sir, if I find my trial's being "scamped" I shall appeal.

THOMSON (*to* SCRUBBY). Take that man away, will you?

SCRUBBY. Certainly, sir. This way, Mr. Lingley.

LINGLEY (*as he goes out centre*). It's disgraceful.

THOMSON. And the rest had better wait *with* him—outside.

SCRUBBY. Very good, sir. Will you all come this way, please?

MRS. C-BANKS (*making a large sweep towards* THOMSON). How do you do? (*Seeing she is ignored she follows the others out*) Oh!
(TOM *goes out, centre, followed by* MRS. MIDGET.)

THOMSON. That's all. (SCRUBBY *follows them off*) Now, we'll get to work.

DUKE. Yes, sir.

THOMSON. Let's see; who have we got on board? (*Reads from his note-book*) Cliveden-Banks, Midget, Prior and the officious gent who spoke to me—yourself.

DUKE. There's an awfully nice quiet young couple.

THOMSON. Oh? I don't remember them. They're not on the passenger list, We'll begin with the officious one. (*Calls*) Scrubby! Where's that fellow got to?

SCRUBBY (*appearing*). Here, sir.

THOMSON. Oh. (*Reading*) Show in Mr. Lingley.

SCRUBBY (*calling off centre*). Mr. Lingley!
(LINGLEY *appears at door centre.*)

THOMSON. Come in. Sit down. There.
(LINGLEY *sits in chair at table right.*)

LINGLEY (*rather truculently*). Well?

THOMSON. Well, sir?

LINGLEY. I am Lingley, of Lingley, Limited.

THOMSON. Never mind the "Limited." You are just Lingley now.

LINGLEY. What am I charged with, anyway?

THOMSON. With just being yourself.

LINGLEY. I am very proud of being myself. From small beginnings I have worked up to great things. I have never hesitated but have always kept to the straight path.

THOMSON. I know. But *how?*

LINGLEY. By hard work—enterprise!

THOMSON. Enterprise! Dishonesty.

LINGLEY (*hotly*). That's a lie!

THOMSON. Very well. Your case is over. Get out.

LINGLEY (*rises, hesitates*). Just a minute. Let's talk this over.

THOMSON. Well? Is it a lie—or is it the truth?

LINGLEY. I—I'm afraid you don't understand *business.*

THOMSON. Not the way *you* conduct it. Why, you've been a rascal from the very start. You commenced your career by breaking a playmate's head against a granite curb because he had a painted tin horse. You wanted to get it.

LINGLEY. Well, I got it.

THOMSON. Oh, I grant you that! That's how you've made that glorious straight path you boast about. By knocking down anyone who came across it or tried to turn you off it. The foundation of Lingley, Limited, was laid when you stole the plans of a turbine engine—and let the inventor die in poverty.

LINGLEY. I've not been wicked. People respect me.

THOMSON. Do they? To your face, perhaps. Some men get found out during their lives, Lingley. You are only found out now. Come; off you get.
(HENRY *and* ANN *appear at the centre door coming from left. They hesitate, looking in for a second, as if awaiting their turn, then pass on right.* DUKE *sees them.*)

LINGLEY. I–I–

THOMSON. There is no appeal. You will suffer as you made others suffer. (*Pause.*)
(THOMSON'S *manner is not hard and vindictive. He is kindly, tolerant and possibly even reluctant to dole out justice. But he is firm and just.*)

LINGLEY (*after a pause*). Give me a second chance.

THOMSON. Did *you* give anybody a second chance? No, you must learn, my son. (*He turns and makes a note in his book.*)
(LINGLEY *looks defiantly for a moment at* THOMSON, *whose back is turned, as if he'd like to strike him.*)

THOMSON (*turning. Quietly*). That's all.
(LINGLEY *slowly turns and goes out centre to left, utterly broken and dejected.*)

DUKE. Thomson!

THOMSON. Don't look so shocked. It must be done. Suffering sometimes works wonderful transformations. Let's hope, boy, let's hope. Scrubby!

SCRUBBY. Sir.

THOMSON (*to* SCRUBBY). Just see he goes the right way.

SCRUBBY. Very good, sir.
(*He follows* LINGLEY.)

DUKE (*rises*). I wish you'd see the young couple next. I know *they* must be suffering.

THOMSON. What young couple is this?

DUKE. I told you about them.

THOMSON. Yes, but I've had no information from any other quarter. It's funny.

DUKE. They seem so devoted. You'll have a pleasant job with them, I know.

THOMSON. But who exactly are they?

DUKE. Well, I used to call them, to myself, "the lovers."
(SCRUBBY *has appeared again in the centre.*)

THOMSON. Steward, do you know anything about a young couple on this boat?

SCRUBBY. Oh, those two, sir! You wouldn't want to see them.

DUKE. Not see them?

THOMSON. Why *shouldn't* I want to see them?

SCRUBBY. They're "half-ways," sir.

THOMSON. Half-ways. Oh, that explains it. No, it wouldn't be much use my seeing them. Show in–Mrs. Cliveden-Banks.

SCRUBBY. Yes, sir. (*He goes out left.*)

DUKE. You're not even going to see them?

THOMSON. I *can't,* old boy.

DUKE (*curiously*). What is a "half-way," Thomson?

THOMSON. You'll learn, Duke, you'll learn in good time.

DUKE. But I wish you would— (SCRUBBY *appears again announcing.*)

SCRUBBY. Mrs. Cliveden-Banks! (*She enters left and gushingly crosses to* THOMSON. SCRUBBY *goes.*)

MRS. C-BANKS. How do you do? How *do* you do? *Very* pleased to meet you.

THOMSON. Delighted to meet you, Mrs. Cliveden-Banks. Come and sit down.

MRS. C-BANKS. Thank you. Very sultry weather for the time of the year, isn't it? Still, we've had a lovely passage, haven't we, *dear* Mr. Duke?

DUKE. Oh, yes, delightful, *dear* Mrs. Cliveden-Banks.
(MRS. CLIVEDEN-BANKS *sits where Lingley sat.*)

THOMSON. I'm glad you enjoyed yourself.

MRS. C-BANKS. Oh, I did, I did. Thanks to your kind friend, Mr. Duke. We clung together like limpets. I really don't know *what* I should have done without him. What wonderful men our church turns out, Mr.—er

THOMSON. Thomson, madam.

MRS. C-BANKS. No; surely not one of the *Berkshire* Thomsons?

THOMSON. Not that I am aware of.

MRS. C-BANKS. Ah! a pity. My great-great-grandfather was a Berkshire Thomson.

THOMSON. Really? My great-great-grandfather was hanged for horse-thieving.

MRS. C-BANKS. How quaint.

THOMSON. Mrs. Cliveden-Banks—

MRS. C-BANKS. Do you play golf?

THOMSON. I play indifferently.

MRS. C-BANKS. I think all men ought to play golf. It keeps them away from home such a lot. My husband, Colonel Cliveden-Banks, is quite an expert, I believe.

THOMSON. Oh, yes, Bunny's hot stuff. I was having a round with him not long ago.

MRS. C-BANKS. I'm so glad to hear it. (*A pause, then suddenly*) *What* did you say? You had a round with my husband not long ago?

THOMSON. He was in terrific form.

MRS. C-BANKS (*alarmed*). When was this?

THOMSON. Oh, about a week ago, I think.

MRS. C-BANKS. But I don't understand. Is he *here?*

THOMSON. He's waiting for you. (*Rises*) Yes, we had a great game. He'll tell you all about it when you land.

MRS. C-BANKS. I *don't land!*—How did *he* get here?

THOMSON. Poor old Bunny died a couple of months ago.

MRS. C-BANKS. How wicked of him. He might have let me know.

THOMSON. Perhaps he didn't think you'd care very much one way or the other.

MRS. C-BANKS. Why not? There was life insurance—how like him, how very like him. Always self-centred. Look at the passage money I've wasted. (*Suddenly*) Benjamin and I are *both* dead then?

THOMSON. Quite dead.

MRS. C-BANKS (*hopefully*). That makes the marriage null and void.

THOMSON. Your marriage is only just beginning.

MRS. C-BANKS. How droll you are. But how nice of you to put it that way.

THOMSON. Now will you go ashore? You'll find everything most comfortable. A villa, servants, all you want—and your husband waiting—with outstretched arms.

MRS. C-BANKS. Yes, I can see him; exactly like a monkey.

THOMSON. I hope you will be able to see his *heart*. I know it's aching for you very badly.

MRS. C-BANKS. How ghastly.

THOMSON. What's the matter?

MRS. C-BANKS. What *right's* he got to bob up again like this?

THOMSON. Every right, and we're very glad to have him here. Your husband is a very useful man.

MRS. C-BANKS. How well I know that phrase! It has always been used of Benjamin in every new office he's undertaken, at the start. Later he invariably got the push. (HENRY *and* ANN *pass the centre door again during this speech, look anxiously in and then pass on left.*)

THOMSON. And do you know why? Because of his wife's malicious tongue.

MRS. C-BANKS (*rises, crosses left*). How dare you? I'm sure I've never said anything bad about Benjamin. I don't know that I've said anything good about him, because there's nothing good *to* say about him. (*Sits.*)

THOMSON. There is a very great deal of good in Bunny. But it was always stifled back by you. He was a staunch, a devoted husband—look what he gave *you*—and what did you give in return? Nothing!

MRS. C-BANKS. But I haven't seen him for years.

THOMSON. It was *your* neglect—not his.

MRS. C-BANKS. Oh, but he looks so funny.

THOMSON. The only funny thing about him is that he wants to see you. Why he should *want* to see you is beyond me. But he does, and he's going to.

MRS. C-BANKS. And what shall I be exactly?

THOMSON. You'll be his wife; and in time you will learn to be a *good* wife.

MRS. C-BANKS. I refuse absolutely.

THOMSON. You *can't* refuse. (*With finality.*)
(*A long pause.*)

MRS. C-BANKS. I won't do it! I won't, I won't.

DUKE. Why won't you, Mrs. Cliveden-Banks?

MRS. C-BANKS. *He* knows—ask him. (*Indicating* THOMSON.)

DUKE. Mr. Thomson—?
(THOMSON *is silent, waiting.*)

MRS. C-BANKS (*to* THOMSON). You know as well as I do, it's his eyes. The look in his eyes. You know I couldn't face them any more—

THOMSON. Yes;—you never could look him in the eyes. You're a thoroughly bad lot. You trapped him; you were grasping, you made him marry you. You—you—you—

MRS C-BANKS. Don't let me down before *him.* (*Indicating* DUKE.)

THOMSON. I wouldn't if you'd been a *good* harlot; but you weren't, you were a bad one.

MRS. C-BANKS (*pause*). Rather a vulgar way of putting it!

DUKE. Dear, dear, only a poor unfortunate after all.

THOMSON. No, Duke, *not* a poor unfortunate. This old woman was once a beautiful young girl, outwardly, but she was never an unfortunate, never. She's been just a schemer. And somehow she's always managed to fall on her feet. There were two other men before she met Cliveden-Banks, richer men too than he was then. But she saw something *steady* in Bunny, so she made him marry her. He found out all about it later—and he's never told her. Too unselfish—too "big"—too loyal.—So she goes back to him. I hope he *beats* her—but I know he won't. Anyway, she'll get her punishment. The eyes that made her run away.—Only remember, Mrs. Cliveden-Banks, it won't be Bunny who'll know now, it will be you and I and everybody *except* Bunny. He'll have forgotten. (*Over to left of table.*)

MRS. C-BANKS. Um! Now let me see. A villa—servants. And you really think Benjamin would idealise me? Oh, well, I suppose it might be worse. I'll go.

THOMSON. Of *course* you will.

MRS. C-BANKS. For his sake, yes. I see it's my duty to. Ah, duty, duty, such a compelling thing. Speaking of duties, there are no *customs,* I suppose? No. Good. Perhaps you'll both come and dine with the Colonel and me—one night. Goodbye, Mr.—(*moves up centre to door*)—er—Tomkins. (*Pause*) You swine.
(*She goes out.*)

THOMSON. Phew! this place wants fumigating.

DUKE. Thomson—what *are* "halfways"?
(*Before* THOMSON *can reply* PRIOR *enters left excitedly.*)

TOM. Duke—Duke!

DUKE. Yes. (*Crosses left.*)

TOM. Make him see *me* next.

DUKE. Really, Prior—

TOM. You must, I can't stand the suspense. My nerves aren't right—and I can't stand it.

DUKE. There's nothing to worry about.

TOM (*shouts*). I tell you I can't stand it. I want to be put out.

THOMSON (*turning and coming down*). What's the matter, boy?

TOM. Oh, sir, if you please, I want you to deal with me next. It isn't fair treating me like the others—I'm very highly strung.

THOMSON. Come in, boy, come in and don't be frightened. (*Passes* TOM *to chair at table right*) We're not going to hurt you. (*Leading him over*) There, sit down there. Now, what's the trouble?

TOM. I want to be dealt with, sir. I want to *know.*

THOMSON. Calm yourself, boy, calm yourself. (*Giving him glass*) Drink this. You're fond of your drink, I know.

TOM. Thanks, sir. (*Drinks and then holds out glass again.*)

THOMSON. Well, what do you want? (*Goes right of table and sits.*)

TOM. I want to be killed—I want to be killed.

THOMSON. Um! Healthy outlook you've got, haven't you?

TOM. No, I haven't. I'm a weak character. I want to be let off lightly. I want to be hit over the head with a stone and finished.

THOMSON. Duke, send ashore for a bag of stones, will you?

TOM. Oh, don't joke! I'll drop all sarcasm—it's the only thing that kept me going up till now—but I'll drop it now if you will.

THOMSON. Certainly.

TOM. I know—at least I guess what you're doing with the others. You're keeping them going, keeping them going with punishment and promises and things. Well, *I* don't want to be kept going. I want blank.

THOMSON. Impossible.

TOM. But I'm dead. (*Rises*) And I demand the right to be properly dead. I've always dreamt about being dead—when I've slept at all.

THOMSON. How old are you?

TOM (*sits*). Oh, hundreds of years—I must be. Give me blank.

THOMSON. You're going on like the others. You've got to.

TOM. I won't, I won't!

THOMSON. You'll find it quite easy to forget here, you know.

TOM. Easy to forget what? You're not suggesting I'm to go on, and without *this*? (*The glass.*)
(MRS. MIDGET *appears centre.*)

THOMSON. Yes.

TOM. Is that all I'm to forget?

THOMSON. Yes.

TOM. As if I could! As if I would anyway. You damned torturer. I see what you want me to do. You want me to chuck drink, develop a nice clean brain and remember all the other horrors! No, I won't do it. It's all I've got, it's my only comfort and if I'm to go on I won't give it up. See? But I'm not going to go on. Kill me! There, it's not asking much. And look at all the trouble it will spare you. I'm not worth saving. I'm not really.

THOMSON. You've suffered.

TOM. Ha! (*As if to say "Haven't I?"*)

THOMSON. Can't I do *anything*?

TOM. No, you can't.

MRS. MIDGET (*quietly from the back*). Perhaps *I* could, sir.

THOMSON (*facing sharply*). What do you want?

MRS. MIDGET. My name's Midget, sir. Excuse me bargin' in as it were, but—

THOMSON. I'm very pleased to meet you—yes, yes, I know all about you. But you've no business here yet.

MRS. MIDGET. Oh, but I *have*. You see, yer Reverence, when I first got on to this big boat nobody would speak to me. I was lost as it were—was—and then young Mr. Prior was very kind to me. '*E* spoke to me and broke the icicles, as is said, and if he is in trouble I really don't feel I could put my 'ead on my pillow tonight—if I 'ave one—after what 'e done for me. (*Goes to* TOM, *touches him*) Now what is all this fluster and to do, anyway? It's about the booze, ain't it?

TOM. Booze—eh? Oh, well—yes—drink *is* certainly mixed up with it.

MRS. MIDGET. Nasty 'orrid stuff.

TOM. Beautiful stuff, Mrs. Midget.

MRS. MIDGET. Mind you I don't say there's any 'arm in a man 'aving 'is beer if he wants 'is beer, but the man I does object to is the man who's *always* wanting it. I shouldn't think you've ever 'ad much of a *chance*, though, 'ave you, sir?

TOM. I've had every chance, Mrs. Midget. I was spoilt. I was ungrateful. I ruined— Please drop it.

MRS. MIDGET (*pause*). There was a girl, too, wasn't there?

TOM. Be quiet.

MRS. MIDGET (*another pause*). There *was* a girl, though, wasn't there?

TOM. Oh, yes, there was. How did you know?

MRS. MIDGET. She was the final old 'ow do you do, I take it?

TOM. As you so poetically express it, she *was*.
(HENRY *and* ANN *appear at door centre and unseen by the others stand listening apprehensively.*)

MRS. MIDGET. She chucked you, didn't she? But you'll be different now. I know something about girls and—your Reverence (*behind* TOM *to* THOMSON), I daresay this particular one might come along here some day?

THOMSON. It's quite possible. But it doesn't always follow, Mrs. Midget, that just because a boy and girl are sweethearts, they always go on together here. On the contrary, they're sometimes *separated*—so much depends—so much depends.
(ANN *utters a faint wail and* HENRY *leads her further back into the shadows up left where they remain enviously watching the rest of the scene.* MRS. MIDGET *looks sympathetically at* HENRY *and* ANN, *then resumes to* TOM.)

MRS. MIDGET. What a triumph it would be for you if *your* girl suddenly appeared 'ere and found you —mind yer, it *might* 'appen—settled down and smart and respectable like, with a good job and a decent salary reg'lar every Saturday. (*To* THOMSON) I suppose you've got jobs 'ere, 'aven't you?

THOMSON. Plenty.

MRS. MIDGET. Now what you want is a nice, good, honest, steady respectable housekeeper who'd take care of you.

TOM (*annoyed*). Mrs. Midget—!

MRS. MIDGET. Yes, *she* might do. Then all your things would be properly looked after. With everything mended and darned ready for yer to put on. Someone to see yer didn't sit up too late, too often. No fussing mind, and call you in the morning with a nice 'ot cup of tea. What time do you get up?

TOM. Oh, don't!

MRS. MIDGET. Oh, you can 'ave your drinks, as long as you don't let them interfere with your meals or take away your appetite. I'm a good cook I am, and if you left anything untouched it would upset me awful.

THOMSON. Mrs. Midget, you're suggesting.

MRS. MIDGET. I was *thinking* of it, yes.

THOMSON. Very fine, very fine of you. There's a litle cottage waiting for you, with a garden by the sea.

MRS. MIDGET (*enthusiastic*). There we *are* then! The very spot. (*Sudden change to the practical*) 'As it got a good sink?

THOMSON. You don't quite follow. True, Mr. Prior is free to do as he chooses but he has not yet arrived on the same plane as you have. He would not be allowed to live there to begin with anyway.

MRS. MIDGET. Then why can't I go where *he's* going? That's simple enough.

THOMSON. It would mean going back to the *slums*.

MRS. MIDGET. And what's the matter with the slums? They're all right.

TOM. I won't listen to the idea.

MRS. MIDGET (*pleading*). You can always give me a week's notice.

TOM. I'm not worth bothering about.

MRS. MIDGET. I'm willing to 'ave a shot.

TOM. I can't understand this extraordinary interest anyway.

MRS. MIDGET. One good turn deserves another. Sir, wouldn't the people who spoilt you be glad if they knew you was in capable 'ands?

TOM. They would be, I suppose.

MRS. MIDGET. *And* doing well? (*With growing fervour.*)

TOM. Er—yes—of course.

MRS. MIDGET. That might ease those 'orrid thoughts of yours a bit too, mightn't it?

TOM. It might.

MRS. MIDGET. Well then, ain't it worth it, sir?

TOM. Please don't keep on calling me "sir." I'm not a gentleman really.

MRS. MIDGET. Aren't you, sir?

TOM. No, I'm not. If I were, I shouldn't be hesitating as I am. Mr. Examiner, help me. *You* must be experienced in making decisions.

THOMSON. No, boy, I can't help you in this. It's your own choice.

TOM. Duke, I—

DUKE. You know what Mr. Thomson said, it's for you to speak.

TOM. Very well then. (*Pause*) I'll go. (*Rising. Another Pause*) By myself!

DUKE. Prior!

TOM. *I'm not worth bothering about.*

THOMSON. And in those very words you've proved you are! Because you really meant 'em. Humility, my boy, humility! Take him away, Mrs. What's—er—name and do the best you can with him.

TOM. Mind you, I won't promise—I won't promise to be good.

MRS. MIDGET. No, sir, we'll just 'ope—mutual like.

TOM (*fingering his glass*). It's going to be difficult—yes, it's going to be difficult.

THOMSON. *That's* the way.

TOM. Thanks awfully. (*Sets down glass*) And I will try.
(*He goes out on to the deck and off right.* MRS. MIDGET *overjoyed starts to follow him.*)

THOMSON. Good day, Mrs. Prior—you're a good mother.

MRS. MIDGET (*turning on* THOMSON *ferociously*). Blast you, how did you find out? Blast you! (*Then suddenly changing to pleading piti-*

fully) You'll never tell 'im, will you? Promise you'll never let him know.

THOMSON. I promise.

MRS. MIDGET (*going to* DUKE *and clutching him*). And you too, sir?

DUKE. I promise, of course.

MRS. MIDGET (*turning back*). Thank you, both. You see he mustn't even guess. Oh, sirs, ain't it wonderful? He doesn't know me, and I've got him to look after at last— Without any fear of me disgracing him, it's 'Eaven, that's what it is, it's 'Eaven!

TOM (*off*). Mrs. Midget.

MRS. MIDGET. He wants me at last —yes, dearie, I'm coming. (*She goes out centre in ecstasy, and off right.*)
(THOMSON *and* DUKE *watch her off, then with a pleased chuckle,* THOMSON *picks up his hat and goes up to door centre.*)

THOMSON. Come along, Duke. (*Starts out door.*)
(DUKE *follows but hesitates as he sees* HENRY *and* ANN *who have drawn up toward door, mystified, fearful and appealing, as if to say, "What about us"?* DUKE *looks at them sympathetically and stops* THOMSON, *calling his attention to them.*)

DUKE. Thomson, can't you?

THOMSON (*coming back a step*). Oh—is this the—young couple?

DUKE. Yes, sir. Can't you?
(HENRY *and* ANN *stand silently appealing.*)

THOMSON (*gazes at them thoughtfully then shakes his head as if regretfully, and most tenderly*). Not *yet*, my children.
(THOMSON *goes out, followed by* DUKE. HENRY *and* ANN *stand hopeless and bewildered, they look from one to the other curiously; then she, terror-stricken in awful apprehension of the uncertainty of their plight, at their being ignored, at the mystery of it all, suddenly clutches* HENRY'S *arm and holds to him tightly.*)

CURTAIN

SCENE II

The scene is now as it was before, the small table which was used for the meeting having been removed. It is moonlight outside. The moonlight pours in through the portholes and through the centre door which is wide open.

SCRUBBY *enters from the left. He collects a few glasses, and places them on a tray. He is tidying up. He then goes through the door behind the bar. Once more the mysterious drum is heard, and* ANN *appears from the deck.*

ANN. Henry! (*Goes to left*) Henry! Henry, where are you? I want you! (*Up again*) Henry! Henry! (*Left.*)

HENRY (*from centre opening*). Yes, dear?

ANN. Where have you been?

HENRY. Looking at the sea—

ANN. You know we've sailed again.

HENRY. Yes.

ANN. Why have we both been left behind?

HENRY. I don't know, dear. But what does it matter, we've been left together.

ANN. Yes, you and I.

HENRY. The lights of that place have gone now. (*At porthole.*)

ANN (*up to* HENRY *up centre*). Where were you just now? Where were you?

HENRY. Looking at the sea.

ANN (*arm in arm down centre*). I've taken a dislike to the sea, husband. It seems to me we should keep terribly close.

HENRY. Why, dear?

ANN. Can't you ever feel when things are passing over you? Bad things, I can. They're round us now, all round. They've been round us since we left that harbour.

HENRY. Why weren't *we* judged?

ANN. I don't know—and I don't know why you left me for a while. (*Sits.*)

HENRY. I thought I heard a dog bark. It was Jock. What's that?

ANN. What?

HENRY. Something seemed to touch my hand. (*He is uneasy*) We should have insisted on being heard, we were cowards.

ANN. Not because we are ashamed of our love.

HENRY. No. Because we were afraid of being separated.

ANN. Yes.
(*A faint, very faint, sound of breaking glass off right.*)

HENRY (*pause—listens*). It's strange, that tinkling noise like glass—sharp pieces of glass falling on stone. Do you hear it, Ann?

ANN. No, dear.

HENRY. My nerves are all on edge. I'd have sworn I did. Ann, where are we going to?

ANN. I can't think. (*Rises, pause*) Perhaps it's the dreadful house with the double staircase in the hall, you know.

HENRY. The stairs I run up and down trying to find you.

ANN. Perhaps it isn't a dream place at all.

HENRY. And since we left that harbour I feel we are bound for some dimly remembered place. . . . Ann, I feel—a breeze like a breath of new—of different air.

ANN. They didn't question us. Perhaps it's freedom.

HENRY. Ann, Ann, wife, wife. Don't let's get away from each other. We don't know where we are, we don't know what's becoming of us, or where we're going.

ANN. I don't really care what's becoming of me as long as I am with my husband. What else matters? But if *you* went away from me—

HENRY. It seems you're rather leaning on me now!

ANN. Shares, Henry.

HENRY. Shares, Ann.

ANN. You see, I love you. I love you so much. I love the way you walk, the way you hold your head. I love *you.* I love your mouth. (ANN *sits down.* HENRY *kneels with arm round her.*)

HENRY. My wonderful Ann. They won't separate us now, will they, Ann? Nothing can take one from the other now?

ANN. Nothing—nothing.

HENRY. Keep close though, keep close . . . Are *you* cold?

ANN (*takes hold of him*). No, I've got you, darling, I've got you.

HENRY. Never let go.

ANN. Why aren't we closer? I thought we *would* be when we're dead.

HENRY. I thought there would be no need for speech. That *we,* the *real* you and I would drift away together. Where is the utter completeness?—Oh, Ann—Ann—

ANN. Supposing, after all, we were wrong.

HENRY. Wrong?—how wrong? What was that? (*Rises.*)

ANN. Just supposing—

HENRY. Ann— (*Listening.*) (SCRUBBY *comes in quickly. He puts down the empty tray on bar.*)

SCRUBBY. Good evening, madam, good evening, sir. (*Goes left.*)

ANN. Good evening, Scrubby.

HENRY. Ann!!

ANN. Yes, dear?

HENRY. There's Jock barking. (*Stepping right a pace.*)

ANN. Don't be silly.

SCRUBBY. Who's Jock, ma'am?

ANN. Our dog—at home.

HENRY. Listen! Listen! (*Stepping further right.*)

ANN. Don't be silly, Henry.

HENRY. I'd like *him* to be with us. Jock!

SCRUBBY. Keep close to him, miss, if you'll take my advice.

HENRY. You can tell us, you can help, can't you? Where are we going to?

SCRUBBY. We just go on like this, sir—forwards and backwards—backwards and forwards.

HENRY. For ever?

ANN. Alone?

SCRUBBY. Yes, quite alone. Until—

HENRY (*slightly excited*). Until what? Why is this happening to us?

SCRUBBY. It happens to all half-ways like—like we are.

ANN. But what are we, Scrubby? We—we half-ways?

SCRUBBY. We're the people who ought to have had more courage.

ANN. For what?

SCRUBBY. To face life.

ANN. Do you remember how you became a half-ways?

SCRUBBY. Oh, no. I've been allowed to forget. I hope you'll be allowed to forget. It would be too cruel if they didn't let you forget in time that you killed yourselves.

ANN. Scrubby! (*A pause—rises.*)

HENRY (*cries out*). My God! *that's* it! Now I remember! Suicide!

SCRUBBY. Keep closer to him, madam.

HENRY. The people who ought to have had more courage! I see. *That's* what we've done that wasn't right.

ANN. Henry! (*Goes to him.*)

HENRY. The little bits are fitting together.

ANN. Dear, don't worry.

HENRY. Ann, I wanted to forget. (*Collapses on chair above table*) Oh, don't say the damned torture's going to start all over again. We'd reached the end of our tether as it was. Ann—

ANN. I'm with you still. (*She stands behind his chair and puts her arms round him.*)

HENRY. But you can't face it, Ann, you can't stand it any more. I won't let you suffer—not another second. We'll kill ourselves, dear, and forget in each other's arms. Then we'll be so happy, sweet, so happy for ever. (*Pause*) Oh, but it's over. We *have* killed ourselves. And we're *not* happy.

ANN. No—we're not. (*Sits down.*)

HENRY. We can't stand it, Ann.

ANN (*after a pause*). We've got to.

SCRUBBY. Why did you kill yourselves?

ANN (*pause*). We weren't married, Scrubby.

SCRUBBY. Weren't you, madam? Oh, you two poor dears. Pardon my familiarity.

HENRY. I was trapped into a marriage.

ANN. He's so guileless, Scrubby.

HENRY (*indicating* ANN). Ann came to me in such a wonderful way. It was like dawn.

ANN. They'd been so cruel to him, Scrubby. Never an atom of love in his whole life before, was there, Henry?

HENRY. Never. Ann was the only true and good thing I've ever met. We loved. We loved. I gave my soul for love as Ann gave hers. We got so *near* each other that we *knew* that there was only one minute spiritual barrier between us, and that we believed was Death. Death can unify utterly. We believed that—and yet we are just as if we had never died.

SCRUBBY. You killed *yourselves.*

ANN. We should have waited?

SCRUBBY. Yes.

ANN. Oh, Scrubby—you don't know the agony we've been through. The way people talked—the things they said.

HENRY. Lies—such bloody lies! (*Rises.*)

ANN. They smeared our love—smeared—

HENRY. With their dirty tongues.

ANN. You see, Scrubby, we didn't conceal it—we didn't pretend.

HENRY. We weren't ashamed. We started so proudly, so proudly.

ANN. Till we were beaten down so bruised, so hurt.

HENRY. But we should have gone on?

ANN. Yes.

SCRUBBY. And now you children are faced with memories.

HENRY. I remember the long sweep into the dark. The last thing I saw was Jock's face against the window. I can see him now—almost feel him—Jock! (*Stooping as if to pet the dog*) Jock!

SCRUBBY. *Outside* the window, sir?

HENRY. Yes—outside. (*To* ANN) And then you, Ann—I haven't taken care of you well enough, and I've been a coward. (ANN *rises*) Oh! to be given back even a little while—to try again. Our future here isn't Hell, it isn't Heaven, it's past imagination.

SCRUBBY. Eternity.

HENRY. Ann, Ann, I must save you. I promise that I will. I'm the man. Oh, it's my fault, it's all my fault. We didn't understand, dear, that we should have been true and brave and fearless. Then nothing could have hurt us wherever we were, whatever we have been, or may be.

ANN. It's too late now.

HENRY (*moving away*). Let me think, dear. There must be a way out. Let me think. The air seems fresher out here.
(*Walks slowly to the deck and leans over rail. After a few seconds during the following dialogue, walks slowly up and down, passing and re-passing the entrance. Gradually a bigger pause between each pass till he doesn't come past.*)

SCRUBBY (*below settee*). Don't let him go too far, madam. Call him now.

ANN. Henry!

HENRY. Ann!

ANN. Don't go too far away.

HENRY (*off*). No, dear!

ANN (*crosses to* SCRUBBY). Why aren't people kinder to each other, Scrubby?

SCRUBBY (ANN *sits left*). Being unkind comes more natural to most people, I'm afraid.

ANN. I'd try to be kinder if I had it over again. How sad there's no one left here to be kind to.

SCRUBBY (*crosses right to table*). Present company excepted. What did you like best in life?

ANN. I liked so many things. I loved the earth, the scent of the earth, of newly cut grass, after rain; and the trees, and all clear things like water. Are you very lonely, Scrubby?

SCRUBBY. Oh no, ma'am, not on the whole. I've all sorts of comforting little thoughts locked up in my brain, so when I get a bit monotonous I just turn the key and out come the thoughts to dance in front of me. Very whimsical and entertaining some of them are, too, I must say.

ANN. I do hope we'll get on together. When I was living I did want people to look after, but I had so few friends. Now I've none excepting you.

SCRUBBY. You'll find lots of new friends, ma'am. Not quite the same, but most consoling. The birds come on board occasionally—and the sky appreciates a clean, good morning, and the sea's in a good temper sometimes. Don't always think of nature as men and women. If you're kind to nature, nature will understand. These are some of my comforts. You want the earth again. Well, the sea will tell your wish to the clouds, maybe, and perhaps some little drifting cloud will float with the news over to the land, and rest above the cool trees and the yellow gorse and the grass near the chalk pits. So though you can't get the earth again, ma'am, the earth may know. And let's hope she will, and send back her kind regards and very best wishes. Call him again.

ANN. Call him? Why? He won't be far from me.

SCRUBBY. *Call him!*

ANN. Henry! (*A pause*) Henry! (*Long pause. Rises and goes up centre, exits and returns*) Henry! Henry! Henry! (*Another pause—goes out left and re-enters. At opening left cries out*) Henry! Henry! (*Pause*) He must be here. He must be here. (*She dashes on to the deck again. Looks round. Then returning cries once more, wildly, "Henry!" There is no answer. She looks at* SCRUBBY *questioningly.*)

SCRUBBY. He has gone.

ANN (*screams*). Henry!! You haven't looked.

SCRUBBY. Useless.

ANN. What do you mean? (*Quiet now.*)

SCRUBBY. I know what's happened to him.

ANN. What?

SCRUBBY. *He lives again!*

ANN. Lives! Henry gone back?

SCRUBBY. The dog, ma'am, outside the window.—Perhaps broke through.

ANN. Henry is gone back, alone.

SCRUBBY. The dog, ma'am, outside the window! to resist the fumes, maybe.

ANN. Gone back. I'll follow him.

SCRUBBY. You can't.

ANN. Henry wouldn't leave me alone.

SCRUBBY. He couldn't help himself, madam.

ANN. But we've been dead a week—

SCRUBBY. A week! A century! A moment! There's no time here. He's gone back, madam.

ANN. Then I'll go too.

SCRUBBY. You can't.

ANN. I will. I must!

SCRUBBY. It's impossible.

ANN. *I will follow.* Henry. Henry. (*Comes down right in front of table, facing front*) Henry dear, where are you? It's Ann, dear. Where are you, baby? Just tell me where you are? *Where are you?* I'll come, darling. Just tell me. Henry! Henry!

SCRUBBY. He won't answer. (*Standing in shadows left.*)

ANN. Henry. Henry, are you in the flat? I believe you are, Henry; you mustn't be there by yourself—you won't know how to manage anything.

SCRUBBY. It's useless.

ANN. I will follow him. I *will.* I will. Henry, listen, Henry. Our love, our great love. (*The drum is heard again*) It's speaking, Henry, the little wedding ring, that wasn't a wedding ring at all—put it on my finger again. It's on the mantelpiece. Henry, don't leave me alone for ever. It's Ann, your Ann, who wants you. Henry! Henry dear!
(*The drum stops.*)

SCRUBBY. Quiet. Quiet. I heard something out there—on the deck. (*Another pause, then* HENRY *appears in the centre doorway.*)

ANN (*without seeing him, still facing front*). Hello, Henry.

HENRY (*coming down to her partly*). Hello, Ann. Quick, dear, be very quick. There's only a second or two. I've come to fetch you home, dear. Ready, sweetheart? (*Holding out his hand.*)

ANN. Ready, Henry, ready! (*Turning up and taking his hand.*)

HENRY. We've such a lot to do, my love. And such a little time to do it in. Quick. Quick.
(*They go out together. The drum starts again very softly.* SCRUBBY *watches them go.*)

CURTAIN

Cavalcade

BY NOEL COWARD

TO

G. B. STERN

DEAR PETER—

I am dedicating *Cavalcade* to you in gratitude for a friendship maintained through many of its years.

NOEL

Cavalcade was first produced in America at the Pasadena Playhouse, Pasadena, California, by the Pasadena Community Playhouse Association on June 6, 1934. The following is the original cast:

Jane Marryot	Doris Lloyd
Robert Marryot	Ralph Freud
Ellen	Sharley Simpson
Bridges	Eric Snowdon
Edward Marryot (*child*)	Dick Quine
Joe Marryot (*child*)	Bill Martin
Edith Harris (*child*)	Pearl Hays
Fanny Bridges (*child*)	Anita Dennison
Edward Marryot (*grown*)	Richard Ritchie
Joe Marryot (*grown*)	Alex Courtney
Edith Harris (*grown*)	Alma Lloyd
Fanny Bridges (*grown*)	Barbara Sheldon
Margaret Harris	Judith Evelyn
Cook	Janet Murdock
Mrs. Snapper	Dora Mayfield
Annie	Cybel Hallam
Flo Grainger	Iris Moore
George Grainger	J. H. Hastie
Mirabelle	Olive Hyatt
Lieut. Edgar	Leslie Abbott
Tom Jolly	Paul Regan Maxey
Ada (Rosa Darling)	June Shafer
Dairy Maid	Edith May Kinney
Stage Manager	Willard Davis
Daisy Devon	Carolyn Bellamy
Marion Christie	Ireta Newport
Netta Lake	Edith May Kinney
Connie Crawshay	Gertrude McCain
Tim Bateman	Phil Ormsby
Douglas Finn	Avery Graves
Lord Martlett (*chubby*)	Madison Goff
First Woman	Doris Brealy
Second Woman	Muriel Bodwell
Uncle George	Cyril Thornton
Uncle Dick	Jack Harling
Policeman	Edmond Kearns
Cabby	Steve Massall
Franklin	Joseph Tomes
Gladys	Jimmie James
Pianist	Pauline Garner

Gilmor Brown, *Supervising Director*
Morris Ankrum, *Director* Willard Davis, *Assistant Director*
Robert Lee, *Art Director* Collenette, *Dance Director*
Mrs. Samuel B. Morris, *General Production Chairman*
Murray Yeats, *General Production Manager*

SCENES

PART I

Scene 1	Sunday, December 31st, 1899	Drawing-room
Scene 2	Saturday, January 27th, 1900	Dockside
Scene 3	Friday, May 18th, 1900	Drawing-room
Scene 4	Friday, May 18th, 1900	Theatre
Scene 5	Monday, January 21st, 1901	Kitchen
Scene 6	Sunday, January 27th, 1901	Park
Scene 7	Saturday, February 2nd, 1901	Drawing-room
Scene 8	Thursday, May 14th, 1903	Ball-room

PART II

Scene 1	Saturday, June 16th, 1906	Bar Parlour
Scene 2	Saturday, June 16th, 1906	Street
Scene 3	Wednesday, March 10th, 1909	Restaurant, Private Room
Scene 4	Monday, July 25th, 1910	Seaside
Scene 5	Sunday, April 14th, 1912	Ship
Scene 6	Tuesday, August 4th, 1914	Drawing-room
Scene 7	1914–1915–1916–1917–1918	Marching
Scene 8	Tuesday, October 22nd, 1918	Restaurant
Scene 9	Tuesday, October 22nd, 1918	Railway Station
Scene 10	Monday, November 11th, 1918	Drawing-room
Scene 11	Monday, November 11th, 1918	Trafalgar Square

PART III

Scene 1	Tuesday, December 31st, 1929	Drawing-room
Scene 2	Tuesday, 1930	CHAOS

CAVALCADE

PART ONE

NOTE ON PART ONE

In the interim of darkness between Scenes I and II, II and III, III and IV, newsboys are heard shouting latest news from the front.

SCENE I

Principals—1899

JANE MARRYOT (aged 31)
ROBERT MARRYOT (aged 35)
ELLEN (aged 25)
BRIDGES (aged 40)

SCENE—*The drawing-room of a London house. The room is charmingly furnished in the taste of the period. There are two windows at the back with a small balcony in front of each of them; apart from this structural necessity the decoration and furniture, etc., can be left to the discretion of the designer.*

TIME—*About 11.45 p.m. Sunday, December 31st, 1899.*

When the curtain rises, ELLEN, *the parlourmaid, is discovered setting the table with a light supper consisting of sandwiches and cake. She is a pleasant-looking woman of twenty-five.*

Enter BRIDGES, *the butler, with a bottle of champagne in a bucket of ice. He is older than* ELLEN, *about forty, with iron-grey hair.*

ELLEN. They won't need champagne if they've got 'ot punch, will they?

BRIDGES. You never know; best to be on the safe side.

ELLEN. How was Cook when you come up?

BRIDGES. Running round that kitchen like a cat on a griddle; New Year's Eve's gone to 'er 'ead, and no mistake.

ELLEN. She's been queer all day, she says she feels like as if it was the end of everything. So do I, for that matter.

BRIDGES. Don't start all that over again.

ELLEN. Oh, Alfred!

BRIDGES. What?

ELLEN. I can't bear to think what it's going to be like when you've gone.

BRIDGES. Well, don't.

ELLEN. I can't 'elp it.

BRIDGES. It's no use upsetting yourself; think of the missus, think of all the other soldiers' wives. You're in the same boat as wot they are.

ELLEN. You was never cut out for a soldier.

BRIDGES. Never mind what I was cut out for. I am one now.

ELLEN. What's going to 'appen to me and Fanny if anything 'appens to you?

BRIDGES (*putting his hands on* ELLEN'S *shoulders*). Look 'ere, old girl, you married me for better or for worse, didn't you?

ELLEN. Yes, but——

BRIDGES. Well, if this turns out to be worse, so much the worse, see? And if it turns out to be better——

ELLEN. So much the better—yes, a fat lot of comfort that is.

BRIDGES. Look at the missus, with a brother out there ever since the beginning, and now 'er 'usband going, and two growing boys to look after.

ELLEN. What's the war for, anyhow? Nobody wanted to 'ave a war.

BRIDGES. We've got to 'ave wars every now and then to prove we're top-dog——

ELLEN. This one don't seem to be proving much.

BRIDGES. 'Ow can you tell sitting at 'ome 'ere safe and sound? 'Ow can you tell what our brave boys are suffering out there in darkest Africa, giving their life's blood for their Queen and country?

ELLEN. Africa looks very sunny and nice in the *Illustrated London News.*

BRIDGES. If this wasn't New Year's Eve, I'd lose my temper, and that's a fact.

ELLEN. Well, it wouldn't be the first time. You'd better go and get the 'ot punch, they'll be in in a minute.

BRIDGES. You mark my words, Ellen, if we didn't go out and give them Boers wot for, they'd be over 'ere wreakin' 'avoc and carnage before you could say Jack Robinson.

ELLEN. Oh, get along with you.

(BRIDGES *goes out.*)

(ELLEN, *puts the finishing touches to the table and then, going to the windows, she pulls back the curtains.*)

(*Enter* JANE MARRYOT. *She is a handsome woman of about thirty-one. She is wearing an evening gown and cloak.*)

(*Enter* ROBERT, JANE'S *husband, following her. He is older, about thirty-five, also in evening dress.*)

JANE (*throwing off her cloak*). I thought we should never get here in time. I'm sure that cabby was tipsy, Robert. How nice the table looks, Ellen. Where did those flowers come from?

ELLEN. They're from Bridges and me, ma'am, with our very best wishes, I'm sure.

JANE. Thank you, Ellen, very much indeed.

ROBERT. A charming thought, Ellen. Thank you both.

ELLEN. Not at all, sir—it's—it's a pleasure indeed.
(ELLEN *withdraws from the room covered with respectful embarrassment.*)
(JANE *smiles at* ROBERT.)

JANE. Small things are so infinitely touching, aren't they? I feel I want to cry. Just a few gentle tears to usher in the new century.

ROBERT. Do, by all means, dearest: this evening was planned sentimentally.

JANE. Just the two of us saying, "Hail and Farewell."

ROBERT. Not farewell quite yet.

JANE. Soon—dreadfully soon.

ROBERT. You looked so beautiful at dinner.

JANE. Did I, Robert?

ROBERT. You look so beautiful now.

JANE. Do I, Robert?

ROBERT. I expect it's only that dress, really. Very deceiving.

JANE. Yes, Robert.

ROBERT. And that ornament in your hair.

JANE. Yes, Robert.

ROBERT. And the fact that I love you so dearly.

JANE. After so long. How can you?

ROBERT. Perhaps you're hideous and ill-dispositioned and tedious, really, and I never knew.

JANE. Perhaps.

ROBERT. Well, it's too late now. I'm set in the habit of loving you. I shall never know the truth.

JANE. I wonder if the boys are asleep.

ROBERT. Snoring, I expect.

JANE. Oh, no, Robert; not snoring. They both have perfect tonsils. Doctor Harrison said so.

ROBERT. Inherited from their mother, dear. You have the most exquisite tonsils in the world.

JANE. You're in a very facetious mood, Robert. It shocks me a little. This should be a solemn occasion. Your bow is crooked, too, and you look raffish.

ROBERT. Raffish?

JANE (*suddenly running into his arms*). Oh, my darling, my darling, why must you leave me? I shall miss you so.

ROBERT (*smiling and holding her tenderly*). The Bugle Call, dear, the Red, White and Blue——

Britons never, never, never
shall be slaves.

JANE. Don't tease me—not about that. What does it matter about the Boers—it can't matter, really.

ROBERT (*seriously*). It matters about Jim, doesn't it? He's out there.

JANE. Yes, I know, I know, but——

ROBERT. But what?

JANE (*leaving his embrace*). I'm sorry, dear. I was nearly behaving badly.

ROBERT. You couldn't behave badly.

JANE (*lightly*). Give him my love if you ever see him, if he's alive.

ROBERT. Of course he's alive. They're all alive. They're bound to be relieved soon.

JANE. Everyone has been saying that for weeks.

ROBERT. Baden Powell's a fine man.

JANE. How long will it last, the war, I mean?

ROBERT. It can't last more than a few months.

JANE. Perhaps it will be over before you get there.

ROBERT. Perhaps.

JANE. I suppose you'd hate that. Wouldn't you?

ROBERT. Bitterly.

JANE. Thank Heaven for one thing. The boys are too young. They won't have to fight; Peace and Happiness for them. Oh, please God, Peace and Happiness for them, always. (*She leans against the window and looks out.*)

(*Enter* BRIDGES *with a bowl of punch, followed by:*)
(ELLEN *entering, carrying a tray of punch glasses and almonds and raisins.*)

BRIDGES. It's started, sir. Just twelve o'clock now.

ROBERT. Open the windows quick.
(ROBERT *takes the punch from* BRIDGES *and fills two glasses.*)
(BRIDGES *opens the windows wide.*)
(*Outside can be heard the growing noise of sirens and chimes of bells.*)
(ELLEN *and* BRIDGES *are about to go.*)

JANE (*suddenly*). Stay and drink with us, won't you? Robert, two more glasses.

BRIDGES. Thank you very much, ma'am.

ELLEN. Thank you, ma'am.

ROBERT (*pouring them two glasses of punch*). Here you are, Jane, Ellen, Bridges. 1900–1900.

JANE. 1900.

ELLEN and BRIDGES (*together*). 1900.
(*Suddenly* JANE *hears a sound upstairs. She puts down her glass hurriedly and:*)
(JANE *runs out of the room.*)

ELLEN. It sounded like Master Joe.

ROBERT (*going to the door and calling after* JANE). Dearest, bring them down here. Bring them both down. (*Coming slowly back into the room, smiling*) How very impolite of the twentieth century to waken the children.

(The lights fade as the noise of chimes and sirens grows louder.)

SCENE II

Principals

ROBERT
JANE
ELLEN
BRIDGES

SCENE—*A Dockside.*
TIME—*About twelve noon, Saturday, January 27th, 1900.*

Before the stage becomes visible to the audience, down stage on the left BRIDGES *and* ELLEN *appear in a pool of light.* BRIDGES *is wearing the uniform of a Private in the C.I.V.* ELLEN *is gaily dressed, but weeping.*

BRIDGES. Be brave, old woman.

ELLEN. Oh, Alfred, Alfred, my 'eart's breaking.

BRIDGES. There, there—I'll soon be back—you see.

ELLEN. I can't bear it.

BRIDGES. Think of the missus—you'll 'ave to look after 'er, you know.

ELLEN. I can't think of anything but you going out among all them awful Boers and lying bleeding yer 'eart out on the battlefield.

BRIDGES. That's a cheerful outlook, I will say.

ELLEN. And Fanny 'aving no father and me being widowed for life.

BRIDGES. You're getting morbid, you know. Fanny'll be all right, and so will you and so will I. She was right as rain when I kissed her good-bye. See her laugh, eh?

ELLEN. She didn't mean to laugh; she's too young to understand.

BRIDGES. All the better, I say. I could do with a bit of a smile from you, now you mention it.

ELLEN. All right—I'll try.

BRIDGES. That's a girl—— *(He kisses her as):*
(The lights fade on them and a steamer siren sounds loudly.)
(Down stage on the right ROBERT *and* JANE *appear in a pool of light.)*
*(*ROBERT *is in the uniform of a C.I.V. officer.)*
*(*JANE *is quietly dressed.)*

ROBERT. I think I'd better be getting aboard.

JANE. It's come at last, hasn't it—this moment?

ROBERT. You'll be very brave, won't you?

JANE. Take care of yourself, my dearest.

ROBERT. I shall probably be sea-sick.

JANE. Lie down flat on every possible occasion.

ROBERT. I'll try to remember.

JANE. Bridges will look after you.

ROBERT. Perhaps he'll be lying down flat, too.

JANE. You mustn't worry about me being unhappy when you've gone. I'm going to keep myself very busy. Lady Brandon is organizing an enormous relief fund matinée in February. She asked me to help her, and there'll be lots of other things, too. I shan't give myself time to feel anything except just very proud.

ROBERT. I'll write and telegraph whenever it's possible.
(*Pause.*)

JANE. This is horrid, isn't it?

ROBERT. I really must go.

JANE. Not just for a minute.

ROBERT. I'm going to kiss you once more now, and then I want you to turn away and go on talking, so that you won't see me actually leave you.

JANE (*in a stifled voice*). Very well, my darling.
(ROBERT *kisses her lingeringly.*)
(*Turning away and talking rapidly*) Edward and Joe were terribly anxious to come, too, but I'm glad I didn't bring them really. Joe gets over-excited so easily, and he's had a very bad cold, anyhow. Edward could have come, I suppose, really, but that would have upset Joe so dreadfully, being left alone. Take care of yourself, my own dear—you're not here any more, so I can break down a little—I felt you go when I said about Joe being over-excited—Robert—Robert——
(ROBERT *has disappeared into the surrounding darkness. As she turns the lights go up and* ROBERT *is seen threading his way through the crowd to the ship's gangway.* BRIDGES *is waiting for him, and they go aboard together.* JANE *walks over to* ELLEN, *who is sobbing bitterly, and puts her arms round her. The crowd is cheering wildly, although several mothers and sweethearts and wives are weeping.*)
(*The steamer gives a short blast on its siren.*)
(*A band strikes up "Soldiers of the Queen."*)
(*The decks of the ship are lined with waving soldiers.*)
(*The gangway is pulled away. Slowly the ship begins to move as:*)
(*The lights fade.*)

SCENE III

Principals

JANE MARRYOT
MARGARET HARRIS
EDITH HARRIS (aged 10)
EDWARD (aged 12)
JOE (aged 8)
ELLEN

SCENE—*The same as* SCENE I.
TIME—*About five o'clock on the afternoon of Friday, May 18th, 1900.*

When the lights go up EDWARD *and* JOE MARRYOT *and* EDITH HARRIS *are discovered playing soldiers on the floor.* EDWARD *is aged twelve,* JOE *eight, and* EDITH HARRIS *about ten.*

JOE (*shooting off a cannon*). Bang—bang, bang, bang.

EDITH (*giving a little squeak*). Oh—oh, dear!

EDWARD. How many?

EDITH. Seven.

EDWARD (*curtly*). Good! You'd better retreat.

EDITH. I don't know how.

JOE. I'm going to shoot again.

EDITH. I do wish you wouldn't. I've only got fourteen left.

JOE (*yelling*). Bang, bang, bang! Dirty old Kruger—dirty old Kruger——

EDWARD. Shut up! How dare you fire without orders.

JOE (*saluting*). I'm sorry, Bobs.

EDITH. Edward.

EDWARD. What?

EDITH. Need I always be the Boers?

EDWARD. Yes.

EDITH. Why?

JOE. Because you're a girl—only a girl. Bang, bang, bang!

EDITH (*struggling with her cannon and ammunition*). I'll teach you, you mean little pig! Bang, bang, bang! There! Bang——
(*The cannon sticks, so* EDITH *throws it at* JOE'S *battalion, annihilating about fifty soldiers.*)

JOE (*yelling*). It's not fair.

EDWARD. Be quiet. Edith, that was cheating.

EDITH (*in tears*). I'm sick of being the Boers—I'll never be the Boers again, never as long as I live!
(*The door opens.*)
(*Enter* JANE, *looking obviously worried and nervy.*)
(*Enter* MARGARET HARRIS, *following* JANE. *She is a nicely dressed woman of about thirty.*)

JANE. Children, why on earth are you making such an awful noise? I heard you right down in the hall. Edith, what's the matter? Joe be quiet.

EDWARD. Edith doesn't like being the Boers—she's mutinied.

JANE. So I should think.

JOE. Bang, bang, bang!
(JOE *throws* EDITH's *cannon back at her and hits her on the knee.*)
(EDITH *screams.*)
(JANE *slaps* JOE *sharply.*)

JANE. You're a naughty, wicked, little boy. You go upstairs this minute.
(MARGARET *rushes to* EDITH *and proceeds to comfort her.*)

MARGARET. Edith, don't cry—it couldn't have hurt you so very much.

JANE. I can't bear it. Go away, all of you. Edward, take Joe away.

EDWARD. Sorry, mum.

JANE. Can't you play any other game but soldiers, soldiers—soldiers hurting each other—killing each other? Go away from me—go away—go away—go away——
(MARGARET, *seeing that* JANE *is in a bad state of nerves, bustles all three children out of the room.*)

MARGARET. Go along, all of you. Edith, I'm ashamed of you, making such a fuss. It's only a tiny little scratch. Go upstairs and ask nurse to put some Pommade Devigne on it. Go along, now.
(*Exeunt* EDITH, EDWARD *and* JOE.)
(MARGARET *shuts the door after the children and comes back to* JANE.)
(JANE *is wearily removing her hat in front of a mirror.*)
(*A barrel organ in the street strikes up "Soldiers of the Queen."*)

JANE. There's no escape anywhere, is there?

MARGARET. Shall I throw him something?

JANE. Make him go away.
(MARGARET *goes to the window and out on to the balcony.*)

MARGARET. Hi! Hi!
(*The organ stops.*)
Will you please go away further down the street? (*Throwing some money out and returning into the room*) He's moving off. Do sit down, Jane dear, you've been standing up all the afternoon.

JANE (*sitting down*). Will these days never end?
(*The barrel organ starts again, but much further off.*)

MARGARET. News will come soon.

JANE. I don't believe I shall see either of them ever again.

MARGARET. Don't give way to despair, Jane. It's foolish. You must have courage.

JANE. It's much easier to be brave when there's something to hear, something definite; this long suspense, these dragging, dragging weeks of waiting are horrible. The two people I love best in the world, so remote from me, beyond reach of my love, probably suffering—it's dreadful, dreadful——

MARGARET. Mafeking is bound to be relieved within the next few days, all the papers say so.

JANE. They've been saying so for months—meanwhile Jim is dying there slowly, by inches, starvation and disease and horror. I can't bear to think of it and yet I can't stop thinking. I wake at night and see his face, as he was when he was a little boy. He was always awfully plucky, my little brother, and so very, very dear to me. (*She breaks down.*)
(*Enter* ELLEN *with tea. She places it on the table and looks enquiringly at* MARGARET.)
(MARGARET *shakes her head.*)

MARGARET. No news yet, Ellen. We've been standing outside the Mansion House for hours, and then we went to Fleet Street to the newspaper offices.

ELLEN (*to* JANE). Have a nice cup of tea, ma'am, it'll make you feel better.

JANE. Thank you, Ellen.

ELLEN. There ain't no cause to worry about the master, ma'am; he's all right. I feel it in me bones. You see, he's got my Alfred with 'im, and if anything 'appened to either of them we'd be bound to 'ear from one of them, if you know what I mean.

JANE. You must be fearfully worried, too, Ellen.

ELLEN. Well, on and off, I am, but I say to myself—no news is good news, and what must be must be, and you'd never believe how it cheers me up.
(ELLEN *goes out.*)

MARGARET. Poor Ellen!
(*A newsboy runs by, shouting.*)

JANE (*jumping up*). Quick! Quick! Give me a halfpenny.
(JANE *rushes on to the balcony and leans over.*) What is it, Ellen—what is it?
(ELLEN *apparently answers "nothing much," and* JANE *returns wearily*). Ellen's up those area steps like lightning every time a paper boy passes. No news is good news. What must be must be. Oh, God!
(MARGARET *gets up with an air of determination.*)

MARGARET. Now, look here, Jane. I'm going now, and I shall be back at a quarter to seven.

JANE. A quarter to seven—why?

MARGARET. We're going out to dine at a restaurant and we're going to a theatre.

JANE. A restaurant! A theatre! I couldn't!

MARGARET. You could and you will—it's senseless sitting at home all by yourself fretting and worrying, and it doesn't do any good. I'll get Ronnie James to take us, and if he can't, we'll go by ourselves, and I don't care what people say. We'll go to something gay—they say "Mirabelle" is very good.

JANE. I can't, Margaret—it's very sweet of you, but I really can't.

MARGARET. I am now going home to have a bath and put on my new Redfern model, and I shall be back at a quarter to seven.

JANE. Margaret—no, really, I——

MARGARET (*kissing* JANE). Don't argue—just do what you're told.

JANE. I haven't anything to wear.

MARGARET. Nonsense! You have your blue "Worth" and if that won't do, put on your presentation gown, feathers and all!

JANE. Margaret, don't be so silly.

MARGARET. I mean it—it's a gesture. Robert and Jim would hate to think of you weeping and wailing. They're being gallant enough. We'd better try and be gallant, too. We'll dine at the Café Royal.

JANE. Margaret!

MARGARET. Be ready at a quarter to seven.

(MARGARET *goes out.* JANE *makes a movement to call* MARGARET *back and then subsides into her chair. Suddenly directly under the window another barrel organ strikes up "Soldiers of the Queen."* JANE *jumps up and runs to the window.*)

JANE (*on balcony*). Go on, then—play louder—play louder! Soldiers of the Queen—wounded and dying and suffering for the Queen! Play louder, play louder!

(*She comes back into the room laughing hysterically and proceeds to kick the children's toy soldiers all over the room; finally collapsing on to the sofa in a storm of tears as:*)

(*The lights fade.*)

SCENE IV

Principals

JANE
MARGARET
MIRABELLE
ADA
EDGAR
TOM JOLLY
SIX C.I.V. GIRLS
CHORUS
STAGE MANAGER

SCENE—*A theatre.*
TIME—*About 9 p.m. Friday, May 18th, 1900.*

Before the lights go up, a spotlight illuminates JANE *and* MARGARET *in evening cloaks and gowns sitting in a stage box left. When the lights go up, it is seen that they are watching a typical musical comedy of the period.*

A Sextette of ample girls are singing a song called "The Girls of the C.I.V.," dressed rakishly in C.I.V. uniforms.

We're the girls of the C.I.V.
Form fours, get in line, one two three.
For our bravery is such
That the Boers won't like it much
When we chase them across the veldt and teach them double Dutch
We're the girls of the C.I.V.
And we're out for a lark and a spree
In our uniforms so stunning
We shall soon have Kruger running
From the girls of the C.I.V.

The Scene on the stage is excessively rural, with apple blossom predominating. When the girls have finished their number, they bounce off and:

The leading lady, MIRABELLE, *enters. She is in reality a Princess, but has disguised herself as a farm girl in order that she might conceivably find a young man to love her for herself alone. Her costume is charming but slightly inappropriate for manual labour.*

She is met down stage by LIEUT. EDGAR TYRELL, R.N., *a wooden young man with an excellent tenor voice.*

EDGAR (*saluting*). We meet again.

MIRABELLE (*curtseying*). Yes, indeed.

EDGAR. It seems a sin that beauty so rare should be hidden for ever in this small country village.

MIRABELLE. Flatterer!

EDGAR. No, no, I mean it.

MIRABELLE. You are a sailor, sir, and I have been warned about sailors.

EDGAR. What have they told you?

MIRABELLE. That sailors are fickle, and that when they have loved a maid they sail away and leave her lonely.

EDGAR. Do you believe that?

MIRABELLE. I hardly know.

EDGAR. Dearest, dearest Mirabelle —my heart is at your feet.

MIRABELLE (*gaily*). Pick it up, sir, pick it up.

EDGAR. Ah, do not tease me. Look into my eyes—can you not see the lovelight shining there?

MIRABELLE. I know nothing of love.

EDGAR. Let me teach you.

MIRABELLE. I know nothing of life.

MIRABELLE WALTZ

LOVER OF MY DREAMS

SHE. *A simple country maid am I,*
As innocent as any flower.
The great big world has pass'd me by,
No lover comes my way to greet me shyly in my bower.

HE. *Oh, say not so!*
Such modesty enchants me:
Could I but stay to while away with you a happy hour.

SHE. *It must be Spring that fills my heart to overflowing,*
Ah, whither am I going?
What is the voice that seems to say:
Be kind to love, don't let him call to you unknowing.

HE. *If true love comes to you don't turn your face away.*

SHE. *Maybe 'tis something in the air;*
For Spring is made for lovers only.

HE. *Live for the moment and take care*
Lest love should fly and leave us lonely.

BOTH. *Ah, if love should leave us lonely.*

REFRAIN

SHE. *All my life I have been waiting*
Dreaming ages through;
Until today I suddenly discover
The form and face of he who is my lover.
No more tears and hesitating;
Fate has sent me you.
Time and tide can never sever
Those whom love has bound forever,
Dear lover of my Dreams come true.

HE. *All my life I have been waiting,*

SHE. *All my life I have been waiting,*

HE. *Dreaming ages through;*

SHE. *Dreaming ages through;*

HE. *Until today I suddenly discover*

SHE. *Until today I suddenly discover*

HE. *The form and face of she who is my lover.*

SHE. *The form and face of he who is my lover.*

HE. *No more tears and hesitating;*

SHE. *No more tears and hesitating;*

HE. *Fate has sent me you—Time and tide can never sever,*

SHE. *Fate has sent me you and tide can never sever*

HE. *Those whom love has bound for ever,*

SHE. *Those whom love has bound for ever,*

HE. *Dear lover of my Dreams come true,*

SHE. *Dear lover of my Dreams come true,*

BOTH. *Dear lover of my*
Dreams come true,
Dear lover of my Dreams come true,
Dear lover of my Dreams come true.

(*Enter* TOM JOLLY, *comedian. He is dressed as a common sailor.*)

(*Enter* ADA *with* TOM (*soubrette*). *She is dressed as a dairymaid.*)

TOM. If I make a noise like a cow —would you kiss me?

ADA (*laughing*). Perhaps.

TOM. Moo—moo. (*He tries to kiss her.*)

ADA. No, no! I'm frightened of bulls.

TOM. If I make a noise like a sheep —then?

ADA. Who knows!

TOM. Baa, baa, baa——

ADA. No, no—no good at all.

TOM. I'll sing, then. Sailing, sailing, over the bounding main!

ADA. I'll kiss you now. I love donkeys!

FUN OF THE FARM

VERSE

ADA. *Tho' sailors are so brave and bold,*
It really must be dreadfully cold
To sail across the sea.

TOM. *I quite agree,*
I quite agree,
I'm sick of the ocean wild and free,
Heigho, heigho, this is the place for me.

ADA. *Now I am weary of the town*
And feel inclined to settle down
A milk pail on my arm.

TOM. *I feel afraid,*
A London maid
Would never know how the eggs are laid.

ADA. *I'd find a cow*
And milk 'til the pail was full,

TOM. *I'd shear the sow*
And probably milk the bull.

BOTH. *You must agree*
That it would be
The height of true rusticity
If you and I should settle on on a farm.

REFRAIN

BOTH. *Oh, the Fun of the Farmyard,*
The roosters are crowing,
The cattle are lowing,
The turkeys go gobbly gobbly goo;
This really is an alarm yard.

ADA. *Like little Bo-Peep,*
I lose my sheep,
And cannot find them anywhere.

TOM. *I ought to be shot,*
For I forgot
To coax the horse to meet the mare.

BOTH. *Who left the canary*
Locked up in the dairy?

ADA. *Cheep, cheep, cheep, cheep,*

TOM. *Snort, snort, snort, snort,*

ADA. *Moo, moo, moo, moo,*

TOM. *Cock a doodle doodle do!*

BOTH. *Oh, dear, far from being a calm yard,*
Quack, quack, quack, quack,
All the fun of the farm.

TOM. Tell me something, Ada.

ADA. What?

TOM. You're no dairymaid, are you?

ADA. Mr. Inquisitive.

TOM. What are you?

ADA (*curtseying*). Lady's maid to the Princess Mirabelle.
(MIRABELLE *enters unobserved at the back.*)

TOM. The Princess! Then he'll win his bet, after all.

ADA. Who? What bet?

TOM. Lieutenant Edgar. All the officers of the ship wagered him that he would not win the hand of the Princess Mirabelle. He said he'd marry her if she was ugly as sin; he needs the money.
(EDGAR *enters.*)

EDGAR. What are you doing here, Tom?

TOM. Just farming! (*Laugh.*)

MIRABELLE. Stop!
(*Enter full* CHORUS.)

FINALE

CHORUS. *What is—what is the matter here?*

MIRABELLE. *Kind friends, you heard my call,*
And so I thank you all
For while you chatter here
My heart has been betrayed.

EDGAR. *Ah, no—not so.*
What foolish words you scatter here.
'Tis naught but your pride that's hurt
I am afraid.

CHORUS. *Who can he be,*
'Tis plain to see,
He seems to know her well.
Who is this man
Who dares offend
The Princess Mirabelle?

MIRABELLE. *You've lied to me and cheated me.*

ADA. *Madame, don't let him see*
Your poor heart breaking.

EDGAR. *Whate'er the future be,*
True love you are mistaking.

WALTZ REFRAIN FINALE

All my life I have been dreaming,
Now my dreams must die.

Within my heart I felt a song awaken,
And now I find a melody forsaken.
All your vows were base and scheming,
All our Love's a lie.
Cruelly you would deceive me,
All I say to you is . . .

(*Enter* STAGE MANAGER, *who raises his hand for silence.*)

STAGE MANAGER. Ladies and gentlemen—Mafeking has been relieved.

(JANE *in her box utters a cry of relief.*)

(*The players on the stage cheer wildly and the lights fade.*)

(*The cheering is heard through the darkness; when the lights come up the audience is discovered cheering, waving hats and handkerchiefs, and programmes are fluttering from the crowded balconies; some of the audience join hands and sing "Auld Lang Syne." The lights fade.*)

SCENE V

Principals

MRS. SNAPPER
COOK
ANNIE
ELLEN
BRIDGES
CABBY

SCENE—*The kitchen of a London house. It is a typical basement kitchen. There is a door at the back opening on to the area steps, also two windows. Another door communicating with the upper parts of the house, and a small door leading into the scullery.*

TIME—*About 5 p.m. Monday, January 21st, 1901.*

When the lights go up COOK *is making toast in front of the range.*

MRS. SNAPPER (ELLEN'S *Mother*) *is sitting on a chair beside a mail-cart in which reposes (mercifully invisible to the audience) the infant* FANNY.

ANNIE, *a scullery-maid, stands about with her mouth open, obviously in a state of considerable excitement, occasionally putting ineffective finishing touches to the table.*

COOK. 'Ere, Annie, 'old this fork a minute, or we'll have to call the Fire Brigade to put my face out. (ANNIE *takes the fork.* COOK *fans herself with her apron.*)

MRS. S. I once knew a woman whose front 'air caught fire when she was making toast, and before you could count ten the 'ole room was ablaze. They'd never 'ave been able to recognise her remains if it 'adn't been for 'er cameo brooch.

COOK. They must 'ave known who she was. (*Coming over to the mail-cart*) And 'ow's her ladyship—who's a lovely girl, eh? Don't burn that toast, Annie. (*She clicks her tongue at the infant* FANNY) Yer dad's comin' 'ome, ducks, safe and sound. (*She chants in order to entertain* FANNY) Safe and sound, safe and sound.

MRS. S. I only 'ope 'e is safe and sound, I'm sure.

COOK. The telegram said 'e was.

MRS. S. Maybe it was a lie to spare Ellen's feelings.

COOK. You're a cheerful one, I must say.

MRS. S. When I was a girl a friend of mine's 'usband come back unexpected from the Crimea with no legs at all.
(*This is too much for* ANNIE, *who drops the toast and goes off into snuffles of laughter.*)

COOK. Stop it, Annie—now look what you've done—cut another piece, quick, they'll be 'ere in a minute.

MRS. S. I do 'ope Ellen didn't cry at the station, it does make her nose so red.

COOK. Alfred will be so pleased to see 'er 'e won't mind if it's red or blue. Come on, Annie, 'urry.

ANNIE. 'Ere they are.

COOK. 'Ere, quick! The rosette for baby. (*She rushes to the dresser and snatches up a red, white and blue rosette*) You pin it on 'er, Mrs. Snapper, while I tidy me 'air.

ANNIE (*at window*). They've come in a cab. Oo-er!
(*There is a great air of tension and excitement in the kitchen, while* ELLEN'S *and* BRIDGES' *legs appear down the area steps. The* CABBY *follows with* BRIDGES' *kit-bag, which is dumped in the passage.* BRIDGES *enters first, looking very hale and hearty.*)

BRIDGES (*entering*). You settle the cab, Ellen, I want to see my love-a-duck. 'Allo, Cook—'allo, Ma—where's my girl? (*He kisses* COOK *and* MRS. SNAPPER, *and then puts his head inside the pram*) 'Allo, Fanny. Coo, 'aven't you grown. Ma, you 'aven't 'arf bin feedin' 'er up. (*He makes delighted gurgling noises and prods the baby with his finger*) See 'er laugh—she knows 'er dad. (*He puts his head inside again apparently kissing her heartily.* ELLEN *comes in flushed and happy.*)

ELLEN. I thought that train would never come—an whole hour I waited—an' all the people yellin' and screamin'. 'Ere, Alfred, take yer great 'ead out of that pram, you'll frighten 'er.

BRIDGES (*withdrawing*). She knows me, that's wot—she knows 'er old dad. Look at 'er rosette and all, smart as my eye. (*He turns and sees* ANNIE) 'Ere, who's this? We 'aven't 'ad the pleasure.

ELLEN. This is Annie.

BRIDGES. 'Ullo, Annie.

ANNIE (*giggling*). Welcome 'ome, Mr. Bridges. (ANNIE *and* BRIDGES *shake hands.*)

BRIDGES (*putting his arm round* MRS. SNAPPER). Well, Ma, 'ow's everything?

MRS. S. I mustn't grumble.

BRIDGES. So I should just think not. I got a surprise for you.

MRS. S. What is it?

BRIDGES. Ellen knows; I told 'er in the cab. Tell 'er, Ellen.

ELLEN. No, you. Go on.

BRIDGES. Well, you know I said in my letters about a lad called Smart —'Erbert Smart.

COOK. Yes. Ellen read your letters aloud.

BRIDGES. Not all of 'em, I 'ope.

ELLEN. Get on with you, you never let yourself go further than a P.S. and a couple of crosses.

BRIDGES. Well, 'Erbert Smart's got a pub, see, and he's staying out in Africa, and I've bought it from 'im cheap, see? So much a year until it's paid off. We always wanted to 'ave somewhere of our own, and you can come and live with us, Ma—'ow's that suit?

MRS. S. A pub—is it a respectable pub?

BRIDGES. All depends 'ow you behave, Ma, you know what you are when you've 'ad a couple.

MRS. S. (*sniggering*). Oh, Alfred, 'ow can you?

BRIDGES. Well, what d'you think about it?

MRS. S. It sounds lovely—but 'ow about them upstairs?

BRIDGES. That's all right. I took the master into me confidence. He wished me luck.

MRS. S. (*breaking down*). Oh, dear, I can 'ardly believe it, not 'aving to live alone any more—oh, dear!

BRIDGES. 'Ere, cheer up, Ma. Come on, 'ave a cup of tea. There ain't nothing to cry about. Let's all 'ave tea, for God's sake. Come on, Cook, me old girl—'ow'd you like to be a barmaid, eh?
(*They all sit down to tea, a grand tea with eggs and shrimps. Everybody is talking at once. Suddenly the cry of a* NEWSBOY *outside cuts through their conversation.*)

BRIDGES. What's 'e yelling about?

COOK (*giving* ANNIE *a halfpenny*). 'Ere, Annie, go and get one, quick. (ANNIE *runs out of the area steps. There is silence in the kitchen.*)

BRIDGES. What's up? What's the matter?

ELLEN. It isn't anything to concern us.

COOK. Ellen, 'ow can you—it concerns the whole country.
(ANNIE *comes clattering back with the paper.* BRIDGES *snatches paper from* ANNIE *and reads it.*)

BRIDGES (*reading*). Whew! The Queen—it says she's sinking!

MRS. S. There now—I told you so.

COOK (*taking paper*). Let's 'ave a look.

ANNIE. She's very old, ain't she?

COOK. Be quiet, Annie. What's that got to do with it?

ANNIE. Well, I never seen 'er.

BRIDGES. I 'ave—driving along Birdcage Walk once—years ago. Coo! England won't 'arf seem funny without the Queen!
(*The lights fade out.*)

SCENE VI

Principals

ROBERT
JANE
MARGARET
EDITH
EDWARD
JOE

SCENE—*Kensington Gardens. There is a row of high railings down stage so that the audience can see through them the trees and shrubs and seats and people and dogs.*
TIME—*About noon, Sunday, January 27th, 1901.*

During the course of this scene there should be no word spoken. Everyone is in black and they walk slowly as though perpetually conscious of the country's mourning. Even the children are in black and one WOMAN *leading a large brown dog has tied an enormous black crepe bow on to his collar.*

ROBERT *and* JANE *walk slowly from the left, followed by* EDWARD *and* JOE.

MARGARET HARRIS *and* EDITH *come from right.*

They all meet and carry on a subdued conversation for a moment centre, and then part and go their different ways as:

The lights fade on the scene.

SCENE VII

Principals

JANE
MARGARET
EDWARD
JOE
EDITH
ELLEN
BRIDGES
COOK
ANNIE

SCENE—*Drawing-room of a London House.*
TIME—*About noon, Saturday, February 2nd, 1901.*

When the lights go up, the children, EDWARD, JOE *and* EDITH, *all in black, are discovered out on the balcony.*

MARGARET *and* JANE *are seated on the sofa.*

There is a small table beside MARGARET *and* JANE *on which there is hot cocoa and cake.*

JOE (*on balcony*). Mum, mum, there's a policeman on a lovely white horse!

JANE. Don't jump about, darling, and get hot and excited. Edward, keep Joe as quiet as possible.

EDWARD. All right, mum.

JANE. More cocoa, Margaret?

MARGARET. No, thank you, dear.

JANE. I feel listless and sad, as though her death were a personal grief. Strange, isn't it?

MARGARET. I think everyone feels that. (*She rises and goes to the window*) All those crowds and crowds of people; they've been waiting for hours so patient and quiet. There's hardly a sound.

JOE (*running in*). Mum, could I ever be a policeman?

JANE. Perhaps, darling—if you're good.

JOE. Are all policemen good?

JANE. Yes, dear, as good as gold.

JOE. Why did Queen Victoria die, mum?

JANE. Because she was a very old lady, and very tired.

JOE. Could I have another piece of cake?

JANE. You won't be able to eat any luncheon.

JOE. I'd rather have the cake.

JANE (*smiling*). Very well, then—a small piece. Take some out to Edward and Edith.

JOE. Thanks, mum. (JOE *dashes out on to the balcony with the cake.*)

MARGARET. How proud you must feel, Jane. All your troubles are over—Robert's home, Jim's home. Robert has a V.C.

JANE. Jim ought to have a V.C. too. All those dreadful months.

EDWARD (*rushing in*). They're coming! They're coming! Quick—quick!

JANE (*rising*). Run and fetch Ellen and Bridges and Cook.
(EDWARD *tears out of the room.* JOE *rushes in.*)

JOE. Mum, please come out. I dropped a bit of cake. I couldn't help it—Edward pushed me.
(JANE *goes out and looks over. An unintelligible voice is heard below.*)

JANE (*leaning over*). I'm very sorry, it was an accident. (*The voice mumbles something*) He didn't throw it—he dropped it. It was an accident. (*She comes in again*) Did you throw it, Joe, on purpose? (JOE *hangs his head*) You're a very naughty little boy indeed, and I've a very good mind not to let you see the procession at all.
(EDITH *comes in. Following* EDITH *are* EDWARD, ELLEN, BRIDGES, COOK *and* ANNIE, *very smartened up.*)

EDWARD. Mum, will father be riding in the beginning part or the end part?

JANE. The beginning, I think. Cook, you'd better come out here, Annie, too. Ellen, look after them, will you? Bridges, oughtn't you to be wearing a coat, it's very cold?

BRIDGES. I'm all right, thank you, ma'am. Warm as toast.

EDWARD (*on balcony*). Here they come—quickly, mum!
(*Everybody crowds out on to the two balconies. There is dead silence and then far away the solemn music of the Dead March is heard. As it draws nearer the children jump about excitedly.*)

JOE (*suddenly*). Look, look—there's father—there's father!

JANE. Shhh! Joe, be quiet—keep still. (*The procession continues. Suddenly there is an outburst of cheering from the crowd which is instantly subdued*) That's Lord Roberts. He held up his hand to stop them cheering.

JOE. Is that Bobs, mum—is that Bobs?

EDWARD. Look, look—one-armed Giffard. Oh, mother, look——

JANE. Shhh! Now then, Joe, Edward, stand absolutely still—to attention, like father showed you.
(*The* BOYS *stand rigid with their hands to their sides.* BRIDGES *stands rigid with his hands to his side, on the other balcony. The music swells as the band passes directly underneath them. As it begins to die away* COOK *bursts into tears.*)

JANE. Five kings riding behind her.

JOE. Mum, she must have been a very little lady.
(*The lights fade.*)

SCENE VIII

Principals

ROBERT
JANE
DUCHESS OF CHURT
MAJOR DOMO

SCENE—*The Grand Staircase of a London house. The head of the staircase is down stage. The stairs descending downwards and out of sight. Behind the well of the staircase, can be seen between columns, the beautifully decorated ballroom in which an orchestra is playing the popular waltzes of the day and people are dancing. The Ball is in full swing.*
TIME—*About 11 p.m. Thursday, May 14th, 1903.*

When the lights go up, the full splendour of a typical Edwardian Ball should, if possible, burst upon the audience.

On the right and left of the staircase a balustraded balcony leads to the ballroom at the entrance of which FOOTMEN *stand with programmes to hand to the guests.*

The DUCHESS OF CHURT *stands near the head of the stairs.*

Near the DUCHESS OF CHURT *stands the* MAJOR DOMO, *who announces each guest in stentorian tones.*

There is a steady babel of conversation and music, but above it all can be heard the names of guests as they are announced. One by one, or sometimes escorted, come the great beauties of the day. They are all received by the DUCHESS *and then make their way towards the ballroom. Finally the* MAJOR DOMO *announces: "*SIR ROBERT *and* LADY MARRYOT*" and:*

ROBERT *and* JANE *appear,* ROBERT *with full decorations, and* JANE *in an elaborate ball gown. As they are received by their hostess:*

The lights fade and the curtain falls.

END OF PART I

PART TWO

SCENE I

Principals

JANE
EDWARD (aged 18)
ELLEN
FANNY (aged 7)
MRS. SNAPPER
GEORGE
FLO
BRIDGES

SCENE—*The Bar Parlour of a London pub.*
TIME—*About 5 p.m. Saturday, June 16th, 1906.*

When the curtain rises High Tea is just over. Seated round the table are JANE, EDWARD, MRS. SNAPPER, FLO *and* GEORGE GRAINGER. FLO *and* GEORGE *are very smartly got up.* ELLEN *is seated at the piano with her back to the room.* FANNY *(aged 7) is dancing. When the dance is finished everyone applauds.*

JANE. She dances beautifully, Ellen. Come here, dear. (FANNY *goes to her*) I knew you when you were a little tiny baby.

FLO. She's a born dancer, if you ask me—haighly talented, haighly.

ELLEN (*leaving the piano*). She certainly does love it. On the go all day she is, jigging about.

MRS. S. Can I press you to another cup, your ladyship?

JANE. No, thank you, we really must be going in a moment.

FLO (*to* EDWARD). 'Ow was Hoxford when you left it, Mr. Marryott?

EDWARD. Awfully nice.

FLO. I've never been there mayself, but George 'as, haven't you, George?

GEORGE. Oh, yes, nice place, Oxford. Very antique—if you know what I mean.

ELLEN. I'm so glad to 'ear the master, Sir Robert, is well.

JANE. He was so sorry not to be able to come down, but as you know, he's a very busy man these days. He wished very specially to be remembered to you and your husband. He'll be sorry to hear that he's ill.

GEORGE. Ill! Alf ill! What's wrong with him?
(MRS. SNAPPER *nudges* GEORGE *violently.* ELLEN *speaks hurriedly.*)

ELLEN. Before you and Flo come, George, I was explaining to 'er Ladyship about poor Alfred's bad leg.

GEORGE. Bad leg?

MRS. S. (*frowning at* GEORGE). Yes, very bad—'e's been in 'orrible agony since Sunday.

GEORGE. Where is 'e?

ELLEN. Upstairs in bed.

GEORGE. I'll pop up and see 'im.

ELLEN. He's asleep now.

FLO. 'Ow did 'e come to 'ave the haccident?

MRS. S. (*firmly and with great emphasis*). Cycling, Flo. He was cycling and 'e fell orf.

FLO. I didn't know 'e 'ad a cycle.

MRS. S. 'E 'asn't any more.

JANE (*rising*). Well, you will tell him how sorry we were not to have seen him, won't you? And I do hope he'll soon be quite well again. Come along, Edward. We really must go now.

EDWARD (*rising*). All right, Mother.

ELLEN. It was so kind of you, ma'am, to come all this way to see us and to bring Fanny that lovely doll, and everything. Fanny, come and say good-bye to 'er ladyship.
(FANNY *makes an abortive effort at a curtsey.* JANE *bends down and kisses* FANNY.)

JANE. Good-bye, Fanny. (*To* MRS. SNAPPER) Good-bye, Mrs. Snapper. (*She shakes hands*) Good-bye. (*She bows to* FLO *and* GEORGE.)

FLO. Pleased to 'ave made your acquaintance, I'm sure.

JANE (*to* ELLEN). Good-bye, Ellen, it's been delightful seeing you again, and to find you well and happy. Don't fail to remember me to Bridges; my husband and I miss you both still; it seems only yesterday that you were with us.

ELLEN. We miss you, too, ma'am.

JANE. Time changes many things, but it can't change old friends, can it?

ELLEN (*emotionally*). No, ma'am. Oh, no, ma'am.
(EDWARD, *who has been saying his good-bye to* MRS. SNAPPER *and* FLO *and* GEORGE, *joins* JANE.)

EDWARD. Good-bye, Ellen. Good luck.

ELLEN. Good-bye, Master Edward. Thank you for coming——
(JANE *and* EDWARD *are about to leave when the street door bursts open and* BRIDGES *staggers into the room. He looks unkempt and unshaven, and is obviously drunk. There is a moment of horrible silence.* BRIDGES *sees* JANE *and* EDWARD *and pulls up short.*)

ELLEN (*in agonised tones*). Oh, Alfred!

BRIDGES. Ow! So that's why you wash trying to get me out of the way——

MRS. S. Alfred Bridges, be'ave yourself and take yer 'at orf.

BRIDGES (*bowing low to* JANE). Pleashed to see you again, milady, I'm shure—welcome to our 'ovel. (*He lurches toward* JANE. JANE *makes an instinctive movement away from* BRIDGES. BRIDGES *draws himself up unsteadily*) Ow! I shee proud and 'aughty, are we——

ELLEN (*wildly*). Alfred, stop it! Stop it!

JANE (*suddenly coming forward and taking both* ELLEN'S *hands in hers*). Ellen—dear Ellen—I'm so very, very, sorry, and I quite understand. Please don't be upset and let me come and see you again soon. (JANE *goes out with* EDWARD. *Again there is silence.* ELLEN *bursts into hopeless sobbing.*)

MRS. S. You drunken great brute!

BRIDGES. Shut yer mouth. You mind yours and I'll mind mine.

GEORGE. Look 'ere, 'ole man, you'd better come up and 'ave a lie down. (*He takes* BRIDGES' *arm.*)

BRIDGES (*pushing* GEORGE *away*). Leave me alone. Lot of shnobs—that's wot—lot of bloody shnobs. I'm not good enough to be 'ome when the quality comes. Ow, no—we'll see who'sh good enough.

ELLEN (*wailing*). Oh, oh, oh! I'll never be able to raise me 'ead again—never—never——

BRIDGES. 'Oo give Fanny that doll? 'Er noble ladyship?

MRS. S. (*stepping forward*). You let the child alone.

BRIDGES (*pushing* MRS. SNAPPER *so hard that she falls against the table*). I can buy me own child a doll, can't I? Don't want any bloody charity 'ere. (*He snatches the doll from* FANNY *and pitches it into the fire.* FANNY *screams.* FLO *makes a dart at the fireplace and finally gets the doll out.* FANNY *continues to scream.* ELLEN *goes for* BRIDGES. BRIDGES *hits* ELLEN. FLO *and* GEORGE *grab* BRIDGES *and push him out of the room.* ELLEN, *sobbing, takes* FANNY *in her arms.* MRS. SNAPPER *sinks into a chair.*)

ELLEN. She was right—she was right. Time changes many things—(*The lights fade.*)

SCENE II

Principals

FANNY
FLO

SCENE—*A London street. The exterior of the public house—the bar parlour of which was the preceding scene—is down stage left. There is a street leading away into darkness up left, and another turning a corner up right. A wedge of houses separates the two streets. There are people at most of the windows of the houses. Down stage right are more houses.*
TIME—*About 10 p. m. Saturday, June 16th, 1906.*

The centre of the stage is crowded with people and barrows lit by naphtha flares. There is another pub up right from which comes the sound of a penny-in-the-slot piano and the sound of singing and laughter. Everyone is moving about and talking. Women with caps and shawls and string bags are shopping at the booths. Some sailors come out of the left pub with two flashily dressed girls and roll across to the pub opposite, into which they disappear. A policeman walks through the crowd and goes off. A German band assembles down stage left and begins to play, effectively drowning the noise of three Coster youths playing mouth-organs. A few Costers in pearlies start dancing, a ring is made round them, and people applaud and yell from the windows. A Salvation Army Band marches on right and proceeds to play and sing hymns, against the German band. A few people make a ring round them and begin singing.

FANNY *comes out of the pub left and begins to dance by herself.*

Some of the crowd laugh and those who are dancing stop and applaud her. A Coster darts forward and puts his pearly cap on FANNY'S *head.*

BRIDGES *comes reeling out of the pub—sees* FANNY, *and tries to grab hold of her. He is prevented by the crowd and*

BRIDGES *is pushed off the stage up right.*

Suddenly from just where BRIDGES *has gone there comes a shout and then an agonising scream. The policeman runs across in the direction of the noise. All the crowd, scenting a street accident, surge off, including the German band.*

Exeunt crowd and German band.

FLO *comes flying out of the pub and*

FLO *disappears with the crowd.*

FANNY *continues to dance in pool of light shed by a street lamp, to the rather dismal music of the Salvation Army.*

FLO *comes rushing back and hammers on the door of the pub.*

FLO. Ellen! Ellen! It's Alfred—'e's been run over—'e's dead. Ellen! Ellen! (*The lights fade.*)

SCENE III

Principals

EDWARD (aged 21)
JOE (aged 17)
TIM BATEMAN
DOUGLAS FINN
LORD MARTLET (Chubby)
MARION CHRISTIE
NETTA LAKE (pianist)
ROSE DARLING (Ada in "Mirabelle")
CONNIE CRAWSHAY
DAISY DEVON

SCENE—*Private room in a popular London restaurant. A supper table set for ten is on one side of the stage. There is a sofa up at the back and another down stage right, and an upright piano.*
TIME—*About 1 a.m. Wednesday, March 10th, 1909.*

Round the table are seated EDWARD *(twenty-one),* TIM BATEMAN, DOUGLAS FINN, MARION CHRISTIE, NETTA LAKE, *and* ROSE DARLING.

On the sofa up stage in a more or less amorous attitude are seated LORD MARTLET (Chubby) *and* DAISY DEVON.

On the down stage sofa is seated JOE *(aged seventeen) with* CONNIE CRAWSHAY, *a very fat blonde.*

Everyone is very gay. They are all in evening dress. The men in white ties and the women elaborately and slightly theatrically fashionable.

JOE *is obviously the youngest present and appears well on the way to being very drunk.*

ROSE (*rising, with a glass of champagne in her hand*). I want to propose a toast—to our host!

EVERYONE. Hear, hear! (*Etc.*)

MARION. A lovely little toastie to our lovely little hostie.

ROSE. Health, wealth and happiness to our Eddie!

EVERYONE (*repeating*). Health, wealth and happiness! Eddie! (*Etc. They clink glasses.*)

CONNIE (*to* JOE). Here, sit up. They're drinking your brother's health.

JOE (*rising unsteadily*). Hear, hear—a thousand times hear, hear!
(*They all sing "For he's a jolly good fellow," which tails off into cries for "speech."*)

EDWARD (*rising*). Ladies and gentlemen——

JOE (*loudly*). Hurray!

EDWARD. Shut up, Joe.

JOE. I won't shut up. Connie agrees with me, don't you, Connie?

CONNIE. Yes, dear, completely, dear. Shut up, dear.

JOE. Good old Connie. (*He subsides on* CONNIE's *lap.*)

EDWARD (*continuing*). First of all, in response to your charming toast, I want to apologise for the presence here tonight of my scrubby little brother Joe.
(*Laughter.*)

JOE. Here—I say!
CONNIE *puts her hand over* JOE's *mouth.*)

EDWARD. He is a crawling, loathsome little creature, as you see, and he really ought not to be here at all, but in his little cot at Eton. I felt, however, that as his elder brother, it was my duty to show him how grown-up people behave. Bring him over here, Connie—he must be christened in Clicquot.

CONNIE. He's almost confirmed in it already. (CONNIE *drags* JOE *over to the table where, protesting loudly, he is anointed by* EDWARD *with champagne.*)

JOE. I must speak now. I want to speak.

CONNIE. Let him speak, dear, he's having a lovely time.

JOE. Ladies and gentlemen—I have always looked up to my elder brother Edward. He has always been my ideal of what a great big gas-bag should be, and I take this opportunity of asking Connie to marry me.
(*Laughter.*)

CONNIE. Oh, isn't he sweet!

ROSE. You can't have Connie, Joe, she's married already; you'd better choose me. I'm a widow.
(*Everybody chants "The Merry Widow" waltz for a moment.*)

JOE. But I love Connie.

CONNIE. Very well, dear, come back to the sofa, dear. (*She leads* JOE *back.*)

EDWARD (*to* LORD MARTLET). Chubby, come out of that corner, you've been there long enough.

DAISY (*coming down*). Quite long enough. This takes me back to the old days of private hansoms. (*She fans herself*) Give me a drink, somebody.

MARION (*gloomily*). I was once sick in a private hansom.

ROSE. That must have been lovely, dear; tell us about it.

MARION. Well, it was the two hundredth performance of "Florodora."

ROSE. By God, she's going to!

MARION. And they suddenly put me in the sextette without a rehearsal, and I suppose the excitement went to my stomach.

ROSE. I was in "Mirabelle" then, with poor old Laura Marsden.

EDWARD. "Mirabelle"! I was taken to see that. Mother was there on Mafeking night. She took me a few weeks later to a matinée.

MARION. *Taken* to see it, were you! That dates us a bit.

EDWARD. I remember now. You were Ada——

ROSE. Yes, I was Ada.

MARION. And Laura Marsden was Mirabelle, and Mikey Banks was Tom. What a cast that was!

TIM. What happened to Laura Marsden?

ROSE. She died. (*She makes a significant drinking gesture.*)

TIM. Oh, I see.

ROSE. Nine years ago. Give me another drink, or I shall get reminiscent like Marion. (NETTA *goes over to the piano and starts thumping the Mirabelle waltz*) Oh, shut up!

EDWARD. Sing it, Rose.

ROSE. I can't—haven't got any voice.

EVERYONE. Come on, Rose—sing it. Come on, you're among friends.

ROSE. I can't sing it like Laura used to. (*She sings the refrain of the waltz, occasionally forgetting a word or two. Everybody applauds.*)

MARION. They do take you back, don't they, those old tunes.
(NETTA *strikes up "Keep off the Grass." The girls sing it together. None of the men are really old enough to remember it.*)

CHUBBY. Play something we all know.
(NETTA *starts "Mary" from "Miss Gibbs." Everyone joins in. They all go into "The Merry Widow" waltz and sing it lustily as the lights fade.*)

SCENE IV

Principals

JANE
ROBERT
JOE
MARGARET
ELLEN
FANNY
MRS. SNAPPER
FLO
GEORGE
1ST WOMAN
2ND WOMAN
UNCLE GEORGE
UNCLE DICK

SCENE—*The beach of a popular seaside resort.*
TIME—*About 6 p.m. Monday, July 25th, 1910.*

The Parade runs along the back about 10 feet above stage level. Down stage left a bandstand on the same level as the Parade juts out on to the beach. On the right the high supports of a swimming enclosure.

There are bathing machines and huts and deck chairs—in fact, all the paraphernalia of a popular seaside town in July.

The beach is crowded with people, some paddling, some playing games, and a lot clustered round an open-air stage, listening to UNCLE GEORGE'S *concert party.*

The Concert Party consists of six men: UNCLE DICK, UNCLE BOB, UNCLE HARRY, UNCLE JIM, UNCLE JACK *and* UNCLE GEORGE *himself. They are all dressed in straw hats, coloured blazers and rather grubby white flannel trousers.*

People are constantly passing to and fro along the Parade, and leaning on the railing, looking down on to the beach.

When the curtain rises UNCLE GEORGE *is singing "Put a little bit away for a rainy day." He finishes with a great flourish, then steps forward.*

UNCLE GEORGE. Ladies and gentlemen and kiddies—I am very happy to announce that the winner of this week's Song and Dance Competition is little Miss Fanny Bridges. (*Everyone applauds*) And it gives me great pleasure to present her with this handsome prize as a souvenir of Uncle George and his merry men. Come on up, my dear. (ELLEN (*in black*) *hoists* FANNY *up from the front row.* FANNY *is hoisted up by* ELLEN. *She is wearing a white dress with a black sash.* UNCLE GEORGE *kisses* FANNY *and presents her with a box of chocolates. The audience clap and one little girl is led away yelling, apparently an unsuccessful competitor.*)

UNCLE GEORGE. And now, to conclude this programme Uncle Dick will sing "Take me back to Yorkshire."

(UNCLE DICK *rises and sings. All the rest join in the chorus, and then, after perfunctory applause, the crowd round the booth disperses.* UNCLE GEORGE *and his* MERRY MEN *pack up their props and disappear in due course up the steps on to the Parade. Exeunt* UNCLE GEORGE *and his* MERRY MEN. ELLEN *and* FANNY *walk across the beach with* MRS. SNAPPER, FLO *and* GEORGE. *They meet* MARGARET HARRIS, JANE *and* JOE.

JANE. Why, it can't be—Ellen—what a surprise!

(*They shake hands.*)

ELLEN. Oh, Ma'am—I'd no idea—fancy you being here!

JANE. Margaret, Joe, you remember Ellen, don't you?

MARGARET (*shaking hands*). Of course! yes—how do you do, Ellen?

JOE. Hullo, Ellen.

ELLEN. You remember mother—Mrs. Snapper—and Flo and George, my cousins by marriage?

JANE. Yes, indeed.

MRS. S. Delighted, I'm sure.

(*Everyone shakes hands and talks politely.*)

ELLEN. Well, Master Joe, 'ow you 'ave grown. Quite the young man about town! How's Master Edward?

JOE. He's here. He and Edith have been to a concert on the pier. They'll be along soon.

ELLEN (*to* JANE). I got your letter, ma'am, when my Alfred died; it was kind of you to write.

JANE. How is your business going?

ELLEN. Oh, very well, really. I've managed to save quite a bit one way and another, and now I've closed the 'ole place for a month so as to give Fanny a holiday. She goes to dancing school now. She's going on the stage.

MARGARET. Surely she's very young.

MRS. S. She's set on it—plain set on it.

(ROBERT *comes down on to the beach. He has grey hair now and looks very distinguished.*)

ROBERT. Jane—there you are—Why, Ellen! (*He shakes hands. All the introductions start all over again. Two elderly women pass in front of them, talking.*)

1ST WOMAN. She went on board the ship dressed as a boy, and that's how the Captain recognised them.

2ND WOMAN. 'Er 'air probably come down under 'er cap.

1ST WOMAN. I don't know 'ow she managed at meals. She couldn't wear 'er cap then.

2ND WOMAN. It's Mrs. Crippen that gets on my mind, poor dear, being all chopped up into little tiny pieces— (*They pass on and up the steps. Meanwhile the* MARRYOTS *and* ELLEN *are parting company.*)

ELLEN. It's been lovely seeing you again, ma'am, and you, too, Mrs. Harris. I expect your Edith has grown into a great big girl by now. I remember her when she was ever so small. (*To* ROBERT) Good-bye, sir—good-bye, Master Joe.

ROBERT. Good-bye, Ellen.

JOE. Good-bye.

JANE. You must come and see us one day—bring Fanny to tea.

ELLEN. Thank you, ma'am—I'd like to see the 'ouse again. I was very 'appy there——

(*The* MARRYOTS *and* MARGARET *go off.* MRS. SNAPPER, ELLEN *and* FANNY *rejoin* FLO *and* GEORGE, *who have been standing waiting for them a little way off. The Band, having assembled, breaks into a gay march. A man walks along with a tray of pink rock, yelling. All dialogue is drowned in the noise of the band. Several children dodge in and out, playing Tag. One child falls down and screams. Suddenly there is the noise of an aeroplane. Everyone screams and surges down to the beach, staring upwards. The band stops abruptly and cranes out of the bandstand. People half dressed rush out of bathing machines. Somebody starts cheering—then everyone takes it up. The aeroplane noise grows fainter. The Band strikes up again. A troop of Boy Scouts with a very sour six-piece band march along the Parade. Suddenly there is a roll of thunder. Everyone looks up apprehensively, people on the beach begin to collect their children and belongings. It starts to rain, gently at first, then develops into a downpour. People put their coat collars up and run. Several umbrellas go up, then more, until the whole beach becomes a sea of umbrellas. Gradually everyone scurries off. The bandstand has by now let down its weather blinds. One fat old woman is left asleep in a deck chair. A tremendous roll of thunder wakes her abruptly and she struggles to get up, and falls back into the chair, which collapses.*)

SCENE V

Principals

EDWARD
EDITH

SCENE—*The deck of an Atlantic liner. This is quite a small inset scene. The rail of the Promenade Deck faces the audience. Behind it can be seen the lighted windows of the lounge. Above can be seen vaguely the Boat Deck, with ventilators and a funnel silhouetted against the stars.*
TIME—*About 7 p.m. Sunday, April 14th, 1912.*

EDWARD *and* EDITH, *he in dinner-jacket, she in evening dress, are leaning on the rail.*

EDITH. It's too big, the Atlantic, isn't it?

EDWARD. Far too big.

EDITH. And too deep.

EDWARD. Much, much too deep.

EDITH. I don't care a bit, do you?

EDWARD. Not a scrap.

EDITH. Wouldn't it be awful if a magician came to us and said: "Unless you count accurately every single fish in the Atlantic you die tonight?"

EDWARD. We should die tonight.

EDITH. How much would you mind—dying, I mean?

EDWARD. I don't know really—a good deal, I expect.

EDITH. I don't believe I should mind so very much now. You see, we could never in our whole lives be happier than we are now, could we?

EDWARD. Darling, there *are* different sorts of happiness.

EDITH. This is the best sort.

EDWARD (*kissing her*). Sweetheart!

EDITH. Don't darling, we don't want any more of the stewards to know we're on our honeymoon.

EDWARD. Why not? It gives them so much vicarious pleasure. Most of them have forgotten what it was like.

EDITH. Are all honeymoons like this?

EDWARD (*firmly*). Exactly.

EDITH. Oh, Edward—that's rather disheartening, isn't it? I do so want this to be unique.

EDWARD. It is, for us.

EDITH. Did you ever think when we were children, going to the pantomime, and going to the Zoo, and playing soldiers, that we should ever be married?

EDWARD. Of course I didn't.

EDITH. Was I nice as a child?

EDWARD. Horrible!

EDITH. So were you, and so was Joe—vile. You always used to take sides against me.

EDWARD. And yet we all liked one another really.

EDITH. I think I liked Joe better than you, but then he was younger and easier to manage. Dear Joe, he was awfully funny at the wedding, wasn't he?

EDWARD. Ribald little beast!

EDITH. He has no reverence, I'm afraid.

EDWARD. Absolutely none.

EDITH. He's passing gallantly through the chorus-girl phase now, isn't he?

EDWARD. Gallantly but not quickly.

EDITH. Well, darling, you took your time over it.

EDWARD. Now then, Edith——

EDITH. You had several affairs before you married me, didn't you?

EDWARD. Light of my life, shut up!

EDITH. You'd be awfully cross if *I* had, wouldn't you?

EDWARD. Had what?

EDITH. Affairs—love affairs—before you.

EDWARD. Did you?

EDITH. Hundreds.

EDWARD. Liar!

EDITH. I rather wish I had, really. Perhaps I should have learnt some tricks to hold you with when you begin to get tired of me.

EDWARD. I never shall, tricks or no tricks.

EDITH. Yes, you will one day. You're bound to; people always do. This complete loveliness that we feel together now will fade, so many years and the gilt wears off the gingerbread, and just the same as the stewards, we shall have forgotten what it was like.

EDWARD (*seriously*). Answer me one thing, truly, dearest. Have you ever seen gingerbread with gilt on it?

EDITH. Never!

EDWARD. Then the whole argument is disposed of. Anyhow, look at father and mother; they're perfectly happy and devoted, and they always have been.

EDITH. They had a better chance at the beginning. Things weren't changing so swiftly; life wasn't so restless.

EDWARD. How long do you give us?

EDITH. I don't know—and Edward —(*she turns to him*) I don't care. This is our moment—complete and heavenly. I'm not afraid of anything. This is our own, for ever. (EDWARD *takes* EDITH *in his arms and kisses her.*)

EDWARD. Do you think a nice warming glass of sherry would make it any more heavenly?

EDITH. You have no soul, darling, but I'm very attached to you. Come on——

(EDITH *takes up her cloak which has been hanging over the rail, and they walk away. The cloak has been covering a life-belt, and when it is withdrawn the words "S. S. Titanic" can be seen in black letters on the white. The lights fade into complete darkness, but the letters remain glowing as The orchestra plays very softly and tragically "Nearer My God to Thee."*)

SCENE VI

Principals

JANE
ROBERT
JOE
MARGARET

SCENE—*The drawing-room of a London house. The room is dark; the blinds are down over the windows.*
TIME—*About 11.16 p.m. Tuesday, August 4th, 1914.*

There is the sound of voices outside.
Enter JANE *and* MARGARET, *both in travelling clothes.*
JANE *turns on the lights and the room is seen to be enshrouded in dust-sheets.*

JANE (*shuddering*). Why is it that a house that's been shut up for a little while feels so awful? (*She goes to the windows, pulls up the blinds, and opens the windows wide*) There! That's better. It's stifling.

MARGARET (*taking off her hat and coat*). That was definitely the most uncomfortable journey I've ever experienced.
(JOE *rushes in. He still has his hat and coat on.*)

JOE. Mum, have you got any change? Father and I have both run out.

MARGARET. I have — here — (*she fumbles in her bag*). How much d'you want?

JOE. Four bob.

MARGARET. There's half-a-crown and two shillings.

JOE. Thanks, Aunt Margaret. (JOE *goes out again.*)

JANE. Help me with these dust-sheets, Margaret. Put them anywhere. We'll get a char in to-morrow to clean up. (*They proceed to pull the dust-sheets off the furniture*) I shall never go on a holiday again, ever. It's horrid when you're there, and much worse when you come back.

MARGARET. It's better to be here in London if anything's going to happen.

JANE. It's going to happen all right. I'm afraid there's no doubt about it, now.

MARGARET (*glancing out of the window*). There seem to be lots more people in the streets than usual—where on earth do they all come from?
(JOE *comes in, this time without his hat and coat.*)

JOE. Well, that's that!

JANE. Where's father?

JOE. Groping about in the wine cellar like an angry old beetle. He says strong drink is essential in a crisis.

JANE. We must have something to eat, too. I wonder if there is anything.

JOE. There's a strong bit of cold tongue in the larder. I just put my head in and it sang the Marseillaise.

JANE. There must be some biscuits, or something. (JANE *goes out hurriedly.*)

JOE (*to* MARGARET). Cigarette? (*He offers her his case.*)

MARGARET (*taking one*). Thank you, Joe.

JOE (*lighting them*). This is pretty thrilling, isn't it?

MARGARET. Yes, I suppose so. I must really go and help Jane. (MARGARET *runs out, almost colliding with* ROBERT, *who is entering with two bottles and some glasses.*)

ROBERT. I could only find hock and port, and port's far too heavy at this time of night; so we'll have to drink to the downfall of Germany in their own damned wine.

JOE. I rather like Germans, don't you, Father?

ROBERT. Enormously. Move these things off the table, and help me open the bottles.

JOE (*doing so*). Got a corkscrew?

ROBERT. In my left pocket.
(JOE *gropes for the corkscrew while* ROBERT *puts the bottles and glasses on the table.*)

JOE (*wrestling with a bottle*). If there is a war, how long do you think it will last?

ROBERT. Three months, at the outside.

JOE. I suppose we shall win, shan't we?

ROBERT. Yes—we shall win.

JOE (*hopefully*). Maybe it will last six months.

ROBERT. Leaving everything else aside, that would be economically quite impossible. Have you any idea of what a war costs, Joe, in actual money?

JOE. Hell of a lot, I should think.

ROBERT. You're quite right. And the Germans can afford it even less than we can. And then there's Russia.

JOE. Good old Russia!

ROBERT. And France and Italy and America.

JOE. And Japan and China and Finland—why, by God! we've got 'em licked before we start.

ROBERT. Don't be silly, Joe.

JOE. Are you glad you left the Army, Father, or sorry?

ROBERT. Absolutely delighted.

JOE. Will you go back again?

ROBERT. I expect so.

JOE. How will you feel about that?

ROBERT. Absolutely delighted.

JOE. I suppose I shall have to do something about it, too.

ROBERT. Do you want to?

JOE. Terribly.

ROBERT. Why?

JOE. I don't know. It's—it's sort of exciting, isn't it?

ROBERT. Yes, but don't set your hopes too high, Joey—it takes a lot of training to make a soldier. It will all be over before you get far.

JOE. I wish Edward hadn't been drowned, we could have started off together.

ROBERT (*after a slight pause*). Don't be too impulsive and patriotic and dashing, Joey. Think of your Mother. Think of me, too, you're all we've got left. (ROBERT *abruptly puts down the bottle he is holding and goes out on to balcony.* JOE *stands staring after him thoughtfully.* JANE *enters carrying a tray.* MARGARET *enters following* JANE, *with some plates.*)

JANE. We found some potted meat and biscuits and Worcester Sauce; and the tongue doesn't look too bad.

JOE (*taking the tray from* JANE). It isn't its looks I object to, it's its personality. (JOE *puts the tray on the table. A newsboy runs by outside shouting.* ROBERT *shouts from the balcony and goes hurriedly from the room.* JOE, JANE *and* MARGARET *stand stock still, waiting.* ROBERT *returns with the paper.*)

ROBERT. We're at war, my dears.

JOE (*grabbing the paper*). Let me see—let me see——

MARGARET. Listen—listen!
(*From far away comes the sound of cheering.* MARGARET *runs out on the balcony for a moment, and then returns.* JANE *sinks down on a chair.*)

JANE. It's very hot, isn't it?

JOE. Don't look sad, mum. It won't last long; Father says it can't possibly; and it's terribly exciting.

JANE. I didn't mean to look sad; I feel rather tired.

JOE (*handing* JANE *a glass of wine*). Here, mum dear—have a nice sozzle. We ought all to get drunk really, and go roaring about the streets——

JANE. Edward missed this, anyhow. At least he died when he was happy, before the world broke over his head.

ROBERT. Don't take that view, dearest, it's foolish. We've had wars before without the world breaking.

JANE. My world isn't very big.
(*A group of people pass along under the balcony laughing and cheering. Some of them start singing the Marseillaise and the others*

down them with Rule Britannia. JANE *gets up suddenly.*)

JANE. Drink to the war, then, if you want to. I'm not going to. I can't! Rule Britannia! Send us victorious, happy and glorious! Drink, Joey, you're only a baby, still, but you're old enough for war. Drink like the Germans are drinking, to Victory and Defeat, and stupid, tragic sorrow. But leave me out of it, please! (JANE *goes abruptly from the room. The lights fade.*)

SCENE VII

Above the proscenium 1914 glows in lights. It changes to 1915-1916, 1917 and 1918. Meanwhile, soldiers march uphill endlessly. Out of darkness into darkness. Sometimes they sing gay songs, sometimes they whistle, sometimes they march silently, but the sound of their tramping feet is unceasing. Below the vision of them brightly dressed, energetic women appear in pools of light, singing stirring recruiting songs—"Sunday I walk out with a soldier," "We don't want to lose you," etc., etc. With 1918 they fade away, as also does the vision of the soldiers, although the soldiers can still be heard very far off, marching and singing their songs.

SCENE VIII

Principals

JOE
FANNY

SCENE—*A restaurant.*
TIME—*About 7.30 p.m. Tuesday, October 22nd, 1918.*

JOE *and* FANNY *are seated at a table; they have just finished dinner.* JOE *is in officer's uniform.*

FANNY *is in very charming day clothes. She is now nineteen and extremely attractive.*

JOE (*pouring some champagne into* FANNY'S *glass*). Have some more.

FANNY. Darling, I shall be tight. You don't want me to fall down during my first number, do you?

JOE. How much do you love me?

FANNY. Now, then, dear, we've had all this out before.

JOE. Will you send me a telegram to Dover?

FANNY. Of course I will. I promised, didn't I?

JOE. Once you get into the theatre, with all those changes, you might forget.

FANNY. I'll send Maggie out with it.

JOE. Dear old Maggie. Say good-bye to her for me, won't you?

FANNY. Aren't you coming down to talk to me while I make up?

JOE. No, I promised to go home. Mother's waiting for me.

FANNY. I shall have to give it to you now, then.

JOE. What?

FANNY. Just a little something I had made for you.

JOE. Oh, Fanny—what is it?

FANNY. Hold on a minute, dear. It's in my bag. (*She searches in her bag and produces a small packet*) Here—with my love.

JOE (*opening it*). Oh, it's lovely.

FANNY. It's nothing really. Just a little souvenir of all the fun we've had.

JOE. You are a darling!

FANNY (*grabbing it from* JOE). Here, silly, you've missed the whole point. It opens—there.
(FANNY *opens the little locket and discloses a minute photograph of herself.*)

JOE (*taking it*). It will be with me always, to the end of my days.

FANNY. You won't want it that long.

JOE. I almost wish I didn't love you quite so awfully. It makes going back much worse.

FANNY. I shall miss you dreadfully.

JOE. It has been fun, hasn't it?

FANNY. Lovely.

JOE. You don't regret it—any of it?

FANNY. Not a moment of it.

JOE. How wonderful you are. Do you really love me, I wonder, deep down inside, I mean?

FANNY. Yes, I think so.

JOE. Enough to marry me?

FANNY. Yes, but I wouldn't.

JOE. Why not?

FANNY. It would be too difficult. We shouldn't be happy married. Your Mother wouldn't like it.

JOE. She'd be all right.

FANNY. Don't let's talk about it now. Let's wait until you come back.

JOE. Very well.
(*There is silence for a moment.* FANNY *puts her hand on* JOE'*s across the table.*)

FANNY. Listen, dear. I love you and you love me, and I've got to go now or I shall be late; and you've got to go, too, but I'm not going to say good-bye. We've had fun, grand fun, and I don't want you to forget me, that's why I gave you the locket. Please keep it close to you, Joey—darling Joey.
(FANNY *goes as the lights fade.*)

SCENE IX

Principals

JANE
JOE

SCENE—*A railway station. The station is foggy and very dimly lit on account of air raids. The ticket barrier can be vaguely discerned and beyond it, the back of a train. Just above the barrier a lamp shines downwards partially illuminating a recruiting poster. On the right is an empty platform, but there are people moving about on it, and several Red Cross orderlies and nurses. There is a crowd of people, mostly women, clustered around the left barrier—occasionally a door in the train opens and a shaft of light falls on to the platform.*
TIME—*About 11 p.m. Tuesday, October 22nd, 1918.*

A crowd of soldiers comes on from the left, wearing full equipment. They are greeted by some of the women. Presently a Sergeant enters, and after their good-byes have been said, the Sergeant gets them in line and marches them through on to the platform, where they can be seen getting into the train.

JANE *and* JOE *come on from the left.*

JOE (*breathlessly*). Whew: I thought we were going to miss it, didn't you, mum?

JANE. Yes.

JOE. Not much time for long good-byes, darling.

JANE. I know. I'm glad, really—aren't you?

JOE. Yes. I never know what to say.

JANE. I'm almost hardened to it by now. This has happened so often.

JOE. Dearest mum, you are marvellous. You never make a fuss.

JANE. Don't be too sweet to me, Joey, I don't want to disgrace you, to behave badly.

JOE. You couldn't behave badly.

JANE. How funny! Do you know that Robert said that to me years and years ago. I must be very dull and unimaginative to be so reserved. It was the Boer War, then. This is very, very different. (*A whistle blows.* JOE *takes* JANE *in his arms.*)

JOE. Good-bye, darling.

JANE. Good-bye, darling—take care of yourself.

(JOE *rushes through the barrier and jumps into the train just as it starts to move.* JANE *stands under the lamp looking after him. Two or three of the women at the barrier burst into loud sobbing, some soldiers in the train start singing. A big steaming locomotive comes slowly to a standstill at the right hand platform. Almost immediately Red Cross Orderlies begin to walk off the platform carrying wounded men on stretchers.* JANE *stands watching them; her face is quite expressionless. Then with a trembling hand she takes a cigarette out of her bag and lights it. The lights fade.*)

SCENE X

Principals

JANE
ELLEN
GLADYS (A parlourmaid)

SCENE—*The drawing-room of a London house. The decoration of the room has changed slightly with the years, but not to any marked extent. It looks very much the same as it has always looked.*
TIME—*About 11 a.m. Monday, November 11th, 1918.*

As the lights go up on the scene, a PARLOURMAID *shows* ELLEN *into the room.* ELLEN *has certainly changed with the years. She is very well dressed, almost smart.*

GLADYS. Her Ladyship will be down in a moment, madam.

ELLEN. Thanks.
(GLADYS *goes out.* ELLEN *wanders about the room. There is a photograph of* EDWARD *on the table, and also one of* JOE. *She looks at them both and sighs.* JANE *enters. She is dressed in street clothes.*)

JANE. Ellen! Gladys said Mrs. Bridges, but I couldn't believe it was you.

ELLEN. I just thought I'd call. It's rather important, as a matter of fact.

JANE. Do sit down. I'm delighted to see you again.

ELLEN. Thanks. (*She sits down.*)

JANE. How's Fanny?

ELLEN. Oh, very well. She's in "Over the Moon," now, you know.

JANE. Yes. I went the other night. She was splendid, I felt very proud to know her.

ELLEN. It's about her I've come to see you, really.

JANE. Oh! Well?

ELLEN. It's—it's—er—rather difficult.

JANE. What is it? What on earth is the matter?

ELLEN. About her and Master—her and Joe.

JANE. Joe?

ELLEN. Yes. They've been—well—er—to put it frankly, if you know what I mean, they've been having an affair.

JANE. My Joe?

ELLEN. Yes—your Joe. His last two leaves he spent a lot of time with Fanny.

JANE (*slowly*). Oh, I see.

ELLEN. I wouldn't have come to see you about it at all, only I think Fanny's very upset about it, and now that the war's over—or almost over, that is—and he'll be coming home—I thought——

JANE (*coldly*). What did you think?

ELLEN. Well, I thought they ought to get married.

JANE. Does Fanny want to marry him?

ELLEN. No—er—not exactly. That is—I haven't talked about it to her. She doesn't know I know.

JANE. How do you know?

ELLEN. I found a letter from him——

JANE. And you read it?

ELLEN. Yes—it's here. I've brought it with me. (*She fumbles in her bag.*)

JANE. I don't wish to see it, thank you.

ELLEN. I only brought it because——

JANE (*cutting* ELLEN *short*). Is Fanny in any sort of trouble?

ELLEN. Oh, no. Nothing like that.

JANE (*rising*). Then I think we'd better leave it until Joe comes home. Then he and Fanny can decide what they wish to do.

ELLEN (*also rising*). I—I didn't mean to upset you.

JANE. I'm not in the least upset.

ELLEN. It's been on my mind—it's been worrying me to death.

JANE. I think you should have spoken to Fanny before you came to me. I never interfere with my son's affairs.

ELLEN. Well, I'm sure I'm very sorry.

JANE. Please don't let's discuss it any further. Good-bye, Ellen.

ELLEN. I suppose you imagine my daughter isn't good enough to marry your son; if that's the case I can assure you you're very much mistaken. Fanny's received everywhere; she knows all the best people.

JANE. How nice for her; I wish I did.

ELLEN. Things aren't what they used to be, you know—it's all changing.

JANE. Yes, I see it is.

ELLEN. Fanny's at the top of the tree now; she's having the most wonderful offers.

JANE. Oh, Ellen!

ELLEN. What is it?

JANE. I'm so very, very sorry.

ELLEN. I don't know what you mean.

JANE. Yes, you do—inside, you must. Something seems to have gone out of all of us, and I'm not sure I like what's left. Good-bye, Ellen.
(GLADYS *enters with a telegram.* JANE *takes telegram.*)
Excuse me, will you. (*She opens it and reads it, and then says in a dead voice*) There's no answer, Gladys.

GLADYS (*excitedly*). It's all over, milady—it's eleven o'clock—the maroons are going off.

JANE. Thank you, Gladys, that will do.

GLADYS. Yes, milady.
(GLADYS *goes out.* JANE *stands holding the telegram. She sways slightly.*)

ELLEN. What is it? What's happened? Oh, my God!

JANE. You needn't worry about Fanny and Joe any more, Ellen. He won't be able to come back after all because he's dead. (*She crumples up and falls to the ground. Maroons can be heard in the distance and people cheering. The lights fade.*)

SCENE XI

Principal

JANE

SCENE—*Trafalgar Square.*
TIME—*11 p.m. Monday, November 11th, 1918.*

Before the scene begins JANE *appears far up stage in a pool of light. Her hat has been pushed on to one side, her clothes look dishevelled, and her handbag hangs on her arm wide open. Twined round her neck and over her hat are coloured paper streamers. She holds in her left hand a large painted wooden rattle, in her right hand a red, white and blue paper squeaker. Her face is dead white and quite devoid of expression.*

The lights go up.

JANE *can be seen threading her way like a sleepwalker through dense crowds of cheering, yelling people. They push her and jostle her. One man blows a long squeaking paper tongue into her face. There is a motor bus festooned with people and a Rolls-Royce and one or two taxis and a hansom cab, all equally burdened with screaming humanity. They move at a snail's pace.* JANE *finally arrives down stage under a lamp-post in the centre. She stands there cheering wildly, with the tears rolling down her face. The lights dim and the yelling crowds fade away.* JANE *is left, still cheering and occasionally brandishing the rattle and blowing the squeaker. But she can't be heard at all because the full strength of the orchestra is playing "Land of Hope and Glory."*

END OF PART II

PART THREE

SCENE I

Principals

ROBERT
JANE
MARGARET

SCENE—*Drawing-room of a London house.*
TIME—*11.45 p.m. Tuesday, December 31st, 1929.*

MARGARET *and* JANE, *both old women, are sitting by the fire.* MARGARET *is very made up, with dyed hair.* JANE'*s hair is white.* MARGARET *is wearing a coloured evening gown.* JANE *is in black.*

MARGARET. I assure you he's the most marvellous man I've ever met. I'd never go to another doctor in the world. He has the most wonderful touch—he's completely cured me, and anyhow the hotel is divine. It's really more a Hydro really, although, thank God, not in the English sense. You can eat what you like and do what you like——

JANE. And what do you like?

MARGARET (*laughing*). Enjoying myself.

JANE. And you do.

MARGARET. Certainly I do.

JANE. Good!

MARGARET. Jane, dear, you really are hopeless.

JANE. I refuse to be jostled, Margaret. I'm perfectly comfortable where I am, without going gallivanting about the Continent taking cures for ailments I haven't got.

MARGARET. How do you know you haven't got any ailments?

JANE. Because I'm sane and active, and as strong as a horse. So is Robert. We've both outstayed our welcome, that's the only thing that's wrong with us.

MARGARET. I don't see any sense in sitting waiting for the grave.

JANE. I'm not waiting for anything. I have a perfectly good time. You're not the only one who enjoys yourself. I go to the Opera. I go to theatres, I go to the Zoo, and I must say, so far I've found the Zoo infinitely the most entertaining.

MARGARET. Dearest Jane—you really are amazing!
(ROBERT *enters. His hair is also white, but he is otherwise hale and hearty.*)

ROBERT. It's nearly time.

MARGARET. Good heavens, I must fly. I wouldn't interfere with your little ritual for the world.

JANE. You wouldn't interfere—you're an old friend.

MARGARET (*kissing* JANE). That's very sweet, Jane, but all the same I must go. I promised I'd be at the Embassy at eleven-thirty. Good night, dear. Good night, Robert. No, don't see me down—the car's outside, isn't it?

ROBERT. Yes, it's been there for a long while.

MARGARET. Happy New Year to you both. Remember you're both dining with me on Thursday.

ROBERT. Good night, Margaret—same to you.
(MARGARET *goes out.* ROBERT *goes over to* JANE.)
Did Franklin bring the champagne up?

JANE. Yes, it's by the table.

ROBERT. Good!

JANE. Well, Robert—here we go again.

ROBERT. I believe you laugh at me inside—for my annual sentimental outburst.

JANE. No dear, I don't laugh at you.

ROBERT. One more year behind us.

JANE. One more year before us.

ROBERT. Do you mind?

JANE. Oh, no—everything passes—even time.

ROBERT. It seems incredible, doesn't it? Here we are in this same room!

JANE. Yes. I've hated it for years.

ROBERT. Do you want to move?

JANE. Of course not.

ROBERT. We might have some new curtains.

JANE. We have, dear.

ROBERT. Good God, so we have! I never noticed.

JANE. They've only been up a week.

ROBERT. They look very nice.

JANE. Dear Robert. (*She pats* ROBERT'S *hand*) What toast have you in mind for tonight—something gay and original, I hope?

ROBERT. Just our old friend—the future. The Future of England.

JANE. It's starting—the champagne, quick!
(ROBERT *gets a champagne bottle out of the bucket and struggles with it.* JANE *opens the window.*)

ROBERT. I can't get the damned thing open.

JANE. Let me try.

ROBERT (*doing it*). There!
(JANE *holds the glasses.* ROBERT *fills the glasses. Meanwhile the chimes and sirens are beginning outside.*)

JANE (*holding up her glass*). First of all, my dear, I drink to you. Loyal and loving always. (*She drinks*) Now, then, let's couple the Future of England with the past of England. The glories and victories and triumphs that are over, and the sorrows that are over, too. Let's drink to our sons who made part of the pattern and to our hearts that died with them. Let's drink to the spirit of gallantry and courage that made a strange Heaven out of unbelievable Hell, and let's drink to the hope that one day this country of ours, which we love so much, will find dignity and greatness and peace again.
(*They both lift their glasses and drink as the lights fade.*)

SCENE II

Principals

ROBERT
JANE
FANNY
MARGARET
ELLEN
FULL COMPANY

SCENE—*A Night Club.*
TIME—*Evening—1930.*

This Scene begins with a night club in which FANNY *is singing, seated on a piano. The decoration is angular and strange, and the song she is singing is oddly discordant.*

TWENTIETH CENTURY BLUES

VERSE

Why is it that civilised humanity
Must make the world so wrong?
In this hurly burly of insanity
Your dreams cannot last long.

We've reached a headline—
The Press headline—every sorrow,
Blues value is News value tomorrow.

REFRAIN

Blues, Twentieth Century Blues, are getting me down.
Who's escaped those weary Twentieth Century Blues.
Why, if there's a God in the sky, why shouldn't he grin?
High above this dreary Twentieth Century din,
In this strange illusion,
Chaos and confusion,
People seem to lose their way.
What is there to strive for,
Love or keep alive for? Say—
Hey, hey, call it a day.
Blues, nothing to win or to lose.
It's getting me down.
Blues, I've got those weary Twentieth Century Blues.

When the song is finished, people rise from the table and dance without apparently any particular enjoyment; it is the dull dancing of habit. The lights fade away from everything but the dancers, who appear to be rising in the air. They disappear and down stage left six "incurables" in blue hospital uniform are sitting making baskets. They disappear and FANNY *is seen singing her song for a moment, then far away up stage a jazz band is seen playing wildly. Then down stage* JANE *and* ROBERT *standing with glasses of champagne held aloft, then* ELLEN *sitting in front of a Radio loud speaker; then* MARGARET *dancing with a young man. The visions are repeated quicker and quicker, while across the darkness runs a Riley light sign spelling out news. Noise grows louder and louder. Steam rivets, loud speakers, jazz bands, aeroplane propellors, etc., until the general effect is complete chaos.*

Suddenly it all fades into darkness and silence and away at the back a Union Jack glows through the blackness.

The lights slowly come up and the whole stage is composed of massive tiers, upon which stand the entire Company. The Union Jack flies over their heads as they sing "God Save the King."

Journey's End

BY R. C. SHERRIFF

Journey's End was first produced in America at the Henry Miller Theatre, New York City, by Gilbert Miller on March 22, 1929, and closed on September 13, 1930.

The following is the original cast:

CAPTAIN HARDY	Evelyn Roberts
LIEUT. OSBORNE	Leon Quartermaine
PRIVATE MASON	Victor Stanley
2ND LIEUT. RALEIGH	Derek Williams
CAPTAIN STANHOPE	Colin Keith-Johnston
2ND LIEUT. HIBBERT	Jack Hawkins
COMPANY SERGEANT-MAJOR	Sydney Seaward
THE COLONEL	Eric Stanley
2ND LIEUT. TROTTER	Henry Wenman
GERMAN SOLDIER	Sol Dowday

Directed by James Whale

SCENE

A dug-out in the British trenches before St. Quentin.

A few rough steps lead into the trench above, through a low doorway. A table occupies a good space of the dug-out floor. A wooden frame, covered with wire netting, stands against the left wall and serves the double purpose of a bed and a seat for the table. A wooden bench against the back wall makes another seat, and two boxes serve for the other sides.

Another wire-covered bed is fixed in the right corner beyond the doorway.

Gloomy tunnels lead out of the dug-out to left and right.

Except for the table, beds, and seats, there is no furniture save the bottles holding the candles, and a few tattered magazine pictures pinned to the wall of girls in flimsy costumes.

The earth walls deaden the sounds of war, making them faint and far away, although the front line is only fifty yards ahead. The flames of the candles that burn day and night are steady in the still, damp air.

ACT ONE

Evening on Monday, the 18th March, 1918

ACT TWO

SCENE I

Tuesday morning

SCENE II

Tuesday afternoon

ACT THREE

SCENE I

Wednesday afternoon

SCENE II

Wednesday night

SCENE III

Thursday, towards dawn

JOURNEY'S END

ACT ONE

The evening of a March day. A pale glimmer of moonlight shines down the narrow steps into one corner of the dug-out. Warm yellow candle-flames light the other corner from the necks of two bottles on the table. Through the doorway can be seen the misty grey parapet of a trench and a narrow strip of starlit sky. A bottle of whiskey, a jar of water, and a mug stand on the table amongst a litter of papers and magazines. An officer's equipment hangs in a jumbled mass from a nail in the wall.

CAPTAIN HARDY, *a red-faced, cheerful-looking man is sitting on a box by the table, intently drying a sock over a candle-flame. He wears a heavy trench-boot on his left leg, and his right foot, which is naked, is held above the damp floor by resting it on his left knee. His right boot stands on the floor beside him. As he carefully turns the sock this way and that—feeling it against his face to see if it is dry—he half sings, half hums a song—humming when he is not quite sure of the words, and marking time with the toes of his right foot.*

HARDY. One and Two it's with Maud and Lou;
Three and Four, two girls more;
Five and Six it's with—hm—hm—hm—
Seven, Eight, Clara and Caroline——

(*He lapses into an indefinite humming, and finishes with a lively burst.*)

Tick!—Tock!—wind up the clock,
And we'll start the day over again.

(*A man's legs appear in the moonlit trench above, and a tall, thin man comes slowly down the dug-out steps, stooping low to avoid the roof. He takes his helmet off and reveals a fine head, with close-cropped, iron-grey hair. He looks about forty-five—physically as hard as nails.*)

HARDY (*looking round*). Hullo, Osborne! Your fellows arriving?

OSBORNE (*hitching off his pack and dropping it in a corner*). Yes. They're just coming in.

HARDY. Splendid! Have a drink.

OSBORNE. Thanks. (*He crosses and sits on the left-hand bed.*)

HARDY (*passing the whiskey and a mug*). Don't have too much water. It's rather strong today.

OSBORNE (*slowly mixing a drink*). I wonder what it *is* they put in the water.

HARDY. Some sort of disinfectant, I suppose.

OSBORNE. I'd rather have the microbes, wouldn't you?

HARDY. *I* would—yes——

OSBORNE. Well, cheero.

HARDY. Cheero. Excuse my sock, won't you?

OSBORNE. Certainly. It's a nice-looking sock.

HARDY. It is rather, isn't it? Guaranteed to keep the feet dry. Trouble is, it gets so wet doing it.

OSBORNE. Stanhope asked me to come and take over. He's looking after the men coming in.

HARDY. Splendid! You know, I'm awfully glad you've come.

OSBORNE. I heard it was a quiet bit of line up here.

HARDY. Well, yes—in a *way*. But you never know. Sometimes nothing happens for hours on end; then —all of a sudden—"over she comes!" —rifle grenades—Minnies—and those horrid little things like pineapples —you know.

OSBORNE. I know.

HARDY. Swish—swish—swish—swish —BANG!

OSBORNE. All right—all right—I know.

HARDY. They simply blew us to bits yesterday. Minnies—enormous ones; about twenty. Three bang in the trench. I really *am* glad you've come; I'm not simply being polite.

OSBORNE. Do much damage?

HARDY. Awful. A dug-out got blown up and came down in the men's tea. They were frightfully annoyed.

OSBORNE. I know. There's nothing worse than dirt in your tea.

HARDY. By the way, you know the big German attack's expected any day now?

OSBORNE. It's been expected for the last month.

HARDY. Yes, but it's very near now; there's funny things happening over in the Boche country. I've been out listening at night when it's quiet. There's more transport than usual coming up—you can hear it rattling over the *pavé* all night; more trains in the distance—puffing up and going away again, one after another, bringing up loads and loads of men——

OSBORNE. Yes. It's coming—pretty soon now.

HARDY. Are you here for six days?

OSBORNE. Yes.

HARDY. Then I should think you'll get it—right in the neck.

OSBORNE. Well, you won't be far away. Come along, let's do this handing over. Where's the map?

HARDY. Here we are. (*He gropes among the papers on the table and finds a tattered map*) We hold about two hundred yards of front line. We've got a Lewis gun just here—and one here, in this little sap. Sentry posts where the crosses are——

OSBORNE. Where do the men sleep?

HARDY. *I* don't know. The sergeant-major sees to that. (*He points off to the left*) The servants and signallers sleep in there. Two officers in here, and three in there. (*He points to the right hand tunnel*) That is, if you've *got* five officers.

OSBORNE. We've only got four at present, but a new man's coming up tonight. He arrived at transport lines a day or two ago.

HARDY. I hope you get better luck than I did with *my* last officer. He got lumbago the first night and went home. Now he's got a job lecturing young officers on "Life in the Front Line."

OSBORNE. Yes. They do send some funny people over here nowadays. I hope we're lucky and get a youngster straight from school. They're the kind that do best.

HARDY. I suppose they are, really.

OSBORNE. Five beds, you say? (*He examines the one he is sitting on*) Is this the best one?

HARDY. Oh, no. (*He points to the bed in the right corner*) *That's* mine. The ones in the other dugout haven't got any bottoms to them. You keep yourself in by hanging your arms and legs over the sides. Mustn't hang your legs too low, or the rats gnaw your boots.

OSBORNE. You got many rats here?

HARDY. I should say—roughly—about two million; but then, of course, I don't see them all. (*He begins to put on his sock and draw on his boot*) Well, there's nothing else you want to know, is there?

OSBORNE. You haven't told me anything yet.

HARDY. What else do you *want* to know?

OSBORNE. Well, what about trench stores?

HARDY. You *are* a fussy old man. Anybody'd think you were in the Army. (*He finds a tattered piece of paper*) Here you are: 115 rifle grenades—I shouldn't use them if I were you; they upset Jerry and make him offensive. Besides, they are rusty, in any case. Then there's 500 Mills bombs, 34 gum boots——

OSBORNE. That's seventeen pairs——

HARDY. Oh, no; 25 right leg, and 9 left leg. But everything's down here. (*He hands the list to* OSBORNE.)

OSBORNE. Did you check it when you took over?

HARDY. No. I think the sergeant-major did. It's quite all right.

OSBORNE. I expect Stanhope would like to see you before you go. He always likes a word with the company commander he's relieving.

HARDY. How *is* the dear young boy? Drinking like a fish, as usual?

OSBORNE. Why do you say that?

HARDY. Well, damn it, it's just the natural thing to ask about Stanhope. (*He pauses, and looks curiously at* OSBORNE) Poor old man. It must be pretty rotten for you, being his second in command, and you such a quiet, sober old thing.

OSBORNE. He's a long way the best company commander we've got.

HARDY. Oh, he's a good chap, I know. But I never *did* see a youngster put away the whiskey he does. D'you know, the last time we were out resting at Valennes he came to supper with us and drank a whole bottle in one hour fourteen minutes—we timed him.

OSBORNE. I suppose it amused everybody; I suppose everybody cheered him on, and said what a splendid achievement it was.

HARDY. He didn't want any "cheering" on——

OSBORNE. No, but everybody thought it was a big thing to do. (*There is a pause*) Didn't they?

HARDY. Well, you can't help, somehow, *admiring* a fellow who can do that—and then pick out his own hat all by himself and walk home——

OSBORNE. When a boy like Stanhope gets a reputation out here for drinking, he turns into a kind of freak show exhibit. People pay with a bottle of whiskey for the morbid curiosity of seeing him drink it.

HARDY. Well, naturally, you're biased. You have to put him to bed when he gets home.

OSBORNE. It rather reminds you of bear-baiting—or cock-fighting—to sit and watch a boy drink himself unconscious.

HARDY. Well, damn it, it's pretty dull without *something* to liven people up. I mean, after all—Stanhope really *is* a sort of freak; I mean it *is* jolly fascinating to see a fellow drink like he does—glass after glass. He didn't go home on his last leave, did he?

OSBORNE. No.

HARDY. I suppose he didn't think he was fit to meet papa. (*A pause*) You know his father's vicar of a country village?

OSBORNE. I know.

HARDY (*laughing*). Imagine Stanhope spending his leave in a country vicarage sipping tea! He spent his last leave in Paris, didn't he?

OSBORNE. Yes.

HARDY. I bet it was *some* leave!

OSBORNE. Do you know how long he's been out here?

HARDY. A good time, I know.

OSBORNE. Nearly three years. He came out straight from school—when he was eighteen. He's commanded this company for a year—in and out of the front line. He's never had a rest. Other men come over here and go home again ill, and young Stanhope goes on sticking it, month in, month out.

HARDY. Oh, I know he's a jolly good fellow——

OSBORNE. I've seen him on his back all day with trench fever—then on duty all night——

HARDY. Oh, I know; he's a splendid chap!

OSBORNE. And because he's stuck it till his nerves have got battered to bits, he's called a drunkard.

HARDY. Not a drunkard; just a—just a hard drinker; but you're quite right about his nerves. They *are* all to blazes. Last time out resting we were playing bridge and something happened—I don't remember what it was; some silly little argument—and all of a sudden he jumped up and knocked all the glasses off the table! Lost control of himself; and then he—sort of—came to—and cried——

OSBORNE. Yes, I know.

HARDY. You heard about it?

OSBORNE. He told me.

HARDY. Did he? We tried to hush it up. It just shows the state he's in. (*He rises and puts on his pack. There is a pause*) You know, Osborne, you ought to be commanding this company.

OSBORNE. Rubbish!

HARDY. Of course you ought. It sticks out a mile. I know he's got pluck and all that, but, damn it, man, you're twice his age—and think what a dear, level-headed old thing you are.

OSBORNE. Don't be an ass. He was out here before I joined up. His experience alone makes him worth a dozen people like me.

HARDY. You know as well as I do, you ought to be in command.

OSBORNE. There isn't a man to touch him as a commander of men. He'll command the battalion one day if——

HARDY. Yes, if! (*He laughs.*)

OSBORNE. You don't know him as I do; I love that fellow. I'd go to hell with him.

HARDY. Oh, you sweet, sentimental old darling!

OSBORNE. Come along. Finish handing over and stop blithering.

HARDY. There's nothing else to do.

OSBORNE. What about the log-book?

HARDY. God! you are a worker. Oh, well. Here we are. (*He finds a tattered little book among the papers on the table*) Written right up to date; here's my last entry: "5 p.m. to 8 p.m. All quiet. German airman flew over trenches. Shot a rat."

OSBORNE. Did he?

HARDY. No, I shot the rat, you ass. Well, finish up your whiskey. I want to pack my mug. I'll leave you that drop in the bottle.

OSBORNE. Thanks. (*He drinks up his whiskey and hands* HARDY *the mug.*)

HARDY (*tucking the mug into his pack*). I'll be off.

OSBORNE. Aren't you going to wait and see Stanhope?

HARDY. Well, no, I don't specially want to see him. He's so fussy about the trenches. I expect they *are* rather dirty. He'll talk for hours if he catches me. (*He hitches his pack over his shoulders, hangs on his gas satchel, map-case, binoculars, compass-case, until he looks like a travelling pedlar. As he dresses:*) Well, I hope you have a nice six days. Don't forget to change your clothes if you get wet.

OSBORNE. No, papa.

HARDY. And don't forget about the big attack.

OSBORNE. Oh, Lord, no, I mustn't miss that; I'll make a note in my diary.

HARDY (*fully dressed*). There we are! Do I look every inch a soldier?

OSBORNE. Yes. I should get quite a fright if I were a German and met you coming round a corner.

HARDY. I should bloody well hope you would.

OSBORNE. Shouldn't be able to run away for laughing.

HARDY. Now don't be rude. (*He leans over to light a cigarette from a candle, and looks down on the table*) Well, I'm damned. Still at it!

OSBORNE. What is?

HARDY. Why, that little cockroach. It's been running round and round that candle since tea-time; must have done a mile.

OSBORNE. I shouldn't hang about here if I were a cockroach.

HARDY. Nor should I. I'd go home. Ever had cockroach races?

OSBORNE. No.

HARDY. Great fun. We've had 'em every evening.

OSBORNE. What are the rules?

HARDY. Oh, you each have a cockroach, and start 'em in a line. On the word "Go" you dig your cockroach in the ribs and steer him with a match across the table. I won ten francs last night—had a *splendid* cockroach. I'll give you a tip.

OSBORNE. Yes?

HARDY. Promise not to let it go any farther?

OSBORNE. Yes.

HARDY. Well, if you want to get the best pace out of a cockroach, dip it in whiskey—makes 'em go like hell!

OSBORNE. Right. Thanks awfully.

HARDY. Well, I must be off. Cheero!

OSBORNE. Cheero!

HARDY (*goes up the narrow steps into the trench above, singing softly and happily to himself*).

"One and Two, it's with Maud and Lou;
Three and Four, two girls more——"

(*The words trail away into the night.*)

(OSBORNE *rises and takes his pack from the floor to the bed by the table. While he undoes it a* SOLDIER SERVANT *comes out of the tunnel from the left with a table-cloth over his arm and a plate with half a loaf of bread on it.*)

MASON. Excuse me, sir. Can I lay supper?

OSBORNE. Yes, do. (*He shuffles up the papers from the table and puts them on the bed.*)

MASON. Thank you, sir. (*He lays the table.*)

OSBORNE. What are you going to tempt us with tonight, Mason?

MASON. Soup, sir—cutlets—and pineapple.

OSBORNE (*suspiciously*). Cutlets?

MASON. Well, sir—well, yes, sir—cutlets.

OSBORNE. What sort of cutlets?

MASON. Now, sir, you've got me. I shouldn't like to commit meself too deep, sir.

OSBORNE. Ordinary ration meat?

MASON. Yes, sir. Ordinary ration meat, but a noo shape, sir. Smells like liver, sir, but it 'asn't got that smooth, wet look that liver's got.
(MASON *leaves the dug-out.* OSBORNE *sits up to the table and examines the map. Voices come from the trench above; a gruff voice says:*) "This is 'C' Company 'Eadquarters, sir."

(*A boyish voice replies.*) "Oh, thanks."
(*There is a pause, then the gruff voice says:*) "Better go down, sir."
(*The boyish voice replies.*) "Yes. Righto."
(*An* OFFICER *comes groping down the steps and stands in the candlelight. He looks round, a little bewildered. He is a well-built, healthy-looking boy of about eighteen, with the very new uniform of a 2nd lieutenant.* OSBORNE *looks up from the trench map, surprised and interested to see a stranger.*)

OSBORNE. Hullo!

RALEIGH. Good evening (*he notices* OSBORNE'S *grey hair and adds*) sir.

OSBORNE. You the new officer?

RALEIGH. Er—yes. I've been to Battalion Headquarters. They told me to report here.

OSBORNE. Good. We've been expecting you. Sit down, won't you?

RALEIGH. Thanks. (*He sits gingerly on the box opposite* OSBORNE.)

OSBORNE. I should take your pack off.

RALEIGH. Oh, right. (*He slips his pack from his shoulders.*)

OSBORNE. Will you have a drink?

RALEIGH. Er—well——

OSBORNE. You don't drink whiskey?

RALEIGH (*hastily*). Oh, yes—er—just a small one, sir.

OSBORNE (*pouring out a small whiskey and adding water*). Whiskey takes away the taste of the water——

RALEIGH. Oh, yes? (*He pauses, and laughs nervously.*)

OSBORNE.—and the water takes away the taste of the whiskey. (*He hands* RALEIGH *the drink*) Just out from England?

RALEIGH. Yes, I landed a week ago.

OSBORNE. Boulogne?

RALEIGH. Yes. (*A pause, then he self-consciously holds up his drink*) Well, here's luck, sir.

OSBORNE (*taking a drink himself*). Good luck. (*He takes out a cigarette case*) Cigarette?

RALEIGH. Thanks.

OSBORNE (*holding a bottle across so that* RALEIGH *can light his cigarette from the candle in it*). Ever been up in the line before?

RALEIGH. Oh, no. You see, I only left school at the end of last summer term.

OSBORNE. I expect you find it a bit strange.

RALEIGH (*laughing*). Yes—I do—a bit——

OSBORNE. My name's Osborne. I'm second in command of the company. You only call me "sir" in front of the men.

RALEIGH. I see. Thanks.

OSBORNE. You'll find the other officers call me "Uncle."

RALEIGH. Oh, yes? (*He smiles.*)

OSBORNE. What's *your* name?

RALEIGH. Raleigh.

OSBORNE. I knew a Raleigh. A master at Rugby.

RALEIGH. Oh? He may be a relation. I don't know. I've got lots of uncles and—and things like that.

OSBORNE. We've only just moved into these trenches. Captain Stanhope commands the company.

RALEIGH (*suddenly brightening up*). I know. It's a frightful bit of luck.

OSBORNE. Why? D'you know him?

RALEIGH. Yes, rather! We were at school together—at least—of course —I was only a kid and he was one of the big fellows; he's three years older than I am.

(*There is a pause;* OSBORNE *seems to be waiting for* RALEIGH *to go on, then suddenly he says.*)

OSBORNE. He's up in the front line at present, looking after the relief. (*Another pause*) He's a splendid chap.

RALEIGH. *Isn't* he? He was skipper of football at Barford, and kept wicket for the eleven. A jolly good bat, too.

OSBORNE. Did you play football—and cricket?

RALEIGH. Oh, yes. Of course, I wasn't in the same class as Dennis —I say, I suppose I ought to call him Captain Stanhope?

OSBORNE. Just "Stanhope."

RALEIGH. I see. Thanks.

OSBORNE. Did you get your colours?

RALEIGH. I did for football. Not cricket.

OSBORNE. Football and cricket seem a long way from here.

RALEIGH (*laughing*). They do, rather.

OSBORNE. We play a bit when we're out of the line.

RALEIGH. Good!

OSBORNE (*thoughtfully*). So you were at school with Stanhope. (*Pause*) I wonder if he'll remember you? I expect you've grown in the last three years.

RALEIGH. Oh, I think he'll remember me. (*He stops, and goes on rather awkwardly*) You see, it wasn't only that we were just at school together; our fathers were friends, and Dennis used to come and stay with us in the holidays. Of course, at school I didn't see much of him, but in the holidays we were terrific pals.

OSBORNE. He's a fine company commander.

RALEIGH. I bet he is. Last time he was on leave he came down to the school; he'd just got his M.C. and been made a captain. He looked splendid! It—sort of—made me feel——

OSBORNE. —keen?

RALEIGH. Yes. Keen to get out here. I was frightfully keen to get into Dennis's regiment. I thought, perhaps, with a bit of luck I might get to the same battalion.

OSBORNE. It's a big fluke to have got to the same company.

RALEIGH. I know. It's an amazing bit of luck. When I was at the base I did an awful thing. You see, my uncle's at the base—he has to detail officers to regiments——

OSBORNE. General Raleigh?

RALEIGH. Yes. I went to see him on the quiet and asked him if he could get me into this battalion. He bit my head off, and said I'd got to be treated like everybody else——

OSBORNE. Yes?

RALEIGH. —and next day I was told I *was* coming to this battalion. Funny, wasn't it?

OSBORNE. Extraordinary coincidence!

RALEIGH. And when I got to Battalion Headquarters, and the colonel told me to report to "C" Company, I could have cheered. I expect Dennis'll be frightfully surprised to see me. I've got a message for him.

OSBORNE. From the colonel?

RALEIGH. No. From my sister.

OSBORNE. Your sister?

RALEIGH. Yes. You see, Dennis used to stay with us, and naturally my sister (*he hesitates*)—well—perhaps I ought not——

OSBORNE. That's all right. I didn't actually know that Stanhope——

RALEIGH. They're not—er—officially engaged——

OSBORNE. No?

RALEIGH. She'll be awfully glad I'm with him here; I can write and tell her all about him. He doesn't say much in his letters; can we write often?

OSBORNE. Oh, yes. Letters are collected every day.
(*There is a pause.*)

RALEIGH. You don't think Dennis'll mind my–sort of–forcing myself into his company? I never thought of that; I was so keen.

OSBORNE. No, of course he won't. (*Pause*) You say it's–it's a good time since you last saw him?

RALEIGH. Let's see. It was in the summer last year–nearly a year ago.

OSBORNE. You know, Raleigh, you mustn't expect to find him–quite the same.

RALEIGH. Oh?

OSBORNE. You see, he's been out here a long time. It–it tells on a man–rather badly——

RALEIGH (*thinking*). Yes, of course, I suppose it does.

OSBORNE. You may find he's–he's a little bit quick-tempered.

RALEIGH (*laughing*). Oh, I know old Dennis's temper! I remember once at school he caught some chaps in a study with a bottle of whiskey. Lord! the roof nearly blew off. He gave them a dozen each with a cricket stump. (OSBORNE *laughs*) He was so keen on the fellows in the house keeping fit. He was frightfully down on smoking–and that sort of thing.

OSBORNE. You must remember he's commanded this company for a long time–through all sorts of rotten times. It's–it's a big strain on a man.

RALEIGH. Oh, it must be.

OSBORNE. If you notice a–difference in Stanhope–you'll know it's only the strain——

RALEIGH. Oh, yes.
(OSBORNE *rouses himself and speaks briskly.*)

OSBORNE. Now, let's see. We've got five beds here–one each. Two in here and three in that dug-out there. I'm afraid you'll have to wait until the others come and pick the beds they want.

RALEIGH. Righto!

OSBORNE. Have you got a blanket?

RALEIGH. Yes, in my pack. (*He rises to get it.*)

OSBORNE. Better wait and unpack when you know where you are sleeping.

RALEIGH. Righto! (*He sits down again.*)

OSBORNE. We never undress when we're in the line. You can take your boots off now and then in the day-time, but it's better to keep pretty well dressed always.

RALEIGH. I see. Thanks.

OSBORNE. I expect we shall each do about three hours on duty at a time and then six off. We all go on duty at stand-to. That's at dawn and dusk.

RALEIGH. Yes.

OSBORNE. I expect Stanhope'll send you on duty with one of us at first—till you get used to it.
(*There is a pause.* RALEIGH *turns, and looks curiously up the steps into the night.*)

RALEIGH. Are we in the front line here?

OSBORNE. No. That's the support line outside. The front line's about fifty yards farther on.

RALEIGH. How frightfully quiet it is!

OSBORNE. It's often quiet—like this.

RALEIGH. I thought there would be an awful row here—all the time.

OSBORNE. Most people think that. (*Pause.*)

RALEIGH. I've never known anything so quiet as those trenches we came by; just now and then I heard rifle firing, like the range at Bisley, and a sort of rumble in the distance.

OSBORNE. Those are the guns up north—up Wipers way. The guns are always going up there; it's never quiet like this. (*Pause*) I expect it's all very strange to you?

RALEIGH. It's—it's not exactly what I thought. It's just this—this quiet that seems so funny.

OSBORNE. A hundred yards from here the Germans are sitting in *their* dug-outs, thinking how quiet it is.

RALEIGH. Are they as near as that?

OSBORNE. About a hundred yards.

RALEIGH. It seems—uncanny. It makes me feel we're—we're all just waiting for something.

OSBORNE. We are, generally, just waiting for something. When anything happens, it happens quickly. Then we just start waiting again.

RALEIGH. I never thought it was like that.

OSBORNE. You thought it was fighting all the time?

RALEIGH (*laughing*). Well, yes, in a way.

OSBORNE (*after puffing at his pipe in silence for a while*). Did you come up by trench tonight—or over the top?

RALEIGH. By trench. An amazing trench—turning and twisting for miles, over a sort of plain.

OSBORNE. Lancer's Alley it's called.

RALEIGH. Is it? It's funny the way it begins—in that ruined village, a few steps down into the cellar of a house—then right under the house and through a little garden—and then under the garden wall—then alongside an enormous ruined factory place—then miles and miles of plains, with those green lights bobbing up and down ahead—all along the front as far as you can see.

OSBORNE. Those are the Very lights. Both sides fire them over No Man's Land—to watch for raids and patrols.

RALEIGH. I knew they fired lights. (*Pause*) I didn't expect so many—and to see them so far away.

OSBORNE. I know. (*He puffs at his pipe*) There's something rather romantic about it all.

RALEIGH (*eagerly*). Yes, I thought that, too.

OSBORNE. You must always think of it like that if you can. Think of it all as—as romantic. It helps.
(MASON *comes in with more dinner utensils.*)

MASON. D'you expect the captain soon, sir? The soup's 'ot.

OSBORNE. He ought to be here very soon now. This is Mr. Raleigh, Mason.

MASON. Good evening, sir.

RALEIGH. Good evening.

MASON (*to* OSBORNE). I've 'ad rather a unpleasant surprise, sir.

OSBORNE. What's happened?

MASON. You know that tin o' pineapple chunks I got, sir?

OSBORNE. Yes?

MASON. Well, sir, I'm sorry to say it's apricots.

OSBORNE. Good heavens! It must have given you a turn.

MASON. I distinctly said "pineapple chunks" at the canteen.

OSBORNE. Wasn't there a label on the tin?

MASON. No, sir. I pointed that out to the men. I said was 'e *certain* it was pineapple chunks?

OSBORNE. I suppose he said he was.

MASON. Yes, sir. 'E said a leopard can't change its spots, sir.

OSBORNE. What have leopards got to do with pineapple?

MASON. That's just what *I* thought, sir. Made me *think* there was something fishy about it. You see, sir, I know the captain can't stand the sight of apricots. 'E said next time we 'ad them 'e'd wring my neck.

OSBORNE. Haven't you anything else?

MASON. There's a pink blancmange I've made, sir. But it ain't anywhere near stiff yet.

OSBORNE. Never mind. We must have the apricots and chance it.

MASON. Only I thought I'd tell you, sir, so as the captain wouldn't blame me.

OSBORNE. All right, Mason. (*Voices are heard in the trench above*) That sounds like the captain coming now.

MASON (*hastening away*). I'll go and dish out the soup, sir.
(*The voices grow nearer; two figures appear in the trench above and grope down the steps—the leading figure tall and thin, the other short and fat. The tall figure is* CAPTAIN STANHOPE. *At the bottom of the steps he straightens himself, pulls off his pack, and drops it on the floor. Then he takes off*

his helmet and throws it on the right-hand bed. Despite his stars of rank he is no more than a boy; tall, slimly built, but broad-shouldered. His dark hair is carefully brushed; his uniform, though old and war-stained, is well cut and cared for. He is good-looking, rather from attractive features than the healthy good looks of RALEIGH. *Although tanned by months in the open air, there is a pallor under his skin and dark shadows under his eyes. His short and fat companion* —2ND LIEUTENANT TROTTER—*is middle-aged and homely looking. His face is red, fat, and round; apparently he has put on weight during his war service, for his tunic appears to be on the verge of bursting at the waist. He carries an extra pack belonging to the officer left on duty in the line.*)

STANHOPE (*as he takes off his pack, gas satchel, and belt*). Has Hardy gone?

OSBORNE. Yes. He cleared off a few minutes ago.

STANHOPE. Lucky for him he did. I had a few words to say to Master Hardy. You never saw the blasted mess those fellows left the trenches in. Dug-outs smell like cess-pits; rusty bombs; damp rifle grenades; it's perfectly foul. Where are the servants?

OSBORNE. In there.

STANHOPE (*calling into* MASON'S *dug-out*). Hi! Mason!

MASON (*outside*). Coming, sir! Just bringing the soup, sir.

STANHOPE (*taking a cigarette from his case and lighting it*). Damn the soup! Bring some whiskey!

OSBORNE. Here's a new officer, Stanhope—just arrived.

STANHOPE. Oh, sorry. (*He turns and peers into the dim corner where* RALEIGH *stands smiling awkwardly*) I didn't see you in this miserable light. (*He stops short at the sight of* RALEIGH. *There is silence.*)

RALEIGH. Hullo, Stanhope!

(STANHOPE *stares at* RALEIGH *as though dazed.* RALEIGH *takes a step forward, half raises his hand, then lets it drop to his side.*)

STANHOPE (*in a low voice*). How did you—get here?

RALEIGH. I was told to report to your company, Stanhope.

STANHOPE. Oh. I see. Rather a coincidence.

RALEIGH (*with a nervous laugh*). Yes.

(*There is a silence for a moment, broken by* OSBORNE *in a matter-of-fact voice.*)

OSBORNE. I say, Stanhope, it's a terrible business. We thought we'd got a tin of pineapple chunks; it turns out to be apricots.

TROTTER. Ha! Give me apricots every time! I 'ate pineapple chunks; too bloomin' sickly for me!

RALEIGH. I'm awfully glad I got to your company, Stanhope.

STANHOPE. When did you get here?

RALEIGH. Well, I've only just come.

OSBORNE. He came up with the transport while you were taking over.

STANHOPE. I see.
(MASON *brings in a bottle of whiskey, a mug, and two plates of soup —so precariously that* OSBORNE *has to help with the soup plates on to the table.*)

STANHOPE (*with sudden forced gaiety*). Come along, Uncle! Come and sit here. (*He waves towards the box on the right of the table*) You better sit there, Raleigh.

RALEIGH. Right!

TROTTER (*taking a pair of pince-nez from his tunic pocket, putting them on, and looking curiously at* RALEIGH). You Raleigh?

RALEIGH. Yes.
(*Pause.*)

TROTTER. I'm Trotter.

RALEIGH. Oh, yes?
(*Pause.*)

TROTTER. How *are* you?

RALEIGH. Oh, all right, thanks.

TROTTER. Been out 'ere before?

RALEIGH. No.

TROTTER. Feel a bit odd, I s'pose?

RALEIGH. Yes. A bit.

TROTTER (*getting a box to sit on*). Oh, well, you'll soon get used to it; you'll feel you've been 'ere a year in about an hour's time. (*He puts the box on its side and sits on it. It is too low for the table, and he puts it on its end. It is then too high. He tries the other side, which is too low; he finally contrives to make himself comfortable by sitting on his pack, placed on the side of the box.*)
(MASON *arrives with two more plates of soup.*)

OSBORNE. What kind of soup is this, Mason?

MASON. It's yellow soup, sir.

OSBORNE. It's got a very deep yellow flavour.

TROTTER (*taking a melodious sip*). It wants some pepper; bring some pepper, Mason.

MASON (*anxiously*). I'm very sorry, sir. When the mess box was packed the pepper was omitted, sir.

TROTTER (*throwing his spoon with a clatter into the plate*). Oh, I say, but damn it!

OSBORNE. We must have pepper. It's a disinfectant.

TROTTER. You must have pepper in soup!

STANHOPE (*quietly*). Why wasn't it packed, Mason?

MASON. It—it was missed, sir.

STANHOPE. Why?

MASON (*miserably*). Well, sir, I left it to——

STANHOPE. Then I advise you never to leave it to anyone else again—unless you want to rejoin your platoon out there. (*He points into the moonlit trench.*)

MASON. I'm—I'm very sorry, sir.

STANHOPE. Send one of the signallers.

MASON. Yes, sir. (*He hastens to the tunnel entrance and calls*) Bert, you're wanted!
(*A* SOLDIER *appears, with a rifle slung over his shoulder. He stands stiffly to attention.*)

STANHOPE. Do you know "A" Company Headquarters?

SOLDIER. Yes, sir.

STANHOPE. Go there at once and ask Captain Willis, with my compliments, if he can lend me a little pepper.

SOLDIER. Very good, sir.
(*He turns smartly and goes up the steps,* MASON *stopping him for a moment to say confidentially:* "A *screw* of pepper, you ask for.")

OSBORNE. We must have pepper.

TROTTER. I mean—after all—war's bad enough with pepper—(*noisy sip*)—but war without pepper—it's —it's bloody awful!

OSBORNE. What's it like outside?

TROTTER. Quiet as an empty 'ouse. There's a nasty noise going on up north.

OSBORNE. Wipers, I expect. I believe there's trouble up there. I wish we knew more of what's going on.

TROTTER. So do I. Still, my wife reads the papers every morning and writes and tells me.

OSBORNE. Hardy says they had a lively time here yesterday. Three big Minnies right in the trench.

TROTTER. I know. And they left the bloomin' 'oles for us to fill in. (MASON *arrives with cutlets on enamel plates*) What's this?

MASON. Meat, sir.

TROTTER. I know that. What sort?

MASON. Sort of cutlet, sir.

TROTTER. Sort of cutlet, is it? You know, Mason, there's cutlets and cutlets.

MASON. I know, sir; that one's a cutlet.

TROTTER. Well, it won't let me cut it.

MASON. No, sir?

TROTTER. That's a joke.

MASON. Oh. Right, sir. (*He goes out.*)

OSBORNE (*studying the map*). There's a sort of ruin marked on this map—just in front of here, in No Man's Land—called Beauvais Farm.

TROTTER. That's what we saw sticking up, skipper. I wondered what it was.

STANHOPE. Better go out and look at it tonight.

TROTTER. I 'ate ruins in No Man's Land; too bloomin' creepy for me.

OSBORNE. There's only about sixty yards of No Man's Land, according to this map—narrower on the left, from the head of this sap; only about fifty.

TROTTER (*who has been looking curiously at* STANHOPE, *eating his meal with lowered head*). Cheer up, skipper. You *do* look glum!

STANHOPE. I'm tired.

OSBORNE. I should turn in and get some sleep after supper.

STANHOPE. I've got hours of work before I sleep.

OSBORNE. I'll do the duty roll and see the sergeant-major—and all that.

STANHOPE. That's all right, Uncle. I'll see to it. (*He turns to* RALEIGH *for the first time*) Trotter goes on duty directly he's had supper. You better go on with him—to learn.

RALEIGH. Oh, right.

TROTTER. Look 'ere, skipper, it's nearly eight now; couldn't we make it 'alf-past?

STANHOPE. No. I told Hibbert he'd be relieved at eight. Will you take from eleven till two, Uncle?

OSBORNE. Right.

STANHOPE. Hibbert can do from two till four, and I'll go on from then till stand-to. That'll be at six.

TROTTER. Well, boys! 'Ere we are for six days again. Six bloomin' eternal days. (*He makes a calculation on the table*) That's a hundred and forty-four hours; eight thousand six 'undred and forty minutes. *That* doesn't sound so bad; we've done twenty of 'em already. I've got an idea! I'm going to draw a hundred and forty-four little circles on a bit o' paper, and every hour I'm going to black one in; that'll make the time go all right.

STANHOPE. It's five to eight now. You better go and relieve Hibbert. Then you can come back at eleven o'clock and black in three of your bloody little circles.

TROTTER. I 'aven't 'ad my apricots yet!

STANHOPE. We'll keep your apricots till you come back.

TROTTER. I never knew anything like a war for upsetting meals. I'm always down for dooty in the middle of one.

STANHOPE. That's because you never stop eating.

TROTTER. Any'ow, let's 'ave some coffee. Hi! Mason! Coffee!

MASON. Coming, sir!

TROTTER (*getting up*). Well, I'll get dressed. Come on, Raleigh.

RALEIGH (*rising quickly*). Right!

TROTTER. Just wear your belt with revolver case on it. Must have your revolver to shoot rats. And your gas mask—come here—I'll show you. (*He helps* RALEIGH) You wear it sort of tucked up under your chin like a serviette.

RALEIGH. Yes. I was shown the way at home.

TROTTER. Now your hat. That's right. You don't want a walking-stick. It gets in your way if you have to run fast.

RALEIGH. Why—er—do you have to run fast?

TROTTER. Oh, Lord, yes, often! If you see a Minnie coming—that's a big trench-mortar shell, you know—short for *Minnywerfer*—you see 'em coming right out of the Boche trenches, right up in the air, then down, down, down; and you have to judge it and run like stink sometimes.
(MASON *comes in with two cups of coffee.*)

MASON. Coffee, sir?

TROTTER. Thanks. (*He takes the cup and drinks standing up.*)

RALEIGH. Thanks.

TROTTER. You might leave my apricots out, Mason. Put 'em on a separate plate and keep 'em in there. (*He points to* MASON's *dug-out.*)

MASON. Very good, sir.

TROTTER. If you bring 'em in 'ere you never know *what* might 'appen to 'em.

MASON. No, sir.

TROTTER. "B" Company on our right, aren't they, skipper?

STANHOPE. Yes. There's fifty yards of undefended area between. You better patrol that a good deal.

TROTTER. Aye, aye, sir.

STANHOPE. Have a look at that Lewis gun position on the left. See what field of fire they've got.

TROTTER. Aye, aye, sir. You don't want me to go out and look at that blinkin' ruin?

STANHOPE. I'll see to that.

TROTTER. Good. I don't fancy crawling about on my belly after that cutlet. (*To* RALEIGH) Well, come on, my lad, let's go and see about this 'ere war.
(*The two go up the steps, leaving* STANHOPE *and* OSBORNE *alone.* MASON *appears at his dug-out door.*)

MASON. Will you take apricots, sir?

STANHOPE. No, thanks.

MASON. Mr. Osborne?

OSBORNE. No, thanks.

MASON. I'm sorry about them being apricots, sir. I explained to Mr. Osborne——

STANHOPE (*curtly*). That's all right, Mason—thank you.

MASON. Very good, sir. (*He goes out.*)

OSBORNE (*over by the right-hand bed*). Will you sleep here? This was Hardy's bed.

STANHOPE. No. You sleep there. I'd rather sleep by the table here. I can get up and work without disturbing you.

OSBORNE. This is a better one.

STANHOPE. You take it. Must have a little comfort in your old age, Uncle.

OSBORNE. I wish you'd turn in and sleep for a bit.

STANHOPE. Sleep?—I can't sleep. (*He takes a whiskey and water. A man appears in the trench and comes down the steps—a small, slightly built man in the early twenties, with a little moustache and a pallid face.*)

STANHOPE (*looking hard at the newcomer*). Well, Hibbert?

HIBBERT. Everything's fairly quiet. Bit of sniping somewhere to our left; some rifle grenades coming over just on our right.

STANHOPE. I see. Mason's got your supper.

HIBBERT (*gently rubbing his forehead*). I don't think I can manage any supper tonight, Stanhope. It's this beastly neuralgia. It seems to be right inside this eye. The beastly pain gets worse every day.

STANHOPE. Some hot soup and a good tough chop'll put that right.

HIBBERT. I'm afraid the pain rather takes my appetite away. I'm damn sorry to keep on talking about it, Stanhope, only I thought you'd wonder why I don't eat anything much.

STANHOPE. Try and forget about it.

HIBBERT (*with a little laugh*). Well —I wish I could.

STANHOPE. Get tight.

HIBBERT. I think I'll turn straight in for a rest—and try and get some sleep.

STANHOPE. All right. Turn in. You're in that dug-out there. Here's your pack. (*He picks up the pack that* TROTTER *brought down*) You go on duty at two. I take over from you at four. I'll tell Mason to call you.

HIBBERT (*faintly*). Oh, right—thanks, Stanhope—cheero.

STANHOPE. Cheero. (*He watches* HIBBERT *go down the tunnel into the dark.*)

HIBBERT (*returning*). Can I have a candle?

STANHOPE (*taking one from the table*). Here you are.

HIBBERT. Thanks.
(*He goes out again. There is silence.* STANHOPE *turns to* OSBORNE.)

STANHOPE. Another little worm trying to wriggle home.

OSBORNE (*filling his pipe*). I wonder if he really is bad. He looks rotten.

STANHOPE. Pure bloody funk, that's all. He could eat if he wanted to; he's starving himself purposely. Artful little swine! Neuralgia's a splendid idea. No proof, as far as I can see.

OSBORNE. You can't help feeling sorry for him. I think he's tried hard.

STANHOPE. How long's he been out here? Three months, I suppose.

Now he's decided he's done his bit. He's decided to go home and spend the rest of the war in comfortable nerve hospitals. Well, he's mistaken. I let Warren get away like that, but no more.

OSBORNE. I don't see how you can prevent a fellow going sick.

STANHOPE. I'll have a quiet word with the doctor before *he* does. He thinks he's going to wriggle off before the attack. We'll just see about that. No man of mine's going sick before the attack. They're going to take an equal chance—together.

OSBORNE. Raleigh looks a nice chap.

STANHOPE (*looking hard at* OSBORNE *before replying*). Yes.

OSBORNE. Good-looking youngster. At school with you, wasn't he?

STANHOPE. Has he been talking already?

OSBORNE. He just mentioned it. It was a natural thing to tell me when he knew you were in command. (STANHOPE *is lounging at the table with his back to the wall.* OSBORNE, *sitting on the right-hand bed, begins to puff clouds of smoke into the air as he lights his pipe*) He's awfully pleased to get into your company. (STANHOPE *makes no reply. He picks up a pencil and scribbles on the back of a magazine*) He seems to think a lot of you.

STANHOPE (*looking up quickly at* OSBORNE *and laughing*). Yes, I'm his hero.

OSBORNE. It's quite natural.

STANHOPE. You think so?

OSBORNE. Small boys at school generally have their heroes.

STANHOPE. Yes. Small boys at school do.

OSBORNE. Often it goes on as long as——

STANHOPE. —as long as the hero's a hero.

OSBORNE. It often goes on all through life.

STANHOPE. I wonder. How many battalions are there in France?

OSBORNE. Why?

STANHOPE. We'll say fifty divisions. That's a hundred and fifty brigades —four hundred and fifty battalions. That's one thousand eight hundred companies. (*He looks up at* OSBORNE *from his calculations on the magazine cover*) There are one thousand eight hundred companies in France, Uncle. Raleigh might have been sent to any one of those, and, my God! he comes to mine.

OSBORNE. You ought to be glad. He's a good-looking youngster. I like him.

STANHOPE. I knew you'd like him. Personality, isn't it? (*He takes a worn leather case from his breast pocket and hands a small photograph to* OSBORNE) I've never shown you that, have I?

OSBORNE (*looking at the photograph*). No. (*Pause*) Raleigh's sister, isn't it?

STANHOPE. How did you know?

OSBORNE. There's a strong likeness.

STANHOPE. I suppose there is.

OSBORNE (*intent on the picture*). She's an awfully nice-looking girl.

STANHOPE. A photo doesn't show much, really. Just a face.

OSBORNE. She looks awfully nice. (*There is silence.* STANHOPE *lights a cigarette.* OSBORNE *hands the photo back*) You're a lucky chap.

STANHOPE (*putting the photo back into his case*). I don't know why I keep it, really.

OSBORNE. Why? Isn't she—I thought——

STANHOPE. What did you think?

OSBORNE. Well, I thought that perhaps she was waiting for you.

STANHOPE. Yes. She is waiting for me—and she doesn't know. She thinks I'm a wonderful chap—commanding a company. (*He turns to* OSBORNE *and points up the steps into the line*) She doesn't know that if I went up those steps into the front line—without being doped with whiskey—I'd go mad with fright.
(*There is a pause.* OSBORNE *stirs himself to speak.*)

OSBORNE. Look here, old man. I've meant to say it, for a long time, but it sounds damned impudence. You've done longer out here than any man in the battalion. It's time you went away for a rest. It's due to you.

STANHOPE. You suggest that I go sick, like that little worm in there—neuralgia in the eye? (*He laughs and takes a drink.*)

OSBORNE. No. Not that. The colonel would have sent you down long ago, only——

STANHOPE. Only—what?

OSBORNE. Only he can't spare you.

STANHOPE (*laughing*). Oh, rot!

OSBORNE. He told me.

STANHOPE. He thinks I'm in such a state I want a rest, is that it?

OSBORNE. No. He thinks it's due to you.

STANHOPE. It's all right, Uncle. I'll stick it out now. It may not be much longer now. I've had my share of luck—more than my share. There's not a man left who was here when I came. But it's rather damnable for that boy—of all the boys in the world—to have come to *me.* I might at least have been spared that.

OSBORNE. You're looking at things in rather a black sort of way.

STANHOPE. I've just told you. That boy's a hero-worshipper. I'm three years older than he is. You know what that means at school. I was skipper of football and all that sort of thing. It doesn't sound much to a man out here—but it does at school with a kid of fourteen. Damn it, Uncle, you're a schoolmaster; you know.

OSBORNE. I've just told you what I think of hero-worship.

STANHOPE. Raleigh's father knew mine, and I was told to keep an eye on the kid. I rather liked the idea of looking after him. I made him keen on the right things—and all that. His people asked me to stay with them one summer. I met his sister then——

OSBORNE. Yes?

STANHOPE. At first I thought of her as another kid like Raleigh. It was just before I came out here for the first time that I realised what a topping girl she was. Funny how you realise it suddenly. I just prayed to come through the war—and—and *do* things—and keep absolutely fit for her.

OSBORNE. You've done pretty well. An M.C. and a company.

STANHOPE (*taking another whiskey*). It was all right at first. When I went home on leave after six months it was jolly fine to feel I'd done a little to make her pleased. (*He takes a gulp of his drink*) It was after I came back here—in that awful affair on Vimy Ridge. I knew I'd go mad if I didn't break the strain. I couldn't bear being fully conscious all the time—*you've* felt that, Uncle, haven't you?

OSBORNE. Yes, often.

STANHOPE. There were only two ways of breaking the strain. One was pretending I was ill—and going home; the other was this. (*He holds up his glass*) Which would you pick, Uncle?

OSBORNE. I haven't been through as much as you. I don't know yet.

STANHOPE. I thought it all out. It's a slimy thing to go home if you're not really ill, isn't it?

OSBORNE. I think it is.

STANHOPE. Well, then. (*He holds his glass up to* OSBORNE) Cheero, and long live the men who go home with neuralgia. (*He puts his glass down*) I didn't go home on my last leave. I couldn't bear to meet her, in case she realised——

OSBORNE. When the war's over—and the strain's gone—you'll soon be as fit as ever, at your age.

STANHOPE. I've hoped that all the time. I'd go away for months and live in the open air—and get fit—and then go back to her.

OSBORNE. And so you can.

STANHOPE. If Raleigh had gone to one of those other one thousand eight hundred companies.

OSBORNE. I don't see why you should think——

STANHOPE. Oh, for Lord's sake don't be a damn fool. *You* know! You know he'll write and tell her I reek of whiskey all day.

OSBORNE. Why should he? He's not a——

STANHOPE. Exactly. He's not a damned little swine who'd deceive his sister.

OSBORNE. He's very young; he's got hundreds of strange things to learn; he'll realise that men are—*different*—out here.

STANHOPE. It's no good, Uncle. Didn't you see him sitting there at supper?—staring at me?—and wondering? He's up in those trenches now—still wondering—and beginning to understand. And all these months he's wanted to be with me out here. Poor little devil!

OSBORNE. I believe Raleigh'll go on liking you—and looking up to you—through everything. There's something very deep, and rather fine, about hero-worship.

STANHOPE. Hero-worship be damned! (*He pauses, then goes on, in a strange, high-pitched voice*) You know, Uncle, I'm an *awful* fool. I'm *captain* of this company. What's that bloody little prig of a boy matter? D'you see? He's a little prig. Wants to write home and tell Madge all about *me*. Well, he won't; d'you see, Uncle? He *won't* write. Censorship! I censor his letters—cross out all he says about me.

OSBORNE. You can't read his letters.

STANHOPE (*dreamily*). Cross out all he says about me. Then we all go west in the big attack—and she goes on thinking I'm a fine fellow for ever—and ever—and ever. (*He pours out a drink, murmuring "Ever—and ever—and ever."*)

OSBORNE (*rising from his bed*). It's not as bad as all that. Turn in and have a sleep.

STANHOPE. Sleep! Catch *me* wasting my time with sleep.

OSBORNE (*picking up* STANHOPE'S *pack and pulling out the blanket*). Come along, old chap. You come and lie down here. (*He puts the pack as a pillow on* STANHOPE'S *bed, and spreads out the blanket.*)

STANHOPE (*with his chin in his hands*). Little prig—that's what he is. Did *I* ask him to force his way into my company? No! I didn't. Very well, he'll pay for his damn cheek. (OSBORNE *lays his hand gently on* STANHOPE'S *shoulder to persuade him to lie down*) Go away! (*He shakes* OSBORNE'S *hand off*) What the hell are you trying to do?

OSBORNE. Come and lie down and go to sleep.

STANHOPE. Go sleep y'self. I censor his letters, d'you see, Uncle? You watch and see he doesn't smuggle any letters away.

OSBORNE. Righto. Now come and lie down. You've had a hard day of it.

STANHOPE (*looking up suddenly*). Where's Hardy? D'you say he's gone?

OSBORNE. Yes. He's gone.

STANHOPE. Gone, has he? Y'know, I had a word to say to Master Hardy. He *would* go, the swine! Dirty trenches—everything dirty—I wanner tell him to keep his trenches clean.

OSBORNE (*standing beside* STANHOPE *and putting his hand gently on his shoulder again*) We'll clean them up tomorrow.
(STANHOPE *looks up at* OSBORNE *and laughs gaily.*)

STANHOPE. Dear old Uncle! Clean trenches up—with little dustpan and brush. (*He laughs*) Make you little apron—with lace on it.

OSBORNE. That'll be fine. Now then, come along, old chap. I'll see you get called at two o'clock. (*He firmly takes* STANHOPE *by the arm and draws him over to the bed*) You *must* be tired.

STANHOPE (*in a dull voice*) God, I'm bloody tired; ache—all over—feel sick—
(OSBORNE *helps him on to the bed, takes the blanket and puts it over him.*)

OSBORNE. You'll feel all right in a minute. How's that? Comfortable?

STANHOPE. Yes. Comfortable. (*He looks up into* OSBORNE'S *face and laughs again*) Dear old Uncle. Tuck me up.
(OSBORNE *fumbles the blankets round* STANHOPE.)

OSBORNE. There we are.

STANHOPE. Kiss me, Uncle.

OSBORNE. Kiss you be blowed! You go to sleep.

STANHOPE (*closing his eyes*). Yes—I go sleep. (*He turns slowly on to his side with his face to the earth wall.*)
(OSBORNE *stands watching for a while, then blows out the candle by* STANHOPE'S *bed.* STANHOPE *gives a deep sigh, and begins to breathe heavily.* OSBORNE *crosses to the servant's dug-out and calls softly.*)

OSBORNE. Mason!

MASON (*appearing with unbuttoned tunic at the tunnel entrance*). Yessir?

OSBORNE. Will you call me at ten minutes to eleven—and Mr. Hibbert at ten minutes to two? I'm going to turn in for a little while.

MASON. Very good, sir. (*Pause*) The pepper's come, sir.

OSBORNE. Oh, good.

MASON. I'm very sorry about the pepper, sir.

OSBORNE. That's all right, Mason.

MASON. Good night, sir.

OSBORNE. Good night.
(MASON *leaves the dugout.* OSBORNE *turns, and looks up the narrow steps into the night, where the Very lights rise and fade against the starlit sky. He glances once more at* STANHOPE, *then crosses to his own bed, takes out from his tunic pocket a large, old-fashioned watch, and quietly winds it up. Through the stillness comes the low rumble of distant guns.*)

THE CURTAIN FALLS

ACT TWO

SCENE I

Early next morning.

A pale shaft of sunlight shines down the steps, but candles still burn in the dark corner where OSBORNE *and* RALEIGH *are at breakfast.* MASON *has put a large plate of bacon before each, and turns to go as* TROTTER *comes down the steps, whistling gaily and rubbing his hands.*

TROTTER. What a lovely smell of bacon!

MASON. Yes, sir. I reckon there's enough smell of bacon in 'ere to last for dinner.

TROTTER. Well, there's nothing like a good fat bacon rasher when you're as empty as I am.

MASON. I'm glad you like it fat, sir.

TROTTER. Well, I like a bit o' lean, too.

MASON. There *was* a bit of lean in the middle of yours, sir, but it's kind of shrunk up in the cooking.

TROTTER. Bad cooking, that's all. Any porridge?

MASON. Oh, yes, sir. There's porridge.

TROTTER. Lumpy, I s'pose?

MASON. Yes, sir. Quite nice and lumpy.

TROTTER. Well, take the lumps out o' mine.

MASON. And just bring you the gravy, sir? Very good, sir.

(MASON *goes out.* TROTTER *looks after him suspiciously.*)

TROTTER. You know, that man's getting familiar.

OSBORNE. He's not a bad cook.

(TROTTER *has picked up his coffee mug, and is smelling it.*)

TROTTER. I say, d'you realise he's washed his dish-cloth?

OSBORNE. I know. I told him about it.

TROTTER. Did you really? You've got some pluck. 'Ow did you go about it?

OSBORNE. I wrote and asked my wife for a packet of Lux. Then I gave it to Mason and suggested he try it on something.

TROTTER. Good man. No, he's not a bad cook. Might be a lot worse. When I was in the ranks we 'ad a prize cook—used to be a plumber before the war. Ought to 'ave seen the stew 'e made. Thin! Thin wasn't the word. Put a bucketful

of 'is stew in a bath and pull the plug, and the whole lot would go down in a couple of gurgles.
(MASON *brings* TROTTER'S *porridge.*)

MASON. I've took the lumps out.

TROTTER. Good. Keep 'em and use 'em for dumplings next time we 'ave boiled beef.

MASON. Very good, sir. (*He goes out.*)

TROTTER. Yes. That plumber was a prize cook, 'e was. Lucky for us one day 'e set 'imself on fire making the tea. 'E went 'ome pretty well fried. Did Mason get that pepper?

OSBORNE. Yes.

TROTTER. Good. Must 'ave pepper.

OSBORNE. I thought you were on duty now.

TROTTER. I'm supposed to be. Stanhope sent me down to get my breakfast. He's looking after things till I finish.

OSBORNE. He's got a long job then.

TROTTER. Oh, no. I'm a quick eater. Hi! Mason! Bacon!

MASON (*outside*). Coming, sir!

OSBORNE. It's a wonderful morning.

TROTTER. Isn't it lovely? Makes you feel sort of young and 'opeful. I was up in that old trench under the brick wall just now, and damned if a bloomin' little bird didn't start singing! Didn't 'arf sound funny. Sign of spring, I s'pose. (MASON *arrives with* TROTTER'S *bacon*) That looks all right.

MASON. If you look down straight on it from above, sir, you can see the bit o' lean quite clear.

TROTTER. Good Lord, yes! That's it, isn't it?

MASON. No, sir; that's a bit o' rust off the pan.

TROTTER. Ah! *That's* it, then!

MASON. You've got it, sir. (*He goes out.*)

TROTTER. Cut us a chunk of bread, Uncle.
(OSBORNE *cuts him off a chunk.*)

OSBORNE. How are things going up there?

TROTTER. I don't like the look of things a bit.

OSBORNE. You mean—the quiet?

TROTTER. Yes. Standing up there in the dark last night there didn't seem a thing in the world alive—except the rats squeaking and my stomach grumbling about that cutlet.

OSBORNE. It's quiet even now.

TROTTER. Too damn quiet. You can bet your boots the Boche is up to something. The big attack soon, I reckon. I don't like it, Uncle. Pass the jam.

OSBORNE. It's strawberry.

TROTTER. Is it? I'm glad we've got rid o' that raspberry jam. Can't stand raspberry jam. Pips get be-'ind your plate.

OSBORNE. Did Stanhope tell you he wants two wiring parties out to-night?

TROTTER. Yes. He's fixing it up now. (*He pauses, and goes on in a low voice*) My goodness, Uncle, doesn't he look ill!

OSBORNE. I'm afraid he's not well.

TROTTER. Nobody'd be well who went on like he does. (*There is another pause*) You know when you came up to relieve me last night?

OSBORNE. Yes?

TROTTER. Well, Raleigh and me came back here, and there was Stanhope sitting on that bed drinking a whiskey. He looked as white as a sheet. God, he looked awful; he'd drunk the bottle since dinner. I said " 'Ullo!" and he didn't seem to know who I was. Uncanny wasn't it, Raleigh?

RALEIGH (*with lowered head*). Yes.

TROTTER. He just said, "Better go to bed, Raleigh"—just as if Raleigh'd been a chool kid.

OSBORNE. Did he? (*There is a pause*) Look at the sun. It'll be quite warm soon.
(*They look at the pale square of sunlight on the floor.*)

TROTTER. It's warm now. You can feel it on your face outside if you stand in it. First time this year. 'Ope we 'ave an 'ot summer.

OSBORNE. So do I.

TROTTER. Funny about that bird. Made me feel quite braced up. Sort of made me think about my garden of an evening—walking round in me slippers after supper, smoking me pipe.

OSBORNE. You keen on gardening?

TROTTER. Oh, I used to do a bit of an evening. I 'ad a decent little grass plot in front, with flower-borders—geraniums, lobelia, and calsularia—you know, red, white, and blue. Looked rather nice in the summer.

OSBORNE. Yes.

TROTTER. 'Ad some fine 'olly'ocks out the back. One year I 'ad one eight feet 'igh. Took a photer of it. (*He fumbles in his pocket case*) Like to look at it?

OSBORNE. I would. (*He looks at the photo*) By Jove, it's a beauty.

TROTTER (*looking over* OSBORNE'S *shoulder*). You see that, just there?

OSBORNE. Yes?

TROTTER. That's the roof of the summer-'ouse.

OSBORNE. Is it really!

TROTTER. Just shows the 'ite of the 'olly'ock.

OSBORNE. It does. (*He shows the photo to* RALEIGH) A beauty, isn't it?

RALEIGH. Rather!

TROTTER. It never wanted no stick to keep it straight, neether. (*There is a pause*) You keen on gardening?

OSBORNE. Yes. A bit. I made a rockery when I was home on leave. I used to cycle out to the woods and get primroses and things like that, and try and get 'em to grow in my garden.

TROTTER. I don't suppose they would!

OSBORNE. They would if you pressed a bit of moss round them——

TROTTER. —to make 'em feel at 'ome, eh? (*He laughs.*)

OSBORNE. They'll be coming out again soon if they've got this sun at home.

TROTTER. I reckon they will. I remember one morning last spring—we was coming out of the salient. Just when it was getting light in the morning—it was at the time when the Boche was sending over a lot of that gas that smells like pear-drops, you know?

OSBORNE. I know. Phosgene.

TROTTER. That's it. We were scared to hell of it. All of a sudden we smelt that funny sweet smell, and a fellow shouted "Gas!"—and we put on our masks; and then I spotted what it was.

OSBORNE. What was it?

TROTTER. Why, a blinkin' may-tree! All out in bloom, growing beside the path! We did feel a lot of silly poops—putting on gas masks because of a damn may-tree! (*He stretches himself and tries to button his tunic*) Lord! I *must* get my fat down. (*He gets up*) Well, I better go and relieve Stanhope. He'll curse like hell if I don't. I bet he's got a red-hot liver this morning.

OSBORNE. I relieve you at eleven.

TROTTER. That's right. I don't like this time of day in the line. The old Boche 'as just 'ad 'is breakfast, and sends over a few whizz-bangs and rifle grenades to show 'e ain't forgotten us. Still, I'd rather 'ave a bang or two than this damn quiet. (*He puts on his helmet and gas mask satchel and goes up the steps*) Cheero!

OSBORNE. Cheero!

RALEIGH. Cheero!

OSBORNE. (*to* RALEIGH). I expect Stanhope'll let you go on duty alone now.

RALEIGH. Will he? About what time?

OSBORNE. Well, after me, I expect. From about two till four.

RALEIGH. I see.
(*There is a pause. Then* OSBORNE *looks at* RALEIGH *and laughs.*)

OSBORNE. What do you think about it all?

RALEIGH. Oh, all right, thanks. (*He laughs*) I feel I've been here ages.

OSBORNE (*filling his pipe*). I expect you do. The time passes, though.

RALEIGH. Are we here for six days?

OSBORNE. Yes. Seems a long time, doesn't it?

RALEIGH (*laughing shortly*). It does rather. I can't imagine—the end of six days here——

OSBORNE. Anyhow, we've done twelve hours already. It's fine when you are relieved and go down the line to billets, and have a good hot bath, and sit and read under trees.

RALEIGH. Good Lord, I feel I haven't seen a tree for ages—not a real tree with leaves and branches—and yet I've only been here twelve hours.

OSBORNE. How did you feel—in the front line?

RALEIGH. Oh, all right. It seemed so frightfully quiet and uncanny—everybody creeping about and talking in low voices. I suppose you've *got* to talk quietly when you're so near the German front line—only about seventy yards, isn't it?

OSBORNE. Yes. About the breadth of a football field.

RALEIGH. It's funny to think of it like that.

OSBORNE. I always measure distances like that out here. Keeps them in proportion.

RALEIGH. Did you play football?

OSBORNE. Yes. But mostly reffing at school in the last few years.

RALEIGH. Are you a schoolmaster, then?

OSBORNE. Yes. I must apologise.

RALEIGH. Oh, I don't mind schoolmasters. (*Hastily*) I—I mean, I never met one outside a school.

OSBORNE. They do get out sometimes.

RALEIGH (*laughing*). Who did you play for?

OSBORNE. The Harlequins.

RALEIGH. I say, really!

OSBORNE. I played for the English team on one great occasion.

RALEIGH. What! For *England!*

OSBORNE. I was awfully lucky to get the chance. It's a long time ago now.

RALEIGH (*with awe*). Oh, but, good Lord! that must have been simply topping. Where did you play?

OSBORNE. Wing three.

RALEIGH. I say, I—I never realised—you'd played for England?

OSBORNE. Tuppence to talk to me now! Anyhow, don't breeze it about.

RALEIGH. Don't the others know?

OSBORNE. We never talk about football.

RALEIGH. They ought to know. It'd make them feel jolly bucked.

OSBORNE (*laughing*). It doesn't make much difference out here!

RALEIGH. It must be awfully thrilling, playing in front of a huge crowd—all shouting and cheering——

OSBORNE. You don't notice it when the game begins.

RALEIGH. You're too taken up with the game?

OSBORNE. Yes.

RALEIGH. I used to get wind up playing at school with only a few kids looking on.

OSBORNE. You feel it more when there are only a few. (*He has picked up a slip of paper from the table; suddenly he laughs*) Look at this!

RALEIGH (*looking at it curiously*). What is it?

OSBORNE. Trotter's plan to make the time pass quickly. One hundred and forty-four little circles—one for each hour of six days. He's blacked in six already. He's six hours behind.

RALEIGH. It's rather a good idea. I like Trotter.

OSBORNE. He's a good chap.

RALEIGH. He makes things feel—natural.

OSBORNE. He's a genuine sort of chap.

RALEIGH. That's it. He's genuine. (*There is a pause. He has been filling a new pipe.* OSBORNE *is puffing at his old one*) How topping—to have played for England!

OSBORNE. It was rather fun.
(*There is a pause.*)

RALEIGH. The Germans are really quite decent, aren't they? I mean, outside the newspapers?

OSBORNE. Yes. (*Pause*) I remember up at Wipers we had a man shot when he was out on patrol. Just at dawn. We couldn't get him in that night. He lay out there groaning all day. Next night three of our men crawled out to get him in. It was so near the German trenches that they could have shot our fellows one by one. But, when our men began dragging the wounded man back over the rough ground, a big German officer stood up in their trenches and called out: "Carry him!"—and our fellows stood up and carried the man back, and the German officer fired some lights for them to see by.

RALEIGH. How topping!

OSBORNE. Next day we blew each other's trenches to blazes.

RALEIGH. It all seems rather—*silly*, doesn't it?

OSBORNE. It does, rather.
(*There is silence for a while.*)

RALEIGH. I started a letter when I came off duty last night. How do we send letters?

OSBORNE. The quartermaster-sergeant takes them down after he brings rations up in the evenings. (STANHOPE *is coming slowly down the steps.* RALEIGH *rises.*)

RALEIGH. I think I'll go and finish it now—if I go on duty soon.

OSBORNE. Come and write it in here. It's more cheery.

RALEIGH. It's all right, thanks; I'm quite comfortable in there. I've rigged up a sort of little table beside my bed.

OSBORNE. Righto.

(RALEIGH *goes into his dug-out.* STANHOPE *is slowly taking off his equipment.*)

STANHOPE. What a foul smell of bacon.

OSBORNE. Yes. We've got bacon for breakfast.

STANHOPE. So I gather. Have you told Raleigh about rifle inspection?

OSBORNE. No.

STANHOPE (*at the entrance to* RALEIGH'S *dug-out*). Raleigh!

RALEIGH (*appearing*). Yes?

STANHOPE. You inspect your platoon's rifles at nine o'clock.

RALEIGH. Oh, righto, Stanhope. (*He goes again.*)

STANHOPE (*sitting at the table*). I've arranged two wiring parties to begin at eight o'clock to-night—Corporal Burt with two men and Sergeant Smith with two. I want them to strengthen the wire all along the front.

OSBORNE. It's very weak at present.

STANHOPE. Every company leaves it for the next one to do. There're great holes blown out weeks ago.

OSBORNE. I know.

STANHOPE. Next night we'll start putting a belt of wire down both sides of us.

OSBORNE. Down the sides?

STANHOPE. Yes. We'll wire ourselves right in. If this attack comes, I'm not going to trust the companies on our sides to hold their ground.

(MASON *has come in, and stands diffidently in the background.*)

MASON. Would you like a nice bit o' bacon, sir?

STANHOPE. No, thanks. I'll have a cup of tea.

MASON. Right, sir. (*He goes out.*)

STANHOPE. I've been having a good look round. We've got a strong position here—if we wire ourselves right in. The colonel's been talking to me up there.

OSBORNE. Oh. Has he been round?

STANHOPE. Yes. He says a German prisoner gave the day of attack as the 21st.

OSBORNE. That's Thursday?

STANHOPE. Yes. Today's Tuesday.

OSBORNE. That means about dawn the day after tomorrow.

STANHOPE. The second dawn from now.

(*There is a pause.*)

OSBORNE. Then it'll come while we're here.

STANHOPE. Yes. It'll come while we're here. And we shall be in the front seats.

OSBORNE. Oh, well——

(*In the silence that follows,* MASON *enters with a cup of tea.*)

MASON. Would you like a nice plate of sardines, sir?

STANHOPE. I should loathe it.

MASON. Very good, sir. (*He goes out.*)

OSBORNE. Did the colonel have much to say?

STANHOPE. Only that when the attack comes we can't expect any help from behind. We're not to move from here. We've got to stick it.

OSBORNE. I see.

STANHOPE. We'll wire ourselves in as strongly as possible. I've got to arrange battle positions for each platoon and section this afternoon.

OSBORNE. Well, I'm glad it's coming at last. I'm sick of waiting.

STANHOPE (*looking at* TROTTER'S *chart*). What's this extraordinary affair?

OSBORNE. Trotter's plan to make the time pass by. A hundred and forty-four circles—one for each hour of six days.

STANHOPE. How many hours are there till dawn on the 21st.

OSBORNE. Goodness knows. Not many, I hope.

STANHOPE. Nearly nine o'clock now. Twenty-four till nine tomorrow; twelve till nine at night—that's thirty-six; nine till six next morning; that's forty-five altogether. (*He begins to count off forty-five circles on* TROTTER'S *chart.*)

OSBORNE. What are you going to do?

STANHOPE. At the end of the forty-fifth circle I'm going to draw a picture of Trotter being blown up in four pieces.

OSBORNE. Don't spoil his chart. It took him an hour to make that.

STANHOPE. He won't see the point. He's no imagination.

OSBORNE. I don't suppose he has.

STANHOPE. Funny not to have any imagination. Must be rather nice.

OSBORNE. A bit dull, I should think.

STANHOPE. It must be, rather. I suppose all his life Trotter feels like you and I do when we're drowsily drunk.

OSBORNE. Poor chap!

STANHOPE. I suppose if Trotter looks at that wall he just sees a brown surface. He doesn't see into the earth beyond—the worms wandering about round the stones and roots of trees. I wonder how a worm knows when it's going up or down.

OSBORNE. When it's going down I suppose the blood runs into its head and makes it throb.

STANHOPE. Worms haven't got any blood.

OSBORNE. Then I don't suppose it ever does know.

STANHOPE. Rotten if it didn't—and went on going down when it thought it was coming up.

OSBORNE. Yes, I expect that's the one thing worms dread.

STANHOPE. D'you think this life sharpens the imagination?

OSBORNE. It must.

STANHOPE. Whenever I look at anything nowadays I see right through it. Looking at you now there's your uniform—your jersey—shirt—vest—then beyond that——

OSBORNE. Let's talk about something else—croquet, or the war.

STANHOPE (*laughing*). Sorry! It's a habit that's grown on me lately—to look right through things, and on and on—till I get frightened and stop.

OSBORNE. I suppose everybody out here—*feels* more keenly.

STANHOPE. I hope so. I wondered if there was anything wrong with me. D'you ever get a sudden feeling that everything's going farther and farther away—till you're the only thing in the world—and then the world begins going away—until you're the only thing in—in the universe—and you struggle to get back—and can't?

OSBORNE. Bit of nerve strain, that's all.

STANHOPE. You don't think I'm going potty?

OSBORNE. Oh, Lord, no!

STANHOPE (*throwing back his head and laughing*). Dear old Uncle! you don't really know, do you? You just pretend you do, to make me feel all right.

OSBORNE. When people are going potty they never talk about it; they keep it to themselves.

STANHOPE. Oh, well, that's all right, then. (*There is silence for a while*) I had that feeling this morning, standing out there in the line while the sun was rising. By the way, did you see the sunrise? Wasn't it gorgeous?

OSBORNE. Splendid—this morning.

STANHOPE. I was looking across at the Boche trenches and right beyond—not a sound or a soul; just an enormous plain, all churned up like a sea that's got muddier and muddier till it's so stiff that it can't move. You could have heard a pin drop in the quiet; yet you knew thousands of guns were hidden there, all ready cleaned and oiled—millions of bullets lying in pouches—thousands of Germans, waiting and thinking. Then, gradually, that feeling came——

OSBORNE. I never knew the sun could rise in so many ways till I came out here. Green, and pink, and red, and blue, and grey. Extraordinary, isn't it?

STANHOPE. Yes. Hi! Mason!

MASON (*outside*). Yessir!

STANHOPE. Bring some mugs and a bottle of whiskey.

MASON. Yessir.

OSBORNE (*smiling*). So early in the morning?

STANHOPE. Just a spot. It's damn cold in here.

OSBORNE (*turning over the pages of a magazine*). This show at the Hippodrome has been running a long time.

STANHOPE. What? *Zig-zag?*

OSBORNE. Yes. George Robey's in it.

STANHOPE. Harper saw it on leave. Says it's damn good. Robey's pricelessly funny.
(MASON *brings whiskey and mugs and water.*)

OSBORNE. Wish I'd seen a show on leave.

STANHOPE. D'you mean to say you didn't go to any shows?

OSBORNE (*laughing*). No. I spent all the time in the garden, making a rockery. In the evenings I used to sit and smoke and read—and my wife used to knit socks and play the piano a bit. We pretended there wasn't any war at all—till my two youngsters made me help in a tin-soldier battle on the floor.

STANHOPE. Poor old Uncle! You can't get away from it, can you?

OSBORNE. I wish I knew how to fight a battle like those boys of mine. You ought to have seen the way they lured my men under the sofa and mowed them down.

STANHOPE (*laughing and helping himself to a drink*). You going to have one?

OSBORNE. Not now, thanks.

STANHOPE. You go on duty at eleven, don't you?

OSBORNE. Yes. I relieve Trotter.

STANHOPE. Raleigh better go on at one o'clock and stay with you for an hour. Then he can stay on alone till four. Hibbert relieves him at four.

OSBORNE. Righto.

STANHOPE. What's Raleigh doing now?

OSBORNE. Finishing a letter.

STANHOPE. Did you tell him?

OSBORNE. About what?

STANHOPE. Censorship.

OSBORNE. You don't mean that seriously?

STANHOPE. Mean it? Of course I mean it.

OSBORNE. You can't do that.

STANHOPE. Officially I'm supposed to read all your letters. Damn it all, Uncle! Imagine yourself in my place—a letter going away from here—from that boy——

OSBORNE. He'll say nothing—rotten—about you.

STANHOPE. You think so? (*There is a pause*) I heard you go on duty last night. After you'd gone, I got up. I was feeling bad. I forgot Raleigh was out there with Trotter. I'd forgotten all about him. I was sleepy. I just knew something beastly had happened. Then he came in with Trotter—and looked at me. After coming in out of the night air, this place must have reeked of candle-grease, and rats—and whiskey. One thing a boy like that can't stand is a smell that isn't fresh. He looked at me as if I'd hit him between the eyes—as if I'd spat on him——

OSBORNE. You imagine things.

STANHOPE (*laughing*). Imagine things! No need to imagine!

OSBORNE. Why can't you treat him like any other youngster?

(RALEIGH *comes in from his dug-out with a letter in his hand. He stops short as he notices the abrupt silence that follows his entry.*)

RALEIGH. I'm sorry.

OSBORNE. It's all right, Raleigh. Going to inspect rifles?

RALEIGH. Yes.

OSBORNE. You needn't bother if the wood's a bit dirty—just the barrels and magazines and all the metal parts.

RALEIGH. Righto.

OSBORNE. See there's plenty of oil on it. And look at the ammunition in the men's pouches.

RALEIGH. Right. (*He crosses towards the door and turns*) Where do we put the letters to be collected?

OSBORNE. Oh, just on the table.

RALEIGH. Thanks. (*He begins to lick the flap of the envelope.*)

STANHOPE (*in a quiet voice*). You leave it open.

RALEIGH (*surprised*). Open?

STANHOPE. Yes. I have to censor all letters.

RALEIGH (*stammering*). Oh, but—I haven't said anything about—where we are——

STANHOPE. It's the rule that letters must be read.

RALEIGH (*nervously*). Oh, I—I didn't realise that. (*He stands embarrassed; then gives a short laugh*) I—I think—I'll just leave it, then. (*He unbuttons his tunic pocket to put the letter away.*)

(STANHOPE *rises, crosses slowly and faces* RALEIGH.)

STANHOPE. Give me that letter!

RALEIGH (*astonished*). But—Dennis——

STANHOPE (*trembling*). Give me that letter!

RALEIGH. But it's—it's private. I didn't know——

STANHOPE. D'you understand an order? Give me that letter!

RALEIGH. But I tell you—there's nothing—(STANHOPE *clutches* RALEIGH'S *wrist and tears the letter from his hand*) Dennis—I'm——

STANHOPE. Don't "Dennis" me! Stanhope's my name! You're not at school! Go and inspect your rifles.

(RALEIGH *stands in amazement at the foot of the steps.*)

STANHOPE (*shouting*). D'you understand an order?

(*For a moment* RALEIGH *stares wide-eyed at* STANHOPE, *who is trembling and breathing heavily, then almost in a whisper he says:* "Right," *and goes quietly up the narrow steps.* STANHOPE *turns toward the table.*)

OSBORNE. Good heavens, Stanhope!

STANHOPE (*wheeling furiously on* OSBORNE). Look here, Osborne, *I'm* commanding this company. I ask for advice when I want it!

OSBORNE. Very well.
(STANHOPE *sinks down at the table with the letter in his hand. There is silence for a moment. Then he throws the letter on the table and rests his head between his hands.*)

STANHOPE. Oh, God! I don't want to read the blasted thing!

OSBORNE. You'll let it go then?

STANHOPE. I don't care.
(*There is a pause.*)

OSBORNE. Shall I glance through it —for you?

STANHOPE. If you like.

OSBORNE. I don't *want* to.

STANHOPE. You better. I can't.
(OSBORNE *takes the letter from the table and opens it.* STANHOPE *sits with his head in his hand, digging a magazine with a pencil. After a while,* OSBORNE *glances up at* STANHOPE.)

OSBORNE. D'you want to hear?

STANHOPE. I suppose I better know.

OSBORNE. He begins with a description of his getting here—he doesn't mention the names of any places.

STANHOPE. What does he say then?

OSBORNE. The last piece is about you.

STANHOPE. Go on.

OSBORNE (*reading*). He says: "And now I come to the great news. I reported at Battalion Headquarters, and the colonel looked in a little book, and said, 'You report to "C" Company—Captain Stanhope.' Can't you imagine what I felt? I was taken along some trenches and shown a dug-out. There was an awfully nice officer there—quite old—with grey hair"—(OSBORNE *clears his throat*)—"and then later Dennis came in. He looked tired, but that's because he works so frightfully hard, and because of the responsibility. Then I went on duty in the front line, and a sergeant told me all about Dennis. He said that Dennis is the finest officer in the battalion, and the men simply love him. He hardly ever sleeps in the dug-out; he's always up in the front line with the men, cheering them on with jokes, and making them keen about things, like he did the kids at school. I'm awfully proud to think he's my friend." (*There is silence.* STANHOPE *has not moved while* OSBORNE *has read*) That's all. (*Pause*) Shall I stick it down?
(STANHOPE *sits with lowered head. He murmurs something that sounds like* "Yes, please." *He rises heavily and crosses to the shadows by* OSBORNE'S *bed. The sun is shining quite brightly in the trench outside.*)

THE CURTAIN FALLS

SCENE II

Afternoon on the same day. The sunlight has gone from the dug-out floor, but still shines brightly in the trench.

STANHOPE *is lying on his bed reading by the light of a candle on the table beside him. A burly* FIGURE *comes groping down the steps and stands blinking in the shadows of the dug-out. A huge man, with a heavy black moustache, a fat red face, and massive chin.*

STANHOPE *puts the magazine down, rises and sits up to the table.*

STANHOPE. I want to talk with you, sergeant-major.

S.-M. (*standing stolidly by the steps*). Yes, sir?

STANHOPE. Sit down. Have a whiskey?

S.-M. (*a suspicion of brightness in his voice*). Thank you, sir. (*The* SERGEANT-MAJOR *diffidently takes a small tot.*)

STANHOPE. I say. You won't taste that. Take a proper one.

S.-M. Well—sir—(STANHOPE *reaches over, helps the* SERGEANT-MAJOR *to a large tot, and takes one himself*) Turning chilly again, sir. Quite warm this morning.

STANHOPE. Yes.

S.-M. Well, here's your very good health, sir. (*He raises his glass and drinks.*)

STANHOPE. Cheero. (*He puts down his glass and abruptly changes his tone*) Now, look here, sergeant-major. We must expect this attack on Thursday morning, at dawn. That's the second dawn from now. (*The* SERGEANT-MAJOR *takes a very dirty little notebook from his pocket and jots down notes with a very small stub of pencil.*)

S.-M. Thursday morning. Very good, sir.

STANHOPE. We're to hold these trenches, and no man's to move from here.

S.-M. Very good, sir.

STANHOPE. It may happen that companies on our sides will give way, leaving our flanks exposed; so I want a screen of wire put down both flanks till it meets the wire in the support line.

S.-M. (*writing hurriedly*). Both flanks—yes, sir.

STANHOPE. When the attack begins, I shall take charge of the left, and Mr. Osborne the right. You will be with Mr. Osborne, and Sergeant Baker with me; 9 and 10 Platoons will move over here. (*He points out the position on the trench map*) 11 and 12 Platoons to the left.

S.-M. I see, sir.

STANHOPE. Is there anything you're not clear about?

S.-M. (*looking at his notes*). Seems all clear, sir.

STANHOPE. Anything you want to know?

S.-M. Well, sir (*clears his throat*) —when the attack comes, of course, we beat 'em off—but what if they keep on attacking?

STANHOPE. Then we keep on beating them off.

S.-M. Yes, sir. But what I mean is —they're bound to make a big thing of it.

STANHOPE (*cheerily*). Oh, I think they will!

S.-M. Well, then, sir. If they don't get through the first day, they'll attack the next day and the next——

STANHOPE. They're bound to.

S.-M. Then oughtn't we to fix up something about, well (*he gropes for the right words*)—er—falling back?

STANHOPE. There's no need to—you see, this company's a lot better than "A" and "B" Companies on either side of us.

S.-M. Quite, sir.

STANHOPE. Well, then, if anyone breaks, "A" and "B" will break before we do. As long as we stick here when the other companies have given way, we can fire into the Boche as they try and get through the gaps on our sides—we'll make a hell of a mess of them. We might delay the advance a whole day.

S.-M. (*diffidently*). Yes, sir, but what 'appens when the Boche 'as all got round the back of us?

STANHOPE. Then we advance and win the war.

S.-M. (*pretending to make a note*). Win the war. Very good, sir.

STANHOPE. But you understand exactly what I mean, sergeant-major. Our orders are to stick here. If you're told to stick where you are you don't make plans to retire.

S.-M. Quite, sir.
(OSBORNE'S *voice is calling down the steps.* SERGEANT-MAJOR *rises.*)

OSBORNE. Are you there, Stanhope?

STANHOPE (*rising quickly*). Yes. What's the matter?

OSBORNE. The colonel's up here. Wants to see you——

STANHOPE. Oh, right, I'll come up.

COLONEL (*from above*). All right, Stanhope—I'll come down.

S.-M. (*who has risen*). Anything more, sir?

STANHOPE. I don't think so. I'll see you at stand-to this evening.

S.-M. Very good, sir. (*He stands back a pace and salutes* STANHOPE *smartly.* STANHOPE'S *eye falls on the* SERGEANT-MAJOR'S *nearly finished drink on the table. He points to it.*)

STANHOPE. Hoy! What about that?

S.-M. Thank you, sir. (*He finishes the drink. The* COLONEL *comes down the steps.*)

COLONEL. Good morning, sergeant-major.

S.-M. Good morning, sir. (*The* SERGEANT-MAJOR *goes up the steps.*)

STANHOPE. Hullo, sir!

COLONEL. Hullo, Stanhope! (*He sniffs*) Strong smell of bacon.

STANHOPE. Yes, sir. We had some bacon for breakfast.

COLONEL. Hangs about, doesn't it?

STANHOPE. Yes, sir. Clings to the walls.

COLONEL. Lovely day.

STANHOPE. Splendid, sir.

COLONEL. Spring's coming. (*There is a pause*) I'm glad you're alone. I've got some rather serious news.

STANHOPE. I'm sorry to hear that, sir. Will you have a drink?

COLONEL. Well, thanks—just a spot. (STANHOPE *mixes a drink for the* COLONEL *and himself*) Here's luck.

STANHOPE. Cheero, sir. (*Bringing forward a box*) Sit down, sir.

COLONEL. Thanks.

STANHOPE. What's the news, sir?

COLONEL. The brigadier came to see me this morning. (*He pauses*) It seems almost certain the attack's to come on Thursday morning. They've got information from more than one source—but they don't know where it's going to fall the hardest. The Boche began relieving his frontline troops yesterday. They're bound to put in certain regiments where they intend to make the hardest push——

STANHOPE. Naturally——

COLONEL. And the general wants us to make a raid to find out who's come into the line opposite here. (*There is a pause.*)

STANHOPE. I see. When?

COLONEL. As soon as possible. He said tonight.

STANHOPE. Oh, but that's absurd!

COLONEL. I told him so. I said the earliest would be tomorrow afternoon. A surprise daylight raid under a smoke screen from the trench-mortar people. I think daylight best. There's not much moon now, and it's vitally important to get hold of a Boche or two.

STANHOPE. Quite.

COLONEL. I suggest sending two officers and ten men. Quite enough for the purpose. Just opposite here there's only seventy yards of No Man's Land. To-night the trench-mortars can blow a hole in the Boche wire and you can cut a hole in yours. Harrison of the trench-mortars is coming in to dinner with me this evening to discuss everything. I'd like you to come too. Eight o'clock suit you?

STANHOPE. Very good, sir.

COLONEL. I'll leave you to select the men.

STANHOPE. You want me to go with them, sir?

COLONEL. Oh, no, Stanhope. I—I can't let you go. No. I want one officer to direct the raid and one to make the dash in and collar some Boche.

STANHOPE. Who do you suggest, sir?

COLONEL. Well, I suggest Osborne, for one. He's a very level-headed chap. He can direct it.

STANHOPE. And who else?

COLONEL. Well, there's Trotter—but he's a bit fat, isn't he? Not much good at dashing in?

STANHOPE. No. D'you suggest Hibbert?

COLONEL. Well, what do *you* think of Hibbert?

STANHOPE. I don't think so.

COLONEL. No.
(*There is a pause.*)

STANHOPE. Why not send a good sergeant, sir?

COLONEL. No. I don't think a sergeant. The men expect officers to lead a raid.

STANHOPE. Yes. There is that.

COLONEL. As a matter of fact, Stanhope, I'm thinking of that youngster I sent up to you last night.

STANHOPE. Raleigh?

COLONEL. Yes. Just the type. Plenty of guts——

STANHOPE. He's awfully new to it all——

COLONEL. All to the good. His nerves are sound.

STANHOPE. It's rotten to send a fellow who's only just arrived.

COLONEL. Well, who else is there? I could send an officer from another company——

STANHOPE (*quickly*). Oh, Lord, no. We'll do it.

COLONEL. Then I suggest Osborne to direct the raid and Raleigh to make the dash—with ten good men. We'll meet Harrison at supper and arrange the smoke bombs—and blowing a hole in the wire. You select the men and talk to Osborne and Raleigh about it in the meantime.

STANHOPE. Very well, sir.

COLONEL. Better send Osborne and Raleigh down to me in the morning to talk things over. Or, better still—I'll come up here first thing tomorrow morning.

STANHOPE. Right, sir.

COLONEL. It's all a damn nuisance; but, after all—it's necessary.

STANHOPE. I suppose it is.

COLONEL. Well, so long, Stanhope. I'll see you at eight o'clock. Do you like fish?

STANHOPE. Fish, sir?

COLONEL. Yes. We've had some fresh fish sent up from railhead for supper tonight.

STANHOPE. Splendid, sir!

COLONEL. Whiting, I think it is.

STANHOPE. Good!

COLONEL. Well, bye-bye. (*The* COLONEL *goes up the steps.*)
(STANHOPE *stands watching for a moment, then turns and walks slowly to the table.* HIBBERT *comes quietly into the dug-out from the tunnel leading from his sleeping quarters.*)

STANHOPE. Hullo! I thought you were asleep.

HIBBERT. I just wanted a word with you, Stanhope.

STANHOPE. Fire away.

HIBBERT. This neuralgia of mine. I'm awfully sorry. I'm afraid I can't stick it any longer——

STANHOPE. I know. It's rotten, isn't it? I've got it like hell——

HIBBERT (*taken aback*). *You* have?

STANHOPE. Had it for weeks.

HIBBERT. Well, I'm sorry, Stanhope. It's no good. I've tried damned hard; but I must go down——

STANHOPE. Go down—where?

HIBBERT. Why, go sick—go down the line. I must go into hospital and have some kind of treatment. (*There is a silence for a moment.* STANHOPE *is looking at* HIBBERT—*till* HIBBERT *turns away and walks towards his dug-out*) I'll go right along now, I think——

STANHOPE (*quietly*). You're going to stay here.

HIBBERT. I'm going down to see the doctor. He'll send me to hospital when he understands——

STANHOPE. I've seen the doctor. I saw him this morning. He won't send you to hospital, Hibbert; he'll send you back here. He promised me he would. (*There is silence*) So you can save yourself a walk.

HIBBERT (*fiercely*). What the hell——!

STANHOPE. Stop that!

HIBBERT. I've a perfect right to go sick if I want to. The men can—why can't an officer?

STANHOPE. No man's sent down unless he's very ill. There's nothing wrong with you, Hibbert. The German attack's on Thursday; almost for certain. You're going to stay here and see it through with the rest of us.

HIBBERT (*hysterically*). I tell you, I can't—the pain's nearly sending me mad. I'm going! I've got all my stuff packed. I'm going now—you can't stop me! (*He goes excitedly into the dug-out.* STANHOPE *walks slowly towards the steps, turns, and undoes the flap of his revolver holster. He takes out his revolver, and stands casually examining it.* HIBBERT *returns with his pack slung on his back and a walking-stick in his hand. He pauses at the sight of* STANHOPE *by the steps.*)

HIBBERT. Let's get by, Stanhope.

STANHOPE. You're going to stay here and do your job.

HIBBERT. Haven't I *told* you? I *can't!* Don't you understand? Let—let me get by.

STANHOPE. Now look here, Hibbert. I've got a lot of work to do and no time to waste. Once and for all, you're going to stay here and see it through with the rest of us.

HIBBERT. I shall die of this pain if I don't go!

STANHOPE. Better die of pain than be shot for deserting.

HIBBERT (*in a low voice*). What do you mean?

STANHOPE. You know what I mean——

HIBBERT. I've a right to see the doctor!

STANHOPE. Good God! Don't you understand!—he'll send you back here. Dr. Preston's never let a shirker pass him yet—and he's not going to start now—two days before the attack—

HIBBERT (*pleadingly*). Stanhope—if you only *knew* how awful I feel——Please do let me go by—— (*He walks slowly round behind* STANHOPE. STANHOPE *turns and thrusts him roughly back. With a lightning movement* HIBBERT *raises his stick and strikes blindly at* STANHOPE, *who catches the stick, tears it from* HIBBERT'S *hands, smashes it across his knee, and throws it on the ground.*)

STANHOPE. God!—you little swine. You know what that means—don't you? Striking a superior officer! (*There is silence.* STANHOPE *takes hold of his revolver as it swings from its lanyard.* HIBBERT *stands quivering in front of* STANHOPE) Never mind, though. I won't have you shot for that——

HIBBERT. Let me go——

STANHOPE. If you went, I'd have you shot—for deserting. It's a hell of a disgrace—to die like that. I'd rather spare you the disgrace. I give you half a minute to think. You either stay here and try and be a man—or you try to get out of that door—to desert. If you do that, there's going to be an accident. D'you understand? I'm fiddling with my revolver, d'you see?—cleaning it—and it's going off by accident. It often happens out here. It's going off, and it's going to shoot you between the eyes.

HIBBERT (*in a whisper*). You daren't——

STANHOPE. You don't deserve to be shot by accident—but I'd save you the disgrace of the other way—I give you half a minute to decide. (*He holds up his wrist to look at his watch*) Half a minute from now—

(*There is silence; a few seconds go by. Suddenly* HIBBERT *bursts into a high-pitched laugh.*)

HIBBERT. Go on, then, shoot! You won't let me go to hospital. I swear I'll never go into those trenches again. Shoot!—and thank God——

STANHOPE (*with his eyes on his watch*). Fifteen more seconds——

HIBBERT. Go on! I'm ready——

STANHOPE. Ten. (*He looks up at* HIBBERT, *who has closed his eyes*) Five.

(*Again* STANHOPE *looks up. After a moment he quietly drops his revolver into its holster and steps towards* HIBBERT, *who stands with lowered head and eyes tightly screwed up, his arms stretched stiffly by his sides, his hands tightly clutching the edges of his tunic. Gently* STANHOPE *places his hands on* HIBBERT'S *shoulders.* HIBBERT *starts violently and gives a little cry. He opens his eyes and stares vacantly into* STANHOPE'S *face.* STANHOPE *is smiling.*)

STANHOPE. Good man, Hibbert. I liked the way you stuck that.

HIBBERT (*hoarsely*). Why didn't you shoot?

STANHOPE. Stay here, old chap—and see it through——

(HIBBERT *stands trembling, trying to speak. Suddenly he breaks down and cries.* STANHOPE *takes his hands from his shoulders and turns away.*)

HIBBERT. Stanhope! I've tried like hell—I swear I have. Ever since I came out here I've hated and loathed it. Every sound up there makes me all—cold and sick. I'm different to—to the others—you don't understand. It's got worse and worse, and now I can't bear it any longer. I'll never go up those steps again—into the line—with the men looking at me—and knowing—I'd rather die here. (*He is sitting on* STANHOPE'S *bed, crying without effort to restrain himself.*)

STANHOPE (*pouring out a whiskey*). Try a drop of this, old chap——

HIBBERT. No, thanks.

STANHOPE. Go on. Drink it. (HIBBERT *takes the mug and drinks.* STANHOPE *sits down beside* HIBBERT *and puts an arm round his shoulder*) I know what you feel, Hibbert. I've known all along——

HIBBERT. How *can* you know?

STANHOPE. Because I feel the same—exactly the same! Every little noise up there makes me feel—just as you feel. Why didn't you tell me instead of talking about neuralgia? We *all* feel like you do sometimes, if you only knew. I hate and loathe it all. Sometimes I feel I could just lie down on this bed and pretend I was paralysed or something—and couldn't move—and just lie there till I died—or was dragged away.

HIBBERT. I can't bear to go up into those awful trenches again.

STANHOPE. When are you due to go on?

HIBBERT. Quite soon. At four.

STANHOPE. Shall we go on together? We know how we both feel now. Shall we see if we can stick it together?

HIBBERT. I can't——

STANHOPE. Supposing I said *I* can't—supposing we *all* say we can't—what would happen then?

HIBBERT. I don't care. What does it matter? It's all so—so beastly—nothing matters——

STANHOPE. Supposing the worst happened—supposing we were knocked right out. Think of all the chaps who've gone already. It can't be very lonely there—with all those fellows. Sometimes I think it's lonelier here. (*He pauses.* HIBBERT *is sitting quietly now, his eyes roving vacantly in front of him*) Just go and have a quiet rest. Then we'll go out together.

HIBBERT. Do please let me go, Stanhope——

STANHOPE. If you went—and left Osborne and Trotter and Raleigh and all those men up there to do your work—could you ever look a man straight in the face again—in all your life? (*There is silence again*) You may be wounded. Then you can go home and feel proud—and if you're killed you—you won't have to stand this hell any more. I might have fired just now. If I had you would have been dead now. But you're still alive—with a straight fighting chance of coming through. Take the chance, old chap, and stand in with Osborne and Trotter and Raleigh. Don't you think it worth standing in with men like that?—when you know they all feel like you do—in their hearts—and just go on sticking it because they know it's—it's the only thing a decent man can do. (*Again there is silence*) What about it?

HIBBERT. I'll—I'll try——

STANHOPE. Good man!

HIBBERT. You—you won't say anything, Stanhope—about this?

STANHOPE. If you promise not to tell anyone what a blasted funk *I* am.

HIBBERT (*with a little laugh*). No.

STANHOPE. Splendid! Now go and have ten minutes' rest and a smoke—then we'll go up together and hold each other's hands—and jump every time a rat squeaks. (HIBBERT *rises and blows his nose*) We've all got a good fighting chance. *I* mean to come through—don't you?

HIBBERT. Yes. Rather. (*He goes timidly towards his dug-out, and turns at the doorway*) It's awfully decent of you, Stanhope—(STANHOPE *is pouring himself out a whiskey*) And thanks most awfully for——

STANHOPE. That's all right.
(HIBBERT *goes away.* STANHOPE *takes a drink and sits down at the table to write.* MASON *comes in.*)

MASON. Will you have a nice cup of tea, sir?

STANHOPE. Can you guarantee it's nice?

MASON. Well, sir—it's a bit oniony, but that's only because of the saucepan.

STANHOPE. In other words, it's onion soup with tea-leaves in it?

MASON. Not till dinner-time, sir.

STANHOPE. All right, Mason. Bring two cups of onion tea. One for Mr. Hibbert.

MASON. Very good, sir. (*Going towards the door, he meets* OSBORNE *coming in*) Will you have a nice cup of tea, sir?

OSBORNE. Please, Mason—and plenty of bread and butter and strawberry jam.

MASON. Very good, sir.

STANHOPE. Well, Uncle—how are things going on up there?

OSBORNE. Two lonely rifle grenades came over just now.

STANHOPE. I heard them. Where did they pitch?

OSBORNE. Just over the front line on the left. Otherwise nothing doing.
(*Pause.*)

STANHOPE. The colonel's been talking to me.

OSBORNE. About the attack?

STANHOPE. Partly. We've got to make a raid, Uncle.

OSBORNE. Oh? When?

STANHOPE. Tomorrow afternoon. Under a smoke screen. Two officers and ten men.

OSBORNE. Who's going?

STANHOPE. You and Raleigh.
(*Pause.*)

OSBORNE. Oh. (*There is another pause*) Why Raleigh?

STANHOPE. The colonel picked you to direct and Raleigh to dash in.

OSBORNE. I see.

STANHOPE. The brigade wants to know who's opposite here.

OSBORNE. Tomorrow? What time?

STANHOPE. I suggest about five o'clock. A little before dusk——

OSBORNE. I see.

STANHOPE. I'm damn sorry.

OSBORNE. That's all right, old chap.

STANHOPE. I'm dining with the colonel to arrange everything. Then I'll come back and go through it with you.

OSBORNE. Where do we raid from?

STANHOPE. Out of the sap on our left. Straight across.

OSBORNE. Where's the map?

STANHOPE. Here we are. Look. Straight across to this sentry post of the Boche. Sixty yards. Tonight we'll lay out a guiding tape as far as possible. After dark the toch-emmas are going to break the Boche wire and we'll cut a passage in ours.

OSBORNE. Will you fix up the men who are to go?

STANHOPE. Are you keen on any special men?

OSBORNE. Can I take a corporal?

STANHOPE. Sure.

OSBORNE. May I have young Crooks?

STANHOPE. Righto.

OSBORNE. You'll ask for volunteers, I suppose?

STANHOPE. Yes. I'll see the sergeant-major and get him to go round for names. (*He crosses to the doorway as* MASON *comes in with the tea.*)

MASON. Your tea, sir!

STANHOPE. Keep it hot, Mason.

MASON. Will you take this cup, Mr. Osborne?

STANHOPE. Take the other in to Mr. Hibbert, in there.

MASON. Very good, sir. (*He goes in to* HIBBERT'S *dug-out.*)

STANHOPE. Shan't be long, Uncle. (*He goes up the steps.*)

OSBORNE. Righto.
(MASON *returns.*)

MASON. Will you have cut bread and butter—or shall I bring the loaf, sir?

OSBORNE. Cut it, Mason, please.

MASON. Just bringing the jam separately?

OSBORNE. Yes.

MASON. Very good, sir.
(MASON *goes out.* OSBORNE *takes a small leather-bound book from his pocket, opens it at a marker, and begins to read.* TROTTER *appears from the sleeping dug-out looking very sleepy.*)

TROTTER. Tea ready?

OSBORNE. Yes.

TROTTER. Why's Hibbert got his tea in there?

OSBORNE. I don't know.

TROTTER (*rubbing his eyes*). Oh, Lord, I do feel frowsy. 'Ad a fine sleep, though.
(MASON *brings more tea and a pot of jam.*)

MASON. Bread just coming, sir. 'Ere's the strawberry jam, sir.

TROTTER (*reciting*).
"'*Tell me, mother, what is that*
That looks like strawberry jam?'
'*Hush, hush, my dear; 'tis only Pa*
Run over by a tram——'"

OSBORNE. The colonel came here while you were asleep.

TROTTER. Oh?

OSBORNE. We've got to make a raid tomorrow afternoon.

TROTTER. Oh, Lord! What—All of us?

OSBORNE. Two officers and ten men.

TROTTER. Who's got to do it?

OSBORNE. Raleigh and I.

TROTTER. Raleigh!

OSBORNE. Yes.

TROTTER. But 'e's only just come!

OSBORNE. Apparently that's the reason.

TROTTER. And you're going too?

OSBORNE. Yes.

TROTTER. Let's 'ear all about it.

OSBORNE. I know nothing yet. Except that it's got to be done.

TROTTER. What a damn nuisance!

OSBORNE. It is, rather.

TROTTER. I reckon the Boche are all ready waiting for it. Did you 'ear about the raid just south of 'ere the other night?

OSBORNE. Nothing much.

TROTTER. The trench-mortars go and knock an 'ole in the Boche wire to let our fellers through—and in the night the Boche went out and tied bits o' red rag on each side of the 'ole!

OSBORNE. Yes. I heard about that.

TROTTER. And even then our fellers 'ad to make the raid. It was murder. Doesn't this tea taste of onions?

OSBORNE. It does a bit.

TROTTER. Pity Mason don't clean 'is pots better. (MASON *brings some bread on a plate*) This tea tastes of onions.

MASON. I'm sorry, sir. Onions do 'ave such a way of cropping up again.

TROTTER. Yes, but we 'aven't 'ad onions for days!

MASON. I know, sir. That's what makes it so funny.

TROTTER. Well, you better do something about it.

MASON. I'll look into it, sir. (*He goes out.*)

(OSBORNE *and* TROTTER *prepare themselves slices of bread and jam.*)

TROTTER. Joking apart. It's damn ridiculous making a raid when the Boche are expecting it.

OSBORNE. We're not doing it for fun.

TROTTER. I know.

OSBORNE. You might avoid talking to Raleigh about it.

TROTTER. Why? How do you mean?

OSBORNE. There's no need to tell him it's murder——

TROTTER. Oh, Lord! no. (*He pauses*) I'm sorry 'e's got to go. 'E's a nice young feller—— (OSBORNE *turns to his book. There is silence*) What are you reading?

OSBORNE (*wearily*). Oh, just a book.

TROTTER. What's the title?

OSBORNE (*showing him the cover*). Ever read it?

TROTTER (*leaning over and reading the cover*). *Alice's Adventures in Wonderland*—why, that's a kid's book!

OSBORNE. Yes.

TROTTER. You aren't *reading* it?

OSBORNE. Yes.

TROTTER. What—a *kid's* book?

OSBORNE. Haven't you read it?

TROTTER (*scornfully*). No!

OSBORNE. You ought to. (*Reads*):
"*How doth the little crocodile*
Improve his shining tail,
And pour the waters of the Nile
On every golden scale?

"*How cheerfully he seems to grin*
And neatly spread his claws,
And welcomes little fishes in
With gently smiling jaws!"

TROTTER (*after a moment's thought*). I don't see no point in that.

OSBORNE (*wearily*). Exactly. That's just the point.

TROTTER (*looking curiously at* OSBORNE). You are a funny chap!

(STANHOPE *returns.*)

STANHOPE. The sergeant-major's getting volunteers.

OSBORNE. Good!

TROTTER. Sorry to 'ear about the raid, skipper.

STANHOPE (*shortly*). So am I. What do you make the time?

TROTTER. Just on four.
(MASON *brings in more tea.*)

STANHOPE (*taking the mug of tea*). Was Hibbert asleep when you came out of there?

TROTTER. No. 'E was just lying on 'is bed, smoking.

STANHOPE (*going to the sleeping dug-out*). Hibbert!

HIBBERT (*coming out*). I'm ready, Stanhope.

STANHOPE. Had some tea?

HIBBERT. Yes, thanks.

TROTTER. I reckon Raleigh'll be glad to be relieved. Rotten being on dooty for the first time alone.

OSBORNE. I don't think he minds.

STANHOPE. I shall be up there some time, Uncle.

OSBORNE. I say, why don't you have a rest—you've been on the go all day.

STANHOPE. There's too much to do. This raid's going to upset the arrangements of the wiring party tonight. Can't have men out there while the toch-emmas are blowing holes in the Boche wire. (*He drinks up his tea*) Ready, Hibbert? Come on, my lad.
(STANHOPE *and* HIBBERT *leave the dug-out together.* TROTTER *looks after them curiously, and turns to* OSBORNE.)

TROTTER. Can't understand that little feller, can you?

OSBORNE. Who?

TROTTER. Why, 'Ibbert. D'you see, 'is eyes? All red. 'E told me in there 'e'd got 'ay-fever.

OSBORNE. Rotten thing, hay-fever.

TROTTER. If you ask me, 'e's been crying——
(OSBORNE *is writing at the table.*)

OSBORNE. Maybe.

TROTTER. Funny little bloke, isn't 'e?

OSBORNE. Yes. I say—d'you mind? I just want to get a letter off.

TROTTER. Oh, sorry. They 'aven't collected the letters yet, then?

OSBORNE. Not yet.

TROTTER. I'll get one off to my old lady. (*He goes towards his dug-out*) She's wrote and asked if I've got fleas.

OSBORNE. Have you?

TROTTER (*gently rotating his shoulders*). I wish it *was* fleas.
(TROTTER *goes into his dug-out;* OSBORNE *continues his letter.* RALEIGH *comes down the steps from the trench.*)

RALEIGH (*excitedly*). I say, Stanhope's told me about the raid.

OSBORNE. Has he?

RALEIGH. Just you and me, isn't it —and ten men?

OSBORNE. Yes, tomorrow. Just before dusk. Under a smoke cloud.

RALEIGH. I say—it's most frightfully exciting!

OSBORNE. We shall know more about it after Stanhope sees the colonel tonight.

RALEIGH. Were you and I picked—specially?

OSBORNE. Yes.

RALEIGH. I—say!

THE CURTAIN FALLS

ACT THREE

SCENE I

The following day, towards sunset. The earth wall of the trench outside glows with a light that slowly fades with the sinking sun.

STANHOPE *is alone, wandering to and fro across the dug-out. He looks up the steps for a moment, crosses to the table, and glances down at the map. He looks anxiously at his watch, and, going to the servants' dug-out, calls:*

STANHOPE. Mason!

MASON (*outside*). Yessir!

STANHOPE. Are you making the coffee?

MASON. Yessir!

STANHOPE. Make it hot and strong. Ready in five minutes. I'll call when it's wanted.

MASON. Very good, sir.
(*Again* STANHOPE *wanders restlessly to and fro. The* COLONEL *comes down the steps.*)

COLONEL. Everything ready?

STANHOPE. Yes, sir. (*There is silence*) You've no news, then?

COLONEL. I'm afraid not. It's got to be done.

STANHOPE (*after a pause*). I see.

COLONEL. The brigadier says the Boche did the same thing just south of here the other day.

STANHOPE. I know; but didn't you suggest we altered our plans and made a surprise raid farther up the line after dark?

COLONEL. Yes. I suggested that.

STANHOPE. What did he say?

COLONEL. He said the present arrangements have got to stand.

STANHOPE. But surely he must realise——?

COLONEL (*impatiently breaking in*). Look here, Stanhope, I've done all I can, but my report's got to be at headquarters by seven this evening. If we wait till it's dark we shall be too late.

STANHOPE. Why seven?

COLONEL. They've got some conference to arrange the placing of reserves.

STANHOPE. They can't have it later because of dinner, I suppose.

COLONEL. Lots of raids have taken place along the line today. With the attack tomorrow morning, headquarters naturally want all the information they can get as early as possible.

STANHOPE. Meanwhile the Boche are sitting over there with a dozen machine-guns trained on that hole—waiting for our fellows to come.

COLONEL. Well, I can't disobey orders.

STANHOPE. Why didn't the trench-mortars blow a dozen holes in different places—so the Boche wouldn't know which we were going to use?

COLONEL. It took three hours to blow that one. How could they blow a dozen in the time? It's no good worrying about that now. It's too late. Where's Osborne and Raleigh?

STANHOPE. They're up in the sap, having a last look round. What d'you make the time, sir?

COLONEL. Exactly nineteen minutes to.

STANHOPE. I'm thirty seconds behind you.

COLONEL. Funny. We checked this morning.

STANHOPE. Still, it's near enough. We shan't go till the smoke blows across.

COLONEL. The smoke ought to blow across nicely. The wind's just right. I called on the trench-mortars on the way up. Everything's ready. They'll drop the bombs thirty yards to the right.

STANHOPE. Are you going to stay here?

COLONEL. I'll watch from the trench just above, I think. Bring the prisoners straight back here. We'll question them right away.

STANHOPE. Why not take them straight down to your headquarters?

COLONEL. Well, the Boche are bound to shell pretty heavily. I don't want the risk of the prisoners being knocked out before we've talked to them.

STANHOPE. All right. I'll have them brought back here.
(*There is a pause. The* COLONEL *sucks hard at his pipe.* STANHOPE *roves restlessly about, smoking a cigarette.*)

COLONEL. It's no good getting depressed. After all, it's only sixty yards. The Boche'll be firing into a blank fog. Osborne's a cool, level-headed chap, and Raleigh's the very man to dash in. You've picked good men to follow them?

STANHOPE. The best. All youngsters. Strong, keen chaps.

COLONEL. Good. (*Another pause*) You know quite well I'd give anything to cancel the beastly affair.

STANHOPE. I know you would, sir.

COLONEL. Have these red rags on the wire upset the men at all?

STANHOPE. It's hard to tell. They naturally take it as a joke. They say the rags are just what they want to show them the way through the gap.

COLONEL. That's the spirit, Stanhope. (OSBORNE *and* RALEIGH *come down the steps*) Well, Osborne. Everything ready?

OSBORNE. Yes, I think we're all ready, sir. I make it just a quarter to.

COLONEL. That's right.

OSBORNE. The men are going to stand by at three minutes to.

COLONEL. The smoke bombs drop exactly on the hour. You'll give the word to go when the smoke's thick enough?

OSBORNE. That's right, sir.

STANHOPE (*at the servants' dug-out*). Mason!

MASON. Coming, sir!

STANHOPE. Were the men having their rum, Uncle?

OSBORNE. Yes. Just as we left. It gives it a quarter of an hour to soak in.

COLONEL. That's right. Are they cheerful?

OSBORNE. Yes. Quite.
(MASON *brings in two cups of coffee and puts them on table.*)

STANHOPE. Would you like to go up and speak to them, sir?

COLONEL. Well, don't you think they'd rather be left alone?

STANHOPE. I think they would appreciate a word or two.

COLONEL. All right. If you think they would.

OSBORNE. They're all in the centre dug-out, sir.

COLONEL. Right. You coming, Stanhope?

STANHOPE. Yes. I'll come, sir.
(*The* COLONEL *lingers a moment. There is an awkward pause. Then the* COLONEL *clears his throat and speaks.*)

COLONEL. Well, good luck, Osborne. I'm certain you'll put up a good show.

OSBORNE (*taking the* COLONEL'S *hand*). Thank you, sir.

COLONEL. And, Raleigh, just go in like blazes. Grab hold of the first Boche you see and bundle him across here. One'll do, but bring more if you see any handy.

RALEIGH (*taking the* COLONEL'S *offered hand*). Right, sir.

COLONEL. And, if you succeed, I'll recommend you both for the M.C. (OSBORNE *and* RALEIGH *murmur their thanks*) Remember, a great deal may depend on bringing in a German. It may mean the winning of the whole war. You never know. (*Another pause*) Well, good luck to you both. (*Again* OSBORNE *and* RALEIGH *murmur their thanks. The* COLONEL *and* STANHOPE *go towards the door.*)

COLONEL (*over his shoulder*). Don't forget to empty your pockets of papers and things.

RALEIGH. Oh, no. (*He goes into his dug-out, taking letters and papers from his pockets.*)
(STANHOPE *is about to follow the* COLONEL *up the steps when* OSBORNE *calls him back.*)

OSBORNE. Er–Stanhope–just a moment.

STANHOPE (*returning*). Hullo!

OSBORNE. I say, don't think I'm being morbid, or anything like that, but would you mind taking these?

STANHOPE. Sure. Until you come back, old man.

OSBORNE. It's only just in case—— (*He takes his watch and a letter from his tunic pocket and puts them on the table. Then he pulls off his ring*) If anything should happen, would you send these along to my wife? (*He pauses, and gives an awkward little laugh.*)

STANHOPE (*putting the articles together on the table.*) You're coming back, old man. Damn it! what on earth should I do without you?

OSBORNE (*laughing*). Goodness knows!

STANHOPE. Must have somebody to tuck me up in bed. (*There is a pause*) Well, I'll see you up in the sap, before you go. Just have a spot of rum in that coffee.

OSBORNE. Righto.
(STANHOPE *goes to the steps and lingers for a moment.*)

STANHOPE. Cheero!
(*For a second their eyes met; they laugh.* STANHOPE *goes slowly up the steps. There is silence in the dug-out.* OSBORNE *has been filling his pipe, and stands lighting it as* RALEIGH *returns.*)

OSBORNE. Just time for a small pipe.

RALEIGH. Good. I'll have a cigarette, I think. (*He feels in his pocket.*)

OSBORNE. Here you are. (*He offers his case to* RALEIGH.)

RALEIGH. I say, I'm always smoking yours.

OSBORNE. That's all right. (*Pause*) What about this coffee?

RALEIGH. Sure. (*They sit at the table.*)

OSBORNE. Are you going to have a drop of rum in it?

RALEIGH. Don't you think it might make us a–a bit muzzy?

OSBORNE. I'm just having the coffee as it is.

RALEIGH. I think I will, too.

OSBORNE. We'll have the rum afterwards–to celebrate.

RALEIGH. That's a much better idea. (*They stir their coffee in silence.* OSBORNE'*s eyes meet* RALEIGH'*s. He smiles.*)

OSBORNE. How d'you feel?

RALEIGH. All right.

OSBORNE. I've got a sort of empty feeling inside.

RALEIGH. That's just what I've got!

OSBORNE. Wind up!

RALEIGH. I keep wanting to yawn.

OSBORNE. That's it. Wind up. I keep wanting to yawn too. It'll pass off directly we start.

RALEIGH (*taking a deep breath*). I wish we could go now.

OSBORNE (*looking at his watch on the table*). We've got eight minutes yet.

RALEIGH. Oh, Lord!

OSBORNE. Let's just have a last look at the map. (*He picks up the map and spreads it out*) Directly the smoke's thick enough, I'll give the word. You run straight for this point here——

RALEIGH. When I get to the Boche wire I lie down and wait for you.

OSBORNE. Don't forget to throw your bombs.

RALEIGH (*patting his pocket*). No. I've got them here.

OSBORNE. When I shout "Righto!" –in you go with your eight men. I shall lie on the Boche parapet, and blow my whistle now and then to show you where I am. Pounce on the first Boche you see and bundle him out to me.

RALEIGH. Righto.

OSBORNE. Then we come back like blazes.

RALEIGH. The whole thing'll be over quite quickly?

OSBORNE. I reckon with luck we shall be back in three minutes.

RALEIGH. As quick as that?

OSBORNE. I think so. (*He folds up the map*) And now let's forget all about it for—(*he looks at his watch*)—for six minutes.

RALEIGH. Oh, Lord, I can't!

OSBORNE. You must.

RALEIGH. How topping if we both get the M.C.!

OSBORNE. Yes. (*Pause*) Your coffee sweet enough?

RALEIGH. Yes, thanks. It's jolly good coffee. (*Pause*) I wonder what the Boche are doing over there now?

OSBORNE. I don't know. D'you like coffee better than tea?

RALEIGH. I do for breakfast. (*Pause*) Do these smoke bombs make much row when they burst?

OSBORNE. Not much. (*Pause*) Personally, I like cocoa for breakfast.

RALEIGH (*laughing*). I'm sorry!

OSBORNE. Why sorry? Why shouldn't I have cocoa for breakfast?

RALEIGH. I don't mean that. I—mean—I'm sorry to keep talking about the raid. It's so difficult to—to talk about anything else. I was just wondering—will the Boche retaliate in any way after the raid?

OSBORNE. Bound to—a bit.

RALEIGH. Shelling?

OSBORNE.
"'*The time has come,' the Walrus said,*
'*To talk of many things:*
Of shoes—and ships—and sealing-wax—
Of cabbages—and kings.'"

RALEIGH.
"'*And why the sea is boiling hot—*
And whether pigs have wings.'"

OSBORNE. Now we're off! Quick, let's talk about pigs! Black pigs or white pigs?

RALEIGH. Black pigs. In the New Forest you find them, quite wild.

OSBORNE. You know the New Forest?

RALEIGH. Rather! My home's down there. A little place called Allum Green just outside Lyndhurst.

OSBORNE. I know Lyndhurst well.

RALEIGH. It's rather nice down there.

OSBORNE. I like it more than any place I know.

RALEIGH. I think I do, too. Of course, it's different when you've always lived in a place.

OSBORNE. You like it in a different way.

RALEIGH. Yes. Just behind our house there's a stream called the Highland; it runs for miles—right through the middle of the forest. Dennis and I followed it once as far as we could.

OSBORNE. I used to walk a lot round Lyndhurst.

RALEIGH. I wish we'd known each other then. You could have come with Dennis and me.

OSBORNE. I wish I had. I used to walk alone.

RALEIGH. You must come and stay with us one day.

OSBORNE. I should like to—awfully.

RALEIGH. I can show you places in the forest that nobody knows about except Dennis and me. It gets thicker and darker and cooler, and you stir up all kinds of funny wild animals.

OSBORNE. They say there are ruins, somewhere in the forest, of villages that William the Conqueror pulled down to let the forest grow.

RALEIGH. I know. We often used to look for them, but we haven't found them yet. (*Pause*) You must come and help look one day.

OSBORNE. I'll find them all right!

RALEIGH. Then you can write to the papers. "Dramatic Discovery of Professor Osborne!"
(OSBORNE *laughs.*)

OSBORNE. I did go exploring once—digging up Roman remains.

RALEIGH. Where was that?

OSBORNE. Near my home in Sussex there's a Roman road called Stane Street; it runs as straight as a line from the coast to London.

RALEIGH. I know it.

OSBORNE. Near where I live the road runs over Bignor Hill, but in recent times a new road's been cut round the foot of the hill, meeting the old road again farther on. The old road over the hill hasn't been used for years and years—and it's all grown over with grass, and bushes and trees grow in the middle of it.

RALEIGH. Can you still see where it runs?

OSBORNE. Quite easily, in places.

RALEIGH. Did you dig a bit of it up, then?

OSBORNE. Yes. We got permission to dig out a section. It was in wonderful condition.

RALEIGH. Did you find anything?

OSBORNE. We found a horseshoe—and a Roman penny.

RALEIGH (*laughing*). Splendid!

OSBORNE. It's awfully fascinating, digging like that.

RALEIGH. It must be. (OSBORNE *glances at his watch*) Is it time yet?

OSBORNE. Two minutes. Then we must go up. I wish we had a good hot bath waiting for us when we get back.

RALEIGH. So do I. (*Pause*) We're having something special for dinner, aren't we?

OSBORNE. How did you know? It's supposed to be a secret.

RALEIGH. Mason dropped a hint.

OSBORNE. Well, we've had a fresh chicken sent up from Noyelle Farm.

RALEIGH. I say!

OSBORNE. And a most awful luxury—two bottles of champagne and half a dozen cigars! One each, and one spare one in case one explodes.

RALEIGH. I've never smoked a cigar.

OSBORNE. It's bound to make you sick.
(RALEIGH *notices* OSBORNE's *ring on the table; he picks it up.*)

RALEIGH. I say, here's your ring.

OSBORNE. Yes. I'm—I'm leaving it here. I don't want the risk of losing it.

RALEIGH. Oh! (*There is silence. He puts the ring slowly down.*)

OSBORNE (*rising*). Well, I think perhaps we ought to get ready.

RALEIGH. Yes. Righto. (*He also rises.*)

OSBORNE. I'm not going to wear a belt—just my revolver, with the lanyard round my neck.

RALEIGH. I see. (*He puts his lanyard round his neck and grips his revolver*) I feel better with this in my hand, don't you?

OSBORNE. Yes. Something to hold. Loaded all right?

RALEIGH. Yes.
(*They put on their helmets.* OSBORNE *takes his pipe from his mouth and lays it carefully on the table.*)

OSBORNE. I do hate leaving a pipe when it's got a nice glow on the top like that.

RALEIGH (*with a short laugh*). What a pity!

(*There is another pause.* OSBORNE *glances at his watch as it lies on the table.*)

OSBORNE. Three minutes to. I think we'd better go.

RALEIGH. Righto.
(*Their eyes meet as* OSBORNE *turns from the table.*)

OSBORNE. I'm glad it's you and I—together, Raleigh.

RALEIGH (*eagerly*). Are you—really?

OSBORNE. Yes.

RALEIGH. So am I—awfully.

OSBORNE. We must put up a good show.

RALEIGH. Yes. Rather!
(*There is a short pause.*)

OSBORNE. Let's go along, shall we?

RALEIGH. Righto. (*They go towards the steps.* MASON *comes to the entrance of his dug-out as they pass.*)

MASON. Good luck, sir.

OSBORNE. Thanks, Mason.

MASON. It's a lovely chicken for dinner, sir.

OSBORNE (*slowly going up the steps*). Splendid!

MASON. Good luck, Mr. Raleigh.

RALEIGH. Thanks.
(OSBORNE *and* RALEIGH *go up to-*

gether into the pale evening sun. MASON *tidies the papers on the table; picks up the two coffee mugs, and goes away. There is silence in the trenches above the deserted dug-out. Then, suddenly, there comes the dull "crush" of bursting smoke bombs, followed in a second by the vicious rattle of machine-guns. The red and green glow of German alarm rockets comes faintly through the dug-out door. Then comes the thin whistle and crash of falling shells; first one by itself, then two, almost together. Quicker and quicker they come, till the noise mingles together in confused turmoil. Yet the noise is deadened by the earth walls of the tiny dug-out, and comes quite softly till the whine of one shell rises above the others to a shriek and a crash. A dark funnel of earth leaps up beyond the parapet of the trench outside; earth falls and rattles down the steps, and a black cloud of smoke rises slowly out of sight. Gradually the noise dies away—there is a longer pause between the crash of each bursting shell. The machine-guns stop—rattle again and stop—rattle for the last time—and stop. Voices are calling in the trench outside;* STANHOPE'S *voice is heard.*)

STANHOPE. All right, sir. Come down quickly!

COLONEL. How many?

STANHOPE. Only one. (*Another shell whines and shrieks and crashes near by. There is silence for a moment, then* STANHOPE *speaks again*) Hurt, sir?

COLONEL. No. It's all right.
(STANHOPE, *pale and haggard, comes down the steps, followed by the* COLONEL.)

STANHOPE (*calling up the steps*). Bring him down, sergeant-major.

S.-M. (*above*). Coming, sir.

STANHOPE (*to the* COLONEL). You won't want me, will you?

COLONEL. Well—er——

STANHOPE. I want to go and see those men.

COLONEL. Oh, all right.
(STANHOPE *goes to the door, making way for the* SERGEANT-MAJOR *to come down, followed by a bareheaded* GERMAN BOY, *in field grey, sobbing bitterly. Behind come two* SOLDIERS *with fixed bayonets.* STANHOPE *goes up the steps. The* SERGEANT-MAJOR *takes the* GERMAN BOY *by the arm and draws him into the centre of the dug-out to face the* COLONEL, *who has seated himself at the table. The two* SOLDIERS *stand behind.*)

S.-M. (*soothingly to the* GERMAN BOY). All right, sonny, we ain't going to 'urt you.
(*Suddenly the* BOY *falls on his knees and sobs out some words in broken English.*)

GERMAN. Mercy—mister—mercy!

S.-M. Come on, lad, get up. (*With a huge fist he takes the* BOY *by the collar and draws him to his feet.*) (*The* BOY *sobs hysterically. The* COLONEL *clears his throat and begins in somewhat poor German.*)

COLONEL. Was ist sein Regiment?

GERMAN. Wurtembergisches.

COLONEL. Was ist der nummer von sein Regiment?

GERMAN. Zwanzig.

COLONEL (*making a note*). Twentieth Wurtembergers. (*He looks up again*) Wann kommen sie hier?

GERMAN. Gestern abend.

COLONEL (*making a note and looking up again*). Wo kommen sie her?

GERMAN (*after a moment's thought*). Mein Geburtsort?

COLONEL (*forgetting himself for a moment*). What's that?

GERMAN (*in halting English*). You —wish—to know—where I was—born?

COLONEL. No! What town did you come up to the line from?

GERMAN (*after a little hesitation*). I—do not tell you.

COLONEL. Oh, well, that's all right. (*To the* SERGEANT-MAJOR) Search him.
(*The* SERGEANT-MAJOR'S *big fists grope over the* BOY'S *pockets. He produces a small book.*)

S.-M. (*giving it to the* COLONEL). Looks like 'is pay-book, sir.

COLONEL (*looking eagerly into the book*). Good.
(*The* SERGEANT-MAJOR *has found a pocket-book; the* GERMAN BOY *clutches at it impulsively.*)

S.-M. 'Ere, stop that!

GERMAN. Lass mich! (*He pauses*) Let—me—please—keep—that.

S.-M. (*very embarrassed*). You let go! (*He wrenches the case away and gives it to the* COLONEL.)

COLONEL (*glancing at the papers in the case*). Look like letters. May be useful. Is that all, sergeant-major?

S.-M. (*looking at a few articles in his hands*). 'Ere's a few oddments, sir—bit o' string, sir; little box o' fruit drops; pocket-knife; bit o' cedar pencil—and a stick o' chocolate, sir.

COLONEL. Let him have those back, except the pocket-knife.

S.-M. Very good, sir. (*He turns to the* GERMAN BOY *with a smile*) 'Ere you are, sonny.
(*The* GERMAN BOY *takes back the oddments.*)

COLONEL. All right, sergeant-major. Send him straight back to my headquarters. I'll question him again there.

S.-M. Very good, sir. (*He turns to the* GERMAN) Come on, sonny, up you go. (*He points up the steps.*)
(*The* GERMAN BOY, *calm now, bows stiffly to the* COLONEL *and goes away, followed by the two* SOLDIERS *and the* SERGEANT-MAJOR. *The* COLONEL *is deeply absorbed in the* GERMAN'S *pay-book. He mutters "Splendid!" to himself, then looks at his watch and rises quickly.* STANHOPE *comes slowly down the steps.*)

COLONEL (*excitedly*). Splendid, Stanhope! We've got all we wanted —20th Wurtembergers! His regiment came into the line last night. I must go right away and 'phone the brigadier. He'll be very pleased about it. It's a feather in our cap, Stanhope.

(STANHOPE *has given one look of astonishment at the* COLONEL *and strolled past him. He turns at the table and speaks in a dead voice.*)

STANHOPE. How awfully nice—if the brigadier's pleased.

(*The* COLONEL *stares at* STANHOPE *and suddenly collects himself.*)

COLONEL. Oh—er—what about the raiding-party—are they all safely back.

STANHOPE. Did you expect them to be all safely back, sir?

COLONEL. Oh—er—what—er——

STANHOPE. Four men and Raleigh came safely back, sir.

COLONEL. Oh, I say, I'm sorry! That's—er—six men and—er— Osborne?

STANHOPE. Yes, sir.

COLONEL. I'm very sorry. Poor Osborne!

STANHOPE. Still it'll be awfully nice if the brigadier's pleased.

COLONEL. Don't be silly, Stanhope. Do you know—er—what happened to Osborne?

STANHOPE. A hand grenade—while he was waiting for Raleigh.

COLONEL. I'm very sorry. And the six men?

STANHOPE. Machine-gun bullets, I suppose.

COLONEL. Yes. I was afraid—er—— (*His words trail away; he fidgets uneasily as* STANHOPE *looks at him with a pale, expressionless face.* RALEIGH *comes slowly down the steps, walking as though he were asleep, his hands are bleeding. The* COLONEL *turns to the boy with enthusiasm*) Very well done, Raleigh. Well done, my boy. I'll get you a Military Cross for this! Splendid! (RALEIGH *looks at the* COLONEL *and tries to speak. He raises his hand to his forehead and sways. The* COLONEL *takes him by the arm*) Sit down here, my boy. (RALEIGH *sits on the edge of* OSBORNE'S *bed*) Have a good rest. Well, I must be off. (*He moves towards the steps, and turns once more to* RALEIGH *as he leaves*) Very well done. (*With a quick glance at* STANHOPE, *the* COLONEL *goes away.*)

(*There is silence now in the trenches outside; the last shell has whistled over and crashed. Dusk is beginning to fall over the German lines. The glow of Very lights begins to rise and fade against the evening sky.* STANHOPE *is staring dumbly at the table—at* OSBORNE'S *watch and ring. Presently he turns his haggard face towards* RALEIGH, *who sits with lowered head, looking at the palms of his hands.* STANHOPE *moves slowly across towards the doorway, and pauses to look down at* RALEIGH. RALEIGH *looks up into* STANHOPE'S *face, and their eyes meet. When* STANHOPE *speaks, his voice is still expressionless and dead.*)

STANHOPE. Must you sit on Osborne's bed?

(*He turns and goes slowly up the steps.* RALEIGH *rises unsteadily, murmurs "sorry"—and stands with lowered head. Heavy guns are booming miles away.*)

THE CURTAIN FALLS

SCENE II

Late evening on the same day.

The dug-out is lit quite festively by an unusual number of candles. Two champagne bottles stand prominently on the table. Dinner is over.

STANHOPE, *with a cigar between his teeth, lounges across the table, one elbow among the plates and mugs. His hair is ruffled; there is a bright red flush on his cheeks. He has just made a remark which has sent* HIBBERT *and* TROTTER *into uproarious laughter; he listens with a smile.* TROTTER *is sitting on the box to the right of the table, leaning back against the wall. A cigar is embedded in his podgy fingers; his face is a shiny scarlet, with deep red patches below the ears. The three bottom buttons of his tunic are undone, and now and then his hand steals gently over his distended stomach.* HIBBERT *sits on the bed to the left, his thin white fingers nervously twitching the ash from his cigar. His pale face is shiny with sweat from the heat of the candles; his laugh is high-pitched and excited.* TROTTER *speaks in a husky voice as the laughter dies away.*

TROTTER. And what did she say to that?

STANHOPE. She said, "Not in these trousers"—in French.
(TROTTER *and* HIBBERT *burst into laughter again.*)

TROTTER (*coughing and wheezing*). Oh—dear-o-dear!

STANHOPE. I simply drew myself up and said, "Very well, mam'sel, have it your own way."

TROTTER. And she did?

STANHOPE. No. She didn't.
(*Again the others laugh.* TROTTER *wipes a tear from his eye.*)

TROTTER. Oh, skipper, you *are* a scream—and no mistake!

HIBBERT. I never forget picking up a couple of tarts one night and taking 'em out to dinner.

TROTTER (*winking at* STANHOPE). 'E's orf again.

HIBBERT. We drank enough bubbly to sink a battleship——

STANHOPE. To *float* a battleship.

HIBBERT. Well—to float a battleship. Then I took 'em for a joy-ride out to Maidenhead—did sixty all the way. We danced a bit at Skindles, and drank a lot of port and muck. Then damned if I didn't lose the way coming back—got landed miles from anywhere. And those tarts began cursing me like hell—said I'd done it on purpose. I said if they didn't damn well shut up I'd chuck 'em both out in the road and leave 'em.

STANHOPE (*ironically*). Hurrah! That's the idea! Treat 'em rough!

HIBBERT (*giggling*). That shut 'em up all right! Then I started doing about sixty down all sorts of roads—I went round a corner on two wheels with those girls' hair on end—didn't have any more trouble from *them!* (*He chuckles at the memory, and takes an unsteady gulp of champagne.*)

STANHOPE. You're the sort of fellow who makes girls hard to please.

TROTTER (*heavily*). Well, I never 'ad no motorcar; my old lady and me used to walk; legs is good enough for me.

STANHOPE. You satisfied with legs?

TROTTER. *I* am—yes!

STANHOPE. Much cheaper.

HIBBERT (*laughing delightedly*). That's damn good!

STANHOPE (*raising his mug*). Well, here's a toast to legs—God bless 'em!

HIBBERT (*raising his mug*). Good old legs!

TROTTER (*raising his mug*). Shank's mare.

STANHOPE. Shank's *what?*

TROTTER. Shank's mare, they call 'em.

STANHOPE. Call what?

TROTTER. Why—legs.

HIBBERT (*almost screaming with delight*). Oh, Trotter! you're a *dream!*

TROTTER (*turning a baleful eye on* HIBBERT). You've 'ad too much champagne, you 'ave.

(HIBBERT *takes a leather case from his pocket and produces some picture post-cards.*)

HIBBERT. I say, I've never shown you these, have I? (*He hands them one by one to* STANHOPE, *smiling up into* STANHOPE'S *face for approval.*)

STANHOPE. Where did you get these from?

HIBBERT. In Bethune. (*He hands up a card*) She's all right, isn't she?

STANHOPE. Too fat.

HIBBERT (*looking over* STANHOPE'S *shoulder*). Oh, I don't know.

STANHOPE. Much too fat. (*He hands the card to* TROTTER) What do you think, Trotter?
(TROTTER *takes a pair of pince-nez from his pocket, balances them on his fat nose, and looks at the picture.*)

HIBBERT. All right, isn't she?

TROTTER. Well, I don't know. If you ask me I'd rather 'ave a decent picture of Margate Pier.

HIBBERT (*impatiently*). Oh, you don't understand *art.* (*He hands another card to* STANHOPE) There's a nice pair of legs for you.

STANHOPE. Too thin—aren't they, Trotter? (*He hands* TROTTER *the card.*)

TROTTER (*after some thought*). Scraggy, I call 'em.

HIBBERT (*handing* STANHOPE *another card*). *That's* the one I like best.

STANHOPE. Not bad.

HIBBERT. Glorious bedroom eyes.

STANHOPE. She's all right.

HIBBERT. Ever seen that show *Zip* at the Hippodrome? Couple of damn fine girls in that—twins. Did you see 'em, skipper?

STANHOPE (*wearily*). I don't know —seen stacks of shows—can't remember them all. (*He brightens up*) Now then, swallow up that bubbly! Hi! Mason!

MASON. Yessir!
(MASON *appears.*)

STANHOPE. Bring some whiskey.

MASON. Yessir. (*He disappears.*)

TROTTER. What? Whiskey on top of champagne?

STANHOPE. Why not? It's all right.

TROTTER. Well, I don't know; doesn't sound right to me. I feel as if somebody's blown me up with a bicycle pump.

STANHOPE. You look it, too.

TROTTER (*blowing a stream of cigar smoke up to the dark ceiling*). Any-'ow, it was a jolly bit o' chicken—and I'd go a mile any day for a chunk o' that jam pudding.
(MASON *brings a bottle of whiskey.*)

STANHOPE. Your pudding's made Mr. Trotter feel all blown out, Mason.

MASON. I'm sorry, sir; it wasn't meant, sir.

TROTTER. It was all right, Mason, take it from me. I know a decent bit o' pudden when I see it.

MASON. It was only boiled ration biscuits and jam, sir. (*He turns to* STANHOPE) I thought I better tell you, sir—this is the last bottle.

STANHOPE. The last bottle! Why, damn it, we brought six!

MASON. I know, sir. But five's gone.

STANHOPE. Where the devil's it gone to?

MASON. Well, sir, you remember there was one on the first night—and then one——

STANHOPE. Oh, for Lord's sake don't go through them one by one; this'll last till sunrise. (*He turns to* TROTTER *and* HIBBERT) Sunrise to-morrow, my lads!

TROTTER. Oh, forget that.

STANHOPE. You bet we will! Now then! Who's for a spot of whiskey?

TROTTER. I reckon I'm about full up. I'd like a nice cup o' tea, Mason.

MASON. Very good, sir. (*He goes out.*)

STANHOPE. Tea!

TROTTER. Yes. That's what I want. Decent cup o' tea. Still, I'll just 'ave about a spoonful o' whiskey—got a touch of pulpitations.

STANHOPE. Here you are—say when!

TROTTER. Wo! That's enough!

STANHOPE. You'll have a decent spot, won't you, Hibbert?

HIBBERT. Yes. I'm game!

TROTTER (*stifling a hiccup*). Just a cup o' tea—then I'll go and relieve young Raleigh. Pity 'e didn't come down to supper.

STANHOPE. I told him to. I told him to come down for an hour and let the sergeant-major take over.

TROTTER. I wonder why 'e didn't come.

HIBBERT. That lad's too keen on his "duty." He told me he liked being up there with the men better than down here with us.

STANHOPE (*quietly*). He *said* that?

HIBBERT. Yes. I told him about the chicken and champagne and cigars —and he stared at me and said, "You're not having that, are you?" —just as if he thought we were going to chuck it away!

TROTTER. I reckon that raid shook 'im up more'n we thought. I like that youngster. 'E's got pluck. Strong lad, too—the way he came back through the smoke after that raid, carrying that Boche under 'is arm like a baby.

HIBBERT. Did you see him afterwards, though? He came into that dug-out and never said a word—didn't seem to know where he was.

TROTTER. Well, 'e's only a lad.

STANHOPE (*to* HIBBERT). He actually told you he preferred being up with the men better than down here?

HIBBERT. That's what he said.

TROTTER. Well, I 'ope 'e gets the M.C., that's all; 'e's just the kid I'd like if ever I 'ave a kid—strong and plucky.

STANHOPE. Oh, for God's sake forget that bloody raid! Think I want to talk about it?

TROTTER (*surprised*). No—but, after all——

STANHOPE. Well—shut up!

TROTTER (*uneasily*). All right—all right.

STANHOPE. We were having a jolly decent evening till you started blabbing about the war.

TROTTER. *I* didn't start it.

STANHOPE. You did.

TROTTER. You began it about——

STANHOPE. Well, for God's sake stop it, then!

TROTTER. All right—all right.

HIBBERT. Did I ever tell you the story about the girl I met in Soho?

STANHOPE. I don't know—I expect you did.

HIBBERT (*undismayed*). It'll amuse you. I'd been to a dance, and I was coming home quite late——

STANHOPE. Yes, and it's late now. You go on duty at eleven. You better go and get some sleep.

HIBBERT. It's all right. I'm as fresh as a daisy.

STANHOPE. You may be. But go to bed.

HIBBERT. What?

STANHOPE (*louder*). I said, "Go to bed!"

HIBBERT. I say, that's a nice end to a jolly evening!

STANHOPE. I'm sorry. I'm tired.

HIBBERT (*perkily*). Well, *you* better go to bed!
(*There is silence.* STANHOPE *looks at* HIBBERT, *who sniggers.*)

STANHOPE. What was that you said?

HIBBERT. I was only joking.

STANHOPE. I asked you what you said.

HIBBERT. I said, "*You* better go to bed."
(STANHOPE'S *flushed face is looking full into* HIBBERT'S. HIBBERT *gives the ghost of a snigger.*)

STANHOPE. Clear out of here!

HIBBERT (*rising unsteadily*). What—what d'you mean?

STANHOPE. Get out of here, for God's sake!

HIBBERT (*blustering*). I say—look here——

STANHOPE. Get out of my sight! (*With a frightened glance at* STANHOPE, HIBBERT *sneaks quietly away into his dug-out. There is silence, and the guns can be heard—deep and ominous*) Little worm gets on my nerves.

TROTTER. Poor little bloke. Never seen 'im so cheerful before out 'ere.

STANHOPE. Doesn't he nearly drive you mad?

TROTTER. I reckon 'e only wanted to keep cheerful.

STANHOPE. Doesn't his repulsive little mind make you *sick?* (MASON *brings* TROTTER'S *mug of tea and goes away*) I envy you, Trotter. Nothing upsets you, does it? You're always the same.

TROTTER. Always the same, am I? (*He sighs*) Little you know——

STANHOPE. You never get sick to death of everything, or so happy you want to sing.

TROTTER. I don't know—I whistle sometimes.

STANHOPE. But you always *feel* the same.

TROTTER. I feel all blown out now. (*There is a pause.* TROTTER *sips his tea and* STANHOPE *takes a whiskey*) 'Ere's 'Ibbert's post-cards. Funny a bloke carrying pictures like this about. Satisfies 'is lust, I s'pose—poor little feller. (*He rises*) Well, I'll go and relieve young Raleigh. Pity 'e didn't come down to supper. (*He tries to button his tunic, without success. He buckles his webbing belt over his unbuttoned tunic, puts on his helmet, and slings his respirator over his shoulder*) Well, cheero!

STANHOPE. You realise you're my second-in-command now, don't you?

TROTTER. Well, you 'adn't said nothing about it, but——

STANHOPE. Well, you are.

TROTTER. Righto, skipper. (*He pauses*) Thanks. (*He goes towards the door*) I won't let you down.

STANHOPE. After your duty, have a decent sleep. We must be ready at half-past five.

TROTTER. Righto, skipper. Well, I'll be going up. Give me a chance to cool off up there. It's as 'ot as 'ell in 'ere, with all them damn candles burning.

STANHOPE. I suppose it is. My head's nearly splitting. (*He blows out three of the candles, leaving the dim light of one.*)

TROTTER (*half up the steps*). There's a bit of a mist rising.

STANHOPE (*dully*). Is there? (TROTTER *disappears into the night.* STANHOPE *broods over the table*) Mason!

MASON (*outside*). Yessir!

STANHOPE. You can bring Mr. Raleigh's dinner.

MASON. Very good, sir.
(MASON *brings a plate of steaming food, gathering up and taking away some of the used crockery. Presently* RALEIGH *comes slowly down the steps. He pauses at the bottom, takes off his helmet, and hesitates.* STANHOPE *is sitting at the table puffing at the remains of his cigar. There is silence except for the rumble of the guns.*)

STANHOPE. I thought I told you to come down to dinner at eight o'clock?

RALEIGH. Oh, I'm sorry. I didn't think you—er——

STANHOPE. Well? You didn't think I —er—what?

RALEIGH. I didn't think you'd—you'd mind—if I didn't.

STANHOPE. I see. And why do you think I asked you—if I didn't mind?

RALEIGH. I'm sorry.

STANHOPE. Well, we've kept your dinner. It's ready for you here.

RALEIGH. Oh, it's awfully good of you to have kept it for me, but—I—I had something to eat up there.

STANHOPE. You—had something to eat up there? What do you mean, exactly?

RALEIGH. They brought the tea round while I was on duty. I had a cup, and some bread and cheese.

STANHOPE. Are you telling me—you've been feeding with the men?

RALEIGH. Well, Sergeant Baker suggested——

STANHOPE. So you take your orders from Sergeant Baker, do you?

RALEIGH. No, but——

STANHOPE. You eat the men's rations when there's barely enough for each man?

RALEIGH. They asked me to share.

STANHOPE. Now, look here. I know you're new to this, but I thought you'd have the common sense to leave the men alone to their meals. Do you think they want an officer prowling round eating their rations, and sucking up to them like that? My officers are here to be respected—not laughed at.

RALEIGH. Why did they ask me—if they didn't mean it?

STANHOPE. Don't you realise they were making a fool of you?

RALEIGH. Why should they?

STANHOPE. So you know more about my men than I do?
(*There is silence.* RALEIGH *is facing* STANHOPE *squarely.*)

RALEIGH. I'm sorry then—if I was wrong.

STANHOPE. Sit down.

RALEIGH. It's all right, thanks.

STANHOPE (*suddenly shouting*). *Sit down!* (RALEIGH *sits on the box to the right of the table.* STANHOPE *speaks quietly again*) I understand you prefer being up there with the men than down here with us?

RALEIGH. I don't see what you mean.

STANHOPE. What did you tell Hibbert?

RALEIGH. Hibbert? I—I didn't say——

STANHOPE. Don't lie.

RALEIGH (*rising*). I'm not lying! Why should I—lie?

STANHOPE. Then why didn't you come down to supper when I told you to?

RALEIGH. I—I wasn't hungry. I had rather a headache. It's cooler up there.

STANHOPE. You insulted Trotter and Hibbert by not coming. You realise that, I suppose?

RALEIGH. I didn't mean to do anything like that.

STANHOPE. Well, you did. You know now—don't you? (RALEIGH *makes no reply. He is trying to understand why* STANHOPE'S *temper has risen to a trembling fury.* STANHOPE *can scarcely control his voice. Loudly*) I say—you *know* now, don't you?

RALEIGH. Yes. I'm sorry.

STANHOPE. My officers work *together*. I'll have no damn prigs.

RALEIGH. I'll speak to Trotter and Hibbert. I didn't realise——
(STANHOPE *raises his cigar. His hand trembles so violently that he can scarcely take the cigar between his teeth.* RALEIGH *looks at* STANHOPE, *fascinated and horrified.*)

STANHOPE. What are you looking at?

RALEIGH (*lowering his head*). Nothing.

STANHOPE. Anything—*funny* about me?

RALEIGH. No. (*After a moment's silence,* RALEIGH *speaks in a low, halting voice*) I'm awfully sorry,

Dennis, if—if I annoyed you by coming to your company.

STANHOPE. What on *earth* are you talking about? What do you mean?

RALEIGH. You resent my being here.

STANHOPE. Resent you *being* here?

RALEIGH. Ever since I came——

STANHOPE. I don't know what you mean. I resent you being a damn fool, that's all. (*There is a pause*) Better eat your dinner before it's cold.

RALEIGH. I'm not hungry, thanks.

STANHOPE. Oh, for God's sake, sit down and eat it like a man!

RALEIGH. I can't eat it, thanks.

STANHOPE (*shouting*). Are you going to eat your dinner?

RALEIGH. Oh! Good God! Don't you understand? How *can* I sit down and eat that—when—(*his voice is nearly breaking*)—when Osborne's—lying—out there——
(STANHOPE *rises slowly. His eyes are wide and staring; he is fighting for breath, and his words come brokenly.*)

STANHOPE. My God! You bloody little swine! You think I don't care—you think you're the only soul that cares!

RALEIGH. And yet you can sit there and drink champagne—and smoke cigars——

STANHOPE. The one man I could trust—my best friend—the one man I could talk to as man to man—who understood everything—and you think I don't care——

RALEIGH. But how can you when——?

STANHOPE. To forget, you little fool—to forget! D'you understand? To forget! You think there's no limit to what a man can bear? (*He turns quickly from* RALEIGH *and goes to the dark corner by* OSBORNE'S *bed. He stands with his face towards the wall, his shoulders heaving as he fights for breath.*)

RALEIGH. I'm awfully sorry, Dennis. I—I didn't understand. (STANHOPE *makes no reply*) You don't know how—I——

STANHOPE. Go away, please—leave me alone.

RALEIGH. Can't I——
(STANHOPE *turns wildly upon* RALEIGH.)

STANHOPE. Oh, get out! For God's sake, get out!
(RALEIGH *goes away into his dugout, and* STANHOPE *is alone. The Very lights rise and fall outside, softly breaking the darkness with their glow—sometimes steel-blue, sometimes grey. Through the night there comes the impatient grumble of gunfire that never dies away.*)

THE CURTAIN FALLS

SCENE III

Towards dawn. The candles are no longer burning. The intense darkness of the dug-out is softened by the glow of the Very lights in the sky beyond the doorway. There is no sound except the distant mutter of the guns.

A man comes from the servants' dug-out; for a moment his head and shoulders stand out black against the glowing sky, then he passes on into the darkness by the table. There comes the rasp of a striking match—a tiny flame—and a candle gleams. MASON *blinks in the light and turns to* STANHOPE'S *bed.* STANHOPE *lies huddled with his blanket drawn tightly round him.*

MASON (*softly*). Sir—— (STANHOPE *does not move;* MASON *shakes him gently by the knee. A little louder*) Sir——

STANHOPE. Yes? (*There is a pause*) That you, Mason?

MASON. 'Arf-past five, sir.

STANHOPE. Oh, right. (*He raises himself on his elbow*) I was only half asleep. I keep on waking up. It's so frightfully cold in here.

MASON. It's a cold dug-out, this one, sir. I've made some 'ot tea.

STANHOPE. Good. You might bring me some.

MASON. Right you are, sir.

STANHOPE. And take some to the officers in there—and wake them up.

MASON. Very good, sir.
(MASON *goes to his dug-out.* STANHOPE *rises stiffly from his bed, shudders from the cold, and slowly begins putting his equipment on.* TROTTER *wanders in from his dug-out vigorously lathering his face. He is dressed, except for his collar.*)

TROTTER. Wash and brush-up, tuppence!

STANHOPE (*looking up, surprised*). Hullo! I thought you were asleep.

TROTTER. I 'ad a decent sleep when I come off dooty. What's the time?

STANHOPE. Half-past five. It'll be getting light soon. You better buck up.

TROTTER. All right. *I* shan't be long. Sounds quiet enough out there.

STANHOPE. Yes.
(MASON *brings four mugs of tea.*)

TROTTER. Ah! that's what I want. A decent cup of tea.

MASON (*putting a mug on the table for* STANHOPE). Nice and 'ot, sir. I've cut a packet of sambridge for each gentleman, sir.

STANHOPE. Good.
(MASON *takes the other mugs of tea into the right-hand dug-out.* TROTTER *follows, lathering with gusto.*)

STANHOPE. You might give Hibbert and Raleigh a call.

TROTTER. I woke 'em up, skipper. They're getting their things on.
(MASON *returns.*)

STANHOPE. When you've cleared up your kitchen, you must dress and join your platoon in the line.

MASON. Very good, sir.

STANHOPE. If things are going well at eleven o'clock, come down here and do your best to get some lunch for us. We shall come down in turn as we can.

MASON. Very good, sir.
(STANHOPE *sits at the table and begins to write a short report. The first sign of dawn is beginning to gleam in the dark sky.* STANHOPE *calls "Runner!" as he writes. A* SOLDIER *comes from the servants' dug-out.*)

STANHOPE (*folding the note*). Take this to Battalion Headquarters. There's no reply.

SOLDIER. Yessir.
(*The* SOLDIER *salutes and goes up the steps. A plaintive noise comes from the other dug-out.* TROTTER *is singing "There's a long, long trail a-winding."* STANHOPE *listens for a moment, then rises, takes a few small coins from his pocket, and throws them into* TROTTER'S *dug-out. The singing stops abruptly. After a moment* TROTTER'S *voice comes.*)

TROTTER. Thank you kindly, gov-'nor!
(*The* SERGEANT-MAJOR *comes down the steps.*)

STANHOPE. Morning, sergeant-major.

S.-M. Morning, sir. Wiring parties are just in, sir. Made a decent job of it—right down to the support line.

STANHOPE. Good. Everything quiet?

S.-M. It's all right opposite 'ere, sir, but the guns are goin' 'ard down south. 'Eavy bombardment. Not sure if it ain't spreading up this way, sir.

STANHOPE. Very likely it is. The officers are coming up in a minute. They'll stand by with their platoon. I must stay here awhile in case of messages. I shall come up directly things begin to happen.

S.-M. Very good, sir.

STANHOPE. Are the men having their tea?

S.-M. Yessir.

STANHOPE. Let 'em have a decent drop of rum.

S.-M. About 'arf again, sir?

STANHOPE. Yes.

S.-M. If the attack don't come, sir, 'ow long are we to stand-to?

STANHOPE. We must expect the attack any time up till midday. After then I don't think it'll come till to-morrow.

S.-M. Very good, sir.

STANHOPE. We must naturally make our plans to meet things as they happen.

S.-M. Quite, sir.

STANHOPE. All right, sergeant-major. I'll see you up there soon.

S.-M. Yessir. (*He salutes and goes away.*)
(MASON *brings in four little packets of sandwiches, and puts one packet on the table for* STANHOPE.)

MASON. Your sambridges, sir. 'Arf bully beef and 'arf sardine. Sardine on top, sir.

STANHOPE. How delicious. No *pâté de foie gras?*

MASON. No what, sir?

STANHOPE. No *pâté de foie gras?*

MASON. No, sir. The milkman 'asn't been yet.
(MASON *takes the other parcels to the left-hand dug-out.* STANHOPE *pours a little whiskey into his tea and the remainder of the contents of the bottle into his flask.* MASON *returns.*)

STANHOPE. Get dressed as soon as you can.

MASON. Yessir.
(MASON *goes out.* TROTTER *comes in, fully dressed for the line.*)

TROTTER. All ready, skipper. Want me to go up?

STANHOPE. Yes. I think so. Go right round the line and see everything's all right. I'll be up soon.

(*Suddenly there comes the faint whistle and thud of falling shells—a few seconds between each.* STANHOPE *and* TROTTER *listen intently, four shells fall, then silence.*)

TROTTER. 'Ullo, 'ullo.
(STANHOPE *strides to the doorway, goes up a few steps, and looks out into the night. He comes slowly back.*)

STANHOPE. Over on Lancer's Alley—somewhere by the reserve line.
(*There comes the louder thud of three more shells.*)

TROTTER. That's nearer.

STANHOPE. Better go up, Trotter. Call the others.

TROTTER (*at the left-hand dug-out*). 'Ibbert! Raleigh! come on! (*He lights a cigarette over the candle—lingers a moment, and slowly goes up the steps*) Cheero, skipper. See you later.

STANHOPE. Send your runner down to tell me how things are going.

TROTTER. Righto.
(TROTTER *disappears into the dark. A vague white line of dawn is broadening above the dark trench wall outside.* STANHOPE *sits at the table and sips his tea. He takes a cigarette and lights it with a quivering hand.* RALEIGH *comes from his dug-out.* STANHOPE *lowers his head and writes in his note-book.*)

RALEIGH. Do you want me to go up?

STANHOPE (*without looking up*). Yes. Trotter's gone.

RALEIGH. Right. (*He goes to the steps and turns shyly*) Cheero—Stanhope.

STANHOPE (*still writing with lowered head*). Cheero, Raleigh. I shall be coming up soon. (RALEIGH *goes up the steps.* STANHOPE *stops writing, raises his head, and listens. The shells are falling steadily now. He glances towards the left-hand dug-out and calls*) Hibbert! (*There is no reply. He slowly rises and goes to the left-hand dug-out doorway. He calls again—louder*) Hibbert!! (*He looks into the doorway and says*) What are you doing? (HIBBERT *appears. He is very pale; he moves as if half asleep*) Come along, man!

HIBBERT. You want me to go up now?

STANHOPE. Of course I do. The others have gone.

HIBBERT. Got a drop of water?

STANHOPE. What d'you want water for?

HIBBERT. I'm so frightfully thirsty. All that champagne and stuff—dried my mouth up.
(STANHOPE *pours a drop of water into a mug and gives it to* HIBBERT.)

STANHOPE. Here you are. Didn't you have any tea?
HIBBERT. Yes. It was a bit sweet, though.
(*The shelling is steadily increasing, and now, above the lighter "crush" of the smaller shells, there comes the deep, resounding "boom" of Minenwerfer.* HIBBERT *sips his water very slowly, rinsing his mouth deliberately with each sip.* STANHOPE *is by the doorway, looking up into the trench. He has just turned away as a sonorous drawn-out call comes floating through the dawn:* "Stretcher bear-ers!" STANHOPE *half turns, then faces* HIBBERT.)

STANHOPE. Come on. Buck up.

HIBBERT. There's no appalling hurry, is there?

STANHOPE. No hurry! Why d'you think the others have gone up?

HIBBERT (*slowly*). What? Trotter and Raleigh?

STANHOPE (*sharply*). Wake up, man! What the devil's the matter with you?
(HIBBERT *slowly puts down his mug.*)

HIBBERT. Champagne dries the mouth up so. Makes the tongue feel like a bit of paper.
(*There is a slight pause.*)

STANHOPE. The longer you stay here, the harder it'll be to go up.

HIBBERT. Good Lord! You don't think I'm——

STANHOPE. You're just wasting as much time as you can.

HIBBERT. Well, damn it, it's no good going up till I feel fit. Let's just have another spot of water.
(HIBBERT *takes the jug and pours out a little more water. He is the picture of misery.* STANHOPE *stands impatiently beside him.* MASON *appears from his dug-out, fully dressed for the line, his rifle slung over his shoulder.*)

MASON. I'll go right along, sir. I've made up the fire to last a good three hours—if you don't mind me popping down about nine o'clock to 'ave a look at it.

STANHOPE. All right, Mason. Mr. Hibbert's coming up now. You can go along with him.

MASON (*to* HIBBERT). I'd like to come along of you if you don't mind, sir. I ain't bin up in this part of the front line. Don't want to get lorst.

STANHOPE. Mr. Hibbert'll show you the way up. (*He turns to* HIBBERT) Keep your men against the back wall of the trench as long as the shells are dropping behind. Cheero! (HIBBERT *looks at* STANHOPE *for a moment, then with a slight smile, he goes slowly up the steps and into the trench,* MASON *following behind. A dark figure stands out against the pale sky; comes hurrying down the steps—a* PRIVATE SOLDIER, *out of breath and excited*) Yes?

SOLDIER. Message from Mr. Trotter, sir. Shells falling mostly behind support line. Minnies along front line.

STANHOPE. Who's just been hit?

SOLDIER. Corporal Ross, I think it was, sir. Minnie dropped in the trench at the corner—just as I come away.
(*The* SERGEANT-MAJOR *comes down the steps, very much out of breath.*)

STANHOPE (*to the* SOLDIER). All right, thanks.
(*The* SOLDIER *salutes, and goes up the steps slower than he came.*)

S.-M. Beginning to get 'ot, sir.

STANHOPE. Corporal Ross hit?

S.-M. Yessir.

STANHOPE. Badly?

S.-M. Pretty badly, sir.

STANHOPE. Most of the shelling's going over, isn't it?

S.-M. Most of the *shells* is be'ind, sir, but there's Minnies and rifle grenades along the front line. Pretty 'ot it's getting, sir. They're attacking down south—there's rifle fire.

STANHOPE. All right, sergeant-major; thanks.

S.-M. What I come to ask, sir—what about the wounded—getting 'em down, sir? The shelling's pretty thick over Lancer's Alley.

STANHOPE. What about Fosse Way?

S.-M. Pretty bad there, too, sir.

STANHOPE. Don't try then. Take anyone badly hit down into the big dug-out on the right. Let the stretcher-bearers do what they can there.

S.-M. Very good, sir.

STANHOPE. Only Corporal Ross hit?

S.-M. That's all, sir——

(*Again there comes the drawn-out call—several times as it is passed from man to man:* "Stretcher bearers!" *The* SERGEANT-MAJOR'S *eyes meet* STANHOPE'S. *He turns and goes up the steps.* STANHOPE *is alone. Flying fragments of shell whistle and hiss and moan overhead. The sharp "crack" of the rifle grenades, the thud of the shells, and the boom of the Minenwerfer mingle together in a muffled roar.* STANHOPE *takes his belt from the table and buckles it on, puts his revolver lanyard round his neck, and drops his flask and sandwiches into his pocket. The* SERGEANT-MAJOR *reappears and comes hurrying down the steps.*)

STANHOPE (*turning quickly*). What is it, sergeant-major?

S.-M. Mr. Raleigh, sir——

STANHOPE. What!

S.-M. Mr. Raleigh's been 'it, sir. Bit of shell's got 'im in the back.

STANHOPE. Badly?

S.-M. 'Fraid it's broke 'is spine, sir; can't move 'is legs.

STANHOPE. Bring him down here.

S.-M. Down 'ere, sir?

STANHOPE (*shouting*). Yes! Down here—quickly!
(*The* SERGEANT-MAJOR *hurries up the steps. A shell screams and bursts very near. The* SERGEANT-MAJOR *shrinks back and throws his hand across his face, as though a human hand could ward off the hot flying pieces. He stumbles on again into the trench, and hurriedly away.* STANHOPE *is by* OSBORNE'S *bed, fumbling a blanket over it. He takes a trench coat off the wall and rolls it for a pillow. He goes to his own bed, takes up his blanket, and turns as the* SERGEANT-MAJOR *comes carefully down the steps carrying* RALEIGH *like a child in his huge arms.*)

STANHOPE (*with blanket ready*). Lay him down there.

S.-M. 'E's fainted, sir. 'E was conscious when I picked 'im up.
(*The* SERGEANT-MAJOR *lays the boy gently on the bed; he draws away his hands, looks furtively at the palms, and wipes the blood on the sides of his trousers.* STANHOPE *covers* RALEIGH *with his blanket, looks intently at the boy, and turns to the* SERGEANT-MAJOR.)

STANHOPE. Have they dressed the wound?

S.-M. They've just put a pad on it, sir. Can't do no more.

STANHOPE. Go at once and bring two men with a stretcher.

S.-M. We'll never get 'im down, sir, with them shells falling on Lancer's Alley.

STANHOPE. Did you hear what I said? Go and get two men with a stretcher.

S.-M. (*after a moment's hesitation*). Very good, sir.
(*The* SERGEANT-MAJOR *goes slowly away.* STANHOPE *turns to* RALEIGH *once more, then goes to the table, pushes his handkerchief into the water-jug, and brings it, wringing wet, to* RALEIGH'S *bed. He bathes the boy's face. Presently* RALEIGH *gives a little moan, opens his eyes, and turns his head.*)

RALEIGH. Hullo—Dennis——

STANHOPE. Well, Jimmy—(*he smiles*)—you got one quickly.

(*There is silence for a while.* STANHOPE *is sitting on a box beside* RALEIGH. *Presently* RALEIGH *speaks again—in a wondering voice.*)

RALEIGH. Why—how did I get down here?

STANHOPE. Sergeant-major brought you down.
(RALEIGH *speaks again, vaguely, trying to recollect.*)

RALEIGH. Something—hit me in the back—knocked me clean over—sort of—winded me—— I'm all right now. (*He tries to rise.*)

STANHOPE. Steady, old boy. Just lie there quietly for a bit.

RALEIGH. I'll be better if I get up and walk about. It happened once before—I got kicked in just the same place at football; it—it soon wore off. It—it just numbs you a bit. (*There is a pause*) What's that rumbling noise?

STANHOPE. The guns are making a bit of a row.

RALEIGH. Our guns?

STANHOPE. No. Mostly theirs.
(*Again there is silence in the dug-out. A very faint rose light is beginning to glow in the dawn sky.* RALEIGH *speaks again—uneasily.*)

RALEIGH. I say—Dennis——

STANHOPE. Yes, old boy?

RALEIGH. It—it hasn't gone through, has it? It only just hit me?—and knocked me down?

STANHOPE. It's just gone through a bit, Jimmy.

RALEIGH. I won't have to—go on lying here?

STANHOPE. I'm going to have you taken away.

RALEIGH. Away? Where?

STANHOPE. Down to the dressing-station—then hospital—then home. (*He smiles*) You've got a Blighty one, Jimmy.

RALEIGH. But I—I can't go home just for—for a knock in the back. (*He stirs restlessly*) I'm certain I'll be better if—if I get up. (*He tries to raise himself, and gives a sudden cry*) Oh—God! It does hurt!

STANHOPE. It's bound to hurt, Jimmy.

RALEIGH. What's—on my legs? Something holding them down——

STANHOPE. It's all right, old chap; it's just the shock—numbed them.
(*Again there is a pause. When* RALEIGH *speaks, there is a different note in his voice.*)

RALEIGH. It's awfully decent of you to bother, Dennis. I feel rotten lying here—everybody else—up there.

STANHOPE. It's not your fault, Jimmy.

RALEIGH. So—damn—silly—getting hit. (*Pause*) Is there—just a drop of water?

STANHOPE (*rising quickly*). Sure. I've got some here. (*He pours some water into the mug and brings it to* RALEIGH. *Cheerfully*) Got some tea-leaves in it. D'you mind?

RALEIGH. No. That's all right—thanks—— (STANHOPE *holds the mug to* RALEIGH's *lips, and the boy drinks*) I say, Dennis, don't you wait—if—if you want to be getting on.

STANHOPE. It's quite all right, Jimmy.

RALEIGH. Can you stay for a bit?

STANHOPE. Of course I can.

RALEIGH (*faintly*). Thanks awfully. (*There is quiet in the dug-out for a long time.* STANHOPE *sits with one hand on* RALEIGH'S *arm, and* RALEIGH *lies very still. Presently he speaks again—hardly above a whisper*) Dennis——

STANHOPE. Yes, old boy?

RALEIGH. Could we have a light? It's—it's so frightfully dark and cold.

STANHOPE (*rising*). Sure! I'll bring a candle and get another blanket. (STANHOPE *goes to the left-hand dug-out, and* RALEIGH *is alone, very still and quiet, on* OSBORNE'S *bed. The faint rosy glow of the dawn is deepening to an angry red. The grey night sky is dissolving, and the stars begin to go. A tiny sound comes from where* RALEIGH *is lying—something between a sob and a moan.* STANHOPE *comes back with a blanket. He takes a candle from the table and carries it to* RALEIGH'S *bed. He puts it on the box beside* RALEIGH *and speaks cheerfully*) Is that better, Jimmy? (RALEIGH *makes no sign*) Jimmy——
(*Still* RALEIGH *is quiet.* STANHOPE *gently takes his hand. There is a long silence.* STANHOPE *lowers* RALEIGH'S *hand to the bed, rises, and takes the candle back to the table. He sits on the bench behind the table with his back to the wall, and stares listlessly across at the boy on* OSBORNE'S *bed. The solitary candle-flame throws up the lines on his pale, drawn face, and the dark shadows under his tired eyes. The thudding of the shells rises and falls like an angry sea. A* PRIVATE SOLDIER *comes scrambling down the steps, his round, red face wet with perspiration, his chest heaving for breath.*)

SOLDIER. Message from Mr. Trotter, sir—will you come at once. (STANHOPE *gazes round at the* SOLDIER—*and makes no other sign*) Mr. Trotter, sir—says will you come at once! (STANHOPE *rises stiffly and takes his helmet from the table.*)

STANHOPE. All right, Broughton, I'm coming.
(*The* SOLDIER *turns and goes away.* STANHOPE *pauses for a moment by* OSBORNE'S *bed and lightly runs his fingers over* RALEIGH'S *tousled hair. He goes stiffly up the steps, his tall figure black against the dawn sky. The shelling has risen to a great fury. The solitary candle burns with a steady flame, and* RALEIGH *lies in the shadows. The whine of a shell rises to a shriek and bursts on the dug-out roof. The shock stabs out the candle-flame; the timber props of the door cave slowly in, sand-bags fall and block the passage to the open air. There is darkness in the dug-out. Here and there the red dawn glows through the jagged holes of the broken doorway. Very faintly there comes the dull rattle of machine-guns and the fevered spatter of rifle fire.*)

THE PLAY ENDS

The Barretts of Wimpole Street

BY RUDOLF BESIER

TO

HUGH WALPOLE

The Barretts of Wimpole Street was first produced in America at the Empire Theatre, New York City, by Katharine Cornell on February 9, 1931, and closed on October 3, 1931. The following is the original cast:

DOCTOR CHAMBERS	George Riddell
ELIZABETH BARRETT MOULTON-BARRETT	Katharine Cornell
WILSON	Brenda Forbes
HENRIETTA MOULTON-BARRETT	Margaret Barker
ARABEL MOULTON-BARRETT	Joyce Carey
OCTAVIUS MOULTON-BARRETT	John Halloran
SEPTIMUS MOULTON-BARRETT	William Whitehead
ALFRED MOULTON-BARRETT	Vernon Downing
CHARLES MOULTON-BARRETT	Frederick Voight
HENRY MOULTON-BARRETT	Basil Harvey
GEORGE MOULTON-BARRETT	Leslie Denison
EDWARD MOULTON-BARRETT	Charles Waldron
BELLA HEDLEY	Dorothy Mathews
HENRY BEVAN	John D. Seymour
ROBERT BROWNING	Brian Aherne
DOCTOR FORD-WATERLOW	Oswald Marshall
CAPTAIN SURTEES COOK	John Buckler
FLUSH	By Himself

Directed by Guthrie McClintic

SCENES

ACT ONE

Porter in a Tankard

ACT TWO

Mr. Robert Browning

ACT THREE

Robert

ACT FOUR

Henrietta

ACT FIVE

Papa

This Comedy was played in Elizabeth Barrett's bed-sitting-room at 50, Wimpole Street, London, in 1845.

THE BARRETTS OF WIMPOLE STREET

ACT ONE

PORTER IN A TANKARD

ELIZABETH BARRETT'S *bed-sitting-room at Number 50, Wimpole Street, London. A window overlooking the street at the back. A door on the left. Fireplace on the right. It is best to give a description of the room in Elizabeth's own words from a letter to a friend:*

". . . The bed like a sofa and no bed: the large table placed out in the room, towards the wardrobe end of it; the sofa rolled where a sofa should be rolled—opposite the armchair: the drawers crowned with a coronal of shelves (of paper, deal, and crimson merino) to carry my books; the washing-table opposite turned into a cabinet with another coronal of shelves; and Chaucer's and Homer's busts on guard over their two departments of English and Greek poetry; three more busts consecrate the wardrobe. . . . In the window is fixed a deep box full of soil, where are springing up my scarlet-runners, nasturtiums, and convolvuluses, although they were disturbed a few days ago by the revolutionary insertion among them of a great ivy root with trailing branches so long and wide that the top tendrils were fastened to Henrietta's window of the higher storey, while the lower ones cover all my panes. . . ."

It is evening; blinds and curtains are drawn; the fire glows dully; lamplight.

ELIZABETH *lies on her sofa, her feet covered with a couvre-pieds. Seated beside her is* DOCTOR CHAMBERS, *an elderly, white-whiskered man. He is feeling her pulse, watch in hand.* FLUSH—*Elizabeth's dog—lies asleep in his basket. On the table is a tray with the remains of a meal, and a pewter tankard.*

CHAMBERS (*dropping her wrist and pocketing his watch*). Hm—yes. It's this increasingly low vitality of yours that worries me. No life in you—none. . . . What are we going to do about it?

ELIZABETH (*lightly*). Well, Doctor, if you shut a person up in one room for years on end, you can't very well expect to find her bursting with life and vigour! Why not prescribe something really exciting for a change?

CHAMBERS. Exciting, eh?

ELIZABETH. A gallop three times round the Park every morning—dumb-bell exercises—a course of calisthenics—a long sea voyage . . .

CHAMBERS. How I wish I could, my dear!

ELIZABETH. It's funny to think of it now—but you know, Doctor, as a child I was a regular tomboy!

CHAMBERS. Yes, I've heard all about that—and, mentally, you're a tomboy still! To tell you the truth, Miss Ba— oh forgive me, my dear Miss Elizabeth, that quaint nickname of yours slipped out unawares! I'm always hearing it from your brothers and sisters. . . .

ELIZABETH (*smiling*). Oh, please . . .

CHAMBERS. To tell you the truth, I'm not sure that brain of yours isn't altogether too active. The trouble with you is that you never will do anything in moderation—not even playing the invalid! Seriously, aren't we, perhaps, overdoing our studies?

ELIZABETH. Of course not.

CHAMBERS. Still hard at Greek?

ELIZABETH. Oh, not more than two or three hours a day.

CHAMBERS. Hm. Are you engaged on any literary work at the moment?

ELIZABETH. Only a few articles for the *Athenæum* and other papers.

CHAMBERS. The *Athenæum*—dear, dear! . . . Now why not give all these heavy labours a rest, and turn your mind to something light and easy for a change? . . . Poetry! You're not neglecting your poetry, I hope?

ELIZABETH. Meaning something—light and easy! (*Laughs*) Oh, Doctor, I must remember to tell that to Mr. Robert Browning when I see him tomorrow!

CHAMBERS. Robert Browning? A brother bard, eh?

ELIZABETH. Don't tell me you've never heard of him!

CHAMBERS. Well, my dear, poetry isn't much in my line, you know.

ELIZABETH. That's evident! All the same, read Mr. Browning's "Sordello"—and then come back and tell me that poetry's—light and easy!

CHAMBERS. I'll make a note of it. . . . Well, well, I suppose we mustn't rob you of your mental exercises if they keep you contented.

ELIZABETH. Contented! Oh, Doctor, I shudder to think what my life would be like if I hadn't a turn for scribbling and study!

CHAMBERS. Hm, yes. Quite so. Yes. . . . And this isn't the liveliest house for any one to live in—let alone an invalid.

ELIZABETH. No, I suppose not. . . . I wish dear Papa were a happier man! It would make such a world of difference to all of us. . . .

CHAMBERS. Happier, eh? It's no business of mine, but when a man has good health, plenty of money, and a jolly family of boys and girls, I can't see why he should make life a burden to himself and others! . . . It's amazing—incredible, and—well, as I said, it's no concern of mine. But you *are*, my dear—and a very worrying concern, too! Of course, the winter has been abominable, and these spring months are always trying. The fact is you oughtn't to live in England at all. Italy's the place for you.

ELIZABETH. Italy! Oh, Doctor, what a heavenly dream!

CHAMBERS. Yes—and must remain a dream, I fear. . . . But if only I could prescribe some sort of change for you—something—anything—to get you out of these dismal surroundings for a time. . . . Tell me now, Miss Elizabeth, have you ventured on your feet at all lately?

ELIZABETH. No, hardly at all. I rather lost my nerve after that fall I had last Christmas.

CHAMBERS. I remember.

ELIZABETH. Papa, as you know, or one of my brothers, carries me from my bed to the sofa in the morning, and back to bed again at night. Sometimes, when I'm feeling venturesome, my maid supports me across the room.

CHAMBERS. Feeling venturesome at the moment?

ELIZABETH. Not particularly. . . .

CHAMBERS. All the same, I think we'll try a step or two. (*Rising, he takes both of her hands*) Quietly now—slowly—there's no hurry. (*With his assistance she gets on to her feet*) There we are. (*She sways a little. He supports her*) Feeling giddy, eh?

ELIZABETH. A little. . . .

CHAMBERS. Close your eyes and lean against me. It will pass in a minute. . . . Better?

ELIZABETH. Yes. . . . Oh, yes. . . .

CHAMBERS. Take your time now, and step carefully. Don't be nervous; I won't let go your hands. . . . (*She takes a couple of faltering steps, he walking backwards, holding her hands*) No—don't look at the floor. Look straight ahead. . . . That's first rate—that's fine—splendid—splendid. . . .
(*After taking half a dozen steps she falters and sways.*)

ELIZABETH. Oh, Doctor! . . .
(*He quickly catches her in his arms and carries her back to the sofa.*)

CHAMBERS. Feeling faint?

ELIZABETH. No, no, I'm all right. . . . I—I am really. . . . It's only my knees—they don't seem able to—to support me.

CHAMBERS. Well, if they can't do that, they're a pretty useless pair! Why, there's no more to you than to a five-year-old! . . . How's the appetite? Just peck at your food, I suppose?

ELIZABETH. I always try to eat what I'm given. But I'm never very hungry. (*With sudden animation*) Doctor, that reminds me! Do you remember Papa suggesting to you that a kind of beer—called porter—might do me good?

CHAMBERS. Yes—and an excellent suggestion too!

ELIZABETH. Oh, but forgive me, it was nothing of the kind! I have to drink it twice a day out of a pewter tankard—and my life, in consequence, has become one long misery!

CHAMBERS. God bless my soul!

ELIZABETH. I am not exaggerating *—one long misery!*

CHAMBERS. But, my dear child, quite apart from its invaluable blood-making properties, porter is generally considered a most palatable beverage. There's nothing I enjoy more than a pint of porter with my steak or chops at breakfast.

ELIZABETH (*in a shocked whisper*). With your breakfast! . . . All I can say is that to me porter is entirely horrible. . . . Horrible to look at, more horrible to smell, and most horrible to drink. Surely something one abominates so intensely can't possibly do one any good! It's no use *my* appealing to Papa —especially as the dreadful idea originated with him. But if *you*, dear, dear Doctor Chambers, were to suggest to him that something else—anything—I don't mind what it is—might be equally efficacious . . .

CHAMBERS (*laughing*). You poor little lady! But of course I will!

ELIZABETH. Oh, thank you a thousand times!

CHAMBERS. What do you say to a couple of glasses of hot milk as a substitute?

ELIZABETH. I dislike milk—but I'll drink it all day long, if only you'll rescue me from porter! (*A knock at the door*) Come in. (WILSON, ELIZABETH'S *maid, enters. She is a fine, capable-looking girl in the middle twenties*) Yes, Wilson?

WILSON. Begging your pardon, Miss, but (*turning to the* DOCTOR) the Master wishes most particularly to see you before you leave, sir.

CHAMBERS. Of course, of course. . . . (*Looks at his watch*) And high time I were off! Is your Master in his study?

WILSON. Yes, sir.

CHAMBERS. Well, good-bye, Miss Elizabeth, good-bye. (*Takes her hand.*)

ELIZABETH. Good-bye, Doctor. (*In a low voice*) And you won't forget?

CHAMBERS. Eh?

ELIZABETH (*spelling the word*). P-O-R-T-E-R.

CHAMBERS (*laughing*). I'll speak to him about it now.

ELIZABETH. Oh, thank you! thank you!

CHAMBERS (*still laughing*). Good night. (*To* WILSON, *as he goes to the door*) You needn't see me downstairs, I know my way.

WILSON. Thank you, sir. (DOCTOR CHAMBERS *goes out*) I'm just going to post your letters, Miss Ba. Shall I take Flush with me?

ELIZABETH (*excitedly*). Quick, Wilson—away with it! (*Points at the tankard of porter.*)

WILSON (*bewildered*). What, Miss? . . .

ELIZABETH. I hadn't the courage to drink it at dinner. I was putting off the dreadful moment as long as I could. . . .

WILSON. Your porter, Miss?

ELIZABETH. And now dear Doctor Chambers tells me I needn't drink it any longer. Take it away! Quick! Quick! And never mention the word porter to me again!

WILSON. Lor', Miss! Very good, Miss. But since you haven't had your porter, won't you——

ELIZABETH (*covering her ears*). I told you never to mention the word again! Take it away! Please! Please!

WILSON. Very good, Miss Ba. Come, Flush. (*She picks up the dog and puts him out of the room; then returns for the tray, with a rather concerned glance at* ELIZABETH, *who starts laughing.* HENRIETTA *enters suddenly. She is a beautiful, high-spirited, blooming girl.*)

HENRIETTA. What are you laughing at, Ba?

ELIZABETH. Wilson thinks I've gone mad.

WILSON. Mad, Miss? What things you do say!

ELIZABETH (*still laughing*). Will you, or won't you, take away that —that black beer?

WILSON. Very good, Miss. (WILSON *goes out.*)

HENRIETTA. I don't know why you're laughing, Ba, and you needn't tell me. Only don't stop! I'll tickle you if you think you can't keep it up without being helped! . . . Oh, dinner was awful!

ELIZABETH. But, Henrietta——

HENRIETTA. Awful! Awful!

ELIZABETH. Was Papa——

HENRIETTA. Yes, he was. It was awful. He was in one of his moods—the worst kind. The nagging mood is bad enough, the shouting mood is worse—but don't you think the *dumb* mood is the worst of all?

ELIZABETH. Yes, perhaps, but——

HENRIETTA. I don't believe there were more than a dozen remarks all through dinner—and most of them were frozen off at the tips! Papa would just turn his glassy eyes on the speaker. . . . You know? For the last twenty minutes or so the only sound in the room was the discreet clatter of knives and forks. Directly dinner was over he ordered his port to be taken to the study—and, thank Heaven! he followed it almost at once.

ELIZABETH. Doctor Chambers is with him now.

HENRIETTA. Oh, Ba, I do hope, for all our sakes, his report of you isn't *too* good.

ELIZABETH. But, Henrietta . . .

HENRIETTA (*all sudden contrition, kneeling at the sofa and putting her arms round* ELIZABETH). Forgive me, dearest! It was odious of me to say that! You know I didn't mean it, don't you? Nothing in the whole world matters to me if only you get better. You know that, don't you?

ELIZABETH. Of course I do, you silly child. But what you said makes Papa an inhuman monster. And that's wickedly untrue. In his own way—he cares for all his children.

HENRIETTA. In his own way . . . ! No, dear, what I meant was that good news of any kind would be certain to aggravate him in his present mood. I don't know why it should, but it does. (*With sudden anxiety*) Ba, Doctor Chambers isn't dissatisfied with you? You're not worse?

ELIZABETH. No, no, dear; I am just the same—neither better nor worse. . . .

(ARABEL *enters. She is a tall, dark, serious woman.*)

ARABEL. Oh, you're here, Henrietta! I've been looking for you everywhere. Papa has just sent you this note from his study.

HENRIETTA. Me? Oh dear! When he starts sending out notes from his study look out for squalls! (*Opens the note and reads*) "*I have heard this morning that your Aunt and Uncle Hedley, and your Cousin Bella, have arrived in London earlier than was expected. They are staying at Fenton's Hotel. Your Cousin Bella and her fiancé, Mr. Bevan, propose to call on you tomorrow at 3 o'clock. You and Arabel will, of course, be here to receive them, and if Elizabeth is well enough, you will bring them upstairs to see her. I have written to invite your Uncle and Aunt and Cousin to dinner next Thursday.—Papa.*" Well!

ARABEL. I understand now why Papa seemed so—so displeased at dinner.

HENRIETTA. Vile-tempered you mean.

ARABEL. Is it necessary always to use the ugliest word?

HENRIETTA. Yes, Arabel—when you're describing the ugliest thing. Oh, but Papa is quite impossible! He got that letter from the Hedleys at breakfast. Why couldn't he have spoken then? Why couldn't he have spoken at dinner? Heaven knows he had opportunity enough!

ARABEL. I'm afraid he was too displeased.

HENRIETTA (*with a grimace*). Displeased. . . . Oh, of course, we all know that he hates being ordinarily polite to any one—and now he's simply bound to show some kind of hospitality to the Hedleys! No wonder he was—*displeased.*

ELIZABETH. Are you quite fair, dear? Papa seldom objects to us receiving our friends here.

HENRIETTA. For a cup of tea and a bun—and so long as the house is clear of them before he's back from the City! Has *any* one of us *ever* been allowed to ask *any* one to dinner? Or even to luncheon? But that's an old story! What enrages me is that I was expecting a friend tomorrow at three—and now I shall have to put him off somehow.

ARABEL (*archly*). Why?

HENRIETTA. Why what?

ARABEL (*as before*). Why must you put your friend off? Bella and her *fiancé* won't eat—your friend.

HENRIETTA (*angrily*). What—what business is that of yours?

ARABEL (*dismayed*). But, Henrietta——

HENRIETTA. I hate people prying into my affairs! . . . (*She goes quickly out of the room, slamming the door behind her.*)

ARABEL (*distressed*). Oh, dear! Oh, dear! What can be the matter with her tonight? Usually she quite enjoys being quizzed about Captain Surtees Cook.

ELIZABETH. Perhaps she may have begun to take his attentions seriously.

ARABEL. Oh, Ba, I hope not! You remember when young Mr. Palfrey wanted to marry her two years ago —those dreadful scenes with Papa?

ELIZABETH. I should rather forget them.

ARABEL. Oh, why can't Henrietta realise that if there's one thing Papa will never, *never* permit, it's a marriage in the family? It doesn't worry *me* at all, as gentlemen never attracted me in that way. Nor you, dear . . .

ELIZABETH (*with a laugh*). Me!

ARABEL. Of course, my poor darling, today anything of that kind is quite out of the question—Papa or no Papa. But even when you were younger and stronger, I don't ever remember your having had . . . little affairs with gentlemen.

ELIZABETH (*whimsically*). Perhaps the gentlemen never gave me the chance.

ARABEL. Oh, but you were quite pretty as a young girl.

ELIZABETH. What is Captain Surtees Cook like? Is he nice?

ARABEL. Yes, I think so. Yes, quite nice. But he never says much. He just sits and looks at Henrietta.

ELIZABETH. She's very lovely. . . .

ARABEL. But Papa would never countenance any kind of understanding between them. Captain Cook would be forbidden the house at the least mention of such a thing —and it's dreadful to think what would happen to Henrietta! Even if he came offering her a coronet, instead of being an officer with a small allowance in addition to his pay, it would make no difference. You know that as well as I do.

ELIZABETH. Poor Henrietta. . . . (HENRIETTA *reënters. She goes quickly up to* ARABEL *and kisses her.*)

HENRIETTA. I'm sorry.

ARABEL. Oh, my dear, I never meant to annoy you.

HENRIETTA. You didn't—you *displeased* me! (*With a laugh*) Oh, I'm Papa's daughter all right!

ELIZABETH. When Bella and her *fiancé* call to-morrow, Arabel will bring them up here to see me—and you can entertain Captain Cook in the drawing-room.
(ARABEL *looks distressed.*)

HENRIETTA. What a thing it is to be a genius! You darling! (*Embraces* ELIZABETH.)

ELIZABETH. But I must have the room to myself at half-past three, as Mr. Robert Browning is calling then.

HENRIETTA (*excitedly*). No!

ARABEL. But I thought——

HENRIETTA. Of course, I know you've been corresponding with Mr. Browning for months as I've posted any number of your letters to him. But then you write to so many literary people whom you absolutely refuse to see, and——

ARABEL. Has Papa given his permission?

ELIZABETH. Of course.

HENRIETTA. But why—why have you made an exception of Mr. Browning? I've heard he's wonderfully handsome, but——

ELIZABETH (*laughing*). Oh, Henrietta, you're incorrigible!

ARABEL. I know he's been most anxious to call. Mr. Kenyon told me so.

HENRIETTA. But you said yourself, only a short time ago, that you didn't intend to receive him!

ELIZABETH. I didn't—and I don't particularly want to now.

HENRIETTA. But why?

ELIZABETH (*lightly*). Because, my dear, at heart I'm as vain as a peacock! . . . You see, when people admire my work they are quite likely to picture the poetess as stately and beautiful as her verses. At least, that's what I always tell myself. . . . And it's dreadfully humiliating to disillusion them!

HENRIETTA. Don't be silly, Ba. You're very interesting and picturesque.

ELIZABETH (*laughing*). Isn't that how guidebooks usually describe a ruin?

HENRIETTA. Oh, Ba, I didn't mean——

ELIZABETH. Of course not, dear! . . . As a matter of fact, Mr. Browning has been so insistent that, out of sheer weariness, I've given way. But I don't want an audience to witness the tragedy of his disillusionment! So mind, Arabel—Bella and her Mr. Bevan must have left the room before he arrives. (*A knock at the door*) Come in. (OCTAVIUS BARRETT *enters. He is about eighteen, and he stammers slightly*) Come in, Occy.

OCTAVIUS. I've j-just come to see how you are, and to wish you g-good-night. (*Bends down and kisses her*) Doctor satisfied?

ELIZABETH. Oh, yes, I think so.

HENRIETTA (*handing* OCTAVIUS *Barrett's note*). Read that, Octavius.

ARABEL (*while* OCTAVIUS *reads*). Oh, dear! I quite forgot that I was to attend a lecture on the Chinese Wesleyan Mission at Exeter Hall tomorrow afternoon!

OCTAVIUS. Well, you can't attend it. (*Flourishes* BARRETT's *letter*) This is undoubtedly a Royal D-decree!

HENRIETTA (*dramatically*). Given at Our study at 50, Wimpole Street, on this 19th day of May, 1845. God save Papa!

ARABEL (*reprovingly*). Henrietta dear!
(*A knock at the door.*)

ELIZABETH. Come in. (SEPTIMUS BARRETT *enters. He is a year older than* OCTAVIUS. *Like* OCTAVIUS *and the other Barrett brothers who subsequently appear, he is in evening dress*) Well, Septimus?

SEPTIMUS. How are you, Ba? (*Kisses her*) I hope the Doctor is satisfied with you?

ELIZABETH. Oh, yes, I think so.

OCTAVIUS. I say, Septimus, the Hedleys are d-dining here in force next Thursday.

SEPTIMUS. Bai Jove! Not really?
(*A knock at the door.*)

ELIZABETH. Come in. (ALFRED BARRETT *enters. He is older than* SEPTIMUS) Come in, Alfred.

ALFRED. And how's our dear Ba tonight? I hope the Doctor was happy about you?

ELIZABETH. Oh, yes, I think so. (*A knock at the door*) Come in. (CHARLES BARRETT *enters. He is somewhat older than* ALFRED) Come in, Charles.

CHARLES. How are you feeling tonight, Ba? (*Kisses her*) I hope Doctor Chambers' report was good?

ELIZABETH. Oh, yes, I think so. (*A knock at the door*) Come in. (HENRY BARRETT *enters. He is slightly older than* CHARLES) Come in, Henry.

HENRY. Well, Ba? How are you, my dear? (*Kisses her*) Was the Doctor pleased with his patient?

ELIZABETH. Oh, yes, I think so.

HENRY. That's good. I must say I think you are looking a little better. What d'you say, Charles?

CHARLES. Eh?

HENRY. Looking better, don't you know. More herself, what?
(*A knock at the door.*)

ELIZABETH. Come in. (GEORGE BARRETT *enters. He is slightly older than* HENRY) Come in, George.

GEORGE. Well, and how's Ba tonight? (*Kisses her*) The Doctor's just been, hasn't he? I'm afraid he wasn't too pleased with you.

ELIZABETH. Oh, yes, I think so. . . . I mean—why?

GEORGE. You're not looking so well. Is she, Henry?

HENRY. On the contrary, I think she's looking considerably better. So does Charles. Don't you, Charles?

CHARLES. Eh?

OCTAVIUS. I say, George, the Hedleys have arrived unexpectedly in town. Bella and her swain are c-calling on the girls tomorrow afternoon. And on Thursday she and her parents are d-dining here in state.

ALFRED, HENRY, SEPTIMUS (*simultaneously*). Dining *here!*

GEORGE. Well, I hope they'll enjoy their dinner as much as we did tonight!

HENRY. You have met this Mr. Bevan, haven't you?

GEORGE. I have.

HENRY. What is he like?

GEORGE. Pompous ass. But warm—a very warm man. Ten thousand pounds a year, if he has a penny.

HENRIETTA. No!

GEORGE. And ten thousand more when his grandmother dies.

ARABEL. Oh!

HENRIETTA. It's grossly unfair! What has Bella done to deserve such luck?

OCTAVIUS. George says he's a p-pompous ass.

HENRIETTA. Oh, that's jealousy! No man with ten thousand a year can be (*imitating his stammer*) a—p-p-p-p-pompous ass!

GEORGE. I think it's just possible that you'll all be interested to hear that Papa is going to Plymouth on business next week, and—(*Excited exclamations from all except* ELIZABETH.)

HENRIETTA. Go on, George, go on! *And—?*

GEORGE. And that he's not expected to return—for at least a fortnight. (*Murmurs of satisfaction and smiling faces.*)

HENRIETTA. Oh, George! (*She flings her arms round his neck*) How wonderful! How glorious! Do you polk, George?

GEORGE. Don't be childish.

HENRIETTA. Well, I polk! (*She dances the polka round the room, humming a polka measure. The others look on amused.* OCTAVIUS *claps his hands. The door is opened quietly and* EDWARD MOULTON-BARRETT *enters. He is a well-set-up handsome man of sixty.*)

ELIZABETH. Papa . . . (*An uneasy silence falls.* HENRIETTA, *in the middle of the room, stops dead.* BARRETT *stands for a moment just beyond the threshold, looking before him with a perfectly expressionless face*) Good evening, Papa. . . .

(*Without replying,* BARRETT *crosses the room and takes his stand with his back to the fire place. A pause. No one moves.*)

BARRETT (*in a cold, measured voice*). I am most displeased. (*A pause*) It is quite in order that you should visit your sister of an evening and have a few quiet words with her. But I think I have pointed out, not once, but several times, that, in her very precarious state of health, it is inadvisable for more than three of you to be in her room at the same time. My wishes in this matter have been disregarded—as usual. (*A pause*) You all know very well that your sister must avoid any kind of excitement. Absolute quiet is essential, especially before she retires for the night. And yet I find you romping around her like a lot of disorderly children. . . . I am gravely displeased. (HENRIETTA *gives a nervous little giggle*) I am not aware that I have said anything amusing, Henrietta?

HENRIETTA. I—I beg your pardon, Papa.

BARRETT. And may I ask what you were doing as I came into the room?

HENRIETTA. I was showing Ba how to polk.

BARRETT. To . . . polk?

HENRIETTA. How to dance the polka.

BARRETT. I see.
(*A pause.*)

OCTAVIUS (*nervously*). Well, B-Ba, I think I'll say g-good-night, and——

BARRETT. I should be grateful if you would kindly allow me to finish speaking.

OCTAVIUS. Sorry, sir. I—I thought you'd d-done.

BARRETT (*with frigid anger*). Are you being insolent, sir?

OCTAVIUS. N-no indeed, sir—I assure you, I——

BARRETT. Very well. Now——

ELIZABETH (*quickly, nervously*). As I am really the cause of your displeasure, Papa, I ought to tell you that I like nothing better than a—a little noise occasionally. (*A slight pause*) It—it's delightful having all the family here together—and can't possibly do me any harm. . . .

BARRETT. Perhaps you will forgive my saying, Elizabeth, that you are not the best judge of what is good or bad for you. . . . And that brings me to what I came here to speak to you about. Doctor Chambers told me just now that you had persuaded him to allow you to discontinue drinking porter with your meals.

ELIZABETH. It needed very little persuasion, Papa. I said I detested porter, and he agreed at once that I should take milk instead.

BARRETT. I questioned him closely as to the comparative strength-giving values of porter and milk, and he was forced to admit that porter came decidedly first.

ELIZABETH. That may be, Papa. But when you dislike a thing to loathing, I don't see how it can do you any good.

BARRETT. I said just now that you are not the best judge of what is good or bad for you, my child. May I add that self-discipline is always beneficial, and self-indulgence invariably harmful?

ELIZABETH. If you think my drinking milk shows reckless self-indulgence, Papa, you're quite wrong. I dislike it only less than porter.

BARRETT. Your likes and dislikes are quite beside the point in a case like this.

ELIZABETH. But, Papa—

BARRETT. Believe me, Elizabeth, I have nothing but your welfare at heart when I warn you that if you decide to discontinue drinking porter, you will incur my grave displeasure.

ELIZABETH (*indignantly*). But—but when Doctor Chambers himself—

BARRETT. I have told you what Doctor Chambers said.

ELIZABETH. Yes, but—

BARRETT. Did you drink your porter at dinner?

ELIZABETH. No.

BARRETT. Then I hope you will do so before you go to bed.

ELIZABETH. No, Papa, that's really asking too much! I—I can't drink the horrible stuff in cold blood.

BARRETT. Very well. Of course, I have no means of coercing you. You are no longer a child. But I intend to give your better nature every chance of asserting itself. A tankard of porter will be left at your bedside. And I hope that tomorrow you will be able to tell me that—you have obeyed your Father.

ELIZABETH. I am sorry, Papa—but I sha'n't drink it.

BARRETT (*to* HENRIETTA). Go down to the kitchen and fetch a tankard of porter.

HENRIETTA. No.

BARRETT. I beg your pardon?

HENRIETTA (*her voice trembling with anger and agitation*). It's—it's sheer cruelty. You know how Ba hates the stuff. The Doctor has let her off. You're just torturing her because you—you like torturing.

BARRETT. I have told you to fetch a tankard of porter from the kitchen.

HENRIETTA. I won't do it.

BARRETT. Must I ask you a third time? (*Suddenly shouting*) Obey me this instant!

ELIZABETH (*sharply*). Papa . . . Go and fetch it, Henrietta! Go at once! I can't stand this. . . .

HENRIETTA. No, I——

ELIZABETH. Please—please . . .
(*After a moment's indecision,* HENRIETTA *turns and goes out.*)

BARRETT (*quietly, after a pause*). You had all better say good night to your sister.

ARABEL (*in a whisper*). Good night, dearest. (*She kisses* ELIZABETH *on the cheek.*)

ELIZABETH (*receiving the kiss impassively*). Good night.
(ARABEL *leaves the room. Then each of the brothers in turn goes to* ELIZABETH *and kisses her cheek.*)

GEORGE. Good night, Ba.

ELIZABETH. Good night.
(GEORGE *goes out.*)

ALFRED. Good night, Ba.

ELIZABETH. Good night.
(ALFRED *goes out.*)

HENRY. Good night, Ba.

ELIZABETH. Good night.
(HENRY *goes out.*)

CHARLES. Good night, Ba.

ELIZABETH. Good night.
(CHARLES *goes out.*)

SEPTIMUS. Good night, Ba.

ELIZABETH. Good night.
(SEPTIMUS *goes out.*)

OCTAVIUS. G-good night, Ba.

ELIZABETH. Good night.
(OCTAVIUS *goes out.* BARRETT, *standing before the fireplace, and* ELIZABETH, *on her sofa, look before them with expressionless faces. A pause.* HENRIETTA *enters with a tankard on a small tray. She stands a little beyond the threshold, glaring at her father and breathing quickly.*)

ELIZABETH. Give it to me, please.
(HENRIETTA *goes to her.* ELIZABETH *takes the tankard and is putting it to her lips, when* BARRETT *suddenly, but quietly, intervenes.*)

BARRETT. No. (*Putting* HENRIETTA *aside, he takes the tankard from* ELIZABETH. *To* HENRIETTA) You may go.

HENRIETTA. Good night, Ba darling. (*She moves forward to* ELIZABETH, *but* BARRETT *waves her back.*)

BARRETT. You may go.

ELIZABETH. Good night.
(HENRIETTA, *with a defiant look at her father, goes out.* BARRETT *puts the tankard on the mantelpiece; then goes to the sofa and stands looking down at* ELIZABETH. *She stares up at him with wide, fearful eyes.*)

BARRETT (*in a gentle voice*). Elizabeth.

ELIZABETH (*in a whisper*). Yes?

BARRETT (*placing his hand on her head and bending it slightly back*). Why do you look at me like that, child? . . . Are you frightened?

ELIZABETH (*as before*). No.

BARRETT. You're trembling. . . . Why?

ELIZABETH. I—I don't know.

BARRETT. You're not frightened of me? (ELIZABETH *is about to speak —he goes on quickly*) No, no. You mustn't say it. I couldn't bear to think that. (*He seats himself on the side of the sofa and takes her hands*) You're everything in the world to me—you know that. Without you I should be quite alone—you know that too. And you—if you love me, you can't be afraid of me. For love casts out fear. . . . You love me, my darling? You love your father?

ELIZABETH (*in a whisper*). Yes.

BARRETT (*eagerly*). And you'll prove your love by doing as I wish?

ELIZABETH. I don't understand. I was going to drink——

BARRETT (*quickly*). Yes—out of fear, not love. Listen, dear. I told you just now that if you disobeyed me you would incur my displeasure. I take that back. I shall never, in any way, reproach you. You shall never know by deed or word, or hint, of mine how much you have grieved and wounded your father by refusing to do the little thing he asked. . . .

ELIZABETH. Oh, please, please, don't say any more. It's all so petty and sordid. Please give me the tankard.

BARRETT (*rising*). You are acting of your own free will, and not——

ELIZABETH. Oh, Papa, let us get this over and forget it! I can't forgive myself for having made the whole house miserable over a tankard of porter.
(*He gives her the tankard. She drinks the porter straight off.* BARRETT *places the tankard back on the mantelpiece; then returns to the sofa and looks yearningly down at* ELIZABETH.)

BARRETT. You're not feeling worse tonight, my darling?

ELIZABETH (*listlessly*). No, Papa.

BARRETT. Just tired?

ELIZABETH. Yes . . . just tired.

BARRETT. I'd better leave you now. . . . Shall I say a little prayer with you before I go?

ELIZABETH. Please, Papa.
(BARRETT *kneels down beside the sofa, clasps his hands, lifts his face, and shuts his eyes.* ELIZABETH *clasps her hands, but keeps her eyes wide open.*)

BARRETT. Almighty and merciful God, hear me, I beseech Thee, and grant my humble prayer. In Thine inscrutable wisdom Thou hast seen good to lay on Thy daughter Elizabeth grievous and heavy afflictions. For years she hath languished in sickness; and for years, unless in Thy mercy Thou take her to Thyself, she may languish on. Give her to realise the blessed word that Thou chastisest those whom Thou lovest. Give her to bear her sufferings in patience. Give her to fix her heart and soul on Thee and on that Heavenly Eternity which may at any moment open out before her. Take her into Thy loving care tonight; purge her mind of all bitter and selfish and unkind thoughts; guard her and comfort her. These things I beseech Thee for the sake of Thy dear Son, Jesus Christ. Amen.

ELIZABETH. Amen.

BARRETT (*rising to his feet, and kissing her forehead*). Good night, my child.

ELIZABETH (*receiving his kiss impassively*). Good night, Papa.
(BARRETT *goes out.* ELIZABETH *lies motionless, staring before her for a moment or two. A knock at the door*) Come in.
(WILSON *enters, carrying* FLUSH.)

WILSON (*putting* FLUSH *in his basket*). Are you ready for your bed now, Miss Ba?

ELIZABETH. Oh, Wilson, I'm so tired—tired—tired of it all. . . . Will it never end?

WILSON. End, Miss?

ELIZABETH. This long, long, grey death in life.

WILSON. Oh, Miss Ba, you shouldn't say such things!

ELIZABETH. No, I suppose I shouldn't. . . . Did Flush enjoy his run?

WILSON. Oh, yes, Miss. (*A short pause.*)

ELIZABETH. Is it a fine night, Wilson?

WILSON. Yes, Miss, and quite warm, and there's such a lovely moon.

ELIZABETH (*eagerly*). A moon! Oh, do you think I can see it from here?

WILSON. I don't know, I'm sure.

ELIZABETH. Draw back the curtains and raise the blind.
(WILSON *does so; and moonlight, tempered by the lamplight, streams on* ELIZABETH'S *face.*)

WILSON. There you are, Miss! The moon's right above the chimleys. You can see it lovely!

ELIZABETH (*dreamily*). Yes. . . . Yes. . . . Please put out the lamp and leave me for a little. I don't want to go to bed quite yet.

WILSON. Very well, Miss Ba. (WILSON *extinguishes the lamp and goes out.* ELIZABETH *is bathed in strong moonlight. She stares, for a while, with wide eyes at the moon. Then her quickened breathing becomes audible, and her whole body is shaken with sobs. She turns over on her side and buries her face in her arms. The only sound is her strangled weeping as the Scene closes.*)

ACT TWO

MR. ROBERT BROWNING

The afternoon of the following day. The curtains are drawn aside, the blinds are up, and sunshine pours into the room. On a little table near Elizabeth's sofa is a tray, with an untouched sweet on it.

ELIZABETH *lies on the sofa, her couvre-pieds over her feet. She is reading a small book with intense absorption; now and again running her fingers through her ringlets or tossing them back from her face.* FLUSH *lies in his basket.*

ELIZABETH (*with puzzled emphasis*).
"With flowers in completeness,
All petals, no prickles,
Delicious as trickles
Of wine poured at mass-time."
(*A knock at the door.* ELIZABETH, *absorbed, takes no notice. She re-*

peats, clutching her forehead)

"All petals, no prickles,
Delicious as trickles—"

(*The knock repeated*)

"Of wine—"

Come in. . . . (WILSON *enters*) Oh, yes, Wilson . . . I'm quite ready for lunch.

WILSON (*stolidly*). You've had your lunch, Miss Ba.

ELIZABETH. Oh, yes, of course. . . . And I enjoyed it very much!

WILSON. You only picked at the fish, Miss Ba. An' I took away the best part of that nice chop. An' I see you haven't touched the pudding—cornflour blammonge too, with raspberry jam.

ELIZABETH (*wonderingly regarding the tray*). Oh. . . . Anyhow, it's too late now. . . . (*She once more plunges into her book.* WILSON *carries out the tray and reënters immediately, shutting the door after her.*)

WILSON (*going to the mantelpiece and measuring out some medicine into a medicine glass*). And now, Miss Ba, if you're all nice and comfortable, I'll take Flush out for his airing. (ELIZABETH, *absorbed in her reading, takes no notice.* WILSON *holds the glass of medicine towards her*) Your physic, Miss Ba.

ELIZABETH (*taking the glass, with her eyes still fixed on her book*). Thank you. (*With the glass in her hand she continues reading.*)

WILSON (*going to the window*). I think, p'raps, I'd better pull down the blind a bit. Too much sun isn't good for you, Miss. . . . (*She half draws down the blind.*)

ELIZABETH (*holding out the untouched glass, her eyes still on the book*). Thank you. . . .

WILSON. You haven't drunk it yet, Miss.

ELIZABETH. Oh. . . . (*She swallows the medicine and, with a little grimace, hands the glass back to* WILSON) Please open the door, Wilson. I am expecting visitors this afternoon, and I want the room to be quite fresh for them. How I wish we could open the window!

WILSON (*shocked*). Open the window, Miss Ba!

ELIZABETH (*with a sigh*). Yes, I know it's strictly forbidden. . . . Well, open the door *wide*.

WILSON. I'd best cover you well up first of all. (*Fetches a rug*) Visitors, Miss Ba? . . .

ELIZABETH (*while* WILSON *covers her up to her chin*). Yes, my cousin, Miss Bella Hedley. I haven't seen her since she was a child—such a lovely slip of a child! And now she's just become engaged.

WILSON. Indeed, Miss. And is she bringing her young gentleman with her?

ELIZABETH. Yes. (WILSON *opens the door*) And Mr. Robert Browning is calling later.

WILSON. Indeed, Miss? The gentleman who's always sending you such lovely boukeys?

ELIZABETH. Yes.
(*Starts reading again.*)

WILSON. Sure you don't feel a draught, Miss Ba?

ELIZABETH (*without looking up*). Quite, thanks.

WILSON. Hadn't you better keep your arms covered? These spring days the air is that treacherous.

ELIZABETH (*to herself, with despairing emphasis*). No—it's quite beyond me! I give it up!

WILSON. Beg pardon?

ELIZABETH (*speaking intensely*). Wilson.

WILSON. Yes, Miss.

ELIZABETH (*as before*). Have you noticed anything—*strange* in me today?

WILSON. Strange, Miss?

ELIZABETH. Yes, strange. I mean—dull-witted—thick-headed—stupid—idiotic. . . .

WILSON. Lor'! No! P'raps a bit absent-minded like—but that isn't anything for you to worry about, Miss Ba.

ELIZABETH. Then you don't think I'm going—*mad?*

WILSON. Mercy on us! Mad!

ELIZABETH. Very well. But now, listen carefully and tell me what you make of this: (*She reads*)

"And after, for pastime,
If June be refulgent
With flowers in completeness,
All petals, no prickles,
Delicious as trickles
Of wine poured at mass-time,—
And choose one indulgent
To redness and sweetness:

Or if, with experience of man and of spider,
June used by June-lightning, the strong insect-ridder,
To stop the fresh film work,—why June will consider."

Well?

WILSON (*enthusiastically*). I call that just lovely, Miss Ba!

ELIZABETH. But do you know what it means?

WILSON. Oh, no, Miss.

ELIZABETH. Does it convey *anything* at *all* to your mind?

WILSON. Oh, no, Miss.

ELIZABETH (*with a sigh of relief*). Thank Heaven for that!

WILSON. But then po'try never does, Miss. Leastways, not real po'try, like what you make.

ELIZABETH (*laughing*). But *I* didn't write that! It's by Mr. Browning.

WILSON. He must be a clever gentleman!

ELIZABETH. Oh, yes! He's all that! (WILSON *has picked up* FLUSH) Well, Flush dear, are you going to behave nicely today? (*She holds out her arms for the dog and* WILSON *gives it to her*) I shall ask Wilson for a full report when she gets home. (*To* WILSON) Where are you taking him to?

WILSON. Well, Miss, being so fine, I thought of a little walk in the Park.

ELIZABETH. Oh, yes. And mind you notice the flowers! I shall want to hear all about them. The laburnum is over, of course. But there ought to be still some pink May, and tulips, and wall-flowers. And perhaps some early roses. . . . Oh, Flush, I'd give almost anything to be going with you instead of Wilson!

OCTAVIUS (*outside*). May I c-come in?

ELIZABETH. Occy, dear! (OCTAVIUS *enters.* ELIZABETH *gives* FLUSH *to* WILSON) What on earth are you doing at home at this time of the day?
(WILSON *goes out, carrying* FLUSH.)

OCTAVIUS. Papa's b-bright idea. Suggested I should take a half-holiday to help you feed and entertain the l-lovebirds.

ELIZABETH (*laughing*). But why? Henrietta and Arabel are socially quite competent. So am I.

OCTAVIUS. But you labour under the d-disadvantage of being all the same sex. Papa appears to think that at least one male B-Barrett ought to show up. He seems fully determined to do the p-polite thing by the Hedleys. And when Papa is fully d-determined on a thing, that thing is done. Or am I wrong?

ELIZABETH (*sighing*). No—that thing is done. . . . But now—I want you to be diplomatic. Captain Surtees Cook is calling at the same time as Bella and Mr. Bevan. He's coming to see Henrietta. . . .

OCTAVIUS. Is he, by Jove! And won't the gallant fella rejoice when he finds Henrietta chaperoned f-four times over!

ELIZABETH. I've arranged for Arabel to bring Bella and Mr. Bevan up here to see me. *You* must come with them.

OCTAVIUS. Must I indeed? And why?

ELIZABETH. So that Henrietta may have Captain Cook to herself for a little while.

OCTAVIUS. Oh. Ah. Yes. Quite so. I see. . . . And you d-don't look in the least ashamed of yourself!

ELIZABETH. I'm not.

OCTAVIUS. But does it occur to you, my dear Ba, that we may be doing Henrietta an uncommonly b-bad turn by encouraging this b-budding romance?

ELIZABETH. Yes. But I think we ought to chance that. . . . (*He looks at her questioningly*) Occy, when you six boys wished me good night yesterday, a queer thought came into my mind. You weren't alive at all—just automata.

OCTAVIUS. By Jove!

ELIZABETH. Like automata, you get up at half-past seven every morning. Like automata, you eat your breakfasts. Like automata, you go to work. Like automata, you return home. You dine like automata. You go to bed like automata.

OCTAVIUS. But I say——

ELIZABETH. And though she works on different lines, Arabel is as automatic. You all seem to me to have cut out of life everything that makes life worth living—excitement, adventure, change, conflict, frivolity, love. . . .

OCTAVIUS. *We* haven't cut 'em out, my dear! That operation was performed by dear P-Papa.

ELIZABETH. I know, but——

OCTAVIUS. Oh, I admit we're a pretty spineless lot! But what would you? We're none of us particularly g-gifted—and we're all of us wholly dependent on Papa, and must obey, or be broken. You're not c-counselling sedition?

ELIZABETH. No—but not resignation. Keep your souls alive. What frightens me is that you may become content with a life which isn't life at all. You're going that way—all of you—except Henrietta.

OCTAVIUS. And what does she get by t-trying to be herself? More kicks than ha'pence!

ELIZABETH. Yes—but being kicked keeps one alive! So don't let us do anything, just for the sake of peace and quiet, to hinder her little romance. Even if it should come to grief.

OCTAVIUS. It will.

ELIZABETH. Grief is better than stagnation.

OCTAVIUS. All very f-fine, my dear Ba—but what about you?

ELIZABETH. Me?

OCTAVIUS. Yes, you. We may all, with the possible exception of young Henrietta, be drifting with the stream. But I don't notice that you make much of a struggle against it? Where did that p-porter finally g-get to last night?

ELIZABETH (*with a dreary little laugh*). Oh, but I don't count! I am quite out of it. You have your lives before you. My life is over.

OCTAVIUS. Rubbish!
(HENRIETTA *enters.*)

HENRIETTA. Why, Occy, what are you doing here?

OCTAVIUS. Papa's n-notion. He somehow got wind that Surtees Cook was p-prowling around this afternoon and sent me home to head the f-feller off.

ELIZABETH. Occy!

HENRIETTA (*in breathless consternation*). How did he hear? He couldn't have heard—(*to* ELIZABETH) unless you, or Arabel——

ELIZABETH. Occy, you idiot! No, dear——

OCTAVIUS. Sorry! My little joke, you know. . . .

HENRIETTA (*hotly*). I hate you!

OCTAVIUS. Quite right, too. (*Puts his arm around her*) I repeat, I'm sorry. You may s-slap me if you like.

HENRIETTA (*half mollified*). I've a good mind to.

OCTAVIUS (*sitting down and drawing her on to his knee*). No, my che-ild, it's like this. His Majesty sent me home to represent His Majesty at the reception. I don't intend to leave Bella's side—not even when she and her beloved come up her to emb-brace Ba. Meanwhile you'll amuse Cook—j-just as you're amusing me now. (*Kisses her*) In fact, we may take this as a l-little rehearsal.

HENRIETTA (*jumping up from his knee*). Occy! how can you be so vulgar! (*She listens*) What's that? (*Runs to the window*) Oh, Ba, they've arrived! And in state! The Bevan family barouche, powdered footman and all! (OCTAVIUS *joins her at the window*) Look at Bella! What a gown! What a bonnet! Lovely! Oh, and Mr. Bevan's whiskers! (*Gestures round her chin*) Aren't you green with envy, Occy?

OCTAVIUS. Positively verdant.

HENRIETTA (*pushing* OCTAVIUS *to the door*). Go and help Arabel receive them. Off with you! Quick! I'll wait here till Captain Cook arrives. I'm going to let him in. And then you and Arabel can bring Bella and Mr. Bevan up here.

OCTAVIUS. All c-cut and dried, what? But l-look here——

HENRIETTA. Go along with you! (*Pushes him out of the room and shuts the door. Then runs again to the window and looks eagerly down into the street*) What's the time?

ELIZABETH (*smiling*). Five minutes past three.

HENRIETTA. *Past* three?

ELIZABETH. Past three.

HENRIETTA. I don't understand. . . . He said *three*. . . . (*With sudden anxiety*) Ba! Today *is* Thursday, isn't it?

ELIZABETH. Yes, dear.

HENRIETTA (*with a sigh of relief*). Oh . . . (*turns again to the window*) I wish he were able to come in his uniform. That would take the curl out of Mr. Bevan's whiskers! (ELIZABETH *laughs*) Oh, there he comes! (*She runs out of the room, leaving the door open.*)

ELIZABETH. Please shut the door. (*But* HENRIETTA *has gone.* ELIZABETH *smilingly shrugs her shoulders, picks up her book and starts reading. After a moment one hears voices outside; then approaching footsteps.* OCTAVIUS *reënters.*)

OCTAVIUS. Are you ready to receive them?

ELIZABETH. Yes, quite. What are they like, Occy?

OCTAVIUS. Oh, *she's* a dream of l-loveliness! And *he*—isn't. (*He goes out. A pause. The voices grow nearer. Then* BELLA HEDLEY *flutters in. She is an exquisitely pretty, exquisitely turned-out little creature, voluble, affected, sentimental, with a constitutional inability to pronounce her r's. She is followed by* ARABEL, MR. HENRY BEVAN, *and* OCTAVIUS. MR. BEVAN *is a model of deportment, inwardly and outwardly. He affects a magnificent Kruger beard, and his voice and manner are as beautifully rounded as his legs.*)

BELLA (*ecstatically*). Cousin Elizabeth!

ELIZABETH (*stretching out her hand*). Bella, dear. . . .

BELLA. Ba! (*Drops on her knees at the sofa and embraces* ELIZABETH) Deawest Ba! After all these years! . . . But oh, my poor, poor Ba, how sadly you've changed! So pale, so fwagile, so etheweal!

ELIZABETH. And you, Bella, are even lovelier than you promised to be as a child.

BELLA. Flattewer! (*She kisses* ELIZABETH'S *hand, and still holding the hand, rises to her feet*) You hear that, Ha'wy? This is my dear, dear Ha'wy. Mr. Bevan—Miss Elizabeth Ba'wett.

BEVAN (*bowing*). Delighted, Miss Barrett, charmed. . . .

BELLA (*stretching out her free hand to* BEVAN. *He takes it*). No, no, Ha'wy, you must take her hand. . . . (*Tenderly to* ELIZABETH) Such a little hand! So fwail! So spiwitual!

BEVAN (*taking* ELIZABETH'S *hand and bowing over it*). And the hand that penned so much that is noble and eloquent! . . . I am honoured, Miss Barrett.

ELIZABETH. Thank you. And may I congratulate you?—both of you? I hope you will be very happy.

BEVAN. Thank you, Miss Barrett. I am indeed a fortunate man!

BELLA. Dear Ha'wy. Dear Ba.

ELIZABETH. But won't you sit down? . . .
(BELLA, ARABEL, *and* BEVAN *seat themselves.* OCTAVIUS *stands near the window.*)

BELLA. I adore your poems, Ba—especially when dear Ha'wy weads them! He wead me "Lady Gewaldine's Courtship" the day after we became engaged. He weads so beautifully! And he *too* adores your poems—which ought to please you, as he is dweadfully cwitical!

BEVAN. Oh, come, come, my pet!

BELLA. Oh, but Ha'wy, you are! He doesn't quite approve of even Mr. Alfwed Tennyson's poems.

ELIZABETH. Really, Mr. Bevan?

BEVAN. I have nothing against them as poetry, no, indeed. Mr. Tennyson always writes like a gentleman. What grieves me, Miss Barrett, is that his attitude towards sacred matters is all too often an attitude tinged with doubt.

ARABEL. How sad. . . .

BEVAN. Sad indeed, Miss Arabel! and I grieve to say a very prevalent attitude among the younger men of today. Loss of faith, lack of reverence, and a spirit of mockery, seem to be growing apace. Of course, I am not alluding to Mr. Tennyson when I say this. His work is always reverent even when expressing doubt. Now your poems, my dear Miss Barrett, show no touch anywhere of these modern tendencies. There's not a line in one of them that I would disapprove of even dear Bella reading.

ELIZABETH. That—that's very satisfactory. . . .

BELLA. Dear Ha'wy is so fwightfully earnest!

BEVAN. Oh, come, come, my pet. . . .

OCTAVIUS. I say, Mr. B-Bevan, you've not yet met my father, have you?

BEVAN. No, that pleasure is yet to come.

OCTAVIUS. I think you and he would g-get on famously together!

BEVAN. Indeed?

BELLA. Oh, yes! for dear Uncle Edward is fwightfully earnest as well! Mamma has often told me so. . . . But there is one matter on which they are bound to differ. Like Mamma and Papa, dear Uncle Edward is a stwict Nonconformist, Ha'wy.

BEVAN (*sadly*). Ah, ah, indeed. . . .

ELIZABETH. Then you are a member of the Church of England, Mr. Bevan?

BEVAN. I am indeed, Miss Barrett. Like Bella, I was brought up in Dissent. But Oxford changed all that. A dear friend of mine persuaded me to attend the services at St. Mary's, where Doctor Newman preaches, you know; and to study Pusey's works. . . . Two years ago I was received into the Church.

ARABEL (*in a scared voice*). Pusey . . . Doctor Pusey. . . . But, Mr. Bevan, you're not—you're not——

BELLA. Oh, but he is, dear Awabel, and so am I! We're both Puseyites! Of course, dear Mamma and Papa were fwightfully distwessed about it at first, and feared my change of faith was entirely due to dear Ha'wy's influence. But in weality, I had long felt a lack of *something* in Nonconformity. . . . Don't you think it lacks *something,* dear Ba? Don't you feel it's a form of worship less suited to people in our walk of life than to the lower orders?

ELIZABETH (*with a quickly suppressed little laugh*). No, I—I can't say it ever struck me quite like that. . . . But now tell me, dear, when is the wedding to be? Or am I being indiscreet?

BEVAN. Not at all, dear Miss Barrett, not at all. We——

BELLA (*excitedly*). Oh, that weminds me! Where's dear Henwietta? . . . The wedding? Early in August. (*Looks round the room*) Where's Henwietta?

OCTAVIUS. At the moment she's d-downstairs entertaining a friend.

BELLA. Oh, I wanted to ask her ——A fwiend? Not that tall gentleman we passed in the hall?

ELIZABETH. Yes, Captain Surtees Cook.

BELLA. Oh, in the Army? How thwilling! I thought his ca'wiage was militawy! So he's a fwiend of dear Henwietta?

ELIZABETH. Yes. . . . You wanted to ask Henrietta something?

BELLA. Oh, yes! Oh, Ba, I do so want her to be one of my bwidesmaids! Do you think—— (HENRIETTA *enters. She is visibly distraite.* BELLA *jumps to her feet*) Henwietta! (*Taking both her hands*) Henwietta darling, I was just saying —— Oh, you must be one of my bwidesmaids! you simply must!

HENRIETTA. Bridesmaids? Oh, yes—at your wedding. I should love to, Bella. It's sweet of you to ask me. And of course I will—if Papa—— But I'm sure he won't mind. . . .

BELLA. Mind? Uncle Edward? Why should he mind?

HENRIETTA. No, no, I'm sure it will be all right. I don't see how he could possibly object.

BELLA. Object? But I don't understand! . . . Isn't she funny, Ba? You're only asked to be a bwidesmaid, darling—not a bwide!

HENRIETTA. Yes, I know, but—— Oh, it's so hard to explain. . . .

BEVAN (*gravely helpful*). Perhaps Mr. Barrett looks on bridesmaids as frivolous irrelevancies at so solemn a sacrament as marriage . . . ?

HENRIETTA. No, no, Mr. Bevan. It's not that. It's—(*the words suddenly rush out*) It's simply that nothing—nothing at all in this house must happen without Papa's sanction. You know he once owned slaves in Jamaica. And as slavery has been abolished there, he carries it on in England. I'm quite serious. We are all his slaves here.

ARABEL. Henrietta!
(BEVAN *and* BELLA *look astonished and embarrassed.*)

HENRIETTA. Well, aren't we? Aren't we, Occy? Aren't we, Ba? We can't move hand or foot without his permission. We've got to obey his least whim and fall in with his moods—and they're as changeable as the weather! We haven't a soul of our own, not one of us . . . ! I tell you, Bella, it's more than likely that he'll refuse to let me be your bridesmaid, for no rhyme or reason—except that he's out of temper!

OCTAVIUS. I say, what about t-tea?

ARABEL (*rising quickly*). Oh, yes, yes!

HENRIETTA. Tea is quite ready. I'm sorry—I—I forgot to tell you.

OCTAVIUS. Good Heavens, let's h-hurry or Captain Cook will have swallowed it all! (*Crosses to the door and opens it.*)

HENRIETTA. He's gone. . . . (*She moves to the window and stands there, her face half averted.*)

BELLA. *A wivederci*, deawest Ba! (*Kisses her*) It's been so lovely seeing you! May I come soon again? And next time I shall want you all to myself—without Ha'wy, I mean.

ELIZABETH. Come whenever you like, dear.

BEVAN. But why must I be excluded?

BELLA. Because I've heaps and heaps to tell dear Ba about a certain big, big man who might easily gwow conceited if he heard me!

BEVAN. Oh, come, come, my pet. (BELLA *takes* ARABEL'S *arm.* BEVAN *bows over* ELIZABETH'S *hand*) Good-bay, dear Miss Barrett.

ELIZABETH. Good-bye. It was nice of you to come and see me.

BEVAN. Not at all. I have long been looking forward to the honour of meeting you. Good-bay.
(BELLA, *her arm still in* ARABEL'S, *kisses her hand to* ELIZABETH.)

BELLA. *Au wevoir,* darling!

ELIZABETH. *Auf wiedersehen.*
(BELLA *and* ARABEL *go out.*)

BEVAN (*turning and bowing at the door*). Good-bay.

ELIZABETH. Good-bye.
(BEVAN *goes out.* OCTAVIUS, *turning at the door, bows to* ELIZABETH, *in imitation of* BEVAN, *and follows him.* ELIZABETH *smiles, and glances at* HENRIETTA, *who still stands with averted face at the window; then she takes up a book and starts reading. A pause. Suddenly* HENRIETTA *turns on her.*)

HENRIETTA (*vehemently*). Well, why don't you say something?

ELIZABETH (*coldly*). What do you want me to say?

HENRIETTA. Nothing. . . . Oh, Ba, don't scold me! (*Goes to* ELIZABETH, *and sits on the floor beside her sofa*) I know I deserve it. I have been dreadful. But I couldn't help it. I'm so miserable.

ELIZABETH (*quickly*). Miserable, dear?

HENRIETTA. Yes—and so—so wildly happy! . . . Ba dear, may I tell you about it? I oughtn't to, I know. Because if it should ever come to anything, and Papa asks if you had any idea of what was going on, you'll have to lie—which you hate doing—or admit that you knew. And then he'd vent half his rage on you for not warning him in time.

ELIZABETH. Never mind, dear. Go on.

HENRIETTA. Surtees has just asked me to marry him.

ELIZABETH. Oh, Henrietta! But——

HENRIETTA. And, of course, I accepted him—and said that I couldn't. And I had to tell him that we must never see each other again. When he calls here tomorrow, we shall have to——

ELIZABETH. You're not talking sense, child. What really *has* happened?

HENRIETTA. I don't know . . . except that we both love each other terribly. . . . Oh, Ba, what *are* we to do? Surtees has only just enough money to keep himself decently. And, of course, I haven't a penny of my own. If only I had your four hundred a year, I might defy Papa and leave the house and marry Surtees tomorrow!

ELIZABETH. And what earthly good is that money to me? I'd give it to you, and how gladly——

HENRIETTA. I know you would, darling! But that's utterly impossible! Just think what your life would be like if Papa knew that you had made it possible for me to marry! No. But isn't it a cruel irony that the only one of the family with the means to be free and happy hasn't any use for it? (*With sudden urgency*) Ba dear, is there anything—anything at all—to be said for Papa's attitude towards marriage? Can it possibly be wrong to want a man's love desperately—and—and to long for babies of my own?

ELIZABETH. No. . . . But who am I to answer a question like that? Love and babies are so utterly remote from my life. . . .

HENRIETTA. Yes, I know, dear. You're a woman apart. But love and babies are natural to an ordinary girl like me. And what's natural can't be wrong.

ELIZABETH. No. . . . And yet the holiest men and women renounced these things. . . .

HENRIETTA. I daresay. But I'm not holy. And come to that, neither is Papa—not by any means! Didn't he marry, and—— (*A knock at the door.*)

ELIZABETH. Come in. (WILSON *enters.*)

WILSON. Mr. Robert Browning has called, Miss.

ELIZABETH (*breathlessly*). Mr.—Mr. Browning . . . ?

WILSON. Yes, Miss.

HENRIETTA. Then I'd better be off!

ELIZABETH (*agitated. Quickly*). No—no, stay here. I can't see him. I—I don't feel up to it. I can't——

HENRIETTA. But Ba, what on earth is the matter? You told me yesterday——

ELIZABETH. I know. I know. But I really don't feel that I can see him now. (*To* WILSON) Tell Mr. Browning I am very sorry but I am not well enough to receive him.

HENRIETTA. But that's not true, Ba! You can't send him away like that, dear. It would be too rude and unkind after having asked him to call, and all the efforts he has made to get here. (*To* WILSON) Where is Mr. Browning?

WILSON. I showed him into the library, Miss.

ELIZABETH. But I—I'd much—much rather not see him. . . .

HENRIETTA. Oh, fudge! You're not a silly schoolgirl! I'll bring him up myself. Mr. Kenyon says he's wonderfully romantic-looking, and quite the dandy. (HENRIETTA *goes out.*)

ELIZABETH. Is—is my hair tidy?

WILSON. Yes, Miss Ba.

ELIZABETH. Oh, please arrange the *couvre-pieds*. . . . (WILSON *arranges the couvre-pieds*) Thank you. . . . And, Wilson—no. . . . Thank you, that will do. . . .

WILSON. Yes, Miss.
(*She goes out.*)
(ELIZABETH, *obviously in a state of strained nerves, awaits the coming of* ROBERT BROWNING. *A pause.* HENRIETTA *enters.*)

HENRIETTA. Mr. Robert Browning. (ROBERT BROWNING *enters. He is a dark, handsome man in the middle thirties, faultlessly, perhaps even a trifle foppishly, dressed. Over his shoulder he wears a cape fastened with a chain at the throat. He carries his high hat, lemon-coloured gloves, and clouded cane. Browning's manner is sincere and ardent; his speech rapid, voluble, and emphasised by free gestures.* HENRIETTA *goes out.*)

BROWNING (*pausing for a moment a few steps beyond the threshold*). Miss Barrett?

ELIZABETH (*stretching out her hand*). How-do-you-do, Mr. Browning?

BROWNING (*quickly lays aside his hat, cane and gloves, and crossing to the sofa, takes her hand in both of his*). Dear Miss Barrett—at last! (*Raises her hand to his lips*) At last!

ELIZABETH (*still all nerves, and rather overcome by the ardour and unconventionality of his manner*). I—I've had to put off the pleasure of meeting you much longer than I wished. . . .

BROWNING (*still holding her hand*). Would you ever have received me if I hadn't been so tiresomely insistent?

ELIZABETH. As you know from my letters, I've not been at all well during the winter, and I—— (*Realising that her hand is still in his, she gently withdraws it*) But won't you take off your cape?

BROWNING. Thank you. (*Unfastens his cape and lays it aside.*)

ELIZABETH. I—I hope you don't find the room very close, Mr. Browning?

BROWNING. No, no. . . .

ELIZABETH. My doctor obliges me to live in what I am afraid must be to you a—a hot-house temperature. . . .

BROWNING (*who has thrown a quick glance round the room*). Wonderful! You may think, Miss Barrett, that this is the first time I've been here. You're quite wrong, you know!

ELIZABETH. But——

BROWNING. Quite wrong. I have seen this room more times than I can remember. It's as familiar to me as my own little study at home! Before I came in, I knew just how your books were arranged, just how that tendril of ivy slanted across the window panes—and those busts of Homer and Chaucer are quite old friends, and have looked down on me often before!

ELIZABETH (*smilingly protesting*). No, really——!

BROWNING. But I could never make out who the other fellows were on the top of the wardrobe, and——

ELIZABETH (*laughing, and now quite at her ease*). Oh, come, Mr. Browning! I know that dear Mr. Kenyon is never tired of talking about his friends; but I can't believe that he described my poor little room to you in detail!

BROWNING (*seating himself beside her*). I dragged all the details I possibly could out of him—and my imagination supplied the rest. Directly after I had read your brave and lovely verses I was greedy for anything and everything I could get about you.

ELIZABETH (*smilingly*). You frighten me, Mr. Browning!

BROWNING. Why?

ELIZABETH. Well, you know how Mr. Kenyon's enthusiasms run away with his tongue? He and I are the dearest of friends. What he told you about poor me I quite blush to imagine!

BROWNING. You mean, Miss Barrett, about you—you *yourself*?

ELIZABETH. I feel it would be hopeless for me to try to live up to his description.

BROWNING. He never told me anything about you—personally—which had the slightest interest for me.

ELIZABETH (*puzzled*). Oh?

BROWNING. Everything he could give me about your surroundings and the circumstances of your life I snatched at with avidity. But all he said about *you* was quite beside the point, because I knew it already—and better than Mr. Kenyon, old friend of yours though he is!

ELIZABETH. But—— Oh, Mr. Browning, do my poor writings give me so hopelessly away?

BROWNING. Hopelessly – utterly – entirely—to *me!* . . . I can't speak for the rest of the world.

ELIZABETH (*smilingly*). You frighten me again!

BROWNING. No?

ELIZABETH. But you do! For I'm afraid it would be quite useless my ever trying to play-act with you!

BROWNING. Quite useless!

ELIZABETH. I shall always have to be—just myself?

BROWNING. Always.

ELIZABETH. Oh . . . (*quickly*) And you too, Mr. Browning?

BROWNING. Always—just myself! (*He stretches out his hand; she takes it with a smile. Then, with a sudden laugh*) But really, you know, Miss Barrett, I sha'n't be able to take much credit for that! Being myself comes to me as easily as breathing. It's play-acting I can't manage—and the hot water I've got into in consequence . . . ! If life's to run smoothly we should all be mummers. Well, I can't mum!

ELIZABETH. Yes, I can well believe that now I know you. But isn't it extraordinary? When you are *writing* you never do anything else but —play-act.

BROWNING. I know——

ELIZABETH. You have never been yourself in any one of your poems. It's always somebody else speaking through you.

BROWNING. Yes. And shall I tell you why? I am a very modest man. (*Quickly, after a slight pause*) I am really!

ELIZABETH (*with suppressed amusement*). I didn't question it, Mr. Browning.

BROWNING. So modest, I fully realise that if I wrote about myself—my hopes and fears, hates and loves, and the rest of it—my poems would be intolerably dull.

ELIZABETH (*laughingly, vivaciously*). Well—since we are pledged to nothing but the truth, I won't contradict that—until I know you better!

BROWNING (*with a laugh*). Bravo!

ELIZABETH (*ardently*). Oh, but those poems with their glad and great-hearted acceptance of life—you can't imagine what they mean to me! Here am I shut in by four walls, the view of Wimpole Street my only glimpse of the world. And they troop into the room and round my sofa, those wonderful people of yours out of every age and country, and all so tingling with life! life! life! No, you'll never begin to realise how much I owe you!

BROWNING (*with emotion*). You—you really mean that?

ELIZABETH. Why, why, Mr. Browning——

BROWNING. But of course you do, or you wouldn't say it! And you'll believe me when I tell you that what you have said makes up to me a thousand times over for all the cold-shouldering I've had from the public?

ELIZABETH (*fiercely*). Oh, it infuriates me! Why can we never know an eagle for an eagle until it has spread its wings and flown away from us for good? Sometimes—I detest the British public !

BROWNING (*lightly*). Oh, no, no! Dear old British public! At least it gives us generously the jolly pastime of abusing it! And mind you, Miss Barrett, I've an uneasy feeling that my style is largely to blame for my unpopularity.

ELIZABETH (*a little too eagerly*). Oh, surely not!

BROWNING. Didn't we agree never to play-act with each other?

ELIZABETH (*with a laugh*). *Touché!* Well, perhaps, there *are* passages in your work a little invol—I mean a little too—too profound for the general reader.

BROWNING. Oh, no! it's not what I say, but how I say it.

ELIZABETH. Oh, but——

BROWNING. And yet to me it's all simple and easy as the rule of three! And to you?

ELIZABETH. Well . . . not *quite* always. Sometimes there *are* passages. . . . (*She picks up a book*) I have marked one or two in your "Sordello" which rather puzzle me. Here, for instance . . .
(*She opens the book and hands it to him.*)

BROWNING (*taking the book*). Oh, "Sordello!" Somebody once called it "a horror of great darkness!" I've done my best to forget it. However—— (*He reads the passage to himself, smiling. The smile fades; he passes his hand over his brow and reads it again. She watches him, covertly smiling. He mutters*) Extraordinary. . . . But—but a passage torn from its context. . . . (*He rises and goes to the window, as though to get more light on the subject, and reads the passage a third time.* ELIZABETH *has some difficulty in suppressing her amusement. He turns to her with an expression of humorous chagrin.*)

ELIZABETH. Well? . . .

BROWNING. Well, Miss Barrett—when that passage was written only God and Robert Browning understood it. Now only God understands it. (*She laughs, and he joins in*) What do you say—shall we lighten this great darkness by pitching it on the fire?

ELIZABETH (*indignantly*). No, indeed! We shall do nothing of the kind! Please give me back the book. (*He does so*) Such passages are only spots on the sun. I love "Sordello."

BROWNING (*eagerly*). You would! Of course you would! And shall I tell you why? Because it's a *colossal failure.*

ELIZABETH. If by a failure you mean an attempt—yes! you're right! That's just why "Sordello" appeals to my very heart. I too am always making colossal attempts—and always failing.

BROWNING. Isn't one such failure worth a hundred small successes?

ELIZABETH. Oh, a thousand and more!

BROWNING (*eagerly*). You think so too? But, of course, I knew that! . . . Miss Barrett, you smiled when I told you that Kenyon had no need to describe you because I knew you through and through already. And what you have just said about success and failure proves to me finally how right I was. All Kenyon did was to fill in the background. I—I had painted the portrait—with the true soul of you, ardent and lovely, looking out of it.

ELIZABETH. Ardent and lovely! And you think you know me! (*With a bitter smile*) Oh, Mr. Browning—too often impatient and rebellious. . . .

BROWNING. Well, what of it? I've no love for perfect patience under affliction. My portrait is the portrait of a woman, not a saint. Who has more right to be impatient and rebellious than you?

ELIZABETH. Did Mr. Kenyon paint my background with a very gloomy brush?

BROWNING. Old Rembrandt would have envied him!

ELIZABETH (*smilingly*). Poor dear Mr. Kenyon! He is more Royalist than the Queen herself! I assure you my afflictions worry him a great deal more than they worry me. . . . I suppose he told you that I am a—a dying woman?

BROWNING. We are all of us—dying.

ELIZABETH. And that our family life was one of unrelieved gloom?

BROWNING. Yes, he hinted at something of the sort.

ELIZABETH. He really shouldn't say such things! Frankly now, Mr. Browning, do you find me such a very pitiable object?

BROWNING. I find you, as I expected to find you, full of courage and gaiety. . . . And yet, in spite of what you say, I'm not at all sure that Kenyon's colours were too sombre.

ELIZABETH. But——

BROWNING (*eagerly interrupting*). No, no, listen to me. Those colours are not yet dry. They must be scraped off! The whole background must be repainted! . . . And if only you'll allow it—I must have a hand in that splendid work.

ELIZABETH. But, Mr. Browning——

BROWNING (*carried away*). No, listen! I'll dip my brush into the sunrise and the sunset and the rainbow! You say my verses have helped you—they're nothing. It's I—I who am going to help you now! We have come together at last—and I don't intend to let you go again.

ELIZABETH. But——

BROWNING. No, listen. Give me your hands. (*Bends forward and takes them*) I've more life than is good for one man—it seethes and races in me. Up to now I've spent a little of all that surplus energy in creating imaginary men and women. But there's still so much that I've no use for but to give! Mayn't I give it to you? Don't you feel new life tingling and prickling up your fingers and arms right into your heart and brain?

ELIZABETH (*rather frightened and shaken*). Oh, please . . . Mr. Browning, please let go my hands. . . .

(*He opens his hands; but she still leaves hers lying on his palms for a moment. Then she withdraws them, and clasping her cheeks, looks at him with wide, disturbed eyes.*)

BROWNING (*softly*). Well?

ELIZABETH (*a little shakily, with forced lightness*). You—you are really rather an overwhelming person, and in sober truth, I'm——

BROWNING. No—don't tell me again that you are afraid of me! You're not. It's life you're afraid of—and that shouldn't be.

ELIZABETH. Life?

BROWNING. Yes.

ELIZABETH. Well, when life becomes a series of electric shocks!

BROWNING (*smiling*). Was it as bad as all that?

ELIZABETH (*smiling*). Indeed, yes! Do you affect other people in the same way?

BROWNING. They've often told me so.

ELIZABETH (*lightly*). No wonder I hesitated about meeting you, much as I wanted to! Something of your disturbing vitality must have come to me from your letters and poems. . . . You'll laugh at me, Mr. Browning, but do you know we very nearly didn't meet today after all! When my maid told me you had arrived I was so panic-stricken that I all but sent down a message that I was too unwell to receive you. And it was a big effort to pull myself together, and behave like a sensible woman, when you came into the room!

BROWNING. I think I must have been quite as nervous as you at that moment.

ELIZABETH. You, Mr. Browning!

BROWNING. Yes—and I'm anything but a nervous man as a rule. But that moment was the climax of my life—up to now. . . . Miss Barrett, do you remember the first letter I wrote to you?

ELIZABETH. Yes, indeed! It was a wonderful letter.

BROWNING. You may have thought I dashed it off in a fit of white-hot enthusiasm over your poems. I didn't. I weighed every word of every sentence. And of one sentence in particular—this sentence: *"I love your books with all my heart—and I love you too."* You remember?

ELIZABETH (*lightly*). Yes—and I thought it charmingly impulsive of you!

BROWNING (*almost with irritation*). But I tell you there was nothing impulsive about it. That sentence was as deeply felt and anxiously thought over as any sentence I've ever written.

ELIZABETH. I hope I have many readers like you! It's wonderful to think I may have good friends all the world over whom I have never seen or heard of.

BROWNING. I am not speaking of friendship, but of love. (ELIZABETH *is about to make a smiling rejoinder*) No, it's quite useless your trying to put aside the word with a smile and a jest. I said love—and I mean love——

ELIZABETH. But really, Mr. Browning, I must ask you——

BROWNING (*swiftly interrupting her*). I'm neither mad nor morbidly impressionable—I'm as sane and level-headed as any man alive. Yet all these months, since first I read your poems, I've been haunted by you. And today you are the centre of my life.

ELIZABETH (*very gravely*). If I were to take you seriously, Mr. Browning, it would, of course, mean the quick finish of a friendship which promises to be very pleasant to both of us.

BROWNING. Why?

ELIZABETH. You know very well that love—in the sense you, apparently, use the word—has no place, and can have no place, in my life.

BROWNING. Why?

ELIZABETH. For many reasons—but let this suffice. As I told you before, I am a dying woman.

BROWNING (*passionately*). I refuse to believe it! For if that were so, God would be callous, and I *know* that He's compassionate—and life would be dark and evil, and I *know* that it's good. You must never say such a thing again. I forbid you to.

ELIZABETH. Forbid, Mr. Browning? . . .

BROWNING. Yes—forbid. Isn't it only fair that if you forbid me to speak of you as I feel, and I accept your orders, as I must, that I should be allowed a little forbidding as well?

ELIZABETH. Yes, but——

BROWNING (*breaking in with sudden gaiety*). Dear Miss Barrett, what a splendid beginning to our friendship! We have known each other a bare half hour and yet we've talked intimately of art and life and death and love, and we've ordered each other about, and we've almost quarrelled! Could anything be happier and more promising? . . . With your permission, I'm going now. Mr. Kenyon impressed upon me to make my first visit as short as possible, as strangers tire you. Not that I'm a stranger!—still I can see that you are tired. . . . When may I call again?

ELIZABETH (*a little dazed*). I don't quite know . . . I——

BROWNING. Will next Wednesday suit you?

ELIZABETH (*as before*). Yes, I—I think so. But perhaps it would be better——

BROWNING. Next Wednesday then.

ELIZABETH. But——

BROWNING. At half-past three again?

ELIZABETH. Yes—but I——

BROWNING (*bowing over her hand*). *Au revoir* then.

ELIZABETH. Good-bye.

BROWNING (*gently masterful, retaining her hand*). *Au revoir.*

ELIZABETH (*a little breathlessly, after a slight pause*). *Au revoir.*

BROWNING. Thank you.

(*He kisses her hand, turns and picks up his hat and cape, etc., and goes out.*)

(*The moment after the door has closed behind him* ELIZABETH *sits up and clasps her face with both her hands. Then she slips off the sofa and unsteadily gets on to her feet. With the help of the table and the chairs, she manages to cross the room to the window. Grasping the curtain to support herself, she stands looking down into the street after the departing* BROWNING, *her face as alive with excitement and joy as though she were a young girl. And the Scene slowly closes.*)

ACT THREE

ROBERT

Some three months later.

DOCTOR CHAMBERS *stands by the fireplace.* DOCTOR FORD-WATERLOW *sits on the sofa. He is sharp-featured, sharp-tongued old man. Both* DOCTORS *are intently watching* ELIZABETH *as she walks with firm and sure tread across the room to the window and back again.* FLUSH *lies on the sofa.*

FORD-WATERLOW. Once again, if you please. (ELIZABETH *walks across the room again*) My dear Miss Barrett, I congratulate you. Now sit down. (*She sits close to him, and he feels her pulse while talking*) When exactly was it you last called me in for consultation, Doctor Chambers.

CHAMBERS. Three months ago almost to a day.

FORD-WATERLOW. Yes, yes—and your patient was in a very low condition at the time. Well, you've done wonders, Doctor.

CHAMBERS. Oh, mine was just the ordinary spade-work. Honesty compels me to give most of the credit to another.

FORD-WATERLOW. Eh?

CHAMBERS. The real healer is no one but Miss Barrett herself.

ELIZABETH. But, Doctor . . . !

CHAMBERS. I mean it, my dear, I mean it. Three months ago you seemed more than a little inclined to let life and the world slip through your pretty fingers. Then slowly the change began. Oh, believe me, I was watching you like a lynx! Life and the world became more and more worth grasping. The wish to live is better than a dozen physicians—as I think even my distinguished friend will admit.

FORD-WATERLOW. The wish to live. . . . Hm, yes. . . . And you are able to get about and take the air occasionally nowadays?

ELIZABETH. Oh, yes, Doctor. I have visited some of my friends, and been for several delightful drives round the Park. The only bother is getting up and down stairs. I'm inclined to lose my head going down, and I'm not yet able to undertake the upward journey.

FORD-WATERLOW. Quite so. Quite so.

CHAMBERS (*smilingly*). Fortunately it doesn't need a very strong man to carry you.

ELIZABETH. Oh, but that's where you're wrong! (*To* FORD-WATER-

LOW) You have no idea how I am putting on weight!

FORD-WATERLOW. Is that so indeed?

CHAMBERS (*solemnly*). So much so, that I have seriously thought of docking Miss Barrett's porter—a beverage, I may say, of which she is inordinately fond.

ELIZABETH (*laughing*). I wonder you're not ashamed to mention that subject, Doctor Chambers!

FORD-WATERLOW. Well now, about the future, Miss Barrett. I fully agree with Doctor Chambers that another winter in London must, if possible, be avoided. If you continue picking up strength as you are doing, I see no reason against your travelling South by October, say.

ELIZABETH (*with barely controlled eagerness*). Travelling . . . South? . . .

FORD-WATERLOW. To the Riviera, or, better still, to Italy.

ELIZABETH (*breathlessly*). Italy . . . ! Oh, Doctor, do you really mean it?

FORD-WATERLOW. Why not? You could travel there by easy stages. I have been given to understand that you have set your heart on Italy, and that there are no—er—practical difficulties in the way of your going there.

ELIZABETH. If by practical, you mean financial—none at all. I have my own little income, and——

FORD-WATERLOW. Quite so, quite so.

CHAMBERS. I've taken the liberty to tell Doctor Ford-Waterlow of the only real difficulty in the way of your wintering abroad, and he is quite prepared to deal with—him.

FORD-WATERLOW. Quite—and drastically.

ELIZABETH (*quickly*). Oh, I am sure that won't be necessary! Papa may not raise any kind of objection. It depends how he is feeling at the time, and——

FORD-WATERLOW (*testily*). Fiddlesticks, my dear young lady! Mr. Barrett's feelings are neither here nor there. All that matters is his daughter's health and happiness, as I intend to make clear to him. Quite clear.

ELIZABETH. Oh, you mustn't think that Papa isn't kindness and generosity itself. But gentlemen have their moods. . . . Italy! Oh, it's hard to take in even the bare possibility of going there! My promised land, Doctor, which I never thought to see otherwise than in dreams!

FORD-WATERLOW (*rising*). Well, well, let us hope realisation won't bring disillusion along with it! A grossly overrated country to my mind. Nothing but heaps of rubbish, dust, flies, stenches, and beggars! Good-bye, my dear Miss Barrett. No, please don't get up. (*Takes her hand*) I'm delighted with your improvement. Delighted. And now for a little talk with your father. Good-bye.

ELIZABETH. Good-bye, Doctor.

CHAMBERS. Good-bye, Miss Elizabeth.

ELIZABETH. Good-bye. (*Both* DOCTORS *go out.* ELIZABETH *clasps her cheeks and whispers*) Italy—Italy—Italy. . . . (*She picks up* FLUSH) And you're coming with us, too, Flushy! We'll see Rome together, Florence, Venice, Vesuvius—— (ARABEL *enters.* ELIZABETH *puts* FLUSH *down and jumps to her feet*) Arabel! (*Embracing* ARABEL *impetuously*) It's all but settled, my dear! I'm to go to Italy! He says that I shall be quite fit to travel by October! . . . Rome! Florence! Venice! Vesuvius! Raphael! Dante! "Sordello!" . . . Oh, I don't know what I'm saying—I'm quite off my head with excitement!

ARABEL. How wonderful for you! I'm so glad! . . . And you think Papa will consent?

ELIZABETH. But of course he will! Both the Doctors are putting it before him as strongly as they can. Oh, surely he'd never have the heart to refuse when he realises all this Italian trip means to me. . . .

ARABEL (*without conviction*). No, dear, no. . . .

ELIZABETH. Have you seen him this afternoon?

ARABEL. Yes.

ELIZABETH (*quickly*). What was he like?

ARABEL (*eagerly*). Oh, quite sunny! He called me "Puss"—and he never does that when he's in one of his moods. And afterwards, when Bella came in, he was really merry.

ELIZABETH. Thank Heaven for that!

ARABEL. Which reminds me, dear—Bella has brought the gown Henrietta is to wear as bridesmaid. They want you to see it. They're trying it on now. . . .

ELIZABETH. Oh, I should love to! (*She pulls the bell rope*) I want badly some distraction to help me over the suspense of waiting for Papa's decision. . . .

ARABEL. Somehow I feel, Ba, that it wasn't altogether wise of you to keep this Italian plan secret from Papa, and then spring it suddenly on him.

ELIZABETH. Yes, I know, but—— (*A knock at the door*) Come in. (WILSON *enters*) Please tell Miss Hedley and Miss Henrietta I shall be delighted to see them now.

WILSON. Yes, Miss.

ELIZABETH. Oh, and take Flush out. He gets so excited when there are several people in the room. (WILSON *picks up* FLUSH *and goes out with him*) It was Doctor Chambers himself who advised me to say nothing to Papa until *both doctors* were satisfied that I was absolutely fit to travel. I quite agreed with him at the time. But now—oh, Arabel, I'm not so sure now! I'm so afraid Papa may think—— (*Voices and laughter outside*) Don't say anything about this to them. . . . (ARABEL *nods.*)

BELLA (*outside*). May we come in?

ELIZABETH (*rising*). Come in, dear. (BELLA *flutters in, followed by* HENRIETTA, *shy but radiant, in her bridesmaid's array*) Bella dear!

BELLA (*embracing* ELIZABETH). Darling, darling! Oh, but you weally shouldn't get up to weceive little me!

ARABEL (*contemplating* HENRIETTA). How perfectly lovely!

ELIZABETH. Delicious!

BELLA. Yes, isn't it? Isn't she, I should say! Dear Henwietta will be quite the pwettiest of my bwidesmaids. Indeed, I'm afwaid she'll dwaw all eyes from the little bwide! At any wate, all the gentlemen's! . . . But, darling Ba, you weally mustn't stand about like this! (*Leads her to the sofa.*)

ELIZABETH. But I'm as well able to stand as any one nowadays.

BELLA (*as* ELIZABETH *submits to be laid on the sofa*). No, no . . . ! One has only to see your dear face, so twanspawent and spiwitual, to know how near you are to Heaven. You always have a look in your eyes, darling, as though you alweady saw the angels!

HENRIETTA. She's looking at me, Bella—and I'm no angel!

BELLA. No, I'm afwaid you're not. . . . But you're vewy, vewy beautiful! . . . And fancy, Ba, if I hadn't spoken to Uncle Edward myself, I should never have had her for my bwidesmaid!

ELIZABETH. Yes, my dear, you certainly have a way with you.

HENRIETTA. *Spoken* to Papa! I like that! Why, you sat on his knee and stroked his whiskers.

ARABEL (*reprovingly*). Henrietta dear! (ELIZABETH *laughs.*)

BELLA. And why not? Isn't he my Uncle? . . . Besides that, I think he's most fwightfully thwilling! I adore that stern and gloomy type of gentleman. It's so exciting to coax and manage them. And so easy—if you know how! And I weally think I do. . . . But what I can't understand is his extwaordinawy attitude towards love and ma'wiage, and all that. It isn't as if he were in any way a mis—mis—oh, what's the howwid word?

ELIZABETH. Misogynist?

BELLA. Yes, and——

HENRIETTA. Well, *I* should describe him as the king of misogynists!

BELLA. But he *isn't*, I tell you.

HENRIETTA. How do *you* know?

BELLA. Never mind. But I *do* know. . . . Besides, didn't he mawwy himself—and, what's more, have eleven childwen? . . . (*An uncomfortable silence*) Oh, have I said anything—vewy dweadful?

ARABEL. No, dear—but, perhaps, not quite nice. When God sends us children it's not for us to enquire how and why. . . .

BELLA. I'm so sowwy! I didn't mean to be i'wevewent. . . . But I *do* find dear Uncle Edward's attitude extwaordinawy—and so useless! For in spite of it—and wight under his nose—and all unknown to him—his whole house is litewally seething with womance!

ARABEL. Bella!

HENRIETTA (*sharply*). What on earth do you mean?

BELLA. *You* ought to know, darling.

HENRIETTA. I?

BELLA (*enthusiastically*). I think Captain Surtees Cook is quite fwightfully thwilling! The way he looks at you, dear—and looks—and looks—and looks! . . . If he ever looked at *me* like that my knees would twemble so that I shouldn't be able to stand, and I'd get the loveliest shivers down my back!

ARABEL. Really, Bella!

HENRIETTA (*vexed and embarrassed*). I've never met any one who was able to pack more sheer nonsense into a couple of sentences than you.

BELLA. Haven't you, darling? . . . And then, there's George! *You* may not believe it, but *I'm* absolutely certain he has a thwilling understanding with your little cousin Lizzie. . . . And you weally mean to tell me that Charles and Miss what's-her-name are just mere fwiends? As for poor Occy—well, I don't mind telling you, in confidence, that my dear, dear Ha'wy is fwightfully jealous of him. . . .

ARABEL. Mr. Bevan jealous of Occy! But why?

BELLA. Why indeed? Aren't gentlemen silly?

ELIZABETH (*laughing*). What an extraordinary girl you are, Bella!

BELLA. Oh, I'm a fwightfully observant little thing! F'winstance, though you hardly ever mention his name, I know that Mr. Wobert Bwowning comes here to see you at least once evewy week. And at other times he sends you flowers. And he often bwings little cakes for dear Flush. . . . Flush! Oh, wouldn't it be fwightfully intewesting if only dear Flush could speak!

ARABEL. Good gracious, why?

ELIZABETH (*coldly*). But not so interesting as if Bella were occasionally silent.

BELLA. *Touché*, darling! I know I'm a dweadful little wattle—but you don't weally mind my quizzing you, do you?

ELIZABETH. Not in the least.

BELLA (*to* ARABEL). You see, dear Flush is the only witness of all that goes on at Ba's weekly *tête-à-tête* with the handsomest poet in England. He—Flush, I mean—ought to know a wonderful lot about poetwy by this time! For when two poets are gathered together they talk about whymes and whythms all the time? Or don't they? . . . I'm fwightfully ignowant.

ELIZABETH. Oh, no, my dear! On the contrary—you're "fwightfully" knowing.

BELLA. Me?

HENRIETTA. I hope to goodness you won't chatter any of this outrageous nonsense in front of Papa.

BELLA. Nonsense, is it? Well, I've my own little opinion about that! . . . But, of course, I won't bweathe a word of it to Uncle Edward. I'm all on the side of womance, and the path of twue love, and all that. . . .

ARABEL (*solemnly*). Bella, I regret to say it, but I think you are one of the few girls I know who would have benefited entirely under Papa's system of upbringing.
(ELIZABETH *and* HENRIETTA *laugh.*)

BELLA. Ooh . . . what a thwilling thought! He was always fwightfully stwickt, wasn't he? Did he whip you when you were naughty? How fwightfully exciting to be whipped by Uncle Edward!
(*A knock at the door. The* BARRETT SISTERS *are on the alert at once.*)

ELIZABETH. Come in.
(BARRETT *enters.* BELLA *jumps to her feet with a little scream and runs up to him.*)

BELLA. Oh, Uncle Edward! (*She thrusts her hand through his arm and snuggles against him*) Uncle dear, if I had been your little girl instead of Papa's would you have been te'wibly severe with me? . . . You wouldn't, would you? Or would you?

BARRETT. Would–wouldn't–would–would? Are you trying to pose me with some silly riddle?

BELLA (*drawing him into the room*). No, no, no. Sit down. (*Pushes him into a chair and perches herself on his knee*) It's like this—— But why that gloomy fwown, Uncle Edward? . . . (*She passes her fingers lightly over his forehead*) There–there–all gone! (BARRETT *has slipped his arm round her waist*) Awabel says it would have done me all the good in the world to have been bwought up by you. She thinks I'm a spoilt, fwivolous little baggage, and——

ARABEL. Bella! I never said anything of the sort!

BELLA. I know you didn't. But you *do!* (*Points to* HENRIETTA *and* ELIZABETH) And *you* do. And *you* do. . . . But *you* don't, Uncle, do you?

ARABEL. Really, Bella——

BARRETT (*speaking to* BELLA, *but at the others*). If my children were as bright and open and affectionate as you are I should be a much happier man.

BELLA. Oh, you mustn't say such things, or they'll hate me . . . !

BARRETT (*drawing her close. The two seem to be quite withdrawn from the others and oblivious of them*). And you're a distractingly lovely little creature. . . .

BELLA. Anything w'ong in that?

BARRETT. I didn't say so. . . .

BELLA. Then why do you look at me so fiercely? Do you want to eat me up?

BARRETT. What's that scent you have on you?

BELLA. Scent? Me? (*Giggling and snuggling up to him*) Don't you like it?

BARRETT. I abominate scent as a rule–but yours is different.

BELLA. Nice?

BARRETT. It's very delicate and subtle. . . . Still, I should prefer you not to use it.

BELLA. Why?

BARRETT. Never mind. (*Gently but audibly smacks her thigh.*)

BELLA. Ooh—that hurts!

BARRETT. Nonsense.

BELLA (*triumphantly*). But I never use scent! I haven't a dwop on me. I think it's ho'wid and common! (*With her arms round his neck*) Oh, Uncle, you're a darling! You've called me bwight and open and affectionate, distwactingly lovely and fwagwant all within a few minutes! You may kiss me!
(BARRETT *kisses her twice so roughly on the mouth that she gives a little cry. Then he pushes her abruptly off his knee and gets to his feet. She looks a little frightened.*)

BARRETT (*brusquely*). There, there, child, run away now. I want to speak to Ba. (*To the others*) You can go too.
(*He crosses to the window and stands looking out, with his back to the room.*)

BELLA (*in a rather injured voice*). Good-bye, Uncle.

BARRETT (*without turning*). Good-bye.

BELLA. Good-bye, Ba.
(*With a little toss of her head, she goes out.*)

ELIZABETH. Good-bye.
(HENRIETTA *and* ARABEL *go out. A pause.* ELIZABETH *looks with nervous expectancy at her father, who still stands at the window with his back to the room.*)

BARRETT (*without turning*). When is the wedding?

ELIZABETH. The wedding? Oh, Bella's . . . On the twenty-seventh.

BARRETT (*turning, and speaking half to himself*). Good. Less than a fortnight. . . . We are not likely to see much of her till then. And afterwards—well, she'll be living in the country most of the year.

ELIZABETH. But I thought you were so fond of her, Papa.

BARRETT (*sharply*). Fond of her? Why not? Isn't she my niece? . . . But she's a disturbing influence in the house. To see your brothers following her about with their eyes—especially Octavius. . . . Faugh! the room is still full of her! I shall be glad when she's gone. But I don't want to talk about Bella. Your doctors have just left me.

ELIZABETH (*expectantly*). Yes, Papa . . . ?

BARRETT (*with forced heartiness*). Their report is excellent. Astonishing. I'm more than gratified. I'm delighted. . . . Of course, my poor child, it's unlikely that you will ever be a normal woman. Even Chambers—optimistic fool though he is—was forced to admit that. . . . By the way, who *is* this Doctor Ford-Waterlow?

ELIZABETH. I've been told he is one of the cleverest physicians in London.

BARRETT. Really? . . . Well, he needs some amazing qualities to counterbalance his execrable manners. But even this medical phenomenon is unable to account for the sudden improvement in your health. Puts it down to Chambers' ministrations—which is, of course, arrant nonsense.

ELIZABETH. Perhaps the wonderful weather we've been having has most to do with it. I always thrive in warmth and sunshine.

BARRETT. Rubbish. Last summer was sweltering, and you have never been worse than then. No, to my mind, there is only One whom we have to thank—though this Doctor what's-his-name was pleased to sneer when I mentioned—Him.

ELIZABETH. Him?

BARRETT. I mean Almighty God. . . . It amazes me, Elizabeth, that you, on whom this miracle of recovery has been worked, should ascribe it to mere earthly agencies. Haven't I knelt here night after night and implored our all-loving Father to have compassion on His child? . . . It amazes me. It grieves me unspeakably. That is all I have to say for the present.
(*He turns to the door.*)

ELIZABETH. Papa.

BARRETT. Well?

ELIZABETH. Didn't Doctor Ford-Waterlow speak to you about—about next winter?

BARRETT. Doctor Ford-Waterlow talked, if I may say so, a great deal of nonsense.
(*He turns to go.*)

ELIZABETH. But Papa——

BARRETT (*testily*). What is it?

ELIZABETH. Didn't he tell you that I should avoid spending next winter in England?

BARRETT. Well?

ELIZABETH. And that he thinks I shall be fit to travel to Italy in October, if you——

BARRETT. So! It's out at last! And how long has this precious plot been hatching, may I ask?

ELIZABETH. It's now several weeks since Doctor Chambers first mentioned Italy as a real possibility.

BARRETT. I see. And do your brothers and sisters know anything of this delightful project?

ELIZABETH. I believe I mentioned it to them.

BARRETT. You believe you mentioned it to them. And Mr. Kenyon, and Mr. Horne, and the Hedleys, and that charlatan Browning—all your friends and relations in short—you've discussed your plans with the lot of them, I suppose?

ELIZABETH. Oh, Papa, what does it matter? My only reason——

BARRETT. Matter? Not in the least! It's nothing at all that I alone should be shut out of my favourite daughter's confidence—treated like a cipher—ignored—insulted——

ELIZABETH. Insulted?

BARRETT. Grossly insulted. When that fellow, Ford-Waterlow, sprung your carefully prepared mine on me and I naturally expressed my astonishment and displeasure, he became extremely offensive, and——

ELIZABETH. Believe me, Papa, my one reason for not worrying you with this Italian idea before was——

BARRETT. The fear that I should nip it in the bud at once. Exactly. I quite understand.

ELIZABETH. But——

BARRETT. No. I beg you to spare me explanations and excuses. The whole miserable business is abundantly clear. I am cut to the heart that *you*—the only one of my children whom I trusted implicitly—should be capable of such underhand conduct.

ELIZABETH. No—no——

BARRETT. If returning health must bring with it such sad change of character I shall be driven to wish that you were once more lying helpless on that sofa. There is nothing more to be said.
(*He turns to the door.*)

ELIZABETH (*with restrained anger*). But there is more to be said, and I must beg you to listen to me, Papa. How many years have I lain here? Five? Six? It's hard to remember—as each year has been like ten. And all that time I've had nothing to look forward to, or hope for, but death.

BARRETT. Death . . . ?

ELIZABETH. Yes, death. I was born with a large capacity for happiness—you remember me as a young girl?—and when life brought me little happiness and much pain, I was often impatient for the end, and——

BARRETT (*outraged*). Elizabeth! I'm shocked that——

ELIZABETH (*swiftly*). And now this miracle has happened! Day by day I am better able to take and enjoy such good things as every one has a right to—able to meet my friends, to breathe the open air and feel the sun, and see grass and flowers growing under the sky. . . . When Doctor Chambers first spoke to me of Italy I put the idea from me—it seemed too impossibly wonderful! But as I grew stronger, it came over me, like a revelation, that Italy wasn't an impossibility at all, that nothing really stood in the way of my going, that I had every right to go——

BARRETT. Right?

ELIZABETH. Yes! every right—if only I could get your consent. So I set about consulting my friends, meeting all obstacles, settling every detail, so as to have a perfectly arranged plan to put before you after the doctors had given you their opinion. In my eagerness I may have acted stupidly, mistakenly, tactlessly. But to call my conduct underhand and deceitful is more than unkind. It's unjust. It's cruel.

BARRETT (*more in sorrow than in anger*). Self! Self! Self! No thought, no consideration, for any one but yourself, or for anything but your pleasure.

ELIZABETH (*passionately*). But Papa——

BARRETT (*with a silencing gesture*). Didn't it even once occur to you that all through those long, dark months you proposed to enjoy yourself in Italy, your father would be left here utterly alone?

ELIZABETH. Alone?

BARRETT. Utterly alone. . . . Your brothers and sisters might as well be shadows for all the companionship they afford me. And you—oh, my child, don't think that I haven't noticed that you too, now that you are stronger and no longer wholly dependent on me, are slowly drawing away from your father. . . .

ELIZABETH. It's not true!

BARRETT. It is true—and, in your heart, you know it's true.

ELIZABETH. No!

BARRETT. New life, new interests, new pleasures, new friends—and, little by little, I am being pushed into the background—I who used to be your whole world, I who love you—who love you——

ELIZABETH. But Papa——

BARRETT (*with a silencing gesture*). No. There is nothing more to be said. (*He crosses to the window, looks out, then turns*) You want my consent for this—Italian jaunt. I shall neither give it nor withhold it. To give it would be against my conscience as encouraging selfishness and self-indulgence. To withhold it would be a futile gesture. You are your own mistress. Even if I refused to pay your expenses, you have ample means of your own to carry out your intentions. You are at liberty to do as you wish. . . . And if you go, I hope you will sometimes spare a thought for your father. Think of him at night stealing into this room which once held all he loved. Think of him kneeling alone by the empty sofa and imploring the Good Shepherd to—— (*A knock at the door*) Eh . . . ?

ELIZABETH (*with a start, her hand going to her heart*). Oh. . . .

BARRETT (*testily*). Who's that? Come in.
(WILSON *enters.*)

WILSON. If you please, Mr. Browning has called.

BARRETT (*under his breath*). That fellow again. . . .

WILSON. I showed Mr. Browning into the drawing-room, Miss, seeing as you were engaged.

ELIZABETH. Would you like to meet Mr. Browning, Papa?

BARRETT. Certainly not. I should have thought you knew by this time that I never inflict myself on any of my children's friends. (*To* WILSON) You may show Mr. Browning up.

WILSON. Very good, sir.
(*She goes out.*)

BARRETT. Mr. Browning appears to consider this his second home.

ELIZABETH. I have not seen him since last Wednesday.

BARRETT. Indeed.
(*He goes out.*)

(ELIZABETH *sits quite still, breathing quickly, her eyes fixed on the door.* WILSON *enters.*)

WILSON. Mr. Browning.
(BROWNING *enters and* ELIZABETH *rises to receive him.*)
(WILSON *goes out.*)

BROWNING (*taking her hands*). Oh, but how splendid! This is the fourth time you've received me—standing!

ELIZABETH (*her whole manner has changed: she is all sparkle and life*). If ever I receive you from my sofa again you may put it down to my bad manners and nothing else!

BROWNING. I will, with all my heart, I will! And now, tell me quickly. I've been dithering with suspense all day. You've seen them? What do they say?

ELIZABETH. Doctor Ford-Waterlow was quite taken out of his grumpy self with astonished delight at my improvement.

BROWNING (*delightedly*). Say that again!

ELIZABETH. Oh, must I? The whole sentence?

BROWNING. I should like to see it in letters of fire burning at me from each of these four walls! This is the best moment I've had since I got your note giving me permission to call on you! How many years ago was that?

ELIZABETH. Three months.

BROWNING. Absurd! We've always been friends! I've known you a lifetime and over! So, he was quite taken out of his grumpy self with astonished delight, was he? Splendid! Of course, *I* never once doubted that you would turn the corner some day. The world isn't rich enough to afford the waste of such a life as yours! But even *I* little dreamt recovery would be so rapid. And Italy? Are both Doctors agreed about your wintering there?

ELIZABETH (*with a note of reserve in her voice*). Yes.

BROWNING. And when do they think you'll be fit for travelling?

ELIZABETH. The middle of October—unless there's a relapse.

BROWNING. Relapse? There isn't such a word! October! Extraordinary! For you know, October suits my own plans to perfection.

ELIZABETH. *Your* plans?

BROWNING. Don't you remember my telling you that I had thought of wintering in Italy myself? Well, now I am quite decided. You see, I have practically made up my mind to remodel "Sordello." I should never be able to grapple with the task satisfactorily in England. Impossible to get the Italian atmosphere in a land of drizzle and fog! May I call on you often in Italy? Where do you intend to stay? (ELIZABETH *laughs*) Why are you laughing?

ELIZABETH. In Italy I'm afraid you'll need seven-league boots—when you call on me!

BROWNING. What do you mean?

ELIZABETH. I shall be at 50, Wimpole Street next winter.

BROWNING. Here?

ELIZABETH. Yes.

BROWNING. But didn't you tell me that both doctors——

ELIZABETH. Doctors may propose; but the decision rests—elsewhere.

BROWNING. Your father?

ELIZABETH. Yes.

BROWNING. He—he has vetoed the plan?

ELIZABETH. No—not exactly. But I am quite sure that he—that it will be impossible for me to go.

BROWNING. But—didn't the doctors make it clear to him that this move of yours may mean all the difference between—life and death?

ELIZABETH. I believe Doctor Ford-Waterlow spoke very forcibly.

BROWNING. Then, in Heaven's name——

ELIZABETH (*quickly, nervously*). Oh, it's rather hard to explain to some one who doesn't know all the circumstances. . . . You see, Papa is very devoted to me, and——

BROWNING. Devoted? . . .

ELIZABETH. Very devoted to me—and depends a lot on my companionship. He hasn't many points of contact with my brothers and sisters. If I were away for six months, he——

BROWNING (*visibly and audibly putting restraint on himself*). Miss Barrett—may I speak plainly?

ELIZABETH (*nervously*). Oh, do you think you'd better? I know—more or less—how you feel about this. But you don't quite understand the situation. How should you?

BROWNING. Very well. Then I'll say nothing. . . . (*His control suddenly gives way: his words pour out in a furious torrent*) You tell me I don't understand. You are quite right. I don't. You tell me he is devoted to you. I don't understand a devotion that demands favours as if they were rights, demands duty and respect and obedience and love, demands all and takes all, and gives nothing in return—I don't understand a devotion that spends itself in petty tyrannies and gross bullying—I don't understand a devotion that grudges you any ray of light and glimpse of happiness, and doesn't even stop at risking your life to gratify its colossal selfishness! Devotion! Give me good, sound, honest hatred rather than devotion like that?

ELIZABETH. Mr. Browning—I must ask you——

BROWNING. Forgive me—but I won't be silent any longer! Even before I met you, I knew that sickness wasn't the only shadow on your life. And all these months—though you never once breathed a syllable of complaint—I felt that other shadow deepening, and I've stood by, and looked on, and said nothing. Who was I to step in between you and the man nature, as an ugly jest, chose for your father? A mere friend! I might find you tired and sick after hateful scenes I could picture only too vividly—and I must pretend to know nothing, see nothing, feel nothing. Well! I've done with pretence from today on! I refuse any longer to let myself be gagged and handcuffed! It's not just your comfort and happiness which are at stake now. It's your very life. And I forbid you to play with your life. And I have the right to forbid you.

ELIZABETH (*desperately*). No—no—no . . . Oh, please don't say any more!

BROWNING (*with compelling ardour*). The right. And you won't deny it—you're too utterly candid and true. At our first meeting you forbade me to speak of love—there was to be nothing more than friendship between us. I obeyed you. But I knew well enough—we both knew—that I was to be much more than just your friend. Even before I passed that door, and our eyes first met across the room, I loved you—and I've gone on loving you—and I love you now more than words can tell—and I shall love you to the end, and beyond. You know that? You've always known?

ELIZABETH (*brokenly*). Yes—yes—I've always known. . . . And now for pity's sake—for pity's sake—leave me.

BROWNING (*seizing both her hands*). No.

ELIZABETH. Oh, please . . . please . . . let me go. Leave me. We must never see each other again.

BROWNING. I shall never let you go. I shall never leave you. (*He draws her into his arms*) Elizabeth . . . Elizabeth . . .

ELIZABETH (*struggling feebly in his embrace*). No—no. . . . Oh, Robert, have mercy on me. . . .

BROWNING. Elizabeth, my darling. . . .
(*He kisses her; and at the touch of his lips, her arms go round his neck.*)

ELIZABETH. Oh, Robert, I love you —I love you—I love you.
(*They kiss each other again. Then she sinks into a chair, and he kneels beside her, holding her hands.*)

BROWNING. And yet you ask me to take my marching orders and go out of your life?

ELIZABETH. Yes, Robert, for what have I to give you? I have so little of all that love asks for. I have no beauty, and no health, and I'm no longer young. . . .

BROWNING. I love you.

ELIZABETH (*with restrained spiritual passion*). I should have refused to see you again after our first meeting. For I loved you then, though I would have denied it—even to myself. . . . Oh, Robert, I think Eve must have felt as I did when her first dawn broke over Paradise—the terror, the wonder, the glory of it! I had no strength to put up any kind of resistance except the pitiful pretence of mere friendship. I was helpless, I was paralysed, with happiness I had never dreamt it was possible to feel. . . . That's my only excuse—and God knows I need one!—for not having sent you away from me at once.

BROWNING. I love you.

ELIZABETH. My life had reached its lowest ebb. I was worn out, and hope was dead. Then you came. . . . Robert, do you know what you have done for me? I could have laughed when Doctor Chambers said that I had healed myself by wanting to live. He was right! Oh, he was right! But he little knew what lay behind his words! I wanted to live—eagerly, desperately, passionately—and only because life meant you—you—and the sight of your face, and the sound of your voice, and the touch of your hand. Oh, and so much more than that! Because of you the air once more was sweet to breathe, and all the world was good and green again.

BROWNING (*kissing her hands*). And with those words singing in my ears, I'm to turn my back on you and go?

ELIZABETH. But, Robert, can't you —can't you see how impossible——

BROWNING. I've never yet turned my back on a friend or an enemy. Am I likely to turn it on you?

ELIZABETH. But how is it all to end? What have we to look forward to? And how——

BROWNING. I love you—and I want you for my wife.

ELIZABETH. Robert, I can't marry you. How can I when——

BROWNING. Not today or tomorrow. Not this year, perhaps, or next. Perhaps not for years to come——

ELIZABETH. I may never be able to marry you.

BROWNING. What then? If you remain to the last beyond my reach, I shall die proud and happy in having spent a lifetime fighting to gain the richest prize a man was ever offered.

ELIZABETH. No—no! Oh, Robert, put aside your dream of me—and look on me as I am. I love you too well to let you waste your manhood pursuing the pale ghost of a woman.

BROWNING. Do you think I'm a boy to be swept off my feet by an impulse? Or a sentimental dreamer blind to reality? There's no man alive who sees things as they are with clearer eyes than I do, and has his feet more firmly planted on the earth. And I tell you, in all soberness, that my need of you is as urgent as your need of me. If your weakness asks my strength for support, my abundant strength cries out for your weakness to complete my life and myself.

ELIZABETH (*after a pause*). Robert, have you thought what your position here would be like if you went on seeing me after today?

BROWNING. Yes.

ELIZABETH (*quickly*). We should have to keep our love secret from every one lest a whisper of it get to my father's ears.

BROWNING. I know.

ELIZABETH. If he had the least suspicion that you were more than a friend, the door would be slammed in your face, my letters supervised, and my life made unbearable.

BROWNING. I know.

ELIZABETH. And you, my dear—you're as frank and open as the day—how would you enjoy coming here under false pretences, and all the deceits, subterfuges, intrigues we'd be forced to use?

BROWNING (*with an exultant laugh*). I shall *detest* it—I shall *hate* it with all my heart and soul. And I thank God for that!

ELIZABETH. But Robert——

BROWNING. For it's splendid and right that I should suffer some discomfort, at least, for such a reward as you! The immortal garland was never run for without dust and heat!

ELIZABETH (*bitterly*). Immortal! Oh, Robert, fading, if not already faded! (*He is about to protest*) No, don't speak! don't speak! . . . (*She rises and goes to the window and looks, with unseeing eyes, into the street. After a moment she turns to him*) Robert, if we were to say good-bye today, we should have nothing but beautiful memories of each other to last to the end of our lives. We should be unhappy: but there are many kinds of unhappiness. Ours would be the unhappiness of those who have put love away from them for the sake of love. There would be no disillusion in it, or bitterness, or remorse.

BROWNING (*in a low, tense voice*). Is it *you* who are speaking?

ELIZABETH. What do you mean?

BROWNING. I don't know you. I thought yours was the courage that dared the uttermost, careless of defeat. Here's life—*life*—offering us the best that life can give, and you dare not grasp at it for fear it will turn to dust in your hand! We're to dream away the rest of our lives in tepid sadness rather than risk utter disaster for utter happiness. I don't know you. I never thought you were a coward!

ELIZABETH (*proudly, indignantly*). A coward? I? (*With a sudden change of voice*) Yes, I'm a coward, Robert—a coward through and through. . . . But it's not for myself that I'm afraid.

BROWNING (*going swiftly up to her and taking her in his arms*). I know that, my darling.

ELIZABETH. What's another disaster, great or small, to me who have known little but disaster all my life? But you're a fighter—and you were born for victory and triumph. If disaster came to you through me——

BROWNING. Yes, a fighter. But I'm sick of fighting alone. I need a comrade-at-arms to fight beside me—and——

ELIZABETH. Not one already wounded in the battle. . . .

BROWNING. Wounded—but undefeated, undaunted, unbroken.

ELIZABETH. Yes, but——

BROWNING. What finer comrade could a man ask for?

ELIZABETH. But Robert——

BROWNING. No.

ELIZABETH. But Robert——

BROWNING. No.
(*And he kisses the protest from her lips as the Scene closes.*)

ACT FOUR

HENRIETTA

Some weeks later.

ARABEL *enters, carrying* FLUSH. *She is in outdoor clothes and has her bonnet on.*

ARABEL (*standing in the open doorway and speaking*). You had really better let Wilson help you up the last few stairs, Ba.

ELIZABETH (*outside*). No! No, Wilson, don't touch me!

ARABEL. But, my dear . . .
(ELIZABETH *enters, bonneted and in outdoor clothes. She is breathless but triumphant.* WILSON *follows at her heels.*)

ELIZABETH. There! All the way up, and without one pause or help of any kind! And I feel splendid—just a little out of breath, that's all. . . . (*She sways a little on her feet. Both* WILSON *and* ARABEL *stretch out hands to support her*) No, don't touch me! I'm perfectly all right. . . . (*She walks to the sofa and sits down, and takes her bonnet and gloves off during the following*) Now wasn't that a glorious triumph? And you know, Wilson, I got out of the carriage and walked quite—two miles in the Park!

WILSON. Lor', Miss!

ARABEL. Ba, *dear* . . . !

ELIZABETH. Well, one mile then. Anyhow, that's what I'm going to tell Doctor Chambers.

ARABEL. *Really,* Ba . . . !

ELIZABETH. Oh, my dear, Flush has muddied your gown disgracefully! What a filthy state you're in, Flushy! . . . You had better take him, Wilson, and get Jenny to bath him. He's not been properly washed for ages.

WILSON (*taking* FLUSH *from* ARABEL). Very good, Miss Ba.
(WILSON *goes out carrying* FLUSH.)

ELIZABETH (*pointing to a little heap of letters*). Oh, the post has come. Please give me those letters, dear.

ARABEL (*handing her the letters*). Why, that's Mr. Browning's handwriting! I'm sorry, I couldn't help seeing it, Ba. But aren't you expecting him this afternoon?

ELIZABETH (*absently*). Yes. . . . (*She tears open the letter and reads it, smiling to herself*) Yes, dear, he should be here very soon now. . . . This was just to wish me good night.

ARABEL. To wish you good night . . . ?

ELIZABETH. Yes, it was written yesterday evening.

ARABEL. Oh. . . .

ELIZABETH (*turning over the letters*). Mr. Haydon—Miss Martineau—Mr. Horne—Oh! . . . (*A sharp change coming into her voice*) This is from Papa.

ARABEL (*anxiously*). From Papa! But he's returning today. . . .

ELIZABETH. Perhaps he's been detained. . . .
(*She opens the letter.*)

ARABEL (*hopefully*). Oh, do you think so?

ELIZABETH (*she quickly scans the letter; then in a voice of consternation*). Oh! . . . Oh, Arabel! . . .

ARABEL. What is it, dear?

ELIZABETH. We're leaving.

ARABEL. Leaving?

ELIZABETH. Yes—leaving this house. Leaving London. Listen——
(*A knock at the door and* HENRIETTA'S *voice.*)

HENRIETTA (*outside*). May I come in, Ba?

ELIZABETH. Come in, dear. (*In a hurried whisper to* ARABEL) Don't speak of this yet. . . .
(HENRIETTA *enters.*)

HENRIETTA (*in great excitement*). Oh, Ba, you must see him at once! You positively must!

ELIZABETH. Him . . . ?

HENRIETTA. He's in his full regimentals. He's just been to St. James' to receive—or whatever you call it—his adjutancy—or something—from Queen Victoria herself. He's wonderful! He's gorgeous! May I bring him up here for you to look at?

ELIZABETH. But——

HENRIETTA. Papa need never know. Oh, Ba, do let me! You've never seen him yet—it's high time you met—and you couldn't see him to better advantage than now! . . . I'm talking of Captain Cook, you know.

ELIZABETH. Yes, so I've gathered. But I can't see him now, dear. I'm expecting Mr. Browning any minute.

HENRIETTA (*crestfallen but resigned*). Oh . . . then of course it's impossible. . . . But I tell you what, Ba! I'll try to keep him until Mr. Browning goes. I don't think he'll mind. (*She hurries to the door, and throws over her shoulder*) You can keep your poet here as long as you like.
(*She goes out.*)

ELIZABETH (*with a short laugh that ends in a sigh*). Yes, she had best make the most of her soldier while she can, poor darling. She is not likely to see much of him in the future.
(*She takes up* BARRETT'S *letter.*)

ARABEL. Oh, Ba, tell me quickly. . . .

ELIZABETH. He writes from Dorking. (*She reads*) "*This is to let you know that we shall be leaving London on Monday, the 22nd of this month. I have taken a furnished house at Bookham, in Surrey, some twenty miles from London and six miles from Leatherhead, the nearest railway station. Whether we shall eventually make it our permanent home I have not yet decided. At any rate, we shall spend the winter there. You will benefit by the country air and the complete seclusion of your new surroundings. I have felt for some time now that your present feverishly restless mode of life in London will, if continued, affect you harmfully both physically and morally. I am writing this letter so that you may inform your brothers and sisters of my decision and tell them that I decline absolutely to discuss it when I return home tomorrow.*" —That's today.—"*The matter is finally settled, and you and they will make such preparations as are needful for the move.*"

ARABEL. Oh, Ba! . . .

ELIZABETH (*bitterly*). That's not quite all. He finishes up with a characteristic touch of humour.

ARABEL. Humour?

ELIZABETH. Yes. He signs himself—"*Your loving Papa.*"

ARABEL. The twenty-second. That gives us barely a fortnight longer here.

ELIZABETH (*stormily*). My "feverishly restless mode of life"!—a few drives, a few calls on my friends, a few visitors. . . . I wonder he doesn't describe me as a recklessly dissipated woman! He made my going to Italy impossible. And now I am to be cut off any little pleasures I have begun to find here. (*She crumbles up the letter and tosses it into the grate.*)

ARABEL. I know, dear, I understand —and I'm very sorry for you. . . . The change won't hit me so hardly. My only ties in London are my Mission work and district visiting. But you and Henrietta—— (*She hesitates.*)

ELIZABETH. Well?

ARABEL (*with sudden earnestness*). Oh, Ba, don't be angry with me if I tell you that this move may, in the long run, be a blessing in disguise for you.

ELIZABETH. A blessing in disguise! I seem to have been brought up on that pious *cliché!* What do you mean?

ARABEL. We all pretend to be ignorant of each other's affairs in this house—except poor Henrietta's. It's safer so. And yet we know—we all know—that you and Mr. Browning——

ELIZABETH. Well?

ARABEL. Oh, Ba, one has only to look at your face when you're expecting him—and again after he has left you. . . .

ELIZABETH (*proudly*). I love him and he loves me. What of it? Haven't I as much right to love and be loved as any other woman?

ARABEL. Oh, yes, dear—but how is it all to end? So long as Papa's alive none of us will ever be able to marry with his consent—and to marry without it is unthinkable. And, in your case it isn't only a question of Papa's consent. . . . Of course it's—it's wonderful how much stronger and better you are—you walked upstairs splendidly just now. . . . But—but——

ELIZABETH. But even if I can manage to walk up a few steps it doesn't mean that I shall ever be fit to marry—is that what you're trying to say?

ARABEL. Oh, Ba, darling, it's because I love you so dearly, and don't want you to suffer, that I'm forcing myself to speak. I know very little about gentlemen—except that they all want to marry the ladies they fall in love with. I—I don't know Mr. Browning at all—but—— But even great poets want to settle down in time, and have a home of their own, and a wife, and—and little ones. . . . It would be so dreadful if——

ELIZABETH (*springing to her feet*). Oh, be quiet! be quiet! Do you suppose I haven't thought of all that a thousand times already?
(*She goes to the window and looks out.*)

ARABEL. I am sorry. . . . I—I didn't mean to interfere. All I want is to save you any—— (*She notices that* ELIZABETH *is no longer listening, but is waving her hand to some one in the street, her face transformed with joy*) Oh . . .
(*She rises and slips softly out of the room, unnoticed by* ELIZABETH.)

ELIZABETH (*turning*). Mr. Browning has just—— (*Realises the empty room*) Oh. . . . (*Her eyes light on* BARRET'S *crumpled letter in the grate. She picks it up and smooths it out, her face emptied of joy. She puts it on the mantelpiece. A knock at the door*) Come in.
(BROWNING *enters. They look at each other in silence for a moment; then he goes up to her and takes her in his arms.*)

BROWNING. My love.

ELIZABETH. Robert. . . .
(*They kiss.*)

BROWNING (*holding her at arm's length*). You look tired, sweetheart. What have you been doing today?

ELIZABETH (*with forced lightness*). I went for a drive—and a walk in the Park. And afterwards I ran all the way upstairs—without help, and without one stop.

BROWNING. Oh, but you know——! Of course, dearest, it's a splendid feat, and I'm proud of you! . . . Come and sit down. (*Leads her to the sofa, and they sit down*) Now, aren't you being a trifle too ambitious?

ELIZABETH. I don't think so. . . . I'm feeling wonderfully well. . . .

BROWNING. Look at me. (*She looks at him*) What's the matter, Ba?

ELIZABETH. Nothing. . . .

BROWNING. Has your father returned?

ELIZABETH. No. We expect him today.

BROWNING (*taking her face in his hands*). Those talking eyes of yours give you hopelessly away. Something has gone wrong. What is it? You must tell me.

ELIZABETH. Read that letter on the mantelpiece, Robert.

BROWNING (*goes to the mantelpiece and takes* BARRETT'S *letter*). From your father?

ELIZABETH. Yes. (*He reads the letter; then looks at her with a strange smile on his face*) Well?

BROWNING (*still smiling*). I think, by the look of it, you crumpled up this letter furiously in your little hand—and I'm quite sure you pitched it into the grate.

ELIZABETH. Yes, I did. But——

BROWNING. Why?

ELIZABETH. Oh, Robert, don't you see what this means to us?

BROWNING. Yes—and perhaps better than you do.

ELIZABETH. Better than I? Oh, you mustn't deceive yourself! You think this move will make little difference to us. You think you'll be able to ride over from London and see me almost as often as we see each other here. But you're wrong! you're wrong! You don't know Papa as I do. He's grown jealous of my life here, my pleasures and my friends—and I'm slowly and surely to be parted from them. I've felt this coming for some time now. Oh, Robert, it will soon be made impossible for me to see you at all. . . .

BROWNING. This precious letter may mean all that. But it means a great deal more that you haven't as yet been able to grasp.

ELIZABETH. A great deal more . . . ?

BROWNING. It means that you will be in Italy before the month is out.

ELIZABETH (*in a whisper*). Italy . . . ?

BROWNING. Yes—and with me.

ELIZABETH. Robert . . .

BROWNING. It means that we must be married at once.

ELIZABETH (*standing up*). Do you know what you're saying?

BROWNING. Yes, I know what I am saying. And I repeat it. We must be married at once. (*He goes up to her*) My darling, listen to me—— (*He is about to take her hands.*)

ELIZABETH (*starting back*). No! Don't touch me! What you say is madness! . . . I can't marry you—I can never marry you.

BROWNING (*with a sudden blaze of passion*). You can, and you shall! You'll marry me if I have to carry you out of this house and up to the altar! (*Controlling himself*) Do you seriously imagine I'm going to allow myself to be elbowed out of your life now? And just to satisfy the selfish jealousy of a man whom I no longer believe to be sane? You ought to know me better by this time——

ELIZABETH (*quickly breaking in*). Oh, Robert, it's not only Papa who stands between us. It's I—it's I . . .

BROWNING. We've gone into that a hundred times already, and——

ELIZABETH. Yes, and now we must go into it once again, and frankly, for the last time.

BROWNING. But——

ELIZABETH (*silencing him with a gesture*). Robert, it's no use deceiving ourselves. However much stronger I may become, I shall always remain an invalid. You tell me that you want me sick or well—and it's wonderful of you to say that, and I know you believe it. . . . But I—Robert, I'm not generous enough—I'm too proud, if you like —to accept what I feel through and through, in spite of anything you say, to be a sacrifice of your life and your manhood. As your wife I should be haunted day and night by thoughts of all the glorious things you would have enjoyed but for me—freedom, ease, adventure, and passionate love I—I could never really satisfy. . . .

BROWNING. No—no—listen——

ELIZABETH (*with all her soul in her voice*). Oh, Robert, I should be haunted by the ghosts of your unborn children. . . . When I read that letter my world seemed to fall to pieces. . . . But now I thank God that it came while we're still free, and have the strength to shake hands and say good-bye. . . . (*She stretches out her hand.*)

BROWNING (*with a complete change of manner, ignoring her hand, and speaking in a quiet, matter-of-fact voice*). On the whole I think this will be our best plan of campaign. The family leave here on the—(*he consults the letter*)—on the twenty-second. So we have barely a fortnight to get everything done in. You told me last week that Mr. Hedley had invited your sisters to picnic in Richmond Park next Saturday. So the house will be conveniently empty. We'll meet at Mary-le-Bone Church and be married quietly some time in the morning. I'll see about a licence at once, and interview the Vicar.

ELIZABETH (*who has been staring at him with bewilderment and fear*). Robert——

BROWNING (*as before*). It would be madness to leave England on the same day. You'll need all the rest and quiet you can get before the journey. So, directly after we are married, I think you had better return here and take things very easily for a day or two. You'll have six days if we leave on Saturday week. Now——
(*He takes a paper out of his pocket.*)

ELIZABETH. Oh, stop! I can't listen to you!

BROWNING (*as before, consulting the paper*). For some time now I've kept careful note of the sailings from Southampton in case of just such an emergency as this. The Packet leaves the Royal Pier on Saturdays at nine o'clock. We must catch the five o'clock express at Vauxhall. It arrives at Southampton at eight.

ELIZABETH. Oh . . . (*She laughs wildly, the laugh changing into sobs.* BROWNING *takes her into his arms and draws her down beside him on the sofa. Her sobs gradu-*

ally subside. She says brokenly) And—and I always believed Papa was the most overbearing man in the world. . . .

BROWNING (*smiling*). And yet you've known me for some time now!

ELIZABETH. But I mustn't give way, Robert—I mustn't—I daren't. . . .

BROWNING. There's one other thing, my darling, of the utmost importance that we must settle at once. You can't possibly travel without a maid. Wilson must have a pretty shrewd idea of our relations. You say she is entirely devoted to you. But do you think she will be willing to come abroad with us?

ELIZABETH (*after a pause, in a low voice*). Robert . . . have you ever thought that my strength may break down on the journey?

BROWNING. Yes.

ELIZABETH. Suppose I were to—to die on your hands?

BROWNING (*softly, after slight pause*). Are you afraid, Ba?

ELIZABETH (*proudly, indignantly*). Afraid? I? You know that I am not afraid! You know that I would sooner die with you beside me than live a hundred lives without you. . . . But—but how would *you* feel if I were to die like that? And what would the world say of you?

BROWNING (*quietly*). I should be branded as little better than a murderer. And what I should feel I—I leave you to imagine.

ELIZABETH. And yet you ask me to come with you?

BROWNING. Yes. I am prepared to risk your life—and much more than mine—to get you out of this dreadful house into the sunshine, and to have you for my wife.

ELIZABETH. You love me like that?

BROWNING. I love you like that. (*A long pause.*)

ELIZABETH. Robert . . . will you—will you give me a little time?

BROWNING. Time is short, my dear.

ELIZABETH. Yes, I know. But I must have a little time. I can't decide now. I daren't. . . . I feel something *must* happen soon to show me definitely the way. . . . Give me a few hours. Before I sleep tonight I'll write and tell you my decision. . . . Please, Robert.

BROWNING. You promise me that?

ELIZABETH. I promise.

BROWNING. Very well.

ELIZABETH. Thank you.

BROWNING. Shall I go now?

ELIZABETH. Please. . . . (*He kneels and takes both her hands and presses them passionately to his lips. She receives the caress passively. He rises and leaves the room in silence. She sits motionless, staring before her. A pause. Then a light knock at the door. Another pause. Then a louder knock.* ELIZABETH *starts out of her thoughts*) Come in.

(HENRIETTA *enters.*)

HENRIETTA. I saw Mr. Browning going down the stairs. . . . May I bring him in?

ELIZABETH. Him?

HENRIETTA. He's standing on the landing outside. . . . (*She gives* ELIZABETH *a little shake*) Wake up, Ba! I'm talking of Surtees.

ELIZABETH. Oh, yes, of course. . . . But won't some other time do as well?

HENRIETTA. No! No! I told you he was in uniform. You promised to see him, Ba!

ELIZABETH (*with a sigh*). Very well, dear. . . .
(HENRIETTA *kisses* ELIZABETH *impulsively; then goes to the door and opens it.*)

HENRIETTA (*speaking into the passage*). Come in, Surtees. (CAPTAIN SURTEES COOK *enters: a huge, handsome, whiskered, frank-faced man. He is arrayed in the full splendour of his "regimentals" and carries his headgear under his arm*) Captain Surtees Cook, Ba.—My sister, Elizabeth.
(ELIZABETH *has risen to receive him.* COOK *clicks his heels together and bows stiffly.*)

COOK. Your servant, Miss Barrett.

ELIZABETH (*offering him her hand*). How-do-you-do?

COOK (*taking her hand and bowing over it*). Greatly honoured, 'pon my word I am, Miss Barrett. Understand not every one received here,

HENRIETTA. No indeed, Surtees! With the exception of the family, very few gentlemen have ever been allowed in Ba's room.

COOK. Twice honoured in one day, y'know. First by Her Majesty; now by you, Miss Barrett. Can't think what I've done to deserve it.

ELIZABETH. Oh, I had forgotten! You've just come from the Palace. I have never seen the Queen. What is she like?

COOK. Very little lady, Ma'am; but royal, every inch of her.

HENRIETTA. Surtees, you haven't got your sword on!

COOK. Not etiquette, as I told you, to wear it indoors.

HENRIETTA. Oh, bother etiquette! I want Ba to see you in full warpaint. Where did you leave it?

COOK. In the hall.

HENRIETTA. I'll fetch it. (*Runs to the door.*)

COOK. No, but really—Miss Barrett doesn't want——
(HENRIETTA *goes out.*)

ELIZABETH. But indeed I do, Captain Cook! I don't think I've ever seen an officer in . . . full warpaint before, except at reviews and ceremonies—and that was years ago.

COOK. Indeed? (*After a short pause*) Er—Miss Barrett . . .

ELIZABETH. Yes?

COOK. Miss Barrett . . .

ELIZABETH (*encouragingly*). Yes, Captain Cook?

COOK. I say, Miss Barrett. . . .

ELIZABETH. You want to tell me something about Henrietta?

COOK (*eagerly*). Just so, Miss Barrett, just so. Exactly. You know, Miss Barrett—you know—— (*He is unable to go on.*)

ELIZABETH (*very kindly*). Yes, Captain Cook, I know. And though I'm quite powerless to help, believe me, you have my heartfelt sympathy. (*She gives him her hand.*)

COOK (*taking it in both of his*). Thank you. Thank you. More than I deserve. Thank you, Miss Barrett. Never was such a girl, y'know—Henrietta, I mean. Dunno what I've done to deserve——

(HENRIETTA *enters with the sword.* ELIZABETH *and* COOK *are still holding hands.*)

HENRIETTA. Oh, yes, I thought he'd seize the opportunity to tell you something while I was out of the room. Did he really manage to get it out?

ELIZABETH (*smiling*). Perhaps, not quite. Did you, Captain Cook?

COOK. Well—ah—y'know. . . . Still, like most ladies—quick in the uptake. . . .

ELIZABETH. Yes, I understood. (*Kissing* HENRIETTA) My dear, how I wish I could do something for you both!

HENRIETTA. Well, you can't, favourite daughter though you are! Nobody can. (*She sits down with the sword across her lap*) Surtees wants to ask Papa for my hand and all that—quite like the conventional suitor. I can't get it into his poor head that such things are simply not possible at 50, Wimpole Street.

ELIZABETH (*earnestly*). Oh, believe me, Captain Cook, it would be more than useless! You would be peremptorily ordered out of the house—and I don't know what would happen to Henrietta!

COOK. Quite aware that I'm not much of a match, Miss Barrett. Poor man, y'know. Little else than my pay. Still, quite respectable and all that. Decent family and all that. Should be more than willing, if necessary, to throw up soldiering and take to some money-making business, but——

HENRIETTA. And a fine mess you'd make of it, my poor dear!

COOK. Well, I'm not so sure about that. Admit, of course, that soldiering's my special job. Haven't the brain for much else, I'm afraid. Still, you never know what a fella can't do with a prize like Henrietta to reward his efforts. What d'you say, Miss Barrett?

HENRIETTA. Oh, Ba, can *you* make him understand? I can't!

ELIZABETH (*very impressively*). Captain Cook, if you were a Prince of Eldorado and came here courting, with a pedigree of lineal descent from some signory in the Moon in one hand, and a ticket of good behaviour from the nearest Independent Chapel in the other—

even then, Papa would show you the door! *Now* do you understand?

COOK. Can't say I do.

HENRIETTA. Well, anyhow, you're not to speak to Papa, and I forbid you to give up soldiering. Now that I've seen you in your glory, do you suppose I should ever take you without your uniform? Get up. I want to buckle on your sword.

COOK. Aw, I say—— (*Stands up, smiling rather sheepishly.*)

HENRIETTA (*getting to work*). Ba thinks poets are the flower of manhood—a certain poet, at any rate. I mean to show her that she's mistaken. . . .

COOK. I say, you've got it wrong. Sword hangs from the left hip, y'know.

HENRIETTA. Why?

COOK. Well——
(BARRETT *enters, and taking in the scene with a look of amazement, his face immediately hardens into a mould of freezing displeasure. Both* GIRLS *stare at him in consternation.* COOK *stands rigid.*)

ELIZABETH. Papa. . . . You're—you're home earlier than I expected, Papa.

BARRETT. I don't think I have the privilege of this gentleman's acquaintance.

HENRIETTA. Captain Cook, may I introduce my father? Papa—Captain Surtees Cook.

COOK. Your servant, sir.
(BOTH MEN *bow stiffly.*)

HENRIETTA (*after a short pause*). Captain Cook is a great friend of George and Occy.

BARRETT. Indeed? (*To* COOK) My sons are very rarely at home at this time of the day.

COOK. Fact is—just passing the house—thought I'd look in on the off chance, y'know, sir—finding one of them in and all that. . . .

BARRETT. I see.

ELIZABETH (*breaking a pause*). Captain Cook has just come from Buckingham Palace . . . and Henrietta thought I should like to see him in all the splendour of his regimentals.

BARRETT. Indeed. (*Takes out his watch and looks at it.*)

COOK. Nothing much to look at, of course—but ladies like a bit of colour, and er—— By Jove, must be getting late!

BARRETT (*pocketing his watch*). It's nineteen-and-a-half minutes past five.

COOK. By Jove! High time I were moving. . . . (BARRETT *pulls the bell rope twice*) Good-bye, Miss Barrett.

ELIZABETH. Good-bye, Captain Cook.
(*She gives him her hand.* BARRETT *crosses to the door and holds it open.*)

COOK. Good-bye, Miss Henrietta.

HENRIETTA. I'll see you out.
(COOK *moves to the door, followed by* HENRIETTA.)

COOK (*to* BARRETT). Your servant, sir.

(BARRETT *returns his bow in silence.* COOK *goes out and* HENRIETTA *is about to follow.* BARRETT *stays her with a gesture.*)

HENRIETTA. I am seeing Captain Cook to the door.

BARRETT. The servant will attend to that. (*He closes the door, and, in silence, crosses to the fireplace and takes up his stand in front of it. When he speaks he looks straight before him*) Your list of gentlemen visitors appears to be lengthening, Elizabeth.

ELIZABETH. This is the first time I have had the pleasure of meeting Captain Cook.

BARRETT. Indeed. But I infer, from what I saw as I came into the room, that Henrietta's acquaintance is of somewhat longer standing? Or am I mistaken?

HENRIETTA. I have known Captain Cook for some time now.

BARRETT. Ah. And since when has it been your custom to buckle on his accoutrements?

HENRIETTA. I have never seen him in uniform before.

BARRETT. And I think it improbable that you will see him in uniform, or in mufti, very frequently in the future.

HENRIETTA (*in a strained voice*). Why?

BARRETT (*ignoring the question*). Again I may be mistaken, but I was under the impression, Elizabeth, that notice should be given me before strangers visited you here.

ELIZABETH. One can hardly describe a friend of George and Occy as a stranger, Papa.

HENRIETTA. Is Captain Cook to be forbidden the house because I helped him on with his sword?

BARRETT (*to* ELIZABETH, *ignoring* HENRIETTA). You received my letter?

ELIZABETH. Yes, Papa.

BARRETT. What has just happened fully confirms me in the wisdom of my decision. This house is fast becoming a *rendezvous* for half London. I have neither time nor inclination to find out whether all the persons visiting here are desirable acquaintances for my children. Fortunately our new home is so far from town that your London friends are not likely to trouble us —at least, during the winter.

HENRIETTA (*blankly*). Our new home? . . .

BARRETT (*to* ELIZABETH). You have not told your sisters?

ELIZABETH Arabel knows.

HENRIETTA. I don't understand. Are we—are we leaving Wimpole Street?

BARRETT (*without looking at* HENRIETTA). I have taken a house at Bookham, in Surrey. And we move in on the twenty-second.

HENRIETTA. Why?

BARRETT. I am not in the habit of accounting for my actions to any one—least of all, to my children.

HENRIETTA. But one thing I have a right to ask you, Papa. If Captain Cook is to be forbidden to visit us, is it because you found him here in Ba's room and saw me fastening on his sword?

BARRETT (*after a slight pause, looking fixedly at her*). I understood you to say that Captain Cook is George's friend and Occy's.

HENRIETTA. Yes . . . and my friend too.

BARRETT. Ah.

HENRIETTA. Yes, and since it was I who suggested his seeing Ba, and I who asked him to show me how to buckle on his sword, it's unjust to penalise him for——

ELIZABETH (*warningly*). Henrietta . . .

BARRETT (*to* HENRIETTA *in a sharp low voice*). Come here.

HENRIETTA (*she takes a few steps towards him, and speaks, a little breathlessly*). Yes, Papa . . . ?

BARRETT (*looks at her steadily under lowered brows for a moment, then points to the floor at his feet*). Come here. (*She goes right up to him, breathing quickly and fearfully. He keeps his eyes fixed on her face. Then in a low, ominous voice*) What is this fellow to you?

HENRIETTA. I—I've told you. . . . He's a friend of ours.

BARRETT. What is he to *you*?

HENRIETTA. A—a friend. . . .

BARRETT. Is that all?

HENRIETTA. Yes.

BARRETT (*suddenly grasping her wrist, his voice like the crack of a whip*). You liar!

ELIZABETH (*sharply*). Papa!

HENRIETTA (*gaspingly*). Let me go!

BARRETT (*tightening his grip*). What's this man to you? Answer me. (*She tries to free herself and cries out*) Answer me.

HENRIETTA. Oh, Papa . . . please . . .

BARRETT. Answer me.

HENRIETTA. Oh, don't . . . don't . . .

BARRETT. Answer me.

HENRIETTA (*in a strangled voice*). He's—he's—oh, Papa, I love him——

BARRETT. Ah . . . (*between his teeth, seizing her other wrist and forcing her to her knees*) ah—you—you—you—— (*She gives a cry of pain.*)

ELIZABETH (*seizing* BARRETT'S *arm*). Let her go, Papa! I won't have it! Let her go at once!

(BARRETT *flings* HENRIETTA *off. She collapses in a heap on the floor, sobbing, her face buried in her hands.*)

BARRETT (*turning on* ELIZABETH). And you—you knew of this—filthiness?

ELIZABETH. I've known for some time that Henrietta loved Captain Cook, and I've given her all my sympathy.

BARRETT. You dare to tell me——

ELIZABETH. Yes. And I would have given her my help as well, if I had had it to give.

BARRETT. I'll deal with you later. (*To* HENRIETTA) Get up.

HENRIETTA (*suddenly clasping his knees and speaking in a voice of passionate entreaty*). Oh, Papa, please listen to me—please. I—I'm not a bad girl—I swear to you I'm not. I know I've deceived you—and I'm sorry—I'm sorry. . . . But I couldn't help it. I—I love him—we love each other—and if you'd known you would have turned him from the house. . . . Oh, can't you understand—won't you try to understand? . . . He's poor—we don't expect to be married yet—but he's a good man—and it can't be wrong to love him. Other women love—why must I be forbidden? I want love—I can't live without love. Remember how you loved Mamma and how she loved you—and—and you'll understand and pity me. . . .

BARRETT (*inexorably*). Get up.

HENRIETTA. Have pity on me, Papa. . . .

BARRETT. Get up. (*He forcibly loosens her hold of his knees, and she staggers to her feet*) Sit there. (*He points to a chair. She drops into it, and sits listlessly with drooped head*) How long has this been going on? (HENRIETTA *says nothing*) Do you hear me? How long have you been carrying on with this fellow?

HENRIETTA. I—I've known him a little over a year.

BARRETT. And you've been with him often?

HENRIETTA. Yes.

BARRETT. Alone?

HENRIETTA. Yes.

BARRETT. Where?

HENRIETTA. We—I—I've met him in the Park, and—and——

BARRETT. And—here?

HENRIETTA. Yes.

BARRETT. Here. And alone? (HENRIETTA *is silent*) Have you met him in this house alone?

HENRIETTA. Yes.

BARRETT. So! Furtive unchastity under my own roof—and abetted by one whom I believed to be wholly chaste and good. . . .

HENRIETTA. No—no——

ELIZABETH (*fiercely*). How dare you, Papa!

BARRETT. Silence! (*To* HENRIETTA, *his voice hard and cold as ice*) Now attend to me. Something like this happened a year or two ago, and I thought I had crushed the devil in you then. I was wrong. It needed sterner measures than I had the courage to use. . . . So now, unless I have your solemn word that you will neither see nor in any way communicate with this man again, you leave my house at once, as you are, with nothing but the clothes you have on. In which case, you will be your own mistress, and can go to perdition any way you please. But of this you may be certain. Once outside my doors you will never again be admitted, on any pretext whatever, so long as I live. I think by this time you have learnt that it's not my habit to make idle threats, and that I never go back on my word. Very well. You have your choice. Take it.

HENRIETTA (*after an agonised mental struggle*). Is it nothing to you that I—that I shall hate you for this to the end of my life?

BARRETT. Less than nothing.

HENRIETTA. But—but I must let Captain Cook know that——

BARRETT. I will deal with Captain Cook.

HENRIETTA (*desperately*). But Papa——

BARRETT. Will you give me your word neither to see nor to communicate with this man again?

HENRIETTA (*after a pause, in a dead voice*). I—I have no choice.

BARRETT. Give me your Bible, Elizabeth.

ELIZABETH. Why?

BARRETT. I am not prepared to accept your sister's bare promise. But I think even she would hesitate to break an oath made with her hand resting on the Word of God. Give me your Bible.

ELIZABETH. My Bible belonged to Mamma. I can't have it used for such a purpose.

BARRETT. Give me your Bible.

ELIZABETH. No.

BARRETT. You refuse?

ELIZABETH. Yes.
(BARRETT *pulls the bell rope. A pause. No one speaks or moves.* WILSON *enters.*)

BARRETT. I want you to go to my bedroom and fetch my Bible. Are your hands clean?

WILSON (*looking at her hands*). My hands, sir?

BARRETT. Are they clean?

WILSON (*with a touch of asperity*). Yes, sir. I've just been helping to bathe Flush.

BARRETT. You will find the Bible on the table beside my bed.

WILSON. Very good, sir.
(*She goes out. All three are silent and motionless until she returns.* WILSON *reënters with* BARRETT'S *Bible. She gives it to him and goes out.*)

BARRETT (*to* HENRIETTA, *placing the Bible reverently on the table*). Come here. (HENRIETTA *rises and goes to the table*) Place your hand upon the Book. (*She does so*) Repeat after me: "I give you my solemn word that I will neither see, nor have any communication with, Captain Cook again."

HENRIETTA (*in a toneless voice*). I give you my solemn word that I will neither see, nor have any communication with, Captain Cook again.

BARRETT. You will now go to your room and remain there until you have my permission to leave it. (*Without a word, but with her head held high,* HENRIETTA *goes out. . . . After a pause*) Have you anything to say to me, Elizabeth?

ELIZABETH. No.

BARRETT. Then I must leave you under my extreme displeasure. I shall not see you again, I can have nothing to do with you, until God has softened your heart, and you repent of your wickedness, and ask for His forgiveness, and . . . mine. (*He takes his Bible and goes out. The moment he has closed the door* ELIZABETH *gets up and pulls the bell rope. She does so with an air of decision. A pause.* WILSON *enters.*)

ELIZABETH. Shut the door. please. (*Impulsively*) Wilson, are you my friend?

WILSON (*bewildered*). Your . . . friend, Miss?

ELIZABETH. Yes, my friend. I am in dire need of friendship and help at the moment.

WILSON. I—I don't quite understand, Miss Ba. . . . But I'm that fond of you—I'd do anything to help you.

ELIZABETH. You would? And I know I can trust you?

WILSON. Yes, indeed, Miss.

ELIZABETH. Wilson, next Saturday, I am going to marry Mr. Browning.

WILSON (*with a gasp*). Marry . . . !

ELIZABETH. Hush. . . . Yes. Of course nobody in this house knows —and nobody must know.

WILSON. Lor', Miss, I should just think not indeed!

ELIZABETH. We're to be married secretly at Mary-le-Bone Church. Will you come with me?

WILSON. Me, Miss? Yes, Miss—and gladly.

ELIZABETH. Directly afterwards I shall return here for a few days, and——

WILSON (*in boundless amazement*). Here! With Mr. Browning . . . !

ELIZABETH (*with an hysterical laugh*). No—no—no! Just alone with you. . . . Then, on the following Saturday, I shall join Mr. Browning, and we're going abroad. . . . We're going to Italy. . . . Will you come with us?

WILSON (*in a whisper*). To Italy . . . ?

ELIZABETH. Yes. . . . Will you come with me?

WILSON. Well, Miss, I can't see as how I can help myself. Not that I hold with foreign parts—I don't. But husband or no husband, you'd never get to Italy alive without me.

ELIZABETH. Then you'll come? Then you'll come! Oh, I am so glad! I'll tell Mr. Browning—I'm writing to him now. And I shall want you to take the letter to the post at once. Go and put on your things—I'll have finished by the time you're ready.

WILSON. Yes, Miss.

(WILSON *goes out, and* ELIZABETH *takes pen and paper and starts writing rapidly as the Scene closes.*)

ACT FIVE

PAPA

SCENE I

ELIZABETH *is kneeling beside Flush and fastening a lead on to his collar. She pats his head abstractedly, rises, and picks up a little heap of letters in their envelopes from the table, runs through them and places them on the mantelpiece. Then, with a shuddering sigh, she walks to the window, clasping and unclasping her hands in agitation. After standing at the window for a moment, she sighs again and returns to the mantelpiece, picks up the letters and replaces them one by one on the table. Her cloak and bonnet and gloves, etc., are on the bed.*

WILSON *hurries into the room with two travelling rugs on her arm.*

WILSON. Oh, Miss Ba, I'm that sorry! In my flurry to get the luggage off to the railway station yesterday I clean forgot to pack these rugs. And there was heaps of room in the carpetbag.

ELIZABETH. Never mind.

WILSON (*placing the rugs across the back of a chair*). I do hope we haven't forgotten nothing else.

ELIZABETH. And if we have it won't matter much. Mr. Browning insisted that we should travel as lightly as possible. We shall be able to get all we need in Paris.

WILSON. Lor', Miss, it don't seem possible we'll be in Paris tomorrow!

ELIZABETH. No. . . . (*She consults her watch*) Oh, how the time crawls! We've still an hour and a half of this dreadful waiting. . . . You're sure, Wilson, they quite understood at the livery stables exactly when, and where, the cab was to meet us?

WILSON. Oh, yes, Miss, I was most particular to see that the young man took it all down—the cab to be at the corner of Wimpole Street at ha'-past three punctual. It won't take us more than ten minutes to get to Hodgson's Library—and then Mr. Browning will have us in his charge. (*Her voice drops to a warm confidential tone*) Your husband, Miss Ba, dear . . .

ELIZABETH. Oh, hush! hush! Don't breathe that word here.

WILSON. But, Miss Ba——

ELIZABETH. I'm foolishly nervous, but I can't help it. The very walls seem to be listening. There is no one in the house, I know, except Miss Henrietta—and she should have gone out by now. Still——

WILSON. Miss Henrietta was putting on her bonnet as I came along the passage.

ELIZABETH. Oh, Wilson, it's impossible to believe that in little more than an hour I shall have left this room, never, in all likelihood, to see it again. . . .

WILSON. And glad you'll be to see the last of it, I'm sure, Miss Ba.

ELIZABETH. Yes—and no. . . . I've been very miserable here, and very happy. . . . Oh, I wish it were time to go! This waiting is killing me!

WILSON. Have you finished writing your letters, Miss?

ELIZABETH (*almost hysterically*). Yes. Yes. I've written to them all to tell them what I've done and to wish them good-bye. I've just been reading over my letter to Mr. Barrett to see if there was something I could add—something—anything. But I can't think—I can't think.

WILSON. Least said, soonest mended, Miss. (*With a chuckling laugh*) Oh, Miss Ba, I know I shouldn't say such things—but there's a lot I'd give to be here tonight when the Master reads your letter and knows you've been a married lady for almost a week. . . .

ELIZABETH (*quickly*). Don't, Wilson, don't! The very thought terrifies me! I can see his face—I can hear his voice. . . . Thank God, we shall be miles and miles away. . . . (*She looks at her watch*) An hour and twenty minutes still. Will time never pass?

WILSON (*after a pause*). Why don't you write some po'try, Miss?

ELIZABETH (*dumbfounded*). Poetry . . . ?

WILSON. Yes, Miss. That 'ud make the time pass nicely, I'm sure.

(ELIZABETH *breaks into rather hysterical laughter.* HENRIETTA *enters in her shawl and bonnet. She has a letter in her hand.* ELIZABETH *abruptly stops laughing and looks at her with frightened eyes.*)

ELIZABETH (*hastily turning her letters on to their faces*). I—I thought you had gone out.

HENRIETTA. Wilson, I want to speak to Miss Ba.

WILSON. Yes, Miss. (*She goes out.*)

HENRIETTA. I was just going when I ran into a messenger at the door. He brought this letter. It's for you.

ELIZABETH (*anxiously, reaching out her hand*). For me?

HENRIETTA (*retaining the letter*). Yes. But it's in—in *his* hand-writing.

ELIZABETH. Captain Cook's?

HENRIETTA. Yes.

ELIZABETH. Open it, dear.

HENRIETTA (*tears open the letter and reads*). "*Dear Miss Barrett, I know I am doing very wrong in drawing you once again into my, and Henrietta's, affairs. But the matter is so urgent I am sure you will forgive me. My regiment has been ordered to Somerset at short notice—and I must positively see Henrietta before I go. If I wrote to her direct, my letter would certainly be read by Mr. Barrett. I understand he opens all her correspondence. Hence my trespass on your kindness. Will you please give Henrietta the enclosed letter, and believe me your grateful and obedient servant, Surtees Cook.*" . . . Somerset . . . (*She drops the letter, opens the enclosure and reads it eagerly.* ELIZABETH *picks up the letter and tears it into little pieces*) What is the time?

ELIZABETH. A quarter past two.

HENRIETTA (*in a low, tense voice*). You remember Papa threatened to turn me out of the house unless I swore on the Bible not to write to or see Surtees?

ELIZABETH. Yes.

HENRIETTA (*defiantly*). Well, I'm going to break that "Bible oath" today.

ELIZABETH (*quietly*). Are you, dear?

HENRIETTA (*more defiantly still*). Yes—and I shall glory in breaking it! Surtees says he'll be at—never mind where!—between four and six —the only free time he has—*every* day until he leaves next Wednesday. We shall all have left here on Monday: so I must meet him either today or tomorrow. I shall meet him *both* days. And if Papa asks me where I have been—I shall go out of my way to lie to him as often and as grossly as I can.

ELIZABETH (*quietly*). I see. Why do you tell me all this?

HENRIETTA (*belligerently*). Because I want you to say that I'm a wicked, deceitful, perjured, *loose* woman, so that I can fling the words back in your face! (*Suddenly throws her arms round* ELIZABETH) Oh, Ba, darling, forgive me! I'm not myself these days. I am all love and hate—and I don't know which is the worse torture. . . .

ELIZABETH (*with passionate tenderness*). My dear, my dear, you think I don't understand! Oh, but I do! I do! And I feel for you and pity you with all my heart! . . . I can do nothing to help you. I daren't even advise you. . . . But never lose hope—never lose courage —never—

(WILSON *flashes into the room. She is in a state of uncontrolled agitation.*)

WILSON (*gaspingly*). Oh, Miss Ba —Miss Ba . . . !

(*Both sisters stare at her,* HENRIETTA *astonished,* ELIZABETH *in terror.*)

ELIZABETH. What is it, Wilson? (*To* HENRIETTA) Shut the door.

WILSON. The Master, Miss! He—he's just come in. . . .

ELIZABETH (*in a whisper*). Papa. . . .

WILSON. Yes—just this minute. . . . He must 'ave 'eard—some one must have told him——

ELIZABETH. Be quiet.

HENRIETTA (*who has been looking in bewilderment from one to the other*). But Ba, what on earth is the matter?

ELIZABETH. Nothing. Nothing. It's—it's only that Papa hasn't been to see me for ten days now—ever since—you remember——? And—and scenes of forgiveness are always trying. . . . (*To* WILSON, *sharply*) Put away my hat and cloak. Quick. (WILSON *does so.*)

HENRIETTA. I don't believe that's all. You're as white as a sheet. What did Wilson mean? Ba, is there anything I can——

ELIZABETH (*softly, intensely*). No, no, no! Don't speak—don't ask me anything. . . . You know nothing—you understand?—nothing—nothing.

HENRIETTA. But——

ELIZABETH. No. (*To* WILSON) Those rugs . . . (WILSON *picks them up. There is a knock at the door.* WILSON *gasps.* ELIZABETH *speaks in a whisper*) Come in. (*She clears her throat, then louder*) Come in. (BARRETT *enters. They are all standing in tense attitudes.* ELIZABETH *commands her voice*) You're home early, Papa. . . .

(BARRETT, *without replying, looks at each of the three in turn; then crosses to the fireplace.* WILSON, *obviously terror-stricken, slips out of the room, the rugs over her arm.*)

BARRETT (*to* ELIZABETH). What's the matter with that girl?

ELIZABETH. Wilson?

BARRETT. Yes. . . . And with you?

ELIZABETH. Nothing, Papa. . . .

BARRETT (*after staring broodingly at her for a moment, he turns to* HENRIETTA). Where have you been?

HENRIETTA. Nowhere.

BARRETT. Where are you going?

HENRIETTA. To tea with Aunt Hedley.

BARRETT. Is that the truth?

HENRIETTA. Yes.

BARRETT. You remember your oath?

HENRIETTA. Yes.

BARRETT. Have you kept it?

HENRIETTA. Yes.

BARRETT. Are you going to keep it?

HENRIETTA. Yes.

BARRETT (*after staring at her for a moment*). I want to speak to your sister. You can go. (*Without a glance at either of them,* HENRIETTA *goes out.* ELIZABETH *sits per-*

fectly still, waiting. BARRETT *walks to the window; then turns and goes up to her*) Do you know why I am back so early?

ELIZABETH (*in a whisper*). No, Papa.

BARRETT (*in a low, intense voice*). Because I could bear it no longer. . . . It's ten days since last I saw you. . . .

ELIZABETH. Am I to blame for that, Papa?

BARRETT (*with restrained fury*). You dare to ask me such a question? Weren't you a party in your sister's shameless conduct? Haven't you encouraged her? Haven't you helped her? Haven't you defended her? And did you expect to go scot-free of my displeasure? (*Stopping himself with a violent gesture*) I've not come to speak about that—but to put it behind me—to forget it—to forget it. . . . I wonder, my child, have you been half so miserable these last ten days as your father?

ELIZABETH. Miserable, Papa?

BARRETT. Do you suppose I'm happy when I'm bitterly estranged from all I love in the world? Do you know that night after night I had to call up all my will power to hold me from coming here to forgive you?

ELIZABETH. Papa——

BARRETT. All my will power, I tell you—all my sense of duty and right and justice. . . . But today I could bear it no longer. The want of your face and your voice became a torment. I had to come. I am not so strong as they think me. I had to come. And I despise myself for coming—despise myself—hate myself. . . .

ELIZABETH. No—no! (*Suddenly rises and puts her hands on his shoulders*) Oh, Papa, can't you see, won't you ever see, that strength may be weakness, and your sense of justice and right and duty all mistaken and wrong?

BARRETT (*hoarsely, taking her hands from his shoulders*). Mistaken and wrong? What do you mean? . . . (*Quickly stopping her from speaking*) No, be silent. Don't answer me. . . . Mistaken and wrong? You don't know what you're saying.

ELIZABETH. If you'll only listen to me, Papa, I——

BARRETT. No.

ELIZABETH. But, Papa——

BARRETT. No. (*He moves to the window and stands there, his face half averted from her. A pause. He turns*) If there were even a vestige of truth in what you say, my whole life would be a hideous mockery. For always—through all misfortunes and miseries—I've been upheld by knowing, beyond a doubt, what was right, and doing it unflinchingly, however bitter the consequences. . . . And bitter they've been—how bitter, only God knows! It's been my heavy cross that those whom I was given to guide and rule have always fought against the right that I knew to be the right—and was in duty bound to impose upon them. . . . Even you. Even your mother.

ELIZABETH (*in a whisper*). My mother?

BARRETT. Yes, your mother. . . . But not at first. . . . You—you, my eldest child, were born of love and only love. . . . But the others—long before they came the rift had begun to open between your mother and me. Not that she ever opposed me—never once. Or put into words what she felt. She was silent and dutiful and obedient. But love died out—and fear took its place—fear. . . .

ELIZABETH (*sharply*). No! No!

BARRETT. And all because I saw the right—and did it.

ELIZABETH (*in a low voice, staring before her*). Oh . . . oh, dear God, what she must have suffered.

BARRETT. She? — She? . . . And what of me? What of me?

ELIZABETH. You? . . . Oh, Papa, then you—you still loved her—after her love for you had died?

BARRETT (*in a muffled voice, looking aside*). Love? . . . What's love? . . . She was my wife. . . . You—you don't understand. . . .

ELIZABETH (*in a horrified whisper*). And all those children . . . born in fear. . . . Oh, it's horrible—it's horrible—it's horrible. . . . (*With a shuddering sob, she covers her face with her hands.*)

BARRETT (*aghast and embarrassed*). Ba, my dear—don't—don't . . . I—I shouldn't have spoken—I shouldn't have told you all that. . . . Forget it, child. . . . (*He goes up to her*) Take your hands from your face. . . . (*He gently touches her wrists. She starts away from him, looking at him with wide, frightened eyes*) Don't look at me like that. (*In a low, thick voice, averting his eyes*) You don't understand. How should you? You know nothing of the brutal tyranny of—passion, and how even the strongest and best are driven by it to hell. Would you have abetted your sister in her——

ELIZABETH (*fiercely*). Henrietta's love—how dare you speak of it in the same breath as——

BARRETT (*brutally*). Her *love*? *You* ignorant little fool! What do *you* know of love? Love! The lust of the eye—the lowest urge of the body——

ELIZABETH (*springing to her feet*). I won't listen to you!

BARRETT (*seizing her wrist and forcing her back to her seat*). You must—you shall! It's time a little reality were brought into your dream of life. Do you suppose I should have guarded my house like a dragon from this so-called love if I hadn't known, from my own life, all it entails of cruelty and loathing and degradation and remorse? . . . (*He pulls himself together*) With the help of God, and through years of tormenting abstinence, I strangled it in myself. And so long as I have breath in my body, I'll keep it away from those I was given to protect and care for. You understand me?

ELIZABETH (*in a low voice, looking him full in the face*). Yes—I understand you . . . I understand you. . . .

BARRETT. Very well. (*A pause.* ELIZABETH *sits quite still, looking before her. When he speaks again his voice has changed*) This has been a hateful necessity. I had to speak—plainly—lest your very innocence should smirch the purity I am utterly resolved to maintain in my home. . . . And because I feel that you acted in innocence and ignorance, I—I forgive you freely, my child. . . . We must turn over this ugly page—and forget what was on it. . . . (*He takes her hand*) You're—cold as ice. . . . Why are you trembling?

ELIZABETH (*drawing her hand from his*). I shall never forget what you have said.

BARRETT. Never forget—but——And yet, perhaps that's as well. . . . (*With sudden urgency*) But, for God's sake, my darling, don't let this raise any further barrier between us! I've told you how all these past months I've seemed to feel you slipping little by little away from me. . . . Your love is all I have left to me in the world.

ELIZABETH. You had Mamma's love once. You might have had the love of all your children.

BARRETT. Yes, if I'd played the coward's part, and taken the easier way, and shirked my duty. I'd rather be hated by the whole world than gain love like that.

ELIZABETH (*in a broken voice*). Oh, Papa, you—you don't know how I pity you. . . .

BARRETT (*roughly*). Pity? I don't want your pity. . . . But if I should ever lose you or your love—— (*He seizes her unwilling hands*) My darling, next week we shall have left this house, and I hope we shall never return here. I've grown to loathe it. In our new home we shall draw close to each other again. There will be little to distract you in the country—nothing and no one to come between us. (*He draws her stiffening form into his arms*) My child, my darling, you want me to be happy. The only happiness I shall ever know is all yours to give or take. You must look up to me, and depend on me, and lean on me. You must share your thoughts with me, your hopes, your fears, your prayers. I want all your heart and all your soul. . . . (*He holds her passionately close; she leans away from him, her face drawn with fear and pain.*)

ELIZABETH (*sobbingly*). I can't bear it—I can't bear any more. . . . Let me go, Papa—please let me go. . . .

(*He loosens his embrace, and she falls away from him, her arm covering her face. He rises and bends over her.*)

BARRETT. Forgive me, dear. I've said too much. I was carried away. I'll leave you now.

ELIZABETH (*in a whisper*). Please . . .

BARRETT. Shall I see you again tonight?

ELIZABETH (*as before*). Not tonight. . . .

BARRETT. I shall pray for you.

ELIZABETH (*half to herself*). Pray for me? . . . Tonight. . . . (*She *turns and looks up at him*) Yes, pray for me tonight—if you will. . . . (*He kisses her forehead gently, and goes out. She sits for a moment looking before her, and then, with frightened eyes, round the room. She whispers*) I must go at once—I must go—I must go. . . . (*She gets up quickly, and fetches her cloak and bonnet from the wardrobe.* WILSON *enters, stealthily and hurriedly, the rugs on her arm.*)

WILSON. He's gone to the study.

ELIZABETH (*putting on her bonnet*). We must go. Now. At once.

WILSON. But, Miss Ba——

ELIZABETH. At once. Help me on with my cloak.

WILSON (*doing so*). But the cab won't be there yet—not for an hour. Besides——

ELIZABETH. Then we must walk about the streets. I can't stay here any longer. I'm frightened. I'm frightened. Fetch your cloak and bonnet.

WILSON. Walk about the streets, Miss? You can't—you can't. Besides—the Master's at home. He may see us leaving. For God's sake, Miss——

ELIZABETH. Where did I put those letters? Ah, here. . . . (*Spreading them out on the table*) Fetch your cloak and bonnet. Quick.

WILSON. But if he saw us leaving——

ELIZABETH. We must chance that.

WILSON. But, Miss Ba——

ELIZABETH. He can't stop me. I don't belong to him any more. I belong to my husband. Papa can kill me. But he can't stop me.

WILSON. I daren't, Miss, I daren't.

ELIZABETH. Then I must go alone.

WILSON. You can't do that.

ELIZABETH (*with compelling earnestness*). Wilson, things have passed between my father and me which force me to leave this house at once. Until today I didn't realise quite how unforgivably I have been driven to deceive him. Until today—I've never really known him. He's not like other men. He's—dreadfully different. . . . I—I can't say any more. . . . If you want to draw back you need never reproach yourself. This, after all, is no affair of yours. But I must go now.

WILSON. I'll fetch my cloak and bonnet at once, Miss. (ELIZABETH *puts her arm round* WILSON'S *neck and kisses her*) Oh, Miss Ba . . . (WILSON *goes out quickly.* ELIZABETH *spreads the letters on the table. Then, from a ribbon on which it is hung, she draws her wedding ring from her bosom. She slips it on to her finger; looks at it for a moment; then pulls on her gloves.* WILSON *reënters, softly and quickly, in cloak and bonnet.*)

ELIZABETH. I am quite ready. You take the rugs, Wilson. I had better carry Flush.

WILSON (*breathlessly*). Yes, Miss.

ELIZABETH. And now slip downstairs and see whether the study door is shut.

WILSON. Yes, Miss.

(WILSON *goes out, leaving the door open.* ELIZABETH *picks up* FLUSH, *and stands with him under her arm, and looks round the room with an indescribable expression on her face.* WILSON *reënters.*)

WILSON (*in a whisper*). The door's shut—and all's quiet.

ELIZABETH. Very well. (*She passes out, and* WILSON *follows, closing the door softly after her. For a moment the room stands empty. Then the Scene slowly closes.*)

SCENE II

The curtain rises on the still empty room. An hour or two has elapsed. The sky, seen through the window, is full of colour from the afterglow. A pause. ARABEL *enters.*

ARABEL (*on entering*). Ba, dear, I want—— (*She realises the room's emptiness and stares bewildered around her. Her eyes light on the letters* ELIZABETH *has left. Leaving the door open, she goes to the table and looks at them. She picks up a letter, and whispers, visibly agitated*) For me. . . . What can it mean . . . ? (*She tears open the letter, and reads it with little gasping exclamations*) Oh . . . ! No, no . . . ! Married . . . ! No . . . ! Oh . . . Oh . . . !

(*She looks up from the letter, her face transformed with terror and excitement; then suddenly sits back on the sofa and goes into shrieks and peals of hysterical laughter. The noise is appalling. After a moment there are voices, and steps outside, and* GEORGE, CHARLES, *and* OCTAVIUS *enter almost simultaneously.* GEORGE *is dressed for dinner; but the other two have not yet finished their toilet.*)

GEORGE. Arabel!

CHARLES. For God's sake!

GEORGE. Arabel! What on earth——

OCTAVIUS. High-strikes! B-by Jove! (ARABEL *laughs on.*)

GEORGE (*taking one of her hands and slapping it*). Stop that, Arabel! Stop it at once!

ARABEL (*half gasping, half shrieking*). Married—gone—married—gone —— (*She goes into another wild peal of laughter.*)

GEORGE. Be quiet! (*Slaps her hand again*) Fetch some water some one . . .

OCTAVIUS. Eau-de-Cologne . . . (ALFRED, SEPTIMUS, *and* HENRY, *two of them dressed, the other without coat and collar, enter hurriedly.*)

ALFRED. What's the matter?

HENRY. Is Ba ill? Arabel!

ARABEL (*gaspingly*). She's married —she's gone—married—gone . . .

(HENRIETTA *enters in her cloak and bonnet. She stands for a moment, wide-eyed, taking in the scene*) Married and gone—Married and gone. . . .
(*She moans and sobs. Realisation begins to dawn on the brothers.*)

CHARLES. What does she mean? Where's Ba?

SEPTIMUS. Married and gone—she's mad!

GEORGE (*taking* ARABEL *by the shoulder*). Arabel—what do you mean?

OCTAVIUS. Married . . . !
(HENRIETTA *suddenly pushes them aside, seizes* ARABEL *by the shoulders and vigorously shakes her.*)

HENRIETTA. Arabel! Arabel! Pull yourself together at once! . . . Where's Ba? . . . Answer me! . . . Where's Ba?

ARABEL (*gaspingly*). She—she's m-m-married Mr. Robert Browning. . . .

HENRIETTA (*in a whisper*). Married . . .
(*Consternation among the brothers and amazed exclamations:—"Married!" — "Married!" — "It can't be true!"—"Robert Browning!"—"Good God!"* . . .)

HENRIETTA (*to* ARABEL, *who is still sobbing*). Where is she?

ARABEL. She—she's gone. . . . Those letters—— She's written to—to all of us. . . . She—she's gone. . . . (OCTAVIUS *has pounced on the letters.*)

OCTAVIUS. F-for you. (*Hands a letter to* HENRIETTA. *She tears it open and reads*) George—Henry—Alfred—Septimus—Charles.
(*He hands them each a letter which is quickly torn open and read with muttered exclamations:—"Good God!"—"Impossible!"—"Married!"—"A week ago—"*)

GEORGE. Yes, she was married last Saturday.

OCTAVIUS (*holding up a letter*). And this letter is for P-papa.
(*A frightened silence falls on them. Only* HENRIETTA *looks before her with an inscrutable smile on her face.*)

ARABEL (*in a shuddering whisper*). P-P-papa. . . .

SEPTIMUS. Is he in?

GEORGE. Dressing for dinner.

OCTAVIUS. What's to be d-done?

HENRY. Some one must give him Ba's letter.

HENRIETTA (*in a clear voice*). Let me. I should love to.

ARABEL (*in a terrified whisper*). Oh, hush—hush . . .
(*She points tremblingly to the door. They all hold their breath. In the pause one hears the sound of approaching footsteps. Then* BARRETT, *in evening dress, appears on the threshold. He looks at his assembled family in stern amazement. No one stirs.*)

BARRETT. What is the meaning of this? (*No one stirs or replies*) Who was making that hideous noise just now? (*No one stirs or replies*) Why are you gentlemen half-dressed? (*No one stirs or replies. A pause. Then sharply*) Where is Elizabeth? (*A silence. He passes into the room. With a stifled cry,* ARABEL *rises and clings on to* HENRIETTA'*s arm*) Do you hear me? . . . (*To* HENRIETTA) Where is your sister?

HENRIETTA (*freeing herself from* ARABEL *and picking up the letter*). She left you this letter.

BARRETT (*without touching it, in a low voice, his face becoming a mask*). Left me. . . . What do you mean?

HENRIETTA. She left letters for all of us. This is yours.

(*His eyes fixed on her face, he slowly takes the letter from her. He is about to open it when she suddenly seizes his arm. . . . Passionately, entreatingly*) You must forgive her, Papa—you must forgive her—not for her sake—but for yours! I thought I hated you, but I don't. I pity you—I pity you. . . . And if you've any pity for yourself—forgive her. . . .

(*He looks at her steadily for a moment; then puts her away from him. He opens and reads the letter. Nothing but his quickened breathing betrays the fury of emotions seething in him. His face, when at last he raises it from the letter, is a white mask. He stands motionless, staring before him and mechanically folding and refolding the letter. He turns and walks to the window, and his gait somehow gives the impression that he is blind. He throws open the window and stands in front of it with his back to the room and his hands clasped behind him, grasping the letter. The movement of his shoulders shows that he is breathing quickly and heavily. No one stirs.*)

BARRETT (*half to himself, turning from the window*). Yes—yes. . . . Her dog. . . . (*A smile of indescribable ugliness flickers across his face*) Yes—I'll have her dog. . . . Octavius.

OCTAVIUS. Sir?

BARRETT. Her dog must be destroyed. At once.

HENRIETTA. But——

BARRETT (*slightly raising his voice*). You will take it to the vet—tonight. . . . You understand me? . . . Tonight. (*A pause*) You understand me?

OCTAVIUS (*desperately*). I really d-don't see what the p-poor little beast has d-done to——

BARRETT (*ominously*). You understand me?

HENRIETTA (*vainly trying to control the triumph in her voice*). In her letter to me Ba writes that she has taken Flush with her. . . .

(*A silence.* BARRETT *stands perfectly still, staring straight before him and mechanically tearing* ELIZABETH'*s letter into little pieces, which drop to his feet.*)

THE CURTAIN FALLS

Dangerous Corner

BY J. B. PRIESTLEY

Dangerous Corner was first produced in America at the Empire Theatre, New York City, by Harry Moses on October 27, 1932, and closed on May 10, 1933. The following is the original cast:

MAUD MOCKRIDGE, a novelist	Jane Wheatley
OLWEN PEEL, secretary to the publishers	Mary Servoss
FREDA CHATFIELD, Robert's wife	Jean Dixon
BETTY WHITEHOUSE, Gordon's wife	Barbara Robbins
CHARLES STANTON, one of the publishers	Stanley Ridges
GORDON WHITEHOUSE, Freda's brother	Cecil Holm
ROBERT CHATFIELD, head of the publishing firm	Colin Keith-Johnston

Directed by Elsa Lazareff

Setting by Woodman Thompson

SCENE: *Living room of the Chatfield country home, after dinner.*

DANGEROUS CORNER

ACT ONE

Living room of the Chatfield country home, after dinner. FOUR WOMEN *discovered sitting and talking.*

MISS MOCKRIDGE (*seated chair Left of table lighting cigarette*). And what do you say this novel is called?

OLWEN (*seated down Left*). *The Sleeping Dog.*

MISS MOCKRIDGE. *The Sleeping Dog.* I must remember that. When will you publish it?

OLWEN. Next spring, I suppose.

MISS MOCKRIDGE. I must look out for it.

OLWEN. We'll send you a copy. If you're here when it comes out, I'll give you a ring about it.

MISS MOCKRIDGE. Oh, of course you're in the city office now.

OLWEN. Yes, I am. Though I still come up here as often as I can.

MISS MOCKRIDGE. You know you people make such an intimate little group that you confuse me. I can't make out who's here and who's in the city office.

FREDA (*seated chair Right of table smoking cigarette*). It's very simple. It's so arranged now that the married ones—my brother Gordon and Betty and Robert and I are here—and the single ones, Olwen and Stanton, are in the city office.

OLWEN. And come back here every time there's the smallest excuse. Only I haven't the luck to have as many excuses as Charles Stanton has. But I do my best.

MISS MOCKRIDGE. I'm sure you do. So would I. (*To* OLWEN) Miss Peel, I think you ought to marry Mr. Stanton. (OLWEN *laughs. To the other two*) Don't you think she ought to marry Mr. Stanton?

OLWEN. Oh? Why shuld I?

BETTY (*seated Left arm of chair Right of table*). I didn't know you were a match-maker, Miss Mockridge.

MISS MOCKRIDGE. I'm not. In the ordinary way, I consider it a disgusting business. But I like things symmetrical. I like a neat pattern. And you see, if you married Mr. Stanton, that would complete the pattern here. Then you'd have your three directors, and also three pairs of adoring husbands and wives.

FREDA. I must say the adoring husbands don't seem in a hurry to join their wives tonight.

BETTY (*turning head Right*). Aren't they pigs! What's keeping them?

FREDA. Well, I think I know one thing that's keeping them. Robert has just acquired some old brandy that he's terribly proud of (*sudden burst of laughter from* MEN *off*), and I suppose they're sampling that.

MISS MOCKRIDGE. They're probably laughing at something very improper.

BETTY. No. I know them. It's just gossip. Men like gossip.

FREDA. Of course they do.

OLWEN. Well, why shouldn't they?

MISS MOCKRIDGE. Exactly. Why shouldn't they? People who don't like gossip aren't interested in their fellow creatures. So I insist upon my three publishers gossiping.

BETTY. Yes, but they always say it's business. I don't mind Gordon drinking Robert's old brandy—and I don't mind him gossiping. But I do object to him coming in—as he will, you'll see—looking very important and pretending he knows all the secrets of the publishing business.

FREDA. Well, Betty, you may know Gordon better than I do, but even if he is your husband, he's my brother and I've known him long enough to realise he has to look important now and again about *something* rather absurd.

MISS MOCKRIDGE. I hope you don't mean by that, Mrs. Chatfield, that you think the publishing business absurd. As a woman who gets her living through it, I protest.

OLWEN. And as another woman who also gets her living by it—though in a humbler capacity—I also protest.

MISS MOCKRIDGE. Meanwhile, I'm almost prepared to marry Mr. Stanton myself to be one of your charmed circle here. What a snug little group you are!

FREDA. Are we?

MISS MOCKRIDGE. Well, aren't you?

FREDA. Snug little group! How awful.

MISS MOCKRIDGE. Not awful at all. I think it's charming.

FREDA. It sounds disgusting.

BETTY. Yes, like Dickens or a Christmas card.

MISS MOCKRIDGE. And very nice things to be like, too, let me tell you. In these days almost too good to be true.

BETTY. Oh, why should it be?

OLWEN. I didn't know you were such a pessimist, Miss Mockridge.

MISS MOCKRIDGE. Didn't you? Then you don't read the reviews of my books—and you ought to, you know, being an employee of my publishers. I shall complain of that to my three directors when they come in. Certainly I'm a pessimist. I'm an intelligent woman. (*Snuffling*) But I didn't mean in that way, of course. I think it's wonderful here.

FREDA. It is rather nice here. We've been lucky.

OLWEN. It's enchanting. I hate to leave it.

MISS MOCKRIDGE. I'm sure you do. It must be comforting to be all so settled.

FREDA. Quite the cosy little nest!

BETTY. Oh, talking about nests! What about that white bird that comes into your garden nearly every night? (*Rising*) Do you suppose we might see it now?

FREDA (*rising*). We might try. It usually comes about this time. Perhaps we might get a glimpse of it. (*Crosses up to Right side of window*) That is, if it's condescending to visit us tonight.

MISS MOCKRIDGE (*rising*). That sounds interesting. (*Crosses up to window Centre*) What does it look like?

FREDA (*pulling curtains open*). I suppose it's a white owl. But it looks like the ghost of a bird.
(OLWEN *rises and crosses up to window.*)

MISS MOCKRIDGE. How exciting!

BETTY. I can't see anything at all.

FREDA (*crosses Right to light switch*). Just a second, I'll turn out the lights. (FREDA *switches off the lights and the stage is in complete darkness, except for the moonlight which silhouettes the four women against the window, and a light from the hall coming through the half-open door up Right. After a moment's pause there is the sound of a revolver shot off stage Right.* BETTY *gives a sharp little scream. Startled exclamations from the other three women.* FREDA *advances toward the door*) Robert, Robert, what was that! (*Pause*) ROBERT!!!

ROBERT'S VOICE (*off Right*). It's all right. I was showing them my gun and took a crack at a flower pot.
(FREDA *switches on the lights.*)

GORDON'S VOICE (*off Right*). Pretty good shot. . . .

ROBERT'S VOICE. And what's more I hit it!

STANTON'S VOICE (*off Right*). Pretty lucky I'll say. . . .

ROBERT'S VOICE. We'll be in in a minute!

FREDA. I should hope so. Those idiots firing Robert's revolver out of the window!
(*Crosses Left. When the lights go up,* BETTY *is discovered Right Centre.*)

BETTY (*crosses down to below couch*). You ought to take it away from him. They nearly frightened the life out of me.
(MISS MOCKRIDGE *above chair Right. Moves down and sits as Betty speaks.*)

FREDA (*crosses Left*). There's no chance of seeing our bird *now.* If it was there, it must have cleared out pretty quickly.

BETTY. I should say so—after all that racket. (*Sits on sofa Right.*)

OLWEN (*Left chair Left of table, moves down below chair Left of table*). Perhaps it will come back later. (*Sits.*)

FREDA (*crosses down Left between piano and chair Left of table*). No, no, I hardly think so. I've never caught sight of it much after ten.

MISS MOCKRIDGE. I suppose you all miss your brother-in-law. He used to be up here with you too, didn't he?

FREDA (*stopping Left of chair Left of table and turning Right*). You mean Robert's brother, Martin?

MISS MOCKRIDGE. Yes.

FREDA (*crosses down Right*). What made you think of Martin just then?

MISS MOCKRIDGE. Well, I don't quite know. He just came into my head, I suppose.

FREDA (*sits Right end settee*). It must have been the shot.

MISS MOCKRIDGE. Oh, surely not. I was away at the time and never quite understood what happened. Something rather dreadful, wasn't it? I'm sorry if I—

FREDA. No. It's all right. It was very distressing for us at the time, but it's done with now. Martin shot himself. It happened a year ago—last October in fact—at his own cottage about twenty miles from here.

MISS MOCKRIDGE. Oh, yes. Dreadful business, of course. I only met him twice, I think. I remember I thought him very amusing and charming. He was very handsome, wasn't he? (*Enter* STANTON *and* GORDON.)

OLWEN. Yes, very handsome.

STANTON (*on platform*). Who's very handsome?

FREDA. Not you, Charles.

STANTON (*crosses down steps Left and continues Left to up Centre*). Well, who is it? Or is it a secret?

GORDON (*crosses down step Right*). They must have been talking about me. Betty, why do you let them rave about your husband like that? (*Crosses to Left end of sofa.*)

BETTY. Darling, I'm sure you've had too much manly gossip and old brandy. (STANTON *crosses Right Centre*) You're beginning to look purple in the face and bloated—a typical financier.
(GORDON *crosses up Left to piano. Enter* ROBERT. *Closes door.*)

ROBERT. Why so dim?— (*Switching on extra light*) Sorry about that gun, Freda. (*Crosses down steps Right*) It was stupid. I hope it didn't frighten anybody. (*Crosses to below sofa.*)

FREDA. As a matter of fact, it did. All of us.

MISS MOCKRIDGE. Yes, and I'd just been saying what a charming little group you've made here, all of you.

ROBERT. I'm glad you think so.

MISS MOCKRIDGE. I think you've all been lucky.

ROBERT (*sits sofa Right of* BETTY). I agree, we have.

STANTON (*Left of chair Left*). It's not all luck, Miss Mockridge. You see, we all happen to be nice easy-going people.

ROBERT. Except Betty— She's terribly wild.

STANTON. That's only because Gordon doesn't beat her often enough—yet.

MISS MOCKRIDGE. You see, Miss Peel, Mr. Stanton is still the cynical bachelor. I'm afraid he rather spoils the picture.

STANTON. Oh. You must have a dark relief— (*Crosses to chair down Left and sits.*)

GORDON (*crosses Left. Picks up radio section of Times from piano, crosses Right to Left of sofa*). I wonder if there's any dance music on the radio tonight?

ROBERT. I hope not. Let's be quiet. (GORDON *crosses up to radio*) What have you people been talking about?

FREDA. Olwen has been telling us about *The Sleeping Dog*.

ROBERT. *The Sleeping Dog?* Oh yes—that novel we're going to publish, the one she's so keen on.

STANTON. Why does he call it that?

OLWEN. Don't you know the proverb—Let Sleeping Dogs Lie?

STANTON. Where does that come into it?

FREDA. From what Olwen says, the sleeping dog represents truth.

OLWEN. Yes, and the chief character—the husband—insisted upon disturbing it.

ROBERT. Well, he was quite right to disturb it.

STANTON. Was he? I think it a very sound idea—the truth as a sleeping dog.

MISS MOCKRIDGE. But of course we do spend too much of our time telling lies and acting them.

BETTY. Oh, but one has to. I'm always fibbing. I do it all day long.

GORDON (*still at radio*). You do, darling. You do.

BETTY. It's the secret of my charm.

MISS MOCKRIDGE. Very likely. But we meant something more serious.

ROBERT. Serious or not, I'm all for it coming out. It's healthy.

STANTON (*picks up puzzle from table*). I think telling the truth is about as healthy as skidding round a corner at sixty.

FREDA. And life's got a lot of dangerous corners—hasn't it Charles?

STANTON. It can have—if you don't choose your route well. To lie or not to lie—what do you think, Olwen? You're looking terribly wise.

OLWEN. I agree with you. I think telling everything is dangerous. The point is, I think—there's truth *and* truth.

GORDON. I always agree to that. Something *and* something.

STANTON. Keep quiet, Gordon. (GORDON *sits arm of chair up Left*) Go on, Olwen.

MISS MOCKRIDGE. Yes—go on.

OLWEN. Well—the real truth—that is, every single little thing, with nothing missing at all, wouldn't be dangerous. I suppose that's God's truth. But what most people mean by truth is only half the real truth. It doesn't tell you all that went on inside everybody. It simply gives you a lot of facts that happened to have been hidden away and were perhaps a lot better hidden away. It's rather treacherous stuff.

GORDON (*rises, crosses down Left of* MISS MOCKRIDGE). Yes, like the muck they drag out of everybody in the law courts. Where were you on the night of the 27th of November? Answer yes or no.

MISS MOCKRIDGE (*looking at* GORDON). Yes! (*Turns to* OLWEN *as* GORDON *crosses up to radio*) I'm not convinced, Miss Peel. I'm ready to welcome what you call half the truth—the facts.

ROBERT. So am I. I'm all for it.

FREDA. You would be, Robert.

ROBERT. What do you mean by that, Freda?

FREDA. Anything, nothing. (*Rises*) Let's talk about something more amusing. (*Crosses to table down Left*) Who wants a drink? Drinks, Robert. And cigarettes. (ROBERT *rises, crosses to drinks.* FREDA *takes up musical cigarette box from table Left, being careful to keep it closed. Turns towards* MISS MOCKRIDGE) A cigarette, Miss Mockridge? (*Offering the box.*)

MISS MOCKRIDGE (*rises*). No, thanks, I'm a slave to my own brand. (*Crosses up to piano. Picks up her bag and continues to chair up Left.*)

FREDA (*crosses to* OLWEN). Cigarette, Olwen? (OLWEN *rises.*)

OLWEN (*as* FREDA *crosses. Taking the box*). Oh, I remember that box. It plays a tune, doesn't it? I remember the tune. (*Opens the box*) Yes, it's the Wedding March, isn't it? (*She takes a cigarette, as the box plays.*)

ROBERT (*crosses to Right arm of chair Right of table*). Good, isn't it?

FREDA (*taking the box from* OLWEN *and snapping it shut*). It can't have been this box you remember. (MISS MOCKRIDGE *sits chair up Left*) This is the first time I've had it out.

OLWEN. It belonged to Martin, didn't it? He showed it to me.

FREDA. He couldn't have shown it to you, Olwen. He hadn't got it when you saw him last.

STANTON. How do you know, Freda?

FREDA (*turning Left*). That doesn't matter. I know. Martin couldn't have shown you this box, Olwen. (*Crosses up to piano and puts box down.*)

OLWEN (*to* FREDA's *back*). Couldn't he? . . . (*Turns to* ROBERT) No, perhaps he couldn't. (*Sits chair Left of table*) I suppose I got mixed up. I must have seen a box like this somewhere else and then pushed it on to poor Martin because he was always so fond of things like this. (*Sits chair Left of table.*)

ROBERT (*crosses to* OLWEN). Olwen, I'm going to be rather rude, but I know you won't mind. You know you suddenly stopped telling the truth then, didn't you? (*Strikes match and lights cigarette for* OLWEN) You're absolutely positive that this is the box Martin showed you, just as Freda is equally positive it isn't.

OLWEN. Well, does that matter?

GORDON (*fiddling with radio*). Not a hoot. I'm trying to find some dance music, but this thing has suddenly decided not to function.

ROBERT. Then don't fiddle about with it.

BETTY. Don't bully Gordon.

ROBERT. Well, you stop him.

BETTY. Stop it, Gordon! (GORDON *turns off radio.*)

ROBERT. No. I don't suppose it does matter, Olwen, but after what we'd been saying, I couldn't help thinking that it was rather an odd, provoking situation.

MISS MOCKRIDGE. Just what I was thinking—it's all terribly provoking—. More about the cigarette box, please!

FREDA (*crosses down*). It's all perfectly simple. . . .

OLWEN. Wait a minute, please, Freda. I don't think it is all perfectly simple, but I can't see that it matters now.

FREDA. I don't understand you.

ROBERT. Neither do I. First you say it can't have been the same box and now you say it's not all perfectly simple and begin to hint at grand mysteries. I believe you're hiding something, Olwen, and that isn't like you. Either that box you saw was Martin's or it wasn't—

STANTON. Oh, damn that box. (FREDA *turns, moves up to piano.*)

MISS MOCKRIDGE. Oh, but Mr. Stanton, we'd like to hear—

STANTON. Sorry—but I hate a box that plays tunes. Let's forget it.

GORDON (*crosses down Right above chair Right*). Yes, and Martin too. He isn't here—and we are.

ROBERT. Gordon, please— (*Turns out up below piano bench.*)

GORDON. Don't let's mention Martin or think about him. He's dead.

FREDA. Well, there's no need to be tragic about it, Gordon. One would think you owned Martin, to hear you talk.

BETTY (GORDON *turns Right*). Instead of which, nobody owned Martin. He belonged to himself. He had some sense.

ROBERT (*crosses down Centre to above table*). What does all that mean, Betty?

BETTY. It means that I'm being rather stupid and that you're all talking a lot of rot and that I think I'm going to have a headache any minute.

ROBERT (*crosses to chair Right of table*). Is that all?

BETTY. Isn't that quite enough?

ROBERT (*sits chair Right of table*). More about the box, Freda. (GORDON *sits arm of sofa.*)

FREDA (*crosses down*). I wish you wouldn't be so absurdly persistent, Robert. It came to us with some other of Martin's things from the cottage. I put it away and this is the first time it's been out here. Now the last time Olwen was at Martin's cottage was that Saturday when we all went over—you remember, at the very beginning of October. (*Sits Left end of settee facing Right.*)

GORDON. Gosh—yes. What a day that was. And a marvellous night, wasn't it? That was the time we all sat in the garden for hours and Martin told us all about those ridiculous people he'd stayed with in Cornwall—the handwoven people.

BETTY. Yes—and the long, long thin woman who always said "Do you belong?"

GORDON. I don't think I ever had a better day. We'll never have another like that.

ROBERT (*rises, crosses up to drinks*). Yes, it was a good day. Though I'd no idea you felt so deeply about it, Gordon. (*Pours drink.*)

FREDA. Neither had anybody else. Gordon seems to have decided that he ought to be sentimental every time Martin is mentioned.

BETTY. I suspect it's Robert's old brandy. And those enormous glasses. They go to his head.

GORDON. Well, where do you want them to go to?

ROBERT (*crosses to back of chair Right of table with drink*). The point is then, that that first Saturday in October was the last time Olwen was at Martin's cottage—

FREDA. Yes, and I know that he hadn't got this cigarette box then.

ROBERT. No, he'd have shown it to us if he'd had it then. As a matter of fact, I never remember seeing the thing at the cottage. So there you are, Olwen.

OLWEN. There I am.

ROBERT. Yes, but—hang it all—where are you?

OLWEN. You *are* a baby, Robert. I don't know where I am. Out of the dock or the witness box, I hope.

MISS MOCKRIDGE. Oh, no, that would be too disappointing.

BETTY. You know, that *wasn't* the last time you were at the cottage, Olwen. Don't you remember, you and I ran over the next Sunday afternoon, to see Martin about those little etchings?

OLWEN. Yes.

ROBERT. Yes, that's true.

BETTY. But I don't remember his showing us this cigarette box. In fact, I've never seen it before.

STANTON. Neither have I, and I don't think I ever want to see it again. I never heard such a lot of fuss about nothing.

FREDA (*to* STANTON). I agree with you, Charles. (*To* OLWEN) But I may as well tell you—if only to have done with it—that Martin couldn't have shown it to you that Sunday anyhow, because he hadn't got it then.

STANTON. You seem to know a lot about that box, Freda.

GORDON. That's just what I was going to say. Why are you so grand and knowing about it?

BETTY. I know why. You gave it to him.

ROBERT. Did you, Freda?

FREDA. Yes, I gave it to him.

ROBERT. That's queer. I don't mean it's queer your giving it to him—why shouldn't you? But your never mentioning it. When did you give it to him? Where did you pick it up?

FREDA. That's easily explained. You remember the day before that awful Saturday? You were staying in town, and I came up for the day. Well, I happened to see the cigarette box in a shop. It was amusing and rather cheap, so I bought it and had it sent parcel post to Martin.

ROBERT. Oh! so that he never got it until that last Saturday.

FREDA. Yes.

ROBERT (*crosses Right to platform Left, puts down glass*). Well, that's that.

GORDON. I'm sorry, Freda, but it's not quite so simple as all that. You mustn't forget that I was with Martin at the cottage that very Saturday morning.

ROBERT. Well, what about it?

GORDON. Well, I was there when the parcel post came, with the letters in the morning. I remember Martin had a parcel of books—I don't forget anything about that morning, and neither would you if you'd been dragged into that hellish inquest (*rises*), as I was. (*Crosses Right end of table Centre*) But he didn't have that cigarette box.

FREDA. I suppose it must have arrived by the afternoon post then. What does it matter?

GORDON. It doesn't matter at all, Freda darling, except that parcels are never delivered there by the afternoon post.

FREDA. Yes, they are.

GORDON. No.

FREDA. How do you know? (ROBERT *crosses down Left of Left arm of sofa.*)

GORDON. Because Martin used to grumble about it and say that he always got books and manuscripts a day late. That cigarette box didn't arrive in the morning, because I saw the post opened, and it couldn't have been delivered in the afternoon. Freda, I don't believe you ever sent the box. You took it to Martin yourself. You did, didn't you?

FREDA. You are a fool, Gordon.

GORDON. Possibly. But, you did take it to Martin, didn't you?

ROBERT. Did you?

FREDA. Well, if you must know—I did.

ROBERT. Freda!

GORDON. I thought so. (*Crosses up Left to back of chair Left of table.*)

ROBERT (*crosses Left to table Centre*). But, Freda, if you went to the cottage to give Martin the box after Gordon had left, you must have seen Martin later than anybody, only a few hours before he—before he shot himself.

FREDA. I did. I saw him shortly before dinner.

ROBERT. But why have you never said anything about it? Why didn't you come forward at the inquest? You could have given evidence.

FREDA. I could, but why should I? What good would it have done? It was bad enough Gordon having to do it—

GORDON. It was hell.

FREDA. If it could have helped Martin, I'd have gone. But it couldn't have helped anybody. (GORDON *crosses up Left to radio.*)

STANTON. That's true. You were quite right.

ROBERT. Yes, I can understand that. But why didn't you tell me? Why did you keep it to yourself, why have you kept it to yourself all this time? You were the very last person to talk to Martin.

FREDA. Was I the last person?

ROBERT. You must have been.

FREDA. Then what about Olwen?

ROBERT. Olwen? Oh—the cigarette box.

FREDA. Yes, of course—the cigarette box. (STANTON *rises, turns out Left*) Martin didn't get that box until late Saturday afternoon, and Olwen admitted that he showed it to her.

BETTY. No, she didn't. She said it was some other box, and I vote we believe her and have done with it.

MISS MOCKRIDGE. No, no—Mrs. Whitehouse—

BETTY. Yes, I do. It's all wrong going on and on like this.

STANTON (*crosses up Left piano bench*). And I second that.

ROBERT. And I don't.

BETTY. Oh! But Robert.

ROBERT. I'm sorry, Betty. After all you don't come into this. Martin was my brother and I don't like all these mysteries and I've a right to know.

OLWEN. All right, Robert. But must you know now?

FREDA. I don't see the necessity. (*Rises*) But then I didn't see why I should have been cross-examined, with the entire approval of the company, apparently. But now that it's your turn, Olwen, I've no doubt that Robert will relent. (*Turns out Left.*)

ROBERT. I don't see why you should say that, Freda.

FREDA (*turning in*). You might as well admit it, Olwen. Martin showed you that box, didn't he? So you must have seen him, you must have been at the cottage that Saturday night.

OLWEN. Yes, he did show me the box. That was after dinner—about nine o'clock—on that Saturday night.

ROBERT. You were there? But this is crazy. First Freda—then you. And neither of you has said a word about it.

OLWEN. I'm sorry, Robert. I couldn't.

ROBERT. But why were you there?

OLWEN. I'd been worried about—something – something that I'd heard—it had been worrying me for days. I felt I had to see Martin to ask him about it. So I motored up to see him. I had some dinner on the way, and got to the cottage just before nine. Nobody saw me go and nobody saw me leave—you know how quiet it was there. Like Freda, I thought it wouldn't serve any good purpose to come forward at the inquest—(FREDA *crosses to chair down Left and sits*) so I didn't. That's all.

ROBERT. But you can't dismiss it like that. You must have been the very last person to talk to Martin. You must know something about it.

OLWEN (*rises*). Please Robert! It's all over and done with! Let's leave it alone! (*Crosses Left*) We don't mean to discuss it, do we, Freda? There's nothing to discuss. It's all over.

ROBERT (OLWEN *turns Right*). But look here, Olwen, you must tell me this. Had your visit to Martin that night anything to do with the firm? You said you'd been worried about something.

FREDA. Oh, Robert, please.

ROBERT. I'm sorry, but I must know this. Was that *something* to do with that missing money?

GORDON (*crosses down Right*). Oh —for God's sake—don't drag that money into it. We don't want that all over again. Martin's gone. Leave him alone, can't you, and shut up about the rotten money.

FREDA. Gordon, be quiet. You're behaving like an hysterical child tonight. I'm sure we must be boring Miss Mockridge with all this!

MISS MOCKRIDGE. No, no, I'm enjoying it very much!

GORDON (*crosses up*). I'm sorry! I beg your pardon, Miss Mockridge.

FREDA. I think we'd better change the subject, Robert.

MISS MOCKRIDGE (*rising*). Not at all. Well, I think—I'd better be going! It must be getting late.

FREDA (*rises*). Oh, no.

ROBERT (*turning up*). Oh, don't go yet.

MISS MOCKRIDGE (*crosses*). The Pattersons said they'd send their car over for me to take me back. It hasn't arrived yet, do you know?

ROBERT. Yes, I heard it when we left the dining room and I told the man to wait in the kitchen. I'll get hold of him for you. (*Turns, crosses up to door and exits.*)

FREDA (*crosses Centre*). Oh, must you really go?

MISS MOCKRIDGE. Yes, I really think I ought. It's at least half an hour's run to the Pattersons', and I don't suppose they like their car and chauffeur to be kept out too late. (FREDA *crosses Right to platform. To* FREDA) Thank you so much. (*To* OLWEN) It's been so delightful seeing you all again.

STANTON. Good-night Miss Mockridge.

MISS MOCKRIDGE (*crosses up steps Left. To* BETTY). Good-bye, Mrs. Whitehouse. Good-bye.

BETTY. Good-night.

FREDA. I think you left your wrap in my room. I'll get it for you. (MISS MOCKRIDGE *exits.* FREDA *follows and shuts door.* STANTON *crosses down Right to drinks.*)

GORDON (*crosses to chair Left of table*). I'm glad she's gone. (OLWEN *sits chair down Left.*)

BETTY. I am too! I can't bear that woman. (*Crosses to table Centre*) She reminds me too much of a geometry teacher I used to have. (*Sits chair Right of table.*)

STANTON. I've always suspected your geometry, Betty. (*Picks up glass*) Drink, Gordon?

GORDON (*lighting cigarette*). No, thanks.

STANTON (*fixing drink*). That was mean—. Because after all she's not at all a bad novelist. I don't mean she's just a good seller, but she's a good novelist too. Why is it there seems to be always something rather unpleasant about good novelists?

GORDON (*sits chair Left of table*). I give it up. But I don't call Maud Mockridge a good novelist, Charles!

BETTY. I'll bet she's a good gossiper.

STANTON (*crosses down*). She is. She's notorious for it. She'll embroider that cigarette box story and have it all around town within a week. The Pattersons will have it tonight, to begin with. It must have been agony for her to go away and not hear any more. (*Sits Right end of sofa facing Left.*)

GORDON. She wouldn't have gone if she'd thought she'd have heard any more. But she's got enough to go on with. She'll probably start a new novel in the morning and we'll all be in it.

BETTY. Well, she'll have to use her imagination a bit about me.

STANTON. And me. Perhaps she'll invent the most frightful vices for us, Betty.

BETTY. She can't really do much with what she's just heard, you know. After all, why shouldn't Freda have taken Martin a cigarette box, and why shouldn't Olwen have gone to see him?

OLWEN (*reading magazine*). Yes, why not?

BETTY. I'd forgotten you were there, Olwen. May I ask something? After all I don't think I've asked anybody anything, so far, have I?

OLWEN. You may ask. I don't promise to answer.

BETTY. I'll risk it then. Were you in love with Martin, Olwen?

OLWEN. Not in the least.

BETTY. I thought you weren't.

OLWEN. As a matter of fact, to be absolutely candid, I rather disliked him.

BETTY. Yes, I thought so.

GORDON (*rises, crosses Left to* OLWEN). Oh—rot. I'll never believe that, Olwen. You couldn't dislike him. Nobody could. I don't mean he hadn't any faults or anything, but with him they just didn't matter. He was one of those people. You had to like him. He was Martin.

BETTY. In other words—your god. (GORDON *turns Right*) You know, Gordon literally adored him. Didn't you darling?

STANTON (*rises, crosses to table Centre and puts down glass*). Well, he could be fascinating. And he was very clever. I must admit the firm's never been the same without him. (*Crosses to Right end of sofa.*)

GORDON. I should think not.

BETTY. How could it be?
(*Enter* ROBERT *followed by* FREDA *who closes door.*)

ROBERT (*crosses Centre between two chairs*). Now we can thrash this out.

OLWEN. Oh, no, please, Robert.
(GORDON *turns up to piano and puts out cigarette.*)

ROBERT. I'm sorry, Olwen. But I want to know the truth now. There's something very queer about all this. First Freda going to see Martin, and never saying a word about it. Then you going to see him, too, Olwen, and never saying a word about it either. It's not good enough. (FREDA *crosses down steps Left*) You've both been hiding this all along. You may be hiding other things too. It's about time some of us began telling the truth—for a change.

FREDA (*between sofa and chair Right of table*). Do you always tell the truth, Robert?

ROBERT. I try to.

STANTON. Noble fellow. But don't expect too much of us ordinary mortals. Spare our weaknesses. Please!

FREDA (*crosses Right*). What weaknesses?

STANTON. Anything you like, my dear Freda. Buying musical cigarette boxes, for instance. I'm sure that's a weakness.

FREDA. Or making rather too much use of one's little country cottage. I think that too under circumstances might be described as a weakness. (*Turns out Left.*)

STANTON. Do you mean Martin's cottage? I hardly ever went there.

FREDA. No, I wasn't thinking of Martin's. (*Sits couch Left.*)

STANTON. I'm afraid I don't understand.

ROBERT. Look here, what's all this about? Are you starting now, Stanton?

STANTON (*turning out Right*). Certainly not.

ROBERT. Well, I want to get to the bottom of this Martin business. And I want to do it now.

GORDON. Oh, Lord, is this going to be another inquest?

ROBERT. Well, it wouldn't be necessary if we'd heard more of the truth perhaps when there was an inquest. And it's up to you, Olwen. You were the last to see Martin. Why did you go to see him like that? Was it about the missing money?

OLWEN. Yes, it was.

ROBERT. Did you know then that Martin had taken it?

OLWEN. No.

ROBERT. But you thought he had?

OLWEN. I thought there was a possibility he had.

GORDON (*turning up*). You were all damned ready to think that.

BETTY. Gordon, I want to go home now.

ROBERT. So soon, Betty?

BETTY. I'm going to have an awful headache if I stay any longer. I'm going home— (*Rises.*)

GORDON. All right. Just a minute.

STANTON. I'll take you along, Betty, if Gordon wants to stay on.

BETTY (*crosses up Right to steps*). No, I want Gordon to come along too.

GORDON (*crosses up Right*). All right. But hang on a minute.

BETTY. I tell you I want to go now. Take me home.

ROBERT (*taking her hand*). Why, what's the matter, Betty?

BETTY. I don't know. I'm stupid, I suppose. (*Crosses up steps.*)

GORDON. All right. We'll go.

ROBERT. But, Betty, I'm awfully sorry if all this stuff has upset you.

BETTY (*on second step*). Oh, don't go on and on about it. Why can't you leave things alone? (*She rushes out.*)

GORDON. Well—good-night, everybody. (*Exits.*)

STANTON (*crosses up steps and turning*). I'll see these infants home and then turn in myself.

OLWEN. Very good of you.

STANTON. Yes, isn't it? Good-night. (*Closes door.*)

FREDA. Good-night. (STANTON *exits.*)

ROBERT (*crosses down Right of chair Right of table*). Now, Olwen, you can tell me exactly why you rushed to see Martin like that about the missing money.

OLWEN (*rises*). We're all being truthful now, aren't we?

ROBERT. I want to be.

OLWEN. What about you, Freda?

FREDA (*rises, crosses Left above table Centre*). Yes, yes, yes. I don't care. What does it matter?

ROBERT. Queer way of putting it.

FREDA. Is it? Well sometimes, Robert, I'm rather a queer woman. You'd hardly know me. (*Crosses below chair up Left.*)

OLWEN. You started all this, you know, Robert. (*Crosses up Right to below chair Left of table*) Now it's your turn. (*Rises*) Will you be truthful, with me?

ROBERT (*crosses step down*). Good God. Yes—of course I will. I loathe all these silly mysteries. (FREDA *sits chair up Left*) But it's not my turn. I asked you a question that you haven't answered yet.

OLWEN. I know you have. But I'm going to ask you one before I answer yours. I've been waiting to do it for some time but I've never had the chance or never dared. Now I don't care. It might as well come out. Robert—did you take that money?

ROBERT. Did I take the money?

OLWEN. Yes.

ROBERT. Of course not. You must be crazy, Olwen. Do you think even if I had taken it, I'd let Martin shoulder the blame like that? But Martin took it, of course. We all know that.

OLWEN (*sits chair Left of table*). Oh, what a fool I've been.

ROBERT. I don't understand. Surely you must have known that Martin took it. You can't have been thinking all this time that I did.

OLWEN. Yes, I have. And I've not been thinking it—I've been torturing myself with it.
(FREDA *rises, turns up to piano.*)

ROBERT. Damn it all—it doesn't make sense. I might have taken the money—I suppose we're all capable of that, under certain circumstances—but never on earth could I let somebody else—and especially Martin, take the blame for it. How could you think me capable of such a thing? I thought you were a friend of mine, Olwen—one of my best and oldest friends.

FREDA. You might as well know, Robert—

OLWEN. Oh, no, Freda. Please. Please.

FREDA (*crosses to back of chair Left of table*). Why not? What does it matter! (*To* ROBERT) You might as well know, Robert, and how you can be so dense baffles me, that Olwen is not a friend of yours.

ROBERT. Of course she is!

FREDA. She's not! She's a woman who's in love with you. A very different thing! She's been in love with you for ages!

OLWEN. Freda, that's damnably unfair! That's cruel!

FREDA. It's not going to hurt you, and he wanted the truth. Let him have it!

ROBERT. I'm terribly sorry, Olwen. We've always been very good friends and I've always been very fond of you.

OLWEN. Stop! Freda, that's unforgivable! You'd no right to say that!

FREDA. But it's true, isn't it? (*Crosses Right between two chairs*) You wanted the truth, Robert, and here it is—some of it. Olwen's been in love with you for ages. I don't know exactly how long, but I've been aware of it for the last eighteen months. Wives always are aware of these things. And, I'll tell you now what I've longed to tell you for some time. I think you're a fool for not being aware of it yourself, for not having responded to it, for not having done something drastic about it long before this. If somebody loves you like that, for God's sake enjoy it, make the most of it, hold on to it, before it's too late. (*Turns out Left.*)

OLWEN. Freda, I understand now.

FREDA. Understand what?

OLWEN. About you. I ought to have understood before.
(FREDA *turns out up Left.*)

ROBERT (*crosses up below chair up Right*). If you mean by that, that you understand now Freda doesn't care for me very much—you're right. We've not been very happy together—somehow our marriage hasn't worked. Nobody knows.

FREDA (*crosses Right to* ROBERT). Of course they know.

ROBERT. Do you mean you've told them?

FREDA. Of course I haven't. If you mean by them the people we know intimately—our own group here—(*Crosses down Right to Left arm of sofa*) they didn't need to be told.

ROBERT (*crosses step*). But Olwen has just said she understood about it for the first time.

OLWEN. No, I knew about that before, Robert. It was something else I've just—

ROBERT (*crosses Center*). Well, what is it?

OLWEN. I'd rather not explain.

FREDA (*facing Right*). Being noble, now, Olwen? You needn't, you know. We're past that.

OLWEN. No, it's not that. It's—it's because I can't talk about it. There's something horrible to me about it. And I can't tell you why.

FREDA. Something horrible!

OLWEN. Yes, something really horrible. Don't let's talk about that side of it!

FREDA. But Olwen . . .

OLWEN. I'm sorry I said I understood. It just slipped out! Please!

FREDA. Very well. But you've got to talk about that money now. You said you believed all along Robert had taken it.

OLWEN. It looked to me as if he must have.

ROBERT (*steps down to* OLWEN). But if you believed that, why didn't you say something?

FREDA (*sits platform above sofa*). Oh, Robert—can't you see why she couldn't?

ROBERT. You mean—she was shielding me?

FREDA. Yes, of course.

ROBERT. Olwen—I'm terribly sorry. I'd no idea. Though it's fantastic, I must say, that you could think I was that kind of man and yet you go on caring enough not to say anything.

OLWEN. But it's not fantastic at all.

FREDA. If you're in love with somebody, you're in love with them, and they can do all sorts of things, be mean as hell, and you'll forgive them or just not bother about it. At least, some women will.

ROBERT (*crosses up to piano bench*). I don't see that in you, Freda.

FREDA. Don't you? But there are a lot of things about me you don't see. (*To* OLWEN) But this is what I wanted to say, Olwen. If you thought that Robert had taken that money, then you knew that Martin hadn't.
(ROBERT *turns in Left.*)

OLWEN. Yes, I was sure—after I had talked with him that last night—that Martin hadn't taken it.

FREDA. But you let us all think he had.

OLWEN. I know. But it didn't seem to matter then. It couldn't hurt Martin any more. He wasn't there to be hurt. And I felt I had to keep quiet.

ROBERT (*crosses down Centre*). Because of me?

OLWEN. Yes, because of you, Robert.

ROBERT. But Martin *must* have taken it.

OLWEN. No.

ROBERT (*crosses down Centre*). That's why he shot himself. He thought he'd be found out. He was terribly nervous—always was. And he simply couldn't face it.

OLWEN (*rises, crosses*). No, it wasn't that at all. You *must* believe me. I'm positive Martin never touched that money.
(*Turns out up Left.*)

FREDA. I've always thought it queer that he should. It wasn't his style at all—doing some sneaky work with a check. I knew he could be wild—and rather cruel sometimes. But he couldn't be a cautious cunning little sneak-thief. It wasn't like him and he didn't care at all about money.

ROBERT. He spent enough of it. He was badly in debt.

FREDA (*rises*). Yes, but that's just the point. He didn't mind being in debt. He could have cheerfully gone on being in debt. Money simply didn't matter. Now, you loathe it. You're entirely different. (*Crosses Right below sofa.*)

OLWEN (*crosses to back of chair Left of table*). Yes, that was one of the reasons I thought that you—

ROBERT. Yes, I see that. Though I think those fellows who don't care about money, who don't mind being in debt, are just the sort who might help themselves to other people's.

FREDA. Yes, but not in a cautious sneaky way. That wasn't like Martin at all.
(*Crosses up to platform above sofa.*)

ROBERT (*crosses Left*). . . . Olwen, where did you get the idea that I'd taken it?

OLWEN. Because Martin himself was sure that you had taken it. He told me so.

ROBERT. Martin told you so?

OLWEN. Yes. That was the first thing we talked about.

ROBERT. Martin thought I had taken it.

OLWEN. Yes.

ROBERT. But he knew me better than that. Why should he have thought that?

FREDA. You thought he'd been the thief. You didn't know him any better, it seems.

ROBERT. There were special circumstances, I'd been told something. Besides, I wasn't at all sure. It wasn't until after he shot himself that I felt certain.

OLWEN. You say you'd been told something? But then Martin had been told something too. He'd practically been told that you'd taken that check.

ROBERT. What!

OLWEN. And do you know who told him?

ROBERT. I can guess now.

FREDA (*crosses to chair Right of table*). Who?

ROBERT. Stanton, wasn't it?

OLWEN. Yes, Stanton.

ROBERT. But he told me that Martin had taken that check.

FREDA. Oh, but he—
OLWEN. Oh!

ROBERT. He practically proved it to me. He said he didn't want Martin given away—said we'd all stand in together, all that sort of thing.

OLWEN. But don't you see—he told Martin all that too. And Martin would never have told me if he hadn't known—well, that I would never give you away.

ROBERT. Stanton.

FREDA. Then it was Stanton himself who got that money?

OLWEN (*turning in*). It looks like it.

FREDA. I'm sure it was. He played Martin and Robert against each other. Could anything be more vile?

ROBERT. You know, it doesn't follow that Stanton himself was the thief.

FREDA. Of course he was.

ROBERT. Wait. Let's get this clear. (*To* OLWEN) That check made payable to bearer was on your father's desk, Freda, in his private office. Remember, only three of us had access to his office. Martin, Stanton and I. The check disappeared. Cashed at one of the branch banks where none of us were known. The teller was rather vague about it all except that the person who cashed it was about the age and build of Martin or myself, so it couldn't have been Stanton.

FREDA. How could you believe Martin had taken the check?

ROBERT. The evidence pointed to him or to me, and I knew I hadn't taken it.

FREDA. And Stanton told you—?

ROBERT. That he'd seen Martin coming out of your father's office.

OLWEN. Stanton told Martin he'd seen you coming out of that office.

FREDA. Stanton took that money himself.

ROBERT (*fiercely*). Whether he took the money or not, Stanton's got to explain this. (*Crosses Right up steps to phone and dials*) No wonder he didn't approve of this business and was glad to get out of it. He's got too much to hide.

OLWEN (*crosses Centre between two chairs*). We all have too much to hide.

ROBERT. Then we'll let some daylight into it for once, if it kills us. Stanton's got to explain this.

FREDA (*crosses up above Left*). Not tonight.

ROBERT. Tonight!

OLWEN. They've probably all gone to bed.

FREDA. Are you going to get them all back, Robert?

ROBERT. Yes. Hello, is that you, Gordon? . . . He is, is he? Well, I want you both to come back here. . . . Yes, more and more of it. . . . It's damned important. . . . Oh, no, we can keep Betty out of it. All right, then. Be as quick as you can. (*Puts back receiver*) They're coming back.

CURTAIN

(*Quickly as he says the last line.*)

ACT TWO

ROBERT, FREDA *and* OLWEN *are discovered in exactly the same position as they were at the end of Act I.*

FREDA (*above steps Left*). Are they all coming back?

ROBERT (*on platform*). No, not Betty. She's going to bed.
(FREDA *crosses down to drinks, throws* OLWEN *a look—then takes cigarette.*)

OLWEN (*on* FREDA'S *look*). Wise little Betty.
(*Turns and sits Left arm chair Right of table.*)

ROBERT (*crosses down steps Left*). What do you mean, Olwen? You know very well she's not mixed up in this business.

OLWEN. Do I?

ROBERT (*turning in Centre between two chairs*). Well, don't you?

FREDA. Poor Robert, look at him now. (*Sits platform above sofa*) This is really serious, he's saying to himself. How we give ourselves away. It's a mystery we have any secrets at all.
(*Lights cigarette.*)

ROBERT. No, but—hang it all, Olwen—you've no right to sneer at Betty like that. You know very well it's better to keep her out of all this.

OLWEN (*rises*). No, we mustn't soil her pure young mind.
(*Crosses Right.*)

ROBERT. Well, after all, she's younger than we are—and she's terribly sensitive. You saw what happened to her just before they went. She can't stand the atmosphere of all this.

OLWEN. I suppose not.
(*Sits Right end of sofa.*)

ROBERT. Obviously you dislike her, Olwen. I can't imagine why. She's always had a great admiration for you.

OLWEN (*takes cigarette from box on platform*). Well, I'm sorry, Robert, but I can't return her admiration—except for her looks. I don't dislike her. But—well, I can't be as sorry for her as I'd like to be or ought to be.
(*Lights cigarette.*)

ROBERT. Is it necessary for you or anybody else to be sorry for her? You're talking wildly now, Olwen.
(*Crosses down to table Center.*)

FREDA (*rises, crosses to chair Right of table*). I suspect not. And anyhow it seems to be our evening for talking wildly. Also, I'm now facing a most urgent problem, the sort of problem that only women have to face. If a man has been dragged back to your house to be told he's a liar, a cad and a possible thief, oughtn't you to make a few sandwiches for him?

ROBERT (*sits, chair Left of table*). He'll get no sandwiches from me.

FREDA. No sincerity, no sandwiches —that's your motto, is it? No? Oh, dear—how heavy we are without Martin. (*Sits Right arm chair Right of table*) And how he would have adored all this. He'd have invented the most extravagant and incredible sins to confess to. Oh, don't look so dreadfully solemn, you two. You might be a bit brighter—just for a minute.

ROBERT. I'm afraid we haven't your light touch, my dear Freda.

FREDA. I suppose I feel like this because, in spite of everything I am a hostess expecting company, and I can't help thinking about bright remarks and sandwiches. (*A bell rings out in the hall.* ROBERT *rises*) And there they are! (*Rises*) You'll have to let them in yourself, Robert.
(OLWEN *puts out cigarette.* ROBERT *goes out.*)

OLWEN. Freda.

FREDA. Yes.

OLWEN (*rises, crosses to Right arm of chair Right*). Have you really known a long time?

FREDA. Yes. More than a year. I've often wanted to say something to you about it.

OLWEN. What would you have said?

FREDA. I don't quite know. Something idiotic. (*Crosses steps Right*) But friendly, very friendly.

OLWEN. And I only guessed about you tonight, Freda. And now it all seems so obvious. I can't think why I never guessed before.

FREDA. Neither can I.

OLWEN. This is quite mad, isn't it?

FREDA. And rapidly getting madder. (*Turns out*) I don't care, do you? It's rather a relief.
(*Centre above to chair.*)

OLWEN. Yes, it is—in a way. But it's rather frightening too. Like being in a car when the brakes are gone.
(*Noise of* MEN *outside.* STANTON *enters first,* GORDON *follows.* ROBERT *follows closing door.*)

STANTON (*as he enters*). I can't see why. (OLWEN *sits chair Right of table*) I'm sorry about this, Freda. But it's Robert's doing. He insisted on our coming back.
(*Crosses down steps Left.*)

FREDA. I think Robert was right.
(*Crosses Left to piano.*)

GORDON (*crosses down step Right*). That's a change, anyhow. Well, what's it all about?

ROBERT (*on platform*). Chiefly about that money.

GORDON. Oh—hell—I thought as much. Why can't you leave poor Martin alone?

ROBERT. Wait a minute, Gordon. Martin didn't take that check.

GORDON. What? Is that true? Are you sure?

FREDA. Yes.

GORDON. You know, I never could understand that. It wasn't like him.

STANTON (*to* FREDA *and* ROBERT). Do you really believe that Martin didn't get that money? If he didn't, who did? And if he didn't, why did he shoot himself?

ROBERT (*crosses down steps Left*). We don't know, Stanton. But we're hoping that you'll tell us.

STANTON (*up Left Centre*). Being funny, Robert?

ROBERT. Not a bit. I wouldn't have dragged you back here to be funny. You told me—didn't you—that you were practically certain that Martin took that check?

STANTON. Certainly I did. And I told you why I thought so. All the evidence pointed that way. And what happened afterwards proved I was right.

ROBERT. Did it?

STANTON. Well, didn't it?

FREDA (*by piano*). If it did, then why did you tell Martin you thought Robert had done it?

STANTON. Don't be ridiculous, Freda. Why should I tell Martin I thought Robert had done it?

FREDA. Yes, why should you? That's exactly what we want to know.

STANTON. But of course I didn't.

OLWEN. Yes, you did.

STANTON (*crosses down to between two chairs*). Olwen. Are you in this too?

OLWEN. Yes, I'm in it too. (*Rises*) Because you lied like that to Martin, telling him you were sure Robert took the cheque. You've given me hours of misery.

STANTON (*crosses down to above table*). But I never meant to, Olwen. How could I know that you would go and see Martin and he would tell you?

OLWEN. It doesn't matter whether you knew or not. It was a mean vile lie. After this I feel that I never want to speak to you again.
(*Crosses Right to sofa.*)

STANTON. I'm sorry, Olwen. I'd rather anything had happened than that. You do believe that, don't you?
(*Turns out up to piano.*)

FREDA (*crosses down to chair down Left*). Apparently the rest of us don't matter very much. But you owe us a few explanations.

ROBERT. You'd better stop lying now, Stanton. (OLWEN *sits sofa Centre*) You've done enough. Why did you play Martin and me against each other like that?

FREDA. There can only be one explanation. Because he took that check himself.

GORDON. My God—you didn't, did you, Stanton?

STANTON (*turning*). Yes, I did.

GORDON. Then you're a rotten swine, Stanton. I don't care about the money. But you let Martin take the blame. You let everybody think he was a thief.

(*Closes in on Stanton to back of chair Right.*)

STANTON. Don't be such a hysterical young fool.

ROBERT (*seizes* GORDON'S *Right hand, pins it on back of chair Right*). Keep quiet, Gordon.

GORDON. I won't keep quiet!

STANTON. Sit down and behave yourself. We don't want this to develop into a free fight.

GORDON. But you let—

STANTON (*back to piano*). I didn't let Martin take the blame, as you call it. He wasn't the sort to take the blame, and you ought to know that. (GORDON *turns out Right to platform and faces Left*) It happened that in the middle of all the fuss about this money, he shot himself. You all jumped to the conclusion that it was because he had taken the money and was afraid of being found out. I let you go on thinking it, that's all. You might as well think he shot himself for that as for anything else. And anyhow he was done with it, out of it. Besides—where he's gone, it doesn't matter a damn whether people here think you've stolen money or not. (*Turns out up.*)

ROBERT (*closes in step*). But you deliberately tried to fasten the blame on to Martin or me.

FREDA. Of course he did. That's what makes it so foul.
(*Sits down Left.*)

STANTON (*turns back*). Not really. I'd not the least intention of letting anybody else be punished for what I'd done. I took that check because I needed some money quickly and I didn't know where to turn. I knew I could square it up in a week. But when it all came out, I had to play for time, and that seemed to me the easiest way of doing it.

ROBERT. But you couldn't have cashed the check at the bank yourself.

STANTON. No, I got somebody else to do that—a fellow who could keep his mouth shut. It was pure coincidence that he was about the same age and build as you and Martin. Don't go thinking there was any deep-laid plot. There wasn't. It was all improvised and haphazard and damned stupid.
(*Turns up.*)

ROBERT. Why didn't you confess to this before?

STANTON (*turning Right*). Why the devil should I?

FREDA. If you can't understand why, it's hopeless for us to try and show you. But there is such a thing as common honesty and decency.

STANTON (*crosses down to* FREDA *back of chair Left of table*). Is there? Don't forget—before you become too self-righteous—that you happen to be taking the lid off me. It might be somebody else's turn before we've finished.

ROBERT. Possibly. But that doesn't explain why you've kept so quiet about all this.

STANTON (*crosses up Centre to* ROBERT). I should have thought it

did. Martin's suicide put paid to the whole thing. Nobody wanted to talk about it after that. Dear Martin must have done it, so we won't mention it. That was the line. It wasn't the money. I'd have been glad to replace that. But I knew damned well that if I confessed, the old man would have had me out of the firm in two minutes. I wasn't one of his pets like you and Martin. I had to work myself up from nothing in the firm. I hadn't been brought in because I had the right university and social backgrounds. If the old man had thought for a minute that I'd done it, there'd have been none of this hush-hush business. He'd have felt like calling in the police. Don't forget, I'd been a clerk in the office. You fellows hadn't. It makes a difference, I can tell you.
(*Turns out Left.*)

FREDA. But my father retired from the firm six months ago.

STANTON. Well, what if he did? The whole thing was over and done with. Why open it up again? It might never have been mentioned if this damn fool inquisition hadn't been started tonight. Robert, Gordon and I were all working well together in the firm. What would have happened if I'd confessed? Where are we now? Who's better off because of this?

FREDA. You're not, it's true. But Martin is. And the people who cared about him.

STANTON. Are they?

FREDA. Of course they are.

STANTON. Don't be too sure.

FREDA. At least we know now that he wasn't a mean thief.

STANTON. And that's all you do know. But for all that he shot himself. And you don't suppose he did it for fun, do you?

FREDA (*rises*). Oh—you—you—!

GORDON. You are a rotter, Stanton.

ROBERT. Drop that sort of talk, Stanton.

STANTON (*crosses up Centre to* ROBERT). Why should I? You wanted the truth, and now you're getting it. I didn't want to come back here and be put in the witness box. It's your own doing. I'll say what I damn well like. Martin shot himself, and he did it knowing that he'd never touched the money. So it must have been something else. Well, what was it? You see what you've started now.
(*Turns out Left.*)

FREDA (*crosses up to piano*). What have we started? You're talking now as if you knew a lot more about Martin than we did.

STANTON. What I *do* know is that he must have had some reason for doing what he did, and that if it wasn't the money, it must have been something else. You're probably a lot better off for not knowing what that something is, just as you'd have been a lot better off if you'd never started poking about and prying into all this business.
(*Crosses up Left to piano bench.*)

ROBERT. Perhaps he did it because he thought I'd taken the money.

STANTON (*turning back*). And then again—perhaps not. If you think that Martin would have shot himself because he thought you'd taken some money—then you didn't know your own brother. Why, he laughed when I told him. It amused him. A lot of things amused that young man.
(*Crosses down to chair down Left.*)

OLWEN. That's true, I know. He didn't care. He didn't care at all.

ROBERT. Look here—do you know why Martin did shoot himself?

STANTON (*back to fireplace*). No. How should I?

FREDA. You talk as if you do.

STANTON. I can imagine reasons.

FREDA. What do you mean by that?

STANTON. I mean he was that sort. He'd got his life into a mess, and I don't blame him.

FREDA. You don't blame him! Who are you to blame him or not to blame him? You're not fit to mention his name. You hung your mean little piece of thieving round his neck, tried to poison our memory of him, and now when you're found out and Martin's name is clear of it, you want to begin all over again and start hinting that he was a criminal or a lunatic or something.

ROBERT. The less you say now, the better.

STANTON. The less we all say, the better. You should have thought of that before. I told you as much before you began dragging all this stuff out. Like a fool, you wouldn't leave well enough alone.
(*Turns out up.*)

ROBERT. Anyway, I've cleared Martin's name.

STANTON (*turning back*). You've cleared nothing yet, and if you'd a glimmer of sense you'd see it. But now I don't give a damn. You're going to get all you ask for.

FREDA. One of the things we shall ask for is to be rid of you.

GORDON. Do you think you'll stay on with this firm after this?

STANTON. I don't know and I don't care.

FREDA. You did a year ago.

STANTON. Yes, but now I don't. I can get along better now without the firm than they can without me.
(*Turns out down.*)

GORDON. Well, after this, at least it will be a pleasure to try. You always hated Martin, and I knew it.

STANTON (*swinging back Right*). I had my reasons. Unlike the Whitehouse family—father, daughter and son—who all fell in love with him.

ROBERT. Does that mean anything, Stanton? If it doesn't just take it back—now. If it does, you'll kindly explain yourself.

STANTON. I'll take nothing back.

OLWEN (*rises, crosses up above chair Right of table*). Stanton—

please. Don't let's have any more of this. We've all said too much already.

STANTON. I'm sorry, Olwen. But you can't blame me.
(OLWEN *moves up to window Right.*)

ROBERT. I'm waiting for your explanation.

FREDA. Don't you see, he's getting at me.

ROBERT. Is that true, Stanton?

STANTON. I'm certainly not leaving her out.

ROBERT. Be careful.

STANTON. It's too late to be careful. (FREDA *sits chair up Left*) Why do you think Freda's been so angry with me? There's only one reason, and I've known that reason for a long time. She was in love with Martin.
(*Turns out Left.*)

ROBERT. Is that true, Freda? I must know, because if it isn't I'm going to kick Stanton out of this house.

STANTON (*turning in*). Don't talk like a man in a melodrama. I wouldn't have said it if I hadn't known it was true. (*Crosses up back of chair Left of table*) Whether she admits it or not is another matter. But even if she doesn't admit it, you're not going to kick me out of the house. (*Crosses up to piano bench*) I'll go in the ordinary way, thank you.
(GORDON *sits platform above sofa.*)

ROBERT (*crosses Left to* FREDA). Freda, is it true?
(OLWEN *sits.*)

FREDA. Yes.

ROBERT. Has that been the trouble all along?

FREDA. Yes. All along.

ROBERT. When did it begin?

FREDA. A long time ago. Or it seems a long time ago, ages.

ROBERT. Before we were married?

FREDA. Yes. I thought I could—break it—then. I did for a little time. But it came back, worse than ever.

ROBERT. I wish you'd told me. Why didn't you tell me?

FREDA. I wanted to. Hundreds of times I tried to. . . . I said the opening words to myself so often—Sometimes I've hardly known whether I didn't actually say them out loud to you.

ROBERT. I wish you had. But why didn't I see it for myself? It seems plain enough now. I know now when it began. It was when we were all up at the lake that summer.

FREDA. Yes, it began then. Oh, that lovely, lovely summer! Nothing's ever been quite real since then.

ROBERT. Martin went away, and you said you'd stay a few days with the Hutchinsons. Was that—?

FREDA. Yes, Martin and I spent that little time together. It was the only time we really did spend together. It didn't mean much to him—a sort of experiment, that's all.

ROBERT. Didn't he care?

FREDA. No, not really. If he had, it would have been all so simple. That's why I never told you. And I thought when we were married, it would be—different. It wasn't fair to you, I know, but I thought it would be all right. But it wasn't. You know that too. It was hopeless. But you don't know how hopeless it was—for me.

ROBERT. But why didn't Martin tell me? He knew how unhappy I was.

FREDA. He couldn't. He was rather afraid of you.

ROBERT. Martin afraid of me?

GORDON. Yes, he was.

ROBERT. Nonsense. He wasn't afraid of anybody—and certainly not of me.

FREDA. Yes, he was, in some strange way.

GORDON. I know that. He told me that when you're really angry, you'll stop at nothing.

ROBERT. Queer. I never knew he felt like that. (*To* FREDA) It couldn't have been—this—

FREDA (*rises, crosses Left to fireplace*). No, no. He didn't care. Oh, Martin, Martin—

OLWEN (*rises*). Freda—don't. (*Steps down Centre.* ROBERT *turns out up Left.*)

STANTON (*crosses down Right*). That's how it goes on, you see. A good evening's work.

ROBERT (*facing Right*). I'm not regretting it. I'm glad all this has come out. I wish to God I'd known earlier, that's all.

STANTON. What difference would it have made? You couldn't have done anything.

ROBERT. To begin with, I'd have known the truth. And then something might have been done about it. I wouldn't have stood in their way.

STANTON (*crosses up Right to radio*). You didn't stand in their way.

GORDON (*rises*). No, it was Martin himself. As Freda says he didn't care. He told me about it. (*Crosses down to sofa.* OLWEN *crosses to piano bench.*)

FREDA (*turns Right*). Gordon, I don't believe you.

GORDON (*crosses Left to table Centre*). Why should I lie about it? Martin told me. He used to tell me everything.

FREDA. Rubbish. He thought you were a little nuisance—always hanging about him.

GORDON. That's not true.

FREDA (*crosses Right to table Centre*). It is. He told me so that—that very last Saturday, when I took him the cigarette box. He told me then he'd had to do everything he could to get rid of you.

GORDON. Freda—you're making this up, every word of it. I know you are. Martin would never have said that about me. He knew how fond I was of him, and he was fond of me too in his own way.

FREDA. He wasn't.

GORDON. You're just saying this because you're jealous.

FREDA. I'm not.

GORDON. You've always been jealous of Martin's interest in me.

FREDA. Gordon, that's a disgusting lie.

GORDON. It isn't.

FREDA. It is. He told me himself how tired he was of having you around him and suddenly becoming hysterical. I see what he meant now. Every time he's been mentioned tonight, you've been hysterical. What are you trying to make me believe you are?

ROBERT (*crosses down*). Freda, you're mad.

GORDON. It's all jealousy, jealousy. If he'd thought I was a nuisance, he wouldn't have kept asking me down to the cottage. (*Turning to* FREDA) But he was tired of you, pestering him and worrying him all the time. He didn't care for women. He was sick of them. He wanted me to tell you so that you'd leave him alone.

FREDA (*sits settee*). You're making me feel sick.

GORDON. Well, you just leave me—

OLWEN. Stop it. Stop it, both of you.

GORDON. And I was going to tell you too. Only then—he killed himself.

FREDA (*rises, crosses Left*). I don't believe it. I don't believe it. Martin couldn't have been so cruel. (OLWEN *sits piano bench.*)

GORDON. Couldn't he? What did he say to you that afternoon when you took him the cigarette box?

FREDA (*facing Right*). What does it matter what he said? You're just making up those abominable lies.

ROBERT (*crosses down between* FREDA *and* GORDON). Look here, I'm not having any more of this. I understand about you, Freda, and I'm sorry—(FREDA *turns out Left to fireplace*) but for God's sake keep quiet about it now. I can't stand any more. As for you, Gordon—you must be tight or something—

GORDON. I'm not. I'm as sober as you are. (*Crosses Right.*)

ROBERT. Well, behave as if you were. You're not a child. I know Martin was a friend of yours— (*Crosses up to piano.*)

GORDON (*turning on* ROBERT *hotly and scornfully*). Of course he was. Martin was the only person on earth I really cared about. I couldn't help it. There it was. I'd have done anything for him. Money, my God, I'd have stolen ten times the amount from the firm if Martin had asked me to. He was the most marvellous person I'd ever known. Sometimes I tried to hate him. Sometimes he gave me a hell of a time. But it didn't really matter. He was Martin, and I'd rather be with him, even if he was jeering at me all the time, than be with anybody else I've ever known. I'm like Freda—since he died, I haven't really cared a damn. He didn't really care for women. He tried to amuse himself with them, but he distrusted them, disliked them. He told me so, many times. (*Turns out Right*) Martin told me everything. And that was the finest thing that ever happened to me. (*Sits sofa*) And now you can call me any name you like, I don't care.

ROBERT. But what about Betty?

GORDON. You can leave her out of this.

ROBERT. I want to. But I can't help thinking about her.

GORDON. Well, you needn't. She can look after herself.

ROBERT. That's just what she can't do and she shouldn't have to. You ought to see that.

GORDON. Well, I don't see it. And I know Betty better than you do.

FREDA. You know everybody better than anybody else does, don't you? (OLWEN *rises.*)

GORDON. You would say that, wouldn't you? I can't help it if Martin liked me better than he liked you.

FREDA. How do you know that he—

OLWEN. Stop it, both of you. (*Crosses down*) Can't you see that Martin was making mischief, just to amuse himself?

GORDON. No, I can't. He wasn't like that.

STANTON (*crosses down to drinks*). Oh, no. Not at all like that. You couldn't ask for a quieter, simpler, more sincere fellow. (*Turns in Centre.*)

FREDA (*crosses to chair Left of table*). Nobody's going to pretend he was that. But at least he didn't steal money and then try to put the blame on other people. (*Sits.*)

STANTON. We could all start talking like that, Freda. Just throwing things at each other's heads. But I suggest we don't. (*Turns out up Right.*)

OLWEN (*up Centre*). I agree. But I do want Freda and Gordon to understand that it's simply madness quarrelling over anything Martin ever said to them. He was a born mischief-maker, cruel as a cat. That's one of the reasons why I disliked him so much.

ROBERT. Olwen!

OLWEN. Yes, I'm sorry, Robert, but I didn't like Martin. I detested him. You ought to have seen that.

STANTON (*turning in Left*). And you were quite right, Olwen. I'm afraid you always are.

OLWEN (*turns out up Centre*). No, I'm not.

STANTON. I'd trust your judgment. And you're the only one of us who

will come out of this as sound as you went in.
(*Turns up.*)

OLWEN. No, that's not true.

GORDON. No—it was Olwen and that damned cigarette box that began the whole business.

STANTON (*turns Right*). Oh, that was nothing. I knew about that all along.

OLWEN. You knew about what?

STANTON (*crosses Left to* OLWEN). I knew you'd been to see Martin that Saturday night.

OLWEN. You knew?

STANTON. Yes.

OLWEN. But how could you? I don't understand.

STANTON. I was spending that week-end at my own cottage. You remember that garage, where the road forks? You stopped there that night for some gas.

OLWEN. Yes, I believe I did.

STANTON. They told me, and said you'd taken the old road, and so I knew you must have been going to see Martin. You couldn't have been going anywhere else, could you? Quite simple.

OLWEN. And you've known all this time?

STANTON. Yes, all this time.
(OLWEN *turns up stage and crosses to window platform.*)

ROBERT. I suppose, Stanton, it's no use asking you why you've never said a word about it?

STANTON. I'm afraid not. I think I've done my share in the confession box tonight.
(OLWEN *sits window Left.*)

GORDON. Well, I wish I'd known a bit more, that's all. There was I dragged into that foul inquest. Did I know this? Did I know that? My God—and all the time, I wasn't the last person he'd talked to at all. (*Rises*) Freda had been there some time in the afternoon. And Olwen was there that very night, at the very moment—for all we know.

STANTON (*crosses down*). Don't talk rubbish.

GORDON. Well, is it rubbish? After all, what do we know? What was Olwen doing there?

ROBERT. She's told us that. She was there to talk to Martin about the money.
(*Crosses up Left to piano bench.*)

GORDON. And how far does that take us?

STANTON. What do you mean by that?

FREDA. He means—I imagine—that Olwen hasn't told us very much so far. We know she went to Martin to talk to him about the missing money. And that he thought Robert had taken it and that she thought so too. And that's all we do know.

GORDON (STANTON *crosses down Left*). Yes, we don't know how long she was there or what Martin said to her, or anything. It's a good thing she wasn't pushed in front of that coroner or they'd have had it out of her in no time. (*Crosses up Right*) I think it's up to her to tell us a little more.

STANTON (*crosses Left to piano*). Well, there's no need to sound so damned vindictive about it.
(OLWEN *looking out through the window suddenly starts back and says as* FREDA *rises.*)

OLWEN. Somebody's out there.

ROBERT (*opens window and looking out*). There's no one there now.

OLWEN. No, they darted away. But I'll swear there was somebody. They'd been listening.

STANTON (*crosses down Left*). Well, they couldn't have chosen a better night for it.

ROBERT (*closing window*). It's impossible, Olwen. And there isn't a sign of anybody.

GORDON (*crossing down Right*). Thank the Lord for that.
(*There are several short rings of a door bell heard from off.* FREDA *rises.*)

ROBERT. Who on earth can this be?

FREDA (*crosses down above settee*). Don't ask me. I haven't the slightest idea. Go and see.

ROBERT. Yes, I know. But we don't want anybody interrupting us now.

FREDA. Well, don't let them interrupt us, whoever they are. But you'll have to see who it is.

(*The bell rings again and* ROBERT *goes out.* GORDON *crosses to below steps Right.*)

ROBERT (*heard outside*). But we haven't, I tell you. You've never been mentioned.

BETTY (*outside*). I know you have. I can feel it. That's why I had to come back.

ROBERT (*outside*). I tell you we haven't.
(ROBERT *opens the door and* BETTY *is seen in front of him.*)

GORDON (*as* BETTY *enters*). I thought you'd gone to bed, Betty. What's the matter?

BETTY (ROBERT *enters and shuts door. On the platform*). You're talking about me, all of you. (*Looking round them all*) I know you are. I wanted to go to bed. I started to go. And then I couldn't. I knew you were all talking about me. I couldn't stand it. I had to come.

FREDA (*crosses up to back of chair Left of table*). Well, you were wrong. As a matter of fact, you're the one person we haven't been talking about.

BETTY. Is that true?

ROBERT. Yes, of course.

OLWEN (*to* BETTY). You were outside just now, weren't you? Outside the window, listening.

BETTY. No, I wasn't listening. I was trying to look in, to see exactly who was here and what you all looked like. You see, I was sure you were all saying things about me. I meant to go to bed and I was tired, but I felt too excited to sleep and now I'm so damn nervous. (*Crosses down steps Left*) God knows what I shall be saying in a minute. You mustn't mind me. (*Sits chair Right of table.*)

ROBERT (*crosses down step Left to Right of chair Right of table*). I'm so sorry, Betty. (OLWEN *crosses up to window and sits Right*) Not a word's been said about you. In fact, we all wanted to keep you out of this. It's all rather unpleasant.

FREDA. Seeing that Betty has married into one of the families concerned, I think she ought not to be too carefully protected from the sordid truth.

ROBERT. Keep quiet, Freda.

FREDA. I thought we should see a different Robert now.
(*Crosses down.*)

ROBERT. After what you've said tonight, I can't see that it matters much to you how different I may be.

FREDA. Perhaps not, but I still like reasonably decent manners.
(*Sits on settee.*)

ROBERT. Then set us an example.
(*Crosses up Right below chair up Right.*)

GORDON. Oh, be still, both of you.

BETTY. But what have you been talking about then?

GORDON (*crosses Left*). It began with the money.

BETTY. You mean that Martin took?

GORDON (*back of* BETTY'S *chair*). Martin didn't take it. We know that now. Stanton took that money. He's admitted it.
(*Crosses up to piano bench and leans against piano.*)

BETTY. Admitted it! Stan—Stanton. Oh, surely—it's impossible.

STANTON (*crosses to back of chair Left of table*). It sounds impossible, doesn't it, Betty, but it isn't. I'm sorry to go down with such a bump in your estimation, my dear Betty, but this is our night for telling the truth, and I've had to admit that I took that money. Terrible, isn't it?

ROBERT (*crosses down*). What did you mean by that, Stanton?

STANTON. I meant what I said. I nearly always do.

ROBERT. Why did you use that tone of voice to Betty?

STANTON. Perhaps because I think that Betty has not a very high opinion of me—and so need not have sounded so surprised and shocked.
(*Crosses out Left.*)

ROBERT. I don't quite understand that.

FREDA. I'm sure you don't, Robert.

ROBERT. Do you?

FREDA. Yes, I think so.

BETTY. But if Martin didn't take the money—then why—why did he shoot himself?

GORDON. That's what we want to know. Olwen saw him last of all, that very evening, and she knew he hadn't taken the money, but that's all she's told us.

OLWEN. I've told you that he thought Robert had taken the money.

ROBERT (*crosses down to arm of sofa*). And that was enough—in the state he was in then—to throw him clean off his balance. All that stuff about his merely being amused is nonsense. That was just his bluff. Martin hated anybody to think he was really moved or alarmed by anything.

GORDON. That's true.

ROBERT. And he depended on me. He used to laugh at me a lot, but that was nothing. He depended on me. You've told me yourselves—that he was secretly rather frightened of me. It was because Martin had a respect for me. He thought I was the solid steady one. I tell you, it must have been a hell of a shock to poor Martin.

OLWEN. I don't think it was, Robert.

STANTON. Neither do I.

ROBERT. But neither of you knew him as I did. What's the good of talking. He was in a wretched state, all run down and neurotic, and when he heard that I'd taken the check he must have felt that there was nobody left he could depend on, that I'd let him down. He'd probably been brooding over it day and night—he was that sort. He wouldn't let you see it, Olwen. He wouldn't let anybody see it. But it would be there all the time, giving him hell. Oh! what a fool I was. I ought to have gone straight to him and told him what Stanton has told me.

GORDON (*crosses down Left to* STANTON). If this is true, then the person really responsible is Stanton.

FREDA. Yes.

STANTON (*crosses up*). Rubbish.

FREDA. It isn't. Don't you see what you did?

STANTON (*turning down at corner of piano*). No, because I don't believe it.

GORDON. No, because you don't choose to, that's all.

STANTON. Oh, talk sense. Can't you see Martin had his own reasons?

ROBERT (*crosses Left*). No. What drove him to suicide was my stupidity and your damned lying, Stanton. That settles it once and for all!

STANTON. You're not in a state to settle anything.

ROBERT. Listen to me, Stanton—

STANTON. Oh, drop it, man.

GORDON. You've got to answer.

ROBERT. I'll never forgive you for telling Martin what you did—by God! I won't.

STANTON. You've got it all wrong.

GORDON (*crosses up to* STANTON). They haven't, you rotten liar. You made Martin shoot himself.

OLWEN. Wait a minute, Gordon. Martin didn't shoot himself.

MEDIUM CURTAIN

ACT THREE

ALL *are discovered in exactly the same positions as they were at the end of Act II.*

FREDA (*rising*). Martin didn't shoot himself?

OLWEN (*on window platform*). No. I shot him. (*Crosses down to Left of drinks.* BETTY *rises.*)

FREDA (*crosses up between table and chair Left of table*). Olwen!

ROBERT (*crosses up Right of piano bench*). That's impossible, Olwen. You couldn't have done it.

GORDON (*below chair up Left*). Are you joking?

OLWEN. I wish I were.

GORDON. Olwen!

ROBERT. She must be hysterical.

STANTON (*by piano crosses Right Centre*). Olwen's not hysterical. She means it.

BETTY (*crosses up to piano bench*). Oh, Lord!—She can't mean—she murdered him? Can she?

STANTON (*crosses in up Right Centre*). You might as well tell us exactly what happened now, Olwen. And I might as well tell you—before you begin—that I'm not at all surprised. I suspected this from the first.

OLWEN (*turning Left*). You suspected I had done it? But why?

STANTON. For three reasons. The first was, that I couldn't understand why Martin should shoot himself. You see, I knew he hadn't taken the money, and though he was in every kind of mess, he didn't seem to me the sort who'd get out of it that way. Then I knew you'd been with him quite late, because—as I said before—I'd been told you'd gone that way. And the third reason—well, that'll keep. You'd better tell us what happened now. (OLWEN *sits on platform above sofa*) It was an accident, wasn't it? (BETTY *sits on piano bench.*)

OLWEN. Yes, it was really an accident. (FREDA *sits on chair Left of table*) I'll tell you what happened but I can't go into details. It's all too muddled and horrible. But I'll tell you the complete truth. I won't hide anything more, I promise you.

I think we'd all better tell everything we know now, really speak our minds.

STANTON. Yes, of course.

OLWEN. I went to see Martin that Saturday night, as you know, to talk to him about the missing money. Mr. Whitehouse had told me about it. He thought that either Martin or Robert must have taken it. I gathered it was more likely Robert. So I went to see Martin. I didn't like Martin and he knew it but he knew too what I felt about Robert, and after all, he was Robert's brother. He believed that Robert had taken the money and he wasn't a bit worried about it. I'm sorry, Robert, but he wasn't. I hated him for that too. He was rather maliciously amused. The good brother fallen at last—that sort of thing.

FREDA. I can believe that. I hate to, but I know he could be like that!

OLWEN. I've never seen him as bad as he was that night. He wasn't really sane.

ROBERT. Olwen.

OLWEN. I'm sorry, Robert. I didn't want you to know all this, but there's no help for it now. You see, Martin had been taking some sort of drug!

ROBERT. Drug!

OLWEN. Yes. He'd had a lot of it.

ROBERT. Are you sure? I can't believe it.

GORDON. It's true. You remember when he went to Berlin and how nervous he was just then? Well, a fellow he met there put him on to it—some new drug that a lot of the so-called Bohemians were doping themselves with—

FREDA. But did Martin . . . ?

GORDON. Yes, he liked it, and took more and more of it!

ROBERT. But how could he get it? (*Cross Left to above chair Left.*)

GORDON. Through some one he knew in town. When he couldn't get it, he was pretty rotten.

STANTON. But didn't you try to stop him?

GORDON. Of course—but he only laughed. (*Crosses down*) I don't blame him really. None of you can understand what life was like to Martin—he was so sensitive. He was one of those people who are meant to be happy. (*Sits on settee facing up.*)

STANTON (*crosses up Right. Leans on radio*). We're all those people who are meant to be happy. Martin's no exception.

ROBERT. Yes, that's true. But I know what Gordon means.

FREDA. You couldn't help knowing what he means, if you knew Martin. There was no sort of middle state, no easy jog-trot for him. Either he had to be gay—and when he was gay, he was gayer than anybody else in the world—or he was intensely miserable.

ROBERT (*back to piano*). But what about this drug, Olwen?

OLWEN. He took some—while I was there and it had a terrible effect on him. It gave him a sort of devilish gaiety. I can see him now. His eyes were queer. Oh—he really wasn't sane. (*Stops.*)

ROBERT. What happened?

OLWEN. I've tried not to think about it. He knew I disliked him, but he was so frightfully conceited that he couldn't believe it. He seemed to think that everybody young, male or female, ought to be falling in love with him. He saw himself as a sort of Pan.

FREDA. Yes, he did. And he'd every reason to.

OLWEN. He began taunting me. He thought of me or pretended to—as a priggish spinster, full of repressions, who's never really lived. All rubbish, because I'm really not that type at all. But he pretended to think I was and kept telling me that my dislike of him showed that I was trying to repress a great fascination he had for me. And of course that all these repressions were bad for me. I'd never lived, never would live, and all the rest of it. He talked a lot about that. I ought to have run out and left him, but I felt I couldn't while he was in that state. In a way I was sorry for him, because really he was ill, sick in mind and body, and I thought perhaps I could calm him down. I might dislike him, but after all he wasn't a stranger. He was one of our own set, mixed up with most of the people I liked best in the world. I tried to stop him. But everything I said seemed to make him worse. I suppose it would when he was in that excited abnormal state. Well, he talked about my repressions, and when I pretended to laugh at him, he got more and more excited. And then he tried to show me some beastly foul drawings he had—horrible obscene things by some mad Belgian artist—

FREDA (*rises*). Oh—my God— (*Crosses up to back of chair Right of table.*)

OLWEN (*rises*). Oh, Freda, I'm so sorry. Please forgive me. I know how this thing must be hurting you.

FREDA. Martin. Martin.

OLWEN (*crosses Left to back chair Right of table*). Don't listen to any more. I'll stop if you like.

FREDA. Oh—he wasn't like that really. If you'd known him as I'd known him—before.

OLWEN. I know that. We all do. He was different. He was ill.

FREDA (*crosses up Centre, turns*). Go on, Olwen. (*Crosses up to window platform Left, holds on to curtains.*)

ROBERT. Yes, Olwen. You can't stop now.

OLWEN (*back of chair Right of table*). There isn't a lot to tell you. When I pushed his beastly drawings away and was rather indignant about them, he got still more excited, completely unbalanced, and shouted out things about my repressions. And then I found he was telling me to take my clothes off. (FREDA *sits*) I told him not to be a fool and that I was going. But then he stood between me and the door. And he had a revolver in his hand and was shouting, something about danger and terror and love. He wasn't threatening me with it or himself. He was just waving it about—being dramatic. I didn't even believe it was loaded. (*Crosses Right to drinks*) But by this time I'd had more than enough of him—I couldn't be sorry for him any more—and I told him to get out of the way. When he wouldn't, I tried to push him out of the way. And then we had a struggle. He tried to tear my clothes. We really fought one another. It was horrible He wasn't any stronger than I was. I'd grabbed the hand with the revolver in it. I'd turned the revolver towards him. His finger must have been on the trigger. I must have given it a jerk. The revolver went off. Oh— Horrible— (*Sits on platform above sofa*) horrible. I've tried and tried to forget that. If he'd just been wounded, I wouldn't have left him alone. But he wasn't. He was dead.

ROBERT. Yes, we understand that. You needn't tell us.

OLWEN. When I realised what had happened, I rushed out and sat in my car for I don't know how long. I couldn't move a finger. There was nobody about. It was fairly late and you know how lonely that cottage was. I just sat on and on in the car, shivering, and it was so quiet in the cottage, so horribly quiet. I've gone through that over and over again. (FREDA *rises.*)

ROBERT. You can't be blamed, Olwen.

(FREDA *opens the windows and sits Centre.*)

STANTON (*crosses Left below chair up Left*). Of course she can't be blamed. And there must never be a word spoken about this—not to anybody. We must all promise that.

OLWEN. Give me a cigarette, Robert. (ROBERT *crosses to* OLWEN, *gives her a cigarette and lights it for her.*)

GORDON (*rises, crosses up Left between table and chair Right of table*). It's a pity we can't all be as cool and business-like about this as you are, Stanton.

STANTON. I don't feel very cool and business-like about it. But you see, it's not as big a surprise to me as it is to you people. I guessed long ago that something like this had happened. (*Turns out Left.*)

ROBERT. But it looked so much like suicide that nobody bothered to suggest it wasn't. It never seemed to me to be anything else. All the evidence pointed that way. I can't think how you could have guessed even though you knew Olwen had been there.

STANTON (*crosses Right above Left end of settee*). I told you I had a third reason. I was over fairly early next morning— The postman rang me up—and I was there before anybody but the village constable and the doctor. And I found something on the floor (OLWEN *rises*) that they had overlooked, (OLWEN *crosses down Left before table Centre*) I've kept it ever since. (*Brings out pocketbook and produces a small square of patterned silk.*)

OLWEN (*crosses down Left to settee*). Let me see. Yes, that's a piece of the dress I was wearing. It was torn in the struggle we had. So that's how you knew?

STANTON. Yes.

OLWEN. But why didn't you say something?

GORDON. I can tell you that. He didn't say anything because he wanted everybody to think that Martin had shot himself. (*Crosses up to Radio*) You see, that meant that Martin must have taken the money.

(OLWEN *sits on settee,* STANTON *turns out Left.*)

ROBERT. That's about it, I suppose. It falls into line with everything we've heard from him tonight.

STANTON (*turning Right*). No, there happened to be another reason, much more important. I knew that if Olwen had had a hand in Martin's death, then something like that must have happened, and so Olwen couldn't be blamed. I knew her better than any of you—or I felt I did. And I trusted her. She's about the only person I would trust. She knows all about that. I've told her often enough. She's not interested, but there it is. (*Turns down Left.*)

OLWEN. And you never even hinted to me that you knew.

STANTON (*turns Right to* OLWEN). Surprising isn't it? What a chance I missed to capture your interest for a few minutes! But I couldn't take that line with you. I suppose even nowadays, when we're all so damned tough, there has got to be one person that you behave to always as if you were Sir Roger de Coverley, and with me you've been that person for a long time now. And I knew all along that you were saying nothing because you thought Robert had taken the money and that he was safe after everybody assumed it was Martin. And that didn't always make it any easier for me. (*Turns out Left.*)

BETTY (*rises*). No? What a shame. But what a fine romantic character you are, aren't you? (*Crosses below piano.*)

ROBERT. Betty. You don't understand.

FREDA. How could she?

BETTY (*turning up*). Why do you say that—in that tone of voice?

FREDA (*rises*). Why does one say anything—in any tone of voice? (*Turns out up.*)

OLWEN (*to* STANTON). You know, I nearly did take you into my confidence. And that might have made a difference. But I chose a bad moment.

STANTON (*steps Right*). Why? When was this? Tell me.

OLWEN. I told you I sat in my car that night for some time not able to do anything. But then, when I felt a little better, I had to tell somebody, and you were the nearest person.

STANTON. But you didn't go there—that night?

OLWEN. Yes, I did. (STANTON *turns out Left*) I drove over to your cottage that very Saturday night. I got there about eleven o'clock or just afterwards. I left my car at the bottom of that tiny narrow lane and walked up to your cottage. And then—I walked back again.

STANTON. So that's when you came. After that, it was hopeless.

OLWEN. Quite hopeless, I think that added the last touch to that night. I don't think I've ever felt the same about people—not just here, but everybody, even the people who walk into the office or sit opposite one in buses and trains—since that night. I know that's stupid, but I couldn't help it. And you must all have noticed that I've been completely off country cottages.

FREDA. Yes, even Betty's noticed that.

ROBERT (*crosses Left to* BETTY). Why, what's the matter, Betty?

GORDON. What a little liar you are, Betty!

BETTY. Haven't we all been liars?

ROBERT. But you haven't, Betty.

GORDON (*crosses down to Left of sofa*). Oh, don't be a fool, Robert. Of course she has. She's lied like fury.

ROBERT. What about?

FREDA. Why don't you ask her?

OLWEN. Oh, what does it matter? Leave the child alone.

BETTY. I'm not a child. That's the mistake you've all made.

ROBERT. Not you—and Stanton? Is that what they mean? Why don't you tell them it's ridiculous?

FREDA. How can she? Don't be absurd.

STANTON. Oh, drop this. I'm going.

BETTY. You're not going!

STANTON. Don't be a fool. It's no business of yours.

FREDA. That's where you're wrong, Stanton.

ROBERT. I'm waiting for an answer, Betty.

BETTY. What do you want me to say?

ROBERT. Were you with Stanton at his cottage?

BETTY. Yes.

ROBERT. Were you his mistress?

BETTY. Yes.

ROBERT. Betty—in God's name—Stanton—how could you?

BETTY. How could I? Because I'm not a child. You would drag all this out and now you can damned well have it. Yes, I stayed with Stanton that night, and I've stayed with him other nights. And he's not in love with me and I know it, and I'm not in love with him. I wouldn't marry him if I could. But I had to make something happen. Gordon was driving me mad. If you want to call someone a child, then call him one, for that's all he is. (ROBERT *turns out up*) This damned marriage of ours that you all get so sentimental about is the biggest sham there's ever been. It isn't a marriage at all. It's just nothing—pretence, pretence, pretence. Betty darling and Gordon darling, the very sight of him makes me want to scream. (*Head turns out up.*)

FREDA. Betty, you mustn't go—

BETTY. It's not my fault. (*Turns down*) I was in love with him when we were married and I thought everything was going to be marvellous. I wouldn't have looked at anybody else if he'd been —real. But he just isn't. He can't even talk to me.

GORDON. For God's sake, keep quiet, Betty.

BETTY. I won't. They want to know the truth and they can have it. I don't care. I've had nothing, nothing out of my marriage. If I were the child you all thought me, perhaps it wouldn't have mattered. But I'm not. I'm a woman. And Stanton was the one person who guessed what was happening and treated me like a woman.

GORDON. I wouldn't have blamed you if you'd fallen in love with someone, but this was just a low sordid intrigue, a dirty little affair, not worth all your silly lies. I suppose Stanton gave you all those fine presents?

BETTY. Yes, he did. You couldn't even be generous, though you'd have given your precious Martin everything we'd had. I know Stanton didn't really care for me. But men who say they're in love with one woman and spend their weekends with another deserve all they get.

FREDA (*to* STANTON). Is that why you suddenly had to have that money?

STANTON. Queer, how it works out, isn't it?

GORDON. Then Betty is responsible for all this misery, for Martin!

BETTY. Always Martin. If I was responsible for all that, then it's your fault really, Gordon. Because you're responsible for everything that happened to me. You never should have married me.

GORDON. I didn't know. It was a mistake. (*Sits platform above sofa.*)

FREDA. We seem to make that kind of mistake in our family.

BETTY. I ought to have left you long before this. That was my mistake—staying on—trying to make the best of it—pretending to be married to one who wasn't there —simply dead!

ROBERT (*turning down. To* BETTY). I suppose you knew how I felt about you!

BETTY. Yes. But I didn't care very much.

ROBERT. No, why should you?

BETTY. No. It isn't that. But I knew you weren't in love with me. You didn't know me. You were only worshipping somebody you'd invented, who looked like me. And that's not the same thing at all.

ROBERT. Yes, I even thought that you and Gordon were happy together—

BETTY. Yes, we put up a good show, didn't we?

ROBERT. You did. (*Turns out up above piano bench.*)

GORDON. Yes, we did. What would have happened if we'd gone on pretending like hell to be happy together?

BETTY. Nothing.

GORDON. No. If we'd gone on pretending long enough, I believe we might have been happy together, some time. It often works out like that.

BETTY. Never.

OLWEN. Yes, it does. That's why all this is so wrong, really. The real truth is something so deep you can't get at it this way, and all this half truth does is to blow everything up. It isn't civilised.

STANTON. I agree.

ROBERT (*crosses down between two chairs*). You agree. You might as well.

STANTON. You'll get no sympathy from me.

ROBERT. Sympathy from you? I never want to set eyes on you again, you're a thief, a liar, and a dirty seducer.

STANTON (*back to fireplace*). And you're a fool. You look solid but you're not. You've a good deal in common with that cracked brother of yours. You won't face real things. You've been living in a fool's paradise, and now, having got yourself out of it by tonight's efforts—all your doing—you're busy building yourself a fool's hell to live in.

ROBERT. I think this was your glass, Stanton. (*Crosses to table and picks up glass. Moves up to window and throws it out*) And now take yourself after it. Get out.
(FREDA *turns out up.*)

STANTON (*crosses Centre and stops*). Good-night, Olwen. I'm sorry about all this.

OLWEN. So am I. Good-night.

STANTON (*crosses Right to steps*). Good-night, Freda.

FREDA. Good-night.

GORDON (*as* STANTON *crosses up steps to platform*). Don't forget, Stanton, we expect your resignation.

STANTON (*turning*). Oh, you're going to take it that way, are you?

GORDON. Yes, I'm going to take it that way.

STANTON. Good-night. No, don't trouble. I can find my way out. (*He exits and closes door.*)

OLWEN. Don't be too hasty, Gordon. (GORDON *rises*) Whatever his faults, Stanton's a first-class man at his job. If he goes, the firm will suffer.

GORDON (*crosses Right*). I can't help it. I couldn't work with him after this. The firm will have to suffer, that's all.

ROBERT. Don't worry. It's not a case of the firm suffering. The firm's smashed to hell now.

FREDA (*steps down from platform*). Nonsense.

ROBERT. Is it? I don't think so.

GORDON. Well, Betty darling, I think we'd better return to our happy little home, our dear little nest. (*Crosses up steps.* FREDA *crosses Right.*)

BETTY. Oh, don't, Gordon.

FREDA (*crosses up steps Left*). I'll let you out.
(*Exit* GORDON. *Exit* FREDA. BETTY *picks up coat and starts for door.*)

ROBERT (*to* BETTY). Good-bye. (*Staring at her.*)

BETTY (*stops Centre*). Why do *you* look like that?

ROBERT. I'm not saying good-bye to you. I don't know you. I never did, it seems.
(BETTY *crosses up steps Left and exits.* ROBERT *turns, crosses down Right to drinks. As* ROBERT *pours drink,* OLWEN *rises and speaks:*)

OLWEN. Robert, please don't drink any more tonight. I know how you feel, but it'll only make you worse —really it will. (*Crosses up to Left arm of chair Left of table.*)

ROBERT (*crosses Left to back of chair Right of table*). What does it matter? I'm through, anyway. (*He drinks.*)

OLWEN. Robert, I can't bear seeing you like this. You don't know how it hurts me.

ROBERT (*crosses Left to Right arm of chair Left of table*). I'm sorry, Olwen, I really am sorry. You're the only one who's really come out of this. I know that. Strange, isn't it—that you should have been feeling like that about me all the time. I'm sorry. (*Faces down.*)

OLWEN (*back of chair Left of table*). I'm not. I mean about myself. I suppose I ought to be, but I'm not. It hurt at times but it kept me going.

ROBERT. I know. And you see, now I've stopped going. Something's broken—inside.

OLWEN. It won't seem bad tomorrow. It never does.

ROBERT. All this isn't going to seem any better tomorrow, Olwen.

OLWEN. Freda will help you. After all, Robert, she's fond of you.

ROBERT. No, not really. It isn't that she dislikes me steadily, but every now and then she hates me—and now I see why, of course. She hates me because I'm Robert and not Martin, because he's dead and I'm alive.

OLWEN. She may feel differently—after tonight.

ROBERT. She may. I doubt it. She doesn't change easily—that's the trouble. And then again, you see, I don't care any more. That's the point. Whether she changes or doesn't change I don't care now.

OLWEN. You know there's nothing I wouldn't do for you, Robert.

ROBERT. I'm terribly grateful, Olwen. But nothing happens here—inside. (FREDA *enters*) That's the damned awful cruel thing. Nothing happens. (*Sits Right arm chair Left of table*) All hollow, empty.
(FREDA *closes door.* OLWEN *turns up to piano.*)

FREDA (*on top step*). I'm sure, it's not at all the proper thing to say at such a moment, but the fact remains that I feel rather hungry. (*Crosses down steps Left*) What about you, Olwen? You, Robert? Or have you been drinking too much? (*Crosses Left to* ROBERT.)

ROBERT. Yes, I've been drinking too much.

FREDA. Well, it's very silly of you. (*Takes empty glass from* ROBERT.)

ROBERT. Yes.

FREDA (*puts her hand on* ROBERT's *shoulder*). And you did ask for all this.

ROBERT. I asked for it. And I got it.

FREDA. Though I doubt if you minded very much until it came to Betty.

ROBERT. That's not true. But I can understand your thinking so. You see, as more and more of this rotten stuff came out (FREDA *takes hand away from* ROBERT's *shoulder*), so more and more I came to depend on my secret thoughts of Betty—as someone who seemed to me to represent some lovely quality of life.

FREDA. I've known some time, of course, that you were getting very sentimental about her. And I've known some time too all about Betty (*Turns Right*), and I've often thought of telling you. (*Crosses Right to drinks.*)

ROBERT. I'm not sorry you didn't.

FREDA (*puts glass down*). You ought to be.

ROBERT. Why?

FREDA (*sits arm of sofa*). That kind of self-deception's rather stupid.

ROBERT. What about you and Martin?

FREDA. I didn't deceive myself. I knew everything—or nearly everything—about him. I wasn't in love with somebody I'd made up!

ROBERT. I think you were. Probably we always are.

OLWEN (*crosses down back of chair Left of table*). Then it's not so bad. You can always build up another image for yourself to fall in love with.

ROBERT. No, you can't. That's the trouble. You lose the capacity for building. You run short of the stuff that creates beautiful illusions, just as if a gland had stopped working.

OLWEN. Then you have to learn to live without illusions.

ROBERT. Can't be done. Not for us. We started life too early for that. Possibly they're breeding people now who can live without illusions.

I hope so. But I can't do it. (*Rises*) I've lived among illusions. (*Turns up.*)

FREDA. You have.

ROBERT (*turns back*). Well, what if I have? They've given me hope and courage, they've helped me to live. I suppose we ought to get all that from faith in life. But I haven't got any. No religion or anything. Just this empty damned shell to live in. And a few damn glands and secretions and nerves to do it with. But it didn't look too bad. I'd my little illusions, you see. (*Turns out up.*)

FREDA (*rises, crosses up Left above chair Right of table*). Then why didn't you leave them alone, instead of clamoring for the truth all night like a fool?

ROBERT (*turning on* FREDA). Because I am a fool. Stanton was right. That's the only answer. I had to meddle, like a child, with fire. I began this evening with something to keep me going. I'd good memories of Martin. I'd a wife who didn't love me (FREDA *half turns out down*) but at least seemed too good for me. I'd two partners I liked and respected. There was a girl I could idealise. And now—

OLWEN. No, Robert—please. We know.

ROBERT. But you don't know, you can't know—not as I know—or you wouldn't stand there like that, as if we'd only just had some damned silly little squabble about a hand at bridge.

OLWEN. This is mad!

ROBERT. Don't you see, we're not living in the same world now. Everything's gone. My brother was an obscene lunatic—

FREDA. Stop that. (*Crosses up Centre.*)

ROBERT (*following* FREDA). And my wife doted on him and pestered him. (*Turns Left to* OLWEN) One of my partners is a liar and a cheat and a thief. (*Turns to out*) The other—God knows what he is—(*Crosses Right to steps and up steps. The lights begin to dim*) And the girl's a greedy little cat.

FREDA (*grabs his hand*). Robert, please!

OLWEN (*crosses to back of chair Right of table*). No, Robert. It won't be like this tomorrow!!

ROBERT (*on platform*). Tomorrow. Tomorrow. I tell you, I'm through, I'm through. There can't be a tomorrow. (*Runs out. As* ROBERT *goes through the door the lights dim out except moonlight and light in hall.*)

FREDA. He's got a revolver in his bedroom.

OLWEN. Stop, Robert. Stop. Stop! (*In the darkness* MISS MOCKRIDGE *and* BETTY *enter through invisible door Left end of window platform and take the same positions as in the blackout in Act I. After a moment's pause there is the sound of a revolver shot off stage Right.* BETTY *gives a sharp little scream. Startled exclamations from the other three women.* FREDA *advances towards the door.*)

FREDA (*calling*). Robert, Robert, what was that! (*Pause*) Robert!!

ROBERT'S VOICE (*off Right*). It's all right. I was showing them my gun and took a crack at a flower pot. (FREDA *switches on the lights.*)

GORDON'S VOICE. Pretty good shot. . . .

ROBERT'S VOICE. And what's more I hit it!

STANTON'S VOICE. Pretty lucky, I'll say. . . .

ROBERT'S VOICE. We'll be in in a minute!

FREDA. I should hope so. Those idiots firing Robert's revolver out the window! (*Crosses Left. The positions and movement identical with Act I.*)

BETTY. You ought to take it away from him. They nearly frightened the life out of me.

FREDA. Well, we've no hope of seeing our ghost bird now. If it was there, it must have cleared out pretty quickly.

BETTY. I should think so after all that racket.

OLWEN. Perhaps it will come back later.

FREDA. No, I hardly think so. I've never caught sight of it much after ten.

MISS MOCKRIDGE. I suppose you all miss your brother-in-law. He used to be up here with you too, didn't he?

FREDA. You mean Robert's brother, Martin?

MRS. MOCKRIDGE. Yes.

FREDA. What made you think of Martin just then?

MISS MOCKRIDGE. Well, I don't quite know. He just came into my head, I suppose.

FREDA. It must have been the shot.

MISS MOCKRIDGE. Oh, surely not. I was away at the time and never quite understood what happened. Something rather dreadful, wasn't it? I'm sorry if I—

FREDA. No, it's all right. It was very distressing for us at the time, but it's done with now. Martin shot himself. It happened a year ago—last October, in fact—at his own cottage, about twenty miles from here.

MISS MOCKRIDGE. Oh, yes, dreadful business, of course. I only met him twice, I think. I remember I thought him very amusing and charming. He was very handsome, wasn't he?
(*Enter* STANTON *and* GORDON.)

OLWEN. Yes, very handsome.

STANTON. Who's very handsome?

FREDA. Not you, Charles.

STANTON. Well, who is it, or is it a secret?

GORDON. They must have been talking about me. Betty, why do you allow them to rave about your husband?

BETTY. Darling, I'm sure you've had too much manly gossip and old brandy. You're beginning to look purple in the face and bloated —a typical financier.

(*Enter* ROBERT, *switching on extra light as he enters.*)

ROBERT. Why so dim? Sorry about that gun, Freda. It was stupid. I hope it didn't frighten anybody.

FREDA. As a matter of fact, it did. All of us.

MISS MOCKRIDGE. Yes, and I'd just been saying what a charming little group you've made here, all of you.

ROBERT. I'm glad you think so.

MISS MOCKRIDGE. I think you've all been lucky.

ROBERT. I agree, we have.

STANTON. It's not all luck, Miss Mockridge. You see, we all happened to be nice easy-going people.

ROBERT (*smiling at her*). Except Betty—she's terribly wild.

STANTON. That's only because Gordon doesn't beat her often enough —yet.

MISS MOCKRIDGE. You see, Miss Peel, Mr. Stanton is still the cynical bachelor. I'm afraid he rather spoils the picture.

GORDON. I wonder if there's any dance music on the radio tonight?

ROBERT. I hope not. Let's be quiet. What have you people been talking about?

FREDA. Olwen had been telling us about *The Sleeping Dog.*

ROBERT. *The Sleeping Dog?* Oh—that novel we're going to publish, the one she's so keen on.

STANTON. Why does he call it that?

OLWEN. Don't you know the proverb—Let Sleeping Dogs Lie?

STANTON. Where does that come into it?

FREDA. From what Olwen says, the sleeping dog represents truth.

OLWEN. Yes, and the chief character—the husband—insisted upon disturbing it.

ROBERT. Well, he was quite right to disturb it.

STANTON. Was he? I wonder. I think it a very sound idea—the truth as a sleeping dog.

MISS MOCKRIDGE. Still we do spend too much of our time telling lies and acting them.

BETTY. Oh, but one has to. I'm always fibbing. I do it all day long.

GORDON (*still at radio*). You do, darling. You do.

BETTY. It's the secret of my charm.

MISS MOCKRIDGE. Very likely. But we meant something more serious.

ROBERT. Serious or not, I'm all for it coming out. It's healthy.

STANTON. I think telling the truth's about as healthy as skidding round a corner at sixty. What do you think, Olwen . . . you're looking terribly wise?

OLWEN. I agree with you. I think telling everything is dangerous. What most people mean by the truth is only half the truth.

FREDA. Well, let's talk about something else. Who wants a drink? Drinks, Robert, and cigarettes. (*Crosses to table down Left, picks up cigarette box*) Cigarette, Miss Mockridge.

MISS MOCKRIDGE (*rising*). No, thanks, I'm a slave to my own brand!

FREDA (*crosses to* OLWEN). Cigarette, Olwen?

OLWEN (*taking box from* FREDA). Oh, I remember that box. It plays a tune, doesn't it? I remember the tune. (*Opens box*) Yes, it's the Wedding March.
(*As it plays.*)

ROBERT. Good, isn't it!

GORDON (*who has been fiddling with the radio suddenly says*). Wait a minute. Listen to this.
(*"Can't We Talk It Over?" gradually fades in on the radio set.*)

BETTY (*rising*). Oh, I adore that tune.

STANTON. What is it?

BETTY. "Can't We Talk It Over?"

MISS MOCKRIDGE. What?

GORDON (*he starts to dance with* BETTY). "Can't We Talk It Over?" (OLWEN *moves up Centre.* STANTON *crosses up to her and they start to dance.* MISS MOCKRIDGE *takes a cigarette from her case and* FREDA *lights it for her.* ROBERT *crosses down to them and they stand talking as the*

CURTAIN

falls. The CURTAIN *goes up again,* OLWEN *and* STANTON *continue dancing;* GORDON *and* BETTY *continue to dance; the* GROUP *by the fireplace watch them in animated conversation. The* CURTAIN *falls. The music is cut off and*

CURTAIN

The Green Bay Tree

BY MORDAUNT SHAIRP

TO

MY WIFE

The Green Bay Tree was first produced in America at the Cort Theatre, New York City, by Jed Harris on Oct. 20, 1933, and closed on March 10, 1934. The following is the original cast:

(In the order of their appearance)

TRUMP	Leo G. Carroll
MR. DULCIMER	James Dale
JULIAN (his adopted son)	Laurence Olivier
LEONORA YALE	Jill Esmond
MR. OWEN	O. P. Heggie

Directed by Jed Harris

Settings by Robert Edmond Jones

ACT ONE

SCENE I

At Mr. Dulcimer's flat in Mayfair. May.

SCENE II

The same. Some hours later.

ACT TWO

SCENE I

At Mr. Owen's house in Camden Town. August.

SCENE II

At Mr. Dulcimer's. The same evening.

ACT THREE

SCENE I

At Mr. Dulcimer's. The next morning.

SCENE II

The same. Six months later.

Time—The Present.

THE GREEN BAY TREE

ACT ONE

SCENE I

At MR. DULCIMER'S *flat in Mayfair, London.*
An evening in May.

The atmosphere of the room is one of luxury and fastidiousness. The owner is an artist in the sense that everything in the room has been chosen for its intrinsic value and given its absolutely right position in the general scheme of decoration. He never puts up anything because of its associations, nor leaves anything about because the room has been well-used. To the outsider the room is artificial, but it excites curiosity about the owner. To him, it is a constant source of pleasure. It reflects his personality, his sensitiveness, and delicate appreciation of beauty.

The room has a large semi-circular window on the right. This is curtained and fitted with cushioned seats, and looks out on to the tops of trees of a London Square. In the centre of the back wall is the entrance to the roof-garden. This is approached up a couple of steps and through handsome wrought-iron gates. When necessary these gates have close-fitting, opaque glass screens behind them, which open out on either side on to the roof-garden, being then out of sight, and thus making it possible to see the roof-garden through the gates. In the left-hand wall is the only entrance to the room, through large double doors.

The roof-garden can be treated in many ways, and can be as large or small as space permits. It should look out over a parapet on to an expanse of sky.

The furniture is arranged in this way. On the right, down stage, below the window, is a small table against the wall with a flower vase on it. On the other side of the window, up stage, is a radio-gramophone. By the window is an arm-chair.

Against the back wall, on the right-hand side of the gates, is an old embroidery frame with a stool in front of it. On the left-hand side of the roof-garden is a small rostrum on which stands a grand piano placed at such an angle that when MR. DULCIMER *sits at it he can survey the whole room. On the piano stands a bowl of flowers. The dais and piano fill up the left-hand corner. On the other side of the doors into the room, down stage, is the fireplace. Below this is a writing bureau with telephone on top of it, and a small stool in front. The rest of the furniture consists of a couch at right angles to the fireplace, but as the piano is on a dais, the couch does not mask* MR. DULCIMER, *when playing, from the audience.*

Behind the couch is a table useful as a side-table at dinner and for drinks. It should be as high as the back of the couch. In the middle of the room is a round dining-table with a chair on either side.

There are very few ornaments in the room, but it is suggested that the walls should be painted and not papered, and that over the mantelpiece should be a decorative painting by a modern artist.

When the curtain rises the room is empty and TRUMP, *an immaculate butler, enters with three evening papers in his hand. He places two on the bureau below the fireplace, and then opens the "Evening Standard" and reads it for a moment. Hearing steps in the passage, he places it hurriedly on the other two. He then goes to the table in the centre which is laid for dinner for two people, and appears to be putting the finishing touches to the things on it.*

The doors open again, and MR. DULCIMER *enters. He is a man of about forty-five, immaculately turned out, and wearing at present a double-breasted dinner jacket. He speaks exquisitely, in a clear voice, and with now and then a slight drawl. He has a habit of looking at you from under his eyes, and though a complete dilettante, he has an alert, vibrating personality. A man who could fascinate, repel, and alarm. Instantly we know that he is the one thing missing in the room, and he seems to know it, too, for he stands a moment inside the doors, almost as if he were "taking a call" for having created it. He walks to the end of the Knowle couch and stands looking round the room.*

(TRUMP *is still busied with the table.*)

DULCIMER. Trump!

TRUMP. Yes, Sir!

DULCIMER. The room looks very naked!

TRUMP (*standing to attention*). I didn't get any fresh flowers, Sir.

DULCIMER (*drawlingly*). And why didn't you get any fresh flowers?

TRUMP. You haven't used the ones from Silver Gates, Sir. The gardener sent them up this morning.

DULCIMER. Why didn't you tell me sooner? I'm terribly overdressed for doing flowers.

TRUMP (*gravely, as he begins to move towards door*). Shall I get you an apron, Sir?

DULCIMER (*meditatingly, as he comes down to the hearth*). No. I don't think I'll have an apron.

TRUMP. Could you trust me to arrange them?

DULCIMER. What flowers has Paget sent?

TRUMP. Tulips, Sir! . . . And irises and a rose or two.

DULCIMER. I don't think I could trust you with a tulip.

TRUMP. Perhaps not, Sir.

DULCIMER (*decisively*). I'll do them. Get me that little table and my gloves.

TRUMP. Very good, Sir.
(TRUMP *goes to the small table, right, below the window, and moves it opposite the window-seat.*

DULCIMER *has moved to the bureau below the fireplace and has picked up the "Evening Standard." He holds it between his finger and thumb.*)

DULCIMER. Someone's been tampering with the papers, Trump!

TRUMP (*innocently*). Really, Sir? (*Fetches a vase from the piano.*)

DULCIMER. I hate sharing a newspaper. (*Drops paper on couch.* TRUMP *places the vase on the small table by the window*) Is Mr. Julian in yet? (*Coming to the centre of the room.*)

TRUMP. Not yet, Sir!

DULCIMER. I do hope he's not going to be late again.

TRUMP. Perhaps he won't be in to dinner, Sir?

DULCIMER (*with a drawl*). And why shouldn't he be in to dinner?

TRUMP (*with a slight suggestion that he knows more*). No reason, Sir.

DULCIMER. Very well. Get me the flowers.

TRUMP. Yes, Sir. (*Moves to the door.*)

DULCIMER. Trump!

TRUMP (*turning round*). Yes, Sir?

DULCIMER (*taking a cigarette case out of his pocket*). You let me go out today without my cigarette case! I had to smoke Lady Pelham's. Unfiltered! I believe she smokes them for the coupons.

TRUMP. It shan't occur again, Sir! (*Exits.* DULCIMER *walks across to the small table by the window and lights a cigarette.* TRUMP *returns with a tray of flowers, scissors, and a pair of gloves. He places the tray on the table.*)

DULCIMER (*as he puts on the gloves*). Thank you. I hope Paget has been careful this time about the stalks. (*Takes out an iris and examines it*) That's better. (*Puts it in a vase*) Get me an ash-tray. (TRUMP *takes an ash-tray from the centre table and puts it by him*) We'll have the irises on the piano, and the tulips on the dinner table.

TRUMP. Very good, Sir. (*Hearing sound of door slamming*) I think that must be Mr. Julian!

DULCIMER (*petulantly*). I've only just started these. I thought I had taught him how to time things properly.
(*Enter* JULIAN, *a handsome boy in the early twenties, charming and well-made, but self-assured and self-indulged. Like* MR. DULCIMER *he is dressed perfectly. He has just a suspicion of knowing that he is late for dinner. He is opening a couple of invitations.*)

JULIAN. Hullo! Dulcie! I'm frightfully sorry I'm late!
(*Exit* TRUMP. JULIAN *comes over to* DULCIMER'S *side.*)

DULCIMER. My dear boy. I'd almost given you up. What have you been doing with yourself?

JULIAN. I've been out all the afternoon. I've absolutely fallen in love with the new car.

DULCIMER. Have you? I'm so glad. I thought you'd like it.

JULIAN. I've been taking it for a run in Richmond Park. (*Moves over to fireplace and puts invitations on bureau.*)

DULCIMER. How terribly healthy! I've been to a heart-rending private view.

JULIAN. Did you buy anything? (*Picks up paper off couch.*)

DULCIMER. No. I missed you. You're always so instinctively right about modern art. (JULIAN *looks pleased*) As a matter of fact, you promised to come.

JULIAN. Did I? I forgot all about it.

DULCIMER. You've been forgetting a good many things lately. Don't forget that we're going to the opera tomorrow night.

JULIAN (*not altogether pleased*). Are we? (*Sits on couch and looks at paper.*)

DULCIMER. Yes. Edward Trammle has offered me his box. Fortunately I was out when he brought it in. I only hope he won't come too. I shall never forget how he fidgeted through the whole of *Götterdämmerung*.

JULIAN. What is it tomorrow?

DULCIMER. *Tristan*.

JULIAN. That means early dinner.

DULCIMER. Not at all. I never arrive at *Tristan* till the second act.

JULIAN (*with meaning*). I shall be in the mood for *Tristan* tomorrow.

DULCIMER (*carrying the bowl of tulips to the piano*). It's the most exquisite love-story ever imagined. Quite perfect. I'll go through the score again with you in the morning.

JULIAN (*moving to window*). Aren't these first spring days marvellous?

DULCIMER (*from the piano*). Don't use that dreadful word! "Marvellous" is the expletive of the ignorant and unimaginative. When you hear anyone describe an experience as "marvellous," you can be sure that it has made no impression on them whatever. (*Comes back to the table and does the other vase.*)

JULIAN (*by the window*). I don't know how to describe what I felt this afternoon.

DULCIMER. Don't try then. Only poets can do justice to the Spring, that cruel, terrifying time.

JULIAN. Terrifying?

DULCIMER. There is always something terrifying in the remorselessness of nature, something shattering in all this re-assertion of the principle of life. Trump has got it badly. He rumpled the *Evening Standard*.

JULIAN (*laughing*). I believe I've got it too.

DULCIMER. There is a distinctly bucolic look in your eye. In another moment you'll tell me you've been to the Westminster Baths.

JULIAN (*moving round below centre table and up to the roof-garden gates*). I felt very like it.

DULCIMER. When the really warm days come, we'll go down to Silver Gates. You'll find the amber pool preferable to the sweaty transports of the Westminster Baths. (*Reflectively*) I think I shall have amethyst cushions this year in the seats round the edge of the pool. Tomorrow we'll go and choose (*he makes a lot of the word*) the material together.

JULIAN. How you love the word "choose"! (*Moves down below the couch.*)

DULCIMER. Choice is what separates the artist from the common herd. Nobody knows how to choose nowadays. I hope you will never forego your prerogative of choice. Never do anything that is unconsidered, or take what is second best.

JULIAN. But supposing one is carried away? There are moments when one just can't choose.

DULCIMER. Rise above those moments with a colossal assertion of your individuality. (*Pointing through the open window*) Look at those colours down there in the Square. That is how I like to see Nature, controlled and at my feet. Don't wallow in her.

JULIAN. I don't think I've quite got your detachment.

DULCIMER. It's the result of sensitiveness. But then, I think I've made you sensitive.

JULIAN. I'll rush into a dinner jacket. (*He goes out gaily.*)

DULCIMER (*as* TRUMP *enters*). Trump! Trump!

TRUMP. Yes, Sir?

DULCIMER (*pointing to table*). When on earth are you going to take all this away? I look like a wayside shrine! (TRUMP *puts the tulips on the table*) I hate being lagered in with tables. (TRUMP *puts the table back by the window.* DULCIMER *takes off his gloves and puts them on the table. He then goes to the piano, sits down at it and plays softly.*)

DULCIMER (*pointing to roof-garden gates*). I think we'll have those closed.

TRUMP. These light evenings are deceptive, Sir. (*Closes the doors*) Shall I draw the curtains?

DULCIMER. Not yet. But we'll dine by candle-light.

TRUMP. Very good, Sir. (*Goes to the bureau, takes a taper and a box of matches; lights taper. At that moment the sun goes in.*)

DULCIMER (*playing*). How obliging of the sun to go in! (*Watches* TRUMP *light the candles*) That looks very attractive. The whole room looks attractive.

TRUMP. Shall I turn up the lights as well?

DULCIMER. No, thank you. I hate a glare.

TRUMP (*having collected tray and gloves from table below window*). I've got the cocktails outside, Sir!

DULCIMER. Very well; we'll drink cocktails till Mr. Julian is ready. He deserves to miss them.

TRUMP. I've got a "side-car" for Mr. Julian. Perhaps you would prefer sherry?

DULCIMER. Perhaps I should. (*Exit* TRUMP. MR. DULCIMER *plays for a moment, then comes to the table and eats an olive meditatively.* TRUMP *returns with the drinks on a tray.*)

TRUMP (*as* MR. DULCIMER *takes his sherry from the tray*). Perhaps this is the moment to break a piece of bad news to you, Sir.

DULCIMER. You mean that you've done the breaking already?

TRUMP (*behind the table*). Oh, no, Sir, it's much worse than that.

DULCIMER (*a shadow crossing his face*). It's nothing about Mr. Julian?

TRUMP. Oh dear, no, Sir.

DULCIMER. Let me sit down first. (*Sits down on the couch. Sips his sherry.*)

TRUMP (*by the corner of the couch*). It's only this, Sir. I'm afraid the drill is coming to the Square.

DULCIMER. The drill?

TRUMP. The pneumatic drill. They're going to have the road up.

DULCIMER (*deploringly*). Am I never to be left in peace?

TRUMP. I knew it would be a shock. I hardly knew how to tell you, Sir.

DULCIMER. I shan't eat a thing at dinner.

TRUMP. It's a short dinner, Sir.

DULCIMER. You've got an ice for Mr. Julian?

TRUMP. Coupe "Evelyn Laye."

DULCIMER. Why?

TRUMP. It looks so beautiful, Sir.

DULCIMER. I could have managed a plover's egg. How long are they to be kept away from me?

TRUMP. I'm afraid for ever, Sir.

DULCIMER. Good God!

TRUMP. I had hoped the authorities would be satisfied with a year or two. But I'm afraid it's "never again"! They're eating sea-gulls' eggs in some restaurants, Sir.

DULCIMER. Where do they find them? On the Embankment? (*Enter* JULIAN, *also in a double-breasted dinner jacket. There is now a rather grotesque likeness between him and* MR. DULCIMER.)

JULIAN (*coming over to* TRUMP *behind table, and taking his cocktail*). I'm ready, Trump. (*Exit* TRUMP.)

DULCIMER. Julian, which would you rather, go to Silver Gates or to Margherita?

JULIAN. Must we go to either?

DULCIMER. I'm afraid we must. The road's coming up.

JULIAN. But I can't take Peter if we go to Italy.

DULCIMER. I suppose you can tear yourself away from your dog for a month or two?

JULIAN (*over by the window*). I don't much want to tear myself away from London. The nicest time of the year is just beginning.

DULCIMER. You know that they always mend the roads at the nicest time of the year.

JULIAN. Would that matter very much?

DULCIMER (*rising*). Would it matter? I refuse to stay here with the Square full of men frying bacon in tarpaulin huts. (*Puts his glass on table behind couch. Moves back to dining-table and eats another olive.*)

JULIAN. Well, I like the next couple of months in London. (*Puts his glass on the table behind couch. Comes to the dining-table and eats an olive.*)

DULCIMER. Shall we sit down? This isn't a quick-lunch counter. (*They sit on either side of the table.*)

JULIAN. It's going to be decent weather, too. We haven't had a fine season for ages.

DULCIMER. Supposing we go to Silver Gates? That's not far from London, and you can take your beloved Peter.
(JULIAN *is silent.* TRUMP *comes in with the dinner on a trolley-waiter. The dinner can be made to seem natural and not too hurried if the first course is something easily disposed of, like tomato-juice cocktail, so that the second course follows at once, and if there are the pauses indicated by* JULIAN'*s silence, in the dialogue that follows.*)
I looked forward to dining with you tonight. I've been so bored all day. I had a most miserable lunch.

JULIAN (*curtly*). With whom?

DULCIMER. Millicent Armstrong. She would talk about the fourth dimension. All I got was a couple of quails. In the end I had to tell her that I was a very coarse feeder. (TRUMP *opens a bottle of champagne with a pop*) What an exquisite noise! I didn't actually order it, Trump. Are you a thought-reader?

TRUMP. I thought that everything pointed to it, Sir. (*Fills* DULCIMER'S *glass, then goes to* JULIAN.)

DULCIMER. Mr. Julian will want a magnum if his melancholia continues. I hate people who eat in silence. It's so bestial. We shall end by having wireless during dinner.

JULIAN. The last thing I want to do is to spoil your dinner.

DULCIMER. I'm just devouring what's put in front of me simply because it's there. That's such a pity, because nobody else knows anything about food nowadays. It doesn't matter! Trump will stay and talk to me.

JULIAN. Don't be an ass!

DULCIMER. I knew it! You have been to the Westminster Baths and stayed in too long!

JULIAN. I'm sorry! I want to talk to you. I've got something to tell you. I daresay it will be rather a surprise.

DULCIMER (*to* TRUMP). Farewell! A long farewell!
(*Exit* TRUMP *with the trolley-waiter, having cleared away the used crockery on to it.*)

JULIAN. I've a very good reason for wanting to stay in town.

DULCIMER (*conciliatory*). My dear boy, I'm sure you have!

JULIAN (*after a drink*). I've fallen in love!

DULCIMER. So you remarked just now. I think you said it was with your car.

JULIAN. I don't mean the car this time.

DULCIMER (*cautiously*). You mean?

JULIAN (*nodding his head*). I do.

DULCIMER. All I can say is that I'm very sorry for the lady.

JULIAN. Thank you!

DULCIMER. Isn't a lover supposed to idle in "the wanton summer air" and do something or other with gossamer? You look as if you'd formed an attachment for a policewoman.

JULIAN. I'm depressed at having to go away and (*with slight reluctance*) I thought you might be annoyed about it.

DULCIMER. My dear boy, you ought to know me better. After all the training I've given you in observation! Besides, it's quite . . . what shall I say? Quite an ordinary thing to do. You've played with the idea once or twice before.

JULIAN. I'm not playing this time. (*Firing up*) I'm desperately in love. It wasn't the real thing before. I can't fight this. It's something outside myself. I can't find words to express it.

DULCIMER. Be as lyrical as you please! I shan't mind. The poorest lover has something of the poet about him.

JULIAN. It's no good my telling you about it unless you're going to be sensible.

DULCIMER. Of course I may have been half-witted all these years without knowing it. (*Conciliatory, as* JULIAN *rises*) My dear Julian, I can see that you're in earnest. I've known for some time that something was absorbing you. Haven't I been discretion itself in asking no questions?

JULIAN. I suppose I have been a bit secretive.

DULCIMER. Never mind if you have. Tell me about it. I'm probably responsible for the good impression you have made. I take it that the lady returns your passion?

JULIAN. I think so, but you've had nothing to do with this!

DULCIMER (*humouring him*). Perhaps not. Every lover likes to think that he is original.

JULIAN (*rising and moving to fireplace*). I mean you might not quite understand what I feel. I don't think you've ever been in love! (MR. DULCIMER *winces, but* JULIAN *is not looking at him and so does not see him*) Her name is Leonora Yale. Her people are retired Army and live somewhere in the country. She's a Veterinary Surgeon. (*A moment's silence.*)

DULCIMER. I suppose that Peter introduced you?

JULIAN. I suppose he did in the first place.

DULCIMER. Another argument against dogs. They create unsubstantial intimacies.

JULIAN. Why unsubstantial?

DULCIMER. Everything seems durable while it lasts. May I put this crude question? How long will your passion for Miss Yale last?

JULIAN. You're certainly crude. I thought you'd be a little out of your depth over this.

DULCIMER. Out of my depth! Because I ask the old question that has echoed down the ages! Very well then, I won't probe any further, but I must make my arrangements. You take your ecstasy to Silver Gates and I'll go to Margherita. That seems the best arrangement as you're both attached to animals.

JULIAN. I knew you wouldn't understand. (*Quietly*) I want to marry Leo. (DULCIMER *lets his knife and fork fall on to his plate with a slight jarring sound.*)

DULCIMER (*his face full of shadows but his voice controlled*). You never mentioned the word "Marry." (*Leaning forward*) My dear boy, are you serious?

JULIAN. Perfectly.

DULCIMER. How long have you known her?

JULIAN. About three months.

DULCIMER. Why didn't you tell me before?

JULIAN. I kept quiet until I was sure.

DULCIMER. And when did you feel sure?

JULIAN. Last night.

DULCIMER (*after a drink*). Julian?

JULIAN. Yes.

DULCIMER. You don't think you'd like to give it another three months and then open the question again?

JULIAN. Ten years won't make any difference. I've made up my mind. I've seen Leo nearly every day. I've been to her Surgery, I've met her under a variety of circumstances, and always felt the same.

DULCIMER. In another moment you'll tell me that you were made for each other.

JULIAN. Perhaps we were. But nothing you can say will laugh me out of it. This isn't just a matter of "choosing." It's got to be. That's the part I don't expect you to understand.

(*Enter* TRUMP *with* JULIAN'S *ice, coffee, and brandy.*)

DULCIMER (*irritably*). Put the things on the table, Trump. We'll help ourselves. (TRUMP *does so.*)

TRUMP. Will that be all, Sir?

DULCIMER. That will be all for the moment. (*Exit* TRUMP. *Taking a cigarette*) Really! Trump is very exasperating. He's forgotten the lighter!

JULIAN (*coming from entrance to roof-garden*). I've got a match. (*Takes a box out of his pocket. Lights* DULCIMER'S *cigarette*) You see, Leo's got this Canine Infirmary at Notting Hill, and she's made a great success of it.

DULCIMER. Does she have to do this?

JULIAN (*sitting at table again*). No, but she's got a flair for animals. So has Ranulf, her partner.

DULCIMER (*craftily*). So she's got a partner?

JULIAN. Yes. They've worked it up together.

DULCIMER (*dreamily*). I believe there was an Archbishop Ranulf in the Middle Ages. I think he got into trouble with the Pope.

JULIAN. She's a little older than I am.

DULCIMER. Is she beautiful?

JULIAN. I think so.

DULCIMER. And so you want to marry her? But of course you do. Lovers are always impulsive. That's why they make so many mistakes.

JULIAN. I know what I am doing. But I realise what this means to you . . . to us both. I shall hate leaving you, Dulcie. You've given me a wonderful life.

DULCIMER. You've been my son since you were eleven years old. Does Leonora know that I'm not your real father?

JULIAN. Yes, of course. I've told her I owe everything to you. My real father couldn't have done as much for me as you have.

DULCIMER (*grimly*). That's certainly true. He couldn't have done anything at all. You mean to get married quite soon?

JULIAN. If possible. (*A look at him*) Then while Ranulf carries on at the Surgery, I want to take Leo abroad. There are heaps of places I'd like to show her. She'd adore Italy.

DULCIMER. You might go to Italy for your honeymoon?

JULIAN. I'm quite keen to stay there for several months.

DULCIMER. Why not? There is Scriptural warrant for it. Old Testament honeymoons lasted a year.

JULIAN (*hopefully*). You approve?

DULCIMER. Entirely. And then?

JULIAN. Then I suppose we must settle down somewhere. Leo wants to get on with her work and I'd like to be able to help her. She needs a better Surgery in a more central place. I'd like to be able to give it her.

DULCIMER (*quietly*). Have you told her you will?

JULIAN. No. (*With a smile at him*) Not exactly. We've naturally built a few castles. She's very keen on my getting a *job*.

DULCIMER. And what do you say to that?

JULIAN. I haven't encouraged it enormously. (*With another delightful smile.*)

DULCIMER (*rising and filling their glasses with brandy, then sitting down again. Craftily*). Well, I'm bound to say I think you've handled the whole situation with tact and imagination.

JULIAN. But I know quite well that everything does really depend on you. I can't move a step without you.

DULCIMER. I shall buy you a trousseau and give you away at St. Paul's, Knightsbridge.

JULIAN. That's lovely of you! (*Feeling embarrassed*) But I am just a little anxious to know what's going to happen after that!

DULCIMER. What do you imagine will happen?

JULIAN (*with charm*). I did rather hope that you'd increase my allowance.

DULCIMER. I've always loved your ingenuousness. It's one of your greatest charms. (*Then, like a steel trap, all his silkiness gone*) I shouldn't dream of increasing it. In fact, if you leave me, I don't propose to make you any allowance whatever.

JULIAN (*laughingly*). Then you're just turning me adrift?

DULCIMER. That's hardly how I should describe a young man who proposes to support a wife.

JULIAN. Support a wife? That sounds rather dreary.

DULCIMER. It's an ugly middle-class term, but you force me to use it. After all, it will be a great novelty for you to earn your own living.

JULIAN (*grimly*). Yes, I suppose it will. (*Rises from the table and goes to the window.*)

DULCIMER. Aren't you going to finish your brandy?

JULIAN (*without looking round*). No thanks. (*Then turning round quickly*) Do you mean that as soon as I marry Leo, I become penniless?

DULCIMER (*getting up from the table*). Come and sit over here (*pointing to couch*), and let us try and understand one another. (*He takes* JULIAN'S *arm and they go towards the hearth*) Will you let me put the case from my own point of view?

JULIAN (*by the fire*). Of course. I know that I haven't got any rights. As I'm not your own son I can't expect to have any.

DULCIMER (*standing at the left-hand corner of the couch*). What are rights? You've had privileges. You've been my constant companion. Have you ever appreciated the compliment?

JULIAN. Of course I have. You've given me everything I could possibly want.

DULCIMER. I did more than that. I created you. I've made you what you are because I rescued you from a life of squalor. I chose you instinctively, just as I have chosen everything else in my life. It was a bold experiment, but I didn't make a mistake. You have always been a very delightful son and companion to me. But life with me and life with Leo are two very different things. You can't expect them to overlap.

JULIAN (*sitting on couch*). I suppose I can earn my own living like anyone else?

DULCIMER (*craftily*). What's to stop you. You're personable and accomplished. You've travelled. Above all, you've got my training and experience behind you. The blossoming time has come a little earlier than I expected. Never mind! All I ask is that in return for my careful nurture I may be allowed to watch you flower. That will interest me enormously, and I shall be very proud if you succeed. If you fail, I can always rescue you again.

JULIAN. I shan't fail.

DULCIMER (*craftily*). You'll be a poor advertisement for me if you do. (*Sits beside him*) My dear boy, people will be only too glad to get you!

JULIAN (*eagerly*). Do you think they will?

DULCIMER. I'm sure of it. We must look out for an opening immediately.

JULIAN (*quite impressed by all this*). You didn't mind my—asking you?

DULCIMER. Of course I didn't.

JULIAN. I believe I can do anything I want to.

DULCIMER. Then I should be very wrong to smother your initiative with a few hundreds a year.

JULIAN. I shall have to put off marrying Leo for a bit. I'll explain that to her when she comes. She'll understand that. By the way—she'll be here in a few minutes.

DULCIMER (*springing up*). What?

JULIAN. We're going to the Ballet. I asked her to pick me up.

DULCIMER. She's coming here tonight?

JULIAN. I want you to meet her.

DULCIMER (*in his usual ecstasy of protestation*). I do wish you wouldn't spring surprises on me. I'm as shy as an antelope when I'm surprised. (*Rings the bell. The room is now in the imaginary confusion created by* MR. DULCIMER.)

JULIAN (*coming to the table*). I may as well finish my ice. (*Carries it to window seat.*)

DULCIMER (*ecstatically*). By all means, let us carry our food about the room. I dislike this Bohemian way of dining. I can see the end of all this. I shall sit on a cherry. (*Enter* TRUMP *with trolley-waiter*) Clear away, Trump, as quickly as you can. We're expecting a lady here at any moment. (TRUMP *begins to put everything on the trolley-waiter.*)

JULIAN. There's plenty of time. Here you are, Trump! I've had enough. (*Hands him the ice.*)

DULCIMER (*to* TRUMP). Needless to say, she's visiting Mr. Julian. (*The bell rings.*)

JULIAN. All right, Trump! I'll go. (*Exit.*)

DULCIMER. There! I knew that would happen! Caught in the middle of a vulgar shuffle! I feel as if I had been to the Aldershot Tattoo. Why doesn't he hurry up? If someone doesn't relieve the tension I shall snap!
(JULIAN *returns with* LEONORA YALE. *Enter* LEONORA YALE. *She is a beautiful girl, clean-cut, charming, strong-willed, decisive, quite free from pose, does not take other people's opinions or judge things on their face value. She is modern in the best sense of the word. She can wear clothes and knows how to wear them. As usual she makes an impression, and she makes it on* DULCIMER. *She is not quite what he expected. There is nothing middle-class about her. There is something about her of the thing well done, well turned out, that appeals to him. She speaks well and decisively. She comes into the room.* JULIAN *brings her to* DULCIMER.)

JULIAN. Dulcie, this is Leo!

DULCIMER. I'm delighted to meet you. Julian has kept you dark for too long. I never even knew of your existence till dinner this evening.

LEONORA. I've known you for ages. I always watch you coming into the stalls on "First Nights."

DULCIMER. Are you a "First Nighter"?

LEONORA. Not a real one, but whenever I go, I always enjoy your entrance.

DULCIMER. We'll make an entrance together at the Opera tomorrow. Won't you sit down? (*She sits in left-hand corner of couch.*)

JULIAN. That's a good idea! (*To* LEONORA) It's *Tristan.*

LEONORA. Lovely! By the by, is my car safe in the square?

JULIAN (*sits on left-hand chair of centre table*). Perfectly. Trump will see to that. (*Exit* TRUMP *with trolley-waiter.*)

LEONORA. Was that Trump? (*Nodding.*)

DULCIMER. Have you fallen for him as well?

LEONORA. He's nearly as intriguing as you, isn't he? Quite the prelude to adventure.

DULCIMER. I'm dreading the day when my friends prefer to stay and talk to him instead of coming in here. One afternoon I shall find them all with him having kitchen tea. (*They laugh. He sits beside her.*)

LEONORA. What a jolly window! I love looking down on to trees.

DULCIMER. I have to be high up. I can't stand noise.

LEONORA. You wouldn't like my waiting-room.

DULCIMER. Julian's been telling me about your work.

JULIAN. He wasn't interested. He hates dogs.

DULCIMER. He means that I won't let his terrier rampage about in here.

LEONORA. Well, of course not! This is much too exquisite a room for dogs, unless you had something that would keep very still on that rug over there. (*Points.*)

JULIAN. You mean a toy dog?

LEONORA. I was thinking of a Borzoi. They're so decorative.

DULCIMER. Well, perhaps! Have you a discarded Borzoi?

JULIAN. It's not a dog's home.

DULCIMER (*going over to the rug*). Yes. I think I can see something on that rug. Something graceful and slender! (*Seeing her look*) That amuses you, doesn't it? But you professional people can never understand the artist.

LEONORA. I suppose it's all right if you've got the time. I wonder you've never gone in for decoration.

DULCIMER. I couldn't endure planning rooms for other people. My taste would have to be theirs.

LEONORA. I wish I could run my business that way.

DULCIMER. Do your clients interfere?

LEONORA. Not with the treatment, of course, but a lot of my time is taken up with humouring them. You should hear my bedside manner. (*Imitating herself*) "The little patient has passed a fairly good night!" Meaning some overfed Pekinese!

DULCIMER (*amused*). I shall consult you about the Borzoi!

LEONORA. I'll give you your money's worth.

DULCIMER. I hope you're very expensive? (*Coming and sitting beside her again.*)

LEONORA. Very. . . . To you!

DULCIMER. Are you very professional? Do you wear a white coat?

LEONORA. Oh, yes, always. A spotless one.

JULIAN. If we're going to the Ballet, I must go and put on my coat and a spotless white tie. I shan't be long, darling. (*Throws her a kiss and exits.*)

LEONORA (*going over to the embroidery frame*). What a beautiful old frame!

DULCIMER (*from the couch*). It belonged to my grandmother.

LEONORA. And what lovely work!

DULCIMER (*pleased*). It's mine. Some of my happiest hours are spent there while Julian plays the piano.

LEONORA (*with a touch of sarcasm*). Is he good with his needle, too?

DULCIMER. No. I tried to teach him, but such gifts are not easily acquired. (*Sensing her thought*) It doesn't quite meet with your approval, does it?

LEONORA. I'm bound to say that I'm glad he won't want to embroider. But then, I'm so poor at sewing myself.

DULCIMER (*indignantly*). Sewing? Is that all you see in my work? (*Rising and coming towards her*) I don't believe it! There's nothing of the Philistine about you, even though you have this dreadful obsession for dumb animals. That's the Leo part of you. Leo's so fierce and hostile. I shall always call you Leonora.

LEONORA (*from the window*). Do. If you'll let me off calling you Dulcie!

DULCIMER. That's only Julian's pet name for me. (*As he walks back to the couch*) Tell me, Leonora! If you hadn't known, you'd have taken us for father and son?

LEONORA. I think I should. I see now that Julian has many of your mannerisms. Is he at all like his real father?

DULCIMER. I hope not. I got him in time to prevent that.

LEONORA. I should rather like to meet Julian's father.

DULCIMER. There's nothing to stop you. He plies his trade in Camden Town.

LEONORA. What does he do?

DULCIMER. He has a dairy or a drapery or something dreadful.

LEONORA (*interested*). Really?

DULCIMER. That's enthralling, isn't it? Well, when you go, I hope he'll be sober. (*They are now seated again.*)

LEONORA. Is that the trouble?

DULCIMER. It used to be. I believe he's a reformed character now. Of course, I've never seen him since I adopted Julian.

LEONORA. It was very decent of you to rescue him.

DULCIMER. I shall never forget the day I first heard him sing at an Eisteddfod in Wales.

LEONORA (*quietly*). You fell in love with his voice?

DULCIMER (*after a tiny pause*). If you like to put it that way. He had the most exquisite treble voice I've ever heard. I had a record made of it. Some day I'll put it on when he isn't here.

LEONORA. Doesn't he like it?

DULCIMER. It's not that. I don't want to remind him of his beginnings. I pursued that voice to a back alley in some unpronounceable Welsh town, and there I found Julian with a drunken father and no mother. It would have been sacrilege to have left him there, but no one else had sensibility enough to see that.

LEONORA. Did you send him to school?

DULCIMER. I thought of doing so, but my interviews with headmasters were not encouraging.

LEONORA. I wish you had a record of them.

DULCIMER. He may not have had a public school education, but Julian is as much at home in Paris or in Rome as he is in London.

LEONORA. That will be very useful. I love going abroad.

DULCIMER. He can paint. He knows something about music. He's cultured and charming, because I've taught him to be so.

LEONORA. Yes, I see you've taken a lot of pains with him. (*She realises what she's up against.*)

DULCIMER (*slowly*). He's my creation. I've succeeded where any ordinary "father" would have failed. He's more than a son to me, and it will mean more to me to give him up. Perhaps that won't be necessary immediately?

LEONORA. Perhaps not quite immediately. (*She understands what he means.*)
(*Enter* JULIAN. *He has changed into "tails."*)

DULCIMER (*to* JULIAN). Leonora and I have been getting to know each other. (*Rising to go. To* LEONORA) Do you think we're going to be friends?

LEONORA (*without enthusiasm*). I hope so.

DULCIMER. I hope so, too. Well, as it seems I'm going to spend the evening alone, I'll go and slip into something comfortable, if you'll excuse me. (*Exit.*)

JULIAN (*coming and sitting beside her*). Well, what have you been talking about? I hope you haven't been bored?

LEONORA. He'd never bore anybody.

JULIAN. No. He's pretty stimulating to live with.

LEONORA. He made me feel terribly wholesome and ordinary.

JULIAN. Did he talk about me?

LEONORA. He's been telling me what a wonderful education he's given you.

JULIAN. I've got something to tell you—something beastly.

LEONORA. Julian!

JULIAN. At dinner this evening, after I'd told him about you, he suddenly got all Victorian, and said that if I married anybody I must earn my own living. He cut me clean off without even a shilling. I never felt such a fool in my life.

LEONORA (*cheerfully*). Oh, well, we'll have to wait a bit, that's all.

JULIAN. It never entered my head that he wouldn't make me an allowance. It was quite natural to expect it. But he made it sound so unreasonable that I hadn't the nerve to argue about it.

LEONORA. Isn't it because your guardian doesn't want you to marry at all? He thinks you belong to him, and he knows you are under more of an obligation to him than if he was your real father.

JULIAN. I don't see that. I didn't ask him to adopt me. All the same, I'm glad he did.

LEONORA. Well, now, it's up to us to carry on without him. What do you think you'd like to do?

JULIAN. Let me see. I can drive a car. I can paint a bit, and play a bit, and I've got an eye for colour.

LEONORA. There isn't a sixpence in any of them.

JULIAN. I hate sixpences, anyway. They're no use except in cloakrooms.

LEONORA (*getting up under a sudden feeling that the situation is hopeless*). I wonder if we'd better call the whole thing off?

JULIAN (*getting up*). Do you mean, not get married?

LEONORA. It seems so unfair to you. There's no earthly reason why you should suddenly have to become like everybody else and slave and grind out a living.

JULIAN. Look here, Leo! I haven't any illusions about myself. I know it's laughable at my age to be wondering what I'm going to be, like a boy in a fourth form, but I do know I'm going to be something so that I can marry you. And I will marry you, Leonora! I love you more than anything in the world. You ask me what I want to do. Well, something that will make the time before we can get married as short as possible.

LEONORA (*with great sincerity and a touch of wistfulness*). Darling! That's the real you! Isn't it?

JULIAN. No more talk of calling the whole thing off!

LEONORA. I was only thinking of you when I said that, and if I'd seen the slightest flicker of relief in your face when I did say it . . .

JULIAN. Well?

LEONORA. Never mind!

JULIAN. Tell me!

LEONORA. I should have felt as if the end of everything had come. I love you so much that I don't mind how long I wait! I love you so! (*A long kiss.*)

LEONORA. Now let's be sensible! (*Sitting on chair left of centre table*) Julian, how would you like to be a vet?

JULIAN. Doesn't it mean passing exams and things?

LEONORA. Well, why not? I could help you tremendously with your work, and when you were qualified, you could join us.

JULIAN. Is it a long business? Will it take a year?

LEONORA. More like five. Nearly as long as being a doctor. (JULIAN *groans.*)

JULIAN. Oh, Leonora! Five years? It's a life-time!

LEONORA. I don't see why we shouldn't get married after you've passed your first exam.

JULIAN (*coming to her side*). I'll pass *that* exam all right.

LEONORA. Of course you will.

JULIAN. When can I start?

LEONORA. You've got to break away from here first. I mean really break away.

JULIAN. Live on my own? How can I?

LEONORA. Haven't you got any money?

JULIAN. I've got some of this quarter's allowance. A good bit in fact. And I've got some things I can sell. That'll keep me going for a while. Why must I leave here?

LEONORA. Can you honestly see yourself doing any work here?

JULIAN. Dulcie wouldn't let me dissect cats, or anything of that kind. Otherwise I don't see what's to stop me.

LEONORA. He wouldn't let you do a stroke. He despises work, and he'd never understand your wanting to be a vet. A man who doesn't like having a terrier in the sitting-room!

JULIAN. I wish he could hear you calling it a sitting-room! I'm afraid you don't like my guardian!

LEONORA. No. I don't like him. But I'm going to take him very seriously. We can't afford to trifle with him. Whatever you decide to do, he'll try to prevent it. Don't you feel that?

JULIAN (*gloomily*). Yes, I do.

LEONORA. I know what you'll be giving up and that you'll be giving it up for me. I adore you for it. (*Kiss.*)

JULIAN. I shall clear out of here as soon as I can. I'll tackle Dulcie about it tonight.

LEONORA. You will choose the right moment, won't you?

JULIAN. Trump and I are geniuses at that. We can tell the wrong moment a mile off. It will give him a shock to see me working. Well, now that we've made this marvellous start, what about going to the Ballet?

LEONORA. I should love it. (*They move*) By the way, there's one question I haven't asked you. Who are you?

JULIAN. Who am I?

LEONORA. What's your real name?

JULIAN. Dulcie didn't tell you?

LEONORA. No, he brushed your father aside rather hurriedly.

JULIAN. My original name was Owen—David Owen.

LEONORA. You're not even Julian?

JULIAN. No. I'm plain David.

LEONORA. And very nice, too.

JULIAN. But I'm patented "Julian Dulcimer," or naturalised, or whatever it is.

LEONORA. When we're married, shall I be Mrs. Owen or Mrs. Dulcimer?

JULIAN. Which would you like to be?

LEONORA. Mrs. Owen!

JULIAN. I knew you'd say that. We'll have to see about it. I suppose I can be "rendered down" again or something.

LEONORA. I must meet my father-in-law.

JULIAN. You'll see him at the wedding. At least I suppose you will.

LEONORA. Suppose they both come? (*They laugh. At this moment the door opens.* DULCIMER *sees them, and coughs a little ostentatiously.*)

DULCIMER. Did I do that well? I've been practising coughing for the last ten minutes. What a lot you lovers have to say to each other.

JULIAN. We're just off.

DULCIMER. Julian can take you in his car and bring you back here for a drink. There's a wonderful atmosphere about this room in the small hours of the morning.

LEONORA. They mustn't be too small. I'm a working woman, Mr. Dulcimer!

DULCIMER. When you come back, we'll think of a name for you to call me by. We'll all write things down on pieces of paper.

JULIAN (*at the door*). Come on, Leo!
(*They go out, closing the door behind them.* DULCIMER *stands in the middle of the room, looking after them.*)

CURTAIN

SCENE II

The same. Some hours later. Nearly all the lights are turned out.

MR. DULCIMER *is sitting in the arm-chair facing the window. A dance band is coming over the radio.* TRUMP *enters with a plate of sandwiches.*

DULCIMER (*without looking up*). What time is it, Trump?

TRUMP (*putting sandwiches on table*). About a quarter to twelve, Sir. (*He moves to turn on the lights.*)

DULCIMER. Leave the lights.

TRUMP. I've brought in a few sandwiches.

DULCIMER (*with his frequent habit of repeating remarks in the form of a question*). And why have you brought in a few sandwiches?

TRUMP. Mr. Julian didn't have much dinner, Sir, and as Miss Yale's car is still outside, I daresay she'll like one too.
(*The dance band stops, and there is heard the usual babel of voices and shuffling of feet.*)

DULCIMER (*pointing to the radio*). I expect Mr. Julian and Miss Yale are in there by now!

TRUMP (*with a startled look at* MR. DULCIMER). In there, Sir? Oh, I see what you mean! At the Dorchester.

DULCIMER. Can you distinguish Mr. Julian's voice?

TRUMP (*going up to the radio and listening*). No, Sir! But then they never sound to me like voices.
(*The band begins again.*)

DULCIMER (*with a tinge of regret*). I expect Miss Yale dances well.

TRUMP. I'm sure she does, Sir!

DULCIMER (*angrily*). Turn it off, Trump! (TRUMP *does so.*)

TRUMP. Is there anything more I can get you?

DULCIMER. No, thank you.

TRUMP. Good-night, Sir.

DULCIMER. Good-night!
(*Exit* TRUMP, *meeting* JULIAN *in the doorway in top-hat and dress overcoat.*)

JULIAN. Hullo, Dulcie! Had a dull evening? (*Puts hat on table and overcoat and scarf on left-hand chair. Then he turns up the other lights.*)

DULCIMER. Not at all. Where is Leonora?

JULIAN. She sent her apologies and wouldn't come in, after all! She's tired, and gets up earlier than we do. (*He is standing by the table and eating sandwiches.*)

DULCIMER (*regarding him curiously*). Did you have a good time?

JULIAN. Rather!

DULCIMER. I saw you both at the Dorchester.

JULIAN (*stopping in the middle of his sandwich, and looking at him in amazement*). However did you manage that?

DULCIMER (*moving across the room*). "In my mind's eye, Horatio!" Dear me! I'm very full of quotations tonight. It's always a sign that something's disagreed with me when I'm full of quotations. I must find out what it is. (*Rings the bell.* JULIAN *at the table watches him, wondering what sort of a mood he is in.*)
(*Enter* TRUMP.)

TRUMP. Yes, Sir?

DULCIMER. Something has disagreed with me, Trump. What is it?

TRUMP. I can't think of anything particular, Sir. If I may say so, Sir, we ate our dinner rather thoughtlessly.

DULCIMER. Did I gobble?

TRUMP. Oh, no, Sir! But the arrival of Miss Yale keyed us up a little beyond our usual concert pitch.

JULIAN (*amused*). Well done, Trump. Jolly good for this hour of the night. (*He goes to* DULCIMER, *takes him by the arm, and puts him on the couch*) Sit down, Dulcie! I'll get some brandy! (*Goes back to the table.*)

DULCIMER (*surprised at his confident manner*). We're quite the assured lover, aren't we?

JULIAN (*ignoring this*). You don't want to keep Trump out of bed, do you?

DULCIMER. Do I want to keep you out of bed, Trump?

TRUMP. Probably, Sir!

DULCIMER (*murmuring*). Go to your truckle-bed, Trump! I would willingly change places with you, but I feel like King Henry IV in his nightgown. "Get you to rest, cramm'd with distressful bread!" There I go again! (*Then, as* JULIAN *approaches him with brandy, he says icily*) I'm not in need of brandy, thank you.
(TRUMP *is trying to suppress a yawn.*)

JULIAN (*shrugging his shoulders and putting brandy on the table*). Very well! (*To* TRUMP) Go on, Trump! Don't stand there swallowing yawns!
(*Exit* TRUMP.)

DULCIMER (*coldly*). Since when have you taken to ordering my servants about?

JULIAN. I only wanted to get rid of him. (*Taking the sandwiches and sitting by his side*) I want to talk to you, and you're generally at your best at this time. I haven't offended you, have I?

DULCIMER (*thawing*). No, my boy! Of course you haven't. But I don't know that I'm particularly sparkling tonight.

JULIAN. I don't want you to sparkle. I want you to be serious.

DULCIMER. What a dreadful request!

JULIAN. I mean I don't want you to be witty, just for a minute or two. You see, I've got a suggestion to make, and you may be a little surprised at it. To begin with, Leonora and I didn't go to the Ballet.

DULCIMER. Why not?

JULIAN. We did rather an extraordinary thing. (*Pause*) We went to see my father instead.

DULCIMER. What?

JULIAN. We went to see my father instead. (DULCIMER *gets up in agitation and walks about the room*) I liked him. So did Leo. I don't know why we went tonight. We had been talking about him before we left here.

DULCIMER. So you were impressed by your father?

JULIAN. I think I've had a wrong idea of him before.

DULCIMER. Do you mean that I've given you that wrong idea?

JULIAN. Perhaps he's changed. There's nothing disreputable about him. He was sitting quietly at home, reading the Bible.

DULCIMER. Good Heavens! Don't I read the Bible? Haven't I told you that you can't form your style without it?

JULIAN. He's a preacher in some local chapel. Well, Leo and I have been mapping out our future this evening. We can't be married till I've got a job, and I've decided to become a "vet."
(*A tiny pause.*)

DULCIMER (*in hard, loud tones from the roof-garden steps*). Go on! I've not the least desire to be witty.

JULIAN. It'll mean a lot of hard work, and I've got to live somewhere while I'm doing it. I think it will be possible to live with my father. He rather liked the idea. Apparently he feels he's got something to make up to me.

DULCIMER. He's been a little slow at feeling that.

JULIAN. The college is close to where he lives. Everything just happens to fit. That's all.

DULCIMER. You asked me to be serious just now. I'm going to be. I think you're quite mad and rather uncouth.

JULIAN. I knew you wouldn't see it!

DULCIMER. I can see it quite clearly! (*Coming close to him*) An impetuous boy, because he has fallen in love, wants to rush headlong out of my house at a moment's notice, without giving a thought to my wishes or plans!

JULIAN. That's not fair! I have thought about you.

DULCIMER. Then you certainly haven't thought about yourself. Do you really imagine that you'll find living with your father congenial?

JULIAN. I shall have too much to do to worry about that. I think we shall get on, and we shan't see very much of each other.

DULCIMER. Has he spacious apartments?

JULIAN. He can give me a room.

DULCIMER. I believe I was right. You *are* insane! I shall have you certified tomorrow.

JULIAN. You'll never see my point, but I can see yours. To you I must be as mad as a hatter.

DULCIMER. Not only mad, Julian, but rather cruel. A little vindictive perhaps.

JULIAN. Dulcie, I don't want to offend you, but surely you must see that I couldn't work here.

DULCIMER. Why not? You can pore over diagrams of dogs' intestines to your heart's content!

JULIAN. You'd loathe it if I did. (*Going to bureau*) Look at this! (*He picks up a large quill pen, exquisitely feathered in jade green*) That's your idea of a pen! I couldn't work with that! (*Throws it down on bureau*) And that is typical of everything here! I don't want to be uncouth or ungrateful, but I know that the only sensible thing to do is to get away on my own.

DULCIMER (*with a penetrating voice*). On your own? Julian, are you hinting that I am the obstacle to your success?

JULIAN. We should get on each other's nerves a thousand times a day.

DULCIMER. Did Leonora make you think that?

JULIAN. No, not exactly. She agrees with me, though.

DULCIMER. You mean that you agree with her. (*As if thinking*) I see. She's determined to get you away from me, and she's not wasting any time about it.

JULIAN. Well, I think I shall go to bed now. I've got a lot of things to arrange tomorrow. (*Coming up to* DULCIMER) We're friends about this, aren't we? (DULCIMER *turns aside and refuses to take his hand*) Oh, all right! But you're behaving very childishly!

DULCIMER (*turning round on him*). You fool! You little, self-confident fool!

JULIAN. I'm not going to quarrel with you. You'll see things differently in the morning. (*Exits.*)

(*For a moment or two* MR. DULCIMER *paces the room like a tiger. Then he goes to the gramophone and puts on the "Mars" record from Holst's "Planets." The music is a dramatisation of his mood. Then he goes to the window, opens it, and breathes in the air, afterwards turning off the lights turned on by* JULIAN. *Then, with his quick resolute stride, he walks back to the gramophone. He puts on a second record, and a boy's treble voice comes floating into the silent room. He returns to the arm-chair and sits listening.*)

CURTAIN

ACT TWO

SCENE I

MR. OWEN'S *sitting-room in Camden Town.*
Three months later. August.

A small, neat, simply furnished room. It can be set inside the Dulcimer flat. It is comfortable and contains good solid furniture, but the wallpaper is crude and the pictures and ornaments are chosen without taste. MR. OWEN *is proud of it.* JULIAN *detests it.*

The room has a fireplace on the right, the door is in the back wall towards the right and opens into a small hall with hat-stand. On the other side of the door is a sash window looking out on to the street and giving a good view of some posters advertising Guinness. "GUINNESS IS GOOD FOR YOU."

The furniture of the room is arranged in this way. On either side of the fireplace is an arm-chair. Between the door and the window stands a small American organ, symbolic of a great deal of MR. OWEN'S *soul. It is open and a large volume of hymns rests on the music stand. In the window is a small table with a plant on it.*

In the left-hand corner, up stage, stands an open bureau, correspondence and business papers lying about on it. Above is a single shelf that now contain's JULIAN'S *scientific books. By the bureau is a waste-paper basket, and below it, down stage, a horsehair sofa. In the middle of the room is a solid square table with a coloured cloth and four chairs.*

It is suggested that there might be photographs of MR. OWEN'S *family, and perhaps one of* JULIAN *as a child, on the mantelpiece and elsewhere, but any decorations should be in keeping with the atmosphere of the room.*

JULIAN (*lolling in the arm-chair with a notebook in his hand*). I've got no brain this afternoon. I try to make it function but nothing happens. I've read that passage through three times and haven't taken in a word.

LEONORA (*coming over from the window*). Darling, give me the book! I'll read it out to you. Put your legs straight. (*Sits on the arm of his chair*) Now, where's the place?

JULIAN. Somewhere on that page. (*Pointing and giving her book.*)

LEONORA. Boyle's law?

JULIAN. That's it.

LEONORA (*reading*). "When the temperature of a gas . . ."

JULIAN (*interrupting*). Wait a minute! Let's get comfortable before we start. (*Draws her into the arm-chair beside him*) There! That's better! (*Kissing her*) This is the perfect way to coach for any exam.

LEONORA (*trying to be serious*). Now, listen!

JULIAN. Angel, I could listen for ever. (*Looks at her adoringly.*)

LEONORA. This is Boyle's law.

JULIAN. Who was Boyle?

LEONORA. Never mind who he was. He formulated this law, which you've got to remember.

JULIAN. I believe he formulated that wallpaper, too, which I'm very anxious to forget.

LEONORA. Darling, it's miraculous of you to stand it. I do know what it means to you. I shouldn't mind myself, but then I'm not so desperately sensitive.

JULIAN. Don't tell me you'd ever live in a room like this!

LEONORA. Of course not! Our flat's going to be lovely—I've got all sorts of ideas.

JULIAN. Tell me about them.

LEONORA. Well, they'll include a refrigerator. (*Moves a little in the chair as if hot.*)

JULIAN (*surprised*). Of course they will.

LEONORA (*amused at him*). Every flat hasn't got one.

JULIAN. Good God! Hasn't it?

LEONORA. Certainly not. They're still considered luxuries.

JULIAN. "Luxury" is a word invented by people with no imagination. It's only another word for decency. Baths were luxuries once.

LEONORA. At any rate, you've got a bathroom.

JULIAN. Only just. I wouldn't keep a goldfish in it. The whole scheme of things is preposterous. It's natural to be clean, it's natural to be cool. They ought either to be free or subsidized.

LEONORA. Darling, I'm afraid you've left your perfect world for a very imperfect one.

JULIAN. Which I gladly accept because you're in it, but it shan't hold us a second longer than is absolutely necessary, shall it?

LEONORA. Not one second, darling, I promise you that.

JULIAN. Good. Let us Boyle!

LEONORA. This is the law. (*Reads*) "When the temperature of a gas does not alter, the product of its volume and pressure is constant."

JULIAN. Isn't that nonsense? I love your voice, Leo. It rises and falls over those ridiculous words and the whole room is full of music.

LEONORA. Yes, but have you taken in what it's about?

JULIAN. Not a syllable, darling! Anyone who wants to "take in" Boyle's law with you sitting there, looking so adorable, is a frosty-minded wretch.

LEONORA. Then there's "Dalton's Law of Partial Pressures."

JULIAN. "Partial Pressures!" Parcel Post!

LEONORA (*reading*). "By partial pressure is meant the pressure that any one gas would exert if it alone were present, filling the whole space."

JULIAN. It sounds like a word picture of father!

LEONORA (*laughing and getting up and putting the book down on the table*). Well, I don't think we'll do any more this afternoon.

JULIAN (*gravely*). I think it is that I'm a little "off" physics. Let's have a look at anatomy. (*Rises and goes to bookcase above writing-table, from which he takes a book. As he passes the window, he pauses and looks at the poster on the opposite wall*) Guinness is good for you! (*Coming to* LEONORA'S *side*) I've rather taken to anatomy.

LEONORA (*encouragingly*). You ought to know a lot about it already. You couldn't draw unless you did.

JULIAN. Anatomy's got pictures. Look at that dear little rabbit all pinned out with A's and B's and C's. (*Showing her.*)

LEONORA. Isn't he a pet?

JULIAN. Go ahead. Ask me some questions. I do know something about bones.

LEONORA (*taking book*). Let me see. What's the sacrum?

JULIAN (*putting his arm round her waist*). The sacrum, my angel, is the triangular bone at the back of the pelvis.

LEONORA. Splendid!

JULIAN. Though I can't conceive how one earns a living by knowing that. (*Sits in arm-chair again.*)

LEONORA (*eagerly*). And what is the carpus? (*She is in the arm-chair opposite him.*)

JULIAN (*frowning*). The carcase?

LEONORA. Carpus! C-A-R-P-U-S!

JULIAN. Well, that's funny now! That seems to have slipped away. Have I got a carpus?

LEONORA. Yes.

JULIAN. Has everybody?

LEONORA. Certainly.

JULIAN. I've missed it, somehow. (*Sings to the tune of "Today I feel so Happy."*)

You say I've got a carpus!
A carpus! A carpus!
I know I've got a carpus!
I don't know where it is!

LEONORA (*pointing to her hand*). It's that part of the skeleton which unites the hand to the forearm.

JULIAN (*with deep interest*). Is it? Let me see. (*Goes on his knees in front of her and takes her hand*) Just there! (*Pointing to the spot.*)

LEONORA (*showing him*). A little higher up.

JULIAN (*kissing her wrist*). That's the exact spot. (*Naïvely*) I don't think I should ever get bored by anatomy. It's the only red letter in my alphabet. (*Counting off wearily*) Anatomy, Botany, Biology, Chemistry. Then there's a ghastly leap and we land on physics.

LEONORA. It's only about Heat, Light, and Sound.

JULIAN. Why learn about them? Heat, a thing I detest; Light, which ought to be shaded always; Sound! Well, there's too much in the streets already. No, darling, I wish to go no further into the matter!

LEONORA (*taking the book from him*). All right, we won't do any more today. You'll pass it on your head. (*She puts it back in the shelf.*)

JULIAN (*standing by centre table*). I suppose I shall! It's all so new to me not to be certain of myself. Anything I've done before I've done, and there's an end of it. I don't take to this competing business. (LEONORA *comes to him.*)

LEONORA (*seriously*). Don't you think, darling, that that's the difference between an amateur and a professional? It doesn't really matter whether the amateur gets there or not.

JULIAN. I don't know so much about that. Amateurs take themselves very seriously.

LEONORA. Well, at any rate, you can't live an amateur life.

JULIAN. I think that's just what I've been doing, and I've got a deuce of a lot of fun out of it.

LEONORA. Yes, but I know that you're worth ever so much more than that. (*A long kiss.*)

JULIAN. D'you think I'm an amateur lover?

LEONORA. No!

JULIAN (*going back to fireplace*). Even Isaiah would admit that I've had a hell of a day. I've had three hours with a crammer, taken down his blasted notes, and read Boyle at home.

LEONORA. You're beginning to feel that this is home?

JULIAN. No. I can't quite say that. I haven't been trained to live with a minor prophet.

LEONORA. I admire him for having the courage of his convictions.

JULIAN. Yes, but I do wish he'd stop calling me Davy!

LEONORA. David's a good name!

JULIAN. Yes, but "Davy"! It doesn't go with me at all. What's he up to this afternoon?

LEONORA (*with a "cod" Welsh accent*). It's Thursday. Early closing!

JULIAN. And sermon night!

LEONORA. Let's try and keep off the chapel for once. It always leads to trouble.

JULIAN. Not a hope! The chapel's like drink to him.

LEONORA. Not a very fortunate remark!

JULIAN. It was quite unconscious. Sometimes I wish he would drink a bit! It might cheer him up!
(*The front door bangs.*)

LEONORA. There he is! Now be careful what you say!

JULIAN. Woe unto the ungodly!
(*Enter* WILLIAM OWEN. *He is a wiry man with a beard, a determined face, and uncompromising eyes. His hair is grey and his clothes workaday clothes. He is a man who has suffered a good deal and who might have gone to the bad altogether had it not been for religion. Through religion he has pulled himself together and is proud of the fact. Through the chapel he finds an outlet for his poetry, his fanaticism, and capacity to preach. He is not a hard man, but he has not much understanding of or tolerance for* JULIAN DULCIMER. *To him he is just "Davy," his extravagant son, who ought to think only of passing his exams. He comes in with a file of bills in his hand.*)

OWEN (*as he hangs his hat and coat up on the stand outside*). Hullo, Leo! Hullo, Davy my boy!

How are your studies? Have you done well today? (*Sits in arm-chair.*)

JULIAN (*teasing him*). Top in everything. The teachers were awfully pleased. I mean this one is.

LEONORA. What have you been doing, Isaiah?

JULIAN (*teasing him*). Been to the pictures?

OWEN (*putting his bills on the bureau*). I flatter myself that I've a higher idea of recreation than that.

JULIAN. Wait a minute! You don't know what the stage show is this week.

OWEN. What should I be doing with stage shows?

JULIAN. You'd enjoy this one. It's not the Rhumba Girls. It's grand opera. The whole of *Cavalleria Rusticana.* Will you go to Hell for an hour for the sake of grand opera?

LEONORA. Do, Isaiah! It would do you a world of good.

OWEN (*sitting in arm-chair above fire place*). I don't like jokes about Hell, Leo. It's a very real place.

LEONORA. I didn't mean to shock you, but I'm sure you don't have half enough pleasure in your life.

OWEN. Principle before pleasure, I should have said.

LEONORA (*regretfully*). Always?

OWEN. Goodness gracious, yes! (*Getting out his pipe.*)

LEONORA. You lead such a model life with that dear little dairy downstairs, full of fresh eggs and glasses of milk.

JULIAN. Watered.

OWEN. Don't you dare to say that to me, Davy!

JULIAN. Anyhow, Leo's quite right. You ought to unbend sometimes.

OWEN. And supposing I couldn't straighten up again? Besides, do you know what the picture is? Rosalind Turner in *Outraged.* What would the chapel say if they saw me going to see that?

LEONORA. You could preach a wonderful sermon next Sunday on the Evils of Hollywood.

OWEN. I did that last Sunday, so it would fall rather flat. I preached for an hour on the "lure of the screen." I should like to have heard the music, though! Never mind. At Christmas the chapel is doing the "Messiah." That will be grand. (*Moves to bureau to get his tobacco.*)

LEONORA. Have you had some tea?

OWEN. Yes, thank you. I've been over to Brixton to see my sister-in-law. (*To* JULIAN) Your Aunt Lily is very anxious to see you.

JULIAN. What, again? (OWEN *goes back to arm-chair and fills his pipe.*)

OWEN. She asks about you every time I go there.
(LEONORA *sits in the arm-chair below the fireplace.* JULIAN *is at the table reading the "Methodist Times."*)

JULIAN. What an awful thought.

OWEN (*a little annoyed*). I'm sorry you find your family uncongenial.

JULIAN. I've come to it rather late in life. I'm afraid of it. Honestly I am. Aunt Lily's got a laugh like a double bass.

OWEN. You be thankful she wants to make you welcome.

JULIAN. And as for my cousin Trevor!

OWEN. You needn't patronise Trevor, either. He's doing very well for himself.

JULIAN. He let me know that all right.

OWEN. You didn't like him because he said you looked like something out of Hope Brothers.

JULIAN (*turning to* LEO). Now I ask you, Leo! Could I have been more grossly insulted?

LEO. I think it is rather a libel.

OWEN. I thought it hit the nail on the head.

JULIAN. My "family" as you call it, may be doing very well for itself, but it does not know anything about clothes.

OWEN. Whenever I see Trevor, he is always tidily turned out.

JULIAN. Yes, that's just about it. (*Moves to sofa.*)

OWEN. You could learn a lot from him! He'd smarten you up no end!

JULIAN (*aghast*). Smarten me up?

OWEN. Make a man of you instead of a tailor's dummy!

LEONORA (*seeing the look on* JULIAN'S *face*). Now you two, it's waste of time arguing about clothes. We can't all look alike.

OWEN. Julian can dress up as much as he pleases, but he's got to be more affable all round. It's not my sister only. It's anybody who comes here. (*To* JULIAN) It's no use being uppish when you've nothing to be uppish about. This isn't the Hotel Camden, you know. If you're not satisfied, you can go to the Ritz!

LEONORA. Julian's perfectly satisfied, Isaiah. You mustn't imagine things.

OWEN. I've a pretty good ear for undertones. However, he'll soon have a chance of turning over a new leaf. Lily and Trevor are coming here this evening. (*To* JULIAN) Now, mind you don't call me Isaiah in front of them!

JULIAN. There's no fear of that! We shan't be here! Leo and I are going out! (*Coming back to table.*)

OWEN (*shaking his finger at* LEONORA). More pleasure, I suppose?

LEONORA (*charmingly*). Lots more, I hope!

OWEN. I'm afraid, Leo, you're like all the rest. Pleasure, pleasure, pleasure!
(*A knock at the front door.*)

LEONORA. I'll go.
(*Exit.*)

OWEN (*coming to table and sitting opposite him. In a conciliatory mood*). Davy, my boy, I don't want to seem inquisitive, but when you've spent your money, where will you get any more from?

JULIAN. I'll settle that when the day comes.

OWEN. But you can't go over the abyss with your eyes open. Save your money. You've got nothing to spend it on. Your home isn't so bad, is it?

JULIAN. No, of course it isn't.

OWEN. I didn't mean what I said about the Hotel Camden, but I can't bear to see you wasting your money on rubbish. How much did that tie cost? Nearly five shillings, I suppose?

JULIAN. Nearly fifteen.

OWEN (*awed in spite of his convictions*). Did it now? It's wicked. I'd rather wear a bootlace than pay so much. I want you to take life more seriously. It doesn't take much to lead you away from the right path. Do you know what will keep you on it?

JULIAN. A good balance at the bank.

OWEN (*gravely*). No, Davy, it's not that. Prayer and Purpose, my boy! That's what you want. Prayer and Purpose! They've been the backbone of my life for the last fifteen years.

JULIAN. I'm afraid they haven't exactly come my way.
(*Enter* LEONORA.)

LEONORA. Telegram for you, darling! (*Hands it to* JULIAN. *He opens it.*)

JULIAN. Splendid! Dulcie's back. (LEONORA *and* OWEN *look at each other*) He arrived this afternoon! There's no answer! Why ever didn't he tell me? I'd have met him. (LEONORA *goes off and dismisses the telegraph boy, returning at once.*)

OWEN. He'll keep all right till tomorrow.

JULIAN. I expect he's had a marvellous time at Silver Gates. I can see it all stretched out there in the sun!

OWEN (*getting up*). I must begin to collect my thoughts for Sunday. Where did I leave my Bible? I know, it's by my bedside. (*Exit.*)

JULIAN. That sounds rather ominous.

LEONORA (*who has been watching him*). Darling, you're not too terribly pleased at Dulcie's coming back, are you?

JULIAN. I can't help being glad, but (*Taking her hands*) you've got nothing to be afraid of.

LEONORA. You won't let the old life come between us and spoil our plans?

JULIAN. Of course not. I'm glad he's back, though. I'll tell you why presently. (*Crosses over to fireplace. Enter* OWEN *with large Bible under his arm.*)

OWEN. I've got something this week that'll make them sit up! (*Puts Bible on table and opens it. He stands in front of Bible*) Now listen to this!

LEONORA. That's right, Isaiah! You try it on us first!

OWEN (*a little taken aback*). I'm not sure that I was including you, Leo. It's about the ungodly.

JULIAN. I thought it would be.

OWEN. Listen! (*Declaiming*) "I myself have seen the wicked in great power and spreading himself like a green bay tree."

JULIAN (*regretfully*). Happy days!

OWEN (*getting worked up and turning on him quite fiercely*). Do you think so? (*With uplifted hand*) Wait! Listen to the Psalmist's conclusion! "Yet he passed away, and lo, he was not: yea, I sought him, but he could not be found."

JULIAN. Come now, Isaiah, I'm not quite ripe for passing away yet!

OWEN. Perhaps not. But you're on the way if you don't look out. Remember, it's watching you that has sent me to that text. "He passed away, and lo, he was not!" (*With a sweep of his hand*) Wiped out completely!

LEONORA. Do you believe, Isaiah, that that actually happens?

OWEN. It's true enough! It's happening every day! Look at those earthquakes! God moves in a mysterious way to bring about His will.

JULIAN. Isaiah, you're a barbarian! You belong to the Old Testament! I believe you'd enjoy being an instrument of destruction.

OWEN. If it was the Lord's will, He would not find me wanting! I've seen the day of reckoning come time and time again.

LEONORA. But Julian doesn't deserve a reckoning!

OWEN. Not if he comes to chapel!

JULIAN. I'll come next Sunday. I wouldn't miss hearing you expound that for worlds. It's a new sensation being preached at by one's own father.

OWEN. It will be hot, I promise you. I've only given you a taste of what is to come! I'm no light-weight in the pulpit.

JULIAN. You must give us a gala show on Sunday. Something more terrific than you've ever done before.

OWEN. You may humbug now. You won't feel like humbugging when you come out of chapel!

JULIAN. All right. I must have a last ungodly fling! I'm going out to buy twenty "Player's."
(*Exit.* OWEN *turns after him with an exasperated "Davy!"*)

LEONORA (*reassuringly*). He's just being naughty, Isaiah!

OWEN (*sitting at table while she sits at the other side, confidentially*). I want him to take a pull at himself in time. That's why I'm trying to put the fear of God into him. He won't stick to his books. I can't make him see the importance of it.

LEONORA. He's made a very good start.

OWEN. He's not done so badly, but he doesn't put enough will power into it. He doesn't concentrate.

LEONORA. I hope Dulcimer won't make it more difficult for him. I wish he'd stayed at Silver Gates. Julian has had nothing to distract him whilst his guardian was away.

OWEN. You've a great respect for Dulcimer, haven't you?

LEONORA. I've no illusions about his attraction for Julian. I can see that by the way Julian likes getting his letters. Dulcimer's got a huge personality, and he's rotten to the core.

OWEN. I remember all you told me about him.

LEONORA (*rising*). We'll get the better of him.

OWEN. We'll fight him together! (*Wistfully*) You don't blame me for handing Davy over?

LEONORA (*having moved over to the window*). Of course I don't.

OWEN. I blame myself sometimes. It wasn't a very creditable transaction. There was more in it than I've told you. (*With shame*) I got £500 for David, on condition that I had no more to do with him, but I didn't know so much about Mr. Dulcimer then as I do now. I was an awful drunkard at that time. I've wondered over and over again how I could have brought myself to sign that document. I must have been blind drunk at the time. I had come back from the War and my wife had died, and everything had gone to pot. (*Naïvely*) And yet, do you know, from the moment I got that £500, everything flourished.

LEONORA (*with a smile*). Like a green bay tree!

OWEN (*ruefully*). Perhaps the cap fits me after all. I tell you, Leo, I get in an awful muddle sometimes as to who are the ungodly and who aren't! Anyhow, I can't get away from it. I should never have got on and ended up by buying this business in London, if I hadn't had that start twelve years ago!

LEONORA. Don't worry over it. Julian will be all right. (*More to herself than to him.*)

OWEN. At any rate, I've set him an example. I've pulled myself together. (*He sees what she is looking at out of the window and joins her*) Do you see that old poster there? Fifteen years ago I would rather have sat in a charnel-house than sat opposite that! Now it's the symbol of my triumph! I could gaze at it unmoved for ever!

LEONORA. Have you told Julian all about yourself?

OWEN. No. I can't talk to him like I can talk to you, Leo.

LEONORA. I think he'd like to know, and I think it would help him to understand.

OWEN. I'm afraid not. He doesn't want to join up with me in any way. You see, Dulcimer has made him think himself a gentleman. That's where we are poles apart. I've no use for that sort of gentleman.

LEONORA. But you've very proud of him, all the same, aren't you?

OWEN. He's my son! My home is his as long as he cares to stay. He doesn't know how often I've wanted him, but that old Dulcimer kept him so close. Directly he was twenty-one I asked for him back, but it was no good.

LEONORA. We're allies over Dulcimer.

OWEN. No doubt he told Davy the tale about me. Still, I'm not a great catch.

LEONORA. You love him as I do.

OWEN. There's nothing I wouldn't do to help him, but a father's love hasn't much of a look in after twelve years of luxury. The best thing that ever happened to him was to fall in love with you.

LEONORA (*with great sincerity*). I'm terribly fond of him, Isaiah. (*He kisses her lightly on the forehead.*)

OWEN. Let's have some music. (*Sits at the organ*) This old organ has been my solace many a time.

LEONORA. Play one of your old Welsh airs.

OWEN. I'll play you *Tone Botel.* It's an old tune that was found in a bottle washed up out of the sea. (*He plays that fine but sombre air.*)

LEONORA (*after the first bars are over*). There's a wonderful roll in it, isn't there?

OWEN (*playing*). You want to hear a thousand people singing it up at Mountain Ash on Sunday evening. There's the strength of the mountains in it.
(*While he is playing,* JULIAN *comes back and stands listening on the right.* OWEN *sees him in a minute and stops.*)

OWEN. I didn't see you, Davy!

JULIAN. Don't stop! Something prehistoric in me stirs at that!

OWEN (*playing*). It's the music of your country, Davy! You can't help being stirred.

JULIAN. I've left all that that stands for a long way behind. I think it is like you, Isaiah! Rugged and rather sad! (*A knock at the front door*) Who on earth can that be?

OWEN. Run and see, my boy. It can't be your Aunt Lily yet.

JULIAN (*confidentially to* LEONORA). If it is, remember, we're going out!
(*Exit* JULIAN. *When he is gone,* OWEN *plays again.*)

LEONORA (*going to centre table*). I think we'll get off soon. I don't want to be caught!

OWEN. What are you going to see?

LEONORA (*looking down the advertisements in the paper*). Some show or other. Something gay. I think Julian wants to see *Spangles on Europe.*

OWEN. What does that mean?

LEONORA. God knows! I don't! (*Voices are heard on the stairs. Enter* JULIAN *followed by* TRUMP, *looking neat and rather sinister, with his hat in his hand.* OWEN *stops playing.*)

JULIAN. Leo! Here's Trump with a message from Dulcie!

TRUMP. Mr. Dulcimer presents his compliments, Miss, and hopes that you and Mr. Julian will dine with him this evening?

LEONORA (*wanting to get out of it*). Haven't we an engagement already, Julian?

JULIAN. No. We can easily go to a show another evening.

TRUMP. He's looking forward to seeing you both, Sir.

JULIAN. How is he?

TRUMP. Very fit, Sir. A little bored with the country, I fancy. Shall I tell him you're coming, Sir?

JULIAN (*to* LEONORA). We are coming, aren't we?

LEONORA. I suppose so.

TRUMP. The car will be round here at a quarter-to-eight, Sir.

JULIAN. Make it seven-thirty, and then I can go and call for Miss Yale.

TRUMP. Very good, Sir.

JULIAN. Seven-thirty. (*Exit* TRUMP.)

OWEN (*who has been taking in* TRUMP *during this conversation*). How does that fellow justify his existence?

JULIAN. By knowing what Dulcie wants almost before he knows it himself.

OWEN. He's Mr. Dulcimer's keeper, is he?

JULIAN (*smiling*). Not exactly. Look here, Isaiah, would you mind frightfully letting me have a word with Leo?

OWEN. Not at all, my boy. I'll take my Bible into the other room. (*Gets it*) But do you know what I should do this evening, if I were you? I'd go to *Spangles on Europe.* (*Exit.*)

JULIAN (*to* LEONORA). Darling, you look as if you'd seen the Devil!

LEONORA. Why on earth couldn't he have left us alone a little bit longer?

JULIAN (*coming to join her on the left-hand side of the table*). It's only natural he should want to see us.

LEONORA. He doesn't want to see me. That's quite certain.

JULIAN (*coaxingly*). Yes, he does.

LEONORA. No, Julian. And you know that perfectly well. He has no use for me whatever. (*Firmly.*)

JULIAN (*a little irritably*). Well, do you want me to ring him up and get out of it?

LEONORA. I should love you to.

JULIAN. Don't you think it would be rather rude?

LEONORA. I shouldn't care how rude it was. It would be so good for him to see that he can't just send for you whenever he pleases.

JULIAN. Are you jealous of Dulcie?

LEONORA (*protesting, but without conviction*). No! Of course I'm not!

JULIAN. It would be rather a ridiculous situation if you were!

LEONORA (*again with that unhappy note in her voice*). Wouldn't it? (*Sits on chair.*)

JULIAN. I'll tell you why I particularly want to go tonight. He hasn't seen me for nearly three months, and he's sure to be amiable. It's an excellent moment for reöpening the subject of an allowance.

LEONORA. Darling, he'll never change his mind about that.

JULIAN. I'll make him change it. (*Moving round to the other side of the table*) There's no earthly reason why I shouldn't have an allowance. From every point of view, I'm entitled to it. I think he was just testing me. He'll be quite different when he sees I've had a shot at working.

LEONORA. You mean to give up the idea of being a vet. If he consents?

JULIAN (*leans across the table*). If he consents I've got all sorts of schemes.

LEONORA. And if he refuses?

JULIAN. Then I stay here and go on with what I am doing. But if he consents it means that we can get married tomorrow!

LEONORA. That's worth risking anything for. (*He doesn't see what is behind her words.*)

JULIAN. Darling Leo! Happier now?

LEONORA. I'll go with you, Julian.

JULIAN. It won't be a very pleasant evening for me because I shall have this on my mind. After dinner I want you to invent some engagement, and leave me to tackle him. I couldn't do it with you there.

LEONORA. No, of course you couldn't. All right. I'll clear out early.

JULIAN. Splendid! Now you must go home and dress, and put on your prettiest frock. This is my idea if tonight comes off. . . .
(*They go out together, talking.*)

CURTAIN

SCENE II

At MR. DULCIMER'S *flat. The same evening.*
The gates into the roof-garden are without their screens.

The dinner, which has been unusual in its arrangement, is drawing to a close. The centre table has gone and MR. DULCIMER *sits at a small table in the middle of the room separated from* JULIAN *and* LEONORA, *who are at a similar small table near the window, but so placed that* MR. DULCIMER *can see both their faces. There is yet a third table, up stage left, with a chair on each side but without diners. Each table is identical, with lace cloth, flowers, and shaded candle lamp.*

This arrangement is one of MR. DULCIMER'S *jokes, but it serves to isolate* JULIAN *and* LEONORA. *The dinner has been excellent. Throughout it* MR. DULCIMER *has communicated with them through* TRUMP, *who acts up to* MR. DULCIMER'S *whim by posing as a magnificent Maître d'Hôtel.*

The joke has amused JULIAN, *who has entered into the game and has ordered every item of the dinner with the utmost gravity from* TRUMP'S *menu card.* LEONORA *has also entered into the spirit of it, but she has been a little embarrassed, for she knows that all through the meal* MR. DULCIMER *has been watching her.*

When the curtain rises TRUMP *is obsequiously attending to the imaginary diners at the third table.* MR. DULCIMER *is scribbling a note in pencil.*

LEONORA (*attracting his attention*). Julian! Have you enjoyed your dinner? (*She unconsciously lowers her voice.*)

DULCIMER. Trump! (TRUMP *leaves the imaginary diners and comes to him*) Will you give this to the gentleman at the other table?

TRUMP. Certainly, Sir. (*Takes note to* JULIAN.)

JULIAN. Thank you. (*Reads note, laughs, and scribbles reply.* TRUMP *takes it to* DULCIMER) I haven't had a dinner like this since . . . well, not since I left home.
(*He casts half an eye on* DULCIMER *who is sipping brandy meditatively.* DULCIMER *reads note. Exit* TRUMP.)

LEONORA. But I mean, have you enjoyed having it this way?

JULIAN. I haven't minded. In fact, it's been rather fun. As if I really had been taking you out to dinner. We'll have lots of these later on.

LEONORA. Shall we have to go on playing this game all the evening?

JULIAN. Good Lord, no! Dulcie will suddenly call it off, especially as we've played up to him so well. He can't bear anyone not to enter into a joke or to seem stupid and awkward over it.

LEONORA. I'm beginning to feel self-conscious now. It's gone on too long, and I know he's watching me. He's been watching me all the time.

JULIAN. Don't give in! You've been splendid! It hasn't spoiled your dinner, has it?

LEONORA. Not a bit. (*Enter* TRUMP) As long as I don't think he's done it just to annoy me, and make me look a fool.

JULIAN. Rather not. He used to spring all sorts of surprises on me when I was a boy, and see how I reacted to them. It was his idea of education. Whatever the occasion, never be gauche or nonplussed! It did smarten one up. Here comes the ice pudding!
(TRUMP *is entering with a large and very exquisitely designed ice pudding shaped like a small rose tree in bloom. The roses are made of strawberry ice. He carries it round the room showing it to the diners at the imaginary table as well.* MR. DULCIMER *comes out of his apparent reverie and gazes at it languidly.*)

TRUMP (*coming up to* LEONORA). Will madame take ice pudding?

LEONORA (*who has already exclaimed as the pudding came into the room*). Yes, please, if you can bear cutting it.

TRUMP. We like our guests to pick the flowers. I will give madame a little of this one. (*He helps her.*)

JULIAN (*to* LEONORA). Have a liqueur, darling?

LEONORA. No, thanks.

JULIAN (*to* TRUMP, *as he helps him*). I seem to remember a very fine old brandy when I was here in the old days.

TRUMP. The 1796, Sir?

JULIAN. That must be it.

TRUMP. Certainly, Sir.

JULIAN. Your face seems familiar, too.

TRUMP. Thank you, Sir. (*Moves away with the pudding to* DULCIMER.)

DULCIMER. Not for me, thank you. (*Taking a couple of roses from the bowl in front of him*) Do you think I dare interrupt that charming couple once more?

TRUMP. I'm sure they'll only be too delighted, Sir.

DULCIMER. You really think so? Then give the lady these roses with my compliments. Tell her that they will add to the illusion.
(TRUMP *puts the pudding on* DULCIMER'S *table and takes the roses to* LEONORA.)

TRUMP. With the compliments of the gentleman at the centre table, madame.

LEONORA (*taking roses*). Aren't they exquisite? Thank him very much.

DULCIMER. Maître d'hôtel!

TRUMP. Yes, Sir?

DULCIMER. Remove the rose bush and bring me some more brandy.
(TRUMP *takes pudding to side table behind couch and gets brandy from there.*)

LEONORA. We can't keep it up much longer. I shall laugh in a minute.

JULIAN. I've known him pretend to be someone else for a whole day. Have some more pudding to keep you going?

LEONORA. No, thanks. (*Then, after a moment*) Do you think we can play it out to the very end? I mean, pretend to pay for the dinner and then go off somewhere together?

JULIAN. I'm afraid we can't do quite that, but it'll help to bring matters to a head. (*To* TRUMP, *who has given* MR. DULCIMER *his brandy*) Waiter!

TRUMP (*turning to* JULIAN *and feigning indignation of an exquisite kind*). Maître d'hôtel, Sir!

JULIAN (*with a smile*). I beg your pardon! Anyhow, let me have my bill!

TRUMP. Certainly, Sir! (*Pretends to go and fetch the bill.*)

JULIAN. Bring me a cheque form will you?

TRUMP (*nonplussed for a moment*). A cheque form, Sir?

JULIAN. Good Heavens, you know me well enough for that, don't you?

TRUMP. We should do, Sir! (*Under his breath*) That's torn it!

JULIAN. Well, look sharp, we're going to the Paramount to see *The Man About Town*. We're late as it is.

TRUMP. I believe it's a good second act, Sir! (*To himself*) Oh well, here goes! (*Walks over to the bureau and looks for* MR. DULCIMER'S *cheque book.*)

LEONORA. Is he going to let him get it?

JULIAN (*watching* DULCIMER *out of the corner of his eye*). Wait a minute!

DULCIMER (*speaking over his shoulder to* TRUMP). When you've quite finished rummaging among my papers, Trump, will you please bring coffee?

TRUMP (*relieved that the game is over*). Yes, Sir! (*Exit.*)

JULIAN (*smiling*). I think we win, Dulcie?

DULCIMER (*getting up*). Your game, my boy. Very neatly played.

JULIAN. Now say "How do you do?" to Leo, and stop acting.

DULCIMER (*coming over to them*). I shan't say anything so banal after admiring you both for the last half-hour. A delightful couple! (*To* LEONORA *in explanation*) It's so refreshing to see people sometimes from an unusual angle.

LEONORA. I think it's a marvellous game. I can imagine all kinds of possibilities.

DULCIMER. It's a relief from the obvious and monotonous. They are the ghosts that haunt modern civilisation. Nowadays everybody does everything and nobody does it well. I can't join in the great display of uninspired competence, so I contrive little originalities of my own.

JULIAN. You're a "bright" old thing, aren't you?

DULCIMER. Let's sit and smoke! (*Sits at their table, taking the spare chair from his own table*) So the course of love runs smoothly even though it runs through Camden Town.

LEONORA (*emphatically*). It runs beautifully, Mr. Dulcimer.

DULCIMER (*after a tiny pause*). I left my cigarette-holder in the roof-garden, Julian. I wish you'd get it for me.

JULIAN (*getting up after a quick look at* LEONORA). Right you are! (*Exit.* DULCIMER *gets up and shuts the gates of the roof-garden.*)

LEONORA (*getting up and continuing her remark*). I shall win.

DULCIMER (*turning round and smiling innocently*). What a fierce little thing it is! Of course you'll win as you call it, if by that you mean that you'll marry Julian. (*Coming to her.*)

LEONORA (*firmly*). I do mean that!

DULCIMER. Well, then, that's all right. (*Pats her hand. She withdraws it*) Still determined to see me as an enemy just because I didn't fling you at each other's heads like any ordinary parent would have done. (*Sits again at her table on the same chair. She takes the chair* JULIAN *sat in before*) By the way, how is the official parent?

LEONORA. He's very fit. He's awfully pleased to have Julian back.

DULCIMER. He wants to resume parenthood you know. He wrote to me about it.

LEONORA. He's very anxious to be a real father to Julian.

DULCIMER. Perhaps the moment has come for that too.

LEONORA. Do you really mean that? Would you let him go?

DULCIMER. Let him go! You really must disabuse yourself of this notion that I wish to detain him. It's simply that I don't suddenly expose sensitive hot-house plants to harsh winds, not even when you're the Lady of the Garden. I took a certain amount of risk in doing what I did.

LEONORA. But he's survived all right.

DULCIMER. I can see that. I was watching you both carefully just now.

LEONORA. I knew you were.

DULCIMER. Again that note of suspicion! Just because I go out of my way to test things to make quite sure. You both had a theory that you were in love . . .

LEONORA. It was never a theory with me!

DULCIMER (*protestingly*). I know! But it might have been! Isn't that true?

LEONORA. I suppose it is.

DULCIMER. The last time you were here you were both very impetuous. You wanted me to cover you with large allowances . . .

LEONORA. No. I never wanted that. I knew that Julian could do without it!

DULCIMER. And that part of the experiment is working, too?

LEONORA. He's made a splendid start!

DULCIMER. And knows all about Foot and Mouth Disease?

LEONORA. Very nearly all.

DULCIMER. I can see the change in him. He's got a purpose in his life.

LEONORA (*enigmatically*). I'm glad you see that.

DULCIMER. And don't you think that an allowance two months ago might have undermined him? Now, of course . . .

LEONORA (*almost afraid to put her thought into words*). You mean that you feel differently about it now?

DULCIMER. I mean that at every crisis in Julian's life, I want to be behind him with just that bias in the right direction that a real father never seems able to give. You can't believe that, can you?

LEONORA. I should like to believe it very much.

DULCIMER. I remember the moment so well, when you suddenly took it into your head to dislike me. You were standing over there. (*Pointing.*)

LEONORA. I couldn't help myself then. I can't help myself now.

DULCIMER. And yet, quite a number of people have liked me! Some have even said that I was fascinating! (*With that disarming drawl of his*) Do I fascinate you, Leonora?

LEONORA. Yes. Shall I tell you how? I'm afraid it won't sound very complimentary. (*Rising*) You fascinate me like a snake fascinates.

DULCIMER (*seemingly horrified*). You mean that you're afraid of me?

LEONORA (*firmly*). Not for a second. You see, I'm not under the spell. I mean that I like watching you, just as much as you like watching me.

DULCIMER (*rising and walking about the room*). Oh, dear! Why wasn't I born ordinary? Ordinary people aren't accused of casting spells, or turned into things at the Zoo. (*Indignantly*) I know what it is. You'd have liked a nice suburban wooing! High tea and then the Upper Circle at *Cavalcade*. I'm sorry! I don't know how to set about it. I just don't!

(*Enter* JULIAN *from roof-garden.*)

JULIAN. I can't find your cigarette-holder anywhere on the roof.

DULCIMER (*moving to fireplace*). It doesn't matter. I must have dropped it down a chimney.

JULIAN. What are you standing on your hind legs for?

DULCIMER. Begging, my dear boy! Begging for a little of the milk of human kindness.

LEONORA. Mr. Dulcimer has started another game now. This time he's the great misunderstood, and he's annoyed with me because I won't play.

JULIAN. I've no misunderstandings about anything. I'm just happy and comfortable.

DULCIMER. You mustn't be happy or comfortable! You must sit up to the table and have a nice cup of cocoa! (*Sits on couch.*)

JULIAN. That's not a bad idea! (*Goes to table behind couch and helps himself to another glass of brandy*) Here's to comfort!
(DULCIMER *and* LEONORA *are both watching him.*)

LEONORA. As a matter of fact, Mr. Dulcimer and I understand each other perfectly. Whatever we say, we both see into each other's minds quite a long way.

JULIAN (*languidly*). How simple!

LEONORA (*firmly*). I think it is, too! (*Rises*) At any rate I'm going to leave it to you now.

DULCIMER (*surprised, not understanding*). You're not going?

LEONORA (*chaffing him*). My suburban habits again! Bed early!

JULIAN. Don't go yet!

LEONORA. You know that I've got to. I only hope that Mr. Dulcimer won't think me rude. I've got a couple of sick dogs to look after. (DULCIMER *winces.*)

JULIAN (*earnestly*). Don't go, Leo! Not quite yet! (*He is struggling mentally between her and his old life.*)

LEONORA. All right! I'll stay a little longer!
(*Enter* TRUMP *with coffee.*)

JULIAN (*pushing brandy bottle away*). I'm as firm as a rock.

LEONORA. Darling, don't be absurd.

JULIAN. I mean that and all it symbolises. I can't actually push the whole room away, but I do.

LEONORA (*in whisper*). Darling, I love you!
(TRUMP *hands coffee.*)

DULCIMER (*turning round*). You must stay till you've had your coffee.
(TRUMP *hands it round.*)

LEONORA. I'll be delighted to.

DULCIMER (*to* TRUMP, *as he hands him coffee*). Clear away the Monseigneur! (*Pointing to the two tables.*)

TRUMP. Yes, Sir. (*He moves centre table bodily from the room after having turned out the light. Then he returns with the trolley-waiter, and during the following dialogue puts the other two tables out of the way, and clears the things from them.*)

DULCIMER. I'm afraid we must be obvious for once and turn on that dreadful wireless. (JULIAN *does so*)

You see, Leonora, I'm much more ordinary than you think, I've just this single room. Here I am and here I have to stay.

LEONORA (*coming over to him and sitting by his side. Amused*). Poor dear! So hampered and hemmed in!

DULCIMER. So few rooms mean anything, and I could just do something with this one, and then of course there was the roof-garden. That counted for something.

JULIAN (*coming near them. Joking*). It's not a bad little common room.

DULCIMER. It has its drawbacks of course. One can never "join the ladies."

LEONORA. Well, you asked me to stay!

DULCIMER (*kindly*). I want you to stay! I always remember your appreciation of this room the first time you saw it.

LEONORA. You don't forget things, do you?

DULCIMER. I make vivid mental notes of anything I like or dislike. (*To* TRUMP *who is clearing away*) What's that tune?

TRUMP. I think it's a new fox-trot, Sir. "I like her for liking her baby."

DULCIMER. Don't you think you ought to dance?

LEONORA. I don't feel like it, do you, Julian?

JULIAN. Come on! Let's try! (*They dance.*)

DULCIMER (*tormenting himself with the sight*). You were right, Trump!

TRUMP (*stopping in his work*). Was I, Sir?

DULCIMER. You said that Miss Yale danced well.
(*They are now on the other side of the room.* MR. DULCIMER *gets up.*)

TRUMP. Is anything wrong, Sir?

DULCIMER. Yes. (*Puts his coffee cup on mantelpiece.*)

TRUMP. I'm sorry, Sir!

DULCIMER. I've lost my cigarette-holder. It's on the roof somewhere.

TRUMP. Let me look, Sir!

DULCIMER (*harshly*). No, you get on with your work. I shall call down every chimney. (*Exit quickly on to roof-garden.* TRUMP *watches him and smiles. He knows.*)

JULIAN (*stopping dancing*). Has he gone? (*Speaks over* LEONORA'S *shoulder.*)

TRUMP (*pointing to roof-garden*). Out there, Sir! (*Exit with trolley-waiter.*)

JULIAN. You really think he's come round?

LEONORA. I couldn't tell. He never came to the point.

JULIAN. I'll bring him to the point.

LEONORA. But if nothing comes of it, you won't let him undermine us, will you? Even if these two months haven't meant a huge amount of work, they've brought us still closer together, haven't they?

JULIAN. Closer than ever, darling!

LEONORA (*moving to roof-garden*). Is he watching us?

JULIAN (*following her*). He's out there in the darkness.

LEONORA. I know. Watching!

JULIAN. Darling, what a bogy you make of him!

LEONORA. It's not himself. It's everything he stands for! It's this room, and luxury, and comfort . . . and idleness . . .

JULIAN. And everything that's mine by right. Why shouldn't I have it? I shall work then, with security behind me, instead of this void stretching out for centuries.

LEONORA. Yes, but supposing he won't?

JULIAN. Then we just go on as we are.

LEONORA. Promise?

JULIAN. Promise!

LEONORA. We'll think of something.

JULIAN. Of course, darling Leo! (*He puts his arm round her.*)

LEONORA (*seeing that* DULCIMER *is coming back*). Take care!

JULIAN. Let him see that we mean business.

(*A long embrace.* DULCIMER *returns from the roof. He switches off the radio. They break.*)

JULIAN. Well, Dulcie, is it a starry night?

DULCIMER. The Coliseum appears to be in the ascendant at the moment.

LEONORA. Now, I really must be off. Can I ring you up before I go to bed?

JULIAN. Rather!

LEONORA. Here? You won't be going at once?

JULIAN. Not for ages.

LEONORA. I don't want to bring your father down to answer it.

JULIAN. Ring me here.

LEONORA. Just to say "good night" (*and to hear the result of his talk*).

JULIAN. I'll get your wrap. (*He goes out of the room.*)

DULCIMER (*to* LEONORA). Don't forget your roses. (*Gets them from the table*) Would you hate me to pin them into your dress?

LEONORA. I've nothing to fasten them with.

DULCIMER (*looking at her earnestly*). Will you carry them? Wait a minute. (*He gets a silver penknife from the bureau and strips the thorns from the stalks*) There! Now they are as harmless as I am. (LEONORA *takes them, looking at him steadily.*)

LEONORA. They're delicious. (*Smells them.* JULIAN *returns with cloak.*)

JULIAN (*putting it round her*). Same time as usual, tomorrow? (DULCIMER *rings the bell.*)

LEONORA. Yes, darling. Don't come down. (*To* DULCIMER) Good night!

JULIAN. I'll see you to the lift. (*He goes out with her.* DULCIMER *watches them go, then turns down some of the lights, and going to the piano, plays softly.* JULIAN *comes back, wanders round the room, and leans on piano.*)

JULIAN. Have you ever played the harmonium, Dulcie? (*Dreamily*) It's not an instrument you can stroke like you're stroking that piano. Is that Chopin?

DULCIMER. Sonata in B Minor.

JULIAN. It seems to call out all the peacefulness of the room, but you make it seem magical. (*Coming to couch and sitting down*) Who was the person who heard "sounds and sweet airs" and "cried to sleep again"?

DULCIMER (*quoting*). "Sounds and sweet airs, that give delight, and hurt not . . ."

JULIAN. Yes! That's it!

DULCIMER. "and then in dreaming,
The clouds, methought would
open, and show riches,
Ready to drop upon me; that,
when I waked,
I cried to dream again."

JULIAN. You read it to me once. "Riches ready to drop upon me," and Leo . . . (*Then he suddenly springs to his feet.* MR. DULCIMER *stops playing*) I was nearly passing out. (*He braces himself up*) I expect the room's hot.

DULCIMER. Go on to the roof and get some air. (*He comes towards him.*)

JULIAN. I'm all right. I haven't been used to anything soft for such a long time. I felt as if I was drowning.

DULCIMER. You were always very imaginative. Sit down again. I won't play any more if my playing makes you swoon. (JULIAN *sits on couch again, this time a little apprehensively.* DULCIMER *stands behind him*) Perhaps you need a restorative? (*Takes up brandy from table behind.*)

JULIAN. No, thanks.

DULCIMER. It is rather too good to take medicinally. (*Sits beside* JULIAN) So things haven't lost their glamour?

JULIAN. I've missed everything horribly, and it's marvellous to be back. Why did you have that freak dinner tonight?

DULCIMER. I was just thinking of you and Leonora. You might have hated the thought of this place and of me and of everything to do with it. Then the formality, the removal to a distance, would have reassured you. You would have eaten your dinner, perhaps we should have smiled at each other once or twice, like one does, you'd have paid your bill and departed.

JULIAN. That's just what Leo wanted to do!

DULCIMER. And by now you'd have been peacefully enjoying Continuous Variety. (*Springing up*) What a fool I've been! An ill-mannered fool! To start a game and then refuse to play it out! You wanted to go! But then you found that the prison door wasn't really open! Like the captives in the Bastille you reached the last corridor only to rush into your gaoler's arms! (*He has worked himself up into a fine passion.*)

JULIAN (*half-amused and half-alarmed*). You know quite well that I didn't think anything of the kind! I was thankful to get back here, and hated not being able to talk to you all through dinner. Now sit down, and as I said before, stop acting!

DULCIMER (*sitting down beside him*). At least you can never say that I kept you against your will, even though I have no respect for natural ties.

JULIAN. I've had an eye-opener over them, I can assure you. Do let me enjoy myself a little bit! I'm going back to "natural ties" soon enough!

DULCIMER (*interested and inwardly anxious*). Do you find they count for much?

JULIAN. More than I expected. I suppose that's because he is my father. I suppose he got a footing inside me during those first eleven years.

DULCIMER (*indignantly*). He never bothered about you at all.

JULIAN. Well, there it is! He's utterly impossible, but he exists. I don't suppose you can understand. You never knew your father, did you?

DULCIMER. No.

JULIAN. But you adored your mother.

DULCIMER. She was the only woman who ever meant a thing to me.

JULIAN. And then of course I have some strange affinity with him over the past. He plays those ghastly Welsh hymns, and I listen to them, and something happens to me. I don't know what it is.

DULCIMER. Some of those melodies are extraordinarily fine.

JULIAN. It isn't anything aesthetic. It isn't even pleasure. It calls from somewhere very far off and makes me feel I belong to something very old. I thought what a contrast it was just now. You at the piano and father at the harmonium. But they both speak. . . . Now let's forget Camden Town.

DULCIMER. I should like you to have been at Silver Gates this time. I took your advice about the music room. It now faces the swimming pool.

JULIAN. I always told you it ought to.

DULCIMER. You were perfectly right. I've had the pool floodlighted. Now at night the box hedges enclose a lagoon of deep Mediterranean blue. Ruinously expensive!

JULIAN. Marvellous! I mean—how exquisite! (*They laugh.*)

DULCIMER. We must give a fancy-dress bathing party. Venetian and very slippery. (*All the time he is watching* JULIAN *closely.*)

JULIAN. My God! So while you're splashing in the moonlight, I shall be sweating in Camden Town!

DULCIMER (*realising that the spell is working, and getting up*). Now, won't you change your mind? (*Goes to table behind and holds up brandy bottle.*)

JULIAN. Well, I don't see why I shouldn't! (DULCIMER *gives him some brandy and takes some himself*) Yes! That's not for invalids!

DULCIMER (*standing*). Leonora tells me that you settled down to work wonderfully!

JULIAN. Did she say that? But I don't think I've taken her in! Not really! She knows that I'm not getting on, but she's a fine encourager.

DULCIMER. She certainly made me think you'd made a good start.

JULIAN. I've tried. I genuinely have. But I can't get up any interest in the stuff. What's the point in reading up a lot of flapdoodle in order to give some filthy little Pekinese an emetic?

DULCIMER. I should hate to give anyone an emetic. I could never get into the right frame of mind. But then, I haven't the call! (*Moves right.*)

JULIAN. Nor have I. Dulcie, it is no good shirking the fact any longer. I'm no good at it.

DULCIMER (*coming back to him*). We won't despair after two months.

JULIAN (*firmly*). I despaired after a fortnight. I knew then.

DULCIMER (*with assumed surprise*). You give it up?

JULIAN. I'm afraid so. As far as exams are concerned.

DULCIMER (*sitting beside him after showing relief*). Shall I make a suggestion?

JULIAN (*earnestly and hopefully*). I wish you would.

DULCIMER. Take a rest and then come back to it. Come for a holiday.

JULIAN. I could do with a holiday.

DULCIMER. Come to the Villa at Margherita.

JULIAN. Can I bring Leo?

DULCIMER. Of course.

JULIAN. I know she won't though. (DULCIMER *shows relief in his face*) She'll never leave her work just now, especially after giving up so much time to me.

DULCIMER. Can't you tear yourself away from her for a week or two?

JULIAN. I suppose I could. (*Gets up and moves a little away to the right.*)

DULCIMER. You're so adhesive, Julian. First it was Peter. Now it's Leonora.

JULIAN. They're not quite the same thing.

DULCIMER. For Heaven's sake don't you begin to misunderstand me. I was merely admiring your loyalty, but I don't want to drag you there.

JULIAN. You know I'd adore to come! (*The struggle in him is now definitely beginning.*)

DULCIMER (*sprawling on couch*). I daresay I was only going to make a convenience of you. The ceiling wants touching up badly. The Cupids on it look like very old charwomen. It's delicate work, but no doubt I can get it done.

JULIAN (*coming and standing at head of couch*). Dulcie! You know perfectly well that I'd give my head to come to Italy. The point is, I've got to earn a living. (DULCIMER *sits straight and* JULIAN *beside him*) Dulcie, I've never asked you for anything much before. I've never had to ask you. Now I must put it into words, though I hate doing it. Can't you reconsider your decision?

DULCIMER. What decision?

JULIAN. I've been screwing up my courage all the evening to ask you for an allowance. The fact is I simply cannot earn.

DULCIMER (*suavely*). Supposing I do reconsider my decision?

JULIAN (*eagerly*). Then that would make everything all right. I don't want to be idle. I never have been idle. I like having something to do all the time. You see, my idea is to live in the country, away from all this that I can't afford.

DULCIMER. You think you could endure the country—always?

JULIAN. I'd like to run kennels or something of the kind. I haven't the slightest intention of vegetating . . . we've got all sorts of schemes. We thought it might be possible to run polo ponies.

DULCIMER. What sum of money do you think would make it possible?

JULIAN. Well, we'd have to make a start. That costs a good bit, I know.

DULCIMER. It's no good underestimating that. By the time you'd bought your house and equipped it with livestock, you'd have spent the best part of four or five thousand pounds.

JULIAN (*on tenterhooks*). I'm afraid I should. But then we could live on very little. I think that five hundred a year would do us well. That would mean a home and security, and I should be delivered for ever from this nightmare of daily bread.

DULCIMER. It almost seems a pity I didn't make you a plumber.

JULIAN (*smiling ruefully*). I rather wish I had been taught something. (DULCIMER *sighs and is silent*) What are you thinking?

DULCIMER. I was thinking that six months hence, or a year hence, you'll find that your allowance isn't enough and that your menagerie doesn't pay, and you'll come and ask for more.

JULIAN. I promise you I'll never ask you for a penny again!

DULCIMER. Like the tiger, you'll have tasted blood and you'll be greedy to taste more!

JULIAN. Then you mean that you won't help me?

DULCIMER (*looking at him gravely*). I won't give you any money, Julian. (*He gets up and walks away to window as* JULIAN *did in Act One.* JULIAN *watches him.*)

JULIAN (*after a moment*). Dulcie?

DULCIMER. Well?

JULIAN. You want me to be happy, don't you?

DULCIMER (*turning round fiercely*). Want you to be happy? You've always been happy. I've made you happy!

JULIAN. Yes, but I must go on. I can't just stand still.

DULCIMER. You must be as you are. You must develop naturally. (*Standing by couch*) Listen, Julian! There is nothing to be ashamed of or disappointed over in not being able to earn a living. You aren't made that way, that's all. I delivered you for ever from what you call "the nightmare of daily bread." You have a home and security that nothing can take from you, and you won't recognise it.

JULIAN (*emphatically*). I want to get married, I tell you!

DULCIMER. For goodness' sake, don't be strident!

JULIAN. I can't always pick and choose my words, just to please you!

DULCIMER. I'm not complaining of your language yet. I only ask you not to shout!

JULIAN. You seem to think that what is soft and expensive and luxurious is everything!

DULCIMER (*quickly*). And, don't you? Haven't you proved it tonight? Haven't the last two months proved it? What matters to you most is to be comfortable, to have pleasant rooms and pleasant meals, and money in your pocket. You have tried the other thing, and hated it, haven't you? (*Sits in armchair near window*) Very well, then. Be honest with yourself. Don't try to be some other person. Be Julian Dulcimer.

JULIAN. But I'm not Julian Dulcimer!

DULCIMER. Do you want me to believe that you're David Owen just because you were stirred a little at some crude revivalist hymn?

JULIAN (*getting up*). You can't understand what I am or what I want!

DULCIMER (*also getting up*). By all means let us talk this out standing up. It's very fatiguing, but I can see that you mean to be emphatic!

JULIAN (*coming over to him*). Dulcie, do for one moment be human! Can't you try to understand what I'm struggling against?

DULCIMER. I do, perfectly. But why struggle with no chance of succeeding?

JULIAN. Why shouldn't I succeed?

DULCIMER. Because you can't be two people at the same time. You cannot be Julian Dulcimer and a married man. They have been fighting with each other from the first moment they met. My dear boy, it's quite natural that you should want to include Leonora in your scheme, but unfortunately there isn't room for her.

JULIAN (*surprised*). Why?

DULCIMER. Well, you don't want her to have to keep you, do you?

JULIAN (*moving away*). I haven't the slightest intention of her doing so! (*Sits on couch.*)

DULCIMER. Yet, that is what it will come to! You want me to let you pretend for a while that you are what is known as a bread-winner, but in the end you'll depend on your wife. All these dreams of dogs and polo ponies and other country nonsense will crumble into dust the first morning you don't feel like getting up, or fancy a day in town. You couldn't stand up to your inclination for a second, and why should you?

JULIAN (*turning round*). You think you know me, but you're wrong!

DULCIMER. Very well, then! Go and get married! (*Vehemently*) Disregard your temperament, your disposition, your everything that cries out against it! Beat out a living from the world and fashion a home for your wife, and live in it, and be happy ever after! Can you do it?

JULIAN. Why do you torment me like this?

DULCIMER. Can you say, "Leonora comes before everything else? I don't care what I do and where I live so long as she is with me!" Of course you can't! But you haven't the courage to admit it, and it's only a fool who won't recognise his own limitations. (*A silence*) However, I suppose that your silence means that you do recognise them, so we won't use any more harsh names. You're not really the fool you're trying so hard to be. (*Passing in front of him to the hearth.*)

JULIAN (*turning on him fiercely*). By God, I'm not! I'm not fool enough to be one thing, and that is, your slave!

DULCIMER. Don't be ridiculous!

JULIAN (*trembling*). You think my life is yours to arrange as you please, but you're wrong again. I'm damned well going to do what I like with it! I think I detest you and your luxurious ways, and your beastly superior air about everything. I shall live where I like and how I like, and you can go to Hell! (*The telephone bell rings.*)

DULCIMER. Prove it, then! Now's your chance! (*Holding receiver towards him*) Tell her! You little canting fool! You know that luxury is the breath of your life. You couldn't do without it for a second. What you are feeling is a childish revulsion against yourself. You wanted to be noble and romantic, and you're disappointed because you can't be! Self-loathing is always painful, but fortunately one outgrows it. Tell her that I won't help you, and that you'll fight your way to her through poverty and struggle and self-denial! Don't keep her waiting! (*Holds receiver nearer to him.*)

(JULIAN *takes receiver and tries hard to answer* LEONORA, *then with an exclamation of despair drops the receiver on the floor and falls on the couch in a fit of weeping.* DULCIMER *picks up the receiver and replaces it, then goes to the bell and rings it. He then walks quickly to the piano, seats himself at it and plays the Chopin Sonata. Enter* TRUMP.)

DULCIMER (*playing as the 'phone rings again*). Get Mr. Julian's room ready, please!

TRUMP. Very good, Sir! (*He glances at the 'phone, then at* DULCIMER, *then goes. The 'phone continues to ring.*)

CURTAIN

ACT THREE

SCENE I

At MR. DULCIMER'S *flat. Next morning.*

The arrangement of the room is as in Act I. The centre table is now back in its place; on it stands an open attaché case, but the audience cannot see the contents. The table behind the couch is gone.

MR. DULCIMER *is seated at the bureau.* TRUMP *enters carrying a brown paper parcel which he puts on the table near the case.*

DULCIMER (*looking up*). Oh, there you are, Trump! I want you to send off this wire. We're going abroad. Do you like the idea? (*Hands him wire.*)

TRUMP. Shall we be away long, Sir? (*He seems a little perturbed at the news.*)

DULCIMER. About six months, I think.

TRUMP. Really, Sir?

DULCIMER. Yes. Mr. Julian and I both want a change. He's been overworking. I'm anxious about him. (*Seeing his face*) You look a little dashed at my news. *You've* not been forming any attachments, have you?

TRUMP. No, Sir. I'm quite heart-whole.

DULCIMER. Good. For a moment I thought that you'd been tainted.

TRUMP. No, Sir. Quite immune, as yet.

DULCIMER. That's right. We shall be passing into a more temperate zone in a day or two, beyond the ravages of this terrible disease.

We'll take sanctuary first at Margherita. That's why I want Michele to get that wire as soon as possible. So that he may get the villa ready. Later on, I dare say, we shall be moving about. (*Moves across the room, picking up parcel from table. He takes off the paper, throws it on to the window seat, and puts the book on the centre table.*)

TRUMP. When are we starting, Sir?

DULCIMER. Tonight.

TRUMP. Shall I make the usual travelling arrangements?

DULCIMER. Please. And tell Mortimer I'm taking the car. We need movement and distraction.

TRUMP. Very good, Sir.
(*Exit* TRUMP. DULCIMER *goes to bureau, gets pass-port, etc., unlocks drawer, takes out a revolver, and puts them all in attaché case. Enter* JULIAN *a moment later, in a very elaborate dressing-gown.* DULCIMER *is now by the roof-garden and is carolling "O, Sole Mio."*)

JULIAN. You sound very gay this morning.

DULCIMER. My dear boy, I've gone all holiday. The Blue Train is in my blood. Tomorrow evening we shall be by the Mediterranean. Don't you think that a little of Italy will be rather fun?

JULIAN (*sitting down by the window in the arm-chair*). I shall be glad to get away anywhere. (*Not with very great enthusiasm.*)

DULCIMER (*handing him the book*). This came for you, just now.

JULIAN. What is it? (*Taking it.*)

DULCIMER. It's Deller's "*Impressions of the Umbrian Towns.*" There's a picture of Perugia in the early morning that's rather lovely.

JULIAN (*opening the book*). Are we going to the Umbrian Towns?

DULCIMER. Would you like to?

JULIAN. I don't care where we go as long as it's somewhere new, something I haven't seen before.

DULCIMER. We'll take the car and break new ground.

JULIAN (*looking at the pictures*). That's refreshing.

DULCIMER. I thought you knew Deller's work? I've been meaning to give you this for a long time. I sent down for it directly after breakfast this morning. I wanted something to blot out yesterday evening.

JULIAN. It's awfully kind of you, Dulcie.

DULCIMER. Let me have it for a moment. (*He takes the book and writes in it with his pen*) There! (*Hands it back.*)

JULIAN (*reading*). "Addio to all misunderstandings." (*Smiles, but just a little sadly.*)

DULCIMER (*lightly*). It will do to read in the train. (*Goes back to roof-garden.*)

JULIAN. Yes. For God's sake, let's be off!

DULCIMER. Trump's fixed everything up.

JULIAN. I should like to get into the car and go at once.

DULCIMER. I think everything points today to a very good lunch somewhere and then a little shopping. You'll want to get some things, won't you?

JULIAN. One or two, I suppose.

DULCIMER. A super-lunch and then a little agreeable spending in Bond Street or thereabouts. We won't get back till it's time to start.

JULIAN. I've got to see Leo some time for a minute.

DULCIMER (*cautiously*). Perhaps you'll write?

JULIAN. No. I must see her.

DULCIMER. I can drop you at the Surgery for five minutes.

JULIAN. Yes. That will do.

DULCIMER (*ingratiatingly and coming to him*). Don't be too hard on yourself. Six months' probation before you finally make up your mind is a most reasonable request.

JULIAN. I shall be glad to get it over, all the same.
(*Enter* TRUMP.)

DULCIMER. What is it?

TRUMP. Miss Yale would like to see Mr. Julian.

JULIAN (*getting up*). Where is she?

TRUMP. In the hall, Sir. I didn't know whether you had time to see people.

JULIAN (*crossing to couch*). Show her in.

TRUMP. Very good, Sir.
(*Exit* TRUMP.)

DULCIMER. Would you like me to tackle this?

JULIAN (*very pale*). No thanks, Dulcie.

DULCIMER. All right. I'll clear out and leave you together. (*Putting his hand on his shoulder*) I'm sure she'll understand.

JULIAN (*simply*). I hope she will. (DULCIMER *goes to the door. As he gets to it,* TRUMP *opens it and shows in* LEONORA.)

TRUMP. Miss Yale.

DULCIMER (*unpleasantly agreeable*). Good morning, Leonora! (*As she ejaculates "Julian!"*) Now you mustn't scold him. We got very late last night and hadn't the heart to disturb you.

LEONORA. But I rang you quite early and couldn't get any reply.

DULCIMER. We were here all the evening. However, Julian will tell you all about it. (*Exit.*)

LEONORA (*coming to* JULIAN). Good morning, darling! (*They kiss uncomfortably*) What did happen? I rang up Isaiah this morning and found that you hadn't been home last night.

JULIAN. No. I stayed here.

LEONORA (*seeing that there is something different about him*). I see. Isaiah is rather worried. He came along with me. He's waiting outside in the square. (*Taking hold of his hand and drawing him down on to the couch*) Julian, darling, don't mind! What's it matter if he won't give you any money? That's why you didn't answer the 'phone, wasn't it?

JULIAN. I couldn't get a penny out of him, Leo.

LEONORA. I knew that was it. Well, we're not going to let money stand between us and our happiness, are we? I expect we've worried too much about it. Last night when I didn't hear from you, I made up my mind what we'd do. We'll get married at once and damn the money. I've got enough for two, with a squeeze.

JULIAN (*in misery*). I can't let you do that, Leo. It's lovely of you to suggest it, but I can't.

LEONORA. You wouldn't mind skimping a little with me, would you? Until something turned up. I think we'd better put the idea of exams out of our heads, don't you?

JULIAN (*almost amused, in spite of himself*). Darling, I do.

LEONORA. Everybody who's got a job hasn't passed an exam. Something will come along.

JULIAN. One can always tout notepaper round to people's front doors.

LEONORA. We've not come to that yet. We'll get uncertainty out of our life first and then set to work to build it up. You'll feel far more confident of yourself when you're married to me.

JULIAN. Leo, I can't marry you!

LEONORA. Julian!

JULIAN. Not yet. I couldn't come and live on you. I should be miserable every minute of the time.

LEONORA (*lightly*). Darling, you're not turning me down, are you? It's a firm offer.

JULIAN. Of course I'm not turning you down. It was marvellous of you to have thought of it. It's just unthinkable to me, that's all. You can't imagine what a drag I should be.

LEONORA. Darling, don't go on apologising for yourself. I can see all the drawbacks perfectly well.

JULIAN (*nerving himself*). I'm not apologising, but I won't pretend any more. It's like this. I've been accustomed to living in one way too long to give it up. I must have comfort. I must have pleasure. I must have money to spend. I must. (*Moving to centre table*) I tried to do without them, but it's been hell all the time. When I came back here last night, I knew what hell it had been.

LEONORA. So that was why you didn't go to your father's?

JULIAN. That was it. The moment I came back here, everything began to get hold of me again. I tried to fight it, but it was too strong. I suppose one must be as one is made. You don't know what it means to me to sleep in a comfortable bed again, with decent sheets.

LEONORA (*kindly*). Don't you think you've rather got the idea that you're the only person who's ever been comfortable? (*Coming to him*) I have quite a fair amount of comfort, but I don't make it my God.

JULIAN. I hate and detest everything that's cheap and ugly and second-best.

LEONORA. That I can understand, but it's a terrible thought to me that you don't mind how you get your luxury or who gives it you so long as you get it.

JULIAN. I don't think I do mind. Not much. (*Moves to window and stands with his back to her.*)

LEONORA. You don't realise what you're saying. If you think that, it means that you're just a taker, a parasite. You're not really worth keeping alive.

JULIAN (*turning round*). I'm sorry you think so poorly of me!

LEONORA. I'm only taking you at your own valuation. Do you think it's pleasant for me to find out that the man I love isn't a man at all, but only a bundle of sensations?

JULIAN (*coming back to table*). I've done my best to control circumstances. If I'm so worthless, you'll soon be able to forget me.

LEONORA. My God, I hope so! I'll do my best, I promise you. To think of all that I've been offering you and you haven't even begun to understand what I was saying.

JULIAN. Can't you see that it's the thought of you that's been making me so desperately miserable?

LEONORA. Desperately miserable! You don't know what the words mean! You haven't any feelings, not real feelings. If you cared anything for me, if you'd ever cared, you'd have chucked all this to the winds, really chucked it. Not just gone a little way off and hankered after it all the time. I've been fool enough to imagine that there was something more in you, something that hadn't a chance to get out, and that my love would set it free. I ought to have known last night when you didn't answer the 'phone that you'd succumbed to all this again . . . and to him.

JULIAN. I can't help it. He's been the biggest thing in my life.

LEONORA. Anyone can see that. I wonder how much you really care about him? I hope I shan't meet you one day in Piccadilly with a painted face, just because you must have linen sheets!

JULIAN. You needn't be blatant just because I've been honest with you. I'm sick to death of being talked at. (*Moves to hearth.*)

LEONORA. Poor Julian, I won't talk any more or plan or scheme or try to put energy and self-respect in you. But if ever you can come to me and prove that what I've loved exists, I'll marry you.

JULIAN. If you haven't married someone else.

LEONORA. Quite. But you don't realise that you chose a faithful one. God! That makes me angry and bitter. What a pitiful waste!

JULIAN (*turning to her*). I'll prove to you yet that I'm not as rotten as you think.

LEONORA. I hope so!

JULIAN (*sitting on couch*). I'm going away for six months just to get a breather, and I'm going to do some hard thinking about myself.

LEONORA. I wonder why you like to go on playing with the idea of me? That's the part I can't understand. You know you don't want me. You've said so, and yet you can't quite cut yourself off.

JULIAN. I do want you.
(*At this moment the door opens and* MR. DULCIMER *enters. He is very conscious that everything has turned out as he expected. He comes between them, standing at the corner of the couch with his hand on* JULIAN'*s shoulder.*)

DULCIMER (*to* LEONORA). Well, has Julian explained everything to you?

LEONORA. Oh, yes. (*Moving away*) He's made it all perfectly clear.

DULCIMER. I don't want to break in on any intimacies, but (*to* JULIAN) I do think that you ought to finish your toilet. (*Meaning the dressing-gown*) That's a dressy little garment, Julian, but they are still very conservative at the Ritz, especially about lunch-time. (*Moves to roof-garden.*)

JULIAN. I shall be ready in a few minutes.

DULCIMER. Don't rush into your clothes. There's plenty of time. I've told the car to be here in half an hour. Will that do?

JULIAN. Yes.

DULCIMER. Tell Trump to bring a glass of champagne to your dressing-room. There's nothing like a glass of champagne for giving a fillip to the tie. (*Goes into the roof-garden.*)

JULIAN (*coming to* LEONORA). Good-bye, Leo.

LEONORA. Good-bye, Julian.

JULIAN. I suppose there's nothing more to be said.

LEONORA. No. I suppose there isn't. (*He goes out quickly. When he has gone, she makes a move to go.*)

DULCIMER (*returning and standing on the top step into the roof-garden*). Must you go for a minute?

LEONORA (*turning round*). I can't think of anything to say to you, Mr. Dulcimer. At least, nothing adequate. I know you're pleased with the way things have gone.

DULCIMER. Can one be pleased at the inevitable? I knew what would happen. I foresaw it from the start. My comment is merely *La Commédia è finita.* I'm glad you take it philosophically. I should have been sorry if you had been really hurt.

LEONORA. And I should have loathed your pity!

DULCIMER. And yet I do pity you. There is something definitely pathetic in the way you have set yourself up against me. You really thought that you could succeed! Even now that you've failed I feel that you would like to have a real tilt at me. We have carried on a subconscious warfare. We've never come to the surface and fought in the open.

LEONORA. I've made no secret of what I've thought of you, how utterly I've loathed and despised you. I knew from the first that you were a deadly enemy. Yet, even now, I'm wondering how you dare to destroy Julian as you have done. Why couldn't you have let him go?

DULCIMER. Because he is to me, youth and charm and companionship. I admit the claims of these indefinable things. I must have them.

LEONORA. And yet, I doubt if he really cares any more for you than he does for me. He stays with you for the sake of what you can give him. If we were both penniless, he'd come to me.

DULCIMER (*stepping down to her*). You're welcome to think so. We can't put it to the proof. But I can see what brought you together. You're both dreamers, idealists. There's not much of it in Julian. But I shall quite probably have a lot of trouble still with you, with the idealised picture of you as his wife. It will only be a faint stirring of course, but I shall have to quiet him.

LEONORA. Haven't you any conscience at all about keeping him from what is normal and healthy, what is best for him?

DULCIMER. I didn't adopt him to please my conscience, if I have one, or to give him what was best for him. My aim was to make him like, and to be unable to do without, what was best for me. That makes you open your eyes wide, doesn't it? You see I'm not like you good people, with one eye on an ideal and the other on reality, a feverish urge towards goodness and then a degraded relapse towards what your natures clamour for insistently. I am a materialist and I glory in it. But I never have to struggle to maintain my position. I know exactly what I want out of life and I get it.

LEONORA. You get what you want out of life simply because you can pay for it. Your foundations are entirely in the sand. Another convulsion in the world and you might vanish tomorrow.

DULCIMER. Certainly. I admit that money isn't the rock it used to be. But I like to have it to use. I like the power of money. I have created comfort and beauty and constant change of scene out of money, and a cage for Julian's soul in which he sings to me as sweetly as in that stuffy Welsh schoolroom all those years ago. And if the convulsion comes, which you no doubt are praying for, there is always this. (*He puts his hand into the attaché case and takes out an exquisitely jewelled revolver, replacing it at once.*)

LEONORA. You wouldn't have the pluck to face things, then! Not even with Julian!

DULCIMER. He wouldn't stay with me, then, why should he? I should have nothing to offer him. As you admit, he's coming back to me because I've made him a better offer. You can only offer him your love, and the so-called "demands" made by love, another foolish, futile little marriage. . . .

LEONORA (*fiercely*). I offer him life and everything that makes life worth having and worth living. You can only talk and make your words seem very plausible. On your own confession you've no real hold on life!

DULCIMER. Life is bearable so long as I have Julian. You made me very angry when you first came into our lives. I thought for one moment that you might succeed and then I saw myself alone and demanding human sympathy. That made me feel very degraded.

LEONORA. Degraded?

DULCIMER. Yes. You see, I don't think I've ever asked for anything for years. But I must have a focusing point for all my activities and interests and self-expression. That focusing point is Julian. If you take him away, I'm lost. I admit that. Like you, I have feelings, but with Julian in my life I am never troubled by them. He keeps them constant and satisfied. (*Moves as he says this to the window.*)

LEONORA. And so he's just to minister to your emptiness and vanity and self-esteem. His mission is to make you think that you are really alive. You shan't keep him! Even if he doesn't come to me, he shall know what you've done to him! (*She is making for the door when he intercepts her.*)

DULCIMER (*with a voice that cuts like a whip*). Come back! (*He walks quickly to her*) I can assure you that the repulsion you feel is mutual. You have forced your way into my life and into my house and I won't have vulgar scenes in either! I have gone to the trouble of explaining myself to you because you will insist that you have a foothold in my affairs. You haven't! Understand that once and for all! This discussion has taken place partly because it amuses me, but more to make certain that it shall never take place again. From now on you will cease interfering with me and with Julian! I gave you an opportunity of making good and you have failed. I knew you would fail and I have told you why. (*Moving away to table and speaking calmly*) There is nothing more to be said, and I hope you will now have the good taste to leave my house as quietly as you came.

LEONORA. I'm not going! Not like this! If I went now, I should be just surrendering. I don't care if it's your house or what your wretched susceptibilities are! I'm not beaten yet! I won't be beaten! What I'm fighting for is worth a scene and I'm not afraid of making one!

(*Voices are heard outside. Enter* TRUMP.)

TRUMP. There's a gentleman, Sir, in the hall. He wants to know if Miss Yale's ready.

LEONORA (*running to the door before* TRUMP *has finished speaking*). Isaiah! Come in! I want you to help me! Isaiah!

(*She returns, almost dragging* MR. OWEN. *Exit* TRUMP.)

OWEN. What are you doing, Leo? I thought you were never coming!

LEONORA. Listen, Isaiah! This man has got hold of Julian body and soul! He's going to take him abroad, and if we let him go we'll never see him again.

DULCIMER (*coming up to them*). How do you do, Mr. Owen! We seem destined to meet under very peculiar circumstances. (*Holds out his hand.* OWEN *does not take it*) I hear that you've gone up in the world since I saw you last. (*Goes and sits at writing-table.*)

OWEN. Wait a minute, Leo! I haven't got my bearings yet! I'm taking it all in as fast as I can! (*Horrified*) Is it all over between you and David? (DULCIMER *is addressing labels.*)

LEONORA. Yes. That's all been a mistake. Don't think about me. What we've got to do is to save him from Dulcimer.

OWEN. Very well, then, all I've got to say to him is this. (*Going to him*) I want my son!

DULCIMER (*turning round*). I'm grateful to you for being concise, Mr. Owen! Leonora has positively battered me with words. You at any rate have a point and come to it quickly; "I want my son!" How admirably put!

OWEN. Perhaps you'll be as brief in your answer!

DULCIMER. I will, with pleasure. You can't have him!

OWEN. Why not?

DULCIMER. Because I don't wish it! Now that must really do! I've got a lot of letters to finish and arrangements to make. (*Turns back to bureau.*)

OWEN. And you think that will satisfy me!

DULCIMER (*writing and not looking round*). I'm afraid it will have to!

OWEN. Well, it won't! (*Coming closer.*)

DULCIMER (*turning round again*). Mr. Owen, I think that you're a business-man first and a prophet second. Let's stick to business! Twelve years ago we made a contract, and you did very well under it. That contract still holds good.

OWEN. No, it doesn't, then! Julian's of age now, and if he wasn't, there was nothing in our agreement to say that you might corrupt him altogether!

DULCIMER. Ah! I was afraid I'd overestimated your common sense. The prophet is stronger than the milkman, I see! (*Turns back to the table.*)

OWEN. You won't impress me with your nasty insults!

DULCIMER. Mr. Owen! I've really been very tolerant and extremely courteous, but your time is up. Please leave me in peace.

OWEN (*to* LEONORA). What am I to do, Leo?

LEONORA (*coming to him*). Don't give in yet! We've got to get Julian away, somehow!

OWEN (*to* LEONORA). I must see him before I go!
(*Enter* TRUMP.)

TRUMP. The car is at the door, Sir!
(LEONORA *runs to the window and looks down at the car.*)

DULCIMER (*getting up and giving the labels to* TRUMP, *who goes out*). At last! Now that really must be the end. I've got to go out, and I can't leave you two in possession. (*Moves to centre.*)

OWEN. Before I go, I'm going to see my son!
(JULIAN *is heard calling,* "Dulcie!")

LEONORA. He's coming now!
(*Comes to the centre.*)

DULCIMER. You're a remarkable man, Mr. Owen! You've only to utter a wish and it is instantly gratified!
(JULIAN *hurries in and stands at end of couch.*)

JULIAN. Dulcie! Where on earth have you been? I've been sitting in the car for nearly five minutes. Aren't you . . . (*He sees* LEONORA *and* OWEN) What on earth is going on now?

DULCIMER. Another crisis, my boy! But I'm afraid we've reached a deadlock!

JULIAN (*irritably to* LEONORA *and* OWEN). What do you want?

OWEN (*coming to* JULIAN). I want to speak to you, David! Just a word!

LEONORA (*to* JULIAN). Do listen to him!

JULIAN. Well, what is it?

OWEN. David, I'm not making up grand sentences now! I'm speaking to you from my heart. I want you to believe me when I say that this man is wicked. He's evil. You don't realise how evil he is! I want you to get away before he destroys your soul altogether!

JULIAN. I don't know anything about my soul, but I'll be thankful to get away! I'm wearied to death of being ordered about by each one of you in turn! (*To* OWEN) You want me to be one thing, and Leo another, and Dulcie a third. Well, I'm sick of it! What I should like to do would be to go off by myself away from all of you, and find out who I really am and what I really want to do.

LEONORA (*eagerly*). Julian, why don't you? What a splendid idea! We'll help him to do it, won't we Isaiah?

OWEN. Yes. Come on, my boy! It's the best possible thing you can do! Be quick, now!

JULIAN. By God! I will! (*Turns to the door, and begins to go.*)

DULCIMER (*with all the will power he can command*). Julian! (*Going quickly to him*) Come back! (JULIAN *turns and during the speech comes slowly towards him*) You can't choose! You haven't any choice! You know perfectly well what you want and where your happiness lies!

LEONORA (*pleadingly*). Darling! Please!

DULCIMER. Don't let them torment you with their miserable misgivings! They're a relic of your race and your early upbringing.

OWEN (*pleadingly*). Davy!

DULCIMER. I delivered you from all that, long ago! (*Gripping his arms*) Stay here, Julian! (JULIAN *struggles in agony for a moment, then half collapses across the back of the couch.*)

JULIAN. I can't! (MR. OWEN'S *eye lights on the revolver in the attaché case.*)

DULCIMER (*turning round in triumph and facing the others*). There! Now, are you satisfied? Perhaps you'll . . . (*But before he can say any more,* MR. OWEN *has picked up the revolver and fired.* MR. DULCIMER *drops dead, clutching at the couch as he falls.* LEONORA *and* JULIAN *drop on to their knees beside him.*)

OWEN (*with deep emotion*). There! Davy! You're free at last!

CURTAIN

SCENE II

The same. Six months later, about five o'clock in the afternoon.

The gates to the roof-garden are closed and the glass screens are in position. A fire is burning, and on the wall over the piano facing the audience is a death-mask of MR. DULCIMER.

LEONORA *is standing by the arm-chair near the window.*

JULIAN *hurries in. He wears an overcoat and scarf. He puts his hat on the piano as he passes.*

JULIAN. Hullo! Leo! It's lovely of you to come! I hope I haven't kept you waiting a frightful time. I've been tearing along from the lawyer's as hard as I could. (*He has thrown his coat and scarf over the arm-chair.*)

LEONORA (*quietly*). I've only been here about five minutes.

JULIAN. Oh! Good! I know I ought to have come to you, but I couldn't face the Surgery today. I wanted to see you alone. (*Smiling*) Well, Leo?

LEONORA (*looking at him steadily*). Well, Julian?

JULIAN (*confidently*). It's all right, now. (*With childish pride*) I'm a very rich man. We can get married tomorrow.

LEONORA (*still looking at him steadily*). Are you going to keep this money?

JULIAN (*surprised*). Keep it? What else should I do?

LEONORA. Do? Get a hundred miles away from all that it stands for, from all it has meant in your life, from all it has done to me!

JULIAN. Are you serious? Dulcie wanted me to have it. He left me everything.

LEONORA (*quietly*). I know.

JULIAN. He looked on me as his son. Why shouldn't I keep it? You're not going to be peculiar now? Surely at last we're going to be happy?

LEONORA. Happy? With your father in prison?

JULIAN. Poor old Isaiah! He'd always got a bee in his bonnet.

LEONORA. You really think that he killed Dulcimer because he was mad?

JULIAN. Didn't everybody think so? Judge and jury and all the rest of them. I don't see how you can get away from it. Religious mania.

LEONORA. He knew exactly what he was doing. You know perfectly well that he killed him because he thought he could save you.

JULIAN. Really, Leo, I don't know what you do want! We couldn't be married unless I had money, and now you're being difficult because I've got it. I only wanted the money to give to you.

LEONORA. I couldn't touch it! Not after all the unhappiness it has brought! Don't have anything to do with it! Give it up!

JULIAN. Leonora! Don't be a fool.

LEONORA. Are you going to let Isaiah's sacrifice be wasted?

JULIAN. Don't be fantastic!

LEONORA (*turning to go*). Then I've nothing to stay for. In a day or two you'll be thankful I've gone!

JULIAN. Now you're just being brutal!

LEONORA. I'd rather be brutal than so utterly callous as you! You've got rid of your guardian, your father's at Broadmoor, and now you're getting rid of me! (JULIAN *turns round and tries to speak*) No! don't say anything! I expect I'm well out of it! (*As she moves to the door, her eye falls on* DULCIMER's *death-mask over the piano*) What's that?

JULIAN. That's his death-mask. He wanted it done. He left instructions in his will.

LEONORA (*after another look*). I don't wonder he's smiling!
(*Exit.* JULIAN *goes to the piano and leans on it looking at the mask. He is ruffled and irritated.* TRUMP *comes in with tea on a tray.*)

TRUMP. Are you alone for tea, Sir?

JULIAN. Yes, Trump. Miss Yale has gone. (*A second's pause*) We're not going to be married, after all.

TRUMP (*looking up at mask*). Mr. Dulcimer always said, Sir, that a man could never settle down until he'd got women out of his life.

JULIAN. I expect he was right. (*Moves to couch*) He nearly always was.

TRUMP (*putting tea on centre table*). If you're not going to be married, Sir, perhaps you will reconsider my "notice." I should be proud to serve you as a bachelor, Sir, but a married establishment means women servants. And that . . . (*He makes an eloquent pause.*)

JULIAN. I hope I shall keep you for life, Trump. You understand my ways.

TRUMP. Thank you, Sir. (*Moves to door.*)

JULIAN. I don't think I want any tea. I'll just have a cocktail.

TRUMP (*coming back to table and removing tray*). A "side-car," Sir? Very good. By the way, the flowers have come from Silver Gates.

JULIAN (*with a* DULCIMER *drawl*). Do you think I ought to do them now, Trump.

TRUMP. Just as you please, Sir.

JULIAN (*rises*). Perhaps I ought. The room does look rather naked.

TRUMP. I'll fetch you the flowers, Sir.
(*Exit* TRUMP. JULIAN *lights a cigarette and goes to the window.* TRUMP *returns with the tray of flowers, scissors, and gloves. Then he gets the small table, as in Act I, and places it in front of* JULIAN. JULIAN *picks up the gloves.* TRUMP *gets a vase from the piano and puts it on the small table.*)

JULIAN. Not the green vase, Trump!

TRUMP. Mr. Dulcimer always preferred the green vase for iris, Sir.

JULIAN (*putting on the gloves*). I like to make my own choice. Choice, Trump, is what distinguishes the artist from the common herd. I prefer the amber vase. (*This is already on the table in front of him.*)

TRUMP. Very good, Sir.
(*Replaces the green vase on the piano.*)

JULIAN (*examining the flowers*). Some of these irises are rather poor, Trump. Badly chosen.

TRUMP. I'm sorry, Sir. I'll fetch you some water. (*Exit.*)

JULIAN (*with a flower in his hand*). I must tell Paget to be more careful about the stalks. (*He begins to arrange the flowers. The death-mask continues to smile.*)

SLOW CURTAIN

Victoria Regina

BY LAURENCE HOUSMAN

Victoria Regina was first produced in America at the Broadhurst Theatre, New York City, by Gilbert Miller on December 26, 1935, and closed on May 29, 1937. The following is the original cast:

(*In the order of their appearance*)

A Footman	Alfred Helton
Lord Conyngham	E. Bellenden-Clarke
Archbishop of Canterbury	Harry Plimmer
A Maidservant	Mary Austin
Duchess of Kent	Babette Feist
Victoria	Helen Hayes
Lord Melbourne	Charles Francis
Prince Albert	Vincent Price
Prince Ernest	George Macready
Mr. Richards (Albert's valet)	Albert Froom
Mr. Anson (Albert's secretary)	Oswald Marshall
1st Queen's Gentleman	Arthur Gould-Porter
Royal Footman	Alan Bandler
A Court Usher	Edward Martin
Lady Muriel	Mary Heberden
Lady Grace	Renee Macredy
Lady-in-Waiting	Mary Newnham-Davis
2nd Queen's Gentleman	Fothringham Lysons
Mr. Oakley	James Bedford
Duchess of Sutherland	Cherry Hardy
Lady Jane	Helen Trenholme
General Grey (The Queen's secretary)	Tom Woods
3rd Queen's Gentleman	Edward Jones
John Brown	James Woodburn
Benjamin Disraeli (Earl of Beaconsfield)	Abraham Sofaer
A Footman	Robert Von Rigel
Sir Arthur Bigge	Herschel Martin
An Imperial Highness	Felix Brown
His Royal Highness	Gilbert McKay
1st Princess	Mary Forbes
2nd Princess	Shirley Gale
3rd Princess	Elizabeth Munn

Members of the Royal Family, Footman and Court Officials: Jean Stephenson, Willis Duncan, Guy Moneypenny, Shirley Poirier, Buddy Buehler.

Staged by Gilbert Miller

Designed by Rex Whistler

SCENES

ACT ONE

SCENE I–The Six O'clock Call. 1837.
Entrance hall of Kensington Palace.

SCENE II–Suitable Suitors. 1838.
A sitting room at Windsor Castle.

SCENE III–Woman Proposes. 1839.
The same as Scene II.

SCENE IV–Morning Glory. 1840.
Prince Albert's dressing room at Windsor Castle.

ACT TWO

SCENE I–A Good Lesson. 1842.
Prince Albert's writing room at Buckingham Palace.

SCENE II–Under Fire. 1842.
A room in Buckingham Palace, overlooking the Park.

SCENE III–The Rose and the Thorn. 1846.
An ante-chamber at Windsor Castle.

SCENE IV–Intervention. 1861.
Prince Albert's writing room at Buckingham Palace.

ACT THREE

SCENE I–The Queen, God Bless Her! 1877.
A garden tent at Balmoral Castle.

SCENE II–Happy and Glorious! 1897.
Buckingham Palace.

VICTORIA REGINA

ACT ONE

SCENE I

THE SIX O'CLOCK CALL

1837

It is still dark; for in the entrance hall of Kensington Palace the shutters have not yet been unclosed. Behind a wide archway at centre burns a dim light: there is the staircase lobby. To the left of the archway one sees the foot of the stairs.

In the dark emptiness goes the clanging of a bell, followed by knocks. A FOOTMAN, *not quite dressed as he should be, enters carrying a light. He crosses from left to right, and passes out of view. You hear unchaining and unbolting of a door; then, indistinctly, voices, which grow louder as the visitors enter and become visible. Heavily cloaked,* LORD CONYNGHAM *comes in, followed by the* ARCHBISHOP OF CANTERBURY.

CONYNGHAM. Tell them to take the message at once! Say the matter is urgent.

FOOTMAN. Yes, my Lord. But Her Royal Highness isn't up yet, my Lord.

CONYNGHAM. "Up?" Of course she's not up at this hour! Send Her Royal Highness's maid to call her.
(*The* FOOTMAN, *having the only candle, is busy now lighting others. But the urgency of his lordship stops the business half-way; and only one set of candles gets lighted before he goes.*)

FOOTMAN. Yes, my Lord.

CONYNGHAM. And say His Grace the Archbishop of Canterbury, and Lord Conyngham are here to see Her Royal Highness on important business.

FOOTMAN. Yes, my Lord.

CONYNGHAM. Hurry, man! Hurry!

FOOTMAN. Yes, my Lord; but I'll have to call the maid first.

CONYNGHAM. Well, call her!

FOOTMAN. Yes, my Lord; but the maids sleep where I'm not supposed to go; and the door up to it is locked. I shall have to throw up at the window.

CONYNGHAM. Isn't there a bell?

FOOTMAN. Yes, my Lord; in Her Royal Highness the Duchess's room there is a bell.

CONYNGHAM. Well, go and ask that it may be rung!

FOOTMAN (*aghast*). I daren't go to Her Royal Highness the Duchess's room, my Lord: not now. Her Royal Highness the Princess is there too.

CONYNGHAM. Well, go and do the best you can. But say Her Royal Highness *must* come—

FOOTMAN. Yes, my Lord.
(*Exit* FOOTMAN.)

CONYNGHAM (*finishing his sentence*).—at once! . . . Good Lord! What a house! Sleeps with the old Cat, does she?

ARCHBISHOP (*corrective, but suave*). I beg your pardon?

CONYNGHAM. I—I beg yours! Yes; I suppose one oughtn't to say that now. But your Grace knows that the Duchess has been a difficulty all along.

ARCHBISHOP. The Duchess is a determined character.

CONYNGHAM. Yes.

ARCHBISHOP. It has had its advantages.

CONYNGHAM. They have escaped my observation, I'm afraid.

ARCHBISHOP. The Princess has not seen a great deal of her uncles. Her education has been—safeguarded.

CONYNGHAM (*extenuatingly*). Well, of course, I know—I know—I know.

ARCHBISHOP (*less extenuatingly*). Yes, my Lord, we *know*.

CONYNGHAM. Had we not better sit down? We may have to wait. If that man's stone-throwing is not good—we may have to wait a long time. . . . So this is how history gets written!

ARCHBISHOP. *This* won't get into history, my Lord.

CONYNGHAM. No . . . Your Grace? —may I? . . . (*He offers a flask-cup, after filling it.*)

ARCHBISHOP. Ah, no. I thank you.

CONYNGHAM. It's a chilly hour to be up. I never go about, late at night, or early—without *something*. (*Drinks.*)

ARCHBISHOP. For you, my Lord, very wise, I've no doubt. But I never go out at night, you see; at least, not late.

CONYNGHAM. Ah! I often wish I didn't, when the night is over.

ARCHBISHOP. That is—understandable.

CONYNGHAM (*missing the note of sympathy*). It's only human nature, your Grace.

ARCHBISHOP. Yes, I suppose so. I don't know . . . My office . . . There is a good deal of human nature that I have to avoid.

CONYNGHAM. Rather difficult to avoid at the Court of the Regency, wasn't it?

ARCHBISHOP. Oh, of course, sometimes I had to—well—look the other way. Still, I attended so seldom; only when called on officially.

CONYNGHAM. Your Grace has officiated on a similar painful though auspicious occasion, I believe?

ARCHBISHOP. Yes. Yes. I announced his accession to His late Majesty King William. But he was only in the next room waiting.

CONYNGHAM. Ah! How did he take it?

ARCHBISHOP. With alacrity . . . "Bless my soul! you don't say so!" were his first words. And then—"Well, well, though I'm less of a figure-head, I shall make a better King than poor George."

CONYNGHAM. But he didn't, you know.

ARCHBISHOP. No; a better character, but not a better King. That sometimes happens, I'm afraid.

CONYNGHAM. Yes, kings often manage to do quite well without morals. Brain is more important.

ARCHBISHOP. Not too much of that either, I should have thought. Don't those with brain give much more trouble to their Ministers?

CONYNGHAM. Oh, they manage to do that without any! His late Majesty was a conspicuous example of it. You wouldn't believe—no, you wouldn't believe the trouble we sometimes had with him. They say you can make a donkey go by tying a carrot in front of its nose. Well, he was like a donkey with a carrot tied to its tail.

ARCHBISHOP. Really?

CONYNGHAM. Just like that. Over the Reform Bill, you know, we almost had a Revolution—almost. Not *his* fault that we didn't.

ARCHBISHOP (*discreetly*). Was he just a little—like his Father, you know?

CONYNGHAM. Mad, eh? No, not mad. It was the shape of his head, I think. It was pear-shaped, you know—just like a pear. "The weakest fruit drops earliest to the ground," says Shakespeare. Well, his head was weak fruit distinctly—amazing how it *hung on*: one can't exactly say "lasted." (*The* FOOTMAN *re-enters*) Well? What have you done?

FOOTMAN. I've called the maid, my Lord. Would your Lordship like more light?

CONYNGHAM. Oh yes; a little more light would, I suppose, be better. (*Then to the* ARCHBISHOP) For so auspicious an occasion.

FOOTMAN. The windows, my Lord?

CONYNGHAM. No, no, not the windows, I think. *The blinds—the blinds* must stay down at any rate. (*The* FOOTMAN *lights more candles.*)

ARCHBISHOP (*confidentially*). Very sad, very sad, you know! Good old King George—such a large family—so many sons, and not one of them what he should be.
(*Exit* FOOTMAN.)

CONYNGHAM (*grimly*). And she—the daughter of one of them.

ARCHBISHOP. Ah, but women are different—so different, you know. Let's hope! Let's hope!

CONYNGHAM. Well, we must get her married, and then—married to the right man—the difference won't so much matter—her Cousin, Prince George of Cambridge, would be very suitable—same age, and can talk English now, so I'm told, like a native.

ARCHBISHOP. Over that you will have difficulty with the Duchess.

CONYNGHAM. Oh yes; the Duchess is going to be difficult whatever's proposed. She will regard this as her own succession almost.

ARCHBISHOP (*wisely*). It almost will be.

CONYNGHAM. That is what we must *prevent*.

ARCHBISHOP. The Duchess has privately planned a marriage more to her own liking, I'm told.

CONYNGHAM. Eh? Who?

ARCHBISHOP. She has two nephews —through her brother the Duke of Saxe-Coburg—Prince Ernest, and Prince Albert.

CONYNGHAM. But that won't do! Tainted blood! Tainted blood!

ARCHBISHOP. Indeed!

CONYNGHAM (*disgustedly*). Ye-es: bleeding skins—haemophilia. It's in the family. Cousins. No; it won't *do*.

ARCHBISHOP. But Prince George is her cousin, also.

CONYNGHAM. Ah, but it's not on that side. It's on the mother's—the Coburgs. And, you know, it comes through the women. The males have it: the women don't; but they pass it on. Do you know her brother, the Duke, once nearly bled to death?

ARCHBISHOP. Dear me! Is that so?

CONYNGHAM. Marrying her daughter to *his* son would be fatal! You know, it's all very well, in one way, Royalty to make itself a class all by itself. But it's a German notion: 'tisn't English. And when it leads to so much inbreeding, it gets dangerous. English kings have married commoners in the past; they'd better do it again—or into the peerage. Do you know—if the Duke of Wellington had been—well, twenty years younger, I'd have married her to him.

ARCHBISHOP. You don't mean it!

CONYNGHAM. I do. 'Twould have been very popular; and a foreign marriage won't be. (*He looks at his watch*) Tut, tut! That girl's a very long time coming!

ARCHBISHOP (*correctively*). The Queen?

CONYNGHAM (*plausibly covering his mistake*). No, no; I mean the maid. I'm wondering whether she has called her . . . It's a pity, you know, a pity! I don't know what to think of it!

ARCHBISHOP. "It" meaning what?

CONYNGHAM. A female on the throne; a King would have been so much better.

ARCHBISHOP. I don't know, my Lord. Heirs male of the last generation have not been a conspicuous success.[1]

CONYNGHAM. No English King has been a conspicuous success since Edward I.

ARCHBISHOP. Yet the monarchy has —gone on.
(*Enter* MAID-SERVANT.)

CONYNGHAM. Yes; but it's gone off.

MAID. I beg your pardon, my Lord.

CONYNGHAM. Yes? Well?

MAID. Her Royal Highness, my Lord. I went in, but Her Royal Highness was asleep.

CONYNGHAM. Well, you must wake Her Royal Highness up, then.

MAID. Such a beautiful sleep, my Lord: I didn't like to.

CONYNGHAM. Even the most beautiful sleep must give way to affairs of State. You know who I am?

MAID. Yes, my Lord.

CONYNGHAM. You know His Grace?

MAID. Yes, my Lord.

CONYNGHAM. Then go at once: wake Her Royal Highness, and tell her that we are here, waiting—for an audience. (*Awestruck and submissive, the* MAID *goes. A clock strikes*) Six o'clock. There is to be a Council at ten.

ARCHBISHOP. Where? Here?

[1] This remark having been ruled out of one of my plays by the Lord Chamberlain, now goes into another.

CONYNGHAM. At St. James's, I imagine. No, perhaps it will have to be here. She mustn't appear in public yet. 'Twouldn't be quite decent. People might cheer.
(*Enter the* DUCHESS OF KENT: *she is robed rather than dressed; but her heavy negligé has a certain dignity about it. She enters, a conscious "Presence." They rise and bow.*)

DUCHESS. Your Grace, my Lord Conyngham, you have news for us?

CONYNGHAM. For her Royal Highness the Princess, we have news, Madam.

DUCHESS. Ah! The King then—?

CONYNGHAM. Is dead.

DUCHESS. Then my daughter is now—?

CONYNGHAM. Queen.

DUCHESS. It has come, then—at last! And I—I am the Queen Mother!

CONYNGHAM. No, Madam: your Royal Highness is not the Queen Mother.

DUCHESS (*affronted*). *Not?*

CONYNGHAM. Your Royal Highness is the Queen's Mother; that is the distinction. Only had your Royal Highness been Queen in the first place, would that other title now follow.

DUCHESS. Then, if it is not mine by your laws, she shall give it me.

CONYNGHAM. That, Madam, I fear, will be impossible.

DUCHESS. Ah! I will go myself and speak to her at once. That shall settle it!

CONYNGHAM. Madam, we are here to see Her Majesty the Queen on urgent business; and we must not be delayed. Your presence at the interview, Madam, will not be required, unless Her Majesty sends for you.

DUCHESS. Ah! This is not to be borne!

ARCHBISHOP (*conciliatory*). Madam, this is a very historic occasion. We are here officially only. Etiquette and immemorial tradition prescribe certain rules which have to be observed. Your Royal Highness would not wish to break them.

CONYNGHAM (*at centre*). Your Grace, she's coming!

ARCHBISHOP. Then, Madam, for a moment—for a moment only!
(*He opens a side-door and bows the* DUCHESS *through it. She goes, compelled, but reluctant. The shadow of* QUEEN VICTORIA *is projected upon the wall of the lobby as she descends. She enters: the* ARCHBISHOP *and the* LORD CHAMBERLAIN *kneel and kiss her hand. The side-door opens again; the* DUCHESS *thrusts in her head; she watches spell-bound.*)

CONYNGHAM. Your Majesty, it is our painful duty to announce to your Majesty—

DUCHESS (*not waiting for the sentence to finish*). Ah! my daughter, she is Queen—Queen!
(*The curtain slowly descends; after a few seconds it rises again.* VICTORIA *stands alone at the foot of the stairs. Away to the right, ceremoniously backing from the Presence, the* ARCHBISHOP *and the* LORD CHAMBERLAIN *make their last bow and go. Into this solemn scene no* FOOTMAN *intrudes; they let themselves out. At the sound of the shutting door, the side-door opens fully: the* DUCHESS *enters, and advances rapturously to claim her daughter's homage.*)

VICTORIA (*still a little mazed at the wonder of it all*). Mamma!

DUCHESS (*embracing her*). My child! My child! Oh, my child!

VICTORIA. They came to tell me that I am Queen.

DUCHESS. Yes: you are Queen at last!

VICTORIA. But really Queen—*now*: before I have been crowned?

DUCHESS. Yes: now, at once! The King is dead: you are Queen!

VICTORIA. Then my reign has already begun? I can do—as I like?

DUCHESS. Yes; as you like! Do not mind what anyone says. If you want to do it—do it!

VICTORIA. Oh! . . . Then . . . Mamma. There is something I would like.

DUCHESS. Ah, yes! Say it! It shall be done.

VICTORIA. How strange that it should have all come—so suddenly!

DUCHESS. Yes, so suddenly—after we have waited so long. But now, my love—do not stay here to catch cold. Come back to your own Mother's bed!

VICTORIA. No, Mamma dear. As I may now do as I like, I wish in future to have a bed, and a room of my own!

DUCHESS (*stupent*). *Of your own?*

VICTORIA. Yes—please, Mamma.

DUCHESS. Oh! so you have been waiting—for *that!*

VICTORIA. I should be glad, if you don't mind—now that I am my own mistress. Yes, I would rather be alone.
(*She does not wait to hear more.*)

DUCHESS. Mind! . . . Glad! . . . Alone! . . . O God! What is going to become of me?
(*She stands and watches, while* VICTORIA, *mistress henceforth of her own destiny, turns and goes quietly upstairs again, having imposed, even now, her wish to be alone for a while.*)

SCENE II

SUITABLE SUITORS

1838

THE QUEEN *is still in mourning, but she does not mourn. Animated and happy, she sits listening to what, in earlier youth, she was never allowed to hear—the conversation of a gentleman of breeding, worldly, witty, and to a certain extent wise. This she thoroughly enjoys. And* LORD MELBOURNE, *her Prime Minister, enjoys talking to her. She is not clever; she cannot say clever things; but the mingled strain of artlessness and self-possession, of dignity and simplicity, which he finds in his Royal Mistress's character—a character which he is artfully moulding, not so much to his own ends as his own convenience—attracts and delights him. They are now on such intimate terms that* THE QUEEN, *when he comes for an audience, does not keep him long standing. They are seated now; and as an indication of their pleasant relations,* THE QUEEN *is going on with her woolwork.*

VICTORIA. How do you begin the day, Lord Melbourne?

MELBOURNE. Begin it, Ma'am?

VICTORIA. Yes. What do you do first—you, who have so many things to do in the day? I find it difficult to know myself where to begin.

MELBOURNE. Well, starting at the very beginning, Ma'am, I breakfast—if I may be allowed to say so—in bed.

VICTORIA. Oh I should never have thought of that!

MELBOURNE. Try it, Ma'am, try it!

It makes an invaluable break between sleeping and waking. Sleeping is one thing: it takes time. Waking is another: it takes more time. Working is another: and takes more time than all the others put together.

VICTORIA. And after breakfast, what then?

MELBOURNE. Well, let me think! . . . First, I rise, Ma'am. Over that I need not go into details.

VICTORIA. No?

MELBOURNE. Or—would you like me to, Ma'am?

VICTORIA (*a little disappointed*). No, oh, no. You rise?

MELBOURNE. I rise from my bed. Then I ride in the Park; when I come home I write. So I begin with the three R's.

VICTORIA. But "write" begins with a W.

MELBOURNE. I am corrected, Ma'am. "Write" *does* begin with a W. Your Majesty is right, as usual.

VICTORIA (*laughing*). Oh! you are funny, Lord Melbourne.

MELBOURNE. Funny?

VICTORIA. So witty, I mean. You always say something amusing. Yes; please go on!

MELBOURNE. That, Ma'am, is all the beginning of my day. When that is done, the day is half over.

VICTORIA. And when do you say your prayers, Lord Melbourne?

MELBOURNE. My prayers? Oh, I say them whenever I have time for them.

VICTORIA (*a little shocked*). But—Lord Melbourne!

MELBOURNE. As often, and as long as possible.

VICTORIA. That seems to me a little irregular.

MELBOURNE. Did your Majesty never hear the story of the holy monk who had a Vision vouchsafed to him: a Vision of—well, of a very high character? And just as the Vision appeared, the chapel-bell began ringing. Duty—discipline—required the monk to leave the seraphic Vision and go into chapel with the rest: a function which, in these circumstances, was so like praying to the Vision behind its back, that it seemed almost foolish. It was a hard thing to do; but the monk did it. In great anguish of spirit, he left the Vision to itself, and went and did his duty. The service seemed intolerably long; he was dying to get back to his Vision. At last he was able to do so. The Vision was still there; and as he fell down before it in renewed adoration, the Vision made this remark: "If you had not answered that bell, I should not have stayed" —or words to that effect. Ma'am, my position as Prime Minister is very similar to that of the pious monk. I am constantly having to leave the vision to answer the *bell*.

VICTORIA. I thought, Lord Melbourne, that visions were rather superstitious things.

MELBOURNE. They are, Ma'am. In these days they are! Do your best to avoid them. They savour too much of Roman Catholicism. And so, Ma'am, with your Majesty's permission, let me, for the moment, leave visions and come down to facts, and the affairs of State. There are certain things which will have soon to be decided, and one or two in which delay—delay of preparation at all events—is inadvisable.

VICTORIA. Oh yes; there are many, I'm sure.

MELBOURNE. There is one especially, which your Majesty graciously deigned to mention the other day. You then said, Ma'am—with a courage which I thought remarkable in one so young—"Some day we must marry" . . . Has your Majesty given that matter any further thought?

VICTORIA. Oh yes, Lord Melbourne, I have thought of it a great deal.

MELBOURNE. Is your Majesty prepared yet to take me into your Majesty's gracious confidence?

VICTORIA. You mean?

MELBOURNE. As to the possible recipient of so overwhelming an honour.

VICTORIA. Oh, I have not thought of any person—in particular. I mean, I have made no decision.

MELBOURNE. I am relieved to hear it, Ma'am. Then your Majesty has still an open mind!

VICTORIA. An open mind? Oh, *of course,* I shall make my own choice, Lord Melbourne.

MELBOURNE. Why, of course, Ma'am. I would not suggest otherwise, for a moment.

VICTORIA. But there are certain things as to which I am quite resolved.

MELBOURNE. As for instance?

VICTORIA. My marriage, Lord Melbourne, must be a marriage of affection.

MELBOURNE. That, I am sure, Ma'am, can be arranged without difficulty.

VICTORIA. Someone, I mean, whose character I can respect: one whom I can love and look up to.

MELBOURNE. Look up to?

VICTORIA. Yes, Lord Melbourne, it may sound strange to you; but I must have as my husband one whom I can eventually look up to—when I have trained him for the position he will have to occupy.

MELBOURNE. Oh, quite so, quite so. I trust that such a person will be found. And as your Majesty has owned to an open mind on the subject, I have here with me a list of—of possibles.

VICTORIA. Oh, Lord Melbourne, how interesting! . . . How many?

MELBOURNE. Well, at present, Ma'am, only five. But more are coming.

VICTORIA. Coming?

MELBOURNE. That is, I am making inquiries about them.

VICTORIA. What kind of inquiries?

MELBOURNE. All kinds of inquiries, Ma'am: my bounden duty. I would not wish to present your Majesty with one to whom there could be any possible objection.

VICTORIA. And you have already found *five!* Lord Melbourne, how clever of you!

MELBOURNE. "Possibles," I said. The inquiry is still going on; I am making it now. After inquiry of your Majesty, possibly there will be only one left.

VICTORIA. I would like to see your list, Lord Melbourne.

MELBOURNE. If your Majesty will pardon me a moment. When I have fully explained the considerations which guided me in my selections, I will submit my list for your Majesty's judgment, and (as I hope) approval.

VICTORIA. I cannot approve all five!

MELBOURNE. Just as a preliminary, Ma'am, why not? From five in the running select your favourite—the winner.

VICTORIA. Perhaps I shall not choose one for a long time. But go on; I am quite interested and excited.

MELBOURNE. The conditions, Ma'am, for a suitable consort to your Majesty's throne are necessarily special and particular—I might even say, peculiar. He must, of course, be of Royal blood; on the other hand, he must not be the direct or likely heir of any foreign king or reigning prince.

VICTORIA. But why not, Lord Melbourne?

MELBOURNE. Political complication might arise, Ma'am. The crown of Hanover has passed from your Majesty to another, because of the law which limits the succession to males only: a circumstance which I regard as fortunate. We want no more crowns of Hanover; the country is better without them. To proceed, then: he must be a Prince of some Royal House, not too petty, not too important. We must avoid entangling alliances. He must also be of the Protestant faith.

VICTORIA. Oh yes, *I couldn't* marry a Papist.

MELBOURNE. You could not, Ma'am. The Act of Settlement forbids it. He must be sufficiently young to be a suitable life-partner to your Majesty. He must know, or be capable of learning the English language; capable also of adapting himself to English customs, habits, and prejudices. The last is the most difficult of all, since the English have a prejudice against foreigners.

VICTORIA. But, Lord Melbourne, that makes it impossible!

MELBOURNE. No, Ma'am. It only rather restricts the choice. Someone must be found who, once naturalised, is able to share the prejudice. I've known it done. Your Majesty's cousin, Prince George of Cambridge, for instance, is rapidly acquiring a thoroughly British outlook. In another five years or so he will have learned to dislike foreigners as much as we do.

VICTORIA. But do *you* dislike foreigners, Lord Melbourne?

MELBOURNE. No, Ma'am, no: of course not! But sometimes, for political reasons, one has to pretend to.

VICTORIA. Well, and what more?

MELBOURNE. It would be well, Ma'am, if he had some means of his own; though they need not be large. Parliament will provide whatever addition is necessary. He must have presence suited to his station; also a certain amount of brain, but not too much. He must not expect to interfere in politics.

VICTORIA. Indeed, no! I should never allow it.

MELBOURNE. Finally, he must have health, and a sound constitution; he must—that is to say—come of good stock. And that, Ma'am, has been our main difficulty. Good stock, in the Royal Families of Europe, is rare.

VICTORIA. Please explain, for I don't quite understand. "Good stock"—I thought that meant cattle.

MELBOURNE. It does, Ma'am, in certain connections. But it also means—what comes from father to son. You find it referred to in the Second Commandment, where we are told that the sins of the fathers are visited on the children: also their virtues. In certain Royal lines the sins and the virtues have been mixed; and one has to be careful that they shall not be more mixed. For that reason the marriage of Royal cousins is generally inadvisable.

VICTORIA. Oh.

MELBOURNE. Generally, I say. In the case of a certain branch of your Majesty's family connections it is unfortunately true in a rather special degree. For that reason, in the list I am about to submit, I have not included—though it was suggested to me—two of your Majesty's cousins, who might otherwise have been desirable candidates—their Serene Highnesses Prince Ernest and Prince Albert of Saxe-Coburg Gotha.

VICTORIA. But they both looked quite strong and healthy when I last saw them two years ago.

MELBOURNE. Apparently, Ma'am. But appearances are sometimes deceptive. It is, of course, a delicate—even a painful subject. But, acting under medical advice, and with a due sense of my responsibility, I have not included either of those young Princes in the list which I have now the honour to present to your Majesty. (*He rises, and puts the list into her hand: hurriedly she glances down the names.*)

VICTORIA. Oh, but do I know any of them?

MELBOURNE. Your Majesty knows one of them very well.

VICTORIA. Oh—I didn't see. But Prince George is my cousin too.

MELBOURNE. By another branch, your Majesty. There is not there the same objection.

VICTORIA. Oh, but I couldn't marry my Cousin George! He is so—so—

MELBOURNE. Nobody wishes to decide your Majesty's choice. There are others.

VICTORIA. But, as I say, I don't know any of them.

MELBOURNE. That, Ma'am, can easily be remedied. You ask them to your Court in turn, saying nothing. And you let them go away again—saying nothing; or you *do* say something; and then—either they stay, or they come again.

VICTORIA. But it is for me to decide, is it not?

MELBOURNE. It is for your Majesty to decide. Your Majesty need not marry at all.

VICTORIA. Oh, but I must marry. Mamma always said so.

MELBOURNE. So I have been told. But in so important a matter, even devoted filial affection should not be allowed to influence your *choice*. I have merely indicated, Ma'am, that were any attempt to be made to influence your choice in a certain direction, that choice—for reasons already given, I should have to oppose.

VICTORIA. Lord Melbourne, I should not allow any opposition in a matter of that kind. It would not influence me for a moment.

MELBOURNE. No?

VICTORIA. Indeed, rather the other way.

MELBOURNE. I see. I understand, Ma'am. I sympathise. I shall say no more. I will only commend the matter to your Majesty's good sense—and conscience.

VICTORIA. Oh, how kind you always are to me, Lord Melbourne! What a lot you are teaching me!

MELBOURNE. What a lot you are teaching *me*. I have served under older sovereigns—under two. But I have never served under one who listened to advice so wisely or so well.

VICTORIA (*rising*). Good-bye, Lord Melbourne. Will you keep the list, or shall I?

MELBOURNE. By your leave, Ma'am; let what I have said be either remembered or forgotten. (*He tears the list and throws it into the fireplace*) The choice must be your own.

VICTORIA. Yes; but you haven't yet shown me—any portraits.

MELBOURNE. Portraits, Ma'am? Why portraits?

VICTORIA. I can't decide about anyone—till I know what they are like. It wouldn't be fair to them—or to me.

MELBOURNE. But your Majesty can send for them, and see.

VICTORIA. Oh no. I'm not going to send for any, if I don't like the look of them.

MELBOURNE. Portraits are sometimes deceptive, Ma'am.

VICTORIA. Yes; I saw a portrait of my Cousin George of Cambridge the other day: quite handsome he looked.

MELBOURNE. I can get their portraits, Ma'am, if you wish. But Court Painters, like Prime Ministers, know their duty; and they only do what is expected of them. If they can't do that, they have to go.

VICTORIA (*going toward a table, on which stands a framed portrait*). Here is a portrait that was sent to Mamma, the other day—of my Cousin, Prince Albert.

MELBOURNE (*who has followed to the table*). Oh! Ah! Yes. H'm.

VICTORIA. Surely *he must* have grown very handsome! It would not be possible for a Court Painter to imagine anyone like that.

MELBOURNE. You never know, Ma'am, you never know. Imagination sometimes goes a long way. Well, the list having gone, am I now to make a collection of portraits for your Majesty?

VICTORIA. Oh no, Lord Melbourne. I wasn't speaking seriously when I said that.

MELBOURNE. No more was I, Ma'am. But I do ask your Majesty to *think* seriously. The future welfare of this country is now in this little hand. (*He stoops and kisses it.*)

VICTORIA. Indeed, Lord Melbourne, I pay great attention to everything that you say. And I shall continue to take your advice, whenever I find it—possible. Good-bye. (LORD MELBOURNE *bows himself out. She goes and takes up the portrait and kisses it*) Albert . . . Albert . . . Albert . . . will you marry me?

SCENE III

WOMAN PROPOSES

15th October 1839

In a sitting-room at Windsor Castle PRINCE ALBERT *of Saxe-Coburg Gotha stands looking rather sadly out of the window. The outside prospect is beautiful; but some other prospect seems to depress him. Still very young, he has already a full-grown conscience, which at times becomes too much for him.*

The door opens, his brother, PRINCE ERNEST, *enters, shuts the door, and stands looking at him. After a pause he speaks: his English is good, but he has a foreign accent.*

ERNEST. Well, Albert?

ALBERT (*not turning*). Jawohl, mein Bruder?

ERNEST. We must speak English.

ALBERT (*turning*). Why?

ERNEST. For practice. One of us—you or I—will have to always.

ALBERT (*sighing*). I suppose!

ERNEST (*guardedly*). Which of us, do you "suppose," it is going to be?

ALBERT. That is not for me to say. The decision will not be ours.

ERNEST. But we shall have to say *something*—one of us—presently.

ALBERT. Yes, presently. And only one answer will be possible.

ERNEST. You mean it must be "yes"?

ALBERT. Since it cannot possibly be "no."

ERNEST. Then—you do not wish—?

ALBERT. I have given up "wishing," Brother. Wishes might hinder.

ERNEST. You don't seem very happy about it. . . . No?

ALBERT. This foreign land terrifies me. Look! (*He indicates the landscape.*)

ERNEST. Rather beautiful, don't you think?

ALBERT. Beautiful? Yes, but all the same it means exile—to live in it.

ERNEST. But then—to be almost a King!

ALBERT. No! The English people will never allow a foreigner—you or me—to be King: nor anything like one.

ERNEST. We are hardly more foreigners than are some of their own Royalty. We speak as good English.

ALBERT. But we were not *born* in England.

ERNEST. What real difference does that make to a man—where he was born?

ALBERT. Real? None. But—to the English—*all* the difference. Has it never struck you, Ernest, that the English are a very romantic nation?

ERNEST. Rather materialistic, I should say.

ALBERT. Yes, but very romantic over their material—some of it. Their history—their wars—their royal successions—their revolutions. I have been reading English history lately. It is all a romance. Their lost battles? Where are they? Except for one or two—they do not exist.

ERNEST. What about their lost countries—France, and America?

ALBERT. They don't know they have lost them—till it is such old history that it means to them—nothing. For three hundred years after they had been driven out, their Kings still called themselves Kings of France. That is true, Ernest. Don't laugh!

ERNEST. Of France? Yet don't like foreigners, you say?

ALBERT. Oh, they like *ruling* them. They do that as a favour. Here you or I will only be—a puppet, kept to breed by. If it is *you,* are you going to resign yourself to that—willingly?

ERNEST. If it is to be *me,* you say? It is time that I speak, Albert. It *must* be me. Did not Papa tell you?

ALBERT. Tell me? No! What?

ERNEST. Oh, well: perhaps he found it more difficult to tell—you. I do not know. But this is quite sure. He wishes it shall be *me*.

ALBERT. *You?*

ERNEST. Are you sorry?

ALBERT (*resentfully*). Then—why did he make me come?

ERNEST (*with a touch of sarcasm*). Oh, she has to choose, she has to choose! But she has to choose—*me*.

ALBERT. Why?

ERNEST. It is Papa's wish. He says—that there are family reasons.

ALBERT. Why did he not tell *me* so?

ERNEST. I do not know, Albert; I do not know. But you were always our Mamma's favourite. So, perhaps, that is why I am his.
(*Some new thought seems to have come to* ERNEST. *He looks at* ALBERT *curiously.*)

ALBERT. What was their quarrel about, Ernest?

ERNEST. It was more than a quarrel. I am thinking. (*Evidently he is*) . . . Do you remember our Mamma at all, Albert?

ALBERT. Oh yes. I remember her, just once, very well. She was crying. She took me into her arms and cried, and cried, till I cried too.

ERNEST. You were very young when she—went away from us. . . . I wonder . . . (*ponderingly*).

ALBERT. She used to write me letters.

ERNEST. Ah! She never wrote one to me!

ALBERT. They came secretly, by hand. I was to let nobody know.

ERNEST. Did you answer those letters?

ALBERT. Yes.

ERNEST. Secretly?

ALBERT. Yes.

ERNEST. So you never told *me*.

ALBERT. I was not to do so, lest it should be found out.

ERNEST. Though I was your Brother? Oh yes! You were always more to her than I. She wanted to take you with her—did you know? *Me*—she did not want.

ALBERT. When she went to live in Paris—alone, you mean?

ERNEST (*scoffingly*). Oh! not alone. . . . (*Suddenly a thought strikes him*) Ah! So *that* is it? Now I understand! . . . Yes. . . . Listen, Albert. . . . *It has got to be me!* You are my Brother, but you are not the son of my Father. I have just come to be sure of it.

ALBERT. I am not—? (*He stands dumbfounded.*)

ERNEST (*with more emphasis*). *You are not the son of my Father.* And *that* is why he says now it must be *me*. . . . Forgive me, Albert! You are very dear to me. But you must obey my Father.

ALBERT. If what you tell me is true, why should I obey—*your* Father?

ERNEST. Oh, well, Albert, because—whatever you are *not*—he is still your Reigning Prince. You owe him loyal duty and obedience, like all the rest.

ALBERT. No!

ERNEST. No?

ALBERT (*touched in his pride*). He did not tell *me!* Had he wished for my obedience, he should have told *me,* not *you.*

ERNEST. The explanation would have been rather difficult.

ALBERT. No doubt. That he did not choose to explain—removes the difficulty—so far as it concerns *me.*

ERNEST (*startled*). What, then, do you mean to do, Albert?

ALBERT. If she asks me, I shall accept.

ERNEST. Then she shall *not* ask you! Albert, we have the same Mother, and your honour is mine, and this shall never be known. But I must see that my Father's wishes are obeyed. I shall have you sent home.

ALBERT. Sent home!

ERNEST. Yes, at once. You shall be ordered to return. I shall send word today.

ALBERT. And what if I refuse to go?

ERNEST. My dear Albert, we are not English, we are German. If the Duke, my Father, your Sovereign Prince, sends for you to return, you *will* return. You know that perfectly well. (*Albert looks at him in silence for a while; then turns slowly away*) I am not taking away from your happiness, Albert. You will be happier than I.

ALBERT. Happiness is not everything.

ERNEST. Almost.

ALBERT. Live for it, and you lose it! To be happy has never been my thought—about life. I have not aimed for that.

ERNEST. No? What, then?

ALBERT. To do something that shall be worth doing.

ERNEST. Just now you said—to be a "puppet." I save you from *that.*

ALBERT (*coldly*). I would rather save myself.

ERNEST. Ah! So you have ambition?

ALBERT. Ambition? . . . I wonder. . . . Is it ambitious to give oneself—up?

ERNEST. No, Brother; but you will not have to give up yourself. Only, in this, do as you are told.

ALBERT. As *you* tell me?

ERNEST. As your Reigning Prince tells you. As you will be told—very soon.

ALBERT. Well, about that—we shall see!

ERNEST. *Yes,* Albert.

(*Hearing a step, they turn.* VICTORIA *has entered. She has already taken in something of a situation which she is not to understand. And since she is to be denied its explanation, she intends to terminate it.*)

VICTORIA. What are you two looking so serious about?

ERNEST. The rain.

VICTORIA. Oh, but it will clear presently; then we will go for a ride in the Park.

ERNEST. Oh, that will be very nice, to be sure!

VICTORIA. I hope you are going to enjoy your stay, Cousin.

ERNEST. Very much. I shall find it most delightful.

VICTORIA. And you too, Albert?

ALBERT. You are very kind, dear Cousin. How could I help enjoying myself while I am with you?

VICTORIA. Albert, that is the first pretty speech you have ever made me!

ALBERT. I am sorry, Cousin.

VICTORIA. Oh, but I like it!

ALBERT. I mean—that it should be only the first.

VICTORIA. Well, so long as it's not the last, I don't mind.

ERNEST. The rain is clearing. It has stopped. Shall we go out now?

VICTORIA (*correctively*). Cousin Ernest, I have made all necessary arrangements. We shall go out when we do go out—and not before. Besides—have you practised your music yet? At home, I was told, you practise every day.

ERNEST. But here one cannot find the time.

VICTORIA. Go, and do it now; and there will be time.

ERNEST. I tried one of the pianos the day we arrived, Cousin. It was not in very good tune.

VICTORIA. But that doesn't matter. You will be alone. No one will hear you.

ERNEST. Generally, when we practise, Albert and I practise together.

VICTORIA. Duets, you mean? Oh, but if the piano is out of tune, duets would be dreadful. Go and practise by yourself, Ernest; and Albert shall practise by *him*self, another time.

ERNEST. Is it a command, Cousin?

VICTORIA. My dear Ernest, I wouldn't think of commanding you. But I do want you to be quite at home here; and as you *always* practise at home, I want you to practise here, and now. We shall not start our ride for an hour. That gives you just time; so do go—now.

(COUSIN ERNEST *is not pleased; but the little creature is so born to rule that she gets her way.*)

ERNEST. Very well, Cousin . . . Albert, *remember!* (*He goes out, with a jerk of the head towards*

ALBERT, *which conveys a meaning.*)

VICTORIA. How strangely Ernest spoke to you, then! Is anything the matter?

ALBERT (*with reserve*). Oh no; nothing serious.

VICTORIA. You haven't been quarrelling, I hope?

ALBERT. We never quarrel.

VICTORIA. I think it would be very hard to quarrel with *you*, Albert. *I* couldn't.

ALBERT. Please, don't ever try!

VICTORIA. Some people are able to quarrel without trying.

ALBERT. Yes.
(*A pause.*)

VICTORIA. I suppose they like it.

ALBERT. Yes, I suppose so.
(*A pause.*)

VICTORIA. Won't you sit down, Albert? (*He takes a distant seat*) Why don't you sit nearer? Talking then is so much easier. (*He comes towards her.*)

ALBERT. You are very kind, Cousin, ever since we came: to both of us, I mean.

VICTORIA. I am very fond of—Ernest.

ALBERT. Yes, so am I. (*He sits down.*)

VICTORIA. You've always been together, haven't you?

ALBERT. We've never been apart yet.

VICTORIA. How very nice that has been—for both. (*A pause*) Would it be a great trial to you, if you had to live away from him?

ALBERT. Of course, the parting would be a trial. But one would get used to it—as to other things—if it had to be.

VICTORIA. My life has been so different from yours. I have never had anyone always with me like that—one of my own age. All my life I have been so much alone, except, of course, with Mamma. I don't know what it can be like—to have a brother.

ALBERT. One gets very fond of a brother.

VICTORIA. Yes; but one can get fonder of someone else—can one not?

ALBERT. It happens, sometimes.
(*A pause.*)

VICTORIA. Albert! What are you doing?

ALBERT. I was listening to Ernest, practising. I can just hear him; it is Beethoven.

VICTORIA. Don't listen to Ernest! You must listen to me!

ALBERT. I beg your pardon, Cousin; I was listening. Please don't think I am inattentive.

VICTORIA (*after a long pause*). Albert . . . I have something to say to you.

ALBERT. Yes . . . what is it, Cousin?

VICTORIA. In my position, it is I who have to say it—unfortunately. Ordinarily it is not what a woman would wish to say herself. She would rather—*he* said it.

ALBERT. Is there anything you wish me to say—that I can say?

VICTORIA (*tremulously*). To hear you say you *can* love me, is all I can hope—yet. If you could say that you already *do* love me, that would be—almost like Heaven.

ALBERT. I do . . . love you, Cousin.

VICTORIA. Enough to marry me?

ALBERT. More than enough to marry you. For people in our position often marry without any love at all.

VICTORIA. I couldn't do that—Albert.

ALBERT. Nor could I—Victoria.

VICTORIA. Then you will marry me?

ALBERT. If it is still your wish—when you know me—I will, very gratefully and humbly, accept this dear hand that you offer me.

VICTORIA. When I know you?

ALBERT. Yes; for I, too, have something to say. A few minutes ago, I did not know about myself what I know now. Even now I have no proof. Yet something tells me that it is true.

VICTORIA. Don't tell me—if it is anything I shouldn't wish to know, Albert.

ALBERT. But I must. My brother Ernest and I had the same mother; but not the same father.

VICTORIA. I don't understand.

ALBERT. I am sorry you should have to. . . . My Mother and my Father (Ernest's Father) separated —after I was born. They did not love each other. . . . My Mother must have loved someone else.

VICTORIA. While she was married? (*His head makes silent assent*) Before you were born—or after?

ALBERT. Before.

VICTORIA. Who?

ALBERT. I don't know. So neither do I know who *I* am. Perhaps I shall never know. Yet there must still be someone who could tell me —more than I have been able to tell you. . . . Shall I—? Do you wish me to go now? I had to tell you this.

VICTORIA. Yes . . . of course.

ALBERT. Then now—you wish me to go?

VICTORIA. No. . . . No. . . . I wish you to stay. It makes no difference to *me*. . . . And besides, who knows?

ALBERT. Somebody must know. Ernest knows.

VICTORIA. Ernest?

ALBERT. It was he who told me. And his Father knows.

VICTORIA. But his Father sent you here—let you come.

ALBERT. Yes. But he hoped it would be Ernest.

VICTORIA. How very silly of him!

ALBERT. Why?

VICTORIA. How could it possibly be Ernest, after I had seen you? . . . Oh, Albert! Albert! What does it matter? It is not your Father that I shall marry: it is you!
(*And as she speaks they are in each other's arms. Her passionate abandonment awakens response, though of a more restrained nature.*)

ALBERT. My very dear Cousin! My sweet Wife that is to be.

VICTORIA. Aren't you going to kiss me?

ALBERT. If I may. (*The kiss is given.*)

VICTORIA. Again, please! . . . Again!

ALBERT. I pray God you do not ever have to repent of this.

VICTORIA. Repent? How could I repent! It is not in my nature, Albert. Besides, there isn't going to be time. We must be married quite soon. Everybody expects it.

ALBERT. Expects it? They don't know!

VICTORIA. Expects me to marry, I mean. I had to choose *some*body. But I wasn't going to choose *any*body.

ALBERT. Not even Ernest?

VICTORIA. Oh, I liked Ernest very much, from the first. . . . I do still.

ALBERT (*with a touch of humour*). Is that why you sent him to practise? . . . He *knew*.

VICTORIA. That this was going to happen?

ALBERT. No; he did not know *that*.

VICTORIA. What, then?

ALBERT. That you were going to ask me.

VICTORIA. Well, then, what else could he suppose *would* happen?

ALBERT. He expected me to say no.

VICTORIA (*almost affronted*). But you couldn't have said "No" to a Queen—could you, Albert?

ALBERT. No, dear; one couldn't say "No" to a Queen.

VICTORIA. But did you want to?

ALBERT. No, Dearest One. All it means is that Ernest will be disappointed.

VICTORIA. Oh, I see. Poor Ernest! . . . Well, we must both try to be very nice and kind to him. . . . And now it is quite time that we went for our ride.

ALBERT. Isn't Ernest to come, too?

VICTORIA. Why, yes, of course!

ALBERT. Then won't you send and say he may stop practising? This hasn't taken an hour, you know.
(*Enter* ERNEST.)

VICTORIA. Nor has he, either; for here he is. Are you ready to come riding, Ernest?

ERNEST. Quite, if you are, Cousin.

VICTORIA. Oh yes, we are quite ready *now*. Everything has been settled. Tell him, Albert.

ALBERT. Ernest. . . . You told me to remember. . . . I *forgot*.
(ERNEST *has only to look at them, and the awful situation is explained. It will also have to be explained elsewhere. For when* VICTORIA *says that a thing is settled, it is settled—for good.*)

SCENE IV

MORNING GLORY

11th February 1840

A bell has just sounded. Into THE PRINCE'S *dressing-room at Windsor, where two candles are already burning, comes an elderly Valet. With deft movement, and the utmost correctitude of deportment, he places hot water, razors, soap, shaving-brush, and towel. He then proceeds to lay out in orderly sequence* THE PRINCE'S *clothing for the day; then goes to the window, draws back the curtains, raises the blind, and puts out the candles. The sun is already well up, for the hour is late. Having done all, he stands to attention, and waits. A door opens;* PRINCE ALBERT *enters, in a fine brocaded dressing-gown, and a silk night-cap of rather Eastern design, in which he looks well.*

ALBERT. That will do. I will shave myself this morning. When I want you, I will ring.
(*The Valet makes a short bow, and retires.* THE PRINCE *goes to the glass, throws off his night-cap, and, taking up a comb, passes it through the long locks of his rather disordered hair. He then uncords his dressing-gown, sits down, and, removing his fur-edged slippers, draws on a pair of pantaloons. He rises, resumes his slippers, and advances to the dressing-table. Opening the collar of his night-shirt, he prepares to shave himself, and is already applying the lather, when there comes a light tabbering on the door by which he has just entered. He turns a little surprised; the door opens: it is* THE QUEEN. *At first we only see her head, in a pretty frilled night-cap, with the strings hanging loose; but presently she is all there, wearing a rose-coloured dressing-gown, and over it a white Cashmere shawl with long fringes. She looks very happy and charming.*)

THE QUEEN. Albert, may I come in?

ALBERT. Yes, Dearest, if you wish to.
(She gazes in pleased astonishment at a spectacle she has never seen before: the solid foam of shaving-soap on a human countenance is something quite new to her.)

THE QUEEN. What *are* you doing?

ALBERT. Shaving.

THE QUEEN. Oh! How exciting! May I stay, and watch you?

ALBERT. If it would interest you, Weibchen.

THE QUEEN. But, of course! to see you shaving is wonderful! Something I never thought of.

ALBERT. Oh? Did you think one did not have to shave at all?

THE QUEEN. I never thought about it—till now. . . . You see, Albert, I have never seen a man shave himself before.

ALBERT. No, I suppose not.

THE QUEEN. How often do you have to do it? Once a week?

ALBERT. Every day.

THE QUEEN. Every day! But how absurd! It can't grow as fast as all that.

ALBERT. Oh yes, it does.

THE QUEEN. How very troublesome! Why, I only cut my *nails* once a week.

ALBERT. Nails can wait longer; beards won't.

THE QUEEN. I wouldn't like you to have a beard, Albert!

ALBERT. Nor would I. That's why I am taking it off now.
(Having sufficiently lathered, he now begins to shave.)

THE QUEEN. How strange it looks! . . . and how interesting!—fascinating! . . . Is it dangerous?

ALBERT. Not if you don't talk to me—

THE QUEEN (*a little startled*). Oh!

ALBERT. —not just while I am stroking myself.

THE QUEEN. Stroking yourself! Oh, Albert, you are funny!

ALBERT. Is that not the right word? Ought I to have said "wiping myself"—or what?

THE QUEEN. Really, I'm not sure, Albert. It's a part of the English language, which—from not having to know—I've not been taught.

ALBERT. Ah, Vicky! It is nice to hear you say that! Then you, too, do not know the English language quite like a native. For that—if it were not for the soup—I would kiss you.

THE QUEEN. The soup?

ALBERT. This, I mean.

THE QUEEN. Oh! not "soup," Albert darling. *Soap!*

ALBERT. Ah! Soap, then.

THE QUEEN. But I don't mind the soap, Albert—*your* soap—if you would like to.

ALBERT. Very well, then; now I will.
(*Having wiped his lips, he kisses her, and then goes on with his shaving.*)

THE QUEEN. Let me see what you do it with.
(*He gives her a razor; she takes it, and examines the edge.*)
Oh! how sharp it is!

ALBERT. Yes, it does have to be sharp—always.

THE QUEEN. Does it hurt?

ALBERT. No.

THE QUEEN. Do you ever cut yourself?

ALBERT. No; not when I am alone. I had a valet once, that used to shave me, before I knew how for myself. One day, he cut me, rather badly. After that, I had to learn; and for a long time, shaved only myself.

THE QUEEN. And what happened to him?

ALBERT. Oh, he had his head cut off, I suppose. . . . I did not inquire. I sent him out of the room, and told him never to come back. And oh, how he ran!
(*He laughs.*)

THE QUEEN. And then?

ALBERT. Then the Court Physician came running in a terrible fright, for the man having told him. He thought to find me bleeding to death.

THE QUEEN. To death? Why?

ALBERT. Because, my Dear, my brother Ernest—and his father—once so nearly did. But that did not happen to *me*. . . . I am not that way, you see. What I told you makes the difference.

THE QUEEN. Oh, Albert! Then that "difference" has, perhaps, saved your life?

ALBERT. Possibly.

THE QUEEN. Then, how thankful I really ought to be.

ALBERT. To my Mother, and my Father, you mean?

THE QUEEN. Yes. . . . Albert, suppose you had died before we got married, *could* I have married anyone else?

ALBERT. Of course, Dearest. You had to marry someone. You could not disappoint your people by not giving them an heir to the Throne.

THE QUEEN. Oh, Albert! Shall I? Will that really happen?

ALBERT. We will hope so, Dearest—in time.

THE QUEEN. In time? I hope it will be very soon. Oh, isn't it wonderful? We really are—married now, aren't we?

ALBERT (*covertly amused*). Yes, Weibchen, I think so.

THE QUEEN. Yesterday seems almost like another world—so different. All the crowds, and the cheering, and the firing, and the bells: and thousands and thousands of people all looking at us, as if we belonged to them: as, of course, in a way, we do. . . . And now we are all by ourselves—all alone—just we two.

ALBERT. Yes, all alone—just we two. Shall I be able to make you happy, —you think? . . . You *are* happy?

THE QUEEN. Happy? So happy, I can't—I can't tell you, Albert! . . . And to think that this will go on, and on, for years and years . . . It's like Heaven!

ALBERT. No, Vicky, not just like this—that is not possible . . . That is not human nature.

THE QUEEN. But I shall never love you less than I do now, Albert.

ALBERT. No, Dearest, perhaps not. But you will be less excited about it—less romantic, perhaps. I shall have become less strange to you. We love each other, but we are still both rather strangers. We have to learn each other's characters—and ways. That will take time. . . .
(*She shakes her head fondly, confident that she knows him already—by heart.*)

ALBERT. Oh yes. . . . You have come to see me shave today—for the first time. That pleases—that excites you. But it will not always excite you as much as today. You will not come, I think, to see me shave every day—for the next twenty years.

THE QUEEN. Why not?

ALBERT. Because, Dearest, you will have too much else to do. Also you will know so well what it looks like, which today you see only the first time. So, that it should become less of a spectacle, is only reasonable.

THE QUEEN. I don't want to be reasonable with *you*, Albert!

ALBERT. But you *will* want—in time, I hope, Vicky. So shall I. You have a great life of duties to perform, in which I am to share. Is that not so?

THE QUEEN. We can't share everything, Albert. Some things I shall have to do alone—affairs of State, in which it would not be right for you to concern yourself.

ALBERT (*a little sharply*). So?

THE QUEEN. Yes. You must take great care, Dearest. The English are jealous; and to them you are still a foreigner.

ALBERT. And—to *you?*

THE QUEEN. To me you are everything—life, happiness, peace, and comfort! When I am with you, I shall want to forget everything—except our love.
(*It is a prospect over which, as she flings herself into his arms, she looks more happy than he does. All at once, from the Terrace outside, comes a burst of music. With the happy excitement of a child, she draws him to the window, and points.*)

Hark! Look! That is the Band of my Royal Life Guards. I gave orders for it to be here this morning an hour earlier—so that we might hear it before we came down. . . . I thought you would like it.

ALBERT. Oh yes; it is very good music.

THE QUEEN. What is it they are playing?

ALBERT. You do not know?

THE QUEEN. No. I only said that some suitable pieces were to be chosen—it being such a special occasion. What is it?

ALBERT. That, my Vicky, is Mendelssohn's *Wedding March,* from his new setting to Shakespeare.

THE QUEEN. Mendelssohn! Oh, I'm glad. He is one of the world's greatest composers, is he not? . . . No, I have never heard it before. But now it is going to be my favourite piece.

ALBERT. You could not choose better. But you will not want to hear it every day, Weibchen.

THE QUEEN. Perhaps not quite every day.

ALBERT. Any more than you will want to see me shave—every day.

THE QUEEN. Now you are laughing at me.

ALBERT. Just a little, Dearest; because you—and I, are both today so young.

THE QUEEN. And so happy! Look how the sun is shining!
(*She goes and stands in the window.*)

ALBERT. Ah, do not stand so near to that window, Vicky!

THE QUEEN. Why not?

ALBERT. The people might see you.

THE QUEEN. Well, but why shouldn't they? It would please them.

ALBERT (*uncomfortably*). Yes: too much. . . . That is why I say—*don't!*

THE QUEEN. Albert, darling, we have got to appear in public again almost at once. It's no use being shy. And why should we, when I'm so proud of having got you?

ALBERT (*rescuing modesty with common sense*). I want my breakfast, Vicky! Please to go and get yourself ready—quick. I am going to ring now for my dresser to come.

THE QUEEN (*revelling in wifely submission*). Order me to go, Albert! . . . *Order* me!

ALBERT (*playing up*). *Go,* woman! He says to you, *Go!*
(*Gazing at him adoringly, she drops a deep mocking curtsy, and retires. He stands looking fondly after her: then, with a sigh, turns, and rings the bell. His Valet enters. The Band plays on.* THE PRINCE *proceeds to dress himself with formal correctness for the very difficult new life which now awaits him.*)

ACT TWO

SCENE I

"A GOOD LESSON!"

1842

It is ten o'clock, and a bright morning. In THE PRINCE'S *writing-room at Buckingham Palace,* MR. ANSON, *his Private Secretary, stands by the table, sorting correspondence; opened letters he places in one heap, unopened in another. The door opens; one of* THE QUEEN'S GENTLEMEN *enters.*

GENTLEMAN. Her Majesty wishes to know whether the Prince has yet returned?

ANSON (*in a quiet, matter-of-fact tone*). No. . . . At least, so far as I know, he has not.

GENTLEMAN (*hesitating*). Oh? . . . Do you know, Mr. Anson, where the Prince *is?*

ANSON (*with studied nonchalance*). Now? . . . No, I don't.

GENTLEMAN (*with embarrassment*). You know, I suppose, that His Highness did not return to the Palace, last night?

ANSON (*as before*). From the Royal Academy Dinner? Oh, indeed . . . didn't he?

GENTLEMAN (*making a plunge*). Did he *go,* Mr. Anson?

ANSON. Oh yes, I think so. The papers *say* that he did. Here is his speech, fully reported, in this morning's *Times;* and a very good one, too.

GENTLEMAN. Very strange, Mr. Anson!

ANSON. Not at all. His speeches generally are.

GENTLEMAN. I meant—his not returning.

ANSON (*coldly*). Hadn't you better report to Her Majesty that His Highness has *not* yet returned? That, I believe, was all you were sent to find out.

GENTLEMAN (*stiffly*). Certainly. I will.

(*He goes.* ANSON *continues sorting the letters. There comes a knock at the door; and permission given —in comes* THE PRINCE'S *Valet,* MR. RICHARDS.)

RICHARDS. I beg pardon, Sir. I heard you were alone: so I came to see you, Sir.

ANSON. Yes? What is it, Richards?

RICHARDS. His Royal Highness, Sir. . . . He hasn't sent for me this morning, Sir: and didn't last night, either. He doesn't seem to have been in his dressing-room at all, Sir: not since I dressed him last night, for the Dinner.

ANSON. Oh, it's all right, Richards. His Royal Highness was unexpectedly called elsewhere, at a late hour last night, so did not return.

RICHARDS (*re-assured*). Oh, very good, Sir.

ANSON. I expect His Royal Highness to be back before long. So you be ready for him.

RICHARDS. Yes, Sir. Very good, Sir. (*He goes.* ANSON, *left to himself, can no longer conceal his anxiety.*)

ANSON. But is it "all right," I wonder? . . . God!
(*Nervously he snatches up the paper, then throws it down again. He moves restlessly to the window, and back again. The door opens; in comes* PRINCE ALBERT, *looking very calm and collected.*)

ALBERT (*quietly*). Good morning, Anson.

ANSON. Good morning, Sir.

ALBERT. Is there any news this morning?—anything special?

ANSON. In the papers, Sir? A full report of the Academy Banquet. (*He takes up* The Times, *and offers it*) Did that go off well, Sir?

ALBERT (*not taking it*). Very well.

ANSON. I was just reading your Highness's speech.

ALBERT. Yes, Anson; of which you wrote for me the notes.

ANSON. At your Highness's dictation.

ALBERT. Well, I did not make it too long, I hope?

ANSON. It reads very well, Sir. And it seems to have been well received.

ALBERT. Yes; it was altogether a very well managed affair. And I found the company quite interesting. We were talking of the decorations for the walls of the new Houses of Parliament; and I was proposing that there should be a Competition and a Fine Arts Commission to decide it. They thought it was a good idea.

ANSON. Well, Sir, if a Competition will produce the right artists, it certainly will be. But we have not had much practice of mural art in this country, Sir, I'm afraid; we don't run to it.

ALBERT. We must begin, then, and try.

ANSON. Yes, Sir.

ALBERT. That was Sir Francis Chantrey's objection. But when I said to him—"How would it do, then, to employ foreign Artists?" he said that if they came, their heads would be broken; and that—old as he was—he would himself lend a hand for the purpose.

ANSON. Indeed, Sir?

ALBERT. Yes, indeed! So you see! . . .
(THE PRINCE *seats himself at his writing-table.*)

ALBERT. Letters?

ANSON (*handing some*). These, Sir, I think, are all that your Highness need see for the present.

ALBERT. Thank you.

(THE QUEEN'S GENTLEMAN *again enters.*)

GENTLEMAN. Her Majesty sent me to inquire if your Royal Highness was disengaged?

ALBERT. Oh yes. Tell Her Majesty I am quite free, if she wishes to see me. (*The* GENTLEMAN *bows, and retires.* THE PRINCE *continues to look over his correspondence*) Now you may go, Anson. Take all those other letters, and leave me these. (ANSON *retires.* THE PRINCE *goes on opening his correspondence. A minute passes; suddenly the door is flung open, and* THE QUEEN *makes a flamboyant entry.*)

THE QUEEN. Albert! Where have you been?

ALBERT. To Windsor, Victoria.

THE QUEEN. Windsor? Impossible! Why did you not come back last night?

ALBERT. I did not come back last night, Victoria, because of the way in which you sent for me.

THE QUEEN. I told you before you went, that I wished you to be back by half-past ten at the latest.

ALBERT. Yes.

THE QUEEN. At half-past ten you had not come; so I sent for you.

ALBERT. Yes, I received from you this note. (*He produces it*) . . . "Albert, it is quite time you were back. Please to come at once!"

THE QUEEN. Yes; I wrote it; I sent it; and my orders were that it should be put into your hand by the Messenger to whom I gave it.

ALBERT. It was put into my hand. I sent back word to say that I had received it.

THE QUEEN. Yes; but you did not come!

ALBERT. I did not come, because I was not then ready to come.

THE QUEEN. Albert! when you go anywhere without *me* (as you *had* to do on this occasion), I do not expect you to be late.

ALBERT. No. But when I do go without you, you must leave it for me to decide, myself, when I shall return.

THE QUEEN. But this time I had already told you my wishes, and had decided *for* you. . . . I sent again.

ALBERT. Yes. At eleven o'clock, I received this. (*He produces it*) "Albert, I order you to return at once! V.R."

THE QUEEN. And still you did not!

ALBERT. I did not.

THE QUEEN. So you disobeyed your Queen!

ALBERT (*serenely*). Yes, my Dear; I disobeyed my Queen. Send me to the Tower for it, and cut off my head.

THE QUEEN. I do not regard this as a subject for amusement and jest, Albert.

ALBERT. No? Then it is lucky that *I* do. For if neither of us thought it amusing, we might have quite a serious quarrel about it. But now—as it is only you who do not think it amusing—the quarrel will not be so serious.

THE QUEEN. Albert, what did you do, after I had ordered you to return? Where did you spend the night?

ALBERT. At Windsor, as I have told you.

THE QUEEN. I don't believe it!

ALBERT. Don't you?
(*Quietly he turns back to his letters.*)

THE QUEEN. Albert, I will not be treated like this! Please to remember that, though I am your Wife, I am also your Queen.

ALBERT (*kindly*). Sit down, my Dear, sit down! there is nothing to stand up about. . . . Last night there was; so I had to. But now I am ready to sit here and talk it over, quite reasonably and comfortably: just you and me, Weibchen—with the Queen left out. . . . Please! (*With a gesture he gets her seated*) Listen to me, my Dear. When you married me, you made a promise that was strange for a Queen to make: but you made it. . . . To love, honour, and obey. And because it was so strange—so unlikely—I have never once told you to obey me—except for fun, when you wished it. Now, my Dear, as I have not expected *you* to obey *me* in anything—so there are some things in which you must not expect *me* to obey *you.*

THE QUEEN. When you do things for me in public—officially, that is to say—then I *do* expect you to obey me.

ALBERT. When I do things for you in public, my Dear, I obey you by doing them. But you must trust me to do them in my own way—

THE QUEEN. No, Albert.

ALBERT. —not to interfere with me, while I am doing them, as you did last night. That is why, when I started back—after having received your "orders"—I told the Coachman to drive—not to Buckingham Palace, but to Windsor.

THE QUEEN. The Coachman! You told him that! What must he have thought?

ALBERT. I will tell you what he thought. . . . At first he thought it was very strange. But when we got to Windsor, he thought that he knew the reason.

THE QUEEN. Why, only then?

ALBERT. It was rather late: almost half-past one. But when we got there, there were lights, and music, and dancing.

THE QUEEN. Music! . . . Dancing! . . . *In* the Castle?

ALBERT. In the Castle. . . . Behind our backs—so sure that we should be away—the servants were having a fancy-dress ball.

THE QUEEN (*her anger quite diverted*). What an improper liberty! Most extraordinary! And how fortunate that you should have caught them!

ALBERT. Yes; a curious coincidence, was it not? So, of course, the Coachman thought that I had got wind of the affair, and had come there to catch them at it.

THE QUEEN. Where were they dancing, Albert?

ALBERT. In the great Hall.

THE QUEEN. And in fancy-dress, you say?

ALBERT. Yes. Two of them had dressed up to look like you and me.

THE QUEEN. Albert! Did you see who they were?

ALBERT. No. They ran too quick! I went in, and stood. . . . They were all very much surprised to see me.

THE QUEEN. Indeed, I should think so! . . . What happened then?

ALBERT. First, the dancing all stopped; then all the music. . . . I stood there and looked at them. It was very funny: I tried not to laugh.

THE QUEEN. I hope you did not, Albert!

ALBERT. No; I composed myself to look as though I was very angry.

THE QUEEN. I hope you did. And then, what did you do?

ALBERT. I told them that they might go on for just five minutes more; but that it was not to happen again.

THE QUEEN. No, indeed!

ALBERT. And it will not, I am sure.

THE QUEEN. Did you get any explanation, as to why they had *dared* to do such a thing?

ALBERT. Oh yes; it was explained. You see, they were to have had a ball soon after Christmas; but on the very date the Court had to go into mourning; so it was put off, and forgotten. And as they had got all the dresses, they were naturally disappointed.

THE QUEEN. But, Albert, that such a thing *could* happen without our knowing—well, it means that such a lot of other things may be happening too.

ALBERT. Yes; I am afraid so . . . I think, my Dear, that you had better make me your Manager of Windsor—factotum, you call it? They will not like it, because I have too much of a head for business; but it will be good for them. And for you, a great saving of unnecessary expense.

THE QUEEN. Yes; and if I do it at once, everybody will understand *why*.

ALBERT. It was a good thing, Vicky, was it not, that I was brought up rather poor?

THE QUEEN. So was I.

ALBERT. Yes? But you had not to manage much for yourself, had you? What for are you smiling at?

THE QUEEN. The Coachman, Albert! It *was* funny! I'm so glad you went; for now they will all be thinking how clever it was of you to find out! And what a good lesson it was for them, to be sure!

ALBERT. Yes, my Dear, a good lesson. . . . But Weibchen, you have not kissed me "Good Morning" yet. . . . Please!

(*And he says it so simply and sweetly, that, quite forgetting now what she first came about, she kisses him with true wifely affection, very fondly and contentedly.*)

SCENE II

UNDER FIRE

30th May 1842

In a room of Buckingham Palace overlooking the Park, PRINCE ALBERT *moves impatiently to the window, and back again. He looks at his watch: a slight sound of annoyance escapes him. The door opens; his Private Secretary enters.*

ALBERT (*stiffly*). Mr. Anson, you are late.

ANSON. I am sorry, Sir. I was just coming, when the Chief Inspector of Police sent word that he wished to see me.

ALBERT (*sharply*). Has he news?

ANSON. None, Sir. They can't trace the man. So he very urgently begs that Her Majesty shall not drive out today.

ALBERT. But that is nonsense! If Her Majesty does not drive in the Park as usual, the man will suspect that we know. So we shall not catch him.

ANSON. It is a great risk, Sir.

ALBERT. It is a risk. It has to be taken. It will be a greater risk if we leave him to choose his own time later, when the Police will not be so ready for him as they are today.

ANSON. He will choose his own time in any case, Sir.

ALBERT. Yes; but now it will be the earliest possible. Yesterday, when his pistol missed fire, he did not know that he was seen by anyone. Her Majesty herself was looking the other way.

ANSON. That was very fortunate, Sir.

ALBERT. Perhaps. . . . Why?

ANSON. Had Her Majesty shown any alarm, it would have told him.

ALBERT. Her Majesty would have shown no alarm. You may be quite sure of that. When I told Her Majesty afterwards, what had happened, she was not alarmed at all; only rather surprised that one of her subjects should have done anything so wicked and foolish.

ANSON. Ah, yes, Sir; that is, indeed, how it might well—

ALBERT *(continuing)*.—Nor is Her Majesty alarmed now. It was her own decision, not mine, that we should go out today. When I told her that the man was sure to make another attempt, she said that he had better make it at once then, and get it over.

ANSON. That was very courageous of Her Majesty.

ALBERT. And very sensible. Sense is sometimes more valuable than courage—and much rarer where Kings are concerned. It is so here. I have no doubt that this afternoon the man will try again. It is better that he should try again, when we expect it, than at some later time when we do not. And that, Mr. Anson, is why—if the Inspector is so stupid that he must have it explained—that is why Her Majesty drives out again today, at her usual time. You will go and tell him that at once. (*He moves to the window*) Out there are the people, waiting to see Her Majesty start. Tell him that we shall be punctual.

ANSON. I will, your Highness. . . . I hope—

ALBERT (*cutting him short*). We *all* hope, Mr. Anson. It is the only sensible thing to do. Ah, here is Her Majesty.

(THE QUEEN *enters in bonnet and shawl.* MR. ANSON *stands aside for her to pass, then bows himself out. A little nervous, but very self-controlled,* THE QUEEN *advances towards* THE PRINCE.)

ALBERT (*approvingly*). You are very punctual, my Dear.

THE QUEEN. Yes; we mustn't be late today.

ALBERT. You look very well—very charming! That bonnet suits you.

THE QUEEN. Kiss me, Albert.

ALBERT (*as he does so*). You make a very good Queen, my Dear.

THE QUEEN. With you to help me.

ALBERT. Even by yourself, I think, you would not do so badly.

THE QUEEN. That will never happen, Albert. I couldn't live without you.

ALBERT. You can do very unexpected things, my Dear. You never expected that you would have to do anything like this. But you are going to. It is having to do it that makes it possible.

THE QUEEN. Doing it with you, Dearest, I *like* doing it.

ALBERT. So do I. It makes our life mean so much more to us. . . . Look at all those friendly people, waiting for you to smile on them. . . . Rather amusing, is it not?—that none of them knows in the least—what *we* know.

THE QUEEN (*tremulously*). Albert, this must be rather like going into battle.

ALBERT. Just a little, my Dear. But we have to do it in cold blood, without any excitement. That makes it rather more difficult, perhaps.

THE QUEEN. Oh, but it excites me very much, Albert. For this is really to be a Queen. And with you I feel quite safe that I can behave like one.

ALBERT. Yes; so do I, Weibchen; so do I.
(*The door opens; a* COURT USHER *enters to make formal announcement.*)

USHER. May it please: your Majesty's Ladies are in attendance.

THE QUEEN. Oh yes. . . . Tell them to come in. (THE USHER *retires.* THE QUEEN *turns quickly to* THE PRINCE) Albert, I didn't say anything to them before; I thought it was better not. But *they* mustn't come with us today; it wouldn't be safe.

ALBERT. You are quite right, my Dear. It would be, for them, an unnecessary risk. We must go alone.
(*The two Ladies-in-Waiting enter, dressed for going out. They make their curtsies, and stand to receive orders.*)

THE QUEEN. Lady Muriel, Lady Grace, I do not require either of you this afternoon. I and the Prince are going out alone.
(*The two Ladies receive this information with perfect correctness; but there is a suspicion of offended coldness in* LADY MURIEL'S *tone as she speaks.*)

LADY MURIEL. And your Majesty will not require us again—later?

THE QUEEN. No; not this afternoon. You can wait till we have gone. And then I shall not require your further attendance till this evening. . . . And now, Albert, I am quite ready to start. . . . I wonder if it is going to rain?

ALBERT. I think not. Just now it looked quite promising.
(*And so, talking of the weather, they go out, to give Fate and its Fool their opportunity for ending the Victorian Era before it has earned its name.*
And now the two Ladies-in-Waiting are alone; and, defrauded of her afternoon ride with Royalty, before admiring crowds (for which, with bonnet and shawl, she has so elaborately prepared herself), LADY MURIEL *breaks out.*)

LADY MURIEL. Well! I do think that's too bad! Here have we been kept waiting all for nothing; and if I'd known, I could have got off for the whole afternoon, as I very much wanted to do. I do call that inconsiderate of her!

LADY GRACE. It's what she is, my dear. I suppose she can't help it. It's being a Queen. When you are so important yourself, you can't think much about other people. Oh, it's happened before; and it'll happen again! It's what we are here for.

LADY MURIEL. Oh, there! I've torn my glove. Dear, dear! My own fault, I suppose, taking it off in a temper.

LADY GRACE (*at the window*). Now, they're off. There they go! . . . No cheering this afternoon; the crowd isn't big enough. It always takes a certain number to cheer;—haven't you noticed? . . . But we bow, all the same. Oh, how he does take his hat off!—So like a foreigner! He'll never learn to be English.

LADY MURIEL. Which way are they going?

LADY GRACE. Which way? Why, there's only one way to the Park that I know of, my dear: up Constitution Hill.

LADY MURIEL. If they are only going to the Park, isn't it rather strange that they should choose to go alone? The Prince so insists on the Queen being properly attended. It's my belief they've been quarrelling about something; and she wants to have it out with him.

LADY GRACE. But she can't do that in the Park, with people staring at them.

LADY MURIEL. Oh, *can't* she? She can say anything she wants to say, without moving a muscle of her face! She can whip you with a word, while she's smiling to someone else across the room. It's happened to me; so I know. She'll be able to say *all* she intends to say while they are driving in the Park. Yes; he's going to catch it about something.

LADY GRACE. But does he ever "catch" it?

LADY MURIEL. My dear! She adores him, as we all know; but she can be jealous. And when she *is* jealous, she lets him know—you may depend on it.

LADY GRACE. Well, of course, he *is* dangerously handsome. It's a wonder we don't all fall in love with him: but we don't.

LADY MURIEL. Oh, he could be much more dangerous, if he chose, my dear. But it isn't manners that makes the man with him—it's morals.

LADY GRACE. I suppose that's why he's so stiff when he talks to us. Oh, I've seen her watching him. I've been told that once, in the early days, he gave one of her Ladies a present. There was a frightful row. He never did it again!

LADY MURIEL. Perhaps it was something more than a present.

LADY GRACE. Oh, my dear, I don't think you ought to say that!

LADY MURIEL. I know I oughtn't! And that's why it's such a relief to say it! He's so good, he irritates me. Everything so proper! Life here is just a row of "oughts," all standing to attention—rules, rules, rules! I wonder he puts up with it.

LADY GRACE. I think it's just as much his doing as hers. It's the way he was brought up: he doesn't know how to be natural.

LADY MURIEL. Just as well, perhaps. . . . I don't believe he loves her a little bit.

LADY GRACE. But he *must!*

LADY MURIEL. Why?

LADY GRACE. Well, he's stiff; but he's got a heart. And not to love one who loves him so terribly well, would be heartless.

LADY MURIEL. She only loves him selfishly.

LADY GRACE. No, my dear, not selfishly—jealously, perhaps. But she knows how much he's her superior; and a selfish person wouldn't. . . . What's that?

LADY MURIEL. I didn't hear anything.

LADY GRACE. It sounded like a shot. (*But to neither of them does a chance shot seem a matter of importance; so talk goes on.*)

LADY MURIEL. Well, my dear, I suppose we've been wasting time in a very ignoble conversation—running down our betters, which, after all, we have to admit they are. . . . What are you going to do?

LADY GRACE. I don't know: it's too late to go anywhere now. But I don't want to stay here and watch them come back.

LADY MURIEL. Isn't it funny how people *do?* Look, there's the crowd still waiting. They've seen them once; but they want to see them again. And I believe that sometimes it's the same people who come day after day—day after day.

LADY GRACE. Oh, well, Royalty are one of the sights of London. Country Cousins expect to see them; and if you read your Court Circular, they can always be seen *here* at the stated hours.

LADY MURIEL. My dear! What are all those people running for? Look! Constitution Hill is full of them! What can have happened?

LADY GRACE. Has there been an accident?

LADY MURIEL. No, no! Not an accident. They are cheering, waving, shouting! And here come mounted police—such a lot of them.

LADY GRACE. They are coming back! They are coming back!

LADY MURIEL. Who?

LADY GRACE. The Queen! Something exciting must have happened! Has there been a declaration of War?

LADY MURIEL. There's no one just now to declare war against, that I know of.

LADY GRACE. Well, they must have done something very popular, anyhow. Look! The crowd's quite crazy.
(*And then in bursts another of the Ladies-in-Waiting, panting, and flapping her hands with excitement.*)

LADY-IN-WAITING. She's been shot at! She's been shot at!

LADY MURIEL AND LADY GRACE. Who?

LADY-IN-WAITING. The Queen!

LADY MURIEL AND LADY GRACE. Where? When?

LADY-IN-WAITING. Just now; on Constitution Hill.

LADY GRACE (*highly excited*). I heard it!

LADY MURIEL. Was she hurt?

LADY GRACE. Who did it?

LADY-IN-WAITING. No; not hurt. A man—a madman, they think.

LADY GRACE. Caught? Was he caught?

LADY-IN-WAITING. Yes; they were expecting it. He'd tried to do it before—yesterday.

LADY MURIEL. How do you know?

LADY-IN-WAITING. I don't know. It mayn't be true. But everybody says so.

LADY GRACE. Look! now they're coming in. The police are pushing the crowd back—such a lot of them on duty, they *must* have known.

LADY MURIEL. Oh! Then—*She* must have known too!

LADY-IN-WAITING. Yes; I suppose so.

LADY MURIEL (*catching hold of* LADY GRACE). Then that was *why!* Oh, my dear! She *knew!*—went, knowing that she was going to be shot at—*so didn't take us!* Oh! what a worm I feel myself now!

LADY GRACE (*sharing the feeling*). Yes, dear.

LADY MURIEL. I want to run away, and hide; I'm so ashamed of myself!

LADY GRACE. You can't go! They are coming.

(*The door opens;* THE QUEEN *enters, followed by* PRINCE ALBERT. *The Ladies curtsy with an emotional reverence which makes the formality almost beautiful.*)

LADY MURIEL. Oh! your Majesty!

THE QUEEN. Lady Muriel, why are you here still? Didn't I tell you that I should not want you again till this evening? Now go at once.

LADY MURIEL. Oh, your Majesty! before I go, may I—may I—kiss your Majesty's hand?

THE QUEEN. Why, certainly, if you wish to. Now don't cry: don't be silly! It's all over.

LADY MURIEL. Oh, I'm so sorry, Ma'am: so sorry! So ashamed of myself!

THE QUEEN. Ashamed? Why?

LADY MURIEL. When your Majesty said we were not to come out with you this afternoon, I was foolishly cross: I didn't understand.

THE QUEEN. Of course not. It was not necessary that you should. But now you *do.* So that will help you to know better—another time.

ALBERT (*turning sharply*). Another time!

THE QUEEN. Go, please, Lady Muriel. I don't want you any more now. (*And* LADY MURIEL *curtsies herself out after the others who have already gone*) Why, yes, Albert: there *may* come another time. Why not?

ALBERT (*taking her in his arms*). Oh, my Dear, my Dear And you can say that *now*—as if you did not mind if it *should* come again! Is that really true?

THE QUEEN. Yes, Albert: it was wonderful! For, with you, I felt—so safe. . . . Didn't you?

ALBERT. No, Weibchen. I was afraid!

THE QUEEN. Afraid?

ALBERT. I was afraid that—if he missed *one* of us, it might be *me* that he missed. Ah, no, no, no! do not talk of another time! I could not bear it—another time!

THE QUEEN (*startled*). Oh, Albert, had I thought for a moment that it might be *you*—I *couldn't* have gone! But that *that* could happen I didn't think!

ALBERT. What a very good thing it was, then, my Dear, that you did *not* think. Queens must not think too much about others—only about themselves! (*And having made that little joke, very much to his own satisfaction, he kisses her.*)

THE QUEEN. Dearest! Have I pleased you?

ALBERT. Very much. You have more than *pleased* me. You have behaved —like a Queen!

THE QUEEN. Then now I must go and take off my things. Oh, dear! what a lot of letters I shall have to write *now!* To Uncle Leopold, and to everybody! (*And with this added inconvenience of attempted assassination upon her mind, off she goes, for there is no time to lose.*)

SCENE III

THE ROSE AND THE THORN

1846

THE QUEEN *is holding her Court at Windsor. A Footman opens the folding-doors of a small ante-chamber; and from its softly illumined interior one sees across the broad corridor, through looped curtains, the large music-room (where presently performance is to take place) brilliantly lighted. Under its crystal chandeliers, the Ladies and Gentlemen of the Court are beginning to gather. The small room has in it little furniture: away from the wall, on one side of the door, stands a small settee; on the other, a grand-piano. On the same side, lower down, is a smaller door. Into the room come four musicians, carrying their instruments: their conductor, the future* SIR JOHN OAKLEY—*now only* "MR."—*leading them.*

OAKLEY. We must come in here, for a moment. Her Majesty does not allow any tuning-up to be done in her presence. (*He opens the piano, and strikes notes and chords for the musicians to tune by*) So. . . . You are all ready? Come, then!

(*They go out, leaving the folding-doors open, and cross the corridor to the music-room. A little later, the doors of the music-room are closed, and one hears from within, very softly, the performance beginning. And now two Ladies of the Court enter: the one a very *beautiful* DUCHESS *of middle age,* THE QUEEN'S *Mistress of the Robes; the other her cousin,* LADY JANE, *small, young, and pretty.* THE DUCHESS, *leading the way, lays down on the settee a richly embroidered shawl, and a feather fan. Meanwhile the younger lady is speaking.*)

LADY JANE. But, your Grace, it's so difficult!

DUCHESS. My dear, Court life *is* difficult. Its difficulties are the larger part of its duties.

LADY JANE. But to be suspected—and for nothing—is so humiliating!

DUCHESS. Yes, my dear; high positions, when they are not the highest, involve humiliation for all of us. Do you think *I* never feel humiliated?

LADY JANE. You! Your Grace?

DUCHESS. When I am sent out of the room, as if I were a servant, I feel it.

LADY JANE. But you do it so grandly—with such an air!

DUCHESS. Yes: that is how one covers the humiliation. After all, Court life is mainly made up of formalities; and being sent out of the room is one of them. Ministers are dismissed, and so are we. Even Lord Palmerston had a narrow escape the other day.

LADY JANE. Lord Palmerston!

DUCHESS. Yes; and quite right, too!

LADY JANE (*who has gone to the mirror, to re-arrange the flowers in her hair*). What for?

DUCHESS. Well, it wasn't the Queen who told me, or I shouldn't repeat it. He told me himself—cross, but half-laughing. He wanted the Prince out of the room, while he discussed Foreign Affairs with her. And, to avoid it, he sent off some despatches without first submitting them. So there was trouble.

LADY JANE. I should think so!

DUCHESS. Yes, my dear; anyone who touches the Prince, touches a bomb, which goes off. She's the bomb: *He* isn't.

LADY JANE (*reverting to her grievance*). But I haven't touched him!

DUCHESS. No; but you've looked at him. That's enough.

LADY JANE. But, your Grace, he's there to be looked at! And how can one help admiring him, when he's so handsome?

DUCHESS. You needn't help it; but you mustn't be admired in return.

LADY JANE. Oh, why doesn't she only have *plain* women about her?

DUCHESS. Even that wouldn't always meet the difficulty. Plain women have often a way with them. And it wants something more than mere looks to attract *him.*

LADY JANE (*with a touch of spite*). He isn't a bit in love with *her!*

DUCHESS. No; but he's very fond of her. The Prince is—what is so rarely found amongst Royalty—the domestic man; and he's not only domestic, he's conjugal.

LADY JANE. Then why is she so jealous of him?

DUCHESS. My dear, she can't help it: she's possessive, and she's in love with him.

LADY JANE. But *I'm* not!

DUCHESS. Of course not, my dear. I know you wouldn't take such a liberty.

LADY JANE. I wish she'd send me away! If this goes on, I shall ask to resign my appointment.

DUCHESS. No, no, my dear! Don't do anything so out of character. "Hold your ground!" is the motto of our family. Hold it! . . . What, exactly, happened today?

LADY JANE. We were out riding in the Park; and the Prince came and rode beside me, just for a moment. My reins had got caught, and he was putting them straight for me. And the Queen pushed her horse right in between us; and she said, "Lady Jane, if you don't know how to ride properly, you had better not come out with us!" And the Prince said, "Lady Jane rides very nicely and well." Oh, you should have seen the Queen's look then! And it's true; I *do* ride nicely—better than she does; and she knows it!

DUCHESS. And was that all that happened?

LADY JANE. All that happened to *me*. But the Prince left the Queen, and went straight off, and rode with one of his Gentlemen. And then the Queen suddenly turned round, and we all had to ride back to the Castle. And of course everybody knew that something was the matter, for we hadn't gone half our usual round. And now, I believe, she has put Lady Maud to spy on me.

DUCHESS. Oh, I don't think that's likely, my dear. The Queen wouldn't say anything to anyone —she's too proud.

LADY JANE. Well, she *is* spying anyway—hoping perhaps to tell tales presently. If I catch her, I'll slap her face!

DUCHESS. My dear, I think I'd better arrange for you to take a little holiday—change of air. You shall see your doctor, and he will advise it. But don't give up your post. If the Queen proposes to dismiss you, I shall say something. She won't dismiss *me*.

LADY JANE. No; but perhaps she will send you out of the room.

DUCHESS. Perhaps she will, my dear. She has done it before; and I have continued the conversation the next day, with the Prince there to help me.

LADY JANE. To help you?

DUCHESS. Oh yes; she's always much more easy to reason with when he's there.

LADY JANE. He has such beautiful manners to every one, hasn't he?

DUCHESS. He is a very good corrective; and she knows it. I'm very fond of her; but she needs managing; and he is the only person who can do it.

LADY JANE. He didn't manage her this morning!

DUCHESS. He didn't try. . . . You wait!

LADY JANE. Oh, dear! I don't know that I *can* wait. Everybody knows I'm in disgrace; so they won't speak to me.

DUCHESS. Now be brave, my dear, be brave! The unfortunate thing has happened, and now it's over. You keep under my wing; and you shan't look as if you've been sent to Coventry by anyone. . . . There's the music coming to an end. We must go back, or she will be missing us. (*Forgetting her shawl and fan, she goes towards the door of the music-room, followed by* LADY JANE. *At that moment the doors open: from within comes a polite murmur of applause. The musicians come out, carrying their instruments, and pass down the corridor. Behind them comes* MR. OAKLEY; *in the doorway he turns and bows. He, also, is retiring, when one of* THE QUEEN'S GENTLEMEN *comes after him.*)

GENTLEMAN. Her Majesty wishes to speak to you, Mr. Oakley.
(THE QUEEN *appears in the doorway. She is followed by* PRINCE ALBERT, *who, with stiff formality, crosses the corridor, and enters the ante-room, while* THE QUEEN *stays to speak to* MR. OAKLEY.)

THE QUEEN. That was very beautiful, Mr. Oakley. Thank you. It was your own composition, I believe?

OAKLEY. It was, your Majesty.

THE QUEEN. We should very much like to hear another piece presently.

OAKLEY. Most honoured, your Majesty.
(*Leaving* MR. OAKLEY *to receive the congratulations of other members of his audience,* THE QUEEN *follows* THE PRINCE *into the ante-room.*)

THE QUEEN. Albert, why are you so cold to me?

ALBERT. It is a cold day, my Dear. And this morning we did not take enough exercise.

THE QUEEN. You did not come to me afterwards. I have hardly seen you since—except with others.

ALBERT. (*stiffly*). No; that is so.

THE QUEEN. Albert, have I offended you?

ALBERT. My Dear, you must not try to give me riding lessons—before others. (*He moves away.*)

THE QUEEN. I want to speak to you, Albert.
(*Paying no attention, he returns to the corridor, and seeing* MR. OAKLEY, *pauses to speak to him. The other members of the Court draw back respectfully. Meanwhile* THE QUEEN, *after standing for a few moments, angry and undecided, turns and goes quickly past them. At the music-room door she stops to exchange words with some of her Ladies. Meanwhile* THE PRINCE *is speaking.*)

ALBERT. Ah, Mr. Oakley, I have some news that I hope will please you. We are expecting to have the great Mendelssohn with us again soon. He is coming to England in the Spring.

OAKLEY. That is great news indeed, Sir. Will he also be coming to Windsor?

ALBERT. We hope so. We have invited him to come.

OAKLEY. For all who love music, as does your Royal Highness, it will be a great occasion.

ALBERT. It will, indeed.
(*Dismissing* MR. OAKLEY *with a courteous gesture,* THE PRINCE *turns towards the music-room; but at sight of* THE QUEEN *standing in the doorway, he re-enters the anteroom, where* THE DUCHESS, *followed by* LADY JANE, *has returned to pick up her fan and shawl. Just as* LADY JANE *is entering, a rose falls from her hair.* THE PRINCE, *with courtly grace, stoops and picks it up for her.*)

ALBERT. Lady Jane, here is something that you have dropped. (*He presents the flower.*)

LADY JANE (*nervously*). Oh, your Highness, I am sorry!—sorry to have given your Highness the trouble!

ALBERT (*gallantly*). No trouble . . . a pleasure. . . . It is a colour that suits you.
(*Meanwhile* THE DUCHESS *has moved to the door, and is looking back with an amused smile, when* THE QUEEN, *pushing past her, comes swiftly into the room. Trembling with rage, she advances upon* LADY JANE, *and snatches the flower from her hand. With an instinct for the emergency,* THE DUCHESS *closes the folding-doors: such a scene must have no spectators.*)

LADY JANE (*with tremulous courage*). Your Majesty must pardon me: that flower is mine.

THE QUEEN. How dare you speak to me! Go! Go, instantly!
(LADY JANE, *her head very erect, makes a swift, deep curtsy, and goes out of the room. Meanwhile* THE DUCHESS *is speaking to* THE PRINCE.)

DUCHESS (*urgently*). I beg your Royal Highness to allow me to explain. I saw just what happened.
(THE PRINCE *hesitates for a moment, then turns abruptly, and goes out of the room by the other door. There is a pause.* THE QUEEN *stands crushing the flower in her hands.*)

THE QUEEN. Go and tell the Prince to come back! I wish to speak to him.

DUCHESS. Will your Majesty—

THE QUEEN. At once! Do as I tell you!

DUCHESS. Yes, Ma'am, yes; in a moment. But first I beg your Majesty to allow me to speak—to explain.

THE QUEEN. There is nothing to explain.

DUCHESS. But there is! There is! I saw everything.

THE QUEEN. So did I. I saw the Prince give her this flower—this rose. Do you mean to deny it?

DUCHESS. No, your Majesty, no; he did not give it her. She had dropped it.

THE QUEEN (*suspiciously*). Dropped it? Ah, yes!

DUCHESS. No, Ma'am; quite by accident. It fell out of her hair. The Prince only picked it up and returned it to her.

THE QUEEN. You saw that, you say? You know that—for certain?

DUCHESS. I assure your Majesty it was so.

THE QUEEN. Do you know, also, what happened this morning?

DUCHESS. I do, Ma'am. My Cousin has told me everything.

THE QUEEN. Did she try to explain it?

DUCHESS. There was hardly anything to explain, Ma'am. It might have happened to anyone.

THE QUEEN. Then why did she tell you about it?

DUCHESS. She was very much upset at the way your Majesty had taken what was a mere accident.

THE QUEEN. It may have been an accident: I don't know. What has happened now is much more serious.

DUCHESS. *Very* much more serious, your Majesty.
(THE QUEEN *looks at her in surprise:* THE DUCHESS *does not flinch. There is a pause.*)

THE QUEEN (*defensively*). It was all so sudden—so unexpected. One hadn't time to think.

DUCHESS. That is so. Your Majesty gave yourself no time—to think.

THE QUEEN. I was too hasty, you mean?

DUCHESS. Does your Majesty wish me to say more than I have said?

THE QUEEN. I only wish you to tell me the honest truth.

DUCHESS. I will, Ma'am. . . . At least, I will try. But the truth is sometimes difficult.

THE QUEEN. It should not be.

DUCHESS. Not even when it is—to a Queen, Ma'am?

THE QUEEN. A Queen may need it sometimes, far more than others.

DUCHESS. If she knows that she needs it, Ma'am, she is already on the side of truth.

THE QUEEN. I do know it—I do! . . . Tell me!—is it possible that I have been unjust?

DUCHESS. It is possible, your Majesty.

THE QUEEN. I did not intend to be.

DUCHESS. No one, who knows your Majesty, would think that for a moment.

THE QUEEN. Thank you, dear Duchess, for saying that! In my position, I would wish never to be unjust to anyone. . . . Will you—will you ask your Cousin—Lady Jane—to come and speak to me?

DUCHESS (*hesitating*). I am not

sure, Ma'am, that she will come—now.

THE QUEEN. Will you say "please" for me?

DUCHESS. If I can say it, Ma'am, as you have said it— (*Her voice breaks; she kisses* THE QUEEN'S *hand, and goes.* THE QUEEN, *left to herself, sits rigid—facing an ordeal which, for her, is of an almost unbelievable character. Nevertheless, she faces it. Presently the door opens, and* LADY JANE *enters. She halts at the door, and curtsies: the word "please," which has brought her, has been left unexplained, and the expression of her face does not make things easier for* THE QUEEN.)

THE QUEEN. Lady Jane . . . I have sent for you to say . . . I am sorry. . . . Forgive me. . . . I was quite wrong.
(LADY JANE *curtsies deeply, but does not speak. Slowly* THE QUEEN *reaches out her hand.* LADY JANE *goes quickly forward, kisses it, and bursts into tears.*)

THE QUEEN. I am sorry, so sorry to have upset you. You had better go to bed now, and rest. . . . And, Lady Jane, if you would like—only if you would like—to go away for a little, for a change—pray do so. I'm not asking you to go; but should you at all wish to do so, you have my permission.

LADY JANE. I thank your Majesty for so kindly suggesting it.

THE QUEEN. Then that shall be arranged. . . . And now will you tell the Prince—I mean, will you ask someone to tell the Prince that I wish to see him?
(LADY JANE *makes her final curtsy, and goes.* THE QUEEN *sits with bowed head, motionless: time passes.* THE PRINCE *does not come. Her head sinks lower; she is shaken by sobs. Then, very quietly, the door opens, and* THE PRINCE *enters. He comes gently towards her, stands at her side, and reaching down his hand, begins softly to stroke her hair. Neither of them makes any attempt to speak, or any further move. Presently, leaving her, he goes to the piano, seats himself, and begins playing. It has to be something very simple and familiar—otherwise she might miss its meaning. He plays a few bars; then, in a low undertone, sings words which she already knows by heart.*)

ALBERT.

Drink to me only with thine eyes,
And I will pledge with mine;
Or leave a kiss but in the cup,
And I'll not look for wine.
The thirst that from the soul doth rise,
Doth ask a drink divine:
But might I of Jove's nectar sup,
I would not change for thine.

(*As the first verse draws to its close,* THE QUEEN *rises, crosses slowly, and stands behind him. As he begins the second verse, timidly she lays a hand upon his shoulder; and when the verse is half-way through, she lets her head fall upon his; and is so standing, with her cheek resting against the beautiful hair, which is already beginning to grow thin, when the verse ends.*)

I sent thee late a rosy wreath,
Not so much honouring thee,
As giving it a hope that there
It could not withered be.
But thou thereon didst only breathe,
And sent'st it back to me:

Since when it grows and smells,
I swear,
Not of itself, but thee.

(*The song ends. What happens then—who knows? As the last chords are played, the* CURTAIN *falls slowly; but neither of them has moved.*)

SCENE IV

INTERVENTION

30th November 1861

On THE QUEEN'S *writing-table a Government Despatch-box lies open.* GENERAL GREY, THE QUEEN'S *Private Secretary, stands reading to Her Majesty the despatch which* LORD RUSSELL, *the Foreign Secretary, has addressed to Lord Lyons, the British Ambassador at Washington, on the seizure upon the High Seas, from the British ship* Trent, *of the two Confederate officers, Slidell and Mason.*

THE QUEEN. Before you go on, General Grey, will you ring, please. (THE GENERAL *rings, and continues reading. . . . One of* THE QUEEN'S GENTLEMEN *enters.*) Has His Royal Highness not returned from Sandhurst yet?

GENTLEMAN. A few minutes ago, he had not, your Majesty.

THE QUEEN. But it is so late! Was not the ceremony to have been over by midday?

GENTLEMAN. I believe so, your Majesty. It is possible that His Royal Highness *may* have just returned.

THE QUEEN. Please go and see; and, if he has, bring back word at once. . . . General Grey, this looks very serious indeed! Is the Messenger who brought it still waiting?

GENERAL GREY. I am not sure, Ma'am.

THE QUEEN. Will you please to find out? And if he has not gone, say that he is to wait. . . . I do wish the Prince would come! It is so urgent; and with Lord Palmerston Prime Minister, one never knows what he may not do next, without waiting for *our* instructions.

GENERAL GREY. Indeed no, Ma'am.

THE QUEEN. At once, please! (*As* THE GENERAL *goes, the* GENTLEMAN *returns.*)

GENTLEMAN. His Royal Highness has just returned, your Majesty. He has gone up to his room.

THE QUEEN. Then go and ask His Royal Highness to come at once. Say that the matter is most urgent.

(*The* GENTLEMAN *goes.* THE QUEEN *takes up the despatch, and is re-reading it when* GENERAL GREY *returns.*)

GENERAL GREY. The Messenger has gone, your Majesty.

THE QUEEN. Without waiting!

GENERAL GREY. He waited for an hour, Ma'am, I'm told.

THE QUEEN. An hour! He should have waited all day, if necessary. Messengers from my other Ministers know that they have to wait. Why do not Foreign Office Messengers wait too? This is what is always happening: and then they pretend that the delay it causes is our fault, not theirs.

GENERAL GREY. Cannot one of your Majesty's Messengers go, Ma'am—the matter being so urgent?

THE QUEEN. Yes, he must. Tell one of them to be ready to start instantly.
(*As* THE GENERAL *is going,* THE PRINCE CONSORT *enters. He looks haggard and tired.*)

THE QUEEN. Oh, Albert, why did you wait to change? I have been so wanting you!

ALBERT. My uniform was wet through, my Dear; and I was feeling very cold.

THE QUEEN (*taking his hand*). You are cold still, Dearest! your hand is like ice. Oh, why did you go in such weather, when I begged you not to?

ALBERT. I had to, my Dear. . . . What is the matter?

THE QUEEN. It's about that trouble with America, for having taken the Confederate Envoys off one of our ships. And most wrong of them it was! This is the despatch Lord Russell is sending to our Ambassador in Washington about it. He wants it to go tonight.

ALBERT (*taking it*). Is the Messenger waiting?

THE QUEEN. No; he's gone.

ALBERT (*sharply*). Gone? Ah! That is what one has now to expect, I suppose!

THE QUEEN. Yes; it's that Pilgerstein again. Troublesome man!

ALBERT. Yes; though this time it is Lord Russell that does it; that Go-between, who was always so apologetic and nice to us. Hah! But it is Pilgerstein—as you say—still. Oh yes!

THE QUEEN. Read it quickly, Albert. I want to know what you think about it.
(GENERAL GREY *re-enters.*)

GENERAL GREY. I have given your Majesty's order. A Messenger is ready and waiting.

THE QUEEN. Very well. And now that the Prince is here, General Grey, I shall no longer need you.
(THE GENERAL *goes.* THE QUEEN *sits watching* THE PRINCE CONSORT *as he reads. Not till he has finished it does he speak.*)

ALBERT. This means War.

THE QUEEN. Yes; I was afraid so. How foolish of them not to give in!

For they must know they are in the wrong. And everything that Lord Russell says is true, is it not?

ALBERT (*deep in thought*). Quite. . . . Quite. . . . But—it won't do.

THE QUEEN. But, Albert, as we are in the right, what else can we do?

ALBERT. Alter a few words. . . . Say it; but say it differently. Often it is just the way a thing is said that decides whether it shall be peace or war. It is the same when two people quarrel. You and I, Weibchen, might often have quarrelled, had we said the same thing that we did say—differently. . . . Russell? Oh no: this is Pilgerstein, I think! He is the man that would *like* to have war with America. He has worked for it; and this is his opportunity—that we are in the right! . . . He shall not have it! War? Oh yes; and this time we should win. But another time would come, and we should *not* win.

THE QUEEN. But we could always beat America now, Albert.

ALBERT. Ah, so? What if we were fighting someone else, Vicky; and America chose her time then? No; that is what these "patriots" never think about. . . . It is always—"*This* time, *this* time! We are *right*, and we shall do what we like!" What fools their patriotism makes clever men to be! And Pilgerstein the cleverest fool of them all! . . . And when he dies, they will say of this man—"Oh yes; he had his faults; but he always upheld the Honour of his country." And when they say "Honour," they mean Pride. Again and again he has been ready to sacrifice the Honour of his Country to its Pride. For Honour means that you are too proud to do wrong; but Pride means that you will not *own* that you have done wrong—at all. *That* is the difference.

THE QUEEN. Then that applies to America, now.

ALBERT. Yes. Here is America: she has done wrong, and she knows it. . . . Invite her to reconsider—a mistake: something done by her agents without her instructions. She will think, and will behave reasonably. . . . But say "I order you!" and she will *not*.

THE QUEEN. But, Albert, ought we to make it so easy for them as all that?

ALBERT. Yes; because we should do just the same ourselves, if we were ordered. And we should call it "Honour." And for that Honour we should send thousands and thousands to die! What a wicked black thing Honour can become—when men make use of it—*so!*

THE QUEEN. Then what are we going to do, Albert?

ALBERT. We are going to alter this, *now*. . . . Sit down at once, and write! Say that this despatch is not to go, till he has heard from you. . . . And your Messenger must go now, at once, and must see Lord Russell himself. . . . This will take me more time; but you write your letter at once!

THE QUEEN. Yes, Albert, yes!

(THE QUEEN *seats herself at one writing-table.* THE PRINCE CONSORT *goes to another.* THE QUEEN *begins to write, then rings, and continues writing. A* GENTLEMAN *enters, and stands waiting, while the letter is being finished.*)

THE QUEEN. Tell the Messenger to take this to Lord Russell, at the Foreign Office. He is to see him, and is to bring an answer.
(*The* GENTLEMAN *takes the letter, and goes.* THE QUEEN *goes across to* THE PRINCE CONSORT. *She puts her hand on his shoulder, and leans over him.*)

ALBERT (*gently*). Will you leave me alone, my Dear, while I do this? I shall try not to be long.

*

(*As the scene closes, the clock on the mantelpiece strikes four. When it opens again, some hours have passed. Candles are lighted.* THE PRINCE *is still at his desk, writing. He sits up; the pen falls from his hand.*)

ALBERT. That is done . . . *done!*
(*Slowly he reaches out, takes up a hand-bell, and rings. A* GENTLEMAN *enters.*)
Tell Her Majesty that I have finished. . . . Ask Her Majesty to come.
(*The* GENTLEMAN *bows, and goes out.* THE PRINCE *tries to rise, sinks back into his seat; resting his hands on the table, he bends slowly forward; his head drops to the table.*)

(THE QUEEN *enters.*)

THE QUEEN. Albert, what is the matter? Are you ill?

ALBERT (*raising himself with difficulty*). I have done. Read it! If you approve, send it!
(THE QUEEN *takes up the amended despatch and reads it. While she does so, the clock strikes seven.*)

THE QUEEN (*reading*). Yes. . . . Yes. . . . Yes. . . . I do—I do approve—every word.

ALBERT. Then let it go—*now!*
(THE QUEEN *rings. She puts the paper into the Despatch-box, and locks it. A* GENTLEMAN *enters.*)

THE QUEEN. See that this goes at once!
(*The* GENTLEMAN *goes.* THE PRINCE *has once more taken up his pen; he tries to write. The pen falls from his hand. He reaches out to* THE QUEEN, *with a gesture of helplessness.*)

ALBERT. Take me to bed! . . . Take me to bed, Weibchen! . . . Ich bin so schwach. Ich habe kaum die Feder halten können!
(*Again he tries to rise, fails, and falls back into his chair.* THE QUEEN *throws her arms round him.*)

THE QUEEN. Albert!

ACT THREE

SCENE I

"THE QUEEN! GOD BLESS HER!"

1877

A Scene from Home-Life in the Highlands

The august Lady is sitting in a garden-tent on the lawn of Balmoral Castle. Her parasol leans beside her. Writing-materials are on the table before her, and a small fan, for it is hot weather; also a dish of peaches. Sunlight suffuses the tent interior, softening the round contours of the face, and caressing pleasantly the small plump hand busy at letter-writing. The even flow of her penmanship is suddenly disturbed; picking up her parasol, she indulgently beats some unseen object, lying concealed against her skirts.

QUEEN. No: don't scratch! Naughty! Naughty!
(*She then picks up a hand-bell, rings it, and continues her writing. Presently a fine figure of a man in Highland costume appears in the tent-door. He waits awhile, then speaks in the strong Doric of his native wilds.*)

MR. J. BROWN. Was your Majesty wanting anything, or were you ringing only for the fun?
(*To this brusque delivery Her Majesty responds with a cosy smile, for the special function of* MR. JOHN BROWN *is not to be a courtier; and, knowing what is expected of him, he lives up to it.*)

QUEEN. Bring another chair, Brown. And take Mop with you: he wants his walk.

MR. J. B. What kind of a chair are you wanting, Ma'am? Is it to put your feet on?

QUEEN. Oh, no. It is to put a visitor on. Choose a nice one with a lean-back.

MR. J. B. With a lean back? Ho! Ye mean one that you can lean back in. What talk folk will bring with them from up south, to be sure! Yes, I'll get it for ye, Ma'am. Come, Mop, be a braw little wee mon, and tak' your walk! (*And while his Royal Mistress resumes her writing, taking Mop by his "lead," he prepares for departure*) Have ye seen the paper this morning yet? Ma'am. (*The address of respect is thrown in by way of after-thought, or, as it were, reluctantly. Having to be in character, his way is to tread heavily on the border-line which divides familiarity from respect.*)

QUEEN. Not yet.

MR. J. B. (*departing*). I'll bring it for ye, now.

QUEEN. You had better send it.

J. B. (*turning about*). What did ye say? . . . Ma'am.

QUEEN. "Send it," Brown, I said. Mop mustn't be hurried. Take him round by the stables.
(*He goes: and* THE QUEEN, *with a soft, indulgent smile, that slowly flickers out as the labour of composition proceeds, resumes her writing. Presently enters a liveried* FOOTMAN, *who stands at attention with the paper upon a salver. Touching the table at her side as an indication,* THE QUEEN *continues to write. With gingerly reverence the man lays down the paper and goes. Twice she looks at it before taking it up; then she unfolds it; then lays it down, and takes out her glasses; then begins reading. Evidently she comes on something she does not like; she pats the table impatiently, then exclaims*)
Most extraordinary! (*A wasp settles on the peaches*) And I wish one could kill all wicked pests as easily as you. (*She makes a dab with the paper-knife, the wasp escapes*) Most extraordinary! (*Relinquishing the pursuit of wasps, she resumes her reading. In a little while* MR. JOHN BROWN *returns, both hands occupied. The chair he deposits by the tent door, and hitches Mop's "lead" to the back of that on which* THE QUEEN *is sitting. With the small beginnings of a smile she lowers the paper, and looks at him and his accompaniments.*)

QUEEN. Well, Brown? Oh yes; that's quite a nice one. . . . I'm sure there's a wasps' nest somewhere; there are so many of them about.

J. B. Eh, don't fash yourself! Wasps have a way of being aboot this time of year. It's the fruit they're after.

QUEEN. Yes: like Adam and Eve.

J. B. That's just it, Ma'am.

QUEEN. You'd better take it away, Brown, or cover it; it's too tempting.

J. B. (*removing the fruit*). Ah! Now if God had only done that, maybe we'd still all be running aboot naked.

QUEEN. I'm glad He didn't, then.

J. B. Ye're right, Ma'am.

QUEEN. The Fall made the human race decent, even if it did no good otherwise. Brown, I've dropped my glasses. (*He picks them up and returns them.*)

QUEEN. Thank you, Brown.

J. B. So you're expecting a visitor, ye say?

QUEEN. Yes. You haven't seen Lord Beaconsfield yet, I suppose?

J. B. Since he was to arrive off the train, you mean, Ma'am? No: he came early. He's in his room.

QUEEN. I hope they have given him a comfortable one.

J. B. It's the one I used to have. There's a good spring-bed in it, and a kettle-ring for the whisky.

QUEEN. Oh, that's all right, then.

J. B. Will he be staying for long? Ma'am.

QUEEN. Only for a week, I'm afraid. Why?

J. B. It's about the shooting I was thinking: whether it was the deer or the grouse he'd want to be after.

QUEEN. I don't think Lord Beaconsfield is a sportsman.

J. B. I know that, Ma'am, well enough. But there's many who are not sportsmen that think they've got to do it—when they come north of the Tweed.

QUEEN. Lord Beaconsfield will not shoot, I'm sure. You remember him, Brown, being here before?

J. B. Eh! Many years ago, that was; he was no but Mr. Disraeli then. But he was the real thing, Ma'am: oh, a nice gentleman.

QUEEN. He is always very nice to me.

J. B. I remember now, when he first came, he put a tip into ma hand. And when I let him know the liberty he had taken, "Well, Mr. Brown," he said, "I've made a mistake, but I don't take it back again!"

QUEEN. Very nice and sensible.

J. B. And indeed it was, Ma'am. Many a man would never have had the wit to leave well alone by just apologising for it. But there was an understandingness about him, that often you don't find. After that he always talked to me like an equal—just like yourself might do. But Lord, Ma'am, his ignorance, it was surprising!

QUEEN. Most extraordinary you should think that, Brown!

J. B. Ah! You haven't talked to him as I have, Ma'am: only about politics, and poetry, and things like that—where, maybe, he knows a bit more than I do (though he didn't know his Burns so well as a man ought that thinks to make laws for Scotland!). But to hear him talking about natural facts, you'd think he was just inventing for to amuse himself! Do you know, Ma'am, he thought stags had white tails like rabbits, and that 'twas only when they wagged them so as to show, that you could shoot them? And he thought that you pulled a salmon out o' the water as soon as you'd hooked him. And he thought that a haggis was made of a sheep's head boiled in whisky. Oh, he's very innocent, Ma'am, if you get him where he's not expecting you.

QUEEN. Well, Brown, there are some things you can teach him, I don't doubt; and there are some things he can teach you. I'm sure he has taught me a great deal.

J. B. Ay? It's a credit to ye both, then.

QUEEN. He lets me think for myself, Brown; and that's what so many of my Ministers would rather I didn't. They want me to be merely the receptacle of their own opinions. No, Brown, that's what we Stuarts are never going to do!

J. B. Nor would I, Ma'am, if I were in your shoes. But believe me, you can do more, being a mere woman, so to speak, than many a king can do.

QUEEN. Yes; being a woman has its advantages, I know.

J. B. For you can get round 'em, Ma'am; and you can put 'em off; and you can make it very awkward for them—very awkward—to have a difference of opinion with you.

QUEEN (*good-humouredly*). You and I have had differences of opinion sometimes, Brown.

J. B. True, Ma'am; that *has* happened; I've known it happen. And I've never regretted it, never! But the difference there is, Ma'am, that I'm not your Prime Minister. Had I been—you'd 'a been more stiff about giving in—naturally! Now there's Mr. Gladstone, Ma'am; I'm not denying he's a great man; but he's got too many ideas for my liking, far too many! I'm not against temperance any more than he is—put in its right place. But he's got that crazy notion of "local option" in his mind; he's coming to it, gradually. And he doesn't think how giving "local option" to them that don't take the wide view of things may do harm to a locality. You must be wide in your views, else you do somebody an injustice.

QUEEN. Yes, Brown; and that is why I like being up in the hills, where the views *are* wide.

J. B. I put it this way, Ma'am. You come to a locality, and you find you can't get served as you are accustomed to be served. Well! you don't go there again, and you tell others not to go; and so the place gets a bad name. I've a brother who keeps an inn down at Aberlochy on the coach route, and he tells me that more than half his customers come from outside the locality.

QUEEN. Of course; naturally!

J. B. Well now, Ma'am, it'll be bad for the locality to have half the custom that comes to it turned away, because of local option! And believe me, Ma'am, that's what it will come to. People living in it won't see till the shoe pinches them; and by that time my brother, and others like him, will have been ruined in their business.

QUEEN. Local option is not going to come yet, Brown.

J. B. (*firmly*). No, Ma'am, not while I vote Conservative, it won't. But I was looking ahead; I was talking about Mr. Gladstone.

QUEEN. Mr. Gladstone has retired from politics. At least, he is not going to take office again.

J. B. Don't you believe him, Ma'am. Mr. Gladstone is not a retiring character. He's in today's paper again—columns of him; have ye seen?

QUEEN. Yes; quite as much as I wish to see.

J. B. And there's something in what he says, I don't deny.

QUEEN. There's a great deal in what he says I don't understand, and that I don't wish to.

J. B. Now you never said a truer thing than that in your life, Ma'am! That's just how I find him. Oh, but he's a great man; and it's wonderful how he appreciates the Scot, and looks up to his opinion. (*But this is a line of conversation in which his Royal Mistress declines to be interested. And she is helped, at that moment, by something which really does interest her.*)

QUEEN. Brown, how did you come to scratch your leg?

J. B. 'Twas not me, Ma'am; 'twas the stable-cat did that—just now while Mop was having his walk.

QUEEN. Poor dear Brown! Did she fly at you?

J. B. Well, 'twas like this, Ma'am; first Mop went for her, then she went for him. And I tell ye she'd have scraped his eyes out if I'd left it to a finish.

QUEEN. Ferocious creature! She must be mad.

J. B. Well, Ma'am, I don't know whether a cat-and-dog fight is a case of what God had joined together; but it's the hard thing for man to put asunder! And that's the scraping I got for it, when I tried.

QUEEN. You must have it cauterised, Brown. I won't have you getting hydrophobia.

J. B. You generally get that from dogs.

QUEEN. Oh, from cats too; any cat that a mad dog has bitten.

J. B. They do say, Ma'am, that if a mad dog bites you—you have to die barking. So if it's a cat-bite I'm going to die of, you'll hear me mewing the day, maybe.

QUEEN. I don't like cats: I never did. Treacherous, deceitful creatures! Now a dog always looks up to you.

J. B. Yes, Ma'am; they are tasteful, attractive animals, and that, maybe, is the reason. They give you a good conceit of yourself, dogs do. You never have to apologise to a dog. Do him an injury—you've only to say you forgive him, and he's friends again.
(*Accepting his views with a nodding smile, she resumes her pen, and spreads paper.*)

QUEEN. Now, Brown, I must get to work again. I have writing to do. See that I'm not disturbed.

J. B. Then when were you wanting to see your visitor, Ma'am? There's his chair waiting.

QUEEN. Ah, yes, to be sure. But I didn't want to worry him too soon. What is the time?

J. B. Nearly twelve, Ma'am.

QUEEN. Oh! then I think I may. Will you go and tell him: the Queen's compliments, and she would like to see him, now?

J. B. I will go and tell him, Ma'am.

QUEEN. And then I shan't want you any more—till this afternoon.

J. B. Then I'll just go across and take lunch at home, Ma'am.

QUEEN. Yes, do! That will be nice for you. And, Brown, mind you have that leg seen to!
(MR. JOHN BROWN *has started to go, when his step is arrested.*)

J. B. His Lordship is there in the garden, Ma'am, talking to the Princess.

QUEEN. What, before he has seen *me*? Go, and take him away from the Princess, and tell him to come here!

J. B. I will, Ma'am.

QUEEN. And you had better take Mop with you. Now, dear Brown, do have your poor leg seen to, at once!

J. B. Indeed, and I will, Ma'am. Come, Mop, man! Come and tell his Lordship he's wanted. (*Exit* MR. JOHN BROWN, *nicely accompanied by Mop.*)
(*Left to herself,* THE QUEEN *administers a feminine touch or two to dress and cap and hair; then with dignified composure she resumes her writing, and continues to write even when the shadow of her favourite Minister crosses the entrance, and he stands hat in hand before her, flawlessly arrayed in a gay frock suit suggestive of the period when male attire was still not only a fashion, but an art. Despite, however, the studied correctness of his costume, face and deportment give signs of haggard fatigue; and when he bows it is the droop of a weary man, slow in the recovery. Just at the fitting moment for full acceptance of his silent salutation, the Royal Lady lays down her pen.*)

QUEEN. Oh, how do you do, my dear Lord Beaconsfield! Good morning; and welcome to Balmoral.

LORD B. (*as he kisses the hand extended to him*). That word from your Majesty brings all its charms to life! What a prospect of beauty I see around me!

QUEEN. You arrived early? I hope you are sufficiently rested.

LORD B. Refreshed, Madam; rest will come later.

QUEEN. You have had a long, tiring journey, I fear.

LORD B. It was long, Madam.

QUEEN. I hope that you slept upon the train?

LORD B. I lay upon it, Ma'am. That is all I can say truly.

QUEEN. Oh, I'm sorry!

LORD B. There were compensations, Ma'am. In my vigil I was able to look forward—to that which is now before me. The morning is beautiful! May I be permitted to inquire if your Majesty's health has benefited?

QUEEN. I'm feeling "bonnie," as we say in Scotland. Life out of doors suits me.

LORD B. Ah! This tent light is charming! Then my eyes had not deceived me; your Majesty is already more than better. The tempered sunlight, so tender in its reflections, gives—an interior, one may say—of almost floral delicacy; making these canvas walls like the white petals of an enfolding flower.

QUEEN. Are you writing another of your novels, Lord Beaconsfield? That sounds like composition.

LORD B. Believe me, Madam, only an impromptu.

QUEEN. Now, my dear Lord, pray sit down! I had that chair specially brought for you. Generally I sit here quite alone.

LORD B. Such kind forethought, Madam, overwhelms me! Words are inadequate. I accept, gratefully, the repose you offer me. (*He sinks into the chair, and sits motionless and mute, in a weariness that is not the less genuine because it provides an effect. But from one seated in the Royal Presence much is expected; and so it is in a tone of sprightly expectancy that his Royal Mistress now prompts him to his task of entertaining her.*)

QUEEN. Well? And how is everything?

LORD B. (*rousing himself with an effort*). Oh! Pardon! Your Majesty would have me speak on politics, and affairs of State? I was rapt away for the moment.

QUEEN. Do not be in any hurry, dear Prime Minister.

LORD B. Ah! That word from an indulgent Mistress spurs me freshly to my task. But, Madam, there is almost nothing to tell: politics, like the rest of us, have been taking holiday.

QUEEN. I thought that Mr. Gladstone has been speaking.

LORD B. (*with an airy flourish of courtly disdain*). Oh yes! He has been—speaking.

QUEEN. In Edinburgh, quite lately.

LORD B. And in more other places than I can count. Speaking—speaking—speaking. But I have to confess, Madam, that I have not read his speeches. They are composed for brains which can find more leisure than yours, Madam—or mine.

QUEEN. I have read some of them.

LORD B. Your Majesty does him great honour—and yourself some inconvenience, I fear. Those speeches, so great a strain to understand, or even to listen to—my hard duty for now some forty years—are a far greater strain to read.

QUEEN. They annoy me intensely. I have no patience with him!

LORD B. Pardon me, Madam; if you have read *one* of his speeches, your patience has been extraordinary.

QUEEN. Can't you stop it?

LORD B. Stop?—stop what, Madam? Niagara, the Flood? That which has no beginning, no limit, has also no end: till, by the operation of nature, it runs dry.

QUEEN. But, surely, he should be stopped when he speaks on matters which may, any day, bring us into war!

LORD B. Then he would be stopped. When the British nation goes to war, Madam, it ceases to listen to reason. Then it is only the beating of its own great heart that it hears: to that goes the marching of its armies, with victory as the one goal. Then, Madam, above reason rises instinct. Against that he will be powerless.

QUEEN. You think so?

LORD B. I am sure, Madam. If we are drawn into war, his opposition becômes futile. If we are not: well, if we are not, it will not be his doing that we escape that—dire necessity.

QUEEN. But you *do* think it necessary, don't you?
(*To the Sovereign's impetuous eagerness, so creditable to her heart, he replies with the oracular solemnity by which caution can be sublimated.*)

LORD B. I hope it may not be, Madam. We must all say that—up till the last moment. It is the only thing we *can* say, to testify the pacifity of our intention when challenged by other Powers.

QUEEN (*touching the newspaper*). This morning's news isn't good, I'm afraid. The Russians are getting nearer to Constantinople.

LORD B. They will never enter it, Madam.

QUEEN. No, they mustn't! We will not allow it.

LORD B. That, precisely, is the policy of your Majesty's Government. Russia knows that we shall not allow it; she knows that it will never be. Nevertheless, we may have to make a demonstration.

QUEEN. Do you propose to summon Parliament?

LORD B. Not Parliament; no, Madam. Your Majesty's Fleet will be sufficient.
(*This lights a spark; and the Royal mind darts into strategy.*)

QUEEN. If I had my way, Lord Beaconsfield, my Fleet would be in the Baltic tomorrow; and, before another week was over, Petersburg would be under bombardment.

LORD B. (*considerately providing this castle in the air with its necessary foundations*). And Kronstadt would have fallen.

QUEEN (*puzzled for a moment at this naming of a place which had not entered her calculations*). Kronstadt? Why Kronstadt?

LORD B. Merely preliminary, Madam. When that fortified suburb has crumbled—the rest will be easy.

QUEEN. Yes! And what a good lesson it will teach them! The Crimea wasn't enough for them, I suppose.

LORD B. The Crimea! Ah, what memories—of heroism—that word evokes! "Magnificent, but not war!"

QUEEN. Oh! There is one thing, Lord Beaconsfield, on which I want your advice.

LORD B. Always at your Majesty's disposal.

QUEEN. I wish to confer upon the Sultan of Turkey my Order of the Garter.

LORD B. Ah! how generous, how generous an instinct! How like you, Madam, to wish it!

QUEEN. What I want to know is, whether, as Prime Minister, you have any objection?

LORD B. "As Prime Minister." How hard that makes it for me to answer! How willingly would I say "None"! How reluctantly, on the contrary, I have to say, "It had better wait."

QUEEN. Wait? Wait till when? I want to do it *now*.

LORD B. Yes, so do I. But can you risk, Madam, conferring that most illustrious symbol of honour, and chivalry, and power, on a defeated monarch? Your royal prestige, Ma'am, must be considered. Great and generous hearts need, more than most, to take prudence into their counsels.

QUEEN. But do you think, Lord Beaconsfield, that the Turks are going to be beaten?

LORD B. The Turks *are* beaten, Madam. . . . But England will never be beaten. We shall dictate terms—moderating the demands of Russia; and under your Majesty's protection the throne of the Kaliphat will be safe—once more. That, Madam, is the key to our Eastern policy: a grateful Kaliphat, claiming allegiance from the whole Mohammedan world, bound to us by instincts of self-preservation—and we hold henceforth the gorgeous East in fee with redoubled security. His power may be a declining power; but ours remains. Some day, who knows? Egypt, possibly even Syria, Arabia, may be our destined reward.

(Like a cat over a bowl of cream, England's Majesty sits lapping all this up. But, when he has done, her commentary is shrewd and to the point.)

QUEEN. The French won't like that!

LORD B. They won't, Madam, they won't. But has it ever been England's policy, Madam, to mind what the French don't like?

QUEEN *(with relish)*. No, it never has been, has it? Ah! you are the true statesman, Lord Beaconsfield. Mr. Gladstone never talked to me like that.

LORD B. *(courteously surprised at what does not at all surprise him)*. No? . . . You must have had interesting conversations with him, Madam, in the past.

QUEEN *(very emphatically)*. I have never once had a conversation with Mr. Gladstone in all my life, Lord Beaconsfield. He used to talk to me as if I were a public meeting—and one that agreed with him, too!

LORD B. Was there, then, any applause, Madam?

QUEEN. No, indeed! I was too shy to say what I thought. I used to cough sometimes.

LORD B. Rather like coughing at a balloon, I fear. I have always admired his flights—regarded as a mere *tour de force*—so buoyant, so sustained, so incalculable! But, as they never touch earth to any serviceable end, that I could discover—of what use are they? Yet if there is one man who has helped me in my career—to whom, therefore, I should owe gratitude—it is he.

QUEEN. Indeed? Now that does surprise me! Tell me, Lord Beaconsfield, how has he ever helped you?

LORD B. In our party system, Madam, we live by the mistakes of our opponents. The balance of the popular verdict swings ever this way and that, relegating us either to victory or defeat, to office or to opposition. Many times have I trodden the road to power, or passed from it again, over ruins the origin of which I could recognise either as my own work or that of another; and most of all has it been over the disappointments, the disaffections, the disgusts, the disillusionments—chiefly among his own party—which my great opponent has left me to profit by. I have gained experience from what he has been morally blind to; what he has lacked in understanding of human nature he has left for me to discover. Only today I learn that he has been in the habit of addressing—as you, Madam, so wittily phrased it—of addressing, "as though she were a public meeting," that Royal Mistress, whom it has ever been my most difficult task not to address sometimes as the most charming, the most accomplished, and the most fascinating woman of the epoch which bears her name. (*He pauses, then resumes*) How strange a fatality directs the fate of each one of us! How fortunate is he who knows the limits that destiny assigns to him: limits beyond which no word must be uttered.

(*His oratorical flight, so buoyant and sustained, having come to its calculated end, he drops deftly to earth, encountering directly for the first time the flattered smile with which* THE QUEEN *has listened to him.*)

Madam, your kind silence reminds me, in the gentlest, the most considerate way possible, that I am not here to relieve the tedium of a life made lonely by a bereavement equal to your own, in conversation however beguiling, or in quest of a sympathy of which, I dare to say, I feel assured. For, in a sense, it is as to a public assembly, or rather as to a great institution, immemorially venerable and august that I have to address myself when, obedient to your summons, I come to be consulted as your Majesty's First Minister of State. If, therefore, your royal mind have any inquiries, any further commands to lay upon me, I am here, Madam, to give effect to them in so far as I can.

(*This time he has really finished, but with so artful an abbreviation at the point where her interest has been roused that* THE QUEEN *would fain have him go on. And so the conversation continues to flow along intimate channels.*)

QUEEN. No, dear Lord Beaconsfield, not today! Those official matters can wait. After you have said so much, and said it so beautifully, I would rather still talk with you as a friend. Of friends you and I have not many; those who make up our world, for the most part, we have to keep at a distance. But while I have many near relatives, children and descendants, I remember that you have none. So your case is the harder.

LORD B. Ah, no, Madam, indeed! I have my children—descendants who will live after me, I trust—in those policies which, for the welfare of my beloved country, I confide to the care of a Sovereign whom I revere and love. . . . I am not unhappy in my life, Madam; far less in my fortune; only, as age creeps on, I find myself so lonely, so solitary, that sometimes I have doubt whether I am really alive, or whether the voice, with which now and then I seek to reassure myself, be not the voice of a dead man.

QUEEN (*almost tearfully*). No, no, my dear Lord Beaconsfield, you mustn't say that!

LORD B. (*gallantly*). I won't say anything, Madam, that you forbid, or that you dislike. You invited me to speak to you as a friend; so I have done, so I do. I apologise that I have allowed sadness, even for a moment, to trouble the harmony—the sweetness—of our conversation.

QUEEN. Pray, do not apologise! It has been a very great privilege; I beg that you will go on! Tell me—you spoke of bereavement—I wish you would tell me more—about your wife.
(*The sudden request touches some latent chord; and it is with genuine emotion that he answers.*)

LORD B. Ah! My wife! To her I owed everything.

QUEEN. She was devoted to you, wasn't she?

LORD B. I never read the depth of her devotion—till after her death. Then, Madam—this I have told to nobody but yourself—then I found among her papers—addressed "to my dear husband"—a message, written only a few days before her death, with a hand shaken by that nerve-racking and fatal malady which she endured so patiently—begging me to marry again.
(THE QUEEN *is now really crying, and finds speech difficult.*)

QUEEN. And you, you—? Dear Lord Beaconsfield; did you mean—had you ever meant—?

LORD B. I did not then, Madam; nor have I ever done so since. It is enough if I allow myself—to love.

QUEEN. Oh, yes, yes; I understand—better than others would. For that has always been my own feeling.

LORD B. In the history of my race, Madam, there has been a great tradition of faithfulness between husbands and wives. For the hardness of our hearts, we are told, Moses permitted us to give a writing of divorcement. But we have seldom acted on it. In my youth I became a Christian; I married a Christian. But that was no reason for me to desert the nobler traditions of my race—for they are in the blood and in the heart. When my wife died I had no thought to marry again; and when I came upon that tender wish, still I had no thought for it; my mind would not change. Circumstances that have happened since have sealed irrevocably my resolution—never to marry again.

QUEEN. Oh, I think that is so wise, so right, so noble of you!
(*The old Statesman rises, pauses, appears to hesitate, then in a voice charged with emotion says*)

LORD B. Madam, will you permit me to kiss your hand!
(*The hand graciously given, and the kiss fervently implanted, he falls back once more to a respectful distance. But the emotional excitement of the interview has told upon him, and it is in a wavering voice of weariness that he now speaks.*)

LORD B. You have been very forbearing with me, Madam, not to indicate that I have outstayed either my welcome or your powers of endurance. Yet so much conversation must necessarily have tired you. May I then crave permission, Madam, to withdraw? For, to speak truly, I do need some rest.

QUEEN. Yes, my dear friend, go and rest yourself! But before you go, will you not wait, and take a glass of wine with me? (*He bows and she rings*) And there is just one other thing I wish to say before we part.

LORD B. Speak, Madam, for thy servant heareth.
(*The other* SERVANT *is now also standing to attention, awaiting orders.*)

QUEEN. Bring some wine. (*The* ATTENDANT *goes*) That Order of the Garter which I had intended to confer upon the Sultan—have you, as Prime Minister, any objection if I bestow it nearer home, on one to whom personally—I cannot say more—on yourself, I mean.
(*At that pronouncement of the Royal favour the Minister stands, exhausted of energy, in an attitude of drooping humility. The eloquent silence is broken presently by* THE QUEEN.)

QUEEN. Dear Lord Beaconsfield, I want your answer.

LORD B. Oh, Madam! What adequate answer can these poor lips make to so magnificent an offer? Yet answer I must. We have spoken together briefly today of our policies in the Near East. Madam, let me come to you again when I have saved Constantinople, and secured once more upon a firm basis the peace of Europe. Then ask me again whether I have any objection, and I will own—"I have none!"
(*Re-enters* ATTENDANT. *He deposits a tray with decanter and glasses, and retires again.*)

QUEEN. Very well, Lord Beaconsfield. And if you do not remind me, I shall remind you. (*She points to the tray.*) Pray, help yourself! (*He takes up the decanter.*)

LORD B. I serve you, Madam?

QUEEN. Thank you.
(*He fills the two glasses; presents hers to* THE QUEEN, *and takes up his own.*)

LORD B. May I propose for myself—a toast, Madam?
(THE QUEEN *sees what is coming, and bows graciously.*)

LORD B. The Queen! God bless her! (*He drains the glass, then breaks it against the pole of the tent, and throws away the stem.*) An old custom, Madam, observed by loyal defenders of the House of Stuart, so that no lesser health might ever be drunk from the same glass. To my old hand came a sudden access of youthful enthusiasm—an ardour which I could not restrain. Your pardon, Madam!

QUEEN (*very gently*). Go and lie down, Lord Beaconsfield; you need rest.

LORD B. Adieu, Madam.

QUEEN. Draw your curtains, and sleep well!
(*For a moment he stands gazing at her with a look of deep emotion; he tries to speak. Ordinary words*

seem to fail; he falters into poetry.)
"When pain and anguish wring the brow,
A ministering Angel, thou!"
(It has been beautifully said, they both feel. Silent and slow, with head reverentially bowed, he backs from the Presence. THE QUEEN *sits and looks after the retreating figure, then at the broken fragments of glass. She takes up the hand-bell and rings. The* ATTENDANT *enters.)*

QUEEN. Pick up that broken glass. *(The* ATTENDANT *collects it on the hand-tray which he carries)* Bring it to me! . . . Leave it! *(The* ATTENDANT *deposits the tray before her, and goes. Gently* THE QUEEN *handles the broken pieces. Then in a voice of tearful emotion she speaks)* Such devotion! Most extraordinary! Oh! Albert! Albert!
(And in the sixteenth year of her widowhood and the fortieth of her reign, the Royal Lady bends her head over the fragments of broken glass, and weeps happy tears.)

CURTAIN

SCENE II

HAPPY AND GLORIOUS

20th June 1897

From the "great relief," confirmed by the voice of the electorate two years later, THE QUEEN *passes serenely on to the culminating triumph of her reign. The Diamond Jubilee provides material for a tableau rather than a play; and it is as a tableau that we have here presented to us this gathering together, at Buckingham Palace, of more than fifty of the Queen's direct descendants, together with representatives of all the crowned heads of a Europe still at peace.*

The Triumphal Procession is over, and the large upper chamber becomes filled with Royalty. Bonnets, costumes, uniforms mingle in a moving clash of colours; Orders sparkle, sword-chains clink, spurs jingle. Their owners step delicately, bowing their way from group to group; and—some now encountering for the first time—high form and ceremony are still the rule. But here and there Members of the Royal Family, meeting each other, exchange remarks of a familiar character, though sometimes in a foreign accent. And as all (except an Official or two) who thus mix and converse are Royal Highnesses—if nothing more—there is no need to trouble about names. Nobody today, except THE QUEEN *herself (and perhaps the Heir-Apparent) is individually important. So, not as individuals but in the group, we listen to their* ROYAL HIGHNESSES *chatting among themselves over the events of the day, filling up time till the Chief Character makes her appearance.*

ROYAL HIGHNESSES. Well! So that's over! . . . How beautifully everything went! . . . Excellently! . . . Very well indeed! . . . Nothing could have been better! . . . I hope Mamma enjoyed it as much as we did. . . . Oh, I'm sure she did. . . . What crowds! What cheering! And what perfect order! . . . Yes, the English are a wonderful people. . . . Have you seen Mamma, since she got back? . . . Yes, I have just been with her. . . . How has she borne it? . . . Oh, she's all right. She will be up in a minute. They are getting her into her chair.

AN IMPERIAL HIGHNESS. My dear Uncle Bertie, congratulations! What a glorious landmark in the annals of your great Nation!

HIS ROYAL HIGHNESS. Thank you. Yes, very satisfactory, I think. I am so glad that you were able to be present.

AN IMPERIAL HIGHNESS. Ach! I would not have missed it for anything!

HIS ROYAL HIGHNESS (*to an* OFFICIAL). Sir Arthur, will you please to give orders for the window to be ready? (SIR ARTHUR *bows, and goes to give the order. Presently two Footmen enter, and undo the bolts of the centre window. A Court Official enters, comes to His Royal Highness, bows, and makes a communication.*)

HIS ROYAL HIGHNESS (*to* HIS IMPERIAL HIGHNESS). Excuse me for one moment.

SIR ARTHUR (*to the Footmen*). Do not go; remain.

(*They stand to attention on either side of the window. And now, from the corridor outside, comes an approaching sound—a mingling of voices, foot-steps, and a low rolling of wheels; and* THE QUEEN *enters, seated in her wheeled chair, accompanied by her two Sons. The assembled Family and the Royal Guests, with the formality befitting a great occasion, bow low upon her entrance. The word "Congratulations" emerges from the general hum of voices. Then expressions of affection take the place of ceremony.*)

A ROYAL PRINCESS. Mamma, dear, how are you?

THE QUEEN. Very tired, my dear; but oh, so happy! . . . To think now that it is all over! . . . So glad that I had the strength for it!

PRINCESS. And the courage, Mamma, dear!

ANOTHER PRINCESS. You were quite wonderful, Mamma!

THE QUEEN. Yes, so the Doctor tells me. He has just felt my pulse and taken my temperature. And he says that he could not have believed it possible. Oh, I'm—I'm so thankful!

HIS ROYAL HIGHNESS. So is everybody. And now, Mamma, I think you had better take a glass of wine. It will do you good.

THE QUEEN. Thank you.

HIS ROYAL HIGHNESS. And may we also drink to your good health, Mamma?

THE QUEEN. Certainly; why, yes, certainly! Please, all of you!

(*In the background Attendants have already begun serving wine into glasses. A glass is brought to* THE QUEEN.)

THE QUEEN. What is it?

HIS ROYAL HIGHNESS. Champagne, Mamma.

THE QUEEN. No, no; I will have sherry. (*So sherry is brought*) How long has it taken?

PRINCESS. Nearly three hours, Mamma.

THE QUEEN. Oh, dear me! And it seems like yesterday and tomorrow —almost! . . . Three hours!

HIS ROYAL HIGHNESS. Your Imperial and Royal Highnesses, I have great pleasure in asking you to drink to the health of Her Majesty, the Queen. May she continue long, in health and prosperity, to enjoy the love of her Children and her people.

(*The health is drunk with decorous enthusiasm.* THE QUEEN *sits bowing her acknowledgments to all the assembled Family, with tears and smiles.*)

THE QUEEN. Thank you! Oh, thank you!

PRINCESS. Won't you go and rest now, Mamma?

THE QUEEN. Not yet. . . . That cheering that I hear means that my dear people are expecting to see me again. I must try not to disappoint them.

PRINCESS. It would be nice if you could, Mamma. You think you can?

THE QUEEN. Yes, but I can't get up. I must go as I am. Have the windows opened.

(*The windows are opened by the Footmen; the cheering swells.*)

THE QUEEN. Yes, but over the balustrade, they will not be able to see me. I must be raised. Tell them to bring in the sliding dais.

HIS ROYAL HIGHNESS. It is already there in position, Mamma.

THE QUEEN. Really! How thoughtful! (*And so, when the window is opened, the sliding dais is let down from without into the window-frame. While this is being done with quiet efficiency by the well-trained Footmen, the* QUEEN *continues speaking*) Then, now, will you, Bertie, and some of the others go out, and let them know that I am coming? Not too many, just a few. (*So six members of the Royal Family go out on to the balcony, and the cheering grows louder.* THE QUEEN, *seeing that the dais is now in position, makes a gesture of command, and the chair, slowly propelled, mounts the ramp prepared for it, and passes into the balcony. Immediately the cheering becomes tremendous, and would go on without abatement for much longer than exhausted old human nature can allow.* THE QUEEN *gives the signal for retirement; the chair is withdrawn, and backs into its former central position; and the Royal Family retire, bowing, from the public gaze. The dais is lifted, the window is closed again.*)

THE QUEEN. It's very gratifying, very, to find—after all these years—that they do appreciate all that I have tried to do for them—for their good, and for this great Country of ours. We have been so near together today—they and I: all my dear people of England, and Scotland—*and* Ireland, and the dear Colonies, and India. From all round the world I have had messages. Such loyalty—such devotion! Most extraordinary! Tell Mr. Chamberlain how very much I approve of all the arrangements he made for the proper representation of all parts of my Empire in the Procession. Everything so perfectly in order. Most gratifying! . . . Well, I must go now and rest, or I shall not be able to take my place at dinner tonight, and that would never do! . . . So happy! . . . As we were coming back—you were in front, Bertie, so perhaps you didn't see—it was just by Hyde Park Corner, there was a great crowd there; and a lot of rough men—of course it ought not to have happened, but it didn't matter—broke right through the lines of the police and troops guarding the route; and they ran alongside the carriage, shouting and cheering me. And I heard them say: "Go it, Old Girl! You've done it well! You've done it well!" Of course, very unsuitable—the words; but so gratifying! And oh, I hope it's true! I hope it's true! . . . Hark! They are still cheering. . . . Albert! Ah! if only you could have been here!

(And, having said her say, the great, wonderful, little old Lady gives the signal to her Attendants, and is wheeled slowly away.)

The Corn Is Green

BY EMLYN WILLIAMS

TO

S. G. C.

AND, AT HER REQUEST,

TO ALL TEACHERS.

The Corn Is Green was first produced in America at the National Theatre, New York City, by Herman Shumlin on November 26, 1940. The following is the original cast:

(*In the order in which they speak*)

JOHN GORONWY JONES	Rhys Williams
MISS RONBERRY	Mildred Dunnock
IDWAL MORRIS	Charles S. Pursell
SARAH PUGH	Gwyneth Hughes
A GROOM	George Bleasdale
THE SQUIRE	Edmond Breon
MRS. WATTY	Rosalind Ivan
BESSIE WATTY	Thelma Schnee
MISS MOFFAT	Ethel Barrymore
ROBBART ROBBATCH	Thomas Lyons
MORGAN EVANS	Richard Waring
GLYN THOMAS	Kenneth Clarke
JOHN OWEN	Merritt O'Duel
WILL HUGHES	Terence Morgan
OLD TOM	Sayre Crawley

Boys, Girls and Parents: Julia Knox, Amelia Romano, Betty Conibear, Rosalind Carter, Harda Normann, Joseph McInerney, Marcel Dill, Gwilym Williams, Tommy Dix.

Produced and staged by HERMAN SHUMLIN

Setting designed by HOWARD BAY

Costumes designed by ERNEST SCHRAPPS

SCENES

ACT ONE

SCENE I—An afternoon in June.
SCENE II—A night in August, six weeks later.

ACT TWO

SCENE I—An early evening in August, two years later.
SCENE II—A morning in November, three months later.

ACT THREE

An afternoon in July, seven months later.

The action of the play takes place in the living room of a house in Glansarno, a small village in a remote Welsh countryside.

The time is the latter part of the last century, and covers a period of three years.

THE CORN IS GREEN

ACT ONE

SCENE I

The living room of a house in Glansarno, a small village in a remote Welsh countryside. A sunny afternoon in June, in the latter part of the last century.

The house is old, and the ceiling slants away from the audience. Facing the audience, on the left, narrow stairs lead up to a landing and then on the left to a passage to the bedrooms; we can just see, facing, the door of one bedroom which is later to be Miss Moffat's. A door leads to the kitchen; at the foot of the stairs, an alcove and a door lead to a little room which is later the study. In the back wall, to the right, the front door, with outside it a small stone porch faintly overgrown with ivy, and opening to the left on to a path; in the back wall, to the left, a large bay window with a small sofa seat. In the right wall, downstage, the garden door, and above it a small side window; when the door is open we can just see a trellised porch with a creeper. Through the thickish curtains over the bay window we glimpse a jagged stone wall and the sky.

The floor is of stone flags, with one rug in front of the sofa. Faded sprigged wallpaper.

The furniture is a curious jumble of old Welsh and Victorian pieces. A large serviceable flat-topped desk under the side window, a desk-chair in front of it; a table with a small chair, near the middle of the room; an armchair, between the desk and the table; a sofa, downstage, between the table and the foot of the stairs; in the back wall, near the kitchen door, an old Welsh dresser with plates and crockery; in the left wall, against the staircase, a settle; in the window recess, a small table. In the back wall, to the right of the front door, a small grandfather's clock. An oil lamp on the centre table, another on the desk. Another on the dresser.

The most distinctive feature of the room is the amount of books on the walls, of all sorts and sizes; some in open bookcases, others on newly built shelves, in practically every available space.

The kitchen door is open; there are books on the window seat.

As the curtain rises, MR. JOHN GORONWY JONES *and* MISS RONBERRY *are arranging the last books in their places; she is sitting on a tiny stool taking books out of a large packing case and fitting them on to narrow shelves between the garden door and the side window, flicking each one mechanically with a tiny lace handkerchief. She is a gentlewoman in her thirties, with the sort of pinched prettiness that tends to look sharp before that age, especially when it makes sporadic attempts at coquetry; she wears a hat. He is a shabby Welshman of forty, bespectacled, gloomy and intense; a volcano, harmless even in full eruption. He is perched on top of a step-*

ladder, arranging books on a high shelf between the front door and the bay window, dusting them vigorously before putting them in place.

MR. JONES (*singing*). ". . . Pechudur wyf, y dua'n fyw—'O Uffern!' yw fy nghri; Gostwng dy glust, a'am llefain clyw . . . So—so—so—la—so—so!"

MISS RONBERRY (*seated on stool*). Your voice has given me an agonising headache. And if you must indulge in music, will you please not do it in Welsh?

MR. JONES. I wasn't indulgin' in music, I was singin' a hymn. (*Putting the last book on the shelf and climbing down*) And if a hymn gives you a headache, there is nothing wrong with the hymn, there is something wrong with your head.

MISSS RONBERRY. I still don't see the necessity for it.

MR. JONES (*picking up the empty packing case and moving towards the kitchen*). I sing to cheer myself up.

MISS RONBERRY. What do the words mean?

MR. JONES. "The wicked shall burn in hell." (*Exits into kitchen.*)

(MISS RONBERRY *picks up packing case.* IDWAL MORRIS *comes in from garden, stops at door.*)

MISS RONBERRY. Oh! (IDWAL *is a thin, ragged boy of thirteen, very timid*) Is the garden nice and ready?

IDWAL. 'Sgwelwchi'n dda, d'wi'di torri'r bloda.

MISS RONBERRY. Translation! (*Crosses with box to chair in arch of bay window—then to left of centre table.*)

(MR. JONES *returns, carries two piles of books.*)

IDWAL. Os gwelwchi'n dda, Mistar Jones, d'wi'di torri'r bloda, a mae'r domen yn hogla'n ofnadwy.

(MISS RONBERRY *goes to him and takes flowers.*)

MR. JONES. He says he cut the sweet peas and the rubbish heap is smelling terrible.

MISS RONBERRY. Oh, dear. His father must put something on it. (*Arranges flowers in vase.*)

MR. JONES (*going up ladder*). That's the English all over. The devil is there, is he? Don't take him away, put a bit of scent on him! Gofyn i dy dad i roi rwbeth arno am heddyw.

IDWAL. Diolch, syr. (*He runs into the garden again.*)

MISS RONBERRY. I hope he will have the sense to give the message.

MR. JONES (*still on ladder*). It is terrible, isn't it, the people on these green fields and flowery hillsides bein' turned out of Heaven because they cannot answer Saint Peter when he asks them who they are in English? It is wicked, isn't it, the Welsh children not bein' *born* knowing English—isn't it? Good heavens, God bless my soul, by Jove, this, that and the other!

MISS RONBERRY. Anybody in Wales will tell you that the people in this part of the countryside are practically barbarians. (SARAH PUGH *comes out of the bedroom and down the stairs. She is a buxom peasant woman, with a strong Welsh accent*) Not a single caller for fifteen miles, and even then . . .

SARAH. Please, Miss—I made the bed lovely. And I dust . . .

MISS RONBERRY. That will be all, dear. The Colonel is bound to have his own manservant.

SARAH. Then I better have another sit down in my post office.

MR. JONES. What is the matter with your post office?

SARAH. It has—(*Opens door*)—not had a letter for seven weeks. Nobody but me can write, and no good *me* writin', because nobody but me can read. If I get a telegram I put him in the window and I die straight off. (*She goes, closes door.*)

MISS RONBERRY. You see? I can't *think* why a Colonel should elect to come and live in this place. There. . . . I have never *seen* so many books! I do hope the curtains will not be too feminine. I chose them with such care.

MR. JONES (*darkly*). Why are you taking so much trouble getting somebody else's house ready for them?

MISS RONBERRY (*examines cushion*). You need not have helped me if you did not wish! (*Crosses to settle for needle and thread*) I am frightened of the spinning-wheel, too, and the china; his own furniture is *so* distinctive. The desk. And the wastepaper basket. . . . So . . . so virile.

MR. JONES (*on ladder*). Are you hoping that the Colonel will live up to his wastepaper basket?

MISS RONBERRY. That is horrid.

MR. JONES. And then you will have two on a string: him and the Squire . . .

MISS RONBERRY. Mr. Jones!

MR. JONES. And if I was a bit more of a masher, there would be three. Worldly things, that is your trouble. "Please, Mistar Jones, my life is as empty as a rotten nutshell, so get me a husband before it is too late, double quick!"
(*A knock at the front door; it opens and a liveried* GROOM *appears.*)

MISS RONBERRY. You insulting man . . .

GROOM. The Squire.
(*The* SQUIRE *follows him. He is a handsome English country gentleman in his forties, wearing knickerbockers and gaiters; a hard drinker, bluff, kind, immensely vain; and, when the time comes, obtusely obstinate. The* GROOM *goes out again and shuts the door.*)

MISS RONBERRY (*fluttering eagerly into a handshake*). Squire. . . .

THE SQUIRE (*with exuberant patronage*). Delicious lady, delicious surprise, and a merry afternoon to ye, as our forebears put it. . . . How are you, Jones, making the most of your half-day?

MR. JONES (*sullenly, making an uncertain effort to rise from the ladder*). Good afternoon, sir . . .

THE SQUIRE. Squat, dear fellow, squat . . . No ceremony with me! And why, dear lady, were you not at the Travers-Ellis wedding?
(JONES *starts down the ladder.*)

MISS RONBERRY. Naughty! I sat next to you at the breakfast.

THE SQUIRE. By Jingo! So you did!

MR. JONES. Excuse me . . .
(*He goes into study.*)

THE SQUIRE. Deuced fine breakfast. . . .

MISS RONBERRY. We had a talk about children.

THE SQUIRE. *Did* we? Well, the next wedding we're at, there'll be *no* chance of my forgettin' you, eh?

MISS RONBERRY. Why?

THE SQUIRE. Because—you'll be the stunning, blushing bride!

MISS RONBERRY. And who—will be the—?

THE SQUIRE. Now that's what *I* want to know, because *I'm* going to give you away!

MISS RONBERRY. Oh!
(MR. JONES returns from the study.)

THE SQUIRE. Now who's it going to be?

MISS RONBERRY. Squire, you are too impatient! I am taking my time!

THE SQUIRE. Too bad . . . No sign of the new inhabitant?

MISS RONBERRY. Any moment now, I think! The pony and trap met the London train at a quarter to twelve!

THE SQUIRE. Hasn't the fellow got his own private conveyance?

MISS RONBERRY. I think not.

THE SQUIRE. I hope he's all right.

MISS RONBERRY. He wrote very civilly to Mr. Jones about the house . . .

THE SQUIRE. Oh, yes. Not a club, I remember, but the paper—not bad texture. Funny sort of chap, though, eh?

MISS RONBERRY. Why?

THE SQUIRE. All these books.
(*A timid knock at the front door.* IDWAL *enters, very frightened.*)

IDWAL. Osgwelwchi'n dda, syr, mae Mistar Tomos wedi 'ngyrru i yma ich gweld chi!

THE SQUIRE. Y'know, it's as bad as being abroad. . . . Been among it half my life, and never get used to it.

MR. JONES. The groom told him, sir, that you wanted to see him.

THE SQUIRE. Oh, yes—well, come here where I can see you, eh? (SQUIRE *turns to him*) Now, boy, how old are you—(*To* JONES)—or whatever the Chinese is for it?

MR. JONES. Just turned thirteen, sir.

THE SQUIRE. Thirteen? Well, why aren't you working in the mine over in the next valley? Don't like to see young fellows wasting their time, y'know.

MR. JONES. He has got one lung funny.

THE SQUIRE. Oh, I see. . . . Rough luck. Here, laddy, there's a sixpence for you, and remember all work and no play makes Taffy a dull boy!

IDWAL. Diolch yn faw, syr . . .

THE SQUIRE. And tell your uncle I want Ranger shod . . .

IDWAL. Diolch, syr . . .

THE SQUIRE. And a gate mended . . .

IDWAL. Diolch yn faw, syr . . . (*He runs out.*)

MISS RONBERRY. But he hasn't understood your orders!

THE SQUIRE. Neither he has . . .

MR. JONES. He thought the Squire was havin' a chat. I will tell his uncle—

IDWAL (*offstage, calling shrilly to his friends*). Tomos—Aneurin—dyma'r cerbyd—(JONES *looks out window*)—dewch i wel'd—fe ddwedai wrth y Scweiar—brysiwch!

MISS RONBERRY (*rises*). That must be something . . .
(IDWAL *appears at the front door, panting with expectation.*)

IDWAL. Pliss, syr, dyma'r carbyd! (*He darts back, leaving the door open.*)

MISS RONBERRY (*looks out window*). He must mean the Colonel. How gratifying . . .
(BESSIE WATTY *wanders shyly in. She is an extremely pretty, plump little girl of fourteen; it is a moment before one realises that her demureness is too good to be true. She wears her hair over her shoulders, is dressed very plainly, in a shabby sailor suit and hat, and carries brown-paper parcels. She is followed by* MRS. WATTY, *a middle-aged Cockney servant, dressed for traveling, carrying a hamper in her arms. Her self-confidence is not so overwhelming as the* SQUIRE'S, *but it is quite as complete, and as kindly.*)

THE SQUIRE. Capital . . .

MRS. WATTY (*to the* SQUIRE). D'you speak English?

THE SQUIRE (*taken aback*). I do.

MRS. WATTY. Be a dear an' 'old this! (*She hands him the hamper and hurries out through the front door.*)

THE SQUIRE. Crikey! A Colonel with an abigail! (*Catching* BESSIE'S *owl-like expression and stopping short*) Why don't *you* say something?

BESSIE. I never speak till I'm spoken to.

THE SQUIRE. Oh . . . Well, who was that?

BESSIE. My mummy. (*To* MISS RONBERRY) I never had no daddy. (*Her accent is not as natural as her mother's; she sometimes strains to be ladylike, especially at moments like this.* MRS. WATTY *returns with two large parcels.*)

MRS. WATTY. My Gawd—(*Pause*)—they're heavy. (*Puts them on table.*)

MISS RONBERRY. What are they?

MRS. WATTY. Books.
(*Takes hamper from* SQUIRE.)

THE SQUIRE. Is your employer with you, my good woman?

MRS. WATTY. No, followed be'ind, most of the way. Ought to be 'ere by now, I'll 'ave a see. . . . (*Goes to door*) 'Ere we are! Tally-o! Thought we'd lost you!
(*A pause.* MISS MOFFAT *comes in from the road, wheeling a bicycle. She is about forty, a healthy Englishwoman with an honest face, clear, beautiful eyes, a humorous mouth, a direct friendly manner, and unbounded vitality, which is prevented from tiring the spectator by its capacity for sudden silence and for listening. Her most prominent characteristic is her complete unsentimentality. She wears a straw hat, collar and tie, and a dark unexaggerated skirt; a satchel hangs from her shoulder.*)

MISS MOFFAT. I was hoping to pass you, but that last hill was too much for me. (*Displaying the bicycle*) Good afternoon.

ALL. Good afternoon.

MISS MOFFAT. There's a smallish crowd already, so I thought I'd better bring Priscilla inside. Watty, can you find somewhere for her? (*She gives the room a quick appraising look, peers out of the side window, and nods pleasantly to the* SQUIRE.)

MRS. WATTY. Dunno, I'm sure.

MISS MOFFAT. I think I'll have a look at the garden first. (*She goes out into the garden.*)

MRS. WATTY (*wheeling bicycle gingerly towards the kitchen*). That must be my kitchen in there, we'll 'ave to 'ang 'er with the bacon. (*To* BESSIE) Come on, girl, give us a 'and—don't stand there gettin' into mischief!

BESSIE. I'm frightened of it.

MRS. WATTY. It won't bite you! Most it can do is catch fire, and I'll 'ave a drop o' water ready for it. (*Her voice fades away into the kitchen.*)

BESSIE. Has anybody got a sweetie?

MISS RONBERRY. No.

BESSIE. Oh. . . .
(*She trails after her mother into the kitchen.* MISS MOFFAT *returns very businesslike.*)

MISS MOFFAT. It's bigger than I expected. . . . (*Closes door*) There! (*Puts satchel on desk*) Good afternoon! So this is my house. . . .

THE SQUIRE (*blustering*). No, it isn't!

MISS MOFFAT. Oh? Isn't this Pengrath? The name of the building, I mean?

MISS RONBERRY. Yes, it is. . . .

MISS MOFFAT. That's right, it was left me by my uncle, Dr. Moffat. I'm Miss Moffat. I take it you're Miss Ronberry, who so kindly corresponded with me?

THE SQUIRE. But sure—those letters were written by a man?

MISS MOFFAT. Well, if they were, I have been grossly deceiving myself for over forty years. Now this is jolly interesting. Why did it never occur to you that I might be a woman?

THE SQUIRE. Well—the paper wasn't scented . . .

MISS RONBERRY. And such a bold hand . . .

THE SQUIRE. And that long piece about the lease being ninety-nine years, don't you know . . .

MISS MOFFAT. Was there anything wrong with it?

THE SQUIRE. No, there wasn't, that's the point.

MISS MOFFAT. I see.

MISS RONBERRY. And surely you signed your name very oddly?

MISS MOFFAT. My initials, L. C. Moffat? You see, I've never felt that Lily Christabel really suited me.

MISS RONBERRY. And I thought—it meant Lieutenant-Colonel! But there *was* a military title after it.

MISS MOFFAT. M.A., Master of Arts.

THE SQUIRE. Arts? D'ye mean the degree my father bought me when I came down from the Varsity?

MISS MOFFAT. The very same. Except that I was at Aberdeen, and had to work jolly hard for mine.

THE SQUIRE. A female M.A.? And how long's that going to last?

MISS MOFFAT. Quite a long time, I hope, considering we've been waiting for it for two thousand years.

MR. JONES (*who has been silent since she entered*). Are you saved?

MISS MOFFAT (*starting, turning and taking him in for the first time*). I beg your pardon?

MR. JONES. Are you Church or Chapel?

MISS MOFFAT. I really don't know . . . And now you know all about me, what do *you* do?

THE SQUIRE. I'm afraid I don't do anything. (*He extricates his hat angrily from the table.*)

MISS RONBERRY. Mr. Treverby owns the Hall!

MISS MOFFAT. Really. I've never had much to do with the landed gentry. Interesting.

THE SQUIRE. Au revoir, dear lady. 'Day, Jones. (*He goes frigidly out by the front door.* JONES *closes door.*)

MISS MOFFAT. Well, nobody could say that I've made a conquest there. . . . What's the matter with him? (MRS. WATTY *comes in from kitchen with tea tray.*)

MRS. WATTY. I found the tea, ma'am, it *looks* all right. . . .

MISS MOFFAT. Good!

MRS. WATTY. An' the big luggage is comin' after . . .

MISS MOFFAT (*at study door*). This isn't a bad little room . . .

MRS. WATTY. Where's his lordship?

MISS MOFFAT (*going upstairs*). Took offense and left. (*She disappears down the passage.*)

MRS. WATTY (*looks at them both*). Took offense? At 'er?

MISS RONBERRY. I am afraid so.

MRS. WATTY. I'm jiggered! What d'*you* think of 'er, eh? Ain't she a clinker?

MISS RONBERRY. She is unusual, is she not?

MRS. WATTY. She's a clinker, that's what. Terrible strong-willed, o' course, terrible. Get 'er into mischief, I keep tellin' 'er. Would bring me 'ere. I said no, I said, not with my past, I said.

MISS RONBERRY. Your past?

MRS. WATTY. Before she took me up. But what with 'er, and now I've joined the Corpse, it's all blotted out.

MR. JONES. The Corpse?

MRS. WATTY. The Militant Righteous Corpse. Ran into 'em in the street I did, singin' and prayin' and collectin', full blast; and I been a different woman since. Are *you* saved?

MR. JONES. Yes, I am.

MRS. WATTY. So'm I. Ain't it lovely?

MISS RONBERRY. But what *was*—your past?

MRS. WATTY (*sorrowfully*). Light fingers.

MISS RONBERRY. Light fingers? You mean—stealing?

MRS. WATTY. Everywhere I went. Terrible. Pennies, stockin's, brooches, spoons, tiddly, anything. Every time there was a do, everything went; and I always knew it was me! (MISS MOFFAT *comes downstairs*) I was just tellin' 'em about my trouble.

MISS MOFFAT. Well, don't tell them any more. Is your kitchen all right?

MRS. WATTY. I ain't seed no mice yet. (*She goes into kitchen, takes hamper with her.*)

(*Far away, softly, the sound of boys' voices, singing an old country song, in harmony, in Welsh: "Yr Hufen Melyn."*)

MISS MOFFAT. I agree with the last tenant's taste. . . . You have arranged my things quite splendidly, Miss Ronberry. I do thank you—both of you. . . . I like this house (*As the music grows imperceptibly in the distance*) . . . What's that singing?

MR. JONES. Boys coming home from the mine.

MISS RONBERRY. They burst into song on the slightest provocation. You mustn't take any notice . . .

MISS MOFFAT. I like it . . . And those mountains. That grand wild countryside . . . The foreign-looking people . . . But business . . . I've heard about that mine. How far is it?

MR. JONES. It is the Glasynglo coal mine, six miles over the hills.

MISS MOFFAT. Hm . . .

MISS RONBERRY. We're hoping it will stay the only one, or our scenery will be ruined—such a pretty landscape . . .

MISS MOFFAT. What is the large empty building next door?

MR. JONES. Next door? The old barn belongin' to the Gwalia Farm, before the farm was burnt down. . . .

(*Song fades out.*)

MISS MOFFAT. So it's free?

MR. JONES (*perplexed*). Free? Yes . . .

MISS RONBERRY (*rises*). I am overstaying my welcome. So very charming . . .

MR. JONES. I also. All the volumes are dusted. . . .
(*Starts to go towards her.*)

MISS MOFFAT. I want you two people. Very specially. First you, Miss Ronberry. I used to meet friends of yours at lectures in London. You live alone, you have just enough money, you're not badly educated, and time lies heavy on your hands.

MISS RONBERRY. The Wingroves! How mean! I should never have thought . . .

MISS MOFFAT. Isn't that so?

MISS RONBERRY. Not at all. When the right gentleman appears . . .

MISS MOFFAT. If you're a spinster well on in her thirties, he's lost his way and isn't coming. Why don't you face the fact and enjoy yourself, the same as I do?

MISS RONBERRY. But when did you give up hope? Oh, what a horrid expression. . . .

MISS MOFFAT. I can't recall ever having any hope. Visitors used to take a long look at my figure and say: '*She's* going to be the clever one."

MISS RONBERRY. But a woman's only future is to marry and—and fulfill the duties of . . .

MISS MOFFAT. Skittles! I'd have made a shocking wife, anyway.

MISS RONBERRY. But haven't you ever—been in love?

MISS MOFFAT. No.

MISS RONBERRY. How very odd.

MISS MOFFAT. I've never talked to a man for more than five minutes without wanting to box his ears.

MISS RONBERRY. But how have you passed your time since . . . ?

MISS MOFFAT. Since I had no hope? Very busily. In the East End, for years.

MISS RONBERRY. Social service?

MISS MOFFAT. If you like; though there's nothing very social about washing invalids with every unmentionable ailment under the sun. . . . I've read a lot, too. I'm afraid I'm what is known as an educated woman. Which brings me to Mr. Jones; the Wingroves told me all about you, too.

MR. JONES. My conscience is as clear as the snow.

MISS MOFFAT. I'm sure it is, but you're a disappointed man, aren't you?

MR. JONES (*startled*). How can I be disappointed when I am saved?

MISS MOFFAT. Oh, but you can! You can't really enjoy sitting all by yourself on a raft, on a sea, containing everybody you know. You're disappointed because you're between two stools.

MR. JONES. Between two stools? On a raft?

MISS MOFFAT. Exactly. Your father was a grocer with just enough money to send you to a grammar school, with the result that you are educated beyond your sphere, and yet fail to qualify for the upper classes. You feel frustrated, and fall back on being saved. Am I right?

MR. JONES. It is such a terrible thing you have said that I will have to think it over.

MISS MOFFAT. Do. (*Rises*) But in the meantime—(*Pause*)—would you two like to stop moping and be very useful to me?

MISS RONBERRY. Useful?

MISS MOFFAT. Yes, tell me—within a radius of five miles, how many families are there round here?

MISS RONBERRY. Families? There's the Squire, of course, and Mrs. Gwent-Price in the little Plas Lodge, quite a dear thing . . .

MISS MOFFAT. I mean ordinary people.

MISS RONBERRY. The villagers?

MISS MOFFAT. Yes. How many families?

MISS RONBERRY. I really haven't the faint . . .

MR. JONES. There are about twenty families in the village and fifteen in the farms around.

MISS MOFFAT. Many children?

MR. JONES. What age?

MISS MOFFAT. Up to sixteen or seventeen.

MR. JONES. Round here they are only children till they are twelve. Then they are sent away over the hills to the mine, and in one week they are old men.

MISS MOFFAT. I see. How many can read or write?

MR. JONES. Next to none.

MISS RONBERRY. Why do you ask?

MISS MOFFAT. Because I am going to start a school for them.

MISS RONBERRY (*coldly*). Start a school for them? What for?

MISS MOFFAT. What for? See these books? Hundreds of 'em, and something wonderful to read in every single one. These nippers are to be cut off from all that, for ever, are they? Why? Because they happen to be born penniless in an uncivilised countryside, coining gold down there in that stinking dungeon for some beef-headed old miser!

MR. JONES (*roused*). That's right. . . .

MISS MOFFAT. The printed page, what is it? One of the miracles of all time, that's what! And yet when these poor babies set eyes on it, they might just as well have been struck by the miracle of sudden blindness; and that, to my mind, is plain infamous!

MR. JONES. My goodness, Miss, that's right. . . .

MISS RONBERRY. The *ordinary* children, you mean?

MISS MOFFAT. Yes, my dear, the ordinary children that came into the world by the same process exactly as you and I. When I heard that this part of the world was a disgrace to a Christian country, I knew this house was a godsend. I am going to start a school, immediately, next door in the barn, and you are going to help me!

MISS RONBERRY. I?

MISS MOFFAT. Yes, you! You're going to fling away your parasol and your kid gloves, and you're going to stain those tapering fingers with a little honest toil!

MISS RONBERRY. I couldn't teach those children, I couldn't! They—they smell!

MISS MOFFAT. If we'd never been taught to wash, so would we; we'll put 'em under the pump. . . . Mr. Jones—d'ye know what I'm going to do with that obstinate old head of yours?

MR. JONES. My head?

MISS MOFFAT. I'm going to crack it open with a skewer. And I'm going to excavate all those chunks of grammar-school knowledge, give 'em a quick dust, and put 'em to some use at last.

MR. JONES. I am a solicitor's clerk in Gwaenygam and I earn thirty-three shillings per week. . . .

MISS MOFFAT. I'll give you thirty-four—and your lunch.

MISS RONBERRY. I have an enormous house to run, and the flowers to do. . . .

MISS MOFFAT. Shut it up except one room, and leave the flowers to die a natural death—in their own beds. I've been left a little money and I know exactly what I am going to do with it. . . .

MR. JONES. But those children are in the mine—earning money. How can they . . . ?

MISS MOFFAT. I'll pay their parents the few miserable pennies they get out of it . . . And when I've finished with you, *you* won't have time to think about snapping up a husband, and *you* won't have time to be so pleased that you're saved! Well?

MR. JONES. I do not care if you are not chapel, I am with you.

MISS MOFFAT. Good! I have all the details worked out. I'll explain roughly. . . . Come along—my dears, gather 'round, children—gather round. (*She takes the dazed* MISS RONBERRY *by the arm, seats her beside her on the sofa, and beckons* MR. JONES *to sit on her other side*) Of course, we must go slowly at first, but if we put our backs into it . . . Here we are, three stolid middle-aged folk, settled in our little groove and crammed with benefits; and *there* are those babies scarcely out of the shell, that have no idea they are even breathing the air. . . . Only God can know how their life will end, but He will give us the chance to direct them a little of the way. . . .

MR. JONES (*intoning, seized with religious fervor*). We have the blessed opportunity to raise up the children from the bowels of the earth where the devil hath imprisoned them in the powers of darkness, and bring them to the light of knowledge—

MRS. WATTY (*coming in from the kitchen*). Here's the tea!

MISS MOFFAT. Each of us can take several classes, not only for the children, but their fathers and their mothers, and the older people too.

THE CURTAIN FALLS

SCENE II

A night in August, six weeks later. The window curtains are closed and the lamps lit. The armchair has been pushed away from table, and two small benches face the audience. Red geraniums in pots across the window sills. Miss Moffat's straw hat is slung over the knob of the settle at the foot of the stairs. The big desk, the sofa and the settle are littered with books, exercise books and sheets of paper. Apart from these details the room is unchanged.

Sitting on the bench are five black-faced miners, between twelve and sixteen years of age, wearing caps, mufflers, boots and corduroys embedded in coal; they look as if they had been commanded to wait. They all look alike under their black; the ringleader is MORGAN EVANS, *fifteen, quick and impudent; his second is* ROBBART ROBBATCH, *a big, slow boy, a year or two older; the others are* GLYN THOMAS, WILL HUGHES *and* JOHN OWEN. *They all hum at rise.*

MRS. WATTY *comes downstairs, carrying a basket of washing.*

MRS. WATTY. You 'ere again? (*On stairs, stops halfway down.*)

ROBBART. Be mai'n ddeud?

MRS. WATTY. I said, you 'ere again?

MORGAN. No, Miss.

MRS. WATTY. What d'ye mean, no, Miss?

MORGAN. We issn't 'ere again, Miss.

MRS. WATTY. What are you, then?

MORGAN. We issn't the same lot ass this mornin', Miss.

MRS. WATTY. Ain't you?

MORGAN. Miss Ronny-berry tell us to wait, Miss.

MRS. WATTY. Ma'am! (*Goes to kitchen door.*)

MISS MOFFAT (*in the bedroom*). Yes?

MRS. WATTY. Five more nigger boys for you! (*She goes into the kitchen.* MORGAN *takes a bottle from his pocket and swigs at it. One of the others holds out his hand, takes the bottle, gulps, and gives it back, while another begins to hum, absent-mindedly, a snatch of the same song as before. The rest take up the harmony and sing it to the end.* MR. JONES *comes in.*)

MORGAN. Sh! Good evenin', sir.

MR. JONES. Good evening. (*Tips hat.*)

MORGAN. I seed you and the lady teacher be'ind the door! (*A laugh from him and the others.*)

MR. JONES. You wait till you see Miss Moffat. She will give you what for.

MORGAN (*shaking finger at boys*). You wait till you see Miss Moffat. She will give you what for! (MR. JONES *goes into the kitchen.* ROBBART *repeats: "You wait till you see Miss Moffat, she will give you what for!"*) Shh!
(MISS MOFFAT *comes downstairs from the bedroom.*)

MISS MOFFAT. I told you, the shape of the bedroom doesn't allow for a door into the barn—Oh, she isn't here. . . . Sorry to keep you waiting, boys, but I have to go across to Mr. Rees, the carpenter, and then I'll be able to talk to you. In the meantime, will you go to the pump in the garden shed, and wash your hands? Through there. You'll find a lantern. Did you understand all that?

MORGAN. Yes, Miss.

THE OTHERS. Thank you, Miss.

MISS MOFFAT. Good. (*Starts to go.*)

MORGAN. Please, Miss, can I have a kiss?

MISS MOFFAT (*returns*). What did you say?

MORGAN. Please, Miss, can I have a kiss?

MISS MOFFAT. Of course you can. (*Puts her foot on bench—takes him by the neck and bends him over her knee and spanks him with the plans she carries*) Can I oblige anybody else? (*She goes out by the front door. The others follow her with their eyes, aghast, in silence.*)

ROBBART. Please, Miss, can I 'ave a smack bottom?
(*An uproar of mirth, and a quick tangle of Welsh.*)

WILL. Na-beth of Naw-stee.

MORGAN. Cythral uffarn . . .

GLYN. Be hari hi—hi a'i molchi . . .

JOHN. Pwy sisho molchi . . .

WILL. Welso ti'rioed wraig fel ene—

MORGAN. Mae'n lwcus na ddaru mi mo'i thrawo hi lawr a'i lladd hi . . .

ROBBART. Nawn—(*Rises*)—i drio molchi—dewch hogia— (*All rise—start off*) mae'n well nag eistedd yma—dewch . . .

GLYN. Dynna gusan yti Morgan Bach.

ROBBART. Cymmer yna y corgu fol.

JOHN. Dynna ateb—i—ti.

WILL. Jobin da y diawl.

MORGAN. Cai da geg.

(*They lumber into the garden, close door.* MR. JONES' *head appears timidly from the kitchen. He sees they are gone, gives a sigh of relief, and comes into the room, carrying books.* BESSIE *comes in from the front door, dejected and sulky. She is munching a sweet; her hair is in curls, and one curl is turned around one finger, which she holds stiffly in the air. She lays her hat on the sofa, then decides* MR. JONES'S *company is better than none.*)

BESSIE. Would you like a sweetie?

MR. JONES. No, thank you, my little dear. Have you had another walk?

BESSIE. Yes, Mr. Jones. All by myself.

MR. JONES. Did you see anybody?

BESSIE. Only a lady and a gentleman in the lane—and mother told me never to look. . . . I do miss the shops. London's full o' them, you know.

MR. JONES. Full of fancy rubbish, you mean.

BESSIE. I'd like to be always shopping, I would. Sundays and all. . . .

MRS. WATTY. Bessie!

BESSIE (*slyly*). Mr. Jones, is it true the school idea isn't going on that well?

MR. JONES. Who told you that?

BESSIE. Miss Ronberry was sayin' something to my mum. Oh, I wasn't listenin'! . . . Besides, we've been here six weeks, and nothin's started yet.

MR. JONES. Everything is splendid.

BESSIE (*disappointed*). Oh, I'm glad. Miss Moffat's been cruel to me, but I don't bear no grudge.

MR. JONES. Cruel to you?

BESSIE. She hides my sweets. She's a liar too.

MR. JONES. A liar?

BESSIE. Told me they're bad for me. And it says on the bag they're nourishin'. . . . And the idea of learnin' school with those children, ooh . . .

MR. JONES. Why are you holding your hair like that?

BESSIE. These are my curls. D'you think it's nice?

MR. JONES. It is nice, but it is wrong.

MRS. WATTY (*calling shrilly, in the kitchen*). Bess-ie!

BESSIE. I've been curlin' each one round me finger and holdin' it tight till it was all right. My finger's achin' something terrible. (*She goes into the kitchen. A knock at the front door.*)

MR. JONES. Dewch ifewn.
(IDWAL *appears, drawing a small wooden crate on tiny wheels which he pushes in front of the sofa.* MISS RONBERRY *comes in from the study.*)

IDWAL. Cloch yr ysgol, Mistar Jones.

MR. JONES. Diolch, ymachgeni. (*Pause*) Nosdawch.

IDWAL. Nosdawch, Mistar Jones. (*He leaves through the front door.*)

MISS RONBERRY. It says here that eight sevens are fifty-six. Then it says that seven eights are fifty-six—I can't see that at all. (MISS MOFFAT *returns*) Well?

MISS MOFFAT. No good.

MISS RONBERRY. Oh, dear.

MISS MOFFAT. Mr. Rees says he's had a strict order not to discuss lining the roof till the lease of the barn is signed.

MR. JONES. Who gave the order?

MISS MOFFAT. That's what I want to know.

MISS RONBERRY. And when will the lease be signed?

MISS MOFFAT. Never, it seems to me. Did you call at the solicitor's?

MR. JONES. They have located Sir Herbert Vezey, but he is now doubtful about letting the barn and will give his decision by post.

MISS MOFFAT. But why? He'd already said it was no use to him. And my references were impeccable. . . . *Why?*

MISS RONBERRY. You look tired.

MISS MOFFAT. It's been a bit of a day. A letter from the mine to say no child can be released aboveground—that's all blethers, but still . . . A request from the public house not to start a school in case it interferes with beer-swilling and games of chance. A message from the chapel people to the effect that I am a foreign adventuress with cloven feet; a bit of a day.
(MRS. WATTY *comes in from the kitchen with a cup of tea.*)

MRS. WATTY. Drop o' tea, ma'am, I expect you've 'ad a bit of a day. . . .

MISS MOFFAT. Who was that at the back, anything important?

MRS. WATTY. Only the person that does for that Mrs. Gwent-Price. Would you not 'ave your school opposite her lady because of her lady's 'eadaches.

MISS MOFFAT (*angrily*). What did you say?

MRS. WATTY. I pulverized 'er. I said it would be a shame, I said, if there was such a shindy over the way that the village couldn't hear Mrs. Double-Barrel givin' her 'usband what for, I said. The person didn't know where to put 'erself. (*She goes back into the kitchen.*)

MR. JONES. That has not helped the peace in the community, neither.

MISS MOFFAT. I know, but she does make a tip-top cup of tea. . . . (*Seeing the crate, wearily*) What's that?

MR. JONES. It is the bell, for the school.

MISS MOFFAT. Oh, is it?

MISS RONBERRY (*rising*): The bell? Do let us have a peep . . .

MR. JONES. It was on Llantalon Monastery before it burnt down. . . .

MISS MOFFAT (*opens crate*). Look, it's got the rope, and everything. . . . Well, it's good to see it, anyway.

MISS RONBERRY. The mason finished the little tower for it yesterday. Do let us tell those boys to put it up! It'll bring us luck!

MISS MOFFAT. If it keeps them out of mischief till I'm ready . . .

MISS RONBERRY. Mr. Jones, do go and tell them!
(JONES *gives her a doubtful look and goes towards the garden. As he opens the door,* JOHN OWEN *shouts: "Mai, Mr. Jones, yn dywed." All the boys laugh.*)

MISS MOFFAT. Poor Jonesy, he's terrified of 'em.

MISS RONBERRY. So am I. They're so big. And so black. . . .

(SARAH *runs in, excited, leaving the door open behind her.*)

SARAH. A letter from the gentleman that own the barn. I had a good look at the seal!

MISS MOFFAT. At last . . .

MISS RONBERRY. What does it say?

MISS MOFFAT. Sir Herbert still cannot give a definite decision until the seventeenth. Another week wasted. This is infuriating.

MISS RONBERRY. Does it mean he may not let you have it?

SARAH. Oh. . . .

MISS MOFFAT. He must—it would ruin everything. . . .

MISS RONBERRY. Sarah—isn't there another empty building *anywhere* round here?

SARAH. There is the pigsties on the Maes Road, but they isn't big enough. (*She goes.*)

MISS RONBERRY. Oh, dear! Can't we start afresh somewhere else?

MISS MOFFAT. I've spent too much on preparations here—besides, I felt so right here from the start. . . . I *can't* leave now . . . I'm a Christian woman, but I could smack Sir Herbert's face till my arm dropped off.
(*The front door is opened unceremoniously and the* SQUIRE *strides in; he is in full evening dress.*)

THE SQUIRE. Jolly good evenin', teacher. Remember me?

MISS MOFFAT. Would you mind going outside, knocking, and waiting quite a long time before I say "Come in"?

THE SQUIRE. Jolly good! Parlor games, what?

MISS RONBERRY. But, Miss Moffat, it's the *Squire!* Squire, you must forget you ever saw me in this dress . . . So ashamed . . . I shan't be a moment . . . (*She runs upstairs into the bedroom.*)

THE SQUIRE. Rat tat tat, one two three four come in, one two three four, forward *march!* My dear madam, you're not in class now! (*A knock at the garden door*) Come in!
(ROBBART *and* MORGAN *enter from garden.* MORGAN *has lantern.*)

ROBBART. Please, Miss, for the bell.

THE SQUIRE. Evening, boys! (*Enter* JONES) Evening, Jones. I am appalled to observe, my boys, that you are still soiling your fingers in that disgusting coal mine!

MR. JONES. Excuse me, please. . . . (*He goes into the study.*)

THE SQUIRE. What's that you've got there?

ROBBART. Bell, syr, for the school.

THE SQUIRE. Up with it, boys, up with it! (ROBBART *lifts the crate and carries it out of the garden, door, which* MORGAN *has opened for him.* MORGAN *follows him, shutting the door*) Ding dong bell—teacher's in the well! . . . Now. my dear madam—

MISS MOFFAT. I'm rather irritable this evening, so unless there's a reason for your visit . . .

THE SQUIRE. Oh, but there is! Very important message. Word of mouth. From a gent that's just been dining with me. Sir Herbert Vezey.

MISS MOFFAT. Yes? Oh, do be quick! . . .

THE SQUIRE. He has definitely decided that he has no use for the barn—but he does not see it as a school, and under no circumstances will he let it as such, so he must regretfully decline, et cetera.

MISS MOFFAT (*trying to hide her chagrin*). He implied in his first letter that he would be willing to sell.

THE SQUIRE. Then some bigwig must have made him change his mind, mustn't he?

MISS MOFFAT (*suddenly looking at him, incredulously*). You?

THE SQUIRE (*rising, serious, taking the floor with a certain authority*). I have not called on you, madam, because I have been eyeing your activities very closely from afar. . . . It is with dis—disapproval and —er—dis—

MISS MOFFAT. It is unwise to embark on a speech with the vocabulary of a child of five.

THE SQUIRE (*suddenly aggressive*). I am not going to have any of this damned hanky-panky in my village!

MISS MOFFAT. *Your* village!

THE SQUIRE. *My* village! I am no braggart, but I'd have you know that everything you can see from that window—and you haven't got a bad view—*I own!* Now, my dear madam . . .

MISS MOFFAT (*in an outburst*). And stop calling me your dear madam. I'm not married, I'm not French, and you haven't the slightest affection for me!

THE SQUIRE. Oh. . . . First of all, I'm not one to hit a woman below the belt. If you know what I mean. Always be fair—to the fair sex. . . . All my life I've done my level best for the villagers. They call me Squire, y'know, term of affection, jolly touching. . . . I mean, a hamper every Christmas, the whole shoot, and a whopping tankard of beer on my birthday, and on my twenty-firster they all got a mug . . .

MISS MOFFAT. Go on.

THE SQUIRE. They jabber away in that funny lingo, but bless their hearts, it's a free country! But puttin' 'em up to read English, and pothooks, and givin' 'em ideas . . . If there were more people like you, y'know, England'd be a jolly dangerous place to live in! What d'ye want to do, turn 'em into gentlemen? What's the idea?

MISS MOFFAT. I am beginning to wonder myself.

THE SQUIRE. Anyway, this buyin' 'em out of the mine is a lot of gammon. I own a half share in it.

MISS MOFFAT. That explains a good deal.

THE SQUIRE. Why don't you take up croquet? Keep you out of mischief. (MISS RONBERRY *comes out of the bedroom*) Well, dear lady, anything I can do to make your stay here a happier one . . .

MISS MOFFAT. Thank you.

THE SQUIRE. I must be getting back. If I know Sir Herbert, my best old port will be no more . . .

MISS MOFFAT. Wait a minute.

THE SQUIRE. Yes?

MISS MOFFAT. I know I shall be sticking a pin into a whale, but here are just two words about yourself. You are the Squire Bountiful, are you? Adored by his contented subjects, intelligent and benignly understanding, are you? I should just like to point out that there is a considerable amount of dirt, ignorance, misery and discontent abroad in this world, and that a good deal of it is due to people like you, because you are a stupid, conceited, greedy, good-for-nothing, addle-headed nincompoop, and you can go to blue blazes. Good night! (*She turns away. A frozen pause.*)

THE SQUIRE. I perceive that you have been drinking. (*He goes.*) (MISS RONBERRY *comes downstairs.*)

MISS MOFFAT. That was undignified, but I feel better for it. (*She sits on the bench, intensely depressed.*)

MISS RONBERRY. I am glad, because it *was* plain-spoken, wasn't it? Has he been nasty? So unlike the Squire . . .

MISS MOFFAT. He was kindness itself. He advised me to go and live in a hole in the ground with my knitting. He has persuaded the owner not to sell.

MISS RONBERRY. Oh, dear . . . of course . . . I always think men know best, don't you?

MISS MOFFAT. Yes.

MISS RONBERRY. I'm wearing my mousseline de soie, and he never even noticed. . . . What will you do?

MISS MOFFAT. Sell the house; take this brain child of a ridiculous spinster, and smother it. Have you got a handkerchief?

MISS RONBERRY. Yes, Miss Moffat. Why?

MISS MOFFAT. I want to blow my nose. (*She holds her hand out;* MISS RONBERRY *hands her the handkerchief. She blows her nose, and returns the handkerchief.*)

MISS RONBERRY. You ought to have had a cry. I love a cry when I'm depressed. Such an advantage over the gentlemen, I always think.

MISS MOFFAT (*opening the study door*). Mr. Jones . . .

JONES (*off stage*). Yes . . .

MISS MOFFAT. Will you write letters to the tradespeople and the mine? We are giving up the school . . .

JONES (*off stage*). Oh!

MISS MOFFAT. I suppose we'd better start putting some order into this chaos, and get the business over . . . What are these filthy exercise books doing among my papers . . . ?

MISS RONBERRY. Those hooligans just now. They said Mr. Jones had picked them out because they could write English and would I mind my own some-dreadful-word business.

MISS MOFFAT. I set them an essay on "How I would spend my holiday." I must have been mad. . . . (*Throws one book away and takes one from* MISS RONBERRY.)

MISS RONBERRY (*reading, laboriously*). "If—I has ever holiday—I has breakfast and talks then dinner and a rest, tea then nothing—then supper then I talk and I go sleep."

MISS MOFFAT. From exhaustion, I suppose. (BESSIE *comes in from the kitchen, gets hat from table and starts for door*) Where are you going?

BESSIE. Just another walk, Miss Moffat.

MISS RONBERRY. What's the matter, little dear?

BESSIE. Mum's hit me.

MISS RONBERRY. Oh, naughty mum. Why?

BESSIE. Just because I told her she was common. (*She goes out.*)

MISS RONBERRY. That child *is* unhappy.

MISS MOFFAT. I can't be bothered with her. Another time I'd have been faintly amused by this one's idea of a holiday, judging by a rather crude drawing.

MISS RONBERRY. What is it?

MISS MOFFAT. A bicycling tour with me in bloomers.

MISS RONBERRY. Tch, tch . . .

MISS MOFFAT (*reading*). "'Holiday-time.' That carefree magic word! What shall it be this year, tobogganing among the eternal snows or tasting the joys of Father Neptune?"

MISS RONBERRY. But that's beautiful! Extraordinary!

MISS MOFFAT. I might think so too if I hadn't seen it in a book open on that desk. (*Throws book in wastebasket.*)

MISS RONBERRY. Oh!

MISS MOFFAT. No, your Squire was right. . . . I have been a stupid and impractical ass, and I can't imagine how . . . (*Looks at name on book. She begins to read, slowly, with difficulty*) "The mine is dark . . . If a light come in the mine . . . the rivers in the mine will run fast with the voice of many women; the walls will fall in, and it will be the end of the world."
(MISS RONBERRY *is listening, enquiringly.* MORGAN *enters brusquely. He has made no attempt to wash, but now that he is alone he half-emerges as a truculent, arresting boy with, latent in him, a very strong personality which his immaturity and natural inclination make him shy to display.*)

MORGAN. We put up the bell, Miss.

MISS RONBERRY. Shhh—the garden . . . (MORGAN *moves sulkily towards the door*) Do go on . . .

MISS MOFFAT (*reading*). ". . . So the mine is dark. . . . But when I walk through the Tan—something—shaft, in the dark, I can touch with my hands the leaves on the trees, and underneath . . . where the corn is green." (*Looks at* MORGAN.)

MORGAN. Go on readin'.

MISS MOFFAT (*reading*). ". . . There is a wind in the shaft, not carbon monoxide they talk about, it smell like the sea, only like as if the sea had fresh flowers lying about . . . and that is my holiday." (*She looks at the name on book.* MORGAN *starts off, turns quickly as she speaks*) Are you Morgan Evans?

MORGAN. Yes, Miss.

MISS MOFFAT. Did you write this?

MORGAN (*after hesitation, sullenly*). No, Miss.

MISS MOFFAT. But it's in your book.

MORGAN. Yes, Miss.

MISS MOFFAT. Then who wrote it?

MORGAN. I dunno, Miss.
(MISS MOFFAT *nods to* MISS RONBERRY, *who patters discreetly into the study, closes door.*)

MISS MOFFAT. Did you write this? (*It is difficult to tell from the crisp severity of her manner that she is experiencing a growing inward excitement.* MORGAN *looks at her, distrustfully.*)

MORGAN. I dunno, Miss. . . . What iss the matter with it?

MISS MOFFAT. Sit down. (*He sits*) And take your cap off. (*He takes off his cap*) Spelling's deplorable, of course. "Mine" with two "n's," and "leaves" l, e, f, s.

MORGAN. What wass it by rights?

MISS MOFFAT. A "v," to start with.

MORGAN. I never 'eard o' no "v's," Miss.

MISS MOFFAT. Don't call me Miss.

MORGAN. Are you not a Miss?

MISS MOFFAT. Yes, I am, but it is not polite.

MORGAN. Oh.

MISS MOFFAT. You say "Yes, Miss Moffat," or "No, Miss Moffat." M, o, double f, a, t.

MORGAN. No "v's"?

MISS MOFFAT. No "v's." Where do you live?

MORGAN. Under the ground, Miss.

MISS MOFFAT. I mean your home.

MORGAN. Llyn-y-Mwyn, Miss . . . Moffat. Four miles from 'ere.

MISS MOFFAT. How big is it?

MORGAN. Four 'ouses and a beer-'ouse.

MISS MOFFAT. Have you any hobbies?

MORGAN. Oh, yes.

MISS MOFFAT. What?

MORGAN. Rum. (*He takes a small bottle of rum out of his pocket.*)

MISS MOFFAT. Rum? Do you live with your parents?

MORGAN. No, by my own self. My mother iss dead, and my father and my four big brothers wass in the Big Shaft Accident when I wass ten.

MISS MOFFAT. Killed?

MORGAN. Oh, yes, everybody wass.

MISS MOFFAT. What sort of man was your father?

MORGAN. 'E was a mongrel.

MISS MOFFAT. A what?

MORGAN. 'E had a dash of English. 'E learned it to me.

MISS MOFFAT. D'you go to chapel?

MORGAN. No, thank you.

MISS MOFFAT. Who taught you to read and write?

MORGAN. Tott?

MISS MOFFAT. Taught. The verb "to teach."

MORGAN. Oh, teached.

MISS MOFFAT. Who taught you?

MORGAN. I did.

MISS MOFFAT. Why?

MORGAN. I dunno.

MISS MOFFAT. What books have you read?

MORGAN. Books? A bit of the Bible and a book that a feller from the Plas kitchen nab for me.

MISS MOFFAT. What was it?

MORGAN. *The Ladies' Companion!* (MISS MOFFAT *rises and walks thoughtfully towards her desk, studying him. He sits uncomfortably, twirling his cap between his fingers*) Can I go now, pliss . . .

MISS MOFFAT. No. (MORGAN *sits, taken aback*). Do you want to learn any more?

MORGAN. No, thank you.

MISS MOFFAT. Why not?

MORGAN. The other men would have a good laugh.

MISS MOFFAT. I see. Have you ever written anything before this exercise?

MORGAN. No.

MISS MOFFAT. Why not?

MORGAN. Nobody never ask me to. What iss the matter with it?

MISS MOFFAT. Nothing's the matter with it. Whether it means anything is too early for me to say, but it shows exceptional talent for a boy in your circumstances.

MORGAN (*blinking and hesitating*). Terrible long words, Miss Moffat.

MISS MOFFAT. This shows that you are very clever.

(*A pause. He looks up slowly, not sure if he has heard aright, looks at her searchingly, then away again. His mind is working uncertainly, but swiftly.*)

MORGAN. Oh.

MISS MOFFAT. Have you ever been told that before?

MORGAN. It iss news to me.

MISS MOFFAT. What effect does the news have on you?

MORGAN. It iss a bit sudden. It makes me that I . . . (*Hesitating, then plunging*) I want to get more clever still. I want to know what iss—behind of all them books. . . .

MISS MOFFAT. Miss Ronberry . . . (*To him*) Can you come tomorrow?

MORGAN (*taken by surprise*). Tomorrow—no—I'm workin' on the six-till-four shift.

MISS MOFFAT. Then can you be here at five?

MORGAN. Five—no, not before seven, Miss—six miles to walk . . .

MISS MOFFAT. Oh, yes, of course—seven then. In the meantime I'll correct this for spelling and grammar.

MORGAN (*staring at her, fascinated*). Yes, Miss Moffat.

MISS MOFFAT. That will be all. Good night.

MORGAN. Good night, Miss Moffat.

MISS MOFFAT. Are you the one I spanked? (*He turns at the door, looks at her, smiles, blinks and goes)* Miss Ronberry! Mr. Jones! (MISS RONBERRY *runs in from the study.)*

MISS RONBERRY. Yes?

MISS MOFFAT. I have been a deuce of a fool. It doesn't matter about the barn; we are going to start the school, in a small way at first, in this room. . . . And I am going to get those youngsters out of that mine if I have to black my face and go down and fetch them myself! Get Jonesy before he posts those letters, and tell those others I'll be ready for them in five minutes. We are going on with the school! (MISS RONBERRY *scampers into the study, rather dazed. Her voice is heard, calling: "We are going on with the school!" The door shuts behind her.* MISS MOFFAT *reads from the exercise book)* ". . . and when I walk—in the dark . . . I can touch with my hands . . . where the corn is green. . . ." *(The school bell rings.)*

CURTAIN

ACT TWO

SCENE I

An early evening in August, two years later; the sun is still bright.

The room is now a complete jumble of living room and schoolroom, and there is every sign of cheerful overcrowding. The table in the window recess is replaced by a double school desk; the table and its small chair are pushed behind the sofa; a school desk stands isolated between the big open-top desk and the sofa; between the sofa and the bay window, two rows of four school desks each, squeezed together and facing the audience at an angle. Charts, maps, an alphabet list are pinned up higgledy-piggledy over all the books; a large world globe on the shelf; hat-pegs have been fixed irregularly back of right door above and below kitchen door. Books overflow everywhere, all over the dresser especially, in place of plates; the hat-pegs are loaded with caps and hats; MISS MOFFAT'S *cloak hangs on a hook on the back of the front door; a blackboard lies on the sofa upside down, with "Constantinople is the capital of Turkey" written across in* MISS RONBERRY'S *tremulous handwriting. The lamp on the table has been removed. Potted plants on the window sills.*

Before the curtain rises, voices are heard singing, in harmony, in Welsh, "Bugeilio'r Gwenyth Gwyn"; children, shrill, sweet and self-confident, reinforced by harmony from older boys and parents, especially SARAH.

The room seems full of people; MISS RONBERRY *stands perched on the tiny stool between the sofa and the foot of the stairs, her back to the audience, conducting stiffly;* MR. JONES *is crouched in the desk chair, correcting exercises at the open desk.* SARAH, *two older peasant women in shawls, and three older men in their shabby best stand crowded behind the eight desks and in the window recess. In the front row of desks sit* ROBBART, IDWALL, *a little girl, and* GLYN THOMAS; *in the second sit another little boy, another little girl,* BESSIE *and* WILL HUGHES. *At another desk pushed provisionally next the front row sits* JOHN OWEN, *and at the other isolated one sits* OLD TOM, *an elderly distinguished-looking peasant, his cap and stick before him, carried away by the music. A young girl sits at table.*

BESSIE *is silent, bored, and prettier than ever, though still dressed as a sober little schoolgirl. The boys we saw before as miners are clean and almost spruce; the parents follow every movement of* MISS RONBERRY'S *with avid curiosity. The pupils have slates and slate pencils in front of them.*

The song is sung through to the end.

MISS RONBERRY. Now that was quite better. Full of splendid feeling, and nice and precise as well. Have you all got my English translation? (*She climbs down from her stool.*)

THE PUPILS. Yes, Miss Ronberry.

MISS RONBERRY. Are you all quite sure of the meaning of "Thou lovedest him, fair maid, that doth not love thee back?"
(*Four older people follow with motion of lips.*)

THE PUPILS. Yes, Miss Ronberry.
(*Four people speak the line after the others have said it.*)

OLD TOM (*singing stentoriously, in broken English*). "That doth not luff thee . . . ba-a-ck!"

MISS RONBERRY. Capital, Mr. Tom. (*She takes a small handbell from a hook beneath the stairs, rings it vigorously, and hangs it up again; nobody moves*) Home sweet home, children! Boys and girls, come out to play!
(MISS PUGH *nudges* IDWAL.)

IDWAL. Please, Miss Ronberry, can we have some more?

MISS RONBERRY. Well, just the tiniest lesson. We must keep to the curriculum. (*Steps upon stool again*) Now what would you like?

IDWAL. Please, Miss Ronberry, how do you spell it?

MISS RONBERRY. What, dear?

OLD TOM. Curriculum!

MISS RONBERRY. What would you like? The rivers of Europe or King Alfred and the cakes?

OLD TOM. Multiplication table!
(*Some say "Yes." Others repeat "multiplications."*)

MISS RONBERRY. Well, twice six are twelve!
(*One old man does not recite. He smiles.*)

THE PUPILS. Twice seven are fourteen—twice eight are sixteen—
(*They complete the table.*)

OLD TOM. Twice thirteen are twenty-six!

MISS RONBERRY. Capital—school dismiss!

(IDWAL *crosses front of desk to window. All rise except* BESSIE.)

GLYN THOMAS. Be'di'r gloch, Merry?

1ST GIRL. Chwarter i bump.

A MOTHER. What iss the next thing in the multiplication?

A BOY. Wn i ddim yn wyr—gofyn iddi— (*Rises.*)

A MOTHER. Why issn't there any geography now?

SARAH PUGH. Friday geography, Thursday today . . .

AN OLD LADY. Pnawn dydd Iau, te, hanner awr wedi tri—

IDWAL. Dyma'r fistress!
(MISS MOFFAT *walks in from the garden. All rise but* BESSIE. *She is more alert and businesslike than ever. She is studying an exercise book. She goes into the kitchen.*)

SARAH PUGH. Miss Moffat.

A YOUNG FATHER. Oh, yes.

SARAH PUGH.
Mi ddylaswn fod yn pobi heddyw—
A dwidi gadal y cig yn y popdy—

A MOTHER. Mi fydd eich cegin chi ar dan, Mrs. Pugh—

IDWAL. 'Nhad, gai fynd i chwara yn nghae John Davies—

A FATHER. (*Answering him*) Ddim heddyw—dwisho ti gartre—

1ST GIRL. Yforty d'wi am drio sgwennu llythyr—(*Crossing to* 2ND GIRL.)

2ND GIRL. Os gynnachi steel-pen golew?

WILL HUGHES. Mae'na gymaint o flots!

3RD GIRL. Dwi wedi sgwennu llythyr at fy nain, wni ddim be didi'thi.

WILL HUGHES. Welsochi 'rioed eiriau fel one?

SARAH PUGH. Fedri'thi ddim canu fel Cymraes, digon siwr—

ROBBART ROBBATCH. Mae'r hen ddyn am ofyn rwbeth iddi eto—drychwch arno—

SARAH PUGH.
Mi gollith'o ei Gymraeg cyn bo hir—
Idwal, what you looking so sorry—always wanting to know something—

3RD GIRL.
Mae genni just ddigon o amswer i gyrraedd at y llyn—
Mae'r dwr yn rhy oer i ymdrochi—

SARAH PUGH.
Nag ydi—mae'r haul wedi bod yn rhy boeth heddyw—
(*The crowd finally trickle out, shepherded by* MISS RONBERRY. *Besides* BESSIE, *there are left* OLD TOM, *studying,* MISS RONBERRY *and* IDWAL.)

IDWAL. Miss Ronberry, please, what is four times fourteen?

MISS RONBERRY. Thank you so much for the flowers, Idwal, dear.

IDWAL. Yes, Miss Ronberry. (*He follows the others; leaves door open.*)

MISS RONBERRY. Is there anything you would like to know, Mr. Tom?

OLD TOM. Where iss Shakespeare?

MISS RONBERRY. Where? Shakespeare, Mr. Tom, was a very great writer.

OLD TOM. Writer? Like the Beibl?

MISS RONBERRY. Like the Bible.

OLD TOM. Dear me, and me thinkin' the man was a place. (*Following the others, muttering sadly*) If I iss been born fifty years later, I iss been top of the class.

MISS RONBERRY. Oh, dear . . . (*Tidying the desks.* BESSIE *crawls over seats to small desk*) Miss Moffat has been doing grammar with Form Two under the pear tree for an hour, she must be dead. . . . Why did you not get up when she crossed? (*She takes a pumice stone from a drawer.*)

BESSIE. My foot went to sleep. (*Her manner is more impudent than ever.*)

MISS RONBERRY. That, dear, is a naughty fib.

BESSIE (*sits*). If you want to know, Miss Ronberry, I feel quite faint sometimes, as if my heart'd stopped and the world was coming to an end.

MISS RONBERRY (*with guileless solicitude*). Bessie, dear, how *horrid!*

MR. JONES. It may be in the nature of a premonition.

MISS RONBERRY. A what?

MR. JONES. I had a premonition once. Like a wave of the ocean breakin' on a sea shell. Something had said to me that mornin': "Walk, and think, and keep off the food, for thirteen hours." So I ordered my supper, and I went. Towards the end of the day (MISS MOFFAT *enters from kitchen*) I was sittin' on a stile in a cloak of meditation; and a voice roared at me: "John Goronwy Jones, tomorrow morning is the end of the world!"

MISS MOFFAT. And was it?

MR. JONES (*sadly*). It was eight years ago. It was a splendid experience.

MISS MOFFAT. Which proves how much the gift of prophecy can owe to an empty stomach. . . . Anybody seen a Greek book? (*Picking up a tiny volume*) Here it is . . . (*Starting toward stairs.*)

MISS RONBERRY. Greek, Miss Moffat?

MISS MOFFAT. Morgan Evans is starting Greek this month.

MISS RONBERRY. No! I didn't know you knew Greek?

MISS MOFFAT. I don't; I've just got to keep one day ahead of him and trust to luck. (*She disappears into her bedroom.*)

MISS RONBERRY. To think that two years ago he hardly knew English!

BESSIE. Stuck-up teacher's pet.

MISS RONBERRY. You must not think that, dear, Miss Moffat says he is clever.

BESSIE. He always looks right through me, so I don't know, I'm sure. Stuck-up teacher's pet. . . . I got some scent on my hands, Mr. Jones, like to smell them?

MR. JONES. No, thank you, Bessie, I can smell them from here, thank you.

BESSIE (*sniffing her hands, softly*). Ooh, it's lovely. . . .

MISS RONBERRY. She has some wonderful plans for him—I can tell by her manner. I think she is trying to send him to one of those Church schools so that he can get a curateship. Would not that be exciting?

BESSIE (*indolently*). I think she's ridin' for a fall.
(JONES *turns, looks, and goes back to his work.*)

MISS RONBERRY. Bessie! Why?

BESSIE. All this orderin' 'im about. I've got eyes in my head, if she hasn't, and he's gettin' sick of it. I think a lady ought to be dainty. She's no idea.
(MISS MOFFAT *appears at the top of the stairs.*)

MISS MOFFAT. Evans! (*A pause,* MORGAN *comes in from the study. He is now seventeen. He is dressed in a shabby country suit, and is at the moment the submissive schoolboy, very different from the first act. He carries a sheet of writing and a pen.* MISS MOFFAT'S *attitude to him seems purely impersonal. The others watch them*) Finished?

MORGAN. Yes, Miss Moffat.
(MISS RONBERRY *rubs ink off her hands with pumice stone.*)

MISS MOFFAT. How many pages?

MORGAN. Nine.

MISS MOFFAT. Three too many. Boil down to six. Have you got those lines of Voltaire?

MORGAN. Yes, Miss Moffat.

MISS MOFFAT. It's just five—have your walk now, good and brisk. . . .
(MORGAN, *taking his cap from a peg, starts for the front door.*)

MORGAN. Yes, Miss Moffat. (*Stops.*)

MISS MOFFAT. But kill two birds and get the Voltaire by heart. If you can ever argue a point like that, you'll do. Back in twenty minutes—and take your pen from behind your ear. (*She disappears into her bedroom. Her manner is too matter of fact to be unkind, but* MORGAN *is not taking it well. He throws his pen on to a desk.*)

BESSIE. Now turn a somersault and beg. (*He looks at her with contempt. She returns his stare brazenly. She turns to see if the others are noticing.* MISS RONBERRY *is busy with her pumice stone and* MR. JONES *is engrossed in his work.* BESSIE *looks away from them all, suddenly soft and mysterious*) Can you smell scent?

MORGAN. Yes.

BESSIE (*dreamily*). Nice, isn't it?

MORGAN. I don't know, I never come across scent before. (*Correcting himself unwillingly*) I did never come across—scent before. . . .

BESSIE. Bright, aren't you? Don't you ever get tired of lessons? (JONES *looks in disapproval. She begins to sing "With His Bell Bottom Trousers." He goes to the front door, turns, then goes, banging the door. She flings down her slate*) There we go. And my mummy ought to be back soon, and then we'll know somethin'.

MR. JONES. What is the matter? Where has she gone?

BESSIE. One of her prayer meetings. Twenty miles to shake a tambourine in the open air. I think it's wicked. . . . She ought to be just in time, and then we'll know.

MR. JONES. Know what?

BESSIE. About that horrid Morgan Evans. It's been lessons every night with teacher, hasn't it, since we left the mine? And long walks in between, to blow the cobwebs away? But the last week or two we've been breaking our journey, so we've heard.

MR. JONES. How do you mean?

BESSIE. A glass of rum next door at the Gwesmor Arms and then another, and then another!

MR. JONES (*perturbed*). Oh. . . . Whoever told you that?

BESSIE. A little bird. And if my mummy's sciatica's better she's going to jump up and look over the frosty part, and then we'll *know.* (MRS. WATTY *hurries in through the front door, in high spirits. She wears an ill-fitting Militant Righteousness Corps uniform, and carries an umbrella and a brown-paper parcel.*)

MRS. WATTY. Guess what's 'appened to me!

BESSIE. What?

MRS. WATTY. I'm a Sergeant-Major! (MISS MOFFAT *has come out on to the landing; her hair is down and she is brushing it.*)

MISS MOFFAT. Watty, you're not! (JONES *turns to* MISS MOFFAT.)

MRS. WATTY. Oh, ma'am, I didn't see you . . .

MISS MOFFAT. Tell me more!

MRS. WATTY. You remember Sergeant-Major 'Opkins desertin' in Cardiff and marryin' a sailor?

MISS MOFFAT. Yes?

MRS. WATTY. Well, last week, not two months after she give up the Corpse, she was dead!

MISS MOFFAT. And you've stepped into her shoes?

MRS. WATTY. They're a bit on the big side; but I can put a bit of paper in. The uniform fits lovely, though. I'll get you a cup o' tea and an egg, ma'am, you never 'ad that cold meat, ma'am, I'll be bound?

MISS MOFFAT. Folk eat too much anyway. (*She goes back into her bedroom.*)

BESSIE. Did you jump?

MRS. WATTY (*coming back into the room*). Just caught 'im. (*To* MR. JONES, *sorrowfully*) He was 'avin' a good drink, sir. . . . (*To* BESSIE) Don't you dare tell *'er*, you little dollymop, or I'll rattle your bones. . . .

(MISS MOFFAT *reappears and comes downstairs.*)

MISS MOFFAT. Was it a nice service, Watty?

MRS. WATTY. Beautiful, ma'am. They said they 'oped the late Sergeant-Major was gone where we all want to go, but with 'er having deserted they couldn't be sure. Then we saved three sinners. You ought to been there. . . . And the collection! (*Starts for kitchen*) I 'adn't seed so much oof since the Great Liverpool Exhibition.

MISS RONBERRY. But they didn't make a collection at the Liverpool Exhibition, did they?

MRS. WATTY. No, but I did.

(MR. JONES *takes blackboard to settle.* MISS RONBERRY *gets book from dresser.* MRS. WATTY *goes to kitchen.*)

BESSIE. Please, Miss Moffat, can I have the money for my ticket?

(MR. JONES *draws diagram on blackboard.*)

MISS MOFFAT. What ticket?

BESSIE. For Tregarnar Fair tomorrow. You said I could go.

MISS MOFFAT. On the contrary, I said you couldn't. Not in school hours.

MISS RONBERRY. Are you feeling better, dear?

BESSIE. No, Miss Ronberry. It's all this sittin' down. It's been going on for two years now. I heard tell it ends in everythin' rottin' away.

MISS MOFFAT (*sitting at desk*). What's rotting away?

MISS RONBERRY. Bessie says she's been sitting down for two years.

MISS MOFFAT. She's lucky. My feet feel as if I've been standing for the same length of time. What are these, Ron?

MISS RONBERRY. Two more accounts, I fear.

MISS MOFFAT. Oh, yes. The Liddell and Scott and Evans's new suit. Tch . . . (*Cheerfully*) I shall have to sell out a couple more shares, I expect.

MISS RONBERRY. Oh, dear.

MISS MOFFAT. Not at all. It's easy to squander money, and it's easy to hoard it. The most difficult thing in the world is to use it. And if I've learned to use it, I've *done* something. That's better. . . . My plans are laid, Ron, my dear, my plans are laid! But don't ask me what I'm hatching, because I can't tell you till tomorrow.

MISS RONBERRY. You are wonderful!

MISS MOFFAT. Go to Halifax. (MISS RONBERRY *sits on couch and studies from book*) I'm enjoying myself. (*Huge sigh from* BESSIE) Bessie Watty, what is this dying-duck business?

BESSIE. Yes, Miss Moffat.

MISS MOFFAT. Don't "yes, Miss Moffat" me. Explain yourself.

BESSIE. My mummy said all these lessons is bad for my inside.

MISS MOFFAT. She told me they stop you eating sweets, but perhaps I am telling the lie.

BESSIE. Yes, Miss Moffat.

MISS MOFFAT. What's the matter with your inside?

BESSIE. It goes round and round through sittin' down. P'r'aps what I want is a change.

MISS MOFFAT (*muttering*). "Adelphos, a brother" . . . There is nothing to prevent you going for walks between lessons. You can go for one now, as far as Sarah Pugh Postman, to see if my new chalks have arrived. (*Looking at* BESSIE, *as the latter stares before her without moving*) Quick march.

BESSIE. I'm not goin'.

MISS MOFFAT. What did you say?

BESSIE. I'm not goin'. Everybody's against me. . . . I'm goin' to throw myself off of a cliff, an' kill myself. . . . It'll make a nice case in the papers, me in pieces at the bottom of a cliff! I'm goin' mad, mad, and I'm goin' to kill myself, nothin' goin' to stop me—stone dead at the bottom of a cliff—ah—ah—ah . . .

(MRS. WATTY *strides in from the kitchen with a cupful of cold water which she throws into her daughter's face.*)

MRS. WATTY (*to* MISS MOFFAT). I made a mess o' your rug, ma'am, but it's worth it. She's got bad blood, this girl, mark my word.

MISS RONBERRY. She'll catch her death!

MRS. WATTY. Nothing like cold water, ma'am. I learnt that with her father. 'E was foreign, you know. (*She goes back into the kitchen.* MISS MOFFAT *studies* BESSIE *with distaste.*)

MISS MOFFAT. And how do you feel after that?

BESSIE. I can't remember anything. I'm in a comma.

MISS MOFFAT (*taking her by the arm, starts pushing her upstairs*). We'll sit on our bed for an hour with the door locked, shall we, and *try* to remember? And next week you go away into service and see how we like that. . . . (*She pushes her out of sight into the passage; a door bangs; the noise of a lock turning.* MISS MOFFAT *comes downstairs, tucking the key into her petticoat pocket*) I must count her as one of my failures. Fish out of water, of course. Guttersnipe species—if there is such a fish. She'll be more at home in service. . . . (*Muttering*) "Dendron, a tree—"

MISS RONBERRY. I beg your pardon . . . ? Oh, Miss Moffat, I am bursting with curiosity—your plans for Morgan Evans—is it a curateship?

MISS MOFFAT (*slowly, amused*). No, it isn't a curateship. (*She laughs happily, walks towards the desk and takes up an exercise book.*)

MISS RONBERRY. I really don't see anything funny about curates. (*To* MR. JONES) I mean, there is nothing *wrong* with curates, is there?

MR. JONES. No, except that they ought to go to chapel.

MISS MOFFAT. Who has been writing in here?
(MRS. WATTY *appears at the kitchen door.*)

MRS. WATTY. Your egg, ma'am!

MISS MOFFAT. "Bessie Watty has the face of an angel!"
(JONES *takes hat from peg, goes to door.*)

MISS RONBERRY. What an extraordinary . . .

MISS MOFFAT. But I know the writing. John Goronwy Jones, I'm ashamed of you.

MR. JONES. I shall see you tomorrow if we are spared.

MISS RONBERRY (*shocked*). Oh!

MR. JONES. You all misjudge that little girl. She has the face of a good woman in the melting pot.

MISS MOFFAT. I've got the face of a good woman, too, and well out of the melting pot, but I don't think I'd ever find it in writing. (*She goes into the kitchen.*)

MRS. WATTY. I never thought I'd live to call *you* a naughty old man. (*She follows* MISS MOFFAT *into the kitchen.* MR. JONES *goes out through the front door.* MISS RONBERRY *gets her hat and shawl and crosses to small mirror in bookcase. The front door opens abruptly and* MORGAN *appears. He is dishevelled, and it is fairly apparent that he has been drinking. His manner is defiant. The door bangs behind him.*)

MISS RONBERRY. Oh, it's you, Morgan. . . . (*Back at the mirror*) Miss Moffat is having something to eat.

MORGAN. And I have been having something to drink, so we are quits.

MISS RONBERRY (*looking at him sharply, the unpleasant truth dawning on her*). I will tell her that you are back. . . .

MORGAN. I don't want to see no Miss Moffat.

MISS RONBERRY. You mean "I don't want to see Miss Moffat." The double negative. . . .

MORGAN. Now don't you start! . . . I like the double negative, it says what I want the way I like, and I am *not* goin' to stand *no* interferences from *no*body! Voltaire indeed . . . (*Crumples paper, kicks it savagely into a corner.*)

MISS RONBERRY. Morgan! I've never seen you like this before!

MORGAN. You haven't, have you? (*In a rising torrent of invective*) Well, now I come to think of it, I haven't neither, not for two years, and I'm surprised by meself, and shocked by meself! Goin' inside one o' them public houses and puttin' me nice clean boots on that dirty rail, and me dainty lady fingers on that detestable mucky counter! Pourin' poison rum down me nice clean teeth, and spittin' in a spittoon. What's come over you, Morgan Evans? You come back to your little cage, and if you comb hair and wash hands and get your grammar right and forget you was once the Middle-weight Champion of the Glasynglo Miners, we might give you a nice bit of sewin' to do . . . Where's that Bessie Watty, sendin' her mother to spy on me, I'll knock her bloody block off. . . .

MISS RONBERRY (*outraged*). Morgan Evans, *language!* Don't you dare use an expression like that to me again!

MORGAN (*facing her, leaning over couch*). I got plenty of others, thank you, and they are all comin' out. I am goin' to surprise quite a few . . .
(MISS MOFFAT *enters from the kitchen.*)

MISS MOFFAT. Have a good walk, Evans?

MORGAN. Yes, Miss Moffat.

MISS MOFFAT. Can you repeat the Voltaire? (*Sitting on the sofa, drinking milk.*)

MORGAN. Not yet.

MISS MOFFAT. It's very short.

MORGAN. Paper blowed away.

MISS MOFFAT. Oh. Copy it again, will you, and bring it to me.

MORGAN (*muttering*). Yes, Miss Moffat.

MISS MOFFAT (*holding out the jug*). Would you like a drink? (MORGAN *stops.*)

MORGAN. No, thank you. (*He goes into the study.*)

MISS MOFFAT. I hope he's not going to be slow at French. It'll make the Greek so much more difficult. . . .

MISS RONBERRY. You don't think perhaps all this—in his situation—is rather sudden for him? I mean . . .

MISS MOFFAT. Not for him, my dear. He has the most brilliantly receptive brain I've ever come across. Don't tell him so, but he has.

MISS RONBERRY. I know his *brain* is all right. . . .

MISS MOFFAT. I'm very pleased with his progress, on the whole. . . . (*A knock at the front door.* MISS RONBERRY *moves towards the door.* MISS MOFFAT *stops her*) Wait a minute! (*Crosses to alcove window. Peering out towards the front door*) Yes, it is. . . .

MISS RONBERRY. Who?

MISS MOFFAT. Royalty, the Conservatives and all the Grand Lamas rolled into one. The Squire.

MISS RONBERRY. The Squire! Oh, *my!*

MISS MOFFAT. It is indeed. Oh, my —let me have your shawl.

MISS RONBERRY. But he hasn't been here since that dreadful evening. . . .

MISS MOFFAT. I (*Going upstairs*) behaved more stupidly that night than I ever have in my life, and that's saying something. . . .

MISS RONBERRY. But why is he here now?

MISS MOFFAT. Never you mind. . . . All I can tell you is that it is to do with Morgan Evans, and that it is vital I make the right impression.

MISS RONBERRY (*as* MISS MOFFAT *runs upstairs*). What sort of impression?

MISS MOFFAT (*on last step*). Helpless and clinging, or as near as dammit . . . (*She disappears into her room, as there is a second impatient knock at the front door.*)

MISS RONBERRY. Come in!
(*The door opens and the* GROOM *appears.*)

THE GROOM (*announcing*). The Squire.
(*The* SQUIRE *follows the* GROOM, *who retires and shuts the door.*)

THE SQUIRE. Good afternoon. (*He is dressed in a summer lounge suit, and holds his hat in his hand.*)

MISS RONBERRY. Your hat, Squire . . .

THE SQUIRE. No, thank you, I am not staying.

MISS RONBERRY. Oh, dear, I do look a sketch . . .

THE SQUIRE (*looks around*). So this is the seat of learning.

MISS RONBERRY. We are always on the point of a good spring-clean. How dreadful that we have no refreshment to offer you!

THE SQUIRE. You can tell her from me that I am not here to be insulted again.

MISS RONBERRY. Oh, I'm sure you aren't! I mean . . .

THE SQUIRE. She called me an addle-headed nincompoop.
(MISS MOFFAT *comes downstairs, a lace shawl draped over her shoulder. She carries a bowl of flowers.*)

MISS MOFFAT. Miss Ronberry, dear, my roses are dying. . . . Would you pour out a little water for them, I have such a headache I don't think . . . (*Feigning surprise*) *Squire!*

THE SQUIRE. You wrote to me. Perhaps you have forgotten.

MISS MOFFAT. How could I forget! I only thought that after the overwrought fashion of my behaviour at our last meeting you must ignore my very nervous invitation. Miss Ronberry, a chair, dear, for the Squire. . . .
(*Startled,* MISS RONBERRY *takes a small chair from desk.*)

THE SQUIRE. I have not a great deal of time to spare, I fear.

MISS MOFFAT. Of course you haven't, I was just saying to Miss Ronberry, he's so busy he'll *never* be able to fit it in! Miss Ronberry, dear, would you get some water for them? (*She hands the bowl to* MISS RONBERRY, *who passes the* SQUIRE *and goes into the garden bewildered*) Tell me, Squire, how did your prize-giving fare this afternoon?

THE SQUIRE. Rather a bore, y'know.

MISS MOFFAT. I had so hoped to see you judge. I love flowers.

THE SQUIRE. It wasn't flowers. It was cows.

MISS MOFFAT. Oh. It was your speech I wanted to hear, of course; I heard you made such an amusing one at the Croquet.

THE SQUIRE. Oh, did they tell you about that? Rather a good pun, eh? (*Laughing*) Ha, ha . . . I—may I sit down?

MISS MOFFAT. Do!

THE SQUIRE. I thought Griffith, the butcher, was going to laugh his napper off.

MISS MOFFAT. Indeed . . . Do you know, Squire, that makes me rather proud?

THE SQUIRE. Proud? Why?

MISS MOFFAT. Because he would not have understood a word if his little girls hadn't learnt English at my school.

THE SQUIRE. Oh. Never thought of it like that. . . . (*As she puts her hand to her head, says "Oh"*) Headache?

MISS MOFFAT. Squire, you see before you a tired woman. We live and learn, and I have learnt how right you were that night. I have worked my fingers to the bone battering my head against a stone wall.

THE SQUIRE. But I heard you were a spiffing success.

MISS MOFFAT. Oh, no.

THE SQUIRE (*muttering*). It's fair of you to admit it, I must say.

MISS MOFFAT. You see, in one's womanly enthusiasm one forgets that the qualities vital to success in this sort of venture are completely lacking in one: intelligence, courage and authority. . . . The qualities, in short, of a man.

THE SQUIRE. Come, come, you mustn't be too hard on yourself, y'know. After all, you've meant well.

MISS MOFFAT. It's kind of you to say that.

THE SQUIRE. What about this Jones chappie?

MISS MOFFAT. He's a dear creature, but . . . I have no wish to be fulsome. I mean a man like yourself.

THE SQUIRE. I see.

MISS MOFFAT. One gets into such muddles! You'd never believe!

THE SQUIRE. Well . . . I've never been on your side, but I'm sorry to hear you've come a cropper. When are you giving it up?

MISS MOFFAT. Oh . . . That again is difficult; I have all my widow's mite, as it were, in the venture. . . .

(MORGAN *appears from the study carrying a paper. He has regained his self-control.*)

MORGAN (*stops*). Please excuse me—

MISS MOFFAT. It's all right, Evans. Have you copied it? On my desk, will you?

MORGAN. Excuse me, sir . . . Good afternoon, sir.

THE SQUIRE. Good afternoon, my boy.

MORGAN. Excuse me, sir . . . Thank you. (*He goes.*)

THE SQUIRE. Nice well-spoken lad. Relative?

MISS MOFFAT. No. A pupil. He used to be one of your miners.

THE SQUIRE. No!

MISS MOFFAT. I'm glad you thought he was a nice well-spoken lad.

THE SQUIRE. Yes . . . One of my miners, interesting . . .

MISS MOFFAT. Because he is the problem I should like your advice about.

THE SQUIRE. What's he been up to, poaching?

MISS MOFFAT. No.

THE SQUIRE. A bit o' muslin?

MISS MOFFAT (*amused*). No, no . . . There are none, anyway. . . .

THE SQUIRE (*suddenly shrewd*). What about the little Cockney filly?

MISS MOFFAT. Bessie Watty? Oh, no, I assure you—she's a schoolgirl. . . .

THE SQUIRE. I dunno, all these young people growing up together, y'know—eh?

MISS MOFFAT. I think it's good for them . . . No, there's nothing of that sort—but he's a problem just the same. And like a true woman I have to scream for help to a man. To you.

THE SQUIRE (*completely won*). Scream away, dear lady, scream away!

MISS MOFFAT. Well, he's—clever.

THE SQUIRE. Oh, is he? Good at figures, and all that? Because if he is, there's no reason why I shouldn't put him in my Mine Office, as junior office boy. What d'ye think of that?

MISS MOFFAT. No. Figures aren't his strong point.

THE SQUIRE. Thought you said he was clever.

MISS MOFFAT. To begin with, he can write.

THE SQUIRE. Oh. Well?

MISS MOFFAT. Very well.

THE SQUIRE. Then he could make fair copies. Eh?

MISS MOFFAT. No. (*Choosing her words carefully*) This boy—is quite out of the ordinary.

THE SQUIRE. Sure?

MISS MOFFAT. As sure as one of your miners would be, cutting through coal and striking a diamond without a flaw. He was born with very exceptional gifts. They must be—they ought to be given every chance.

THE SQUIRE. You mean he might turn into a literary bloke?

MISS MOFFAT. He might, yes.

THE SQUIRE. I'm blowed! How d'ye know?

MISS MOFFAT. By his work. It's very good.

THE SQUIRE. How d'ye know it's good?

MISS MOFFAT. How does one know Shakespeare's good?

THE SQUIRE. Shakespeare? What's he got to do with it?

MISS MOFFAT. He was a literary bloke.

THE SQUIRE. Ye-es. *He* was good, of course.

MISS MOFFAT. This little tenant of yours, Squire, has it in him to bring great credit to you.

THE SQUIRE. Yes, he *is* a tenant of mine, isn't he?

MISS MOFFAT. Imagine if you could say that you had known—well, say, Lord Tennyson, as a boy on your estate!

THE SQUIRE. Rather a lark, what? Though it's a bit different, y'know. Tennyson was at Cambridge. My old college.

MISS MOFFAT. Oh . . . Poor Evans. What a pity he was not born at the beginning of the eighteenth century!

THE SQUIRE. Beginning of the eighteenth century . . . . Now when was that . . . ?

MISS MOFFAT. He would have had a protector. (*Takes two books from bookcase.*)

THE SQUIRE. What against?

MISS MOFFAT. A patron. Pope, you recall, dedicated the famous "Essay on Man" to his protector. (*Crosses front of small desk.*)

THE SQUIRE. "To H. St. John Lord Bolingbroke." Mmm . . . I *have* heard of it, now I remember. . . .

MISS MOFFAT. Isn't it wonderful to think that that inscription is handed down to posterity? (*Reading from the other book*) "To the Right Honourable Earl of Southampton . . . Your Honour's in all duty, William Shakespeare."

THE SQUIRE. Oh.

MISS MOFFAT. I often think of the pride that surged in the Earl's bosom when his encouragement gave birth to the masterpiece of a poor and humble writer!

THE SQUIRE. Funny, I never thought of Shakespeare being poor, somehow.

MISS MOFFAT. Some say his father was a butcher. The Earl realised he had genius, and fostered it.

THE SQUIRE. Mmm! If this boy really is clever, it seems a pity for *me* not to do something about it, doesn't it?

MISS MOFFAT. A great pity. And I can tell you exactly how you can do something about it.

THE SQUIRE. How?

MISS MOFFAT. There's a scholarship going.

THE SQUIRE. Scholarship? Where?

MISS MOFFAT. To Oxford.

THE SQUIRE (*staggered*). Oxford?

MISS MOFFAT (*moves closer*). A scholarship to Trinity College, Oxford, open to boys of secondary education in the British Isles. My school hardly comes under the heading of secondary education, and I wrote to your brother at Magdalen; he pulled some strings for me, and they have agreed to make a special case of this boy, on one condition. That you vouch for him. Will you?

THE SQUIRE. My dear lady, you take the cake . . . Can't he be just as clever at home?

MISS MOFFAT. No, he can't. For the sort of future he ought to have, he must have polish—he has everything else. The background of a university would be invaluable to him. . . . (SQUIRE *rises*) Will you?

THE SQUIRE. Well, the 'Varsity, y'know, hang it all . . . Mind you, he'll never get it.

MISS MOFFAT. I know, but he *must* have the chance. . . .

THE SQUIRE. Still, y'know, even the mere prospect of one o' my miners . . .

MISS MOFFAT. Think of Shakespeare!

THE SQUIRE. All serene. (MISS MOFFAT *rises*) I'll drop a line to Henry next week. Rather a lark, what? I must be off . . .

MISS MOFFAT. I should be most obliged if the letter could be posted tomorrow. Would you like me to draft out a recommendation and send it over to the Hall? You must be so busy with the estate. . . .

THE SQUIRE. I am rather. Polka supper tomorrow night . . . Yes, do do that. Good-bye, dear lady!

MISS MOFFAT. Thank you so very much, Squire. . . .

THE SQUIRE. Happier conditions, and all that! Glad you've come to your senses!

MISS MOFFAT. Thank you so very much, Squire!

THE SQUIRE. Not at all, I'm all for giving a writer-fellow a helping hand. Tell my brother that, if you like . . . Good-bye—Good-bye. (*Exits.* MISS MOFFAT *closes door.* MISS RONBERRY *hurries in from the garden, carrying the bowl of roses. The afternoon sun begins to set.*)

MISS RONBERRY. Well? (*Puts vase on desk.*)

MISS MOFFAT. That man is so stupid it sits on him like a halo.

MISS RONBERRY. What happened?

MISS MOFFAT. In ten minutes I have given the Squire the impression that he spends his whole time fostering genius in the illiterate.

MISS RONBERRY. But how?

MISS MOFFAT. Soft soap and curtseying; with my brain, my heart and my soul. I've beaten you at your own game, my dear; at my age and with my looks, I flirted with him! And he is going to write to Oxford; at least, I am going to write to Oxford for him. Hallelujah.

MISS RONBERRY. Oxford?

MISS MOFFAT. I am entering my little pit-pony for a scholarship to Oxford, child, Oxford University!

MISS RONBERRY (*incredulous*). But they don't have miners at Oxford University!

MISS MOFFAT. Well, they're going to. The lad is on this earth for eighty years at the most out of a few millions; let the proud silly ones grovel and be useful for a change, so he can step up on their backs to something better! I was bursting to say that to the Lord of the Manor, so I must vent it on you . . . Thank you for your shawl, my dear—and now you've served your purpose, you can go home—but you'd better watch out, I may beat you to the altar yet. . . . (*She shuts the front door on her, and comes back into the room, gets papers, then crosses to table—moves table, moves milk jug to sideboard and sits at table. Seated before she calls*) Evans! (MORGAN *comes in from the study, carrying a pen, books and papers. His mantle of reserve has descended on him again; his inward rebellion is only to be guessed at from his eyes, which she does not see. He pulls the chair up to the table and sits opposite her. The daylight begins to wane*) Is this your essay on the Wealth of Nations?

MORGAN. Yes.

MISS MOFFAT (*reading briskly*). Say so and underline it. Nothing irritates examiners more than that sort of vagueness. (*She hands him the exercise book*) I couldn't work this sentence out.

MORGAN. "The eighteenth century was a cauldron. Vice and elegance boiled to a simmer until the kitchen of society reeked fulminously, and the smell percolated to the marble halls above." (*Hands paper back.*)

MISS MOFFAT. D'ye know what that means?

MORGAN. Yes, Miss Moffat.

MISS MOFFAT. Because I don't. Clarify, my boy, clarify, and leave the rest to Mrs. Henry Wood. . . . "Watter" with two t's . . . that's a bad lapse. . . . The Adam Smith sentence was good. Original, and clear as well. Seven out of ten, not bad, but not good—you *must* avoid long words until you know exactly what they mean. Otherwise domino. . . . Your reading?

MORGAN. Burke's "Cause of the Present Discontents."

MISS MOFFAT. Style?

MORGAN. His style appears to me . . . as if there was too much of it.

MISS MOFFAT. His style struck me as florid.

MORGAN. His style struck me as florid.

MISS MOFFAT. Again.

MORGAN. His style struck me as florid.

MISS MOFFAT. Subject matter?

MORGAN. A sound argument, falsified by—by the high color of the sentiments.

MISS MOFFAT. Mmm. "The high color of the sentiments" . . . odd but not too odd, good and stylish. . . . For next time. (*Dictating as* MORGAN *writes*) Walpole and Sheridan as representatives of their age; and no smelly cauldrons. (*Opening another book*) By the way, next Tuesday I'm starting you on Greek.

MORGAN (*looking up, feigning interest*). Oh, yes?

MISS MOFFAT (*subduing her excitement*). I am going to put you in for a scholarship to Oxford. (*He looks up at her, arrested.*)

MORGAN. Oxford? Where the lords go?

MISS MOFFAT (*amused*). The same. I've made a simplified alphabet to begin with. It's jolly interesting after Latin. . . . (*The matter-of-factness with which she is controlling her excitement over the scholarship seems to gall him more and more; he watches her, bitterly*) Have a look at it by Tuesday, so we can make a good start. Oh, and before we go on with the lesson, I've found the nail file I mentioned. . . . (MORGAN *slams a book*) I'll show you how to use it. I had them both here somewhere. . . .

MORGAN (*quietly*). I shall not need a nail file in the coal mine.

MISS MOFFAT. In the what?

MORGAN (*turns to her*). I am going back to the coal mine.

MISS MOFFAT. I don't understand you. Explain yourself.

MORGAN. I do not want to learn Greek, nor to pronounce any long English words, nor to keep my hands clean.

MISS MOFFAT (*staggered*). What's the matter with you? Why not?

MORGAN. Because . . . because (*Leans over, both hands on table*) I was born in a Welsh hayfield when my mother was helpin' with the harvest—and I always lived in a house with no stairs, only a ladder—and no water—and until my brothers was killed I never sleep except three in a bed. I know that is terrible grammar but it is true.

MISS MOFFAT. What on earth has three in a bed got to do with learning Greek?

MORGAN. It has—a lot! The last two years I have not had no proper talk with English chaps in the mine because I was so busy keepin' this old grammar in its place. Tryin' to better myself . . . Tryin' to better myself, the day and the night . . . ! You cannot take a nail file into the Gwesmor Arms public bar!

MISS MOFFAT. My dear boy, file your nails at home! I never heard anything so ridiculous. Besides, you don't go to the Gwesmor Arms!

MORGAN. Yes, I do, I have been there every afternoon for a week, spendin' your pocket money, and

I have been there now, and that is why I can speak my mind!

MISS MOFFAT. I had no idea that you felt like this.

MORGAN. Because you are not interested in me.

MISS MOFFAT. Not interested in you?

MORGAN (*losing control*). How can you be interested in a machine that you put a penny in and if nothing comes out you give it a good shake? "Evans, write me an essay; Evans, get up and bow; Evans, what is a subjunctive!" My name is Morgan Evans, and all my friends call me Morgan, and if there is anything gets on the wrong side of me it is callin' me Evans! . . . And do you know what they call me in the village? Ci bach yr ysgol! The schoolmistress's little dog! What has it got to do with you if my nails are dirty? Mind your own business! (*He buries his head in his hands.*)

MISS MOFFAT. I never meant you to know this. I have spent money on you—I don't mind that, money ought to be spent. But time is different. Your life has not yet begun, mine is half over. And when you're a middle-aged spinster, some folk say it's pretty near finished. Two years is valuable currency. I have spent two years on you. Even since that first day, the mainspring of this school has been your career. Sometimes, in the middle of the night, when I have been desperately tired, I have lain awake, making plans. Large and small. Sensible and silly. Plans, for you. And you tell me I have no interest in you. If I say any more I shall start to cry; and I haven't cried since I was younger than you are, and I'd never forgive you for that. I am going for a walk. I don't like this sort of conversation; please never mention it again. If you want to go on, be at school tomorrow. (*Going*) If not, don't.

MORGAN. I don't want your money, and I don't want your time! . . . I don't want to be thankful to no strange woman—for anything!

MISS MOFFAT. I don't understand you. I don't understand you at all. (*Taking her cloak that is hanging on door, she goes out by the front door.* MORGAN *folds his arms, takes a drink, puts bottle on the table. There is a book there. He moves book.* BESSIE *comes in from the garden. She has put her hair half up and wears earrings.*)

BESSIE. Hello! (*She clutches her leg*) Caught my knee climbin' down the rainpipe, ooh. . . . (*As he takes no notice, she crosses to kitchen door*) P'raps I'm invisible. . . . (*She marches into the kitchen, singing "Bell Bottom Trousers" and bangs the door behind her. Far away, the sound of singing: Men returning from the mine, harmonising their familiar melody, "Yr Hufen Melyn."* BESSIE *returns from the kitchen*) Mum's gone out. (*After a pause*) Expect she's gone to tell Mrs. Roberts about her meetin'. Though how she manages with Mrs. Roberts knowin' no English an' deaf as well . . . (*After a pause*) Talking a lot, aren't I?

MORGAN. Yes.

BESSIE. Well, I'm not deaf.

MORGAN. Been spyin'?

BESSIE. If people lock me in and take the key out of the keyhole, they can't blame me for listenin' at it. Ooh, I think she's wicked.

MORGAN. Mind your own business!

BESSIE. I won't. I like to know about everything; I like doin' all the things I like; I like sweets, I don't care if it does make me fat, and I *love* earrings. I like to shake my head like a lady. . . . (*The singing stops. A pause*) It's funny. . . . We never been by ourselves before. (*She begins to sing in Welsh. The tune is "Lliw Gwyn Rhosyn yr Haf"*) Didn't know I knew Welsh, did you? . . . You like that song, don't you? That's why I learnt it.

MORGAN. You are different when you sing.

BESSIE. Am I? . . . What's this, medicine? (*Picks up rum bottle, drinks. He takes bottle from her, takes a drink and puts it in his pocket*) Tastes like rubber. Nice, though. . . . You know—you was quite right to put her in her place. Clever chap like you learnin' lessons off a woman!

MORGAN. That's right. . . .

BESSIE (*soft, persuasive*). You don't 'ave to go to Oxford! Clever chap like you!

MORGAN (*in a whisper*). That's right. . . . (*He turns slowly and looks at her.*)

BESSIE. What a man wants is a bit o' sympathy!
(*He looks at her, his hand on the back of the chair. It is growing faintly darker. She laughs, and begins to sing again; she turns, still singing, looks up at him, and smiles. He pushes away the chair, seizes her with violence, and kisses her passionately. Their arms entwine and the chair crashes to the floor.*)

THE CURTAIN FALLS

SCENE II

A morning in November, three months later. The room is much as it was; the potted plants have been removed; the daylight is so poor that the lamps are lit.

MRS. WATTY *is carrying in from the kitchen a small table, new and light. On it blotter, ink, pens, pencil, a duster and a cup of tea.* MISS RONBERRY *is pushing the armchair in from the study past the sofa into its old place, next to the isolated desk.*

MRS. WATTY (*singing*). "I'm saved I am, I'm saved I am. . . ." (MRS. WATTY *moves the large table a bit, so as to get through, picks up small table, places it well downstage*) What would the armchair be for, miss?

MISS RONBERRY. The Squire's coming. He's invigilating. (*She opens desk drawer, and takes out package with sealed Oxford papers.*)

MRS. WATTY. *What* was that, please, miss?

MISS RONBERRY. The Oxford people have appointed him and Miss Moffat to watch Morgan Evans while he is sitting the scholarship, so that he cannot cheat.

MRS. WATTY. What a shame. . . . (*Still arranging furniture*) You'd never think it was nearly nine in the morning, would you?

MISS RONBERRY. It's stopped snowing.

MRS. WATTY (*peering out of the window*). Only just. The milkman said the road was blocked down by the bridge.

MISS RONBERRY. How terrible if Morgan couldn't get through!

MRS. WATTY. Countin' sheep all night, I was. (*Picking up two envelopes from the floor, near the front door*) She didn't 'ave a wink neither. I could 'ear her thinkin'.

MISS RONBERRY. It is a very important day for her.

MRS. WATTY. Looks like that one's Bessie. Would you mind?

MISS RONBERRY. That means Sarah the Post got through. . . .

MRS. WATTY. She'd come the other way, down the 'ill. . . .

MISS RONBERRY. That's true . . . (*Reading*) "Dear Mum"—to think I taught her to write—"Cheltenham is terrible. Can I have a shilling? I do the steps. Madam is terrible. Your obedient girl."

MRS. WATTY. Obedient. (*Laughs*) I like that. . . . (*Throwing the letter into the wastepaper basket*) She's been away three months now, she ought to be gettin' used to it.

MISS RONBERRY. But do you not miss her?

MRS. WATTY (*emphatically*). No! I don't like 'er, you know, never 'ave.

MISS RONBERRY. But, Mrs. Watty, your own daughter!

MRS. WATTY. I know, but I've never been able to take to 'er. First time I saw 'er, I said, "No." (*Going*) With 'er dad being foreign, you see.

MISS RONBERRY. But couldn't your husband have taken her abroad to his own family?

MRS. WATTY. Oh, my 'usband was quite different. British to the core. (*She goes into the kitchen.* MISS RONBERRY *blinks after her, and places writing pad on the little table.* MISS MOFFAT *comes slowly downstairs. She is alert, but more subdued than the audience has yet seen her.* MISS RONBERRY *takes up the cup of tea, and watches her apprehensively.*)

MISS MOFFAT. It's stopped snowing.

MISS RONBERRY. It's a white world, as they say . . . Do you think he will get through the snow?

MISS MOFFAT. This morning he would get through anything.

MISS RONBERRY. I am so glad. I thought perhaps he—he had not been working satisfactorily. . . .

MISS MOFFAT. At ten o'clock last night I had to take his books away from him.

MISS RONBERRY. I *am* glad.

MISS MOFFAT. I hope he won't get wet—he must not (*Picks up string, plays with it*) be upset in any way. What made you think he wasn't working well?

MISS RONBERRY. Nothing, only . . . you remember the night you went for that long walk, when he might be going back to the mine?

MISS MOFFAT (*after a pause*). Yes?

MISS RONBERRY. The next morning he started studying again, and yet it seemed so different.

MISS MOFFAT. How?

MISS RONBERRY. Almost strained . . . what a silly thing to say . . . I mean, as you did not say anything more about the mine . . .

MISS MOFFAT. He didn't say any more himself. He just turned up. I didn't embrace him on both cheeks, but I said "Righto." Since which time, he has never stopped working.

MISS RONBERRY. I *am* so glad . . . Oh, this arrived from the Penlan Town Hall! It must be his birth certificate. . . .

MISS MOFFAT. Good. . . . I must send it off to the President of Trinity. Rather a nervous post-mortem from him last night; two pages to ask if the youngster's legitimate. (*Opens envelope, looks at birth certificate*) Thank Heaven he is. And no conviction for drunkenness; references have been spotless. That will help, I hope.

MISS RONBERRY. Would it not be splendid if he—won!

MISS MOFFAT (*after a pause*). Not very likely, I am afraid. (*Moving about, nervously*) The syllabus rather attaches importance to general knowledge of the academic sort. His is bound to be patchy—on the exuberant side—I have had to force it; two years is not enough even for him. If he checks himself, and does not start telling them what they ought to think of Milton, with fair luck he might stand a chance. He will have some pretty strong public-school candidates against him, of course. Bound to. It depends on how much the examiners will appreciate a highly original intelligence.

MISS RONBERRY (*seated on couch*). But wouldn't it be *exciting!*

MISS MOFFAT. Yes, it would. People run down the Universities, and always will, but it would be a wonderful thing for him. It would be a wonderful thing for rural education all over the country.

MISS RONBERRY. And most of all, it would be a wonderful thing for you!

MISS MOFFAT (*almost soliloquising*). I suppose so . . . It is odd to have spent so many hours with another human being, in the closest intellectual communion—because it has been that. I know every trick and twist of that brain of his, exactly where it will falter and where it will gallop ahead of me—and yet not to know him at all. I woke up in the middle of the night thinking of Henry the Eighth. I have a feeling there may be a question about the old boy and the Papacy. (*Crosses to bookshelves. Takes book from shelf and makes notations on a piece of writing paper*) I'll cram one or two facts into him, the last minute . . . (*Suddenly, in a sob, with all the inward conviction of which she is capable*) Oh, God, he must win it . . . (MRS. WATTY *comes in from the kitchen, carrying a steaming cup of tea*) He must.

MRS. WATTY (*hands her cup of tea*). Cup a tea! Now, ma'am, don't get in a pucker! Six more Saturday mornin's like this in the next 'alf-year, (*Gets* MISS RONBERRY's *cup from table*) remember!

MISS MOFFAT. The first paper is the important one—I expect we'll get more used to the others. . . .

MISS RONBERRY. Suppose the Squire doesn't come!

MISS MOFFAT. He will. He has got to the point of looking on the lad as a racehorse.

MISS RONBERRY. You don't think the snow might deter him?

MRS. WATTY. I just seed 'is nibs' gardener clearin' a way from the gates. Shame the red carpet gettin' so wet. (MRS. WATTY *goes back into the kitchen.*)

MISS RONBERRY. Surely it is getting brighter this side . . . (*Looks out of the window*) Oh, I can see him! Morgan, I mean!

MISS MOFFAT. Can you?

MISS RONBERRY. Coming up the Nant, do you see? Ploughing through!

MISS MOFFAT. What is the time? (*Looks at her breast watch.*)

MISS RONBERRY. Ten minutes to!

MISS MOFFAT (*sitting at her desk*). He will have just two minutes . . . (*A knock at the front door*) Good. There's the Squire . . .

MISS RONBERRY (*running to the door*). He is as excited as any of us . . . (BESSIE *enters the room, followed by* MR. JONES) Bessie . . . But it cannot be you, your mother has just received . . .

BESSIE. I left the same day I posted it. (*She is shabbily dressed, in semi-grown-up fashion, and wears a cloak. Her manner is staccato, nervy and defiant.* MR. JONES *closes door, leaves* BESSIE's *bag near desk. She faces* MISS MOFFAT, *who stares at her, puzzled.*)

MISS MOFFAT. This is unexpected.

BESSIE. Isn't it just? I have been travellin' all night, quite a wreck. I woke Mr. Jones up and he got the stationmaster to drive us over in his trap, in the snow—nice, wasn't it? (*She is trying not to be frightened, and not succeeding. The conversation from now on quickens and grows more nervous.*)

MISS MOFFAT. You have arrived at an inconvenient time.

(MISS RONBERRY *crosses Left above table.*)

BESSIE. Fancy.

MISS MOFFAT. Have you come to see your mother?

BESSIE. No. (*She plucks up courage and sits suddenly in the arm-chair.* MISS MOFFAT *frowns and rises.*)

MISS MOFFAT. Then why are you here?

BESSIE. Questions and answers, just like school again!

MISS MOFFAT. Why have you brought this girl here this morning?

MR. JONES. I did not bring her, Miss Moffat, she brought me. . . .

MISS MOFFAT. Whom have you come to see?

BESSIE. You.

MISS MOFFAT. Me? (BESSIE *does not speak*) I can give exactly one minute of my time. (*Pause*) Is it money? (*As* BESSIE *does not answer, impatiently to the others*) Will you wait in the study? (MR. JONES *follows* MISS RONBERRY *into the study*) One minute. . . . Quickly!

BESSIE. Why?

MISS MOFFAT. Morgan Evans is sitting for his Oxford examination here this morning.

BESSIE. Well, 'e needn't.

MISS MOFFAT. What do you mean?

BESSIE. Because he won't ever be goin' to Oxford.

MISS MOFFAT. Why not?

BESSIE. Because there's goin' to be a little stranger. (*A pause*) I'm going to have a little stranger. (*She begins to whimper into her handkerchief, half acting, half nerves and excitement.* MISS MOFFAT *stares at her.*)

MISS MOFFAT. You're lying.

BESSIE. Doctor Brett, The Firs, Cheltenham . . . And if you don't believe it's Morgan Evans, you ask 'im about that night you locked me up—the night you had the words with him!

MISS MOFFAT. I see . . . (*With a sudden cry*) Why couldn't I have seen before! (*Her eyes rest on the examination table. She collects herself, desperately*) Does he know?

BESSSIE. I've come to tell 'im! I was ever so upset, of course, and now I've lost me place. Oh, she was artful. He'll have to marry me, or I'll show him up, 'cause I must give the little stranger a name. . . .

MISS MOFFAT (*exasperated beyond endurance*). Stop saying "little stranger"! If you must have a baby, then call it a baby! . . . Have you told anybody?

BESSIE. Mr. Jones, that's all. . . .

MISS RONBERRY (*peering timidly through the study door*). The Squire is coming up the road! (*She goes back into the study.*)

BESSIE. I'll wait here for him.

MISS MOFFAT. For the next three hours, he must not be disturbed. You are not going to see him . . .

BESSIE. You can't bully me, the way I am! (*Rising, and facing her across the examination table, the resentment of two years pouring out, real hysteria this time*) 'Asn't sunk in yet, 'as it? I'm teaching *you* something, am I? You didn't know things like that went on, did you? Why? You couldn't see what was goin' on under your nose, 'cause you're too busy managin' everythin'! Well, you can't manage him any longer, 'cause he's got to manage me now, the way I am, he's got to—
(MR. JONES *pokes his head round the study door; he is in a state of panic.* MISS RONBERRY *hovers behind him.*)

MR. JONES. Morgan Evans has turned the corner up the hill . . .

MISS RONBERRY. So there isn't much time!
(MR. JONES *follows* MISS RONBERRY *back into the study.*)

MISS MOFFAT. I'm afraid I am going to do a little managing now. You are going into the kitchen, where your mother will make you breakfast; you will then lie down, and as soon as this session is finished we will go upstairs and talk it all over when we are a little calmer.
(*A knock at the front door.*)

BESSIE. He's here! I got to see him!
(BESSIE *starts up.* MISS MOFFAT *detains her.*)

MISS MOFFAT. If you try and disobey me, I shall not answer for the consequences. (*Holds her wrist.*)

BESSIE (*cowed*). You wouldn't dare lay a finger on me . . .

MISS MOFFAT. Oh, yes, I would. If you attempt to stay in this room, or to blab to anybody about this before we have had that talk—even your mother . . . I am in a pretty nervous state myself, this morning, and I shall strike you so hard that I shall probably kill you. . . . I mean every word of that.
(*Another knock, more impatient. She quells* BESSIE *with her look; crosses and holds open the kitchen door.*)

BESSIE (*laughs*). I don't mind. Three hours'll go soon enough.
(*She goes into the kitchen.* MISS MOFFAT *shuts the door after her, straightens herself, and opens the front door. The* SQUIRE *enters, in Inverness cape and hat, stamping the snow from his boots; he carries several periodicals, chiefly sporting and dramatic. The rest of the scene is played very quickly.*)

MISS MOFFAT (*takes his coat and hat*). So very sorry—how kind of you—such a dreadful day . . .
(*Hangs* SQUIRE's *coat on door.*)

THE SQUIRE. Not at all, Mistress Pedagogue, anything for a lark. . . . Glad it isn't me, what . . . ? I've got a spiffy bit of news for you.

MISS MOFFAT. Yes?

THE SQUIRE. I've bought the barn from Sir Herbert, and we can move the whole shoot next door by March. What d'ye think?

MISS MOFFAT. Wonderful . . .

THE SQUIRE. We can knock a door straight through here to the barn—aren't ye pleased about it?

MISS MOFFAT (*going to the desk, hardly aware of what she is doing, as* MISS RONBERRY *runs in from the study*). Yes, but you know, this examination, (*Knock at front door*) rather worrying . . .

MISS RONBERRY. Good morning, Squire! Terrible weather . . .

THE SQUIRE. Beastly—
(MISS RONBERRY *opens the front door and lets* MORGAN *in. She closes the door before she takes his overcoat, cap and muffler. He has been hurrying, but he is quiet and calm.*)

MISS MOFFAT. Wet?

MORGAN. No, thank you. Good day, sir . . .

MISS RONBERRY. Let me take your things . . .

MORGAN. Thank you . . .

MISS MOFFAT. Before I open the papers, I have a feeling they may bring up Henry the Eighth. Memorize these two facts, will you? (*Hands him a paper.*)

MISS RONBERRY (*puts down a sprig of white heather*). White heather—just a thought! (*She runs into the study.*)

MORGAN. Thank you . . .

THE SQUIRE. Good luck, my boy.

MORGAN. Thank you, sir . . .

THE SQUIRE. Glad it isn't me!
(MORGAN *hands her the paper.*)

MR. JONES (*pops his head round the study door*). Pob llwyddiant, ymachgeni!

MORGAN. Diolch—
(MISS MOFFAT *throws paper in the basket.* MR. JONES *goes back into the study.* MORGAN *sits at the table.*)

MISS MOFFAT. Name and particulars, to save time. And don't get exuberant.

MORGAN. No.

MISS MOFFAT. Or illegible.

MORGAN. No.
(*Pause.*)

THE SQUIRE. But aren't *you* going to wish my little protégé good fortune?

MISS MOFFAT (*after a pause, to* MORGAN). Good luck.

MORGAN. Thank you.
(*The clock begins to strike nine.*)

MISS MOFFAT. Ready? (MORGAN *nods. She cuts the envelope and places the examination paper in front of him. She looks at the duplicate paper of questions, smiles*) Henry the Eighth! (*She sits in the armchair. The* SQUIRE *embarks on his periodical.* MORGAN *begins to write.* MISS MOFFAT *raises her head, looks anxiously towards the kitchen, then steadfastly at* MORGAN, *her lip trembling. A pause. The only sound is the scratch of a pen.*)

THE CURTAIN FALLS SLOWLY

ACT THREE

SCENE—*An afternoon in July. Seven months later.*

The school has been moved next door, and the room is much less crowded; the small table is back in the window recess, the armchair is in its old position; the large table, however, is no longer behind the sofa with its chair, its place being taken by three small school desks facing the front door; between the front door and the bay window a blackboard on its easel faces the audience at an angle, with "Elizabeth, known as Good Q. Bess" written on it in block letters.

MR. JONES *stands in command beside the blackboard. In two of the school desks sit* IDWAL *and* ROBBART, *each poring over his slate. On the settle sit the* SQUIRE, *downstage, his arms folded like a pupil, his eyes fixed on* MR. JONES, *and next to him* OLD TOM, *upstage, laboriously copying the inscription on to his slate.* MR. JONES *crosses to* IDWAL'S *desk, then to* ROBBART'S *desk; looks at their work.*

OLD TOM (*muttering, as he writes*). Elissabeth – known – as – what in goodness is a "k" doin' there, that iss a pussell for me . . .

MR. JONES. "I wandered lonely as a cloud." From "The Daffodils," by Wordsworth.
(*The boys scratch busily. The* SQUIRE *begins to nod sleepily.* MISS RONBERRY *hurries in from the garden.*)

MISS RONBERRY. What is the capital of Sweden?

MR. JONES. Stockholm.

MISS RONBERRY. Thank you. (*She hurries back into the garden.*)

OLD TOM. Please, sir, how many l's in "daffodils"?

THE SQUIRE. Damned if I know.
(JOHN OWEN *comes in by the study door.*)

JOHN. Please, Mistar Jones, Form Two Arithmetic Report—Miss Moffat says will you come in school with it. (*He goes back.* MR. JONES *follows him through the study after getting book and papers from the sideboard. The* SQUIRE *snores.*)

ROBBART. Mae o'n cysgu. Tyd. Idwal . . .

OLD TOM. Plenty Welsh at home, not in the class, please, by request, scoundrels and notty boys!

IDWAL (*rises*). Squire iss 'avin' a snore. Nai ddangos rwbeth ichi— (*He rises, runs to the blackboard, takes the chalk and the duster, and swiftly rubs out and adds to the inscription till it reads: "NO . . . GOOD . . . BESSIE." The* SQUIRE *grunts. As he strikes the period the* SQUIRE *sticks his foot out. He says "Na-fe."*)

MR. JONES (*returning*). Now history. (*Stumbles over the* SQUIRE'S *foot. Crosses to blackboard*) Excuse me . . . Elizabeth . . . (*He sees the inscription and stops short. He turns on the others, grave and perturbed*) Who did this?

IDWAL. Please, Mr. Jones, perhaps it iss some terrible dunce that want to know what iss Bessie Watty been doin' the last few months.
(*A pause.*)

MR. JONES. Whoever it was . . . (SQUIRE *rises*) I am going to cane him! It was not you, sir, by any chance?

THE SQUIRE. Not guilty. . . . Bessie Watty? Little Cockney thing? Nice ankles?

MR. JONES. I do not know, sir . . . (*Boys snicker*) Silence, boys! Where is my duster?
(SQUIRE *goes to window and looks out.*)

THE SQUIRE. Still no sign of him.

MR. JONES. You mean Morgan Evans, sir? (*Boys look up*) He is not expected before the train leaving Oxford half-past one . . .

THE SQUIRE. There's a sporting chance the Viva finished yesterday, and I sent the wagonette to meet the one-ten.

MR. JONES. Do you think that he may know the result when he arrives?

THE SQUIRE. I doubt it. Miss Moffat said we'll hear by letter in a day or two. . . . (*Rising restlessly and going towards the front door*) Think I'll propel the old pins down the highway, just in case . . .

IDWAL. Please, sir, what sort of a place is Oxford?

THE SQUIRE. Dunno, I'm sure. Cambridge myself. (*He goes. Leaves door open.*)

MR. JONES (*at blackboard*). Now history. Repeat after me . . .

IDWAL. Please, Mr. Jones, tell us about Bessie Watty?

MR. JONES. If you are kept in tomorrow, I will give you religion. Repeat after me . . . (*The school bell rings*) Dismiss! (ROBBART *rises and straps books.* MR. JONES *goes to desk and tidies papers.* SARAH *hurries in from the front door. She is dressed in her best, in the traditional Welsh peasant costume with a steeple hat.*)

SARAH. Please, sir, have you got my father— (*Seeing* OLD TOM) tiddona, 'nhad, ma'dy frwas di'n oeri . . .

OLD TOM. English, daughter, in the class, pliss!

SARAH. You are an old soft, your porridge it iss gettin' cold and you have not got your sleep . . .

OLD TOM. But I got my Queen Elizabeth . . .
(SARAH *takes his slate, puts it on* ROBBART'S *desk.*)

SARAH. And in the mornin' you got your rheumatics—come on! (SARAH *helps* OLD TOM *to rise.* MISS RONBERRY *comes in from the garden.*)

ROBBART. Sarah Pugh, what you all clobbered up for?

SARAH. Because for Morgan Evans.

MR. JONES. Is there some news?

MISS RONBERRY. About Morgan? Oh, quickly!

SARAH. Not yet, Mistar Jones. But when it comes, I know it iss good news, so what do I do? I open the dresser, out the lavender bags and into my Sundays! Home (*Starts to door with* OLD TOM), dada, for Sundays . . .

MR. JONES. Before we have definite news, that is unwise . . .

SARAH. John Goronwy Jones, pliss, sir, you are an old soft. Everybody is ready to meet him by the Nant! The grocer got his fiddle . . .

IDWAL. And William Williams the public got his cornet!

ROBBART. And with me on me mouth organ . . . (*Strikes chord on mouth organ.*)

SARAH. And me singin'!

ROBBART. Tyd, Idwal— (*He runs out by the front door, followed by* IDWAL.)

MISS RONBERRY. Perhaps preparing for news to be good means that it will be.

MR. JONES. Everything is preordained. Morgan Evans has either won the scholarship, or lost it.

MISS RONBERRY. Let us all say together, "Morgan Evans has won the scholarship!"

ALL (*except* MR. JONES). "Morgan Evans has won the scholarship!"

SARAH (*to* OLD TOM). Tiddana, 'nhad—

OLD TOM. I never got a letter yet, and nobody never put Sundays on for me. . . . (*He goes out by the front door.* SARAH *starts to go,* MISS RONBERRY'S *eye catches the blackboard.*)

MISS RONBERRY. "No . . . (SARAH *comes back*) good . . . Bessie." Good gracious!

MR. JONES. Where *is* my duster? (*Looks behind blackboard.*)

MISS RONBERRY. What does that mean?

SARAH. Bessie Watty. Miss Ronberry, where is she?
(MR. JONES *finds duster at* IDWAL'S *desk.*)

MISS RONBERRY. I don't know, dear.

SARAH. Miss Moffat she hears from her, in my post office. (JONES *erases blackboard*) We wass all wonderin'. (*She goes out by the front door.*)

MISS RONBERRY. Well, I have been wondering too! She came back that morning and just went away again. Morgan Evans was telling me only the day he left for Oxford that he didn't even *see* her. Where is she?

MR. JONES. It is more important to know if Morgan Evans has won or not.

MISS RONBERRY. I know . . . If he hasn't, it will break her heart.

MR. JONES. Would she feel it so keen as all that?

MISS RONBERRY. I used not to think so, but since that day they have been so much better friends, it has been a pleasure to hear them conversing. Perhaps it is the strain of all these examinations . . .
(MISS MOFFAT *comes in from the study with exercise book, chuckling.*)

MISS MOFFAT. Gwyneth Thomas, the plasterer's eldest, essay on Knowledge. "Be good, sweet maid, and let who will be clever"—I wonder if the Reverend Kingsley had any idea what a smack in the eye that was for lady teachers? And then Gwyneth Thomas starts (*Reading*): "It is not nice to know too much, I wish to be like Miss Ronberry, Miss Moffat is different, she knows everything." Any news?

MR. JONES. Not yet.

MISS MOFFAT. I thought not. . . . (*A pause*) Where is the Squire?

MR. JONES. Gone to see if there is any sign.

MISS MOFFAT. Thank the Lord. That man is really becoming a nuisance. He gave up Henley to be here this week. Did you know?

MR. JONES. You do not appear nervous?

MISS MOFFAT. I am past being nervous. If he has won, I shan't believe it. Flatly.

MISS RONBERRY. And if he has lost?

MISS MOFFAT. If he has lost . . . (*After a pause*) We must proceed as if nothing had happened. The sun rises and sets every day, and while it does we have jolly well got to revolve round it; the time to sit up and take notice will be the day it decides not to appear. In the meantime, Mr. Jones, your report is on your desk. Miss Ronberry, Form Two are waiting for your music like a jungle of hungry parakeets.

MISS RONBERRY. Yes, Miss Moffat.
(*They retire meekly through the study.* MISS MOFFAT *is alone. She looks at her watch; her armour loosens perceptibly; she is on edge and apprehensive. She goes towards the stairs, but before she reaches them the garden door opens suddenly and* MORGAN *appears. He wears a new dark suit, carries a travelling bag and his cap, and looks dusty and tired. His manner is excited and unstable; he is alternately eager and intensely depressed. She stares at him, not daring to speak.*)

MORGAN. I caught the early train. I knew they would all be watching for me, so I got out at Llanmorfedd and got a lift to Gwaenygam.

MISS MOFFAT. Does that mean . . . ?

MORGAN. Oh, no news. Except that I am not hopeful.

MISS MOFFAT. Why not?

MORGAN. They talked to me for one hour at the Viva . . .

MISS MOFFAT. That doesn't mean anything. Go on.

MORGAN. They jumped down hard on the New Testament question. As you said they would. . . . You are very pale.

MISS MOFFAT. Better than a raging fever. Go on.

MORGAN. I spent five minutes explaining why Saint Paul sailed from a town three hundred miles inland.

MISS MOFFAT. Oh, dear. (*Their manner together has changed since we last saw them together. They are hardly at all teacher and pupil, superior and inferior, adult and child. They are more like two friends held solidly by a bond unsentimental and unself-conscious.* MORGAN's *English has immensely improved, and he expresses himself with ease.*) Parnell?

MORGAN. Parnell . . . (*Smiles*) Oh, yes . . . I was going to stick up for the old chap, but when they started off with "that fellow Parnell," I told the tale against him for half an hour. I wasn't born a Welshman for nothing.

MISS MOFFAT. Ha . . . And the French?

MORGAN. Not good. I said "naturellement" to everything, but it didn't fit every time.

MISS MOFFAT. And the Greek verbs?

MORGAN. They were sarcastic.

MISS MOFFAT. Did the President send for you?

MORGAN. I had half an hour with him . . .

MISS MOFFAT. You did?

MORGAN. Yes, but so did the other nine candidates! He was a very kind and grand old gentleman sitting in a drawing room the size of Penlan Town Hall. I talked about religion, the same as you said . . .

MISS MOFFAT (*correcting him, mechanically*). Just as you advised . . .

MORGAN. Just as you advised. He asked me if I had ever had strong drink, and I looked him straight in the eye and said "No."

MISS MOFFAT. Oh!

MORGAN. I was terrible—terribly nervous. My collar stud flew off, and I had to hold on to my collar with one hand, and he did not seem impressed with me at all. . . . He was very curious about you. (*Rises*) Did you know there was an article in the *Morning Post* about the school?

MISS MOFFAT. Was there? . . . But what else makes you despondent?

MORGAN. The other candidates. They appeared to me brilliant. I had never thought they would be, somehow! Two from Eton and one from Harrow—one of them very rich. I had never thought a scholarship man might be rich. He had his own servant.

MISS MOFFAT. Gosh!

MORGAN. And the servant looked so like my father I thought it was at first. . . . And, as I was leaving, the examiners appeared to be sorry for me in some way, and I received the impression that I had failed. I . . .

MISS MOFFAT. When shall we know?

MORGAN. The day after tomorrow. They are writing to you.

MISS MOFFAT. The villagers are all in their best, and talking about a holiday tomorrow. It is very stupid of them, because if you have failed it will make you still more sick at heart . . .

MORGAN. If I have failed? (*In sudden desperation*) Don't speak about it!

MISS MOFFAT. But we must! You faced the idea the day you left for Oxford . . .

MORGAN. I know, but I have *been* to Oxford, and come back, since then! I have come back—from the world! Since the day I was born, I have been a prisoner behind a stone wall, and now somebody has given me a leg-up to have a look at the other side. . . . They cannot drag me back again, they cannot. They *must* give me a push and send me over!

MISS MOFFAT. I've never heard you talk so much since I've known you.

MORGAN. That is just it! I *can* talk, now! The three days I have been there, I have been talking my head off!

MISS MOFFAT. Ha! If three days at Oxford can do that to you, what would you be like at the end of three years?

MORGAN. That's just it again. It would be everything I need, everything! Starling and I spent three hours one night discussin' the law—Starling, you know, the brilliant one. . . . The words came pouring out of me—all the words that I had learnt and written down and never spoken. I suppose I was talking nonsense, but I was at least holding a conversation! I suddenly realised that I had never done it before—I had never been *able* to do it. (*With a strong Welsh accent*) "How are you, Morgan? Nice day, Mr. Jones! Not bad for the harvest." A vocabulary of twenty words; all the thoughts that you have given to me were being stored away as if they were always going to be useless—locked up and rotting away—a lot of questions with nobody to answer them, a lot of statements with nobody to contradict them. . . . And there I was with Starling, nineteen to the dozen. I came out of his rooms that night, and I walked down the High. That's their High Street, you know.

MISS MOFFAT (*nodding, drinking in the torrent with the most intense pleasure*). Yes, yes. . . .

MORGAN. I looked up, and there was a moon behind Magd—Maudlin. Not the same moon I have seen over the Nant, a different face altogether. Everybody seemed to be walking very fast, with their gowns on, in the moonlight. The bells were ringing, and I was walking faster than anybody and I felt—well, the same as on the rum in the old days!

MISS MOFFAT. Go on.

MORGAN. All of a sudden, with one big rush, against that moon, and against that High Street—I saw this room; you and me sitting here studying, and all those books—and everything I have ever learnt from those books, and from you, was lighted up—like a magic lantern: Ancient Rome, Greece, Shakespeare, Carlyle, Milton. . . . Everything had a meaning, because I was in a new world—my world! And so it came to me why you worked like a slave to make me ready for this scholarship. (*Lamely*) I've finished.

MISS MOFFAT. I didn't want you to stop.

MORGAN. I had not been drinking.

MISS MOFFAT. I know.

MORGAN. I can talk to you too, now.

MISS MOFFAT. Yes. I'm glad.
(THE SQUIRE *comes in from the front door.* MORGAN *rises.*)

THE SQUIRE. No sign of the feller-me-lad, dang it . . . (*Hangs hat on door*) Evans! (*Goes to* MORGAN, *shakes hands*) There you are!

MORGAN. Good day, sir.

THE SQUIRE. Well?

MORGAN. They are sending the result through the post.

THE SQUIRE. The devil they are. (*To* MISS MOFFAT, *as he sits in armchair*) D'ye know I am finding this waiting a definite strain?
(MR. JONES *runs in from the study, stops at foot of stairs.*)

MR. JONES. Somebody said they had seen Morgan . . .

MORGAN. Day after tomorrow.

MR. JONES. Oh. . . .

THE SQUIRE. Examiners all right, my boy?

MORGAN. Rather sticky, sir.

THE SQUIRE. Lot of old fogies, I expect. Miss Moffat, I told you you ought to have made inquiries at the other place. However . . .
(MISS RONBERRY *runs in from the study.*)

MISS RONBERRY. Somebody said they had seen . . .

THE SQUIRE AND MR. JONES. The day after tomorrow!

MISS RONBERRY Oh . . . How are you, Morgan, dear . . . ?

MR. JONES (*wandering out to the porch*). The suspense is terrible.

THE SQUIRE. I know.

MR. JONES. Even the little children are worrying about— (*He stops short; he has seen somebody coming down the village street; he looks again, doubtfully; starts, then peers anxiously into the room. Everybody is preoccupied. He comes into the room, shuts the door, and stands a moment with his back to it*) Morgan, my boy, are you not exhausted after your journey? Would you not like something to eat?

MORGAN. I am rather hungry, yes . . .

MISS MOFFAT. But how stupid of me! Watty will boil you an egg . . . Come along . . .

MORGAN (*rising*). Thank you. Excuse me . . . (*He follows* MISS MOFFAT *out.*)

MISS MOFFAT (*as she goes into the kitchen*). Did they spot the Dryden howler?

MORGAN. No.
(MR. JONES *goes to the kitchen door and closes it after them.*)

THE SQUIRE. You seemed very anxious to get 'em out of the room. What's the matter . . . ?
(*The front door opens and* BESSIE *walks in. She has completely changed; she might be ten years older. Her hair is up; she wears a cheaply smart costume, with a cape, and looks dazzlingly pretty in a loose opulent style. Her whole personality has blossomed. A pause. They stare at her.*)

BESSIE. Hallo!

THE SQUIRE. How d'ye do . . . ?

BESSIE. I'm very well indeed, thanks, and how are you, blooming? (*Her accent is nearer the ladylike than it has been yet.*)

THE SQUIRE. Yes, thanks . . . What *is* this?

MISS RONBERRY. I really couldn't say . . . Good gracious, it's Bessie W—

BESSIE. Right first time. Hello, Miss Ronberry, how's geography, the world still goin' round in circles? Hello, Mr. Jones, flirty as ever?

THE SQUIRE. And to what do we owe this honor?

BESSIE. Well, it's like this . . .

MR. JONES (*desperately*). Miss Ronberry, will you please return to your class . . . ?

MISS RONBERRY. They are quite safe. I left Mary Davies in charge . . .

BESSIE. No, you don't. We've had too many secrets as it is.

MR. JONES. Three days ago she sent money to you. Did you not receive the letter?

BESSIE. Yes, I did, and all the others, till I was sick of 'em.

THE SQUIRE. What *is* all this?

BESSIE. Last week I was glancing through the *Mid-Wales Gazette,* and I'm here to congratulate a certain young gent in case he has won that scholarship.

MR. JONES. Oh!

MISS RONBERRY. But what has that got to do with you?

BESSIE. You see, Miss, it's like this . . .

MR. JONES (*in a last effort to stop her*). Don't say it—don't say it!

BESSIE. Four weeks yesterday, I had a baby.
(*A pause.* MISS RONBERRY *and* THE SQUIRE *stare at her.* MR. JONES *gives a sigh of impotent despair.*)

THE SQUIRE. You had a what?

BESSIE. A baby. Seven pounds thirteen ounces.

THE SQUIRE. Good God, how ghastly.

MR. JONES (*turns to her*). It is a disgustin' subject and . . .

BESSIE. It isn't disgusting at all. If I had a wedding ring you'd think it was sweet.
(MRS. WATTY *hurries in from the kitchen.*)

MRS. WATTY. Morgan Evans's luggage. Excuse me, sir. (*Catches sight of the* SQUIRE'S *serious face*) Oh! . . . (*Fearfully*) Any news?

THE SQUIRE. Well, yes. . . .

MRS. WATTY. Bessie! (*Drops the bag in her excitement*) My, you do look a dollymop! Excuse me, sir . . .

THE SQUIRE. Say anything you like . . .

MRS. WATTY. Where d'you get them bracelets?

BESSIE. Present.

MRS. WATTY. Oh, that's all right. Where 'ave you been, you madam?

BESSIE. Turnin' you into a granny.

MRS. WATTY. A gra– (*Both laugh*) Well, *fancy!*
(MISS MOFFAT *comes in from the kitchen.*)

MISS MOFFAT. And I should try and have a sleep if I were you . . .

MRS. WATTY. You could 'ave knocked me down with a feather!

BESSIE. Hello. (MISS MOFFAT *stops short*) I've just been telling them you-know-what. (*It is plain she is no longer afraid of* MISS MOFFAT. *The latter looks from one to the other, helplessly.*)

THE SQUIRE. And now I think it's time you told us who the fellow is. I am going to take drastic proceedings . . .

MRS. WATTY. That's right, dear. Who is it?

BESSIE. Well, as a matter of fact . . .

MISS MOFFAT (*with a cry*). No! I'll pay you anything . . . Anything!

BESSIE. It's no good, miss. (MISS MOFFAT *turns away*) It's Morgan Evans.
(*A pause.*)

THE SQUIRE. What!

MISS RONBERRY (*dazed*). I don't believe it . . .

MRS. WATTY (*really upset, to* MISS MOFFAT). Oh, ma'am.

MISS MOFFAT. I've been dreading this, for months. In a terrible way it's a relief.

BESSIE. Bamboozlin' me every week he was in the gutter!

MISS MOFFAT. Lies, all lies, and I was glad to be telling them . . .

MISS RONBERRY (*suddenly articulate*). I can't go on listening! I can't bear it! It all comes of meddling with this teaching. She was in my class . . . What *would* Papa have said! This horrible unnatural happening . . .

MISS MOFFAT (*exasperated beyond endurance*). Don't talk nonsense! It isn't horrible, and it isn't unnatural! On the contrary, it's nature giving civilisation a nasty tweak of the nose. The schoolmistress *has* learnt a lesson, but it's a little late now.

BESSIE (*rising*). Where is he?

MRS. WATTY. Over my dead body, my girl . . .

BESSIE. She's right, mum, it's too late. I got a four-weeks-old baby, kickin', healthy and hungry, and I haven't got a husband to keep him, so his father's got to turn *into* my husband. That's only fair, isn't it?

THE SQUIRE (*rises*). I'm sorry, Miss Moffat, but I'm inclined to agree . . .

BESSIE. I'll call him . . .

MR. JONES. There is no need to call him!

THE SQUIRE. What's the matter with you?

MR. JONES. I am sorry to say that I have a strong feeling of affection for this young woman.

BESSIE (*sitting again on the sofa, amused*). Oh, yes—I've got the face of an angel, haven't I?

MR. JONES. And I am willing to do my duty by rehabilitating her in wedlock, and bestowing on the infant every advantage by bringing it up a Baptist.

THE SQUIRE. Are you serious?

MR. JONES. I am always serious.

BESSIE (*to* MISS MOFFAT). You'd like that, wouldn't you?

MRS. WATTY. Now we're not pretendin' it's a windfall, but for a girl who's took the wrong turnin' it's a present! And you'd 'ave your own way in everything—wouldn't she, sir?

MR. JONES (*eagerly*). Of course . . .

MRS. WATTY. Well, will you?

BESSIE. No. I won't. I'd like to oblige . . . (*Laughs*) but, really, I couldn't! (MR. JONES *turns away*) Besides, my friend would be furious.

MRS. WATTY (*clutching at straws*). Your friend?

BESSIE. Ever such a nice gentleman, sporting, quite a swell, owns a racecourse. (MRS. WATTY *looks suspicious*) You needn't look like that. I only met him ten weeks ago. I'd started servin' behind a bar for fun. I was the picture of health and ever so lucky in the counter bein' very high.

THE SQUIRE. I have never heard such a conversation outside a police court. I am seeking the safety of my own quarters. Anything I can do, Miss Moffat . . .

BESSIE. I suppose *you* wouldn't care to stake a claim?

THE SQUIRE. Good gracious . . . (*Exits.* BESSIE *laughs.*)

MISS MOFFAT. Doesn't this man of yours want to marry you?

BESSIE. 'E won't talk of anything else, but he won't have the baby. He says it would be different if the father'd been a pal of his—you can understand it, really, can't you? So I've got to give up my friend and marry Morgan Evans. Pity, 'cos my friend worships me. Ever since I left he keeps on sending me telegrams. I just got two at the station, and I expect I'll get some more tonight, isn't it rich? (*Laughs*) Mr. Jones wouldn't consider the baby without me?

MISS RONBERRY. The baby without you! Your child! What about your—your mother love?

BESSIE. I expect you'll think I'm a wicked girl, but d'you know, I haven't got any!

MISS RONBERRY. Oh, what a vile thing to say, vile . . .

BESSIE (*rising*). Now listen, dear. . . . You're seeing this baby as if it was yours, aren't you—you'd think the world of it, wouldn't you?

MISS RONBERRY. It would mean everything to me— (*Turns away*) my whole life. . . .

BESSIE. I have a pretty near idea how old you are. When I'm your age I'll love the idea of a baby, but life hasn't begun yet for me. I'm just getting a taste for it. What do *I* want with a baby?

MRS. WATTY. That's what we all want to know!

BESSIE. Yes, mum, but you know what it is . . .

MISS RONBERRY. You're inhuman, that's what you are! To think you don't want it. . . . (*She is on the point of bursting into foolish tears, and runs into study.*)

BESSIE. I didn't mean to be nasty—but inhuman indeed! I didn't want the baby, nobody would have, but I was careful so it'd be all right, and now it is all right I want it to have a good time. But *I* want a good time too! I *could* have left it on a doorstep, couldn't I? But I must see it's in good hands—and that's why I've come to Morgan Evans.

MISS MOFFAT. You want to make him marry you, on the chance he will become fond enough of the child to ensure its future—your conscience will be clear and later you can go off on your own?

BESSIE. I shouldn't be surprised . . .

MISS MOFFAT. In the meantime, it's worth while to ruin a boy on—on the threshold of . . .

BESSIE. I don't know anything about that, I'm sure. (*Calling*) Morgan!

MISS MOFFAT (*intercepting her, desperately*). Ssh! Wait a minute, wait. . . . There may be a way out—there must be . . .

MRS. WATTY. Gawd bless us, ma'am —I got it!

MISS MOFFAT. What?

MRS. WATTY. Why can't you adopt it? (BESSIE *and* MR. JONES *stare from her to* MISS MOFFAT.)

MISS MOFFAT. Don't be ridiculous.

MRS. WATTY. Would that do you, Bessie?

BESSIE. Well! I never thought . . .

MRS. WATTY. Would it, though?

BESSIE (*after consideration*). Yes, it would.

MISS MOFFAT. It *would?* . . . But . . . But what would *I* do with a baby? I—I don't even know what they look like!

MRS. WATTY. They're lovely little things. Now it's all arranged . . .

MISS MOFFAT. But it would be fantastic . . .

BESSIE (*going up to her, eagerly*). Oh, do, please, it'd put *everything* to rights! I would know the baby was safe. Morgan Evans need never know a thing about it. I can marry my friend, and it will all be beautiful! He might grow like his father and turn out quite nice, and anyway I'm not really so bad, you know. And he's on the bottle now—and I could give all the instructions before I go. And you could have it straight away, see, because if it's going I don't want to have it with me longer than I can help, see, because I'd only start gettin' fond of it, see . . .

MRS. WATTY. Come on, ma'am, you've been pushin' us about for three years, now we'll give *you* a shove!

MISS MOFFAT. But it's mad—I tell you . . .

MRS. WATTY. Not as mad as takin' *me* in was, with my trouble! You've allus been like that, you might as well go on . . .

MISS MOFFAT. But I was never meant to be a mother. I'm not like Miss Ronberry. Why, *she* is the one to do it . . .

MR. JONES (*hastily*). She would never agree. We were discussin' Marged Hopkins going to the workhouse—and she said she could never hold with any child born like that.

MISS MOFFAT. Oh . . . I suppose it would worry some folk. . . . But, Watty, you're the grandmother, and surely you . . .

MRS. WATTY. Oh, I couldn't! I don't bear it no ill-will, but every penny I get goes to the Corpse. You're the one, dear, really you are.

MISS MOFFAT. Bessie Watty, do you mean that if I do not adopt this child, you . . .

BESSIE. I will have to tell Morgan Evans, and he will have to marry me, I swear that.

MISS MOFFAT. And do you swear that you would never let Morgan Evans know the truth?

BESSIE. I swear. If there are any questions, I'll say it was my friend's.
(*A pause.*)

MISS MOFFAT. Then—I give in.

BESSIE. That's lovely. My friend *will* be pleased. I'll pop back to the public-house for his telegram and send him a nice one back. Goodbye, all, we'll arrange details later, shall we? My friend gave me this buckle, isn't it nice? He offered me a tiny one, real, but I think the false is prettier, don't you?

MR. JONES (*as she turns to go*). Are you going to take up a life of sin?

BESSIE (*smiling*). I shouldn't be surprised. I'm only really meself with a lot of gentlemen round me, y'know, and a nice glass o' port will never come amiss, neither. (*To* MRS. WATTY) That cold water didn't really do the trick, mum, did it? . . . (*To* MISS MOFFAT, *serious for a moment*) Good-bye . . . I only did it to spite you, y'know.

MR. JONES. You are not fit to touch the hem of her garment.

BESSIE. Oh, yes, I am! Just because she's read a lot o' books. Books, books! Look at 'em all! I got more out of life at my age than she has out o' them all her days—and I'll get a lot more yet! What d'you bet me? (*She goes out by the front door, leaves door open.* MRS. WATTY *closes the door after her.*)

MRS. WATTY. That's settled . . . (*Comes down.*)
(*The voices of children, in the barn, singing "Dacw'n-ghariad."*)

MR. JONES (*making for the study door*). For which we must be truly thankful . . .
(MORGAN *walks in quickly from the kitchen. He goes straight to* MISS MOFFAT; *his face is white and shocked. They stare at him, instinctively silent.*)

MORGAN. Has she gone?

MISS MOFFAT. Why?

MORGAN. The Squire just came in to see me.

MISS MOFFAT. The fool! The idiotic fool . . .

MORGAN. Then it's true . . . ! He thought I knew. (*Laughs*) Then he said it was for the best—that I ought to be told. . . . (*The singing stops in the barn*) It is funny. She and I, we do not know each other at all. It was a long time ago, and I never thought again about it —and neither did she. I know she didn't . . . And here we are . . . It is funny, too, because if you and I had not made that bad quarrel, it would never have happened . . . It ought to make me feel older—but I feel more—young than I have ever done before . . . Oh, God, why should this happen. . . .

MISS MOFFAT. Steady . . .

MR. JONES. There is no need for you to upset yourself, my boy. Miss Moffat is going to take care of—of—

MORGAN. What?

MISS MOFFAT. I am going to adopt it.

MORGAN (*his old truculent self emerging*). What in hell do you take me for?

MR. JONES. Morgan, swearing! Be haru ti . . .

MORGAN (*in a rage*). I will swear some more too, if people talk to me like that! (*To* MISS MOFFAT) What do you take me for?

MR. JONES. Then what would you like to do, my boy . . . ?

MORGAN. What would I like to do? (*Getting more and more Welsh*) It is not a question of what I would like to do, or what I might be allowed, but what I am *going* to do—what any fellow with any guts in him must do! I am going to marry her!

MISS MOFFAT (*with a cry*). I knew this would happen, I knew . . .

MORGAN. What else is there, when I have made a fool of myself and of her, and of the poor—the poor—I am not going to talk about any of it to anybody. All I will say is that Bessie Watty and I are going to get married as soon as we can, and that is final! (*He flings himself into the armchair.*)

MISS MOFFAT (*hopelessly*). I see. (*A knock at the front door.* SARAH *hurries in agog with excitement. She runs to* MRS. WATTY.)

SARAH. Bessie's telegram from her friend, they send it from Penlan . . . I never seed one before!

MRS. WATTY. Poor chap, 'e'll be disappointed again. . . . (*Opens the telegram, and hands it to* MISS MOFFAT) What does it say, ma'am? . . . Read it, ma'am, take your mind off things . . .
(MISS MOFFAT *glances halfheartedly at the telegram. A pause. She looks up at* MORGAN.)

MISS MOFFAT. You have won the scholarship. (*Reading*) "First, Evans, Second, Fayver-Iles, Third, Starling. Congratulations." (SARAH *claps her hands and runs out by the front door, closes it.* MORGAN *laughs bitterly and turns away. Folding the telegram carefully, she tucks it into her belt, still quiet, burning with a slow-mounting and deliberate fervour*) Lock the school door, Watty, will you?

MRS. WATTY (*to* MR. JONES, *tremulously*). Go in there, sir, I'll make you a cup of tea. . . . (MR. JONES *goes into the kitchen.* MRS. WATTY *locks the study door and follows him.*)

MISS MOFFAT. Look at me, Morgan. (MORGAN *faces her in the armchair, defiantly*) For the first time, we are together. Our hearts are face to face, naked and unashamed, because there's no time to lose, my boy; the clock is ticking and there's no time to lose. If ever anybody has been at the crossroads, you are now. . . .

MORGAN. It is no good. I am going to marry her.

MISS MOFFAT. And I am going to speak to you very simply. I want you to change suddenly from a boy to a man. I understand that this is a great shock to you, but I want you to throw off this passionate obstinacy to do the right thing. . . . Did you promise her marriage?

MORGAN. No, never . . .

MISS MOFFAT. Did you even tell her that you were in love with her?

MORGAN (*repelled*). No, never . . .

MISS MOFFAT. Then your situation now is the purest accident; it is to be regretted, but it has happened before and it will happen again. So cheer up, you are not the central figure of such a tragedy as you think . . .

MORGAN. That does not alter the fact that I have a duty to—to them both. . . .

MISS MOFFAT. She has her own plans, and she doesn't want the child; and I am willing to look after it if you behave as I want you to behave. If you marry her, you know what will happen, don't you? You will go back to the mine. In a year she will have left you—both. You will be drinking again, and this time you will not stop. And you will enjoy being this besotted and uncouth village genius who once showed such promise; but it will not be worth it, you know.

MORGAN. There is a child, living and breathing on this earth, and living and breathing because of me. . . .

MISS MOFFAT. I don't care if there are fifty children on this earth because of you! . . . You mentioned the word "duty," did you? Yes, you have a duty, but it is not to this loose little lady, or to her offspring either.

MORGAN. You mean a duty to you?

MISS MOFFAT. No. A year ago I should have said a duty to me, yes; but that night you showed your teeth—you gave me a lot to think about, you know. You caught me unawares, and I gave you the worst possible answer back. I turned sorry for myself and taunted you with ingratitude. I was a dolt not to realise that a debt of gratitude is the most humiliating debt of all, and that a little show of affection would have wiped it out. I offer that affection to you, today.

MORGAN. Why are you saying this to me now?

MISS MOFFAT. Because, as the moments are passing, and I am going to get my way, I know that I am never going to see you again. (*A pause.*)

MORGAN. Never again? But why?

MISS MOFFAT. If you are not to marry her, it would be madness for you to come into contact with the child; so if I am adopting the child, you can never come to see me; it is common sense. You have been given the push over the wall that you asked for.

MORGAN. But you—will be staying here . . . How can I never come back—after everything you have done for me?

MISS MOFFAT. D'you remember, the last six months, I've gone for a long walk over Moel Hiraeth, every morning at eight, like clock-work, for my health?

MORGAN. Yes?

MISS MOFFAT. There's one bit of the road, round a boulder—and there's an oak tree, and under it the valley suddenly drops sheer. Every morning regularly, as I was turning that corner, by some trick of the mind, I found myself thinking of you working for this scholarship, and winning it. And I experienced something which must after all be comparatively rare: A feeling—of complete happiness. I shall experience it again. No, Morgan Evans, you have no duty to me. Your only duty—is to the world.

MORGAN. To the world?

MISS MOFFAT. Now you are going, there is no harm in telling you something. I don't think you realise quite what your future can become if you give it the chance. I have always been very definite about the things I wanted, and I have always had everything worked out to a T. P'r'aps that's the trouble with me, I dunno . . . I've got *you* worked out, and it's up to you whether it will come right or not. . . .

MORGAN (*eagerly*). Go on.

MISS MOFFAT. I rather made out to the Squire that I wanted you to be a writer—the truth might have sounded ridiculous; but stranger things have happened. You have a great deal now and Oxford will give you the rest.

MORGAN. For what?

MISS MOFFAT. Enough to become a great man of our country. "If a light come in the mine" you said, remember?

MORGAN. Yes.

MISS MOFFAT. Make that light come in the mine and some day free these children. And you could be more, much, much more; you could be a man for a future nation to be proud of . . . Perhaps I'm mad, I dunno. We'll see. It's up to you.

MORGAN (*rises before speaking*). Yes.
(MR. JONES *appears timidly from the kitchen.*)

MR. JONES. Is it all right to ring the bell to say holiday tomorrow?

MISS MOFFAT. Yes. (MR. JONES'S *face lights up; he hurries to the study door, unlocks it, and disappears*) I think that's all.

MORGAN. But—I—I do not know what to say.

MISS MOFFAT. Then don't say it.

MORGAN. I have been—so much time in this room.

MISS MOFFAT. And the lessons are over.

MORGAN (*impulsively*). I shall—always remember.

MISS MOFFAT. Will you? Well, I'm glad you think you will. (*She presses the bag and cap into his unwilling hands.* IDWAL *runs in from the study, very excited.* ROBBART *appears behind him.*)

IDWAL. Please, Miss Moffat, the band is out, and they say Morgan got to come down to Penlan Town Hall for Wales to see a real toff!

MORGAN. Na, ddim diolch . . .

ROBBART. Tyd, man, tyd, they never forgive you! (*An afterthought*) And, please, Miss Moffat, Mr. Jones say is he to say school day after tomorrow, nine o'clock same as usual?

MISS MOFFAT. Nine o'clock. The same as usual. . . .

ROBBART. Yes, Miss Moffat. (*He runs back into the study, followed by* IDWAL.)

MISS MOFFAT (*she offers her hand,* MORGAN *takes it*). Good-bye. And

I had my heart set on coming up to London and having tea on the Terrace.
(*Voices mixed with singing off stage.*)

IDWAL (*putting his head round the barn door, and disappearing again*). Brysia, Morgan Evans, brysia!
(MORGAN *tries to say something, fails, and hurries into the study. The kitchen door opens, and* MRS. WATTY *appears cautiously.*)

MRS. WATTY (*whispering*). Has he gone?

MISS MOFFAT. Yes. It's all over.

MRS. WATTY. Bessie's sent a gentleman over to see you from the public-house . . . (*Hands her birth certificate.*)

MISS MOFFAT. Tell him I can't see anybody . . . (*Taking certificate*) What's this?

MRS. WATTY. His birth certificate, ma'am.

MISS MOFFAT. I had forgotten—all about that.
(MRS. WATTY *starts to kitchen.*)

MRS. WATTY. Come on, ma'am, you got to start sometime!

MISS MOFFAT. Just coming.
(MRS. WATTY *goes into the kitchen. The sound of the village people singing and cheering down the road. A pause.*)

MISS MOFFAT (*looks down at the birth certificate. The singing and cheering die down and stop. A pause*). Moffat, my girl, you mustn't be clumsy this time. You mustn't be clumsy . . . (*The school bell begins to ring, clear and confident. She looks up, as she did once before, listening, smiling faintly. A vociferous burst of cheering and singing in the village. She turns and walks towards the kitchen.*)

CURTAIN

APR 1970